APPALACHIA

Social Context
Past and Present
Third Edition

Edited by

Bruce Ergood
Bruce E. Kuhre

Ohio University
Athens, Ohio

Foreword by Loyal Jones

KENDALL/HUNT PUBLISHING COMPANY
2460 Kerper Boulevard   P.O. Box 539   Dubuque, Iowa 52004-0539

Cover design by Patricia Light
Photographs by James L. Hart

Contents

Foreword by Loyal Jones   v
Preface to the Third Edition   vii

I. What Is Appalachia?—Geographically and Sociologically   1

    1. "Why Study Appalachia" by People's Appalachian Research Collective   3
    2. "Harry Caudill in the Cumberlands" by Wendell Berry   7
    3. "Regional Definitions" by Karl B. Raitz and Richard Ulack   10
    4. "Finding Ourselves: Reclaiming the Appalachian Past" by Ronald D. Eller   26
    5. "The Southern Highlands and the Southern Highlander Defined" by John C. Campbell   31
    6. "Freedom in the Mountains" by Don West   37
    7. "Toward a Definition of Appalachia" by Bruce Ergood   39
    8. "The Sociology of Southern Appalachia" by David S. Walls and Dwight B. Billings   49

II. Historical Background of Appalachia   61

    9. "Pioneer Routes of Travel and Early Settlements" by John C. Campbell   63
  10. "Appalachia and the Idea of America: The Problem of the Persisting Frontier" by Henry D. Shapiro   **74**
  11. "The Passing of Provincialism" by Thomas R. Ford   80
  12. "Cash Is a Four-Letter Word" by Paul Salstrom   104

III. Demographic Characteristics of the Region (Jenny's Gone Away)   113

  13. "Looking in the Mirror" by Jack Russell   115
  14. "Appalachia's Decade of Change—A Decade of Immigration" by Jerome Pickard   123
  15. "Comparing Appalachia's Counties with the Nation's" from Appalachia   127
  16. "Living City, Feeling Country: The Current Status and Future Prospects of Urban Appalachians" by Phillip J. Obermiller and Michael E. Maloney   133
  17. "America's Soweto: Population Redistribution in Appalachian Kentucky, 1940–1986" by Stephen E. White   139

IV. Appalachian Culture and a Sense of Community   147

  18. "The Search for Community in Appalachia" by Ron D. Eller   149
  19. "Appalachia and the Concept of Culture: A Theory of Shared Misunderstanding" by Allen Batteau   **153**
  20. "Appalachian Values" by Loyal Jones   169
  21. "The Image of Appalachian Poverty" by Walter Precourt   173
  22. "Victim-Blaming in Appalachia: Cultural Theories and the Southern Mountaineer" by Stephen L. Fisher   185
  23. "Coaltowns: The Company Town and Southern Appalachian History" by Crandall Shifflett   194
  24. "Traditional Appalachian Music/Early Commercial Country Music: Continuity and Transition" by Ivan Tribe   198

Institutional Analysis of the Region

V. **Economy (Which Side Are You on Boys, Which Side Are You On)** 207

25. "The Poverty of Abundance Revisited" by John Gaventa 209
26. "The Economy of Appalachia in the National Context" by Salim Kublawi 215
27. "Fatalism or the Coal Industry" by Helen Lewis 221
28. "Alliance Releases Land Ownership Study Findings: Land Task Force Urges Community Response" from Mountain Life and Work 230
29. "The Kentucky Way: Resistance to Dependency upon Capitalism in an Appalachian Region" by Rhoda H. Halperin 237
30. "Environmental Threats in Appalachia" by Paul J. Nyden 243

VI. **Polity** 255

31. "What the New Frontier and Great Society Brought" by James Branscome 257
32. "Power and Powerlessness in Appalachia: A Review Essay" by Steve Fisher 266
33. "The Worst Last: The Programs of the Appalachian Regional Commission" by David Whisnant 271
34. "Appalachian Culture As Reaction to Uneven Development: A World Systems Approach to Regionalism" by Roberta McKenzie 284
35. "An Alternative Development Strategy for Appalachia's Future: Applications of 'Another Development' and 'Sustainable Society' Themes to a Region in Crisis" by John G. McNutt 290

VII. **Family** 297

36. "Family, Land, and Community" by Patricia Duane Beaver 299
37. "Gender, Family Structure, and Poverty in Central Appalachia" by Ann R. Tickamyer and Cecil Tickamyer 307
38. "Marriage and the Family" by Janet M. Fitchen 315

VIII. **Education** 325

39. "Educating Appalachia's Poor" by James Branscome 327
40. "To Make a Life: Settlement Institutions of Appalachia" by Jim Stokely 330
41. "Progress Is Our Most Important Product: Decline in Citizen Participation and the Professionalization of Schooling in an Appalachian Rural County" by Tom Boyd 337
42. "Family and Education in Southern Appalachia" by Susan E. Keefe, Una Mae Lange Reck, and Gregory G. Reck 345

IX. **Religion (Just a Closer Walk With Thee)** 353

43. "Grace and the Heart of Appalachian Mountain Religion" by Deborah Vansau McCauley 355
44. "Traditionalism, Antimissionism, and the Primitive Baptist Religion: A Preliminary Analysis" by Melanie L. Sovine 362
45. "Holiness People" by Yvonne Snyder Farley 369

X. **A Selective Bibliography for Appalachian Studies (Revised, Summer 1990)** by Steve Fisher 375

XI. **Audio-visual Materials Available from Appalshop Films** 419

XII. **Appendix of Demographic Characteristics, U.S. and Appalachia** 425

Foreword to the Third Edition

I have used the two previous editions of Ergood's and Kuhre's book for fourteen years in a course called Appalachian Problems and Institutions. It has been a good text. The second edition was much better than the first. This third edition promises to be better still and reveals an attempt to bring more recent essays, while retaining some of the ageless ones that impart an understanding of the Appalachian past. Also the new edition includes articles that show changes in the region and the growth in, and the maturing of, Appalachian Studies. This edition should be effective as a text in a variety of courses relating to sociology, education, community and regional development, political science or government, regional economics, resource management, and the like. The articles herein were written by some of the most knowledgeable persons who have tried to describe and analyze the region and its people in relation to forces and influences from the nation and the world.

Appalachia—land and people—is one of the most complex subjects any writer ever attempted to understand, let alone explain to others. John C. Campbell, one of the earliest writers to take on the task, said more is known about the place *that isn't so* than about any other place, and the stereotypes had not fully taken hold at the time he wrote. Since then many newspaper and magazine articles, a dozen popular movies, numerous television shows and hundreds of brochures from "helping" agencies have appeared, telling interesting but not always accurate stories about us mountaineers. Some have appeared as recently as the last couple of years. For complex reasons their authors have presented their views of the region, and for equally complex reasons, readers and viewers have accepted these images of mountain people with little critical adjustment. Mainstream Americans have been fascinated by Appalachian people for more than a century and have avidly read or watched widely disparate descriptions. Thus, they carry pictures derived from the various media in their heads, and it has been difficult for them to take a new look, unencumbered by the distorted pictures, to look afresh at the facts and at our own version of ourselves.

Appalachia: Social Context Past and Present gives an opportunity for the earnest seekers of truth to study the region anew. The essays reflect thoughtful definitions and analyses by natives of the region, who have risen on the Appalachian literary scene in fairly recent years. It also contains sophisticated theoretical analyses of the region and of similar places worldwide, showing the influence of academic enclaves from which some of the writers observe the region. Together, these essays show not an isolated region and insular people but rather Appalachia as a part of the global order—or disorder as the case may be. The careful reader cannot escape the truth that the industrial world thrives on Appalachian coal, oil, and gas, builds with Appalachian wood and utilizes Appalachian intellect and labor all over the country and the world. The reader will grasp the fact that the weaknesses of Appalachia are the weaknesses of the industrial system and the failure of governmental policies. Appalachia is a part of the modern world with all of its advantages and problems. Many Appalachians have prospered along with advantaged people elsewhere, but conversely, like disadvantaged people throughout the country, many here in the mountains, especially single-parent families and children, have lost ground and are very poor by American standards. Some Appalachia states and counties offer at least adequate government, good schools, enough support payments to provide minimum shelter and food. Others, depending on how political or how inept, offer services that would be unacceptable in most parts of the country.

We are in ways distinctive—perhaps more traditional than some others, more personal in our relationships, more willing to mind our own business even to the point of letting others run things in a way that serve some better than others. Describing the distinctive qualities of Appalachians gets us writers in trouble. In order to show how we are different, we generalize. When we do, we also create stereotypes. Scholars devise interviewing instruments to elicit information in an objective way, in the hope of settling certain controversial subjects. Even these studies, however, do not always bring agreement because we each have differing ideologic orientations and seek information for our own reasons, seeing facts, data or opinion through our own biases. Thus, there is no single book or essay (although I am frequently asked to recommend such) that can give us the real and true Appalachia. We must examine an expanding literature, written by people with varying views, in order to understand that this region is complex and that we must form our own views after diligent study.

Many students come to class with their biases well in place. Some see the "problems" of Appalachia as being the result of Appalachian culture. If people are unemployed, then they must be "sorry," that is, lazy. Whatever problems they face must be their own fault. Don't we all know numerous people who have overcome difficulties with the right values and by hard work? One of the first points to try to teach is that it is more complicated than this. Many factors bear on Appalachian poverty. What has been the effect of parts of the region being treated as a raw materials colony? What is the effect on a county of the major portions of land being owned by outside economic interests? What happens to initiative if there are not enough jobs in a county? What effect does bad or inadequate education have on a child? Can the effects of poor medical care be computed? How are people affected by vicious stereotypes and by being classed as inferior because of their accents or manner? This book will lead students into considering some of these difficult questions. They will learn different descriptions and definitions of the region. They will learn some of the history necessary to an understanding, learn about the demographics, the culture, the institutions, the politics, the family, the problems in education and something about complicated religious beliefs. The book also offers a valuable bibliography, prepared by Dr. Stephen Fisher, and information on helpful audio-visual materials from the Appalachian Film Workshop in Whitesburg, Kentucky.

Loyal Jones
Appalachian Center
Berea College

Preface to the Third Edition

Appalachia simply will not go away. With the renewed interest in coal as a basic energy source for the nation, the controversy concerning the environmental effects of burning high sulfur coal, and the persistent high levels of poverty, the media has once again brought Appalachia to the attention of the American public. We are again faced with selective reporting about specific and often very local issues in this large geographic area of the Eastern United States. The image projected may be locally accurate but erroneously interpreted as representative of the larger Region.

Many earlier works describing the Region and critically discussing issues within the Region are now dated. The monumental study of the *Southern Appalachian Region* is out of print, the excellent work of Campbell is now over 50 years old. Even *Appalachia in the 60s* presents material most of which is now over two decades old. There is a continuing need to provide materials which are both contemporary and current. For while certain historic and descriptive accounts are timeless, the ever changing boundaries of the Region and the changing social conditions call for sharing information which is current. This Third edition provides both historic documents and current information and analysis of the region.

The problem faced by both students of Appalachia and the intellectually curious (and many of the former are included among the latter) is to find a handle—an unchanging definition—by which to grasp Appalachia. After a long search we have concluded that if there is an Appalachia it is a varied thing, and no single handle will serve very well. The geographic area has been defined, redefined and will undoubtedly be redefined again. The economy of the area is both industrial *and* extractive, as well as agricultural. The people are rural *and* urban, some poor, some very adequately provided for. They came from early settler families and more recent immigrants. They exhibit many regional characteristics which vary greatly from northeast Mississippi to near Albany, New York.

Thus our decision has been to present an overview of a varied Region. We have tried to include articles which show a variety of conditions in an Appalachia whose boundaries have varied as well. Many selections are taken from journals and papers which are not readily available in most libraries. Some articles appear for the first time and sixty percent of the selections are new in this edition. Some are from magazines which are published by organizations working in the Region. We have intentionally omitted selections by many of the popular and well-known writers. Their works are easy to come by and we recommend that the reader become familiar with this body of monographs.

This book is divided into nine different sections, each of which deals with a subject that has provoked a great deal of discussion on the part of those interested in Appalachia. The articles in the first four sections serve to give the reader a general introduction to the Region. The focus of attention in these articles is upon such things as the nature of Appalachia geographically and sociologically, an examination of the historical background of present day Appalachia; demographic information relative to migration, characteristics of the population, and employment and income; and finally, a discussion of the nature of the Appalachian culture. The issues raised in this last section revolve around the question of whether it is possible to arrive at a meaningful characterization of an Appalachian culture or subculture.

The five remaining sections of the volume contain articles which provide an analysis of selected social institutions and in many cases their interrelationship. A great deal of emphasis is placed upon a critical analysis of the Region relative to the economy, both historically and at the present time. The nature of the economy and the concomitant social conditions are reflected both directly and indirectly in the other institutional structures dealing with family, education, religion, and polity.

The work concludes with an extensive bibliography of works considered relevant to a general introduction and understanding of the Region. It lists works covering such diverse areas as data sources, history, agents of socialization, political setting, coal mining and many others. A listing of Appalshop's extensive film resources with a brief description and film length is also included.

The general reader may find *Appalachia: Social Context Past and Present* a basic and useful survey of events and descriptive of traditional Appalachia. The student of social change and institutions may find our collection to be an "Appalachian variations on a theme." If we are able to satisfy both groups we have achieved our goal. In the meantime we have published a collection which we have found most useful in our own work with Appalachian studies courses.

We wish to thank those whose willingness to write original articles or to allow reprinting of their articles has made this volume possible, and to our colleagues in several states whose helpful suggestions and criticism has substantially contributed to the form and content of the collection which follows.

Bruce Ergood
Bruce E. Kuhre
Ohio University 1990

I. What Is Appalachia? Geographically and Sociologically

Illegal whiskey, feuding families, sect members, speaking in tongues, impoverished living conditions and hillbillies. These are conditions of life in, where, in New York City, Chicago, and Los Angeles. True, these conditions do exist in our major cities but one would hardly expect a responsible description of urban life to center on these conditions alone. Yet that is exactly what seems to have occurred in the mass media description of the Appalachian Region. We have been misled by the atypical *and carry in our minds a grossly distorted and highly misrepresentative picture of mountain life.*

Until very recently the historian, social scientist and even the novelist have presented the Appalachia we wanted to know. We have been given the social and fictitious results of a complex process which includes both the intra-regional socio-political interactions and, as Harry Shapiro argues in his highly regarded discussion of how social descriptions are often created to fill social needs, the interregional interactions as well. [1] But as workers for social change—including teachers—became more critical of the contemporary disparities between the traditional Southern Highland region and its immediate neighbors, they began a public dialogue. The printed pages from that dialectic process, of which this book is but one, now provide a more balanced, hence accurate, view of the region.

The many monographs which document the atypical are not to be faulted however. Those reports often represent careful social scientific work. Too often they have been taken to represent the total social description of the region while this was probably never the intent of the writers (although the same cannot always be said for the preface guest writers and book jacket journalists). The careful student will not make that mistake. The atypical should never be confused with the dominant life-style. As reviewer John Opie has noted ". . . only by truly knowing Appalachia, which is not *of the heart (emphasis added) of the American mainstream, can we know wider national values and priorities"[2]*

In this volume we present a collection of articles which call attention to both the variety of social conditions found in what has been traditionally considered Appalachia, and by focusing on some of the strengths inherent in those social conditions.[3] It is only through a more accurate

---

[1] *Appalachia On Our Mind*, Chapel Hill: University of North Carolina Press, 1978.

[2] In a review of *Apples on the Flood* in *Appalachian Journal*, Summer, 1987, p. 397.

[3] Two volumes which present the traditional "Appalachian" or mountaineer in what we consider to be a more balanced view are W. D. Weatherford and Earl C. C. Brewer, *Life and Religion in Southern Appalachia*, 1962 and Thomas R. Ford, editor, *The Southern Appalachian Region: A Survey*, 1962.

understanding of the variety of background factors which helped to shape the Region, and a knowledge of the many definitions which have been imposed on it that we can put an end to the widely held stereotypes about the Region.

In a sense we cannot define Appalachia except in geo-political terms. Travelers in the Southern Mountains early recorded distinct life-styles and social conditions, and an isolation which helped perpetuate it. Early in this century John C. Campbell, an educator and what today might be called a "social service organizer," was one of the first to clearly demark its geo-political boundaries.[4] Since that time the Region has been "rediscovered" several times, to use Robert Munn's apt term. Harry Caudill awakened many to the dormant yet very much alive issues of exploitation and the legacy of "King Coal" with his Night Comes to the Cumberlands *(1962). The Appalachian Regional Commission, too, brought a new geographic description, created by a political formula, one that included so much that had never before been considered Appalachia that a regional description has now been rendered both inaccurate and inappropriate. Raitz and Ulack's recent regional definition (included in the section) may be the last attempt at presenting the region as a geographic "place".*

Thanks then to the ARC, what was once a commonly agreed on Appalachian description has become so diffuse and heterogeneous that, except to state house and federal bureaucrats, a recognizable region no longer exists. This is probably a blessing in disguise since the earlier fixed geographic region was never the uniform social configuration it was misrepresented to be. This loss of an "easy" definition in part accounts for the decreased interest in defining the region, and opens the study of Appalachia to its more important purpose: to describe and analyze the social conditions found therein in order to both build knowledge and correct injustices.[5]

Recognizing this "latest discovery of Appalachia" we introduce the reader to the old, and to the new Region. In so doing we lay stress on the variety of social and cultural traditions found therein, even though the distribution of cultural traits generally defy the fixing of geographic limits. We present several viewpoints on the general subject, What is Appalachia, in the hope that the reader will appreciate the fact of continued change in social definition and what that means in establishing and working with fixed regional descriptions. But in the final analysis, we must leave it up to you, the reader to decide on the definition which best suits the many and varied avenues of inquiry.

---

[4] An excellent discussion of the many definitions of this geographic region is found in David S. Walls article, "On the Naming of Appalachia" in *An Appalachian Symposium*, edited by J. W. Williamson, 1977, pp. 56–76.

[5] Professor Thomas Ford has suggested that this characteristic may help explain the lessening interest in trying to define the Region. Personal correspondence.

1. WHY STUDY APPALACHIA?

Perhaps the Appalachians who in recent months have been most vocal in demanding "Appalachian Studies" are its potential teachers. This is true, just as the prime movers behind Appalachian development programs and plans have been private corporation and government developers. However, there has been a growing restlessness among mountain youth about the usual "American Studies" in Appalachia and among Appalachian workers and community people about the trickle-down "American Development Plan" for Appalachia (dig now, pay later; bulldoze now, move later; get ye children to a big city ghetto instead).

There are thus many vital reasons why people who live in Appalachia (or who personally carry it with them) might want to seize the "means of instruction" as if their own lives depended on it—to start listening to each other and to their own true history and potential.

As James Branscome, director of Appalachian Regional Commission youth leadership programs, has put it:

> There is not one Appalachian studies program in the region which could begin to rival the offerings in Far Eastern studies or astronomy. English majors seldom if ever hear a word—much less whole courses—on Appalachian literature. Art majors seldom or never study about the beauty and value and history of Appalachian crafts. Economics majors sitting right in the middle of the strip-mining country never hear about the economics of Appalachia and what stripmining and the outside corporations mean to the economy of the region and how economists might address these problems. Sociology majors spend four years in institutions in the heart of Appalachia and seldom hear a word about the different life patterns of the Appalachian people. Political science majors graduate without studying Appalachian politics and the effect or noneffect it has had on the plight of the people of the region. Education majors never get instruction on the special problems of Appalachian youth and how to meet these problems with their teaching. Medical students are taught to treat medulla tissue on the brain, but know next to nothing about how to practice in rural areas. Nursing students graduate with experience in urban and local hospitals, but few have real training in public health with field work in the region. History majors learn about English history, "American" History, Indian History, Russian History, Latin American History, and lately sometimes Black History, but not a word about Appalachian History. Home economics majors are taught to cook fine French dinners and to prepare receptions for New York society, but not a word about the dishes of the mountains or nutrition training for poor mothers. In fact, no institution of American society is more divorced from Appalachia than the higher educational system which resides within it.

WHY STUDY APPALACHIA?

1. *Hillbilly is beautiful.* There are many inherent reasons—the history, the people, the land, and even the latest national discovery and official government designation of Appalachia as a depressed area—for studying the region. We have some ideas we'd like to share with you about why study Appalachia, perhaps beyond some of the usual perceptions and designations, as follows:

There is uniquely compelling quality about being Appalachian in America that turns the hillbilly stereotype on its head. It rings out in history, landscape (what's left of it), song, dance, craft, poetry. It is profoundly touched with tragedy, pride, spirit, determination, deeply etched beauty. Behold the heart-felt feelings of outrage with which mountain people have historically resisted the ravages of capital coal, and today resist black lung, mine disasters such as Hyden and Mannington, strip mining, profit export. Behold the pride of regional "cultural nationalist" Billy Best, of the North Carolina mountains, now a professor at Berea College, Kentucky, who writes:

> I believe that the worst thing that has happened to Appalachians in the past is that we have been deprived of our identity. We have been defined by missionaries for their purposes; coal, timber, and railroad barons for their purposes; government bureaucrats for their purposes; and lately by middle-class radicals for their purposes. . . . In the final analysis, we will probably have to attempt our own liberation in our own special way, and, I think, this will involve the development of our own leadership.

2. *Appalachia is America.* As far back as 1958, the editors of the *Wall Street Journal* admitted that America was on "the wrong side of a social revolution" that was even then gripping the globe in a new vision, the quest for what historian W. A. Williams calls "a true human community based far more on social property than upon private property." For America, this global crisis is uniquely represented in Appalachia—where domestic parallels of imperialism are starkly present in the social and environmental destruction of a coal and energy "company region," and where there are perhaps fewer "middle-class" privileges and preoccupations to cloud the true causes of the crisis.

*Appalachia is a predominantly white, working, middle-American region ghetto, although Appalachian blacks and women doubly experience American ghetto-ization.

*Appalachia has been experiencing a unique domestic AID program under the Appalachian Regional Commission which, although it might soon lose its formal tenure, has been seen as a national model of federal-state relations, revenue-sharing, functional

Reprinted from *Appalachia's People Problems Alternatives: An Introductory Social Science Reader,* Vol. I, Rev. Ed. 1972, pp. 10–22. Used by permission.

public administration, promoted urbanization, and creating new state and local "development districts," all now part of President Nixon's proposed "New American Revolution."

*Appalachia is dramatically experiencing central national crises of the environment (stripping and pollution); of the fiscal system (bankrupt state and local governments and public services), and of the workplace (severe occupational health problems, particularly in coal and energy; new public employee and industrial worker rebellion and union organizing; and what *Fortune* magazine calls "anarchy" in the coal fields). Appalachia's people feel heavily the personal impact of the War in Vietnam (estimates show West Virginia has an extraordinary death and casualty rate) and are among the "first fired" in the War-recessed general economy. Its youth are caught in the turbulent generational revolt with more systematic insults, fewer material resources, and a unique regional folk patriotism.

*It can be projected that Appalachia may contain "Tomorrow's People" in terms of what a radical reconstruction of American society might entail—certain cultural and political consciousness and struggle preconditions, and prophetic actions for a truly New American Revolution as part of a global intercommunity revolution against colonialism. The "company region" aspect emerges from the fact that most basic problems can be traced at least partly to the operations of the private, primarily externally and monopoly-owned, international coal and oil-energy industry. Living in "company regions," Appalachians can perhaps come to understand better than most Americans some of the problems of Third World "underdeveloped" countries in the wake of imperialist exploitation. However, at the same time, Appalachians can perhaps be seen as experiencing the more "advanced social contradictions" of neo-capitalism in America—those special kinds of "alienation" that only living in the "mother country" of the most wealthy, centralized, socialized, and integrated, yet socially irrational, system in history can produce. This ranges from (a) economic depression and balance; to (b) the social costs of occupational health and safety and environmental destruction (stripping, air pollution, acid mine water pollution, etc.); to (c) individual low-income (unemployment and little real security against accident, illness, and old age) and public lost income and services (taxes prevented or evaded); to (d) the permeation and capturing of local and state political and social institutions such as political parties, universities, law enforcement agencies, schools, medical centers, even United Fund drives.

3. *Conventional social science and public policy approaches are severely limited as a result of the American global system crisis.* Thus, an opportunity exists for students themselves to fill a vacuum in the social sciences and in public consciousness, particularly in the case of Appalachia, as they are applied to the wavering laws of "regional development." The Appalachian experience provides a most direct way of learning systematically about both conventional and unconventional modes of social science analysis and description and of policy-planning diagnoses and prescriptions that grow out of these. This becomes a head-on question of which systems, assumptions and methods to use. The student is confronted very specifically with the limits of conventional hypotheses and methods and with questions about the relevance of much of their empirical evidence. The paradox is discovered that little of relevance has been written though "ordinary" people appear to know basic things about what are the root problems and necessary responses. This reflects a broader crisis of established social theory and of the credibility of the American university that is just beginning to be fully felt. As Cornell University economist Douglas Dowd wrote recently about his discipline with application to all the social sciences:

> It is a *system* that has produced our economics, and that system is today in deep trouble. Therefore, economics, which was developed to serve a system that was growing in strength and confidence, is also in deep trouble. The crisis in economics, as in the rest of education, will be resolved if and when, and in the same directions as we resolve our deeper social crisis. (*Liberation* magazine, November 1970, p. 35.)

Thus, sensitive students now enter not into a great hall of easily established frameworks and facts, but into a cacophony of controversy and redefinition. Alternatives are being sought to social science based on the strict "behavioral" assumptions of a once seemingly triumphant neo-capitalist economic, political, and social system in which "self-regulating" order and managed consensus were achieved. More relevant knowledge often appears to flow out of peoples' underground history of self-expression, from historian-reporters and journalists, radical pamphleteers, independent prophets and social philosophers, the people's "PhDs"—pursuers of human democracy. As John McDermott wrote a year ago, after a tour of American college campuses:

> It is no longer only the Harvards and the Berkeleys which suffer serious student unrest; some of the most interesting and militant activity occurs at the nonelite schools. In addition, scores of young men and women continue to be exiled by their elite graduate schools into a lifetime of work in the nonelite universities. The narrowest interests of these teachers and their most lofty professional and political aspirations lie in the same direction. It is to take up the task in common with their students, of rebuilding the vitality of a popular resistance culture—that is, of a culture which will "enhance the capacity of ordinary Americans to identify their social interests and to struggle successfully in their behalf." (*Nation* magazine, March 10, 1969, p. 301.)

4. *It is in your interest to be part of a regional movement to change global America basically.* Such a movement is necessary for youth/students/"new class" white collar and service workers, as well as for poor, black, Third World, and industrial working people. Analytically participating in the Appalachian experience might help you to see that such a "revolution" is in your interest, is both necessary and possible, and that your own "action-research" involvement can make a vital contribution to such change.

(a) There are special public and private "regional plans" for you on which your life does depend. You too might see yourself as an exploited regional worker being channeled and trained—most likely, to be a channeler. Your own true liberation might require that you be part of such basic democratic change.

(b) Appalachia could provide a basis for a relevant, all-generations and all-"working classes" commonwealth of communities and workplaces in cooperative struggle and a relevant counter-culture to global "colonial" hegemony. It could be part of an America and a world where revolution is happening if people know how to listen and to participate in it. Many Appalachians know from their own experiences the need for natural cultural and community unity and defense against a colonial pattern. An underlying spirit of "Hillbilly is beautiful" if made manifest could bring new confidence and unity that make "Yesterday's People" tomorrow's. Prophetic forms of struggle in workplaces, communities, youth groups, and among new class people are already developing in the region.

(c) Because of growing crises of the global colonial system, total and basic popular challenge is becoming increasingly necessary and possible in all places. In Appalachia there might be convergent awareness of the general global contradictions of the colonial system—both "underdevelopment" in terms of resource denial and "overdevelopment" in terms of the social and qualitative content of personal and community life.

(d) Not only is being part of the struggle increasingly an obvious necessity for the life and self-interests of the sensitive young person, but the most vital way for you to be a student is to be part of efforts to change things basically with growing clarity and commitment about your own interests, hypotheses, and contributions. You should be exposed to and support all peoples and classes in democratic social struggle around you, especially Third World people (blacks) and industrial workers (coal miners); but you can and should wage major struggle in your own arenas of life, work and thought—the university, institutions, professions, "white collar" workplaces. That can and should begin to happen now as a student; indeed, an important way to be part of changing things basically is to see yourself as a continuous learner. As historian Staughton Lynd has charged:

> The intellectual's first responsibility is, as Noan Chomsky says, "to insist upon the truth, . . ." But what truth we discover will be affected by the lives we lead . . . to hope that we can understandingly interpret matters of which we have no first-hand knowledge, things utterly unproved upon the pulses . . . is intellectual hubris . . . I think the times no longer permit this indulgence, and ask us, at the very least, to venture into the arena where political parties and workingmen, and young people do their things, seeking to clarify that experience which becomes ours as well, speaking truth to power from the vantage-point of that process of struggle. (New Univ. Conference Newsletter, Chicago, May 24, 1968, pp. 5–6.)

WHAT IS APPALACHIA?

There is, perhaps, no single definition of Appalachia which will satisfy everyone; geographers, economists, sociologists, political scientists, administrators and politicians all have their own definitions for their own purposes. Most of these definitions do share a common characteristic, however, in that they are externally imposed by social scientist "observers" of the region or by policymakers and program developers whose job it has become to "administer" the region.

Perhaps the most commonly used definition is the one used by the Appalachian Regional Commission, a federal-state agency which administers a multi-billion dollar economic development program under the 1965 Appalachian Redevelopment Act. ARC defines the region as parts of twelve states plus all of West Virginia; for ARC Appalachia stretches from a few counties in northern Mississippi to southern New York state.

The region can be defined in terms of its physical geographic features, its economic relationship to metropolitan American, its demographic characteristics, and the homogeneous nature of its coal-based economy. It can also be defined in terms of certain shared indexes of low incomes, poor health, inadequate housing and substandard education. The region has frequently been defined as a subculture within the broader context of mainstream America.

Whether or not any of these standard definitions are acceptable or real to people who live in Appalachia is open to question. But in the pages to follow we have presented some of them for your consideration.

THE REGION DESCRIBED[1] . . .

The Appalachian region is characterized by certain unifying features which are important considerations in any program of regional development. These fea-

1. From Maryland Department of Economic Development. *The Appalachian Region, A Preliminary Analysis of Economic and Population Trends in an Eleven State Problem Area,* May, 1960.

tures are shared to a greater or lesser extent by virtually all parts of the Region.

1. The Appalachian Mountain chain is the single most distinctive feature of the Region. The mountainous topography creates conditions of difficult accessibility, limits the amount of level, buildable land, and increases flood dangers. The general north-south orientation of the Appalachian mountains tends to make for difficult east-west access across the mountains and divides the Region into a number of north-south valleys.

2. A considerable portion of the nation's bituminous coal mining and virtually all of its anthracite resources are found in the Appalachian Region. Drastic reductions in the employment level of the Region's mines have left many communities and areas of the Region in serious economic straits. This has been equally true of both hard and soft coal areas.

3. The agriculture of the Appalachian Region, consisting largely of intensive cultivation of steep slopes and narrow valleys, has nearly always been at a disadvantage as compared to the more level, richer soil areas of the nation. The relatively high population per acre of cropland, the short growing season, the lack of level land and the loss of topsoil through erosion of cutover hillsides are some of the factors which have resulted in a continuing decline in the Region's agricultural economy. Most Appalachian farms are small, undercapitalized operations yielding low incomes to their owners.

4. Another unifying feature of the Appalachian Region lies in the characteristics of its inhabitants. To a significant degree, the Region's people are of Anglo-Saxon extraction, descendants of many generations of native-born Americans.

5. A fifth unifying feature of the Appalachian Region is its chronic economic and population problems. In most of the Region's 260 counties incomes are relatively low and unemployment and underemployment rates are high. Serious labor surpluses have led to a high rate of out-migration of persons seeking economic opportunities elsewhere in the nation.

Differentiation within the Region

It must be recognized that all of the Appalachian area does not share in these unifying features to the same degree. Among the more significant differences within the Region the following can be mentioned:

1. The topography of the Region varies greatly from place to place. In some areas large, reasonably level and accessible land is found, while in others steep hillsides and narrow, flood-prone valleys present awesome difficulties to either urban or rural development.

2. The economies of component parts of the Region vary considerably. Coal mining, which characterizes much of the area, is wholly absent in some places. The agriculture of the Region also differs considerably throughout its length and breadth, in response to variations in climate, soils and topography.

3. The urban centers of the Region vary in the nature and strength of their economies and differ sharply from the rural areas. Manufacturing activities and services and trades employment are concentrated in the urban centers, which are generally much better off in terms of job opportunities, income levels, living conditions and levels of educational attainment than the rural areas and mining settlements.

4. The Southern Appalachians can generally be differentiated from the Northern Appalachians by virtue of a greater dependence on agriculture and by the fact that the problems of the southern part of the Region tend to characterize a great portion of the southeastern United States. In contrast, the Northern Appalachians tend to differ sharply from the more level lands not far distant to the east and west which contain most of the nation's largest cities.

These brief statements on the nature of the Appalachian Region indicate that the Region has sufficient identity to justify its consideration as an interstate area with distinctive unifying features.

3 APPALACHIAS: 5,000,000 YEARS OLD

. . . Not only are there three regional divisions of Appalachia, but three topographical ones as well. The main range, sometimes called the Older Appalachians, extends from Maine to Georgia under a variety of names. Actually, it is not a single range but a chain of mountain groups known by various names, such as the Green Mountains in Vermont and the Unaka Mountains in Tennessee. West of the older Appalachians, a newer range extends from southern New York to Alabama. This spur range boasts a variety of local names such as the Cumberland Mountains in Kentucky, Sand Mountain in Alabama, and Lookout Mountain in Georgia. However, it is usually known as the Allegheny Mountains. The Alleghenies are bolstered by hundreds of miles of plateau areas. A third, lesser known portion of the Appalachians consists of the many buttressing cross ranges which stand at right angles to the main ranges, particularly in the southern mountains. One of these cross ranges, the Black Mountains of North Carolina, contains the tallest peak east of the Rockies, Mt. Mitchell (6,684 ft).

. . . . .

But how were the Appalachians formed? Though they are impressive in height and length, the Appalachians are only the eroded remains of what geologists consider to be the oldest and perhaps once the tallest range in North America. The ancient Appalachian chain lay in an unbroken line from Newfoundland to Alabama, and perhaps extended even farther southwest into Oklahoma. The main backbone now extends only from Maine to Georgia, with a small extension into Alabama. Still, traces of the northern range are found in Newfoundland, Prince Edward Island, New Brunswick, and Nova Scotia. . . .

One would hardly expect mountains along the Mississippi-Alabama border, but in northeastern Mississippi and northwestern Alabama, scattered amid cotton lands, are the last of the southern Appalachians. They may be seen as 1,000- to 1,500-foot ridges along U.S. Highway 43 near Hamilton, Alabama, and as Mississippi's highest "mountain," Mt. Woodall (806 ft), south of U.S Highway 72 near Iuka.

These ancient Appalachians were the product of what some writers have termed the Appalachian Revolution, a great upheaval that thrust the mountains from the sea some 500 million years ago. Even then, the Appalachians were old. Geologists have discovered that one layer of Appalachian rock, known as the Ocoee series, is considered to be 600 million years old—so old that the rocks have no trace of fossils.

After millions of years of compressing layers of mud, sand, gravel, plant and animal life into rock form, the mountains themselves were formed by a series of violent motions. These upheavals were of various types.

New England's mountain ranges, such as the White Mountains, were shaped from molten rock which seeped from a crack in the earth's crust. Instead of reaching the surface, this rock formed large blisters directly beneath the surface. Through thousands of years, the outer layer eroded to expose the dome-shaped inner layer, which meantime had hardened into granite. Thus were produced such domed, granite peaks as Mt. Washington in New Hampshire's White Mountain National Forest.

The southern Appalachians were created in a somewhat different fashion. During this same revolution, the stress placed on large quantities of subterranean rock caused the earth to buckle, much as one might cause a loose rug to buckle into parallel ridges by pushing on one end. This parallel feature explains many things, such as the immense width of the Blue Ridge and Unaka ranges in North Carolina and Tennessee. From Black Mountain in North Carolina's Mount Mitchell State Park, or from Roan Mountain in Tennessee's Cherokee National Forest, the seemingly endless wave of ridges may be viewed.

The newer Appalachians, called the Alleghenies, form the western wall of the Great Appalachian Valley, which extends from the St. Lawrence Valley in Canada to Alabama. Most of the valley is coursed by U.S. Highway 11 and Interstate 81. The Great Appalachian Valley was once the floor of a great shallow sea. This sea covered the land west of the main Appalachian range. Over millions of years, huge, deep layers of rock were gradually formed. The sea then receded, the earth buckled, and the Alleghenies were the result. The best example of the Alleghenies' parallel nature is the outlying Allegheny ranges west of Harrisburg, Pennsylvania. Here the beautiful Juniata River flashes repeatedly through parallel mountains to join the Susquehanna near Duncannon.

2. HARRY CAUDILL IN THE CUMBERLANDS*

Wendell Berry

On July 15, 1965, a friend then living in Hazard gave me my first look at the strip mines of eastern Kentucky. The strip miners at that time were less "regulated" than they are now, and under the auspices of the notorious "broad form deed" they frequently mined without compensation to the surface owners. The result was wreckage on an unprecedented scale: the "overburden" was simply pushed off the coal seam onto the mountainside to go wherever gravity would take it; houses with their families still in them were carried down the slopes by landslides, wells polluted by acid from the exposed coal seams, streams poisoned and choked with rubble; and the whole establishment of the people on the land was treated simply as so much more "overburden." There could have been no better demonstration of the motives and the moral character of the business of energy.

That night we attended a meeting of the Appalachian Group to Save the Land and the People in the courthouse at Hindman. The occasion of the meeting was the arrest the day before of Dan Gibson, a respected farmer and lay preacher who had gone onto the mountain with a gun and turned back the strip miners' bulldozers. He was acting on behalf of a younger member of his family then in the service; he was past eighty years old, he said, and had nothing to lose by dying. Thirteen state police, a sheriff, and two deputies had been sent to rescue the thus-threatened free enterprise system, and a shooting was averted only by the intervention of several members of the Group, who persuaded the police to allow *them* to take the old man before the local magistrate. The magistrate, an employee of the mining company, placed Mr. Gibson under a bond of $2,000. He did not stay long in jail, but the whole affair was so clearly an outrage as to give a vivid sense of injury, identity, and purpose to the assemblage in the Knott County courtroom the following night.

The meeting was called to order, the events of the preceding day were described by various witnesses, and then Harry Caudill was called upon and came to the front of the room. I had read *Night Comes to the Cumberlands* perhaps two years before, and was full of respect for it, but until then I had never seen its author. I do not expect to forget him as I saw and heard him that night. He spoke with the eloquence of resolute intelligence and with the moral passion of a lawyer who understood and venerated the traditions of justice.

They are destroying our land under our very households, he said. They are going to drive us out as the white men drove out the Indians. And they have prepared no reservation to send us to. The law has been viciously used against us, and it must be changed. We have been made fools of for sixty years, and now at last maybe we are going to do something about it. And he spoke of "the gleeful yahoos who are destroying the world, and the mindless oafs who abet them." It was a statement in the great tradition that includes the Declaration of Independence and the Bill of Rights. And it was a statement, moreover, to which Harry Caudill had dedicated his life; he had outlined it fully in *Night Comes to the Cumberlands,* and in the coming years he would elaborate it in other books, in many speeches, articles, and public letters. The statement—the indictment, the plea for justice—has, I think, remained essentially the same, but the *case* has been relentlessly enlarged by the gathering of evidence, by thought, reading, and research. For twenty years his has been

an able public voice recalling us to what, after all, we claim as "our" principles.

In that same twenty years, hundreds of spokesmen in the same cause have come and gone, hundreds of protests have flared and burned out, hundreds of "concerned" officials have made wages or made hay and gone on. Harry Caudill is one of the few who have endured. As recently as January 5, 1981, a long letter to the editor of the *Louisville Courier-Journal* set his argument yet again before the people of his native state. A few quotations from it will suggest the quality both of the argument and of the man.

First, the indictment:

> The state taxes coal in the ground at the rate of 1/10 cent per $100 of value—a mere 315th part of the rate levied on houses and farms. The severance tax is 4½ percent as compared to rates ranging from 12½ percent to 30 percent in the western fields, and most of it returns to the coalfields to build and repair coal roads. The coal industry enjoys low taxes, public esteem, political power, and immense profits. The people generally carry all the burdens growing out of ruined roads, silted rivers and lakes, polluted water, inadequate housing, poor schools, and low health standards.

And then he calls the roll of the beneficiaries of this curious welfare state:

> . . . Kentucky River Coal, Occidental Oil, Gulf Oil, Ford Motor, Neufinanze AG (of Lichtenstein), KyCoGo Corporation, Stearns Coal and Lumber, U.S. Steel, Royal Dutch Shell, National Steel, Koppers Corporation, Columbia Gas, Equitable Gas, Big Sandy Corporation, Tennessee Valley Authority, Harvard University, Southern Railway, Diamond Shamrock, International Harvester, Howell Oil Company. . . .

And he concludes with the obvious question:

> Why should Kentucky be the nation's leading coal-producing state if all we get out of it is crippled and dead miners, silted streams and lakes, torn up roads, uprooted forests and holes in the ground?

Harry Caudill's frustration has been that this question has never been satisfactorily answered. His triumph is that he has kept asking it, has kept making the same good sense, invoking the same principles, measuring by the same high standards year after year. The passion of his intelligence has been to know what he is talking about, to condescend to no occasion, to indulge in none of the easy pangs of "disillusionment." What has kept him going?

Not, I think, his sense of justice or his capacity for moral outrage—or not only those things. A sense of justice, though essential, grows pale and cynical when it stands too long alone in the face of overpowering injustice. And moral outrage, by itself, finally turns intelligence into rant. To explain the endurance of Harry Caudill, it is necessary to look deeper than his principles.

It is a fact, and an understandable one, I think, that many would-be defenders of the land and people of eastern Kentucky have felt both to be extremely uncongenial. The region is, after all, part of a "national sacrifice area," and has been so considered and so treated by governments and corporations for well over half a century. The marks of the ruin of both land and people are everywhere evident, are inescapable, and to anyone at all disposed to regret them they tend to be depressing. The first article on strip mining I ever read began by saying how delighted the writer had been to leave Hazard, Kentucky, where he had served a protracted journalistic term of, I believe, one week. Harry Caudill, by contrast, can write: "I had the good fortune to be born in 1922 in Letcher County, Kentucky." He did not come there, then, to serve justice. He has been there because he has belonged there; the land and people for whom he has spoken are his own. Because he got his law degree and went home with it, his mind has never made the expedient separation of knowledge from value that has enabled so much industrial pillage, but has known with feeling and so has served with devotion—a possibility long disregarded by modern educators, who believe despite overwhelming evidence to the contrary that education alone, "objective knowledge," can produce beneficent results.

Another thing. As anybody knows who ever got within ear-shot of this man, Harry Caudill is a superb storyteller. A lecture, public or private, on the industrialization of the coal fields is apt to be followed by a string of wonderful tales, each reminding him of another, all riding on a current of exuberant delight and laughter. And this telling and the accompanying laughter do not come, I think, as escape or relief from the oppressive realities of the lecture, but come from the same life, the same long concentration on the same region and people.

And so this book, *The Mountain, the Miner, and the Lord,* which would be welcome enough by itself, is particularly welcome because it is a significant part, until now missing from the printed record, of Harry Caudill's statement about his region. It is not "something different," but belongs innately to the twenty years' work that began with *Night Comes to the Cumberlands* and is a part of its explanation.

In the preface, valuable in itself as a remarkably compact, incisive historical essay on his region, Mr. Caudill tells how these stories came to him: "I practiced law within a mile of my birthplace for twenty-eight years and saw and talked to a daily procession of people . . . I tried to afford them a good listener." Or that is the way most of the stories came; elsewhere in the book he makes us aware that some of them, or some

parts of them, were learned in the years of his childhood and youth. It is evident in places (and is nearly everywhere supposable) that the stories were not heard all together, as they stand here, but were collected in scraps from various other rememberers and tellers and pieced together over the years like quilts.

"These tales," he writes, "are intended to show how the cultural layers were formed and a people fashioned." And they do that, or help to do it. They show again and again, for example, how the parade of national history and power has impinged on the region: the frontier, the Civil War and its various successors, Prohibition and the continuing federal excitement over moonshine, corporations, unions, welfare, et cetera. They show also the influence of cultural inheritance, topography, geography, poor farming, and the oppressions of coal.

But they also do—and are—more than that. They spring, as perhaps the best stories always have, from the ancient fascination with human extremity, from the tendency, apparently native to us all, to remember and tell and tell again the extravagances of human vice and virtue, comedy and tragedy. This book contains a number of examples of the sort of outrageous wisdom that passes endlessly through the talk of rural communities:

One woman ain't hardly enough fer a man if he is any account a-tall.

The worst thing that can happen to a man is to need a pistol and not have it!

There are tales of justice, public and private, heartwarming or hair-raising. There are the inevitable chapters of the region's history of violence. Best of all, to me, is "The Straight Shooter," a political biography of one Fess Whitaker: I don't know how it could be better told.

This book, I fear, is doomed to be classed by those who live by such classification as "folk" material. But they had better be careful. It is, for one thing, very much a lawyer's book. Harry Caudill is master of an art of storytelling that I think could rightly be called "legal," for it has been practiced by country lawyers for many generations. Its distinction and distinctive humor lie in the understanding of the tendency of legal rhetoric to overpower its occasions:

Thereupon he towered above Collins like a high priest at some holy rite and poured forth a generous libation of buttermilk upon the judge's pate, shoulders, and other parts.

For another thing, these stories—though they have to do with people who by a certain destructive condescension have been called "folk"—are the native properties of an able, cultivated, accomplished, powerful, and decent mind.

3. REGIONAL DEFINITIONS

Karl B. Raitz
Richard Ulack

A basic task in regional geography is delimitation of appropriate boundaries. This essential step in regional study is difficult and often not fully acceptable to all critics. That areas can be carved into parcels as many different ways as there are persons to do the carving is not surprising, since there are an almost infinite number of criteria upon which to base a regionalization. The criteria used, of course, depend upon the purpose of the regionalization. Thus, the boundary lines we create might enclose areas that are somewhat homogeneous in terms of culture, physiography, climate, agriculture, or planning jurisdiction. In short, a region is a mental construct: an area that has been bounded in accordance with the goals of those delimiting the region. In a sense, regions do not have truth—they have only utility.

Some areas seem particularly enigmatic and therefore difficult to delimit. In the United States, for example, the Midwest and the South are two such regions. Joseph Brownell and Wilbur Zelinsky have discussed the difficulties in delimiting these two regions and have provided us with solutions. Zelinsky offered the "settlement landscape" (the aggregate pattern of all structures and assemblages of structures in which people house their activities) as a way to bound the South.[1] The solution given by Brownell for the Midwest was based upon responses from postmasters as to whether or not they considered themselves to be located in that rather nebulous region.[2] Clearly, the use of other criteria would have provided very differently bounded regions.

Another major American region for which different regionalizations exist is Appalachia. Our ultimate goal in this chapter is to delimit an Appalachian region that will best suit our purposes. There should be some natural basis for doing this, and in that context it seems appropriate that we begin by discussing the various regionalizations of Appalachia that have been introduced by others.

DEFINING APPALACHIA AS A REGION

Many characteristics could be used to set Appalachia off as a separate region in America. The mere mention of the word *Appalachia* conjures up a variety of impressions depending upon one's perspective or purpose: Appalachia has been variously described as a region of mountains, coal mining, poverty, unique culture, tourism, welfarism, isolation, and subsistence agriculture. Any of these characteristics, or others, could be used to define the Appalachian region.

Physical Geographic Definitions

Some of the earliest regionalizations of the United States were based upon one physical feature or a combination of several features. Natural vegetation, climatic patterns, and especially physiography have been used to delimit physical, or natural, regions. That Appalachia is often defined on the basis of its physiography is not at all surprising, given that it has a high relief relative to the areas surrounding it. Indeed, this high relief has been an effective barrier to historic migrations and according to many writers has been responsible in part for some of the region's less desirable characteristics like "isolation, poverty, and a retarded civilization."[3]

There is evidence to suggest that the Appalachians were first named in the sixteenth century by Spanish explorers (possibly even by Hernando De Soto, one of the first to explore the southern part of the Appalachians) who, so the theory goes, took the name from an Indian tribe (or village), the Apalachee of northern Florida. From that time until the Civil War, *Appalachia* was simply a term for the physiographic mountain system.[4] It was not until the latter part of the nineteenth century that Appalachia began to be viewed as a distinctive social, cultural, and economic region.

Physical geographers—more specifically, geomorphologists—have long been interested in the question of regionalization, and they have developed a number of physiographic regions for the United States. All such physical regionalizations include an Appalachian region. The first of these regional delimitations came from "the geographer Arnold Guyot in 1861 [who] is credited with establishing scientific and popular usage for the entire mountain range."[5] Guyot used the term *Allegheny* on his map (although his paper is entitled "On the Appalachian Mountain System") and discussed the east-to-west division of the system into parallel mountain ranges.[6] He also proposed dividing the system north to south into three subregions. The northern one included that area from the Gaspé Peninsula in southeastern Quebec Province (geologically, the Appalachian system extends from Newfoundland through Oklahoma to Texas) south to the Adirondack Mountains of New York; the middle section extended from the Mohawk River south to the New River; and the southern section included the area from the New River south to Alabama. The entire area covered a north-south distance of some 1,400 mi (2,252.6 km).

A segment of a 1719 map by John Senex, titled "A New Map of the English Empire in America," shows the "Apalitean Mountains" extending from north Florida to the Pennsylvania border. The "Large Savana" in western Carolina may be a section of the Great Valley that was reported to have been cleared by Indian burning (From the American Geographical Society Collection of the University of Wisconsin–Milwaukee.)

Another major effort to define the region was that of John Wesley Powell in 1895.[7] His was the first attempt to divide the entire United States into physiographic regions. Powell delimited three separate regions that, taken together, are generally considered today to be physiographic Appalachia. From east to west Powell named the three subregions the Piedmont Plateaus, the Appalachian Ranges, and the Allegheny Plateaus. Together they encompassed an area that extends southwestward from the Hudson and Mohawk valleys in New York to northern Georgia and Alabama.

To geographers perhaps the best-known physical regionalization of the United States is that by Nevin Fenneman. Originally discussed in 1913 at the annual meeting of the Association of American Geographers, the culmination of Fenneman's regional work came with the publication of his *Physiography of Western United States* in 1931 and *Physiography of Eastern United States* in 1938.[8] Basically, Fenneman's geomorphic regions of the United States are defined by existing differences in topography and elevation as affected by the three control factors of structure, process, and stage.

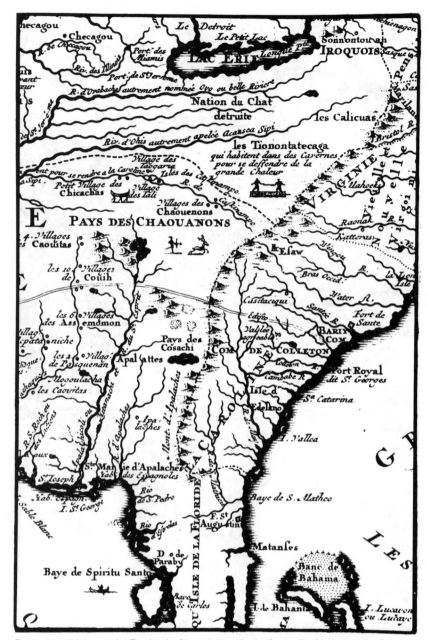

Part of a 1732 map by Zacharie Chatelain, titled "Carte De La Nouvelle France . . ." shows the "Mont. d'Apalaches" in Northern Florida reaching north to "Mariland." River names and place-names north of Ste. Marie d'Apalaches on Florida's Gulf Coast may have been derived from local Indians. (From the American Geographical Society Collection of the University of Wisconsin–Milwaukee.)

Simply stated this means "that given a certain geologic framework [type of rock], the topographic condition or expression of an area is largely determined by its geomorphic history."[9] Fennamen included eight major physiographic divisions in the United States; one of them he called the Appalachian Highlands. This region includes six provinces and extends from the Gulf Coastal Plain to the St. Lawrence River (including the Adirondacks and New England) and from the Atlantic Coastal Plain west to the Central Lowland (Figure 3.1). The Appalachian Highlands takes its name from its most prominent features, but it is by no means all high altitude. Indeed, subdivisions of the region differ greatly and each of these has considerable internal diversity as well. As Fenneman stated, "So far as this extensive region has unity, it is found in the results of repeated

12

Detail from "A Map of the British Empire in America . . ." by Henry Popple, 1733. The "Apalachean Mountains" are shown in western North Carolina and extend north into Pennsylvania. The Potomac River rises west of the mountains, and the "Hohio River" apparently originates just south of Lake Erie. (From the American Geographical Collection of the University of Wisconsin–Milwaukee.)

uplifts, involving for the most part greater altitude and stronger relief than that of adjacent regions."[10] Although Fenneman included six provinces within the Appalachian Highlands, our discussion of physiographic Appalachia will be limited to four of these: the Piedmont, the Blue Ridge, the Ridge and Valley, and the Appalachian Plateaus provinces. These provinces conform more closely with other regional delimitations of Appalachia, including our own (see the last section of this chapter).

Other physiographic, or natural, regions of the United States that have been introduced by geologists and physical geographers correspond very closely to the regional delimitation devised by Fenneman. Two such examples include the physiographic provinces of Atwood and the natural regions discussed by Hunt.[11]

13

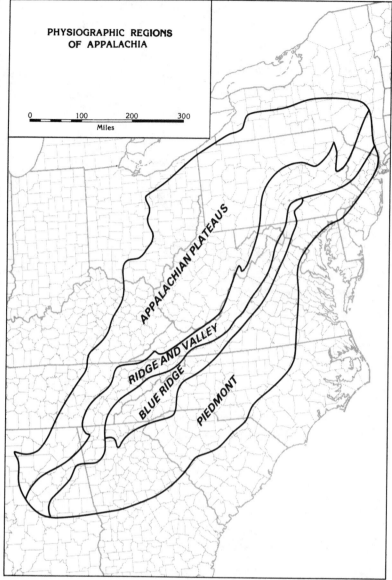

Figure 3.1. After Nevin M. Fenneman, *Physiography of Eastern United States* (New York: McGraw-Hill, 1938), Plates I, II, and III.

Our review of twelve regional textbooks on North America and the United States published between 1934 and 1979 revealed how geographers have delimited the Appalachian region for heuristic purposes. Virtually all of the works include a map showing the physiographic regions of the United States, and in each case Appalachia appears as a distinct, major physiographic region. Generally, these physiographic regions closely follow the Fenneman definition and include the Piedmont, the Blue Ridge, the Ridge and Valley, and Plateau provinces as the major subregions.

There is much less agreement among these twelve regional texts as to the way in which the United States is carved into the geographic regions that are ultimately discussed. Only six of the twelve books included Appalachia as a major region for discussion and devoted at least one entire chapter to the region. Of these six, four texts apparently delimited Appalachia principally on the basis of physiographic criteria, although it is evident that other, nonphysical criteria were considered as well.[12] A fifth delimited Appalachia and the other regions of the United States based on "the total environment both physical and cultural."[13] It was not possible to determine Appalachian regional boundaries for the sixth text because no map of the regions discussed was included. The regionalization in this case

14

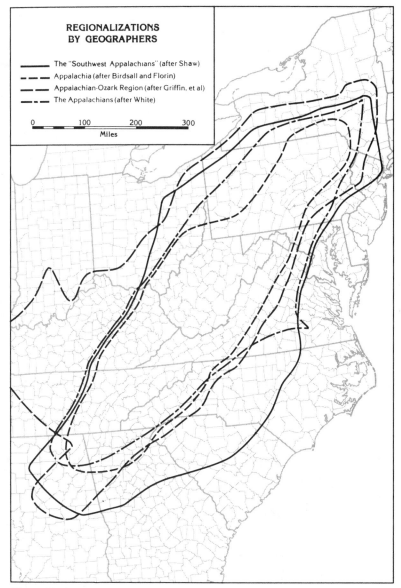

Figure 3.2

was based on the author's selection of whatever criteria he felt best expressed the "personality" of a region. Thus "cultural origins, climate, space relationships, and livelihood are likely to be involved and are given coherence by the writer's perception that they compose an entity."[14]

A composite map comparison of four of the five different Appalachian regions delimited in the texts clearly demonstrates significant variations in boundary definition, even among the three that bound a physiographic region (Figure 3.2).[15] The region used for comparison here was the smallest area that was labeled "Appalachia." The boundary used by Birdsall and Florin excludes the Pittsburgh metropolitan area, which is included in most other regional delimitations of

northern Appalachia. The eastern boundary of this regionalization generally lies farther west than any of the other three and clearly excluded the Piedmont area from Appalachia. The exclusion of both Pittsburgh and the Piedmont suggests that urban and topographic criteria were both important in determining the regional boundaries. The Piedmont, as we shall see in the next chapter, has generally lower average elevations than the three other physiographic provinces. Two of the other regionalizations shown also exclude most of the Piedmont Province.

The northern boundaries of the four Appalachian regions shown generally correspond and in all four cases lie south and west of New York's Hudson and Mohawk valleys. Even though physiographic Appalachia extends north of this area into Canada, geographic definitions of Appalachia that consider nonphysical criteria in drawing regional boundaries rarely extend north of this valley area. At the opposite end of the region the southern boundaries also show some degree of correspondence. Where they do not, the reason is much the same as for disagreement on the eastern boundary: the question of whether or not to include the Piedmont Province. The gently rolling nature of much of the Piedmont cities—Atlanta, Columbia (South Carolina), and Charlotte—are experiencing dynamic growth and change. According to some definitions, such socioeconomic characteristics differentiate this part of physiographic Appalachia from its other provinces.

Except that the Ozark-Ouachita Uplands of southern Missouri, northern Arkansas, and eastern Oklahoma are included within the boundary used by Griffin et al., the western boundaries of the Appalachian region correspond the most closely. In fact, three boundaries virtually overlap in Tennessee and Kentucky. These boundaries clearly are based on the sharp structural differences between physiographic provinces along the "knob" belt and Highland Rim that form the western edge of the Appalachian Plateaus Province.

The regionalization by Griffin, the "Appalachian-Ozark Region," maintains contiguity between the Appalachians and the Ozarks, and thus the western boundary differs from the other three regionalizations. The idea that the Ozarks and Ouachitas should be included as part of the Appalachian physiographic region has some merit, because structurally the two areas are very similar. The Ozark-Ouachita Uplands are also similar to the Appalachians in terms of various nonphysical criteria, and there is both precedent and justification for grouping the two areas together. As there seems to be little physiographic justification, however, for including the area between the Appalachians and the Ozarks within the regional boundaries, apparently the authors wanted to maintain contiguity. The physiographic area included, known as the Interior Low Plateaus, is a gently rolling upland with elevations generally less than 1,000 ft (304 m), considerably less than even the Upland Piedmont. It includes Nashville, Tennessee, and Louisville, Kentucky.

It is clear, then, that the Appalachian region can be delimited on the basis of physiographic (structural) characteristics: The mountains and associated geologic structures extend southwestward from Newfoundland in the north and disappear under the Gulf Coastal Plain to reappear in the Ouachita Mountains of Arkansas and as far west as the marathon Basin region in western Texas. For sociocultural reasons, however, geographic definitions of the region have generally excluded that part of physiographic Appalachia north and east of the Hudson and Mohawk valleys. Generally, the Plateaus,

the Ridge and Valley, the Blue Ridge, and at least a portion of the Piedmont (the upland section) are included within the region's boundaries by geographers. Although the Ozark-Ouachita area is sometimes included we will not consider this area to be a part of Appalachia.

Sociocultural Regionalizations

Appalachia was not recognized as a distinct sociocultural region until the latter part of the nineteenth century. During the 1870s the region began to be popularized through what has been termed the local color movement.[16] Many romantic and colorful accounts of distinctive people and lifeways in the area appeared as novels and as popular-magazine articles. Authors used adjectives such as *isolated, quaint, independent, self-sufficient, violent, poor, simple,* and *strong* to describe the region's residents. It was a time when writers and other visitors from outside the region began to give Appalachia its distinctive reputation. Supplanting the color writers were preachers and teachers who came to Appalachia from elsewhere with their various missions intended to contribute to the health and education of the mountain people.

Gradually, more precise sociocultural definitions of the Appalachian region began to appear in the academic literature. In most cases the early studies that included regionalizations dealt only with the southern portion of physiographic Appalachia, the mountainous areas of West Virginia, Virginia, Kentucky, Tennessee, North Carolina, Georgia, and Alabama—the same areas that the local color writers had found quaint and interesting. According to David Walls, "The first person to give a precise geographic definition to the southern Appalachians as a cultural region was William G. Frost."[17] In 1894 Frost and a former student identified 194 counties in Maryland, West Virginia, Virginia, Kentucky, Tennessee, North Carolina, South Carolina, Georgia, and Alabama that were included in what was later called the Mountain Region of the South, or Appalachian America.[18]

Certainly the most widely recognized of the early sociocultural delimitations of the southern Appalachia region is that of John C. Campbell, which appeared in *The Southern Highlander and His Homeland* in 1921.[19] Campbell called the region the Southern Highlands and included 254 counties in the Blue Ridge, the Allegheny-Cumberland Plateaus, and the Greater Appalachian Valley of 9 states (Figure 3.3). Interestingly, Campbell used historic and political criteria, as well as physical, to arrive at his boundary:

> The lines by which the Southern Highlands are defined are not chosen arbitrarily. They correspond for the most part with boundaries of natural divisions; on the east with the face of the Blue Ridge, which defines the western margin of the Piedmont Plateau, on the south with the

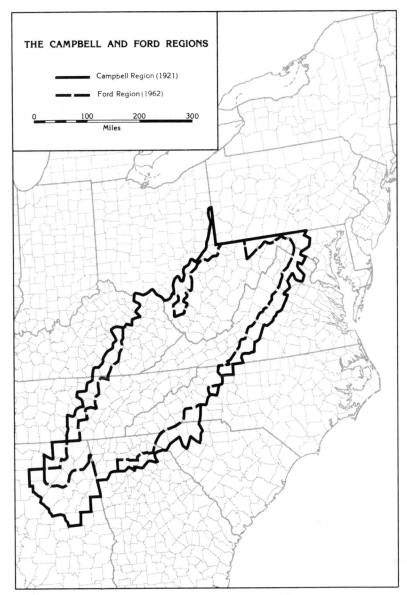

Figure 3.3

upper limits of the Coastal Plain, and on the west with the western escarpment of the Allegheny-Cumberland Plateau. The northern line [known also as the Mason and Dixon Line], in part purely political, was in its beginning a surveyor's line to determine a boundary dispute of long standing, growing out of the claims of [William] Penn and Lord Baltimore.[20]

The next major nongovernmental attempt to delimit boundaries for Appalachia was funded by the Ford Foundation. The results of this study, which reported on the population, economic, political, educational, religious, and folk characteristics of southern Appalachia, were published in 1962 under the editorship of sociologist Thomas R. Ford.[21] Titled *The Southern Appalachian Region: A Survey,* the study bounded a

region that included 190 counties in 7 states (Figure 3.3). Unlike the Campbell region, the Ford region did not include any counties in Maryland or South Carolina. The eastern, western, and southern boundaries of the Ford region generally move inward from the region defined by Campbell by one row of counties. For both regions, of course, county boundary lines yield the precise regional definition. The Ford definition was unique in that it made "use of the new concept of state economic areas [SEA], developed jointly in 1950 by the Bureau of the Census and the U.S. Department of Agriculture"[22] (a state economic area is a grouping of counties whose social and economic characteristics are similar). Some twenty-seven State Economic Areas were included in the Ford region; nineteen of these were

17

rural-farm or rural-nonfarm SEAs, and eight were metropolitan areas. Thus, the Ford region includes the major cities of Huntington, Charleston, Roanoke, Asheville, Knoxville, and Chattanooga. Notably, it excludes Birmingham, Alabama, which is a part of the Appalachian region in virtually all other regional delimitations. The Appalachian region presented in the Ford study is the smallest of the various regional delimitations and according to one author, it "reduced the region to a heartland of Appalachia."[23] This "small" region is more than 600 mi (965.4 km) long and almost 250 mi (402.3 km) across at its widest point and encompasses an area of some 80,000 sq mi (207,200 sq km).

To our knowledge, no cultural geographers or other cultural regionalists have explicitly delimited an Appalachian culture region. Most cultural regionalists, however, do recognize a distinctive "upland" culture subregion, at least in the southeastern portion of the United States. Such a subregion is usually a part of the larger South and is given the name Upland South, Upper South, or sometimes Yeoman South, to distinguish it from the Lowland, or Plantation, South. One of the best-known cultural regionalizations of the United States is that by geographer Wilbur Zelinsky, which appeared in *The Cultural Geography of the United States.*[24] In his regional delimitation, Zelinsky identified a major subregion of the South that he called the Upland South, which "comprises the Southern Appalachians, the Upper Appalachian Piedmont, the Cumberland and other low interior plateaus and the Ozarks and Ouachitas. . . . Within the Upland South, the Ozark segment might legitimately be detached from the Appalachian."[25] Zelinsky's culture areas are defined as "a naively perceived segment of the time-space continuum distinguished from others on the basis of genuine differences in cultural systems."[26] The two characteristics that differentiate this type of region from others are the great variety of ways in which it manifests itself on the landscape (e.g., house type, religion, dialect, dietary preferences) and a self-consciousness on the part of the participants.

Northern physiographic Appalachia (south and west of the Hudson and Mohawk valleys) is included in the two major culture regions that were called the Midland and the Middle West by Zelinsky. The pertinent subregions, for our purposes, are portions of the "Pennsylvania region" and the "New York region" in the former and the extreme eastern segment of the "Lower Middle West" in the latter. The modern cultural imprint of northern Appalachia, as well as southern Appalachia (the Upland South) is largely European in origin and can be traced to two "nuclear nodes along the Atlantic Seaboard: . . . the Midland, based in the Delaware and

Susquehanna valleys; and Chesapeake Bay."[27] Philadelphia and Tidewater Virginia were thus the important origins for Appalachian settlers beginning about 1700.

A second cultural regionalization of the United States was that by Raymond Gastil, who acknowledged the valuable assistance of Zelinsky's work. Gastil's regions were defined "primarily by variations in the cultures of the peoples that dominated the first settlement . . . , and secondarily by variations in the cultures of the peoples that dominated later settlements, as well as cultural traits developed subsequently."[28] Basically, physiographic Appalachia south of the Hudson and Mohawk valleys is a part of three of Gastil's major U.S. cultural divisions: New England, Pennsylvania, and South. Unlike Zelinsky's regional delimitation, Gastil included New York State in cultural New England (rather than with Pennsylvania) and, interesting, specifically labeled the southernmost "district" (the Southern Tier counties of New York) in this region "Appalachian." Two districts in Pennsylvania, called simply Western and Central Pennsylvania, also correspond to physiographic Appalachia. In the South, Gastil included a "Mountain" (Appalachian and Ozark areas) district and an "Upland" district. The latter includes most of the Piedmont and the interior plateaus. In short, the regions identified are similar to those posited by Zelinsky.

The cultural regionalizations of both Zelinsky and Gastil attempt to define areas through a consideration of the totality of cultural artifacts and behavior. Other regionalizations exist that attempt to define geographic regions in the United States on the basis of fewer cultural characteristics. An example of one such study is that by Kevin Phillips, who identified regions through an examination of historic voting-behavior patterns.[29] Though the precise boundaries are not shown, Phillips's Appalachia (also referred to as the Southern Mountains) corresponds rather closely to the Ford region. The Ozarks of Arkansas, eastern Oklahoma, and southern Missouri are also included. The Southern Highlands, according to Phillips, have long been politically and culturally different from the rest of the South. Characteristics that differentiate the Southern Highlands from neighboring areas include a predominantly Scotch-Irish pioneer settlement, relative isolation (and thus little sociocultural cross fertilization), and politics based on tradition. Political independence became apparent during the Civil War when "most of the highlands opposed secession, favored the Union and thereafter voted for the Republican Party. For all practical purposes, the mountain counties were devoid of slaves. . . ."[30] This is an important part of the "tradition" upon which contemporary voting behavior is based.

It is apparent that although most cultural regionalists do not recognize the Appalachia upland areas as a primary region, a distinct "upland" culture is recognized as an important subregion within the South and a portion of the Northeast. The contemporary cultural characteristics of these upland areas can be traced to the Scotch-Irish, English, and German immigrants who came to the uplands from Philadelphia and Tidewater Virginia. Other, more recent immigrant groups who have added to this cultural milieu, and thus to the region's diversity, include East Europeans who populated the Pennsylvania coal-mining and steel-manufacturing areas and blacks who populated the Piedmont areas of Georgia, Alabama, and the Carolinas.

Governmental Regionalization

The first attempt at geographical delimitation of Appalachia by a federal agency (and the first recognition of the region as a social problem area) is found in a 1935 publication by the U.S. Department of Agriculture in which F. J. Marschner defined the region on the basis of its physiography, soil, and climate characteristics.[31] The three major divisions identified were the Blue Ridge Mountains (the eastern division), the Valley and Ridge (the central division), and the Appalachian Plateau (the western division). This region excludes the states of northern Appalachia. In the northern part of the Marschner region, the 3 westernmost counties of Maryland are included; however, the counties of West Virginia that border the Ohio River are excluded. At the southern extreme, the region includes much of northern Alabama to the Mississippi border; both Tuscaloosa and Birmingham are included as a part of Appalachia. In total, Marschner's Appalachia includes 236 counties in 9 states that are divided among sixteen physiographic subregions.[32]

Another attempt on the part of the federal government to delimit an Appalachian region appeared in a 1940 publication by the Works Progress Administration that identified thirty-four "rural cultural regions" in the United States.[33] One of these regions was called Appalachia and included 154 counties in Kentucky, Ohio, West Virginia, Virginia, Tennessee, North Carolina, and Georgia. A second region, called Allegheny, consisted of 125 counties in West Virginia, Pennsylvania, Ohio, Maryland, and Virginia. The basis for regionalization in this study was "type of farming as a point of departure and placed on top of farming pattern such factors as population increase, standard of living, land value, tenancy, and race."[34]

The most recent attempt at regional delimitation of Appalachia by a government agency occurred in 1965 when Public Law 89-4 (the Appalachian Regional Development Act of 1965) established the Appalachian Regional Commission (ARC) and defined, in Section 403, the Appalachian region. As originally defined, the region consisted of 360 counties in 11 states from Pennsylvania to Alabama. Section 403 also included a provision whereby contiguous New York counties could participate, and in August 1965 the commission invited New York to join. In 1967, Public Law 90-103 amended the 1965 legislation and officially added 37 counties to the Appalachian Regional Commission's region. The inclusion of 20 counties in Mississippi, 14 counties in New York, Lamar and Pickens counties in Alabama, and Cannon County, Tennessee, brought the number of ARC-region states to 13 and the total number of counties to the present 397.

The boundaries of the original ARC region were based on both natural environmental and socioeconomic characteristics. The report of the original commission set up by President John F. Kennedy in 1963 stated that the region is "a mountain land boldly upthrust between the prosperous Eastern seaboard and the industrial Middle West. . . . Below its surface lie some of the Nation's richest mineral deposits including the seams which have provided almost two-thirds of the Nation's coal supply. The region receives an annual rainfall substantially above the national average. More than three-fifths of the land is forested. Its mountains offer some of the most beautiful landscapes in eastern America. . . ."[35] In addition to rough terrain and other aspects of the region's physical geography, the president's commission discussed several socioeconomic measures that presented Appalachia as "a region apart." Characteristics of the region included low income, high unemployment, lack of urbanization, deficits in education, and deficits in living standards as indicated by such measures as retail sales, savings, housing conditions, and public assistance. One study that examined how counties included in the ARC region compared with the stated criteria for inclusion observed that the original region was well conceived.[36] However well conceived this original region, subsequent additions tend to be viewed as "political logrolling."[37] In short, "ARC's boundaries . . . increased in response to increasing political pressure as federal money for Appalachia became available."[38]

The Appalachian Regional Commission region was originally divided into four subregions because it was recognized that although the region was basically homogeneous (uniform), there were identifiable subregions, each with distinctive income, population, and employment characteristics and thus with distinctive development needs. These four subregions were called Northern, Central, Southern, and Highlands Appalachia. In 1974, the counties of the Highlands subregion were merged into the other subregions, so that the ARC presently recognizes three subregions (Figure 3.4).[39] The Northern subregion includes 143 counties and is

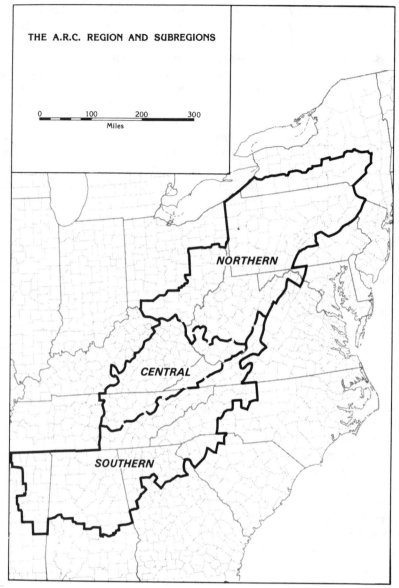

Figure 3.4

described as an old industrial-based economy undergoing modernization. Central Appalachia is characterized as the poorest of the subregions, with coal as its primary resource. It includes 85 counties in eastern Kentucky, southern West Virginia, extreme western Virginia, and a portion of northeastern Tennessee. The 169 counties of the Southern Appalachian subregion have traditionally been agrarian based but are in transition to an urban and industrial economy. In this way the ARC recognized diversity in the region it defined, with the idea that such recognition would facilitate socioeconomic development. Even so, one critic observed, "ARC Appalachia is too large and too heterogeneous physically, economically, and politically to be dealt with effectively, even if sufficient money were available."[40]

The passage of the Appalachian Regional Development Act of 1965 came about after the recognition of Appalachia as a region socioeconomically apart from most of the rest of America. *Appalachia,* the 1964 report by the President's Appalachian Regional Commission (chaired by Franklin D. Roosevelt, Jr.), stated "rural Appalachia lags behind rural America; urban Appalachia lags behind urban America; and metropolitan Appalachia lags behind metropolitan America."[41] As we have seen, the history of the federal government's awareness of Appalachia (or some portion of it) as a social problem area can be traced to the 1930s and to programs instituted by agencies such as the U.S. Department of Agriculture, the Works Progress Administration, and the Tennessee Valley Authority. However, it was not until the 1960s and the establishment of the Appalachian Regional Commission by President John F. Kennedy that the federal government developed a program that was focused on the entire region. The overall goal was region-wide development, so that the social and economic gap between Appalachia and the rest of America might be narrowed. The extent to which the commission has realized this goal is examined in Chapter 10. Certainly, however, we can state that one lasting impact of the Appalachian Regional Commission has been to bring about a general public awareness of the Appalachia region that did not exist before the 1960s. Although the commission appears to be in its final days as a government agency because of the Reagan administration's economic cutbacks, the region it has defined most likely will remain *the* Appalachian regional delimitation to the majority of the public who are cognizant that an Appalachian region exists.

Cognitive Appalachia

Yet another way in which Appalachia has been delimited is through studies in regional perception. Utilizing responses from college students, a study by Kevin Cox and Georgia Zannaras developed a technique that derived perceptions of states from a ranking of state similarities.[42] Analysis of the results revealed that the student sample identified an Appalachian region centered on West Virginia, Kentucky, Tennessee, and Virginia.

In a comprehensive search for America's vernacular regions, another study by Ruth Hale found very limited recognition of the term "Appalachia" among the respondents (in this case individuals such as the county agent, postmaster, and newspaper editor were the respondents). In only two southeastern Ohio counties, Monroe and Noble, did a significant proportion of the sample state that Appalachia was the name for the region in which they lived.[43] The vernacular names given for the region in many other counties in Appalachia were primarily physiographic, such as Mountain, Piedmont, Shenandoah Valley, and Endless Mountains.

Based upon our own analysis of nearly 2,400 student respondents from sixty-three colleges and universities in and adjacent to physiographic Appalachia, we were able to construct an isopleth map that shows the percentage of students who agreed that a certain area was included in the Appalachian region (Figure 3.5). The overall regional pattern has the typical linear orientation along a northeast-southwest axis. The 10 percent cognitive-agreement line was arbitrarily selected as the minimum threshold for establishing a regional boundary. This means, of course, that at least 240 students included the area within this line as a part of the Appalachian region as they perceived it. The 80 percent agreement line is the cognitive core of the Appalachian region and corresponds to Mercer County, West Virginia. The cognitive Appalachian region differs substantially from the ARC region in that a significant portion of the student sample, about 40 percent, included only West Virginia, western Maryland, eastern Kentucky, western Virginia, western North Carolina, extreme northern Georgia, the western tip of South Carolina, a narrow strip in southeast Ohio, and a small portion of southwest Pennsylvania within Appalachia.[44]

By disaggregating the total respondent group we were able to examine how three subgroups that we identified, termed insiders, cognitive outsiders, and residential outsiders, perceived the Appalachian regional boundaries. The first group, *insiders,* included all those who perceived themselves as living in Appalachia. *Cognitive outsiders,* on the other hand, were those respondents who resided in physiographic Appalachia but stated they were not Appalachian. *Residential outsiders* were those who lived outside the region and stated they were not from Appalachia. Examination of the regional delimitations of each of the three subgroups reveals interesting differences (Figure 3.6). We also queried respondents as to what characteristics they associated with Appalachia (poverty and mountains were cited most often) and found, generally, that the insiders associated more positive characteristics with the region, whereas cognitive outsiders were more prone to be negative, and residential outsiders tended to fall somewhere in between.[45]

A NEW APPALACHIAN REGION

Recently Whisnant observed that "Appalachia's boundaries have been drawn so many times that it is futile to look for a 'correct' definition of the region."[46] We have seen that there has been a variety of attempts to delimit the region. Each attempt has had a somewhat different purpose, and therefore varying criteria have been utilized. Notwithstanding Whisnant's observation and the number of Appalachian regionalizations that already exist, we offer another expanded

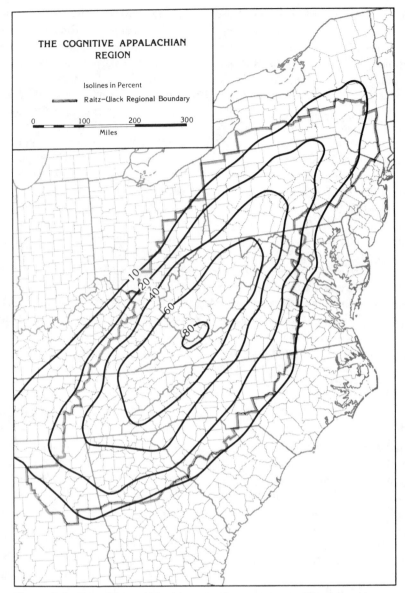

THE COGNITIVE APPALACHIAN
REGION

Isolines in Percent
Raitz–Ulack Regional Boundary

0   100   200   300
Miles

Figure 3.5. From Richard Ulack and Karl Raitz, "Appalachia: A Comparison of the Cognitive and Appalachian Regional Commission Regions." Reprinted with permission from the *Southeastern Geographer* 21, no. 1 (May 1981), p. 45.

version—the Raitz-Ulack region (Figure 3.7). Even though the principal criteria used for our regional delimitation are physiographic boundaries, political (county) boundaries, and contiguity, we are cognizant of the other important criteria that could be used. Indeed, cultural and socioeconomic characteristics were considered in our regional delimitation. For example, the Shenandoah Valley of Virginia (which is excluded from the ARC region) was included not only because it is a part of the physiographic Ridge and Valley Province but also because of its great cultural significance

to the entire Appalachian region. It was the valley into and through which many descendants of Piedmont, Plateau, and Blue Ridge settlers migrated in the late eighteenth century. Indeed, contemporary cultural characteristics of all of Appalachia are intertwined closely with the post-1700 history of the Shenandoah Valley. We have carefully considered all the major attempts at regionalizing Appalachia in drawing our final regional boundary. We do not, of course, suggest this is the "best" Appalachia. We do believe, however, that it is well suited for the purposes of this volume and perhaps for other purposes as well.

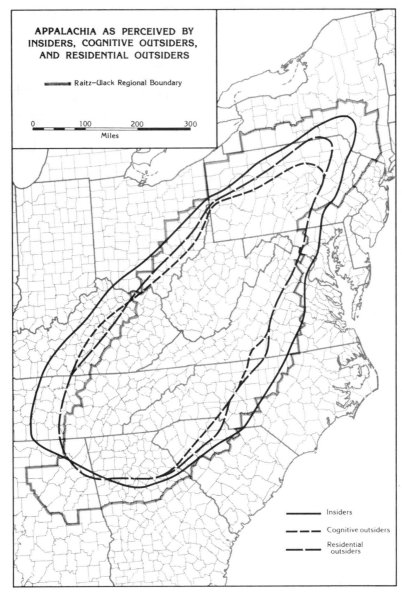

Figure 3.6. After Richard Ulack and Karl Raitz, "Appala-chia," *Environment and Behavior* 14 (November 1982), pp. 742, 743, 744.

The region includes 445 counties and thus is the largest nonphysiographic Appalachian region yet defined.[47] The next-largest such region, that of the ARC, includes 397 counties (Table 3.1). The southern boundary of our region corresponds rather closely to that of the Fenneman region and therefore excludes the 20 counties of Mississippi and 17 counties in central and western Alabama that are a part of the ARC region. We have attempted to keep our regional boundary within that of the Fenneman region; therefore, the western boundary of our region also excludes many of the ARC counties. For example, Clermont County, Ohio (part of the Cincinnati metropolitan area), Green County, Kentucky, and Macon County, Tennessee, are part of the ARC region but excluded from this region. The northern boundary corresponds rather closely with the ARC region and is south and west of the Hudson and Mohawk valleys. We follow more closely the Fenneman boundary than does the ARC and thereby exclude Erie County, Pennsylvania, and Chautauqua County, New York; however, the counties of New York's Catskill Mountains are included. The greatest difference between our proposed region and that of the ARC is in the eastern boundary.

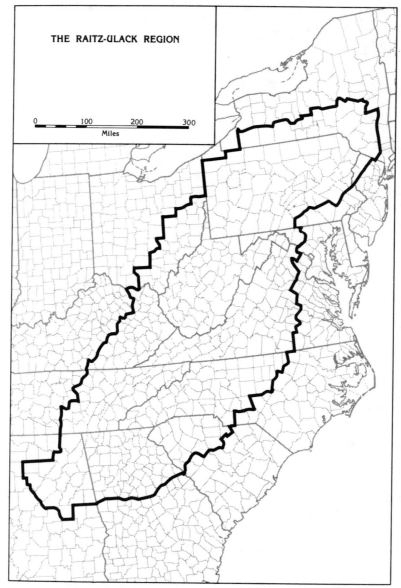

Figure 3.7. The Raitz-Ulack regional boundary shown here is delineated on maps throughout the book.

The ARC excludes most of the Piedmont counties, whereas the majority of the counties in the Upland Piedmont are included here. Our eastern boundary corresponds closely to Fenneman's differentiation of the Piedmont and Coastal Plain along the Fall Line. We have drawn our boundary approximately one row of counties to the west of the Fall Line. Additionally, we have excluded the Lowland Piedmont counties and also those counties in the metropolitan orbits of Baltimore, Washington, D.C., Philadelphia, and New York. We did not include the mountains of Arkansas and Missouri because that area, physiographically, is not contiguous

to the rest of Appalachia. We used county lines for our final boundary because they facilitate the use of census data.

The Raitz-Ulack region includes a 1980 population of some 26.5 million, or 11.7 percent of the United States total (Table 3.1). Its area is 213,217 sq mi (552,232 sq km), or 6.0 percent of that of the United States. It is an area that produces a large share of some of the nation's primary commodities, including coal, tobacco, lumber, and corn. It is also a region with important metropolitan areas that have been, and are becoming, centers of major industrial activity. Pittsburgh,

24

TABLE 3.1

The Appalachian Region: Number of Counties, Area and Population by State, 1980.

State	Redefined Appalachian Region			A.R.C. Region		
	Number of Counties	Area (sq. mi.)	Population (000s)	Number of Counties	Area (sq. mi.)	Population (000s)
Alabama	18	12,650	1,508.4	35	24,600	2,427.0
Georgia	59	17,836	3,087.4	35	10,804	1,103.9
Kentucky	36	12,868	848.7	49	16,942	1,077.1
Maryland	4	2,211	334.4	3	1,546	220.1
Mississippi	0	0	0	20	10,313	482.7
New Jersey	2	889	200.6	0	0	0
New York	17	14,370	1,514.9	14	11,806	1,083.3
North Carolina	52	22,950	3,513.2	29	11,884	1,217.7
Ohio	23	11,090	1,063.5	28	13,732	1,262.6
Pennsylvania	58	38,710	7,160.7	52	36,626	5,995.1
South Carolina	16	9,602	1,204.9	6	3,964	791.6
Tennessee	44	17,511	2,002.1	50	19,238	2,073.6
Virginia	61	28,450	2,060.1	21	9,398	549.9
West Virginia	55	24,080	1,949.6	55	24,080	1,949.6
TOTAL	445	213,217	26,448.5	397	194,933	20,234.2

Atlanta, Birmingham, Charleston, Knoxville, Harrisburg, Chattanooga, Charlotte, and Greenville are included among the region's more important cities. As has already been suggested, it is also a region with a varied physiography, a varied past, and a varied culture. In short, it is a region of great diversity, and this characteristic needs to be recognized if we hope to understand the region's past, present, and future.

NOTES

1. Wilbur Zelinsky, "Where the South Begins: The Northern Limit of the Cis-Appalachian South in Terms of Settlement Landscape," *Social Forces* 30 (1951), pp. 172–178.

2. Joseph W. Brownell, "The Cultural Midwest," *Journal of Geography* 59 (1960), pp. 81–85.

3. Ellen Churchill Semple, *American History and Its Geographic Conditions* (New York: Houghton, Mifflin, and Co., 1903), p. 71.

4. David S. Walls, "On the Naming of Appalachia," in J. W. Williamson, ed., *An Appalachian Symposium: Essays Written in Honor of Cratis D. Williams* (Boone, N.C.: Appalachian State University Press, 1977), pp. 56–76.

5. Ibid., p. 66.

6. Arnold Guyot, "On the Appalachian Mountain System," *American Journal of Science and Arts* 31 (1861), pp. 157–187.

7. John Wesley Powell, *Physiographic Regions of the United States* (New York: American Book Co., 1895).

8. Nevin M. Fenneman, "Physiographic Boundaries Within the United States," *Annals,* Association of American Geographers, 4 (1914), pp. 84–134; Nevin M. Fenneman, *Physiography of Western United States* (New York: McGraw-Hill Book Co., 1931); and Nevin M. Fenneman, *Physiography of Eastern United States* (New York: McGraw-Hill Book Co., 1938).

9. William D. Thornbury, *Regional Geomorphology of the United States* (New York: John Wiley & Sons, 1965), p. 9.

10. Fenneman, 1938, op. cit. (footnote 8), p. 121.

11. W. W. Atwood, *The Physiographic Provinces of North America* (Boston: Ginn & Co., 1940); and Charles B. Hunt, *Natural Regions of the United States and Canada* (San Francisco: W. H. Freeman and Co., 1974).

12. Paul F. Griffin et al., *Anglo-America: A Systematic and Regional Geography* (Palo Alto, Ca.: Fearon Publishers, 1968), pp. 226–227; Earl B. Shaw, *Anglo-America: A Regional Geography* (New York: John Wiley & Sons, 1959), p. 147; J. Russell Smith and M. Ogden Phillips, *North America: Its People and the Resources, Development and Prospects of the Continent as the Home of Man* (New York: Harcourt, Brace and Co., 1940), pp. 188–189; and C. Langdon White et al., *Regional Geography of Anglo-America,* 5th ed. (Englewood Cliffs, N.J.: Prentice-Hall, 1979), p. 98.

13. Stephen S. Birdsall and John W. Florin, *Regional Landscapes of the United States and Canada* (New York: John Wiley & Sons, 1978), p. 3.

14. J. H. Paterson, *North America: A Geography of the United States and Canada* (New York: Oxford University Press, 1975), p. 173.

15. The region defined by Smith and Phillips, op. cit. (footnote 12), is not included in Figure 1.2. Their text discussed four "regions" of Appalachia, each in a separate chapter: the Northern Piedmont, the Appalachian Ridge and Valley, the Appalachian Plateau and Upper Ohio Valley, and the Blue Ridge and the Great Smoky Mountains.

16. To appreciate the flavor of these writings, the reader is urged to sample the following examples: Will Wallace Harney, "A Strange Land and Peculiar People," *Lippincott's Magazine* 12 (1873), pp. 429–438; Rebecca H. Davis, "The Rose of Carolina," *Scribner's Monthly* 8 (1874), pp. 723–726; Edward King, "The Great South: Southern Mountain Rambles: In Tennessee, Georgia, and South Carolina," *Scribner's Monthly* 8 (1874), pp. 5–33; David H. Strother, "The Mountains," *Harper's Magazine* 51 (1875), pp. 475–485; Mary N. Murfree, "The Romance of Sunrise Rock," *Atlantic Monthly* 46 (1880), pp. 775–786; Mary N. Murfree, *In the Tennessee Mountains*

(Boston: Houghton, Mifflin, and Co., 1884); J. M. Davies, "Scotch-Irish Stock in the Central South," *The Church at Home and Abroad* 2 (1887), pp. 128–129; Charles D. Warner, *On Horseback: A Tour through Virginia, North Carolina and Tennessee* (Boston: Houghton, Mifflin, and Co., 1888); and Joseph E. Roy, *Americans of the Midland Mountains* (New York: American Missionary Association, 1891).

17. Walls, op. cit. (footnote 4), p. 67. Frost was president of Kentucky's Berea College from 1892 to 1920. Berea College was established in the mid-nineteenth century as an abolitionist and multiracial institution. The college, located on the western edge of the Appalachian Plateau, has a long and active history with the Appalachian region and its people.

18. William G. Frost, *For the Mountains: An Autobiography* (New York: Revell, 1937).

19. John C. Campbell, *The Southern Highlander and His Homeland* (Lexington: University Press of Kentucky, 1969; originally published by the Russell Sage Foundation in 1921).

20. Ibid., pp. 11–12.

21. Thomas R. Ford, ed., *The Southern Appalachian Region: A Survey* (Lexington: University of Kentucky Press, 1962).

22. Ibid. p. 3.

23. Bruce Ergood, "Toward a Definition of Appalachia," in Bruce Ergood and Bruce E. Kuhre, eds., *Appalachia: Social Context Past and Present* (Dubuque, Ia.: Kendall/Hunt Publishing Co., 1976), p. 34.

24, Wilbur Zelinsky, *The Cultural Geography of the United States* (Englewood Cliffs, N.J.: Prentice-Hall, 1973), pp. 118–199.

25. Ibid., pp. 123–124.

26. Ibid., p. 112.

27. Ibid., p. 83.

28. Raymond D. Gastil, *Cultural Regions of the United States* (Seattle: University of Washington Press, 1975), p. 26.

29. Kevin R. Phillips, *The Emerging Republican Majority* (Garden City, N.Y.: Doubleday & Co., 1970).

30. Ibid., p. 253.

31. U.S. Department of Agriculture (U.S.D.A.), *Economic and Social Problems and Conditions of the Southern Appalachians,* Misc. Pub. no. 205 (Washington, D.C.: U.S. Dept. of Agriculture, 1935), p. 11.

32. The Appalachian region discussed in other portions of the U.S.D.A. report (footnote 31) includes 205 counties in 6 southern states with a total area of over 85,000 sq mi (220,150 sq km).

33. Arthur R. Mangus, *Rural Regions of the United States* (Washington, D.C.: Government Printing Office, 1940), pp. 3–5.

34. Ibid., p. 2.

35. President's Appalachian Regional Commission (P.A.R.C.), *Appalachia* (Washington, D.C.: Government Printing Office, 1964), p. xv.

36. Ann DeWitt Watts, "Does the Appalachian Regional Commission really Represent a Region?" *Southeastern Geographer* 18 (1978), pp. 19–36.

37. Walls, op. cit. (footnote 4), p. 71.

38. David E. Whisnant, *Modernizing the Mountaineer: People, Power, and Planning in Appalachia* (New York: Burt Franklin & Co., 1980), p. 134.

39. Appalachian Regional Commission, "The New Appalachian Subregions and Their Development Strategies," *Appalachia* 8 (1974), pp. 10–27.

40. Whisnant, op. cit. (footnote 38).

41. P.A.R.C., op. cit. (footnote 35), p. xviii.

42. Kevin R. Cox and Georgia Zannaras, "Designative Perceptions of Macrospaces: Concepts, a Methodology, and Applications," in Roger M. Downs and David Stea. eds., *Image and Environment: Cognitive Mapping and Spatial Behavior* (Chicago: Aldine, 1973), pp. 162–178.

43. Ruth F. Hale, "A Map of Vernacular Regions in America." (Ph.D. dissertation, Department of Geography, University of Minnesota, 1971).

44. The topic of congruence between ARC Appalachia and cognitive Appalachia is examined more thoroughly in Richard Ulack and Karl Raitz, "Appalachia: A Comparison of the Cognitive and Appalachian Regional Commission Regions," *Southeastern Geographer* 21 (1981), pp. 40–53.

45. See Richard Ulack and Karl Raitz, "Perceptions of Appalachia," *Environment and Behavior* 14 (1982), pp. 725–752; and Karl B. Raitz and Richard Ulack, "Cognitive Maps of Appalachia," *Geographical Review* 71 (1981), pp. 201–213.

46. Whisnant, op. cit. (footnote 38), p. 134.

47. In addition to the 445 counties there are twenty independent cities in Virginia. All data for these cities are included with the data for the county in which the city is located. In general, statements in the text refer to the Raitz-Ulack regional definition unless it is specifically stated otherwise.

4. FINDING OURSELVES: RECLAIMING THE APPALACHIAN PAST

Ronald D. Eller

The late Cratis Williams once described his life as

. . . an odyssey from the happy innocence of a secure childhood in the cultural and social context of an Appalachian valley through troubling adventures of doubt, challenges to selfhood, denial, shame, and rejection, to understanding, acceptance, and affirmation of self as an Appalachian person who embraces his culture, searches out its history, and is proud of his identity as an Appalachian without feeling that he is therefore something less as an American for being an Appalachian.[1]

For many regional writers who came to Appalachian Studies through their own personal struggle with cultural identity, Williams' odyssey both exemplified a common journey and promised hope for the future. Working at a time when institutions were much less responsive to ethnicity and regionalism, he early recognized the importance of regional pride and self-confidence, and he helped to blaze the way for the rediscovery of Appalachian history and the reshaping of our communities.

We learn from the history of democratic social movements that a people's sense of identity, their understanding of the past, helps to shape their ability to act in the present, to seize control of their own lives. We make decisions in the present partly as a result of how we perceive others before us have acted—based

Reprinted from *The Cratis Williams Symposium Proceedings,* Appalachian Consortium Press, pp. 35–46. Used by permission.

upon what we believe the past to have been. Psychologists and political activists alike have recognized the importance of historical memory to self-determination and to the recognition of alternative paths for individual and collective change. Almost every group—be it class, gender, region, race, or nationality—that has sought freedom from oppression has endeavored to rewrite the story of its past, to redefine the collective memory as a basis for building a new community. What we believe we have been affects what we think we can become.

John Shelton Reed, the sociologist of the South, has argued that regionalism has much more to do with identification with a place than with location in a place. Members of a regional community, he believes, share more than geographic space; they share a common identity, a common history that binds them together as a people.[2] Robert Bellah and his associates have recently defined "real community" as being historically constituted of a "community of memory" that does not forget its past. "In order not to forget that past," Bellah writes, "a community is involved in retelling its story, its constitutive narrative, and in so doing, it offers examples of the men and women who have embodied and exemplified the meaning of the community."[3]

Over the last two decades those of us in Appalachian Studies have been redefining our identity as a people, reclaiming our history as a region, and thus reconstituting ourselves as a community. Twenty years ago there was little which would qualify as a scholarly history of Appalachia. Much of what was written about the region was based on long-standing stereotypes and misconceptions, and the static image of Appalachia had led national historians to neglect the region's past and to relegate the mountaineer to historical obscurity.

I remember the response of a senior professor at the University of North Carolina at Chapel Hill when I first entered graduate school to study Appalachian history. He approached me at one of those departmental functions where the senior faculty meet and size up the new crop of graduate students and after some preliminary small talk, popped the important question "What do you plan to study here, Mr. Eller?" When I responded that I wanted to study the history of my people, the history of Appalachia, he paused, put his hand to his chin and remarked "Uh, yes, that's nice. I've seen a copy of the *Foxfire Book*." He then abruptly turned and walked away to find a student with a more relevant, dynamic, and scholarly interest.

Today Appalachian history is more widely accepted as a legitimate field of study, and a new vision of the region's role in the American experience has appeared. Almost every college and university in the region offers a course in Appalachian history, and many public school teachers incorporate local or regional history into their classrooms. It is now possible to pursue graduate study

with a focus on Appalachian history at several universities, and at least five university presses compete for publications in the field. Research in the history of Appalachia appears regularly in national and regional journals and at professional conferences and symposiums. And while no comprehensive history of the region has yet appeared, the literature is substantial, growing, and academically respectable.

Like that of other minority groups seeking to reclaim their cultural identity, the new history of Appalachia has followed a distinct pattern of growth—moving first from the study of external images of the region (history as perceived by others); to the recollections of mountain folk themselves (history as perceived by participants), then to the analysis of the social, institutional, political and economic factors that have shaped life in the region, and finally to a more complex analysis of the cultural and structural factors influencing the mountaineer's position in the society and the world.

Much of the early research, for example, focused on the attitudes about Appalachia and Appalachians which had emerged over the years in the national consciousness. Cratis Williams' landmark dissertation and, later, Henry Shapiro's book, *Appalachia On Our Mind*, helped to document the origins of the "idea of Appalachia" in the years following the Civil War and to launch a decade of research countering the historical myths and stereotypes about the region.[4] The idea that Appalachia was a "strange land inhabited by a peculiar people . . . a region in but somehow not of America" had developed, Shapiro noted, as a by-product of the local-color literature before the turn of the century and has affected the response of mainstream America to the region down to the present time.

Although Shapiro came to doubt the existence of Appalachia in any reality other than the national mind, other scholars moved beyond the static image to portray mountain people as actors in their own history. With the popularity of oral history in the 1970's came a flood of first-hand accounts demonstrating change and resistance in the mountains and portraying a history that was more diverse, more dynamic and more American. *Our Appalachia*, edited by Lois Shakelford and Bill Weinberg was but one of many efforts to interpret Appalachian history from the bottom up and to provide voice to a people long excluded from the historical stage.[5]

Many of the new accounts were rooted in a political perspective which sought to explain or discover the causes of the social and economic problems which plague the region today. Rejecting the "culture of poverty" explanation which had characterized the earlier literature on Appalachia, these scholars looked to the political and economic history of the region for insight into current conditions. Harry Caudill first suggested a "colonial model" of the region's political-economy in *Night Comes To The Cumberlands* and a host of other scholars have refined and expanded that idea through studies of elites, labor, education, politics, and economic change.[6] Gordon McKinney documented the transformation of the mountain Republican party from a local kinship base to an increasingly business dominated political structure.[7] John Alexander Williams described the ascendancy of the captains of industry in northern West Virginia, and John Gaventa analyzed the impact of the London-based American Company Limited in Bell County, Kentucky.[8] My own work chronicled the arrival of industry throughout the region and the destruction to the traditional way of life that ensued.[9] David Whisnant examined the effects of federal planning in the mountains and the "politics of culture" surrounding the missionary movement, settlement schools, and folk festivals.[10] David Corbin, John Hevener, and others have described the social and political conditions in the coal camps which gave rise to unionization and labor struggle.[11]

Each of these accounts was energized by a politically based inquiry which asked new questions and sought new answers about the region's past while at the same time basing research on rigorous scholarship, primary resources, and systematic analysis. In the process these scholars have helped to change not only the substance of regional research but the level of that research as well. Colorful accounts of feuding, moonshining, and bear hunting have given way to hard-hitting analyses of power relationships, economic growth, social structure, institutional change, ideology, and extra-regional linkages. Appalachian historians are now borrowing heavily from the work of social scientists and from other historians examining the South, women's history, black studies, labor history, Latin-America and other areas of the world. Not only is this broader-based scholarship helping to transform our vision of Appalachians from that of victims to actors, but it is expanding our view of the region's historical setting. More confident of who we are, we are increasingly able to put aside our defensiveness, our regional chauvinism, and to engage in self-criticism and self-analysis. Not all of the exploiters, we have learned, were outsiders.

Indeed, the growing ability of Appalachian scholars to place the region in a broader context and to analyze the mountain community from interdisciplinary and comparative perspectives bodes well for the future of regional studies. For the first time we may be able to ask questions of the region which are not born of defensiveness or the need to explain, and we can approach the region's history holistically, opening up untold areas of rich research. The initial compulsion to explain, to defend, and to create a revisionist base for a new history has left much untold and unexplored, and we must begin to address these needs.

For example, our earlier concentration on the industrialization of the region has left us with only a limited understanding of pre-industrial life in Appalachia. We assume that the advent of industrial capitalism altered the economy, the political system, and social relationships in the region, but we know very little about the nature of those relationships. How did the pre-industrial economy of the mountains compare with other pre-commercial farm economies in New England, the mid-west, and other areas of the United States? How did it relate to the evolving plantation economy in the rest of the South? To what degree was it typical of the herding-based economy that characterized other "plain folk" communities of the upper South? What kind of life did it provide for its adherents? Could it have survived growing population pressures and the expansion of industrial capitalism and commercial agriculture?[12]

Appalachian historians would do well to apply to pre-industrial mountain communities the methodologies which other historians have recently used in the study of colonial New England and the antebellum South. Demographic analysis of census records, wills, deeds, birth and death certificates, marriage records, and other local documents should tell us much about land ownership, family, wealth, agriculture, and other aspects of traditional community life. Just how widespread was land ownership, for example, and how was land passed from one generation to another? How did the pre-industrial system of "family labor" operate, and who received the most benefits? At what point did the arrival of a cash economy alter established patterns of family work? What role did out-migration to the west play in sustaining or threatening the traditional economy and social system?

What were the origins of early mountain settlers and did they bring with them a predisposition toward a particular kind of economy and social system as they migrated into the region? The ancestry of the white mountaineer has been a long debated topic, but we have had little detailed research connecting social and economic patterns in the region with those of particular localities in the old world. The excellent work by Curtis Wood and Tyler Blethen on the Scotch-Irish in Appalachia moves us in this direction, as does the recent research on the "old South" by Forest McDonald, Grady McWhiney, John Solomon Otto and others.[13]

McWhiney and McDonald have been leading forces behind a new evaluation of the "plain folk" of the old South, and they argue that there may have existed two separate agricultural worlds in the South, each stemming from the different origins of its English speaking settlers. While those who came to dominate the low country and to develop a plantation, row-crop economy were predominantly from southern and eastern England, many of the "plain folk" of the backcountry, they argue, were from the high country (Scotland, Ireland, Wales, Cornwall, and the north and west of England), and they brought with them a forest-based type of herding economy.

John Otto has traced the migration of these Celtic people across the woodlands of the upper South from Appalachia to the Ozarks, and describes them as preferring a "labor-saving and capital-saving agriculture," one based upon livestock production for cash and self-sufficiency in foodstuffs. Since they traced their origins to Celtic Britain and not to England, he suggests, they preferred a woodlands environment and practiced a non-row-crop, capital-poor form of agriculture which emphasized leisure time and family ties and substituted land for capital and labor. If these historians are correct, we must look once again at the cultural origins of mountain people in order to explain their reluctance to modernize and accumulate capital, their opposition to slavery, and their resistance to the capitalist work ethic in the twentieth century. Perhaps cultural and political explanations of Appalachian development may yet find common ground in an analysis which considers both cultural heritage and political conditions as part of the same model.

Demographic research of this kind may also shed revealing light on the much ignored social structure of the mountains. American social historians in recent decades have re-examined the role of class and wealth in American society, but we have yet to apply this analysis to Appalachian communities. Philip Paludan's perceptive study of a Civil War tragedy in one mountain county suggests that there were strong ideological as well as class differences in the region by the mid-nineteenth century.[14] These differences helped to intensify conflicts during the War and continued to divide mountain communities into the twentieth century. My own research, moreover, found that the mountain middle class played an important role in bringing industrialization to the region and that class differences became much more conscious and apparent after the arrival of industry than before.

What role the middle class played in Appalachia during critical periods of social change remains to be seen. How did physicians, teachers, merchants, lawyers, and larger farmers respond to the social, cultural, and environmental changes that swept the mountains in the last century? What form, if any, did the Progressive movement take in Appalachia, and how did the educated middle class react to the War on Poverty in the 1960's? Over the past two decades, we have gained a greater understanding of absentee ownership of Appalachian resources, but we know little about the ownership of wealth within the region at any given period in time. How much upward mobility existed in the pre-industrial period? How did modernization affect social mobility, and what were the avenues for changing one's class status? How did the rate of mobility across class and occupational lines compare with that of other regions? Harry Caudill's most recent book, *Theirs Be The Power,* provides some insight into the lives of a few mountain elites, but we have far to go before we understand these mountaineers as a social class.[15]

Much the same can be said of our understanding of political and labor history in Appalachia. No one has yet followed up Gordon McKinney's study of mountain Republicanism with a comparable analysis of Democrats in the region. Nor do we have a history of mountain politics before 1870 or after 1920, nor a comprehensive survey of labor struggles in the mountains. Appalachia has a national reputation for political corruption, and yet no one has examined that image from an historical perspective. Several writers have argued that industrialization brought a decline of democracy to the region, but was the older, family-based system of the nineteenth century any more representative than the machine politics of the twentieth? How has the political system in the mountains reflected the changing nature of community, and who are the men and women who exemplified that community? Who were the regional counterparts of State Senator G. Tom Hawkins of Kentucky, a Pike County Republican at the turn of the century who championed women's suffrage, opposed Jim Crow legislation and defended the right of miners to organize? Indeed, such men and women may have been more numerous than we have been led to believe, but they have hitherto been lost to our collective memory.

A similar fate has fallen to other "invisible Appalachians" whose history has been neglected by regional scholars. Traditional stereotypes of Appalachia have all but eliminated blacks, European immigrants, and native Americans from the historical landscape in the mountains, and the story of women's struggles and contributions has been almost universally ignored. The recent publication of Bill Turner and Ed Cabbell's reader, *Blacks in Appalachia,* is an important step in correcting the historical record, but it is just a beginning, and it raises as many questions about the black experience in the mountains as it provides answers.[16] How does the history of blacks in rural, farming areas of Appalachia compare with that of blacks in industrial centers and coal camps? To what degree were black families and communities in the mountains different from those in other parts of the South, and how did the culture and value system of blacks in Appalachia compare at any given time to that of surrounding whites?

There has been little documentation of slavery in Appalachia or the extent of abolitionist sentiment, and no one has yet struggled with the complex and often contradictory history of race relations in the region. David Corbin and others have argued that racism in Appalachia was more tempered than elsewhere in the

South and that, in the coal fields at least, class loyalties overcame racial prejudice. But there is also evidence of racial hostility, segregation, violence, and discrimination throughout the region. Such contradictions cry out for further research and hold great promise for future scholarship.

Likewise, the history of European immigrants in Appalachia has been relatively unexplored. Except for a few scattered articles, there is little published scholarship on the communities of Slavs, Czechs, Hungarians, and Italians who migrated to the region at the turn of the century. They left a considerable heritage which is still evident in the religion, architecture, and family names in many mountain communities, but they too await their historian. Unfortunately immigrants have not received the attention that recent scholars have provided to the native American experience in the mountains. The excellent work of Theda Perdue and John Finger on the Eastern Band of the Cherokee has revised earlier stereotypes and corrected much of the received knowledge about Indians in Appalachia.[17] We still know little about the Cherokee after 1900 or about other native tribes in the region, but as a result of this scholarship we are now able to incorporate the story of the original Appalachians and their struggle with progress and modernization into our emerging history.

We can also hope that future scholarship will focus greater attention on the roles of women in mountain society and life. To date, most of Appalachian history has been written from a decidedly male perspective and has succeeded in elevating Appalachian men to the historical stage while leaving mountain women off somewhere in the wings. We have described the pre-industrial mountain economy but have failed to explore women's contributions to that economy or their receipt of benefits from it. We have analyzed the plight of coal miners without discussing the impact of powerlessness and the cash economy on the lives of wives and daughters, and we have examined labor struggles and other forms of resistance without regard to gender. Women, for example, have played a vital role in union organizing in the mountains and have had primary responsibility for holding the family together during times of stress. Yet we have no accounts of women in the coal fields, on the farm, or in mountain textile mills. Even the 1929 strikes at Gastonia, Elizabethton, Marion and elsewhere in the mountains—strikes led by female operatives from Appalachia—have been ignored by regional scholars. In the years ahead, we must not only begin to look at women as actors in Appalachian history, but we must begin to document attitudes about women in the region and examine the structural and cultural factors which have influenced and shaped women's positions in our communities.

When we begin to broaden the lens through which we view our past, we may also begin to have a clearer picture of the values and beliefs that have shaped the mountain character. We profess to value community, family, land, religion, and freedom, but we have little understanding of the origins of these values or even how they are manifest in our history and daily lives. What was the meaning of community in the mountains at any given time in our history and how has that meaning changed over the years? How have our values differed from those of other Americans? Which values have persisted? Which values have changed? What do we mean by family and familism? By freedom? What elements of our communities have shared these values, and through what mechanisms have they passed on? Can we truly identify an Appalachian character in the same way that Alexis de Tocqueville sought to capture the American character or that Wilbur Cash sought to delineate the mind of the South? As historians of the mountains, we have been so busy defending ourselves and countering false images about the region that we have failed to document those qualities of the human spirit that have shaped our historical identity as a people. It is one thing to know who we are not; it is another to know who we are. To be able to provide a vision for the future, we must have clearer vision of our past.

There are many other gaps in our collective memory. We have yet to examine the Great Depression in Appalachia, the history of education in the region, or the decline of the mountain farm. Except for several notable studies, the history of public works in the mountains is sparse indeed.[18] We need work on the IVA, CCC, WPA, Forest Service, Resettlement Administration Park Service, ARC, OEO, and a host of other government programs if we are to assess the impact of the federal government in Appalachia. It is past time, moreover, for us to analyze the post World War II years, the great out migration, the War on Poverty, and the expansion of the consumer culture in the mountains in the 1970's. Above all, it is time for us to encourage the writing of comprehensive histories of the mountain experience for use in both college and public school classrooms.

We have come a long way in the last twenty years, but we still have far to go. Appalachian history emerged out of our deep desire to know ourselves and to study the causes of our social problems. Its survival in the future will depend upon our ability to use the past as mortar with which to build a brighter future. If our children are to know that sense of place, that affirmation of self that Cratis Williams came to know in his journey, we must be about the work of restoring that community of memory that Cratis sought to preserve.

In so doing, we can learn to think not only from ridge to ridge but, as Jim Wayne Miller has put it, "from ocean to ocean." Eudora Welty may have said it best. "One place comprehended can make us understand other places better. Sense of place gives equilibrium; extended, it is sense of direction."[19]

NOTES

1. Cratis Dearl Williams, *William H. Vaughan: A Better Man Than I Ever Wanted To Be* (Morehead, Ky.: Morehead State University, 1983).

2. John Shelton Reed, *One South: An Ethnic Approach to Regional Culture* (Baton Rouge: Louisiana State University Press, 1982).

3. Robert N. Bellah, et al., *Habits of the Heart: Individualism and Commitment in American Life* (Berkeley: University of California Press, 1985), p. 153.

4. Cratis D. Williams, "The Southern Mountaineer In Fact and Fiction" (Unpublished Ph.D. Dissertation, New York University, 1961) and Henry David Shapiro, *Appalachia On Our Mind: The Southern Mountains and Mountaineers in the American Consciousness, 1870–1920* (Chapel Hill: University of North Carolina Press, 1978).

5. Laurel Shackleford and Bill Weinberg, eds., *Our Appalachia: An Oral History* (New York: Hill and Wang, 1977).

6. See Harry Monroe Caudill, *Night Comes to the Cumberlands: A Biography of a Depressed Area* (Boston: Little, Brown, 1963) and Helen Mathews Lewis, et al., eds., *Colonialism in Modern America: The Appalachian Case* (Boone, N.C.: The Appalachian Consortium Press, 1978).

7. Gordon Bartlett McKinney, *Southern Mountain Republicans, 1865–1965: Politics and the Appalachian Community* (Chapel Hill: The University of North Carolina Press, 1978).

8. John Alexander Williams, *West Virginia and the Captains of Industry* (Morgantown: West Virginia University Library, 1976) and John Gaventa, *Power and Powerlessness: Quiescence and Rebellion in an Appalachian Valley* (Urbana: University of Illinois Press, 1980).

9. Ronald D. Eller, *Miners, Millhands and Mountaineers: The Industrialization of the Appalachian South, 1880–1930* (Knoxville: University of Tennessee Press, 1982).

10. David Whisnant, *Modernizing the Mountaineer: People, Power and Planning in Appalachia* (Boone N.C.: Appalachian Consortium Press, 1981) and *All That Is Native and Fine: The Politics of Culture in an American Region* (Chapel Hill: University of North Carolina Press, 1983),

11. David Alan Corbin, *Life, Work and Rebellion in the Coal Fields: The Southern West Virginia Miners, 1880–1922* (Urbana: University of Illinois Press, 1981); John W. Hevener, *Which Side Are You On? The Harlan County Coal Miners, 1931–1939* (Urbana: University of Illinois Press, 1978).

12. See Dwight Billings, Kathleen Blee and Louis Swanson, "Culture, Family and Community in Pre-industrial Appalachia," *Appalachian Journal,* Vol. 13, No. 2 (Winter 1986).

13. Curtis Wood and Tyler Blethen, *From Ulster To Carolina: The Migration of the Scotch-Irish to Southwestern North Carolina* (Cullowhee, N.C.: Western Carolina University, 1983); Forest McDonald and Grady McWhiney, "The South from Self-Sufficiency to Peonage: An Interpretation," *American Historical Review,* LXXXV (December 1980); Forest McDonald and Ellen Shapiro McDonald, "The Ethnic Origins of the American People, 1790," *William and Mary Quarterly,* 3rd. Ser., XXXVII (April 1980); Forest McDonald and Grady McWhiney, "The Antebellum Southern Herdsman: A Reinterpretation," *Journal of Southern History,* XLI (May 1975); Grady McWhiney and Forest McDonald, "Celtic Origins of Southern Herding Practices," *Journal of Southern History,* LI (May 1985); James Solomon Otto, "The Migration of Southern Plain Folk: An Interdisciplinary Synthesis," *Journal of Southern History,* LI (May 1985).

14. Philip Shaw Paludan, *Victims: A True Story of the Civil War* (Knoxville: University of Tennessee Press, 1981).

15. Harry M. Caudill, *Theirs Be The Power: The Moguls of Eastern Kentucky* (Urbana: University of Illinois Press, 1983).

16. William H. Turner and Edward J. Cabbell, eds., *Blacks in Appalachia* (Lexington: University Press of Kentucky, 1985).

17. Theda Perdue, *Slavery and the Evolution of Cherokee Society, 1540–1866* (Knoxville: University of Tennessee Press, 1979) and John R. Finger, *The Eastern Band of Cherokees, 1819–1900* (Knoxville: University of Tennessee Press, 1984).

18. See Harley E. Jolley, *The Blue Ridge Parkway* (Knoxville: University of Tennessee Press, 1969); Si Kahn, *The Forest Service and Appalachia* (New York: John Hay Whitney Foundation, 1974); Shelley Smith Mastran and Nan Lowerre, *Mountaineers and Rangers: A History of Federal Forest Management in the Southern Appalachians, 1900–1981* (Washington, D.C.: United States Government Printing Office, Department of Agriculture, 1983); Michael J. McDonald and John Muldowny, *TVA and the Dispossessed: The Resettlement of Population in the Norris Dam Area* (Knoxville: University of Tennessee Press, 1982); and William Bruce Wheeler and Michael J. McDonald, *TVA and the Tellico Dam, 1936–1979: A Bureaucratic Crisis in Post-Industrial America* (Knoxville: University of Tennessee Press, 1986).

19. Jim Wayne Miller, "Brier's Sermon: You Must Be Born Again", in *The Mountains Have Come Closer* (Boone, N.C.: The Appalachian Consortium Press, 1980); Eudora Welty, quoted in Comer Vann Woodward, "District of the Devils," *The New York Review of Books* (October 10, 1985), p. 30.

5. THE SOUTHERN HIGHLANDS AND THE SOUTHERN HIGHLANDER DEFINED

John C. Campbell

Recently, while indulging in the somewhat melancholy pleasure of sorting letters and manuscripts yellowing with age, the writer uncovered an address delivered by him during his first year of acquaintance with the mountain people and mountain country. The address, while not so very bad, yet gave evidence of that comprehensive knowledge which frequently characterizes a limited acquaintance with the subject under discussion. Since that time he has heard many discourses upon mountain questions, builded in the same way, and of similar material. All were permeated with the kindliest feeling for the mountaineer, and were colorful

From *The Southern Highlander and His Homeland* by John C. Campbell. Copyright © 1921 by the Russell Sage Foundation. Reprinted by permission of the Russell Sage Foundation.

with descriptions of local, exceptional, or picturesque conditions, but few told who the mountaineers were, or where they lived. This lack of information was supplied, generally, by a sweeping gesture toward the South, accompanying the statement, "In the mountains of our fair Southland lives a people of purest Anglo-Saxon blood, upon whose cabin walls hang the rifles with which their illustrious ancestors at King's Mountain turned the tide of the Revolution."

Few discourses on mountain questions are complete without this reference. The audiences to whom such addresses are given, unless nurtured on Fiske's misinterpreted and misapplied theory that the mountain people are descendants of mean and indentured whites of colonial days, would feel cheated without it. They look for it as expectantly as the Bostonian does for the closing phrase in the Governor's Thanksgiving Proclamation, "God Save the Commonwealth of Massachusetts."

If the speaker has French blood, there is certain to be some allusion to the Huguenots and the Revocation of the Edict of Nantes; if German, a strong reference to the Palatinate element in this early stream of migration; and if there is a drop of Scotch-Irish blood in his veins, not the least doubt is left in the minds of the audience as to who the mountain people are—they are the worthy scions of this worthy stock, and all, of course, Presbyterians by heritage.

The writer longs for the certitude of knowledge with which he spoke twenty-five years ago. But fortunately his education was not allowed to end there. The mountain hamlet where he lived, learned, and tried to teach, lay on an old route of travel. Occasionally there would straggle through the cross-roads a train of canvas-covered wagons, and at times he had privilege of converse with the hopeful adventurer in search of the Eldorado lying always just beyond. Now and again the stillness of the night would bring the echo of some locomotive threading its way through the mountain defiles, or was it the faint whistle of a packet on the Tennessee? Such experiences served to intensify his desire to know more of the early pioneers of our highlands, of their routes of travel, their successors, and the land in which they dwell.

Associated in memory with these experiences are others of college days in the Berkshire Hills of faraway Massachusetts. Of these, one stands out vividly. On a "mountain day" expedition to the top of Greylock, the return trail had been lost in a gathering storm. Forced to seek shelter, we finally made our way to the door of a log cabin, such a cabin as one may see today nestling near the foot of Graybeard or Grandfather in the Carolina Blue Ridge. Given a cordial welcome by the young mother within, we sought to establish friendly relations with the little daughter cuddled, in fear of the storm and in shyness of strangers, in her mother's arms. The fire lighted up the room furnished with a simplicity one might duplicate in many a mountain cabin of the South. With the passing of the storm came a halloo from the stalwart young husband, as he returned from the clearing with axe gleaming over his shoulder. We lingered at the bend to wave them good-bye as they watched us down the trail—mother, babe now in father's arms, with the rainbow over all.

The beauty of the picture lives fresh in the writer's memory, but in later years there has come to him more than the memory of its beauty. To the haunting, half-asked question of the connection between this family group and the straggling train through the mountain hamlet, between the cabin on the slope of the Berkshires and the cabins in the Southern Highlands, an answer has at last been given. What he saw in the Berkshires, and what one still sees occasionally in the Green Mountains and White Mountains, the Catskills and the Adirondacks, are, as it were, re-enacted scenes of the great drama of settlement once lived from New England to Georgia along the frontier line moving ever toward the West. Physiographic and other natural causes will explain why in our Southern Highlands these scenes persist along lingering segments of that frontier line; and why they are found only at isolated points in the Highlands of the North.

Although we must limit ourselves to a discussion of the Southern Highlands, it is well to keep in mind that Southern and Northern Highlands together constitute a whole, a great upland realm extending twelve hundred miles or more from northeast to southwest. Distinctive social customs and standards of living so interesting to many, are strange only when one forgets that these were common to the daily life of our pioneer fathers North and South alike, but a few decades ago as history is measured. Some, still young though growing gray, whose childhood days were of the West, will recall a share in this life and in these customs.

THE SOUTHERN HIGHLANDS

But where are, and what are the Southern Highlands, and who are the Southern Highlanders? For purposes of discussion, the writer has isolated a part of the great Appalachian province which extends from New York to central Alabama, and has called it the Southern Highlands. Within the boundaries of this territory are included the four western counties of Maryland; the Blue Ridge, Valley, and Allegheny Ridge counties of Virginia; all of West Virginia; eastern Tennessee; eastern Kentucky; western North Carolina; the four northwestern counties of South Carolina; northern Georgia; and northeastern Alabama. Our mountain region, of approximately 112,000 square miles, embraces an area nearly as large as the combined areas of New York and New England, and almost equal to that of England, Scotland, Ireland, and Wales.[1]

The boundary which we have regarded as dividing the Southern Highlands from their northern extension is the famous Mason and Dixon line. More specifically, this boundary line begins at the northeast corner of Frederick County, Maryland, and extends west to the southwest corner of Pennsylvania, thence north along the western boundary of Pennsylvania to the point where the Ohio leaves the state just west of Pittsburgh. For purposes of convenience the southern, or more properly the southwestern boundary, may be considered as a base line running diagonally northwest to southeast, passing through the neighborhood of Birmingham, Alabama, and terminating in the southeast corner of Coosa and the northwest corner of Winston Counties. An approximate eastern boundary for this extended territory is formed by connecting the northern and southern boundaries by a curved line passing in a southwesterly direction slightly to the east of Frederick, Maryland, through Lynchburg, Virginia, a little to the east of Asheville, North Carolina, through Spartanburg, South Carolina, and to the north of Atlanta, Georgia. This line is roughly paralleled by the western boundary which, beginning at Pittsburgh, continues down the Ohio to Kentucky, coinciding with the northwestern boundary of West Virginia, and follows the river nearly to Maysville, Kentucky—the Limestone of pioneer days, where river immigrants disembarked for their cross-country journey.[2] From this point it passes southwest through Tullahoma, Tennessee, and Decatur, Alabama.

The lines by which the Southern Highlands are defined are not chosen arbitrarily. They correspond for the most part with boundaries of natural divisions; on the east with the face of the Blue Ridge, which defines the western margin of the Piedmont Plateau, on the south with the upper limits of the Coastal Plain, and on the west with the western escarpment of the Allegheny-Cumberland Plateau. The northern line, in part purely political, was in its beginnings a surveyor's line to determine a boundary dispute of long standing, growing out of the claims of Penn and Lord Baltimore.

The name Southern Highlands has been chosen for several reasons. Southern Appalachians is a term sometimes used, but inasmuch as this term is limited by geographers to that part of the Appalachian mountain system lying south of the New River Divide in southern Virginia, some other name for the whole territory under consideration is necessary. The designation Southern Mountains has also been used. But because so often descriptions of depressed social conditions, which are true only of limited areas, have been given without qualification as existing throughout the Southern mountains, this term has come to carry with it the implication that such conditions prevail generally throughout the region.

The traveler who follows the trails of this far country, fords its rushing streams, and forces his way through thickets of rhododendron and laurel to rest upon some beech-shaded bank of moss, and who toward sunset checks his horse upon the ridge to trace the thread of smoke which signals welcome, may yet be at a loss for a name to describe the land; but when at dawn he wakes with mist rising from every cove and valley, and echoes still sounding of half-remembered traditions, folk-lore and folk-songs, recited or sung before the fire by "granny" or "grandpap," he knows there is but one name that will do it justice—the Southern Highlands.

It is a land of mountains, valleys, and plateaus. Each of the three parallel belts which lying lengthwise, northeast to southwest, form the Highlands, is characterized by the predominance of one of the physical features just indicated. The outstanding feature of the easternmost belt is the Blue Ridge Mountain Range, and we call this belt therefore the Blue Ridge Belt, though it is often referred to technically as the Appalachian Mountain Belt. The western is known as the Allegheny-Cumberland or Appalachian Plateau. Between these truly upland belts extends the Greater Appalachian Valley, better known in its several parts as the Valley of Virginia, the Valley of East Tennessee, and the Coosa River Valley of Georgia and Alabama.

The use of the term Valley, as applied to the great central zone of depression, is likely to mislead. It is more truly a valley-ridge section, with its true valley feature prominent on its eastern side and with ridges toward the west. The floor of the Valley reaches in southern Virginia an altitude of from 2,600 to 2,700 feet above the sea, descending toward the north to an altitude of 500 feet at Harper's Ferry, West Virginia, and southward to 500 feet or less in Alabama. The whole Southern Highland region is therefore an upland region, with a great central depression, and not merely two separate mountain areas with a dividing valley.

More than one-half of the entire territory is included within the Allegheny-Cumberland Belt, a little more than one-fourth in the Blue Ridge Belt, and something less than one-fourth in the Greater Appalachian Valley.[3]

Blue Ridge Belt

In Maryland and Virginia the Blue Ridge Belt is narrow, varying in width from ten to sixteen miles, until near the headwaters of the Roanoke it begins to expand into a lofty plateau. This plateau, lying for the most part in North Carolina, reaches a maximum width of seventy miles, and a maximum height in Mount Mitchell of 6,711 feet. Passing southward into Georgia, it becomes irregular and indefinite until it is lost in the Piedmont Plateau. In general outline it may be compared to a narrow lance-shaped leaf whose stem is the single Blue Ridge River Range of Virginia, and whose tip rests in the region of Cartersville, Georgia. After an interval of nearly one hundred miles, there is in Alabama a recurrence of the belt for fifty miles in the Talladega Mountains.

The Blue Ridge Range proper, from its point of expansion in Virginia, continues southward under that name as the eastern border of the plateau. It carries the main divide between waters flowing into the Atlantic and into the Gulf, and rises from an average altitude of over 3,000 feet to a height of almost 6,000 feet in Grandfather Mountain, North Carolina.

Its eastern slopes are very precipitous, and the Yadkin, Catawba, Broad, and other streams that rise here and make their way to the Atlantic, dash down to the Piedmont Plateau below in a series of high cascades and deep gorges. To the west the descent is more gradual. Westward flowing streams at first for some distance pass through broad high valleys. Deepening their channels as they go, the rivers—chief among which are the New, Watauga, Nolichucky, French Broad, Pig Pigeon, Little Tennessee, Hiwassee, and Ocoee—cut through the mountains bounding the northwest edge of the plateau in deep narrow gorges, and escape to the Greater Valley and eventually to the Mississippi and Gulf.

This northwest mountain boundary of the plateau has been and still is known locally and popularly as the Great Smokies, from the largest of the segments into which it has been divided by the river gorges, but the general name Unaka is now applied to the whole range as well as to two of its five principal segments. From northeast to southwest, these chief segments are called respectively the Iron, Unaka, Bald, Great Smoky, and Unaka Mountains.

The Unaka Range, although it does not bear the divide, is higher than the Blue Ridge and more rugged on both its eastern and western slopes. In point of fact these are younger mountains which rose so gradually on the western edge of the more ancient plateau as to permit the rivers to keep their early westward direction. While it is difficult to give an average height, owing to the broken character of the range, its general altitude is probably about 5,000 feet. Two of its peaks, Guyot and Clingman's Dome, are but a few feet lower than Mount Mitchell, and numerous others are above 6,000 feet.

The whole plateau section lying between the Blue Ridge and Unakas is cut by ridges and cross-ridges which have no uniform direction, but form for the most part the divides between the main stream basins, and are connected more or less closely with the enclosing ranges to the east and west. The main ridges are the Yellow, Black, Newfound, Balsam, Pisgah, Cowee,

Nantahala, Cheoah, and Tusquitee Mountains, of which the Black (wherein lies Mount Mitchell), the Balsam and Pisgah Ranges are the highest.

In general, the mountains of the Blue Ridge Belt are heavily wooded to the top, and the whole range is one of extreme beauty.

Allegheny-Cumberland Belt

Bordering the Greater Appalachian Valley on the northwest, and facing it in bold escarpment, is the Allegheny-Cumberland Belt. Throughout its extent it is a plateau belt, although to parts of it in both northern and southern Appalachians the name mountains is applied. In the northern Appalachians, the Catskill Mountains of New York and the Allegheny Mountains of Pennsylvania are really misnomers, arising from the fact that the edge of this great plateau wall appears to the traveler approaching from the seaboard as another mountain range. In the southern Appalachians, the Cumberland Mountains of Kentucky and Tennessee are, in popular usage, coming to be known as the Cumberland Plateau, a much more descriptive term.

The plateau character of the belt is much more prominently marked in Tennessee and Alabama than farther north, but throughout its course it may be viewed as a great wall facing the Greater Appalachian Valley and sloping gradually to the northwest toward the Interior Lowlands.

The eastern escarpment of the Allegheny-Cumberland Plateau Belt, or the Allegheny Front as it is here called, enters the northern limiterland Plateau Belt, or the of our field between Cumberland and Frostburg, Maryland. Along the Virginia-West Virginia boundary it rises to commanding heights. It declines farther south, but in the Big Black Mountains of Virginia and Kentucky again attains to a height of 4,000 feet. In Tennessee the plateau is much lower in altitude. At Cumberland Gap, made so famous in early settlement and later civil strife, its altitude is from 3,000 to 3,200 feet, while the height of the Gap itself is but 1,649 feet.

In Alabama the eastern part of the plateau is deeply cut by long narrow valleys, separated by isolated plateaus. The easternmost of these plateaus is Lookout Mountain, the eastern face of which marks the boundary between the Greater Valley and the Allegheny-Cumberland Belt in this state. To the west beyond Lookout and Wills Valley lies Sand Mountain, and still beyond, the deeply dissected remnants of the Cumberland Plateau proper, sloping gently to the southward until they merge into the Gulf Coastal Plain.

The western bounds of the Allegheny-Cumberland Belt are the western boundary of West Virginia, the broken "knob country" of eastern Kentucky into which the western escarpment of the Cumberland Plateau is here worn, and the irregular but more clearly defined line of this escarpment in Tennessee and in part of Alabama.[4]

While less imposing, the wild and rugged ridges of the Allegheny Front are hardly less beautiful than the loftier wooded peaks and slopes of the Blue ridge, which forms the front of the eastern belt.

Greater Appalachian Valley

Between these higher belts, the Blue Ridge on the east and the Allegheny-Cumberland on the west, extends the Greater Valley—itself an upland region—which has played so important a part in the settlement of the Southern Highlands and in the history of our country.

Toward the north the valley character of this great, much fluted valley zone is more marked on its eastern side. In Maryland the distinctively valley portion is an extension of the Cumberland Valley of Pennsylvania. In Virginia it is really a series of valleys' taking their names from their rivers—the Shenandoah, the James, the Roanoke, the Kanawha or New, and the Holston or Tennessee. In general configuration, however, the Valley is continuous. It is often referred to as the Shenandoah, from its most famous part, but is better known in its entirety as the Valley of Virginia.

On the western side of the Greater Valley is a series of ridges known collectively as the Allegheny Ridges, lying between the Allegheny Front which forms the eastern escarpment of our plateau belt, and the true valley section of the eastern part of that Greater Valley. To the southward, especially, in Tennessee, the ridge portion of the Valley becomes less prominent and the valley character of the belt more marked, although in Tennessee there are still prominent ridges or mountains in the Greater Valley.

In Georgia and Alabama the Valley broadens and descends in altitude, the valley ridges and enclosing mountain walls gradually lose their character, and the whole belt becomes indistinguishable from the rolling plateau and coastal plain to the southward.

The gentle beauty of much of the Greater Valley, especially on its eastern side, with its green fields and dark cedars, forms a marked contrast to the ridges that border it, some of which assume true mountain proportions. This belt is the seat of many flourishing cities and is traversed by a number of railroads; yet parts of it are very inaccessible, and almost as isolated as the remote sections of the higher belts to east and west.[5]

Though our study is limited to the territory just described, we would repeat that the Southern Highlands should not be disassociated in thought from their northern extension. The Allegheny-Cumberland Belt is continued in the so-called Allegheny Mountains of Pennsylvania and in the Catskills of New York. The Greater Appalachian Valley finds extension to the northeast in the Cumberland and Lebanon Valleys of Pennsylvania, and the Paulinskill and Walkill Valleys of New Jersey and New York. Though the mountain character of the Blue Ridge Belt loses itself in the modest altitude of South Mountain in Pennsylvania, the belt itself is traceable in the highlands of New Jersey and New York, and its ancient remnants, greatly changed by geologic forces, may be followed to the northeast in the Berkshire Hills and Green Mountains of Massachusetts and Vermont, and on into Canada.

In considering our Highland region, or the entire Appalachian province of which it is a part, it is difficult to resist the lure of the geologist who invites us to witness its first narrow crest emerging from the primordial sea, and to hearken to the roar of the ocean upon its eastern shore, and on the west to the wash of the waves of a once great inland sea. Portions of this empire are indeed exceedingly ancient, and the eastern belt especially includes some of the oldest lands of the continent—a fact which invests the region with peculiar appeal to the imagination, as well as with importance to the student of geology. Equally difficult to resist is the temptation to wander in the fascinating by-paths of its more recent history, and to dwell upon the geographic influences exerted by this great barrier which has been so potent in shaping the political, social, and economic life of both North and South.

Those who would understand a people must know the land in which they dwell, and a careful study of the topography of the Southern Highlands will repay the painstaking student. A study of elevations, depressions, and slopes is a dry task in and of itself, but if the narrow winding valley and broad fertile plain, the isolated mesa and expansive plateau, the steep slope and towering peak be translated into terms of life, the study becomes of absorbing interest as the forces are revealed which have influenced some groups to face the future, and others to linger in the past.

The Southern Highlander

To circumscribe territory and give it a name is one thing; to call people by a name not of their choosing is quite another. Obviously, if the term Southern Highlands be allowed for the land, native-born residents of the region are Southern Highlanders. Yet within the Highland area are many native-born inhabitants of urban or valley residence who do not regard themselves as mountain people. The writer has two friends, one living in the Greater Appalachian Valley and one in a prosperous mountain city, and both devoted to the interests of their own people, who refer in conversation to "those mountain folks," although at other times jocosely alluding to themselves as "mountain whites." This opprobious term, coined as a term of distinction by well-meaning advocates of the mountaineer, is resented by all who dwell in the Highlands, by whatever name they may be designated.

If all that had been accomplished by illustrious men of the mountains, and that now ennobles the history of their several states, had been recorded to the glory of a single Appalachian commonwealth, the matter of nomenclature might be easier. Perhaps, then, residents of the "State of Appalachia" would have been proud to call themselves "Appalachians," "Southern Mountaineers," or "Southern Highlanders." They might even have taken the "typical" mountain cabin, now the cause of so much contention, as their state crest, with encircling wreath of mountain laurel, and underneath have inscribed a Latin motto expressive of their loyalty and pride. The mountain areas of certain states are, to be sure, so large and so influential as to kindle a worthy regional pride, and to win respectful consideration both within and without the state. But the name by which such an area is known indicates merely that the district to which it is applied lies in the eastern or western part of the state. It does not convey the impression that the people who live there are Highland people.

Without at all raising the question as to whether some other division of the mountain region would have been better than the existing one, the fact remains that the Highlands were not welded into one commonwealth, nor are they generally regarded as a continuous tract. They lie within nine Southern states, and too often are called, disparagingly by some and apologetically by others, the "back-yards" of the Southern states. It is not easy to assign a reason for the feeling which has found expression in this phrase, and which makes it difficult to define the Southern Highlander. There are, however, a number of causes which indirectly have contributed to it.

Prominent among these is the relation borne by the mountain region to the states within which it is included. The Highlands as a whole make up about one-third of the total areas of these nine states.[6] Their population is nearly a third of the total population. Their influence is less easily determined. Highlands and Lowlands in each state act upon each other reciprocally, their influence varying with the size and population of the Highland area in proportion to the state area, and somewhat, too, with its topography. In certain states regional differences between the two sections have caused a difference in political alignment. Though some of the mountain areas are admittedly the garden-spots of their states when climate and scenery are considered, and others are contributing largely from their natural resources to the state wealth, the fruits of political power have naturally been most in evidence in the constituencies that have the most votes. There are still echoes of old political struggles for full representation of "east" or "west"—whichever of these localities may indicate the mountain portion of the state—even where one party dominates both sections. These political influences are easily exaggerated, but they are to be considered in a summary of causes affecting mountain life.

Another influence tending to diminish the natural pride in his section felt by the mountain dweller, has been exerted unconsciously by travelers from urban centers in the South, or from Northern states where urban life has been a prevailing influence. By accounts of the simplicity of life in the Highlands, picturesque without qualification, they have unwittingly aroused the antagonism of the people living there by causing them to feel that they have been caricatured. It were well for those from states dominated by urban influences, abounding in wealth and unhandicapped by great regional diversities, to reflect that even within their own borders are large rural areas not different from the mountains in the absence of many of the so-called advantages of city life. The folk dwelling within our Highland country are naturally hospitable, and there is a sense of injury that grows into resentment when former guests in their homes, who need not have come unless they had wished, make sweeping statements that do them and their people gross injustice.

There is another great source of irritation. In earlier days, when public funds were less available for education in the mountains, both Northern and Southern church boards established mission schools in communities not adequately supplied with public schools. Despite all the high endeavor that the word "missions" conveys to us individually, no one of us cares to be regarded, even by implication, as a worthy object of betterment, uplift, or missionary effort.

It has come about, therefore, that the term "Southern Mountaineers" has been made to suggest a peculiar people, with peculiar needs. The South as a whole has shown the natural reaction toward any seeming suggestion of peculiarity on the part of any of its people, though at times it would appear to admit the same implication by its use of the term "Hill-Billy." It is as if two brothers reserved to themselves the right to call each other what they would and when they would, but united in resistance against an outsider who offered affront to a member of the family.

The South holds no monopoly of this sensitiveness. A former classmate of the writer, who twenty years ago described conditions as he viewed them in a northern highland area, aroused the ire of the whole region, urban as well as rural, though writing of only a limited part. Even today, though remedial measures bear witness to the truth of some of his statements, his name is uttered occasionally in country life conferences with a degree of feeling too heated to be mistaken for affection.

Perhaps enough has been said to suggest our difficulty in telling who the Southern Highlanders really are. The reader will, however, allow the use of the term in these pages to cover the population within the region described. We cannot conceal our hope of its ultimate adoption. The people living within the boundaries of the Southern Highlands have too much that is worthy of conservation, both in the past and in the present, to allow themselves to ignore their solidarity or to apologize for it.

NOTES

1. A word of explanation is necessary to those who in earlier years have sought form the writer data for addresses and publications. To the counties previously enumerated by him he has added the four western counties of Maryland, and also Winston and Walker Counties of Alabama. The area and population of the region included under the name of Southern Highlands are therefore slightly larger than previously accounted.

2. More accurately, it is a little east of Maysville, at the point where the western line of Lewis County touches the Ohio.

3. For full data on area of belts, see Table 16 of Appendix E.

4. The Piedmont Plateau region, lying to the southeast of the Blue Ridge Belt, and the Western Piedmont region, or Interior Lowlands, lying to the northwest of the Allegheny-Cumberland Plateau, are not included in the Southern Highlands as defined in this study.

5. A more detailed description of the physiography of the several states will be found in Appendix A.

6. The proportion noted above by no means represents the average proportion of the mountain area in each state to its respective state area. West Virginia, for example, is a mountain state in its entirety, while the mountain section of South Carolina, the smallest state mountain area with the exception of Maryland, is about one-eleventh of the entire state area. In Virginia the mountain area is about one-half, in Tennessee three-sevenths, in Kentucky one-third, in Alabama one-fourth, in Maryland one-fourth, in North Carolina one-fifth, and in Georgia one-seventh of the total state area.

It may be questioned whether the state of West Virginia should be regarded in its entirety as a mountain state. It is to be remembered however, that the characteristics which differentiated it from the "Old Dominion" and which led to its separation from it, were the outgrowth of its topography. The Valley of Virginia, although kept distinct for a while from the eastern part of the state by the narrow barrier of the Blue Ridge, was finally assimilated. The western part of Virginia, because of its mountain character, remained unassimilated, and as a result the state of West Virginia, formed from it, differs from the mother state in its political, social, and economic life. (See Appendix A.)

6. FREEDOM IN THE MOUNTAINS

APPALACHIAN HISTORY

Don West

Introduction

I think history is terribly important. It ought to be the most popular school course. But it's not. Why? Maybe the way it's taught sometimes causes students to be bored. Anyhow, too many students, too many people, don't seem to like history.

In these articles I may speak of some things you haven't heard much about. I'll try to make it plain and simple and down to earth, because I believe writing ought to have those qualities. I shall not bother you with footnote references, either. On this particular subject I think there is much misunderstanding, sometimes distortion in the history writing.

Why Is History Important?

Why is the study and understanding of history important? Why, particularly, is the understanding of our own history important for Southern Mountain folk today?

Well, I think the way a people see themselves in history helps to determine their own self-image. Did you know that what you think of yourself, the image you have of yourself, is very important for you? Did you know that it pretty well decides what you may even try

to do? The same is true for a country, or for a community, an area, a people. If we know where we've come from, why and how, maybe we'll have a clearer view of where we may be able to go, and how.

We've Been Hillbillyized

There have been many unpleasant things written about the southern mountaineer. Some very ugly things. We've been "hillbillyized" and "Tobacco Roaded" so long that sometimes some of us may begin to half believe some of those stereotypes about ourselves. Lil' Abner, Beverly Hillbillies and such are hardly calculated to add to our feeling of dignity and self-respect.

A "hillbilly racist" stereotype has emerged, too. I've heard learned scholars of both colors refer to the "hillbilly psychology" when referring to the tap-root of southern racism. But it "ain't necessarily so," as the man said. In fact, it is downright false. These articles will show why.

So you see, the twisting of people's history and cultural heritage may lead to wrong evaluation by others, and even worse, to a false self-image.

Reprinted from *Mountain Life and Work,* Vol. 46 (December, 1970). Used by permission.

Sort of Johnny-Come-Lately

What kind of people are we anyhow? Who is this hillbilly we've heard so much about?

The Federal Government now classes all the Mountain South as "depressed." That means we're poor, have a hard time making a living because of job scarcity and such. Many national magazines, writers, missionaries and other do-gooders have also discovered us in feature stories detailing our poverty and miseries. None of this is news to many of us, of course. The majority of mountain folk have always worked hard for scanty returns. Some of us wonder why the Government and all these other people were so late discovering what we've known all our lives. It strikes us as being a sort of Johnny-come-lately deal. Not that we don't welcome any aid from anywhere. But some of us have the notion that no problem solution ever really comes from the outside. It comes from within ourselves.

We have many sorts of "welfare" jobs now. Some say we're just plain down no 'count, that we're just too lazy to work. Some "welfare" workers seem to try to make us feel like trash or scum. They act like they think we'll break the Federal Government by the few measly dollars we draw!

Yesterday's or Tomorrow's People?

Others see us as "Yesterday's People." All we need to solve our problems is to listen to them, get rid of our quare notions and quaint ways, accept middle class values like the rest of America.

Some of us doubt this. We hold a notion that maybe, after all, there may be good values in our own cultural heritage worth considering, saving and extending. Most of us are exposed to the cultural product of middle class America via TV and other mass media. We find few values to get excited about here. We know about political machines, poverty, race riots and rats, murder gangs and such in the great centers of America.

We've also had political representatives of the great American family dynasties come to us. We have a Rockefeller now. And when John Kennedy ran in the West Virginia primary, spending a quarter of a million dollars on his way to the White House, there was more free liquor around the polls than we'd seen in a mighty long time. But it didn't wipe out our poverty, and it hasn't. We are also aware that the Al Capone type patriot, Cosa Nostra and underworld political deals are as much a part of the "American Way" as is racial injustice.

So some of us seriously doubt the value of becoming just like the rest of America. We even prefer our square, quaint ways, if nothing else.

But is there anything in our own mountain cultural history worth understanding, appreciating, preserving expanding?

I happen to think there is, I remember back in the 1930s teaching on Troublesome Creek in East Kentucky when the first "welfare" program got under way. One day up the left hand fork of Troublesome visiting with Dan and Mary Pratt, I was told how the social worker came by offering surplus commodities. Now Troublesome's people were poor, alright, and needy. But they said: "We're not paupers. We don't take hand-outs."

That sentiment stemmed from our mountain heritage—self-respect, independence, human dignity.

But a lot of water has gone down Troublesome—and Cabin Creek—since then. Men can only stand to look into the eyes of their hungry children for so long. Troublesome's people, like others in the mountains, were eventually forced to accept hand-outs. Life had changed. Great corporations had reached into the mountains. The squeeze was on. A man could no longer take axe and bull-tongue plow to scratch a living from hill-side patches. That self-respect and pride, once virtually a part of every mountain man, have undergone a massive mauling. Conditions created sharp-toothed destroyers that gnawed away inside men until human dignity itself was almost swallowed. Our people became victims of circumstances they did not create and over which they had no control. From such conditions outside corporations drained millions in great fortunes.

But the mountain people never gave in easily. They fought back every step of the way. The heroic tales of trade union beginnings in Harlan, Gastonia, Marion, Elizabethtown, Cabin Creek, Wilder of the 1930s record that spirit. The current struggles against strip-mining devastation at Pikeville, Clear Creek and Troublesome Creek; and the other struggles of mountain groups—all witness the fact that the mountain man is not defeated. He still has courage to dissent. He is never an establishment creature.

Perhaps it remains for the mountain people to again come to the rescue of the nation as in these articles we propose to show they did in the Civil War.

Perhaps instead of labeling us "Yesterday's People," a more fitting one might be "Tomorrow's People."

With Courage to Dissent

Settlers in the mountains came from a different cultural background than the tidewater cavaliers or lowland slaveholders. Mountain men came from a dissenting, freedom-loving tradition. True, they were of the common folk, mostly Scots (sometimes called Scottish-Irish). They had opposed both religious and political oppression in the old country, fled for a time to northern Ireland, then to the New World. There were also sprinklings of German, French Huguenots, Welch, Swiss and English. But in the main they were hard headed independents with courage to dissent even when unpopular and dangerous. Their values were in men more than in things.

Early mountain religion was strongly Presbyterian, naturally, because of the Scots. Mountain men were intensely devoted to religious freedom. Western Virginia's people strongly resented being taxed to support the Anglican established church of Virginia. This was an early point of dissension between mountains and tidewater. Add unfair tidewater representation (three-fifths of the slaves were counted), slavery and secession, and the new mountain state of West Virginia came to be.

No Witches Were Burned

Despite strong Calvinistic influences, and unlike Puritan New England, the mountaineers never tried to force their beliefs on others. No one was persecuted for holding different beliefs, nor for disbelief. No "witches' were burned. One might be a church member or one might not. One might even be an outspoken unbeliever. That was a free man's right.

As time went on and the mountains continued to be isolated and slighted on internal improvements by their several state governments, education waned. Schools and roads were virtually nonexistent. The Mountain South became literally a great unknown wilderness area inhabited by "quare people," sometimes referred to by tidewater aristocrats as "wild men."

But Never Establishment Men

Perhaps the very "wildness" was part of the dissent. For these hardy hill people were never "establishment men." They never had hit it off very well with royalty, nor with those who traded and bought other men's bodies as slaves.

For these mountains were the home of freedom loving men. This is an emphasis that can't be over stressed. It went back to the earliest settlement and beyond. Here was formed the first Commonwealth with a constitution for self-government written by American born white men—the Watauga Association. Here the State of Franklin was created by men who had fought royal governor Tyron of North Carolina in the Alamance Battle. Many of these same veterans with hog rifles trampled back across the Great Smokies to defeat British General Ferguson at King's Mountain in a victory Thomas Jefferson declared crucial to the American Revolution.

The Cradle of Abolition

It was up the valleys through these mountains that the main line of the Underground Railroad ran with refugees bound for Canada and freedom. Many a humble mountain cabin gave food, shelter and direction on the way to weary black men and women. From here came Helper's great book, *The Impending Crisis,* in 1857, used as campaign literature to elect Lincoln in 1860.

It was also here in the Southern Mountains that the abolitionist movement to free 4 million black slaves was born, nurtured and cradled through infancy to a maturity that eventually broke the chains of chattel bondage to make the Negro a man instead of a thing.

It was here that the first newspaper in America dedicated wholly to abolishing slavery was first published—*The Emancipator.* Elihu Embree was publishing his *Emancipator* when William Lloyd Garrison was only ten years old.

And to these mountains the gentle Lundy came to work and shed his sweat and tears getting out the *Genius of Universal Emancipation* after Embree's death.

7. TOWARD A DEFINITION OF APPALACHIA

Bruce Ergood

"Appalachia is anywhere there's coal under the ground" said mountain novelist Jesse Stuart in a recent interview.[1] James Brown, a widely respected student of Appalachian society, says Appalachia is a politically defined region, making obvious reference to that portion of the United States presently considered Appalachian by the Appalachian Regional Commission.[2] Obviously the two definitions are at odds. But they are not the only two definitions.

In the section that follows, we will present three distinctly defined regions, each describing a geopolitical and social region, some or all of which has at one time been called Appalachia.

Part II of the paper presents the people who inhabit the area traditionally thought to be Appalachian or highland country. The people have been described in many ways, but certain threads of independence of spirit and clannishness run throughout. By close attention to these characteristics as presented in social studies we observe a change in emphasis and description.

WHERE IS APPALACHIA?

The Southern Highlands

Beginning with a survey of mountain conditions and the state of mountain "uplift work," John C. Campbell worked from 1913 to his death in 1919 to adequately describe the conditions of the life in the southern mountains. His extensive travels and his dedication to accuracy combine to give us what Rupert B. Vance has called "the one scientific project fit to serve as benchmark" for later regional comparisons.[4] Those familiar with Campbell's work know of his extensive use of census data, of historic materials and his use of thorough documentation. His is the work of a careful student.

Since Campbell's work is the first scientific description of the area since come to be known as Appalachia, his definition of the area and of its people is of special importance. Evidencing a view that the isolated mountaineer himself could not have, he described the region as those areas of the great Appalachian mountain chain which correspond for the most part with boundaries of natural division.[5] Defining South as below the Mason and Dixon Line, the eastern boundary is the Blue Ridge Mountain chain, the central area is contained in the great Appalachian Valley, and the western edge is the Allegheny-Cumberland plateau. The southern most section trails out in the foothills of northeastern Alabama. To quote Campbell,

> It is a land of mountains, valleys, and plateaus. Each of the three parallel belts which lying lengthwise, northeast to southwest, form the Highlands, is characterized by the predominance of one of the physical features just indicated. The outstanding feature of the easternmost belt is the Blue Ridge Mountain Range, and we call this belt therefore the Blue Ridge Belt, though it is often referred to technically as the Appalachian Mountain Belt. The western is known as the Allegheny-Cumberland or Appalachian Plateau. Between these truly upland belts extends the Greater Appalachian Valley, better known in its several parts as the Valley of Virginia, the Valley of East Tennessee, and the Coosa River Valley of Georgia and Alabama.[6]

Campbell knew all to well that mere geography does not a region make. He reminds the reader of fording the rushing streams, forcing one's way through thickets of rhododendron and laurel, of beech-shaded moss stream banks, of the thread of smoke at dusk evidencing a soon-to-be welcoming and hospitality, of rising morning mist and echoes still sounding, of half-remembered traditions, folklore and folk song. His concern for the living conditions and the health of the people, and his detailed description of the schools and education among them gives further indication that he was describing the people and their society in a particular geographic region.

The Southern Highland Region, Campbell's term, included some 256 counties in nine states.

Maryland	4	counties in the northwestern tip
Virginia	43	counties in center to western Virginia
West Virginia	55	counties, the entire state
Kentucky	37	eastern counties
Tennessee	45	center to eastern counties
North Carolina	24	western counties
South Carolina	4	northwestern counties
Georgia	25	northern counties
Alabama	19	northeastern counties

These counties are divided among three categorical groups following the Blue Ridge Belt on the east, the Greater Appalachian Valley which runs through the central portion of the highlands from Maryland, through Virginia, Tennessee and into Georgia and Alabama, and the Allegheny Cumberland Belt on the West. This latter belt makes up fully 50 percent of the total area and accounts for 46.7 percent of the total 1910 Highland population of 5.3 million.[7] It is this same western belt which has the highest percent native born of native parents, 87.8, compared to 84.1 and 78.9 for the eastern and central belts respectively. Moreover, the western belt has only 5.9 percent Negro population compared to 14.9 and 18.3 for the other two belts. Campbell makes the point that the region as a whole is isolated, homogeneous in cultural heritage, primarily of long residency in the region, and gaining population at a far slower rate than the nonmountain regions of the southern highland states.

It is not surprising to note the rurality of this population. Using the figures of "towns of 2,500 or over" as an urban measure, 83.9 percent of the population is classified as rural. It is even more striking, however, to note that when "incorporated communities of 1,000 or over" is used as a measure of urban or "near-urban fold," to use Campbell's term, still 79.4 percent of the highland population is classified as rural. In the nine-state highland region, only 6.1 percent of the total population reside in its six cities of 25,000 or more. The population is a rural one, residing in scattered hamlets and in isolated homes. They are described as farmers although all do not actively engage in working the land. A few professionals and storekeepers are found amongst their group. Those who live on the smallest, most isolated tracts of poorer land, whose homes are most likely to be one-room log cabins, Campbell describes as the smallest highland group, yet the most hospitable and among the kindest souls in the world. They are either

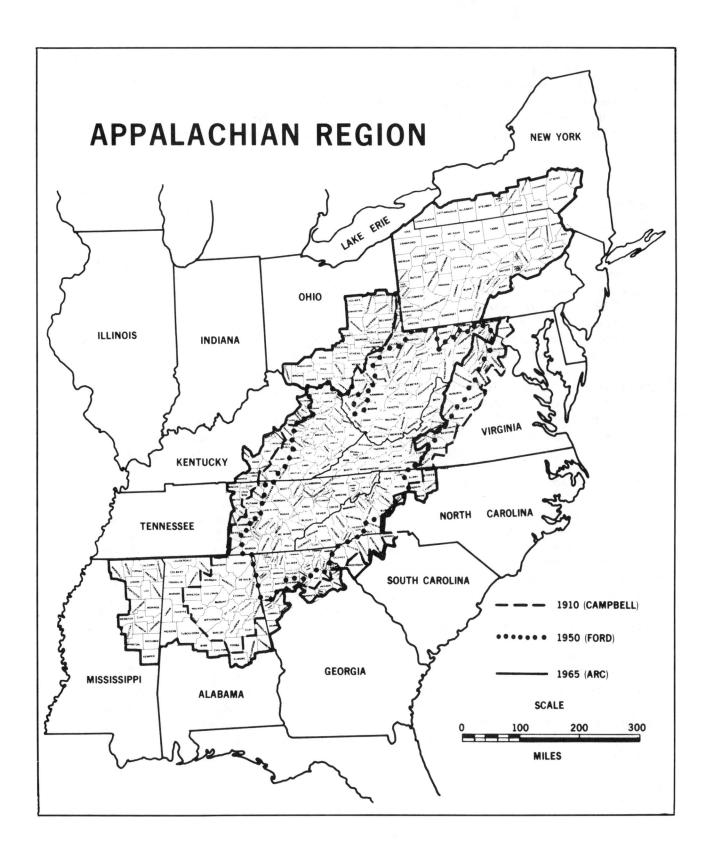

APPALACHIAN REGION

Legend:
- – – – 1910 (CAMPBELL)
- •••••• 1950 (FORD)
- ——— 1965 (ARC)

SCALE

0   100   200   300

MILES

tenant farmers, hollow folk, or families recently bought out by the large mining and lumber companies. It is this group that has been singled out as the typical mountaineer; whose weaknesses and virtues have been exaggerated in the North and Lowland South. While much of their life is picturesque, it is also exceptional, and the distressing conditions found there are cause for great resentment.

The Southern Appalachian Region

Between the publication of Campbell's first social scientific study and the publication of *The Southern Appalachian Region: A Survey*[8] there appeared only a few studies of mountain people and communities.[9] The major study of the period was Howard W. Odum's survey of the *Southern Regions of the United States.*[10] While encyclopaedic in information of a statistical nature the study takes no notice of any particular highland or Appalachian characteristics residing in what is a major portion of the study area. Moreover, the term Appalachian appears only in reference to (1) a portion of the southern mountain states which is losing population at a higher rate than that of the states themselves, and (2) a place ideally formed for the construction of large dams to create power and recreational areas for the urban easterners. Somehow the uniqueness of the area escaped Odum and his team of co-workers.

Appalachia, in the meantime, had not gone unnoticed and was known as a distinct area by both home missions groups, whose efforts by this time were largely translated into support for small missions and settlement schools, and by the Council of Southern Mountains. This latter organization was the continuation of a group of social workers, clergy, educators and health professionals who had been brought together largely through the efforts of John C. Campbell during the years between 1908–1919. Meetings of the annual Knoxville Conference of Southern Mountain Workers slowly became transformed into the Council whose area of concern was the human and social development of the southern mountain people, be they hollow-folk or road-folk, church or unchurched, poor or making it. The Council's executive secretary, self-made sociologist Perley Ayer became the region's best known spokesman and interpreter during his nearly 20 years in that position until his death in 1969. Ayer used the Campbell definition of the area, these 256 highland counties.[11]

Ayer was one of the nonacademicians in attendance at the Berea conference in 1956 which decided to explore the possibility of a new study of the mountain area with a problem-solving purpose in mind. The Ford Foundation undertook the effort and major universities in the region lent cooperation. The final report was published in 1962 as *The Southern Appalachian Region: A Survey* under the general direction and editorship of sociologist Thomas R. Ford. This study was to become the largest single effort to study the cultural, religious, economic, political, educational and recreational life of the mountain people. The study area was defined using a new concept of state economic areas, developed jointly in 1950 by the Bureau of Census and the U.S. Department of Agriculture . . . counties whose livelihood is drawn from the same economic base were grouped to form similar economic base areas. Thus armed with a new definition a new region was carved out of the southern highlands.

The new region is reduced from Campbell's highland region by nearly 60 counties to 190 counties in only seven states. Lost is the western tip of Maryland and northwestern South Carolina. The easternmost part of the region receded westward along a single row of counties from Virginia through North Carolina into Georgia. The western edge of the region moves eastward from Campbell's boundaries and cuts off seven counties in Tennessee and five in Kentucky. The northernmost boundary also shrinks with the loss of some twelve counties in West Virginia. Since the geography and topography of the region had remained constant, and the political subdivisions had not been changed, the area may be said to have been redefined or newly created. Where Campbell had used physical or topographic appearance as his criterion for inclusion, the Southern Appalachian regional study added the socio-economic variable to the geopolitical criterion and reduced the region to a heartland of Appalachia.

To the outsider nothing really had changed. Most of the counties earlier considered highland counties still made up the major portion, indeed 4/5 of the area. The mountains were still the mountains, hillbillies still hillbillies and moonshine still moonshine. Moreover, whatever changes were taking place in the social and economic characteristics of the population (presented in detail later in this article) were not particularly apparent. The one change which is particularly noteworthy is the choice of name for the region. Heretofore, the area had been designated "the mountains," the "hill country," "the highlands" or the "southern mountains." With the publication of the Ford study the name Appalachia was appended to the area, and it was to stick.[12]

The Appalachian Region

Ford's choice of the descriptive term "Southern Appalachia" was probably more of a political choice than one of social definition, for we find Ford himself refers to the people living in the area, not as Appalachians or even Appalachian people, but as "highlanders." The choice of the term is coincidental with the development of a concern on the part of several mountain states; a concern to launch an attack on their similar problems in the mountain areas of their several states. An Annapolis meeting in early 1960 followed by one in Lexington the same year produced a plan to create a "special regional program of development that envisioned combined attack on their problems through the resources of the local, state and Federal governments, and the assistance of private industry, civic groups, and the philanthropic foundations."[13] Responding to a regional study already in process, to university efforts to develop regional plans, and to state economic development offices, the conference of governors called for a federal agency to do for them (and through them) what they themselves were unable to do for themselves; namely to finance the recovery of the mountain region. The plan gave birth to a stoutly funded federal commission, controlled by the participating governors, called the Appalachian Regional Commission (hereafter ARC), created by law in 1965. Shortly before the region was legally defined the governors of Ohio, New York, South Carolina, and Mississippi joined their states to the newly created region.

Again, in less than 50 years, a new Appalachian region was created. This time, however, it was created by men with political power to deliver funds which they do not create through local taxation—to be used for highly visible highway construction and usually noncontroversial aid to health delivery services, educational facilities, sanitary improvements and small business expansion. This new ARC region is one which would be only partially recognizable to Campbell. It includes 397 counties in some 13 eastern states, including portions of Ohio, Pennsylvania, New York and

Mississippi, previously never considered as part of the Appalachian region.

The criteria for inclusion in the ARC Appalachia were determined by the governors and their associates who created the region. The most primary consideration was a simple one: include those portions of the state which had traditionally been weakest in economic development. In words of the Commission's 1970 Annual Report the criteria were a "response to the severe economic and social conditions which existed in large sections of Appalachia in the late 1950s and early 1960s."[14] The report cites a dangerously specialized economy—mining—accounting for 20 percent of the labor force in the central part of the region, a high rate of exodus—2.2 million persons during the 1950s—due primarily to lack of jobs; areas of the barest economic subsistence—four of the five poorest counties in the United States are in the region, and 60 percent of Kentucky's Appalachian portion had annual incomes below $3,000 in 1960; school drop-out rates from 10–20 percent higher than the national rate; a high illiteracy rate; and health conditions paralleling the educational and economic deprivation. The new Appalachia contains 18.8 million people, or 8.8 percent of the nation's 1970 population total.

Thus in a 50-year period the region has been thrice defined, each time using distinct criteria and each time made up of a different mix of geopolitical divisions. Table 7.1 graphically shows these differences. It is apparent that the region experienced shrinkage and expansion depending on the definition used to describe it. Not only are states sometimes Appalachian and sometimes not, e.g., Maryland and South Carolina, but lately four states never before considered Appalachian now

TABLE 7.1

States and Number of Counties Considered to be Appalachian in 1921, 1962, and 1970

	State Considered as Part of the Region in			Number of Counties in the Region in		
	1921	1962	1970	1921	1962	1970
Alabama	X	X	X	19	5	35
Georgia	X	X	X	25	10	35
Kentucky	X	X	X	37	32	49
Maryland	X		X	4	0	3
Mississippi			X	0	0	20
New York			X	0	0	14
North Carolina	X	X	X	24	22	29
Ohio			X	0	0	28
Pennsylvania			X	0	0	52
South Carolina	X		X	4	0	6
Tennessee	X	X	X	45	37	50
Virginia	X	X	X	43	30	21
West Virginia	X	X	X	55	43	55
Totals	9	7	13	256	189 *	397

*The Ford study states 190 as the count. My figures consistently sum to 189.

add a large number of counties to the region. With the inclusion of Mississippi, New York, Ohio and Pennsylvania, 114 counties are added to the Appalachian total.

Population totals for the three periods reflect the expansion and shrinkage of the region. These data are presented for the census years used by Campbell and the Ford study group, namely 1910 and 1950, and for 1970 as the most current ARC descriptive data. In 1910 the highland region population totaled 5.3 million, or slightly over one-third of the total population of states included in the region. By 1950 although smaller in geographic size, due to general population increase the region now numbered 5.8 million. This total, however, was only slightly more than one-quarter of the mountain states' total population. This actual numeric increase is accounted for by two main factors, according to the Ford study: (1) the out-migration which had characterized the region during the first half of the century were drastically slowed due to the depression of the 1930s, and (2) the industrial expansion in the Great Appalachian Valley caused population growth atypical of the region as a whole.[15]

By 1970 the region numbered nearly 18 million people. The inclusion of nearly six million Pennsylvanians, one million Ohioans, one million New Yorkers and four hundred thousand Mississippians did much to increase the figure. The "Appalachian people" now accounted for 27 percent of the Appalachian states' total. Subtracting these four states from the 1970 totals a more useful figure for the regional comparison will be

10.3 million population in the nine Appalachian portions or 30 percent of the Appalachian states' total. Table 7.2 provides the actual data.

It is not our purpose here to make a detailed population analysis from the data presented for the three periods. Our purpose is merely to show by limited use of these data that the region has had many definitions, definitions which when translated into population numbers encompass varying portions of the national and regional totals. Such contraction and, more especially, expansion, has no little impact on who are considered to be "Appalachians."

One further note is of interest. Campbell cited population totals as a primary tool to discriminate the three geographic belts he recognized as natural regional divisions in the highlands. He did not consider (nor even cite) their proportion of the states of which they were a part, nor the nation as a whole. He did, however, cite the number of villages, towns and cities as significant data for comparisons within the region. His main concern was to show intra-regional variation and commonality as it existed in the Southern Highlands. The Ford study is more difficult to categorize. Compiled by hundreds of writers, research assistants and interviewers, the focus varies article by article. However, both intra- and inter-regional comparisons are made, and there is an effort to particularly explain the causes for out-migration, and whatever population increase is found. Needless to say, the Ford group had access to data and personnel of which Campbell could have hardly dreamed.

TABLE 7.2

Appalachian States Population and Selected Portions: 1910, 1950, 1970

	State Population (in 1,000)			Appalachian Population (in 1,000)			Appalachian Population as % of State			Appalachian Population as % of U.S.		
	1910	1950	1970	1910	1950	1970	1910	1950	1970	1910	1950	1970
Alabama	2,138	3,063	3,444	732	207	2,137	34.24	6.76	62.04	0.79	0.13	1.05
Georgia	2,609	3,445	4,590	315	354	814	12.07	10.28	17.73	0.34	0.23	0.40
Kentucky	2,290	2,945	3,219	581	795	876	25.37	26.99	27.21	0.63	0.53	0.43
Maryland	1,295		3,922	185		209	14.28		5.32	0.20		0.10
Mississippi			2,217			419			18.89			0.20
New York			18,191			1,056			5.81			0.52
North Carolina	2,206	4,062	5,082	394	573	1,037	17.86	14.10	20.40	0.42	0.37	0.51
Ohio			10,652			1,129			10.60			0.55
Pennsylvania			11,794			5,930			50.27			2.91
South Carolina	1,515		2,591	205		656	13.53		25.31	0.22		0.32
Tennessee	2,185	3,292	3,924	860	1,321	1,734	39.35	40.12	44.19	0.93	0.87	0.85
Virginia	2,062	3,319	4,648	837	934	470	40.59	28.14	10.10	0.91	0.61	0.23
West Virginia	1,221	2,006	1,744	1,221	1,650	1,744	100.00	82.25	100.00	1.32	1.09	0.85
Total:	17,521	22,131	76,018	5,330	5,834	18,211	30.42	26.36	23.96	5.78	3.86	9.26

U.S. Population: *1910*—92,228,000   *1950*—151,325,000   *1970*—203,212,000

Sources: 1910 Data—Campbell, Appendix E, Table 17, p. 362.
1950 Data—Ford, p. 38 and U.S. Census of Population.
1970 Data—ARC 1970 Annual Report, Appendix A, pp. 103–108.

WHO ARE THE APPALACHIANS?

The best advice on this subject might not be the most useful. Perley Ayer, long time Executive of the Council of Southern Mountains tells us "There is no standard variety of Appalachian mountaineer (to which) urban people can readily relate. . . ."[16] He implies that there is no standard variety at all. Yet the force of the mountain fiction and of the social studies in any given time period seems to press for a standard definition. To most the mountaineer is not a person but a prototype: in one period he's an ornery, independent feuding moonshiner. In another he's a proud, honest, God-fearing subsistence farmer. Still another prototype is the thin, gaunt, black-faced mountain miner. Finally, he is portrayed as a down-hearted, beaten, welfare recipient rocking on his dilapidated porch "just a setten." No prototype is accurate; most are stereotypes and carry the prejudice of ignorance of the true situation and a broad extension to the many of the attributes of the few.

Any accurate picture of mountain people must first clearly define the area of description. With the exception of the studies of a particular place, hollow, or village, most of the Appalachian or mountain studies are either vague on defining the geographic base of their writings or attempt to create *one* characterization from the millions of people who reside therein. We must then accept the fact that most of the social studies of the mountains and mountaineers are not specific as to the mountain region.[17] Given that limitation what does the literature tell us of these people?

Writings dating from the Chicago sociologist George Vincent's visit to the "retarded frontier" up to the present most often note that these people are independent and strong individualists. The independence is usually attributed to either Scotch-Irish Presbyterian "blood" or to the isolated living conditions which are common in the mountains.

Second to the individualism of the people, is their clannishness and family loyalty. We are told of strong family ties, of feuds between families and of respect for members of "one's own." Not only are these people said to be loyal to their kin but much of their total being revolves around dealings with members of both the immediate and extended families. One study even shows how the family operates as a stem, with roots in the mountains and branches to the industrial north with a steady flow or exchange up and down the tree trunk.[18]

A third characteristic often noted, but with far less frequency, is that of a life lived close to or in harmony with nature. Perley Ayer calls it an "easiness with life,"[19] while Edwin White fully describes it in this way: ". . . among far too large a share of the population there is no thought that things can be different. A spirit of passive resignation pervades much of the section."[20] This characteristic is commonly seen as a strength lending support to the Rousseauean notion that living close to the land in a primitive state is a healthy state of being, one to be envied by the hassled urban dweller.

While these three characteristics of independence, clan ties and life in harmony with nature have been consistently cited over the past seventy years, a close look at the general works about Mountain "Appalachian" people indicates that certain features are commonly cited, others not. Moreover, a pattern seems to have developed in these descriptions, particularly since the Ford study's publication. That pattern is the inclusion, starting with Ford, of three other traits, namely fatalism, traditionalism, and religious fundamentalism.

Using information found in 20 books and articles which describe mountain or Appalachian people in general (and omitting several works dealing with particular folk in a specific place, e.g., the Clay County, Kentucky residents of Fetterman's *Stinking Creek,* or the hollow families at the end of Gazeway's *The Longest Mile*), we have found some 11 specific characteristics developed. They are, in order of most frequent citation: Independence, Religious Fundamentalism, Strong Family Ties, Life in Harmony with Nature, Fatalism, Traditionalism, Honor, Fearlessness, Allegiance, Suspicion of Government, and Born Trader. Of the last five cited, Born Trader is found only in Campbell's study, and the others are cited with equal frequency. Table 7.3 presents the works by author and the characteristics cited therein. It also exposes the pattern of recent inclusion of the three traits of fatalism, traditionalism, and religious fundamentalism by writers since Ford. Traditionalism and fatalism are first noted in Ford and have since been commonly cited. Born Trader, noted by Campbell, is not explicitly found in any of the other works used, although it is a common theme in the literature of the mountain regions. Suspicion of Government is first specifically cited in Photoiadis and Schwarzweller as recent as 1970 although it may be inferred in earlier writings.

The rank ordering of these characteristics as shown in table 7.3 changes significantly between the pre-Ford period and that which follows. While Independence continues to rank first, the four other commonly found characteristics are equally ranked. This could be a function of the large number of studies included since Ford's publication—eleven (including Ford) compared to nine pre-Ford. It could be due to the more critical nature of the works of this more recent, more socially conscious, period. Or it could be simply due to the "fall out" syndrome, namely, that once a group is definitively characterized, those who subsequently describe it find these traits said to be characteristics of that population. Given the wide acceptance of the Ford work, and the fact that with it were gathered together articles by acknowledged students of the field of study, it is small wonder that it appears as a watershed for "Appalachian" studies.

TABLE 7.3

Personal Characteristics of Mountain People as Cited in Selected Studies: 1898–1972.[*]

		Family—strong kin ties / a—clan loyalty	Independence—individualism / a—isolated people	Life in harmony with nature	Honor	Fearlessness	Allegiance	Born traders	Traditionalists	Fatalism	Suspicion of gov't	Religious fundamentalism	Terms of usual reference to the people of the area
Vincent	1898	X	a										"mountaineers"
Kephart	1913		X										"highlanders"
Campbell	21	a	X/a			X	X	X				X[1]	"highlanders"
White	37			X									
Ernst and Drake	59		X/a										
Griffin	59		X										
Griffin	pre 60		X	X									"Southern mountain people"
Weatherford	62	a	X/a		X	X							"mountain people"
Brewer	62											X	"Southern Appalachian people"
Ford	62		X	X					X	X		X	"highlander"
Weller	65	X	X			O[2]			X	X		X	"mountaineer"
Powell	66		X	X									"mountain people"
Caudill	66		O[3]										
Jones	6?	X	X		X[4]					X[5]		X	"Appalachian people" and "mountain people"
Ball	68								X				
Ayer	69	X		X									"people"
Photiadis and Schwarzweller	70	X	X/a	X			X		X	X	X	X	"Appalachian people"
Smathers	70										X[6]		"Appalachian people"
Gerrard	70										X	X	"Appalachian people"
Williams	1972		X									X[7]	"Southern mountaineer"
Total: N = 20		X 5 / 7 / a2	X 12 / 17 / a 5	6	2	2	2	1	4	5	2	8	
Pre-Ford		X 1 / 3 / a2	X 6 / 10 / a 4	2	1	2	1	1	0	0	0	2	
Post-Ford		X 4 / 4 / a0	X 6 / 7 / a 1	4	1	0	1	0	4	5	2	6	

This list is not exhaustive of the many articles on or about the people of Appalachia. It includes the better known works describing the larger Appalachian area, and excludes the many excellent monographs about single communities or which specifically treat geographic subregions. Any conclusions drawn from this listing must be, of necessity, merely suggestive, although they might seem compelling.

Harry M. Caudill treats his topic with particular reference to coal miners and Eastern Kentucky, he does not discuss "Appalachia." *Night Comes to the Cumberland,* Boston: Little, Brown and Company, 1962.

Sherman and Henry's *Hollow Folk,* a 1930s study of four levels of community, shows of how little importance religion and kin ties seem to be to the most isolated community. This study also is too geographically specific for inclusion in the list presented here.

Notes:
[1] inferred only.
[2] they are very much afraid, p. 44.
[3] they are losing their independence; all the characteristics cited as usual for those mountain people are vanishing.
[4] substitutes "pride" for honor.
[5] "religious" fatalism.
[6] suspicious of institutions.
[7] a religious nonconformist.
[*] See page 00 for citations of selected studies.

One further note is in order. Most of the specific characteristics cited in Ford are also found in Jack Weller. Due to the nature of the book, its primary audience—the membership of the churches—and its comparative low cost, the Weller book has received far greater popular acceptance. Harry M. Caudill writes in the foreward to Weller's book " . . . (it is an) analysis of the Appalachian mind and personality . . . likely to take its place as an analytical work comparable to *The Mind of the South* by W. J. Cash." An analysis of the life of many mountain people it is, and marked by insights and knowledge. But it is a development of insights and knowledge much of which was undoubtedly gathered from the works of men like W. D. Weatherford, Rupert B. Vance, and Earl D. C. Brewer, to name but the most obvious few, plus Thomas Ford himself. Although the more widely read and known book, *Yesterday's People* is primarily an expression of but one dimension of the mountaineers about whom much data is presented in Ford. Following in the old Biblical studies tradition, only lately discovered by sociologists, Weller's is, in a sense, an exegetical work. This may further explain its popularity in church circles.[21]

In summary then, we find the mountain people described as independent, kin-involved people whose lives are closely bound to their physical environment, whose activities are traditional, and whose beliefs are both fatalistic and religiously fundamentalist. This description has slowly emerged and expanded from the earliest attempts by social scientists to the most recent.

Any attempt at description over time immediately opens up the ever present condition of social change. This is certainly true of the subject at hand, as reflected in the characteristics listed in table 7.3 above. And the greater the amount of description, the greater the probability that change will be noted. This is true not only because of the differential vision or acuity of the several observers, but because social conditions do cause change in attitudes and behavior. Rebecca Caudill laments the loss of that mosaic of characteristics commonly thought to be both unique and peculiar to the mountain people—the loss of independence caused by a new dependence on charity and public welfare for survival, and the loss of a sense of community responsibility and pride.[22] Harry Caudill also notes a similar phenomenon in the same section of the mountains, "myriads of men, women and children . . . gazing with listless unconcern at the world," "(a people whose) fierce pride and sensitive spirit of independence have died . . . ," a broken people.[23] Granted, both these writers are making particular reference to the people of Eastern Kentucky. But others too note the factors of poverty as being widely spread throughout the mountains, and of continual poverty as debilitating, devitalizing, and demoralizing. The collection of articles brought together in Photoiadis and Schwarzweller's *Change in Rural Appalachia,* emphatically makes this point.[24] Our point here is merely to indicate that changing conditions do change the characteristics of the people.

One of the major conditions most commonly cited for the change among the mountain people is their loss of economic power relative to other neighboring parts of America. We have noted above that the ARC definition utilizes this fact as a major determinant of Appalachian status for counties now included as Appalachia. We need not here labor the point that these sections, and the mountain portions particularly, have lower productivity, lower per capita income and, in general, poorer living conditions, than the average for the "Appalachian" states as a whole, or indeed the nation. A quick glance at comparative figures for per capita personal income for the United States, "Appalachian" portions of states, and their "non-Appalachian" portions shows that with but two exceptions the "Appalachian" portions are consistently lower for the thirteen states in the ARC's "Appalachia." Data for 1959 show "Appalachians" to have but 77 percent of the national per capita personal income. That figure was 78 percent nearly a decade later.[25]

However, the per capita income variation within this large region is great. For example, while Virginia's 1967 "Appalachian" portion is only 58 percent of the national average and her non-"Appalachian" portion is 90 percent, nearby Pennsylvania's Appalachian portion has 91 percent of the nation's per capita income while her non-"Appalachian" portion has 111 percent. New York's variation is even greater. Hence poverty is relative in Appalachia, and is greatest in the core sections of the region. The two states with the greatest gap between the "Appalachian" portions of the state are Kentucky with 39 percentage points difference and Ohio with 37. A final indication of the relative nature of this poverty is that Maryland's "Appalachian" portion enjoys 108 percent of the nation's average per capita income while Kentucky's and Georgia's "Appalachians" receive 47 and 59 percent of it, respectively. With such great regional variations it is little wonder that the characteristics of the people who reside therein are varied as well.

Before entering into a discussion of those variations and specific population characteristics, we would like to emphasize one final point related to the change in what has been said to be the Appalachian or mountain characteristics. The isolation which once existed in the mountains is slowly being eroded by improved roads, but it has already fallen in terms of the media invasion. Rural electrification had hardly set the power lines before T.V. sets were daily bringing in the outside world. And with the loss of the previous barrier created by hills and valleys unfriendly to road builders came the loss of innocence. People were less content with their condition when they could see the common luxury of urban living and could hear reports on their own relative conditions of isolation, or poverty, or education, or any of the many media concerns carried during the recently fought "War on Poverty." With greater contact with the "outside" the mountain people have lost much of what had been peculiar to them. John D. Photoidis adds two other causes for the rapid narrowing of the gap between the mountain region and larger American society; namely the availability of employment opportunities in urban centers and changes in formal education.[26] He goes on to develop the point that as greater interaction takes place with urban middle-class Americans the stereotypical homogenous rural Appalachian population will slowly disappear. There is little doubt that change is taking place, and traditional definitions of "Appalachian" characteristics are more and more subject to question.

Identification of Works Cited on Chart Entitled: "Personal Characteristics of Mountain People" from selected studies, 1898–1972

Vincent, George E., "The Retarded Frontier," *American Journal of Sociology* 4:1(7/1898) pp. 1–20.

Kephart, Horace, *Our Southern Highlanders,* New York: The Outing Publishing Co., 1913.

Campbell, John C., *The Southern Highlander and His Homeland,* Lexington: University of Kentucky Press, 1969 (1921).

White, Edwin, *Highland Heritage.* New York: Friendship Press, 1937.

Ernst, Harry W. and Charles H. Drake, "The Lost Appalachians" in *The Nation,* reprinted in David S. Walls and John B. Stephenson (eds.), *Appalachia in the Sixties,* Lexington: University of Kentucky Press, 1972, pp. 3–9.

Giffin, Roscoe, "Newcomers from the Southern Mountains," 1959 speech in Rose, Arnold M. and Caroline B. (eds.), *Minority Problems,* (Second Edition) New York: Harper & Row, 1972, pp. 28–33.

Giffin, Roscoe, cited in Ernst and Drake, (pre-1960).

Weatherford, W. D., and Earl D. C. Brewer, *Life and Religion in Southern Appalachia,* New York: Friendship Press, 1962.

Brewer, Earl D. C., "Religion and the Churches" in Ford, Thomas R., (ed.), *The Southern Appalachian Religion: A Survey,* Lexington: University of Kentucky Press, 1962, pp. 201–218.

Ford, Thomas R., "The Passing of Provincialism" in Ford, *op. cit.,* pp. 9–34.

Weller, Jack E., *Yesterday's People: Life in Contemporary Appalachia,* Lexington: University of Kentucky Press, 1965.

Powell, Levi W., *Who are These Mountain People?,* New York: Exposition Press, 1966.

Caudill, Rebecca and Edward Wallowitch, *My Appalachia: A Reminiscence,* New York: Holt, Rinehart & Winston, 1966.

Jones, Loyal, "Appalachian Values," n.d., (late 60s), Berea College (mimeo).

Ball, Richard A., "The Southern Appalachian Folk Subculture as a Tension-Reducing Way of Life," in Photoiadis and Schwarzweller, *Change in Rural Appalachia,* Philadelphia: University of Pennsylvania Press, 1970, pp. 69–79.

Ayer, Perley, *Seeking a People Partnership,* Berea, Ky.: Council of Southern Mountains, 1969.

Photiadis, John D. and Harry K. Schwarzweller, *Change in Rural Appalachia,* Philadelphia: University of Pennsylvania Press, 1970.

Smathers, Michael, "Suspicion and Community in Appalachia," in Glenn, Max E. (ed.), *Appalachia in Transition,* St. Louis: The Bethany Press, 1970, pp. 69–81.

Gerrard, Nathan L., "Churches of the Stationary Poor in Southern Appalachia," in Photiadis and Schwarzweller, *Change in Rural Appalachia,* op. cit.

Williams, Cratis D., "Who are the Southern Mountaineers?" *Appalachian Journal* Autumn, 1972, pp. 48–55.

NOTES

1. Betty Garrett, "An Appalachian Author Describes His Life Style," *Appalachia,* 6:3 (Dec. 1972–Jan. 1973), 25–28.

2. "A Look at the 1970 Census," *Mountain Life and Work,* July–August, 1970.

3. Jack E. Weller, *Yesterday's People: Life in Contemporary Appalachia* (Lexington: University of Kentucky Press, 1965).

4. In the New Foreword to Campbell's *The Southern Highlander and His Homeland* (Lexington: University of Kentucky Press, 1969(1921)), p. vii.

5. Ibid, pp. 10 ff.

6. Ibid, p. 12.

7. Ibid., pp. 72–89.

8. Thomas R. Ford (ed.), *The Southern Appalachian Region: A Survey* (Lexington: University of Kentucky Press, 1962).

9. Mandel Sherman and Thomas R. Henry coauthor a study of five western Virginia communities from rural to completely isolated in their *Hollow Folks* (New York: Thomas Y. Crowell, 1933). Edwin White's *Highland Heritage* appears in 1937. *Mountain Life and Work,* the magazine of the Council of Southern Mountains published continuously since about 1924, provides some of the best continuous coverage of the social scene. Novels about mountain people appear during this period but it is not until the early 1960s and the New Frontier war on Poverty that Appalachia is rediscovered, as Robert F. Munn so aptly puts it in his article, "The Latest Rediscovery of Appalachia," *Mountain Life and Work,* Fall, 1965. Most of the USDA publications relevant to the Appalachian area appear to be related to the Odum study, discussed below.

10. Howard W. Odum, *Southern Regions of the United States* (Chapel Hill: University of North Carolina Press, 1936).

11. Perley Ayer, *Seeking a People Partnership: Challenges by Perley Ayer* (Berea, Ky.: Council of Southern Mountains, 1969). Ayer uses the figure 257. This writer counts 256. Rupert Vance reports the number to be 216 in his introductory chapter in Ford, and, unfortunately, Campbell nowhere give the total.

12. A half century earlier Berea College President Frost had called attention to "Appalachian America, the mountainous backyards of nine states . . . one of God's grand divisions." His phrase did not catch on until the 1960s. Cited in Munn, *op. cit.*

13. Jerald Jer Horst, "No More Pork Barrel: The Appalachian Approach," *The Reporter,* March 11, 1965, cited in David S. Walls and John B. Stephenson (eds.), *Appalachia in the Sixties* (Lexington: University of Kentucky Press, 1972), p. 32.

14. *Op. cit.,* p. 1.

15. John C. Belcher, "Population Growth and Characteristics" in Ford, *op. cit.,* pp. 37–53.

16. *Op. cit.,* p. 21.

17. Two excellent depictions of specific types of southern people in poverty which do not claim to be "Appalachian specific" but describe the type so often thought of as typical are James Agee and Walker Evans artistic yet tragic portrayals of southern tenant farmers, *Let Us Now Praise Famous Men* (Boston: Houghton Mifflin Co., 1960 (1939)) and Robert Coles' three volumes. *Children in Crisis,* especially vol. 2, *Migrants, Sharecroppers, Mountaineers* (Boston: Little, Brown and Company, 1971 (1967)).

18. Harry K. Schwarzweller, James S. Brown and J. J. Mangalam, *Mountain Families in Transition* (University Park: Pennsylvania State University Press, 1970).

19. Ayer, *op. cit.,* p. 16.

20. White, *op. cit.,* p. 92.

21. Probably the best example of the contemporary discovery of exegesis is Lewis Coser's *The Functions of Social Conflict,* a statement, treatment and restatement of George Simmel's work on conflict.

22. Rebecca Caudill with Edward Wallowitch, *My Appalachia: A Reminiscence* (New York: Holt, Rinehart and Winston, 1966), pp. 64ff.

23. Harry M. Caudill, *Night Comes to the Cumberlands* (Boston: Little, Brown and Co., 1962), pp. 330–350 passim.

24. Photoiadis and Schwarzweller, *Change in Rural Appalachia* (Philadelphia: University of Pennsylvania Press, 1970).

25. *Appalachian Data Book,* Summary Volume (Washington: Appalachian Regional Commission, April, 1970), table 10, pp. 10–11.

26. Photiadis and Schwarzweller, *op. cit.,* pp. 5–7, and the entire opening chapter, "Rural Southern Appalachia and Mass Society."

David S. Walls is Assistant Professor in the College of Social Professions and Planning Coordinator for the Appalachian Center at the University of Kentucky. He is co-editor of *Appalachia in the Sixties.* Dwight B. Billings is Assistant Professor in the Department of Sociology at the University of Kentucky. His *Planters, Capitalists and the Politics of Development in the New South* will be published by the University of North Carolina Press.

8. THE SOCIOLOGY OF SOUTHERN APPALACHIA

David S. Walls
Dwight B. Billings

Sociologists have been fascinated by the Appalachians ever since George Vincent of the University of Chicago took a four-day horseback ride through Breathitt, Perry, and Knott Counties in eastern Kentucky in 1898. Urging study of "this curious social survival . . . now being modified so rapidly," Vincent concluded his descriptive and impressionistic account, "Let students of sociology leave their books and at first hand in the Cumberlands deal with the phenomena of a social order arrested at a relatively early state of evolution."[1] Setting aside questions about the accuracy of Vincent's characterization of the region as a retarded frontier, we can see in his article two themes which predominate in sociological studies of Appalachia from his day to ours: social change and social problems.

Vincent acknowledged his debt to such writers of the "local color movement" as Mary Murfree and John Fox, Jr., for being the first to recognize the Southern Mountains as a distinctive subcultural region. The "discovery" of the Southern Appalachians is itself a problem in the sociology of knowledge and has been addressed by historian Henry Shapiro in *Appalachia on Our Minds,*[2] a brilliant interpretation of the emergence of a national consciousness of Southern Appalachia in the period from 1875 to 1920. Herbert Blumer's comment could well apply to Vincent (and many others) in regard to Appalachia: "Sociological recognition follows in the wake of societal recognition, veering with the winds of the public identification of social problems."[3]

Theories of Social Change and Social Problems

The themes of social change, social problems, and the response of private and public social policy underlie the major social surveys of the Southern Appalachian region: John C. Campbell's *Southern Highlander and His Homeland* in 1921, the U.S. Department of Agriculture's *Economic and Social Problems and Conditions of the Southern Appalachians* in 1935, the section on the "Southern Appalachian Coal Plateaus" in the Study of Population Redistribution in 1936, the Ford Foundation supported study *The Southern Appalachian Region: A Survey* in 1962, and the various studies and annual reports of the Appalachian Regional Commission since 1965.[4] These studies illustrate a major accomplishment of the sociology of Appalachia: the analysis of demographic data from census statistics, including population changes, fertility rates, incomes, unemployment, housing, health, and so on.

David S. Walls is Assistant Professor in the College of Social Professions and Planning Coordinator for the Appalachian Center at the University of Kentucky. He is co-editor of *Appalachia in the Sixties.* Dwight B. Billings is Assistant Professor in the Department of Sociology at the University of Kentucky. His *Planters, Capitalists and the Politics of Development in the New South* will be published by the University of North Carolina Press.

Reprinted from *Appalachian Journal,* Vol. 5, No. 1 (Autumn 1977), pp. 131–144. Copyright Appalachian State University/Appalachian Journal. Used by permission.

Surprisingly, little systematic attention has been devoted by sociologists of Appalachia to fundamental theories of social change or models that explain regional poverty and underdevelopment. Tacit assumptions about the process of social change are more common than explicit models of the roots of regional problems and strategies to overcome the area's difficulties. Description, explanation, and prescription are intertwined in many studies and are not often clearly distinguished. Yet over the years a variety of arguments have been advanced to account for what is variously described as the backwardness, poverty, underdevelopment, and resistance to change of the Appalachian region and its people.

Genes vs. Environment. In the late nineteenth century, historian John Fiske implied a genetic basis for Appalachian poverty and backwardness by suggesting the poor class of mountaineers were the descendants of convicts and indentured servants. The argument of genetic deficiency was elaborated in the 1920's by Arthur Estabrook and Nathaniel Hirsch and revived recently by Harry Caudill.[5] In contrast, the geographic circumstances of isolation and poor communication were emphasized at the turn of the century by William Frost and Ellen Semple.[6] One objective of John Campbell in *The Southern Highlander* was to refute Fiske's argument by providing a correct record of the origins and current status of mountain people and by emphasizing an environmental explanation of mountain problems.[7] In recent years genetic and geographical explanations have generally been superseded by sociocultural and economic theories. During the 1960's, three models were drawn upon to explain Appalachian poverty and underdevelopment: the subculture of poverty, regional development, and internal colonialism models. Each of these three current models was first discovered in the context of underdevelopment in the Third World and applied by analogy to the Appalachian case.

Subculture of Poverty. The subculture of poverty model identifies the internal deficiencies of the lower-class subculture as the source of the problem. Oscar Lewis is the social scientist most closely identified with this model, and the most widely read exposition of the model applied to Appalachia is Jack Weller's *Yesterday's People,* which borrows an analytic framework from Herbert Gans.[8] The subculture of poverty model suggests remedial programs of education, social casework, and clinical psychology. Other studies of Appalachian culture in these terms include David Looff's *Appalachia's Children,* Norman Polansky's *Roots of Futility,* and various articles by Richard Ball.[9]

This model in general has been subjected to devastating criticism, and Steve Fisher has criticized Weller's application of this model to Appalachia.[10] In an empirical test, sociologist Dwight Billings has shown the model to be of little value in explaining the lack of

economic development in the mountain section of North Carolina and the contrasting industrialization of the piedmont. Ironically, it was just when the distinctiveness of the Southern Appalachian traditional subculture was fading that the subculture of poverty model was popularized and applied to the region.[11]

The pejorative viewpoint on Appalachian culture has been answered by an affirmative approach in works from John and Olive Campbell through Loyal Jones' essay on Appalachian values. Mike Maloney and Ben Huelsman have contrasted the affirmative and pejorative approaches in their essay, "Humanism, Scientism, and the Southern Mountaineer."[12] With the humanistic tradition, in their terms, are Robert Coles, John Fetterman, Tony Dunbar, Kathy Kahn, and John Stephenson, who use their subjects' own words to characterize Appalachian life-worlds.[13] Their descriptions of individuals and families manage to capture the strengths as well as the shortcomings of mountaineers and the diversity of personality types within some common subcultural themes.

The subculture of poverty model can be seen as only one approach within a broader framework of explanations rooted in the tradition of cultural idealism. Affirmative cultural approaches toward Southern Appalachia, as exemplified by Frost and the Campbells, are the obverse side of the coin from the pejorative tradition of the subculture of poverty school. The regionalism of the 1930's, as personified by Howard Odum and others, followed in the tradition of affirmative cultural idealism and looked to ties to the land and a sense of place, combined with planning, for regional revitalization. As John Friedmann points out, the new regionalism of the 1960's discarded the grounding in cultural idealism in favor of a regional development model resting within the contemporary technocratic image and ideology of science.[14]

Regional Development. Although the literature on development includes disciplines from social psychology to social ecology, the most influential stream derives from neo-classical economics as amended by central place theory.[15] The resulting regional development model is concerned with providing economic and social overhead capital, training people for skills for new industrial and service jobs, facilitating migration, and promoting the establishment or relocation of privately-owned industries through a growth center. Niles Hansen is probably the best known academic proponent of this approach. The major attempt to apply the model within the United States is the work of the Appalachian Regional Commission (ARC) and its associated programs.[16]

A major sociological contribution to the regional development model is the notion of a modernizing elite as the agent of the developmental process. H. Dudley Plunkett and Mary Jean Bowman elaborate this idea in *Elites and Change in the Kentucky Mountains.* They identify the "interstitial person" as the "cultural bridge" between traditional and modernizing groups and investigate such key occupational groups as bankers, lawyers, public officials, clergy, physicians, and schoolteachers to determine their relative commitments to change. In general, Plunkett and Bowman found the "ministering professionals"—clergy, physicians, and teachers—to have the most modern outlook; businessmen to be intermediate; and the local administrative elite, the "gerontocracy" of bankers, lawyers, and politicians to be the most traditional.[17] The ARC strategy appears to follow the Plunkett and Bowman suggestion of cooperating with the modernizing professionals to coopt or outmaneuver the traditional business elites and the old county political machines. The basic structure for this strategy on the local level is the multi-county Local Development District, which serves as a mechanism for arriving at consensus among regional elites. Through the dual federal-state structure of the ARC, the interests of regional and national elites are reconciled.

With its emphasis on mainstream economic theory and the technical aspects of development, the regional development model lays claim to being a scientific, value-free, non-controversial approach. As such, it is an effective means of providing additional resources to the region without affecting the existing structure of resource control. Actions taken by regional and national planners are defended as technical decisions, rather than political choices among alternative courses of development. Political sociology calls attention to the possibility that the most important decisions may be the "non-decision": the questions that are never raised and the subjects that never make the public agenda. Examples include public ownership of the region's natural resources and worker or community owned and controlled industry.[18]

Internal Colonialism. The issues of power and privilege in Appalachia are seldom faced squarely by the subculture of poverty and regional development advocates. In reaction to this obvious shortcoming, academics and activists looked for a model that emphasized inequality and exploitation. They hit upon the internal colonialism model for reasons that had much to do with the focus of the New Left in the 1960—imperialism abroad and oppression of racial minorities at home. As applied to Appalachia, the internal colonialism model has been used to examine the process by which dominant outside industrial interests established control and continue to prevent autonomous development of the subordinate internal colony. The model suggests the need for an anticolonial movement and a radical restructuring of society, with a redistribution of resources to the poor and powerless.

In his best selling 1962 study *Night Comes to the Cumberlands,* Harry Caudill makes only a passing reference to colonialism; by 1965 he begins to use the *internal* colonial designation. The theme was quickly picked up by activists and radical intellectuals in the Central Appalachian area, particularly the group associated with the Peoples' Appalachian Research Collective and its journal, *Peoples' Appalachia.*[19]

Helen Lewis and her associates have attempted a detailed application to Appalachia of Robert Blauner's model of the process of internal colonization of black Americans. In this analysis, such institutions as the Appalachian family and church emerge as not simply survivals of an earlier traditional subculture but also as defensive institutions whose "closed" characteristics are in part formed in resistance to the process of colonization. By emphasizing such values as "equality, non-competitiveness, and family-neighborhood solidarity," the family and the church resist the social change that would integrate the region into the American mainstream.[20]

Much of the attraction of the internal colonialism model, including its application to Appalachia, derives from its powerful analysis of the destruction of indigenous culture in the process of establishing and maintaining domination over the colonized group. It has also performed a valuable service by focusing attention on the acquisition of the raw materials of the region by outside corporate interests and on the exploitation of the local work force and community at large resulting from the removal of the region's natural resources for the benefit of absentee owners.

Although the internal colonialism model has raised important questions about wealth, power, and exploitation in central Appalachia, it may not offer the most satisfactory characterization of the situation of the region. The analogy with racial minorities in America has serious limitations in any strict definition of internal colonialism.[21] The involuntary entry into the United States of enslaved blacks from Africa or the conquered Native American tribes and the Mexican people of the Southwest presents a substantially different situation from that of most Appalachians. Barriers to the assimilation of Appalachians into mainstream society—prejudice against "hillbillies"— are based on bias against the lower classes, not against all the people of the region. The historical development of Appalachia since the expansion of industrial capitalism may present a better example of class domination than Colonial domination.[22]

Toward a More Comprehensive Theory of Social Change in Appalachia. A comprehensive theory of social change in Appalachia must synthesize and integrate a humanistic approach to culture, the technical aspects of regional development, and an appropriate critique of domination at the present period. Some outlines of such a theory emerge from the work of Frankfurt School theorist Jürgen Habermas. For Habermas there are three fundamental conditions or media through which social systems are maintained: interaction, work, and power or domination. All human societies use these means to resolve the problems of preserving life and culture. Corresponding to each of these media are the human "interests" in mutual understanding, technical control, and "emancipation from seemingly 'natural' constraint."[23] A solution to the problems of Appalachian poverty and underdevelopment would have to be concerned with each of the three modes of culture, technique, and domination. Habermas' distinction provides a basis for viewing cultural adaptation, technical development, and redistribution of power as potentially complementary aspects of social development.

We suggest the history of the Appalachian region is best understood in the context of industrial capitalist development. Currently, Appalachia must be analyzed in the context of advanced capitalism in the United States. In some instances (analyzing the role of the Japanese steel industry in providing capital for opening new coal mines in the region, for example), we may have to expand our horizon to the framework of the world capitalist system. In a recent work Habermas analyzes advanced capitalist societies in terms of their economic, administrative (state), and legitimation systems and the resulting class structures. This framework prompts us to examine the competitive and monopolistic sectors of private industry, the role of state expenditures, the legitimation of the system and the containment of rebellion, and the full complexity of the class structure of the region.[24] It may be fruitful to view Southern Appalachia as a peripheral region, rather than an internal colony, within an advanced capitalist society.[25]

"Middle-Range" Issues in the Sociology of Southern Appalachia

At a less comprehensive level of social theory, in the "middle-range" of sociological investigation, base-line studies have been made in several areas. We have substantial knowledge of kinship and community structures, cultural configurations, and demographic changes. We have much less complete knowledge of Appalachian patterns of social stratification and politics. It is useful to summarize these studies and to point out deficiencies in our knowledge.

Class, Status, and Power in Appalachia. As noted above, the subculture model and the regional development model of Appalachian change have both diverted attention away from certain aspects of social structure and politics and redirected attention to issues of cultural and psychological "modernity"—this, despite the fact that Appalachia was born modern. Two misconceptions about the traditional subculture deserve comment. The traditional subculture of the Southern Appalachians should not be characterized as either a poverty subculture or as a peasant culture. The pre-industrial, pioneer way of life cannot be equated with a subculture of poverty as described by Oscar Lewis; there is no evidence that traditional mountain families felt helpless, dependent, or inferior.[26] The analogy to a peasantry has been used in two senses, both in reference to the traditional subculture and to the type of domination during the company town era.[27] Neither analogy is accurate. Nineteenth-century mountaineers were not descendants of a peasant people, but the children and grandchildren of eighteenth century colonists, most of whom had been landless wage-earners from an agricultural and mercantile capitalist country about to enter into the industrial revolution. In sharp contrast to the *Gemeinschaft* solidarity of traditional peasant society, the Appalachian mountaineer was already the quintessential modern individualist. Further, the situation of the miner in the company town is typical of social relations in the early stage of oligopoly capitalism and should be designated as such, not as a condition of peasantry.

Inappropriate cultural models—as they fix attention on "rich Appalachia" and "poor Appalachia," on "traditional Appalachia" and "modern Appalachia"—obscure the region's complex pattern of social stratification. The expansion of state expenditures has helped create sizeable intermediate groupings of public workers (in education, local government, and public services) and workers in industries heavily subsidized by public funds (health services particularly). These elements of the "new working-class" have taken their places alongside such long-established groups as coal miners, workers in small factories, small farmers, country merchants, county-seat retailers, bankers, professionals, independent coal operators, and managers for the nationally-based coal companies in the monopolistic sector, in addition to the household workers, the welfare poor, and others outside the standard labor force. The occupational structure is obviously complex, and its changes need to be analyzed over time, particulary in relation to changes in the coal industry and the growth of state expenditures.

We have no studies of industrial communities in the mountains and, consequently, we have few accounts of stratification in mining communities and county-seat towns. Rural stratification has frequently been overlooked as well,[28] but some good studies have been made. John Stephenson has pictured a four-level structure in "Shiloh," and Schwarzweller, Brown, and Mangalam[29] have identified a clearly developed stratification system in "Beech Creek," despite the fact that they were studying poor families. Social status differences in Beech Creek were manifested in family reputation, visiting, marital exchanges, and territorial locations. Lower status people retained their ascribed family status—in the authors' words, their "inherited stigma"—despite personal achievements. This suggests that social factors which influence interaction in mountain communities across status boundaries have not been sufficiently studied. Such factors have important consequences for power and participation in local communities and thus for social and economic mobility.

One of the authors of this essay (Billings) first encountered the *process* of stratification when he attended grade school in a Southern West Virginia county-seat town. School property included two buildings and students were segregated by their fathers' occupations. "Coal Camp" students were routinely assigned to an annex, ostensibly because of "special learning difficulties," although every year two or three were assigned to the main building. In the fourth grade, Billings observed that one of these children always turned red and buried her face in her hands when the teacher called on her to participate in class. This same child was once stood up before the class and her chapped hands were shown to her classmates. The teacher explained that her father could not afford to buy her handcream and, in missionary language, she asked if one of the other children would share her bounty and bring her some cream. The undertaker's daughter did. Later, in her absence, the class was told that this was the same child who brought lice into the classroom.

This story suggests that being poor involves a social identity which is learned early and enforced by informal relationships in the local community. We know little about the rule-governed interactions—in the school, the work place, the welfare office, the voting place—which condition the performances of those defined as "the poor" in the mountains. Nor do we know much about the group with whom they have the most direct contact, the mountain middle class, for the latter have been rarely studied. Sociologists who have studied the middle class, such as Plunkett and Bowman, have been chiefly interested in their attitudes. The mountain middle class is typically viewed as a "cultural bridge" between the rural community and mass society. Their role as "gatekeeper," a better functional analogy, has been ignored and their influence on education, social services, political participation, and the economy has not been fully grasped. In fact, community power structure studies in Southern Appalachia are practically non-existent, although we have had Floyd Hunter's work as an exemplar for over 20 years, and a vast amount of subsequent literature.[30]

Richard Ball reported on the power structure of a northern West Virginia mining county; Rod Harless reported on a county in southern West Virginia.[31] Harless found that the county political elite, consisting of bankers and lawyers, were also on retainer for absentee corporations. Harless, however, used only the positional study method, not the reputational or decision-making case study methods. His work is of limited use for understanding the actual exercise of power and influence although it suggests a political structure similar to those found in other economically peripheral or dependent regions.[32] The middle-class role in county politics has also been discussed by Harry Caudill, Richard Couto, Tony Dunbar, and in Huey Perry's *"They'll Cut Off Your Project,"* a description of confrontation in West Virginia during the War on Poverty.[33]

Scholars who developed the colonial model have focused attention on another social group, absentee owners, who are influential in the life of the region, and in the politics of natural resource development. For example, Harless tried to identify a West Virginia ownership establishment and Richard Diehl[34] described an "Appalachian Energy Elite." A field of growing importance is the sociology of natural resource use. The social impact of the Army Corps of Engineers' dam building is beginning to be studied. The social and economic costs of Appalachian coal production have been explored in a series of reports by the Appalachian Resources Project at the University of Tennessee. Si Kahn has opened a discussion of the impact of Forest Service policies on the region.[35] Sue Johnson and Rabel Burdge have outlined a methodology for sociologists making contributions to Environmental Impact Statements under the National Environmental Policy Act of 1969. Another avenue for investigating the social impact of a disaster is explored by Kai Erikson's study of the destruction of community in the wake of the Buffalo Creek Flood.[36]

For the most part, these studies, like the community literature, fail to analyze the actual use of power and influence by absentee owners. An important exception is John Gaventa's analysis of the American Association, an English land-holding corporation in eastern Kentucky and Tennessee.[37] On a related theme, the increasing coordination of government and business in resource development has been described by David Whisnant and by Harry Caudill in the *Watches of the Night.*[38]

Surprisingly little attention has been paid to racial and ethnic minority groups, a shortcoming which has bolstered the old stereotype of Appalachia as a bastion of Anglo-Saxon stock. Racial minorities in Southern Appalachia include blacks, Native Americans, and mixed-race groups. Blacks numbered approximately 1.3 million of the total Appalachian population of 18.2 million according to the 1970 census, some 7.3 percent of the population in the 13-state region as defined by the ARC.[39] The few studies that have been made concerning black Appalachians have been concerned primarily with their participation in the coal industry.[40] Blacks composed a substantial proportion of the work force in coal mining in the Southern states between 1890 and 1930. Since that time the proportion of black miners has declined. The mechanization of the industry that began in the 1950's hit particularly hard at the black miner, who did not receive an equal share of the jobs operating continuous miners and other heavy equipment. As employment in the coal industry declined, blacks were laid off in disproportionate numbers. The increase in strip mining also worked against blacks, who rarely obtained jobs with stripping firms. Black Appalachians have been migrating out of the region at a greater rate than whites.

The Eastern Band of Cherokee Indians is the only organized group of Native Americans living in the Southern Appalachian region. Until recently, the only thorough study of the Eastern Cherokees had been conducted in the late 1950's by the Cross-Cultural Laboratory at the University of North Carolina. The Special Cherokee Issue of the *Appalachian Journal* in 1975, edited by Burt Purrington, has added considerable new material on the Eastern Cherokees.[41] The four counties in western North Carolina which include the Eastern Cherokee reservation lands had a total Indian population of 3,937 in the 1970 census. Several hundred additional Indians live in the North Carolina Piedmont and eastern Tennessee.

Ten major mixed-race or triracial (white, black, and Native American ancestry) groups have been identified in the eastern United States. Two of these, the "Melungeons" and the "Guineas," reside within the Southern Appalachian region. The Melungeons of Tennessee continue to give rise to a considerable quantity of mythology, despite the sober scholarship of Edward Price in the early 1950's. There is little up-to-date information on either group, although a study is underway on the Guineas of West Virginia.[42] An attempt was made to count the mixed-race peoples in the 1950 census, but the figures are highly suspect.[43] Research is needed to determine to what extent these groups have been maintained or have been assimilated.

As with blacks, studies of European ethnic groups in Southern Appalachia have been conducted mainly in terms of their association with the coal industry.[44] And with the notable exception of Kathy Kahn's *Hillbilly Women,* little systematic attention has been given to mountain women.

Finally, in the last few years some excellent theoretical work on social movement organization has been done by sociologists, and we have two exemplary case studies of CORE and SDA.[45] But for Appalachian social movements, social scientists have not kept up with the journalists in describing how occupants of class and status positions organize for cooperative and political action. Brit Hume's *Death and the Mines* provides information on the Black Lung Association and the Miners for Democracy movements. The War on Poverty in Appalachia has prompted many books.[46] David Whisnant has provided historical interpretations of the Council of the Southern Mountains and the Congress for Appalachian Development, and Frank Adams has written a history of the Highlander Center.[47] Most of the literature on the Tennessee Valley Authority written since Philip Selznick's classic *TVA and the Grass Roots* has been historical rather than analytical.[48] Little evaluative research has been done on either the War on Poverty programs or the Appalachian Regional Commission. Attempts by community organizers to create an Appalachian identity among unemployed out migrants in urban contexts and to adapt their communities to the model of inner-city ethnic group politics also deserve more attention.[49]

Culture and Community in Appalachia. Since the time of Frost and the Campbells, students of the Southern Appalachians have been attempting to characterize the subculture of the region. In the major effort to survey the extent to which the traditional subculture has persisted, Thomas Ford in 1962 defined four themes: individualism and self-reliance, traditionalism, fatalism, and fundamentalism. Of these, the people questioned showed a significant difference from national norms only in the direction of greater fundamentalism.[50] It is not clear whether subcultural differences that still persist are distinctive of Southern Appalachia rather than of the rural South, of the rural United States generally, or, as a cultural geographer has suggested, of the Upland South.[51]

Too often, social scientists have erroneously sought to measure Appalachian culture against some standard of urban, middle-class values. This is especially a problem when the former is pejoratively pitted against the latter which is seen as an indicator of "modernity" and, implicitly, of moral health. This prevents an understanding of Appalachian culture in its own terms. In Eugene Genovese's *Roll, Jordan, Roll,* an analysis of slave culture in the American South, and in Richard Sennett and Jonathan Cobb's *The Hidden Injuries of Class,* an analysis of ethnic, working-class culture in contemporary Boston, we have exemplary treatments of the dialectical relationship between class position and culture in history.[52] Unfortunately we lack such a comprehensive historical study of Appalachian culture and society, although James Brown and Helen Lewis have provided much insight.

Brown summarizes the orientation of the pre-industrial Appalachian culture in three themes: familism (social interaction), puritanism (belief system), and individualism (personality system).[53] In *Mountain Families in Transition* the authors abstract cultural traits from their behavioral expressions which exactly counter the pathogenic qualities so often attributed to the culture of "yesterday's people." In a brilliant article entitled "Family, Religion and Colonialism in Central Appalachia; Or: Bury My Rifle at Big Stone Gap," Helen Lewis, Sue Kobak, and Linda Johnson interpret more recent developments in Appalachian culture as a response to "the process of colonialization as it occurred in the Central Appalachians."[54] Family and church institutions, in particular, "became defensive and reverted inward in order to protect members from the sudden influence which came with the development of industrialization." Their work suggests that seen in this context, as a localized response beginning at the turn of the century to the national mobilization of population and resources in America to achieve maximum capitalist industrial development, contemporary Appalachian culture can no longer be seen as that of an "arrested frontier." Rather, one sees functional parallels between contemporary Appalachian culture and other such reactive movements as populism in the South, the emergence of ethnic communities in the industrial Northeast, the flight of the white middle class to suburbia in the 1950's in order to preserve the values of small town and family living,[55] the emergence of a "counterculture" among their children in the 1960's, the subsequent flight of many of these children underground or to Canada to avoid the Vietnam War, the recent protest among working-class communities against busing, and even the opposition to imposed textbooks in the rural sections of West Virginia's Kanawha Valley industrial region. All these may be seen as responses to centralizing tendencies of mobilization and massification.

Studies of communities in Southern Appalachia are less advanced than is first apparent. We have some excellent studies of isolated agricultural communities: Marion Pearsall's *Little Smokey Ridge,* Brown's "Beech Creek." But we also have studies of very poor communities presented as typical: Rena Gazaway's "Duddie's Branch," and Bill Surface's *The Hollow.*[56] And then we have three studies of Celo, North Carolina, done in the early and mid-1960's which make little or no reference to each other.[57]

Studies by John Stephenson, Helen Lewis, and others demonstrate the variety of occupational groupings and life-styles within rural communities.[58] Art Gallaher has suggested a typology of communities ranging from extremely isolated rural, less isolated rural with some

stores and services, company towns, county seat towns, and major urban areas.[59] The diversity of family, life style, and community types is apparent, in contrast to the stereotypes of the uniform subculture of poverty on the one hand, and the polarization of Appalachian society into the rich and the poor on the other.[60] Among aspects of Appalachian culture and community, family organization has received much attention. The importance of the extended family and kinship groups has been noted in most studies of rural regions in Appalachia, in comparison with the relative isolation of the nuclear family in mainstream society. Brown's study of "Beech Creek" over a thirty-year period has made the greatest contribution to the study of mountain families during the great migration out of the region between 1940 and 1970.

The presentation and analysis of census data on the Appalachian region has long been used to describe the characteristics of the population, the differences within the region, and its lag behind the rest of the nation. Campbell presents data from the 1910 census in *The Southern Highlander;* the USDA study presents data through the early 1930's; the Ford study analyzes the data from 1940 to 1960, and Brown has analyzed the 1970 census.[61] Gordon DeJong has made the most detailed analysis of fertility decline in the region.[62] The *Annual Reports* of the ARC bring the income and employment figures up to date. Recently efforts have been made to assess changes in the "quality of life" in the region.[63]

The study of migration out of and into the Appalachians has been developed in considerable detail. Migration from the region has been a feature since the early 1800's; overlooking this pattern contributes to an exaggerated sense of the isolation of the region during the mid-1800's. People left the mountain areas of Kentucky, Tennessee, and the Carolinas and made their way to the Ozarks, southern Illinois, and Oklahoma.[64] A longstanding migration stream from two sources in the Southern Appalachians to two areas of settlement in western Washington state, two thousand miles away, has been described in detail by Woodrow Clevinger.[65] The migration began around 1880, in connection with the timber industry, hit a peak between 1900 and 1917, and continues to a limited extent even to this day. During the 1930's the central Appalachians experienced a net in-migration stream.[66] The work of Clevinger, Brown, and others has demonstrated the importance of the family system in the migration process. While the major migration streams from the region are known, much remains to be done to identify the streams on a detailed, local, or county level. Related to the literature on Appalachian migration is a variety of material on occupational adjustment to industrial work.[67]

An obvious deficiency in the sociological literature on the Appalachian community is the analysis of work. Despite the growing literature on the "single industry community," we have no good studies on industrial communities in the mountains. The only study of a coal mining community in the United States in Herman Lantz's "Coal Town" in southern Illinois.[68] With the exception of the work of Lewis and Knipe, and studies by Ronald Althouse and Keith Dix, little has been done on the industrial sociology of the coal industry by social scientists. Investigative journalists have accomplished far more in analyzing de-developments in the coal industry, mine disasters, and the everyday life of coal miners.[69] A fascinating problem in this area of industrial sociology is explaining the success of unionization in the coalfields and its failure in the textile mills. No comparative studies of coal and textile communities have been made, despite the assertion that both share similar subculture and situation of domination.[70]

Toward a Sociology of the Appalachian Future. Much of the research on Southern Appalachia has sought either to discover a romantic past or to proclaim "the eve of an astonishing development."[71] Instead, we need hard sociological thinking about an Appalachian future. For this we need a more adequate historical society in order to recover an authentic mountain past and to gain a critical perspective on current developments. We also need a more comprehensive sociology of culture in order to articulate the values and goals of Appalachian people, especially those who otherwise lack an institutional basis from which to be heard. Such people have not often been listened to by missionaries, developers, and bureaucrats. Finally, we urgently need a study of the landowning and energy-getting elites in Appalachia whose plans, about which we are always so ignorant, often seem inexorable. The likely emergence of a national energy policy and the importance of coal in that policy make this research agenda and the timely voice of Appalachian people all the more imperative.

NOTES

1. George E. Vincent, "A Retarded Frontier," *The American Journal of Sociology,* 4 (July 1898), 20.

2. Shapiro, *Appalachia on Our Minds* (Chapel Hill: Univ. of North Carolina Press, 1978); the book is a revision of his dissertation, "A Strange Land and Peculiar People: The Discovery of Appalachia, 1870–1920" (Rutgers, 1966). Shapiro's thesis is summarized in his "Introduction" to the reprinted edition of John C. Campbell, *The Southern Highlander and His Homeland* (New York: Russell Sage Foundation, 1921; rpt. Lexington: Univ. Press of Kentucky, 1969).

3. Blumer, "Social Problems as Collective Behavior," *Social Problems,* 18 (Winter 1971), 299.

4. See USDA Miscellaneous Publication No. 205 (1935); Frederick G. Tryon and Bushrod W. Allin, "The Southern Appalachian Coal Plateaus," Ch. 2 in Carter Goodrich, et al., *Migration and Economic Opportunity* (Philadelphia: Univ. of Pennsylvania Press, 1936), pp. 54–123; *The Southern Appalachian Region: A Survey,* ed. Thomas R. Ford (Lexington: Univ. of Kentucky Press, 1962).

5. John Fiske, *Old Virginia and Her Neighbours* (Boston: Houghton, Mifflin, 1897), II, 177–89; Arthur Estabrook, "Presidential Address: Blood Seeks Environment," *Eugenical News,* 11 (August 1926), 106–14; Nathaniel D. Hirsch, "An Experimental Study of the East Kentucky Mountaineers," *Genetic Psychology Monographs* 3 (March 1928), 183–244; Harry M. Caudill, *A Darkness at Dawn: Appalachian Kentucky and the Future* (Lexington: Univ. Press of Kentucky, 1976), Ch. 1.

6. William Goodell Frost, "Our Contemporary Ancestors in the Southern Mountains," *Atlantic Monthly,* 83 (March 1899), 311–19; Ellen Churchill Semple, "The Anglo-Saxons of the Kentucky Mountains: A Study in Anthropogeography," *The Geographical Journal,* 17 (June 1901), 588–623, rpt. *Bulletin of the American Geographical Society,* 42 (August 1910), 561–94.

7. Campbell, *Southern Highlander,* Chs. 3 and 4, Appendix B.

8. Oscar Lewis, *The Children of Sanchez* (New York: Random House, 1961), pp. xxiv–xxvii; Jack E. Weller, *Yesterday's People: Life in Contemporary Appalachia* (Lexington: Univ. of Kentucky Press, 1965); and Herbert J. Gans, *The Urban Villagers: Group and Class in the Life of Italian-Americans* (New York: Free Press, 1962).

9. David H. Looff, *Appalachia's Children: The Challenge of Mental Health* (Lexington: Univ. Press of Kentucky, 1971); Norman A. Polansky, Robert D. Borgman, and Christine DeSaix, *Roots of Futility* (San Francisco: Jossey-Bass, 1972); Richard A. Ball, "New Premises for Planning in Appalachia," *Journal of Sociology and Social Welfare,* 2 (Fall 1974), 92–101; and "The Southern Appalachian Folk Subculture as a Tension-Reducing Way of Life," in *Change in Rural Appalachia,* ed. John D. Photiadis and Harry K. Schwarzweller (Philadelphia: Univ. of Pennsylvania Press, 1970), pp. 69–79.

10. For example, Jack L. Roach and Orville R. Gursslin, "An Evaluation of the Concept 'Culture of Poverty,' " *Social Forces,* 45 (March 1967), 383–92; Charles A. Valentine, *Culture and Poverty: Critique and Counter-Proposals* (Chicago: Univ. of Chicago Press, 1968); the comments on Valentine in *Current Anthropology,* 10 (April–June 1969), 181–201; and the essays in *The Culture of Poverty: A Critique,* ed. Eleanor Burke Leacock (New York: Simon and Schuster, 1971); see Stephen L. Fisher, "Folk Culture or Folk Tale: Prevailing Assumptions about the Appalachian Personality," in *An Appalachian Symposium: Essays Written in Honor of Cratis D. Williams* (Boone: Appalachian State Univ. Press, 1977), a revised and somewhat shortened version of "Victim-Blaming in Appalachia: Cultural Theories and the Southern Mountaineer," in *Appalachia: Social Context Past and Present,* ed. Bruce Ergood and Bruce E. Kuhre (Dubuque: Kendall/Hunt, 1976), pp. 139–148.

11. Dwight Billings, "Culture and Poverty in Appalachia: A Theoretical Discussion and Empirical Analysis," *Social Forces* 53 (December 1974), 315–23; and Thomas R. Ford, "The Passing of Provincialism," Ch. 2 in *The Southern Appalachian Region.*

12. Loyal Jones, "Appalachian Values," in *Voices from the Hills,* ed. Robert J. Higgs and Ambrose N. Manning (New York: Ungar, 1975), pp. 507–17; Mike Maloney and Ben Huelsman, "Humanism, Scientism, and Southern Mountaineers," *Peoples' Appalachia,* 2 (July 1972), 24–7.

13. See Robert Coles, *Migrants, Sharecroppers, Mountaineers,* especially Chs. 5, 6, 9, and 12, and *The South Goes North,* Ch. 6 (Boston: Little, Brown, 1971); John Fetterman, *Stinking Creek* (New York: Dutton, 1967); Anthony Dunbar, *Our Land Too* (New York: Random House, 1969), Part II; Kathy Kahn, *Hillbilly Women* (Garden City: Doubleday, 1973); and John B. Stephenson, *Shiloh: A Mountain Community* (Lexington: Univ. Press of Kentucky, 1968). The methodological basis of the humanistic approach is sketched in John R. Staude, *"The Theoretical Foundations of Humanistic Sociology,"* in *Humanistic Society: Today's Challenge to Sociology,* ed. John F. Glass and John R. Staude (Pacific Palisades: Goodyear, 1972), pp. 262–70.

14. John Friedmann, "Poor Regions and Poor Nations: Perspectives on the Problem of Appalachia," *Southern Economic Journal,* 32 (April 1966), 465–7.

15. On regional development theory, see Harvey S. Perloff et al., *Regions, Resources, and Economic Growth* (Lincoln: Univ. of Nebraska Press, 1960); E. A. J. Johnson, *The Organization of Space in Developing Countries* (Cambridge: Harvard Univ. Press, 1970);

Harry W. Richardson, *Regional Growth Theory* (New York: Wiley, 1973); and *Backward Areas in Advanced Countries,* ed. E. A. G. Robinson (New York: St. Martin's, 1969).

16. Niles M. Hansen's works include *Rural Poverty and the Urban Crisis* (Bloomington: Indiana Univ. Press, 1970); *Intermediate-Size Cities as Growth Centers* (New York: Praeger, 1971); and an edited volume, *Growth Centers in Regional Economic Development* (New York: Free Press, 1972). On the ARC, see Donald Rothblatt, *Regional Planning: The Appalachian Experience* (Lexington, Mass.: Heath, 1971); and Monroe Newman, *The Political Economy of Appalachia* (Lexington, Mass.: Lexington Books, 1972).

17. Plunkett and Bowman, *Elites and Change* (Lexington: Univ. Press of Kentucky, 1973). Two good critical reviews of this work are by Billings in the *American Journal of Sociology,* 79 (May 1974), 1572–4; and Helen M. Lewis in *Social Forces,* 53 (September 1974), 139–40. The notion of a "cultural bridge" is borrowed from Harry K. Schwarzweller and James E. Brown, "Education as a Cultural Bridge between Eastern Kentucky and the Great Society," *Rural Sociology,* 27 (December 1962), 357–73, rpt. in *Change in Rural Appalachia,* ed. Photiadis and Schwarzweller, pp. 129–45.

18. The ideas of "non decisions" is developed in Peter Bachrach and Morton S. Baratz, *Power and Poverty: Theory and Practice* (New York: Oxford Univ. Press, 1970), Ch. 3, pp. 39–51. See also Matthew Crenson, *The Un-Politics of Air Pollution: A Study of Non-Decisionmaking in the Cities* (Baltimore: Johns Hopkins Press, 1971); and Roger W. Cobb and Charles D. Elder, *Participation in American Politics: The Dynamics of Agenda-Building* (Boston: Allyn and Bacon, 1972).

19. Caudill, *Night Comes to the Cumberlands* (Boston: Little, Brown, 1963), p. 325; "Misdeal in Appalachia," *The Atlantic Monthly,* June 1965, p. 44 and his "Appalachia: The Dismal Land," *Dissent,* 14 (November–December 1967), 718–19. See also the entire fourth issue of *People's Appalachia* (August–September 1970), organized around the theme "The Developers: Partners in Colonization."

20. Robert Blauner, "Internal Colonialism and Ghetto Revolt," *Social Problems,* 16 (Spring 1969), 393; revised and reprinted as Ch. 3 in Blauner, *Radical Oppression in America* (New York: Harper and Row, 1972). The Appalachian analogy is first developed in Helen M. Lewis and Edward E. Knipe, "The Colonialism Model: The Appalachian Case," an unpublished paper, revised draft, October 1970 (forthcoming in *The Colony of Appalachia: Selected Readings,* ed. Lewis et al., from The Appalachian Consortium Press); and an expanded version by Lewis, "Fatalism or the Coal Industry? Contrasting Views of Appalachian Problems," *Mountain Life & Work,* 46 (December 1970), 4–15; rpt. in *Appalachia: Its People, Heritage, and Problems,* ed. Frank S. Riddel (Dubuque, Iowa: Kendall/Hunt, 1974), pp. 221–38, and rpt. in *Appalachia: Social Context Past and Present,* ed. Ergood and Kuhre, pp. 153–62. The application is further developed in Helen Lewis, Sue Kobak, and Linda Johnson, "Family, Religion and Colonialism in Central Appalachia; Or: Bury My Rifle at Big Stone Gap," in *Growin' Up Country,* ed. Jim Axelrod (Clintwood, Va.: Council of the Southern Mountains, 1973), pp. 131–56.

21. See, for example, Pablo González-Casanova, "Internal Colonialism and National Development," in *Studies in Comparative International Development,* 1 (1965), 27–37, rpt. in *Latin American Radicalism,* ed. Irving Louis Horowitz et al. (New York: Random House, 1969), especially pp. 130–2; and Pierre van den Berghe, "Education, Class and Ethnicity in Southern Peru; Revolutionary Colonialism," in *Education and Colonialism: Comparative Perspectives,* ed. Philip G. Altback and Gail P. Kelly (New York: McKay, forthcoming).

22. The critique of the internal colonialism model applied to Appalachia is developed at grater length by Walls in "Central Appalachia: A Peripheral Region within an Advanced Capitalist Society," *Journal of Sociology and Social Welfare,* 4 (November 1976), 232–47; "Internal Colony of Internal Periphery?" forthcoming in *The Colony of Appalachia,* ed H. Lewis, et al.; and the paper "Three Models in Search of Appalachian Development: Critique and Synthesis," August 1974, revised May 1976, ERIC no. ED125806.

23. See particularly his Frankfurt inaugural address of June 1965, published as "Knowledge and Human Interests: A General Perspective," in the appendix of Jügen Habermas, *Knowledge and Human Interests,* trans. Jeremy J. Shapiro (Boston: Beacon Press, 1971), pp.

301–17, quoted phrase from p. 311; and the brief explication of Habermas in the epilogue to Joachim Israel, *Alienation: From Marx to Modern Sociology* (1968: Boston: Allyn and Bacon, 1971), pp. 343–7. See also Habermas' essay "Technology and Science as 'Ideology,' " in *Toward a Rational Society* (Boston: Beacon, 1970), pp. 81–122.

24. Habermas, *Legitimation Crisis,* trans. Thomas McCarthy (1973; Boston: Beacon, 1975), pp. 33–41; see also John Kenneth Galbraith, *Economics and the Public Purpose* (1973; New York: Signet, 1975), pp. 38–50; and James O'Connor, *The Fiscal Crisis of the State* (New York: St. Martin's, 1973), especially Ch. 1, "An Anatomy of American State Capitalism," pp. 13–39; and Ralph Miliband, *The State in Capitalist Society: The Analysis of the Western System of Power* (New York: Basic Books, 1969).

25. See Immanuel Wallerstein, "Dependence in an Interdependent World: The Limited Possibilities of Transformation within the Capitalist World Economy," *African Studies Review,* 17 (April 1974) 1–26; and his "Class Formation in the Capitalist World-Economy," *Politics and Society,* 6 (1975), 367–75.

26. To the contrary, careful observers have described this traditional culture as a driving force in the lives of mountain people. Reporting "an urge toward self-improvement" and "a great desire to amount to something" among Beech Creekers, Harry K. Schwarzweller, James S. Brown, and J. J. Mangalam observe that "the omnipresent dissatisfaction of Beech Creek people with their present lot, their inability to be satisfied with the present situation, in a word, their emphasis upon 'becoming' rather than upon 'being,' was a manifestation of their puritan philosophy." See *Mountain Families in Transition: A Case Study of Appalachian Migration* (University Park: Pennsylvania State Univ. Press, 1971), p. 63.

27. See Ingolf Vogeler, "The Peasant Culture of Appalachia and its Survival," *Antipode: A Radical Journal of Geography,* 5 (March 1973), 17–24; and Edward E. Knipe and Helen M. Lewis, "The Impact of Coal Mining on the Traditional Mountain Subculture," in *The Not So Solid South: Anthropological Studies in a Regional Subculture,* ed. J. Kenneth Moreland, Southern Anthropological Society Proceedings, No. 4 (Athens: Univ. of Georgia Press, 1971), pp. 25–37. The concept of peasant is limited to a particular historic type in George M. Foster, "Introduction: What is a Peasant," in *Peasant Society: A Reader,* ed. Jack M. Potter, May N. Diaz, and George M. Foster (Boston: Little, Brown, 1967), p. 7.

28. The only study of a similar (though non-Appalachian, technically speaking) community which purports to have discovered *no* social stratification is Elmora Messer Matthews, *Neighbor and Kin: Life in a Tennessee Ridge Community* (Nashville: Vanderbilt Univ. Press, 1965). She probably didn't ask the right question; compare her "Questionnaire," pp. 153–8, with Stephenson's approach in *Shiloh,* pp. 49–51.

29. *Mountain Families in Transition,* pp. 48–58, 165–74.

30. Floyd Hunter, *Community Power Structure* (Chapel Hill: Univ. of North Carolina Press, 1953); Willis D. Hawley and James H. Svara, *The Study of Community Power: A Bibliographic Review* (Santa Barbara: ABC-Clio, 1972).

31. Richard A. Ball, "Social Change and Power Structure: An Appalachian Case," in *Change in Rural Appalachia,* ed. Photiadis and Schwarzweller, pp. 147–66; Rod Harless, *The West Virginia Establishment* (Huntington: Appalachian Movement Press, 1971).

32. For example, see Susanne Bodenheimer, "Dependency and Imperialism: The Roots of Latin American Underdevelopment," *Politics and Society,* 1 (May 1971), 327–57.

33. Caudill, *Night Comes to the Cumberlands;* Richard A. Couto, *Poverty, Politics and Health Care* (New York: Praeger, 1975); Huey Perry, *"They'll Cut Off Your Project"* (New York: Praeger, 1972).

34. Richard A. Diehl, "Appalachia's Energy Elite: A Wing of Imperialism?" *Peoples' Appalachia,* 1 (March 1970), 2–3.

35. See Joseph F. Donnermeyer, Peter F. Korsching, and Rabel Burdge, "An Interpretative Analysis of Family and Individual Economic Costs Due to Water Resource Development," *Water Resources Bulletin,* 10 (February 1974), 91–100; F. Carlene Bryant, *The Social Impact of Surface Mining in a Rural Appalachian Community,* ARP Publication No. 46 (June 1976); Robert B. Cameron, *An Estimation of the Tangible Costs of Black Lung Disease,* ARP Publication No. 47 (June 1976); Si Kahn, *The Forest Service and Appalachia* (Mineral Bluff, Ga.: Cut Cane Associates, 1974).

57

36. Johnson and Burdge, "Sociologists and Environmental Impact Statements: What Are We Doing Here?" (August 1975), available from Sue Johnson at the Center for Development Change, Univ. of Kentucky; Kai T. Erikson, *Everything in Its Path: Destruction of Community in the Buffalo Creek Flood* (New York: Simon and Schuster, 1976).

37. Gaventa, "In Appalachia: Property is Theft," *Southern Exposure,* 1 (Summer/Fall 1973), 42–51; and his *Power and Powerlessness: Quiescence and Rebellion in an Appalachian Valley* (Oxford: Oxford Univ. Press, forthcoming).

38. Whisnant, *Missionaries, Planners and Developers in Appalachia* (forthcoming); Caudill, *The Watches of the Night* (Boston: Little, Brown, 1976).

39. U.S. Census, *General Population Characteristics, 1970;* State Volumes, Table 34: Race by Sex for Counties. The statistical reports on black Appalachians done by NAACP Legal Defense Fund (1971) and the National Urban League (1972) relied on advance census data which contained numerous minor errors in the figures for the black population in eight of 13 Appalachian states; the figures were corrected only in the final census reports. Figures on minority groups remain one of the least reliable areas within the census.

40. Darold T. Barnum, *The Negro in the Bituminous Coal Mining Industry* (Philadelphia: Univ. of Pennsylvania Press, 1970); Paul Nyden, *Black Coal Miners in the United States* (New York: American Institute for Marxist Studies, 1974).

41. John Gulick, *Cherokees at the Crossroads* (Chapel Hill: Institute for Research in Social Science, Univ. of North Carolina, 1960), reissued in 1973 with an epilogue by Sharlotte Neely Williams; *Appalachian Journal,* 2 (Summer 1975).

42. A popular discussion of mixed-race groups is Brewton Berry, *Almost White* (New York: Macmillan, 1963). For a mixture of fact and fiction, see Bonnie Ball, *The Melungeons: Their Origin and Kin,* 4th ed. (privately printed, 1972); for the facts, see Edward T. Price, "The Melungeons: A Mixed-Blood Strain of the Southern Appalachians," *The Geographical Review,* 41 (April 1951), 256–71. An ongoing study is announced in Avery Gaskins' "An Introduction to the Guineas: West Virginia's Melungeons," *Appalachian Journal,* 1 (Autumn 1973), 234–7.

43. Calvin L. Beale, "American Triracial Isolates: Their Status and Pertinence to Genetic Research," *Eugenics Quarterly,* 4 (December 1957), 187–96; his most dubious figure is a count of 2,420 Melungeons in Knot County, Kentucky!

44. Kenneth R. Bailey, "A Judicious Mixture: Negroes and Immigrants in West Virginia Mines, 1880–1917," *West Virginia History,* 34 (January 1973), 141–61.

45. August Meier and Elliott Rudwick, *CORE: A Study in the Civil Rights Movement, 1942–1968* (New York: Oxford Univ. Press, 1973); Kirkpatrick Sale, *SDS* (New York: Random House, 1973). See John D. McCarthy and Mayer N. Zald, *The Trend of Social Movements in America* (Morristown, N.J.: General Learning Press, 1973).

46. See the articles in *Appalachia in the Sixties,* ed. Walls and Stephenson (Lexington: Univ. Press of Kentucky, 1972), pp. 161–209; Hume, *Death and the Mines* (New York: Grossman, 1971); Bill Peterson, *Coaltown Revisited* (Chicago: Regnery, 1972).

47. David E. Whisnant, "Controversy in God's Grand Division: The CSM," *Appalachian Journal,* 2 (Autumn 1974), 7–45; and "The Congress for Appalachian Development," *Peoples' Appalachia,* 3 (Spring 1973), 16–22. A chapter on the Appalachian Volunteers is also included in his forthcoming collection of essays, *Missionaries, Planners and Developers in Appalachia.* Two doctoral dissertations may lead to books on Appalachian social movements: Paul Nyden on the Miners for Democracy (Columbia, 1974), and Bennett M. Judkins on the Black Lung Associations (Univ. of Tennessee, 1976). On Highlander, see Frank Adams, *Unearthing Seeds of Fire* (Winston-Salem: Blair, 1975).

48. Selznick, *TVA* (1949; New York: Harper and Row, 1966); Whisnant's controversial chapter on TVA has been published in *The Elements,* Nos. 24 and 25 (November and December 1976).

49. See Todd Gitlin and Nanci Hollander, *Uptown: Poor Whites in Chicago* (New York: Harper and Row, 1970); and Tommie Miller, "Urban Appalachians; Cultural Pluralism and Ethnic Identity in the City" (unpublished M. A. thesis, Univ. of Cincinnati, 1976), summarized in the *Research Bulletin* (November 1976) of the Urban Appalachian Council, pp. 3–4.

50. Ford, "The Passing of Provincialism," in *The Southern Appalachian Region: A Survey.* For a methodological critique, see Billings, "Culture and Poverty in Appalachia," *Social Forces,* 53 (December 1974).

51. Wilbur Zelinsky, *The Cultural Geography of the United States* (Englewood Cliffs: Prentice-Hall, 1973), pp. 117–25.

52. Eugene Genovese, *Roll, Jordan, Roll: The World the Slaves Made* (New York: Pantheon, 1974); Richard Sennett and Jonathan Cobb, *The Hidden Injuries of Class* (New York: Vintage, 1973).

53. See *Mountain Families in Transition,* pp. 58–67; these themes reflect the society-culture-personality schema developed by Pitirim Sorokin and Talcott Parsons, with whom Brown studied at Harvard.

54. "Family, Religion and Colonialism," in *Growin' Up Country,* ed. Axelrod.

55. See Roland Warren, *The Community in America,* 2nd ed. (Chicago: Rand McNally, 1972), pp. 75–85, for an interpretation of the move to suburbia "as an attempt to preserve and restore [personalistic and familistic] values threatened with destruction" by the constellation of forces he calls "the great change."

56. *Little Smokey Ridge* (University: Univ. of Alabama Press, 1959); Gazaway, *The Longest Mile* (Garden City: Doubleday, 1969); *The Hollow* (New York: Coward-McCann, 1971). See John Photiadis, *Community Size and Social Attributes in West Virginia,* Appalachian Center Research Report 5 (Morgantown: West Virginia Univ., n.d.), for a comparative study.

57. Stephenson, *Shiloh;* Berton Kaplan, *Blue Ridge* (Morgantown: West Virginia Univ., 1971); George L. Hicks, *Appalachian Valley* (New York: Holt, Rinehart and Winston, 1976).

58. Stephenson, *Shiloh;* Knipe and Lewis, "The Impact of Coal Mining," in *The Not So Solid South,* ed. Moreland, pp. 25–37.

59. Art Gallaher, Jr., "The Community as a Setting Change in Southern Appalachia," in *The Public University in Its Second Century,* ed. Lloyd Davis, Public Affairs Series No. 5 (Morgantown: West Virginia Center for Appalachian Studies and Development, 1967), pp. 17–32; rpt. in *Appalachia,* ed. Riddel, pp. 291–304.

60. On the "two Appalachias," see Harry Caudill, "O, Appalachia!" *Intellectual Digest* (April 1973), 16–19; rpt. in *Appalachia,* ed. Riddel, p. 275; and in *Voices from the Hills,* ed. Higgs and Manning, pp. 524–5. The same conclusion is reached in the face of contrary data in Roman B. Aquizap and Ernest A. Vargas, "Technology, Power, and Socialization in Appalachia," *Social Casework,* 51 (March 1970), 131–9.

61. See John C. Belcher, "Population Growth and Characteristics," and James S. Brown and George A. Hillery, Jr., "The Great Migration, 1940–1960," Chs. 3 and 4 in *The Southern Appalachian Region;* James S. Brown, "A Look at the 1970 Census," in *Appalachia in the Sixties,* pp. 130–144.

62. Gordon F. DeJong, *Appalachian Fertility Decline* (Lexington: Univ. Press of Kentucky, 1968).

63. See C. Milton Coughenour, "Measuring the Quality of Life for Rural Families," *Appalachia,* 9 (February–March 1976), 1–9.

64. Estabrook, "Presidential Address," *Eugenical News,* 11 (August 1926), 106–14; Josiah Henry Combs, *The Kentucky Highlanders from a Native Mountaineer's Viewpoint* (Lexington: J. L. Richardson, 1913), p. 43.

65. Woodrow R. Clevinger, "The Appalachian Mountaineers in the Upper Cowlitz Basin, *Pacific Northwest Quarterly,* 29 (April 1938), 115–34; and "Southern Appalachian Highlanders in Western Washington," *Pacific Northwest Quarterly,* 33 (January 1942), 3–25. See also his *Cascade Mountain Clan: The Clevengers and Stiltners and Related Families* (Seattle: Seattle Univ. Bookstore, 1971). David Looff notes his first contact with Appalachian mountaineers as a boy in the Cascades in Ch. 1 of *Appalachia's Children,* pp. 4–8.

66. Tryon and Allin, "Southern Appalachian Coal Plateaus," in Goodrich, *Migration and Economic Opportunity,* p. 66; Jerome Pickard, "Appalachian Population Estimated at 19 Million," *Appalachia,* 9 (August–September 1975), 1–9.

67. See Schwarzweller et. al., *Mountain Families in Transition,* Chs. 7–9; John Photiadis, *Migration and Occupational Adjustment of West Virginians in the City* (Morgantown: Office of Research and Development, West Virginia Univ., 1974).

68. See, for example, Rex A. Lucas, *Minetown, Milltown, Railtown: Life in Canadian Communities of Single Industry* (Toronto: Univ. of Toronto Press, 1971); Lantz, *People of Coal Town* (New York: Columbia Univ. Press, 1958).

69. Althouse, *Work, Safety, and Life Style among Southern Appalachian Coal Miners* (Morgantown: West Virginia Univ., 1974); the articles in *Appalachia in the Sixties,* pp. 69–119; Thomas N. Bethell, *The Hurricane Creek Massacre* (New York: Harper and Row, 1972); Tom Nugent, *Death at Buffalo Creek* (New York: Norton, 1973); the semi-fictionalized biographical sketch of a coal miner by George Vecsey, *One Sunset a Week* (New York: Dutton, 1974); and Meade Arble, *The Long Tunnel: A Coal Miner's Journal* (New York: Atheneum, 1976). See also the studies by Keith Dix in the Research Series of the Institute for Labor Studies at West Virginia University, and J. Davitt McAteer, *Coal Mine Health and Safety: The Case of West Virginia* (New York: Praeger, 1973).

70. See the work of Broadus and George S. Mitchell in the 1920's and 1930's; Liston Pope, *Millhands and Preachers* (New Haven: Yale Univ. Press, 1940); Glenn Gilman, *Human Relations in the Industrial Southeast* (Chapel Hill: Univ. of North Carolina Press, 1956). Billings is currently working on such a comparison, having just completed an historical analysis of textile industrialization in the Carolina piedmont; see his *Planters, Capitalists, and the Politics of Development in the New South* (Chapel Hill: Univ. of Carolina Press, forthcoming).

71. See John Stephenson's insightful discussion of this second theme in "Appalachia and the Third Century in America: On the Eve of an Astonishing Development—Again," *Appalachian Journal,* 4 (Autumn 1976), 34–8.

II. Historical Background of Appalachia

It might be said that the best introduction to the history of a region is to personally emerse oneself in the place where events have occurred, seeing where the "action" took place. In so doing the sensual limitations become apparent and one is pushed, almost forced, to seek other information to transform the visual and the present into an understanding of the past. Since we are unable to take the reader to the locus of action, as it were, we refer you rather to the many historic accounts of some of the events of the past, some of which are noted in the selected bibliography included in the last section of this volume.

We have included, however, several articles which deal with some significant past events, namely the process of early settlement and cultural roots. We do not attempt an all inclusive survey; we rather highlight such factors as early Indian inhabitants, topographic descriptions, cultural background of settlers, travel routes, migration dynamics and settlement patterns. Some of these same factors apply to the settlement of other regions going on at the same time in America.

We suspect that the travel routes, cultural background and life-styles did not vary greatly in the eighteenth century. Means of transportation, population pools and technology were probably shared by travelers in the Great Valley of Virginia, the National Road (or what was to become the National Road), the Mohawk Trail and the Mississippi Valley. What was to become the distinguishing factor was the isolation of the Southern Mountain settlers from the changes that took place in these other areas due primarily to the topographic fact of extensive mountain ranges, hostile to easy passage. Although other factors are often given credit as cause for the development of so-called unique Appalachian characteristics, there seems to be little disagreement that isolation is a key, if not the key factor.

Our selections are few. We urge the reader to explore the many articles and histories of the development of the Region.

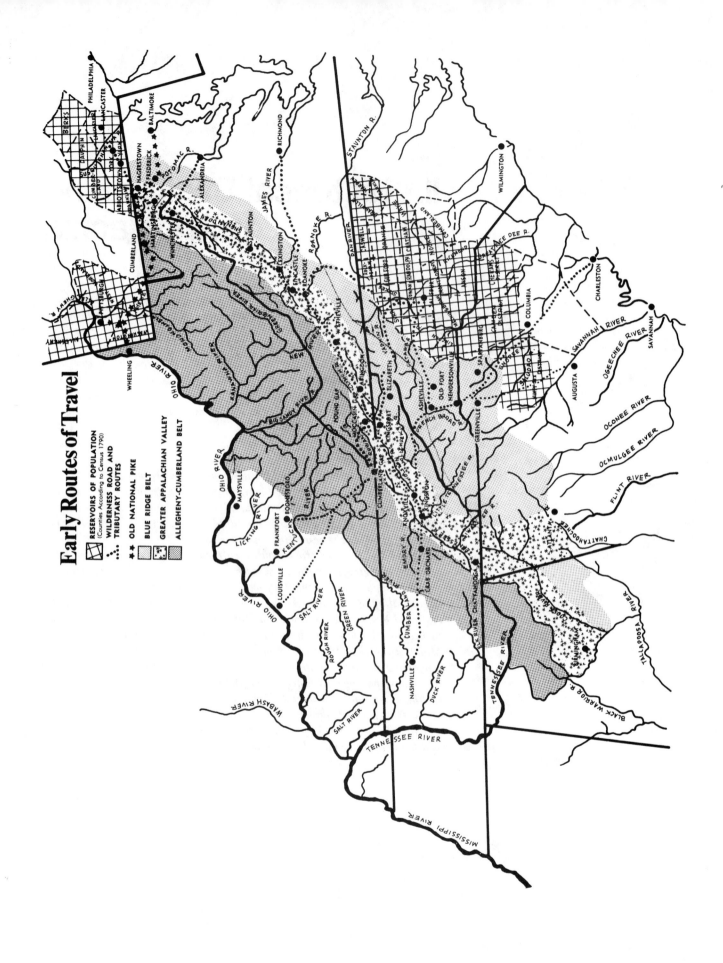

Early Routes of Travel

RESERVOIRS OF POPULATION
(Counties According to Census 1790)

········· WILDERNESS ROAD AND
TRIBUTARY ROUTES

+ + OLD NATIONAL PIKE
BLUE RIDGE BELT
GREATER APPALACHIAN VALLEY
ALLEGHENY-CUMBERLAND BELT

9. PIONEER ROUTES OF TRAVEL AND EARLY SETTLEMENTS

John C. Campbell

The broad expanse of level country that stretches westward from the South-Atlantic seaboard reaches in the Carolinas a width of one hundred to one hundred and fifty miles. As one moves up the leisurely watercourses the land becomes more rolling, a hill country begins to appear, and the rivers issuing from it descend in steep cascades and rapids to the plain below.

One has, according to the geographers, crossed the Coastal Plain, which first appears south of New York harbor as a narrow strip bordering the sea, and extends southward in an ever-widening zone. The cascades mark that famous "fall line" where rivers fall from the Piedmont Plateau to the low-lying lands of the coast. Here in early days were established the first trading posts, and here later grew flourishing cities.

Further separating the Coastal Plain from the Carolina Piedmont extends a broad strip of piney barrens. Beyond these barrens, as one continues westward, the Plateau becomes more rugged, the rivers divide and fork into innumerable branches and rivulets which cut their way through a stiff red soil. The forests change in character, the air grows cooler, until at length against the horizon there lifts a misty blue line. Nearer, it revolves itself into a lofty range of peaks, still hung with blue haze, and fronting the southeast with precipitous rocky cliffs.

Here at last is the Blue Ridge. At its foot the early hunter, eager to add to his string of pelts; paused, fearful of hidden foes beyond the ridges. Here, too, the cattle-driver, following in his steps, stopped to raise his rough shelter in the wilderness. And here, still later, the pioneer settler, gazing up at the formidable barrier, halted his pack-horse or wagon and built his cabin by the side of a rushing stream.

The traveler today, weary from his long train ride, looks out at the railway winding serpent-like up the face of the mountain and no longer wonders why westward expansion from the South Atlantic seacoast was so slow. He wonders rather that the first advance to the Far West was begun across this mountain country at a time when the settlers of New York State had scarce ventured beyond the Valleys of the Hudson and the Mohawk, and when Maine and Vermont formed one frontier of a New England which was just beginning to cross the Berkshire barrier.

History has concerned itself but little with our Southern Highlands, except in incidental fashion as it has dealt with movements, early and later, across the mountain barrier to the west, and with settlements within the mountains, notably in the Valley of Virginia and in the Holston region, which marked or contributed to these western movements. From these movements and settlements, however, came the early population of the Highlands, and a brief review of them and their sources is an integral part of any study of the region.

For an explanation of the first large movement into the mountain country, we must turn from the South to Pennsylvania. Hither, between 1720 an 1770 approximately, came many thousand Germans from the Palatinate, Ulster Scotch or Scotch-Irish[1] from the north of Ireland, and immigrants from other countries. It is not necessary here to enter into the causes, political, religious, and economic, that led to their migrations. They were on the whole a sturdy, virile people, fitted by nature and experience to meet the hardships of pioneer life.

There were few good Atlantic ports in the South: New England did not welcome the strangers;[2] and although many went to New York, by far the greatest number were directed to the great central port of Philadelphia.[3] The lands lying near the coast of Pennsylvania were by this time comparatively well settled, and it seems to be due largely to this fact that to the abundance of cheap territory farther west, that the newcomers pressed on to the frontier. The movement was, however, undoubtedly encouraged by the colonial authorities, as hereby a barrier was established between the seaboard settlements and the Indians.

The Blue Ridge, it will be recalled, which was so formidable an obstacle to early westward expansion from the southern coast, is lost for an interval in Pennsylvania, and a natural entrance is thus afforded into the part of the Greater Appalachian Valley which lies in that state. Following along the lower courses of the Delaware and Susquehanna, and ascending their tributaries, the early immigrants preempted the better lands and entered the Greater Valley. They formed, in Pennsylvania, a great reservoir of population, fed by transatlantic immigration passing through the port of Philadelphia.

That this reservoir, overflowing, should send its first great stream into the Southern Highlands was determined by natural causes. Extending to the Southward, the Greater Appalachian Valley with its vertile limestone soil lay like a great pathway walled between highlands to east and west. Pushing on along this pathway through Maryland and what is now West Virginia, the pioneer entered the Valley of Virginia, out of which flow the waters of the Shenandoah to join those of the Potomac. Continuing southward up the Valley, he was moving up to the headwaters of the Shenandoah.

An examination of the river systems will aid in an understanding of his further movements. Interlocking with the headwaters of the Shenandoah are those of the James, and just beyond lie those of the Roanoke—rivers which both flow diagonally southeast across the Valley, out through the Blue Ridge to the Piedmont Plateau, and thence to the Atlantic. Still beyond, to the southwest, and seeming to terminate the Valley, ridges over 3,000 feet in height separate the waters of the Roanoke from those of the New River flowing northwest to the Ohio.

The southward movement of migration did not at first swell over this divide and continue across New River down the Greater Valley into Tennessee, but as though it were a veritable stream, it was deflected through the Blue Ridge to the southeast, to pour over the lower lying lands of the Carolina Piedmont. It is to be kept in mind that his movement from Pennsylvania to the Carolina Piedmont commonly involved two or three generations of pioneers, each new generation moving on a journey farther into the wilderness. So rapid was the movement, however, that the Virginia Valley, which in 1730 had few inhabitants, by 1750 was well populated; and Mathew Rowan, who in 1746 estimated that in Anson, Orange, and Rowan Counties, which at that time composed the entire section between Virginia and South Carolina, "there was not then one hundred fighting men," in 1753 wrote, "there is now at least 3,000, for the most part Irish Protestants and Germans, and dayley increasing."[4] In 1765 alone, over a thousand immigrant wagons are reported by Governor Tryon to have passed through Salisbury, North Carolina.

The "Great Road from the Yadkin River through Virginia to Philadelphia, distant 435 miles," as indicated on Jeffery's map,[5] or to follow it from north to south, from Philadelphia to the Yadkin, ran through Lancaster and York, Pennsylvania, to Winchester, Virginia, up the Shenandoah Valley, across the upper waters of the James to the Roanoke River, thence down the Roanoke through the Blue Ridge southward, crossing the Dan River, and still farther southward to the headwaters of the Yadkin in what is now Forsyth County, North Carolina.

To the southeast of the Blue Ridge barrier, therefore, grew a second reservoir of population, fed not only from the north but from the south by later and lesser streams of transatlantic migration through the ports of Charleston and Wilmington.

There had been early a seepage of settlers into western and southwestern Pennsylvania from the great reservoir in the Valley of Pennsylvania. In 1750 those who had established themselves on the upper waters of the Monongahela had to be warned back by the colonial authorities, as their presence was a provocation to the Indians, always hostile in this region. After the establishment of Fort Pitt in 1759, and the laying out of Pittsburgh in 1765, the western movement to this region began again, to be largely augmented, in the southwestern counties especially, by streams of settlers from Maryland and Virginia. Thus by the time of the Revolution, to the northwest of our territory was formed a third reservoir of population perhaps best visualized in Pittsburgh which was to influence greatly the settlement of Kentucky and that part of Virginia now known as West Virginia.

While these three reservoirs were forming, two to the north and one to the southeast of the mountain country, the Highlands south of Virginia remained an almost unbroken wilderness. In the region lying west of the Blue Ridge and extending to the Tennessee and Ohio Rivers, even Indian settlements of any size seem to have been infrequent. The country was claimed for the most part by the Cherokee Nation, but it was used as a hunting-ground by other tribes as well. The warpath of both northern and southern Indians ran the entire length of the Greater Valley, branching through Cumberland Gap into Kentucky to the Ohio, and formed the main artery for an intricate network of trails which crossed and recrossed the mountain country.

Into this wilderness hunters and traders had early penetrated. Imagination pictures for us these first daring men who threaded the narrow forrest trails and matched their skill against Indian cunning; but few are the records of these woodsmen, forerunners of the pioneer settlers.

It is impossible to trace with any definiteness the early white settlements in this Indian territory. On Mitchell's map, published in 1755, a number are indicated, "Walker's"[6] in the neighborhood of Cumberland Gap being shown as the most western point of English occupation in 1750. A trail is also indicated across the divide in southwestern Virginia, and the region about the headwaters of the Holston is marked "Settled."[7] While it is probable that this outpost was destroyed, as were most of those in Indian territory indicated by Mitchell, there appear to have been permanent settlers in the Holston region before 1760.

From the early part of the eighteenth century a series of treaties had been made with the Indians, whereby their boundaries were pushed farther and farther west. The new lines established however, did not prevent the encroachments of the white men, who continued to raise their cabins beyond the limits defined by the latest treaty, while a fast growing number of traders and hunters penetrated deeper into the wilderness. Suspicious and alarmed, the Indians were further aroused by the instigations of the French, to whose colonial aspirations the westward advance of the English was a constant menace. The Treaty of Paris in 1763 put an end to French pretensions east of the Mississippi; and King George, to placate the Indians, decreed by royal proclamation that there should be no white settlement beyond the sources of streams flowing into the Atlantic. That this decree was impossible to enforce was apparent from the first, and it was generally disregarded.[8] Not only had lands already been granted and purchases made in good faith to the west of this boundary, but new settlers were not to be restrained from entering in ever increasing numbers the forbidden territory.

Out from among the shadowy figures of this period, whose deeds and even whose names were lost in the dark forest, emerges about this time a youth destined to descend to succeeding generations as the great pioneer of American history. Daniel Boone was born near Reading, Pennsylvania, in 1734, but in 1750 his family left for North Carolina, following the old route up the Valley of Virginia, across the Blue Ridge near the dividing line between Virginia and North Carolina, and on to the forks of the Yadkin in the Carolina Piedmont. A mighty hunter even in those days of mighty hunters, young Boone was fired by the tales of a returned trader[9] to make a trip of exploration into Kentucky—the first of a number of expeditions which were to result in the laying out of the Wilderness Road and the opening of that western land beyond the mountains.[10] There is a tradition, questioned by some, that in the spring of 1769 Boone and James Robertson stood on a mountain path and looked down upon the beautiful Valley of the Watauga. It was in this region in this same year that William Bean, from Virginia, settled in what is now known as the Valley of East Tennessee, but was then supposed to be Virginia, later found to belong to North Carolina, and for a while was embraced within the territory known as the state of Franklin. This was the first permanent settlement of which we have authentic record within the present state of Tennessee.

At first this settlement seems to have been but an extension of that mentioned previously as existing before 1760 in Virginia at the headwaters of the Holston, but it was soon increased by accessions of other settlers. In 1771 came James Robertson with sixteen families from North Carolina; and in 1772 followed Sevier, later to be the first governor of the state of Tennessee. Within a few years of Bean's coming there were a number of hunters, herders, and small farmers with their families in the valleys of the Watauga, Nolichucky, Holston, and Clinch. Just how many came directly from Virginia, and how many from North Carolina, and when they came, is impossible to say, but after the defeat of the Regulators[11] in the Battle of Alamance, 1771, their numbers were largely increased by migrations from the Piedmont counties of North Carolina. In 1772 these scattered settlements were formed into an association known as the Watauga Association.[12]

Writing of this association in his Winning of the West, Theodore Roosevelt says:

> It is this fact of the early independence and self-government of the settlers along the headwaters of the Tennessee, that gives to their history its peculiar importance. They were the first men of American birth to establish a free and independent community on the continent. Even before this date there had been straggling settlements of Pennsylvanians and Virginians along the headwaters of the Ohio; but these settlements remained mere parts of the colonies behind them, and neither grew into a separate community, nor played a distinctive part in the growth of the west.[13]

The next few years witnessed a great influx of hunters and explorers into Kentucky, despite the continued and fierce opposition of the Indians. Boone, in 1773, leading a party of six families which included the first white women and children to enter Kentucky, endeavored to make a settlement, but was attacked and forced to turn back. His eldest son and five others of the party were killed.

The defeat of the Indians north of the Ohio, at the close, in 1774, of Lord Dunmore's War, secured the outposts a brief respite from Indian attack, and with the cession of lands in Kentucky opened the way for the establishment of permanent transmontane settlements. In 1775 Boone was employed by "a number of North Carolina gentlemen"[14] to lay out the Wilderness Road, which offered a direct route from the Watauga Settlement to Cumberland Gap, and thence to the fertile limestone lands of Kentucky. In that same year were laid the foundations of Boonesborough and Harrodsburg.

A review of the population of the Southern Highlands on the eve of the Revolution shows the Valley of Virginia northeast of the divide well populated; scattered clearings follow the valleys on the upper courses of the Greenbrier and Kanawha Rivers in what is now West Virginia, and mark the vicinity of Fort Henry, later the city of Wheeling; and in the Valley in southwestern Virginia and northeastern Tennessee are planted a sturdy group of federated settlements coming to be known as the Holston Settlements. Beyond the Highlands to the west, and separated even from Watauga by over two hundred miles of wilderness, are the feeble beginnings of the state of Kentucky. They all marked, as it were, the first rivulets from the reservoirs banked to northwest and southeast, which after the Revolution were to overflow through the Highlands to that great western country as yet scarcely discovered.

The years of the Revolution were strenuous ones in the frontier. The Indians, whose services were enlisted by the British, continued to harass the whole border, and the settlers, shut away by long miles of ridges, could expect little help from east of the mountains where all were engaged in the struggle for independence. On them alone, therefore, fell the defense of the mountane and transmontane settlements.

One is tempted to dwell upon the many thrilling tales, half-legendary, that have come down to us of these pioneer leaders—Sevier, Robertson, Clark, Shelby, Campbell, and many others whose names are inseparably associated with the history of this period—but it is perhaps enough to say that under their able guidance not only was the foothold already obtained in the west strengthened during the war, but new steps were taken forward into the wilderness. Slowly settlement crept down the valleys of the Nolichucky,[15] Holston, and Clinch; and in 1779 Robertson set out from Watauga for the Cumberland county to make the beginnings of what is now Nashville. Nor must we leave this period without turning to view again those stalwart frontier fighters, who in 1780, the darkest year for American independence, went out by forest trail and gap to dislodge the British from King's Mountain and stem the tide of war.[16] "Rearguard of the Revolution," they have been called, and America owes to them the opening and possession of the great West.

Movement through the mountains had continued even during the Revolution, but at its close the western settlements drew to themselves from all our reservoirs of population; they drew even from the territory north of Pennsylvania, sweeping in their stream some from the frontiers of New York and New England.

The great northwest territory of Ohio, Indiana, Illinois, and Michigan, which in the next century was to be the goal of desire, had not at this time been clearly defined by treaty boundaries and was occupied by hostile tribes. Northern routes, moreover, were dangerous of travel, and not made safe until the British, by Jay's Treaty in 1795, gave over the Lake Forts.

For many years, therefore, the tide of migration to the west flowed along the southern routes. The Kentucky country was widely known for its fertility. It was also accessible, and its government was early organized and stable. To this pioneer land of promise, then, migration flowed in a swollen stream after the Revolution.

A study of this great westward migration shows it moving along two main lines or routes—one the famous so-called Wilderness Road, a large part of whose course lay within our Southern Highlands, and the other the Ohio River, which forms part of the northwest boundary of the mountain region.

The Wilderness Road was the first route to the west to be extensively used. To reach it from the north, emigrants followed the old route up the Valley of Virginia; but instead of turning southeast to the Piedmont, they crossed the divide in southwestern Virginia to Fort Chissell. This rude block-house and outpost in the wilderness, built in 1758 by Colonel Bird as a menace to the Cherokee Indians, was situated near the site of the present Wytheville, on the headwaters of the New or Kanawha River, which flows northwest across the Valley through West Virginia to the Ohio. Here the traveler reached the borders of the "great Wilderness," that dark and mysterious forest which stretched over valley and mountain almost two hundred miles to the Cumberlands, whose cliffs, in the word of Boone, were "so wild and horrid that it is impossible to view them without terror." Thence it was about one hundred and fifty miles to the young transmontane settlements. So dense was this forest wilderness that travelers are said to have moved in a leafy gloom, lightened only where a great tree had fallen and let in the sky.

Interlocking with the headwaters of the New River, those of the Holston flow south until, joining the Clinch, whose source lie not far to the west of its own, they form the Tennessee. The course of the traveler followed down the Holston Valley to the region of the Holston settlements, the first outposts in the wilderness, and later, receiving stations through which passed the great migrations to the Far West. Here was a block-house, and here travelers rested in comparative safety before facing the dangers of the next step in the wilderness.

It might be supposed that the tide would have continued to the junction of the Clinch and Holston,[17] and so on down the Tennessee.[18] Later travelers wishing to reach the Cumberland settlements about Nashville did indeed proceed this way as far as Fort Campbell, situated on the site of the present Kingston, Tennessee. They then struck up the plateau through Crab Orchard, and across and down to Nashville, or on to southwestern Kentucky. After 1783 this route was marked by a well-defined wagon road. Knoxville was not founded and named until 1791, although a fort was there in 1786 "on the extreme border-land of the Indian country."

But the greatest number of travelers turned northward from the Holston settlements, across the Holston River, into Virginia through Moccasin Gap, across the Clinch, over a spur of Powell's Mountain, and down Powell's Valley to Cumberland Gap.[19] This great portal to the west, once probably a river gap, was situated at the point where the boundaries of Virginia, Tennessee, and Kentucky come together, and to it converged many trails. An important contributing route from North Carolina was joined at the French Broad by one from South Carolina, probably just about where the railroad line runs today, and this in turn was joined by another route which led from Augusta, Georgia. From Cumberland Gap the Wilderness Road passed northwest to the Bluegrass region of Kentucky.[20]

Records are few of the great concourse which for many years passed to the west over this rough trail. Usually the travelers formed companies to lessen the danger of Indian attack, and axe and rifle were always ready. Until 1795 the road was but a trace, to be traveled only on foot or horseback. In the years before the road was open to wagons, 75,000 persons at least are estimated to have passed over it.

> Through privations incredible and perils thick, thousands of men, women, and children came in successive caravans, forming continuous streams of human beings, horses, cattle, and other domestic animals, all moving onward along a lonely and houseless path to a wild and cheerless land. Cast your eyes back on that long procession of missionaries in the cause of civilization; behold the men on foot with their trusty guns on their shoulders, driving stock and leading pack-horses; and the women, some walking with pails on their heads, others riding with children in their laps, and other children swung in baskets on horses fastened to the tails of others going before; see them encamped at night expecting to be massacred by Indians; behold them in the month of December, in that ever memorable season of unprecedented cold called the "hard winter," traveling two or three miles a day, frequently in danger of being frozen or killed by the falling of horses on the icy and almost impassable trace, and subsisting on stinted allowances of stale bread and meat; but now lastly look at them at the destined fort, perhaps on the eve of merry Christmas, when met by the hearty welcome of friends who had come before, and cheered by fresh buffalo meat and parched corn, they rejoice at their deliverance, and resolve to be contented with their lot.[21]

The Ohio River route had its great portal at Pittsburgh, situated where the Allegheny and Monongahela unite to form the Ohio. Along the Allegheny came immigrants from Philadelphia; while those from Maryland and Virginia followed the Monongahela. The latter often, however, cut across to Wheeling, ninety miles before Pittsburgh, and took boat there or followed down the Greenbrier to the Kanawha and thence to the Ohio. In any case they were carried in "keel-boats and Kentucky flat-boats and Indian pirogues," generally in flotillas down the Ohio to Limestone, Kentucky, at the site of the present Maysville, and there disembarking, continued across the country by well-marked roads. Returning travelers almost always came overland to avoid the pull against the current.

This route, at first less used because of the greater danger of Indian attack and the difficulty, too, and expense of securing boats, became during the last decade of the century so important as to deflect most of the northern migration from its old channel through the Highlands. "Its complete downfall," says Bruce, speaking of the Wilderness Road, "may be said to have been accomplished with the building of the celebrated national turnpike, the Cumberland Road, which led from Baltimore through Cumberland, Maryland, where unhappy Braddock had marshalled his troops, to Wheeling, in West Virginia, being ultimately extended into Ohio."[22] This new road, which greatly shortened and improved the old Monongahela route to the Ohio, was, during the second quarter of the nineteenth century, one of the great highways between east and west. A description given by Colonel Searight, of its aspect during the height of its use, forms an interesting contrast to the account quoted above of the stream of settlers passing through Cumberland Gap:

> As many as twenty-four-horse coaches have been counted in a line at one time on the road, and large broad-wheeled wagons, covered with white canvas stretched over bows, laden with merchandise and drawn by six Conestoga horses, were visible all day long at every point, and many times until late in the evening, besides innumerable caravans of horses, mules, cattle, hogs, and sheep. It looked more like the leading avenue of a great city than a road through rural districts.[23]

All of these routes, it must be remembered, while undoubtedly affecting the growth of population in the Southern Highlands, were not directed primarily to the mountains, but through them to the west. Some settlements which have been indicated, already existed within the limits of our territory, and these continued to grow and expand, but not by leaps and bounds as was the case in Kentucky.[24] Indeed, many who for awhile shared the fortunes of the mountain settlers joined the westward tide, and, like Robertson of Watauga, moved on to found new cities beyond the ridges.

Early statements within the Southern Highlands were either in parts of the Greater Appalachian Valley, or in the larger river valleys of the upland belts to the east and west of it, on or near what were to become important routes of travel. The relation of these valleys to each other, and to the river systems, suggests the course of further settlement within the mountain country.

South of the New River Divide in Virginia the drainage of the Southern Highlands is into the Ohio and the Gulf, save for the steep eastern slopes of the Blue Ridge, down which plunge streams which are to find their way into rivers flowing across the Piedmont Plateau and Coastal Plain into the Atlantic. Thus to the population massed in the Carolina Piedmont, about the headwaters of the Yadkin, the Catawba, and other eastward flowing streams, and separated by wide piney barrens from the coastal settlements, were offered natural routes of travel up to the sources of these rivers, high in the Blue Ridge Front, and thence to the nearby headwaters of the Nolichucky, French Broad, and other waters which flow northwest down into the major streams of the Greater Valley. The main routes leading from the Valley across the Allegheny-Cumberland Plateau to the west have already been described.

It is not to be understood that the pioneer always followed closely the bed of a river, though the use of water, as defined by a mountain pupil today, "to make a road," was well recognized in frontier times. On the contrary, the Indian and buffalo trails which he commonly used kept often to the high ground, even to the top of the ridges, their general course controlled by the direction of the ranges, location of gaps, and courses of streams.

An inference, however, as to the early importance of rivers, creeks, and branches as routes of travel, may be gathered from a recital of direction actually given to the writer a year ago when he was about to take a ninety-mile ride from one mountain school to another and thence to a county-seat. These directions, it should be explained, were not furnished by one person, the morning informant generally closing his instructions with the advice to "stop by and ask . . . , at the mouth of . . . , and he will tell you how to go."

> "Go up the Trace Branch of the right fork of Troublesome; down Betty's Troublesome to Carr; down Carr to the mouth of Defeated; up to the head of Defeated; over a mountain; down Bull's Creek to the North Fork of the River; down the River for a mile to the mouth of Leatherwood; up Leatherwood four miles to Stony Fork; up Stony Fork to the head, cross the mountain; follow down the least branch on yon side of the mountain to Line Fork; up Line Fork to the headwaters of Greasy; down Greasy to the 'college.'
>
> "From the 'college' go down Greasy six miles to the mouth of Rockhouse; go up Rockhouse and take the right fork over the mountain; across Wolf and Coon to the headwaters of Cutshin; down Cutshin, fording three times; up Flacky, across a right rough little hill to the head of Owl's Nest; down Owl's Nest to Middle Fork, and up Middle Fork a piece to a deep ford; ford the River, and you are at the place you are aiming at."[25]

Clearness of understanding as to progress of settlement will be facilitated if the Highland country be pictured as consisting of two parts: first, the Valley section, which includes the Greater Appalachian Valley and the larger river valleys of the two belts that border it; and secondly, the more rugged portions of the mountain country composed of the ridges and mountains which separate the larger valleys. There are, of course, within the ridge and mountain sections lesser valleys, and the rivulets and branches which find their way down the mountain slopes are tributaries of the larger streams of the major valleys, and also trails or "traces" from minor valley to minor valley, and from minor to greater valley. There is often, too, bordering these lesser streams, much fertile and tillable land, so that settlement has been pushed at times to the springs which feed them.

Viewing the Southern Highlands as a whole, the accessible valleys were first settled. The passage of military expeditions and western settlers over the mountain trails, from the Carolinas into Tennessee, early advertised the fertility of the broader valleys and let toward the close of the eighteenth century to the rise of such mountain communities as Morganton and Ashville,[26] North Carolina. The country along the main routes of travel would naturally be soonest developed, although this was by no means always true. As late as 1790 there was a stretch of one hundred miles on the Wilderness Road with no sign of habitation, and Michaux,[27] in 1796, traveling a much used trace in North Carolina, reports many miles along the road desolate and unpopulated.

The cessions, at different periods, of land held by the Indians were determining factors in settlement. The Highlands were not open to white occupation by one treaty but by a series of treaties. Consequently some mountain areas were available earlier than some valley areas, though it was true that with each cession the valleys were settled earlier than the ridges.

The last treaty of the Colonial Period that affected the Highlands was that of July 20, 1777, when a tract of 6,064 square miles, largely of mountain land within western North Carolina and eastern Tennessee abutting it, was given over by the Cherokees. Including this cession there was thus open to entry by 1777, all of our territory in Maryland, Virginia, West Virginia, Kentucky, almost all of the limited upland section of South Carolina, and about one-fourth of western North Carolina and east Tennessee—in all, an area of approximately 68,000 of the 112,000 square miles of the Southern Highlands.

The first Indian treaty made after the establishment of the Federal Government was that of November 28, 1785, when the boundaries of the Cherokee Nation were defined. These boundaries, however, did not enlarge the amount of land available within the Southern Highlands, save for an area of 550 square miles along the French Broad River in North Carolina, lying just west of the land ceded on July 20, 1777. By successive treaties more of the Highlands was opened to occupation, but it was not until 1805 that Indian claims to the Cumberland Plateau section of Tennessee were extinguished; and not until 1835–1838, when the Cherokees gave over all of their land east of the Mississippi and were finally removed to their reservation beyond it, that the larger part of our territory in northern Georgia and northeastern Alabama and the last mountain lands in western North Carolina and southeastern Tennessee were legally free for entry. Even then a few Cherokees, still unresigned to banishment from the land of their ancestors, refused exile and hid themselves in the wilderness. A small reservation was later set aside for them in western North Carolina, where their descendants still live.

It is not to be supposed, however, that there were no cabins raised on Indian soil prior to the drawing of treaties. Early descriptions of lands, metes, and bounds, were inaccurate, and unintentional transgression often took place. There was also willful transgression in the appropriation of lands, and individual squatters would occupy tracts apparently with the hope that later treaties with the Indians would legalize their holdings. Speaking generally, however, there were few settlements in the mountain-ridge section until the last decade of the century and none in large numbers until after 1800.

The Watauga Settlement in 1769 served as an advance guard to that of the mountain-ridge section. While in general it may be said that the broad central valleys of the Holston, Watauga, and Nolichucky offered sufficient opportunity for the expansion of population for some years, yet, from the time of William Bean's entrance into this mountain region, the valleys of the neighboring ranges began to receive a scattering immigration. Almost contemporaneously, home seekers made their appearance in western North Carolina, which is geographically a part of the same mountain area. These sections were settled partly from the Watauga district of Tennessee, and partly from the North and South Carolina Piedmont frontier.

In eastern Kentucky it is probable that the first settlers entered the border counties somewhat after 1790, and that its mountains as a whole did not receive any great influx of population until after 1800. This was largely due to the fact that in Kentucky the Wilderness Road passed for most of its course to the west of the mountains, and that on account of the Cumberland barrier to the east there were few gateways into the eastern part of Kentucky.

Imlay, whose travels were first published in 1792, referring undoubtedly to the mountainous areas within West Virginia, western Virginia, and eastern Kentucky, says:

> The country that separates the back counties of Virginia from Kentucky is the greater part of it mountainous, and through which to its champaign lands is nearly 250 miles, the whole of that tract of wilderness, extending from Holston nearly north, crossing the Great Sandy River, the Great and Little Kanhaways, quite into the fine lands in the district belonging to Pennsylvania, exclusive of some small tracts in the upper counties of Virginia upon the Ohio, all of which are occupied, is altogether broken into high, rugged, and barren hills, the bottoms excepted, and, in all probability will not be inhabited for centuries to come, by reason of the immense tracts of good lands lying west of the Ohio and Mississippi.[28]

adding:

> that tract of country lying southeasterly from Holston and extending to Cumberland; Powell's Valley, Nolichucky, French Broad, and Clinch excepted, is little better.

This later reference, we may infer, is to the mountainous mass, or at least to a portion of it, which in its entirety includes the mountainous section of eastern Tennessee, western North Carolina, and part of northern Georgia.

It is probable that much of the settlement of the mountain-ridge section was due to the natural increase of families, the rapid succession of generations pushing their clearings farther and farther up creeks and minor valleys away from the land already under cultivation by older members of their families. There was, too, more or less movement back to the mountains by families who had passed through to the west, and who then, for various causes, turned back and took up land in the mountain-ridge section.

This rougher country of itself had certain definite assets which invited immigration. Among these, the discovery of salt springs in Kentucky and West Virginia was a strong inducement to settlement. These "licks" so called from the fact that the spring basins incrusted with salt were the resort of buffalo, elk, deer, and other wild game, had long been familiar to the Indians, who had manufactured salt in early times. The lack of this commodity was keenly felt by the first settlers, and even now there are in the mountains those who tell of the long annual journey to the east, made by their great-grandparents in search of salt.[29]

The rapid growth of population in the region of a salt spring may be illustrated by the early history of Clay County, Kentucky. The first settler of whom there is record in this section, one James Collins, is said to have discovered a salt spring in 1800 while following a buffalo trace, and to have made the first salt ever made in that country. In the court house at Manchester, Clay County, Kentucky, there is on record the sale to James White, of Washington County, Virginia—a quartermaster of General Cox of Tennessee—the salt mines of Ballenger, occupied by outlaw[30] and patented under a grant to Jacob Meyers—4,000 acres. This was in 1804. Two years later the population had so increased as to lead to the organization of the county. As late as 1846, Clay County had fifteen furnaces producing 200,000 bushels of salt annually. So great indeed was the attraction of the salt works as to lead to a back settlement of this section from central Kentucky, and tradition presents the picture of wealthy landlords from the Bluegrass living on baronial mountain estates in almost feudal fashion, surrounded by slaves and retainers.

The discovery of gold in northern Georgia in 1828 brought into that part of the mountains hundreds of people in search of treasure. It will be recalled that this section, then known as Cherokee County, was, together with northern Alabama and parts of North Carolina and southeastern Tennessee, held by the Cherokees until 1838. The inrush of gold seekers into Indian territory, with the drinking, gaming, and brawling that accompanied it, provoked from Governor Gilmer of Georgia the following letter, dated May 6, 1830, and addressed to John McPherson Berrien, then Attorney-General of the United States:

> I am in doubt as to what ought to be done with the gold diggers. They with their various attendants, foragers, and suppliers, make up between six and ten thousand persons.

They occupy the country between the Chestatee and Etowah Rivers, near the mountains, gold being found in the greatest quantity deposited in the small streams, which flow into these rivers.[31]

In spite of the Governor's proclamation prohibiting gold mining in north Georgia, these "paper bullets" as he described them, "had little influence over a people who could not read," and miners managed to continue operations. The first deposit of gold from Georgia, made in 1830, amounted to $212,000; and so important were these fields that a branch of the United States Mint established a Dahlonega, Lumpkin County, in 1838, was maintained for some years. While many of the gold seekers left the country after the first rush was over, some remained to become permanent residents.[32]

Other causes which brought settlers to the mountains were war bounties to soldiers, often taking the form of grants of land, and the opening up of Indian boundaries. In addition, the mountain country was rich in game and timber, and had a cool climate and an abundance of pure water.

For many years, even as late as the middle of the nineteenth century, immigrants in large numbers continued to travel along the mountain trails and passes. The conditions causing these migrations were religious, social, and economic. The struggle of the nonconformists, especially the Baptists,[33] against the Established Church in Virginia; social conditions of the Tidewater; and in particular the Revolution, which freed the western territory from restraint, and thus offered new opportunities to men impoverished by long war, were all factors in the early movements.

By 1800 the great migration from north to west had been deflected almost entirely from the Wilderness Road to the Ohio River route, or was moving overland toward the great northwestern territory of Ohio, Indiana, Illinois, Missouri, and Michigan, then open to settlement and accessible by northern routes. Emigration from Virginia and the Carolinas, especially from the Tidewater sections, however, continued for many years to flow through the mountains both by the old channels and by routes not before available because of danger from Indian attack. Thus in Kentucky, while numbers used the great routes of early days, emigrants later were also able to pass directly from Virginia into Kentucky through gaps in the wall of the Cumberlands and by trails along the Kanawha,[34] Big Sandy, and other rivers. Many now living in the eastern part of the state claim that their ancestors came in through one of the various eastern gaps,[35] and it has often been said that the Kentucky mountains were populated almost entirely by Virginia. This is undoubtedly an overstatement, for the evidence of names, pension lists, and Kentucky traditions as well, point to a large percentage of settlers from North Carolina; yet in connection with the claim just mentioned, it will serve to indicate the later lines of movement through the mountains.

The history of the migrations of one of these Kentucky families, as given by the original pioneer's great-great-grandson, whose grandmother remembered the journey and told him of it, may be suggestive, the more in that it is probably the history of much of the settlement in the mountain section of Kentucky.[36] In 1825 one Ambrose Amburgey came over from the Clinch River, Virginia, into what is now Knott County, Kentucky. The country was exceedingly rough, but he found a couple, James and Priscilla Davis, living near the mouth of Defeated Branch. From them he bought, for $6000, the rights to over 10,000 acres of lands along Carr Creek, a narrow but fertile and lovely valley. He then went back to Virginia, gathered up his wife and two children, his parents, and brothers-in-law, together with their families and their slaves—in all a goodly company. The next year they started for Kentucky, going through the Pound Gap into Letcher County. There they "tented" and made their crop through the summer. In the autumn they moved on to Carr. Amburgey settled the several families along various parts of his purchase. The children were many, ten or fifteen in each household, and in a generation or so there were literally hundreds of the family in that region. Now, in this and neighboring counties, there are thousands of their descendants.

That some settlers came unintentionally into the mountains of Kentucky, through the purchase of land which they had supposed lay in the far-famed limestone region, is also true. William Savage, writing in 1819, mentions the case of an Englishman from Yorkshire who bought 30,000 acres in Kentucky,[37] and who upon this arrival found that:

His land was barren, situated on rocky mountains, far removed from any settlers; no roads, no river in the vicinity; and totally unfit for cultivation or settling. . . . He consoled himself when he found that his land abounded with coal, . . . but this consolation was not of long continuance; his friend, who knew the customs and manners of the people better than himself, assured him that the low price of land enhanced the price of labor, for any man could purchase a few acres by working a few months, and everyone preferred living upon his own property, however poorly, to being a servant; so that it was difficult to procure laborers to work even above ground; and he would find it impossible, while land continued so plentiful, to find men who would work in the bowels of the earth. Nay, that if it were possible to raise coal, to transport it to Lexington and pitch it in the marketplace; then to send the bell-man round the town to inform the inhabitants there was coal to distribute gratis to those who would fetch it, that it would still remain on his hands, as the inhabitants would not burn it, preferring wood.

Thus this visionary expectations vanished; his property wasted; he became dissatisfied; the tax collector each year sold a part of the land for nonpayment of the land tax; and this enthusiast in the purchase of land in America died a disappointed man; and his son, anxious to return to England, sold the remainder of his father's purchase, amounting to *many* acres, to a person in America, who knew the lots, for $50.00!

I do not mention the name of this individual who was ruined by his speculation, but it is not the less a fact. It was sufficiently well-known to many in England; and is a matter of notoriety in Kentucky.

From 1830 to 1850, the westward migration from the Southern states received a new impetus. The decline in prices of cotton and tobacco in the South, together with the exhaustion of the soil, sent many thousands, including not only the poorer small farmers but planters caught by the general financial depression, to the northwest and southwest. In this new tide which passed along the old mountain trails,[38] might be seen "every conceivable sort of conveyance, from a handsome family carriage to the humblest sort of ox-cart."

"The Southerner packed up his household goods," says Pooley, "faced the west, and travelled by the most convenient road." An illustration of this characteristic is given in the answer made by a North Carolina man who, travelling westward with all his earthly possessions, was asked where he was going. "No where in pertick'la" he answered. "Me and my wife thought we'd hunt a place to settle. We've no money, nor no plunder—nothin' but just ourselves and this nag—we thought we'd try our luck in a new country." (From Chicago *Weekly American,* June 20, 1835.)[39]

Pooley estimates, moreover, that:

Before 1850, Virginia had lost by emigration 26 percent of her native-born free inhabitants. South Carolina had lost 36 percent, and North Carolina 31 percent. Further examination of statistics will, however, show that the movement was probably almost entirely within the limits of the planting states themselves. From 1831 to 1840, Georgia gained nearly 34 percent in population; Alabama 91 percent; and Arkansas 275 percent. In the next decade, while the percentages of increase were lower, the actual gain in population in these states was little less than in the preceding decade; and if Texas, which appears for the first time in the Census reports, be included, the increase was nearly 200,000 in excess of that of the preceding decade.[40]

Contemporary with and succeeding these later migrations, the mountain trails were also used for transporting merchandise and for moving large droves of stock—horses, cattle, and hogs—from the west to the east. Four or five thousand hogs were driven at a time from Ohio eastward, and the droves passed often through Tennessee, Virginia, and the Carolinas, where the forest mast supplied abundant food. Through Cumberland Gap, mules and horses were driven to the Tennessee Valley, and so southward to supply southern plantations. In 1828 the value of livestock passing through Cumberland Gap was estimated at $1,167,000; while in 1824 at Saluda Gap, the main gap for trails connecting the coasts of South Carolina and Georgia with transmontane regions, the value of horses, cattle, and hogs, brought from the west to supply the south is held to have amounted to more than a million dollars.[41] The chief center for distribution of merchandise into the back regions of the Carolinas and Alabama was Knoxville.

In view, then, of all the various movements through the mountains, and of the fact that the accessible valley regions were early occupied, it seems reasonable to suppose that some, journeying through the mountains in the later migrations, passed by many routes and trails into the less accessible valleys of the mountain-ridge section. That there should be men of inferior stamina and ability among them would seem inevitable; but it can by no means be claimed that as a whole the later settlers were inferior. This period, throughout the United States, has been designated as one of movement. All classes were in motion, and at a time when isolation was a characteristic of frontier life it was not easy for a pioneer to foresee that choice of a home in what has now become a remote part of our mountain-ridge section, would result as the years went on in the separation of the life of his descendants from that of the greater part of the state.

The poorness of mountain roads was probably not as much a deterrent to travel before 1850 as later. All travel was difficult. In Kentucky, until 1830, there was little difference except in grade and the likelihood of washouts between the mountain thoroughfares and those of the Bluegrass region. The rapidly increasing population and wealth of the Bluegrass, however, as well as perhaps the availability of good highway material, soon led to the establishment of macadam turnpikes in that part of the state. It was during this period, from 1830 to 1850, that the mountain country, left to provide for itself in the matter of roads, began to be shut off from the life of the remainder of the state.[42]

What was true of Kentucky was probably true in greater or less degree of the other states in which the Highlands are situated. Road building in the more prosperous, thickly settled portions led to distinctions between Lowlands and Highlands and between valley areas and mountain-ridge sections; and with the gradual subsidence of the streams of migration from east to west and the separation of the new frontier in the northwest and southwest from the old frontier by a belt of more advanced stage of development, the mountains, especially the mountain-ridge areas, became more and more isolated.

After the middle of the nineteenth century no large migrations passed into or through the Southern Highlands. Such movement as there was affected for the most part the valley areas or the sections where industrial development was taking place. Individuals of course made their way from one section to another, but the composition of the population remained on the whole the same.

An intensive study, county by county, would be necessary to determine accurately the date of settlement of different areas. We have been concerned with the broader questions of early and late settlement mainly as a basis of discussion as to the probable nationality of the ancestors of those now living in the Southern

Highlands, and to provide a background for an understanding of some of the aspects of life in the mountains today.

NOTES

1. "From the year 1720 to 1776 this people came on the average of 12,000 a year, or 600,000 people from the Revolution."—Scotch-Irish Society of America, Vol. III, p. 132. Proceedings of the 1st–8th Congress, 1889–1896. Cincinnati, R. Clarke & Co., 8 vols.

Kuhns estimates that the grand total of German immigration was probably 110,000.—Kuhns, Arthur: The German and Swiss Settlements of Colonial Pennsylvania, New York, 1901.

2. "The explanation of the antipathy excited by the Scotch-Irish immigration lies not in the character of the arrivals, but in the character of the economic system of the community."—Ford, Henry Jones: The Scotch-Irish in America, Ch. VII, p. 224. Princeton University Press, 1915.

3. "Emigrants usually landed either at Lewes or at Newcastle in Delaware, or in Philadelphia."—Hanna, Charles A.: The Scotch-Irish, Vol. II, p. 60. G. P. Putnam's Sons, 1902.

4. North Carolina Colonial Records, Vol. V, pp. 17–18. Mathew Rowan was President and Commander-in-Chief of the Province of North Carolina, 1753–1754.

5. A map printed many times first about 1760 and last about 1790.

6. "Dr. Thomas Walker, who lived at Castle Hill, Albemarle County, Virginia, penetrated these wilds in 1750. He went by Staunton and up the Valley, crossing the Alleghany on the watershed at the present site of Blackberry, crossed New River at Horseshoe, went down the river to the mouth of Walker's Creek, and up the creek along the face of Walker's Mountain to the headwaters of the Clinch River. Passing down the Clinch he made his way to the Gap to which he gave the name of Cumberland."—Speed, Thomas: The Wilderness Road, p. 14. Louisville, Ky., John P. Morton & Co., 1886.

7. This settlement may perhaps be that made by the Inglis and Draper families somewhere about 1750 near the present Blackberry, Virginia, which was raided in 1775 by the Shawnee Indians. Blackberry, however, lies at the headwaters of the Roanoke, and the Roanoke and Holston systems are clearly distinguished on Mitchell's map despite its poor perspective.

8. An attempt was made to adjust matters by a number of new treaties, of which that of Stanwix, New York, in 1768, with the Iroquois, and of Lockabler, South Carolina, with the Cherokees, in 1770, were the most important. By these various treaties most of West Virginia, Kentucky, and much of North Carolina and eastern Tennessee were ceded to the English.

9. Probably John Finley, or Findlay, a Scotch-Irish trader with whom Boone is supposed to have first made acquaintance during Braddock's campaign. Finley has been through Ouasioto, or Cumberland Gap about 1752, and recounted to Boone in glowing terms his memories of the immense herds of buffaloes he had seen in Kentucky, the abundance of bears, deer, and elk, the great salt licks where they gathered, and the innumerable flocks of wild turkeys, geese, and ducks. See Henderson, Archibald: The Conquest of the Old Southwest, Ch. X. New York, Century, 1920.

10. See Appendix C.

11. A body of associates in western Carolina, formed to preserve order on the frontier, an to resist the collection of excessive and fraudulent taxes. For fuller information see Ch. VI, p. 91.

12. There was great disappointment among the settlers in the Watauga region when it was found that they were on North Carolina instead of Virginia soil. Under Virginia they could have expected some protection from the Indians, but the government of North Carolina east of the mountains was too unsettled to afford help to any settlers to the west. The formation of the Watauga Association secured for six years not only a peaceful administration of local affairs, but a certain measure of preparedness against Indian attack. When the association came to an end through the creation by North Carolina of Washington County, now Tennessee, the general system of government continued to work successfully for some years longer. When, however, North Carolina ceded her lands lying "west of the mountains and extending to the Mississippi" to the Federal Government, giving the Government two years in which to accept, not only was great doubt felt in the Holston region as to the Government accepting the territory, but the settlers felt that while the matter was pending they would be left unprotected. North Carolina, also, had not acceded to demands which the association felt to be just. The Wataugans therefore set up an independent state which they called Franklin, adopted a constitution, and carried on their own negotiations with the Indians. So scarce was money in this new state that the following according to Haywood (History of Tennessee, p. 150) were recognized as currency: "Good flax linen ten hundred, at three shillings and six pence per yard; good clear beaver skins, six shillings each; racoon and fox skins, at one shilling and three pence; deer skins, six shillings; bacon at six pence per lb; tallow at six pence; good whiskey at two shillings and six pence a gallon." Lack of recognition by the Federal Government, internal dissension, and poverty, led, in two years, to collapse.

13. Roosevelt: Winning of the West, Vol. 1, p. 231.

14. These gentlemen were Colonel Richard Henderson and eight others, who, by a treaty with the Cherokees in 1775, had obtained title to all the land lying between the Kentucky and Cumberland Rivers, some seventeen million acres. The "Proprietors of the Colony of Transylvania," as they called themselves, were not allowed by the Virginia legislature to hold this immense territory, but Henderson, in consideration of his services, was granted 200,000 acres on the Ohio.

15. "In 1778–9 Jonesboro, the oldest town in Tennessee, and county-seat of Washington County, was laid out, and court-house and jail erected."—Rule, William: History of Knoxville. Chicago, Lewis Publishing Co., 1900.

16. Major Ferguson, dispatched by Cornwallis into the western part of North Carolina to "subdue the back counties," sent word to the Watauga settlers that if "they did not desist from their opposition to the British Arms, he would cross the mountains, hang their leaders, and lay waste the country with fire and sword." In characteristic fashion the frontiersmen determined to attack Ferguson at once, before he could move upon them. At Sycamore Shoals of the Watauga River they gathered, over 1,200 men, including some 400 from the Virginia frontier. A draft was taken to provide a guard for the home settlements. Then, after a powerful sermon by the famous Presbyterian pastor, Dr. Doak, in which he exhorted them to "go forth with the sword of the Lord and of Gideon," they set out to cross the mountains. All were armed with the usual rifle, tomahawk, and hunting-knife, and wore sprigs of evergreen in their coon-skin caps; nearly all were well mounted. Ferguson, forewarned of their approach, discreetly retired from Gilbert Town in Rutherford County, and entrenched himself just over the border in South Carolina, on King's Mountain, from which he stoutly asserted that neither "God Almighty nor all the rebels outside hell, could dislodge him." The frontiersmen, under William Campbell, John Sevier, and Isaac Shelby, after thirty hours in the saddle, drenched by rain, and with inferior numbers, proceeded at once to storm the stronghold. They fought with a combination of tactical skill and Indian cunning, taking advantage of every bit of cover. The battle lasted for some hours, during which, the old chronicler tells us "the whole mountain was covered with smoke and seemed to thunder"; but at last Ferguson was killed and his men who were left alive surrendered. Not more than a month later part of this same band of frontiersmen fought the Indians at Boyd's Creek, Kentucky, more than three hundred miles away across the mountains.

17. By Act of the Tennessee legislature, April 6, 1887, the Tennessee River now begins at the junction of the North Fork of the Holston with the Holston at Kingsport, Tennessee. In early descriptions, however, the river was known as the Holston to the point where it united with the Clinch at Kingston.

18. This route was pursued, 1779–1780, by most of Robertson's party, who took boats down the Tennessee, and up the Ohio and Cumberland—a perilous route on account of the hostility of the Chickamaugas. Generally, however, prior to 1783, early travelers came into western Tennessee and Kentucky by the Wilderness Road, through Cumberland Gap as far as Rockcastle Hills, then turned south and

followed a trace which led to the Bluffs on Cumberland River, afterward Nashville! This was the course taken by Robertson himself in 1779.

19. See Appendix C.

20. There are two important branches of the road in Kentucky; one laid out by Boone followed a buffalo trace to Rockcastle River, and thence up Roundstone Creek, through Boone's Gap in Big Hill, through the present county of Madison, down Otter Creek to its mouth at Kentucky River. About one mile below the mouth of Otter Creek, Boone established his fort and called it Boonesborough.

The other branch, laid out by Logan in 1775, left Boone's at Rockcastle River and bore west through Crab Orchard to the falls of the Ohio. This became known especially as "the road leading through the great wilderness."—Speed, Thomas: The Wilderness Road pp. 26–27. Louisville, Ky., John P. Morton and Co., 1886.

21. Chief Justice Robertson, in an address quoted ibid., p. 41.

22. Bruce, H. A. B.: Daniel Boone and the Wilderness Road, p. 298. New York, The Macmillan Company, 1910.

23. Searight, Thomas B.: The Old Pike, p. 16. Uniontown, Pa., 1894.

24. The population in the forks of the Holston in 1790 is variously estimated from "thousands" to 40,000.

Roosevelt (Winning of the West, Vol. III, p. 276) says: "When peace was declared with Great Britain, the backwoodsmen had spread westward in groups almost to the Mississippi, and they had increased in numbers to some 25,000 souls, of whom a few hundred dwelt in the bend of the Cumberland while the rest were about equally divided between Kentucky and Holston. These figures are simply estimates, but they are based on careful study and comparison, and though they must be some hundreds, and maybe some thousands out of the way, are quite near enough for practical purposes."

25. Notes on directions:

Trace Branch. There are a number of "trace" branches or forks in the mountains of Kentucky. They are the branches or forks of streams which the trail or trace follows.

Defeated. According to tradition, some hunters were defeated here by Indians, and several killed.

Leatherwood. So-called from a kind of tree formerly prevalent along its course. As described by our host, it were a tree what sprangles out at the top, kindly like a rosy bush."

Greasy. According to our host, called Licking Branch when Kentucky was part of Virginia then Laurel, from one of its tributaries; later, a hunter killed a bear upon a flat rock, threw the entrails into the creek which became greasy in appearance, asked where the bear was killed, he replied, "Up there on Greasy," and the name stuck.

Rockhouse. So called from the rocky banks being worn away by the action of the stream, with tops overhanging like a roof.

Cutshin. One tradition holds that it was named from an accident woodcutter, who here cut his shin. Another, to the effect that here in winter the stream freezes so hard as to cut the shins of mules and horses which break through the ice.

26. Tradition has it that the earliest settler of Buncombe County came in by way of Old Fort to the headwaters of the Swannanoa River, and down its valley, a route now followed by the Salisbury and Asheville Branch of the Southern Railway.

27. Michaux, vol. III, in Reuben G. Thwaites' Early Western Travels.

28. Imlay, Gilbert: A topographic Description of the Western Territory of North America, p. 239. New York, Samuel Campbell 1793.

29. The importance of the discovery of salt in the development of the United States is thus described by Turner:

"The early settlers were tied to the coast by the need of salt, without which they could not preserve their meats or live in comfort. Writing in 1752, Bishop Spangenburg says of a colony for which he was seeking lands in North Carolina: 'They will require salt and other necessaries which they can neither manufacture nor raise. Either they must go to Charleston, which is 300 miles distant. . . . Or else they must go down to Boling's point in Va. on a branch of the James P is also 300 miles from here. . . . Or else they must go down the Roanoke—I know not how many miles—where salt is brought up from the Cape Fear.' This may serve as a typical illustration. An annual pilgrimage to the coast for salt thus became essential. Taking flocks or furs and ginseng root, the early settlers sent their pack trains after seeding time each year to the coast. This proved to be an important educational influence, since it was almost the only way in which the pioneer learned what was going on in the East. But when discovery was made of the salt springs of the Kanawha, and the Holston, and Kentucky, and central New York, the West began to be freed from dependence on the coast. It was in part the effect of finding these salt springs that enabled settlement to cross the mountains."—Turner, Frederick Jackson: The Frontier in American History, Report of the American Historical Association, 1893.

30. Occupied by squatters until they had obtained title by adverse possession.

31. Quoted in A Preliminary Report on a Part of the Gold Deposits of Georgia, by W. S. Yeates, S. W. McCallie, and F. P. King, Bulletin No. 4 A, Geological Survey of Georgia. Atlanta, Ga., 1896.

32. "Gold was looked for in all these Cherokee counties, and so the lots were only 40 acres in size. When gold was not found, and there was no indication of it, the lands were very cheap; from $10.00 to $20.00 was the price of a single lot, and many a man bought a small farm for the price of an Indian pony. The cheapness of the lands led to rapid and thick settlement. The country was soon filled up with enterprising young people, and numbers who became substantial farmers on large farms began life in one of these Cherokee Counties on forty acres of poor land."—Smith, George Gillman: The Story of Georgia and the Georgia People, 1732 to 1860, pp. 423–424.

33. See Chapter VIII, p. 158 ff.

34. "The main New-Kanawha Trail with which they (the more northern transmontane trails) connected, and its branches, were regarded in Virginia simply as portage paths to the head of navigation on the Kanawha River, whence the Ohio might be gained. . . . It was not until after 1783, when Indian attacks had become less frequent, . . . that serious attention was given to the betterment of the main trail and a Kentucky extension, as a 'short cut' between east and west. . . . Imlay's map, published 1793, gives the 'New Road to Virginia,' extending from Lexington by way of the junction of the two forks of the Big Sandy at Balclutta, now Louisa, to the falls of the Kanawha, where it connects with the main road, which extends along the Kanawha and Greenbrier Rivers to Winchester, situated on the road leading to Richmond, Alexandria, and other cities. Indian attacks rendered this route unsafe until after the close of the period."—Verhoeff, Mary: The Kentucky Mountains, Transportation and Commerce, 1793 to 1911, Ch. III, p. 90 ff. Filson Club Publication No. 26.

35. "The first County Judge was Nat Collins, son of Jim Collins, and a very strong preacher, who came here in 1806 from North Carolina and was making his way for the Bluegrass section. There were eight men and women and Preacher Collins led the bunch. They had come by the way of Cumberland Gap and did not know how to get across the Stone Mountain into the Bluegrass region. There was no Cumberland Gap tunnel then or any railroads, only a wild wilderness. The bunch came up Powell's River to where Wise, Va., is now, and struck out through the Pound Gap and on to the head of Kentucky River and down the river to where Whitesburg is now located. There was not a family living in Letcher County then, as Daniel Boone had left his camp at the mouth of Boone's Fork and went to the fort at Boonesborough, so they passed through where Whitesburg now is and up Sandlick Creek and over a hill on to Camp Branch. It was just before Christmas and they all went up a small dream under a cliff and laid out. The next morning the snow was six feet deep, and they were all covered with snow. The snow lasted about three months, so they lay up all winter, and the men would kill deer and wild turkey, and they all have a very good time camping out."—History of Corporal Fess Whitaker, Life in the Kentucky Mountains, Mexico, and Texas, p. 107. Louisville, Ky., Standard Printing Co., 1918.

36. The old surveys and land patents of eastern Kentucky, dating 1815–1825, were made along either side of the big rivers and creeks; that is to say, they covered the larger valleys. In the beginning when land was plentiful, little importance was attached to the smaller valleys or to the ridge slopes. It is possible that the settlers did not claim these, or it may be that they did not consider it necessary to designate them especially. Later, however, as families increased greatly, the value of land bordering the small streams and on the sides of the mountains became apparent. Many of the original owners moved their patents back, and back again, of their first boundaries, but in the course of time it became commonly accepted that a man holding a patent cov-

ering the valley or bottom land where he lived, owned on either side a straight line to the top of the ridge, even if this was not so entered on his survey. Blazing, or otherwise marking such boundaries, was held sufficient evidence of ownership.

The indefiniteness of such claims gave the rise not only to great confusion but to the practice of "wild-catting," which was at its height from 1860–1870. "Wild-catters" were men who, through familiarity with the country, or through agents or surveyors who were familiar with it, knew the deficiencies of the various land patents. In order to get a title to such territory as had not been legally registered, they would throw a blanket claim over a designated area, usually from the top of a ridge down either side in lots of several thousand acres. In this way they secured a claim to thousands of acres of unpatented ridge lands and irregular tracts of unpatented territory along the smaller branches. For some years much litigation and bitter feeling were engendered by these "wild-cat" claims. Ultimately, little was gained by the practice, as it could be proved in court, generally, that the mountain citizens were using, or tending toward the use of these lands for legitimate purposes, whereas the "wild-catters" had left them undeveloped.

37. Savage, William: Observations on Emigration to the United States of America, illustrated by original Facts, pp. 26–28. London, 1819.

38. "The roads up the Virginia valleys converged at the Cumberland Gap, although some movers preferred to travel towards the Potomac River striking the old National Road there. Still others followed along the road leading through Charlottesville, Lewisburg and Charlestown to Guyandotte on the Ohio. From the Carolinas they followed the Yadkin through Wilkesville, thence northward through Ward's Gap Virginia) across the valley to the Great Kanawha; or turning southwest from Wilkesville some went through the State Gap (North Carolina) and found their way to one of the Ohio River towns by way of the Cumberland Gap. The roads of South Carolina followed the rivers, and converging at the Saluda Gap in the Blue Ridge, passed through Asheville (North Carolina), through the Smoky Mountains and the Cumberland Gap to Kentucky. As a general rule where there was any tendency to follow a beaten line of travel it was towards some point on the Ohio between Cincinnati and Louisville."—Pooley, William Vipond: The Settlement of Illinois from 1830 to 1850, p. 356. Madison, Wis. May, 1908.

39. Ibid., p. 353.

40. Ibid., p. 334.

41. Turner, Frederick Jackson: The Rise of the New West, 1819–1829, in The American Nation, a History, Vol. XIV, p. 100 ff. New York, Harper Brothers, 1906.

42. Verhoeff, Mary: The Kentucky Mountains, Transportation and Commerce, 1750–1911, Ch. IV. Filson Club Publication No. 26.

10. APPALACHIA AND THE IDEA OF AMERICA: THE PROBLEM OF THE PERSISTING FRONTIER

Henry D. Shapiro

Since the 1870's, Americans have regarded Appalachia as a strange land inhabited by a peculiar people. Defined by its culture as well as by geography, Appalachia has seemed an anomaly in an otherwise unified and homogeneous nation, a discrete region, in but not of America. As such it has generally been ignored, or at most viewed as a quaint and interesting land where moonshiners and feudists live in log cabins and speak the stately language of Elizabethan England, while their wives spin and weave and sing traditional ballads of kings and queens and ravens sitting on fences. From time to time, however, the existence of Appalachia has been brought more or less forcibly to the attention of Americans living outside the region. At such times the peculiarities of mountain life, in whatever terms they are defined at the particular moment, have become troublesome facts requiring explanation, and Americans have been forced to consider the possible implications of Appalachia's existence for their own understanding of the nature of American civilization.

Our own is such a time, of course. In the context of our recent discovery of poverty in the United States, Appalachia has come to epitomize that "other America" of which Michael Harrington wrote, the antithesis of an America defined by economic growth and technological achievement. As a symbol of the existence of pockets of poverty in an affluent society, Appalachia has in fact had a clear advantage over more ephemeral examples of the same phenomenon—those populations which we designate in statistical rather than human terms as "the poor" and to which we thereby deny any existence except that in the minds of demographers. Appalachia is physically real as well as statistically real. It has location and a history—and a history of poverty. Its poverty too has a history and, like Appalachia, can not be expected to disappear with increasing national prosperity.

In the last decade, as a consequence, we have rediscovered Appalachia, and have been faced once again with the need to explain the persistent discrepancy between life in the Southern mountain region and life in the rest of the United States. Such explanation has been easy, however. Having defined Appalachia as a land characterized by permanent poverty, we may regard the disparity between Appalachia and America as a difference of degree, not of kind. In Appalachia there is less money, less opportunity for the accumulation of money, and consequently less of what money can provide, to individuals and to the community, than is normal in the rest of the nation. Seen in these terms, Appalachian culture becomes the culture of a depressed area and hence a temporary phenomenon, however permanent the conditions which create it may be. We are thus obliged to deal only with the historical

Reprinted from An Appalachian Symposium, J. W. Williamson (ed.). Copyright Appalachian State University Press, 1977, pp. 43–55. Used by permission.

causes of Appalachia's poverty, and with the anomaly of pockets of poverty in an affluent society. Because we have so severely restricted our vision of the relationship of Appalachia and America, in other words, we need not face the kind of situation which might challenge our conception of America as a land of opportunity, where economic growth is natural, or of American civilization as unified and homogeneous.[1]

America's relationship with Appalachia has not always been so simple, however. From the late nineteenth century, when the mountainous portions of eight Southern states were first recognized as composing a discrete region, at least through the 1920's, the existence of this strange land and peculiar people raised questions about the nature of American civilization itself. Discovered in the 1870's by local color writers who used it as a neutral ground against which to set their stories of upper-class romance and lower-class passion, by the end of the century Appalachia had come to seem a stubborn outpost of that quintessentially American way of life which industrialism and urbanism were destroying. Indeed, Appalachia was unique among the "little corners" of the nation which came to the public's attention via the local color movement, in that its peculiarities, although identified as characteristic of the American past, were observed in the American present. The tendency to glorify America's past, which has been the typical accompaniment of our most assiduous efforts to abandon that past, gave the peculiarities of Appalachian life a rather special meaning and value during the last years of the century, to the degree that these were identified with the culture and customs of earlier days. From this point of view, the transformation of Appalachia by the forces of modernization and homogenization could only be regarded with ambiguity or downright despair, while the persistence of pioneer virtues among the isolated mountaineers made them seem a rebuke to an effete generation and a possible leaven for the nation.[2]

It was the absence of modern economic institutions and modern social patterns which had first attracted the local color writers to Appalachia—physical for purposes of rustication at the resort areas of the New South and imaginatively as a field to be mined for literary material.[3] Between 1870 and 1890, at the very beginning of the literary exploitation of the region, at least one hundred twenty-five short stories and more than ninety sketches dealing with the nature of mountain life were published.[4] As one of the areas of the nation "least affected by the progress of a growing national unity"[5] and yet within close proximity to the very centers of the nationalizing process, Appalachia seemed inherently interesting, even while its topography and natural history, and the peculiar folkways of its inhabitants, made it seem romantic and picturesque.

The dominance of the literary imagination in this first discovery of Appalachia was of great significance.

Not only did it establish as conventional an essentially literary vision of the Southern mountain region as a strange land inhabited by a peculiar people, over the view of those who saw in the mountains only unlimited possibilities for economic development,[6] but it made literary criteria primary in analyses of mountain life and of the relationship of Appalachia and America. Even such non-literary types as Nathaniel Southgate Shaler, the Kentucky-born Harvard geologist, and George E. Vincent, a University of Chicago sociologist, directed their efforts more at achieving an elegance of style than at careful and complete discussion of mountain conditions. Among the literary folk, on the other hand, Charles Dudley Warner, from the security of an established literary reputation and with an image as Connecticut sophisticate to maintain, was virtually alone in daring to admit that mountain poverty was as dull and unpleasant as any other kind of poverty, from the point of view of participants and observers both.[7] In the literature of Appalachia, as a consequence, metaphor characteristically did the work of exposition. Because it was more interesting, the "as if" was preferred to the "is," and came eventually to be identified as reality.

It was this tendency which may be said to have given America's image of Appalachia its particular form. Those first on the scene noted with some surprise that the mountaineers lived under the rude conditions of a pioneer generation. Those next on the scene sought to turn a literary trick, and in emphasizing the picturesque qualities of life in the region suggested that a journey there was like a journey into America's past— "you detach yourself from all that you have experienced, and take up the history of English speaking men and women at the point it had reached a hundred or a hundred and fifty years ago."[8] It was an easy next step to the identification of the Appalachian present with the American past as a matter of fact, not merely of metaphor. By the end of the century, the literature on Appalachia asked with all seriousness how this enclave of pioneer culture has been preserved against the ravages of time and of progress, and how most effectively to assist the mountaineers in leaping a hundred years from their present to the present of the rest of the nation. The mountaineers had become "our pioneer ancestors."[9]

It is at this point that one may speak of the emergence of a tension between Appalachia and America. Appalachia had come to represent America's past, a past of heroism and self-sacrifice, hard work and commitment, by which independence had been won and preserved, the Union defended, a continent subdued. It was a past in which giants walked the earth, with axe and Bible in hand. It was in any case America's own past, and hence not to be discredited lightly. From the late 1880's on, as a consequence, one may see a persistent ambiguity toward the peculiarities of mountain life in the literature on Appalachia. To the degree that these were conceived as the undesirable consequences of poverty and isolation, they were regarded with contempt, or with that "sympathetic understanding" which precedes remedial action. To the degree that they were conceived as survivals of an earlier pattern of culture, however, they were respected as different but acceptable, or even held up for emulation by a modern generation out of touch with its past and hence with the essential national temper. Ambiguity towards the peculiarities of Appalachian life involved more than America's response to the existence of this particular region, however. Ultimately it precipitated a confrontation with the fact of social and geographic diversity in the present.

Perhaps the most striking aspect of Appalachia's strangeness to those Americans who discovered the region at the end of the nineteenth century was the apparent absence in mountain culture of conceptions of law and order, and of "correct" notions of the relationship of the individual and society, as manifested by the apparent prevalence of feuding and the manufacture of blockade or "moonshine" whiskey. The disregard for duly constituted authority which these phenomena implied was an overt indication of the disparity between mountain life and the more normal life of the rest of America. "A shock falls across the . . . mind to realize that such a community of lawlessness should exist in a country that calls itself civilized," one commentator noted after reading John Fox, Jr.'s fictional reconstruction of "A Cumberland Vendetta."[10] More important, the occurrence of feuding and moonshining helped crystallize a growing sense, based originally on the impressionistic accounts of travellers and short-story writers, that Appalachia was indeed a discrete region, in but not of America.

Conflicts between mountaineers and revenue officers over enforcement of the excise tax on whiskey were reported in the periodical press as early as 1867. It was in the next two decades, however, as the more general interest in Appalachia developed, that real attention was paid to moonshining as one of the peculiarities of mountain life.[11] At issue was not so much the illegality of unlicensed distilleries, however, but the quaintness of this aspect of domestic economy as it persisted in the mountains. By the 1890's, moonshining had become so integral an element in the popular concept of Appalachia that discussion of the phenomenon, often coupled with a defense of such illegal activities on historical grounds, became virtually a requirement in descriptive pieces dealing with the region, while an escape from, or an attack by "revenooers" similarly became a conventional incident in mountain fiction. Suggestive of conventional literary images of banditti or outlaws caught in a historical process which they could neither understand nor control, these fictional confrontations

between moonshiners and "foreigners" representing the legal and social standards of the larger community functioned to epitomize the tension between Appalachia and America, while reinforcing the accepted notion of Appalachia's historical character.

Feuds in the Southern mountains aroused less interest outside the region during this early period, at a time when such private wars could be dismissed as natural extensions of hostilities engendered by the Civil War. By the mid-1880's, feuding incidents began to appear with some frequency in short fictional pieces set in the mountains, as well as in descriptive sketches of mountain life, and by the end of the century the prevalence of feuding had become a conventional element in the popular conception of Appalachia as a strange land inhabited by a peculiar people. Like moonshining, feuding was viewed as a picturesque if somewhat unfortunate aspect of life in that isolated region of the nation, and was explained in historical terms as the result of the persistence of primitive social conditions and a correspondingly primitive form of social control, or else as the result of a persisting tendency toward violence among Southerners.

The outbreak of a new series of family wars around the turn of the century, and the subsequent extension of what had first appeared as private conflict into the arena of public affairs, involving local and then state and interstate politics, brought feuding as an aspect of mountain life to the attention of the nation in a new way.[12] Like moonshining, this new outbreak of feuds involved the mountaineers in a direct confrontation with the world of more normal American behavior, and in particular with the outsiders' institutions of social control. While the possibility of romanticization existed, then, to the degree that the feuds involved persons outside the immediate mountain community, the requirements of the social order in maintaining its viability demanded that this particular aspect of mountain life be defined pejoratively as "lawlessness," even as it demanded that the feudists themselves be convicted as lawbreakers and sentenced to terms in the penitentiary. More important from our point of view, however, accounts of the feuds which flourished around the turn of the century, when combined with the widely accepted notion of the prevalence of illegal distilling in the mountains, precipitated a redefinition of Appalachia as a land of violence and lawlessness.[13]

In and of itself this new emphasis involved nothing more than a more sharply focused conception of the nature of Appalachian otherness. A kind of aesthetic distance continued to separate the mountaineers as objects of popular interest from the writers and social workers who went among them and described their peculiar habits to the rest of America. In the context of a conventional description of the mountaineers as "our contemporary ancestors" and of mountain violence as a survival from an earlier stage of historical development, however, the identification of Appalachia as a lawless land created a dilemma within the American dialogue on the meaning of Appalachia's existence, and raised questions concerning the nature of American civilization as well. Over against an idyllic vision of mountaineers as hard-working pioneers, dependent on their own resources and initiative, was placed what seemed to be a more realistic picture, of pioneer individualism as anarchy, and self-help as anti-social behavior. If private justice yielded public chaos, if private enterprise involved the rejection of public morality, were our pioneer ancestors like our "contemporary ancestors," merely brawlers and brigands?

By the beginning of the twentieth century, of course, there were many who were quite prepared to admit that America's pioneer past was one of violence and anarchic individualism, preferring for that very reason the more civilized present in which egoism had given way to altruism. Indeed, that may well be said to have been the point of much of the rhapsodizing over vanishing frontiers which took place around the turn of the century. It was in any case a position commonly taken by writers on Appalachia in the early years of the twentieth century, and especially by those connected with agencies of social uplift for whom the persistence of the past into the present created irony rather than ambiguity. To them the historical character of mountain life was a kind of bad joke on the mountaineers, as well as a sign of their pressing need for assistance so that they might cast off a discredited or at least a useless past, and join the rest of the nation in the present.[14]

The identification of violence and lawlessness in the Southern mountains as a survival of the American past, which consistent definition of the mountaineers as "our contemporary ancestors" demanded, did create a dilemma nonetheless. What this meant in practice was that explanation of feuding and moonshining by reference to an historical situation came to be seen as inadequate or, to the degree that it unbalanced the equation of a known present and a presumed past, unsatisfactory. In the early twentieth century, as a consequence, two new emphases appeared in discussions of mountain life, which may be seen as responses to the conceptual dilemma which conditions of lawlessness in Appalachia created. The first of these involved identification of the more violent aspects of mountain life as European rather than American in origin, thus permitting continued utilization of the doctrine of survivals while maintaining a traditional conception of the American past as rude but law-abiding. The second involved abandonment of the doctrine of survivals entirely and a new emphasis, in accord with general trends of early twentieth-century social theory, on environment as the determinant of social and cultural patterns. In these terms, Appalachia was seen to be characterized by frontier conditions but was no longer defined as The Frontier.

From the publication in 1878 of Rev. James Craighead's *Scotch and Irish Seeds in American Soil,*[15] the mountaineers of Appalachia were conventionally assumed to be the descendants of Scottish and Scotch-Irish settlers from western North Carolina and Pennsylvania. This was a view which appealed particularly to the home-mission propagandists of the Presbyterian Church, who were enabled thereby to add the responsibilities of blood relationship to the humanitarian appeal of need in requesting funds for benevolent work among the mountaineers. Non-Presbyterians found the notion equally appealing, however. In part this was because it agreed with conventional notions about the patterns of westward migration during the last eighteenth century, but in part this was also the case because it identified the independent mountaineer with that group of colonists conventionally assumed to be the most "independent" in America's eighteenth-century population. The definition of mountain life as a survival of pioneer life was thus reinforced, albeit in a slightly different way.

It was with particular reference to the occurrence of feuds in the mountains that the somewhat ambiguous designation of the mountaineers as "American Highlanders" occurred, however, in an address by Secretary Charles J. Ryder of the Congregationalist American Missionary Association. "No other term so aptly describes these mountaineers as does Highlanders," Ryder noted in 1897:

> They have Highland clans with Highland chieftains at the head of them. Highland feuds flame out now and again, often bringing death and ruin. Not only topographically but also socially the term of the American Highlanders fittingly describes these mountaineers. The relationship between the Lowlanders of the South and the Highlanders is also much the same as that which obtained [N.B.] between the same classes in Scotland. . . . In general character and in physical endurance the comparison between the Highlanders of Scotland and America holds good.[16]

During the early years of the twentieth century, an increasing consciousness of violence as a characteristic of mountain life facilitated the transformation of Ryder's metaphor into a picture of reality, and the mountaineer as Highlander took his place alongside the mountaineer as contemporary ancestor in discussions of Appalachia. B 1916, John M. Moore's classic mission-study text, *The South To-Day,* could complain that "the peculiarities of an individualistic people have been interpreted as hideous deficiencies." In fact, Moore asserted, the mountaineer was "the pure Scotch-Irishman, and in manners, beliefs, and speech his lineage can be traced. . . . I found that Scott and Stevenson in their tales of the Campbells and MacGregors were describing the parties that were appearing in the later roles of feudists in Kentucky. The heads of feuds were no ordinary men in Kentucky than in Scotland."[17] Feuding and moonshining, and a general proclivity to violent and lawless behavior, were thus explained as the result of a particular ethnic heritage rather than of an essentially lawless strain in the American national character, which the identification of violence as a survival of pioneer ways seemed to suggest. More desirable aspects of mountain life might continue to be identified with the American past, and hence be seen as quintessentially American, while the mountaineer himself was maintained in the morally neutral ground of middle-class romanticism.

The use of an environmental explanation for the peculiarities of Appalachia functioned in a similar way, as response to the dilemma which the occurrence of feuds and moonshining presented. Unlike explanation in terms of survivals, however, it did not emerge from within the American dialogue on the meaning of Appalachia as a result of the transformation of metaphor into a statement of reality. It involved instead the introduction of a kind of cultural relativism as a point of view into the literature on Appalachia, and of a new model of social change as a matter of adaptation rather than of development pure and simple. For the environmentalists, as a consequence, while "normal" American culture remained preferable, the legitimacy of a peculiar and indigenous mountain culture was neither denied nor denigrated by its identification with some earlier phase in the evolution of the normal American form. In "The Anglo-Saxons of the Kentucky Mountains: A Study in Anthropogeography," for example, Ellen Churchill Semple argued in what was to become the characteristic way that the apparent persistence of historical forms in the mountains might be better understood as a matter of adaption to a particular environment. Utilitarian ethics, an independence of spirit bred by isolation and the necessity for self-reliance, an economy "severely limited in its possibilities" by lack of transportation facilities, were the circumstances in which feuding and moonshining developed as appropriate means of obtaining justice and disposing of a corn crop, respectively. "The same conditions which have kept the ethnic type pure have kept the social phenomena primitive," she noted "with their natural concomitants of primitive ethics and primitive methods of social control."[18]

For the environmentalists, the critical fact which set Appalachia off from America was not the occurrence of feuding and moonshining, the peculiarities of speech which had received such attention from the local color writers, the persistence of traditional folk song and traditional handicrafts, or even the log cabins which dotted the hillsides, but the absence of community. This was the cause from which all else, including the prevalence of violence in the region, followed. "Lack of good roads has caused an undue isolation, has prevented co-operative activity and the realization of the ideals of a modern community life," one commentator argued. An "over-developed individualism" has resulted "where there is no cohesive community life . . . [and] where local agencies are non-existent and non-local agencies inoperative," said another.[19] Especially in the hands of Warren H. Wilson of the Presbyterian Department of Church and Country Life and John C. Campbell, Secretary of the Russell Sage Foundation's Southern Highland Division, the use of an environmentalist explanation for the peculiarities of Appalachia facilitated a redefinition of the region as "hyper-rural" and the perception of fundamental similarities among all such hyper-rural sections of the nation. "The question of the mountain dwellers is a national question," Campbell told the Home Missions Council in 1916. "You have it in your New England Hills, with less hope of solution it is sometimes felt, and although it is a larger question in the South, it is, after all, only a question of intensified rural conditions."[20]

In such terms, the conflict between Appalachia and America became not a conflict between past and present but between rural and urban ways, and the occurrence of feuds and moonshining became social problems of a kind to be expected in rural regions were community was absent. Although substantial disagreement over how the much-needed sense of community might be provided in Appalachia characterized the environmentalists' discussion of the region—Campbell and Wilson for example urged education appropriate to rural conditions in order to establish a viable mountain culture, while Walter Hines Page, like Wilson a former member of Roosevelt's Country Life Commission, favored removal of the mountaineers to the industrial centers of the New South where the development of community would be natural rather than artificial[21]—so far as feuding and moonshining were concerned there was agreement. Unfiltered through the haze of romance, private justice was seen to yield public chaos, and individualism, in the absence of the controls which community provides, to breed lawlessness. The occurrence of violence in the Southern mountains, when explained as adaptation to environment, thus became an undesirable yet ultimately a temporary and remediable phenomenon, a distortion of the more basic and desirable qualities of independence and self-reliance characteristic of rural life generally and of that special case of rural life which was Appalachia.

Resolution of the dilemma which the occurrence of feuding and moonshining in the Southern mountains posed did not eliminate violence from mountain life, of course, any more than it resolved the tension which the very existence of this strange land and peculiar people generated. Feuding and moonshining persisted as social problems, becoming in fact more acute as prohibition made the manufacture of whiskey increasingly profitable and as the so-called clan wars were complicated by the emergence of class conflict in the region during the later 1920's.[22] Violence continued as a consequence to point up the distance between Appalachia and America. Even after the era of violence had ended, however, Appalachia remained an "other" America in the American consciousness, defined now in terms of one set of characteristics, now in terms of another. And as such, Appalachia has continued to prick our consciences and to challenge the notions of what American civilization is and what is ought to be. If we continue to respond ambiguously, it is better than that we fail to respond at all.

NOTES

1. The principal documents of our recent "rediscovery" of Appalachia, and our redefinition of Appalachian otherness as a matter of economic rather than cultural differences, include Michael Harrington, *The Other America: Poverty in the United States* (New York: The Macmillan Co., 1962); Harry M. Caudill, *Night Comes to the Cumberlands: A Biography of a Depressed Area* (Boston: Little, Brown & Co., 1962); Thomas R. Ford, ed., *The Southern Appalachian Region: A Survey* (Lexington: Univ. of Kentucky Press, 1962); and Jack E. Weller, *Yesterday's People: Life in Contemporary Appalachia* (Lexington: Univ. of Kentucky Press, 1965). On the first discovery of Appalachia, see Henry D. Shapiro, "Strange Land and Peculiar People: The Discovery of Appalachia, 1870–1920" (Ph.D. dissertation, Rutgers University, 1966). On the first discovery and its consequences, see Henry D. Shapiro, *Appalachia on Our Mind: The Southern Mountains and Mountaineers in the American Consciousness, 1870–1920* (Chapel Hill: Univ. of North Carolina Press, 1977).

2. E.g., Thomas Wilson Humes, *The Loyal Mountaineers of Tennessee* (Knoxville: Ogden Bros. & Co., 1888); Joseph E. Roy, *Americans of the Midland Mountains* (New York: American Missionary Assn., 1891); "A Scotch-Irishman [pseud.]," *The Mountain Whites of the South* (Pittsburgh: [Banner Publishing Co.], 1893); Mrs. S. M. Davis, "The 'Mountain Whites' of America," *Missionary Review of the World,* 8 (June 1895), 422–26. A late example is William Goodell Frost, "God's Plan for the Southern Mountains," *Biblical Review,* 6 (July 1921), 405–25.

3. John Dwight Kern, *Constance Fenimore Woolson, Literary Pioneer* (Philadelphia: Univ. of Pennsylvania Press, 1934); Rayburn S. Moore, *Constance Fenimore Woolson* (New York: Twayne Publishers, 1963); James Lane Allen, "Local Color," *The Critic,* n.s., 5 (Jan. 9, 1886), 13–14, and "H. M. Alden," *The Bookman,* 50 (November 1919), 330–36; Grant Knight, *James Lane Allen and the Genteel Tradition* (Chapel Hill: Univ. of North Carolina Press, 1935); Edd Winfield Parks, *Charles Egbert Craddock (Mary Noailles Murfree)* (Chapel Hill: Univ. of North Carolina Press, 1941); Charles Dudley Warner, "On Horseback," *Atlantic Monthly,* 56 (July–October 1885), 88–100, 194–207, 388–98, 540–54, and C. D. Warner correspondence, Century Collection, New York Public Library Manuscript Division; David Hunter Strother, "The Mountains," *Harper's Magazine,* April 1872–September 1875, *passim;* Cecil D. Eby, Jr., *"Porte Crayon": The Life of David Hunter Strother* (Chapel Hill: Univ. of North Carolina Press, 1960).

4. Carvel E. Collins, "Nineteenth Century Fiction of the Southern Appalachians" *Bulletin of Bibliography,* 17 (October 1942 and January 1943), 186–90, 215–17; Henry D. Shapiro, "Strange Land and Peculiar People," 250 ff.

5. Horace Spencer Fiske, *Provincial Types in American Prose Fiction* (Chautauqua, N.Y.: The Chautauqua Press, 1903), 1 Cf. Elizabeth Haven Appleton, "Half-Life and Half a Life," *Atlantic Monthly,* 13 (February 1864), 157–82; Edward H. Pollard, "The

Virginia Tourist," *Lippincott's Magazine,* 5 (May 1870), 48–97; James Esten Cooke, "Owlet," *Harper's Magazine,* 57 (July 1878), 199–211.

6. E.g., William D. Kelley, *The Old South and the New: A Series of Letters* (New York: G. P. Putnam's Sons, 1887).

7. N. S. Shaler, "Peculiarities of the South," *North American Review,* 151 (October 1890), 477–88; George H. Vincent, "A Retarded Frontier," *American Journal of Sociology,* 4 (July 1898), 1–20; Charles Dudley Warner, "On Horseback" (1885).

8. James Lane Allen, "Through Cumberland Gap on Horseback," *Harper's Magazine,* 73 (June 1886), 50–66.

9. Cf. Joseph E. Roy, *Americans of the Midland Mountains;* William Goodell Frost, "Our Contemporary Ancestors in the Southern Mountains," *Atlantic Monthly,* 83 (March 1899), 311–19; Lillian Walker Williams, "In the Kentucky Mountains: Colonial Customs that Are Still Existing in that Famous Section of the Country," *New England Magazine,* n.s., 30 (March 1904), 37–45. It was to the problem posed by the apparent persistence of pioneer culture in the face of rapid economic and social change elsewhere in the nation that Ellen Churchill Semple and the environmentalists of the early twentieth century addressed themselves.

10. Unsigned, "Novel Notes," *The Bookman,* 2 (January 1896), 434. "A Cumberland Vendetta" was first published in *The Century,* 48 (June–August 1894), 163–78, 366–73, 496–505, and was subsequently issued as *A Cumberland Vendetta and Other Stories* (New York: Harper & Bros., 1895). On Fox's treatment of mountain lawlessness generally see the excellent short study *John Fox, Jr.,* by Warren I. Titus (New York: Twayne Publishers, 1969).

11. On mountain violence in literature, see Carvel E. Collins, "The Literary Tradition of the Southern Mountaineer, 1824–1900" (Ph.D. dissertation, University of Chicago, 1944); Isabella D. Harris, "The Southern Mountaineer in American Fiction, 1824–1910" (Ph.D. dissertation, Duke University, 1948). Early reports of feuds and moonshining include: A. H. Gernsey, "Illicit Distillation of Liquors," *Harper's Weekly,* 11 (Dec. 7, 1867), 773, and "Hunting for Stills," *Harper's Weekly,* 11 (Dec. 21, 1867), 811; unsigned, "The Moonshine Man: A Peep into His Haunts and Hiding Places," *Harper's Weekly* 21 (Oct. 21, 1877), 820–22; Young E. Allison, "Moonshine Men," *Southern Bivouac,* n.s., 2 (February 1887), 528–34; Francis Lynde, "The Moonshiners of Fact," *Lippincott's Magazine,* 57 (January 1896), 66–76; unsigned, "The Knell of the Kentucky Feud," *Scribner's Magazine,* 21 (May 1897), 660; J. Stoddard Johnston, "Romance and Tragedy of the Kentucky Feuds," *Cosmopolitan,* 27 (September 1899), 551–58; John Fox, Jr., "Manhunting in the Pound," *Outing,* 36 (July 1900), 344–50.

12. On the Kentucky feuds, see Hartley Davis and Clifford Smyth, "Land of Feuds," *Munsey's Magazine,* 30 (November 1903), 161–72; R. L. McClure, "Mazes of a Kentucky Feud," *The Independent,* 55 (Sept. 17, 1903), 2216–24; O. O. Howard, "The Feuds in the Cumberland Mountains," *The Independent,* 56 (April 7, 1904), 783–88; *New York Times,* 1901–1905, *passim;* Charles G. Mutzenberg, *Kentucky's Famous Feuds and Tragedies: Authentic Histories of the World Renowned Vendettas of the Dark and Bloody Ground* (New York: R. F. Fenno, 1917). While Kentucky was not all of Appalachia, it had traditionally received the most attention from local color writers, denominational home-mission personnel, and travel-writers, and provided the basis upon which generalizations about the region as a whole were made, at least until the organization of the Russell Sage Foundation's Southern Highland Division in 1908.

13. Carvel E. Collins notes this in "Nineteenth Century Fiction of the Southern Appalachians" (see note 4). The shift is apparent in, e.g., the emphases of William Goodell Frost's articles of 1899 and 1900. The first, "Our Contemporary Ancestors in the Southern Mountains," asks for a sympathetic understanding for "these eighteenth century neighbors and fellow countrymen of ours"; the second, "The Southern Mountaineer: Out Kindred of the Boone and Lincoln Type," *American Monthly Review of Reviews,* 21 (March 1900), 303–11, seeks to explain away the feuds by identifying mountaineer "individualism" as an historical trait.

14. Frost, "Our Contemporary Ancestors." Cf. his "Educational Pioneering in the Southern Mountains," National Education Association, *Addresses and Proceedings,* 14 (1901), 555–60, and "Our

Southern Highlanders," *The Independent,* 72 (April 4, 1912), 708–14; John Fox, Jr., *The Kentuckians* (New York: Harper & Bros., 1898), and "The Southern Mountaineer," *Scribner's Magazine,* 29 (April–May 1901), 387–99, 557–70.

15. James G. Craighead, *Scotch and Irish Seeds in American Soil* (Philadelphia: Presbyterian Board of Publication, 1878).

16. Charles J. Ryder, "Our American Highlanders: Problems and Progress," *Education,* 18 (October 1897), 67, 69. Ryder coined the term in an address to the American Missionary Association in 1892 (ibid., 67), published as *The Debt of Our Country to the American Highlanders During the War* (New York: American Missionary Association, [1896]).

17. John M. Moore, *The South To-Day* (New York: Missionary Education Movement of the U.S. and Canada, 1916), 127–28, 132–33.

18. Ellen Churchill Semple, "The Anglo-Saxons of the Kentucky Mountains: A Study in Anthropogeography," *Geographical Journal* (London), 17 (June 1901), 616; reprinted in *Bulletin of the American Geographical Society,* 42 (August 1910), 561–94. See also George E. Vincent, "A Retarded Frontier," *American Journal of Sociology,* 4 (July 1898), 1–20; James Mooney, "Folk-Lore of the Carolina Mountains," *Journal of American Folk-Lore,* 2 (April–June 1889), 95–104; S. S. MacClintock, "The Kentucky Mountains and their Feuds," *American Journal of Sociology,* 7 (July–September 1901), 1–28, 171–87; McClure, "Mazes of a Kentucky Feud"; Howard, "The Feuds in the Cumberland Mountains."

19. Mary Verhoeff, *The Kentucky Mountains. Transportation and Commerce, 1750–1911: A Study in the Economic History of a Coal Field,* Filson Club Publication No. 26 (Louisville: John P. Morton & Co., 1911), 183–84; John C. Campbell, "Social Betterment in the Southern Mountains," National Conference of Charities and Correction, *Proceedings,* 36 (1909), 137.

20. John C. Campbell, "Mountain and Rural Fields in the South," [*Annual Report of the*] *Home Missions Council, 1916* ([New York, 1916]), 180. On Campbell, see John M. Glenn et al., *Russell Sage Foundation, 1907–1946* (New York: Russell Sage Foundation, 1947), I, 62 ff.; Henry D. Shapiro, "Introduction," in John C. Campbell, *The Southern Highlander and His Homeland* (Lexington: Univ. Press of Kentucky, 1969), xxii–xxxi, and *Appalachia On Our Mind,* esp. ch. 7. Some discussion of Wilson's activities will be found in Betty Carol Clutts, "Country Life Aspects of the Progressive Movement" (Ph.D. dissertation, Ohio State University, 1962).

21. Walter Hines Page, ["Editorial Note"], *The World's Work,* 19 (March 1910), 12704. See also Thomas Dawley, "Our Southern Mountaineers: Removal the Remedy for the Evils that Isolation and Poverty Have Brought," *The World's Work,* 19 (March 1910), 12704–14; Walter A. Dyer, "Training New Leaders for the Industrial South," *The World's Work,* 28 (July 1914), 285–92; William L. Hall, "To Remake the Appalachians: A New Order in the Mountains that is Founded on Forestry," *The World's Work,* 28 (July 1914), 321–38.

22. Conditions in Appalachia since the 1920's are conveniently summarized in Caudill, *Night Comes to the Cumberlands.*

11. THE PASSING OF PROVINCIALISM

Thomas R. Ford

Even the most casual observer of conditions in the Southern Appalachian Region during the past three decades cannot fail to be aware of the tremendous material changes. The sprawling growth of the Region's metropolitan areas and the abandoned cabins up narrow hollow roads provide impressive evidence of major population shifts. Brush cover and second-growth timber reclaiming mountain slopes once cultivated to the very ridges, and unfamiliar silhouettes of industrial smokestacks in the Great Appalachian Valley bear equally eloquent testimony of a transforming economy. Hardsurface highways along mountain streams which themselves a scant generation ago served as roadbeds, and television antennas clustered on mountain tops are functional symbols of the intrusion of contemporary mass culture into even the most isolated areas. That the twentieth century has come to the people of the Southern Appalachians is unquestionable. But whether the people of the Southern Appalachians have come to the twentieth century is, at least in the minds of many observers, a moot question.

To some the question may seem anomalous, even absurd. Yet sociologists and anthropologists have long recognized that all parts of culture do not change at an equal rate. As a general rule, at least in our time, the technological aspects are the first to change, followed more slowly by adaptations of social organization to new techniques. Most resistant to change are the fundamental sentiments, beliefs, and values of a people, the ways they feel their world is and should be ordered. So it is not implausible to suppose that the value heritage of the Appalachian people may still be rooted in the frontier, even though the base of their economy has shifted from subsistence agriculture to industry and commerce and the people themselves have increasingly concentrated in towns and cities.

In the early planning of the Southern Appalachian studies it was decided that some attempt should be made to probe beneath the statistics that measure social and economic changes in order to gain some insight into the relationships between those changes and the values, beliefs, and attitudes of the people affected by them. Have the Appalachian people clung to their frontier-agrarian traditions, resisting the philosophical premises of industrial society? Or are they willing to accept the social consequences of a new economy whose benefits must be purchased at the price of a radical alteration of an accustomed way of life? Are there evidences of major discrepancies between new modes of behavior and old patterns of thought? If so, what do these portend in the way of future social problems? And what implications do the beliefs and values of the Appalachian people, whatever they may be, hold for those who are actively working to promote social and economic change in the Region? For as the late Howard Odum

Reprinted from Ford, Thomas R. (ed.), *The Southern Appalachian Region: A Survey.* University of Kentucky Press, 1967. Used by permission.

observed a quarter of a century ago with reference to the entire South: "to attempt . . . to reconstruct its agriculture and economy without coming to grips with its folk culture and attitudes would be quite futile."[1]

The means selected for collecting information that would help to answer these questions was a survey of Appalachian residents drawn from a representative sample of households in the Region. Obviously one cannot gain from even a great many survey interviews the depth of sympathetic understanding that a John C. Campbell was able to acquire from a quarter century of living and traveling through the Region. Neither is it possible to reduce to cold statistics the subtle complexities of warm humans. Yet, despite its limitations, the survey method offered a number of advantages for a study of the type contemplated. For one thing, it could be conducted quickly, and time was at a premium. More important, it could be designed to secure information from a cross section of the heterogeneous Appalachian population. To a considerable extent the popular but erroneous impression of a homogeneous mountain culture stems from the fact that most contemporary studies have been of relatively isolated communities, often selected because they still preserved a way of life that was rapidly disappearing from the remainder of the Region. Not only has this bias created a false impression of homogeneity, but it has also tended to obscure the tremendous cultural changes that have been taking place for many years. Even forty years ago, John C. Campbell, whose authoritative work *The Southern Highlander and His Homeland* became a classic in the field, was disturbed by "the difficulties in the way of writing of a people who, while forming a definite geographical and racial group, were by no means socially homogeneous."[2] He was particularly concerned that his readers might not realize that many of his statements "applicable to the remote rural folk who were the particular object of his study were not true of their urban and valley kinsfolk."

The survey was seen as a way to secure data for different social groups (which Campbell had seen as desirable but infeasible), although not necessarily the same groups that Campbell might have chosen. The selection of major groups was implicit in the method used to choose the sample households. The Region was divided into residential areas of three types: (1) metropolitan, which included counties containing cities of 50,000 or more and adjacent counties within the zone of metropolitan influence; (2) smaller towns and cities with populations between 2,500 and 50,000, designated for purposes of simplicity as urban places; and (3) rural areas, containing both village and open-country population. Nearly, 1,500 sample households were then selected, each type of area contributing to the sample in numbers roughly proportionate to the total population of such areas in the Region.

A primary reason for grouping the population in this manner was to see if there was any "apparent" change in values with increasing industrialization. It was not possible to measure any real change with only one survey, of course, and no comparable surveys had been made at an earlier period. It was reasoned, however, that industrialization would have its greatest impact on the metropolitan population and affect least the rural population. The difference between the beliefs and attitudes of metropolitan residents and those of rural residents would give some indication of a value shift that would be particularly significant because of the increasing concentration of the Appalachian population in metropolitan areas.

The actual interviewing of respondents from selected households took place during the summer of 1958, and 1,466 completed interview schedules were obtained. Of these, 31.5 percent were from metropolitan households, 19.1 percent from other urban households, and 49.1 percent from rural households. Some of the characteristics of these households are shown in Table 11.1. In addition, interviews were held with 379 individuals named as community leaders by respondents in the sampled localities. About these more will be said later.

Once the interviews were completed, it was possible to divide the residential groups into other subgroups, or statistical categories, for purposes of comparison. All household respondents were classified on the basis of sex, age, educational level, and socioeconomic status. To measure socioeconomic status, a composite index was devised from data on household income, occupation and education of the household head, possession of various items of household equipment, and the respondent's identification of himself as a member of the upper, middle, or working class.[3] The population was then divided according to index score into four status categories arbitrarily labeled upper, upper middle, lower middle, and lower. This made it possible to compare different socioeconomic groups within the same type of residential area as well as to compare equal-status groups in residential areas of different types. Similar comparisons could also be made of respondents classified by the other characteristics.

There was still the crucial issue of which specific culture traits should be examined. No culture is simply a collection of traits, of course, yet each has it distinctive attributes and emphases. The distinctive themes of Appalachian culture in an earlier day were not difficult to identify, inasmuch as they attracted the attention of practically all who wrote about life in the Region. The problem, then, was to select those which seemed most significant in view of the social changes taking place. Since a major focus of interest was in the persistence of frontier-agrarian values, the selection was largely

TABLE 11.1

Selected Characteristics of the Survey Households, 1958

Characteristics	Rural	Urban	Metropolitan	All Areas
Percentage of survey population	54.1	16.4	29.5	100.0
Percentage white	97.9	95.0	93.6	96.1
Average number persons per household	3.9	3.1	3.3	3.5
Median household income, 1957	$2,830	$4,478	$5,475	$3,951
Percentage incomes under:				
$ 1,000	12.9	4.8	3.1	8.3
3,000	53.2	25.4	15.8	36.2
5,000	81.6	59.6	43.4	65.4
7,000	94.2	78.5	70.2	83.6
10,000	98.0	91.9	83.6	92.3
Percentage dwellings with:				
gas or electric stove	75.3	97.5	99.8	86.4
washing machine	88.5	85.4	83.3	86.3
television set	65.6	84.6	93.9	78.2
flush toilet	48.3	100.0	93.9	72.6
deep freeze	23.9	17.5	27.5	23.8
Percentage respondents classified by socioeconomic status as:				
upper	5.0	12.5	22.1	11.8
upper middle	14.4	25.4	33.5	22.5
lower middle	30.2	23.6	21.4	26.2
lower	20.7	7.5	5.2	13.3
unknown	29.7	31.1	17.7	26.2

guided by the literature on the isolated rural highlander in the late nineteenth and early twentieth centuries.

From a considerable variety of themes, a number were chosen for analysis of which four will be discussed in this essay: (1) individualism and self-reliance; (2) traditionalism; (3) fatalism; (4) fundamentalist religion containing a powerful strain of Puritanism. In examining the web of mountain life, one finds these themes intertwined and generally, though not always, mutually supporting. Most so-called "mountain traits" are to be found in one form or another throughout the nation, particularly in rural areas. At the same time, each of them has its antithesis in contemporary industrial society. The self-reliant individualist, at least as an "ideal type," stands at the far end of the scale from the much berated "organization man." Traditionalism, not only in the sense of clinging to an earlier heritage but also in the exaltation of resistance to social change, is viewed as both anachronistic and vaguely immoral by a larger society that values progress through rational, scientific endeavor. Even more reprehensible to a culture that stresses achievement, self-betterment, and mastery over nature is a passive resignation to one's situation in life, particularly if it is a situation viewed as both undesirable and remediable. Less subject to censure by the larger society, perhaps, but contrasting

as sharply with its dominant values—and not immune from ridicule—is the rigid, pervasive religious ethos of the Region.

Although it may not be possible to state with any high degree of precision what the current position of Appalachian culture is with respect to any of these values, one may judge whether current attitudes and beliefs seem to reflect the values ascribed to the highlander by such men as Campbell, Horace Kephart, W. G. Frost,[4] and others who studied him in his isolated environment near the turn of the century. Or, moving to a different point of reference, one may compare the apparent values of Appalachian society with those of the encompassing national society as depicted in recent times by scholars such as Robin Williams, Clyde and Florence Kluckhohn, Robert Lynd, Lloyd Warner,[5] and others.

Of necessity the interpretation of the survey data as the relate to the various cultural themes reflects the judgment of the author. Because of space limitations, no attempt has been made to present all the data upon which the judgments have been made, although some of the materials are presented in graphic and tabular form to illustrate certain points. Other relevant tables are presented in the statistical supplement to the main volume. It should also be noted that a supplementary objective of the survey was to secure data, both factual and attitudinal, on specific subjects of interest to those who were making studies of special topics. Consequently, various references to the survey and analyses of question responses will be found in the chapters dealing with population, education, social welfare, local government, religion, and health. Some of the same questions are dealt with in this analysis, but with a different objective in mind. The concern of the other authors is with the topics themselves; the concern here is with tracing the warp threads of culture themes through the several topics that provided the rest of the interview schedule, or questionnaire.

Individualism and Self-Reliance

"Remote from ordered law and commerce, the Highlander learned by hard necessity to rely upon himself," John C. Campbell wrote four decades ago. "Each household in its hollow lived its own life. The man was the provider and the protector. He actually was the law, not only in the management of affairs within the home, but in relation to the home to the outside world. Circumstances forced him to depend upon his own action until he came to consider independent action not only a prerogative, but a duty."[6]

The fierce independence and proud self-reliance of the highlander, a heritage of frontier life, were viewed with mixed feelings even by so sympathetic an observer as Campbell. On the one hand they symbolized the courage and resourcefulness of the pioneer—qualities to be valued in any age. On the other hand, independence carried to its extreme became a major obstacle to the establishment of the law and order necessary for the functioning of a more complex society. And the attachment of supreme value to self-reliance was seen by Campbell as anachronistic in "a new age, one that calls for cooperative service and community spirit." Horace Kephart, writing a few years earlier than Campbell, had felt a similar conflict in his assessment of the highlander, observing that "the very quality that is his strength and charm as a man—his staunch individualism—is proving his weakness and reproach as a citizen."[7]

Individualism has many facets, and in mountain culture the aspects which received greatest emphasis were independence from social restraints or at least legal norms, and abstention from cooperative endeavors in any sustained form, with the possible exception of those that involved kin. During frontier days there were, of course, numerous cooperative ventures involving mutual aid, such as cabin raisings, corn huskings, and the like, but they were activities of special occasions, not daily routines. Complete economic independence was the mark of a successful man, and self-reliance, like many other frontier necessities, was elevated into a virtue.

Whatever their intrinsic moral virtues, independent economic operations are frequently inefficient, as many nineteenth-century craftsmen learned in their losing struggle against competing factories. In an industrial economy, purchasing power, not self-sufficiency, is the standard of success. More because of the changing standards of a nation than because of any deterioration of living conditions, the Appalachian Region came to be viewed as an economic problem area. Consequently, during the Great Depression of the 1930s, when the federal government openly assumed as a responsibility of the state the economic welfare of its citizens, the rural highlanders found themselves eminently qualified to become the recipients of public relief and welfare assistance.

If there were those who supposed that the traditional value accorded self-reliance by the highlanders would lead them to reject the welfare offerings of the national government, they were doomed to early disappointment. "Reputed to be the most individualistic of all the regions," wrote Howard Odum of the southern people, "they cooperate most fully with New Deal techniques."[8] His observation applied with equal validity to the residents of the Southern Appalachians.

There is little evidence that the acceptance of public assistance was ever seen as incompatible with the value themes of individualism and self-reliance as they were defined by the average highlander. "It is interesting to see how accepting welfare and charity has been fitted into local values of pride and independence" Marion Pearsall has observed in a recent study of an isolated mountain community in Tennessee. "It is clear that acquiring money from a welfare agency is not in itself considered degrading. Indeed, accepting welfare money seems almost as legitimate as earning it by some other method. As one woman puts it, 'It's the good Lord taking care of me because I've worked hard all my life and prayed to Him.' "[9]

The data from the survey provide incontrovertible evidence that public assistance measures and programs are endorsed by the great majority of Southern Appalachian residents (Table 11.2). Six out of seven respondents gave an affirmative reply to the question, "Do you think the present relief and welfare program is a good thing?" even though no specification of "the present program" was provided. Two out of three respondents indicated there was little stigma attached to a family's being "on relief," and most of the remaining third thought that only in some cases was a family's reputation jeopardized. Despite real differences in the proportions of rural, urban, and metropolitan residents dependent upon public assistance, and presumed differences in their evaluation of individualism and self-reliance, there was surprisingly little difference in their appraisal of existing welfare philosophy and practice. Most residents in all areas believed it to be "a good thing."

TABLE 11.2

Attitudes Toward Relief and Welfare:
Percentage Distribution of Replies to Selected Questions

Question and Response	Rural	Urban	Metropolitan	All Areas
Do you think the present relief and welfare program is a good thing?				
Yes	86.0	88.2	82.7	85.4
No	7.0	6.1	5.8	6.5
Don't know and no reply	7.0	5.7	11.5	8.0
Do you think relief payments are too high, too low, about right?				
Too high	1.8	2.5	2.8	2.3
Too low	33.7	34.3	32.5	33.4
About right	41.4	34.6	40.0	39.7
Don't know and no reply	23.1	28.6	24.7	24.6
Do you think it reflects badly on a family if they are receiving relief?				
Yes	10.2	13.9	9.7	10.8
No	64.4	63.9	68.6	65.6
In some cases	22.0	20.0	20.3	21.1
Don't know and no reply	3.4	2.2	1.4	2.5

It was quite conceivable, especially in this Region that has a long history of political support of the Republican Party, that government subsidies to community agencies might be regarded quite differently from welfare assistance to individuals and families. So far as the survey data are indicative, however, shifting the benefits from the individual to the community and its institutions only slightly reduced the support accorded federal subsidization programs (Table 11.3).

Most respondents (51 percent) agreed that in general the government was doing "enough" for the people. Significantly, however, more than twice as many thought the government was doing "too little" (21 percent) as thought it was doing "too much." Questioned about specific kinds of government support, the enthusiasm of the respondents picked up considerably. Seventy-two percent said they were in favor of *"Federal aid to help local government provide more and better services."* Sixty-nine percent expressed themselves in favor of federal aid to education. The question concerning federal aid to local government was intentionally loaded to emphasize the benefits in an effort to identify the size of the hard-core group inalterably opposed to federal grants and subsidies, while the question concerning federal aid to education was neutrally worded. The loading seemed to have little effect. Only 17 percent openly opposed aid to local government and 15 percent opposed aid to education. The remaining respondents in both cases were either unsure or unwilling to voice an opinion.

Was the overwhelming endorsement of federal subsidization of local institutions attributable to a failure to perceive such assistance as a threat to independence and self-reliance? Apparently not. At least, when asked, *"Do you think federal aid to local areas makes the people less self-reliant?"* considerably more respondents said they thought it did not (32 percent). About a fifth of the respondents said they didn't know. Apparently self-reliance is not so highly cherished as to generate a strong opposition to federal aid programs that a great many Appalachian residents believe will ultimately weaken it.

It has already been noted that the differences in attitudes of rural, urban, and metropolitan respondents toward welfare assistance were relatively small. The differences were somewhat larger with respect to other programs of Federal aid. Strongest support for these came from rural residents, weakest from residents of metropolitan areas. It is possible that rural areas would receive the greatest benefits from programs of the type proposed, and rural residents as well as those of urban and metropolitan areas are well aware of this fact. Second, the rural population contains a considerably higher proportion of poor people than either the urban or metropolitan populations, and whether poverty breeds dependency or vice versa, the two characteristics are closely related.

The relationship between socioeconomic status and attitudes toward federal assistance is clearly evident in the survey data. For example, in response to the question of whether the federal government was doing

TABLE 11.3

Attitudes Toward Federal Assistance:
Percentage Distribution of Replies to Selected Questions

Question and Response	Rural	Urban	Metropolitan	All Areas
Do you think the government is doing enough for the people or too much or too little?				
Enough	51.5	53.2	48.5	50.9
Too much	5.7	10.7	15.1	9.6
Too little	24.9	21.1	15.1	21.1
Don't know and no reply	17.9	15.0	21.2	18.4
Are you in favor of Federal aid to help local governments provide more and better public service?				
Yes	75.4	72.1	66.0	71.8
No	10.4	23.6	23.2	16.9
Don't know and no reply	14.2	4.3	10.8	11.2
We do not at present have a program of Federal aid to education. What do you think of such a program?				
Favor	74.4	69.3	61.7	69.4
Oppose	11.3	18.9	19.5	15.3
Don't know and no reply	14.2	11.8	18.8	15.2
Do you think Federal aid to local areas makes the people less self-reliant?				
Yes	44.1	50.0	56.5	49.1
No	32.6	35.3	27.9	31.6
Don't know and no reply	23.3	14.6	15.6	19.2

enough, too much, or too little for the people, 38 percent of the upper status respondents but less than 1 percent of the lower status group said "too much." Federal aid to assist local government and education was endorsed by slightly more than half of the upper status respondents but by three-fourths of the lower status respondents. Finally, the percentage of respondents who said they believed federal aid reduced local self-reliance dropped steadily and sharply from 71 percent of the upper status category to only 36 percent of the lower status group. Since schooling level was closely related to socioeconomic status, the response variation followed a roughly similar pattern. Differences between extreme groups (those with seven or fewer years of schooling and those who had gone beyond high school) were somewhat smaller, however. In fact, there was little difference between categories with less than 12 years of schooling, but generally a relatively large gap between high school graduates and those with some college training, the latter being considerably less enthusiastic about the expansion of federal programs. However, a majority of respondents in all categories

endorsed both the existing welfare programs and the proposed federal assistance to local government and education.

The variations of responses with age of respondent may offer one clue to the changes in values over time. So far as attitudes toward public assistance are concerned, the changes were small and inconsistent. The strong approval accorded relief and welfare activities by old and young alike suggests that either there has been little recent change or that older persons have changed their previous views about as rapidly as the younger generation has acquired its current set of beliefs. There were consistent variations with age in the responses concerning expanded federal assistance programs, however. The proportion of respondents who thought the government was doing "too much" for the people, for example, declined from 21 percent of those 65 years old or over to only 4 percent of the respondents under 30 years of age. Furthermore, endorsement of federal aid to local government declined from 83 percent of the youngest group to 67 percent of the oldest, while support of federal aid to education dropped from

80 percent to 56 percent. Finally, only 40 percent of the youngest group compared with 56 percent of the oldest considered federal assistance a threat to local self-reliance. The same pattern, it should be noted, was found in all three types of residential areas, although the actual percentages varied. While it is possible that other factors (such as increasing conservatism with age) may account for the impressive and consistent pattern of differences, the evidence at least does not contravene the conclusion that the value attached to individualism and self-reliance has been on a decline in the Region.

If there has been a weakening of these traits in mountain culture, as the evidence suggests there has, has it been accompanied by a strengthening of the spirit of cooperation and a growing realization of the advantages of organized group action? There is at least some evidence in the survey data that this has been the case.

One of the specific indicators of an increasing appreciation of social organization is to be found in the strength of organized labor in the Region. Half a century ago, when coal mining was a well-established industry in West Virginia but just getting underway in Kentucky, the organization of labor unions was a difficult business, not only because of the violent opposition of the mining companies but also because the highlanders themselves had little concept of and less taste for organization. As Kephart reported at the time, "they simply will not stick together."[10] This difficulty was not easily overcome, and the history of labor organization in the mines and mills of the Appalachian Region is one of blood and violence. Perhaps even more than the mines and industries themselves, labor unions were viewed as an intrusion of an alien way of life.

Considering the general economic character of the Region and the early difficulties of union organization, it came as a distinct surprise that 42 percent of the surveyed households reported that the male wage earner was currently or had previously been a union member. It does not necessarily follow, of course, that they were active members or strong supporters of the unions in which they held membership. Yet there can be no doubt that the general impression of unions in the Region is favorable. Questioned as to whether they thought workers in industry were better off because of unions, three out of every five respondents said they were; only one said they were not; and one said he didn't know. Union membership, past or current, was reported most frequently in metropolitan households (47 percent) compared with 34 percent in urban areas and 42 percent in rural areas. Metropolitan respondents also had the most favorable impression of unions so far as worker benefits were concerned. Seventy-one percent claimed that industrial workers were better off because of unions compared with 59 percent of the urban respondents and 56 percent of the rural respondents.

Responses to various other survey questions appeared to substantiate a growing recognition of the advantages of organized group action. For example, more than 90 percent of the respondents in all areas endorsed the idea that "people should get together and try to bring industry to the community or country" in which they lived. Parent-teacher organizations and 4-H clubs were given highest approval in the ratings of various school-related organizations and activities. And even in the ratings of church activities, substantial majorities approved most of those that implied some considerable degree of organization. One cannot fail to be impressed by the fact that in this region where religion has traditionally stressed personal salvation and other-worldliness, four out of five respondents in rural as well as urban and metropolitan areas endorsed "community improvement programs" as a legitimate church activity. Even if this is only a token recognition, it is symbolic of a changing attitude.

If we are to accept these responses as evidence of a developing sense of cooperation, we must also note the survey evidence (further discussed in Chapter X) that most Appalachian residents appear not in favor of programs that must be supported by local taxes. As a plausible but oversimplified explanation of the conflicting attitudes of highlanders toward cooperation and taxes, it is suggested that the average highlander does not really see in government an extension of himself and his neighbors. The government is "they," not "we." He looks to a beneficent federal government to ease his lot with little consideration that what is provided must be paid for by someone, but this realization comes sharply home when the support of local government activities is at issue. In both cases he perceives government through the eyes of the individualist—"I" or "they," one or the other, but never both. Willing to accept the benefits of tax-supported services, he is not yet ready to assume the obligation of helping to finance them. His concept of democratic government has expanded to include an expectation of economic and social assistance, if not security, but this broadening of perceived rights has not been accompanied by a commensurately developed perception of responsibilities. If this is to be regarded as a flaw in the social perspective of the Appalachian residents it is surely one that he shares with a great many of his fellow citizens in other regions.

Traditionalism and Fatalism

Turning to other aspects of the value system of the Region, there is considerable logic in examining traditionalism and fatalism together. This is not to imply that all traditionalism is attended and supported by a fatalistic philosophy for this is clearly not the case, even in the mountains. However, much of the traditional-istic thinking that is of greatest concern to those who would seek to improve mountain life is of this variety, and, as has already been noted, it is a culture trait that seems strangely out of place in a national society that so highly prizes progress, achievement, and success.

It seems unlikely that fatalism and traditionalism were as closely linked in frontier days as they later came to be. The frontier settler, after all, was seeking to better his lot, and his approach to this end was one that required both high motivation and strenuous activity. Fatalism developed in response to the same circumstances that were largely responsible for the other-worldly emphasis of mountain religion. Both fatalism and other-worldliness share the premise that life is governed by external forces over which humans have little or no control, an outlook which seems peculiar only where advanced technology has given men confidence in their own ability to master nature.

If the early mountain settlers possessed such a confidence, they could not have long retained it in the face of the harsh realities of mountain life. Neither the frontiersmen nor their descendants possessed the resources necessary to gain control over an environment that at times must have seemed merciless. Under the circumstances, their development of a philosophy of fatalism appears eminently reasonable, for after generations of relatively fruitless efforts, what hope could be placed in continued strivings? To some extent one must suppose that many of those who still believed their work should be attended by rewards tempered their hopes with reason and moved on to seek more benevolent circumstances. Of those who remained, many turned to God in the faith that He would provide recompense in a future life for their earthly misery. And others, lacking both hope and faith, simply resigned themselves to fate. "Sometimes it seems that the greatest obstacle of all is lack of desire," wrote Edwin White in his *Highland Heritage*. "People in general simply do not rebel against what ought not to be, do not demand more of life; among far too large a share of the population there is no thought that things can be different. A spirit of passive resignation pervades much of the section."[11]

Not all resistance to change was in the form of passive resignation. Some highlanders, having learned to cope with their situation or at least to subsist with a minimum of effort, actively opposed all measures aimed at altering their way of life by those who sought to improve their social and economic conditions. In many instances they saw in such measures a threat to their inheritance of the Kingdom of Heaven, for which poverty was a necessary if not sufficient condition. In other cases their antagonism reflected nothing more than fear, skepticism, and distrust of strangers and unfamiliar ways.

However strong and prevalent the values of traditionalism and fatalism were a generation ago, and we have no way of measuring them, there is considerable evidence that they have weakened considerably in recent decades. The migration of hundreds of thousands of Appalachian natives to other regions is in itself indicative that at least for them the motivation to improve their lot in life outweighed whatever reasons that they may have had for remaining. At the same time, it is not an illogical proposition that migration drains off those who are energetic and highly motivated to succeed, leaving behind only those who still value tradition above change or who are too apathetic to take action even in their own behalf.

The survey data indicate that this proposition, as plausible as it may seem, is not sound. It is not possible here to review all the evidence in detail, but responses from a few questions from various sections of the questionnaire will serve for illustrative purposes.

One technique that is frequently employed to elicit the values and attitudes of adults is to see what aspirations they hold for their children. In the survey a number of questions were asked concerning children, either actual or hypothetical, and the responses were in most cases quite revealing. A typical question was *"What type of work would you like to see a son of yours go into?"* One value apparently tapped by this particular question was individualism, for a fairly high proportion—almost a third—of the respondents said this matter should be left to the son and refused to give a specific reply. Of those who did reply, though, about eight out of ten named a white collar job, and seven out of ten specified a profession. Respondents of comparable status seemed to have about the same distribution of choices, white collar or blue collar, regardless of where they lived. The higher their status and the more schooling they had received, the more often respondents said they would like for a son to go into some white collar occupation, but only lower status men more often specified a blue collar job (Fig. 11.1).

Women generally held higher aspirations for their children than did men, possibly because the accomplishments of children are more often considered to reflect credit or discredit upon the mother than upon the father. It is probably of some significance that both younger groups of respondents (under 30 years and 30–44 years) named white collar over blue collar jobs by a ratio of six to one compared with a ratio of less than three to one for the two older groups. The aspirations of the latter may have been tempered to some degree, however, by the actual jobs which their grown children held, a mitigating condition which had not yet affected the ambitions of younger parents and prospective parents. Even so, the relatively high aspirations expressed by the younger groups in all areas indicate that they

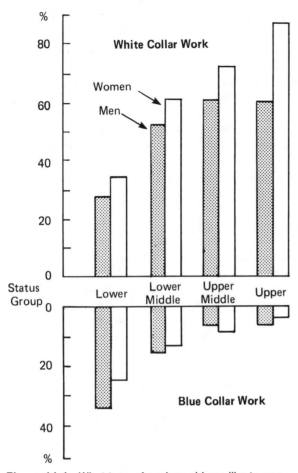

Figure 11.1. What type of work would you like to see a son of yours go into? Percentage of respondents naming white collar and blue collar occupations, by sex and socioeconomic status.

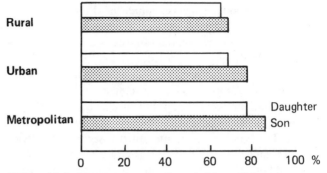

Figure 11.2. How much schooling would you like a son of yours to get? A daughter? Percentage of respondents, by residence, indicating four or more years of college.

responses indicate that Appalachian residents view higher education in much the same way as do people in other parts of the nation, and are cognizant of its value in an industrial society. And the fact that they believe their children *should* receive a good education, whether or not they actually believe they will, is indication not only of the willingness to accept industrial society but also of the hope that an oncoming generation will be able to participate in it effectively.

Larger proportions of metropolitan respondents expressed desires for their children to have a college education (Fig. 11.2). Even so, about two-thirds of the rural residents stated such a desire, and the actual differences between comparable socioeconomic groups in the three residential areas were quite small. With rising socioeconomic status and educational level, increasing proportions of respondents specified a college education as the desired amount of schooling for a child. Less to be expected, perhaps, is that more than half of even the lowest status and least schooled respondents expressed the same aspiration.

Even those who would argue that such expressions are merely fantasies must concede the existence of strong social and cultural forces to make this particular fantasy so prevalent.

As in the case of occupational aspirations for children, there were appreciable differences in the educational aspirations expressed by older and younger respondents. Conceivably the older respondents had adjusted their goals downward to correspond more closely with reality, although they were dealing with hypothetical cases and the number who said they would like for a son or daughter to get a college education was manifestly greater than the number who had actually seen such an aspiration realized. But the higher proportion of younger respondents who expressed the desire that their children go to college supports the proposition that a change in values has taken place, particularly in the rural and urban areas where the differences between age groups was the largest.

are neither tradition-bound nor lacking in hopes for a better future, at least so far as their children are concerned.

The achievement aspirations of Appalachian residents were also evident in their responses to questions about how much education they would want a son or daughter to get. Three out of four said they would like for a son to complete college and two out of three expressed a similar hope for a daughter. Less than 1 percent indicated that they would be satisfied for a son or daughter to have less than a high school education. More than 90 percent said they would want a son or daughter to take advantage of an opportunity to go to college in preference to remaining at home to help the family, and almost all of those said they would be willing to borrow money to help pay part of the college expenses. Such aspirations are obviously unrealistic in this Region where in 1950 only one adult in twenty-five had completed four or more years of college, but it would be a mistake to dismiss them as representing nothing more than the pathetic attempts of the respondents to win the approval of their interviewers. More likely, the

A somewhat more complex pattern of responses was obtained from a third question concerning children: *"If a child of yours was considering where to live, would you want him to stay here or go elsewhere?"* A great many considerations other than economic ones are involved in the reply to such a question, and it is not possible to determine what influence various ones may have had in shaping the pattern of replies. On purely "rational grounds" (in the economic sense) one would expect the percentage of "go elsewhere" replies to decrease with improved economic conditions. Specifically, relatively more rural residents would be expected to answer "go elsewhere" and relatively more metropolitan residents to answer "stay here." This expectation was borne out in that in both rural and urban areas the respondents who said they would wish their children to leave slightly outnumbered those who said they would want the child to remain in the area. In contrast, metropolitan residents favored their children's remaining by a ratio of more than two to one.

More than three-fourths of those who said they would want their children to move elsewhere gave lack of economic opportunity in their home locality as the reason. In both rural and urban areas, the proportion of respondents who said they would want their children to stay at home declined with rising socioeconomic status. This would seem to suggest that lower status respondents may not be as strongly interested in the achievement of their children as their replies to the questions concerning occupational and educational aspirations would indicate. However, of those who gave a definite reply, about as many lower and lower middle status respondents said they would want their children to go as to remain. Family affection was most frequently cited as the reason for desiring them to stay in the community.

In metropolitan areas the division of "stay" and "go" responses for the two lower status groups was about the same as in rural and urban areas, but this was not true of the two upper status groups. On the contrary, upper and upper middle status residents in metropolitan areas favored their children's remaining in the community by a ratio of five to one, while in rural and urban communities they clearly favored their leaving, although by a ratio of less than two to one.

But if most of the population has adopted the American norm of striving for success, there is still a significant lack of accord concerning the best means to this end. One of the more revealing questions asked in this connection was *"What would you say is the most important factor in a man's being successful in his work: natural ability, good education or training, hard work, good luck, knowing the right people, or liking his work?"* Of the six factors listed, *liking his work* and *good education or training* were most frequently

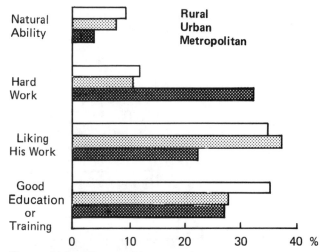

Figure 11.3. What would you say is the most important factor in a man's being successful in his work? Percentage of respondents, by residence, naming specified factors.

named, each by 31 percent of the respondents. Eighteen percent said *hard work* and 7 percent *natural ability*. Less than 1 percent chose either *good luck* or *knowing the right people*. The remainder named factors not listed or said they didn't know.

Several features of the distribution of replies seem significant. Relatively more rural than urban or metropolitan residents named *natural ability* (Fig. 11.3). Metropolitan residents saw *hard work* (which is presumably subject to individual control) as the key to success far more often than did either rural or urban residents. Rural residents more frequently attributed success to good education, which, through little fault of their own, most of them lack. In their own minds, then, they are absolved of personal responsibility for their relative poverty. Urban residents, like rural residents, place little stock in hard work and, perhaps because they are relatively well-schooled, rate liking one's work as more important than good education or training. It is difficult to say whether liking work is subject to personal control or not, and one wonders how many urban respondents who gave this reply really like their own work.

One interpretation of this pattern of responses is that the less successful tend to attribute success to factors beyond their control (but not necessarily beyond all human control) while the more successful see achievement as a product of individual effort. This interpretation is supported by the fact that upper socioeconomic status respondents named *hard work* more often than any other factor while other respondents rated *hard work* well below both *liking work* and *good education and training*, which were chosen with about equal frequency. It is equally noteworthy that respondents with less than nine years of schooling most often attributed

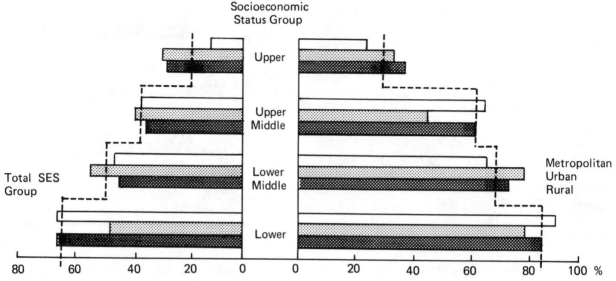

Statement: Nowadays a person has to live pretty much for today and let tomorrow take care of itself.

Statement: No matter how much or how little you take care of yourself, you are going to die when your allotted time is up.

Figure 11.4. Indicators of fatalism in the Southern Appalachian population: percentage of respondents, by residence and socioeconomic status, endorsing specified statements.

success to *good education* while respondents with the most schooling gave less success credit to *education* and more to *hard work* than did any other category. One must take into account, however, that success is largely judged with reference to one's associates, and when all of them are relatively well educated, other factors may seem more important in explaining differential success.

The proportion of respondents attributing primary importance to hard work declined steadily from 23 percent of the oldest group to only 12 percent of the youngest. A reverse pattern of association was found in the selection of *liking one's work* as the most important factor. The younger the respondent group, the more often they selected it as the most important factor. Good education was considered most important by relatively more middle-aged respondents than by either older or younger ones. One could conjecture on the basis of this evidence that the value attached to honest industry has declined in recent times while the pursuit of happiness in work has become an increasingly important goal. But even among the oldest respondents, less than one in four rated hard work most important. And whatever its intrinsic worth, it must be conceded that a tremendous amount of hard work has been expended in the mountain region with very little material return or spiritual gratification.

Passive acceptance of the status quo no longer seems to be a dominant motif of Appalachian culture, if it ever was, but it probably still serves as the major adjustment mechanism for many of those less able to cope with their life circumstances. For that matter, a trace of fatalism is possessed by most of the population, to

judge from responses to two statements included in a list of seven to which respondents were asked to express agreement or disagreement. The two statements designed to test the prevalence of a fatalistic outlook were:

(1) *Nowadays a person has to live pretty much for today and let tomorrow take care of itself.*
(2) *No matter how much or how little you take care of yourself, you are going to die when your allotted time is up.*

Almost half (45 percent) of the respondents agreed with the first statement, with considerably more agreement in rural areas (51 percent) than in urban (45 percent) or metropolitan (37 percent). Seventy percent agreed with the second statement, again with rural residents agreeing most often (78 percent) and metropolitan residents least (61.5 percent). In both instances, responses were closely related to socioeconomic status (Fig. 11.4) and differences between urban, rural, and metropolitan residents of comparable status were relatively small. Thus it would appear that fatalism is not so much a direct product of rural life as it is of poverty, although in the highlands the two are highly congruent.

The apparent persistence of this fatalistic outlook, at least among the more impoverished elements, does not necessarily mean that those who profess it are committed to the course of inaction which it logically implies. Indeed, there is much evidence of illogic in their position, for while 70 percent of the respondents agreed that time of death is foreordained, more than 80 percent later claimed to have a family doctor, whose services presumably would be summoned in case of dire

90

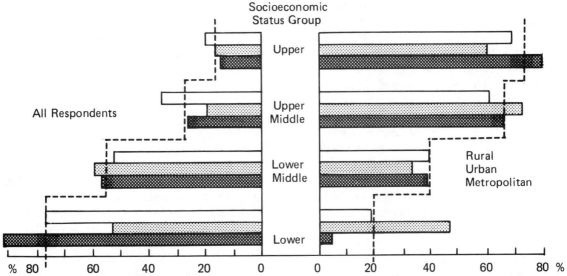

Figure 11.5. Do you think God is more pleased when people try to get ahead or when they are satisfied with what they have? Replies by residence and socioeconomic status of respondent.

illness. And while one might logically suppose that endorsement of a view that tomorrow must take care of itself reflects a desparate and despondent outlook, such apparently was not the case, for three out of four respondents cheerfully agreed that *children today have a wonderful future to look forward to.* Perhaps most amazing of all, the proportion of optimists was practically the same in all categories of respondents—rural and urban, rich and poor, young and old. It is strange that with all the literature devoted to the character of the mountain people, little if any attention has been paid to this spirit of almost Pollyannaish optimism.

There is other survey evidence that many Appalachian residents hold logically conflicting values as to whether they should accept or try to improve their lot in life. Certainly much of what has been reported concerning vocational and educational aspirations would indicate growing acceptance of a philosophy of success-striving that is more in harmony with national norms. Yet over the years the counter philosophy of resigned acceptance has been incorporated into the religious ethic and stamped with divine approval. "Their otherworldliness has been a gigantic obstacle to progress and has prevented wholly or in part the development of a rational control over social conditions," observed John F. Day of Kentucky mountaineers only twenty years ago. "Before each forward step can be taken—in health practices, in living conditions, in education—'The will of God' must be overcome."[12] It is therefore not entirely surprising that even at the present time when many "forward steps" are being taken, apparently with the approval of the great majority of the Appalachian population, many mountain residents still

cling to the perception of God's Will that made bearable the hardships of an earlier day.

The persistence of this outlook is clearly apparent in the responses to the survey question. *Do you think that God is more pleased when people try to get ahead or when they are satisfied with what they have?* The distribution of responses by residence and socioeconomic status are shown in Figure 11.5. Although 57.5 percent of the rural respondents replied "when people are satisfied," compared with 39 percent of the urban respondents and 38 percent of those in metropolitan areas, most of this difference is explained by the rural concentration of lower and lower middle status respondents. The striking shift in responses with changing socioeconomic status lends strong support to the common notion that religiously sanctioned passiveness is the philosophic refuge of the poor. If such passiveness has seemed to be particularly widespread in the Appalachian Region, it has probably been no more prevalent than poverty itself.

The change in interpretation of "God's Will" with varying educational status followed a pattern closely similar to that found for socioeconomic status. This relationship may be of even greater moment to those seeking ways to motivate the apparently apathetic. But the relationship between schooling and belief in striving for improvement is not a simple one in which the former is "cause" and the latter "effect." Even if it were, at least a generation of concentrated effort would be required before the educational level of the younger Appalachian population could be raised to that of the nation.

The survey data that have been presented, sketchy as they may be, are sufficient to illustrate the value confusion and conflict that has developed in the culture of the Region. Almost all of the people in the Region seem willing and indeed eager to accept the economic benefits and material comforts of urban industrial society, but they are not yet willing to abandon completely the philosophy of fatalism which has allowed them to bear hardship and destitution. There is general recognition that formal education is necessary for achievement in the new society, but many see schooling as a substitute for hard work, and for those who define work in terms of physical effort, the dissociation is understandable. It is quite possible that the value ascribed to professional jobs is traceable to the fact they do not appear to require "work." In any case it may be concluded that however traditionalistic they may be in other respects, the impoverished folk of the mountains are not so enamored of their way of life that they wish their children to follow in it. They wish them to acquire more education and to get better jobs, even if it means leaving the mountains, which in most cases it will.

But although all may hope for a better life for themselves and their children, only the economically secure seem to feel that it is within their power to direct the course of events that will lead to the realization of their hopes. Those of average and below average means still see themselves governed by forces over which they have little or no control, and their perception may not be entirely unrealistic. Even so, their apparent resignation to circumstance is not precisely the fatalism of an earlier era. Then destiny was seen as controlled almost exclusively by God; now a larger measure of control is ascribed to men, but more to other men than to themselves. Thus the illiterate miner or subsistence farmer can believe that his children will have a better life if they receive a good education without blaming either himself or God because the schools are poor. He may still ask of God some heavenly recompense for his earthly suffering, but he is less likely to believe that his suffering is divinely ordained and more likely to hope that the state or federal government will do something to alleviate it. Although he views his own role in relation to society as largely passive, he is more than vaguely aware that it is not exclusively so. As a consequence his fatalism is less now than formerly a deterrent to action but rather serves as psychological insurance against failure that he half anticipates and half fears will shatter hopes and ambitions raised too high.

Religious Fundamentalism

Religious values so thoroughly permeate the culture of the Southern Appalachian Region that it is virtually impossible to treat meaningfully any aspect of life without taking them into consideration. Because they underlie so many attitudes and beliefs, they exert complex and frequently subtle influences on secular behavior which are not always apparent to outside observers or even to the people of the Region themselves. Since religious thought and behavior are treated in a separate chapter, the main concern here will be with some of the major influences of religion upon social and economic change in the Region and, to a lesser extent, the effects of change upon religious beliefs.

The basic religious tone of the Region was established during the nineteenth century, which was marked by a series of religious revivals that began with the Great Revival of 1800–1802, and continued almost uninterrupted throughout most of the century. Although the Presbyterian church was the most important religious body on the frontier in the late eighteenth century, it failed to retain its strength or popularity as the line of frontier moved westward into the mountains. Apparently more suited to frontier life were the philosophy and practices of the Baptists and Methodists. These bodies, capitalizing on the spirit of revivalism, gained tremendously in membership, although both groups lost members in turn to numerous smaller sects that sprang up incessantly. The appeal of the Baptist church, or more properly churches, lay in a simple gospel, a democratic congregational organization, and a policy of electing and utilizing lay ministers. These features, ideally suited to frontier conditions, were nearly always retained by the numerous other sects that later arose in the Region. The Methodists were less democratic than the Baptists, as evidenced by their episcopal polity, which significantly was discarded by many sects that splintered off from the Methodist church. However, the Methodists too met frontier needs through their use of circuit riders and their stress on free grace, which was much more in keeping with the democratic spirit of the frontier than was the Calvinist Presbyterians' doctrine of the elect. Most important, the Methodist church was still close enough to its sectarian origins to offer a philosophy that held a strong appeal for the simple and hard-pressed folk of the frontier. Indeed, the main determinant of whether any religious group flourished or waned on the frontier was the extent to which it could provide a plausible and emotionally satisfying explanation of the hardships and sufferings that were the common lot.

As the line of frontier moved westward, some of the religious groups in the more accessible and prosperous areas of the region began to move along the well-traveled route toward becoming formally-organized churches. As they did, they abandoned some of their sectarian traits and with them some of the members for whom such traits held particularly strong appeal. These latter members either joined existing sectarian groups or, not uncommonly, organized a new sect. But since the greater part of the Appalachian region was neither accessible nor prosperous, the sectarian character of most religious groups remained strong throughout the nineteenth century.

Contemporary religion in the Highlands still bears the fundamentalist stamp of its sectarian origins, although only a minority of Appalachian residents could be considered true sectarians. There is no sharp dividing line between sectarian and nonsectarian fundamentalists, but if sectarianism is "a matter of spirit rather than form, organization, or size," as E. T. Clark has suggested,[13] the difference is probably one of disposition. Present day sectarianism, like that of the frontier, offers as its major appeal a psychological escape from the harsh realities of daily living. Consequently it tends to attract those for whom secular life holds few comforts, drawing its adherents predominantly from the lower economic strata. Their orientation is other-worldly, since they seek and are promised divine compensation, contingent upon salvation, for their earthly sufferings. For them as for their frontier forebears, conversion remains the "climax of human experience," while strivings for secular achievement are viewed as vain and fruitless endeavors.[14]

The survey data already presented regarding the aspirations held by Appalachian residents for their children is in itself evidence that earthly achievements are not disparaged by most of the contemporary population. It has also been noted that about as many Appalachian residents believe that striving to get ahead is divinely sanctioned as believe that passive acceptance of one's lot in life is God's will. The survey data contain other evidence of a considerable drift from sectarian practice as well as spirit, such as a surprisingly strong sentiment for a professional ministry.

The increasing rationality of Appalachian religion implied in the predilection for professional ministers is also manifest in responses to the question: *Which is more important in leading a religious life, conversion or religious training?* Only in rural areas did more respondents attribute greater importance to conversion than to training. Conversion is still accorded primary importance by large proportions of the population, ranging from 47 percent in rural areas to 39 percent in urban areas, but considering that it was once viewed as the culmination of religious experience, its decline in significance is striking evidence of the movement away from sectarianism.

If the main body of Appalachian religious philosophy and practice has discarded many of its sectarian attributes, it still adheres strongly to a variety of fundamentalist principles, as Brewer has documented in his chapter on religion and the churches in the Region. Most Appalachian residents still profess belief that the Bible contains the literal and infallible word of God, and the strain of Puritan morality still runs strong. Three out of four survey respondents, for example,

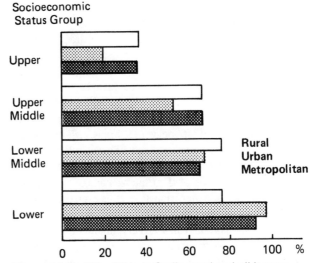

Figure 11.6. "The Bible is God's word and all it says is true." Percentage of respondents, by residence and socioeconomic status, endorsing statement.

stated the belief that drinking is always wrong, 85 percent that gambling is always wrong, and about half were of the opinion that keeping a store open on Sunday is invariably wicked. But even here there has been some adjustment to the norms of secular society, for card playing and dancing—once considered gross iniquities—were characterized as always wrong by less than a third of the respondents, although most Appalachian residents still consider them at least sometimes wrong.

As to be expected, fundamentalism as represented by Biblicism and Puritanism is much stronger in rural areas than in urban and metropolitan areas, where economic conditions are better and where there is greater exposure to the secular values of national society. The profession of fundamentalist beliefs also declined steadily with rising socioeconomic status and educational level, but the only categories in which Biblicists constituted a minority were those of upper socioeconomic status and college-educated respondents (Fig. 11.6).

There seems little doubt that urbanization, increasing contacts with the larger society, and improvements in education have all tended to weaken fundamentalist values in Appalachian society. Nevertheless, they remain impressively strong and it is difficult to evaluate fully their reciprocal influence on social and economic change within the Region. What would seem to be the case is that a working compromise has been effected between religious and secular values of such a nature that social changes once passively (and often actively) resisted are now passively accepted but not actively promoted. One indication of this changed outlook is found in the responses to two survey questions concerning religion and science. The raging conflicts that developed over Biblical accounts of creation and scientific teachings of evolutionary theory are still fresh in the minds of many older Appalachian residents, for it was in a Southern Appalachian county (Rhea) in Tennessee that the dramatic Scopes trial took place in 1924. Although the much publicized "Monkey Trial" was largely a contrived farce, it symbolized the lengths to which the ardent fundamentalists of the day were willing to go in order to denounce any doctrine which appeared to conflict with the revealed word of God. There is little doubt that the attitudinal climate throughout the Southern Appalachian Region at the time was one of ardent fundamentalism. A generation later the prevailing sentiment is still supportive of fundamentalism, but the militant espousal of it has largely subsided.

Responses to questions concerning disagreements between scientific and religious teachings indicate that most Appalachian residents seem to have found, or at least are searching for, some means of conciliating two essentially different systems of value and knowledge. Approximately a third of the respondents claimed that no disagreements exist between science and the teachings of their church. (The proportion is not greatly different from the proportion who had rejected the fundamentalist interpretation of the Bible.) About a fourth of the respondents claimed to be uncertain as to whether there were disagreements, and while this response may be accepted at face value for some, it probably indicated for most the avoidance of an uncomfortable confrontation of issues. A very small proportion of respondents recognized inconsistencies but were unwilling to take a stand as to which position they felt was correct. Militant, antiscientific fundamentalism appears to be supported by only about a third of the population, and even this figure may indicate a stronger opposition to science than exists in reality. One reason for questioning its strength is that 96 percent of the respondents, when asked to rate the importance of various subjects taught in the public schools, rated science as either important or very important. In fact, science received more "very important" ratings than any other academic subject on the list. Even so, there is little evidence that scientific rationalism as a philosophy has many supporters in the Region, for of those who expressed the belief that scientific knowledge and the teachings of their church were in conflict, only about one in eighteen asserted the preeminence of science.

The same spirit of passive acceptance, rather than either rejection or promotion, typified the attitude which most Appalachian residents hold toward church participation in social action programs. There is still some of the older sentiment that religion should be concerned solely with the preaching of the Gospel and the salvation of souls, but it is largely confined to sectarian groups. A more common attitude at the present seems to be that the church should exercise its secular influence indirectly through the "good Christian works" of its members. Still, as has already been noted, eight out of ten survey respondents endorsed participation in community improvement programs as a legitimate activity of the church. Although this activity is not considered as vital as missionary work, revival meetings, Sunday schools, and prayer meetings, to judge by the relative number of endorsers, it was accorded about as much popular approval as fellowship suppers and church picnics, and appreciably more than bazaars, square dances, and activities directed toward raising money to pay the preacher. While it cannot be said that such endorsement is indicative of a demand for such programs or even that they would be strongly supported by most congregations, it does seem to be a tacit concession that churches may, and perhaps should, engage in secular as well as sacred activities.

The same general attitude was apparent in ratings given selected functions of ministers. There is apparently no strong opposition to ministers' engaging in community activities, but there is general belief that his pastoral and preaching functions are more important. And while there seems to be no great enthusiasm for a social gospel, most survey respondents (59 percent) said they thought ministers ought to take a public stand on public issues facing their communities.

There is no gainsaying that fundamentalism remains the main theme of religious thought in the Region, and that it shows few signs of imminent weakening. But to concentrate solely upon fundamentalist traits of Biblicism and Puritan morality as the chief characteristics of conservative Protestantism is to neglect those areas of religious belief and practice where significant changes have taken place, in particular sectarian fatalistic philosophy and exclusive concern for spiritual salvation.

In the Southern Appalachians, past and present—as indeed, in all places at all times—sectarianism has been the companion of privation and emotional insecurity. Its persistence and prevalence are ample evidence of its effectiveness as a mode of adjustment to hardship and suffering, and its decline indicates not so much a reduced efficiency as an abatement of the conditions under which it thrives. It seems almost certain that sectarianism has declined in the Region over the past decades, although it is not possible to say to what degree. In any case, only a minority of the Appalachian population—probably between a fourth and a third, although closer to a half in rural areas—seems to possess a strong sectarian spirit, even though at least two-thirds could be classified as fundamentalists.

What seems to be taking place in the main body of religious thought is a search for a consonance of values, the devising of a new philosophy that will retain the emphasis upon divine ordination of earthly affairs yet accord greater recognition to human control over life circumstances; that will continue to attach paramount importance to spiritual salvation but legitimize secular achievements. In essence the search is for the integration of traditional religious beliefs and values and at least some of the secular norms and goals of contemporary American society. Science is now rarely vilified as subversive of religion except by sectarian minorities. And though not many Appalachian residents would claim that the issues at controversy a generation ago have been resolved, even fewer are desirous of bringing them into conflict again. Most, apparently, would at the present rather consider the claims of science and religion in separate context, thus avoiding the recognition of incompatibilities in their values and beliefs drawn from the two sources. Not many Appalachian residents today view their hopes for eternal salvation and their quests for social and economic improvements as incompatible goals. In fact, to a considerable extent, particularly by those who have achieved or inherited positions of relative comfort and security, they are seen as not only harmonious but complementary.

The translation of God's will for man's earthly well-being into action is not generally perceived as a major function of the church but rather as a duty of Christian individuals. The idea that the church as an organization should undertake programs of social action is accepted, but the social reform activities are not accorded high priority.

It would seem a reasonable conclusion that the religious ethos of the Appalachians no longer poses the barrier to social and economic change that it once did, although it still operates as a restraining force among the depressed classes who continue to use religion as an escape from unpleasant reality. But although religion may no longer serve as a major deterrent to social change in the Region, it can scarcely be considered a strong influence in the promotion of social and economic development. There seems little likelihood for the immediate future that religious values will serve as the main stimulus to usher in a new age or that the churches themselves will play a major role in initiating social reform programs.

Attitudes of Community Leaders

It was earlier mentioned that a number of community leaders were interviewed in addition to the respondents from sample households. There were two major purposes in interviewing these leaders. First, if it may be assumed that leaders actually do lead, in the sense of setting the tone of future thought and action, their beliefs and values would provide an indication of the nature and direction of social and cultural change in the Region. Second, even in the event that the views of today's leaders are not those of tomorrow's masses, it is generally true that such leaders exercise greater influence than the average person in the formulation of institutional plans and in the making of community decisions.

Although the 379 leaders interviewed were selected in each locality from a list of persons named as local community leaders by respondents from sample households, it would be misleading to suggest that they were a statistically representative cross section of local leadership in the Region. Usually the person who was interviewed as a leader was someone who had been named by several respondents in the same community, but in cases where there was no consensus, one of the named persons was arbitrarily selected or, if there was a minister among them, he was interviewed. The latter method of choice was for the benefit of the survey sponsors, who were particularly interested in the beliefs and attitudes of minister-leaders.

The types of persons who are named as leaders in itself provides some insight into the values of a society. Four out of five persons in the Southern Appalachian group were men, and slightly more than half were between 45 and 65 years old. Only 3 percent were under 30 years of age compared with 16 percent aged 65 and over. The fact that only a third of the named leaders were under 45 years of age may be partly explained by the heavy migration of young people from the Region, but it is also indicative of a traditional society in which leadership is acquired with age and, presumably, wisdom. It is particularly significant that the persons named as leaders were considerably above average in education, income, and socioeconomic status. Over half of the metropolitan leaders and a third of the rural leaders had attended college. Less than a third had failed to complete high school, in contrast to 60 percent of the sample survey respondents. Total household income in 1957 reported by leaders averaged nearly $5,700, about 44 percent higher than that reported for sample households. Roughly three-fourths of the leaders were employed in professional occupations or as managers, officials, or proprietors in business or government. To some extent the professional group was inflated by the disproportionate selection of ministers, who constituted about a fourth of the named leaders. It should be remembered, however, that in Southern Appalachian society the influence of ministers is frequently community-wide, and that all of the ministers included had been named as leaders by one or more survey respondents. Since the socioeconomic status index used was based primarily on income, education, and occupation, it is not surprising but nonetheless significant that over half the leaders (51.3 percent) were classified in the upper status category, 30 percent upper middle, 15 percent lower middle, and less than 4 percent lower status. (For the sample population the distribution was 16 percent upper, 30.5 percent upper middle, 35.5 percent lower middle, and 18 percent lower.) In short, the people who were recognized as leaders by the general respondent population were on the average wealthier, better educated, and situated in positions of prestige and influence. Although named by the people, they clearly were not *of* the people in the sense of being typical representatives of the Southern Appalachian population.

To some considerable degree it is possible to infer the attitudes of the leaders from their personal and social characteristics. That is, they would be expected to think much like other residents of comparable education and status. These characteristics in themselves do not make for leadership, however, so some significance must be attached to the ways in which their views differed from those of their status peers. Of particular importance are the ways of thinking which are directly relevant to present and future change in the Region, and again we may focus upon the themes of individualism and self-reliance, traditionalism, fatalism, and religious fundamentalism.

Only leaders of the charismatic type are likely to be true individualists. The average organizational or community leader is both committed to and dependent upon group endeavor. Four out of five leaders expressed themselves, like other residents, as being in favor of current welfare and assistance programs. Only 10 percent expressed the belief that there was any stigma attached to receiving relief, a proportion that was about the same as for the general population and slightly lower than for the upper status group. Despite their relatively liberal attitudes toward public welfare, the attitudes of the leaders toward government subsidies for other purposes were relatively conservative. A fourth of the leaders, compared with less than 10 percent of the sample respondents, held that the government was doing too much for the people, and only 12 percent thought it was doing too little. On the specific issues of federal aid to local government and to education, leaders were more conservative than the average respondent but still most of them favored such subsidies. Five out of eight expressed themselves in favor of aid to local government, two out of three in favor of federal aid to education. Finally, five out of nine leaders compared with less than half of the general respondents but 71 percent of the upper status category said they thought such subsidies reduced local self-reliance.

It has been suggested that leaders by the very nature of the position they occupy in society are in favor of organized activities, and this seems clearly indicated by their attitudes toward organized labor. Although only about a fourth of the leaders reported any current or past union affiliation, nearly three out of four professed the belief that workers in industry were better off because of unions. This was greater support than was accorded either by the general population or by any

socioeconomic status category—even the lower middle status group, in which half the men had held union membership. Practically all other organizational activities, ranging from 4-H clubs to community efforts to attract industry, were overwhelmingly endorsed by the leaders. They were nearly unanimous (97 percent) in their belief that local organized effort should be directed toward attracting industries to their communities. This would seem to indicate not only that Southern Appalachian leaders are staunch believers in "community action" (and perhaps purveyors of "booster spirit") but that as a group they are committed to a policy of economic expansion rather than to the defense of conservative agrarianism.

Nowhere was the difference in the attitudes of leaders toward community enterprises more clearly revealed than in their views toward taxation. Although they could hardly be termed eager to raise taxes, leaders were far more willing to endorse tax increases to improve or provide specified public services than was the general public. The contrast with upper status respondents was particularly striking, for the latter, who were more likely to feel the pinch of increased taxes, were especially reluctant to consider additional taxation except when they perceived some immediate resultant benefit to themselves. Undoubtedly the inclusion of a relatively high proportion of local public officials influenced the responses of the total leader group, but the number of officials was not sufficient to account for the observed differences. It seems at least plausible that leaders, being more attuned to the overall problems of the total community, are more keenly aware of the necessity of an adequate tax program if the problems are to be solved. And while their views in this regard are not likely to receive popular acclaim, their apparent willingness to subordinate class interests to community interests may be one reason why they are recognized as community leaders.

One mark of a truly traditionalistic society is that its leaders are firmly dedicated either to preserving existing patterns of belief and behavior or to restoring earlier patterns considered even more desirable. By this criterion, Southern Appalachian society could hardly be considered traditionalistic. To a far greater degree than the average resident of the Region, persons named as local leaders are devoted to the philosophy of social progress and individual achievement that is a major theme of American culture. They are nearly unanimous in their belief that industrialization would prove of major benefit to the region and, as has already been indicated, that local community efforts should be exerted to attract industry. Their dedication to a philosophy of individual striving and self-betterment is reflected in the aspirations which they hold for their children. Seven out of eight leaders who were willing to express an occupational preference for a son named a white collar job, and three out of four specified a professional occupation. This is not surprising, of course, since nearly half of the leaders were in professional occupations themselves and only about 20 percent were farmers or industrial workers. What is important is that those who were named as leaders by the population cross section are not only relatively successful themselves by purely secular standards but also hold even higher achievement aspirations for their children.

Further evidence of this spirit of achievement is provided by the fact that nine out of ten leaders said they would want a son or daughter to complete college. Nearly a fifth of them said they would want their sons to do graduate work beyond the baccalaureate degree, and 12 percent expressed the same desire for a daughter. Only two of the 379 leaders said they would be content for their children to have less than a high school education, and only one in twenty said he would be willing for them to terminate their educations with a high school diploma. Asked whether they would want a child to stay in the community to live or go elsewhere, there was a five to four preference for remaining in the community, although about a fourth of the respondents said they didn't know. This ratio was about the same as for the total sample of survey respondents, but indicative of a greater preference for the children to seek residence elsewhere than was true of upper status respondents in the general survey.

In their evaluation of "success" factors, also, the views of leaders were somewhat closer to the total population average than to those of upper status respondents. That is, more of them rated *education* and *liking one's work* as the most important factors than rated *hard work* as most important. As was the case with the sample survey group, though, there were important differences by place of residence. Relatively more metropolitan leaders (33 percent) named *hard work* as the most important success factor, as did other metropolitan area residents, but rural leaders, like other rural residents, gave *education* top rating (40 percent), followed by *liking one's work* (33 percent), with only 10 percent giving top rating to *hard work*. Urban leaders named *hard work* more often than *good education* but less often than *liking one's work,* the latter factor being also most frequently named by other urban respondents. It is anomalous, indeed, that hard work, so often considered to be a traditional virtue of rural Americans, is almost disparaged by Appalachian rural residents and their leaders; and that these same rural people, who reputedly have been strongly resistant to formal schooling, more often credit success to good education than do their better educated urban and metropolitan neighbors.

Considering the strong achievement drive of the leaders, one would hardly expect them to be fatalists,

and this expectation is borne out by the survey results. The philosophy of "live for today and let tomorrow take care of itself" was rejected by more than three-fourths of the leader respondents. And only 42 percent endorsed the statement *no matter how much or how little you take care of yourself, you are going to die when your allotted time is up,* a statement with which seven out of ten general survey respondents agreed. Significantly, less than a third of the ministers in the leader group endorsed the latter statement, which would seem to indicate the withdrawal of religious support from the fatalistic doctrine that has no long deterred social action in the Region. This conclusion, at least so far as these particular ministers is concerned, is substantiated in the responses to the question of whether God is more pleased when people try to get ahead or when they are satisfied with what they have. Seventy percent of the minister-leaders and 72 percent of all leaders answered "when people try to get ahead." Even in rural areas, where it would be expected that ministers would be most traditionalistic in their attitudes toward secular achievement, a clear majority of the ministers (56 percent) indicated that they (and God) thought people should try to get ahead.

In summary, Southern Appalachian leaders as represented by the survey are neither fatalists nor reactionaries. Rather, they are "activists" and "progressives" for the most part, committed to a philosophy of individual achievement and social development. If they are distinctive in this regard, they are so largely with respect to the norms and values of the regional past, not those of contemporary national society. But this in itself holds considerable significance, for if their beliefs and behavior are in any way indicative of the direction in which regional values are changing, which seems surely to be the case, they portend an increasing acceptance of national culture traits.

It has been suggested that the aspect of Appalachian culture least affected by social and economic changes has been its system of religious beliefs, although even it has undergone some important modifications. The persistent conservatism that characterized the religious views of the general population was also to be found in those of the leaders, but to a slightly lesser degree, even though about a fourth of the leaders were ministers. Ministers, as to be expected, were generally more conservative than other leaders, but not as conservative as the population cross section. This is not really surprising, since they were selected because they were considered community leaders, not because they were ministers, and religious sectarianism is by its very nature incompatible with the type of secular endeavor generally conceived of as community work. Consequently, the religious beliefs of minister-leaders would not be representative of those of most ministers in the Region and may well represent the "liberal" extreme.

In nearly all respects, including their denominational affiliations, leaders were manifestly nonsectarians. Nevertheless, relatively few of them could be considered religious liberals by most standards except those of the Region itself. Over half (53 percent) of the leaders claimed to believe in the infallibility of the Scriptures as opposed to 46 percent who took a modernist view that the Bible contained some human error. Interestingly, a smaller proportion of ministers (45 percent) than other leaders (56 percent) professed themselves Biblicists. By the criterion of Biblicism, leaders would be considered less fundamentalist than the general population, but more so than other respondents of comparable socioeconomic status and education. With respect to their acceptance of a "Puritan ethic," though, they were about as fundamentalist as the average respondent and considerably more Puritanical than most upper status and college educated respondents. For example, the percentages of leaders and general survey respondents who rated drinking and dancing as "always wrong" were almost the same, about three out of four for drinking and about one in five for dancing. But only 22 percent of the leaders, as compared with 32 percent of the general sample, rated card playing always wrong. Minister-leaders were more conservative than others but, with respect to card playing less so than the general sample.

Among leaders, as among other respondents, there was a considerable weakening of Puritan morality with increasing urbanization, but in all areas the professed beliefs of the leaders were closer to those of the middle classes than to those of upper status and college-educated respondents. Although various interpretations might be placed on this phenomenon, it does suggest that leaders are more likely to respond to the ethical norms of the "total community" rather than to those of the particular social class in which they might be placed by virtue of wealth, occupation, or education.

The closeness of the religious philosophy of leaders to that of the middle classes was also apparent in their responses to questions concerning possible conflicts between science and church teachings. Only 36 percent of the leaders (and only 27 percent of the minister-leaders) acknowledged any disagreements, at least so far as their own churches were concerned. This was very close to the comparable figure (38.5 percent) for the general survey population. Of those leaders who thought there were disagreements, only one in thirty-five said that scientific teachings were probably more nearly right, while four out of five took the side of religion. The remainder, about one in eight, claimed to be unsure as to which was right. It would thus appear that most leaders, like most of the remainder of Appalachian society, are seeking to avoid bringing to the surface any latent conflict stemming from the acceptance of both rational and sacred authority. Cognizant of the current prestige of scientific knowledge but unwilling to deny the preeminence of their religious teachings, many leaders have apparently chosen to ignore conflicting issues while focusing on areas of mutual support.

The social action philosophy of the named leaders finds expression in their beliefs concerning the proper social role of churches and ministers, but there is little evidence that they consider the promotion of social progress a major church function. Nine out of ten leaders endorsed church participation in community improvement programs, and three out of four said they thought ministers should take a public stand on important issues. But other church activities, such as revival meetings, received even more support, and 40 percent of the leaders rated the community service function of the minister as less important than any of his more traditional pastoral and priestly duties. Most leaders considered it more important than administrative duties connected with the church, however. It seems a reasonable inference that leaders, even more so than other respondents, conceive of the churches' role as being broader than mere evangelism and legitimately including the promotion of social and economic improvements. But most leaders do not identify the church as a social action agency and apparently feel that it best serves the cause of social progress through inspiring its members to engage in good works for the glory of God.

To what extent the values and beliefs of those persons identified as local community leaders may signal the future pattern of the Region there is, of course, no way of knowing. It is reasonably certain, however, that their values will figure heavily in local decisions that will shape the course of regional events for at least the near future. The evidence secured in the survey, of which it has been possible to present only fragmentary portions, indicates that the value position of these local leaders lies somewhere between that of the majority of the regional population and that of the more industrialized segment of the national population. The characteristics of the leaders themselves suggest this. They are not the bright young human dynamos that one finds in our industrial metropolises, but neither are they mossbacked rural patriarchs. For the most part they are well educated and hold responsible positions in the business, church, educational, and local governmental institutions of their communities. By national standards, their values would be considered conservative, but not reactionary; by regional standards they seem almost liberal. They have, for the most part, rejected the philosophy of passive acceptance of their social and economic circumstances. They want better conditions for themselves and for their children, and they see industrialization and improved education as primary means to this end.

Perhaps what most distinguishes those who were named as leaders from other residents of comparable education and wealth is their ability and willingness to consider issues from a community standpoint rather than as individuals or representatives of a social class. Yet this fact inevitably creates a moral dilemma which appears time and again in their responses to survey questions. Committed by culture and social position to the values of individual endeavor and free enterprise, they are painfully aware that these in themselves are inadequate to solve the problems of their local communities and of the Region. One senses their reluctance to endorse programs of federal and state assistance which they recognize are probably necessary to the solution of their community problems but simultaneously feel will undermine the traditional virtues of individualism and self-reliance. Forced to a choice, which is already being made through numerous small daily decisions and a few major ones, there is little doubt that community leaders will accept government aid in lieu of a more desirable and less likely economic prosperity created by industrial development. In choosing to tread this unhappy path, they may have whatever solace there is in knowing they have the support of the vast majority of their fellow citizens whom they seek to serve.

Tradition, Change and the Future

At the beginning of this essay, some of the questions that prompted the exploration of values, beliefs, and attitudes of Southern Appalachian people were posed: Have the people clung to their frontier-agrarian traditions, resisting the philosophical premise of industrial society? Are they willing to accept the social consequences of a new economy? Are there evidences of discrepancies between new modes of behavior and old patterns of thought, and, if so, what do they portend in the way of future social problems? And what implications do the current beliefs and values of the Appalachian people hold for those who are actively working to promote social and economic change in the Region? To conclude the chapter, it seems appropriate to return to these questions and attempt to answer them, even though the answers of necessity must be incomplete and to some considerable extent impressionistic. It is to be reemphasized that the very attempt to present conclusions about the values and beliefs of Southern Appalachian people may create an impression of homogeneity that does not in fact exist.

The question of whether the people of the Region have clung to their earlier heritage, steadfastly resisting the secular philosophy of an industrial society, can be answered simply and categorically. The answer is no. But there is some danger both in asking the question and in answering it categorically of perpetuating the widely accepted but misleading assumption of a relatively stable pattern of regional culture introduced

at the time of settlement and persisting well up into the current century. It is the same false assumption that finds currency in reference to the Highlands as an "arrested frontier." In truth the regional way of life has always been in some flux, and there is considerable evidence that there was a rapid decline in so-called "frontier spirit" not long after settlement of the Region was completed.

It is self-evident that the early settlers were not passively resigned to their life circumstances or they would not have exposed themselves to the hardships of frontier life in the first place. Quite possibly, as has been suggested, they were not the doughty pioneers of legend who moved into the mountains undaunted by foreknowledge of the hazardous and rigorous conditions they would encounter, but rather naive romanticists expecting to find a new Garden of Eden or at least a land of milk and honey.[15] In any case, they were actively searching for a better life, which meant in part freedom from the social restraints of the settled seaboard and piedmont and the opportunity to acquire farm land of their own. It is also quite probable that they brought with them and were motivated by the "fundamental pathos of American culture [the belief] that virtue should and will be rewarded—and more particularly that such economic virtues as hard work, frugality, and prudence should receive a proportionate reward."[16]

If such was their belief, they were soon disillusioned. Hard work, frugality, and prudence proved to be not guarantees of prosperity but necessities for sheer survival. Yet they could not accept the harsh verdict that virtue is its own, and often only, reward. Even less willing were they to accept the smug Calvinistic doctrine that prosperity was a sign of the divinely "elect" while poverty was the lot of the uncalled and unchosen. Thus it was no mere coincidence that the gratifying philosophy of sectarian Protestantism found unprecedented acceptance (in the New World) in the mountains. For it defined as virtue not hard work and secular striving but suffering and privation, which the mountain people had in abundance, and offered as reward not mere earthly riches but the inheritance of the Kingdom of God itself. The retreat into fatalism and sectarian religion was not evidence of some peculiar and innate character flaw, but a concession of inadequate skill and resources to control the unyielding forces of nature. Nor was their failure to master the environment, at least during the nineteenth century, because their technical skills were markedly inferior to those of other rural people. Rather, it was because the technology of the age was not adequate to cope with the conditions of their habitat. Once they adjusted psychologically to their situation, though, there was little motivation for many residents to resume the struggle against nature even when ad advancing technology was able to provide them with better weapons.

But it was not the lack of motivation alone that prevented the mountain people from taking full advantage of technological advances. There was also their high degree of individualism, a frontier value strengthened by years of relative isolation. The individualism of the frontier, as many historians have pointed out, was not the individualism of nonconformity but of personal liberty and freedom from civil restraints. Inclined to be suspicious of all extrafamilial social liaisons, the mountain people had little enthusiasm for or experience with the forms of social organization required for the successful functioning of an industrial economy and an urban society. A companion virtue to self-reliance, individualism was easily and often perverted to the cause of social irresponsibility and remained in active force even when the independence which it was supposed to sustain had all but disappeared.

It is difficult to say when the prevailing philosophy of resignation began to be supplanted by a philosophy more in tune with that of the national culture that emphasized work, achievement, and progress. In any event, the transition was not marked by any radical reorientation of values but rather by a gradual shifting of beliefs and sentiments. There were always "activist" individuals and groups in Appalachian society just as there are "passivist" individuals and groups today, but no one has adequately described when or why the activist element began to predominate. The relief program of the New Deal was probably one major force in bringing about the change, but not because it radically affected the value premises of regional society. (Indeed, it challenged those of the national society to a much greater degree.) Many if not most Appalachian residents who received public assistance payments under the New Deal program viewed their relief benefits as *manna,* a direct gift of God disbursed by a beneficent government. For much of the Appalachian Region the Great Depression was a period of relative prosperity, and although there was little in the emergency relief program to spur the people to greater industry, many came to experience for the first time the pleasures of having adequate food, clothing, and housing.

Probably far more effective and enduring in reorienting the value system were the forces and events that served to break down regional isolation. The growth and improvement of public education was one such force, for the schools served as a major communication channel through which the values and norms of national society were introduced into the Region. Rural electrification, too, played an important role, for it made possible material comforts such as electric lights and washing machines that could be afforded by all save the poorest, and even they could aspire to their possession. Perhaps even more important, radios were also widely introduced and by this means the isolated as well as the illiterate residents not only learned more about conditions in other parts of the nation and world but were also exposed to the potent stimuli of mass advertising. The agents of mass communication also served to arouse acquisitive desires and develop emulative tastes—the motion pictures, mail order catalogs, weekly newspapers, and farm journals. The movies were considered particularly threatening to fundamentalist values and were denounced from many pulpits with epithets earlier reserved for drinking, dancing, card playing and other sinful activities. Quite probably such denunciation exaggerated the actual influence of the cinema, but at least in the censure there was recognition that provincial values were at odds with those thought accepted by a more sophisticated society.

Education, mass communication, and improved roads that linked more closely hollows and cities, all contributed to the weakening of traditional values, a process that was greatly accelerated by World War II. Where the other forces had aroused yearnings for new ways, the war provided numerous opportunities to fulfill these desires and created yet others. Even those who did not go into the armed forces were affected by the war. Some migrated to northern cities to find employment in expanded industries at wages earlier undreamed of, and learned to cope with the conditions of urban living. Within the Region itself there were new industries and construction work, while older industries, such as the coal mines, provided employment that was gratifyingly regular and profitable. In short, it was a period of novel experiences, new opportunities, and unprecedented prosperity, and after it was all over there could be no complete return to the old ways. Literally hundreds of thousands left the Region during the postwar period, seeing little opportunity to continue to live as well so long as they remained. But of equal or greater moment, so far as the culture of the Region itself is concerned, is that the great majority of those who did remain, having once experienced flush times, could no longer view poverty as the natural condition of man. Many have since seen poverty return, but they have not, as yet, been able to accept it with the resignation of their forebears, not so much because their faith in God is less but because their faith in man is greater.

The question of whether the mountain people are prepared to accept the social consequences of industrial society along with its economic benefits is more difficult to answer. At least it cannot be answered categorically, for there are many consequences and they cannot be considered as a body.

One obvious social consequence of industrial society is urban living. That this is acceptable to many Appalachian residents is obvious from the patterns of migration that have developed in recent years. But willingness to live in cities is not the same as willingness to adopt the modes of social and civic behavior that urban living implies. Mountain residents who have moved into industrial centers, especially those outside the Region, have frequently been charged with creating a variety of social problems. In this respect, however, they do not differ greatly from European immigrants who settled in many of the same cities in the latter part of the nineteenth century. To a great extent, as Giffin has pointed out in his discussion of the urban adjustment of Appalachian migrants, the behavioral characteristics that create social problems in the cities are attributes of social class rather than of regional culture. If the past history of immigrant assimilation provides a useful guide, the solution of such problems depends in considerable measure upon the types of jobs the migrants are able to fill. Inasmuch as many of them lack the educational or technical qualifications to compete successfully for better paid positions, it seems unlikely that they will be easily absorbed, and complete assimilation will probably not be accomplished within a single generation.

Within the Region itself the adjustment problems are of a somewhat different order. Probably the most serious from the standpoint of regional development are those that stem from the failure to develop a strong sense of civic responsibility. This is evident in the shortage of effective community action organization and in the steadfast reluctance to increase local taxes for purposes that are generally conceded to be worthy. The reasons for this apparent unwillingness to assume social responsibilities are numerous and varied. They include the persistence of individualism as a value, which has already been discussed, and the inherent difficulty of changing from familistic to associational society. To some degree the development of a "relief philosophy" may also have served as a deterrent to community self-reliance, although there has been more emotional assertion than objective evidence to support this case. The growing recognition that the fundamental economic problems of the Region are not likely to be solved by local community action alone and that their deleterious consequences are felt far beyond the Region has also provided for some a rationale for shifting to the national level the total responsibility for seeking effective solution. There seems little doubt that even among the more conservative elements of the Region there is an increasing tendency to view federal assistance as an alternative rather than as a supplement to local efforts to solve community problems. At the same time it must be recognized that numerous towns and cities within the Region have outstanding records of civic enterprise and that many counties have organized effective rural development programs coordinating the services of state and federal agencies and local citizen groups. The question, therefore, is not whether the people of the Region are capable of initiating and organizing local action programs but whether they are yet willing to accept and sustain the fundamental premise that furtherance of the commonweal in a democratic society requires a common effort.

The course of social transition is never smooth, for the adoption of new ways always carries the implication of the inferiority of older ways and the values that have sustained them. It is therefore inevitable that some conflict should develop between the accepters of the new and the defenders of the old. But the people of a society undergoing transition are rarely divided into two sharply distinct categories. More commonly than not, the individuals who compose such a society are internally at odds, accepting some of the new, retaining some of the old, and seeking to resolve or repress whatever logical inconsistencies may arise as a consequence.

Evidence that many members of Appalachian society are faced with internal and unresolved conflicts of various sorts has already been presented and need not be reviewed in detail. Parents with high aspirations for their children frequently do not exert the necessary effort to see that they receive the schooling that the realization of their aspirations requires. Residents of local communities concede the desirability of having better schools, better health facilities, and better government, but reject tax measures needed to provide them. Similarly, there is general recognition that organized social action is more effective than individual efforts, but attempts to organize action groups for purposes that have received popular endorsement often die a-borning. The goals and benefits of industrial society are accepted; the methods of achieving them are endorsed but not supported; and the failure to support them is rooted in the values of agrarian society.

All of these problems of conflicting values, though, have a familiar ring, and one recognizes that they are the same problems that have attended the transition from agrarian to industrial society in other parts of the nation and, indeed, throughout the world. There is little to suggest that the problems of conflicting values, whether the conflict is between groups or within individuals, are radically different in the Southern Appalachian Region. If there is a difference, it is probably more attributable to the greater intensity and persistence of agrarian values in the Region rather than to their nature.

The final question to be considered of those that prompted the attitude survey is *What implications do the current beliefs and values of the Appalachian people hold for those who are actively working to promote social and economic change in the Region?* A major difficulty in handling such a question is that there is not really any general objective or overall program for systematic social change in the Region. Rather, there are many small relatively autonomous programs, with different aspects of social and economic organization and activity, geographically restricted, and each with its own limited objectives. If there is any common thread, it is that of seeking to change the particular local conditions with which each program is concerned to correspond more closely to some real or assumed national standard. That is, the direction in which change is being urged, whether it be in the field of health, education, economics, welfare, or almost any other with the possible exception of religion, is toward the national norm.

It is a generally (although by no means invariably) valid assumption that before the members of a society will move toward the achievement of a specific objective, they must first accept it as legitimate. Most of the people of the Region, according to the evidence of the survey data, have adopted the major goals and standards typical of American society. They, like other people throughout the nation, wish to have larger incomes, greater material comforts, and more prestigeful status. And if it seems unlikely that they will realize these aspirations for themselves, they would at least like to see them realized by their children. In short, the people of the Region have become "progressive-minded" and "achievement-oriented" to a surprisingly high degree, and a large amount of motivation effort, like the preaching, in the Southern Appalachians is expended on the already converted.

In part the continued preoccupation with motivation at the basic value level stems from the value assumptions of the promoters themselves. They believe that acceptance of goals is not only a necessary but a sufficient condition for achieving them. Firmly believing that "where there's a will, there's a way," they persistently attribute lack of achievement to lack of motivation. To support their inference, they can point both to the traditional passivist philosophy of the Region and to not a few contemporary groups and individuals whose lives are still guided by it. Yet the evidence from the attitude survey would indicate that these groups and individuals today constitute a minority of the Appalachian population; but the Region itself continues to lag in its social and economic development. It hardly seems reasonable to ascribe all the backwardness or even most of it to inadequate motivation. While this is not to suggest that motivation efforts are no longer necessary, which is obviously not the case, it is to suggest that the same energies might be more efficiently applied to other tasks.

What might some of these tasks be? Apart from the purely technological considerations of resource development, there are a number of areas of social life that would appear to benefit from rational and concerted action. One of the most obvious deficiencies that has already been discussed is the lack of a strong sense of social responsibility. In large measure this deficiency is a logical consequence of the traditional social organization of Appalachian society based on familism and the cultivation of individualism as a value. There has

been a growing acceptance of the necessity of interdependence for the functioning of an industrial economy and urban society, but it has been viewed as little more than a necessity. There has been little concession that such interdependence entails any greater obligation to or responsibility for one's fellow citizens than what is absolutely necessary to maintain a specific activity. The bonds of loyalty to group or community are often so tenuous as to appear lacking altogether. Not uncommonly projects such as new schools or hospitals that apparently have widespread and even enthusiastic approval fail to receive support when presented as bond issues. Nor can this failure be traced to any belief on the part of the majority of the citizens that education and health are not desirable or that good schools and hospitals do not contribute to their improvement. True, in most such instances numerous rationalizations are offered for the failure—taxes are already too high or the ventures are being promoted by individuals with vested interests or countless others—but the underlying reason is generally the lack of a sense of social responsibility. Certainly the development of this trait would seem to be a worthwhile task for those who are concerned with the improvement of life in the Region. There would appear to be a ready-made basis for such development in the religious ethos, but so far there have been relatively few efforts to establish an explicit linkage between Christ's precept to love one's neighbor as oneself and the solving of community problems. While the appeal to religious values might be considered a hypocritical expediency in some parts of the nation, it need not necessarily be so in the Southern Appalachians, for as our survey data have shown, the leaders themselves seem to be of the same religious persuasion as most of the general population.

Another area in which concerted action could help develop a broader consciousness of social obligations is in the teaching of the techniques of group organization and action. In the criticism of Appalachian residents for their failure to support and participate in organized activities, sight has often been lost of the fact that the social skills required for such participation are not automatically acquired. It is difficult for proud and sensitive people to enter into unaccustomed activities that they feel will reveal them as gauche and inadequate. Consequently many would rather foresake the benefits of group endeavor then endure the humiliation of being considered ignorant and inept. The survey data indicate that the value of organized action is more widely recognized that the low participation rates would indicate. The diffidence that underlies much, although by no means all, of the reluctance to engage in cooperative activities can probably be overcome to some degree through small-scale programs, involving limited numbers of people, that are designed to provide training in the skills and conventions of group action. Many agencies, such as the agricultural extension services of the various states, already incorporate this objective in their programs. But more typically, existing agencies and new organizations concentrate exclusively on the attainment of some concrete program objective and call repeatedly on the services of the overburdened few who are already familiar with the techniques and processes of carrying out group programs. And while most agency and community leaders are aware that program involvement itself generates support, under the pressures of time and circumstance they seldom undertake to broaden the base of support through systematic, long-range plans to train potential participants and develop future leaders.

A third task implicit in the survey findings is in the area of reducing the social conflict and personal confusion arising from the confrontation of different value systems. In recent times the major arena of social conflict arising from the contact of disparate value systems has been in the industrial cities of the north to which Appalachian migrants have flocked by the hundreds of thousands. More often than not the problem has been defined as the inability of the "hill-billies" to adjust to the ways of urban and industrial life. There has been less recognition that the rural provincialism of the mountain migrants is matched by the urban provincialism of city dwellers, and that this latter also figures in the maladjustment.

The most promising approach to the solution of this problem would seem to be one of education. Certainly there is a need to familiarize the mountain migrants, preferably before they migrate, with the requirements and expectations of urban life and the conditions they are likely to face. There is also a need to acquaint the officials, agency workers, teachers, and ordinary citizens of industrial cities with some valid knowledge of the ways and problems of the migrants. Some beginning steps toward meeting this latter need have already been taken through a series of workshops on adjustment problems of Appalachian migrants held at Berea College, Kentucky, under the direction of the Council of the Southern Mountains. As a direct outgrowth of these workshops, a number of groups have been organized in major cities north of the Ohio River to deal with the great variety of complex adjustment problems faced by mountain migrants. No comparable programs have been undertaken within cities of the Region itself to help in the adjustment of rural migrants, however, and there are appreciable adjustment problems there, also, even though the cultural gap is not so great as it is in northern cities. Neither has there been any systematic effort to prepare potential migrants in rural areas for city life, either within or outside the Region, except through the normal educational programs of the public schools.

But of all the implications that may be drawn from the survey of attitudes, values, and beliefs of the Southern Appalachian people, the most important is this: that the old stereotypes that have so long guided social action in the Region no longer apply to the great majority of the residents. The Southern Appalachian people, although they may lag in their social and economic development, are living in the twentieth century. To be sure, they retain the impress of their rural cultural heritage, but for the most part their way of life, their beliefs, their fears, and their aspirations are not radically different from those of most other Americans. If they do not share fully in the larger culture of the nation, which in truth they do not as yet (and, indeed, some of their champions hope they will not), it can hardly be attributed to their lack of willingness to do so. To an appreciable measure their distinctiveness as a people is vested in characteristics that have persisted only because of restricted social and economic opportunities. The economic development of the Region is not so much dependent upon their cultural integration as their cultural integration is dependent upon economic development. Whether or not it is considered desirable, it seems almost certain that as the economic problems are solved, the provincialism of the Region itself will fade.

NOTES

1. Howard Odum, *Southern Regions of the United States* (Chapel Hill, N.C., 1936), p. 499.

2. John C. Campbell, *The Southern Highlander and His Homeland* (New York, 1921), p. xiv.

3. About a fourth of the respondents were excluded from the four socioeconomic status categories (see table 11.1). For the most part these were older persons—retired men, wives of retired men, and widows—from whom meaningful occupational data could not be obtained.

4. Horace Kephart, *Our Southern Highlanders* (New York, 1913); William G. Frost, "Our Contemporary Ancestors in the Southern Mountains," *Atlantic Monthly,* March 1899, pp. 311–19.

5. Robin Williams, *American Society—A Sociological Interpretation* (New York, 1957); Clyde Kluckhohn and Florence R. Kluckhohn, "American Culture: Generalized Orientations and Class Patterns" in *Conflicts of Power in Modern Culture,* ed. Lyman Bryson *et al.* (New York, 1948), pp. 106–28; Robert S. Lynd, *Knowledge for What?* (Princeton, N.J., 1939); Lloyd Warner, *American Life—Dream and Reality* (Chicago, 1953).

6. Campbell, *The Southern Highlander,* p. 93.

7. Kephart, *Our Southern Highlanders,* p. 309.

8. Odum, *Southern Regions,* p. 97.

9. Marion Pearsall, *Little Smoky Ridge* (Tuscaloosa, Ala., 1959), p. 57.

10. Kephart, *Our Southern Highlanders,* p. 309.

11. Edwin White, *Highland Heritage* (New York, 1937), p. 92.

12. John F. Day, *Bloody Ground* (New York, 1941), p. 104.

13. E. T. Clark, *The Small Sects in America,* rev. ed. (Nashville, 1949), p. 20.

14. Elizabeth R. Hooker, *Religion in the Highlands* (New York, 1933), p. 153.

15. Arthur K. Moore, *The Frontier Mind—A Cultural Analysis of the Kentucky Frontiersman* (Lexington, Ky., 1957).

16. Williams, *American Society,* p. 416.

12. CASH IS A FOUR-LETTER WORD

Paul Salstrom

There has been some discussion in the *Appalachian Journal* of fostering communication between "action folk," "creative folk," and "scholarly folk." The shortcut to such communication probably lies in choosing certain subjects rather than others to communicate about.

Last summer, returning to Appalachia after eight years of graduate school in Boston, I tended to see myself in category three, "scholarly folk." Then I was told that a company called Black Gold Inc. had applied for a permit to carry out a "mountaintop removal" on the ridge across from my brother's place in Lincoln County, W.Va., half a mile as the proverbial crow flies.

That had been the first land I'd owned—the catalyst, in my case, of all those subtle inner transmutations E. M. Forster once traced to his own personal acquisition of a freehold.[1] Work there under the pines had been uniquely un-irksome. It was work on "the place," work admixed with dreams and whims. To get cabin logs I cut down the trees most obstructing the view of a similar pine-covered ridge across the branch. That's the ridge which Black Gold Inc. has received permission to start levelling anytime it wants, shoving the scenery down into the branch. In addition to its permit, Black Gold has also received approval from a West Virginia Board of Reclamation review. The company could start bulldozing tomorrow if it wanted.

Soon after getting my Ph.D. last spring and arriving back on the ridge with the view, I went down one evening with a lot of other people to a high school gymnasium for the second official public hearing held under West Virginia Department of Energy auspices on Black Gold's permit application. It still then seemed that the official decision could go either way. Although West Virginia's Department of Energy was run by a strip mining enthusiast, Black Gold itself was run by a virtually bankrupt strip miner from eastern Kentucky who owed over $7 million in unpaid federal reclamation fines in that state. And Black Gold's president, an investor, was also an outsider, an Indianapolis woman who periodically gave John Birch-type press interviews labelling the company's opponents as communists, communist dupes, and drug users.[2]

The first official public hearing, my brother told me, had been packed with strip-mine workers from Logan County, W.Va., whom Black Gold had invited to visit the possible new job site. The atmosphere had been explosive, my brother said. (I took that with a grain of salt since he'd missed the sixties.) At the second hearing June 28, 1988, 21 people got up and delivered statements, all tape-recorded by West Virginia's Department of Energy to ponder at its leisure. Four of the speakers supported Black Gold's permit application and 17 opposed it. One of the opposition statements was delivered by a lawyer (the longest one). Two were delivered by geologists. Several were delivered by people who live in the shadow of the ridge Black Gold proposes to level. But the statement that hit closest to home for me was one delivered by a local high school teacher, Julian Martin:

> It seems real important in Lincoln County to establish where you're from and who you are. A lot of people laugh at you if they think you're from New York or someplace.
>
> I've been a citizen of this state for 52 years. I've lived in this county for 13 years. And I've taught at Duval High School for 12 years. I have to admit I was out of the country a couple of years in Africa. And I was in California a couple of years. Except for that, I've lived here the whole time.
>
> My daddy was a coal miner—lost his eye in the mines. He wasn't a communist. He wasn't an outsider. And he didn't deal in drugs—though he did drink a lot of coffee.
>
> It amazes me at times that we can be so up-tight about "outsiders." And what we have here is a case of a man from Montana threatening to bulldoze—to personally bulldoze—another man's fence down if he finds out the property is on his side of the line. And a man from Kentucky who threatened to kill the same man. And we have a woman from Indianapolis who says we're a bunch of drug dealers and communists.
>
> Now, all three of these people qualify to me as outsiders. I've lived here 52 years. I've got the accent, you know. I can speak the language, okay? I'm not a foreigner, okay?
>
> All my life I've watched the destruction of my native state. I watched Bull Creek disappear. When I was a little boy 40 years ago, I used to walk up Bull Creek over on Coal River. Bull Creek's not there anymore. Any of you guys that have ever worked on strip mines know it's not there anymore. It's gone. My Uncle Ken used to work timber up in the head of that hollow with a mule, and he did the least amount of destruction you possibly could do. That place was beautiful. It's not there anymore. It's just simply gone. It's been destroyed by a strip mine.
>
> My home place over on Coal River—coal companies offered us $250,000 for thirty-two acres. And we turned them down, okay? We don't need the money—by golly—not that bad.
>
> With me this is a spiritual thing. I've always loved the land. I've always loved to walk in the mountains. And the first time I saw a strip mine it absolutely stunned me into silence. I was sad and I was sick. I couldn't believe what people could do with a bulldozer to a piece of land that used to be beautiful.

Paul Salstrom is the former manager of the Appalachian Movement Press and now teaches history part-time at Marshall University. Preparation of this essay was aided by a grant from the Humanities Foundation of West Virginia, a program of the National Endowment for the Humanities.

If it's wrong to love beauty, if it's wrong to love nature, if it's wrong to say that we only have one earth and it will never be reclaimed—you can't reclaim a destroyed mountain—you can put something back there but you can't put that topsoil back on—just try it. You never, never can walk through that little glade where the ferns are growing. And enjoy those cliffs the way they were—the way they were meant to be.

All I see happening is greed. It's money, and where's it going to end? When they get to *your* back door? They're already at some people's back doors right now. Can you strip mine right up to the edge of City Hall? Do the people who own strip mines have strip mines in their back yards? Do they want dynamiting going on where they live? I don't think they do. I think they're going to retreat to their air-conditioned apartments. And I think they're going to send their kids to fine schools out of state.

And if you think strip mining is going to bring jobs, look where they've got strip mining in West Virginia and look where they're got the most unemployment. Mingo County. McDowell County. You go to the counties where they have strip mining—that's where they have the worst of everything. They've got the worst roads, they've got the worst schools, they've got the highest unemployment rate. Everything is wrong with those counties. Is that what we want this beautiful place to become?

My daddy was a coal miner, and I understand being out of work, okay? I've been down that road myself. And I know you've got to provide for your family. But I'm saying they're only giving us two options. They're saying, "Either starve—or destroy West Virginia." And surely to God there must be another option.[3]

"Surely to God there must be another option." Those are the words before me these days. America is facing a prospect of serious economic trauma, and once again Appalachia appears the likeliest candidate to serve the Greater Cause as a national sacrifice area.

Meanwhile, my presence as "scholarly folk" has prompted Home Place Inc. (the local opposition group) to suggest that I look into economic alternatives for Lincoln County. Home Place has secured a $1,000 grant from the West Virginia branch of the National Endowment for the Humanities on which I am to subsist while scholarizing.

When I first came to West Virginia in 1971, I toyed with the idea of setting up a branch of my family's wood-carving business. The business required a semi-trailer load of wood once a week at its Illinois shop (they carve it with machines), and the price of that wood would have been about two-thirds less in West Virginia than in Illinois. I used to go to Illinois and work to get money for buying West Virginia land—and a lot of my friends here began doing the same—but none of us ever embarked on "import substitution" by setting up local production of basic wood products used in Appalachia. After we had managed to pay off our land, we found we could "get by" by farming a little, bartering a lot, exchanging work days with each other, and picking apples in the fall for what cash we needed. Meanwhile,

however, more and more of the natives here were eating out of supermarkets and commuting out of the county to work. Some were commuting to strip-mine jobs in Logan and Boone counties.

My first impulse has been to hastily look again at wood products, and look again at timber stands and lumber prices, and also look into enterprise-feasibility studies by outfits like the Corporation for Enterprise Development in Washington, D.C. That group studies projects underway all over the U.S. to finance motivated people on transfer payments (i.e., on welfare of all sorts, unemployment compensation, etc.) while the recipients are starting up their own businesses—sometimes even using their projected future welfare income as collateral behind bank loans.[4]

In the mid-1980s two woodworking businesses were opened in Lincoln County by newcomers with the help of socially-motivated loan money. And there were already two extant woodworking shops before the newcomers began theirs. As of this writing, however, Lincoln County remains the county with the lowest ratio of bank loans to bank deposits in West Virginia, qualifying for the booby prize as far as enterprise is concerned. And in the nation as a whole, West Virginia remains the state with the lowest ratio of bank loans to bank deposits.

Since receiving my assignment from Home Place, I've basked in the sunshine of last fall's pre-election politicking, and I've shivered in the cold reality that has followed the election. Most business interests and politicians have long seen the Appalachian Plateau (including not only western West Virginia but eastern Kentucky) as a source of coal to be mined as cheaply as possible. The region is expendable.

And in order to save the area from strip-mining shovels, there are two notions that I think Appalachia's activists are going to have to re-examine and toss overboard—two lessons we learned in the past but we now have to un-learn because times have changed. One is our knee-jerk rejection of all economic enterprise and the other is our paranoia about the National Park Service. To hold the strip-mine shovels at bay, we need more economic enterprise and also a much larger presence of the National Park Service.

A lot of people think that something called "tradition" underlies Appalachia's low ranking in enterprise indicators—something called "familism" or "dense collective experience." But family enterprises are flourishing all over the world in all sorts of societies, and collective enterprises are common as well. There is nothing about "familism" that inhibits an enterprising attitude if the material conditions for economic development are indeed available for development. Plenty of street people are individualistic.

When Home Place spelled out my assignment, it said to assess in particular the contribution that Appalachian "traditions" might make toward solving Appalachia's present economic quandary. But in the process of writing a dissertation on this region's past, I've found that although "familism" and "dense collective experience" run through the region's entire history from when white settlers first arrived, nonetheless, up until at least the Civil War, such traits co-existed with very widespread economic enterprise at all levels of society. In other words, economic enterprise was once just as "traditional" as anything else about Appalachia.

Three years ago there was some discussion in the *Appalachian Journal* (in the winter and summer 1986 issues) about whether there was much entrepreneurial thinking among Appalachia's preindustrial farmers. The sociologists Dwight Billings, Kathleen Blee, and Louis Swanson thought there was not, and I thought that there was (and still do). My view is that the thinking of many or most of the region's preindustrial farmers was both subsistence-oriented and profit-oriented, and that it was not until after the Civil War that scarcity began forcing most Appalachian farm families to choose between profit-minded and subsistence-minded ways of thinking.[5]

When I suggested that, I was advised to beware of what analytical structure I might be providing aid and comfort to. I was admonished that "reading the entrepreneurialism of land speculators onto subsistence-oriented farmers contributes to an analysis in which the search for profit is the norm against which Appalachian culture and family practices appear deficient."[6]

The implication here is that Appalachian culture and family practices are not deficient (as Jack Weller once seemed to imply in his notorious *Yesterday's People*)[7] but that they admittedly are different. As evidence continues to accumulate that entrepreneurial activity was extremely widespread in preindustrial Appalachia, we cannot escape the obvious conclusion that "the search for profit" was in fact a "norm" in the region at that time. And as we acknowledge that, the question to be asked is no longer "why hasn't profit-seeking become a norm in Appalachia" but "why did profit-seeking cease being a norm in Appalachia?" That's what we should be asking.

Billings, Blee, and Swanson made reference to "the penetration of capitalist social relations" into Appalachia during the post-Civil War industrialization period.[8] The conception of such a penetration is useful if we realize that market relations were already common in the region prior to industrialization—that market relations pretty much kept pace here with market relations in most of the rest of the country until after the Civil War. What we now label Appalachia's "traditional social relations" were actually an astute expedient worked out in the final third of the nineteenth century by adapting and strengthening extant non-cash relations of exchange. So-called "traditional social relations" were partly an expedient for coping with the cash drought which federal banking legislation imposed on outlying parts of the United States in 1863, 1864, and particularly 1865.

Rather different expedients arose in other financially peripheral parts of the country. In the Deep South, for example, the standard American economic history textbook attributes the post-1865 debt-bondage which storekeepers increasingly exercised over share-croppers and tenant farmers partly to the 1865 federal law which terminated the power of state-chartered banks to issue currency. Without that law, the textbook implies, the direct financing of crops through cash loans could have "atomized" down to the level of small towns, thereby paralleling the atomization of the Deep South's farming units which followed the Civil War.[9] We must not ignore the effects which laws and government policies can have on social formation. Here was an act— the 1865 law that ended state-bank currencies—that passed Congress by a single vote.[10]

It is highly relevant that a technological revolution followed the Civil War and that new economies-of-scale thereby became possible. But my point is that the 1865 banking law had an enormous effect in determining who would and who would not control those new means of production—including who would control their deployment in Appalachia. It determined that their deployment had to be financed by deposit money almost exclusively—that it generally could not be financed by cash. And access to deposit money was virtually monopolized by outsiders.

A few unfamiliar facts: Prior to the Civil War, currency in circulation had expanded far faster than deposit money in the U.S. From 1845 to 1860, currency in circulation grew 244 percent while bank deposits grew only 82 percent.[11] As of 1860, currency exceeded deposits by 3 to 2. By the Civil War's conclusion, deposit holdings had surpassed currency and the ratio stood at 3 to 2 in favor of deposits. From that point, deposits soared while currencies stagnated (sabotaged by the 1865 law that ended state-bank currency-issuing power). By 1914 there would be almost $9 on deposit in the U.S. for every dollar of currency.[12]

The cash drought was most pronounced in the outlying or "peripheral" parts of the U.S., including Appalachia. Paper money in the postbellum period consisted about half of "greenbacks" (issued by the federal government) and the other half of banknotes issued by nationally-chartered banks. As of 1876, the national banks of Connecticut had more banknotes in circulation than the combined banks of Kentucky, Tennessee, Missouri, Kansas, Iowa, Minnesota, and Michigan. In per capita terms, Rhode Island banks were circulating $77.16 per Rhode Islander, whereas Arkansas banks had out only 13 cents per Arkansan. More currency was circulating from merely the banks of New Bedford, Mass., than from any Southern state.[13]

Most financial historians have failed to see anything problematic about this, claiming that deposit money "stepped into the breach" that was created by currency curtailment. But this ignores the social consequences, the regressive social change, enforced by so radical a constriction in available cash. Deposit money simply did not circulate through society in the same way that cash circulated. Cash moved at all levels of exchange, whereas checks were necessarily reserved for relatively large transactions. To receive a check was at best an inconvenience for someone who lacked a bank account in which to deposit it. Checks did not filter down like cash did.

Of course people were still paid for their work, but how were they paid? Looking at Appalachia's coal industry, we find that pay was usually in company scrip. Wages constituted about two-thirds of coal companies' operating costs in the mountains, and there clearly was not enough cash available to most large coal operators to pay miners' wages in cash. Coal companies' income came in the form of checks from financiers (issued against the promissory notes of the companies) and also as checks from the wholesalers who bought their coal. Coal operators deposited those checks in their banks and could then write their own checks to their suppliers, such as the grocery wholesalers who provisioned their company stores. The companies then paid wages in scrip, which functioned as the tokens of an in-company checking system. Until at least the turn of the century in most of Appalachia, there wasn't enough cash available for large coal operators to pay miners in cash.

According to Stuart McGehee (who's an expert on the Flat Top-Pocahontas coalfield), outsiders weren't the first to try to exploit that coalfield. "Locals tried like hell to exploit the coal," he says, "but lacked the necessary means to mount a large-scale operation. The locals acted as middlemen, arranging sales of land and right-of-way to Philadelphia entrepreneurs who financed the thing."[14]

McGehee says there are "boatloads" of primary materials on banking and finance in the Flat Top-Pocahontas coalfield, but apparently no one yet sees the relevance of such data to the shaping of an economic dependency under which Appalachia labors today.

A glance at the first report issued by a West Virginia bank examiner (in 1891) reveals that the largest bank in the West Virginia portion of the Flat Top-Pocahontas coalfield (which extends also into southwestern Virginia) was Isaac T. Mann's Bank of Bramwell, established in 1889. That bank's cash holdings on June 24, 1891 (the day the examiner visited), were only $24,819. The combined cash holdings of the other three West Virginia banks in that coalfield brought the total to a hair above $50,000 for the area.[15]

That same year 3,137,012 tons of coal were mined in the Flat Top-Pocahontas field (including Virginia's tonnage as well as West Virginia's).[16] Since wages ran about 68 cents a ton that year (which incidentally was 75 percent of the coal's value at the mine head),[17] the year's payroll in the coalfield amounted to about $2,133,000. Some of this amount was admittedly dispersed in Virginia rather than West Virginia, but if miners' wages were to be paid in cash, where was even a fraction of that much cash to come from?

The bank examiner's figures for all 49 of West Virginia's state-chartered banks show their combined cash holdings totalling less than $1 million in 1891.[18] Nationally-chartered banks in West Virginia held even less cash.

Later, there was a vast increase in the availability of cash resulting from changes in federal banking laws between 1900 and 1914. Banking reforms of those years multiplied the number of national banks and the amount of currency in circulation.[19] Nonetheless, many coal companies continued paying scrip wages into the 1920s. The pro-labor faction of West Virginia's Democratic Party increased its power in the 1920s but was not able until 1933 to rout conservative Democrats on the scrip issue (not to mention other labor grievances).

All of this history has had a direct role in causing Appalachia's present relative lack of wealth. And it's no secret that America's best schools, best roads, most public amenities, etc. are found in its tax jurisdictions containing the most private wealth. Appalachia's people would have owned a lot more private wealth by now if the financial deck hadn't been stacked against them.

Many of us engaged in Appalachian Studies are in it because the region has given us something, and we want to understand what that is. What has Appalachia given us? Presumably it's something money can't buy, but is it something money would spoil?

My hypothesis is that the Great Divide hindering communication in Appalachian Studies is not actually any significant incompatability among "action folk," "creative folk," and "scholarly folk," but rather the fact that some of us have received a Cause from the region whereas others have received a way of life. For the latter group, the great paradox is that cash is necessary to maintain the way of life, but too much cash, affluence, dissolves the Appalachian way of life.

Altina Waller's *Feud* provides great detail about one preindustrial local mountain entrepreneur—Devil Anse Hatfield—who was first hobbled by the cash drought which followed the Civil War and who was then bought out by people who had plenty of money at their disposal. Devil Anse held 5,000 acres of timber land through most of the 1870s and 80s but was denied any good way to capitalize either his holdings or his crew's labor, so he "lost his shirt."

When first starting his timber business in 1869, Devil Anse had lacked any significant money to invest in it. He operated on credit, promising in 1872 (for instance) to make a large delivery of poplar logs on the Tug Fork's spring (1873) floodwaters in exchange for food and supplies from a storekeeper, John Smith. Waller mentions that Devil Anse was unusual for his generation of Tug Fork Hatfields in that he didn't inherit title to sufficient land to provide a comfortable subsistence for his family. Some personal belt-tightening probably helped motivate him to embark on his timber business, but he also was clearly trying to make more profit than subsistence required.[20]

Altina Waller's great service is to integrate events of the famous feud with the twists and turns of Devil Anse's timber business. By December 1887, for instance, his business had suffered many reverses, and he could only continue operations by mortgaging much of his land to a Logan merchant in order to fend off other merchants who were suing him for nonpayment of previous debts. That's when a coalition of Kentucky McCoys—instigated by Devil Anse's former neighbor and land rival Perry Cline—strategically chose to harass Devil Anse and his entourage, culminating in the January 1888 Battle of Grapevine Creek. This trouble evidently prevented timber deliveries that would have enabled Devil Anse to liquidate his December 1887 mortgage. He then sold his timber lands—not so much to move to another area as to forestall those lands' seizure. Had financial pressures not forced him to sell out, he could have waited for a much higher price, since the Norfolk and Western was planning to place a railroad along either the Tug Fork or the Guyandotte River (40 miles east of the Tug). Later in 1888 the Norfolk and Western would begin surveying a Tug route, and early in 1889 it announced its choice of that route.[21]

But does all the market-oriented behavior of Devil Anse necessarily tell us anything about what he was thinking, what his motives were? Does it necessarily tell us that Devil Anse was clearly trying to make more profit than subsistence required?

Waller tells us that Devil Anse's "shift in emphasis" from farming to timbering was demonstrated by his need to purchase corn in 1873. A list of personal items charged at Smith's store also reveals Anse's interest in what might in the mountains be considered luxury items—"fancy bonnets and combs for his wife and daughters, gold watches, and 'fine' boots, frock coats, and hats for himself and his men." But Waller immediately adds a not-merely-profit-minded interpretation to all of this, theorizing that "this lavish expenditure for clothes and personal possessions indicated a concern with appearance that reflected [Devil Anse's] desire to enhance his status in the community."[22]

Can evidence like this, however, be incorporated into an analytical structure that restricts entrepreneurial thinking to only one "class" in Appalachia's and America's history? No, it cannot. But in those years after the Civil War entrepreneurial success was more and more limited to one class. About the same time that Devil Anse had to sell out, for instance, three Wheeling capitalists bought 2,000 acres for $3,000 in the Tug area. By 1892 they were able to sell 1,568 standing poplar trees on that land for $7,840.[23] Such cases were typical. Wheeling had several large national banks, and people with sufficient financial assets could borrow money there and then invest that money elsewhere in the development and marketing of assets which were inadmissible themselves as national-bank collateral.

Why didn't Devil Anse borrow money from a bank instead of obtaining merchandise on credit and borrowing money from merchants? He lived in what is now (since 1895) Mingo County. In his day it was still part of Logan County, and his affairs often took him to the county seat, the town of Logan.[24] But Logan had no bank until the Guyan Valley Bank opened in 1900.[25] As in the Deep South during the same era, banking failed to "atomize" in Appalachia after state-chartered banks lost the power to issue banknotes. Naturally-chartered banks could issue banknotes, but the minimum paid-in capital stock required to obtain a national-bank charter was $50,000—far beyond the means of most small-town banks. Furthermore, national banks had to back the banknotes they issued 111 percent in federal bonds—which made issuing currency a money-losing proposition. Branch banks, had they not been illegal, could have met some of the banking needs of small towns, but federal law did not allow national banks to operate branches, and only two Appalachian states (Virginia and Georgia) allowed state banks to do so.[26]

The point is that whatever our general theories or our analytical structures may postulate, there have been specific laws which have helped channel us into the social formations we inhabit, and knowing those laws is crucial to getting them reversed and reclaiming our birthright as free people. It will not suffice to sit on the sidelines and condemn anyone who tries to do anything by saying that they're "interfering in Appalachians' native rights." More than such opposition, more than negative action, will be required to stop strip mining. An alternative will be required. As Julian Martin said, "surely to God there must be another option."

Two other statements at the Black Gold hearing went further, sketching out what an alternative might be. First, Lynn Ernest:

> The reason I no longer live in McDowell County, where I grew up, is because it has been totally and utterly destroyed. A "responsible" company called United States Steel came in when I was a kid. My parents worked there

so that they could give me an opportunity to overcome the conditions that the coal company placed on the community.

So here I am in Lincoln County fighting for a way of life that is not the way of the coal companies. Now McDowell County is a ghost county. Ninety percent unemployment in Gary. They pulled out. They were not responsible to the community. Now they're trying to sell landed properties for a nuclear waste dump. Did you know that's what happens to the land after it has become totally raped? There's no place in the nation they want to put it, so they put it in McDowell County.

Seriously, I'm here because of quality of life, and, really, the quality of people. They appreciate cultivation. You have to cultivate things that are worthwhile and take time. You can't do it quickly. Everyone knows what the "fast buck" is all about, right? We don't want it. I'm a native West Virginian. My soul is in these mountains. My soul's in the water. And I don't want anybody to mess with it. . . .

I left McDowell County originally to escape the industrial debris, the foul air, the coal trucks, the noise, the coal dust, the destroyed roads, and the damage to community water. Now we have no community water at all in McDowell County. It's all seeped underground—but also the strip mining allows it to run off quickly.

I find it quite unpleasant to consider a derelict industrialist—such as this company [Black Gold Inc.] represents—to come into this rural farming community where the quality of life and quality of people are so fine. I regret what might happen to the air and water quality and all of those other externalities—the roads, schools.

Those things that you think you might get—forget it! It's not going to be helped. That money can go into someone else's pocket. You know—you're a West Virginian. You know the story. It's been around a long time.

The second thing that I find is the negative effect that this project will have on our community's hope of developing a tourism industry around the Mud River Dam Watershed Project. I and many others have been waiting 15 to 30 years for this to happen, and slowly working toward that. If we are to entertain the idea of offering a respite from the surrounding cities and their industrialism—Logan, Madison, Charleston—we have to maintain and protect our rural farmland, its peace and beauty.

Believe it or not, what you have sells. I've seen it. It can happen. But you've got to sit tight, and then you've got to work hard. The jobs are coming. Just wait a little longer. Don't blow it.

Most of us in this area have been waiting patiently and eagerly for the completion of this project [the Mud River Dam Watershed Project]. And we just did finally hear that it has been backed. It's going to happen.

Don't let the people of the Black Gold industry—of the "fast bucks"—come into our neighborhoods and destroy years of hope and meticulous planning, and eliminate our hopes of developing a clean industry. . . .

Be aware of what is marketed now. You have it. You're sitting on it. And watch it, because you may sell out before you find out what you have. . . .

So don't be fooled. Keep your quality of life. Keep the kind of people that this life attracts here. You're good— if only you knew how good you are. You have to see the other stuff—the slander that goes on of humanity in a mining community. It does not collect the type of people your granddaddy wants to see you around.[27]

Amenities like good schools, good roads, clean air are clearly what the woman from McDowell County envisions in her strip-mine-free alternative for Lincoln County. And another speaker at the same public hearing dealt with drawing in not mere tourists but well-to-do retirees as an alternative to strip mining. Here's Jim Chojnacki's full statement:

We Lincoln Countians must consider how our actions today will affect our future. I believe that we are being tested. Basically our choice is this: if we patiently accept our poverty of today, we will be rewarded with prosperity for our children. But if we impatiently and greedily choose prosperity for ourselves now, we will be punished by witnessing our children in poverty.

So what gives me hope for our children? It comes by simply looking at a well known social fact. In several years the largest segment of America's population will be nearing retirement age. This generation, known as the post-World War II baby boom, will go seeking quiet, secluded, safe places to spend their retirement years and their retirement money. But the Northern states are too cold, and from North Carolina southward is too crowded. The western states will be having great difficulty obtaining enough water. Agricultural states will be polluted with herbicides, pesticides, and nitrates. And industrial states are the ones these boomers will be vacating.

That leaves West Virginia, and particularly Lincoln County with its forested hollows and ridges.

This influx of new money will radically alter our county economically and socially. There is no doubt in my mind that Lincoln County will be the envy of our nation. But strip mine our county now, bring in garbage from out of state, bring in toxic industries, and sell our forests to Ohio and Japan—and we will be leaving this beautiful land locked in poverty forever.[28]

But are these people fooling themselves? Are they trying to jump out of a pot into a fire? Even if tourism and a retiree influx are viable ways to attract money, might they not prove deadly for Appalachia's culture—an embrace that kills? Wouldn't an influx of tourists and retirees in fact breed a living death, a shopping-center wasteland in the hills?

Such a view of tourists and retirees strikes me as overly pessimistic. Would anyone seriously contend that they're worse than strip mining? The value of an influx of tourists and/or retirees is that it can potentially rule out strip mining if accompanied by systematic public education. As of now we're very much on the defensive. The New River Gorge National River, which attracts half a million visitors a year, was opened to strip mining by one of the final acts of the Reagan Administration— an eleventh-hour concession to a lobby that represents holders of alleged mining claims within the National Park System.

What's actually needed isn't just a rearguard action to try to preserve New River Gorge from strip mining. What's needed is a much expanded presence of the National Park Service in southern West Virginia—an "Appalachian National Recreation and Historical

Area" of which the New River Gorge would only be one of several major units.[29] It's the history of the coalfields that could put this across—a history that's both massive and unique, including as it does the histories of labor, entrepreneurs, and ethnic groups. Quite a number of abandoned deep mines, tipples, and the like already lie within the boundaries of New River Gorge, along with the historic coaltown of Kaymoor (which the National Park Service has thought of restoring). Over the past ten years the Park Service has restored historic industrial sites elsewhere and has found the "heritage history" of labor and enterprise of great interest to the public. Americans aren't as charmed as they used to be by the same old "heritage" of 1620 and 1776. It's not only D.A.R. types but the descendants of "ethnic" immigrants who are travelling now to explore their heritage. And the coalfields are full of ethnic history because tens of thousands of families came direct from Ellis Island to the mines with no American acculturation.

Then there's coal mining itself, the most heroic of all major peaceful occupations. Recognition given late is better than recognition never given. Indeed, now that Americans are losing their power to simply command resources with the "almighty dollar," honest recognition of social contributions won't be so easy to withhold. But in the case of coal history, the recognition should come in ways that don't categorize the human spirit by one or another partisan commitment. Along with restoring some coal towns, it should be a job for the National Park Service to establish a museum in which coal's labor leaders, its entrepreneurs, and miners and their families are all given their due under one roof.

Only National Park Service auspices can create such a major new Park Area and new kind of park. To the average tourist, it's only when the Park Service says something is "major" that it then in fact is major and is considered worthy of attention. When the Park Service says that "industrial" or "heritage" history is elevated to National Importance, it thereby is elevated. We ourselves may be sufficiently informed to trust our own personal designations of such things, but most people don't have the time or resources to trust their own judgment in such matters. That's what the National Park Service is for—along with magazines like *National Geographic*.

Are Appalachian scholars willing to work out a version of coalfield history that will place the confrontational, adversarial polarization of the past in a different perspective? Stuart McGehee (who runs the Eastern Regional Coal Archives in Bluefield, W.Va.) thinks that we desperately need "a usable analytical structure."[30] But out in *Appalachian Journal*-land I think I hear a chorus of voices mumbling "usable for what?" And it sounds like the rumble of one of those monster shovels, coming this way.

NOTES

1. Don't ask me to go back and dig up E. M. Forster's essay.

2. For example, "Developer: Dispute Muddled by Communists, Drug Users," Huntington (W.Va.) *Herald-Dispatch,* 29 Feb. 1988.

3. West Virginia Department of Energy surface mine permit application number 509387. Julian Martin statement, transcribed from official W.Va. DOE tape recording of 28 June 1988.

4. The best introduction is Robert E. Friedman (president of the Corporation for Enterprise Development), *The Safety Net as Ladder: Transfer Payments and Economic Development* (Washington: Council of State Policy and Planning Agencies, 1988). The large programs underway in Great Britain and France are especially suggestive—the Enterprise Allowance Scheme in Britain and *Chomeur Createur* in France. See Friedman, pp. 20–1, 99–107. Address: The Corp. for Enterprise Development, 1725 K Street, N.W., Washington, D.C. 20006. Two of CED's recent handbooks are Sara K. Gould and Jing Lyman, *A Working Guide to Women's Self-Employment* (1987); and Alan Okagaki, *Women and Self-Sufficiency: Programs that Work, Policy that Might* (1988).

5. Dwight Billings, Kathleen Blee, and Louis Swanson, "Culture, Family, and Community in Preindustrial Appalachia," *Appalachian Journal,* 13:2 (Winter 1986), 154–70; Paul Salstrom, "To the Editor," *Appalachian Journal,* 13:4 (Summer 1986), 340–50; Dwight Billings, Kathleen Blee, and Louis Swanson, "The Authors Respond," *Appalachian Journal,* 13:4 (Summer 1986), 350–2.

6. Billings, Blee, and Swanson, "The Authors Respond," p. 351.

7. Jack E. Weller, *Yesterday's People: Life in Contemporary Appalachia* (Lexington: University of Kentucky Press, 1965).

8. Billings, Blee, and Swanson, "Culture, Family, and Community," p. 162.

9. Jonathan Hughes, *American Economic History,* expanded ed. (Glenview, Ill.: Scott, Foresman, 1987), pp. 248–9.

10. The banking act in question dates from March 3, 1865. "It passed the House by a vote of only 68 to 67, the majority of one being wholly an accident, and it passed the Senate by a majority of two votes." John M. Chapman and Ray B. Westerfield, *Branch Banking: Its Historical and Theoretical Position in America and Abroad* (New York: Harper and Brothers, 1942), p. 61. These authors add that "those regions where deposits did not circulate easily—the rural parts of the South and West—suffered for want of notes" (p. 61). The original purpose of the law was to stampede state-chartered banks into acquiring charters as national banks. As such, they would be allowed to continue issuing currency if they backed it 111 percent with federal bonds on deposit with the federal government. The underlying aim was to force banks to buy federal bonds and thereby finance the Civil War. The prohibition on state-bank currencies became one of the great grievances of the Greenback Movement, the Grangers, and the Populists. The Democratic Party called for the 1865 law's repeal at its 1892 convention, all to no avail. The "money power" had stumbled onto a good thing and wouldn't let go of it.

11. Hughes, *American Economic History,* p. 199, table 11.2. The term "currency" is used here synonymously with "cash" to mean both metallic and paper money. (Interest-bearing paper, however, is not currency.)

12. John A. James, *Money and Capital Markets in Postbellum America* (Princeton: Princeton University Press, 1978), p. 22.

13. Paul Studenski and Herman E. Krooss, *Financial History of the United States,* 2nd ed. (New York: McGraw-Hill, 1963), pp. 181–2.

14. Stuart McGehee to Paul Salstrom, Dec. 22, 1988. The Flat Top-Pocahontas coalfield was opened in the late 1880s and the 1890s. See Stuart McGehee, "Gary, A First Class Operation," *Goldenseal: West Virginia Traditional Life,* 14:3 (Fall 1988), pp. 28–32. Photos follow on pp. 33–5.

15. "First Report of the State Bank Examiner of the State of West Virginia, for the Year Ending September 30, 1891," in *Biennial Report of the Auditor of the State of West Virginia for the Years 1891 and 1892* (Charleston: Moses W. Donnalley, 1893), pp. 10, 11, 22, 23.

16. I. C. White, State Geologist, West Virginia Geological Survey, Vol. 2, *Levels Above Tide, True Meridians, Report on Coal* (Morgantown: Morgantown Post Co., 1903), pp. 714–15, including table.

17. U.S. Census of 1890, Vol. 7, pp. 356–419.

18. "First Report of the State Bank Examiner of the State of West Virginia," pp. 3–5, 45–8. The banks' cash on hand in 1891 was about 12 percent of their deposits and also about 12 percent of their loans outstanding.

19. Studenski and Krooss, *Financial History of the United States,* pp. 243–9, 254–62.

20. Altina L. Waller, *Feud: Hatfields, McCoys, and Social Change in Appalachia, 1860–1900* (Chapel Hill: University of North Carolina Press, 1988), pp. 36–45.

21. Waller, *Feud,* pp. 153–4, 163–5, 195–201.

22. Waller, *Feud,* pp. 44–5.

23. Waller, *Feud,* p. 280, n. 65.

24. Waller, *Feud,* p. 43.

25. G. T. Swain, *History of Logan County, West Virginia* (Logan: G. T. Swain, 1927), pp. 202–3.

26. James, *Money and Capital Markets in Postbellum America,* pp. 28, 90–1. Had branch banking been legal, many small towns like Logan could have acquired banking services earlier.

27. W.Va. DOE surface mine permit application number 509387. Lynn Ernest statement.

28. W.Va. DOE surface mine permit application number 509387. Jim Chojnacki statement. I regret finding no way to use in this essay's text statements at the public hearing which supported Black Gold's permit application. The longest statement was delivered by J. O. Midkiff and rambled a bit. The three other statements, however, were extremely germane. Unlike the two oppositional statements which are quoted above in the text, the statements supporting strip mining envisioned no major changes ahead in the county's economic possibilities. Indeed, Jack Roy reacted directly to the sort of hypothesizing in which Lynn Ernest and Jim Chojnacki had indulged. "And you mean to try to fool me?" he asked rhetorically, adding that "I've been around too too long" to take at face value "what you tell me you've going to do." Another speaker who supported the proposed strip mine, Michael Abshire, reflected other supporters' views when he said that "West Virginia is known for coal. It's a coal state. And if our people want jobs, they're going to have to let this company come in."

29. The best model on which to pattern a new "Appalachian National Recreation and Historical Area" is northern California's "Whiskeytown-Shasta-Trinity National Recreation Area." The three separate units of that Area are not contiguous, but they share common themes. As for the historical element, the National Park Service already administers 17 national historical parks using highly professional standards. The first large unit of this new "Appalachian" project would be New River Gorge in southern West Virginia. Smaller sites, not only in West Virginia but in southwestern Virginia and in eastern Kentucky, could be added as possible.

30. Stuart McGehee to Paul Salstrom, Dec. 22, 1988.

III. Demographic Characteristics of the Region

"Jenny's Gone Away" or "Goin' Down Cripple Creek . . ."[1]

Demography is literally the graphic description of a population. The usual headings for such descriptions include number and distribution, rural and urban mix, racial and ethnic identification, age and sex distributions, occupations, educational achievement, fertility, mortality and migration.[2] Any complete discussion of the demographic characteristics of the Appalachian Region would include all of these, with the added dimension of analysis and correlations.

The data for many of these population characteristics may be found in the United States Census of Population, several monographs, and many special reports, particularly some issued by the ARC. The factors of Appalachian populations most often discussed, however, are those of migration. This is probably true because of the high rate of out-migration from Central Appalachia experienced during the period 1950–1970. Following usual explanations, the movement was attributed to the reduced need for labor in rural and mountain industries, i.e., lumber and minerals. This migration, true to fashion, was also one dominated by the young, and by males. This high rate of exodus has been slowed, however, and the 7% increase in population noted from 1970 to 1976 can, in part, be attributed to in-migration[3]. It should be noted here that the changing definitions of the Region do effect the rates of migration as well as other demographic descriptions.[4]

Once it is established that people are leaving an area a logical question arises. Where have they gone? We include two articles which present dramatic answers to the question. In a limited, but analytically broad fashion, the answer is provided in the song, "Jenny's Gone Away"—She's gone to O-hi-o. The story of Appalachians in cities, particularly cities on the fringe of the Region, is one which is gaining increased attention. The mid-century immigrant is not Eastern European but Appalachian. For example, Mike Maloney, Executive Director of the Urban Appalachian Council (Cincinnati) has stated that there are a million Appalachians living in Ohio cities.

[1] For material on the majority who stayed, see appropriate other sections of this volume.

[2] T. Lynn Smith and Paul E. Zopf, *Demography: Principles and Methods,* (Second Edition), Port Washington: Alfred Publications, 1976.

[3] Remarks by North Carolina Governor James Hunt at Raising a New Generation in Appalachia Conference, November 1978.

[4] See the article in the section "What Is Appalachia," by Bruce Ergood for comparative state proportions of population in three periods.

They outnumber the Appalachian population in almost half of the Appalachian states' portions presently designated as Appalachia. It is ironic that none of these cities is in the area designated by the federal government as "Appalachia," hence their needs remain essentially unmet by the ARC.

We might add that a very interesting way of highlighting the variety found in the demographic characteristics throughout the region is to pick several variables, e.g., median school years completed, urban/rural mix, per capita income, infant mortality, etc., and do cross-county, cross-state comparisons. This simple exercise will quickly and quite graphically demonstrate the variety which we believe to exist in this large region of the Eastern United States.

13. LOOKING IN THE MIRROR

Jack Russell

We present below the account of another kind of 20th anniversary celebration—a trip to a long-unvisited Appalachian home by a native son. Many of the changes Jack Russell describes will strike a familiar chord for our Appalachian readers, or will seem perceptively observed, but there are things not everyone will agree with. After all, though, this is a personal account. Not all of the changes you are aware of after long absences are external changes; you return home with different eyes and ears and views.

On April 9, 1963, President Kennedy announced the formation of PARC, the federal-state committee that planned the Appalachian Regional Commission. That day I was somewhere in the South China Sea en route to Bangkok, Thailand, as a radioman with the U.S. Navy. I was completely oblivious of anything that was happening in Wythe County, Virginia, of the conditions or people I left behind, or of what was taking place in Washington, D.C. My only concern was whether or not I would be able to transmit an emergency message to the Philippines or Japan. No more Rural Retreat, no more Wytheville, no more carrying coal into the house on cold winter nights, walking with fear on eight-foot snowdrifts or building a fire around the frozen water faucet. This was not part of any grandiose plan or career strategy, but a recognition that a new chapter in my life was beginning.

Wythe County, named for the jurist and Revolutionary War General George Wythe, was organized in 1790. Wythe countians are proud of their military history, and can boast of the county militiamen's involvement in all wars—the French and Indian War, American Revolution, Civil War, World War I and World War II.

The county land area of 460 square miles lies in the Appalachian portion of Virginia. Mountains along its northern border and in the southwestern corner extending up into the central part range in altitude from 2,800 to 4,000 feet. Even the valley parts of the county have altitudes of 2,500 feet. Early settlers were sure its mountains of mineral resources, coal, lead, iron ore and copper, would ensure future development and bring wealth to the area. Jefferson National Forest embraces the mountainous northern border and the southwestern corner.

Wythe County's soil is well suited to farming. In 1960 Rural Retreat, the second largest town in the county, was known as the cabbage capital of the nation. Acre after acre of cabbage, barley, wheat and corn adorned the rolling hills and valleys. The county ranked high among Virginia's counties in cattle, calves and sheep raised and in wool produced. Sixty-two percent of the county land area was in farms. About one-third of farms were part-time or residential, run by people employed in industry or public works. Still, there were almost two times as many people employed in agriculture as in manufacturing, but fewer than in nonmanufacturing positions.

I was born in Rural Retreat, one of two incorporated towns in Wythe County, Virginia. This was home for some 20 years. As a child, I never consciously thought of leaving the area. I never realized we were poor, never thought about being black, never felt isolated, never felt inconvenienced, was never hungry but was always confident. I never recognized around me what today I would probably call deplorable conditions and low socioeconomic status. I daydreamed a lot in my special hideaway called "New Valley," and I was a great storyteller. Always, my fantasies were about going places, about travel and adventure. At times, there was concern about my behavior. My older sister often cautioned me about telling such outrageous stories.

However, there were things that happened or things I did subconsciously that illustrated a desire to leave the area and better myself. Starting around age five, with my mother's help, I entered every mail order word puzzle game or contest available to win money, vacations or other prizes. Later, I spent a great deal of time talking with and listening to the mayor of Rural Retreat, who was a friend of my employer. At first we talked about sports, but this progressed to education and political issues. I realized I was always "talked down to" and often treated abrasively, but I didn't care. Looking back, I received more from him than he from me. The denigration made me more determined to pursue whatever I wanted. Some of the mayor's anger arose because I had rearranged or rumpled the *Roanoke Times* before he had a chance to read it.

The indications of despair in the county were evident, even to the eye of an unconcerned youth such as me. There were families who were carried for years or generations by local grocers. They were always putting off "settling up" for another week. There were the illiterates who could not count money and endorsed their weekly pay checks with their "mark." Miners from the West Virginia coal fields came home to die from coal mine injuries and black lung. People of all ages died at home, but there was little interest in the causes of their

Reprinted from *Appalachia,* Vol. 18, No. 4,5 (June–July 1985), pp. 18–31.

deaths. Many homes were totally inaccessible by automobile; some were as much as a mile from a dirt road. There were no new buildings in the town except for the few new houses built each year.

There were seven members in my family, two sisters, two brothers, Mom, Dad and me. I was the youngest son. Until I was around twelve years old, I was known as a "sickly kid." No illness passed me by. On many occasions Dad carried me down the dirt road to the doctor's office one mile away; on a couple of occasions, he had to find someone with an automobile to take me to the hospital in Wytheville, 15 miles from our house. It seems to me today that we accepted with little thought the conditions that may have been partly responsible for my poor health—unpaved roads, spells of inclement weather when I had to wait for what seemed like hours for the school bus, and, probably even worse, the unsanitary living conditions as a result of no indoor plumbing and running hot water. After all, my grandparents' house and the school had even greater problems since the town's water system did not extend that far. Their water was stored in a cistern from which it was extracted by a hand pump. There was no mechanism to filter or purify the rain water as it drained from the asphalt roof.[1]

As a teenager in the mid to late 50s, I began to think more about work and money. Not in terms, for example, of an occupation or career, but more about how much I could purchase with what I earned and how much money Daddy earned and what this meant to my family. This was probably my first realization of how poor some of my relatives, friends and others in the county really were.

But earnings were not thought of as related to education. We would have said there was little, if any, relationship. To county residents education was for the wealthy. My parents, like most of the other parents in the county, insisted that I attend high school every day, but seldom was there any reference to college or technical education. The top four or five graduating seniors may have been advised in school or counseled on course selection, but for the most part students were on their own. My sister sometimes questioned me on my choice of occupation. More than any other phenomena, people accepted with fatalism the idea that education beyond high school was unlikely. Teachers, administrators, parents and students believed you could not alter the tradition of dropping out of school for work, or going to work after twelve years of school. Usually, if an older brother or sister went to college, then a younger sibling was more likely to follow. Also, the kids of doctors, lawyers and teachers would leave the area to attend college. In my case, an older sister was a college graduate; therefore, the precedent was there for me to attend college. I did, but although I was an above-average student, I had little, if any, academic preparation for a four-year college. I was denied entry to Howard University, Washington, D.C., because I had no biology courses in high school. Bluefield State College accepted me.

On the surface, the conditions were not so bad. If you were "busy" and had "Sunday shoes" to wear to church, those were the social indicators that illustrated you were at least of average wealth. I was "busy" starting at the age of 13 working for one family. First, doing odd jobs, cutting the lawn and hedges, washing windows and waxing floors. The bottom line was, if you were busy, you could not get in trouble. All of the teenagers that I knew were busy in the summer, and most of them were on Saturdays too, all year long. There was work on the farms, in the schools, stores and private homes. Although there was no formal summer jobs program, it seems that anyone who wanted work had it. Some of us also worked on family cabbage farms for wages about equal to the cost of lunch. Later, during my junior year in high school, I went to work in the grocery store owned by the family I had been working for. This no longer classified as "busy"; it was an actual job where I was paid by check.

The overall employment scene, as I saw it, was divided into five categories: teachers, "good jobs," farmers, "working for so-and-so" (usually an individual) and "sorry" people. A "good job" meant working at any state, county or city job, at the milk plant (Pet Milk Company), screw factory (American Screw Company), powder plant (Radford Army Arsenal), block company (Wytheville Block Company), mill (Debord Mill or Reed Creek Mill), plant (Air Reduction Company or New Jersey Zinc Company), railroad (Norfolk and Southern Corporation) or being an auto mechanic or retail clerk. Occupation was not so important as the stability of the employing organization. My father worked at a "good job" (Debord Mill), one of the few blacks who did. Working for "so-and-so" could mean working two or three jobs at the same time, seasonal employment or part-time employment. Like teachers, farmers and "good-job" holders, "so-and-so" work was a sign of stability. By being identified with an individual who had the ability to pay wages or own property and the need for help, you earned a certain amount of respect.

Being "sorry" had several connotations. It could mean someone who changed jobs frequently, was an alcoholic, had some type of mental disability or was illiterate. "Sorry" individuals still managed to work when they so desired. There was always someone who was willing to take a chance and hire them, sometimes for a second or third time.

I never thought about any formal hiring system, about how people were selected for jobs. I knew it was a matter of "place" or knowing your place. Certain families didn't work at some of the "good job" sites, and some others did even though they lacked experience and education or were labeled "sorry." Since there was no technical school within a 35-mile radius, on-the-job training was standard procedure; so qualifications for a job were usually irrelevant. Everyone in the labor market was pretty much equal, or at least they started out that way.

Graduation from high school meant leaving the area, going to work for the same employer as another family member, joining the military or working the family farm, in that order. Seldom was there college or unemployment for any length of time. Outmigration had a distinct pattern, based on family tradition, race and community or location of residence in the county. For example, whites in Rural Retreat migrated to North Carolina or Maryland; blacks in Rural Retreat followed family traditions: some to Ohio, others to Michigan, Washington, D.C., or New Jersey. Whites in Wytheville were more likely to stay within state boundaries while blacks migrated to Michigan, New York, New Jersey and Washington, D.C. Strangely, there was little discussion of leaving, or intent to leave the area. It just happened. You could be looking for someone and notice his or her absence and only later be informed that he or she had left. People simply disappeared.

Joining the armed forces was the "in thing" for males. Returning veterans from the Korean conflict were idolized, at least for a short time. They usually left after about six months. It was fashionable to wear combat boots and fatigues. Carrying an army bayonet on one's belt was as common as wearing a baseball cap. If there was a shortcut to escaping the area, this was it. Everyone had a relative or friend in the service, myself included.

Veterans were extremely popular, almost folk heroes. They had traveled all over the world, and done everything imaginable. Many had been to California and Germany. This was very impressive to someone like myself, even though most of them had dropped out of high school.

We were probably more creative when it came to recreation and leisure than many members of the jet set. This was not a matter of choice. Hunting was the dominant activity in the fall, and fishing in Cripple Creek or Reed Creek in the spring. In between, we constructed basketball goals out of wood pallets and barrel hoops. We cleared cow pastures for baseball (usually without knowing who owned the pasture, much less bothering to inform him). We used car hubcaps for frisbees. We made our own version of skateboards out of discarded roller skates.

New cars and trucks, especially large trucks used for transporting cabbage and iron ore, were symbols of wealth and carried a macho image. If someone purchased such a vehicle or a total stranger arrived with one, it was only a matter of hours before word rippled through the communities. The fascination went even further with some of my friends and relatives. On occasion we used to walk about one mile to U.S. Highway 11 to watch the cars go by. In the event an automobile (especially a new one) driven by someone black passed by, we cheered, hollered and waved—no doubt to the confusion of the driver.

Family activities revolved around two settings. On late summer evenings we all gathered around the front porch of my grandfather's house to hear stories of days gone by. My aunts were home from college but were still intimidated by Granddaddy, who left no doubt that he was boss, and that his intellect was exceeded by none. We kids were not allowed on the porch; so we sat on what grass there was to hear how the "world really was." Any time we got restless and wandered toward the porch, an aunt used a broom or switch to insure that we kept our distance. These evening sessions or rituals were as stimulating as any of my teenage experiences, with the banter and the sometimes argumentative tone of the discussions conveying to me that this way of life had its own frustrations.

The other important focus was church. No one missed going to church on Sunday. You were more conspicuous by your absence than your presence. Church homecomings, or "rallies," as we called them, were the social event of the year. Everyone dressed in his finest on a late summer Sunday to welcome friends, relatives and visitors to a full day of sermons, singing, fried chicken, cakes and pies. For the next two weeks the topic of conversation was how large the bills placed in the collection plate were and who was driving a new car. I always kept close scrutiny on the coalminers from West Virginia to see if they placed a $20 or $50 bill in the offering, because I was under the impression they were rich.

All forms of transportation acted like magnets to many people in the county. The largest Greyhound bus depot between Bristol and Roanoke, Virginia, was located in Wytheville. In 1965 Wytheville was served by 36 buses daily. The "bus station" as we called it, was a favorite place to "hang out," to look at strange people and to get food. Blacks kept to their room; whites congregated in the large lounge and dining area. For those of us from Rural Retreat, Greyhound was our transportation to and from Wytheville. A roundtrip ticket for the 15 miles was 75 cents.

Norfolk and Western Railway also served the county. Five or six freights came through each day. They left fertilizer, coal and grain and sometimes picked up livestock and cabbage. At least eight passenger trains stopped daily in the county, and none went by unobserved. Cars and pickup trucks parked alongside the tracks in close proximity to the train station, to watch to see who got off or who was boarding "Old 42," in the evenings and "14" in the morning or to see the people eating in the dining cars. It was a thrill to receive a wave or friendly nod from the porter.

The trains were important to me and to everyone else. They provided a glimpse of the other side of the world and illustrated to us that there were a few people who managed to get away. Other than in-state travel related to school activities, most people had not traveled more than 100 miles in any direction. Roanoke, Virginia; Beckley, West Virginia; and Winston Salem, North Carolina, were the only places I remember as destinations and places visited. I distinctly remember my first venture outside the state; it was a trip by train from Rural Retreat to Johnson City, Tennessee. I was amazed that we could get there and return in one day. I was to discover later that we had a total misrepresentation of distance outside our little world of Wythe County.

I never forgot the rolling hills, the tall trees, the long, winding roads, and the black dark of the sky at night. Now, the hills are not so high, the paved roads are straighter and seem shorter and the lights from the houses have lightened the sky.

By way of the Great Lakes; San Diego; Pusan, Korea; Danang, RVN; Hawaii and Washington, D.C., I came home to Rural Retreat: nothing special, no military uniform, driving my 12-year-old Datsun. It had been 20 years. I returned to attend my high school reunion and to attend a meeting of the local development district, the Mount Rogers Planning District Commission. Pieces of each event increased my nostalgia. More than anything, I resented the changes, good and bad, and the invasion of my memories. I've changed over the years, and I must accept the fact that everything else has.

Overall, the county has changed drastically, the residents to a lesser extent. Socioeconomic patterns and lifestyles that I remember so well are intact. People are doing basically the same things, just doing them in different places and with variations. The fascination with automobiles is still there; campers and boats for hunting and fishing are highly visible; the same family names are mentioned in conversations; and children are still following family trails to an employer.

People are more private—relatives, former close friends and acquaintances. Still friendly and always a wave from the car or a warm hello. But not so curious about strangers or "outsiders" as I remember. Neither does everyone know everyone else as we used to. At least, I thought we did. I visited my former employer, now in her early 70s. She asked the question I was to hear too frequently, "Where are you now?" I always felt my answer was unimportant, but I responded, "Washington, D.C." Actually, I live in suburban Maryland, but I felt the identification with the nation's capital might generate some interest or stimulate the conversation. It did not. I wanted to be asked about my job, my family and what I had been doing over the years. After all, I was the kid that had stocked the shelves in her store, swept the floor and listened to her stories about how her family made it through the Depression. I was now a stranger, an "outsider," but to me she was the person who bought my senior class ring as a graduation gift, and gave me expensive sweaters for Christmas.

Not wanting to know anything about me today was a common thread. Maybe it was that remembering me as I was 20 years ago made people feel more comfortable or convinced they were still superior. I drove from Wytheville to Washington County on U.S. Route 11 to attend the local development district meeting. I stopped several times to chat with persons I saw outside their homes. I knew these people. It was natural for me to stop and talk for a few minutes. Many did not recognize me, but realized immediately that I was one of Bob Russell's kids, and asked which one. The houses now look livable, warmer and friendlier. Flowers, shrubs, mulch and paved driveways cover what I remember as dirt and mud, car tires, fenders and worn-out appliances. I tried to see if there was a garden or livestock (hogs and cows to butcher), remembering how important they were to our survival and wellbeing. The gardens were there, and seemed much larger than the ones I remember. The outdoor toilets have disappeared.

I thought it a bit ironic that the houses were now heated by oil, when at one time the area was so dependent on coal, as a source both of heat and of employment.

Many of the pastures and green hills have been taken over by hordes of mobile homes. Homes so close to each other that I wondered to myself where the children play or what they could play in such a small area. At dusk it seemed that cars and homes must have been dropped from the sky. Otherwise, there was no way they could be so close. This was quite a contrast to the many renovated bungalows and almost new ramblers I saw. It may have been my imagination, but I felt there was an aura of desperation surrounding the mobile homes. The residents looked tired, harassed and unwilling to wave or speak to a stranger.

Interstates 77 and 81 now intersect a few miles north of Wytheville. With the superior highway system have come motels, hotels, fast food restaurants and industrial parks. Twelve trucking companies provide interstate and intrastate service to industry in the county.

Six of them have terminals here. Also, the distances between all points within the county and the surrounding area seem much shorter. No longer do people feel compelled to shop or bank in their own towns. I checked with the Mount Rogers Planning District Commission and found that 21 percent of all the employed people in the county commute to neighboring counties to work. As I drove around looking for familiar places, I saw signs for McDonalds, Burger Kings and "factory outlets" instead of the memorable Pepsi Cola and farm equipment billboards. Shopping centers now rested on many of the former vacant lots and cow pastures. Most of the small general stores have disappeared. Family enterprises have been taken over by more efficient and highly capitalized "chain" operations. Gone are the days of "settling up" at the end of the month or at a later date. Now there are signs for VISA and Mastercard.

I visited old fishing spots that were barely recognizable; "New Valley," my hideaway and fantasy island, is now home to several families. The section I called the "woods," where we hunted rabbits in the snow, has vanished. These were places with special memories, places I talked about and shared with friends. They were no more. I saw new water-pumping stations and waste treatment plants, and a bright orange water storage tank on the skyline looking down over the town. A beautiful fishing and boating lake took up part of a hillside once covered by corn and cabbage. The churches were the same, and the same family names are associated with the same denomination. I would be attending Mt. Olive Baptist Church if I lived in Rural Retreat.

Main Street in Wytheville is busy, but not the way it used to be. Now all the traffic is local. Leggetts Department Store is still there, but the stately George Wythe Hotel is closed, and Durhams Restaurant, famous for Virginia ham, has moved to a new location more accessible to the Interstate. As I drove past the former hotel and restaurant, I remembered that I had never sat down in either establishment.

The Greyhound bus terminal and the train station are little more than shells. As in urban areas in the north, all the new buidings are in the outlying areas. The landscaping for the new industries, the modern entrances and late model cars could be in Silicon Valley or any other suburban part of America. It was obvious that a great deal of effort, planned and otherwise, had gone into developing the northeast end of town. Along with the beautiful campus of the community college, everything new seemed to me to feed off I-81 and I-77. The industrial growth has made farming less obvious; where I used to see the huge barns and silos along U.S. 11, there are now brick houses, and trailers with satellite discs. The farms that I did see were more sterile, but larger; gone are the small and medium operations that were familiar to the area.

Wythe County is advertised as "a center for good living" in promotional brochures. The Industrial Development Authority and the Mount Rogers Private Industry Council have actively recruited new industry. Adjacent Bland County, once more identifiable with West Virginia, but now closer to Wytheville by means of Interstate 77, has realized the growth potential of its neighbor so much so that the Chamber of Commerce is the Wythe-Bland Chamber of Commerce.

Change or growth in the county is uneven. The town of Rural Retreat as I remember it has almost disappeared. The parking "flat" at midday sits empty of cars and pickups, and just about all the stores I used to frequent are gone. People's Bank, where I opened my first checking account, is now the town hall. I was somewhat taken aback when I walked into the building to find that the huge vault door was wide open, and the vault itself used to store supplies and records. Gone is the town's railroad station; no passenger trains travel through the county. And gone is Vance Hardware, from which my father purchased my first baseball glove. The drug store and landmark, some say the home of a young pharmacist later to be known as "Dr. Pepper," has moved to another location in town. Interestingly, the drug store was not previously identified as being the home of Dr. Pepper. I was under the impression a member of the Gammons family was always the pharmacist. That was the only name I knew. The name change, or identification with Dr. Pepper, took me by surprise. For some reason I never expected Rural Retreat to practice such an adept bit of commercialism.

As I drove around town and into the unincorporated area, I saw brick ramblers and trailers on the former pastures. I saw this as individual progress. The paved roads stretched out to the farms, but they were not like the farms of the past. Barns were dilapidated, silos leaning and the once beautiful white rail fences are now gray. The once cluttered parking lots of the shirt factory and milk plant were vacant. These "good jobs" have been lost to progress.

The people of Rural Retreat do not see their town as dying. Inmigration is on the upswing, and the population has doubled since I left, but outmigration still seems to be a problem. The mayor and town manager both feel that more industry would help keep "young people" in the area. Industrial sites are designated, and one large building is available for occupancy. But the lack of natural gas lines in the area is hindering recruitment efforts. For the most part, residents, especially the newcomers, unconsciously view the town as an extension of Wytheville and Marion (15 miles away in Smyth County). They do not seem to think of the town as a separate entity, subject to economic viability or nonviability. The Interstate has made them closer to jobs, entertainment, retail stores and factory outlets. Rural Retreat, like other small towns in the county, is becoming a bedroom community.

Educational opportunities continue to send mixed messages to county young people. As I asked about individual families, sons and daughters, a clear pattern emerged. Tradition is basically alive and well. Blue-collar work or "good jobs" remain the aspiration and the reality of generations of the county's people, even though the quality of education has improved drastically: the community college (many of whose facilities and equipment received financial support from ARC) offers a variety of technical and occupational courses, and a new voc ed center is available for high school students. I got the distinct impression the facilities are not being taken full advantage of. The old adage still holds true: "if it's good enough for Dad or Mom, it's good enough for me."

The sons and daughters of doctors, lawyers, teachers, managers and other professionals are the ones who attend or have graduated from college. Many return to the area and step into the family business. Others, by their family position and name, garner opportunities not available to many of the county's people. Name is still important, especially to "county and town fathers." You are viewed as thoroughbred, grade horse or a nag. On at least two occasions, I was introduced and described as coming from "good stock; this is Bob Russell's son." "I knew they would go away to school and make something of themselves." But for people like me, with no family business to return to, and not coming from one of the old families, a college degree means leaving the area unless teaching is your goal. Although I was asked several times why I didn't return to the county ("we need people like you"), I could not take the compliment seriously, because I see my "place" much differently than those who asked the question.

I admire those friends, relatives and others I know who have stayed in the area. Not surprisingly, most of the people from my youth had carried on their family traditions of stability and hard work. It was not uncommon to hear "those Johnson brothers are so talented," or "the Houston brothers are moving right up the ladder, and they have good jobs." The son of the owner of the local retail clothing store returned after dental school and is now mayor of Rural Retreat. Many others have succeeded in different fields.

But many have not and will not. With more unskilled jobs available, many young people are leaving school to join the labor force. Some of the work is seasonal and very fluid. Thus, another cycle of uneducated, unskilled people could be in incubation.

Sadly, I found that success brings opposition. In small towns, and especially in rural areas, familiarity breeds contempt. Lifelong residents still know everyone else's background, family history and "skeletons in the closet." I heard many times, "They think they are better than me because they work in Radford." Or "I remember when his daddy sold liquor, but now he thinks

he is something." I realized that some people would rather not deal with such criticism or cope with success. In fact, I was told, "I don't want a job that will make me lose my friends." Or "this might seem irrational, but I remember purposely not trying to be the best student and not wanting attention for being the highest scorer on the high school basketball team." A friend told me of being ostracized for taking a law enforcement position, to the point where he limited his involvement in community social activities. It is not easy to live in a glass house when you move from one with no indoor plumbing.

I got the impression that outmigration is not so popular as it once was. The rate has declined slightly, and I didn't pick up the age-old vibration that "the grass is

Wythe County, Virginia		
Data Summary	1960 and 1980	
	1960	1980
Total Population	21,975	25,522
White	21,014	25,541
Black	955	910
Wytheville	5,634	7,135
Rural Retreat	413	1,083
Balance of County	15,928	17,304
Outmigration at End of Decade	−4,747	2,489 *
Education:		
Percent Less than 4 Years High School	74.0	54.7
Percent 4 Years College or More	4.1	8.6
Median Family Income	$3,235	$15,004
Total Employed Persons	6,936	10,966
Agriculture:		
Number of Farms	1,245	738
Acres per Farm (Average)	147	200
Mobile Homes	54	1,366
Miles of Paved Road	247	400

*Note: Inmigration is attributed to return of Vietnam veterans and construction of Interstates 77 and 81.

always greener on the other side." At least, the impression I got was that leaving was more a family decision in 1985 than when I left the county. Several larger plants have closed: J. Freezer and Son, Pet Milk Company, Air Reduction Company and New Jersey Zinc Company, after 225 years of operation. These were the main employers for Rural Retreat, Ivanhoe and Austinsville. Several new industries are now operating in the county, mostly in Wytheville, adding hundreds of jobs. With this growth some parents do not see a future in "plants" for their children.

The military is still seen as the most viable option. Just as in the days when I was growing up, the uniform is worn with honor and pride. Volunteer service is not restricted to high school graduates; after college, those not wanting to move to another city or state go home to the military. As I was standing outside the county courthouse, a low-flying jet came booming over the mountain. Someone said, "That's so-and-so's son." They knew his outfit, type of airplane and more. People can tell you more specifics about countians in the military (rank, insignia, mission of various bases and units) than the Pentagon itself could.

My return could have been taken from the script of a 1940s movie. I was speaking at the first reunion of my high school, and would attend a meeting with some of the "movers and shakers" of southwest Virginia. I was equally nervous about both. Jackie Russell, me, going home and not to a funeral. I was introduced at the meeting as a local "boy" that went to Washington, D.C., and got a "good job." I received bear hugs and pats on the back. I was on cloud nine, as I received almost as much attention as the U.S. Congressman who spoke at the meeting. The accolades made me feel important for a short time.

Standing before my former schoolmates, former teachers, and the mayor of Wytheville, I felt very humble, and I told my audience this. Apprehensive at the beginning of my speech, I wanted to let them know that I had not changed as a person and that my fondest memories were those we shared.

However, some of the memories were not fond. Those of us from Rural Retreat were the original "cabbage patch" kids. How we resented being called "cabbage" by other students when we transferred from our elementary school to high school in Wytheville! But now I could only see the beauty and warmth in each face I remembered from the past. I spoke for about 20 minutes on the innocence of our youth, our simple satisfactions, our strengths. I pointed out that we had all had an equally good chance to fail. But—although perhaps momentarily for a few of us—we all seemed to

ARC Investment in Wythe County
1966–84

Wythe County

Year	Project	ARC Funds	Total Funds
1966	Wythe County Public Fishing Lake	$ 19,800	$ 66,000
1967	Wythe County Vocational Education School	611,000	940,000
1969	Wythe County Community Hospital	490,172	2,470,256
1969	Wythe County Vocational Education School Overrun	40,000	100,000
1970	Wythe County Community Hospital Overrun	100,000	610,963
1971	Stoney Fork Recreation Access Road	280,000	400,000
1972	Health Center	45,889	206,705
1974	Health Center	25,428	114,540
1976	Wythe County Vocational School Equipment	28,760	40,000
1977	Wythe County Vocational Center Addition	228,642	318,000
1977	Ivanhoe Water System Expansion	203,110	800,000
1978	Wythe County Vocational School Addition	34,776	48,980
1978	Rural Retreat Waterworks Improvement	76,900	677,600
1981	Wytherville Elderly Housing	200,000	$3,449,687
1983	Wythe Housing Opportunity Project	60,000	800,000
1983	Wytheville Water Improvements	500,000	3,403,400
Total		**$2,944,477**	**$14,446,131**

take pride in our small town, our rural heritage and the sacrifices we had made. A period of reflection was good. Most of us felt good about ourselves and home.

As I was leaving, someone I remembered from school as being from an equally poor background but known for the middle-class attitudes she had adopted, approached me. She said, "You are not what I had in mind as a speaker for this occasion, and further I don't remember living in a similar fashion to your family." I did not respond to the comment. Perceptions change over the years, and we sometimes want to forget. I remembered Thomas Wolfe's comment that "there is

nothing in the world that will take the chips off of one's shoulder like a feeling of success." And I remember vividly the exact location of the outdoor toilet of my friend's family.

I've thought about how my children would cope with the rugged lifestyle and inconveniences we lived with every day 20 years ago. My answer is—just think about how much more my son knows and has seen today at age 7 than I knew or had seen at age 16. My conclusion is that for me and many more "ignorance was bliss." We didn't complain; we knew no other way. We asked for nothing because we knew not what to ask for.

Wythe and Carroll Counties

1979	Ivanhoe Industrial Site Expansion	$ 21,300	$ 60,000

Wythe and Grayson Counties

1971	Wythe-Grayson Regional Library	$ 95,814	$ 228,233
1978	Wythe-Grayson Regional Library Equipment	42,185	59,500
Total		**$ 137,999**	**$ 287,733**

Multicounty (Bland, Carroll, Grayson, Smyth, Wythe and Galax Counties): Wytheville Community College

1969	Building Construction	$ 242,855	$ 971,425
1971	Vocational Education Equipment	35,725	50,000
1972	Nursing Building Construction	51,725	321,489
1972	Vocational Education Equipment	35,265	49,322
1974	Vocational Education Equipment	54,735	76,000
1975	Vocational Education Equipment	21,105	30,116
1976	Vocational Education Equipment	44,851	64,000
1977	Vocational Education Equipment	32,511	45,920
1978	Demonstration Program	2,500	5,000
1978	Vocational Education Equipment	156,662	217,980
1980	Vocational Education Equipment	208,623	290,278
1980	Vocational Education Equipment	109,677	152,605
1981	Vocational Education Equipment	87,227	121,367
1982	Vocational Education Equipment	1,000,000	2,834,996
Total		**$2,083,461**	**$ 5,230,498**
Grand Total		**$5,187,237**	**$20,024,362**

14. APPALACHIA'S DECADE OF CHANGE A DECADE OF INMIGRATION

Jerome Pickard

For the first time in many decades, there was sustained inmigration into the Appalachian Region in the 1970s—an inmigration that accounted for 53 percent of the total Appalachian population gain for the decade. This decade was described in the July–August 1981 issue of *Appalachia* as a "decade of change" since a population growth of 2 million persons occurred in the Region in contrast to the previous decade's growth of not quite half a million. The change was due much more to a change in the Region's migration flow than to a change in birth and death rates.

The number of people migrating into the Region for the ten-year period from 1970 to 1980 was 1,074,000, almost as many as had left during the outmigration of the 1960s. In contrast, the Region's rate of natural increase (excess of births over deaths) plummeted during these ten years, as the nation's did; for the decade, the Appalachian natural increase rate was just over 5 percent, only about three-fourths the U.S. average of 7 percent (see Table 14.1). The average birth rate in Appalachia for the decade was 14.8 per 1,000, only 95 percent of the national rate, while the death rate, 9.9 per 1,000, was 110 percent of the U.S. average. As a result, natural increase added only 47 percent of the total Appalachian population gain in the ten-year period, in contrast to the 60 percent that it added to the national gain.

Where Inmigration Occurred

In exactly what parts of the Region did this enormous change in net migration (a swing of over 2 million, from a loss of a million in the 60s to a gain of a million in the 70s) take place?

Appalachia is more rural, less metropolitan and less urban in its population settlement and development patterns than the nation. For several decades prior to 1970, like many predominantly rural regions of the nation, Appalachia had lost population. The Appalachian outflow was relatively large and prolonged, took place over relatively short distances and went predominantly to nearby metropolitan areas outside the Region in the northeastern, north central, and southeastern United States. This shift reflected the national rural-to-urban migration and the attraction of metropolitan areas.

During the 1970s, a new migration pattern developed. People left the larger metropolitan areas and northern areas for less densely populated areas, and predominantly for southern and western areas. The Appalachian Region has also reflected this shift, and very strongly. A large reverse migration into the Region came from many of the areas of earlier attraction, and in addition new population moved into the Region. Nearly all of the net inflow occurred in the southern two-thirds of the Region, south of a line through Appalachian Ohio and West Virginia. This inmigration was at a relatively high rate (13.5 percent into Southern Appalachia and 15.5 percent into Central Appalachia).

In addition to these regional shifts, there were also very important and large-scale local area migrations, with population moving out from older, more congested communities into nearby areas with smaller centers or into rural counties. Within a large number of Appalachian counties, it was not the principal city or cities that showed large population gains, but the fringe around these cities.

Net Appalachian migration in the 1970s flowed into the rural counties, urban counties (containing important smaller centers) and the smaller metropolitan areas, as contrasted with the medium-sized and large metropolises, some of which had net outmigration. It also flowed to the southern areas of Appalachia rather than the northern areas, which, at the beginning of the decade, had a larger proportion of metropolitan and urban population.

The lowest share of net migration in total population growth was in Northern Appalachia (see Table 14.2), and, among county groups, in the major metropolitan counties (Northern Appalachian major metropolitan counties actually experienced net *out*migration). The highest share and most rapid rate of inmigration was found in the peripheral metropolitan counties—the diffusion outward from the core counties was large. Rural Appalachian counties had the largest share and the largest number and rate of inmigration; this was true in all three subregions. The urban counties (which contained the more important submetropolitan centers) had migration and natural increase shares most similar to the Region's.

Of the 69 local development districts, the southern districts generally had the highest rates of net migration over the decade (see Table 14.3), with the Atlanta Region showing the greatest rate of increase (99.2 percent). More northern districts had relatively low rates

Reprinted from *Appalachia,* Vol. 15, No. 1 (Sept–Oct, 1981), pp. 24–28.

Components of Population Change
Appalachian Region and United States
1970-80 and 1960-70

Growth Component	Appalachian Region		United States	
	1970-80	1960-70	1970-80	1960-70
Natural Increase	5.2%	9.0%	6.9%	11.6%
Net Migration	5.9	−6.2	4.5	1.8
Total Change	**11.1%**	**2.8%**	**11.4%**	**13.4%**

TABLE 14.2

Components of Population Change
Appalachian Region and Subregions
1970-80

Geographical Division	Population		Population Change		1970-80 Components of Population Change			
	April 1, 1980	April 1, 1970	1970-80	Percent	Natural Increase	Net Migration	Natural Increase, Percent	Migration, Percent
Appalachian Region	20,234,335	18,216,957	2,017,378	11.07%	943,046	1,074,332	5.18%	5.90%
Northern Appalachia	10,123,604	9,734,022	389,582	4.00	328,543	61,039	3.37	0.63
Central Appalachia	2,114,947	1,744,891	370,056	21.21	133,600	236,456	7.66	13.55
Southern Appalachia	7,995,784	6,738,044	1,257,740	18.67	480,903	776,837	7.14	11.53

Source: Tabulations from 1970 Census of Population (with revisions); and 1980 Census of Population, *Advanced Reports* (PHC-80V series), state bulletins, by ARC staff and data systems. Natural increase calculated from county vital statistics data for the years 1970 through 1979 from state vital statistics reports and tables excepting for Mississippi 1979 data which were estimated from provisional state totals and previous years. Net migration is computed by difference, and is only approximate within the accuracy of Census enumerations and vital statistics.

of increase due to migration, with several Pennsylvania and New York districts experiencing outmigration for the decade.

Net migration was greater than natural increase in Northern Appalachia only for its rural counties; in Central Appalachia, both urban and rural counties had greater net migration than natural growth, while in Southern Appalachia all groups had greater inmigration. Thus, the amount and intensity of net inmigration in the Appalachian Region increased sharply toward the southern two-thirds of the Region, and also in the direction of the rural and urban counties.

The Appalachian Region contains 30 entire metropolitan areas and bordering parts of 10 others (1980 definition), with a total Census population of 10,564,400. The average net inmigration rate for these 40 areas was 3.05 percent, just over half the regional average. Only in Southern Appalachia was the inmigration rate into metropolitan areas above the Region's average. Northern Appalachian metropolitan areas had a total outmigration of 147,700 for the decade. The rate of natural increase in the metropolitan areas of Appalachia was also below that in urban and rural counties in all subregions. As a result of slower population growth, metropolitan Appalachia's share of the Region's population total fell from 53.9 percent in 1970 to 52.2 percent in 1980—a reversal of what had happened from 1960 to 1970. The urban counties of 1980 increased their share slightly from 24.3 to 24.6 percent of regional population, while rural counties made the greatest relative gain, from 21.8 to 23.2 percent of regional population over the decade of the 1970s.

TABLE 14.3
Components of Population Change in Appalachia
1970-80
By State and Local Development District

LDD Code	State and Local Development District	Population		Population Change		1970-80 Components of Population Change			
		April 1, 1980	April 1, 1970	1970-80	Percent	Natural Change	Net Migration	Natural Change, Percent	Migration, Percent
	United States	**226,504,825**	**203,302,031**	**23,202,794**	**11.41%**	**13,967,000#**	**9,236,000#**	**6.87%**	**4.54%**
	Appalachian Region	**20,234,335**	**18,216,957**	**2,017,378**	**11.07%**	**943,046**	**1,074,332**	**5.18%**	**5.90%**
	Alabama	**2,427,024**	**2,137,404**	**289,620**	**13.55%**	**150,085**	**139,535**	**7.02%**	**6.53%**
1A	NW Alabama	215,367	182,118	33,249	18.26	11,108	22,141	6.10	12.16
1B	North Central Alabama	182,043	157,032	25,011	15.93	13,043	11,968	8.31	7.62
1C	Top of Alabama	413,658	363,633	50,025	13.76	30,403	19,622	8.36	5.40
*1D	West Alabama	209,939	180,754	29,185	16.15	13,606	15,579	7.53	8.62
1E	Birmingham	914,431	819,263	95,168	11.62	51,074	44,094	6.23	5.38
1F	East Alabama	448,196	400,943	47,253	11.79	27,944	19,309	6.97	4.82
*1H	Central Alabama	43,390	33,661	9,729	28.90	2,907	6,822	8.64	20.27
	Georgia	**1,103,941**	**813,844**	**290,097**	**35.64%**	**81,634**	**208,463**	**10.03%**	**25.61%**
2A	Coosa Valley	355,115	302,739	52,376	17.30	24,089	28,287	7.96	9.34
2B	Georgia Mountains	225,427	176,784	48,643	27.51	13,812	34,831	7.81	19.70
*2C	Chattahoochee-Flint	62,866	50,758	12,108	23.85	4,913	7,195	9.68	14.17
*2D	Atlanta Regional	221,476	101,008	120,468	119.26	20,265	100,203	20.06	99.20
*2E	Northeast Georgia	64,383	51,469	12,914	25.09	4,082	8,832	7.93	17.16
2F	North Georgia	174,674	131,086	43,588	33.25	14,473	29,115	11.04	22.21
	Kentucky	**1,077,095**	**876,501**	**200,594**	**22.88%**	**72,256**	**128,338**	**8.24%**	**14.64%**
*3A	Buffalo Trace	26,868	23,721	3,147	13.27	1,300	1,847	5.48	7.79
3B	FIVCO	140,734	122,077	18,657	15.28	7,837	10,820	6.42	8.86
*3C	Bluegrass	137,176	113,396	23,780	20.97	8,627	15,153	7.61	13.36
3D	Gateway	66,340	55,678	10,662	19.15	4,287	6,375	7.70	11.45
3E	Big Sandy	181,759	134,307	47,452	35.33	15,468	31,984	11.52	23.81
*3F	Lake Cumberland	149,871	123,933	25,938	20.93	6,368	19,570	5.14	15.79
3H	Cumberland Valley	227,557	184,502	43,055	23.34	15,771	27,284	8.55	14.79
3I	Kentucky River	134,437	107,245	27,192	25.36	12,224	14,968	11.40	13.96
*3J	Barren River	12,353	11,642	711	6.11	373	338	3.20	2.90
	Maryland	**220,132**	**209,349**	**10,783**	**5.15%**	**6,319**	**4,464**	**3.02%**	**2.13%**
4A	Tri-County	220,132	209,349	10,783	5.15	6,319	4,464	3.02	2.13
	Mississippi	**482,712**	**418,644**	**64,068**	**15.30%**	**34,834†**	**29,234†**	**†8.32%**	**6.98%**
5A	Northeast Mississippi	131,683	109,636	22,047	20.11	7,727	14,320	7.05	13.06
*5B	Three Rivers	174,495	150,302	24,193	16.10	11,802	12,391	7.85	8.24
5C	Golden Triangle	166,386	148,473	17,913	12.06	14,685	3,228	9.89	2.17
*5D	East Central Mississippi	10,148	10,233	−85	−0.83	620	−705	6.06	−6.89
	New York	**1,083,266**	**1,056,552**	**26,714**	**2.53%**	**46,081**	**−19,367**	**4.36%**	**−1.83%**
6A	Southern Tier West	284,364	275,429	8,935	3.24	11,712	−2,777	4.25	−1.01
6B	Southern Tier Central	214,477	217,820	−3,343	−1.53	9,921	−13,264	4.55	−6.09
6C	Southern Tier East	584,425	563,303	21,122	3.75	24,448	−3,326	4.34	−0.59
	North Carolina	**1,217,723**	**1,038,956**	**178,767**	**17.21%**	**58,527**	**120,240**	**5.63%**	**11.57%**
7A	Southwestern North Carolina	135,536	115,998	19,538	16.84	5,056	14,482	4.36	12.48
7B	Land-of-Sky	259,758	223,576	36,182	16.18	7,891	28,291	3.53	12.65
*7C	Isothermal	101,906	89,720	12,186	13.58	5,083	7,103	5.66	7.92
7D	Region D	166,018	139,364	26,654	19.13	8,136	18,518	5.84	13.29
*7E	Western Piedmont	165,249	136,529	28,720	21.04	11,763	16,957	8.62	12.42
7-I	Northwest North Carolina	389,256	333,769	55,487	16.62	20,598	34,889	6.17	10.45

Eleven metropolitan areas within Northern Appalachia experienced a total outmigration of 187,200 in the decade of the 1970s. The Pittsburgh metropolitan area accounted for the lion's share of this (137,500), while the ten other areas had only 49,700 net outmigration. The southernmost of the eleven areas was the Charleston, West Virginia, metropolitan area.

The peripheral parts of ten metropolitan areas located just within the Region's borders had rapid population growth—the median rate was 18.4 percent net inmigration, with the range from 79.2 percent in the five-county metropolitan Atlanta fringe to 5.3 percent in Carbon County, Pennsylvania (part of the Allentown-Bethlehem-Easton metropolitan area). None of the 16 counties in these ten areas had net outmigration over the decade.

TABLE 14.3 (cont.)

Components of Population Change in Appalachia
1970-80
By State and Local Development District

LDD Code	State and Local Development District	Population		Population Change		1970-80 Components of Population Change			
		April 1, 1980	April 1, 1970	1970-80	Percent	Natural Increase	Net Migration	Natural Increase, Percent	Migration, Percent
	Ohio	**1,262,558**	**1,129,855**	**132,703**	**11.74%**	**64,239**	**68,464**	**5.68%**	**6.06%**
8A	Ohio Valley	526,682	445,937	80,745	18.11	31,579	49,166	7.08	11.03
8B	Buckeye Hills-Hocking Valley	242,575	219,004	23,571	10.76	11,491	12,080	5.25	5.52
8C	Ohio Mid-Eastern	493,301	464,914	28,387	6.10	21,169	7,218	4.55	1.55
	Pennsylvania	**5,995,097**	**5,930,522**	**64,575**	**1.09%**	**144,066**	**−79,491**	**2.43%**	**−1.34%**
9A	Northwest Pennsylvania	764,425	732,970	31,455	4.29	35,244	−3,789	4.81	−0.52
9B	North Central Pennsylvania	245,254	231,490	13,764	5.94	9,360	4,404	4.04	1.90
9C	Northern Tier	174,550	157,040	17,510	11.15	9,595	7,915	6.11	5.04
9D	Northeastern Pennsylvania	907,819	873,943	33,876	3.88	−5,258	39,134	−0.60	4.48
9E	Southwestern Pennsylvania	2,782,605	2,875,101	−92,496	−3.22	54,103	−146,599	1.88	−5.10
9F	Southern Alleghenies	503,006	490,415	12,591	2.57	16,401	−3,810	3.34	−0.78
*9G	SEDA-COG	617,438	569,563	47,875	8.40	24,621	23,254	4.32	4.08
	South Carolina	**791,587**	**656,325**	**135,262**	**20.61%**	**53,266**	**81,996**	**8.12%**	**12.49%**
10A	SCACOG	791,587	656,325	135,262	20.61	53,266	81,996	8.12	12.49
	Tennessee	**2,073,647**	**1,734,503**	**339,144**	**19.55%**	**111,543**	**227,601**	**6.43%**	**13.12%**
11A	Upper Cumberland	241,516	193,719	47,797	24.67	9,579	38,218	4.94	19.73
11B	East Tennessee	845,039	700,985	144,054	20.55	42,943	101,111	6.13	14.42
11C	First Tennessee-Virginia	418,079	359,441	58,638	16.31	22,080	36,558	6.14	10.17
*11D	South Central Tennessee	70,294	59,861	10,433	17.43	3,762	6,671	6.28	11.14
11E	Southeast Tennessee	498,719	420,497	78,222	18.60	33,179	45,043	7.89	10.71
	Virginia	**549,909**	**470,265**	**79,644**	**16.94%**	**25,539**	**54,105**	**5.43%**	**11.51%**
12A	LENOWISCO	99,644	84,816	14,828	17.48	4,881	9,947	5.75	11.73
12B	Cumberland Plateau	140,067	112,497	27,570	24.51	10,547	17,023	9.38	15.13
12C	Mount Rogers	181,139	159,412	21,727	13.63	5,874	15,853	3.68	9.94
*12D	New River Valley	64,602	56,080	8,522	15.20	2,774	5,748	4.95	10.25
*12E	Fifth District	55,660	49,739	5,921	11.90	1,488	4,433	2.99	8.91
*12F	Central Shenandoah	8,797	7,721	1,076	13.94	−25	1,101	−0.32	14.26
	West Virginia	**1,949,644**	**1,744,237**	**205,407**	**11.78%**	**94,657**	**110,750**	**5.43%**	**6.35%**
13A	Region 1	275,403	238,532	36,871	15.46	17,147	19,724	7.19	8.27
13B	Region 2	291,591	266,766	24,825	9.31	18,165	6,660	6.81	2.50
13C	B-C-K-P (Region 3)	311,307	291,588	19,719	6.76	17,229	2,490	5.91	0.85
13D	Gauley	145,818	122,653	23,165	18.89	5,570	17,595	4.54	14.35
13E	Mid-Ohio Valley	179,564	160,380	19,184	11.96	8,522	10,662	5.31	6.65
13F	Region 6	273,000	243,820	29,180	11.97	10,037	19,143	4.12	7.85
13G	Region 7	118,516	103,460	15,056	14.55	3,883	11,173	3.75	10.80
13H	Region 8	70,251	59,312	10,939	18.44	2,981	7,958	5.02	13.42
13I	Eastern Panhandle	87,788	66,183	21,605	32.64	3,840	17,765	5.80	26.84
13J	Bel-O-Mar	124,871	121,351	3,520	2.90	3,625	−105	2.99	−0.09
13K	B-H-J (Region 11)	71,535	70,192	1,343	1.91	3,658	−2,315	5.21	−3.30

#U.S. totals for components are preliminary and approximate.

*Data are only for the portion of the local development district included in the Appalachian Region.

†Mississippi vital statistics estimated for 1979: deaths from provisional state totals and county trends from preceding years; births from 1979 provisional county data.

**Includes Perry County, Pennsylvania.

Source: See Table 2.

15. COMPARING APPALACHIA'S COUNTIES WITH THE NATION'S

In the years between 1965 and 1980, Appalachia made dramatic strides toward the goal of economic parity with the rest of the nation. Data from a recent Appalachian Regional Commission study indicate that since 1980 Appalachia, as well as other parts of the nation, has been undergoing stressful economic changes and geographic realignments that defy simple Sun Belt/Frost Belt characterizations. The Region has suffered a downturn in its economy since 1980, but it entered 1980 with a sounder economic base and a more diversified economy than it had ever had before.

PROGRESS INTO THE 1980S

When the Commission was established in 1965, a major goal was to connect Appalachia with the more prosperous and highly developed regions on either side of it through a highway system that would link isolated areas of Appalachia to national markets. By 1980 about 1,700 miles of that 3.033-mile highway system were completed or were being constructed through some of the roughest terrain in the nation. A 1981 ARC survey of the 13 Appalachian states and the 69 local development districts established that 801 manufacturing plants with 50 or more employees had located within 30 minutes of the Appalachian corridors. These manufacturing plants added 182,700 jobs to the Region, along with an estimated 32,300 jobs in smaller plants, for a total of 215,000 jobs.

Per capita income had moved up from 78 percent of the national average in 1965 to 82.5 percent in 1980.

The proportion of Appalachian people living in poverty had been cut in half and was approaching the national average.

Health care was within a 30-minute drive of residents of all but about 66 of Appalachia's 397 counties, infant mortality was reduced regionwide from 27.9 deaths per 1,000 live births in 1963 to 11.4 in 1982 and the ration of active nonfederal physicians per 100,000 grew from 90.8 in 1967 to 131.2 in 1981. Nearly 5,000 new physicians opened practices in Appalachia between 1978 and 1982.

The proportion of Appalachians 25 and over with a high school education or more rose from 56 percent of the national average in 1960 to 86.4 percent in 1980.

Outmigration reversed to inmigration in the 1970s, and the Region found itself being an importer of people for the first time since before 1950.

APPALACHIA'S ECONOMY IN THE EARLY 1980S

Shocks to the national and international economies in the first half of the 1980s were reflected even more strongly in the Region's economy.

The 1981 to 1983 recession in particular hit Appalachia more severely than the nation as a whole, due to a heavy concentration of coal-mining and manufacturing industries in the Region, on the one hand, and a smaller service and trade economy (associated with a less urban economy) in the Region, on the other hand.

The Region has more than its proportionate share of the industries which have been experiencing a relative decline in the United States for many years. Such industries found it harder than most to recover their former employment levels after the recessions of the mid 1970s and early 1980s ended.

The high international value of the dollar encouraged imports and adversely affected Appalachian exports of primary and fabricated metals, wood products, chemicals, textiles and apparel, glass products and coal.

From 1982 to 1984, high interest rates, combined with low levels of manufacturing activity and excess plant capacity, retarded investments in plants and equipment and sharply lowered the rate of new construction in many parts of the Region.

THE REGION'S ECONOMY BY 1984–85

Appalachia's unprecedented rate of economic growth during the 1970s slowed in the early 1980s, and the Region's economy began to shrink in relationship to the nation's economy.

Employment

By April 1985 the Region had 7.8 percent of the nation's employment compared with 8.3 percent in 1980. The gain in employment for the Region between April 1980 and April 1985 was almost nil (52,000), compared with a 7.7 percent gain (7,606,000) in the United States.

Labor Force

The Region made up 8.0 percent of the domestic civilian labor force in 1984, compared with 8.3 percent in 1980. The labor force grew 1.9 percent (173,000) in

The following people contributed to this research analysis: Joseph Cerniglia, Robert Decker, Kathleen Gujral, Salim Kublawi, Judith Maher, Monroe Newman, Jerome Pickard.

Reprinted from *Appalachia*, Vol. 19, no. 2–4 (Spring, 1986), pp. 8–15.

Appalachia, compared with 6.2 percent (6,604,000) in the nation between 1980 and 1984; if Appalachia had grown at the U.S. rate, its labor force would have increased by 552,000 (more than three times the actual growth).

Per Capita Income

In 1983 the Region's per capita income was 81.2 percent of the nation's per capita income, compared with 82.5 percent in 1980. Per capita income climbed 21 percent ($7,836 to $9,485) in Appalachia, compared with 23 percent ($9,494 to $11,667) in the nation between 1980 and 1983.

Population

In 1984, the Region had 11.8 percent of the nation's unemployed, compared with 9.9 percent in 1980. Unemployment began to increase faster in the Region than in the nation in 1979 and was still two percentage points higher than the national rate of 7.3 percent in June 1985.

Population

In 1984 the Region had 8.7 percent of the U.S. population, compared with 8.9 percent in 1980. Population increased 1.7 percent (337,000) in Appalachia between 1980 and 1984, compared with a 4.2 percent increase (9,612,000) in the nation.

Although Appalachia grew in absolute numbers, the Region clearly began to lose ground relative to the nation between 1980 and 1985. Aware of the effects national and international events were having on the Appalachian economy, the ARC staff expanded its ongoing analysis beyond the regional level to a nationwide county analysis to see how all U.S. counties were changing and where Appalachia's counties ranked in the nation.

ECONOMIC CHANGES IN THE NATION'S COUNTIES

The ARC staff developed an index to analyze the economic performance of the nation's counties between 1960 and the mid 1980s. Four factors—population, income, unemployment and urbanization—were chosen to measure different aspects of economic change. The factors are sufficiently differentiated that they do not provide multiple measures of the same aspects of economic change. Two of the factors—population and income—were divided into separate indicators measuring level and change over time. (See the box insert on methodology on page 132.)

Each of the factors was ranked and scored, and the scores were added to obtain a combined score for each of the 3,087 counties in the nation. Next, the counties were ranked by combined score from highest to lowest. The counties were then divided into five equal parts, or quintiles. The quintiles were assigned a number from one (highest) to five (lowest).

The ranking, from 1960 to the present, gives a picture of Appalachian counties compared with the nation's counties. Information for 1970, 1980 and the mid 1980s has been completed. The 1960 data will be compiled this summer.

Distribution of Counties in the Highest and Lowest Quintiles

The most visible changes occurred in an area running from both sides of the Great Lakes south to New Orleans, where a wedge of counties is shown to be performing poorly in the mid 1980s. This wedge contains 776 counties in the two lowest quintiles, 241 counties in the middle quintile, 209 counties in the second quintile and only 132 counties in the first or highest quintile.

The majority of counties in the Great Lakes area had been in the first and second quintiles in the 1970 period. By the mid 1980s, a large concentration of counties in the Great Lakes area had shifted to the lowest two quintiles. In 1970, Ohio, Michigan, Indiana, Illinois and Wisconsin had 229 counties in the first and second quintiles. By the mid 1980s the number of counties in these states in the top two quintiles had dropped by more than 50 percent, to 110 counties. At the bottom of the economic profile, this area had 135 counties in the two lowest quintiles in 1970, but by the mid 1980s, 259 counties ranked in the two lowest quintiles.

The Great Lakes area was one of five economically well-off areas in the nation in the 1970s, but it had lost this position by the mid 1980s. There were still five concentrations of counties in the nation ranking in the top two quintiles, but one was a new concentration encompassing Nebraska, Kansas, Oklahoma and Texas. These four states had 182 counties in the two lowest quintiles in 1970. By the mid 1980s, these states had only 88 counties in the two lowest-ranking quintiles. These same states had 209 counties in the first and second quintiles in 1970. The number increased to 315 by the mid 1980s.

Four clusters of counties in the first and second quintiles can be distinguished in both 1970 and mid 1980s. One is in California, stretching from Sacramento in the northern part of the state, south to San Diego. Another is around Atlanta, Georgia; it included 15 counties by the mid 1980s. A third encompasses the coastal counties of Florida. The fourth includes the eastern seaboard megalopolis, stretching from Maine in the north to Richmond, Virginia, in the south. Almost 85 percent of the counties in this area are metropolitan counties.

South of Richmond, the Piedmont area in North and South Carolina is beginning by the mid 1980s to link the Richmond, Virginia, part of the eastern seaboard megalopolis to the Atlanta area. Only a single tier of counties in northeast Georgia forms a small gap between Maine and Atlanta.

Upward and Downward Shifts of Counties among Quintiles

Another way to examine the changes is to look for downward and upward shifts in counties. Only 2,470 counties could shift downward (a county in the lowest quintile could not go any lower), and only 2,470 counties (those in the second, third, fourth and fifth quintiles) could shift upward.

A little over a third of the counties that could shift downward or upward did actually shift: 842 out of 2,470 shifted downward, and 850 out of 2,470 shifted upward. Most of these shifts, however, involved too small a difference in score to be significant. For this analysis, a shift was considered significant if it involved a shift from one quintile to another. There is an exception: a shift from quintile two to quintile three, or from quintile three to quintile four, or the reverse, was not considered significant because the total range of scores in quintiles two, three and four combined is not so large as the range of scores *within* quintile one or *within* quintile five.

This analysis reveals that many counties in some southwestern and western states are shifting upward while many counties in midwestern and eastern states are shifting downward.

Downward Shifts. Of the 2,740 counties that could have shifted downward by the mid 1980s, 842 did shift downward, and 543 (22 percent) had a significant downward shift. As Table 15.1 shows, most of them were in the Midwest and a bordering group of Appalachian states. These counties make up the wedge of poorly performing counties.

Of the 543 counties shifting significantly downward, 275 were in eight midwestern states: Iowa, Illinois, Ohio, Indiana, Wisconsin, Michigan, Missouri and Minnesota. These eight states had 620 counties in the top four quintiles in 1970, so that nearly one-half, that is, 275 out of 620 counties, had a significant shift downward by the mid 1980s.

The next largest group of the 543 significantly downward-shifting counties appeared in six contiguous states, including Pennsylvania, West Virginia, Kentucky, Tennessee, Alabama and Mississippi. These six states had 338 counties in the top four quintiles in 1970. By the mid 1980s, 115 counties (34 percent) had shifted downward significantly.

There were 27 other states in the nation with a total of 153 significantly downward-shifting counties. They were widely scattered throughout the United States from Hawaii, Arizona, Nevada and Idaho in the west to Maine and northern Florida in the east. In these 27 states, only 10 percent of the counties that could have shifted downward significantly did so.

Upward Shifts. There were 2,470 counties in the second, third, fourth and fifth quintiles that could move upward by the mid 1980s. The largest concentration of counties that shifted upward significantly was located in 11 western and south central states: Arkansas, Louisiana, Oklahoma, Texas, New Mexico, Colorado, Utah, Wyoming, California, Oregon and Washington. Nevada and Idaho are excluded from this geographic concentration because their significantly downward-shifting counties outnumbered their significantly upward-shifting counties.

TABLE 15.1

Counties in the United States That Shifted Downward Significantly between 1970 and Mid 1980s

Area	No. of States	Total No. of Counties in Quintiles 1 through 4	Counties with Significant Downward Shift	
			No.	Percent
Midwest	8	620	275	44%
Alabama, Kentucky, Mississippi, Pennsylvania, Tennessee, West Virginia	6	338	115	34
Remainder of United States	27	1,512	153	10
United States	51 *	2,470	543	22%

*Nine states and the District of Columbia (counted in this total as a state) had no downward-shifting counties.

TABLE 15.2

Counties in Appalachia and the United States That Shifted Downward Significantly between 1970 and Mid 1980s

Area	No. of States	Total No. of Counties in Quintiles 1 through 4	Counties with Significant Downward Shift	
			No.	Percent
Appalachian Region	13*	281	84	30%
United States	51**	2,470	543	22%

*Includes all of West Virginia and parts of 12 other states.
**Includes the District of Columbia.

TABLE 15.3

Counties in the United States That Shifted Upward Significantly Between 1970 and Mid 1980s

Area	No. of States	Total No. of Counties in Quintiles 2 through 5	Counties with Significant Upward Shift	
			No.	Percent
Texas	1	206	124	60%
Other South Central and Western States	10	443	143	32
Alaska, North Dakota and Northeastern Seaboard	6	81	47	58
Kansas, South Dakota, Georgia and Florida	4	307	73	24
Remainder of United States	25	1,433	137	10
United States	51*	2,470	524	21%

*Four states (Connecticut, Hawaii, Iowa and Rhode Island) and the District of Columbia (counted in this total as a state) had no upward-shifting counties. The District of Columbia and Rhode Island had no counties outside the first quintile.

As Table 15.3 shows, the highest percent of counties with significant upward shifts occurred in Texas, where 124 of the 206 counties (60 percent) in the lowest four quintiles shifted upward significantly.

Other states with a large percentage of significantly upward-shifting counties included Alaska and North Dakota, along with four small but densely populated northeastern states (New Jersey, Massachusetts, Delaware and New Hampshire), where 47 of the 81 counties (58 percent) in the lowest four quintiles shifted upward significantly.

In four other states—Kansas, South Dakota, Georgia and Florida—24 percent (73 of 307 counties in the four lowest quintiles) shifted upward significantly during the period between 1970 and the mid 1980s.

In the remainder of the United States, there were only 137 scattered counties, or 10 percent of the total counties in the four lowest quintiles, that shifted upward significantly.

With only 44 counties shifting upward significantly, the Midwest was the region with the smallest share of significant upward shifts.

Population and Income Characteristics of the Quintiles

Table 15.5 on page 131 shows the population and average per capita income for each quintile for 1970 and the mid 1980s. The percentage of the nation's population that was in the top two quintiles dropped slightly to just over 81 percent over the period. The gap in per capita income level between the top two quintiles and the lower three narrowed somewhat between 1970 and 1983. The per capita income index for the top two quintiles did not vary appreciably. The per capita income index shows improvement in the third, fourth and fifth quintiles between 1970 and the mid 1980s. The index in the fifth quintile moved from 61.3 in 1970

TABLE 15.4

Counties in Appalachia and the United States That Shifted Upward Significantly between 1970 and Mid 1980s

Area	No. of States	Total No. of Counties in Quintiles 2 through 5	Counties with Significant Upward Shift	
			No.	Percent
Appalachian Region	13*	357	25	7%
United States	51**	2,470	524	21%

*Includes all of West Virginia and parts of 12 other states.
**Includes the District of Columbia.

TABLE 15.5

Population and Average Per Capita Income for Each Quintile in the United States 1970 and Mid 1980s

Quintile	July 1983 Population	Percent of U.S. Population	Per Capita Income	Index (U.S. = 100)
		Quintiles for Mid 1980s		
1	149,603,096	64.0%	$12,833	109.8
2	40,542,152	17.3	10,546	90.2
3	21,390,472	9.1	9,460	80.9
4	13,959,530	6.0	8,575	73.4
5	8,441,173	3.6	7,669	65.6
Total	**233,936,490**	**100.0%**	**$11,687**	**100.0**

Quintile	July 1970 Population	Percent of U.S. Population	Per Capita Income	Index (U.S. = 100)
		Quintiles for 1970		
1	137,025,516	67.2%	$ 4,321	109.5
2	33,640,411	16.5	3,517	89.2
3	16,136,985	7.9	3,052	77.4
4	10,919,029	5.4	2,711	68.7
5	6,076,781	3.0	2,418	61.3
Total	**203,798,722**	**100.0%**	**$ 3,945**	**100.0**

to 65.6 in the mid 1980s. The largest change was in the fourth quintile where the per capita income index moved from 68.7 in 1970 to 73.4 in the mid 1980s.

APPALACHIA BETWEEN 1970 AND THE MID 1980S

With 12.9 percent of the nation's counties, the Appalachian Region should have about 79 counties in each quintile if its performance mirrored that of the nation. In both time periods, it falls short of this in the first and second quintiles and far exceeds its share in the fourth and fifth quintiles. Appalachia had 40 counties in the top quintile in 1970. It lost 20 counties in the first quintile by the mid 1980s. The Region had 61 counties in the second quintile, 68 counties in the third quintile, 106 in the fourth quintile and 142 counties in the fifth quintile by the mid 1980s.

The 142 Appalachian counties in the lowest quintile constituted 23 percent of the 617 worst-off counties in the nation. Although they suffered very high unemployment rates compared with the nation and their per capita income has grown less rapidly in the past few years, almost one-third of these Appalachian counties had above-average population growth in recent years.

Most of the Appalachian counties in the fourth quintile rim the worst-off counties in the Region, with an additional concentration in Alabama and Mississippi. Again, these counties had severe problems with unemployment recently. These 106 counties also had lower incomes and less rapid income growth compared with counties in the nation outside the Region in this quintile.

The counties in the middle quintile are widely dispersed throughout the Appalachian Region except for Appalachian Kentucky and the state of West Virginia, where they are conspicuous for their scarcity. Again, the Appalachian counties in this quintile have markedly high unemployment rates compared to the counties in this group in the rest of the nation.

Almost three-fourths of the 61 Appalachian counties in the second quintile are in the South. Moreover, they tend to be concentrated in the Carolinas and Georgia.

Seventeen of the 20 Appalachian counties in the first quintile are in the southern half of the Region, and 15 are in metropolitan areas. The major cluster on the Region's border adjacent to Atlanta accounts for six of the 20 counties.

Methodology

The index developed by the Appalachian Regional Commission for the nation evolved from an index with 14 variables that was used to test economic changes in the 397 Appalachian counties. The 14 variables were subjected to factor analysis, a statistical technique, to identify how closely one variable related to another. In cases where close relationships existed, for example, between income and poverty, only one—income—was chosen.

This process singled out four factors—population, income, unemployment and level of urbanization—as most suitable to rank the nation's counties for this analysis.

The analyses for 1970, 1980 and the mid 1980s have been completed. Analysis of the 1960 data will be completed this summer.

Indicator Description

Population. Population was split into two indicators—size and percentage change. For the 1970 and 1980 analysis, population size for the latest year in the decade and the percentage change over the decade preceding the latest year were used. For the mid 1980s analysis, population size for 1983 and the percentage change between 1980–83 and 1970–80 were used.

A weight of one was assigned to the population assessment. Since three measures were used in the mid 1980s analysis, the 1983 size was assigned a weight of 0.5, and the two changes over time were each assigned a weight of 0.25. For other years, population size was weighted 0.5, and population change 0.5.

The population data are based on U.S. Bureau of Census estimates for July of each year to correlate with the U.S. Department of Commerce data used in the calculation of per capita total personal income.

Income. The income factor is comprised of two measures: level of income per capita and percentage change in per capita income. Total personal income and population estimates from the U.S. Department of Commerce were used to measure the levels of income per capita for 1970, 1980 and 1983 and to measure the percentage change in per capita income between 1959 (the year measured by the U.S. Department of Commerce instead of 1960) and 1970. For the 1980 analysis, the percentage change in per capita income between 1970 and 1980 was calculated. For the mid 1980s analysis, percentage change in per capita income between 1980 and 1983 was used.

A weight of one was assigned to income. Because each period of study has two income measures, a weight of 0.5 was given to each measure.

Unemployment. The unemployment factor uses data from the 1970 and 1980 censuses. Civilian labor force and employment data from March 1970 and March 1980 were used to derive unemployment rates. For the mid 1980s analysis, unemployment data from the U.S. Department of Labor for March 1983, March 1984 and March 1985 were added together. These rates, the three most current unemployment rates available for March, were chosen to avoid using a single year during the early 1980s when unemployment rates were atypically high.

A weight of one was assigned to the unemployment factor.

Urbanization Level. In the test analysis of Appalachia, an economic diversification index was developed for each of the 397 Appalachian counties. Since the time and cost to develop the same index for the rest of the counties in the nation was prohibitive, the level of a county's urbanization was substituted in the nation as well as Appalachia. Factor analysis showed urbanization to be closely associated with industrial diversification.

Urbanization level was expressed as the percentage of urban population to total population in each area based on data in the censuses of 1970 and 1980.

A weight of one was assigned to this indicator.

Ranking the Counties

All counties in the nation were ranked from highest to lowest on each indicator. The county that was highest was given a score of one, and the county that was lowest was given a score of 3,087.

The scores of each county for each indicator were added to get a combined score. The best possible rank score would be four if a county ranked first in the nation in all indicators, and the worst possible score would be 12,348. The actual extremes in 1970 scores were 1,081 to 11,551, and in the mid 1980s analysis 674 to 11,347. The combined scores for all 3,087 counties were then ranked from highest (smallest summed number) to lowest (largest summed number).

In the case of tie scores, the county with the largest population was ranked higher.

The ranked combined scores for the 3,087 counties were then divided into quintiles. Because 3,087 cannot be evenly divided by 5, the quintile breaks were made as follows: quintile one, 617 counties; quintile two, 618 counties; quintile three, 617 counties; quintile four, 618 counties; and quintile five, 617 counties.

16. LIVING CITY, FEELING COUNTRY: THE CURRENT STATUS AND FUTURE PROSPECTS OF URBAN APPALACHIANS

Phillip J. Obermiller
Michael E. Maloney

The term 'urban Appalachian' was coined in the early 1970s by Appalachians living in midwestern cities to describe themselves after they realized that the term 'Appalachian migrant' was no longer appropriate. Most of these people were not migrants in the sense that they had moved recently from one region to another, or in the sense that applies to migrant farm workers.

'Urban Appalachian' became the favored term to describe those people and their descendants who had come from the Appalachian region to live and work in cities outside of Appalachia. The original migrants are referred to as first-generation migrants, their children as second-generation migrants, their grandchildren as the third generation, and so on. The term 'urban Appalachian' is also used at times to characterize the population of urban centers within Appalachia such as Knoxville or Pittsburgh, but this usage is less frequent.

As used in this chapter, the term 'urban Appalachian' includes both migrants to cities outside of the Appalachian region and their descendants of whatever generation. For simplicity we will refer to the first and second generations as the early generations, and to the third, fourth, and following generations as the subsequent generations.

The phenomenon of Appalachian migration has been well documented over the past twenty years. From 1940 to 1960 more than 7 million people, including most of the rural youth, left Appalachia while only 3 million people moved into the region during the same period. Thus the region lost 4 million people during what is referred to as the Great Migration (Brown, 1961). This mass migration not only depleted the population of Appalachia, but also had the effect of creating large communities of urban Appalachians in metropolitan centers outside of the region (McCoy and Brown, 1981). The cities receiving much of this migration were located primarily in Ohio, Indiana, Illinois, and Michigan. During the 1980s with the decline of employment in the manufacturing industries in the rustbelt and the growth of labor and service employment in the sunbelt, Appalachian migration streams shifted away from the midwestern states towards states in the South and West (Obermiller and Oldendick, 1987).

Much has been written about the social problems, emergent ethnicity, and class status of urban Appalachians. The social problems faced in Appalachian communities are being addressed through cultural,

This article was prepared specifically for the third edition of *Appalachia: Social Context Past and Prsent.* Used by permission of the authors. Phillip J. Obermiller is an associate professor of sociology at Northern Kentucky University and a member of the Urban Appalachian Council's Research Committee. Michael E. Maloney is a native of Breathitt County, Kentucky and an urban consultant for the Appalachian People's Service Organization. He teaches Appalachian studies courses at Xavier University and Chatfield College.

advocacy, and self-help organizations in several cities (Maloney, 1981; Wagner, 1987). Much of the literature on urban Appalachians produced over the past two decades focuses on their emergence as a new urban ethnic group (Obermiller, 1981; Philliber, 1981). More recently researchers have gone beyond the issue of ethnicity to investigate the position of Appalachians in the urban social class structure (Obermiller, 1987; Philliber, 1987).

Most urban Appalachians have now lived outside of the region for all of or the greater portion of their lives. Since millions of Appalachians have made the transition from rural newcomers to long-term residents of urban neighborhoods, new questions are being asked. Given the fact that over three decades have gone by since the peak years of Appalachian migration, how are these people and their children faring in the cities? How do they compare on key social indicators with other urban groups? Are Appalachians assimilating into urban culture or returning to the region? What are some of the key social policy questions they have raised for urban administrators and politicians?

This essay will attempt to shed some light on these questions. To do so it will be necessary to draw on various studies that use a variety of methods. The Cincinnati metropolitan area has an extensive history of Appalachian inmigration and an equally extensive repertoire of current social research on urban Appalachians. Although the studies we refer to focus on Appalachians in the urban counties of Northern Kentucky and Southwestern Ohio, we believe that the findings can be extrapolated to urban Appalachians living in similar metropolitan areas outside of the region.

We will proceed by first discussing the demographic information we have on first- and second-generation of urban Appalachians. We then consider the conditions affecting the subsequent generations of Appalachians. We conclude with an analysis that looks beyond the current status of urban Appalachians to the issues that will affect them in the decade of the 1990s.

THE EARLY GENERATIONS: A DEMOGRAPHIC PROFILE

In both 1980 and 1989 questions were placed on the Greater Cincinnati Survey that allowed for identification of first- and second-generation urban Appalachians. The surveys used a random-digit dialing technique to contact approximately one thousand respondents in Hamilton County, Ohio, the county in which Cincinnati is located. The sampling procedure and response rate allowed for confidence intervals ranging between three and five percent for each question. The respondents were divided into three comparison groups: white non-Appalachians (white), black non-Appalachians (black), and white Appalachians (Appalachian). Because of their relatively small size in the sample (2.3%) and ambiguous status, black Appalachians were not included in either the black or Appalachian cohort (c.f. Philliber and Obermiller, 1987).

The early generations of urban Appalachians make up a substantial portion of Hamilton County's population. In 1980 they constituted a quarter of the people living in the county: nine years later they still accounted for one in five of the county's residents. Although migration has slowed, natural increase is adding to the urban Appalachian cohort and taking into consideration the third and fourth generations, we estimate that the Appalachian component may be as much as 40 percent of the county's total population.

First- and second generation urban Appalachians are about evenly split in terms of cohort size, but, as one would expect, have different age dynamics. The average age of first generation Appalachians in 1989 was 49 while the average age for the second generation was 43. Although the longitudinal data indicate that Appalachians are aging faster than non-Appalachians and that the first generation is aging more slowly than the second generation, we must be cautious in interpreting these figures. First of all, since our sample is comprised of only the first two generations of Appalachians, the Appalachians appear to be older than the non-Appalachian cohort because the latter does not select out particular generations for analysis. Second, because first-generation Appalachians naturally have a higher mortality rate than the second generation, their average ages appears to be rising more slowly over time.

Despite these cautions, the data indicate clearly that first- and second-generation Appalachians form a large cohort that is substantially above the average age of the non-Appalachian groups in the county. In 1989 the average age of blacks was 39, for whites it was 43, and for Appalachians it was 46. The early migrants and their children are growing old, and this fact will have a strong effect on the interpretation of the other Appalachian demographic characteristics.

The ratio of men to women in the urban Appalachian community is shifting over time to a higher proportion of women. By 1989 61 percent of Appalachians surveyed were women and 39 percent were men. This is coherent with an aging population in which men tend to die at an earlier age than women.

The fact that migration has slowed and Appalachians are long-term residents in urban areas is documented in the 1989 figures on length of residence. For blacks the average length of residence in the county was 29, for whites it was 32, and for Appalachians it was 31. Since 1980 this represents a slight increase for blacks, a modest increase for whites, and a large increase for Appalachians. Again, this change can be linked to the age factor; since Appalachians tend to be older overall, they have had a greater opportunity to establish a longer residency period. Nonetheless it is important to note that Appalachians are long-term urban residents with very few recent migrants among them; only 3.5 percent lived in the county two years or less and 67.3 percent have lived there twenty-one years or more.

From another perspective on residency, Appalachians are becoming more urban over time. In 1980 68.6 percent of the Appalachian respondents lived in the suburban areas of the county surrounding the city of Cincinnati and only 31.4 percent were city dwellers. By 1989 a significant shift had taken place with 44.4 percent living in the city and 55.6 percent living in the balance of the county. The comparative statistics show that the proportions of blacks and Appalachians living in the Cincinnati part of Hamilton County have shown large increases in the period between 1980 and 1989. Cincinnati is becoming a city with a growing minority population that is mostly black and Appalachian.

The data on marital status and household size indicate that the urban Appalachian family remains a strong social unit. Appalachians are more likely to be married or widowed than either blacks or whites. Conversely, they are much less likely to have never married than either of the other two groups. The fact that over seven in ten Appalachian respondents reported that they were married can be attributed in part to the higher average age of this group. However, this argument is diminished somewhat by the fact that urban Appalachian divorce rates are about one third of those reported by blacks and on a par with those reported by whites.

The average household size for Appalachians (3.1) remained constant over the nine-year period of the two surveys, and is about the same as that for blacks and whites. The average number of adults in Appalachian households (2.3) has grown slightly from 1980 to 1989, while decreasing for the other two groups. The average number of children under 18 in Appalachian households (.77) has declined between 1980 and 1989, and is lower than that of either blacks or whites. The larger number of adults and smaller number of children in Appalachian households is consistent with the higher average age of the household members.

Urban Appalachians are the least likely among the three groups to report no religious affiliation. Seventy percent of those surveyed reported being Protestant, but nearly 20 percent reported being Catholic, a substantial gain in the latter category since 1980. The proportion of Protestants among Appalachians and blacks is similar and these groups are distinctly different from the whites, half of whom are Catholic and two-fifths of whom are Protestant.

Educational attainment has improved for urban Appalachians in the interval between the two surveys. In 1989 Appalachians had fewer high school dropouts

(17% vs. 27%) and more students in college or graduated from college (45% vs. 36%) than in 1980. However, in 1989 Appalachians held the same relative status in educational attainment as they had in 1980, that is, they fared better than blacks but worse than other whites. The data on educational attainment show that blacks are more likely to drop out of high school and college than Appalachians, while whites are more likely to complete high school and college than Appalachians. When the sample is confined to Appalachians living in inner-city neighborhoods, their educational outcomes are even worse than those for urban blacks (Obermiller and Oldendick, 1989).

The overall occupational status of urban Appalachians declined between 1980 and 1989. During this period Appalachians gained in the number of sales and clerical jobs they held (+14%), but lost ground in the job categories of craftspersons (−10%) and operatives (−7%). Unfortunately, significant employment growth for Appalachians came in the lowest occupational category, that of laborers and service workers (+12%). Blacks also showed substantial growth in the labor and service category, while the growth in this area of employment was only half as large for whites.

The rate of unemployment among Appalachians has dropped slightly from 1980, but is well over double those reported by both whites and blacks in the 1989 survey. This last statistic must be tempered with the knowledge that many Appalachians work outside of the standard employer/employee relationship; they work for themselves in the informal economy doing home maintenance, roofing, hauling, appliance and auto repair, providing child care, and selling goods at flea markets. These individuals may not consider themselves "employed" in the traditional sense, but they are working hard to maintain their family's income.

Between 1980 and 1989 the number of Appalachian families with total incomes of less than $20,000 a year declined, and the number with annual incomes over $30,000 a year rose. However, in the middle-income category, $20,000 to $30,000, Appalachian families lost ground. Overall Appalachian representation across the family income categories is on a par with whites and significantly better than for black families. Although this pattern may vary between inner-city and suburban neighborhoods, it has remained constant at the county level from 1980 to 1989. A significant portion of Appalachian family income is provided by women, some four-fifths of whom are in the labor force.

THE SUBSEQUENT GENERATIONS: PROSPECTS FOR THE FUTURE

The situation of subsequent generations of urban Appalachians can be described in a more qualitative fashion. A minority have obtained a college education, moved away from blue-collar Appalachian neighborhoods, and are largely assimilated into the larger urban culture. Others have moved from the old neighborhoods, but maintain blue-collar lifestyles including their extended family and a group of Appalachian friends as their primary social network. Most urban Appalachians, however, continue to live in working-class neighborhoods whose principal residents are other white Appalachians.

Appalachian neighborhoods vary greatly in their locations within the metropolitan area and in the socioeconomic status of their residents. Some are inner-city neighborhoods characterized by multi-family rental units and high rates of underemployment, unemployment, and poverty. These communities are affected by the social problems typical of such areas: high rates of crime and delinquency, teen pregnancy, substance abuse, child neglect, and family violence. While it is common to think of these neighborhoods as slums, it is more useful to think of them as low-income ethnic neighborhoods or urban villages (Gans, 1962). An urban village is an area of low cost housing in which a group, usually immigrants, rebuilds the family, community, and economic structures that were debilitated by migration. Life in the urban village is more familiar to the earlier generations of Appalachian migrants than to the subsequent generations.

William Philliber (1981) found that the majority of urban Appalachians in Cincinnati do not live in inner-city neighborhoods. Most live in working-class communities, some of which are located in the suburbs. Appalachians also make up a significant part of the population of small towns and cities that surround metropolitan core cities like Cincinnati (Obermiller and Maloney, In press).

Education is a critical issue for the Appalachians of the subsequent generations. Early migrants could obtain manufacturing jobs that merely required physical dexterity and some mechanical aptitude. In an era when most jobs with reasonable salaries require advanced skills, urban Appalachian students drop out of high school in large numbers (Maloney and Borman, 1987). Many reasons have been advanced to explain the high rates of school failures and drop outs among urban Appalachians (Maloney, et. al., 1989). School administrators point to absenteeism and a lack of interest in education among Appalachian parents. Appalachians regard urban public school systems as large, impersonal bureaucracies with little cultural sensitivity. Whatever the explanation, the fact remains that urban Appalachians in Ohio drop out of school at rates even higher than those of other cultural and racial minorities.

The early generations of Appalachians arrived in the cities during an era of industrial expansion and strong unions; semi-skilled jobs were plentiful, wages were rising, and health and retirement benefits were generally available. Because of this blue-collar background, urban Appalachians of the subsequent generations have been devastated by the decline of the automobile, steel, and other manufacturing industries in the Midwest. These workers and their families have adapted in a variety of ways. Some have gone back to the mountains, but this option is limited by the lack of work and housing in rural Appalachia. Others have moved to the urban growth-centers of the South and the West in search of work. Some of those who stayed found replacement jobs in the industrial sector, but many have been forced to settle for lower-paying jobs in the service sector of the formal economy or to resort to work in the informal economy. Family income is maintained by increasing the number of workers; spouses and children all take jobs to supplement the household budget.

Family networks are still heavily used to find employment or to provide a temporary place to live while job searching. Those lacking family support may go on public assistance or get help from their church or a local social agency, but this is considered a strategy of last resort. Appalachians living in inner-city areas who have lost the support of their families and neighborhood social welfare agencies can be found living on the streets, in shelters for the homeless, and in the lines at soup kitchens.

As with education and employment, health conditions among the subsequent generations vary greatly. Urban Appalachians in poverty have high rates of coronary heart disease, diabetes, and work-related disabilities. Their children suffer from lack of perinatal care, poor nutrition, and the effects of urban pollution. Sexually transmitted diseases affect many Appalachian teenagers. Among all generations of urban Appalachians, injuries related to work are common as are illnesses due to stress and diet such as diabetes, hypertension, and heart disease (Obermiller and Oldendick, 1989).

A key question concerning the subsequent generations is whether they are losing their Appalachian identity and assimilating into the cultural mainstream. With some exceptions, most urban Appalachians are concentrated in blue-collar enclaves in urban neighborhoods, suburban communities, and small town settings. Because of their numbers they often form the majority population in these places. In addition to living near relatives and other people with an Appalachian background, they associate with their own kind at work, in their churches, labor unions, civic associations, schools, as well as in local bars and restaurants. Their music, dance, crafts and artistic traditions are constantly being renewed through arts and crafts festivals, bluegrass preservation societies, records, tapes, films, and radio programs. Although there are more Appalachians in

Ohio's Miami Valley (Cincinnati, Hamilton, Middletown, Dayton, Xenia, Troy) than in all of Eastern Kentucky, the residents of these towns make use of the easy access to their homeplaces and kinfolk in the mountains. To a certain extent urban Appalachians resemble Mexican-Americans in the Southwestern U.S. who gain cultural support from visits or frequent communication with their home districts in rural Mexico.

Most studies of migrant groups find that ethnic identity begins to dwindle with the third generation (c.f. Philliber, 1987). However, the process of assimilation is slowed by ethnic organizations with strong leadership that promote the cultural heritage and the political concerns of the group. It is also hindered by the presence of discrimination and the perception by the group of exclusion from the economic and social mainstream. We believe that all the factors we have cited are limiting the absorption of Appalachians into the dominant urban society. There is no danger of the disappearance of Appalachians from the social map of urban America in the 1990s.

COMMENTS AND POLICY RECOMMENDATIONS

We now turn to an analysis of data on urban Appalachians and a commentary on the social policy and program implications of this information. In discussing the data we will again take care to distinguish among urban Appalachians by both age (early generations vs. subsequent generations) and by socioeconomic status (suburban vs. inner-city).

The early generations of urban Appalachians are clearly an aging population. During the 1990s their concerns can be expected to move away from a focus on education and employment and turn to health care. Moreover, many urban Appalachians are aging in place rather than returning to the region for retirement (Obermiller, In press). On the contrary, many elderly Appalachians are being moved from the region by their urban kinfolk to metropolitan areas where access to health care facilities, nursing homes, retirement communities, and the potential for in-home care is much more abundant.

The aging of the early generations also has implications for urban Appalachian women, the traditional caregivers in the Appalachian cultural milieu. At a time when the number of children per household is beginning to fall, and women's educational attainment and labor force participation have begun to rise, care for the elderly will become a larger part of the responsibilities in Appalachian households. Much of this duty will devolve upon the women in the household.

From a policy standpoint, the aging of the urban Appalachian population will require more resources in the area of health care and geriatric services. From a programmatic point of view, social welfare organizations will need to be concerned not only with the Appalachian elderly but also with their caregivers, who for the most part will be working women.

Among the subsequent generations adult education and job training will continue to be important issues. The longitudinal data show urban Appalachians losing way on a socioeconomic treadmill; even as their educational attainment improves, the demand for education in the labor force increases at a higher rate. This explains why members of the early generations who have increased their rates of high school completion are gradually slipping into lower-status job categories over time. In these families, a stable income can be maintained only by maximizing the number of workers in the family. If the cost of living increases while family size remains stable, many working-class urban Appalachians will slip into poverty.

The situation for inner-city Appalachians is even more grim. Half of the adults in these neighborhoods have no more than a high school education, school dropout rates range as high as 75 percent, and youth unemployment is a serious problem. While social problems abide in these neighborhoods, the urban Appalachian community is not without resources to deal with them. In Cincinnati, community schools have been founded to provide onsite G.E.D. programs, adult education courses, and college-level classes. The Appalachian extended family has been battered but not broken as a social unit. It still provides the social and economic resources necessary for its members to survive in an urban setting.

Policy makers need to focus not only on the problems in the urban Appalachian community, but also on its inherent strengths. Every effort should be made to recognize and reinforce the successful survival mechanisms that are operating in low-income Appalachian neighborhoods. Academic and job training projects, for example, should be designed to bolster Appalachian family interaction and local community schooling initiatives. Social welfare programs should support local initiatives among urban Appalachians, rather than attempt to supplant them.

School reform is a critical issue among urban Appalachians (c.f. Maloney, 1990). For the inner-city school systems, stemming the drop-out rates among Appalachian youth continues to be a concern for most of the community but relatively few school administrators. In suburban areas some school systems have better retention rates among Appalachian youth, but these students generally finish in the bottom half of their graduating class. One programmatic suggestion that has yet to be widely implemented is the inclusion of Appalachian studies units in both teacher training sessions and in the school curricula.

Another area of concern implicit in the comparative survey data gathered in Cincinnati and its environs is the relationship between the urban Appalachians, blacks, and whites. As we have noted, blacks and Appalachians are the two largest minorities in the city, yet non-Appalachian whites hold most of the economic and political power in Cincinnati. The black community is frustrated, fearing the loss of hard-won legislative and constitutional gains. Urban blacks are leery of sharing meager power and resources with their Appalachian neighbors; unless new means of cooperation are developed between these two groups, increasing conflict over power and resource allocation will occur.

The policy direction is clear: municipal governments in cities like Cincinnati need to hold mediation sessions with black and Appalachian leaders to discuss cooperation in conflict resolution and resource allocation. Specific areas for mediation include control of community agencies and the allocation of employment and training funds. In the area of education black leaders favor school desegregation plans that entail district-wide busing, while urban Appalachians favor community control of neighborhood schools with local attendance. Resolution of these differences would allow both groups to focus on the quality of education they seek for their children.

Not all issues polarize urban blacks and Appalachians. For instance, they frequently hold similar agendas in opposing police brutality and the displacement of low-income families from their neighborhoods. They share concerns about the inclusion of minority studies in school curricula and about the effects of heavy industrial pollution on their children (c.f. LPH Task Force, 1990). Urban Appalachians and their black neighbors have great potential for either conflict or cooperation. The coming decade may well decide which strategy will prevail.

CONCLUSION

In the next ten years urban Appalachians will continue to deal with issues they have wrestled with in the past, in particular education and employment. Establishing cooperative relations with other racial or ethnic minorities will continue to be a priority in an era of shrinking resources. New concerns will include a stronger emphasis on health care for the elderly population and the very young. Adult education and job retraining will take on increased importance as the decade advances.

The urban Appalachians we have studied do not lack the resources necessary to deal with the changing urban scene. They are maintaining relatively strong family bonds, supporting and using their own cultural institutions and organizations, and devising new ways to deal with old problems. The future for urban Appalachians holds the promise of both great struggles and great successes.

REFERENCES

Brown, James S. and George A. Hillery, "The great migration 1940–1960," in Thomas R. Ford, ed., *The Southern Appalachian Region: A Survey.* (Lexington: University of Kentucky Press, 1962.)

Gans, Herbert, *The Urban Villagers.* (Glencoe, Ill.: The Free Press, 1962.)

Lower Price Hill Task Force, *Report on Health, Education, and Pollution in Lower Price Hill.* (Cincinnati: Urban Appalachian Council, 1990.)

McCoy, Clyde B. and James S. Brown, "Appalachian migration to midwestern cities," in William W. Philliber and Clyde B. McCoy, eds., *The Invisible Minority: Urban Appalachians.* (Lexington: The University Press of Kentucky, 1981.)

Maloney, Michael E., "The prospects for urban Appalachians," in Philliber and McCoy, eds., *op. cit.,* 1981.

———. "Urban Appalachians and school reform," A paper presented at the annual meeting of the Central States Anthropology Association (mimeo) 1990.

Maloney, *et al., The Moraine School District: A Report.* (Cincinnati: Applied Information Resources, 1989.)

Maloney, Michael E. and Kathryn M. Borman, "Effects of school and schooling upon Appalachian children in Cincinnati," in Obermiller and Philliber, eds., *Too Few Tomorrows: Urban Appalachians in the 1980's.* (Boone, NC: Appalachian Consortium Press, 1987.)

Obermiller, Phillip J., "The question of Appalachian ethnicity," in Philliber and McCoy, eds., *op. cit.,* 1981.

———. "Labeling urban Appalachians," in Obermiller and Philliber, eds., *op cit.,* 1987.

———. " 'Ain't goin' back': the aging of Appalachian migrants in urban neighborhoods," in Graham Rowles and John Watkins, eds., *Change in the Mountains: Elderly Migration in Appalachia.* (Lexington: University Press of Kentucky, In Press.)

Obermiller, Phillip J. and Michael E. Maloney "Looking for Appalachians in Pittsburgh: seeking deliverance, finding the deer-hunter," *Pittsburgh History.* (In Press.)

Obermiller, Phillip J. and Robert W. Oldendick "Moving on: recent patterns of Appalachian migration," in Phillip J. Obermiller and William W. Philliber, eds., *op. cit.,* 1987.

———. "Urban Appalachian health concerns," in Appalachian Center, *Proceedings of the Third Annual Conference on Appalachia.* (Lexington: University of Kentucky, 1989.)

Philliber, William W., *Appalachian migrants in urban America: cultural conflict or ethnic group formation?* (New York: Praeger, 1981.)

———. "The future of Appalachians in urban areas," in Obermiller and Philliber, eds., *op. cit.,* 1987.

Philliber, William W. and Phillip J. Obermiller, "Black Appalachian migrants: the issue of dual minority status," in Obermiller and Philliber, eds., *op. cit.,* 1987.

Wagner, Thomas E., "Too few tomorrows," in Obermiller and Philliber, eds., *op. cit.,* 1987.

17. AMERICA'S SOWETO: POPULATION REDISTRIBUTION IN APPALACHIAN KENTUCKY, 1940–1986

Stephen E. White

The Cumberland Plateau of eastern Kentucky experienced substantial population losses due to massive out-migration from 1940 through the late 1960s. Some 615,745 more persons left the area than in-migrated. However, due to high fertility, the total population only declined there from 820,115 to 612,355 inhabitants. But during the 1970s, the region experienced a significant, unprecedented migration reversal which increased the total population to 762,558. Since the early 1980s, it appears that once again out-migration is exceeding in-migration.

Numerous studies have examined the back-and-forth "channelization" of Appalachian migrants to north-central cities (Cincinnati, Chicago, Detroit, for example), the assimilation of mountaineers in those cities (or lack of same), their high propensity to return home, and the economic and sociocultural pushes and pulls that motivate migrants to and from eastern Kentucky.[1] If anything, this region appears to have become a large dormitory community—in fact, an incubator—linked to and responsive to the needs of the urban sector outside the region—a labor supply not unlike but very similar to South Africa's Soweto. Although migrants from the mountains to the cities certainly add to the available labor pool of those cities and may benefit themselves, at least temporarily, from that work, the mountain home counties of eastern Kentucky have not benefitted. Eastern Kentuckians have remained dependent on fluctuations in the external labor demands of the national economy. They have not developed a more internally diversified economic base or gained a greater level of local control over the economic activities within their region.

Though much is known about the social and spatial adjustments of the migrants to the cities, much less is known about the impact of migration streams on the internal redistribution of population within the 32 counties of eastern Kentucky (Figure 1). The study area conforms to Fenneman's Appalachian Plateau physiographic province which is a somewhat smaller, but more socioeconomically uniform area, than that defined by the Appalachian Regional Commission for Kentucky.

REGIONAL POPULATION CHANGE

Between 1940 and 1986, the total population of the area declined slightly from 820,382 to 776,800 residents (Table 17.1); however, these figures hide the real magnitude of population flux. Since 1940, the Kentucky Cumberland Plateau has witnessed tremendous shifts in the magnitude and direction of population movement. During the peak decade of out-migration (1950s), 279,525 more people left the region than arrived. For every 100 persons who resided in eastern Kentucky in 1950, net out-migration produced a loss of 35 people by 1960. The decreased demand for coal, the mechanization of the coal industry and decreased demand for labor, the lack of economic expansion in eastern Kentucky, and the availability of jobs in metropolitan areas of the north-central states are some of the reasons for the massive out-migration.[2]

During the 1960s, net migration loss slowed to a negative 138,702 persons, and an unexpected reversal in the flow dominated the 1970s—92,419 more people migrated to the area than departed, and the net migration rate was a positive 15.1 percent.

The reasons for the reversal are complex. Some have argued that economic conditions in eastern Kentucky improved, particularly in the coal counties, thus providing more attractive economic opportunities than the cities.[3] However, others have placed more emphasis on sociocultural factors such as family ties and economic decline outside the region as important determining reasons for return.[4] For example, survey research by Walker and White suggest that the overwhelming majority of in-migrants during the 1970s were returnees, most of whom returned to the county of their former residence.[5] Clearly, internal economic expansion in eastern Kentucky of the manufacturing sector and the coal industry was not the primary reason for the reversal. In fact, many non-coal counties grew more quickly during the 1970s than coal-producing counties. Importantly, eastern Kentucky gained more manufacturing jobs between 1950 and 1970, a period dominated by massive out-migration, than it did between 1970 and 1980, when it gained population due to in-migration.

The degree to which county-level changes in manufacturing and mining employment have explained changes in net migration between 1940 and 1986 can

Steve White teaches in the department of geography at Kansas State University. He is a native Kentuckian and received his Ph.D. from the University of Kentucky. White's research interests include internal migration, population redistribution, and cognitive maps. He has published several articles on migration in Appalachian Kentucky.

Author's note: I wish to thank the Appalachian Center at Berea College for supporting my research with an Appalachian Studies Fellowship.

Reprinted from *Appalachian Journal*, Vol. 16, No. 4 (Summer, 1989), pp. 350–360. Copyright Appalachian State University/Appalachian Journal. Used by permission.

APPALACHIAN KENTUCKY

STUDY AREA

be statistically estimated by regression analysis. A linear stepwise regression analysis was performed for five different time periods (Table 17.2). Both mining employment and manufacturing employment were collected on a place-of-work rather than a place-of-residence basis.[6] That is, employment changes reflect the availability of jobs in a specific county, not the number of employees who reside there. Place-of-work manufacturing employment data is not available for the 1940–1950 period.

The R-squared values suggest that the massive out-migration of the 1950s was associated with the loss of mining jobs. About 85 percent of the variance in county net migration can be explained by changes in mining employment. However, manufacturing increases during the 1950s explain almost nothing additional about net migration. As out-migration slowed during the 1960s, only about 12 percent of net migration could be explained by a combination of manufacturing and mining employment. During the 1970s, the decade of the reversal, the degree of explanation increased only slightly. This strongly suggests that the internal economic climate was not responsible for the reversals, but that instead a combination of economic stagnation in the north-central states and sociocultural attachments in eastern Kentucky may have been more important considerations. Between 1980 and 1986 manufacturing may, for the first time, be slightly but significantly associated with net migration in the Cumberland Pla-

teau, if 1986 estimates net migration prove to be reliable. The regression for the 1980s indicates that manufacturing change explains about 28 percent of the variance in net migration among the 32 counties, while mining adds very little to the overall explanation.

The lack of association between mining/manufacturing employment changes and net migration may be partially accounted for by the magnitude of unemployment throughout the Cumberland Plateau. For example, an increase in jobs may result in lower unemployment rather than positive net migration, because new jobs may be taken by a large waiting labor surplus rather than by in-migrants. Although official unemployment rates are very high throughout eastern Kentucky, they may greatly understate the magnitude of the potential labor supply. Unemployment statistics miss the "hidden unemployed" who are not searching for jobs locally.

An examination of 1986 marriage licenses in three counties illustrates the degree of under-estimation. While the official 1986 unemployment rate for Clay County was 15.0 percent, 31.1 percent of grooms indicated that they were unemployed at the time of marriage. Over 25 percent of newly-wed males were unemployed in Jackson County, while the rate in Laurel County was about 17 percent. These estimates, while almost double the official estimates of unemployment, are probably also still conservative. While it is likely that some unemployed persons may have optimistically

TABLE 17.1

Population Changes in Eastern Kentucky

Total Population	Total Population					
	1940 820,115	1950 795,016	1960 666,572	1970 612,355	1980 762,558	1986 776,800e
Incorporated places less than 2,500	27,396	30,226	30,410	33,938	38,060	*
Incorporated places 2,500–5,000	51,501	54,238	47,971	49,016	53,548	*
Incorporated places more than 5,000	60,836	68,320	68,356	72,314	74,522	*
Unincorporated	680,382	642,187	519,835	457,087	596,428	*

Total Population	Percent Population Change				
	1940–50 −3.1	1950–60 −16.2	1960–1970 −8.1	1970–1980 24.5	1980–86 1.9e
Incorporated places less than 2,500	10.3	0.6	11.6	12.1	*
Incorporated places 2,500–5,000	5.4	−11.6	2.2	9.2	*
Incorporated places more than 5,000	12.3	0.1	5.8	3.1	*
Unincorporated	−5.6	−19.1	−12.1	30.1	*

	Net Migration				
Cumberland Plateau	−197,518	−279,525	−138,702	92,419	−15,700e

*Not available.

e Estimated (Federal-State Cooperative Estimates, Urban Studies Center, University of Louisville).

TABLE 17.2

Stepwise Regression Results

Decade	Step	R-Squared	Independent Variable	Beta Coefficient
1940–50	1	.033	Mining employment	.033
1950–60	1	.851	Mining employment	.922
	2	.851	Manufacturing employment	−.006
1960–70	1	.077	Mining employment	.300
	2	.117	Manufacturing employment	−.168
1970–80	1	.151	Mining employment	.388
	2	.189	Manufacturing employment	.200
1980–86	1	.283	Manufacturing employment	.532
	2	.310	Mining employment	.166

TABLE 17.3

Net-migration Correlation Coefficients.

	1940–50	1950–60	1960–70	1970–80	1980–86
1940–50	1.000	.806*	.831*	−.305*	.198
1950–60		1.000	.959*	−.504*	.266
1960–70			1.000	−.432*	.354*
1970–80				1.000	.228
1980–86					1.000

*Significant at the .05 probability level.

listed occupations on the marriage certificate, it is unlikely that an employed person would have listed "unemployed." In addition, many persons listed occupations that might suggest part-time employment, such as "handy man," "laborer," and "restaurant worker."

Despite the tremendous fluctuations in the migration volume and direction since 1940, the internal pattern of population change and distribution within the region has been amazingly constant. Correlation coefficients that measure the association between county net migration between decades (Table 17.3) demonstrate that the pattern of net migration in the 1940s was very similar to that during the 1950s (r = +.806), even though the magnitude of population loss was greater in the 1950s. The correlation between net migration in the 1950s and the 1960s increased (r = +.959), even though the total flow of out-migrants declined. During the reversal of the 1970s, counties that had formerly been the biggest population losers became the largest population gainers (r = −.432). The reversal served as a process that brought population distribution on the Cumberland Plateau back into equilibrium.

The Lorenze curves of county population distribution for 1940 and 1980 are very similar. Lorenze curves measure the degree to which a population is concentrated or dispersed on the landscape. A Lorenze curve dissimilarity index of 100 percent indicates that the entire population is concentrated at one location, while 0 percent reveals a maximum uniform distribution; all counties would have the same population. The dissimilarity index for 1940 is 26.5 percent, while that for 1980 is 28.1 percent. This suggests that while the total population has fluctuated for the entire region, the overall distribution of population within the region tends toward uniformity and has changed very little over a 40-year period. The push and pull factors associated with migration change may be common throughout the region, both spatially and temporally. That is, whatever forces seem to cause people to leave the area seem also to influence people on the Cumberland Plateau as a whole. Also, population increases due to the return of former residents tend to occur uniformly throughout the region as well.

INCORPORATED POPULATION CHANGE

Many writers have correctly suggested that Central Appalachia is analogous to a third-world region.[7] The statistical lag in many socioeconomic characteristics such as personal income, educational attainment, housing quality, secondary and tertiary economic activities, health care, and recreational amenities have been well documented. The historical isolation of the region, its dependence on extractive industries, and the control of land and mineral rights by corporations outside Appalachia, and lack of internal investment capital also coincide with the colonization metaphor.[8] However, there is a major demographic difference between third-world regions and Central Appalachia. In most third-world regions there is a major trend toward the centralization of population away from more rural, remote areas to large urban areas and huge, primate cities in particular. A major concern in third-world nations is that substantial urbanization is occurring without corresponding increases in the industrial base. But in Central Appalachia the trend has been toward deconcentration rather than urbanization. The geography of the population in Central Appalachia is an anomaly that conforms to neither first-world nor third-world contemporary demographic processes. The urban cores in the region have remained small and stable. Population fluctuations have affected the unincorporated parts of the Cumberland Plateau—the more rural areas, the countryside—to a much greater extent.

Between 1940 and 1980 the incorporated population of eastern Kentucky grew from 17.0 percent to just 21.7 percent. If we use the Census Bureau definition of "urban," which includes places that have a minimum population of 2,500 residents, this lack of concentration of population is even more pronounced. The urban population grew only from 13.7 percent to 16.7 percent over the same period. Very few areas of the world have such low levels of urbanization. Even India and China have higher levels of urbanization. During the 1970s, when the population increased rapidly due to in-migration, the unincorporated areas grew by 30.1 percent while cities of 5,000 or more inhabitants grew by only 13.1 percent! As a generalization, the smaller the place the greater the growth. Places of 1,000 to 2,500 inhabitants increased by 9.2 percent while places smaller than 1,000 inhabitants increased by 12.1 percent (Table 17.1). These trends suggest that since 1940 the pressures to deconcentrate are far greater than the tendency toward urbanization. At both the 32-county regional level and at the intra-county micro level, population dispersal appears to be more common than pressures toward agglomeration.

Historically, the urban cores in eastern Kentucky, Ashland, Middlesboro, and Paintsville, for example, have suffered very little from population loss during periods of high out-migration, but neither have they experienced major gains during the migration reversal. Urbanization in eastern Kentucky is a group of very small but relatively stable nuclei that are virtually immune to the volatile fulminations of population change that surround them.

A previous study of mine showed that the lack of population increase in urban places in eastern Kentucky can not be attributed to spill-over effects or lack of annexation.[9] Census enumeration districts that bordered incorporated places were examined for 1970 and 1980. The growth rates for these enumeration districts were slightly lower and not significantly different from those that were in more remote areas and that did not adjoin incorporated places.

Several factors may be responsible for the lack of population concentration within eastern Kentucky. Historically, there has been no urban infrastructure on which to build, because the corporate structure that has controlled much of the economy has operated from outside and has reinvested profits far from the region.[10] Lack of urbanization has discouraged the development of basic employment activities that pull capital toward cities. Many return migrants have elected to live near their extended families in proximity to the old homesteads—a characteristic behavior of the "stem family."[11] Most flat bottomland is already settled or is more expensive than more remote locations. High construction costs have increased the dependence on mobile homes which can be easily located in more remote areas. Manufacturing has not expanded significantly throughout the region, and the concomitant industries and services that benefit from the process of agglomeration and urbanization never materialized.

POPULATION REDISTRIBUTION AND THE PROVISION OF PUBLIC SERVICES

One of the Soweto-like drawbacks of population dispersal in Appalachian Kentucky is the increased difficulty that local governments must confront when deciding how to best allocate scarce resources to finance public services. The provision of road maintenance, health care, police protection, sewage treatment, ambulance service, and garbage disposal becomes more difficult as the population is more dispersed rather than concentrated. The lack of urbanization and historical concentration of population around smaller incorporated places and unincorporated settlements produces a more uniform pattern of service demand, thus making the administration and delivery of services more difficult. Not only is this general pattern of population inefficient, but the greatest population changes have occurred in the more remote locations where the costs of service delivery are highest and needs are greatest. (Leithauser and Pickard have discussed the impact of regional and sub-regional population dispersal and have noted that at the state and federal levels, the provision of social services, education, utilities, and fiscal adjustment are difficult issues with which to deal.)[12]

A uniform population distribution exacerbates another dilemma: the lack of an adequate local tax base. Most counties in eastern Kentucky are heavily dependent on infusions of state or federal governmental revenues to support local government. Local tax support is low because family incomes and assessed property valuations are extremely low. For example, the median family income in Wolfe County was $13,700 in 1987, compared to a state-wide median of $23,700.[13] Wolfe County generated a total of $55,166 from property tax assessments in 1986.[14] The median share of revenue generated by local taxation to support county governments in Kentucky is 24.6 percent of the total county budget. Twenty-six of the 32 counties in the study area below the median value (Table 17.4). Wolfe County generates only 5.1 percent of its county budget locally![15] The potential for future increases in the local tax base seems meager in Wolfe County, because only about one in four workers over the age of 25 years (26.8 percent) had a high school diploma in 1986.[16] The probability of economic expansion beyond unskilled, labor-intensive occupations seems low.

One mechanism that has improved county budgets recently has been the return of a portion of severance tax revenues gained from the extraction of minerals (primarily coal) to counties where extraction has occurred. In the major coal-producing counties, the severance tax has proven to be an important contribution to total county revenues. More than 50 percent of the county budget is funded by severance tax revenues in

143

Knott and Martin counties (Table 17.4). Although the severance tax has undoubtedly helped some counties, it has also encouraged inter-regional differences and inequities in total county revenue per capita. In eight counties, less than 10 percent of the budget is funded by severance tax revenues. Counties with little coal have very few dollars per capita to provide basic services.

The combination of a dispersed population, low family income, low property valuation, and variations in government tax distributions insure that many challenges lie ahead for those who want to see an improvement in the magnitude, quality, and equity of services in Appalachian Kentucky.

TABLE 17.4

County Taxation Dependency

County	Local Taxation as a Percentage of Total County Revenue 1986	Total County Revenue Per Capita 1986	Severance Tax as a Percentage of Total County Revenue 1986
Bell	27.1	89.03	18.3
Boyd	38.5	57.84	7.7
Breathitt	13.0	113.08	35.6
Carter	18.3	52.58	11.9
Clay	11.0	86.21	23.3
Elliott	20.4	125.13	19.2
Estill	13.8	81.45	5.0
Floyd	20.6	87.78	47.7
Greenup	36.7	48.32	6.3
Harlan	22.1	75.84	27.8
Jackson	14.0	78.67	2.4
Johnson	21.2	68.97	18.9
Knott	7.7	177.15	52.1
Knox	23.2	64.64	28.1
Laurel	28.0	74.56	5.2
Lawrence	20.7	99.14	28.1
Lee	11.1	172.96	42.0
Leslie	13.2	176.14	42.9
Letcher	16.1	83.81	40.7
Lewis	23.4	74.97	0.9
Magoffin	11.2	118.44	29.7
Martin	13.8	186.71	52.9
McCreary	18.7	99.08	12.2
Menifee	16.7	108.74	4.3
Morgan	17.9	108.91	8.7
Owsley	12.5	120.68	12.8
Perry	16.4	106.94	44.8
Pike	14.0	129.25	35.0
Powell	11.5	110.34	19.9
Rowan	30.4	71.74	0.0
Whitley	24.9	51.65	20.1
Wolfe	5.1	155.64	17.8

RECENT TRENDS

Between 1980 and 1986, manufacturing employment in the area has decreased from 25,898 to 20,985 jobs, reversing a long-term trend of very slow growth since 1950.[17] Mining employment declined from 41,361 to 33,795 over the same period; however, the 1986 job total was still significantly higher than that for 1970.[18] Internal economic decline may again provide the push that will encourage people to leave the region and seek employment elsewhere. According to recent population estimates, the region experienced a population loss of 15,700 due to net migration between 1980 and 1986, reversing the reversal (in other words) of the 1970s.[19] An examination of 1980–81 Internal Revenue Service area-to-area flow data by Obermiller and Oldendick suggested that although many of Appalachia's migration channels were reoriented toward the south, eastern Kentucky streams were still tied to the traditional origins and destinations.[20] Internal population redistribution patterns will not be known until after the 1990 census; however, based on trends since 1940 the hypothesis is that population losses will again occur in the more isolated areas while incorporated places will remain stable. The degree of sociocultural attachment may be reflected by the data; otherwise, a combined loss of 12,479 jobs in manufacturing and mining should have produced more than 15,700 net out-migrants!

Gaventa has noted that Central Appalachia is currently at a regional disadvantage because nationwide economic restructuring to service-based employment from industrially-based employment adversely affects less educated people who have depended on traditional industry.[21] In addition, existing labor-based industries are being exported to foreign countries—not to Appalachia. Population distribution in eastern Kentucky may also be at issue in terms of economic restructuring. A dispersed population prevents the development of urban cores and the agglomerative effects that accrue from a more concentrated population. As Cromley and Leinbach have noted, since 1970 Kentucky cities of between 10,000 and 20,000 inhabitants have been most successful in attracting new industry.[22] Eastern Kentucky has only one city, Middlesboro, in that size class!

While Appalachian Regional Commission policies in general have been to promote the growth center strategy at the expense of more remote areas, population redistribution has simultaneously followed a pattern of decentralization. Importantly, employment opportunities, educational attainment, and other socioeconomic indicators have not improved significantly throughout the region, despite sizeable well-intentioned ARC investments in highways, health care, and vocational education. Perhaps the time has come to implement development strategies that are based on the premise that the distribution of human needs in Appalachian Kentucky are likely to remain decentralized for years to come.

NOTES

1. Appalachian Regional Commission, *A Report to Congress On Migration* (Washington: 1979); James Bohland, "The Influence of Kinship Ties on the Settlement Pattern of Northeast Georgia," *The Professional Geographer,* 22 (1970), 267–9; James S. Brown and George A. Hillery Jr., "The Great Migration: 1940–1960" in *The Southern Appalachian Region: A Survey,* ed. Thomas R. Ford (Lexington: University of Kentucky Press, 1962), pp. 54–78; Lorraine Garkovich, "Kinship and Return Migration in Eastern Kentucky," *Appalachian Journal,* 10 (1982), 62–70; George A. Hillery, James S. Brown, and Gordon F. DeJong, "Migration Systems of the Southern Appalachians: Some Demographic Observations," *Rural Sociology,* 30 (1965), 33–48; William W. Philliber and Clyde B. McCoy, eds., *The Invisible Minority: Urban Appalachians* (Lexington: University Press of Kentucky, 1981); John Vandercamp, "Return Migration: Its Significance and Behavior," *Western Economic Journal,* 10 (1972), 460–5; Wilma J. Walker, "Geographical Analysis of Return Migration: An Eastern Kentucky Case Study," Ph.D. Dissertation, University of Kentucky, 1979; Stephen E. White, "Return Migration to Eastern Kentucky and the Stem Family Concept," *Growth and Change,* 18 (1987), 38–52; and Stephen E. White, "Return Migration to Appalachian Kentucky: An Atypical Case of Nonmetropolitan Migration Reversal," *Rural Sociology,* 48 (1983), 471–91.

2. Brown and Hillery, "The Great Migration"; Gary C. Cox, "An Analysis of Recent Population Changes in Central Appalachia," unpublished paper, 1980; and Clyde B. McCoy and James S. Brown, "Appalachian Migration to Midwestern Cities" in *The Invisible Minority: Urban Appalachians.*

3. Appalachian Regional Commission, *A Report to Congress on Migration;* Thomas R. Ford, "Kentucky and the Great Migration Reversal," *Public Affairs Analyst,* 4 (1978), 1–8.

4. White, "Return Migration to Appalachian Kentucky: An Atypical Case."

5. Walker, "Geographical Analysis of Return Migration"; and White, "Return Migration to Eastern Kentucky and the Stem Family Concept."

6. Kentucky Department of Business Development, *Nonagricultural Employment in Industries Covered by Unemployment Insurance by Place of Work* (Frankfort, Ky.: 1986, 1980, 1970, 1960, 1950); and Kentucky Department of Mines and Minerals, *Annual Report* (Lexington, Ky.: 1986, 1980, 1970, 1960, 1950, 1940).

7. Dwight Billings, Kathleen Blee, and Louis Swanson, "Culture, Family and Community in Preindustrial Appalachia," *Appalachian Journal,* 14 (1986), 154–70; and John Friedmann, "Poor Regions and Poor Nations: Perspectives on the Problem of Appalachia," *Southern Economic Journal,* 32 (1966), 465–73.

8. Harry Caudill, *Darkness at Dawn: Appalachian Kentucky and the Future* (Lexington: University Press of Kentucky, 1976); Harry Caudill, *Night Comes to the Cumberlands* (Boston: Little, Brown and Company, 1963); and Ronald D. Eller, *Miners, Millhands, and Mountaineers: Industrialization of the Appalachian South, 1880–1930* (Knoxville: University of Tennessee Press, 1982).

9. White, "Return Migration to Appalachian Kentucky: An Atypical Case."

10. John Gaventa, "The Property of Abundance Revisited," *Appalachian Journal,* 15 (1987), 24–31.

11. James S. Brown, Harry K. Schwarzweller, and Joseph J. Mangalam, "Kentucky Mountain Migration and the Stem-family: An American Variation on a Theme by Le Play," *Rural Sociology,* 28 (1963), 48–69; and Harry K. Schwarzweller, James S. Brown, and J. J. Mangalam, *Mountain Families in Transition: A Case Study of Appalachian Migration* (University Park: Pennsylvania State University Press, 1971).

12. Gail A. Leithauser, "Population Settlements in the Appalachian Region," paper presented at the meetings of the Population Association of America, Washington, D.C., 1981; and Jerome P. Pickard, "Counting Noses in Region and Nation," *Appalachia,* 13 (1980).

13. Kentucky Department of Business Development, *Nonagricultural Employment in Industries Covered by Unemployment Insurance by Place of Work.*

14. Kentucky Legislative Research Commission, *Annual Report on the Financial Condition of County Governments in Kentucky,* Informational Bulletin No. 163 (Frankfort, Ky.: 1988).

15. Ibid.

16. Kentucky Department of Business Development, *Nonagricultural Employment in Industries Covered by Unemployment Insurance by Place of Work.*

17. Ibid.

18. Kentucky Department of Mines and Minerals, *Annual Reports.*

19. Kentucky Department of Business Development, *Nonagricultural Employment in Industries Covered by Unemployment Insurance by Place of Work.*

20. Phillip J. Obermiller and Robert Oldendick, "Moving On: Recent Patterns of Appalachian Migration" in *The Impact of Institutions in Appalachia,* Proceedings of the 8th Annual Appalachian Studies Conference, 1986, ed. Jim Lloyd and Anne G. Campbell (Boone, N.C.: Appalachian Consortium Press, 1987), pp. 148–65.

21. Gaventa, "The Poverty of Abundance Revisited."

22. Robert G. Cromley and Thomas R. Leinbach, "The Pattern and Impact of the Filter Down Process in Nonmetropolitan Kentucky," *Economic Geography,* 57 (1981), 208–24.

IV. Appalachian Culture and a Sense of Community

As one surveys the vast amount of literature which has been written about the Appalachian region over the years, the concept of "culture" occupies a central theme in much of the material. Two theoretical perspectives have dominated the literature when attempting to describe the distinctive features and characteristics of the region's culture.

The first of these perspectives suggests that the Appalachian region constitutes a distinctive "folk subculture" set apart from the culture of the larger society. The "folk subculture" model of the region implies that there is a relatively homogeneous mountain culture which is the product of unique historical forces and perpetuated by the geographic isolation of the region. As a result of such a characterization, the following features have come to be identified with the culture of the region: traditionalism, group solidarity, social isolation, person-oriented, familism, individualism, self-reliance, and religiousness.

The "folk subculture" model was congruent with another perspective that developed and gained prominence in the 1960's. This was the concept of the "culture of poverty" deriving from the anthropological fieldwork of Oscar Lewis. Lewis' thesis was that there are common cultural traits that are shared by all poor people and these are passed on from one generation to the next. The ideas contained within the "culture of poverty" thesis are clearly reflected in a book written in the mid-sixties by Jack Weller entitled Yesterday's People. *The very title of the book conveys the notion of backwardness as one of the fundamental characteristics of the region. The Appalachians and their culture are marked by passive recognition, traditionalism (regressive outlook), person-oriented and thirty other personal, social, and cultural traits which conveys a negative characterization of them when contrasted with the middle class value orientations of the larger society. Weller's book has helped to perpetuate the stereotypical image of the Appalachian "hillbilly" that continues to the present day.*

More recent attempts to understand the Appalachian culture have begun to question many of these early generalizations and the assumptions from which they derive. It is no longer possible to think of the Appalachian region as a homogeneous entity such as was suggested in much of the earlier literature. It is more appropriate to think of Appalachia as a region of contrasts: rural-urban, poverty-wealth, stability-change, agricultural-industrial, employed-unemployed, young-old, etc. It is also a region made up of many different subregions which show a great deal of variation in their accommodation to social and economic conditions.

Another assumption to come under critical scrutiny is the one-sided emphasis upon cultural explanations as a basis for the persistence of certain behavioral traits. For a long time the "folk subculture" and "culture of poverty" models persisted with relatively little attention given to economic conditions as an explanation for the persistence of certain behavioral characteristics. In recent years there have been a growing number of writers who have critically examined the role of economic development and political structures in creating and sustaining particular social and cultural traits.

The articles in this section express a variety of viewpoints and perspectives concerning the concept of culture and community in Appalachia. Either implicitly or explicitly the majority of authors suggests that there is something distinctive about Appalachia and its inhabitants, but there is considerable diversity of opinion as to what might be labeled the "culture" of Appalachia.

18. The Search for Community in Appalachia

Ron D. Eller

The mountains have much to share with the rest of the country. The story of the mountains is the story of the nation writ small. It is the story of man's relationship to the land, of man's relationship to man—exploitation, racism, sexism, conflict, despair, pride, and triumph. It is the story of democratic people struggling with mass culture, mass thinking, capitalism, and individualism.

In recent years we Americans generally have expressed growing concern about the decline of "community" in our land. Such diverse writers as Simone Weil, Christopher Lasch, Peter Berger, Wendell Barry, and a host of others have lamented the individualizing tendencies of modern culture and have called for a revival of community structures that once provided the safety net for most Americans.[1] The "Roots" phenomenon of the 1970s reflected as much a desire for connectedness in our present lives as it did a desire to rediscover our ancestors. Recently, Robert Bellah and his associates have renewed the debate over our national character with their best seller, *Habits of the Heart.*[2]

We in Appalachian studies should be doubly interested in this debate since the search for community has been central to our work in the region for many years. No theme has been stronger in our literature than the effort to understand the Appalachian character and to explain the nature of the mountain community. If we agree with John Stephenson that Appalachian studies is as much a social movement as an academic enterprise, then that movement itself emerged out of our collective concern for the survival of the mountain community.[3] From another perspective, it is our common search for roots and for meaningful relationships in a rootless society that brings us all together as the Appalachian studies community.

Certainly, no aspect of mountain life has been so frequently studied and yet so misunderstood and maligned as "community." In fact, for over a hundred years observers of mountain life have denied the existence of "community" altogether in our region. Emma Bell Miles, who was otherwise a perspective observer, wrote in 1905 that "there is no such thing as a community of mountaineers. They are knit together, man to man, as friends, but not as a body of men. . . ."[4] Writers from that time to the present—including Horace Kephart, Samuel Tyndale Wilson, James Watt Raine, Jack Weller, Rupert Vance, Thomas R. Ford, and many others—have continued that traditionals view. Jack Weller summarized their attitudes: he wrote in 1965 that the mountaineers "have no community life as such

or life outside their very limited family group. . . . They are virtually impossible to organize into groups and are traditionalistic in the extreme."[5]

Given this perceived absence of community, John C. Campbell concluded that the dominant trait of the mountaineers was independence, "independence raised to the fourth power. . . . Heredity and environment," he wrote, "have conspired to make (the mountaineer) an extreme individualist."[6] Campbell devoted an entire chapter in his classic book to the individualism of the Southern highlanders, and almost every writer since has found individualism to be one of the most powerful, definable traits of "mountain character." According to this received vision, *the mountaineer is the extreme individualist* who cares nothing for cooperation and has no commitment to community beyond what he can get out of it for himself.

This notion of mountain individualism has provided grist for the theoretical mill of those who would see the region as uncivilized, backward, barbaric or degenerate. It has become the popular symbol of the mountaineer in cartoons and the media and has been used to explain everything from labor violence to poor health. In fact, the origins of this individualistic image are deeply rooted in the "idea of Appalachia" itself and lie entwined in the work of turn of the century writers who associated individualism with the passing frontier and community with the progressive and civilizing forces of modern, urban life. Campbell, for example, drew his accounts of the early history of Appalachia from the work of Theodore Roosevelt and Frederick Jackson Turner, men who believed that the frontier had been an individualizing experience, one which had given rise to the great independent spirit of American democracy.[7]

More recent historians, however, have all but turned the "Frontier Thesis" on its head and have pointed to the persistence of community in the westward movement rather than to settlement by independent pioneers. Far from being extreme individualists forced to adapt to a harsh environment, the early frontiersmen were more likely to be part of an extended community of interdependent families, and by practicing communal and cooperative efforts they were able not only to survive but to flourish. Contemporary scholars associate the rise of individualism with the growth of

Reprinted from *Contemporary Appalachia: In Search of a Usable Past: Proceedings of the 9th Annual Appalachian Studies Conference,* Appalachian Consortium Press, 1987, pp. 3–10. Used by permission.

capitalism and modernization, not with the persistence of the frontier.[8] Unfortunately this scholarship has had little effect upon Appalachian studies, and the communal heritage in the mountain character has been all but lost to our collective memory.

Research into the nature of the mountain community, therefore, would undoubtedly reveal a split tradition. In Appalachia, like the rest of the country, individualism and commitment have both been part of our common heritage. As Robert Bellah and others have argued, Americans have always spoken a dual language—one rooted in images of radical individualism, private achievement, personal consumption, and individual success; the other in images of civic responsibility, social equality, public virtue, and commitment. This second, public langauge was central to the republican tradition that dominated the early years of our history, while the voice of individualism emerged to dominate the cultural revolution that accompanied the rise of modern capitalism.[9]

Many contemporary observers of American society believe that this first language of individualism has so displaced our second language of civic virtue that it is undermining our capacity for commitment to one another and threatens the very fiber of our democratic life. "Almost all Americans in the 1980s," writes Harry Boyte, "have experienced some form of wrenching detachment from the communal settings that might nourish a deep and continuous sense of what it means to be an American."[10] Expressive individualism, these critics believe, not only saps us of the connectedness necessary for personal identity, but it weakens the social values of cooperation and responsibility necessary for a democratic society. Individualism separates us from the society around us and causes us to forget our ancestors, to forget our traditions, and to imagine that our whole destiny is in our own hands. We live for the present, lack concern for the well-being of others, and base our actions upon how we feel at the moment because we have little understanding of how others before us have acted. Like Jim Wayne Miller's Brier, "we don't know any more about our history than a dog knows about his daddy. . . . We try to live in somebody else's house. . . . (We're) educated, don't believe in nothing."[11]

But we in Appalachia do profess to believe in something—in our land, in our families, in our traditions, in our God, and in our sense of social justice. Perhaps that is why Appalachian studies has been throughout its history a challenge to the cultural hegemony of modern American life. It allows us to believe that we are doing more with our lives than just serving ourselves. Some of us have focused our challenge to modernism on political and economic relationships that have left our region exploited and impoverished. Others have focused criticism on the loss of certain moral values or

on the modern restraints to self-expression and identity. As a result of these diverse responses to modernism, we in Appalachian studies used to divide ourselves into the "action folk" (politically oriented people) and the "creative folk" (literary and artistic people), as if knowledge, creativity, and politics were somehow separable.[12] But politics and culture are part of the same whole, and any effort to change economic conditions must be considered within a cultural context. We are all engaged in the search for purpose in our lives, in the search for rootedness that gives meaning to our work.

Roots, however, don't exist in a singular vacuum; they require commitment to others—an interconnectedness that gives life to the whole. Thus, the challenge is not simply to abandon our first language in favor of the second, our private world in favor of the public sphere, but to reorient our individual lives for the benefit of the community as a whole. Our pioneer ancestors placed a high value on self-reliance, but that self-reliance had a clearly collective context. It was as a people that they acted independently and a self-reliantly. With the rise of modernism the collective note was muted and our primary obligation has come to be to ourselves. The differences which divide us in Appalachian studies today, therefore, may have less to do with action-seeking vs. creativity than with the reasons for our involvement with this work itself and the level of our commitment to personal and collective goals.

But how do we nourish the collective spirit? For us in the mountains to renew our communities and build a more just and equitable future for our children will require a new commitment and a fundamental realignment of our values. As we have learned in recent years, Appalachia will not be rescued from the outside, whether by the federal government or the private sector. Renewal must begin from within, with the revitalization of communities and of the spirit of self-help and civic virtue. The recovery of community will require that we move beyond a defensive reaction against the things which threaten us and assume a positive initiative to create a new cultural context for democratic change. Such an initiative requires that we relearn old skills and acquire new perspectives: how to talk to each other, how to share with each other, how to recover collective memories, how to discern common values out of diverse traditions, and how to connect personal troubles with social issues.[13]

Central to this process is the restoration of our collective memory. As is true with most social movements, the first step to collective consciousness is the recovery of those common experiences and customs which grant dignity to the individual and an alternative view of the prevailing culture. Martin Luther King recognized the importance of historical memory to the civil rights movement and encouraged his followers not only to recover the lost history of blacks in America, but also to recover the lost meaning of democracy as well. For King the civil rights movement was "not only directed at the transformation of unjust structures; it was also a school for citizenship through which ordinary men and women would acquire "a new sense of somebodyness."[14] Having an understanding of how others before us have acted gives us the confidence to make decisions in the present, to create out of traditions for the past new visions for the future.

Robert Bellah considers historical memory to be essential to community:

> Communities . . . have a history—in an important sense they are constituted by their past—and for this reason we can speak of a real community as a "community of memory," one that does not forget its past. In order not to forget that past, a community is involved in retelling its story, its constitutive narrative, and in so doing, it offers examples of the men and women who have embodied and exemplified the meaning of the community.[15]

We in Appalachian studies have made great strides in the recovery of our collective memory, but we have far to go in beginning to share that memory with ordinary men and women in the region.

Modern culture, with its emphasis on change, has a way of robbing us of historical memory. Appalachians have been especially victimized by that tendency, and until we do a better job recovering and retelling our history, we will be unable to recognize and evaluate the alternative social visions that have existed within our past. Only then can we hope to develop an Appalachian conception of the meaning of a good life and thus an alternative vision for the future.

Recovering our collective memory will also help us to learn once again to talk to each other, to share with each other, and to discern our common values. As the oral history students of the 1970's learned, recording the oral traditions of their neighbors required more than mechanical skills. It taught them how to communicate and how to listen, how to think across time, and how to relate the lives of individuals to the larger social order. Above all it gave them insight into the lives of the men and women who sustained them. In the process, they became tied to that community of memory themselves.

Renewing our individual ties to our communities of memory is a further step toward building active, democratic citizenship. Classical republicanism evoked an image of the active citizen contributing to the public good, and this, notes Bellah, requires us to see the individual within the context of the larger community rather than seeing the "self" as "the only or main form of reality."[16] Remembering our heritage involves accepting our origins—including the painful memories of prejudice, poverty, and exploitation that the pressures to modernize have attempted to deny. Accepting these painful memories is often the wellspring for social consciousness. Thus leaving behind one kind of individualism, Bellah suggests, will help us acquire a new civic individualism, that entails care for the affairs of the community and a new definition of the relationship of individuals to society.

Let us take, for example, the meaning of work in our modern world. How does the way that we define work affect our relationship to community? How does the way in which we in Appalachian studies define our role as scholars, teachers, and activists affect our ability to relate to mountain communities and mountain people? When I was growing up, I was encouraged to "make something of myself" by moving beyond my raising, beyond my family and the cultural community of which I was a part. Success was defined by my teachers as moving up the economic and social ladder, escaping the hillbilly world of "yesterday's people." Education became the utilitarian route to getting a job, and work became simply a way of making money and achieving personal success.

Gone from this modern, individualistic notion of work is the older sense of work as a "calling," wherein one's work was morally inseparable from the needs of the community. In pre-industrial mountain communities, work was a moral relationship between people not just a source of material or personal reward. The work of each person contributed to the good of the whole, and the success of that work was judged by its contribution to the success of the community rather than what the individual could get out of it. I wonder to what extent those of us in Appalachian studies today feel this sense of our work as commitment to that larger community which we profess to study or to what extent we simply use that community to further our own careers and institutional goals or to test our most recent intellectual theory. Is our work in Appalachian studies defined in terms of self-fulfillment or in terms of its contribution to the common good?

If we are to be about the business of nourishing community in our society, we must be more than just a gathering of like-minded individuals whose union depends entirely on spontaneous interest. We must carry a shared sense of civic virtue and committed citizenry into our classrooms and into the communities in which we live and work. We must recognize the many forms of community that still survive in the mountains and support their efforts to bring dignity and meaning to the lives of mountain people: volunteer fire departments, religious organizations, self-help societies, neighborhood associations, reform groups and other associations up and down the ridge which sustain public vitality and the egalitarian spirit. Such associations challenge people to think of themselves as a community—giving, sharing, cooperating,—and they provide living demonstrations of democracy at work.[17]

As for ourselves, we must live out our own understanding of community and bring knowledge and action together in the fulfillment of our professed beliefs. If Appalachian studies is to continue to fulfill its origins as a social movement, it must sustain the power to galvanize widespread political action for reforms of the structures that threaten mountain communities. This means the revival in our own minds of the old Jeffersonian, republican notion of democratic citizenship which requires the active participation of the individual in the political life of the whole. Commitment to community requires both servanthood and servant leadership, and public virtue necessitates political action to right the wrongs created by the excessive exercise of private power. We who profess to believe in Appalachia must work beside our brothers and sisters in the base communities of the region to support their struggles for democracy, jobs, and a better quality of life. We serve only ourselves if we study mountain culture, write mountain history, evaluate mountain conditions without applying that knowledge to the living community and using it to shape an alternative future.

Rebuilding the community will, finally, require more from us in the future than we have provided in the past. It will mean above all that we take seriously the challenge to provide a vision of what things might become in the mountains and in the larger society. It has often been said that we in Appalachian studies have a better idea of what we are against than of what we are for. We have been quick to react to specific threats and issues, but we have been slower to build a collective vision of what life in Appalachia might become. Martin Luther King recognized the importance of vision and dreams to his people, and he constantly reminded them of that dream. King knew the meaning of that verse in Proverbs: "Where there is no vision, the people perish."[18] We might add that where there are no visionaries, the dreams perish as well.

Building a vision of an alternative future based on strong community ties will require a new kind of thinking, a new kind of mind for Americans whose culture has been so strongly shaped by modern individualism. Yet we may have within our own mountain traditions the roots from which new spiritual values may arise: ethics of respect, hard work, family, self-reliance, personal dignity, tolerance, fairness, cooperation, and democracy. Our task is to fashion these strands of individualism and community into a practical ideology that is appropriate for a new era.

Eudora Welty once observed, "One place comprehended can make us understand other places better. Sense of place gives equilibrium; extended, it is sense of direction."[19] Perhaps the search for community in Appalachia may provide a sense of direction for the rebuilding of community in America.

NOTES

1. Simone Weil, *The Need for Roots,* trans. Arthur Wills (New York: Putnam, 1952); Christopher Lasch, "Mass Culture Reconsidered," in *Democracy* (October 1981); Peter Berger, *Facing Up to Modernity: Excursions into Society, Politics and Religion* (New York: Basic, 1977); Wendell Berry, *The Unsettling of America: Culture and Agriculture* (New York: Avon Books, 1978). See also Kirkpatrick Sale, Human Scale (New York: Putnam, 1980).

2. Robert N. Bellah, et al., *Habits of the Heart: Individualism and Commitment in American Life* (Berkeley: University of California Press, 1985).

3. See John Stephenson, "Politics and Scholarship: Appalachian Studies Enter the 1980's," *Appalachian Journal,* Vol. 9, Nos. 2 & 3 (Winter–Spring 1982), pp. 97–104.

4. Emma Bell Miles, *The Spirit of the Mountains* (Knoxville: The University of Tennessee Press, 1975), p. 71.

5. Jack Weller, *Yesterday's People: Life in Contemporary Appalachia* (Lexington: University of Kentucky Press, 1965), p. 88.

6. John C. Campbell, *The Southern Highlander and His Homeland* (Lexington: The University of Kentucky Press, 1969), p. 91.

7. See for example, Campbell, *The Southern Highlander,* pp. 93–94.

8. See for example, Berger, *Facing Up to Modernity;* Rowland Berthoff, "Peasants and Artisans, Puritans and Republicans," *Journal of American History,* 69 (Winter, 1982); Craig Calhoun, "The Radicalism of Tradition: Community Strength or Venerable Disguise and Borrowed Language," *The American Journal of Sociology,* 88 (March 1983); and John Kasson, *Civilizing the Machine: Technology and Republican Values in America* (New York: Penguin, 1977).

9. Bellah et al., *Habits of the Heart,* pp. 27–35 & 142–44.

10. Harry C. Boyte, *Community Is Possible: Repairing America's Roots* (New York: Harper and Row, 1984) p. 31.

11. Jim Wayne Miller, "Brier Sermon: You Must Be Born Again" in *The Mountains Have Come Closer* (Boone, N.C.: Appalachian Consortium Press, 1980).

12. See discussion of this "division" in essays included in "Assessing Appalachian Studies," *Appalachian Journal,* Vol. 9, Nos. 2 & 3 (Winter–Spring 1982).

13. Boyte, *Community Is Possible,* p. 11.

14. Boyte, *Community Is Possible,* p. 217.

15. Bellah et al., *Habits of the Heart,* p. 153.

16. Bellah et al., *Habits of the Heart,* p. 143.

17. See on this subject the work of Harry Boyte and Sara Evans, *Free Spaces: The Sources of Democratic Change in America* (New York: Harper and Row, 1986) and Gar Alperovitz and Jeff Faux, *Rebuilding America* (New York: Pantheon, 1984).

18. *Proverbs,* 29:18.

19. Quoted in C. Vann Woodward, "District of Devils," *The New York Review* (October 10, 1985), p. 30.

19. APPALACHIA AND THE CONCEPT OF CULTURE: A THEORY OF SHARED MISUNDERSTANDINGS

Allen Batteau

More than any other single discipline, anthropology has concerned itself with the systematic, empirical understanding of culture. Despite frequent disagreements over culture's sources, structure, and relationship to behavior, there is a general agreement among social anthropologists that differences between social groups can be accounted for in terms of culture. That is, the differences in behavior between (say) Englishmen and Eskimos are learned and not due to racial or genetic factors. Within this conception, there is assumed a parallel between the distinctions of social groups and the distinctions of traditions, so that one can speak of English culture, Eskimo culture, or Chinese culture. This conception has been modified by the distinction of subcultures to account for cultural variation within one society; hence, one speaks of an Italian-American subculture, the subculture of the lower class, or the subculture of poverty.[1] The conception of subculture assumes a similar parallel between the distinctions of subcultures and distinctions of groups. For clearly delineated ethnic and racial groups, such as blacks, Mexican-Americans, or Puerto Ricans, this assumption creates few problems. One can, without great difficulty, distinguish between blacks and whites in the South and proceed from such an observation to infer certain differences between black and white subcultures.

However, if one is discussing the subculture of a collectivity that is not clearly delineated, such as the Appalachian mountain people, certain problems arise. To discuss "Appalachian culture," one must have some way of telling the difference between the culture of Appalachia and that of other rural groups in the South. With our current understanding of culture, this is difficult. Certain modifications must be made in the underlying assumptions of the culture concept before one can discuss Appalachian culture in any systematic manner.

Culture is a system of shared understandings which provide an orientation for social action. It is a creation of social consciousness and not a historical or psychological precipitate nor simply a summary figure for distinctive behavior. Appalachia exists as a social fact. In discussions of Appalachian culture, we both observe and participate in the emergence of Appalachia as an ethnic entity. Considering this process of emergence, I suggest a new understanding of culture: that it is contingent, negotiated, and politically constituted. Instead of examining Appalachian culture *per se,* my intent here is to place Appalachian culture in a larger social and theoretical context, to suggest that the existence of Appalachian culture poses certain challenges for our understanding both of culture and American society.

I
IMPLICIT THEORIES OF CULTURE IN APPALACHIAN STUDIES

Ever since the term "culture" acquired popular currency, there have been numerous statements concerning the "culture" of Appalachia. Most of these are quite unsystematic in their understanding of culture; they must be examined to clarify in what senses the term "culture" is and is not used here.

"Culture" is usually identified with the learned heritage of a particular group or society. At one time the designation of culture was reserved for the expressive performances of the elite of society: the traditions in music, literature, painting, and the theater. But when anthropologists discovered that social diversity was unexplainable on racial or genetic grounds, this concept had to be elaborated; culture came to include all that is passed on from one generation to the next within a group, whether productive techniques, kinship forms, political institutions, or religious beliefs. Culture is shared by the entire group and not simply by the elite. A second elaboration of this concept, motivated by ethnic revivals, distinguishes among elite, popular, and folk culture. Within this conception, "culture" is still limited to expressive performances, rather than being a direct influence on all areas of life.

The anthropological conception of culture is associated with social diversity. As a result, many writers have ascribed to "culture" any divergence from their own social patterns. The most ill-informed statements about Appalachian culture consist of one individual's local observations of novel behavior patterns, with no explicit statement of his criteria of abstraction, except perhaps a familiarity with sociological jargon. Jack Weller thus finds the mountain subculture to be "regressive," "existence-oriented," and "traditionalistic": "Within the folk culture, fatalism has joined hands with

Allen Batteau has conducted extensive field research in several counties in eastern Kentucky over the past years. Among his recent papers on the region are "The Making of Appalachia in America," "Appalachia as a Metropolitan Problem," and his doctoral dissertation, "Class and Status in an Egalitarian Community."

Reprinted from *Appalachian Journal,* Vol. 7, No. 1–2 (Autumn–Winter 1979–1980), pp. 9–31. Copyright Appalachian State University/Appalachian Journal. Used by permission.

traditionalism to give the mountaineer's outlook a somewhat different cast from that of people in other rural societies in which traditionalism is also a characteristic . . . fatalism can so stultify a people that passive resignation becomes the approved norm. . . ."[2] In Weller's usage, "culture" refers to attitudes, norms, patterns of interpersonal relationships, and entire categories of people.[3] Similarly, Richard Ball discusses the "folk subculture of Southern Appalachia which . . . represents a type of social system built upon . . . *frustration-instigated behavior*." He adds that the "principal components" of this subculture are "fixation, regression, aggression, and resignation," and in another article he terms this an "analgesic subculture."[4] Here "culture" is both a social system and a set of defense mechanisms—non-adaptive behavior designed to reduce anxiety, frequently identified with infantile motivations.

For observers such as Weller and Ball, "culture" (or "folk subculture") becomes a catch-all for anything *they* find distinctive about the region. "Culture" reflects the *observer's* own background, values, and categories, projected onto the screen of a strange and unfamiliar "Appalachia." Weller, for example, highlights only those aspects of mountain life that contrast with the putative pattern of life found in the professional upper middle class.[5] Weller's statements about Appalachian culture have the status of a myth. His is a narrative whose currency is dependent not on its being descriptively accurate but on its being consistent with the preconceptions of the people who believe it. *Yesterday's People* was widely accepted, not because it accurately portrayed Appalachia but because it portrayed Appalachia in a way that middle-class readers *wanted* Appalachia portrayed. Hence, as myth *Yesterday's People* offers a better guide to the preconceptions of the American middle class than to the social life of the Appalachian mountain people. The eager acceptance of this portrayal had its parallel in the eager acceptance 80 years previously of the local colorists' writings about a "strange land and peculiar people."[6] Although the literary conventions have taken a turn for the worse, with sociological jargon replacing romantic imagery, the myth-making process is entirely the same.[7]

Oddly enough, such statements about Appalachian culture recall some of the earliest anthropologists' definitions of culture, which have long since been rejected as vague and inadequate. For instance, the early anthropologist Edward Taylor defined culture as "that complex whole which includes knowledge, belief, art, law, morals, custom, and any other *capabilities* and *habits* acquired by man as a member of society."[8] Clark Wissler stated that culture included "all social activities in the broadest sense, such as language, marriage, property system, etiquette, industries, art, etc. . . ."[9] Such conceptions of culture have been abandoned by

anthropologists because of their imprecision and indefinite boundaries. As Talcott Parsons noted, since "*culture*" was by these early definitions simply a summation of *behavior,* neither could be used to explain or investigate the other.

Instead of ascribing to "culture" whatever strikes one as strange or novel, one might be better advised systematically to collect and catalogue specific traits found in a particular domain of behavior, such as architectural styles, religious rituals, or folktales (as the early ethnographer Franz Boas did with the Central Canadian Eskimo). Although such a procedure has often been used to comment on culture in Appalachia, it does not carry one very far in defining that culture. Folklorists have long collected folktales among the Southern mountaineers, such as the story of Quare Jack collected by Leonard Roberts. In this picaresque tale, Jack, a trickster figure, goes through a number of adventures in which he outwits an old man and proves himself smarter than his two brothers. Roberts annotated Quare Jack in the following way: "This is the most unusual medley of stories and anecdotes that I have ever collected in the mountains. It has at least four story types all of which are somewhat rare in English-American tradition: Type 853, Catching the Princess with her Own Words; Type 1525, The Master Thief; Type 1653, The Robbers under the Tree; and Type 1525R, The Robber Brothers." But such collections do not establish the existence of an Appalachian culture. Folklorist Richard Dorson, commenting on Roberts' annotation of Quare Jack, states: "Type 853 is known in the French and Spanish traditions in North America, Type 1525 to Spanish, French, Polish and Negro storytellers in the United States, and Type 1653 among French, English, Spanish, and Negro groups in North America."[10] This particular item, which in one sense is surely drawn from Appalachian culture, is an assemblage of traits found elsewhere in the Americas. In fact, this turns out to be true for *all* of the trait lists that can be made for Appalachian culture. There is no set or sub-set of cultural traits that is found entirely or exclusively in Appalachia. The only basis for classifying these items of folklore as "Appalachian culture" is their provenance in the mountain region; but, they are found as well elsewhere. As shall be demonstrated later, other Appalachian culture forms, whether kinship structures, religious beliefs, or expressive arts, are found in other locations in the rural South. This is not to deny the existence of Appalachian culture or to argue that all of it is borrowed from other sources. Rather, we need a better way of conceiving of the integrity of Appalachian culture than simply listing cultural traits.

Others who have tried to examine more carefully the cultural distinctiveness of Appalachia have used surveys of attitudes. For instance, Thomas R. Ford inferred that the mountain people are becoming less provincial and less fatalistic by tabulating responses to questions such as the following:

1. Nowadays a person has to live pretty much for today and let tomorrow take care of itself (agree or disagree).
2. No matter how much or how little you take care of yourself, you are going to die when your allotted time is up (agree or disagree).[11]

This process is not rooted in idiosyncratic impressions. Rather, it systematically examines individual traits on a region-wide basis. But such tabulated responses do not yield a complete account of Appalachian culture, because the responses one gets are dependent on the questions one asks. The Ford survey posed questions in those areas of behavior that the middle-class observer usually finds most troubling: fatalism, traditionalism, individualism, religious fundamentalism. The unsurprising result of the survey was that the attitudes of mountain people are not so far off the middle-class mark[12] as some observers have suggested (for example). But such a finding creates a further problem. The Ford survey found that 45% of the respondents agreed with statement number 1 above, while 70% agreed with statement number 2. Is one then to conclude that Appalachian culture is only between 45 and 70 percent fatalistic, or is Appalachian culture essentially fatalistic, but with a near majority of mountain people having abandoned this trait?

The aggregate study of attitudes suffers from the same defect that the equation of behavior and culture does. The expression of attitudes results not only from deeply held values, but also from the actor's understanding of the economic and political circumstances surrounding him. If these circumstances change, so do the apparent attitudes. Hence, to observe that the attitudes of mountain people are becoming less fatalistic is simply to note that mountain people have (correctly) observed that their social, economic, and political environment is changing—not that their culture has changed. In the end, such surveys tells us little about the underlying values which are the substance of culture.

Finally, surveys of attitudes are quite imprecise instruments for observing the shades of nuance and meaning that often form cultural differences. Typically, the survey-taker knocks on the door of a stranger, asks a number of pre-set questions from the schedule, records the responses, and leaves. Since such encounters are not typical in the Appalachian setting, one should not expect the respondents to answer in a manner most typical of their everyday behavior. Often they will hyper-correct their responses to what they think the (middle-class) survey-taker wants to hear or else answer in the most neutral, unemotional manner possible. But the most fundamental meanings of a culture are quite passionately held and are more frequently revealed in informal discourse than in formal interviews by strangers. A mass survey cannot achieve the familiarity and sensitivity required to understand these nuances and meanings.

Frequently I had the experience of asking men in eastern Kentucky, "Have you ever lived up North?" The answer was often "No." I would then sit silently, waiting, studying on that, carefully controlling the urge to fill the conversational void with another question. After a minute's silence, many of the men would add, "I did work in the steel mills in Gary for five years." This was not considered *living* up North; these men had not done any of the actions such as marrying, buying a house, or raising a family that would *signify* that they had *lived* in Gary. To live in a place is to make some permanent commitment to it, to identify with the place in the same manner that one identifies with Irishman Creek or Asheville. One of the cardinal Appalachian values that many have commented on is the *sense of place;* as long as one does not live in Gary, the city does not fulfill that sense of place. Had I been a survey-taker intent on completing the schedule, I would have, after the initial response, simply checked the box marked "no" and moved on to the next question. I would thus have missed not only an important episode in the man's life, but also an understanding of what it meant to live some place. Only by being willing to listen, by providing space for the unexpected, was I able to learn this. Such opportunities are never available within the structured, closed-end survey.

Hence, the better approach to understanding a people's culture, considered a system of significance—the meanings, values, and thoughts that inform their lives—is for the middle-class observer to let the people speak for themselves and to record the results. Some of the recent efforts to do this have produced several oral history surveys of the mountain region. This is an excellent method for obtaining the initial data of cultural inquiry; it does not, however, obviate the usual ethnographic problems of selecting informants, establishing rapport, framing questions and probes, or interpreting texts.

As an example of the results of such studies, we might consider the statement of a farmer, builder, and agricultural laborer describing the old-time institution of the "working":

Back when I was growing up, about February you'd go clearing land, clearing it off for a crop. They'd send one of us old boys out and invite everybody in the whole community to come to the working. They'd come, too. I've seen forty and forty-five and they'd just clean off acres a day, pile it ready to burn. They was grubbing, sawing logs, cutting logs, spreading them, piling them in big grips, and getting them ready to burn. When it got dry they burned it off clean. There was no overseer. They all knowed how to work.[13]

One can infer from this not only patterns of activity and certain social relationships but also specific attitudes toward work and an absence of certain authorities.

One should recognize, however, that oral history collections are narrative history only in a mediated sense. While their truthfulness is unquestionable, they involve, like most history, a selective recollection of facts whose *significance* is consistent with current ways of thinking and a selective forgetting of facts that are too dissonant with current ideas. For learning of the facts of Appalachian life at the turn of the century, oral history and the diaries of people such as Henry Scalf and Verna Mae Slone are about all that we have; they make an important contribution in that respect. In terms of factual accuracy, they are certainly more adequate than the accounts of most travellers, journalists, and sociologists. But the yet greater value of these documents is what they reveal about *current* ways of thinking, about the current system of significance, a rendering of current ideas out of the shreds and patches of an experienced and re-collected past.

The resident's description of the past is thus a statement about the present, and one can understand present cultural concerns by a careful reading of and listening to these statements. The use to which these oral history narratives are put is yet another matter. Typically, they are collected and edited by university-educated historians, in an effort to articulate and preserve a regional or ethnic identity. As a public statement of "our culture," their purpose is to improve the group's public image, contribute to the group's morale, and form a heightened sense of group identity. This is essentially a political approach to culture, similar to that which is behind much of the black culture movement.[14] It stresses certain overt expressive behaviors, whether narratives of the past, folktales, artistic performances, or styles in consumption.[15] Within any group, participation in such rituals and the presentation of such statements are vital for maintaining solidarity and morale. The discovery of a unique culture within any nascent group is an important milestone in the group's emergence.

But there are two dangers to limiting our understanding of a group's culture to these public statements and performances. To the extent that they are deliberate, public, and politically motivated, such statements become secondary rationalizations of the group's basic values and assumptions. For example, in many rural districts of eastern Kentucky, one rarely sees women under the age of fifty wearing bonnets. Yet on the occasion of festivals with an explicitly Appalachian emphasis, the bonnets blossom. The wearing of a bonnet, at least by a woman under fifty, is not a primary trait of Appalachian culture but a secondary expression, a way of saying "I am Appalachian."

Another danger is that in the political approach to culture one examines only the articulate, overt segment of culture, while in fact most groups are inarticulate about their most deeply held values. Most Americans, for example, when asked why children should love their parents or why men are aggressive or why God exists will answer that it is just so, that it is natural, and some perhaps will quote a passage or two of Biblical scripture in support. However, in some societies, it is exceedingly *un-natural* for children to love their parents, or for men to be aggressive.[16] These traits in American culture involve a number of cultural assumptions that seem so "natural" to Americans that most have not bothered to think about them. It is similarly the case with Appalachian culture: the common logic underlying such diverse areas of behavior as food-sharing and religious attendance seem so conventional that they are rarely reflected on.

This is not to say that one therefore needs an anthropologist to discover the deeper meanings of his culture. Poets, novelists, and mystics are usually more adept at this than are social scientists. For instance, Appalachian music, which many ethnomusicologists have categorized as "melancholy" or "morose," was recognized by the mystic Thomas Merton to be apocalyptic—an interpretation far more consistent with other religious themes among fundamentalist Christians than any assumption of melancholia. While one hardly needs an anthropologist to discover the deeper meanings of his culture, we can say that to articulate the inarticulate, a dialogue is preferable to a monologue.

II
SEMIOTICS AND STRUCTURALISM: CONTEMPORARY APPROACHES TO CULTURE

Among all of these ways of examining culture—describing the new and the unfamiliar, listing cultural traits, tabulating attitudes, and presenting certain distinctive performances—there is no one that is "correct"or "incorrect." Rather, how one defines and studies culture is determined by one's larger project. If one is interested in folktales or architectural styles, one will examine culture in one manner; if one is interested in political mobilization, another approach to culture will be used. The anthropological project is an effort to understand what is common to all human groups and the bases of variation between groups. To this end, it seeks to relate a group's culture—its learned heritage—to the other facts of a group's existence: its physical and social environment, its internal structure, and its history. It seeks to derive such an understanding not from speculations or armchair reflections, but from actual observation of, and participation within, the community it examines. In this effort, it has been continually forced to revise its understanding of culture as more is learned about people and their behavior.

The basis for the modern anthropological theory of culture was established by Emile Durkheim's conception of the *moral order:* the shared and integrated set of ideas and values that provide an orientation for behavior within a community.[17] This concept was further developed by Max Weber's distinction between social action and the *orientation* of action: between what people do and the subjective constraints upon, opportunities for, and meanings given to what they do by the acting individual.[18] For example, in American society, we define certain biological relatives as "blood relatives" and believe that we *should* behave in a certain manner toward them, even when we don't. These definitions of who is what, and these shared beliefs of how we should act, are part of our moral order; our actual behavior is often constrained by other matters, such as social mobility, family arguments, or personal idiosyncrasies. These two sets of ideas of Durkheim and Weber are synthesized by Talcott Parsons, in his statement that a shared set of values and understandings provides the basis of group solidarity. A group, according to Parsons, exists on the basis of a moral consensus. The realm of culture is the realm of these shared understandings of the nature of the social world and one's behavior within it.[19]

Within this current anthropological definition of culture, there are two major issues that must be confronted, particularly when one speaks of Appalachian culture. The first is the constitution of the moral order: what is the nature of the shared ideas which provide an orientation for action? The second is the nature of the group or social relationships within which these ideas and values are instituted. The Appalachian data present certain challenges with respect to both our understanding of the moral order and its institutionalization.

Considered as a moral order, culture can be studied in many different ways. Two of the most suggestive for understanding Appalachian culture are the semiotic and the structural approaches to culture. The semiotic approach concentrates on the study of signs and symbols, the meanings given to behavior by the people participating in it. This point of view sees man as

> an animal suspended in webs of significance he himself has spun . . . culture [is] those webs, and the analysis of it [is] not an experimental science in search of laws, but an interpretive one in search of meaning.[20]

The nodal points of these webs are symbols, and their diverse strands, the various referents and relationships of meaning that the symbols encapsulate. On a mundane scale, we can observe that such a gesture as a handshake carries with it the significance of solidarity,

or at least non-aggression. On a grander scale, we can notice how politicians surround themselves with flags and other symbols; how one recent president, when his authority was eroding, gave a television address with a bust of Lincoln displayed prominently in the background; or how advertising skillfully manipulates symbolic media and images of the good life, in order to motivate consumption.

In every community, there are certain areas of behavior that are richly significant, that contain a wide diversity of meanings for the members of the community. In Appalachia, a rich semiotic study can be found on the voting grounds in county elections every four years. The experienced observer can "read" the poll long before it closes: he notes who talks to whom, how close together they stand, who shakes hands and who does not, what pairs of men go around behind the voting house and for how long. Two well-dressed men talking together suggests that a deal is being cut, while a well-dressed man's talking with a poorly dressed man, particularly if their conversation takes place in a hard-to-observe location, suggests a purchase of votes. A hand-waving greeting indicates one sort of relationship, while a cock of the head or the raising of a few fingers suggests another. From such a reading, one can not only calculate the election result; one can also get an insight into the variety and meaning of personal and political relationships in Appalachia. Similarly, in the car one drives there is practically an autobiography: sedan, pickup, or a coupe with the rear end propped up; oversize slicks or mud-and-snow tires on the rear axle; freshly polished or spattered with mud; an umbrella or a shotgun in the gun rack; and, of course, the state license plate displayed. While such symbolism occurs elsewhere in American life, we are obliged to decode it—to understand what it means—before we can understand cars or politics in Appalachia or elsewhere.

If we begin to look for the significance of a people's behavior, we achieve a better understanding of it than by simply assuming that it is mal-adaptive or regressive. If a Presbyterian preacher such as Weller finds it difficult to encourage mountain people to cooperate in group activities, he might, rather than deplore the lack of community spirit, begin wondering what significance such cooperation would have to the men. They might well see it as a form of servility toward an educated outsider.

However, there is a tension within semiotics that is not always appreciated by its practitioners. The signs that people live by are usually unconsciously understood, and few people, anthropologists included, are fully articulate about the codes of meaning that they employ in everyday life. Hence, when we observe another's behavior, we note as symbolic primarily that which is less intelligible to us: if we observe a farmer cultivating his garden with a Roto-tiller, that seems only natural or practical; if he plants that same garden by the phases of the moon, *that* is symbolic. This approach, which we might label "vulgar semiotics," examines the manner in which coal miners decorate their hard hats, but not the use of hard hats or the clashes over safety issues between union and management; it examines only the epiphenomena of social life, the gestures and rituals which decorate behavior.[21] The vulgar semiotic approach examines the ornamental but not the *conventions* of "practical" behavior in economics and politics, because, as Western rationalists, *these are so familiar to us.*

In actuality, though, we construct systems of meaning for all areas of social life, the practical as well as the ornamental. In fact, the very distinction between "practical" and "ornamental" or "expressive" is a conventional distinction; certain behavior, such as stylish dress or speech mannerisms, that might seem impractical for one person, might, for another, be a very practical means of "keeping up appearances" in economic or political competition. The expressive often serves certain practical ends, and, further, practical ends themselves are subject to conventional understanding. Miners construe their interests on the basis of certain learned and shared understandings about the sort of life they are entitled to, the nature of working underground, the impropriety of management "lording it over" the workers, and the actual power that management has. Union/management struggles are part-theater, as heroes and villains play to the galleries of their respective constituencies. Members of a society always order the material forces of their lives—their economic and political relationships—according to certain conventions. The task of social life, in this view, is to understand the many different systems of meaning which inform social life—the codes of political behavior, economic behavior, kinship behavior, religious behavior—and to resolve the inevitable conflicts among them.

At bottom, the tension within semiotics is not between the ornamental and the practical; rather, the tension is between the plethora of models and symbols that have to be invoked to account for diverse domains of behavior. To some extent this tension is overcome by the structural approach to culture. As applied to the study of societies, the structural approach was designed to understand the integration of entire social systems.[22] For the structural approach, any understanding of the world—any categorization of experience and any stipulation of relationships between the categories—is culturally coded. Further, to the extent that the community shares such a common culture and acts accordingly, these categories are *not* simply mental constructions but are realized in the organization of economic activities,[23] in relationships of power and dominance, and even in such concrete forms as housing styles and residential patterns.[24] To the extent that people construct their lives according to such shared understandings, structuralism, when done thoroughly, is not simply a mentalistic approach to culture.

The basic idea of a structure is that of opposition, contrast, or distinction: we can know some entity only by knowing that it is the opposite of that which it is not. As applied to culture, a structural approach seeks those basic distinctions or categories with which people organize their lives, such as the distinction between kinsmen and non-kin, or the distinction between blood relatives (consanguines) and relatives by marriage (affines) in American culture. These fundamental distinctions order many diverse areas of experience. For instance, we might consider the nature of personal relationships in a mountain community. The personalism of mountain people is frequently commented on, and the great value attached to personal relationships frequently influences political behavior and economic transactions. A structural analysis of personalism would begin by asking the question, "What are the different categories or types of personal relationship?" In this regard, I would observe that two of the closest forms of relationship in the area of rural eastern Kentucky where I did fieldwork are those of *neighbors and kinsmen.*[25] Each of these terms denotes not only a status (relatedness by propinquity or by blood and marriage), but also a code for conduct (non-interference and reciprocal sharing make one a good neighbor, while extended solidarity and identification are expected of kinsmen). It is a simple demonstration that many different forms of behavior are normatively directed either toward neighbors or toward kinsmen: transfer of real property is preferably to other kinsmen, while marriage is preferably with neighbors (that is, it is preferred that a spouse be an unrelated person living in the immediate district).

By observing certain rituals we can begin to understand the meaning of this distinction between neighbors and kin and see how it patterns other areas of life. A simple ritual like food sharing is richly suggestive of how mountain people view different relationships. In several years of fieldwork in rural communities in eastern Kentucky, among families that were little exposed to such middle-class acculturating influences as higher education, modern industry, or major roads, I noticed some definite and consistent patterns in the way food was shared among neighbors and kinsmen. Neighbors would share food by passing a dish over the fence, while kinsmen would share food by sitting down at a table together. Outside of somewhat acculturated settings such as colleges and club meetings, and except for one specific form of ritual, I never noticed two unrelated families sitting down together at a table for dinner.

The only occasion in the rural setting where biologically unrelated families ate together was when a church had dinner on the grounds. And there it was the *brothers* and the *sisters* in the church who ate together. (Food and kinship metaphors pervade Appalachian religion: many Old Regular Baptists state that one should attend only his own church, and not those of competing sects, because "You should eat from your own table"; also, preaching is "food from the Lord.") Only in crises such as deaths in the community is it universally accepted to sit down and eat with non-relatives or to attend the services of a sect other than one's own. In short, sharing food among kinsmen emphasizes solidarity and inclusion, the incorporation of a common substance, creating a community of identity. Sharing food among neighbors emphasizes a boundary (the fence), creating a transactional relationship; or else it emphasizes the manner in which neighbors pull together in a crisis.

Both the relationship of propinquity and the relationship of kinship are incorporated into a social form which Brown named the "family group," and which my informants called a "set"—the group of kinsmen, descended from a common ancestor, living at or near the original homeplace.[26] In rural areas of the sort that I studied, the predominant residential pattern is to live near one's own parents or one's spouse's parents after marriage; hence the rural neighborhood is constituted by an array of territorially and genealogically distinct *sets,* spread out across the map. In earlier times, when communities were more isolated, voting behavior was determined by the *set* that one belonged to; entire *sets* would vote as a bloc, and at times neighborhoods would be characterized by a long-standing antagonism between two *sets*. Such antagonisms would surface in family quarrels, boundary disputes, factional voting, and occasionally in violence.

The important feature here is that these two abstract relationships—locality and kinship, encapsulated into the structure of the *set*—form the basic coordinates of personal identity within the rural setting. What creek one lives on and what family name one carries both give one diverse reputations.

A basic feature of Appalachian culture is the distinction between relationships based on proximity (neighborliness) and relationships based on kinship; and great value is attached to each. This value emphasis orders many practical areas of behavior, including economic and political behavior; it is institutionalized in its most permanent form in the residential arrangements of the rural community. It is summarized within the symbolism of a *name,* for a name is both a signifier of individuality and a symbol of social relatedness; a name symbolizes the reputation one has acquired, both from one's own behavior and that of one's neighbors and kinsmen. In both of these senses, a name is inherited from one's ancestors. Walking down rural roads, strangers would often ask me, in an effort to determine what kind of person I was, "Whose boy are you?" Further, having a "big name" and having a "good name" are two of the greatest social values in these communities: factional politics, like basketball, are oriented less toward goals of material advantage and more toward the goal of "making a name."

The structural analysis of Appalachian kinship outlined here suggests that beneath the surface of many different social forms in Appalachian life—religion, neighborhood politics, residential patterns, economic transactions, and marriage—there is a common underlying logic: the emphasis on relationships of inclusion (kinship) and reciprocity (neighborliness), ritualized in certain forms of sharing, and unified within the symbolism of a name. A structural analysis seeks these unconscious logics, these metaphors and symmetries, which order and give meaning to diverse areas of life.

A structural analysis can also provide a clue for the distinctiveness of Appalachian culture. In this great value attached to kinship and to name, and in the solidarity of family groups, Appalachia and the American upper class are more like each other than either is like the middle class. In the middle class, reputations are based on the references given by credit bureaus, employers, and teachers; in Appalachia and the upper class, family name counts far more. In the middle class, the range of effective kinship rarely extends beyond first cousins; in Appalachia and the upper class, it extends as far as third cousins. To be sure, there are some great dissimilarities between Appalachia and the upper class; in the structure of the work situation and the organization of employment, Appalachia is more like the middle class than it is like the upper. The suggestion here is that the surface distinctiveness of life in Appalachia, which many have noted time and again, is actually constituted by a unique assemblage of structures (not traits) institutionalized elsewhere in American society. The logic of Appalachian culture is not a logic of surface forms, or syntagms, as would be suggested if we considered Appalachian culture only in terms of certain expressive forms ("popular culture" and "folk culture"). Rather, the logic of Appalachian culture is a logic of underlying structures, or paradigms. These structures are shared understandings, embodied within social arrangements, which give order to many areas of life. By establishing different categories of groups and activities and the differential values of these categories, and by seeking the shared understandings of the most general (and hence abstract) order, a structural approach can comprehend the most general integration of the society. Thus one can see the construct of *class* as essentially cultural, with our shared understandings providing a categorical map of the class system (bourgeoisie and proletariat; upper, middle, and lower), as well as stipulating certain institutional domains (the economy) whose relationships and whose system of allocation set up the class system.

Structures such as this are the form and meaning of social life. The sort of questions that a structural approach to culture can answer are best subsumed under the question, "What logic or meaning do these people find in their behavior?" It is impossible, though, for this approach to culture to give sufficient answers to such questions as "Why are these people doing what they are doing?" The weakness of the structural approach to culture lies in its inability to explain behavior, even though it is excellent for explaining the meaningful basis of behavior. Rooted as it is in idealism, structuralism necessitates an annihilation of history, an ignoring or assimilating of all historical detail such as war, famine, pestilence, migration, political manipulation, exploitation, and the thousand other events and behaviors that disregard these cultural norms and categories.[27] As has been demonstrated for speech, the underlying grammar or code only partially determines actual performances; contingent states of affairs bear a more direct relationship.[28] Thus the structural approach to culture can better account for fatalism (a world-view) than it can account for labor relations in the coal industry.

III
STRUCTURALISM AND SOCIAL DIFFERENTIATION

The inability of structural and ideational approaches to culture to explain the obvious facts of exploitation and class privilege in contemporary societies has led many writers to reject, or seriously limit, the use of "culture" as a concept for any explanation of "practical" behavior. At first glance such a qualification is attractive, for cultural explanations of the behavior of disadvantaged groups often acquire a blaming-the-victim flavor. The familiar argument that Appalachian poverty results from the fatalism, apathy, or inertia of the mountain people certainly has this character. Further, it is very difficult for a structural approach to culture to account for domains of behavior where there is no consensus on the norms, no shared understandings, but only at best what Marshall Sahlins calls "working misunderstandings." Examples of such situations would include nearly all class relationships, such as those involved in the labor relations of the mining industry. While at one level both the miner and the operator share certain ideas (such as a common lore about the mines), at a more significant level what divides them is their *different* ways of thinking: for many operators, the bottom line on the balance sheet is the

basic goal: anything that enhances profits is good, while anything, such as safety measures, that costs money without yielding a greater return is, at best, a nuisance. The miner, on the other hand, is interested in his life, his family, his safety, and his paycheck. That the miner is not religiously devoted to mining more coal causes some operators to see him as lazy. The miner, on the other hand, often sees the operators as callous and exploitive. Thus, when the two face each other across the picket line, the crucial fact for determining their behavior toward each other is not their common understandings but their common *misunderstandings*.

That such misunderstandings are a relatively stable part of an ongoing relationship justifies characterizing them as "working misunderstandings." Further, as anyone who has spent some time with social workers, mine operators, welfare clients, or coal miners knows, these misunderstandings are *cultivated*. There is considerable lore among social workers and the others, some of it developed by contributions from sociologists, which furthers the misunderstanding of the welfare client in the well-intentioned effort to help him. Yet to characterize such a system of shared misunderstandings as a "culture" is, under our current definitions of culture, disingenuous.

The fallacy lies, of course, in taking one situation and isolating it from its larger context in the entire society. Cultural analysis works only when the entire societal context is taken into account. The same culture that produces mine operators and social workers also produces miners and welfare recipients and the confrontations that develop between them. The diverse world-views of each of these actors can be seen as certain historically created inflections on common cultural concerns. But why class conflict is a typical history of that culture and which specific classes come into conflict at any given period remains to be explained. Events such as a strike in the mines or a quarrel in the welfare office are as much a product of historical contingency as of common culture, yet anthropologists have hardly begin to examine the cultural production of history in modern societies.

The problem is to explain the cultural production and concomitants of social differentiation in modern society: the existence of subcultures (whether class, ethnic, regional, or racial) and the interaction (or conflict and struggle) between subculture-bearing groups. Structural studies in anthropology have avoided this problem in two ways. First, structural studies have concentrated primarily on primitive societies, the so-called "cold" societies, which have neither internal differentiation nor history in the same sense that a modern society has history. Tribal societies, organized primarily by kinship and territory, do not undergo continuous self-generated historical transformation in the same manner that modern societies do. Their history is mostly exogenous—spurred onward by natural calamities and invasions—and cyclical, representing an alternation between war and peace, opposition and coalition with neighboring groups. Their history is standardized, highly patterned, affecting more the society's relationships with other groups rather than the internal structure of the society itself. Their history takes place only at their perimeter.

By contrast, in modern society, social change and history are built into the system. A modern society undergoes a continuous open series of self-generated transformations, whether characterized as revolutions or imperialist expansion. These transformations involve certain cultural redefinitions; one can think of the new cultural currents that resulted from the French Revolution. In modern society, history is involved in cultural production, just as culture is involved in historical production; in modern society, one must come to grips with the manner in which history produces cultural differentiation.

Second, structuralists have been able to avoid studying differentiation in modern societies by examining institutions (such as kinship) that are society-wide in scope. In a well-known example of this approach, David Schneider[29] gives a cultural account of American kinship, in terms of the separate categories of relatives (relatives in nature, relatives in law) and the distinctive features which define a relative as a person and a person as a relative. These are distinctions that few Americans would take exception to, although their connection to actual family behavior and household composition are a bit more difficult to specify. Since there is a general social consensus on the conceptions of kinship in America, one can observe their coercive force upon members of the community: the secrecy and the general horror which accompany incest and spouse abuse are testimony to the validity of these moral conceptions in American society.

When one examines differentiation within a modern society, though, including interaction across group boundaries, the structural approach breaks down. The most notable form that this breakdown takes is the stipulation of "subcultures" for such widely diverse groups and categories as social classes, street gangs, occupational categories, or religious denominations. The concept of subculture poses two problems. First, must one stipulate a new subculture for every different sort of group in the society? What distinguishes subculture-bearing groups from other groups? And second, does one assign a "sub-culture" to every category and collectivity in the society? To demonstrate the existence of a subculture such as the "middle class subculture," one must first demonstrate that there are certain concrete groups, having a similar value consensus, which are predominantly made up of those individuals one would categorize as middle class. Such groups, whether churches, neighborhoods, schools, clubs, workplaces, or visiting circles, must be shown to be sufficiently co-incident and congruent before one can talk about a "middle class sub-culture." This is rarely done, whether in studying Appalachian culture or Appalachian subcultures. For instance, one psychologist, following the lead of his better-educated informants, inferred the existence of three classes in a North Carolina community. The "lower group" (the "sorry class") he identified as having a unique subculture; yet he identified no unique status for the "sorry class" except that of renters (which hardly constitutes them as a group). Indeed, most of his statements about the culture of the "sorry class" come from the mouths of what he labels the "better class."[30] With such an approach, social science becomes a perpetuation of the mythology of the privileged classes.

The collapse of structuralism in the study of social differentiation in modern societies is often hidden by the plausible assumption of ethnic subcultures. From such a perspective, there is a dominant "mainstream" culture, borne by most Americans (but especially the middle class), and various ethnic groups, with their own national origins and heritage, at various stages of assimilation into the "mainstream." Any *differences* between the group subculture and the "mainstream culture" can be ascribed to the diverse national heritages of the ethnic groups, and any similarities between the two are part of the ongoing process of acculturation and assimilation.[31] The ethnic subculture model presumes a clearly delineated group, marked variously by physiognomy, surname, or speech. The two components of this model, group boundary and group heritage, are assumed to be easily discoverable. By this model, Appalachia is often seen as a quasi- (or proto-) ethnic entity, having achieved a distinctive identity by virtue of physical isolation (a boundary) from the developing middle class of the early twentieth century, and hence now possessing a distinctive subculture which is disappearing as Appalachian people are "exposed" to the middle-class mainstream. Hence, the passing of provincialism.[32]

While this model has a certain plausibility, it does not stand up to close scrutiny. Research on ethnicity is beginning to demonstrate that the ethnic subculture model presumes that which is most in need of explanation: the boundaries and heritage of the ethnic group. The heritage of any given ethnic group usually has more to do with contemporary politics—immigration and the contact situation—than national tradition. For instance, various ethnic groups in America, such as Italians and Chinese, had quite diverse cultures in their home countries. Yet these cultures became diluted and unified in most respects once having come to America, with differences in regional cuisine being perhaps the only survival of a rich historical diversity.[33] Defining ethnic boundaries is even more difficult. In most cases, the boundaries of ethnic groups shift to include and exclude various populations, depending on historical accident and political expedient. One of the newest ethnic groups on the American scene, the "Indochinese refugees," are not unified by common language, common nationality, common religion, common policy, or common custom. Their status as an ethnic group is solely a product of the Thirty-Years War in Southeast Asia and the refugee population that war produced.[34]

For most ethnic groups there is some rough coincidence between ethnic identity (i.e., categorization by the larger society), ethnic heritage, and ethnic boundaries. But for Appalachia, the situation is more complex. There is no question that an Appalachian identity has been created in the public consciousness through various media images and embodied in state and federal legislation. Defining an Appalachian heritage and drawing the boundaries of Appalachia, however, are more difficult.

The diversity of subcultures within Appalachia has frequently been noted.[35] Further, if one analyzes the culture of communities in the Appalachian mountains in terms of various *traits,* there are few that are not found elsewhere in the South among certain sectors of the rural population. We might take two examples that are usually considered central to any culture: religion and kinship. The sectarian fundamentalist Baptist congregations that are typical of (rural) Appalachia are found in many areas of the rural South, having been reported by Terry and Sims in Alabama, Matthews in middle Tennessee, West in southern Missouri, and Rubin, Pope, and Morland in the Carolina Piedmont.[36] These areas are not included in even the most generous definitions of Appalachia. Further, the extended kinship groups that are typical of Appalachia were found in many areas of the South before the coming of roads.[37] Campbell's view of Appalachian culture as being simply an intensification of rural forms found throughout the South is supported by these data.[38]

The boundaries of Appalachia present yet a more difficult problem. In terms of media images, Appalachia consists of a depressed area encompassing eastern Kentucky, eastern Tennessee, southwestern Virginia, and most of West Virginia. A more balanced set of boundaries is offered by the Ford study, which includes the Allegheny and Blue Ridge Mountains in addition to the Cumberland Plateau.[39] A very generous bounding of Appalachia was established by the act of Congress which created the Appalachian Regional Commission in 1965. These boundaries have shifted for political reasons: when public attention and sympathy are needed for Appalachian programs, Appalachia is the depressed area of the Cumberland Plateau, the media's Appalachia. When the emphasis is on the folk traditions of the mountain people or the majesty of the landscape, the focus shifts to the Blue Ridge and the Allegheny range; when congressional support is needed for Appalachian appropriations, the boundaries expand to include as many states and congressional districts as plausible; when these appropriations are allocated by the A.R.C., the greater share of the funds goes to the more affluent development districts of the northern and southern extremes of the range, rather than to the depressed area of central Appalachia.

Further, when we consider what populations are considered "authentic" Appalachians, the definitions shift: sometimes it is only the Anglo-Saxons;[40] sometimes it includes the Italian and Hungarian coal miners that came to West Virginia around the turn of the century. Sometimes it is only the poor;[41] sometimes it includes both the poor and the rich. Sometimes it is only the rural dwellers, while at other times it includes "urban Appalachians," whether in Roanoke or Detroit. Sometimes it is only the native-born residents, while at other times it includes both immigrants and emigrants. Sometimes the definitions of who and what is Appalachian seem so confused that all one can say is that "Appalachia is a state of mind" or (as one well-known novelist stated), there are many Appalachias, and everyone must find his own.

IV
CULTURE AS A POLITICAL CREATION

Using contemporary definitions of culture, it appears to make no sense to talk about Appalachian culture except either in the solipsistic sense just mentioned or else at a very abstract level with no apparent relationship to people or their behavior. Yet in the study of simpler societies, the concept of culture has been invaluable in illuminating both the uniquely shared qualities of the community and its members' consciousness and behavior. If the concept of culture is to have such value in the study of a complex region such as the Southern mountains, then certain modifications are necessary. If one wishes for a discussion of culture to have any relevance for peoples' communities or their behavior, one must acknowledge that the relationship between culture and behavior might be different in a modern society from what it is in a primitive society.

In the primitive society, few significant areas of behavior are structured by the shared misunderstandings referred to previously. Only behavior with outsiders, across the boundary of the culture-bearing unit, is so ordered. Within the community, normative behavior is structured by shared understandings. In a modern society, by contrast, these contradictions and negations, which are experienced in the simple society only at its perimeter, are built into the system: class conflict, center/periphery tensions, ethnic rivalries, are all features of modern societies, culturally produced and culturally coded.[42] They create boundaries which are politically reinforced and which restrict shared understandings. Behavior across such boundaries is structured by shared and cultivated *misunderstandings*. In contrast to the primitive society, values in the modern community are often negotiated (rather than given); behavior is, at times, normatively expedient (rather than moral); and the relationship between a group and its members is at times contingent rather than coercive. That is, while still discussing groups, patterned behavior, and values, we must recognize a greater fluidity and variability in a modern society. The model of culture that this indicates adds three dimensions to the structuralist model that has thus far been under discussion.

First, within the conventional model of culture, values are instituted within the group or community. Yet with a modern society, the process of group formation is contingent, and the social-psychological tension between the individual and the group, which exists in all societies, can produce the emergence of new forms of groups, with new values. As such, the coercive force of the moral order, which as Durkheim noted is contingent upon the consensus of the community, is always an empirical question. When groups coalesce, their moral force over individual behavior is great. As noted earlier, it is a significant milestone in the process of group formation to discover or create a moral consensus. But our model of culture must account for the variation between an integrated culture-bearing community and a network of non-communal relationships.

Second, while moral values have their greatest coercive force within a community, they can be articulated in other relationships as well. A sense of value can be created, negotiated, and articulated within a noncommunal relationship. The term *value* has a dual reference: to the relative weight, importance, or propriety of the diverse categories within a structure; and second, to the common standard of evaluation which determines relative values. Value is both a weighing of alternatives and a basis for weighing alternatives. Given this understanding of value, from the actor's point of view, we can distinguish in any particular social relationship between the value *of* the relationship and the values *contained within* the relationship. The former is established by the significance of the relationship vis-a-vis alternative relationships, the latter by the significance of alternative behaviors within the relationship.

Both of these sets of alternatives are determined by historical possibility and cultural propriety.

We might consider, for example, the value of residential location in the early rural community. A hundred years ago in eastern Kentucky, upon getting married, one had essentially two choices about where to establish a residence: at the homeplace of one's parents or of one's spouse's parents. Since there were so few alternatives, the social relationships contained within residence were highly valued. Where there are a large number of alternatives—whether in the cultural definition of what is appropriate, the political awareness of what is possible, or the historical contingency of what is actually present—the relationship *per se* will be less valued. Within any given relationship, there are a large number of alternative behaviors possible; determining what is possible within a relationship can often be a matter of testing, negotiation, and, not infrequently, struggle. The value or significance of these alternatives is not always a matter of consensus between the partners in the relationship. For instance, behaviors within would signal to a social worker a client's desire for self-improvement, might signal self-abasement to the client. For any given actor, there will be an adjustment between these two aspects of the relationship: the greater the value of the relationship *per se*, the less discriminating one will be over the value of its contents (beggars cannot be choosers); conversely, the less the value of the relationship *qua* relationship, the more it will derive its value from its content. In this process of adjustment, continuously provoked by negotiation and testing, relationships, alternatives, and even values are often redefined. In their collective relationship to the mine bosses, coal miners redefined relationships (de-emphasizing personal loyalty to employer and weakening family ties), alternatives (adding peer-group solidarity and emigration to the range of survival strategies available to them), and values (for the first time, for some, placing greater value on economic position than on attachment to place).

The key term in this conception of value (and hence of culture) is the idea of choice, of an alternative. The articulation of values is a weighing of alternatives, and the alternatives one has to weigh, in addition to being culturally defined (as in primitive societies), are a matter of historical contingency and political consciousness. Thus the *third dimension* of this model of culture is that in a modern society the *conscience collective*[43] is political—*consciousness* is political, and *conscience* is political in that it is negotiated. By political consciousness I mean the realization of alternatives: the choices that people receive in their lives constitute their political consciousness. It was a matter of political consciousness when miners saw their only alternatives as either obedience to the boss or black-listing and privation. It was a new political consciousness when a coal miner realized that by allying with other miners he could negotiate a better contract than he could alone. It is a new political consciousness when a consumer realizes that the good life does not depend on buying all that he sees advertised in national media. It is a new political consciousness when a social worker realizes that she need not impose on her client rules that she herself does not agree with. Quite often, such changes in political consciousness are attained by accident (i.e., from historical contingency): an accidental breaking of a rule which is not followed by any sanction, a spontaneous meeting of two individuals who share similar experiences. In short, political consciousness incorporates both cultural necessity and historical contingency.

By political *conscience,* I further need the adjustment of contradictions between the moral and the expedient values of alternatives. The conflict between morality and expediency is typical of all negotiated behavior, yet it is a conflict which must be resolved if one is to act. It is an act of political conscience when one joins a union. It is an act of political conscience to quit a job for moral purposes. Such acts place the general social good ahead of one's immediate advantage.

The first element of this model, the contingency of group formation, is a function of the third; that is, the contingent existence of a moral community with coercive force over individual behavior depends on the political dimension of the *conscience collective.* The awareness by a group of workers that in some important respect they share a similar situation and fate is the first step in the formation of a union; the translation of that awareness from the pursuit of individual advantage to common goals is a step in the transformation from wage- to class-consciousness. Groups are formed when individuals subordinate their expedient interests to the moral dictates of the collectivity. From the standpoint of individual advantage, this is not a rational decision, and it requires a rather unusual set of circumstances, including a new understanding of common interests.[44] Similarly, groups begin to dissolve when individuals place their own advantage ahead of the group's moral imperatives. If individuals are seen violating the moral imperatives of the group with impunity, then the very validity of that moral order comes into question, and the group collapses.

By seeing culture not as *given,* but as historically *emergent* within the negotiation of values in social relationships and the creation of new forms of political conscience and consciousness, we move beyond the dualism that has continually beset culture theory. This is the dualism between economic and political "forces" on the one hand and cultural "influences" on the other. The one, it is sometimes argued, is more "real" than the other; the "material" forces of society somehow eclipse the "cultural." Yet as Sahlins argues,[45] these "material forces" are constituted by an array of social relationships and choices which are culturally structured. And, as I have suggested, these structures are continually tested, negotiated, and redefined within these same relationships. Culture is politically constituted, and politics are culturally structured.

V
THE HISTORICAL MAKING
OF APPALACHIAN CULTURE

The conception of culture developed here unites the classical concerns of culture theory with the distinctive features of a contemporary society which make that classical theory difficult to apply. These classical concerns are with the structure of shared understandings which define a community and with the moral/evaluative qualities of these shared understandings which provide an orientation for and a coercive force influencing social action. This classical model of culture assumes the existence of a moral community, a cyclical process of (culturally structured) history, and a suppression of any historical contingency for the validity of culture. It has been shown that, for contemporary societies, these three assumptions are often the very features most in need of investigation. The model of culture developed here incorporates these contradictions by allowing the existence of a moral community to be a matter of process rather than presumption, by allowing for values to be negotiated rather than accepted, and by allowing for the intervention of historical contingency through the creation of new forms of political conscience and consciousness. Although this model is applicable elsewhere in contemporary societies, its development was provoked by the study of Appalachian culture. It can be demonstrated that the very existence of Appalachia and Appalachian culture is a matter of group formation, the negotiation of values, and the creation of new forms of political conscience and consciousness.

To illustrate this, one needs a statement of Appalachian culture that is independent of, yet can be subsumed within, my exposition here. Thus we might consider Loyal Jones' essay "Appalachian Values":

> Individualism, self-reliance, and pride are perhaps the most obvious characteristics of mountain people. . . . Our forebears were individualistic from the beginning, else they would not have gone to such trouble and danger to get away from encroachments on their freedom. . . .
>
> The pride of the mountaineer is mostly a feeling of not wanting to be beholden to other people.[46]

These values, however, were developed within certain historical social relationships, relationships marked by struggle and negotiation and violence, which led to the initial formation of the mountain community.

The forebears of the mountain people that Jones refers to were primarily Scottish lowlanders. Throughout their history, they occupied a fairly consistent class status with respect to the English government. In the 16th century, they lived in mud huts in the lowlands of Scotland. In order to escape the predation of the Highlanders and the Borderers, they began to migrate to Ulster in 1610. There they also lived on a hostile frontier, providing defensive outposts, and were preyed upon by a hostile indigenous population (the Irish). In the 18th century they began to migrate to Pennsylvania, and from there southward to Virginia. Again they were subordinate to the Royal government, manning frontier outposts, protecting the low country from the Indians. Thus, the Scotch-Irish were, for most of their history, the peripatetic outcasts of the British Empire. They were "undisciplined, emotional, courageous, aggressive, pugnacious, fiercely intolerant, and hard-drinking."[47] Their behavior was kept in check mainly through their church, the Old Side Presbyterian Church.

In the 18th century, loyalty to the government was based on submission to the Church, and the vestries of the Established Church functioned as the Crown's office of religion and public morals: they supervised the behavior of all members of the community and disciplined those who violated the canons of good order. On the frontier, dissenters (such as Presbyterians) were tolerated simply by allowing a dissenting minister to occupy an Anglican puppit, thus satisfying the dissenters' desire for doctrinal purity and the government's desire for civil order. At this time, ideas of a proper hierarchy in society were generally accepted. As one farmer's son, later to become a Methodist minister, wrote: "Such ideas of the difference between *gentle* and *simple* were, I believe, universal among all of my rank and age."[48] According to Bernard Bailyn, at this time, democracy "was identified in the Virginians' minds with the 'popular and tumultuary government' . . . and they wanted none of it; the Assembly as a representative institution was neither greatly sought after nor hotly resisted."[49] Government was exercised through the parallel political, ecclesiastical, and social hierarchies of the county, all accepted by the farmers. These Virginians were neither "freedom-loving" nor "individualistic."

Of these hierarchies, the ecclesiastical hierarchy was the most important for the lives of the ordinary farmers; their religion was taken seriously, since it provided the greatest source of meaning and order in their lives. Yet by the middle of the 18th century, the Anglican clergy had largely abdicated their role as moral arbiters. They quarreled with their parishioners and showed interest mainly in increasing the size of their livings. In many accounts, they failed as paragons of moral virtue. The critical relationship of domination between the Church and the ordinary farmer in the hierarchic society of Colonial Virginia was breaking down. From it and from the emergent awareness of an alternative form of religion in the 1760's there came the values of freedom and individualism.

With the corruption of the Anglican clergy, the ordinary farmers of Virginia, including the Presbyterian Scotch-Irish, turned to the "enthusiastic" preaching of the New Sides and Separate Baptists. The doctrine of these preachers emphasized the direct relationship of the believer with God, unmediated by an ecclesiastical hierarchy of priests and bishops. They preached nonconformity and resistance to the civil authorities who (in the name of the Anglican Establishment) tried to suppress them. They were seen as treasonous by the colonial government and were severely repressed. The wave of enthusiasm and civil resistance that they began flowed directly into the revolutionary violence of the 1770's, and it was from the ranks of these believers that Kentucky and the interior were settled in the next two decades. "Freedom" and "individualism" for these farmers meant, first and foremost, freedom from domination by the planters and the Anglican church which these planters controlled. They sought such freedom on the frontier. The decadence of the Anglican hierarchy and the arrival of these New Sides (both historical contingencies) created an awareness of alternatives to submission to the establishment; those first dissenters who risked bodily harm to defy the Church (an act of political conscience) were the charismatic leaders who created this new order.

Their choice of frontier isolation did not take these settlers very far in developing political consciousness. The groups that were formed as a result of the movement to the interior were highly confined to localities: kinship groups, churches, and neighborhoods were the extent of the Appalachian community in the 19th century. The unification of the mountain people beyond these local groups was contingent upon a second historical accident—the discovery of coal—and the creation of new forms of political consciousness from the industrial development that resulted.

On the Cumberland Plateau, the second major formative period for Appalachian culture (particularly in West Virginia and eastern Kentucky) was that of mining development, spanning roughly the years from 1890 to 1945. For any theory of "folk culture" as a static entity, there are some major challenges here. A new mythology was elaborated in tales told of the union struggles; a new gallery of folk heroes emerged,[50] and some basic shifts in attitudes came about. Family ties became weaker,[51] rates of reproduction became lower,[52] crime rates increased, and, as the mythology would indicate, an awareness of class interests often eclipsed personal ties. A new social relationship was formed, that between the miner and the boss. This relationship combined loyalty, personalism, total domination (which some older miners characterize as "slavery,") and intense work for fairly good pay. We can see this relationship as one of struggle and negotiation in several spheres—the industrial worksite, domestic arrangements, local government, health care, retail trade—mediated only by the total domination of the company and the frequently paternalistic relationship between miner and boss. A redefinition of values (disvaluing loyalty to employer and emphasizing solidarity with peers) became possible when the bosses destroyed the one value that the miners found in their position in the coal camps—security—by laying them off and cutting back on wages. They overplayed their hand in the struggle over jobs and wages by requiring miners to trade at the company store, by shortweighing, and many other such devices. The emergence of a union became possible when the miners realized that they all stood in a similar relationship to the boss. The catalyst creating this new consciousness was the union organizer.

After this major formative episode, a new mythology which codified the new structure of values was created. As but one instance of this mythology, we might consider the legends and imagery that have surrounded Mary Harris Jones since her death. An organizer for several unions, she is best remembered for her work in West Virginia in the 1910's and 1920's. The metonym "Mother" was given to her after she lost her family in a yellow fever epidemic and subsequently "adopted" countless "children" in the coalfields. There are several documents—frequently quoted phrases, photographs, and a ballad ("The Death of Mother Jones")—which illustrate the legend. She had a flair for the dramatic and was adept at playing the trickster role that good myths require.[53] Her exhortation, "Pray for the dead; fight like hell for the living!" is still used by the United Mine Workers as a slogan. The widely circulated ballad commemorating her death was testimony to her mythological status. As Whisnant notes,[54] some of the details of her life have been altered to make a more perfect myth; for example, in legend her family was "killed by company yellow dogs." It is interesting to note the renascence that Mother Jones has experienced in recent years, with her name and legend gaining considerable currency among the New Left.[55] The myth born in the coalfield struggles has become a statement of values, not only for unionists but for other political groups as well.

With this conception of the culture of a modern society as contingent, negotiated, and politically constituted, we can also understand some more recent cultural developments in the region. The various components of the "passing of provincialism" that Ford describes[56] are most strongly correlated with age, education, social class, and urbanism. Each of these demographic abstractions is constituted by a set of enduring social relationships. Social class and urbanism contain relationships of a particular sort with other groups, relationships which often force a group to modify its values. Education is a product of an important social relationship (certainly marked by negotiation and struggle, as any teacher knows) during a formative period in the individual's life. Even attitudinal differences between age cohorts can be shown to bear a relationship to exposure to different socializing agents (television, for instance) at different historical periods. We have here a more concrete specification of the production of cultural change and modernization than is supplied by such abstractions as education and urbanization. The model of culture change implied is not inconsistent with these others, simply less abstract.

VI
CONCLUSION

In suggesting that the contemporary culture of Appalachia is the product of an interaction between local values and external confrontations, one can also suggest a definition of Appalachia. There exists, within certain publics, a clear sense of the *identity* of Appalachia, but, in actuality, Appalachia lacks a clear set of group boundaries and a consistent and unique culture. Rather than defining Appalachia structurally, as a social group, we might instead define it historically: Appalachia represents the convergence of two traditions, each of which contains its own contradiction. The first of these two is the external tradition, those relationships within which the uniqueness of Appalachia was first articulated. For the first part of its history the definition of Appalachia as a region came from outside, as Henry Shapiro has noted.[57] This definition was within a very particular sort of relationship to the region: the local colorists mined the region for literary images, the missionaries mined it for lost souls, and the coal operators mined it for natural resources. The later developers have mined Appalachia as well: the journalists for vivid images of rural white poverty and the technocrats for "human resources"—well-trained workers for America's economy, usually employed away from the region.

This multi-faceted exploitation of the mountain region was the product of the expansive nature of capitalist society. Since the 16th century, capitalist society has accumulated large surpluses, which are re-invested in new markets, new industries, and new regions. Yet this society, in producing the greatest wealth the world has ever seen, has also produced poverty at its periphery and alienation at its center. The production of poverty is the creation of a class having the unrealized alternative of an adequate life: in the absence of an invidious comparison with wealthier classes, there is not poverty, but only hardship; the production of poverty is the creation of great *disparities* of wealth. The production of alienation is the destruction of the myths, legends, and symbols with which societies create meaning. To quote Marx and Engels:

> The bourgeoisie, wherever it has got the upper hand, has put an end to all feudal, patriarchal, idyllic relationships. . . . It has drowned the most heavenly ecstasies of religious fervor, of chivalrous enthusiasm, of philistine sentimentalism, in the icy water of egotistical calculation. It has resolved personal worth into exchange value. . . .[58]

Yet paradoxically, the middle class seeks these illusions, ecstasies, and idyllic relationships just as much as does any other group. It is no historical accident that the most advanced capitalist society in the world looks to its "folk" hinterland for cultural renewal. Such renewal came in the form of local color in the 1870's, and, as noted by several mountain authors, it came in the form of "relevant experiences" for youthful radicals in the 1960's:

> Despite twelve or sixteen years of schooling the youths [who came to Appalachia in the sixties] were astoundingly ignorant. There was a general homogeneity about them which betrayed a shockingly barren background. In the main, they were offspring of World War II veterans who had successfully achieved middle-class status in suburban communities. . . . In eastern Kentucky these visitors found occasional exemplars of an old honest and self-sufficient way of life.[59]
>
> The most all encompassing characteristic of members of the left is the relative absence of what psychologists would call affective development—the development of those characteristics and personality traits which we usually associate with the arts: feelings, intuition, inductive reasoning based on experiential knowledge, and the spiritual dimension of religion. . . . Appalachian culture contains large doses of intuition, and creativity and sensitivity in the arts. . . .[60]

In creating the illusion of a folk-like Appalachia, the metropolitan middle class found the idyllic relationships that it lacked in its daily life. It is a typical sequence in capitalist society to create a poverty population, romanticize them as "folk," and then import their precapitalist "folk" qualities into its own symbolic production, even as the onslaught of commercialism is destroying the few genuine vestiges of folkways that remain.

This is the first tradition that created Appalachia; it also created the Indian (*qua* Noble Savage) and the romantic South of *Gone With the Wind*. But there is a second face to Appalachia which, while not oblivious to, is far less concerned with this ambivalent relationship to the metropolitan middle class. The Old Regular Baptists, intent on proper conduct in this life and salvation in the next, are part of this second face. The craftsman, carefully making baskets and chairs out of oak and walnut and hickory bark, is part of it, as is the family group, "living through and through one another" on the old homeplace. This second face of Appalachia is constituted by those social relationships which have endured, which form the mountain community, and which provide the most important meanings in life for those who were born, raised, and still reside in rural Appalachia.

Yet this second face of Appalachia contains its own contradictions as well. As an undeveloped region in the middle of a developing society, it was ripe for exploitation in the 19th century. Having a high rate of reproduction assured that Appalachia would have a perpetual labor surplus and thus experience the periodic tragedy of emigration. Valuing personal relationships left mountain people vulnerable to exploitation by the personable mineral buyer and mine operator. Strongly attached to localities, mountain people have found it difficult to organize across local boundaries. Just as the second face of Appalachia—the "folk culture"—offers a useful subject for romanticization by the metropolitan society, so, too, do its contradictions leave mountain people vulnerable to commercial exploitation by that same society.

But this "folk culture" was itself born and developed in the context of a particular relationship, marked by negotiation and struggle, with the larger society. This has been demonstrated in my brief discussion of the two formative periods for Appalachian culture. Hence the mountain population and the metropolitan society have always been involved in a struggle with each other; the emergence of Appalachia as a distinctive entity, embodied in federal legislation and articulated by scholars, journalists, and political activists, is simply the latest phase of the struggle. This struggle is similar to, and not distinct from, the struggles of other disprivileged groups in American society.

In defining Appalachia in this manner, one contradicts, it should be noted, the colonialism model that has had considerable currency.[61] "Colonialism" implies the exploitation of a culturally (and perhaps racially) distinct entity. Yet what cultural distinctiveness Appalachia has, as I have argued, is either an adaptation to past forms of exploitation which were more clearly based in class relationships, or else is the romanticized projection of the exploiting class itself. The distinctive culture of Appalachia that many discuss is a product of, and did not exist prior to, the exploitive relationships between Appalachia and the metropolitan society. Appalachia may well be America's energy colony or the last stronghold of Western imperialism; to emphasize the validity and authenticity of local traditions disvalued in the context of oppression is a crucial first step in the struggle against such domination. Yet to dwell, at too great a length, on the cultural distinctiveness of Appalachia, is to limit the political consciousness of the similarity between the domination of Appalachia and other structures of oppression in American society. To the extent that culture is politically constituted, discussions of cultures are, for better or for worse, politically consequential.

NOTES

Acknowledgements: This paper, while prepared expressly for this issue, represents a continuation of a discussion of the interplay of Appalachian history and Appalachian culture that was included in my dissertation, as well as certain later papers. I am grateful to Robert McKinley, Fredric Roberts, Katherine O. See, and David Whisnant, whose comments on various formulations of the argument have contributed much to the paper.

1. Herbert Gans, *The Urban Villagers* (New York: The Free Press, 1962); Walter B. Miller, "Lower Class Culture as a Generating Milieu of Gang Delinquency," *Journal of Social Issues,* 14 (1958), 5–19; Oscar Lewis, *La Vida* (New York: Random House, 1966).

2. Jack Weller, *Yesterday's People* (Lexington: Univ. of Kentucky Press, 1965), p. 37.

3. Weller, p. 140, 154.

4. Richard Ball, "The Southern Appalachian Folk Subculture as a Tension Reducing Way of Life," in *Change in Rural Appalachia,* ed. John D. Photiadis and Harry K. Schwarzweller (Philadelphia: Univ. of Pennsylvania Press, 1970), pp. 69, 73; Richard Ball, "Poverty Case: The Analgesic Subculture of the Southern Appalachians," *American Sociological Review,* 33 (1969), 885–95.

5. Weller, p. 6.

6. Henry Shapiro, *Appalachia on Our Mind* (Chapel Hill: Univ. of North Carolina Press, 1978).

7. Allen Batteau, "The Making of 'Appalachia' in America," paper presented at the Southern Anthropological Assn. Meetings, Memphis, Tenn., 1979.

8. Edward B. Tylor, *Primitive Culture* (London: John Murray, 1873), p. 1, emphasis added.

9. Clark Wissler, *Man and Culture* (New York: Thomas Y. Crowell, 1923), p. 3.

10. Richard Dorson, *Buying the Wind* (Chicago: Univ. of Chicago Press, 1964; rpt. 1974), pp. 172 f.

11. *The Southern Appalachian Region: A Survey,* ed. Thomas R. Ford (Lexington: Univ. of Kentucky Press, 1962).

12. Dwight Billings, "Culture and Poverty in Appalachia: A Theoretical Discussion and Empirical Analysis," *Social Forces,* 53 (1974).

13. Jim Byrd, quoted in *Our Appalachia,* ed. Laurel Shackelford and Bill Weinberg (New York: Hill and Wang, 1976), p. 18.

14. Cf. Robert Blauner, "Black Culture: Myth or Reality?" in *Afro-American Anthropology,* ed. Norman Whitten and John Szwed (New York: The Free Press, 1970).

15. Cuisine, for example: Robert E. Polley, "Appalachian Food: Plenty & Good," *Mountain Review,* 4 (1978), 14–15.

16. Margaret Mead, *Sex and Temperament in Three Primitive Societies* (New York: William Morrow and Co., 1935; rpt. 1963).

17. Emile Durkheim, *The Division of Labor in Society,* trans. George Simpson (New York: Macmillan Co., 1933).

18. Max Weber, *The Theory of Social and Economic Organization,* trans. A. M. Henderson and Talcott Parsons, ed. Talcott Parsons (New York: The Free Press, 1947), p. 120.

19. Cf. Talcott Parsons, *The Structures of Social Action* (New York: The Free Press, 1937). The argument developed in section IV of this paper is based on David Schneider and Marshall Sahlins' elaboration and synthesis of Parsons' conception of culture.

20. Clifford Geertz, *The Interpretation of Cultures* (New York: Basic Books, 1973), p. 5.

21. For an example of this vulgar semiotic approach, in which symbols are discussed with no indication of their relationship to behavior or social reality, cf. Robert J. Higgs, "Versions of 'Natural Man'," in *An Appalachian Symposium,* ed. J. W. Williamson (Boone, N.C.: Appalachian State University Press, 1977). Folkloristic studies at times suffer from this same problem; cf. Richard Bauman, "Differential Identity and the Social Base of Folklore," in *Toward New Perspectives in Folklore,* ed. Americo Paredes and Richard Bauman (Austin: Univ. of Texas Press, 1972).

22. David M. Schneider, "Some Muddles in the Models; or, How the System Really Works," in *The Relevance of Models for Social Anthropology,* ed. Michael Banton (London: Tavistock, 1965).

23. Marshall Sahlins, *Culture and Practical Reason* (Chicago: Univ. of Chicago Press, 1976), pp. 24, 39.

24. Henry Glassie, *Folk Housing in Middle Virginia* (Knoxville: Univ. of Tennessee Press, 1975); Constance Perin, *Everything in Its Place: Social Order and Land Use in America* (Princeton: Princeton Univ. Press, 1977).

25. The analysis given here is essentially a condensation of my earlier analyses of kinship in rural eastern Kentucky found in "Making a Name in Appalachian Kentucky," a paper presented at Michigan State University, March 1, 1977; "Modernisation: Inflections on the Appalachian Kinship System," a paper presented at the Annual Meetings of the Central States Anthropological Society, Cincinnati, Ohio, 1977; and "Class and Status in an Egalitarian Community," unpublished doctoral dissertation, Univ. of Chicago, 1978. Collection of additional data was supported by a grant from the National Institute of Mental Health, No. MH31948–01, which is gratefully acknowledged.

26. James S. Brown, "The Family Group in a Kentucky Mountain Farming Community," Kentucky Agricultural Experiment Station *Bulletin 588* (1952).

27. Claude Levi-Strauss is quite explicit on this point. See his *Structural Anthropology,* trans. Claire Jacobson and Brooke Schoepf (New York: Basic Books, 1963), p. 22.

28. Michael Silverstein, *Shifters, Linguistic Categories, and Cultural Description.* Offset, 1975.

29. *American Kinship: A Cultural Account* (Englewood Cliffs, N.J.: Prentice-Hall, 1968).

30. Berton Kaplan, *Blue Ridge: An Appalachian Community in Transition* (Morgantown: Office of Research and Development, Appalachian Center, West Virginia University, Bulletin, series 71, no. 7–12, 1971), pp. 17, 36.

31. Gans, *The Urban Villagers,* p. 33; Nathan Glazer and Daniel Moynihan, *Beyond the Melting Pot,* 2nd ed. (Cambridge, Mass.: The M.I.T. Press, 1963).

32. *The Southern Appalachian Region: A Survey.*

33. Robert B. Klymasz, "From Immigrant to Ethnic Folklore: A Canadian View of Process and Transition," *Journal of the Folklore Institute,* 10 (1973), 131–40.

34. Kenneth Skinner and Glenn Hendricks, "Indochinese Refugees," paper presented at the annual meeting of the American Anthropological Assn., Los Angeles, Calif., 1978. Cf. Ronald Cohen, "Ethnicity: Problem and Focus in Anthropology," *Annual Review of Anthropology,* 7 (1978), 379–403.

35. Helen Lewis, "Subcultures of the Southern Appalachians," *Virginia Geographer,* 3 (Spring 1968), 2–8; *Our Appalachia.*

36. Paul W. Terry and Verner M. Sims, *They Live on the Land: Life in an Open-Country Southern Community* (University, Alabama: Bureau of Educational Research, University of Alabama, 1939), p. 171; James West (pseud.), *Plainville, U.S.A.* (New York: Columbia University Press, 1945), pp. 149 ff.; Morton Rubin, *Plantation County* (New Haven, Conn.: College and University Press, 1951); Liston Pope, *Millhands and Preachers* (New York: Oxford Univ. Press, 1942); Kenneth Morland, *Millways of Kent* (Chapel Hill: Univ. of North Carolina Press, 1958), pp. 118 ff.

37. West, p. 58; Ray Birdwhistell, "Border County: A Study of Socialization and Mobility Potential," unpub. doctoral dissertation, Univ. of Chicago, 1951; Elmora M. Matthews, *Neighbor and Kin* (Nashville: Vanderbilt Univ. Press, 1965).

38. Shapiro, p. 151.

39. *The Southern Appalachian Region: A Survey.*

40. William G. Frost, "Our Contemporary Ancestors in the Southern Mountains," *Atlantic Monthly,* 83 (1899), 311–19.

41. Weller, *Yesterday's People.*

42. "We arrive thus at a final distinguishing quality of Western civilization: that it responds transformationally to events, incorporates historical perturbations as structural permutations, according to a general code of significance. It is important to stress, however, that this is a quantitative difference within a qualitative identity. History is always structured by society; there are only more or less dynamic modes of effecting this. Nor do the principles of historical structuration differ so much in kind as in locus. The tribal people are capable of the very same transpositions and reformulations of the symbolic code, the generation of new oppositions out of old—only there it goes on mainly between societies and so appears as simple variation, whereas here it goes on within the one system and this presents a compounded growth ('development'). History there takes place at the juncture of societies. . . . For us, by virtue of a different institutional mode of the symbolic process, history is enlisted, in basically the same ways, but in the complication of the one society" (Sahlins, p. 220).

43. *Conscience Collective* is Durkheim's term, for which anthropologists have substituted "moral order" or "culture." Its literal translation is both "collective conscience" and "collective consciousness."

44. Anthony Oberschall, *Social Conflict and Social Movements* (Englewood Cliffs, N.J.: Prentice-Hall, 1973).

45. *Culture and Practical Reason,* p. 39.

46. In *Voices from the Hills,* ed. Robert Higgs and Ambrose Manning (New York: Frederick Ungar, 1975), pp. 509–10.

47. Carl Bridenbaugh, *Myths and Realities* (New York: Atheneum, 1963), p. 133.

48. Devereux Jarratt, *The Life of the Reverend Devereux Jarratt* (Baltimore: Warner and Hanna, 1806), p. 14.

49. Bernard Bailyn, "Politics and Social Structure in Virginia," in *Seventeenth Century America,* ed. James N. Smith (Chapel Hill: Univ. of North Carolina Press, 1959), p. 97.

50. David Whisnant, "The Folk Hero in Appalachian Struggle History," *New South,* 28 (1973), 30–47.

51. Lewis, "Subcultures of the Southern Appalachians," 6.

52. Donald Bogue, personal communications, 1976.

53. Archie Green, *Only a Miner: Studies in Recorded Coal-Mining Songs* (Urbana: University of Illinois Press, 1972), p. 269.

54. Whisnant, "The Folk Hero," p. 36.

55. Green, p. 271.

56. *The Southern Appalachian Region: A Survey.*

57. Shapiro, *Appalachia on Our Mind.*

58. Karl Marx and Friedrich Engels, *The Communist Manifesto,* trans. Samuel Moore (London: Penguin Books, 1967), p. 82.

59. Harry Caudill, *The Watches of the Night* (Boston: Little, Brown & Co., 1976), p. 24.

60. Bill Best, "Stripping Appalachian Soul," *Mountain Review,* 4 (1979), 16.

61. *Colonialism in Modern America: The Appalachian Case,* ed. Helen Matthews Lewis, Linda Johnson, and Donald Askins (Boone, N.C.: The Appalachian Consortium Press, 1978).

20. APPALACHIAN VALUES

Loyal Jones

We mountain people are a product of our history and the beliefs of our forefathers. We are a traditional people, and in the isolated rural setting that was our home, we clung to things of the past, Partly this was because, for so many years, we did not have much truck with the outside world. We became self-reliant. We sought our freedom *from* entanglements. We gained solitude, one of the things we cherish most of all. All of this was both our strength and our undoing.

Our forefathers for the most part came from England, Wales, and Scotland, a few from Germany and France. In the beginning they were mostly English and Scotch-Irish, however, the latter being Scots who settled in the north of Ireland and whose descendants came to America beginning the first part of the 18th century. Most came seeking freedom—freedom from religious and economic restraints, and freedom to do much as they pleased. The patterns of settlement shows

that they were seeking space and solitude. Although considerable numbers of them were literate, as evident from their signing of public documents and their possession of books, they abandoned formal education when they took to the woods. This was a choice of profound significance for mountaineers. They chose freedom and solitude and mainly rejected the accoutrements of civilization.

Life in the wilderness and the continuing isolation of Southern Mountaineers have made us different in many ways from most other Americans. The Appalachian value system that influences attitudes and behavior is different from that which is held by our fellow countrymen, although it seems clear that it is similar to the value system of an earlier America. Let me list

Reprinted from *Twig Magazine.* Used by permission.

some of the values shared by *Appalachian people* that are still important in our lives:

Religion
Individualism, Self-Reliance and Pride
Neighborliness and Hospitality
Family Solidarity
Personalism
Love of Place
Modesty and Being One's Self
Sense of Beauty
Sense of Humor
Patriotism

Religion

Mountain people are religious. This does not necessarily mean that they all go to church, but they are religious in the sense of their values, mostly, and the meaning they see in life spring from religious sources. One has to understand the religion of mountaineers before he can begin to understand mountaineers. In the beginning they were Presbyterians, Episcopalians, and other formally organized denominations, but these churches required an educated clergy and centralized organization, impractical requirements in the wilderness, and so locally autonomous sects grew up. These individualistic churches stressed the fundamentals of the faith and depended on local resources and leadership.

The home mission boards of the mainline denominations have usually looked on these local sect churches as inadequate for us mountaineers, something that we must be saved from, and so they sent hundreds of missionaries to do the job. Many social reformers also view the local sect churches as a hindrance to social progress. What they fail to see is that it was the church which helped sustain us and made life worth living in grim situations. Religion shaped our lives, but at the same time we shaped our religion. Culture and religion are intertwined. There is not enough time to say as much as should be said on this subject, but let me make a few points. The life on the frontier did not allow for an optimistic social gospel. One was lucky if he endured. Hard work did not bring a sure reward. Therefore the religion became *fatalistic* and stressed rewards in another life. The important thing was to get religion—get saved—which meant accepting Jesus as one's personal savior. It was and is a realistic religion which fitted a realistic people. It is based on belief in the Original Sin, that man is fallible, that he will fail, does fail. We mountaineers readily see that the human tragedy is *this,* that man sees so clearly what he should be and what he should do and yet he fails so consistently. Not only does man fail, but he is presumptuous, pretending

to be what he is not, pretending at times *he* is God. But in spite of his failings and presumption, man is still saved if he has accepted Jesus Christ. This is the Good News! Thus, we can look forward to a life better than this one, where we as individuals will be different—better—also. There is strong belief in the ethic of the Golden Rule. These beliefs, and variations on them, have sustained us, have given our lives meaning, and have helped us to rationalize our lack of material success. Every group of people must have meaning in their lives, have to believe in themselves. Religion helps to make this belief possible. There are few Appalachian atheists because Appalachians need God. Many of the values and beliefs which follow have religious origins.

Individualism, Self-Reliance and Pride

These are perhaps the most obvious characteristics of mountain people. Our forebears were individualistic from the beginning, else they would not have gone to such trouble and danger to get away from encroachments on their freedom. This led them to take to the wilderness when they got to the New World. Once in the wilderness they had to be self-reliant or else they perishes. Thus, individualism and self-reliance became traits to be admired on the frontier. The person who could not look after himself and his family was to be pitied. There is a lesson in the mountaineer's all-out search for freedom. He worked so hard to gain it, that eventually he lost it. The mountaineer withdrew from the doings of society, and it passed him by. With the changing of the economy, this free man became a captive of circumstances. But the belief in independence and self-reliance is still there, whether or not the mountaineer is truly independent and self-reliant. That is why so many mountaineers are tragic figures now, bypassed by the economy, often wards of the welfare system, but still believing in independence. We value solitude, whether or not we can always find a place to be alone. We want to do things for ourselves, whether or not it is practical—like make a dress, a chair, build a house, repair an automobile, or play the banjo. There is satisfaction in that, in this age when most people hire other people to do most of their work and a great deal of their living.

The pride of the mountaineer is mostly a feeling of not wanting to be beholding to other people. We want to do everything ourselves, find our own way when we are lost on the road, suffer through when we are in great need. We don't like to ask others for help. Mountain people find it very hard to seek various sources of welfare aid when they are in need. We may pretend to be far better off than we are. I have known Appalachian persons who were in dire economic straits but who pretended that all was well. The value of self-reliance is stronger than the desire to get help.

Neighborliness and Hospitality

The mountaineer's independence is tempered somewhat by basic neighborliness and hospitality. It was necessary to help each other on the frontier, to help each other build houses and barns and to take people in when night caught them on the road. No greater compliment could be paid a mountain family than that they were "clever." As you may know, this did not mean the family was cunning or necessarily superior in intelligence, but that they were hospitable, quick to invite you in and generous with the food. We who were brought up on this value, will always have the urge to invite those who visit to stay for a meal or to spend the night, even though this is not the custom over much of America now, unless a formal invitation is sent out, well in advance.

Family Solidarity

Appalachian people are family centered. As Jack Weller has pointed out in **Yesterday's People,** the mountain person most wants to please his family, and he is more truly himself when he is within the family circle. Loyalty runs deep between family members, and a sense of responsibility for one another may extend to cousins, nephews, nieces, uncles and aunts and to in-laws. Family members gather when there is sickness or death or other disaster. Many supervisors in northern industry have been furious when employees from Appalachia have been absent from jobs because of funerals of cousins or other distant relatives. Appalachian families often take in relatives for extended visits. For example, one of the biggest problems authorities in the cities *think* they have is overcrowding as Appalachian migrants take in relatives until they can jet jobs and places of their own. In James Still's beautiful novel, **River of Earth,** the father brings in relatives, even though there isn't enough food for everyone. The mother finally burns the house down and moves the family into the tiny smokehouse in order to get rid of the relatives whom her husband could not ask to leave. Blood is very thick in Appalachia.

Personalism

One of the main aims in life for Appalachians is to relate well with other persons. We will go to great lengths to keep from offending others, even sometimes appearing to agree with them when we in fact do not. It is more important to us to get along and have a good relationship with other persons than it is to make our true feelings known. Mountaineers will give the appearance of agreeing to attend all sorts of meetings that they have no intention of going to, just because they want to be agreeable. Of course, this personalism is one of the reasons those who work for confrontation politics often fail in Appalachia. We are extremely reluctant to confront anyone and alienate him, if we can get out of it. If, however, the issues are important enough, we will confront him readily enough. The Widow Combs, Dan Gibson, and Jink Ray confronted and stopped strip miners when they came on their land. My point is that mountain people place a high value on their relations with others and it takes something mighty important to cause us to jeopardize these relationships.

Appalachians also respect other persons and are quite tolerant of their differences. James McBride Dabbs, writing about the South, has said that the southerner believes that every man ought to have the right to make a fool of himself. I think that is also a belief here in Appalachia. We let others be themselves, whatever that is. Southern mountaineers have not been saddled with the same prejudices about black people that people from the Deep South have. We have our prejudices, but at least we have not usually made a crusading cause out of them. This is something to be proud of in our history. Indians, whom we fought with bitterly, are accepted in Appalachian society, as contrasted with attitudes in the Southwest. Mountain people tend to accept persons as they are. They may not always like other individuals, but they are able to tolerate them. They tend to judge others on a personal basis rather than on how they look, their credentials or accomplishments.

Love of Place

We mountaineers never forget our native place, and we go back as often as possible. Always, we think of going back for good, perhaps to the Nolichucky, the French Broad, the Big Sandy, the Kanawha, the Holston, or the Oconoluftee, to Drip Rock, Hanging Dog, Kermit, Sandy Mush, Bean Station, Decoy, Pruden Valley, Grannies Branch or Sweetwater. Our place will always be close on our minds. My place is in a valley on the Hiwassee, under Poorhouse Mountain and in view of Tusquittee Bald. And this place is tied in my mind along with my family, and with the people I knew there in the growing process.

Modesty and Being One's Self

We mountaineers believe that we are as good as anyone else, but no better. We believe we should not put on airs, not boast nor try to get above our raising. A mountaineers does not usually extoll his own virtues; there is little competition among mountaineers, except in basketball or in who has the best dog, maybe. Persons who are really accomplished, such as in playing or singing, will be reluctant to perform and will preface a performance with disparaging words about himself or his musical instrument. The mountain preacher will talk of his unworthiness for the task and hint of many others who are far more able. Of course, when these formalities have been dispensed with, the preacher or musician will probably cut loose with a good deal of vigor.

My feeling is that we mountaineers have a pretty realistic view of ourselves. We don't fantasize a lot. We don't take ourselves too seriously. As I said before, we were brought up on the Original Sin. We never believed that man could be perfect. We know that he fails, often, and we are not disillusioned when he does. We don't become as cynical as others may when men fail. When they do not fail we are pleasantly surprised. These beliefs make us somewhat at peace with ourselves. We don't pretend we are something that we are not. Also we see a lot of humor in life. We can laugh at ourselves pretty readily.

Sense of Beauty

We mountaineers have a sense of beauty, and we have many art forms, even though some may seem somewhat crude to others. These expressions are often tied to functional necessities. Great pride was taken in the past in good craftsmanship—in the design, quality and beauty of wood in a chair, the inlay and carving on a rifle, the stitchery, design and variety of color in a quilt, the vegetable dyes in a woven piece. Much time was put into making a household item more attractive. But also there was fine craftsmanship in items which were beyond necessities, such as in the banjos, fiddles, and dulcimers which were made and were played with virtuosity. Appalachian people have perpetuated or created some of the most beautiful songs in the field of folk music. They have preserved some of the great ballads of English literature and passed on old old tales, told with great attention to the dramatic effect. They have also been the masters of the simile and metaphor in song and story and in speech. Such as, "He'd cross hell on a rotten rail to get a drink of likker." Or, "She's cold as a kraut crock." Or, "He looks like the hind wheels of hard times." Those are statements that you can get involved in.

Sense of Humor

We have a good sense of humor, although we may appear to others to be somewhat dour. Humor has sustained us in hard times. We tend to laugh at ourselves

a good deal, saying self-depreciating things like, "I was hiding behind the door when the looks were passed out." Our humor is tied up in our concept of man and the human condition. We see humor in man's pretensions to power and perfection and in his inevitable failures. We may poke a great deal of fun at pompous people and may scheme to get their goat by playing practical jokes on them. We may say, for example, of those who aspire to learning "preachers and lawyers and buzzard eggs—there's more hatched than ever come to perfection." Like every other people, when we mountaineers quit laughing, we're in trouble.

Patriotism

Appalachians have always had a special feeling about the flag of the United States. This is a land that gave them freedom to be themselves, and when this freedom was threatened they led in seeking independence. They took up arms against the British and defeated a British army in the important battle of King's Mountain. Much of Tennessee and Kentucky was settled by Revolutionary War soldiers who were given land in lieu of money after the war and they and their descendants retained intense feelings for the United States. Great areas of Appalachia were loyal to the Union in the Civil War. West Virginia seceded from Virginia and became a Union State. Kentucky was split, and many mountain counties were behind the Union. Jackson County, next door, for example, sent all of its able-bodied men to the Union armies. East Tennessee was a hotbed of Union sympathizers as was north Georgia. Camp Dick Robinson near Berea was an induction center where many mountaineers joined the Union army. It is important to emphasize the fact that mountaineers, except for a few, did not own slaves and thus were not tied up economically with the South. Berea College was founded here because of the attitude against slavery in eastern Kentucky.

Mountaineers have turned out with enthusiasm for all wars except perhaps for the Vietnam Conflict. It is a much noted fact that draft quotas in Appalachia have often been filled by volunteers.

We have an abiding interest in politics. Contrary to popular myth we do turn out in significant numbers to vote. We tend to relate personally to politicians who catch our fancy and appear trustworthy. FDR won over great numbers of formerly Republican counties with his personal charisma. Eastern Kentucky, all of Kentucky, has been able to switch very readily from Alben Barkley, a Democrat, to John Sherman Cooper, a Republican, as Favorite Son, quite aside from political parties. We mountaineers are more closely tied to the national government than we are to the South or to our local and state governments and we are generally supportive of national policies.

*****

I have spoken mainly of the values which I think are good, that I take some pride in knowing are held by my people. Some of these values and beliefs however, are a disadvantage to us, sometimes keeping us from putting our best foot forward, sometimes keeping us from putting either foot forward. Our fatalistic religious attitudes often cause us to adopt a "what will be will be" approach to social problems. Our Original Sin orientation inhibits us from trying to change the nature or practices of people. Our individualism keeps us from getting involved, from creating a sense of community and cooperation and causes us to shy away from those who want to involve us in social causes. Our love of place, sometimes, keeps us in places where there is no hope of creating decent lives. We have been so involved with persons that we have not taken proper notice of ideas and organizations which are important to us in today's society. We have been hospitable and neighborly to strangers who have taken us over and over again. We have been modest and retiring, and thus have let others from the outside do the jobs we should have been doing, and then we have usually decided that they have not done what we wanted done. Finally, we have been so close to the frontier with its exploitive mentality, that we have seen our resources squandered, and we have seen our neighbors exploited without our giving these acts much thought. Our sense of freedom has bordered on license, and we have thrown our trash and allowed our neighbors to throw their trash all over the mountains and in our streams. We allowed strip mining and industrial pollution to add to the mess. In our modest way, we have watched and have not accepted responsibility, and problems have closed in on us. I don't mean to imply that all of our problems are our fault; we have been the victims of plans made outside the region. Many problems, however, we have made or we have allowed to develop.

There are many strengths in the culture, however, strengths which have been lost in much of America. The strengthening qualities must be preserved and nurtured, as we attempt to change the qualities which diminish the chance for a better life. All work in Appalachia must be based on the genuine needs as expressed by mountain people themselves. Whatever work is done must be done with the recognition that Appalachian culture is real and is a functioning culture. This implies that change will not come easily and will not come at all unless the reasons for change are sound.

21. THE IMAGE OF APPALACHIAN POVERTY

Walter Precourt

There is little doubt that the term "Appalachia" is associated with poverty. In the 1960s the Johnson administration categorized Appalachia as a region of "grinding poverty." Appalachia was in turn designated a frontier in the "war on poverty." Literature on Appalachia abounds with statements about the region's poverty. In the *Washington Star* an eleven-part series entitled "Poverty in Appalachia" was published in 1964.[1] The following statement appears in the foreword of *Appalachian Kentucky: An Exploited Region,* "Appalachian Kentucky brings together the factors within the physical environment and the forces within the human geography which have created the conditions of backwardness and poverty associated with 'Appalachia.'"[2] *Poverty: A New Perspective,* published in 1975, focuses almost exclusively on Appalachian Poverty. The book grew out of research on "Poverty in Appalachia" initiated by the Social and Rehabilitation Service of the United States Department of Health, Education and Welfare. According to the author, "some areas, such as Appalachia, appear as massive concentrations of poverty."[3]

What has emerged is an Appalachian poverty image. That is, the term "Appalachian" connotes the idea "poverty." Where did the Appalachian poverty image come from? How did it develop? Does poverty really exist in Appalachia? The latter question may appear ludicrous in light of the barrage of studies and statements on the region's poverty. But if we scrutinize the meaning of "poverty" it is apparent that it rests upon a complex set of cultural assumptions and processes associated with Western economic history. Although most discussions on Appalachian poverty proceed from the assumption that the existence of poverty in the region is a given—that it definitely and concretely exists—there is by no means a consensus among social scientists and policymakers of what poverty actually is. But

Reprinted from *Appalachia and America: Autonomy and Regional Dependence,* Allen Batteau (ed.), pp. 86–110. Copyright 1983 by University Press of Kentucky. Used by permission.

one thing seems clear: "Poverty" as frequently used in America today definitely is *not* a simple synonym for "low income" or "unemployment"; it has complex and far-reaching ideological connotations rooted in the fabric of Western economic and political history.

This paper will critically examine the notion of poverty in Appalachia. It will seek to identify the historical, economic and social processes that underly the image of Appalachian poverty. An attempt will be made to show why the *Appalachian poverty image* developed, not why *Appalachian poverty* developed. The difference between these two terms is very significant, as will become evident in this paper.

CONCEPTUALIZING POVERTY

Poverty, at its extreme, has been defined in terms of absolutes such as starvation, death from exposure, or loss of life due to some total lack of resources. Few definitions, however, define poverty in terms of such extremes. Most definitions use criteria that vary depending upon the social and economic conditions present in a particular geographical region at a particular time in history. According to Louis Ferman, "Definitions of poverty are classification systems, designed to suit the particular policy or program purposes."[4] In the United States this type of definition is utilized by the Council of Economic Advisors, which defines poverty in terms of minimum family income. In fact, income is by far the most frequently used indicator of poverty. Wilber states: "Poverty itself is typically regarded as a lack of income, which in turn is related to poor housing, inadequate education, insufficient medical care, excessive fertility, unemployment, and many other depressing problems."[5] Madden cites a study that lists six broad dimensions of poverty: income, assets or wealth, access to basic services (e.g., health, transportation, legal services), social mobility and education, political power, and status and satisfaction. Income levels is the cornerstone of this poverty classification.[6] Davis reiterates the importance of income as a basic poverty-defining criterion in the United States: "Poverty is defined by the U.S. Department of Labor in terms of the adequacy of current family income in meeting a constant absolute standard of food consumption. The poverty income line is based primarily on family size, with adjustment for farm and nonfarm residency. In the Census Bureau's definition, additional adjustment is made for sex and age differences of the head of household." He cites Department of Labor statistics for 1973 poverty income limits for the continental United States. For a nonfarm family with three persons the poverty income level was $3,450; the level

for a farm family was $2,950. For a family with six persons the poverty income levels were $5,550 and $4,725, respectively.

While there is a great deal of consensus that income is the most widely used criterion for defining poverty, there is little consensus that income level and the associated criteria adequately represent the phenomena of poverty. Wilber attempts to go beyond poverty definitions based primarily on income, which he considers "too simplistic and unrealistic." He views poverty as a complex system: "The system of poverty is defined as the relative lack of resources and/or the inability to utilize resources. At a general level, poverty is treated as a function of resources and mobilization. . . . Thus, instead of treating poverty as a singular entity which is related to a number of additional characteristics of individuals or regions, factors 'related to poverty' are brought into the system."[8]

Wilber divides poverty properties into two categories. Category A includes those properties that relate to the life cycle of the individual. They include health, capability, motivation, personality, and socioeconomic status. Category B includes properties that relate to areas, regions, or collectives of people. These include natural resources, state policy, economic systems, social norms, stratification, community services and facilities, and mass media.

Except for nutritional and biochemical standards, which appear as *absolute* poverty standards, most authors feel that poverty standards are highly *relative*. Lampman states: "It [poverty] is relative rather than absolute, it is essentially qualitative rather than quantitative, it is to a certain extent subjective rather than objective. . . ."[9] Madden cogently discusses the relativity of most poverty standards.

> Prevailing concepts of income adequacy and relative deprivation . . . change over time. Some societies, particularly Western societies, have been characterized as being on a "hedonistic treadmill." That is, as individuals find themselves better off in period two than they were in period one, their aspiration for further improvement in period three tends to make them dissatisfied with the improvement already experienced. This syndrome has serious implications with regard to interpretation of income distribution data. . . . Proponents of the relative standards of poverty recognize that frustration is a function of the gap between aspirations and expectations. Aspirations of the less well-to-do tend to rise as they observe the ever-increasing affluences of their reference groups.[10]

The criticism of some poverty definitions is based on the recognition that most poverty standards are relative. For example, Michael Harrington states that "Poverty should be defined in terms of those who are denied the minimal level of health, housing, food, and education that our present stage of scientific knowledge specifies as necessary for life as it is now lived in the United States."[11] Rose Friedman, in *Poverty: Definition and Perspective,* questions Harrington's use of the idea "minimum levels" in his definition. "Since, except for food, there are no minimum levels specified by scientific knowledge, the only way this quotation can be understood is to take 'necessary' to mean 'customary' or usual—perhaps average in the sense of modal or typical."[12]

In light of the various definitions and concepts of poverty discussed above, it is clear that ideas about poverty deal as much with ideology as they do with material wealth. That is, while physical needs are often considered, cultural values and beliefs are equally significant. Since it is the ideological aspects of Appalachian poverty that are crucial to understanding how Appalachian poverty images have developed, I shall explore in more detail how ideology relates to poverty.

Ideology has been defined as "a general interpretation of reality in terms of a combination of values or preferences and objective descriptions of events."[13] In Karl Mannheim's perspective on ideology, "the whole fabric of institutions of a society must be intimately related to the dominant system of existential belief, which, in turn, not merely rationalizes, but springs from the exigencies of functional organization."[14] The use of ideology in this paper is in line with Mannheim's perspective, but the emphasis here is that ideologies result in a positive or negative interpretation of life experiences. Thus, ideology consists of a basic set of ideas and attitudes shared by members of a society or inhabitants of a geographical area that skews perception at a highly abstract level, placing perceived phenomena into polarities such as good/evil, right/wrong, and desirable/undesirable. Ideological systems are mediated and communicated through complex cultural codes and symbols, e.g., "God" and the "Devil." A fundamental semantic ingredient in the notion of poverty is the idea of good or bad, positive or negative. Thus, to understand the phenomenon of "poverty" we must take into consideration the profound importance of ideology. When we compare ideologies cross-culturally and at different historical periods, the ideological standards by which poverty can feasibly be determined seem potentially as variable as the 862 societies described in the *Ethnographic Atlas.*[15] Any "objective" criteria seem to exist only in terms of the ideological systems that give them meaning.

Even when we consider such basic biological necessities as food and shelter, we cannot overlook the importance of ideology. William Leiss comments on the difficulty of sorting out biological needs from the cultural context.

The symbolizing or cultural activity of human beings is so intense and so complex that the biological-cultural dichotomy is never *present* in the everyday activities of social groups, whether they are primitive societies or industrialized empires. The available anthropological record reveals the great diversity in all the human practices devised in response to physiological requirements, including the instances in which certain individuals will commit suicide by depriving themselves of survival necessities so as to maintain the integrity of the social group. What the individual organism objectively requires is a minimum nutrient intake, proper conditions for retaining or dissipating bodily heat, and socialization experiences to maintain group cohesion in social animals such as man. These are everyone's "existence needs." But such needs can be satisfied under a great variety of circumstances, many of which would be considered abhorrent by most persons today. Indeed these needs can be satisfied most efficiently in a setting where the environment has been ruthlessly simplified and organized for just that purpose. Such a setting is described in Zamyatin's famous dystopian novel *We,* where everyone is assured the necessary nutrients and shelter to sustain life. The sole nutrient is a bland petroleum derivative, however, and the shelter is a small glass-walled cubicle furnished identically for all. . . . All the most interesting and important issues arise when we study how the objective necessities of human existence are filtered through the symbolic processes of culture and of individual perceptions. In short, all the most important issues arise just in that nebulous zone where the so-called objective and subjective dimensions meet.[16]

If aboriginal Eskimo societies didn't regard themselves as poverty stricken, even though they lived in a harsh physical environment, possessed virtually no material wealth, and often were on the brink of starvation, then how can individuals be considered poverty stricken when lack is defined as an inappropriate house-type or style of clothing? This line of thinking may appear like relativism at its extreme, but it does point out the absolute necessity of understanding poverty in a particular context. We must ask why poverty standards exist at all. We must determine how the phenomenon of poverty is manifested and given meaning in different societies. We must identify how a *specific version* of poverty links to *specific* social, economic, and ideological processes. These considerations form the basis of the analysis of Appalachian poverty images which follows below.

IDEOLOGY AND CONTRASTING ECONOMIC SYSTEMS

To understand the origin of Appalachian poverty images it is first necessary to contrast the ideological characteristics of the Appalachian preindustrial economy to those of market capitalism. Between 1800 and 1900 two basic noncapitalistic economic patterns emerged in the Appalachian region. The first can be termed *family-based subsistence farming*. Eller describes this economic pattern:

> Each mountain homestead functions as a nearly self-contained economic unit, depending upon the land and the energy of a single family to provide food, clothing, shelter, and the other necessities of life . . . the family not only functioned as a self-contained economic unit, but it dominated the economic system itself. The mountain farm was a family enterprise, the family being proprietor, laborer, and manager; and the satisfaction of the needs of the family was the sole objective of running the farm.[17]

Eller also points out that by 1880 Appalachia contained a greater concentration of noncommercial family farms than any other area in the nation.

Few commercial items were purchased by those primarily dependent upon the self-sufficient type of economy. Some trading and bartering was done, but these were not interrelated with other aspects of the economy, and were not based on a commercial market system of supply and demand.

The autonomy from the national market economy can in part be explained by the presence of the second economic pattern, *independent commodity production*.[18] The main feature of independent commodity production is that the producer controls the means of production and personally carries out distribution of goods without an intermediary labor market or monetary system. Thus, production and consumption are localized. Banks characterizes independent commodity production in eastern Kentucky during the late 1800s: "Regular household needs, from clothing and food to soap, lamp oil, spirits, sorghum, hand tools, and stoneware, were satisfied through a local trading network based upon the exchange of products from household manufacture, limited farming, and artisanship. The producers and consumers in this setting were virtually one and the same people."[19] Thus, the system of economic exchange was for the most part outside the sphere of the national economy.

It is important to maintain an historical perspective when characterizing the preindustrial, noncapitalistic economic patterns that developed in the Appalachian region. Self-sufficient farming and independent commodity production have been replaced almost entirely by involvement with and dependence on the national market economy. The development of the lumber and coal industry starting at the end of the 1800s is associated with this economic transformation. It would be inaccurate, however, to suggest that the first decades of the twentieth century saw the end of subsistence farming in Appalachia. Even though the size of most farms had decreased, by 1930 self-sufficient farms in Appalachia numbered 150,659.[20] A study initiated by the Department of Agriculture in the 1930s found that 76 percent of the farms in Knott County, Kentucky were self-sufficient.[21] In 1945 Robert Galloway contrasted the social organization of "a typical county in the Northwestern Wheat-fallow sub-region of the Wheat Belt with one in the Southern Appalachian Mountain sub-region." The economy of the wheat farming county, based on mechanized farming, is a large-scale operation with the average gross income in 1945 being $33,000 from wheat alone. In the Appalachian county the farming is essentially domestic. "A typical farmer in this county plants about half of his cropland to corn which is the basic for food for his stock and his family . . . purchases are confined to necessities—principally clothes and a few staple foods that they cannot produce on their farm."[22]

It would also be inaccurate to imply that subsistence farming was the only economic pattern present in the Appalachian region during the nineteenth century. Capitalistic enterprise existed throughout the region in the 1800s in the more urbanized areas, and even in the larger rural settlements. In fact, one must often know the precise date and geographical locale to estimate the relative importance of subsistence farming versus capitalistic enterprise. Early in the 1800s, when the transportation conditions of the Appalachian region were comparable to lowland regions of the United States, commercial enterprise prevailed even in the most remote mountain sections via trade to outside commercial centers. But with the explosion of transportation facilities outside the mountains during the middle of the 1800s, many commercial producers simply could not compete in outside markets because of transportation difficulties. As Arnow observes, "numerous as were the manufacturing establishments of 1803, the Cumberland Country was not destined to become a great industrial center. The small farmer-manufacturer grew less and less able to compete with the mass-produced goods of New England and elsewhere."[23] Banks similarly notes, "Even if the mountain producer could accumulate sufficient surplus goods for export, the mountains themselves presented a formidable barrier, even to the most daring and enterprising individuals."[24]

Although subsistence farming was not universal, Appalachia had by far the greatest percentage of self-sufficient farms in the United States during the late 1800s and early 1900s. But statistics tell only part of the story. The self-sufficient farm economy formed the basis of folklore about the mountains. It was intriguing to outside observers to witness the ability of certain mountain inhabitants to subsist on produce from the farm and forest, and literature on the mountains focused on this type of economy. The self-sufficient economy came to symbolize Appalachia, and the self-sufficing way of life was depicted in novels and eventually in "documentary" works such as the Foxfire series.[25] Thus, whether we consider actual statistics on subsistence economy or works of folklore, the self-sufficient economy became closely associated with Appalachia, and the legacy of the self-sufficient mountaineer exists today.

To understand the relationship between subsistence farming and the emergence of Appalachian poverty images, it is necessary to realize that subsistence farming is much more than a type of economic activity. That is, subsistence farming involves a total system of social relationships and values. Production and consumption are embedded in social institutions, not the commercial market. That is, economic activities are closely tied to the kinship structure and community-wide networks of mutual aid and exchange. James Brown observes this pattern in his Beech Creek study. The family was the primary economic unit:

> Unlike most urban families, and even many rural families in the U.S. today, the Beech Creek family tended to be a unit of economic production and consumption. Consequently the economic roles of the family on the farm could not be separated, except analytically, from the family roles.[26]

Moreover, "most cooperative farming activities were carried on within the family group." In this system the economy does not function as a separate institution as it does in a commercial market system. As a result, many of the values and beliefs associated with a market ideology, i.e., wealth as a basis of prestige, do not exist or, if they do exist, are mitigated by the demands of kinship and community organizations. This is not to say that "status" does not exist; status, however, is defined in terms other than those related to market ideology.

Eller discusses the status system in the self-sufficient farming economy:

> These status distinctions were functions not of economics (wealth, land ownership, or access to natural resources) but of the value system of the community itself. In remote mountain neighborhoods where economic differences were minimal, measures of social prestige and privilege were based on personality characteristics or ascribed traits such as sex, age, and family groups. The rural social order was divided not into upper, middle, and lower classes, but into respectable and non-respectable groups, and each local community determined its own criteria for respectability. This status system, of course, tended to break down in the villages and county seat towns where class distinctions (and thus class consciousness) were more noticeable.[27]

Eller also indicates that the lack of overt class-consciousness "was reflected in the emergence of strong egalitarian attitudes and beliefs."[28]

Many authors have alluded to this value orientation in studies conducted at different times and in different parts of the Appalachian region. Semple states, "Every man recognizes man's equality; there are no different classes" (eastern Kentucky, 1890s).[29] According to Edwards and Jones, there is no discrimination on the basis of dress, language or wealth. "The mountaineer is the same person in overalls, or rags, that he is in a dress suit" (northern Georgia, 1930s).[30] Pearsall similarly observes that the men "feel no special pressure to acquire money and material possessions as status symbols" (eastern Tennessee, 1950s).[31]

These attitudes do not mean that the mountaineer did not put a premium on work. If one refused to contribute his share to family and community, there were definite sanctions against his behavior. But the sanctions were based on standards of the community and not on standards of the marketplace.

Here again, however, it is necessary to point out the "egalitarian ethic" was not universal but limited mainly to those areas where the self-sufficient economy was predominant. But as with self-sufficiency *per se*, the egalitarian value system has become part of folklore on Appalachia, and generalized depictions of Appalachian society have been colored by this ethos.

Market capitalism is essentially different with regard to modes of economic participation and values and beliefs associated with economic behavior. In a market economy, commercial enterprise is a distinct institution. Social institutions such as kinship and community-wide systems of mutual aid no longer control economic behavior. Therefore, the social mechanisms by which the economy functions are no longer effective.

The economy must create another mechanism—one by which members of a society are compelled to function in the market system. Basic physical subsistence is not automatically translated into an incentive to produce. Physical subsistence is linked with production through the need of *earning an income*. That is, the capitalist mode of production is characterized by the "separation of producers from real control over and possession of the means or products of labor, and the contractual exchange of labor power for wages . . . labor itself becomes a commodity."[32] Thus, going from point A, physical need, to point B, commodity, is not direct; the path is mediated by an intermediate agency—wages controlled by a market-based labor system.

Physical needs, however, are never the sole incentive to work in the market system. "An economic system actually relying for its mainspring on hunger would be almost as perverse as a family system based on the bare urge of sex."[33] It is necessary that "higher motives" become rooted in the market ideology and therefore pride, honor, and power become tied to gaining market goods and services.

In the nineteenth century the Protestant ethic was the predominant ideological motivation for market-oriented behavior in Europe and the United States. As the commodities market expanded by the beginning of the twentieth century, conspicuous consumption gradually supplanted the Protestant ethic as an ideological force in the market system. The nature of the commodities market as it developed in the twentieth century must be considered before one can understand the value system associated with the acquisition of consumer goods and services.

Commodities by definition are goods and services designed to fulfill wants, needs, and desires—the demand. The essential point is that market commodities are not geared to fulfilling a stable set of "objective needs"; the market defines existing needs and constantly generates new needs oriented toward the survival and perpetuation of the market system *per se*. Furthermore, "the market is the principal reference framework that defines the prevailing model of rational behavior for the members of society."[34]

In *The Limits to Satisfaction,* William Leiss discusses the commodities market process:

> In this setting wants become less and less coherent, and their objectives less clear and readily identifiable, as individuals continually reinterpret their needs in relation to the expanding market economy. . . . New commodities, which today appear steadily and in great numbers, simultaneously promise the satisfaction of wants and promote a feeling of dissatisfaction with regard to the previously existing array. The dizzy pirouette of wants and commodities presents to the individual an ever-changing ensemble of satisfactions and dissatisfactions in terms of which their is no resolution, but only a continuous movement from a less extensive to a more extensive participation in market activity.[35]

Leiss also argues that commodities themselves become very complex objects. "They are not simply material things but 'material-symbolic' entities—that is, things which embody complex sets of messages and characteristics."[36]

One of the results of the need-commodity treadmill is that each aspect of a person's needs tends to be broken down into progressively smaller component parts. For instance, individuals treat their own bodies as objects made up of component units, each having its own demands. According to Leiss:

> Hair, face, mouth, eyes, hands, axillae, neck, crotch, legs, and feet all require the application of specific and distinct chemical mixtures, which together will make one's body pleasing to others and therefore a means of winning favour. Each of these specific needs in turn can run through potentially infinite permutations in relation to the technological sleight-of-hand embodied in commodities: a deodorant undergoes metamorphosis from paste to powder to spray, is scented with synthetic resemblances to all the fruits of the earth, is packaged in a dazzling variety of shapes and sizes—and so on ad infinitum.[37]

The point of all this is quite simple: the fragmentation of needs requires on the individual's part a steadily more intensive effort to hold together his identity and personal integrity. In concrete terms this amounts to spending more and more time in consumption activities.[38]

In sum, the market/commodity system exerts profound control on virtually every aspect of a person's physical, psychological and emotional being. Individuals socialized in a market-oriented culture are highly sensitive and finely tuned to market-induced demands. Consumption behavior is delicately coordinated and regulated according to the pitch pipe of the market. If we extend the simile further, we can consider physical needs the two lowest notes on a piano keyboard; in addition to these notes, the tune of market control over individual behavior can be played on any of the remaining eighty-six notes—each representing a "needed" commodity. Of course, the number of notes on the piano keyboard continually increases.

An important point to be emphasized here is that the goals concerned with the fulfillment of the market-induced needs are not only those that result in "prosperity," or "luxury." The market also establishes the *subsistence level.* This is a culturally defined level below which a person is not gaining a culturally defined "subsistence." This in no way implies that a person will lack food, shelter, or clothing if he is below this level. The subsistence level I am considering is defined entirely in terms of cultural values oriented around the acquisition of commodities. The subsistence level is therefore the balance point where a person is contributing just enough to meet the market's needs and in return is just "getting by" in terms of the "necessities" as defined by the market culture. The person demonstrates a lifestyle defined as appropriate by market conditions since the lifestyle is functionally linked to the market via consumption patterns that will ensure the market's existence. The market maintains this subsistence level by adapting the culturally defined goals to its needs.

The circumstance of a person's functioning inadequately in terms of the market manifests itself in negative values such as inferiority, shame, and guilt, i.e., the person is below the culturally defined "subsistence level." Poverty is therefore the *stigma* associated with this negative cultural and economic position. It makes members of a culture aware when they dip below a functionally adequate level in the market economy. The flaw in this system, however, is that a person may be defined as functioning inadequately in the economy but may still manage to survive in the society. This may occur among those who disregard the cultural values set accordingly by the market culture. It may also happen when people are incapable of meeting the market demands or unaware of the negative values associated with their economic position.

POVERTY AS A STIGMA

This brings us to the basic concept of poverty. To understand exactly why the label "poverty" is attached to levels of economic functioning deemed inappropriate by market standards we must understand the idea of poverty in an historical context.

Since the fourteenth century in Europe the label "poverty" has been attached to certain groups of people as a stigma for ostracism and the enforcement of oppressive governmental policies designed to control potentially disruptive behavior. Prior to this time the care of the so-called poor was in the province of the Church, which in fact regarded the poor to be of the highest moral status. It was also during the fourteenth century that the collective label "poor" came into wide usage among governmental officials. Waxman notes, "the persistent call for repressive policies to deal with the poor was legitimized by their inherent moral defectiveness and by the belief that they will only cease to be morally defective when they are 'purified' through the process of forced rigid resocialization. . . ."[39] The earliest among these repressive policies were the Statutes of Laborers of 1349, which forbade the giving of alms to those who "refuse to labor, giving themselves to theft and other abominations." A number of Poor Laws were enacted in England during the sixteenth and seventeenth centuries. During the period 1722–1782 a system of workhouses was implemented where men, women, and children who received relief were forced to eat, sleep, and work. The rules in the workhouses were very rigid, and failure to observe them resulted in punishments which "included the stocks, the dungeon, denial of meals, refusal of permission to leave the house."[40]

It was the social Darwinist thinking of Joseph Townsend and Thomas Malthus in the late eighteenth and early nineteenth centuries that influenced attitudes toward poverty at the time of the emergence of capitalism. The "survival of the fittest" mentality fit well into the idea of "laissez-faire" capitalism and influenced the enactment of the Poor Law reforms of 1834.

Central to the Poor Law reforms was the doctrine of *less eligibility,* which meant that persons on relief should be kept in a condition "necessarily worse than that of the lowest paid worker not on relief, the objective being to make relief undesirable and to provide the recipient with a clear and strong incentive to get off the relief rolls."[41]

Chaim I. Waxman discusses the diffusion of attitudes about poverty to the United States:

> In 19th century America, these attitudes and approaches to poverty were transplanted. These were adapted to the prevailing ideologies which, on the one hand, from a religious perspective saw poverty as "a fortunate necessity which led the poor into paths of industry and the rich into acts of charity," and on the other hand, saw poverty as a misfortune, unnecessary in the land of golden opportunity. No one who was willing to work need remain poor. Where it existed, poverty was seen as "punishment meted out to the poor for their indolence, inefficiency or improvidence; or else it was interpreted in terms of heredity, intoxicating drink, "degeneration," partisan politics, or, as in one case, the unrestricted liberty allowed to vagrant and degraded women.[42]

In the twentieth century the fundamental poverty stigma was maintained except the consumption "ante" was steadily "upped": The poverty stigma was applied not just to those who eked out sustenance, but as a sanction for anyone whose behavior did not demonstrate a consumption pattern at the prevailing market level.

EMERGENCE OF AN APPALACHIAN POVERTY IMAGE

Let us now consider how the above perspective on poverty relates to Appalachia. Hicks in *Appalachian Valley* notes, "Since at least 1844, when one of Edgar Allan Poe's short stories mentioned the 'fierce and uncouth races of men' living in western Virginia, there has developed an image of people in Southern Appalachia as slovenly, impoverished, ignorant and sternly individualistic."[43] Thus, by the mid-1800s the process of labeling Appalachians as *different* on the basis of alleged antisocial traits or deprivation of some form set the stage for the development of the clearly established poverty image that emerged in the twentieth century. The labeling of a group as "different" is a significant aspect of the poverty stigma dynamic that had been present in Europe since the 1300s. Also, there were scattered accounts of poverty *per se* in the region. In 1856, a British traveler spoke of the "proverbial poverty" of the people in the "whole region"—due to the excessive time spent on hunting.[44] Missionary groups directly or indirectly fostered a view of impoverishment and deprivation in the region during the late 1800s and early 1900s. As Hicks notes, "missionary efforts of church groups had . . . advertised the mountain people as ignorant and impoverished."[45]

Ideas about Appalachian poverty were, however, relatively sporadic until the economic transformation that occurred between the 1890s and 1930s. During this period the precapitalistic subsistence-oriented economy came under extensive influence and scrutiny by industrial and political agencies of the capitalist system. Let us consider how this process of economic change strengthened and eventually crystallized the image of Appalachian poverty.

Subsistence farming is largely outside the sphere of the commercial market system. In fact, self-sufficient farming is virtually the *antithesis* of a market-based productive system; it is not based on wage labor and cannot possibly provide the monetary means to acquire what the market defines as necessity. In fact, the subsistence economy is integrated according to an entirely different set of principles. Motivation to work is rooted in institutions other than the market, i.e., the family and community-based networks of mutual aid. Thus, prestige is not based on acquiring market goods and services; appropriate productive behavior is defined in terms of an adequate contribution to family and community.

While on the periphery of the capitalist system, Appalachians maintained the integrity of their localized economic system.[46] As Appalachians became more involved with the commercial economy of the United States, the material aspects of their way of life were evaluated by a new set of standards, which was based on the ideology of a self-regulating market system. Economic production and consumption, which by traditional standards was appropriate, represented "poverty" by market standards.

It is true that some authors have viewed the self-sufficient economy in positive terms. For instance, in Eller's historical study of Appalachian preindustrial economy, the perspective is generally positive: "familism, rather than the accumulation of material wealth, was the predominant cultural value in the region, and it sustained a life style that was simple, methodic, and tranquil."[47] But the message communicated by most studies is that subsistence farming is economically unproductive if not disastrous. One reason for this view is simply that most recent studies are based on the standards of contemporary agricultural economics, which measure agricultural productivity in terms of profit and monetary equivalence. Obviously, if the farming system is not geared toward the agricultural market, monetary returns from farming will be negligible, if not entirely absent. For instance, the following statement appears in *The Southern Appalachian Region:* "Data from the 1930 census of agriculture revealed that the Appalachians held the highest concentration of low income farms in the country. Many returned less than $600 value of gross products: subsistence farms sold little on the open market. . . . Every measure used served to indicate the uneconomic returns from Appalachian agriculture."[48]

In the same survey, the conjunction of federal monetary standards and subsistence farming during the depression of the 1930s is discussed. "Without any lowering of the customary live-at-home and do-without economy, the application of federal standards made at least half the population in certain Appalachian areas eligible for relief."[49] Two important points can be made about this statement. One is that a negative connotation was attached to the existing self-sufficient economy; the second is that by the decree of federal monetary relief standards, the subsistence economy became defined as "poverty." Where subsistence farming has persisted, it has generally been associated with poverty. In Bowman's characterization of eastern Kentucky made

in the 1960s, an aspect of the economy is defined as "an extremely poor and largely subsistence agriculture."[50]

I suggest that at least one hillbilly stereotype grew out of a basic misinterpretation of the self-sufficient lifestyle. The stereotype is that of people sprawled out in front of a cabin beside a somnolent bloodhound. The stereotype is now portrayed in the television program "Hee Haw," and has been widespread in numerous depictions of the mountaineer. An observer from outside the mountains might gain an impression from certain activities associated with a self-sufficient way of life that could lead to the fabrication of such a stereotype, especially if the observer were accustomed to a market-based work schedule. Subsistence farming is characterized by periods of productive labor with alternate periods of inactivity. Marion Pearsall discusses time usage among subsistence producers in *Little Smokey Ridge:*

> There are periods of great activity when a man plows, plants, harvests, or perhaps does some building. He may then leave home to wander if he pleases. . . . At home again work is done in spurts, and there are long hours to sit on the porch, relax at the store, or talk and drink with other men. In the course of a year, however, a man does spend a good deal of time and energy in work.[51]

Whether or not it is plausible to link this hillbilly stereotype to a false representation of a subsistence-oriented economy, the stereotype clearly connotes laziness and idleness. These are the characteristics that historically have formed the basis of a poverty stigma.

Thus far I have considered the emergence of Appalachian poverty images in light of general ideological differences between precapitalistic and capitalistic market economies. We must also consider how developments in the coal industry in parts of Appalachia reinforced the emerging poverty image.

Appalachia's rich mineral resources made the region a *resource* in the 1800s from the perspective of American political and economic interests. Valuable raw materials were waiting to be exploited. A major problem, however, faced the outside political and economic interests: Local Appalachians owned the land containing the valuable resources; thus, the local people represented an obstacle to exploiting the resources—they were "in the way."

It is useful to consider this situation in historical and cross-cultural perspective. Whenever a powerful economic and political force demands access to the resources on or under the land of indigenous peoples, a similar pattern seems to emerge in response to the same problem. The problem boils down to this: Something must be done with the people in order to get the resources. One solution to this problem in some cases has been actual genocide. More often, however, indigenous peoples are "corralled" into reservations or otherwise forced off their land.

Such exploitation usually never occurs without a rationale. Most often, the rationale is that, because the exploited peoples are culturally or biologically inferior, they must be "saved" or "modernized." In fact, the term "white man's burden" has been applied to non-Western groups undergoing colonialization.

The same pattern developed with regard to the exploitation of Appalachian resources. In "Property, Coal, and Theft," John Gaventa discusses the ideology and rationale of economic exploitation in the coal industry. "Anyone who had or who wanted any part of the economic benefit of the new society was dependent on the will of those few who controlled it. . . . With the dependency on the economic controllers, though, also came a supporting ideology of progress, civilization, and response to social need. . . . Like other traditional colonialists, the virtues of this 'civilization' were unquestionably better than the past, somehow less-than-human, ways of the 'natives.' "[52] The author notes that articles appeared in the *New York Times* and *Harpers Magazine* in the 1890s that supported this ideology.

The process of denigrating local populations for purposes of exploitation contributed to the poverty stereotype. The process relates directly to the ideological factors associated with the contrasting economic systems discussed above. The Appalachian way of life did not fit the market model; it was therefore lacking; it was therefore in need of salvation by outside industrial interests. Indeed, the poverty label places people, socially, in the need-of-help role. The paternalistic attitudes of early mine operators is indicative of this role relationship. In mining towns practically all economic, political, and legal responsibilities were assumed by the mine operators.

Harry Caudill states: "In return for his labor his employers clothed his back, filled his belly, sheltered and lighted his household, and provided his family with medical treatment, fuel and water."[53] When a mountaineer became dependent on mining, he was placed in a situation virtually the opposite of the self-sufficient way of life. He no longer made his own decisions; rather, the company made them for him. He was now completely dependent upon wages. The company controlled his money by issuing scrip that was made by the company and could be used only in company stores. The company made all decisions concerning political and legal matters, hiring its own law officers and dealing with any legal infraction. The miner was at the mercy of the mine operators, to the extent that he could be evicted from his company house at the company's will.[54]

Paul Cressey describes the transition of the mountaineer from self-sufficiency to dependence upon the industrial market economy in Harlan County, Kentucky, where by 1940, 70 percent of the men were engaged in mining.

Instead of the security provided by the older self-sufficient agriculture there was substituted the instability of industrial employment. A man's livelihood now depended on fluctuations in the national economy which were entirely outside his control. . . . With this change in occupation money assumed a dominant place in the miner's life. The friendly barter system disappeared and human relations came to be measured in terms of wages and profits. . . . The most serious aspect of economic disorganization developed in the relations between the mine operators and the workers. Instead of the older social equality a rigid class system was introduced. . . . More far-reaching than the disruption of the economic organization was the breakdown of the older community structure. . . . Competition and exploitation replaced friendly mutual aid as social relations became casual and impersonal.[55]

The miner had thus become dependent upon the industrial market economy of the United States. However, the coal industry, being so completely specialized, left the miner virtually isolated from other industries and subsequently from access to other forms of wage labor. Morris states: "The mining camp is a one-industry community, usually isolated—cut off from the main currents of industrial life."[56] This left the miner no alternative to mining. During the times of unemployment, therefore, the miner was economically defenseless; he was dependent on, but not well integrated into a market industrial way of life.

PRESENT APPALACHIAN POVERTY IMAGES

The emergence of present poverty images is directly related to the two factors discussed above, which include the denigration of subsistence-oriented economic behavior by market standards, and the exploitation of Appalachian resources. In the context of recent economic trends, these forces help mold the poverty stereotype that prevails today.

Throughout the twentieth century Appalachia faced periods of sporadic unemployment. Where coal mining developed as a major source of employment, fluctuations in the coal market often led to the closing of mines. Furthermore, many mining activities became automated. In these circumstances, large numbers of miners lost their jobs. Because of unemployment, many persons migrated out of the mountains to various cities seeking employment. Many became successfully employed; often, however, there were no jobs available and some of the migrants had to collect welfare. While some of those remaining in the mountains could find employment, many had no alternative but to collect welfare.

It is important to emphasize that not all Appalachians faced these economic problems. Some successfully continued in subsistence and cash-crop farming patterns. Others were employed in occupations that were not affected by unemployment associated with mining.

The conditions of economic depression affected only certain parts of Appalachia; however, that cast a shadow on the entire region: Economic depression was interpreted in terms of the negative ideas already ingrained in the minds of the general populace regarding the nature of Appalachian culture and society. Furthermore, the mass media emphasized the very *worst* economic conditions and, at the same time, it portrayed a picture of the Appalachian as culturally backward, if not actually depraved.

The significance of the mass media cannot be overemphasized. The mass media are highly sensitive to the fluctuations and demands of the national and international market system. Through advertisements, news broadcasts, financial reports, and political messages the key ideological codes of market-appropriate behavior are neatly packed in a highly palatable form. As Leiss notes, "In the high-intensity market setting the number of messages circulating in the social environment is truly staggering. Before reaching the age of twenty a person in the United States will have been exposed on average to 350,000 television commercials."[57]

The rise and fall of the stock market is translated into the emotional well-being of the populace. The interest rate is communicated by news announcers in words and facial expressions as a cause for joy or sorrow. There is virtually no escape from the compulsion to conform to highly variable market standards. Those who do not conform are portrayed in the mass media as exhibiting some form of pathos or deprivation.

Another characteristic of the mass media is to communicate about ethnic groups and regional populations using caricatures, cliches, and highly edited behavioral portraits. The various Appalachian stereotypes portrayed on television are discussed by Horace Newcomb. The programs considered range from the *Beverly Hillbillies* to the *Dukes of Hazzard*.[58]

Poverty images fit well into the mass media scheme of communication. In fact, in certain respects, Appalachian poverty images are a phenomenon of the mass media. Documentary films such as *Appalachia: Rich Land, Poor People* and *Christmas in Appalachia* clearly communicate the message that Appalachia is a poverty-stricken region. But the poverty messages are also part of most dramatized depictions of the "mountaineer." Take for instance, the *Beverly Hillbillies:* the song introducing the program includes the phrase, "poor mountaineer barely kept his family fed." And, of course, the material heritage of the Clampett family is beyond the pale by market standards. *Fantasy Island* had an episode on a "hillbilly" family that was aired on January 10, 1981. The story was about a man who wanted his hillbilly family to experience being millionaires. The

following is from the program narrative: "Ten millionaires and their ladies are going to attend a party hosted by four of the brokest hillbillies ever to set foot on Fantasy Island . . . This is embarrassing Mr. Roarke. A family of poor dirt farmers rubbing shoulders with all that gold and glitter. What have I done?" These and numerous other portrayals of the mountaineer convey a message entrenched in the media perspective of the hillbilly: the mountaineer is poor.

Among social scientists and policymakers another trend of thought has emerged that has reinforced and strengthened the Appalachian poverty image. Conceptions such as "lower-class culture," "low-income lifestyles," "culture of violence," "slum culture," and even "dregs culture" are used to categorize and study groups occupying low income sectors of various regions.[59] Oscar Lewis, in *La Vida,* introduces the concept "culture of poverty" and says essentially that there are certain lifestyles characteristic of the poor.[60] It is generally assumed that poverty-culture traits prevent or inhibit upward mobility in urban economic and social systems. According to Lewis, wherever the culture of poverty occurs," its practitioners exhibit remarkable similarity in the structure of their families, in interpersonal relations, in spending habits, in their value systems and in their orientation in time." Lewis identifies seventy traits that characterize the culture of poverty. For instance one trait is the "disengagement, the nonintegration, of the poor with respect to the major institutions of society. . . . The people do not belong to labor unions or political parties and make little use of banks, hospitals, department stores or museums."[61] The concept has been influential in perspectives on poverty in Appalachia. Appalachians, facing economic difficulties on the one hand and having their way of life stereotyped and denigrated on the other, fit well into the "culture of poverty" mold—Appalachia was now regarded as having a culture of poverty!

Rolland Wright presents a penetrating critique of the culture of poverty concept. His perspective is that of a native of a rural population subject to poverty stereotypes. His analysis has important implications for the present discussion, since it questions the meaning of poverty using criteria that relate to ideological differences between populations. Wright's arguments center around differences between social and economic patterns of individuals living in certain rural areas and those of urban market-oriented groups. According to Wright, the differences are so fundamental that they involve different concepts of the "self." The urban ground rule is that acts are definitive of the self. "Urban people are quite sensitive to any behavioral cues which allow them to locate an individual categorically, whether that cue is overt behavior or some expressive symbol, such as clothes, property, bumper stickers or whatever. . . . This tendency to infer meaning about a man from his acts is so pervasive in urban life I call it the 'urban ground rule.'"[62]

In contrast to this concept of self, Wright argues that among the rural population within which he was socialized, identity tends to be *given*. "They have very little grasp that a man can 'become' anything fundamentally different by the way he acts. . . ." An individual from this group is more likely to think the kind of man he *is* determines what he will accomplish or achieve, not the other way around.

The discussion of different concepts of self is part of Wright's general argument pointing out the inconsistencies in the notion "culture of poverty." The inconsistencies result from the fact the culture of poverty idea stems from one population categorizing another population on the basis of values and judgments meaningful only to the population making the judgments.

According to Wright, poverty culture traits are a series of urban definitions turned inside out. "Being negative constructs, they tend to be empty, something like saying the sea is not the land. It is true, but it doesn't say much about the nature of the ocean. In a similar way, the 'culture of poverty' tells us the [so-called] poor are not urban men, but it says nothing about who they are in their own terms."[63]

Wright's perspective offers support for the basic argument advanced here: that the image of Appalachian poverty is rooted in the interpretations of precapitalistic Appalachian economic and social patterns on the basis of commercial market standards.

Whether or not it is done intentionally, a group labeled poverty-stricken is stigmatized. Authors have voiced the opinion that poverty is just a word—what difference does the word make as long as problems such as low income and unemployment are identified? Use of poverty labels may be justified as a *muckraking* device that will concentrate attention on corruption and injustice. If the poverty label does have utility, it is definitely a double-edged sword. A word such as poverty, especially when incorporated into official policy, is similar to terms such as psychotic, criminal, convict, and traitor. When a person becomes identified with the label the label becomes a stigma having far-reaching emotional, psychological, and social consequences. When the poverty label is attached indiscriminately to an entire region the influence on inhabitants of the region is similar.

Goffman discusses the nature of a stigma:

> While the stranger is present before us, evidence can arise of his possessing an attribute that makes him different from others in the category of persons available for him to be, and of a less desirable kind—in the extreme, a person who is quite thoroughly bad, or dangerous, or weak. He is thus reduced in our minds from a whole and usual person to a tainted, discounted one. Such an attribute is a stigma.[64]

Goffman distinguishes three kinds of stigmas: "tribal stigma of race, nation, and religion," "physical stigma-deformities," and "blemishes of individual character." According to Waxman, a poverty stereotype, when attached to a geographical region or ethnic group, is similar to Goffman's tribal stigma of race. He states that "the stigma of poverty is a special type of stigma which attributes to the poor a status of being 'less than human,' and that the stigma has taken various shapes at different historical stages."[65]

In Appalachia, the poverty image clearly falls into the "tribal stigma of race" category, since the idea of poverty is indiscriminately attached to the group-level category "Appalachian."

Poverty stereotypes can create difficulties for people identified as Appalachian. Such images result in a communication barrier between local Appalachians and those from other regions: This is especially harmful to Appalachians when they migrate to cities. In this situation the problems caused by the negative stereotype far outweigh those associated with such economic factors as unemployment; Appalachians are often socially segregated in residential, educational, and occupational settings. Furthermore, because of the poverty stereotype, it is often assumed that the Appalachian must give up his way of life in order to adapt successfully to "middle-class" urban life. I am aware of inhabitants of the Appalachian region who refuse to be included in literature on the region because they do not want to be considered "poverty-stricken."

For the social scientist and policymaker, poverty images take on another dimension. It is often assumed that if one studies Appalachia, one studies poverty. Thus, it is difficult to formulate research problems that are not biased: The poverty image conveys a perspective for observing Appalachia that compares this population's behavioral, social, and cultural patterns to an arbitrary standard. The poverty image establishes a *mind set* with which to perceive, select, and categorize information about Appalachia.

It is important also to consider the influence of poverty images on public policy. It is often assumed that policy should reflect poverty conditions. Hicks describes the "skirmishes in the war on poverty" that developed in a North Carolina mountain community in the 1960s. "The poverty program in the Little Laurel [Valley] was undertaken by a regional organization, composed of paid and volunteer workers over an area of four counties. Under a well-paid director, this association assigned VISTA workers to various sections of the area, wrote progress reports, and applied for financial grants from the Office of Economic Opportunity in Washington."[66] Hicks notes first of all that the local people resented the flood of poverty propaganda associated with the war on poverty. They simply didn't see themselves as "universally destitute and helpless."

Also, the rhetoric and communication styles of poverty workers were insulting to local people who respected their way of life. But overt conflict erupted when application was made to the Office of Economic Opportunity for a large grant to set up a "poor people's newspaper. . . . Objections from Appalachian newspaper editors and political leaders were overpowering."[67] Hicks concludes his discussion of the impact of the poverty program with the following statement: "Change in the Little Laurel Valley, meanwhile, proceeds at a quickening pace and the outlines of urban America become clearer, but the agencies of change in large part are industrial employment, improved highways, and television, not the poverty program."[68]

I would like to conclude this paper with a quote from *Shiloh: A Mountain Community,* by John Stephenson. John, a native of the Appalachians, is a sociologist and director of the Appalachian Center at the University of Kentucky. I feel his statement captures the essential theme of this paper:

> My interest in the mountains has not always been so problem-centered. In fact, I, like many people raised near the Appalachians, was not so aware that we had such problems until someone informed me. . . . Only gradually did I come to realize that the people referred to by Michael Harrington and Harry Caudill and John F. Kennedy and Vance and the Saturday Evening Post—were the same ones I had as neighbors and school friends when I was a child. In truth, I still think of the mountains as a corner of heaven first and a national disgrace second.[69]

NOTES

1. Haynes Johnson, "Poverty in Appalachia," *Washington Star,* eleven-part series, February 9–14, 16–20, 1964.

2. R. C. Langman, *Appalachian Kentucky: An Exploited Region,* (Toronto: McGraw-Hill Ryerson, 1971), p. v.

3. George L. Wilber, ed. *Poverty: A New Perspective* (Lexington, Ky.: University Press of Kentucky, 1975), p. 5.

4. Louis Ferman, Joyce L. Kornbluh, and Alan Haber, eds., *Poverty in America: A Book of Readings* (Ann Arbor, Mich.: University of Michigan Press, 1968), p. 6.

5. Wilber, *Poverty,* p. 5.

6. J. Patrick Madden, "Poverty Measures as Indicators of Social Welfare," in *Poverty: A New Perspective,* ed. G. Wilber (Lexington, Ky.: University Press of Kentucky, 1975), 26.

7. Carlton G. Davis, "Poverty and Rural Development in the United States: Where Do We Stand?" in *Rural Poverty and the Policy Crisis,* ed. R. O. Coppedge and C. G. Davis, (Ames, Iowa: Iowa State University Press, 1977), p. 12.

8. Wilber, *Poverty,* p. 3.

9. Robert J. Lampman, *Ends and Means of Reducing Income Poverty,* (Chicago: Markham Publishing Co., 1971), p. 26.

10. Wilbert, *Poverty,* pp. 36–38.

11. Michael Harrington, *The Other America: Poverty in the United States* (New York: Macmillan, 1962), p. 179.

12. Rose Friedman, *Poverty: Definition and Perspective,* (Washington: American Enterprise Institute for Public Policy Research, 1965), p. 26.

13. Communications Research Machines, Inc., *Anthropology Today* (Del Mar, Cal.: CRM Books, 1971), p. 546.

14. Anthony F. C. Wallace, *Culture and Personality,* 2nd ed. (New York: Random House, 1970), p. 143.

15. George P. Murdock, *Ethnographic Atlas,* (Pittsburgh: University of Pittsburgh Press, 1967).

16. William Leiss, *The Limits to Satisfaction: An Essay on the Problems of Needs and Commodities.* (Toronto: University of Toronto Press, 1976), pp. 54, 61–62.

17. Ronald D. Eller, "Land and Family: An Historical View of Preindustrial Appalachia." *Appalachian Journal* 6, no. 2 (Winter, 1979): 92, 100.

18. Alan J. Banks, "The Emergence of a Capitalistic Labor Market in Eastern Kentucky," *Appalachian Journal 7,* no. 3 (Spring 1980): 189.

19. Banks, "Emergence," p. 190.

20. United States Department of Agriculture, *Economic and Social Problems and Conditions of the Southern Appalachians,* Miscellaneous Publication no. 205 (Washington: United States Government Printing Office, 1935), p. 46.

21. Faith M. Williams, Hazel K. Stiebeling, Idella G. Swisher, and Gertrude S. Weiss, *Family Living in Knott County Kentucky,* Technical Bulletin no. 576 (Washington: United States Department of Agriculture, 1937), p. 13.

22. Frank D. Alexander and Robert E. Galloway, "Salient Features of Social Organization in a Typical County of the General and Self-Sufficient Farm Region," *Rural Sociology* 12 (December 1947): 396.

23. Harriett S. Arnow, *Seedtime On the Cumberland* (New York: Macmillan, 1960), p. 283.

24. Banks, "Emergence," p. 190.

25. Eliot Wigginton, *The Foxfire Book* (Garden City, N.Y.: Anchor-Doubleday, 1972).

26. James Brown, "The Conjugal Family and the Extended Family Group," *American Sociological Review* 17 (June 1952): 297.

27. Eller, "Land and Family," p. 87.

28. *Ibid.*

29. Ellen C. Semple, "The Anglo-Saxons of the Kentucky Mountains," *Bulletin of the American Geographic Society* 42 (1910): 589.

30. A. S. Edwards and Leslie Jones, "An Experimental and Field Study of North Georgia Mountaineers," *Journal of Social Psychology* 9 (August 1938): 333.

31. Marion Pearsall, *Little Smokey Ridge: The Natural History of A Southern Appalachian Neighborhood* (Birmingham, Ala.: University of Alabama Press), p. 56.

32. Banks, "Emergence," p. 32.

33. Karl Polanyi, "Our Obsolete Market Economy," *Commentary* 3 (February 1947): 111.

34. Leiss, *Limits to Satisfaction,* p. 92.

35. *Ibid.,* p. 27.

36. *Ibid.,* p. 74.

37. *Ibid.,* p. 18.

38. *Ibid.,* p. 19.

39. Chaim, I. Waxman, *The Stigma of Poverty: A Critique of Poverty Theories and Policies* (New York: Pergamon Press, 1977), p. 75.

40. *Ibid.,* p. 78.

41. *Ibid.,* p. 41.

42. *Ibid.,* p. 86.

43. George L. Hicks, *Appalachian Valley* (New York: Holt, Rinehart and Winston, 1976), p. 6.

44. *Ibid.*

45. *Ibid.,* p. 103.

46. See David Walls, "Internal Colony or Internal Periphery? A Critique of Current Models and an Alternative Formulation," in *Colonialism in Modern America: The Appalachian Case,* ed. H. Lewis, L. Johnson and D. Askins (Boone, N.C., Appalachian Consortium Press, 1978).

47. Eller, "Land and Family," p. 106.

48. Thomas R. Ford, ed., *The Southern Appalachian Region: A Survey,* (Lexington, Ky.: University Press of Kentucky, 1962), p. 5.

49. *Ibid.*

50. Mary Jean Bowman and W. Warren Haynes, *Resources and People in East Kentucky: Problems and Potentials of a Lagging Economy* (Baltimore: Johns Hopkins Press, 1963), p. 24.

51. Pearsall, *Little Smokey Ridge,* pp. 89–90.

52. John Gaventa, "Property, Coal, and Theft," in Lewis *et al., Colonialism in Modern America,* pp. 144, 145.

53. Harry Caudill, *Night Comes to the Cumberlands: A Biography of A Depressed Area* (Boston: Little, Brown and Co., 1963), p. 115.

54. Homer Lawrence Morris, *The Plight of the Bituminous Coal Miner* (Philadelphia: University of Pennsylvania Press, 1934).

55. Paul Cressey, "Social Disorganization and Reorganization in Harlan County, Kentucky," *American Sociological Review* 14 (1949): 389–94.

56. Morris, *Plight,* p. 85.

57. Leiss, *Limits to Satisfaction,* p. 82.

58. Horace Newcomb, "Appalachia on Television: Region as Symbol in American Popular Culture," *Appalachian Journal 7,* no. 1–2 (Autumn–Winter 1979): 155–64.

59. Charles Valentine, *Culture and Poverty: Critique and Counter Proposals* (Chicago: University of Chicago Press, 1968).

60. Oscar Lewis, *La Vida: A Puerto Rican Family in the Culture of Poverty,* (New York: Random House, 1966).

61. Oscar Lewis, "The Culture of Poverty," *Scientific American* 215 (1966): 19–25; see Dwight Billings, "Culture and Poverty in Appalachia: A Theoretical Discussion and Empirical Analysis," *Social Forces* 53 (1974): 315–23.

62. Rolland H. Wright, "The Stranger Mentality and the Culture of Poverty," in *The Culture of Poverty: A Critique,* ed. Eleanor B. Leacock (New York: Simon and Schuster, 1971), pp. 320–21.

63. *Ibid.,* p. 325.

64. Erving Goffman, *Stigma: Notes on the Management of Spoiled Identity* (Englewood Cliffs, N.J.: Prentice Hall, 1963), pp. 2–3.

65. Waxman, *Stigma of Poverty,* p. 69.

66. Hicks, *Appalachian Valley,* p. 103.

67. *Ibid.,* p. 104.

68. *Ibid.,* p. 105.

69. John Stephenson, *Shiloh: A Mountain Community* (Lexington, Ky.: University Press of Kentucky, 1968), p. viii.

22. VICTIM-BLAMING IN APPALACHIA: CULTURAL THEORIES AND THE SOUTHERN MOUNTAINEER

Stephen L. Fisher

Emory & Henry College

Social scientists have paid little attention to the Appalachian region. This is due in part to an intellectual snobbery which refuses to recognize the "hillbilly" and his problems as a legitimate area of research and concern, and, relatedly, to a belief that nothing new or significant can be learned by studying this region. Such attitudes are very short-sighted. Appalachia has long been the testing ground for a wide variety of federal and state experiments, the most recent being a novel domestic aid program under the Appalachian Regional Commission. Social scientists are becoming aware that the Appalachian experience is helpful in formulating and testing theories of development, colonialization, socialization, and poverty. By studying Appalachia one can learn much about the causes and impact of many of our national crises—pollution, financially-troubled state and local governments, corporate irresponsibility, inadequate health and education systems, worker rebellion, political corruption, the failure of the welfare state, and mass cynicism toward government at all levels.[1]

As their interest in Appalachia increases, social scientists will no doubt seek background information about the area from two nationally-acclaimed works, Harry Caudill's *Night Comes to the Cumberlands*[2] and Jack Weller's *Yesterday's People.*[3] Caudill's book is designed to be an introduction to contemporary Appalachia, while Weller's study is the most influential work dealing with Appalachian culture. Although based mainly on personal experiences, the conclusions reached by these two authors have frequently been accepted without question by those unfamiliar with the region. This is unfortunate, for, while both provide valuable information about Appalachia, they are seriously flawed works.

Caudill, a lawyer, and Weller, a minister, make an honest effort to understand the mountain people, but one must be very cautious in interpreting and applying their findings. The two books are viewed by many as the most important studies ever written about the Appalachian region, yet *Night Comes to the Cumberlands* deals almost exclusively with developments in eastern Kentucky, while *Yesterday's People* concentrates on a single coal community in West Virginia. Both authors are seen as being sympathetic to the mountaineers, yet Caudill at times displays a patronizing attitude toward them, describing them as "less ambitious," "mental detectives," and "slatterns," while Weller portrays their culture as "unrealistic" and "inadequate." The conclusions of both books are often

Prepared for delivery at the 1975 Annual Meeting of the Southern Political Science Association, Nashville, Tennessee, November 6–8.

A version of this paper was presented at the Appalachian Symposium in honor of Cratis D. Williams (April 7–9, 1976) at Appalachian State University, and it will subsequently appear in the published proceedings of the Symposium. Copyright *Appalachian Journal.* Used by permission.

quoted by scholars and government officials, yet neither work is well-documented. Caudill's study is virtually without footnotes. His assertion that the initial settlers of the region were criminals, homeless orphans, and other wretched outcasts who came as indentured servants from Britain is widely cited without notice that this unsubstantiated statement has come under serious challenge.[4] As will be demonstrated later in this paper, Weller's study is marred by a number of contradictions, stereotypes, and biases.

In spite of these and other shortcomings, Caudill's work has had a positive impact because it has helped to acquaint many Americans with the history and problems of Appalachia. The same cannot be said for *Yesterday's People*. Weller identifies the traits of a Southern Appalachian folk culture which he claims has failed to prepare its people for the cooperative, interrelated, technical society in which they now live. Before the economic, political and social problems of Appalachia can be solved, the people must give up their "defective" folk culture and accept the values of the American middle class. Many of Weller's assumptions and conclusions are similar to those espoused by Oscar Lewis, Edward Banfield, Daniel Moynihan and others who believe the root cause of poverty lies in certain cultural traits shared by the poor. Cultural explanations of poverty have come under increasing attack throughout the social sciences. Nevertheless, Weller's ideas about the mountain personality have continued to dominate the literature on Appalachia and have distracted attention from other explanations for the region's many troubles.[5]

It is not that Weller's hypotheses have gone unchallenged. But, as Helen Lewis points out, the attack on what she calls the Appalachian subculture model has been disjointed and confined mainly to mimeographed underground publications, "movement" newsletters, and obscure journals.[6] By the "Appalachian subculture model," Lewis means the view in which the Southern Appalachians are seen as "a subculture with unique and different customs, values, and style of life which developed historically and is passed on through each succeeding generation."[7] Such a view almost always compares the subculture with the middle-class values of the larger society.

It is important that the debate over the cultural model as it relates specifically to Appalachia receives wide distribution and serious consideration among social scientists. This paper will examine the major points and implications of the Appalachian subculture and then summarize and evaluate the various criticisms which have been leveled against it. It is hoped that this analysis will encourage social scientists to explore alternative models for explaining and coping with Appalachia's problems.

The Appalachian Subculture Model

The first serious attempt to determine whether or not there exists a distinct subculture in Appalachia was by Thomas Ford in an essay entitled "The Passing of Provincialism."[8] Ford set out to determine the strength of four value dimensions—individualism and self-reliance, traditionalism, fatalism, and religious fundamentalism—among the Appalachian people. His survey essentially disproved the existence of a unique Appalachian subculture, but his essay served to focus attention on the cultural values he tested. Although Weller's discussion of the mountain culture is based primarily on his own observations, he was obviously influenced by Ford's study and by Herbert Gans' *The Urban Villagers*.[9] Subsequent studies of the Appalachian personality have, for the most part, accepted Weller's basic assumptions and findings concerning the existence of a distinctive Appalachian folk culture and the traits that make up this culture.[10]

The most important of these traits are:

Individualism. John C. Campbell, an early observer of Appalachia, commented that the dominant trait of the Appalachian mountaineer is "independence raised to the fourth power."[11] Independence is viewed by many as a positive trait, and independent people may work in their own way for a cooperative good. Unfortunately, says Weller, the independent attitude of the Appalachian people has degenerated into a type of self-centered individualism. Today, everything that the mountain man does has the self and its concerns at heart. He is reluctant to join groups and does so only in order to promote his own needs. He judges government as good or bad by the extent to which its policies serve him. This attitude explains why public welfare programs have been welcomed in the mountains and why Appalachians have little conception of the "public good." This independence-turned-individualism, concludes Weller, is a major obstacle for those attempting to promote regional development and cooperation.[12]

Traditionalism. Weller believes the mountain man's static way of life manifests itself in at least two ways. First, most Americans are "progressive"—they plan ahead and look forward to the future with pleasant anticipation. The Appalachian, however, has a "regressive" outlook—he looks backward to a yesterday which is remembered as being happier than today.[13] Such an outlook discourages realistic planning and encourages resistance to outside attempts at change. Second, middle-class America tends to be improvement-oriented while Appalachian America is existence-oriented. Life in Appalachia is geared toward achieving only the very basic goods needed for survival. Secondary goals of beauty, excellence, and refinement are not valued. The mountaineer is contented with just getting along.[14]

Fatalism. While traditionalism and fatalism do not accompany one another in many rural societies, Weller believes there is a direct relationship between them in Appalachia. As the mountaineer's hopes cracked under the weight of depression, floods, and depleted soil, he came to believe that external forces, not man, control human destiny. Such a belief has led to passive resignation and tolerance of undesirable conditions. This fatalism is an important part of the mountain religion. One accepts one's lot in this life in order to gain rewards in the next. There is little questioning, little planning for the future, little complaining.[15]

Action-seeking. The middle-class individual is a routine-seeker. He finds satisfaction in the routine of each day and makes a determined effort to establish a stable way of life by gaining a secure job, attending church regularly, joining clubs, and saving money. The Appalachian, insists Weller, is an action-seeker. For him, routines are something to be avoided or endured; life is episodic. He rejects the routines of education and church attendance. He spends impulsively, often on liquor, gambling, and luxury items. His jobs are often the unstable ones, or those offering excitement, such as coal mining.[16]

Person-orientedness. Weller finds Gans' concepts of person-orientation and object-orientation very helpful in his discussion of Appalachian culture.[17] The object-oriented person strives toward a goal or object outside himself, while the person-oriented individual strives to be liked, accepted, or noticed. The mountaineer is person-oriented. His life goals are achieved in relation to his family and peer groups. Frank Riddel summarizes many of Weller's beliefs about the attitudes and problems which stem from the tendency to be person-oriented:

> The time perspective of many mountain people, their attitudes toward work, the absence of object goals, and the lack of planning for the future are related to their person-orientation. . . . Because the rural Appalachian relies entirely on the reference group as a source of ideas and values, he is not easily reached or influenced by people beyond his group. This not only contributes to the maintenance of a closed society, but it also complicates efforts to promote a spirit of cooperation among different reference groups within the community. Ideas, beliefs, and values are internalized by members of the group to such an extent that new ideas from outside the group or disagreements with outsiders are taken personally rather than in the spirit of intellectual give and take that prevails elsewhere. This supersensitivity to criticism or any hint of criticism in the guise of an opposing idea derives from the person-orientation of the rural Appalachian who equates the rejection of his ideas or beliefs with personal rejection. Thus, it is difficult for the mountaineer to settle grievances with another individual or an agency because every disputed issue involves a deep personal commitment, cooperative activity among different reference groups is hindered, effective leadership does not develop, outsiders remain objects of suspicion, new ideas are rejected, and change does not take place.[18]

Most studies of Appalachian culture are concerned primarily with describing the traits of the culture and give little attention to the questions of why these traits developed and how they have been perpetuated. As a result, family and religious characteristics are frequently discussed as particular traits of the subculture. While certain values of the mountain family and religion clearly differ from dominant American values, analytical reasons suggest that these socialization agents might best be examined as probable causes of a distinct Appalachian folk culture. When explanations for the subculture are mentioned, they most often include

Isolation. As Richard Couto points out, most authors do not view Appalachian culture as a regression; rather it is "arrested" or "dormant," and the people of the region are our "contemporary ancestors."[19] This view stems from a belief that most of the folk cultural traits were brought into the region in the eighteenth and early nineteenth century. After the middle of the nineteenth century, population in the mountains grew largely as a result of natural increase rather than migration. This fact, combined with the continued lack of transportation routes into and out of the mountains, "contributed to the maintenance of a closed society and thus the perpetuation of pre-Civil War cultural traditions."[20] Cratis Williams maintains that the emergence of the mountaineer as a special type is parallel with the increasing differences between his means of communication and those of his relatives who had moved further west.[21] Thousands of persons in the mountains still live a life of isolation, says Weller, and it is these families—isolated by distance, by lack of roads, and by choice—that most clearly display the traits of the Appalachian folk culture.[22]

Family. If isolation has nurtured and preserved an outdated culture, socialization, many believe, has perpetuated it. Rural Appalachia is frequently described as a familistic society, where a person's loyalty is to his extended family before any other group or principle.[23] Rena Gazaway, for example, claims it is the family which "prescribes how members will react toward people, things, or institutions."[24] By monopolizing the individual's allegiance, the family has hindered the development of formal organizations in Appalachia and has been an obstacle to programs promoting change. One might assume that the close-knit nature of the mountain family would lend security to mountain life, but Weller insists that the members of a family are bound to one another by ties of emotional dependence which tend to increase insecurity.[25] Mountain families are adult-centered and children are reared "impulsively," "permissively," and "indulgently." Families socialize children in ways which make them dependent on the reference group and fail to prepare them for the kind of schooling needed in a technical society. Child psychiatrist David Looff even maintains that the strong familistic orientation of the Appalachian culture is responsible for serious emotional disorders in children of the region.[26]

Religion. Initially, the mountaineers were Presbyterians, Episcopalians, and members of other formally organized denominations which required an educated clergy and centralized organization. Since these requirements could not be met in the mountain wilderness, locally autonomous sects developed which stressed religious fundamentalism and other-worldliness, made use of local resources and leadership, and emphasized the importance of conversion and sanctification as the path to salvation.[27] Many view the local sect churches as obstacles to social change since they encourage individualistic, traditionalistic, and fatalistic attitudes. In addition, many of these churches promote an attitude which looks upon political and social participation as almost immoral.

Migration. As the economic situation deteriorated in the mountains, hundreds of thousands of mountaineers fled to Chicago, Cincinnati, Detroit, and other cities where at least the possibility of jobs existed. Who were these people? According to Weller, most were

> the young couples, with strength and ambitions for themselves and their children, who were not content with a marginal existence; they were the better-educated adults who could find in the cities the kind of employment that would enable them to live comfortably . . . ; they were the leaders who had the skills that were useful in the cities—and would have been useful in the mountains.[28]

Who stayed behind? Mostly, it was

> the poorly trained and poorly educated who could find either no jobs or else such poor jobs that life in the cities would have had to be lived in the undesirable slums; the unambitious, who could tolerate a subsistence living at home; those above forty, who found it hard to be retrained . . . ; the aged, the sickly, and the retarded; and the psychologically immobile, who could not move away from the familiar, protective mountain culture.[29]

Thus, the intellectual leadership necessary to provide understanding and information about the complexities of modern life fled Appalachia, leaving behind "Yesterday's People."

Adaptation. Weller and others recognize that many of the values which they describe developed as a result of people adapting to the situation in which they found themselves. The Appalachian's fatalism arose as a realistic response to the hardships he faced and served as a buffer against constant disappointment. The religion which developed in the mountains served to relieve anxieties generated by status deprivation, guilt, and illness, while at the same time supplying recreation in areas where recreation facilities were scarce.[30] The mountaineer's culture, says Weller, "has developed along lines that would allow him to bear up under the crushing loads he had put upon him."[31] This explanation deserves far more attention than proponents of the subculture model have given it. They tend to ignore the significant implications this explanation has for strategies of change in the mountains. These implications will be examined later in this paper.

In sum, Weller and those influenced by him claim that there exists in Southern Appalachia a folk culture that has developed over a long period of time and is passed from generation to generation. This subculture consists of traits quite different from those held by middle-class Americans. These differences are largely responsible for the problems which plague the Appalachian area—poverty, poor health care, low educational achievement, emotional disturbances, violence, poor government, and welfare dependency. Furthermore, efforts to alleviate these problems often fail because of the Appalachian's resistance to new ideas, reluctance to work cooperatively, lack of goals, fatalism, suspicion of outsiders, and distrust of bureaucracies of all types. As a result, simply pumping money into Appalachia will not solve the problems of the area. The folk culture must be changed before substantial social progress can occur. The mountain people are unable and often unwilling to change themselves. Outsiders must provide the stimulus and instruments for revamping the culture. Change agents include ministers, teachers, public health nurses, social workers, recreation leaders, psychiatrists, and government planners. Instruments of change encompass new educational and religious programs, kindergartens, bookmobiles, vocational schools, birth control programs, planning commissions, and an expanded highway system.

Jack Weller's descriptions and prescriptions have dominated the discussion of Appalachia during the past decade and have provided the philosophical underpinnings for the many government programs and church-sponsored activities in Appalachia during this period. This has occurred in spite of the fact that Weller's descriptions are largely unproven and abound with contradictions and that his prescriptions have had some very damaging consequences for the Appalachian people.

Critique of the Appalachian Subculture Model

Criticisms of the Appalachian subculture model can be discussed on five levels: (1) questions concerning the uniqueness of the subculture; (2) questions concerning who is included in the subculture; (3) questions concerning whether the traits of the subculture are accurately portrayed; (4) questions concerning the forces which have given rise to and perpetuated the subculture; and (5) questions concerning the strategies for change suggested by proponents of the subculture model.

Dwight Billings maintains that the distinctiveness and importance of the Appalachian subculture have been overemphasized.[32] As pointed out earlier in this paper, many of the traits attributed to the Appalachian subculture—as well as the best evidence for it—originate in Thomas Ford's essay which appeared in 1962. Yet Ford concluded that the region had become " 'progressive-minded' and 'achievement-oriented' to a surprisingly high degree."[33] His findings do not support the belief that traditionalism, individualism, or fatalism are core cultural values in Appalachia. Billings' own research casts further doubt on the uniqueness of an Appalachian subculture. He produces a scale of "middle-class orientation" from a secondary analysis of data gathered from several thousand respondents in North Carolina. He found that attitudinal differences between respondents from the Appalachian section of that state and from the other regions were quite small and could be attributed to rurality. From his interpretation of this data he concludes that attitudinal characteristics cannot be used to explain the existence of poverty in the mountains. While Billings' evidence is not conclusive, his point is well taken. The burden of proof rests on those who claim that a unique folk culture exists in Appalachia. As of this point in time, they have failed to provide convincing evidence that the folk culture they describe actually exists.

Proponents of the subculture model have also failed to make clear exactly who in the mountains share the traits of the folk culture. Weller and many other students of mountain culture have tended to attribute the traits of the folk culture to the people of Appalachia in a somewhat blanket fashion.[34] This has resulted in much confusion and the perpetuation of harmful stereotypes.

Weller, for example, says that there is a middle class and professional class in the mountains, and that both have the same characteristics of these classes elsewhere. But, he continues, most people living within Appalachia have come out of the folk culture and share its traits to a certain degree.[35] To what degree? Weller gives no answer. Are the characteristics of the Appalachian middle-class closer to American middle-class culture or to the folk culture? Again, no answer is provided.

Confusion also results from the fact that the description of the folk culture is similar in many ways to Oscar Lewis' discussion of the culture of poverty. According to Lewis, the culture of poverty is

a label for a specific conceptual model that describes in positive terms a subculture of Western society with its own structure and rationale, a way of life handed on from generation to generation along family lines. . . . It is a culture in the traditional anthropological sense in that it provides human beings with a design for living, with a ready made set of solutions for human problems and so serves a significant adaptive function.[36]

To scholars like Edward Banfield, the culture of poverty is shared by a lower class which is characterized by "pathological" traits—such as present-orientedness and action-seeking behavior—which combine to keep people poor.[37] The implications of the culture of poverty and the folk culture are the same—people's values must be changed.[38]

Weller describes a lower class in Appalachia that is mired in the culture of poverty. But, he says, this Appalachian lower class differs from the Appalachian folk class. Unfortunately, Weller fails to identify the differences except in the broadest of generalities. The lower class has only disadvantages while the folk class has several advantages. The lower class is worse off, more suspicious of outsiders, and will require more help than the folk class. At the same time, the lower class is less resistant to change than the folk class.[39] It is not surprising that many scholars who rely upon Weller's discussion of Appalachian culture tend to view the lower class and the folk class as one.

The failure to clearly define who participates in the folk culture has given rise to the view that Appalachia has a homogeneous culture. Critics of Weller insist that there exist in Appalachia several life-styles with distinctive group identities and behavior patterns. Certain questions, say these critics, must be answered before an accurate picture of mountain culture is possible. What types of status or class groupings exist in Appalachia? What types of subculture exist? What are the characteristics of the classes and subcultures? What is the relationship between particular classes and subcultures in the mountains? What type of interaction occurs among classes?

Much more research is needed before these questions can be satisfactorily answered. There are, however, several people who have begun to search for some answers. One is Helen Lewis, who tries to document the existence of a rural mountain subculture, a coal mining subculture, and a town subculture in Appalachia.[40] Bill Best believes that both a traditional mountain culture and a culture of poverty exist in Appalachia.[41] The traditional mountain culture, says Best, has been geared to subsistence living. During the early mining period, many mountain families left their small hillside farms and moved into coal camps. The coal companies were very paternalistic and the families became very dependent on them. During the hard times which followed, the families in company towns did not have the farms and farming skills, which had sustained their ancestors, to fall back on. Thus, they migrated to cities or became dependent on private and public welfare and relief organizations. Those who found some type of work and avoided going on welfare constitute what Best calls the traditional mountain culture. Their basic cultural mode is subsistence, which fosters independence. Those who had to go on welfare and remained there, he classifies as a culture of poverty. Their mode is dependency.

> People of both cultures share many of the same values and one uninitiated to the ways of the mountains probably couldn't tell the difference between the two. While both groups are individualistic to a degree, traditionalism is less dominant in the culture of poverty. Those in the culture of poverty have less to lose when change comes to the social order and they can usually be found willing to join many of the new programs which have proliferated in the region since the early sixties.[42]

John Stephenson, using occupation as his criterion, identifies four "family types" in a mountain community he calls Shiloh.[43] What he found in Shiloh, and suspects to be true for similar areas elsewhere, is that the four types of families participate in a traditional mountain subculture in different ways and to different degrees. There are, he says, a number of families in Appalachia today which are living "under two flags," in the midst of a transition from a "traditionalistic kind of cultural background into a modern kind of present and future."[44] Finally, Harry Schwarzweller and his colleagues have conducted a thirty-year longitudinal study of an Appalachian community called Beech Creek. Although all the families in Beech Creek were quite poor, the authors found that social class differences were evident in family reputation, visiting patterns, marital exchanges, and territorial locations.[45]

In spite of Billings' findings and the lack of clarity concerning who possesses what traits, most observers of Appalachian culture are convinced that a distinctive Appalachian subculture exists. Some critics charge that Weller and most other students of the mountain personality have done an inadequate job of portraying this subculture. Roger Lesser points out that while Weller claims to present an objective analysis of Appalachian culture, he emphasizes only the dramatic and destructive elements of the culture.[46] Studies of mountain culture seldom focus attention on such Appalachian traits as neighborliness and hospitality, love of place, modesty, bravery, sense of humor, loyalty, resourcefulness, and patriotism.[47] Such studies often fail to examine the benefits which result from placing a higher value on people over objects, continuity over change, and individualism over group participation. They frequently overlook in Appalachian examples of cooperative activity, routine and stability, and the acceptance of change.

Many of the mountaineer's "negative" or "destructive" traits are negative and destructive only when judged by middle-class standards. For example, Jack Weller claims that "existence-oriented" Appalachian society does not have the secondary goals of "beauty, excellence, and refinement." Yet, as Bill Best points out,

Appalachians do have these goals; they are just expressed in ways different from those of the "improvement-oriented society."[48] The Appalachian individual, rather than striving for excellence in corporate relationships, might turn his drive for excellence into being a good coon hunter, vegetable gardener, or story teller. The mountaineer's sense of beauty is expressed in good craftsmanship, the preservation of the great ballads and tales of English literature, and the use of the simile and metaphor in song, story, and speech. The negativism of many of the studies is revealed by the choice of words used to describe certain traits. Why is the mountaineer's "what will be, will be" attitude most often described as "fatalism" rather than "contentment" or "realism"?[49] In sum, the traits of the Appalachian personality are frequently discussed with little understanding given to the culture in which they are dominant.

Contradictions abound within many analyses of the Appalachian culture. Ernest Austin discusses just a few of the contradictions in *Yesterday's People.*

> Weller tells the reader that mountain people are "place bound," then laments their migratory habits; he states that they are so independent as to disdain group cooperation, then speaks of their emotional dependence upon group and community agreement. . . . Mountain teenagers find life dull partly because they have nothing to do, but there is little delinquency "partly because the rural nature of the area provides plenty of room to work off pent-up emotions" via hiking, fishing, exploring, hunting, etc. . . . The author explains that the people fiercely reject change of any kind, and then he later demonstrates how they readily accept and become attached to changes. . . .[50]

If Appalachians are present-oriented and fatalistic, why have hundreds of thousands left the mountains for the cities in search of a better future? If mountaineers will not cooperate and join groups, why is West Virginia the most unionized state in the nation?[51] If, as David Looff maintains, the problem of the poor white in Appalachia is his "overly close" family, why do other social scientists such as Daniel Moynihan claim that the fundamental black problem is its weak family structure?[52] Proponents of the subculture model should deal with these and other contradictions before their analysis and suggestions for change are accepted.

Some critics, especially Helen Lewis, charge that proponents of the Appalachian subculture model confuse description for analysis. Weller and others begin with the assumption that a unique subculture exists and then proceed to fill in the description of that subculture. This leads to confusion over the purpose of the description. If, as it often appears, the purpose is to explain how the subculture is responsible for poverty and other Appalachian problems, then emphasis should be placed on the factors which have led to the particular behavior patterns described as belonging to those in the

Appalachian subculture. If, on the other hand, the purpose is to identify'the effects of the problems on the subculture, emphasis should be placed on how these behaviors are transmitted from one generation to another. Pure description, says Lewis, does neither. It does not tell us why the problems prevail or why the problems cause certain values, norms, or behaviors of the people.[53]

Culture is more than just description, says Lewis. It refers to a set of normative patterns which arise through a group's interaction with its environment. By discussing culture in isolation from the social, economic, and political setting, most studies portray the Appalachian people as the passive and apathetic carriers of the destructive traits of their culture. Such a picture, insists Lewis, is misleading. The cultural traits of the mountain people cannot be understood apart from the conditions that shaped them and the processes that perpetuate them. Appalachia, she suggests, may be viewed

> as a subsociety structurally alienated and lacking resources due to processes of colonialism and exploitation. Those who control the resources preserve their advantage by discrimination. The people are not essentially passive but these subcultural traits of fatalism, passivity, etc., are adjustive techniques of the powerless; ways in which people protect their way of life from new economic modes and the concomitant alien culture. These values are reactions to powerlessness.[54]

This perspective leads to an interpretation of the Appalachian people and institutions quite different from that of Weller's. For example, some of the characteristics and "problems" attributed to the family and church by Weller and others could be traced to a process whereby the family and church have tried to resist or adapt to a history of colonial exploitation. Helen Lewis, Linda Johnson and Sue Kobak suggest that the family system may have served as a defensive mechanism against outside interference by becoming a refuge for its members, opposing certain changes, developing sabotage techniques, overprotecting children, becoming exclusive and closed, and serving as a center for "underground" mountain culture.[55] Perhaps most importantly, the family may have encouraged biculturalism. Lewis believes that mountain children have been taught to act proper in public and be "hillbilly" at home. When they must,

> Appalachians passively enact the behavior of mainstream culture in settings of formalized intergroup contact: at the welfare office, in court, and at school. It is in such cases that the Appalachian is bicultural and bidialectical.[56]

Colonialism as an explanation for the underdevelopment of Appalachia has been most often applied to the coal mining regions of the mountains. Helen Lewis, relying heavily on Robert Blauner's analysis of colonialism in relation to black Americans, provides the most informative research in this regard.[57] Blauner defines colonialism as "domination over a geographically external political unit most often inhabited by people of a different race and culture, when this domination is political and economic, and the colony exists subordinated to and dependent upon the mother country."[58] While admitting that some characteristics of colonies do not apply to Appalachia, Lewis believes that the history of the region provides evidence to support the view that the four major steps of the colonialization process identified by Blauner have occurred in Appalachia. These are (1) a forced or involuntary entry; (2) a rapid modification of the culture and social organization of the colonized; (3) control by the dominant group; and (4) a condition of racism, social domination by which the colonized are defined as inferior or different and which rationalizes the exploitation, control, and oppression by the superordinate group.

This is not the time nor is there the space to examine Lewis' evidence. She concedes that important questions remain, and that much research is required before they can be answered. It can be said, however, that the colonial analogy is gaining attention and respectability as more becomes known about who controls the resources of Appalachia.[59]

The debate over the Appalachian subculture model would not be of much significance except that the persons and agencies concerned with fighting the conditions of poverty in the mountains have accepted this view of Appalachia and the strategies of change which it implies. The result, as Maloney and Huelsman point out, has been a focus "not on what the rest of society is doing to the Appalachian but rather on what the Appalachian is supposed to be doing to himself through his own defective value system."[60] There has been little questioning of the manner in which the institutions of the region serve and affect the people because there has been agreement that the values of the people are at fault. It is these values which must be changed before poverty can be eliminated.

An acceptance of the colonial analogy implies the need for a radical change in the Appalachian economic and political structure. One need not, however, accept the validity of the colonial model in order to be critical of the subculture model's assumptions about change. The dangers of relying solely upon a cultural explanation for the poverty of a particular group of people has been documented by William Ryan in his book, *Blaming the Victim.*

Ryan is writing primarily about an urban environment, but his remarks are relevant to the Appalachian situation. Victim-blaming, says Ryan, is a warped logic that enables well-meaning middle-class liberals and humanitarians to believe that it is the characteristics of people themselves that are the fundamental causes of problems such as poor education and poor health care. It involves a four-step process. First, identify a social problem. Second, study those affected by the problem and discover in what ways they are different from the rest of us as a consequence of deprivation and injustice. Third, define the differences as the cause of the social problem itself. Fourth, assign a government bureaucrat to invent a humanitarian action program to correct the differences.[61]

It should be obvious that this process is at work with the Appalachian subculture model. Consider just one victim—the miseducated child in an Appalachian school. A problem certainly exists. As many as 65 percent of Appalachian students drop out of school before graduation. A higher proportion of Appalachian students than elsewhere consistently fail the selective service entrance tests.[62] The subculture model blames the child for his inability to read and write well and for his disinterest in school. The child has no interest in books because there are none in his home. He hesitates to talk in class because he soon realizes that his parents have taught him to speak incorrectly. He is unable to relate to the school system or his teacher because he has been overprotected by his family. He is often absent from school because his family encourages him to stay at home. The child, in other words, contains within himself the causes for his miseducation. The solutions implied by this perspective include preschool training in order to weaken family influence, social workers to educate the mother about the value of reading and education, and vocational schools for the many who drop out of school by the ninth grade.

This perspective tends to ignore the effect on students of inadequate facilities, irrelevant texts, insensitive and ill-prepared teachers, misguided curriculum (sic), overcrowded classes, and stingy taxpayers. It tends to overlook a political system in which schools are a source of power and income—a situation which produces local leaders who permit and even encourage irrelevant education.[63] By trying to remedy defects in the child's culture, proponents of the subculture model are treating the symptoms, not the roots of the problem. They are applying what Ryan calls an "exceptionalistic" rather than a "universalistic" approach to the analysis and solution of social problems. They are promoting remedial treatment to a specially-defined category of persons who are afflicted with a unique "disease," rather than trying to prevent a disease that is a result of the social arrangements of the community and is not unique to a special group. The exceptionalist viewpoint is reflected in solutions that are private, voluntary, special, local, and exclusive, while the universalist viewpoint is reflected in solutions that are public, legislated, general, national, and inclusive.[64]

Blaming the victim for his problems can result in a self-fulfilling prophecy. As Helen Lewis points out, the wide acceptance of the Appalachian subculture model may have helped to create an Appalachian subculture by convincing the Appalachian that he is inferior, backward, and has "bad" values.[65] She sums up the feelings of most of the critics of the subculture model when she states that "the wholesale and intemperate acceptance and promulgation" of the subculture model and the strategies of change implicit in it have been "extremely pernicious and wasteful of money." It is, she concludes, "untenable and unjust to characterize Appalachian culture patterns as deficient or pathological versions of mainstream American culture."[66]

Conclusion

The purpose of this paper has been to examine the major parts of the Appalachian subculture model and to summarize and evaluate criticisms of that model. A review of the criticisms does not lead to the conclusion that the model should be discarded—that it has nothing of value to contribute to the analysis of social problems in Appalachia. Indeed, several of the criticisms are contradictory. Each, alone, is incomplete and requires further study. Yet, each identifies a serious deficiency of the subculture model. Together they indicate that one should exercise great caution in accepting, without reservation, the conclusions and recommendations of the proponents of the model.

Many of the myths and stereotypes about blacks and women in our society have been discredited in recent years as a result of both a critical reexamination of the underlying assumptions of earlier studies and in depth scholarly research. The time has now come for a similar effort in regard to the Appalachian. The undocumented observations and implicit assumptions of Jack Weller and other advocates of the Appalachian subculture model should receive serious scrutiny in order to judge their validity. Other models explaining conditions in Appalachia should be tested and different strategies for change should be examined. Social scientists, if they choose, can be of help in this necessary and worthwhile effort. Let us hope that many make this choice.

NOTES

1. "Why Study Appalachia?" in *Appalachia's People, Problems, Alternatives,* comp. by Peoples Appalachian Research Collective, rev. ed. (Morgantown: By the compilers, 1972), p. 12.

2. Harry M. Caudill, *Night Comes to the Cumberlands: A Biography of a Depressed Area* (Boston: Little, Brown & Co., 1962.)

3. Jack E. Weller, *Yesterday's People: Life in Contemporary Appalachia* (Lexington: Kentucky Paperbacks, University of Kentucky Press, 1966).

4. Caudill, pp. 4–7. See the debate on this question in the February (pp. 10–12), March (pp. 18–19), April (pp. 18–19), and June, 1969 (pp. 14–16) issues of *Mountain Life and Work.*

5. For a discussion of Caudill's and Weller's influence on the social science literature related to Appalachia, see Mike Maloney and Ben Huelsman, "Humanism, Scientism and Southern Mountaineers," *Peoples Appalchia,* 2 (July 1972), 24–27.

6. Helen Lewis, "Fatalism or the Coal Industry?" *Mountain Life and Work* (December 1970), p. 6. Helen Lewis was among the first to criticize the underlying assumptions of Weller's analysis and to suggest that the processes of colonialism might be of use in understanding developments in Appalachia. I rely heavily on her analysis in this paper. See also Helen Lewis, Sue Kobak, and Linda Johnson, "Family, Religion and Colonialism in Central Appalachia or Bury My Rifle at Big Stone Gap," in *Growing Up Country,* ed. by Jim Axelrod (Clintwood, Va.: Council of the Southern Mountains, 1973), 131–56; and Helen Lewis and Edward Knipe, "The Impact of Coal Mining on the Traditional Mountain Subculture," in *The Not So Solid South,* ed. by John Moreland (Athens: University of Georgia Press, 1974), 25–37.

7. Lewis, p. 4.

8. Thomas Ford, "The Passing of Provincialism," in *The Southern Appalachian Region: A survey,* ed. by Thomas Ford (Lexington: Kentucky Paperbacks, University of Kentucky Press, 1967), 9–34.

9. Herbert J. Gans, *The Urban Villagers* (New York: Free Press of Glencoe, 1962.) Weller saw many parallels between Southern Appalachia and Gans' description of an urban Italian neighborhood in Boston. See Weller, pp. 4–5.

10. See especially Richard A. Ball, "Poverty Case: The Analgesic Subculture of the Southern Appalachians," *American Sociological Review,* 33 (December 1968), 885–95; Frank S. Riddel, "Related Aspects of the Social and Economic Problems, Cultural Tradition, and Educational System of Rural Appalachia" (Ph.D. dissertation, Ohio State University, 1971); Rena Gazaway, *The Longest Mile* (Garden City, N.Y.: Doubleday, 1969); Berton Kaplan, *Blue Ridge: An Appalachian Community in Transition* (Morgantown: Office of Research and Development, Appalachian Center, West Virginia University, 1971); H. Dudley Plunkett and Mary J. Bowman, *Elites and Change in the Kentucky Mountains* (Lexington: University Press of Kentucky, 1973); John D. Photiadis, "Rural Southern Appalachia and Mass Society," in *Change in Rural Appalachia,* ed. by John Photiadis and Harry Schwarzweller (Philadelphia: University of Pennsylvania Press, 1971), 5–22; David H. Looff, *Appalachia's Children: The Challenge of Mental Health* (Lexington: University Press of Kentucky, 1971); and John B. Stephenson, *Shiloh: A Mountain Community* (Lexington: University Press of Kentucky, 1968). Stephenson is more discriminating than the others in applying Weller's findings and his book is the best of the Appalachian community studies.

11. John C. Campbell, *The Souther Highlander and His Homeland* (New York: Russell Sage Publications, 1921), p. 91.

12. Weller, pp. 29–33; and Riddel, pp. 149–53.

13. Stephenson claims that a more proper label for this phenomenon is present-orientedness. "There is no slavish attempt to live the present exactly as the past. . . . Rather, most persons for whom this traditional outlook is characteristic tend to live in the present, with only occasional backward glances to the past and forward looks to the future." (p. 95).

14. Weller, pp. 33–37.

15. Ibid, pp. 37–40; Riddel, pp. 153–57.

16. Weller, pp. 40–43.

17. Ibid, pp. 49–57.

18. Riddel, pp. 169–71.

19. Richard A. Couto, *Poverty, Politics, and Health Care: An Appalachian Experience* (New York: Praeger Special Studies in U.S. Economic, Social, and Political Issues, 1975), p. 13.

20. Riddel, pp. 146–47.

21. Cratis Williams, "The Southern Mountaineer in Fact and Fiction," 3 vols. (Ph.D. dissertation, New York University, 1961), 1:79.

22. Weller, p. 88.

23. See especially James Brown and Harry K. Schwarzweller, "The Appalachian Family," in *Change in Rural Appalachia,* ed. by John Photiadis and Harry Schwarzweller (Philadelphia: University of Pennsylvania Press, 1971), 85–98; Riddel, pp. 178–89; and Weller, pp. 58–86.

24. Gazaway, p. 94.

25. Weller, p. 88.

26. Looff, pp. 120–27.

27. Loyal Jones, "Appalachian Values," in *Appalachians Speak Up,* comp. by I. Best (Berea Ky.: by the Compiler, 1973), pp. 10–11; Nathan C. Gerrard, "Churches of the Stationary Poor in Appalachia," in *Change in Rural Appalachia,* ed. by John Photiadis and Harry Schwarzweller (Philadelphia: University of Pennsylvania Press, 1971), 99–114; and Weller, pp. 121–33.

28. Weller, p. 21.

29. Ibid.

30. Gerrad, pp. 108–10.

31. Weller, p. 29.

32. Dwight Billings, "Culture and Poverty in Appalachia: A Theoretical Discussion and Empirical Analysis," *Social Forces,* 53 (December 1974), 315–23.

33. Ford, p. 32. See the discussion of Ford's findings in Billings, pp. 316–17.

34. Stephenson, p. 95.

35. Weller, pp. 5–7.

36. Oscar Lewis, "The Culture of Poverty," *Scientific American,* 215 (October 1966), p. 19.

37. Edward C. Banfield, *The Unheavenly City Revisited,* rev. ed. (Boston: Little, Brown & Co., 1974); see the discussion in Couto, pp. 10–17.

38. To the extent that the two models are similar, the Appalachian subculture model is open to the many criticisms which have been leveled against the culture of poverty model, criticisms which have seriously undermined the validity of the model. Since this paper is concerned with Appalachia, a detailed critique of the culture of poverty model will not be presented. There are several books and articles available which do an excellent job of this. See especially Charles A. Valentine, *Culture and Poverty* (Chicago: University of Chicago Press, 1968); William Ryan, *Blaming the Victim* (New York: Pantheon Books, 1971); and Jack L. Roach and Orville R. Gursslin, "An Evaluation of the Concept 'Culture of Poverty,' " *Social Forces,* 45 (March 1967), 383–92. Several of the more important criticisms of the culture of poverty model will be discussed in this paper in relation to the Appalachian subculture model.

39. Weller, pp. 151–52. One source of constant confusion in *Yesterday's People* is Weller's failure to differentiate between the concepts of class and culture. Those in the folk class are the people who exhibit the traits of the folk culture. This practice makes it virtually impossible to correlate behavior patterns with variables such as education, residence, income or occupation.

40. Helen Lewis, "Subcultures of the Southern Appalachians," *Virginia Geographer,* 3 (Spring 1968), 2–8.

41. Bill Best, "From Existence to Essence: A Conceptual Model for An Appalachian Studies Curriculum" (Ed.D. dissertation, University of Massachusetts, 1973), pp. 26–28.

42. Ibid, p. 28.

43. Stephenson, pp. 42–136. See also Kaplan, pp. 31–45.

44. Stephenson, p. 136.

45. Harry Schwarzweller, James Brown and Joseph Mangalam, *Mountain Families in Transition* (University Park: Pennsylvania State University Press, 1971).

46. Roger Lesser, "Culture: Toward Tomorrow's People," *Peoples Appalachia,* 1 (March 1970), p. 6.

47. Three studies that do emphasize these traits are Jones, pp. 101–21, Williams, pp. 315–44, and Best, pp. 8–63.

48. Best, pp. 22–24; see also Jones, p. 118.

49. Stephenson describes this value as "contentment" (pp. 96–99).

50. Ernest H. Austin, Jr. "One View of *Yesterday's People,*" *The Appalachian South,* 1 (Spring/Summer 1966), p. 38.

51. *Appalachian Issues and Resources,* comp. by the Southern Appalachian Ministry in Higher Education (Knoxville: by the Compilers, 1975), p. 22.

52. This point is made by Dwight Billings (p. 317). It appears, says Billings, that the poor can do nothing right in the eyes of middle-class social scientists.

53. Helen Lewis, pp. 4–5.

54. Ibid, p. 6. See also the discussion in Couto, pp. 12–17.

55. Lewis, Johnson and Kobak, pp. 148–53.

56. Helen Lewis, p. 6.

57. Robert Blauner, "Internal Colonialism and Ghetto Revolt," *Social Problems*, 16 (Spring 1969), 393–408. See Helen Lewis, pp. 6–15; and Lewis, Johnson and Kobak, pp. 134–53.

58. Blauner, p. 395.

59. Harry Caudill in 1962 referred to Appalachia as "a colonial appendage of the industrial East and Middle West" (p. 325). Neal Pierce in *The Border South States* (New York: W. W. Norton, 1975) refers to Appalachia as "America's prime economic and political colony of the 20th century" (p. 35). Others describing Appalachia as a colony include William C. Blizzard, "West Virginia Wonderland," *The Appalachian South*, 1 (Spring/Summer 1966), 8–15; Barry Barkan and R. B. Lloyd, "Picking Poverty's Pocket," *Article One* (May 1970); and John Gaventa, "In Appalachia: Property Is Theft," *Southern Exposure*, 1 (Summer/Fall 1973), 43–52. Research that lends support to the colonial analogy includes Rick Diehl, "Appalachia's Energy Elite: A Wing of Imperialism," *Peoples Appalachia*, 1 (March 1970), 2–3; Rick Diehl, "How the Energy Elite Rules," *Peoples Appalachia*, 1 (April–May 1970), 7–12; Keith Dix, "The West Virginia Economy: Notes for a Radical Base Study," *Peoples Appalachia*, 1 (April–May 1970), 3–7; Richard Kirby, "Kentucky Coal: Owners, Taxes, Profits," *Appalachian Lookout*, 1 (October 1969), 19–27; J. Davitt McAteer, *Coal Mine Health and Safety: The Case of West Virginia (New York: Praeger, 1973); Coal Government of Appalachia,* comp. by a Student Task Force for the Appalachian Research and Defense Fund (Charleston, W. Va.: by the Compilers, 1971); and Tom Miller, *Who Owns West Virginia* (Huntington, W. Va.: *The Herald Advertiser* and *The Herald Dispatch*, 1974).

60. Maloney and Huelsman, p. 24.

61. Ryan, p. 8.

62. For a discussion of problems related to education in Appalachia, see Appalachian Regional Commission, *Appalachian Education for Tomorrow* (Washington D.C.: ARC, 1971); Jim Branscome, "A Colonial System of Education," *Mountain Life and Work*, 47 (January 1971), 14–18; Stanley Ikenberry, "Educational Reform in Appalachia: Problems of Relevance, Strategy, and Priority," in *Change in Rural Appalachia*, ed. by John Photiadis and Harry Schwarzweller (Philadelphia: University of Pennsylvania Press, 1971), 195–206; and Franklin Parker, "Appalachia: Education in a Depressed Area," *Phi Kappa Phi Journal*, 50 (Fall 1970), 27–38.

63. Peter Schrag, "The School and Politics," *Appalachian Review*, 1 (Fall 1966), 6–10.

64. Ryan, pp. 16–29.

65. Helen Lewis, p. 5.

66. Ibid.

23. COALTOWNS: THE COMPANY TOWN AND SOUTHERN APPALACHIAN HISTORY

Crandall Shifflett

The coal town was the most enduring symbol of the transformation from a preindustrial to an industrial society in the southern Appalachian Mountains of the United States. Beginning in the 1880's and continuing until the Great Depression of the 1930's, coal companies built facilities for miners in remote and isolated areas close to the supply of coal. The penetration of railroads with spur lines was the first step in opening up previously inaccessible mountain ridges and valleys to coal mining. When the rail line was complete, or nearly so, investors, mostly from the northern United States and Europe eagerly furnished the capital necessary to secure the lease, land or surface rights to seams of coal once cradled in a mountain fastness. Subsequently, company officials contracted local carpenters to build houses, initially of the boarding type for single males, and then recruited laborers to live in the hollows and mine the coal. Little more than encampments at first, these settlements gradually grew into towns.

Most coal towns in southern Appalachia were company towns. The coal company built houses and acted as the landlord; stocked and ran a general store with food, miners' tools, furniture, ice, tobacco, and sundry items; erected schools and churches and hired teachers and preachers to serve them; opened hospitals and infirmatories for the sick and injured and brought in nurses and doctors to staff them; employed sheriffs and deputies to maintain law and order; and provided lodges, meeting halls, baseball diamonds, playgrounds, even graveyards. Not all company towns offered such a full range of services. In general, however, the company town was a cradle to grave existence for thousands of coal miners. According to one estimate, over 600 company towns sprang up in southern West Virginia, eastern Tennessee, northern Georgia, and western North Carolina between 1880 and 1930.[1]

Although not unique to southern Appalachia, the company town typified the coal fields of the South. Town building peaked just before the Great Depression when two-thirds to three-fourths of all miners in southern West Virginia, eastern Kentucky, and southwestern Virginia lived in company towns. In contrast, outside the region, 90 percent of the miners in Indiana and Illinois, about three-fourths of those in Ohio, and a majority of those in Pennsylvania lived in independent towns with privately-owned facilities.[2] Clearly, the company town was a more salient feature of industrial development in the southern coal fields. During the depression years, some southern coal operators apparently began the shift to private ownership, but the company town persisted as a central feature of the southern Appalachian fields into the 1950's.

Reprinted from *Reshaping the Images of Appalachia*, Loyal Jones (ed.), The Berea College Appalachian Center, 1986, pp. 46–53. Used by permission.

The company town did not emerge intentionally to control, exploit, or pacify miners.[3] Unlike the anthracite fields of the northern United States where towns and cities incorporated prior to the opening of the coal mines, in southern Appalachia urbanization and industrialization were twin features of the same process. Few towns existed in the southern fields before the opening of the mines and those that did were often miles from the coal supply. As late as 1925 still 88 percent of the southern miners were two or more miles from the nearest town, and less than 100 non-company towns could be found in the southern Appalachian coal region. Hence, coal developers perforce built houses, cisterns, commissaries, privies for the miners and then gradually expanded the range of services as the labor force grew and changed in nature.[4]

Changes in the composition of the labor forced coal companies to augment the services they offered. World War I brought a dramatic alteration in the sources of labor. The first wave of labor had been recruited from the great pool of southeastern European immigrants entering the United States in the 1890's, especially Italians, Hungarians, Greeks, Poles and Slovaks.[5] When the war broke out, the stream of immigrant labor dried up. Indeed, immigrant miners left the coal fields, and coal companies experienced real shortages of labor at a time of peak demand for coal brought on by the war. Some Negroes left the mines too for the industrial cities of the North but apparently not in such great numbers as the southeastern European immigrants.[6] Increasingly, the operators turned their attention to native whites and blacks. Operators also seized this opportunity to build a more stable labor force by recruiting family men who would presumably be less inclined to pick up and leave. The three to four room single family dwelling soon eclipsed the large boarding house as the most common type of dwelling. Whereas the first wave of labor had been predominantly, although not altogether, single males, the war intensified the search for men with families.

Family labor marked the departure from coal camps to coal towns. Not only did the operators have to provide additional housing, they also had to provide schools and other facilities. Few schools existed nearby, and county governments often could not afford to erect school buildings to serve isolated mining communities. Families also required more churches and recreational facilities. The operators responded with lodge halls, pool rooms, libraries, playgrounds, athletic fields, graveyards, while they expanded existing facilities.[7] Moreover, duplicate, not to say equal, facilities were built in keeping with the custom of segregation along racial and ethnic lines.[8] In this transition from coal camp to company town, three towns actually existed in a single setting: an immigrant town, a Negro town, and an "American" town.[9] More than towns, these were really communities with their separate facilities, organizations, customs, and social life. The immigrant town gradually shrank in importance while the other two grew until the 1920's. Stonega, for example, a company town of the Stonega Coke and Coal Company which employed three-fourths of all Virginia coal miners, was established in 1893. In 1916, Stonega had a population of 2470, of which 500 were listed as "colored." It had 422 houses and 456 families; 1 white grade school with a principal and five teachers; 1 black school with 2 teachers; a Catholic Church with two resident priests; 1 white Methodist, Baptist, and Presbyterian church; 1 Hungarian Presbyterian church; 1 Negro Baptist and Methodist church; 1 segregated theater; two white lodge halls and 1 Hungarian; 3 black lodge halls; and three orders for women. In addition the company hospital was divided into white and black wards, and there were separate baseball teams and white and black first aid squads.[10]

The emergence of communities marked the shift from camps to company towns and was its most significant development. Although the trend was toward white Anglo Saxon dominance, the diversity of the work-force combined with prevailing ethnic and racial prejudice to divide coal towns into separate cultural communities until World War II when large numbers of blacks left the coal fields. As the inventory of churches and organizations at Stonega shows, coal towns were really cultural enclaves, each with its own churches, organizations, social life, values, and lifeways.[11] The enclaves, whether immigrant, Negro, or native white, were waystations between the isolated and weakly organized life of rural agricultural societies and the heavily populated and more organized life of urban industrial societies. Opportunities for recreation, social interaction, worship, and mutual exchanges of information and assistance were never greater than within the company town. Ethnic and racial clustering translated these exchanges into a mutuality of interests out of which grew an understanding of and an appreciation for life in urban industrial society.

Most miners' families appear to have preferred the coal town to the world they had left, or rather, been forced out of. They harbored few misconceptions about the countryside and life on the farm which has been and continues to be idealized in American writing as a wholesome, harmonious, burden-free way of life. In fact, life in the countryside deteriorated in the nineteenth century into a desperate struggle to make a living. One study of the coal mining region of eastern Kentucky described the "monotonous regularity" in population changes, a pattern of "explosive growth and precipitous decline" beginning in 1820 and lasting for 120 years.[12] During part of this period of growth, especially between 1900 and 1930, the expansion of the coal mining industry and the influx of outside labor were

195

responsible for some of the population increase. However, by then the population explosion had done its damage. Indeed, if it had not been for the coming of the coal industry, the population crisis perhaps would have been even greater and starvation a serious regional problem. The preindustrial southern Appalachian farm, which by 1930 had shrunk to an average size of 76 acres, supported families of 8 to 12 people.[13] Farm income in Knott County, Kentucky, in 1930 averaged $215 and two-thirds of that was spent on food, a figure comparable to that of the Belgian working class families studied by Friedrich Engels in 1853. One study of the southern Appalachian region and diet in 1901–04 found diets "below optimum" in protein, calcium, iron and vitamins A and C.[14] A high birth rate, especially in rural Appalachia, was the cause of the population explosion. In 1930 the fertility ratio in the United States was 390 per thousand compared to 339 and 618 per thousand in Appalachian cities and rural areas respectively.[15] The growth was greatest in the poorest areas of hillside farms. Fertility ratios were 747 and 824 in Harlan and Letcher counties respectively, 692 in Hancock County, Tennessee, 667 in Wise County, Virginia and 682 in Mingo County, West Virginia.[16]

In 1974, F. L. Minor of Big Stone Gap, Virginia, a former coal miner, revealed in an interview that his great grandfather had once owned a farm in Hancock County, Tennessee, of 3500 acres. It surprised the interviewer who then inquired why Mr. Minor had left the farm for the coal mines. His answer is a good example of the effects of population growth. He said:

> Well, I'll tell you. My great grandfather, he divided up all this land with his children—he had seven. And some of them had 600 acres of land—some of the boys died— some of the girls had 300 acres and so on like that. Well, they growed up and then they had children, and then, they inherited so much and when we left down there it'd got down to we had 100 acres—my father died—so we decided that, uh, that we'd, uh, try something else, and so we just moved up here in Virginia. At that—at that particular time, of course, Hancock County never did have any industry much.[17]

Such were the backgrounds that shaped the perspectives of the first generation of migrants to the coal fields and company towns of southern Appalachia. Life on the farm was not the Arcadian myth of a care-free, independent, untrammeled yeomanry, but an endless round of work and struggle against the forces of population growth, shrinking farmsteads, and limited opportunities. Work in the coal mines offered new hope. According to the wife of one miner, "People found mining to be a nice way to make money." She compared the opening of the mines to the California gold rush where formerly poor hillside farmers came in search of a better way of life.[18] Melba Kizzire, a coal miner's daughter, contrasted the life she had left with

that of Docena, Alabama, a company town of the Tennessee Coal, Iron, and Railroad Company on the outskirts of Birmingham. She had come to Docena in 1944 with her father from a farm in Nyota in Blount County, Tennessee. "In Nyota," she said, "we lived in just an old wooden house, but here we had it wallpapered, we had running water—it was cold, but we had running water. We had electricity, and we had our sanitation provided for our nice house; [we had] our churches, our teachers." She continued:

> I lived in a wood—a log cabin home in the hills of Blount County, and I came to a brown, painted house. Like, you know, there was paint on *all* four sides and the top. First time I'd ever lived in a painted house. All the rooms were wallpapered with what I thought was the most beautiful wallpaper I had ever seen. . . . The floors were covered in linoleum, and I had been able to see the chickens through the floor where I lived. I mean it was primitive. And the schools had flushing johns; first time I ever saw a flushing john. First time I ever saw a telephone was when I came here. And I had a lot of firsts when I came here. . . . The houses were warm, had a fireplace in every room. . . . And to me it was breathtaking, all the wallpaper. . . . It took me a week to—I was stunned for about a week. . . . It was like I had gone to heaven, you know. . . . In Blount County . . . you didn't see your neighbor's houses. Here you would sit on the front porch . . . and as far as you could see, up the street people were sitting out talking, and blowing their cigarettes at night.[19]

Other, by no means rare, expressions of appreciation for life in the company town appeared in interviews with miners and their families by the Appalachian Oral History Project and the Samford University Oral History Project. They are supported also by a public opinion survey conducted randomly and with anonymity of miners of the Stonega Coke and Coal Company in 1951, and even more recently by the 1980 President's Commission on Coal.[20]

Thus, much evidence indicates that the company town had an impact on its residents quite apart from that which has customarily been associated with it. Contrary to the views that the coal mines and company controlled towns led to social fragmentation, disaffection, and alienation of the workforce, many miners and their families found life in them to be a great improvement over the past. Mines viewed the company town, not in comparison to some idyllic world of freedom, independence, and harmony, but against the backdrop of small farms on rocky hillsides of Tennessee, Kentucky, and Virginia, or a sharecropper's life in the deep South states. They knew firsthand of isolation, disorganization, and real hardship. The coal rush had rescued substantial numbers from poverty. Industrialization was a blessing, not a curse, and many seem to have embraced its benefits of high wages, labor saving conveniences, and a richer social life. Perhaps, the appreciation of miners for the company town explains why southern miners were the last to join the labor movement. Moreover, if the past is important to understanding the first-comers, the second generation—those born in the company town—no doubt developed different perspectives. For these reasons, I intend to compare housing, diet, diseases and medical care, and opportunities for education and social development before and after the opening of the mines. It will also be important to observe generational differences and the major forces of change. I have already shown how World War I altered the composition of the labor force. Equally dramatic were other forces, such as market and technological changes, the union movement, mechanization, the Great Depression, and World War II, all of which sent shock waves through the company town, each altering it in a special way.

In addition, a full description of day-to-day life within the company town is essential to an understanding of the culture of life and work in mining communities. Company towns produced a striking number and variety of voluntary associations. In this regard, the role of churches and religion needs to be examined. How were congregations formed and pastors and priests hired? Were they mere tools of the companies? Or did miners discover in Christianity what slaves in the American South first discovered, i.e., that religion could be a source of strength and a haven of cultural identity? How the culture of work influenced miners and the relationships of miners with outsiders needs much more attention. Some evidence from Stonega, for example, reveals miner awareness and sensitivity to outside feelings. Certainly the nature of mine work set them apart. Miners worked in the dark; they worked underground; the work was dangerous; they often worked unsupervised; many could form their own work groups or buddy system; they had their own unique diseases and injuries; when they came out of the mines they were black with coal dust and had to clean up even before going into their houses. Undoubtedly, these conditions shaped miners' self perceptions as well as those outside the mining communities. The 1951 public opinion survey mentioned above found a high percentage of Stonega employees desirous of a company publication to inform the public about miners and their work as a way of dealing with the ignorance and negative images miners perceived around them. Also, the closeness that miners seem to have felt for one another derived in part from the nature of work. In fact, much evidence suggests that the sense of brotherhood within the mining community emanated, not so much from the labor movement, which more often was a source of conflict and division, but from the common danger of work, the organization of work, and the close contact of families in the company towns. The roles of women and children in this work culture also need elaboration.

In conclusion, the coming and going of the company town was one of the most significant events in Appalachian history. Industrialization came to Appalachia in the form of the company town. Thousands were transformed from farmers and agricultural laborers into industrial workers. The ring of iron and steel replaced the soft cries of livestock; the time clock and production chart, not the sun and the weather, came to regulate the pace and rhythm of work and leisure. Some workers experienced anomie, became discontented, and expressed their discontent by joining the labor movement or drifting from mine to mine. Their story has been told. Significant numbers, however, made peace with urban industrial society. Their story is less well known. They became disaffected too, not with the company town per se, but because its closing signaled the end of steady employment and the demise of close-knit communities. I hope this study will shed additional light on both reactions.

NOTES

The author wishes to thank Berea College, Berea, Kentucky, for an Appalachian Studies Fellowship and the National Endowment for the Humanities for the Fellowship for College Teachers which supported this research.

1. Ronald D. Eller, *Miners, Millhands, and Mountaineers: Industrialization of the Appalachian South, 1880–1930* (Knoxville: The University of Tennessee Press, 1982), XX. Chapter 5 provides a good overview of the company town and its development.

2. Ibid., pp. 162–3. See also David Alan Corbin, *Life, Work, and Rebellion in the Coal Fields; the Southern West Virginia Miners, 1880–1922* (Urbana, Chicago, and London: The University of Illinois Press, 1981), p. 8.

3. For a different view, see Corbin, *Life,* pp. 70–71; Richard M. Simon, "Uneven Development and the Case of West Virginia: Going beyond the Colonialism Model," *Appalachian Journal,* Vol. 8, No 3 (Spring, 1981), pp. 165–86; Eller, *Miners,* pp. 192–8.

4. "Home Environment and Employment Opportunities of Women in Coal-Mine Workers' Families," *Bulletin of the Women's Bureau 45* (Washington: Government Printing Office, 1925), p. 6.

5. Eller, *Miners,* p. 174.

6. Darold T. Barnum, *The Negro in the Bituminous Coal Mining Industry* (Philadelphia: University of Pennsylvania Press, 1970).

7. For the range of services, see interviews with William H. Walker and Frank Bonds (1979), Samford University Oral History Collection, Samford University Library, Special Collections, Birmingham, Alabama; hereafter SUOHC. Also, "Home Environment," pp. 59–61.

8. Evidence of segregation was vast, but see Eller, *Miners,* pp. 170–2; C. G. Duffy to A. H. Reader, March 26, 1913 and Annual Reports, 1915–20, both in Westmoreland Coal Company Records, Stonega Coke and Coal Company, Accession 1765, Series II (Wilmington, Del.: Eleutherian Mills Historical Library), hereafter WCCR: interviews with Cora Frazier, Marvin Gullett (1975), Appalachian Oral History Project, Alice Lloyd College, Pippa Passes, Kentucky, hereafter AOHP and college depository; interviews with Reuben Barnes and William H. Walker (1979), SUOHC.

9. Eller, *Miners,* p. 194.

10. Annual Report, WCCR, 1916.

11. Immigrants, Negroes, and native whites had their own medicines, customs, herbs, dialect and distinct social activities, such as fish and chicken dinners, and Saturday night gatherings. See interview with Marvin Gullett (1975), AOHP, Alice Lloyd; A. H. Reader to W. B. Edwards, May 27, 1913, and Annual Report, WCCR, 1915.

12. George A. Hillery, Jr., "Population Growth in Kentucky, 1820–1960," *University of Kentucky Experiment Station Bulletin 705* (February, 1966), pp. 3–54; for quotes, see p. 25. See also, "Economic and Social Problems and Conditions of the Southern Appalachians," *U.S. Department of Agriculture Miscellaneous Publication 205* (January, 1935), pp. 1–184; Eller, *Miners,* pp. 225–6.

13. Eller, *Miners,* xix–xx, 16–22, 229–31.

14. "Economic and Social Problems," pp. 120–36.

15. Ibid., p. 5. See also, Gordon F. DeJong, *Appalachian Fertility Decline: A Demographic and Sociological Analysis* (Lexington, KY: University of Kentucky Press, 1968).

16. DeJong, *Appalachian Fertility,* Appendix A, 116, 118–9.

17. Interview with L. F. Minor (1974), SUOHC.

18. Interview with Christine Cochran (1979), SUOHC.

19. SUOHC.

20. Public Opinion Survey, WCCR; *The American Coal Miner: A Report on Community and Living Conditions in the Coalfields,* John D. Rockefeller, IV, Chairman, (Washington, 1980).

24. "TRADITIONAL APPALACHIAN MUSIC/EARLY COMMERCIAL COUNTRY MUSIC: CONTINUITY AND TRANSITION"

Ivan Tribe

While Appalachia was never quite as isolated or as self-sustaining as some of the early writers who visited the area would like to have had their readers believe, it could safely be termed more remote than many, if not most, sections of the United States. Making a living through subsistence agriculture on the hillsides and stream bottomland took many hours of hard labor, but folks still found time to make their own entertainment, just as they grew much of their own food and made many of their own household and farm tools. This homemade entertainment included ample amounts of music, both of the instrumental and vocal variety.

Since they constructed many of their working tools, mountain folk also crafted their own instruments—fiddles, banjoes, and in some areas dulcimers—from the native woods that grew in their neighborhoods. Community dwellers would gather and amuse themselves by participating in country dances almost from the time of the earliest settlements. Joseph Doddridge, an early settler of what later became West Virginia, wrote in 1824 of his childhood a generation earlier, that following wedding feasts:

> After dinner the dancing commenced, and generally lasted till the next morning. The figures of the dances were three and four-handed reels, or square sets and jigs. . . . Toward the latter part of the night, if any of the company, through weariness attempted to conceal themselves for the purpose of sleeping, they were hunted up, paraded on the floor, and the fiddler ordered to play 'Hang on till to-morrow morning.'[1]

These practices continued through the nineteenth century. Although by the 1890s, increasing numbers of fiddles and banjoes made in factories found their way into the highlands in addition to such hitherto uncommon instruments as the autoharp, mandolin, and especially the guitar, augmented the sounds of an earlier era. The use of mail order catalogs has often been cited as a reason for the growing number of manufactured instruments. Dulcimers became increasingly scarce, more so in some areas than others. John Day, blunt-spoken and highly critical of romantic writers on the Kentucky hillfolk, stated in his book *Bloody Ground* that mountaineers abandoned dulcimers as soon as the opportunity presented itself, because they realized that there was very little music in the "damn things."[2]

From that point onward, fiddle, banjo, and guitar reigned as the predominant means of making instrumental music in the Appalachian region. Folks played music in their own homes for entertainment, on their porches—if they had them—or in their yards. Any kind of a special event could provide local musicians with an opportunity to display their skills. One oldster recalled that "log rollin's, brush pilin's, burnin's, [and] grubbin's" would often be followed by a dance "when the work had ended." The last day of school in the Spring also provided a time when a festive spirit prevailed. Emmet Lundy an old fiddler from Grayson County, Virginia, told of such an incident involving him and his cousin in the early 1880's at a locale called Hampton School:

> An old fellow named Avery Jones was teachin' the school and we carried our violins over. . . . They wanted us to play some, and this old log house, the floor wasn't nailed down and my cousin had on brogan shoes. He could pat his foot awful heavy and he got to pattin' his foot. Directly the scholars got at it, and the house was in a rock. This old feller Avery Jones, was a Methodist preacher, and he had a mighty savage look and he looked all around. He says 'there's no harm in the fiddle, but it puts the devil in

This article was prepared specifically for the third edition of *Appalachia: Social Context Past and Present.* Used by permission of the author.

the foot and I want this pattin' stopped around here.' Well, after that the kids they did stop, but [cousin] Fields patted the harder and it wasn't long till it was in a rock again. Directly the old preacher got to grinnin' and looked around but he didn't say nothin.'[3]

A decade later, another Lundy kinsman, Burton Stoneman, remembered the country dances held in the Iron Ridge area of neighboring Carroll County:

> We'd go to places, gatherin's, have a good time, all play music, people'd all go home, everybody'd be satisfied, friendly. . . . I recollect you'd go to a party, and they'd bring [whiskey] in a bucket with a dipper in it, set it on a table. People'd come in with their music—banjo and fiddle—that was mostly all they had in that day and time. I never seen a guitar till I was up about twelve years old, I reckon. Just a fiddle and banjo was all we had and you could take a drink of whiskey.[4]

The association of fiddle music with foot "pattin' " which led to dancing and consumption of alcohol led many of the stricter religious folk to refer to the fiddle as the "devil's box." Burton Stoneman's brother George, a noted old-time banjo picker, said that another preacher once referred to his instrument as the "devil's circuit rider." Other church members seemed more tolerant and dances continued to thrive in spite of occasional objections.[5]

In addition to the prevalence of instrumental music for dancing purposes, a tradition of singing ballads and other songs also flourished in the mountains. The lyrics varied in age from those which ancestors had brought with them from the British Isles—some of which had medieval roots—to recently composed songs the highland folk developed themselves. Still other songs originally appeared in published sheet-music form in the cities a generation or two earlier, but persisted in the mountains in oral form long after the urban audiences for whom they had been written and performed forgot about them. Others came from the minstrel stage, the church hymnals, or had even been learned from the flourishing folk music traditions of Afro-Americans. In 1918, a middle class urbanite living in Clarksburg, West Virginia encountered a pair of elderly ladies from the more isolated mountain counties of Upshur and Randolph named Rachel Fogg and Nancy McAtee, respectively. Both had several songs in their repertoire including "A Pretty Fair Maid in a Garden," "The Ship's Carpenter," "Jesse James," "The Little Rosewood Castel" [sic], "My Name is Bill Staffato," and "The Raising of Lazareth." [sic] These numbers managed to encompass virtually all of the aforementioned traditions. The older of the two, Mrs. McAtee remembered that when young she had "heered the soldiers singin' when the war wuz goin' on and pickin' their banjoes and fiddles."[6]

Similar conditions thrived in other parts of Appalachia and not merely among the elderly. When mission school workers like Olive Dame Campbell induced the English folk song scholar Cecil Sharp to visit the mountain regions of North Carolina and Tennessee to collect ballads and songs, the latter expressed some surprise that he could obtain texts "from pretty nearly everyone . . . young and old." Perhaps Sharp exaggerated a little when he said "I found myself for the first time in my life in a community in which singing was as common and almost as universal a practice as speaking," but musical expression was certainly widespread. Later Sharp visited Kentucky, Virginia, and a little of West Virginia, gathering a total of more than 500 texts from the mountain regions of the Bluegrass state alone.[7]

In the days when Cecil Sharp and his colleagues went into the mountains to collect folksongs, vocalists typically performed unaccompanied, without benefit of instrumental music. The English folklorist reported seeing "but one singer who sang to an instrumental accompaniment, the guitar, and that was in Charlottesville, Virginia." He had heard, however, that in Kentucky—which he had yet to visit—that singers sometimes played "an instrument called the dulcimer" while they sang. This suggests that singing to the accompaniment of a stringed instrument may have started to become more common, although it had been an almost unknown custom in earlier days. The advent of the recording industry—within a few years—would alter this condition fairly rapidly.[8]

Skilled musicians in the mountains, with few exceptions, might enjoy a degree of local renown and respect in their communities, but were in the main considered only gifted amateurs, who might receive small tokens of appreciation in either cash or produce for a nights work at a dance or gathering. The few Appalachians who earned their living as musicians tended to be blind persons forced by economic necessity to make the most of their musical talent in order to survive. Street corners, courthouse squares, train stations, tobacco auctions, and county fairs constituted some of the places where a blind musician with a tin cup could solicit donations in exchange for his displays of talent. It is hardly an accident that many of the early musicians from Appalachia who found their way into recording studios were blind street musicians by occupation (this is also true for black blues singers). A dozen examples should prove the point. West Virginia produced four in the persons of John B. Evans, Richard Harold, David Miller, and Alfred Reed; Kentucky had Richard Burnett, Bill Day, and Ed Haley (whose only recordings were released more than twenty years after his death); Tennessee produced G. B. Grayson, Charlie Oaks, and George Reneau; while Georgia could boast of Riley Puckett; and North Carolina, the blind minstrel Ernest Thompson. A few like Haley and Puckett came to enjoy a near legendary status. Burnett and Oaks diversified their professionalism a bit further by having printed sheets and song booklets containing their compositions which they offered for sale. A more atypical type of musical professionalism can be exhibited in the activities of John Carson, fiddler, vocalist, and likely native of the Georgia mountains who migrated to Atlanta. In 1913, Fiddlin' John lost his job in the cotton mill and found that he could support himself and family by playing and singing in the busier sections of working class Atlanta where he gained wide popularity with country folk—mountain and lowland—who had settled in the Georgia metropolis. Although Carson intermittently worked as a housepainter, he would remain a semi-professional musician until his death in 1949.[9]

Carson also became, somewhat by accident, the first in a long series of Appalachian musical figures to make phonograph records and also ranked among the first to appear on radio. Polk Brockman, an Atlanta furniture dealer, knowing the status that Fiddlin' John possessed among folks in Atlanta persuaded Ralph Peer to record his work for the OKeh label. Following the success of this venture in 1923, large numbers of rural white Southerners began making recordings. Many of the most significant of these figures came directly from the Southern mountains. While numerous early artists also came from Piedmont areas and other sections, with three or four exceptions, the most prominent originated either in the highlands or in foothill fringe regions. A few examples will suffice. In addition to Carson, OKeh soon made arrangements to record several Virginia mountaineers. Henry Whitter, a textile mill worker from Fries, on New River in Grayson County, Virginia, journeyed to New York on his own initiative and may have actually cut material prior to Carson, although his modest musical efforts did not appear on disc until later. Limitations on his abilities did not prevent Whitter's work from being well received, and he also initiated an early attempt to record mountain music with a three piece string-band, which eventually became the ultimate personification of quality Appalachian music. His later sessions on Victor, utilizing primarily the talent of the aforementioned G. B. Grayson, also represent something of a zenith in traditional mountain fiddle and vocal work at its best.

At the time, however, Whitter's recordings provided a challenge for neighboring mountaineers who believed they could do as well or better. Ernest Stoneman, a thirty-one year old carpenter from nearby Galax, traveled to New York over Labor Day weekend of 1924 and commenced a recording career that continued—with significant interruptions—until his death in 1968. As Whitter's signature song had been a partially self-composed local ballad about a 1903 railroad accident, "The Wreck on the Southern Old 97," Stoneman fashioned one for himself with a poem clipped from a newspaper about the much better known disaster of 1912, "The Titanic." Another Galax based musical aggregation, calling themselves the Hill Billies made their

initial trip to the studios in January 1925. Inadvertently this group soon found their nickname applied to the entire musical genre they had helped to create. As a word, hillbilly carried both humorous and negative connotations and like other aspects of the life and culture of mountain folk, it evolved into a burden of sorts that its musicians would simply—for better or worse—be forced to bear.[10]

While the OKeh executives busied themselves with the above and a few additional figures, other recording firms also began lining up folks who performed similar types of music. Columbia secured the Georgia fiddler Gid Tanner, and Riley Puckett, a blind vocalist and guitarist, who like Carson had migrated to Atlanta from farther north. They took a fiddle-banjo-vocal combination of ladies named Eva Davis and Samantha Bumgarner from the mountain community of Sylva, North Carolina, whose recording career was, unfortunately, all too brief. Finally, they did several numbers by Ernest Thompson, who hailed from the Appalachian fringe area of Forsyth County, North Carolina, and plied his trade in the Pilot Mountain area all the way from Mount Airy to Winston-Salem. Later Columbia added such authentic mountaineers to their talent roster as the aforementioned Richard Burnett and his guide-musical protege Leonard Rutherford, a pair whose archaic musicianship matched that of G. B. Grayson.

Vocalion Records and its soon to be corporate affiliate Brunswick found east Tennessee talent. The former firm found an elderly fiddler from Morristown named Ambrose Stuart (Uncle Am) and a younger balladeer residing in Knoxville, Blind George Reneau. Brunswick's first Appalachian artists were the fiddle-banjo duo of Bill Chitwood and Bud Landress from Gordon County, Georgia. This pair eventually became the key figures in the band known as the Georgia Yellow Hammers, a Victor attempt to rival Columbia's Skillet Licker band, which had built around the aforementioned Tanner and Puckett. Somewhat later the Hill Billy group (by now alternately known as Al Hopkins and the Buckle Busters) also moved to Vocalion-Brunswick. In 1928, Brunswick added the Kessinger Brothers of St. Albans, West Virginia to their roster. Fiddler Clark Kessinger constituted one of the three or four most outstanding instrumentalists heard on disc during this era.

A smaller but no less significant firm, Gennett (whose masters were often leased to various Sears-Roebuck and Company labels), attracted numerous figures from eastern Kentucky and West Virginia to their studios in Richmond, Indiana. Among the many outstanding mountain figures—including such aforementioned authentics as Grayson, Stoneman, and Burnett—the musical aggregations built around fiddler Doc Roberts deserve some discussion. Roberts ranked with Clark Kessinger as a great fiddler, and usually assisted by guitarist-vocalist Asa Martin, son James Roberts, and sometimes additional musicians, this group produced a large quantity and quality of vocal and instrumental material. Hailing from the western edge of the mountains (Madison and Estill County, Kentucky), their music also reflected a wide variety of influences.

Victor, the most successful record company, entered the field seriously only after Texas-born Vernon Dalhart scored a monumental hit with his cover of "Wreck of the Old 97," and "The Prisoner's Song." Their early efforts in old time music included the Cowan Powers Family of Dungannon, Virginia, but Ernest Stoneman became their major mountain talent in 1926, and persuaded Ralph Peer to hold field sessions in Bristol the following summer. In the meantime Victor recorded another mountain singer from Wythe County Virginia named Kelly Harrell and a string-band built largely around a harmonica instead of a fiddle, the Carolina Tar Heels. Stoneman advocated that holding auditions in an Appalachian town like Bristol would attract mountain talent who would never go to a faraway place like New York City, or Camden, New Jersey—home of Victor records—on their own. Stoneman's argument proved sound for Victor found many musicians of quality who came to Bristol for the tryouts. Unfortunately for him, two of these acts soon displaced Stoneman as Victor's premier hillbilly recording star. One, the Mississippi Blue Yodeler Jimmie Rodgers had almost no Appalachian influence in his style (and no Appalachian roots), but did become something of a significant outside influence on later generations of mountaineers. The other act, the Carter Family of Scott County, Virginia, went on to become the single most significant musical group to come out of the southern mountains. Augmented by a solid guitar and autoharp accompaniment, the Carters would record some 250 songs in the next fourteen years. Their vocal repertoire encompassed virtually all of the diverse origins and traditions that went into Appalachian songmaking. The Carters put their distinct stamp on both British and traditional American ballads, nineteenth century popular songs, sacred lyrics, songs containing Afro-American and minstrel show roots, and even a few items of their own composition. Later generations of naive folksong collectors would gather items from the field that had been learned from Carter Family recordings and accept them as authentic. In their own way, however, the Carters were indeed authentic, as were Grayson and Whitter, Fiddlin' John Carson, Kelly Harrell, Doc Roberts, and Ernest Stoneman. To varying degrees, they made some minor adaptations to commercialism, but never strayed significantly from their Appalachian roots, except perhaps to increasingly combine vocal and instrumental performance. As the comment by Cecil Sharp suggests, this trend predated the commercial recording of Appalachian music, although it seems to have not yet become common.[11]

While Sharp had titled his book *English Folk Songs from the Southern Appalachians,* a few entries reflected purely American origins. For instance "John Hardy" could have been no more than twenty-two years old at the time Ellie Johnson of Hot Springs, North Carolina, sang it for him in September 1916, because Hardy's execution had occurred at Welch, West Virginia in January 1894. Likewise later scholars have concluded that "Wild Bill Jones" lacks British antecedents, although the historical Jones remains to be positively identified. These songs may not have been English, but they did constitute true folk lyrics and remained so when Ernest Stoneman recorded the first for OKeh in 1925, for Gennet in 1928, and when the Carters did it for Victor under the title "John Hardy was a Desperate Little Man" in 1929. Stoneman also put the second song on disc for Edison in 1926. Stella Shelton's singing of "I'm Going to Georgia" at Alleghany, North Carolina for Cecil Sharp was no more or less a folk performance than the one Gid Tanner and Riley Puckett gave for Frank Walker in the Columbia Studio as "Going to Georgia." The same can be said of Frank Blevins and his Tar Heel Rattlers rendition of "Fly Around My Pretty Little Miss" in 1931, which bore strong resemblance to Mrs. Johnson's song "Betty Brown." The five versions of "Giles Collins" collected by Sharp vary but little from the one that Roy Harvey of West Virginia did for Brunswick in 1928. The point is that song and performance whether rendered for a folk song collector or for a record company official, tended to be about as traditional in one instance as they did in the other. The mingling of music and voice was more common on the disc, and technical limitations on record length led to shortened versions of a few of the longer ballads.[12]

Cecil Sharp's definition of folk music had always been more narrow and restricted than the broad range of traditional performances that found their way onto discs in the first decade of recording. While the British scholar had been almost exclusively concerned with material from the old world—a few American originals like "John Hardy" managed to intrude—he totally ignored such key traditions as instrumental and sacred music, both of which were well represented on record. Whether played with a featured solo fiddle or with a fuller sounding string band, virtually every company had at least one or two renditions of old time tunes like "Sally Goodin," "Cripple Creek," "Soldier's Joy," "Ida Red," "Liberty," "Ragtime Annie," "Over the Waves," and "Wednesday Night Waltz" in their catalogs. Other numbers such as "Coal Creek March," "Darlin' Cory," "Shout Little Lulie," and "Little Birdie"—some of which contained vocal refrains—showcased the skills of mountain banjo pickers. "Logan County Blues," "Charlotte Hot-Step," "Spanish Fandango," "Jailhouse Rag," and "Back to the Blue Ridge," on the other hand, illustrated the abilities of Appalachian guitarists.

As religion manifested a significant role in the lives of hillfolk, so too did sacred and gospel song receive its due on early discs. "Amazing Grace," "We Are Going Down the Valley One By One," "Hallelujah Side," "O Come Angel Band," and "Are You Washed in the Blood?" all appeared on records frequently in the twenties as performed by authentic Appalachian singers (seldom in a capella arrangements, however). In addition, many of the Victorian sentimental songs of an earlier generation dealt with the deaths of either children, parents, or other loved ones in a reverent manner that reinforced traditional religious values. Such lyrics as "Two Little Orphans," "The Letter Edged in Black," "Put My Little Shoes Away," and "Shake Hands with Mother Again," all mirrored these prevalent attitudes in song. Chances are that hundreds and possibly thousands of mountain households heard Charles K. Harris's 1901 popular hit "Hello Central, Give Me Heaven" sang by Riley Puckett, David Miller, or the Carter Family on a wind-up phonograph long before they ever heard the actual ring of a telephone.

Two principal points may be made concerning traditional Appalachian music. One is that it came from diverse origins. These included not only cultural baggage brought from the British Isles by early migrants to colonial America, but also material that had been added by later generations of Americans. Some of it reflected authentic folk sources and some had been borrowed from more sophisticated Victorian parlor, minstrel, and hymn composers. A little even derived from Afro-American roots albeit not a great deal because mountain folk had much less contact with blacks than did white folk in the lower South. The second point is that, whether the subject matter of the songs dealt with parted lovers, fun, tragedy, crime, heroics, sin, or sanctity, the music was—on the whole—a reflection of the culture that produced it. That music which first appeared on phonograph records in the 1920s perhaps came as close—with only slight modification—to representing the true essence of Appalachia's rich musical culture as scholars are ever likely to reconstruct.

With the passing of time, commercial influences slowly intruded into the recorded music of Appalachians who performed on recordings and via the radio. As the recording and radio industries relied upon "new material" if an artist wished to sustain even a part-time career, musicians became motivated to write or adapt new songs which fitted their style. Also since very few could earn their living solely from the money they earned from radio or recordings, they became more commercial in order to sustain themselves by giving stage shows, or what one might loosely term concerts. Still, a great deal of the traditional remained in their style. Mainer's Mountaineers who became popular in

the mid-thirties did not sound quite as archaic or authentic as did Grayson and Whitter, or Stoneman's Dixie Mountaineers of a decade earlier but they remained essentially a mountain string band in most of their stylings. So too did Roy Acuff and his group on many of their earlier efforts. The harmony duet singers of the thirties such as the Callahan Brothers and the Blue Sky Boys retained much of the earlier mountain song repertoire and kept their arrangements plain and simple as did Bradley Kincaid, the Kentucky Mountain Boy, who performed fairly authentic renditions of old songs and mountain ballads on both record and major radio stations from the mid-twenties until about 1950, usually with only an uncomplicated guitar accompaniment. Another mountain radio balladeer, Buddy Starcher of Craigsville, West Virginia made no recordings at all until 1946, broadcasting for years from stations extending from Harrisonburg, Virginia to Shenandoah, Iowa, in a simple unadorned mountain style with an uncomplicated guitar accompaniment that appealed to a wide range of listeners.

In the 1940s, the better known Appalachian singers moved a little further from their roots. The war years placed many mountain folks in northern urban environments for the first time, while many thousands of men experienced the cultural mix that accompanied military service. A process of musical amalgamation that started in the late thirties accelerated and the western swing music of Bob Wills and Bill Boyd, the honky-tonk sounds of Ernest Tubb and Jimmie Davis, and the commercialized cowboy songs of Gene Autry and the Sons of the Pioneers began to mingle with and even displace the older mountain influenced music. Newer Appalachian vocalists whose careers flourished from the mid-forties found themselves in the recording studios with electric lead and steel guitars prominent in their accompaniment. Molly O'Day of eastern Kentucky, the Bailes Brothers of West Virginia, and the Louvin Brothers of northeastern Alabama, still exhibited much of the mountain sound in their vocal styles and the subject matter in their songs, but the music while retaining distinct older elements also moved much closer to the mainstream. Roy Acuff managed to keep some of the old sound and the husband-wife team of Wilma Lee and Stoney Cooper even received some recognition from Harvard for their "authentic mountain singing." The most authentic mountaineers like David Akeman of Annville, Kentucky (known on stage as Stringbean) found it necessary to adopt a semi-comic stance in order to gain moderate acceptance. By and large, however, music trends continued toward merging into what increasingly came to be called country and western.

Another generation would see the continuation of this trend. The most prominent Appalachian musical figures of recent decades often display cultural pride in their region and a few of their songs illustrate it. It would be hard to find better examples of an "Appalachian cultural pride manifesto" than either Loretta Lynn's "Coal Miner's Daughter," or Dolly Parton's "Coat of Many Colors." They tell us as much about the culture that produced them as did the music of Dick Burnett, G. B. Grayson, or those mountain folk who sang their songs for Cecil Sharp. Yet, Lynn and Parton perform their material in arrangements, style, and accompaniment that show a much broader (and usually little highland) influence. One suspects that a casual listener might experience great difficulty discerning what the older and the newer music might have in common.[13]

Countertrends exist, but are not likely to replace dominant modes in mainstream country music which competes with rock and other sounds for the ears of contemporary mountain folk. Bluegrass music, developed by Bill Monroe and the musicians he employed, represents a modernized form of the old time sound, and has from the time of its creation in the early and mid-forties. While Monroe and his brother Charlie came from western Kentucky rather than the mountain region, their music found wide acceptance in the highlands and adjacent parts of the Carolina Piedmont. It shared much in common with the music of the Mainers, Blue Sky Boys, Callahans, Roy Hall, the Morris Brothers, the Briarhoppers, and the Hired Hands. Nearly all the pioneer figures in the development of bluegrass—other than the Monroes—came from in or near the southern mountains. For instance, Lester Flatt, Benny Martin, Jimmy Martin, and the Baily Brothers all hailed from east Tennessee; Clyde Moody, Red Rector, Don Reno, Earl Scruggs, Red Smiley, and Carl Story from the western Carolinas; Jim and Jesse McReynolds, Ralph and Carter Stanley, Clarence (Tater) Tate, and Mac Wiseman from western Virginia; Red Allen, Hylo Brown, and the Osborne Brothers from eastern Kentucky; the Lonesome Pine Fiddlers and the Lilly Brothers from West Virginia. Except for the Fiddlers who remained in Bluefield and the Kentucky natives who migrated to Ohio, all of them had extensive radio experience in Asheville, Bristol, and Knoxville, three locales where necessity to please a large Appalachian audience led to both a respect for tradition and desire to be innovative with positive effects.[14]

Despite the modernistic trends to amalgamate Appalachian music with country and western, or in revitalized form as bluegrass, one must admit that old time mountain music remains alive and well. While it has moved from the mainstream to a spot somewhat off center and has undergone a degree of change—no musical culture is or ever has been totally static—it also continues to flourish. Native mountaineers compete in the contests at Galax and other places alongside the Japanese, urban folkies, in-migrants, revivalists, and others who choose to participate. Inspired by the fiddle and banjo skills of authentic oldsters like the late Tommy Jarrell of Surry County, North Carolina, younger enthusiasts procede to take up the sounds and style associated with past generations. Professional performers like Doc Watson, while somewhat eclectic in their musicianship, manage to retain a great deal of the mountain traditions in what they sing and play. The old adage that "the more things change, the more they remain the same," may not be quite true in reference to Appalachian music. However, it isn't exactly wrong either.

NOTES

1. Joseph Doddridge, *Notes on the Settlements and Indian Wars . . . 1824* (Pittsburgh: Ritenour and Lindsey, 1912), p. 104.

2. John F. Day, *Bloody Ground* (Lexington: University Press of Kentucky, 1981 reprint of 1941 edition), p. 242.

3. Elizabeth Lomax, Personal Interview with Emmet W. Lundy, Galax, Virginia, 1941 (Library of Congress, AFS Recording 4938).

4. Elizabeth and John Lomax, Personal Interview with Emory Burton Stoneman, Galax, Virginia, 1941 (Library of Congress, AFS Recording 4936).

5. Elizabeth Lomax, Personal Interview with George W. Stoneman, Galax, Virginia, 1941 (Library of Congress, AFS Recording 4937).

6. Anna Davis Richardson, "Old Songs from Clarksburg, W. Va. 1918," *Journal of American Folk-Lore* 32 (1919): 497–499.

7. Cecil Sharp, *English Folk Songs from the Southern Appalachians* (New York: G. P. Putnam's Sons, 1917), pp. vii–viii. See also Charles K. Wolfe, *Kentucky Country: Folk and Country Music of Kentucky* (Lexington: University Press of Kentucky, 1982), pp. 6–7; and Charles K. Wolfe, *Tennessee Strings: The Story of Country Music in Tennessee* (Knoxville: The University of Tennessee Press, 1977), pp. 3–7.

8. Sharp, *English Folk Songs from the Southern Appalachians,* p. x.

9. For a look at blind musical figures see Wolfe, *Kentucky Country,* pp. 19–24, 66–68, 73–75; Wolfe, *Tennessee Strings,* pp. 8–10, 32, 46–47; Ivan M. Tribe, *Mountaineer Jamboree: Country Music in West Virginia* (Lexington: University Press of Kentucky, 1984), pp. 22–23, 26–28, 31–32, 34; Archie Green, "Hillbilly Music: Source and Symbol," *Journal of American Folklore* 78 (1965), 215. The definitive work on Carson is Gene Wiggins, *Fiddlin' Georgia Crazy: Fiddlin' John Carson, His Real World, and the World of His Songs* (Urbana: University of Illinois Press, 1987).

10. Green, "Hillbilly Music: Source and Symbol." pp. 204–228.

11. The careers of virtually all of the musical figures discussed in this section may be found in Wolfe, *Tennessee Strings, Kentucky Country,* Tribe, *Mountaineer Jamboree;* and Bill C. Malone, *Country Music U.S.A.* Revised Edition (Austin: University of Texas Press, 1985), Chapters 2 and 4.

12. The song examples discussed here may be found in Sharp, *English Folk Songs from the Southern Appalachians,* pp. 100–103, 243, 257–259, 284. Numerous other examples of traditional ballads and songs found on commercial 78 rpm discs by Appalachians in the 1924–1931 era could be cited. For data on John Hardy see John Harrington Cox, *Folk-Songs of the South* (Cambridge: Harvard University Press, 1925), pp. 175–177.

13. The musicians and songs discussed here are discussed in Malone, *Country Music U.S.A.* Revised Edition, Chapters 6 through 9.

14. The definitive work on bluegrass music is Neil V. Rosenberg, *Bluegrass: A History* (Urbana: University of Illinois Press, 1985).

Institutional Analysis
of the
Appalachian Region

V. Economy

"Which Side Are You on Boys, Which Side Are You on"

In recent years considerable national attention has been focused upon the Appalachian region for several reasons. First is the differential economic well-being of the area and its inhabitants relative to most other parts of the nation. Much of the region lags far behind the rest of the nation in terms of economic development. It was this very factor that eventually led to the establishment of the federally funded program known as the Appalachian Regional Commission (ARC) in 1965. The establishment of ARC resulted in drawing up new boundary lines for the designation of the Appalachian region. The new ARC region consists of portions of thirteen states ranging all the way from the Southern most counties of western New York state southward to portions of Mississippi. This geographic region consists of plateau country, great valleys, and highlands—each of which presents unique problems when it comes to economic development. The region presently consists of portions of those states which have been experiencing the weakest economic development, been dominated in many cases by a specialized economy such as coal mining or textiles, subsistence agriculture, high illiteracy, an above average school dropout rate, and general economic deprivation.

The other factor that has increased national interest in Appalachia is the energy crisis. As the nation has become increasingly aware of the energy crisis and our inability to rely upon imported crude oil from the Middle East and other portions of the world, this has brought about a renewed interest in coal as an alternative source of energy.

By the middle of the 70's there was a great deal of optimism in the coal fields of Central and Northern Appalachia. There was the strong belief that the country would once again return to coal as one of the dominant energy sources and this would breathe new economic life into the Appalachian region. The optimism was short lived, however. The recession in the American economy along with problems associated with coal mining in Appalachia such as high sulfur coal, surface mining, and absentee mineral ownership, never really helped in any appreciable way to change the economic conditions of the region.

The articles in this section deal with many of the themes commonly associated with the causes and consequences of the lagging economy and economic development in Appalachia. An explanation that has gained widespread use in the last few years to explain the economic underdevelopment and persistence of below average per capita income, high unemployment rate, and lack of industrial development, and extensive pockets of poverty is the colonization model. This model suggests that a major cause of the deplorable economic conditions in Appalachia can be immediately traceable to the various forms of industrial exploitation that began around the turn of the century and continue up to the present.

The advocates of the colonization model maintain that the region is owned and controlled by corporations outside the region who extract both the natural resources and the wealth from the region. This extraction of wealth is particularly noticeable in the Central Appalachian region with its reliance upon the coal mining industry, but it can be seen in other sections of the region and in other economic activities. The exploitation by the lumbering industry, the controlling of the mineral rights by natural gas and oil industries, and the working conditions in the textile industry are illustrative of the economic imperialism alluded to in the articles. Consequently, the economic exploitation noted by these writers may constitute a very important and major explanation for the economic deprivation and underdevelopment commonly associated with the Appalachian region.

Another model that has received considerable attention in the last few years in an attempt to explain the economic conditions in Appalachia is the "internal periphery model." This model sees the region as an "internal periphery of an advanced capitalist system." According to Plaut it describes the region as ". . . essentially a resource preserve, complete with 'native' leadership that serves the needs of the advanced industrial resources, and recreation-hungry society that surrounds it." (See reference to Plaut article that follows.)

A good discussion of the basic theoretical perspectives in this model can be found in the following two articles, "Internal Colony or Internal Periphery? A Critique of Current Models and an Alternative Formulation" by David Walls and "Extending the Internal Periphery Model: The Impact of Culture and Consequent Strategy" by Tom Plaut.

25. THE POVERTY OF ABUNDANCE REVISITED

John Gaventa

Americans in the Hoover years of the Great Depression, 1929–1933, were a people perplexed by plenty. They saw the nation's magnificent productive plant intact, its ability to produce unimpaired. And yet, in a land celebrated for its abundance, the people were plagued by scarcity. This paradox confounded the age-old notion of poverty. . . . It was the result of rich resources and not of the niggardliness of nature; the outcome of energy and inventiveness, not of indolence and inefficiency; the product of the world's most advanced industrial nation and not of its most backward one. The situation was one peculiar to the modern world of invention and technology. America's poverty was the poverty of abundance.

—Albert Romasco, *The Poverty of Abundance*, 1965

The Current Appalachian Economic Crisis[1]

Today Appalachia is in a state of economic crisis that is as deep as the one which called the War on Poverty into being more than 20 years ago. Yet while the nation's leaders have proclaimed a "recovery" from the recession of the early part of the 1980s, that recovery has rarely reached the people of the region.

During the 1970s, following the War on Poverty, there was a new hope for our region. Though as a whole it still continued to lag behind the rest of the nation, per capita income rose, outmigration was slowed and briefly reversed as in some places new jobs were created.

For many of the region's people, however, the first five years of the 1980s have seen the erosion of whatever gains had been made and an increasing gap between the region and affluent America:

• Since 1970, despite 20 years of economic development activity, almost two-thirds of the counties in the region have actually declined economically, relative to the rest of the nation.

• At the end of 1985, four-fifths of the region's counties had an official unemployment rate higher than the national rate of 6.7%. Eighty-five counties had double the national rate, and 28 had triple the rate for an official unemployment rate of over 20%. Not reflected in the official statistics is the status of the invisible poor who have never been counted on the unemployment rolls or who have given up looking for a job and have dropped off the rolls altogether.

This resurgent Appalachian crisis was dramatized recently by an Associated Press reporter who visited Eureka Hollow, W. Va., the remote community that had stirred John Kennedy 25 years before. The reporter wrote:

> Kennedy's message from Eureka Hollow alerted America to the paradox of wretched poverty in an area teeming with rich resources. It resulted in $15 billion in federal aid to West Virginia and a dozen other states . . . today's message from Eureka Hollow is this: both are still here, the resources and the poverty.[2]

In 1960 Kennedy had visited a disabled coal miner, his wife, and eight children, housed in a mountainside shack without running water. Today the shack is gone, ravaged by strip mining in the valley. One of the miner's children remains. Laid off when the mines started closing in 1982, the son has not had a pay check in four years. Food stamps and "workfare income" amount to $7,668 a year for him, his wife, and three children—well below the national poverty level of $12,500 for a family of five.

The case of Eureka Hollow is not unique. In the last year, a series of reports have warned of a new poverty in Appalachia and across the South, especially in our rural regions. One recent Ford Foundation sponsored study entitled *Shadows Across the Sunbelt* had this to say:

> After two decades of reasonably solid growth, many rural communities are now finding themselves in serious trouble. . . . Instead, it has become increasingly clear that many structural changes are at work in the rural Southern economy, changes which are only intermittently visible, but that taken together promise profound and lasting consequences for the South.[3]

What has happened? Why the failure? At least part of the answer to Appalachia's economic crisis is found

Author's note: This essay is an edited version of the first annual Albert U. Romasco Lecture, presented Feb. 11, 1987, at New York University. Al Romasco wrote two books about the Depression and the role of the presidency in shaping a national response to poverty and economic decline: *The Poverty of Abundance and Politics of Recovery.* When he died he was working on a third book about the War on Poverty of the 1960s. While he never wrote directly about the Appalachian South, the themes of his historical analysis intertwine deeply with the regional experience. Al Romasco was also a friend, one from whom I learned much. He exemplified a human face of scholarship and did so without apology.

John Gaventa is research director at the Highlander Education and Research Center and assistant professor of sociology at the University of Tennessee-Knoxville. His 1980 book, *Power and Powerlessness: Quiescence and Rebellion in an Appalachian Valley,* won the Weatherford Award.

in the profound transformation of the American economy as a whole. Nationally, we are told a reshaping of the economy is occurring. The agricultural and industrial America which was overproducing in the Hoover era, which recovered and thrived under the economic policies of the New Deal, is being transformed to a service-based and finance economy. In the five years between 1979 and 1984, 11.5 million workers nationally lost their jobs as plants shut down or relocated to increase productivity or shrink output. In such economic restructuring, the jobs in traditional sectors like mining, manufacturing, agriculture have declined the most.[4]

Such reshaping will take its heaviest toll upon the Appalachian South, a region which historically has provided the nation with its mines, resources, and low-wage, low-skill workers, whose people are more dependent upon such traditional industries than almost any other. The toll of a restructuring economy is seen in almost every sector, in every area, as we travel through our region.

The experience of Northern Appalachia, traditionally the home of the heavy steel and manufacturing industries, is no better. Plant closings, disinvestment by the nation's largest steel corporations to other industries and to overseas, have left many of these communities virtually paralyzed. In one 20-mile stretch along the Mon Valley alone, over 25,000 basic steel jobs have been lost in the last five years. In the tri-state region surrounding Pittsburgh (encompassing 119 counties of the Northern mountains in western Pennsylvania, eastern Ohio, and West Virginia) almost two-thirds of a million workers were unemployed in 1985. Of these, some 123,000 were the "phantom unemployed" who not only had lost their jobs but had exhausted all benefits and simply dropped off the job rolls altogether. In Pittsburgh, studies show, the unemployment rate has gone down not because the unemployed have received work, but because they have simply stopped being counted.[5]

The de-industrialization of more urban Northern Appalachia is perhaps by now a familiar image in the American landscape. These are the workers who since the Depression had worked, struggled, and in some sense attained the American Dream. Organized into unions, usually male and white, they made decent wages, owned a home, looked forward to a better future for their children. Today their dream is gone.

But if the impact of industrial restructuring is great upon these workers and communities of the Northern region, imagine the impact of de-industrialization on the workers of the mountain hollows, rural farms, and smaller towns further south. These are the workers and communities for whom hard work never meant prosperity. These are the rural people, the women, the minorities, whose experience has always been less visible and voices less powerful, whose hard work has never bought a ticket to the American Dream. These people too are profoundly affected by the restructuring of industrial America.

Think for instance of the coal miners who have been the backbone of the Central Appalachian economy, whose company-town communities and dramatic struggles have written many an important chapter of our nation's social history. Today thousands of these miners throughout West Virginia, eastern Kentucky, Tennessee, and Virginia are without work. Mine closings and lay-offs have silenced whole communities, single-industry communities where there is little left when the company closes.

Recently, for instance, U.S. Steel announced that it was closing the last mine in Gary, W. Va., laying off another 1,000 miners, leaving unemployment in that community above 90%. Gary is but one of the hardest hit communities in a coal-rich state which in recent years has led the nation with the highest state unemployment rate.

For many of the workers and their families such hard times are not new. Their livelihoods have always been dependent upon a boom and bust economy over which they had no control. They know the skills of survival, of waiting. But this decline is not like past busts in Appalachian history. While times are bad for the workers, times are good for the industry. Coal production in the region has reached a ten-year high with over a third fewer miners needed. New technology, increased production, speed-ups at the expense of hard-won safety mean that the workers are simply no longer needed. Moreover, unlike in the 1950s when mechanization sent miners in search of jobs in the North, this time there are no jobs for them there either.

Think of the factory workers, the mill workers of Southern Appalachia. For almost two decades, de-industrialization of the Frostbelt North has meant the growth of the Sunbelt South. Parts of the Appalachian South have benefitted from being on the receiving end of capital mobility i.e., the place where runaway shops from the North came in search of low-wage labor, cheap resources, and community subsidies. Now the trend is changing as the plants here are also closing and/or relocating overseas. According to the Appalachian Regional Commission, in the first four years of the 1980s the Appalachian region lost two and one-half manufacturing jobs for every one that had been created in the 1970s.

An example of the impact of industrial decline may be seen in the textile and apparel industry. While we have heard of the loss of jobs for primarily white skilled males in the industrial heartland of the North, where has been the news of the loss of textile and apparel jobs for women and minorities of the rural South? Nationally the textile industry accounts for one in every eight manufacturing jobs. Primarily low wage, the industry employs a higher percentage of minorities and women than any other industrial sector in the country. Between 1973 and 1983 almost half a million of these jobs were lost. In the last five years over 250 mills closed. The impact has been especially severe in Appalachia where the milltowns of east Tennessee, North Carolina, South Carolina, and Alabama have three and one-half times the average concentration of textile factories and two times the average concentration of garment mills than other parts of America.

Even for workers who have managed to hang on to their jobs the work is often sporadic. As one black woman textile workers recently told a CORA panel:

> I've been with Standard Coosa-Thatcher for about 12 years. . . . I was on quilling, and that was cut back last week, so I'm back in winding. When I received my check last week, I wanted to cry because it was cut from almost $200 to $65. . . . I said "Lord, what can I do with $65, when I got a $200 house note and a light bill over $100?" . . . That's the only income I have coming in. I'm just hoping and praying that my husband will find a job. . . . It's rough. I have two girls in school and just one person working.

Recently I had the opportunity to conduct a survey with some 200 of these displaced workers in the east Tennessee area. Primarily women in middle-age, their story is illustrative of the trends throughout the region. Their employer, the Allied Seat Belt Company (as it is now called), first came to Knoxville in the late 1960s, relocating from the North (one presumes to get away from high-price labor). The shop makes seat belts (a product one would think to be of high value to our automotive society) and employed some 3,000 workers by the late 1970s. It was a union shop and offered among the best wages and benefits for such workers in the area, even though the average wage was only $5.79 an hour for workers with about 15 years experience.

Today employment at the plant is down to only 250 workers. The story is a classic one. Presumably to get non-union and still cheaper labor, the company moved some of its work to Greenville, Ala., in 1980, laying off some 1,500 workers in Tennessee. Later more jobs were transferred still further south to yet cheaper labor in Mexico. Throughout, the company has used the threat—and then the reality—of relocating to Alabama or Mexico as job blackmail for the Knoxville workforce.

Think of the small farmers of the Appalachian South. These are not the full-time mega-farmers of the flat plains of the West but the worker-farmers for whom the land has been insurance against hard times at the mill, and the mill or factory has been supplement to hard times on the land. Now the decline in manufacturing jobs combines with the decline in farm prices to place these farmers in double jeopardy. Unemployed, they cannot subsidize their land; without the land, they cannot survive unemployment.

To offset the bleak picture of industrial decline, we are offered the promises of a new service economy. Nationally about 70% of the new jobs created are in the "service sector," the majority in such growth areas as fast food, health care, business services.

However, reliance on growth of the service sector to solve the economic ills of the nation is problematic at best anywhere in the nation. In our region it is simply a fallacy. While the decline in traditional jobs has been great, the growth in service jobs in the South has been lower than elsewhere in the nation. Where they do come, these industries choose not to locate in these rural, industrial, or minority areas that need the work the most. *After the Factories,* a new study by the Southern Growth Policies Board, shows that these jobs go to the areas that are already the most suburban, the most white, the most educated, and the most affluent. As a result, we are seeing not only the widening of the gap between our region and the rest of the nation but also the rapid splitting of the Two Souths—the urban, growing, somewhat prosperous cities which have generated the Sunbelt image and the declining rural South where unemployment remains 37% greater than in the urban areas.[6]

Yet even for those workers who are able to obtain new employment in the service sectors, new employment may in fact mean downward rather than upward mobility. Take for instance the women textile workers at Allied referred to earlier. Of 174 laid-off workers, slightly more than half had obtained a new job. Of these workers who had obtained jobs, the largest proportion (35%) had obtained "service" jobs—as cleaners, guards or custodians in workplaces or in private homes, as food service workers, or as child or health care workers in workplaces or peoples' homes. Even for the ones who have been able to get some work, over half (53%) are working at part-time jobs. All but one of the workers report that they have taken pay cuts. Average wages have dropped from $5.79 at Allied to $3.70, a loss of $2.09 an hour. Thirty-nine percent are working at minimum wage of $3.35 an hour, and over half are working at $3.45 or less an hour. For 90% of the workers there is no union at their new jobs, and thus one can expect that they have also taken a loss in benefits and job protection.

Human Costs

The economic crisis takes its toll in more than just numbing statistics about jobs, unemployment, and income. Like past economic crises, this one has profound human costs for those who face it. Last year I participated with the Commission on Religion in Appalachia in a project on the new economic crisis that included traveling throughout the region and listening to the words and stories of those who faced economic decline.

The unemployed and underemployed. We heard of the economic hardships—foreclosures, loss of income, increased hunger, lack of health benefits—of persons who have lost their jobs or who are living the uncertainties of part-time insecure work. We heard of the feelings of failure and low self-esteem which arise. We heard of the increase in violence upon one's self with growth in suicides and alcoholism as well as of the violence against others.

The poor. We heard of the increase in poverty resulting from the combination of economic restructuring and federal budget cuts of social programs. The number of Southerners living in poverty increased by two and one-half million between 1979 and 1983, bringing the poverty rate in the region to almost 20%.

Women. We heard of the increasing feminization of poverty which grows from the lack of employment opportunities for women as well as from the occupational segregation and enormous inequities in pay between men and women who do have jobs.

People of Color. We heard repeatedly in the testimony the continuing truth that "blackness in the mountains makes people poorer still." One-third of the black families in Appalachia live below the poverty line, and one-third are unemployed. We also heard of the rise of racial violence especially as blacks compete with low-income whites for jobs and economic survival.

Families and children. We heard testimony of the impact of the economic crisis on our children's futures. Without a clear economic future, educational quality suffers. In West Virginia one speaker told us, "We have children who are going to school hungry who weren't going to school hungry in the '60s and early '70s." We heard fears of increasing school drop-outs, of a growth in illiteracy. Kentucky for instance, a state rich with mineral resources, has the lowest proportion of high school graduates in the country: 800,000 adults have less than an eighth grade education and 400,000 are functionally illiterate.[7]

Natural Resources. We heard of the damage of our natural resources often in the name of economic growth and through the ransom of scarce jobs.

Workers. We heard of the increasing victimization of both workers and communities who fight for their dignity and the increasing fear of those who would like to but dare not. With the specter of unemployment so real, the threat of job loss is also real. "Job blackmail," said one speaker, "is the way that I would capsulize the economic crisis."

It is clear that we are facing a long-term restructuring of the economy with enormous consequences for all aspects of community. While somewhere in the nation the restructuring may offer the hope of new prosperity, for the people at the grassroots of Appalachia it serves to deepen the economic crisis of a people already at the bottom. The nature of the crisis was captured in a story told to us at one of the hearings:

> A miner's son asked his mother: "Why don't you light the fire—it's so cold?" And the mother said, "Because we have no coal. Your father is out of work, and we have no money to buy coal." And the son said, "But why is he out of work, Mother?" And the mother says, "Because there's too much coal."

It is the poverty of abundance revisited.

Appalachia and the Nation: The Contemporary Challenge

Does the Appalachian economic crisis provide a barometer for the rest of the nation? Will the experience of poverty in the Appalachian South contribute to the shaping of a new national politics of poverty and recovery as in the 1930s and 1960s?

National maps of depressed America in the 1960s revealed pockets of poverty, with Appalachia among the largest joined by the Black-belt South and the Indian reservations of the Southwest. The assumption in the 1960s was that the mainstream economy was healthy and the depressed regions were simply those "left behind." Integration into the mainstream, not transformation of that mainstream, was the strategy for recovery.

Today, however, maps of depressed America show that rather than growing smaller the "pockets of poverty" of the 1960s have grown larger. Recent data now show that 80% of the counties which are economically in the bottom fifth of the nation may be found in 17 states in heartland America including those of Appalachia.[8] These counties form a giant V or wedge, stretching from the steel towns of Northern Appalachia down through the coalfields of Central Appalachia and the milltowns of the Southern mountains on through the deeper South and then back up north to encompass the "Rust Belt" areas of the industrial Midwest and the Farm Belt of the Great Plains. Data from these areas reveal a deepening of a two-tier national economy with the developed coasts along the east and the west on the one hand and the depressed heartland on the other.

This picture suggests then that the restructuring economy affects far more than Appalachia. Indeed after 25 years of development activity to bring Appalachia into the mainstream economy, the mainstream economy for many parts of the nation has become more like Appalachia's. Rather than the Americanization of Appalachia we have seen the "Appalachianization" of America. This time the crisis is not of a regional economy "on the outside looking in"; it is of the mainstream economy itself.

Just as one cannot understand Appalachian poverty without understanding the restructuring of the rest of America, neither can one understand it without reflecting on the restructuring of the international economy as well. Again the situation is perhaps more analogous to the 1930s than to the 1960s. Albert Romasco strongly reminded us that the Depression years had to be seen in a global context and that the politics of recovery were shaped in part by a political battle within the Roosevelt administration between the economic internationalists representing multinational corporate interests and the economic nationalists. Roosevelt was faced with proposals to leave international trade and the world money supply alone or to "Buy America," to invigorate the national economy regardless of international interests.

Today similar questions characterize national economic debates. One suspects, however, that there are important differences. First, the five decades since the Depression have seen the enormous growth of transnational corporations and thus a strengthened influence of international capital in national politics. Secondly, with transnationalization of capital has come a changing international division of labor such that much of the agricultural and manufacturing economies which Roosevelt sought to revive has moved to Third World countries. What is left behind here is a financial sector which profits from the control of financial and knowledge resources more than from the extraction of natural resources or the production of goods.

Such corporate transnationalization has a particular significance for the Appalachian South. The corporations which once turned here for raw materials and low-wage labor now easily disinvest and move elsewhere, spreading their exploitative powers abroad while deepening the uncertainty at home. Let us return to the example of the seatbelt factory which came South for the lower wage labor but, as the South developed, moved on to Mexico to make our nation's seatbelts. Side by side with capital mobility has been the conglomeration of the firm. Originally the Jim Robbins Seat Belt Company, the company was bought by the Allied Corporation which in turn merged with the Bendix Corporation, which in its turn merged with the Signal Corporation to become a massive holding company with several hundred subsidiaries throughout the world. Such merger fever gives the image of growth—the *Wall Street Journal* says that the windfalls for the executives in the last merger was the greatest in corporate history. But we have seen what this financial growth produced for the company's manufacturing workers.

There are countless other examples of this interconnection of our regional economy with the international economy. Union Carbide, one recalls, came first to West Virginia for workers and for water to make its pesticides and then on to Bhopal, India. Exxon, the fifth largest producer of coal, disinvests in Appalachia and invests in giant strip mines in Columbia. Meanwhile other U.S.-based companies import coal from South Africa, strengthening that country's apartheid-based economy while weakening Appalachia's regional economy. U.S. Steel buys Marathon Oil and expands its international operations without reinvesting in the productive capacity of its steel mills in the Mon Valley or in its mines in Gary, W. Va.

The points is this: the wealth produced within Appalachia has not come back to develop Appalachia. Rather it has been reinvested by the transnational owners of our region into other regions, industries, countries without regard or commitment to the communities from which the wealth came. The concomitant transnationalization of the economy and the internationalization of the productive processes of the nation have strengthened the ability of capital since the Depression to rise above nationalistic solutions, to pit nation against nation, region against nation, community against community. As a result there is a tendency now as there was in the Depression to blame those overseas for our present crisis, to divide workers and communities who in fact have much in common.

If the nature of the Appalachian economic crisis today is national and international in scope, what does that imply about the nature of the response, of the politics of recovery?

First, we can examine, as Romasco would have done, the question of presidential leadership. In the six short years of the Reagan administration, we have seen the dismantling of much of the New Deal policies which Roosevelt had sought to build, especially the programs of welfare, relief, and economic development. The combination of the destruction of the safety net at the very time that a restructuring economy is tossing more into that net has produced devastating results.

As the crisis deepens, however, one is reminded more of the inaction of Hoover than of the action of Roosevelt—a refusal to acknowledge or see at national levels the depth of the problem in the rest of America, or where seeing, relying on naive faith in market forces, decentralized volunteerism, or governmental laissez faire to produce results. Indeed both the market and the President exhort us to believe that the strategy is working. In recent weeks, the Dow Jones has hit a new high and the President has proclaimed in his State of the Union that the economy is better off than ever before. As in the late 1920s, a celebration of the abundance of America rather than a concern with its poverty seems to characterize the national mood.

The flip side of a national mood of abundance under Hoover was the absence of a politics of poverty. The same is true today. The Roosevelt years brought at least the rhetoric of concern with the "forgotten man" and the "bottom third," and the War on Poverty years brought at least the rhetoric of "maximum feasible participation" of the poor in acting on their own affairs. Though perhaps only rhetoric, the language was believed by many and affected their actions. Today the rhetoric of national leadership is about the absence of hunger in America, about the welfare cheaters not the needy, about the abundance of jobs for those who wish to work. Again the rhetoric helps to set a national mood. With the economic decline of the 1980s has also come a decline at all levels—in government, universities, foundations—in even a *rhetorical* commitment to the capacity, or indeed the right, of the poor and dispossessed to act for themselves. The lack of a national debate *on* the poor translates to the invisibility *of* the poor and to a lack of commitment to the principle of democratic action *by* the poor.

In the Depression, however, the failure of national leadership to respond in time to a deepening economic crisis provided the climate for sweeping actions when the time for action did in fact come. The invisibility of the poor in the Hoover years became the militancy of the farmers, miners, and industrial workers of the Roosevelt era. One cannot help but ask whether beneath the invisibility of poverty on the national agenda today is being built a new politics of recovery for tomorrow.

At the grassroots level, I don't believe the answer is clear. On the one hand the combination of the hard economic times and the withdrawal of national commitment to the affairs of those at the bottom translates to a defensiveness, to the use of energies merely to survive, to hold on to the gains of previous years. On the other hand as that battle is lost, desperation and anger will grow and new ideas for more sweeping action begin to emerge. Throughout the country, in fact, dozens of groups are quietly fighting small skirmishes to save their industries, to build different forms of economic enterprise, to think of a different kind of economy. But without a larger politics these local solutions to what is in fact a larger problem will remain limited.

At the regional political level, governors and politicians are beginning to warn of Two Souths and of the revival of poverty. But the proposals for reform which are being put forward are thus far limited. They rely on old models of helping the region through education, more technology, or enterprise development to compete for more of the national pie, not recognizing that the shape and nature of that pie is also changing.

A new politics of recovery must go beyond the 1960s. As in the 1930s it must recognize that the roots of poverty in Appalachia as elsewhere are national in scope and that the grassroots and regional endeavors need to be strengthened by national action. But unlike in the 1930s, a new politics must recognize that the solution lies not simply in stabilizing the market economy nor, as in the 1960s, in integrating pockets of poverty into the economy. It must change that economy itself. In particular it must recognize that with the restructuring of work and industry in America economic growth no longer necessarily translates into jobs or community prosperity. Policies must be developed which put community climate before business stability, which define economic success not in terms of the profits for the top, but in terms of the well-being of those at the bottom.

In so doing a new politics of recovery must recognize that the futures of communities here and abroad are interconnected and that economic security here can be attained only when there is greater economic justice internationally. We need to look at the role of multinationals and at the role of our international trade agreements, foreign policy, and financial structures which have served to develop and maintain the conditions for capital flight abroad. Policies must be developed which strive to protect American communities and also improve the rights and conditions of overseas workers and communities.

Finally a new politics of recovery will of course require national leadership and the development of new types of expertise. But history has shown us that fundamental changes in economic policy have not originated at that level. If they come, changes will be brought about only as the situation of those at the bottom places these issues before the nation. As always solutions to poverty must involve the poor themselves and a rekindling of the democratic spirit of participation which has been the driving force behind national programs for reform in the past.

The conditions of poverty today call not for a hearkening to past strategies but to a new politics of recovery, one which is more fundamental, which places community stability before capital mobility, which is domestic and international, and which is participatory rather than technocratic. Such a recovery may not yet be in sight but if it were it would definitely be one about which Al Romasco would have loved to have written.

NOTES

1. Parts of the following analysis are drawn from the Report of the Working Group on the Appalachian Economic Crisis to the Commission on Religion in Appalachia, *Economic Transformation: The Appalachian Challenge* (1986), for which I served as principal writer and consultant.

2. Jules Loh, "Life in the West Virginia Hollow is better, but not much," *Roanoke Times Tribune*, 28 Dec. 1986.

3. MDC panel on rural economic development, *Shadows Across the Sunbelt* (Chapel Hill: MDC, Inc., 1986), p. 4.

4. U.S. Congress, Office of Technology Assessment, *Technology and Structural Unemployment: Reemploying Displaced Adults*, OTA-ITE-250 (Washington: Government Printing Office, 1986), p. 5.

5. David Page, "The Phantom Jobless," *New York Times*, 24 Aug. 1984.

6. Stuart A. Rosenfeld and Edward M. Bergman, *After the Factories: Changing Employment Patterns in the Rural South* (Research Triangle Park: Southern Growth Policies Board, 1985).

7. *Shadows Across the Sunbelt*, p. 9.

8. "Comparing Appalachia's Counties with the Nation's," *Appalachia*, Spring 1986.

26. THE ECONOMY OF APPALACHIA IN THE NATIONAL CONTEXT

Salim Kublawi

Regional Economist
Appalachian Regional Commission*

A. NATIONAL PATTERNS

During the last six years there have been profound and rapid changes in the national economy. From 1980 to 1985 the nation's population increased by twelve million people, a growth of 5.4% in five years. From 1980 to mid 1986 national employment increased by 9.7 million jobs, an increase of 9.8%. Moderate economic forecasts for the nation as a whole by the Bureau of Labor Statistics project an increase of 14.5 million jobs between now and the year 1995. This is a remarkable performance for the United States by any standard. The ability of the national economy to continue to create jobs has been, and is projected to be, strong and healthy.

While growth in the aggregate has been high, there have been wide disparities in employment growth, as well as overall economic performance, among the nation's regions. A recent study of the nation's counties by ARC staff showed most of the recent growth in economic performance has been concentrated on the East Coast, the West Coast, and in scattered metropolitan areas and recreational and retirement communities. Comparing the economic performance of the nation's counties in 1970 with the current situation showed a definite reversal of the demographic and economic trends in the 1970s which had favored rural areas (for the first time in 70 years) over urban and metropolitan areas. Recent growth has been more concentrated in counties that are metropolitan but not encompassing the central cities as well as rural counties adjacent to the metro-counties with an accelerating urbanization trend.

In addition to the above, there are the following patterns:

• The much-discussed sunbelt/frostbelt dichotomy is too simple to explain current regional patterns. There appear to be two types of sunbelts. One type is a broad geographic area showing an economically depressed sunbelt extending from Texas in the west to Alabama in the east, and from Louisiana in the south to Kentucky in the north. Here the decline in economic performance is primarily due to decline in agricultural product prices, decline in oil and gas prices, decline in coal prices, and decline in the level of activities in manufacturing such as petrochemicals, leather goods, apparel, wood products, and fabricated metals.

• The second type of sunbelt, which is a prospering area, includes Florida, Georgia, South Carolina, middle and east Tennessee, North Carolina, and parts of Virginia. Here, growth is associated with expansion in construction, manufacturing, trade, banking and finance, and all types of businesses and personal services.

• Another way of looking at the sunbelt is by separating the rural counties from the metropolitan counties. An extensive study by the Southern Growth Policies Board in 1985 showed marked differences in growth and profound discrepancies in economic performance between metropolitan areas and counties adjacent to metropolitan areas on the one hand, and rural or nonmetropolitan counties on the other hand. Most of the economic decline was in the rural counties, and was related not only to a decline in agricultural employment but also due to a decline in manufacturing employment in those rural counties.

• There are at least two frostbelts: the prosperous areas from Boston southward to Washington, D.C., have been experiencing high economic performance recently. On the other hand, the old industrial heartland, stretching from Pennsylvania west to Michigan and Wisconsin has been performing weakly. Thus, there are both better performing and poorer performing counties in the South and in the North.

• It is evident that the benefits of the recovery and prosperity in the United States are not being enjoyed to the same extent in all areas of the country. Some regions are clearly endowed with a higher number of better performing counties than are other regions.

• In each region of the country, the metropolitan areas are outperforming the rural areas. The decade of the seventies saw a short-lived surge in growth in rural counties and small towns, which was a reversal of the farm-to-city movement that started at the beginning of the century. By 1980 the trend reversed and outmigration from rural areas was again the norm.

• The regions lagging behind can be identified as a "wedge" stretching from New York state down a straight line to New Orleans, Louisiana, and up in a

*All views, opinions, and projections in this paper are those of the author only and not of the Appalachian Regional Commission.

Reprinted from the *Proceedings of the Conference on Land and Economy in Appalachia,* Appalachian Center, University of Kentucky (1987), pp. 16–24. Used by permission.

northwest direction to Montana. That wedge contains more than 20 states and most of Appalachia. Within that wedge, however, there were many prospering counties, especially those SMSA (Standard Metropolitan Statistical Area) counties surrounding a central city.

• The effect of the decline in manufacturing employment in the United States is markedly evident. Areas that depend on traditional manufacturing have been shaken by the dwindling relative role of manufacturing as an employer in the U.S. economy. Those areas, including parts of Appalachia, that are still heavily dependent on basic industries, shoes, and wood products as a source of manufacturing growth are also experiencing difficulties.

B. PROFILE OF THE APPALACHIAN ECONOMY

1. Population: Table 26.1 (see page 217) shows the 1980 and 1985 population of the United States, the Appalachian region, and the Appalachian state parts. While the nation gained 12.2 million people (5.4%) between 1980 and 1985, the region gained only 349,000 people (1.7% growth) for the same period.

The table shows eight Appalachian state parts gained population and five states lost population during the 1980–1985 period. Appalachian Alabama, Georgia, Kentucky, Mississippi, North Carolina, Ohio, South Carolina and Tennessee gained population varying from a growth rate of 16.1% for Appalachian Georgia to 1.0% in Appalachian Ohio. Appalachian North Carolina and Georgia grew faster than the United States as a whole.

Five Appalachian state parts lost population during this period, Appalachian Maryland, New York, Pennsylvania, Virginia and the State of West Virginia. The highest rate of population decline was in Appalachian Pennsylvania.

2. Employment: Table 26.2 (see page 217) shows the total employment change profile from 1980 to 1986 of the region. While the nation gained 9.7 million jobs between 1980 and mid-1986, or a 9.8% increase, the region increased by only 182,000 jobs or 2.2% over the 1980 level. Only five Appalachian state parts gained employment during this period: Alabama, Georgia, North Carolina, South Carolina and Tennessee, with Appalachian Georgia gaining 19.1% from 1980 to 1986. Four states grew faster than the U.S. average, Alabama, Georgia, North Carolina and Tennessee.

The remaining eight Appalachian state parts had a net decline in employment, with Pennsylvania losing 75,000 jobs and West Virginia 61,000 jobs during this period. In relative terms, West Virginia declined in employment by 8.5%, followed by Appalachian Kentucky which declined by 7.1%.

Most of the losses in employment were in counties that specialize in coal mining, apparel, shoes, furniture

and other wood products, chemicals, fabricated metals, machine tools, glass, transportation equipment, agricultural products, and certain textile products.

Most of the employment gains were in specialized manufacturing, construction and real estate in second home counties, high technology and space, retail trade, finance, and all types of health, educational, personal, and professional services which are predominantly near large cities.

3. Unemployment: Unemployment is presently a problem for a large part of the Appalachian region. Not only cyclical and seasonal unemployment hit the region hard in the early 1980s, but structural unemployment seems to be persistent in about a fifth of the region's counties, with unemployment rates exceeding twice the national average. On the other hand, there are counties in the region that are outperforming the nation in employment.

In May of 1986, 90 counties in the region had unemployment rates below the national average. These were distributed as follows:

Appalachian State Parts	No. of Counties
Alabama	3 (total 35)
Georgia	27 (total 35)
Kentucky	2 (total 49)
Maryland	1 (total 3)
Mississippi	0 (total 20)
New York	4 (total 14)
North Carolina	21 (total 29)
Ohio	1 (total 28)
Pennsylvania	10 (total 52)
South Carolina	3 (total 6)
Tennessee	8 (total 50)
Virginia	3 (total 21)
West Virginia	6 (total 55)

At the other end of the spectrum there were 176 counties with unemployment rates more than 150% of the national average (and 65 counties with rates more than twice the national average) distributed as follows:

Appalachian State Parts	No. of Counties
Alabama	16 (total 35)
Georgia	0 (total 35)
Kentucky	37 (total 49)
Maryland	0 (total 3)
Mississippi	14 (total 20)
New York	0 (total 14)
North Carolina	2 (total 29)
Ohio	22 (total 28)
Pennsylvania	18 (total 52)
South Carolina	0 (total 6)
Tennessee	22 (total 50)
Virginia	13 (total 21)
West Virginia	32 (total 55)

TABLE 26.1

Population 1980 and 1985 and Population Change—1980 to 1985 U.S., Appalachia and Appalachian State Parts (in thousands)

Areas	1980	1985	1980–1985 Difference	1980–1985 % Change
United States	226,550	238,739	12,189	5.4
Appalachian Region	20,239	20,588	344	1.7
Appalachian State Parts:				
Alabama	2,430	2,511	81	3.3
Georgia	1,104	1,282	178	16.1
Kentucky	1,077	1,102	25	2.3
Maryland	220	216	(4)	−1.8
Mississippi	483	496	13	2.7
New York	1,083	1,072	(11)	−1.0
North Carolina	1,218	1,286	68	5.6
Ohio	1,262	1,275	13	1.0
Pennsylvania	5,994	5,888	(106)	−1.8
South Carolina	793	832	39	4.9
Tennessee	2,074	2,142	68	3.3
Virginia	554	550	(4)	−0.7
West Virginia	1,950	1,936	(14)	−0.7

TABLE 26.2

Employment 1980 and 1986 and Change from 1980 to 1986 U.S., Appalachia and Appalachian State Parts (in thousands)

Areas	1980 Employment	1986 Employment Average	1980–1986 Difference	1980–1986 % Change
United States	98,569	108,233	9,664	9.8
Appalachian Region	8,155	8,337	182	2.2
Appalachian State Parts:				
Alabama	960	1,079	119	12.4
Georgia	498	593	95	19.1
Kentucky	381	354	(27)	−7.1
Maryland	89	86	(3)	−3.4
Mississippi	201	200	(1)	−0.5
New York	447	436	(11)	−2.5
North Carolina	552	611	59	10.7
Ohio	489	483	(6)	−1.2
Pennsylvania	2,417	2,342	(75)	−3.1
South Carolina	368	392	24	6.5
Tennessee	819	901	82	10.0
Virginia	220	207	(13)	−5.9
West Virginia	714	653	(61)	−8.5

It should be emphasized, however, that persistent unemployment for the last five years has been in those counties located in Central Appalachia, the Ohio Valley, Appalachian Mississippi, and Appalachian Alabama as well as some industrial counties in Appalachian Ohio and Pennsylvania. Most of these counties are classified as rural nonfarm. The problem of persistent unemployment in most of these counties seems to be due to the slow recovery of many of the traditional industries in the region as well as a slow rate of development of new employment opportunities in the nationally emerging industries plus slower rates of growth in services and trade.

C. EMPLOYMENT PROJECTIONS

1. Total Employment Projections in 1995: Taking the BLS moderate growth scenario of total employment for the nation to 1995 and extrapolating the region's total employment as a shifting share of that national figure results in a moderate total employment projection for the region of 9,078,000 jobs by 1995 or a net increase over mid 1986 of 741,000 jobs. This will be an increase of 8.9% in the next nine years, compared with the nationally projected increase of 13.4%.

The 1995 level of projected total employment and the net increase from 1986 to 1995 are given in Table 26.3 (see page 219).

As Table 26.3 shows, Appalachian Alabama, Georgia, North Carolina and Tennessee are expected to account for a net increase of 448,000 jobs or 60% of the total net growth in the next nine years. These four Appalachian state parts now account for 38% of the total employment in the region. These four Appalachian state parts are increasing their employment in manufacturing as well as services, trade and other growing sectors. These states are also urbanizing rapidly.

North and Central Appalachia are expected to slowly recover and increase in overall employment during the next nine years.

The three quarters of a million job net increase is expected to be distributed as shown in the attached map. The map reveals the following:

- 32 counties in the region will have a net increase in jobs exceeding 5,000 in the next nine years; all but one county are in SMSAs.
- 128 counties will have employment growth between 1,000 and 5,000 jobs. 55 of these are in SMSAs.
- 165 counties, mostly in Central Appalachia and Ohio will have no change in total employment or an increase of less than 500 jobs.

2. Projections by Sector: Table 26.4 (see page 219) shows employment projections by sector for the region as whole. The main features of the table are the following:

- The region is expected to lose 70,500 jobs in manufacturing; most of the losses will be in non-durable manufacturing.
- The region may gain 131,000 jobs in transportation, communications, and public utility sectors.
- The region may gain 275,000 jobs in the trade sector in 15 years from 1980 to 1995, with two-thirds of the total gain in retail and one-third in wholesale trade.
- The region may gain 148,000 jobs in the finance, insurance, and real estate sector.
- The largest gain may be in the service sector, particularly in health, personal, and professional services.

D. IMPLICATIONS OF THE FORECASTS

The implications of the forecasts are that the region will follow the national trend of the shifts in population, employment, and industrial diversity, but lag slightly behind them. In addition, the movement of people and jobs to areas around the large SMSAs, those with access to the central cities and to all the services and amenities of urban living, will persist in the nation and the region. These forecasts take into account the profound forces affecting the nation's economy. One only has to look back to 20 years ago and compare the current Appalachian experience to realize how much the region has advanced in its economic performance, economic diversification, and the reduction of the number of counties with high levels of poverty. But the Appalachian region is now facing new challenges.

In the last ten years we have seen the emergence of global competition in global markets as a results of: 1) high rates of economic growth in some countries, notably Japan and other southeast Asian countries;[1] 2) application of advanced technology, (a large part of it exported by the United States in the past) to new manufacturing, trade and services processes abroad;[2] and 3) new financing strategies. The results have been an increase in labor productivity of other nations as well as an enhancement of their competitive advantage.

A recent study by SRI (Stanford Research Institute) entitled *Investing in the Future* describes the driving technologies that are currently transforming the U.S. economy:

1. Information technologies such as microelectronics, computer hardware and software, and telecommunications;
2. Factory automation and office automation;

TABLE 26.3

Employment Projections 1995 and Change from 1986 to 1995 U.S., Appalachian Region, and Appalachian State Parts (in thousands)

Areas	1980 Employment	1986 Employment Average	1980–1986 Difference	1980–1986 % Change	1995 Employment	1986–1995 Difference	1986–1995 % Change
United States	98,569	108,233	9,664	9.8	122,760	14,527	13.4
Appalachian Region	8,155	8,337	182	2.2	9,078	741	8.9
Appalachian State Parts:							
Alabama	960	1,079	119	12.4	1,230	151	14.0
Georgia	498	593	95	19.1	695	102	17.2
Kentucky	381	354	(27)	−7.1	366	12	1.0
Maryland	89	86	(3)	−3.4	91	5	5.8
Mississippi	201	200	(1)	−0.5	214	14	7.0
New York	447	436	(11)	−2.5	463	27	6.2
North Carolina	552	611	59	10.7	689	78	12.8
Ohio	489	483	(6)	−1.2	515	32	6.6
Pennsylvania	2,417	2,342	(75)	−3.1	2,479	137	5.8
South Carolina	368	392	24	6.5	431	39	9.9
Tennessee	819	901	82	10.0	1,018	117	13.0
Virginia	220	207	(13)	−5.9	213	6	2.9
West Virginia	714	653	(61)	−8.5	674	21	3.2

*Regional employment projections are based on national employment projections by the Bureau of Labor Statistics; moderate employment projections scenario.

TABLE 26.4

Employment by Sector Appalachian Region 1980 and Projections to 1995

Sector	1980	Percent of Total	1995	Percent of Total	Change 1980–95
Agriculture, Forestry, Fisheries and Mining	427,400	5.3%	363,400	4.0%	−67,900
Construction	490,400	6.1	472,500	5.2	−17,900
Manufacturing	2,335,500	29.1	2,289,600	25.2	−70,500
Durable	1,303,800	16.2	1,353,800	14.9	35,400
Nondurable	1,031,700	12.9	935,800	10.3	−105,900
Transportation, Communications and Public Utilities	569,500	7.1	708,700	7.8	131,500
Wholesale Trade	288,200	3.6	372,500	4.1	80,300
Retail Trade	1,214,600	15.1	1,426,500	15.7	196,500
Finance, Insurance and Real Estate	319,400	4.0	472,500	5.2	148,000
Services	2,049,200	25.6	2,607,682	28.7	530,300
Government	324,900	4.0	372,500	4.1	43,600
Total	8,019,100	100.0%	9,086,000	100.0%	968,900

1995 projections are based on a projected Regional unemployment rate of 7.5 percent and that Appalachia's share of national employment will be 6.91 percent.

3. New materials;

4. Bio-technology; and

5. Health and medical technologies.

These technologies are creating new wealth, new job opportunities, and new entrepreneurial opportunities.[3] In addition, SRI highlights changes in consumer values and lifestyles. The consumer, they say, now demands a better and more durable specialized and customized product. Finally, SRI notes a restructuring of American companies that means that companies are continuously seeking optimum location for different types of operations. SRI stresses a new trend toward decentralization and "unbundling."

SRI outlines five key factors which " . . . appear to differentiate the attractiveness of regions to firms competing on an international level." These factors are:

1. Access to technology;

2. Skilled and adaptable labor force;

3. Adequate physical and social infrastructure;

4. Availability of capital;

5. An entrepreneurial climate.

For Appalachia to continue to develop it must be competitive in these five elements. It is my proposition that many parts of the Appalachian region are or can be competitive in all five. The question is not whether they are available; it is rather to what degree, how fast, and in what location. Most of the ARC investments in the region have been and presently are geared toward upgrading all these five elements.

The Appalachian region has 34 standard metropolitan areas within its boundaries and has over 50 around it. In addition to these, it also has numerous centers of technological advancement in its public and private laboratories, universities and colleges, and other related facilities.

The region has a large pool of labor. Granted, a portion of it is not trained for the new and emerging challenges, but it can adapt a large portion of it to the new tasks ahead through training and retraining. A most promising trend is that many Appalachian governors have been leaders in educational improvement, and they are fully aware that this is a matter of strategic economic importance.[4]

The region has a near-adequate physical infrastructure to capture and sustain new opportunities. The Appalachian corridor system alone, now two-thirds complete, has been a major factor in promoting jobs and access to jobs.

In recent years Commission programs have tried to help states and localities address the need for capital formation for business development. Commission studies have not found any barriers within the region that prevent it from attracting capital for worthwhile private investment.

The last factor, an entrepreneurial climate, is crucial because it is the one that puts all the four previous factors together to foster economic development. Several programs in Appalachian states have proven to be very successful in creating opportunities for entrepreneurs to emerge.

There is a critical role for the public sector involvement in the new emerging challenges for the Appalachian region, especially at the local and state levels. The private investments which are going to generate new job opportunities in Appalachia need a stable environment, adequate infrastructure, and a flexible labor market with commitments for investments in upgrading labor skills to meet the new challenges. The public sector, the states, and multi-county units have the power and opportunity to do that.

There are several possible futures for the Appalachian region. But since rapid change seems to be the constant factor, adaptation to change is certainly an important component of any new strategy for change. A most significant factor is the quality of the labor force. Through proper education and training, the labor force can flexibly adapt to new technologies more rapidly than physical capital or physical infrastructure, which are slow to change. Thus, from the public perspective, any community's economic future will depend heavily on proper training for the emerging industries and services in the region wherever they may occur.

NOTES

1. Last issue of **High Technology** shows that Singapore, Taiwan, South Korea, and Hong Kong have a net export balance of $38 billion with the United States.

2. These four nations mentioned above are not only manufacturers of labor intensive goods but developers and exporters of high technology products such as new materials, micro chips, telecommunication equipment, and pharmaceuticals.

3. AmeriTrust Corporation, "Investing in the Future: A Prospectus for Mid America", September 1986.

4. **High Technology**, issue of November 1986, states that South Korea in 1962 had a per capita gross national product of $80.00 and the World Bank regarded the county as a very poor prospect for investment. Today its per capita gross national product is $2,300, and with a growth rate of GNP of 7% annually, it may surpass Great Britain by the end of the century. This was primarily done as the article indicates by investment in human resources.

27. FATALISM OR THE COAL INDUSTRY?

Helen Lewis

"Pictures in Our Heads"

Walter Lippman, in the introduction to his early treatise on public opinion, spoke of the way men perceive social reality as "the world outside and the picture in our heads."[1] What are the pictures in the heads of those who are interested and involved in the uplift of Appalachia? What are their views of the situation? Unfortunately many of these students, workers, change agents, helpers, organizers and general meddlers are completely unaware of the preconceptions, definitions, and models which guide their proclamations and programs for the area. This has led to conflicts and confrontations concerning programs for Appalachia. Appalachia has been the ground for many battles throughout its history: family and clan feuds, coal mine wars, battles between strip miners and land owners, and now individuals and groups at war over how to solve the problems of Appalachia. Some of the recent confrontations between members of the Council of the Southern Mountains can be seen as confrontations of two different views of Appalachian problems and two different strategies for helping solve the problems. One can also go further, take a step behind the "views" and look to where these protagonists are "located" in the social structure to explain their views.

I would like to outline two opposing views of Appalachia and suggest some of the implications of each for the solution to Appalachian problems. The first view is termed the Appalachian Subculture Model and the second, the Colonialism—Exploitation Model. In simple terms it is either fatalism or the coal industry.

View Number One: Appalachian Subculture

The Appalachian subculture model is what Charles Valentine in *Culture and Poverty* calls a "difference" or "deficiency" model.[2] By this view one sees the Southern Appalachians as a subculture with unique and different customs, values, style of life which developed historically and which is passed on through each succeeding generation. It is almost always compared with the greater society or mainstream America and the differences between the two are pointed out. The Appalachian is fatalistic while mainstream Americans believe they can control their environment and their lives. The Appalachian is impulsive, personalistic and individualistic while mainstream Americans are rational, organized, can handle impersonal role relationships and have a social consciousness.[3]

Some emphasize the subcultural traits as obsolete as indicated by such terms as Yesterday's People, Contemporary Ancestors, Arrested Frontier culture while others emphasize the traits as pathological, disorganized, defeating value system such as Ball's ultra-mainstream-chauvinistic characterization of the Appalachians as an "analgesic" subculture.[4] Some are kinder and use more positive terms in describing the traits as when Stephenson uses "contentment" as contrasted to Weller's "fatalism."[5] Lesser insists that most subculture descriptions emphasize only the dramatic and destructive traits of Appalachia, e.g., traditionalism, fatalism and emphasize the Appalachian people as passive and apathetic carriers of their culture.[6] Mostly these approaches describe and generalize on Appalachian character and general values. Some speak of the adaptive nature of the subculture and explain how such values are tied to conditions of poverty, lack of resources, isolation, powerlessness and the group's location in the total socio-political-economic system.[7]

Problems and Consequences of This Viewpoint

A major problem with this type of view, and the resultant descriptions of Appalachia, is that they emphasize a stereotyped view of Appalachian values with little concern for the socialization process and the content of what is transmitted from one generation to another. It is assumed that middle-class or dominant American values are not transmitted in Appalachia. If we are concerned with the causes of Appalachian problems we must view them differently than if we are concerned with the effects of these problems. In the former case we are concerned with the factors which led to those behaviors described as belonging to those in the Appalachian subculture. In the latter case we want to know how these behaviors are transmitted from one generation to another. Pure description answers neither one of these questions. They do not tell us why these conditions prevail and do not tell us why these conditions cause certain values, norms or behaviors of the people.[8]

Yet many helpers, social workers, community organizers, teachers, preachers accept and operate on this view of Appalachia. In so doing they focus in on the

Reprinted from *Mountain Life and Work,* Vol. 46 (December, 1970), pp. 4–15. Used by permission.

values of the Appalachian and say that these must be changed. Unfortunately, the subcultural model has been the predominant one influencing most of the poverty programs. One seeks to improve the schools, motivate children to achievement, change the values, break down the isolation, bring the area into the "mainstream." One does not question the institutions and avoids recognizing the need for radical change in the society. The wholesale and intemperate acceptance and promulgation of this model and these strategies have been extremely pernicious and wasteful of money. They have, if anything, helped create an Appalachian subculture by convincing the Appalachian that he is inferior, backward, lazy, and has "bad" values. He should catch up, "get with it." This image has been projected upon Appalachians by all major institutions from the mass media to antipoverty programs. It is untenable and unjust to characterize Appalachian culture patterns as deficient or pathological versions of mainstream American culture.

Proponents Isolated in a Middle-Class Culture

Where are these change agents located in the total social structure? They are generally representing and defending institutions. Most fear disruption of services and perhaps their jobs. They say "some services are better than none"; poor schools are better than none and "What will you put in its place?" Although they will reject this contention, they are themselves culturally isolated in a middle class and/or bureaucratic institutional culture and they are ethnocentric about their values. They are upholding their particular subculture which is dominant. Many of them are tolerant, generous, kindly, liberal and want to "help Appalachian people." They accept their differences and their problems and speculate on how many generations before "these people" can be changed into middle-class Americans. There is an arrogance in the subcultural view reflected in such hypocritical strategies and statements as: maximum feasible participation, development of indigenous leadership, preparation for modernization, viability of life-styles, preservation of the "best" of their culture, self-help programs. The Appalachian cause becomes a sort of "city man's burden." Instead of pride or power or positive identity the Appalachian poor folks are allowed maximum feasible participation in a self-help program to preserve the "best" of their culture: cornshuck dolls. They may also be motivated and educated and trained and psychologically readied for nonexistent opportunities or alternatives.

Appalachians Are Bicultural

This is not to say that there are not some different life-styles, values, subcultures in the mountains. There are several Appalachian subcultures which present distinctive group identities and behavior patterns including dialects, aesthetic styles, bodies of folklore, religious beliefs and practices, political allegiances, family structure, food and clothing preferences. There is no single homogeneous Appalachian culture but several subcultures with intergroup commonalities and some sharing of mainstream culture. It might be best to view the Appalachian as bicultural.

Most Appalachians learn and practice both mainstream culture and their mountain subculture at the same time. The Appalachian cannot avoid mainstream culture and is enculturated in dominant culture patterns by mainstream institutions, mass media, television, advertising, public schooling, welfare system, antipoverty programs, modern medicine, national fashions, holidays, heroes, and his association with middle- and upper-class town people in his area. The subculture is focused within family and kinship units, small neighborhoods, churches, older mountain rituals and ceremonies which pass on values and role models. For the poor, isolated Appalachian much of the mainstream culture remains much or less latent or potential rather than being actively expressed in everyday behavior because the structural conditions of poverty, discrimination, and isolation prevent them from achieving most mainstream middle-class values, aspirations, and role models. They may also be aware of contradictions within mainstream culture and refuse to emulate these roles of "uppity, society folk" with "fancy ways," the impersonal bureaucrats, "foolish" teachers and "cold, hard" welfare workers. When they must, Appalachians passively enact the behavior of mainstream culture in settings of formalized intragroup contact: at the welfare office, in court and at school. It is in such cases that the mainstreamer is limited to a single cultural system whereas the Appalachian is bicultural and bidialectical.

The Appalachian may also "drop out," refuse to participate in the alien culture, seeing it as an attack upon his way of life. He reads clearly the definitions of his helpers and the strategies designed to destroy his culture. The helpers see Appalachians with cultural values which impede learning or change and feel that they must wipe out these differences. But his definition of the situation also tells him that this is impossible because the cultural differences make the people impossible to motivate or to teach or to organize or the community to mobilize and he can thus rationalize all the failures of schools or programs by blaming them on the Appalachian culture—for the so-called "culturally deprived or disadvantaged" cannot be reached. This view assumes that the Appalachian culture is not only distinct but pathogenic; there is no recognition that mainstream institutions might be pathogenic and responsible for the Appalachian problems, rather, the difficulty must lie within the family or the noninstitutional community. It becomes a way of blaming poverty on the poor.

View Number Two: Colonialism and Exploitation

Some of the outspoken critics of the subculture model claim that the subculture proponents blame the underdevelopment of the region on the Appalachian character rather than the exploitative conditions institutionalized in the region. In their search for the causes of the problem they see Appalachia as a subsociety structurally alienated and lacking resources due to processes of colonialism and exploitation. Those who control the resources preserve their advantages by discrimination. The people are not essentially passive but these "subcultural" traits of fatalism, passivity, etc., are adjustive techniques of the powerless; ways in which people protect their way of life from new economic modes and the concomitant alien culture. These values are reactions to powerlessness.

There has been a growing interest in using this model to describe the social and economic conditions of the Southern Appalachians and to describe the region along with Harry Caudill as "the last unchallenged stronghold of Western colonialism."[9] It is not a new claim and C. Vann Woodward in *Origins of the New South* in 1951 characterized the whole South as a colony suffering from absentee ownership and economic exploitation and placed the Southern Appalachian colonialism in that context: "As the nineteenth century drew to a close and the new century progressed through the first decade, the penetration of the South and the Southern Appalachians was begun by Northeastern capital and is continuing at an accelerated rate. The Morgans, Mellons, and Rockefellers sent their agents to take charge of the region's railroads, mines, coke furnaces and financial corporations."[10]

The claim of colonialism has become more popular with young "change agents" in the mountains, VISTA workers, students, young professionals, lawyers and churchmen working in the area. The emergence of books on Algerian and Third world colonialism have also encouraged comparisons.[11] Except for Caudill most of the writings stressing this interpretation of Appalachia have been in the mimeographed, underground publications, "movement" newsletters and student press.[12] This speaks to the location in the social structure of those who promote this view. Most are outside the established institutions and many are involved in counter or alternate institutional movements. Many poor also champion this view.

Coal and Colonialism

The colonialism interpretation has been particularly applied to that portion of the mountains in which coal mining developed, that section labeled by the Appalachian Regional Commission as "Central Appalachia."

The following excerpts provide examples of this type analysis:

In West Virginia, then, as throughout the Appalachia, we live in a system of absentee control by large financial and industrial corporations pursuing their economic ends without respect for the lives of the people in the state or region. The responsibility for the damage—political, economic, and social—can be attributed to these colonial exploiters. They have caused the serious lack of public services, because of their unwillingness and tireless opposition to any sort of meaningful tax reform.[13]

West Virginia is a rich state. Yet it is also obvious that West Virginia is a poor state. Much wealth has been extracted from West Virginia natural resources, but little of that wealth has remained in the hands of West Virginians. The reason for this, of course, lies in the exploitation of the Mountain State's natural resources by outside capital. The resemblance of West Virginia (and much of the rest of Appalachia) to the colonial domains created by Great Britain and other powers during the nineteenth century imperialist era has been pointed out. . . . Outside capital . . . milks its victims of natural resources while dominating the native government and treating the natives as contemptible, expendable and a source of cheap labor.[14]

More recently Barry Barkin and R. Baldwin Lloyd claim "the colonizer that rapes the natural resources and saps the spirit of the people is not another nation, but a handful of coal, railroad, and labor barons . . . the net effect is the same. The enormous wealth which could have made a so-called 'depressed area' prosperous continues to be pumped out of the region."[15]

Is This Model Adequate?

Does the Colonialism model fit? Is Appalachia a colony suffering from absentee ownership and economic exploitation? Is it true that the Central Appalachian area was, from its settlement in 1770 until 1890, a land of small landowners; families making their living by subsistence farming until outside "colonizers" or "developers" came into the region. The developers were British investors, Pennsylvania coal operators, Virginia aristocrats, unemployed Confederate generals and New York bankers and railroad men.

Blauner defines classical colonialism as "domination over a geographically external political unit, most often inhabited by people of a different race and culture, when this domination is political and economic, and the colony exists subordinated to and dependent upon the mother country."[16] It is a process and a system of relationships that exist between those dominating and those in a subordinate position. It is a process of oppression or domination which involves (1) a forced or involuntary entry; (2) a rapid modification of the culture and social organization of the colonized; (3) control by the dominant group; and (4) a condition of racism, social domination by which the colonized are defined as inferior or different and which rationalizes the exploitation, control and oppression by the superordinate group.

Blauner sees the main source of domination coming from technological superiority. The colonized have resources and the colonizer has tools and knowledge to harness and exploit these resources. The colonizer's superiority and power increases and is perpetuated ad infinitum.

Is this the story of Appalachia? When the outside colonizers came to the Appalachian region in the latter part of the nineteenth century they found a society approximating an Asian or African country in its economic foundations. The outside speculators bought land, mineral and timber rights from illiterate, simple, mountain farmers who were unable to cope with the representatives of the coal industry or the many fraudulent land deals which were forced upon the settlers.

The Broad Form Deed

A survival of this early relationship is found in the "broad form" deeds that have been supported by Kentucky courts. These deeds included "all minerals and metallic substances and all combinations of the same" and they give the unconditional right to remove them by any method they "deemed necessary or convenient." This has allowed companies to strip or surface mine land in the face of strong opposition by the landowners who had sold only the mineral rights many years before. The state has used the broad form deeds to support arresting landowners who have attempted to block mining operations. Several cases have made the news in the past few years. Widow Combs placed her body in front of dozers and ended up in the Knott County jail. Conspiracy charges were made against Appalachian Volunteers and Southern Conference Educational Fund workers who helped Jink Ray and other local landowners successfully stop stripping operations.

More Documentation Needed

Although many writers on Appalachia speak of the outside control of the wealth, the degree and extent to which this is true has been only slightly and sporadically documented. There are no systematic, thorough studies of the land and mineral ownership for the region.

This "oversight" itself might be considered "evidence" of the protection provided colonizers. Even the Appalachian Regional Commission after a number of years of data collection and analysis of various aspects of Appalachian poverty and economic potential has only lately turned its attention to the Central Appalachian area, first with a study of capital resources and a proposed study of land and mineral ownership and taxation.[17] One must go to the radical student or movement publications to find any studies, or to the Bureau of Mines statistics on such things as coal production to find documentation.

"The Energy Era"

Kirby, in a study of the tax records of eleven major coal producing counties in Eastern Kentucky, found thirty-one people and corporations owned four-fifths of Eastern Kentucky's coal. It is estimated that 70 to 80 percent of the Southwest Virginia minerals are owned by four or five large corporations.[18] And David Walls lists seven firms which produce one-third of the total coal production in Central Appalachia.[19]

More interesting is the fact that many of these "independent" companies are linked together in corporate structures. One study for a two county area in Southwest Virginia found a tightly linked chain of railroad men, industrialists and financiers who own and benefit from the timber and mineral wealth of the area.[20] Diehl has traced some of the interconnections of ownership in Eastern Kentucky and West Virginia. These connections take us in some cases beyond the borders of America to such places as South Africa and to such diversified industries as electronic equipment, chemicals, oil, banks, and auto manufacturing.[21]

The absorption of coal companies by fuel and energy industries reflects the major changes in dominant industries in the United States in general. The early coal companies were controlled by shipping and railroads; later they were dominated by the steel and automobile manufacturers. Beginning in the 1960s and the "Energy Era" fuel and electrical powers began their present domination.

Another indication of outside control of this area is seen when looking at taxation and economic development. David Brooks talks of the role of the coal industry in regional development.[22] He points to the limited ability of mining to provide economic development in a region. Unlike manufacturing or industries in which materials are fabricated or value is added through a production process, mining processes add little value and do little to stimulate other types of economic activities. Since mining is immobile, fixed in space, limited in its one product, and work is arduous and dangerous, it must develop means of attracting or controlling labor. It is to the advantage of coal mining to operate in isolation without competing companies. These characteristics of mining lead to a one-industry area with labor tied to the one industry and little development outside the extraction of the minerals. This also leaves no development when the minerals are gone.[23]

Colonial Character of Coal Companies

Without intervention mining itself tends to develop certain exploitative or colonial characteristics. Resources generated by coal mining for the local area are low. In other industries surplus is used for capital investments and this creates new corporations, associations, and other businesses and develops a middle-stratum of technicians and specialists. This does not happen with coal mining.

Except for wages paid to workers and local taxes paid to the area, coal mining offers little. At one time large numbers were employed in the mines of the area. In 1932 there were 705,000 miners in 1940 there were 439,000 miners and today there are only 132,000.[24] The mechanization of coal mining and the resultant decline in mining employment in the Southern Appalachian region in the 1950s resulted in a wholesale migration from the area and a high degree of unemployment which continues into the 1970s.

In Virginia there are still 8,862 miners in a six county area. Coal mining is still the main source of employment accounting for approximately one-third of the total labor force. The coal companies paid in wages in 1968 $56,361,577. During this same year this area produced 36,865,703 tons of coal which if valued at $4.50 a ton would total $165,956,000.[25] The total taxes paid to the area are not known. But one can draw some conclusions from the record of one company. This company in 1967 employed 448 men and mined approximately 2,500,000 tons of coal in four mines. Wages, if all the men worked full time, would have been approximately $3,240,000; royalties to the corporation owning the mineral rights to the land at $1.42 per ton would amount to $360,000, and 40 cents a ton to the United Mine Workers Health and Welfare Fund would amount to $1,000,000. The land holding company and the mining company paid $207,533 in county taxes in 1968. This tax amount represents taxes on land under development, land not under development, buildings and equipment. In addition to the four mines, land was leased for stripping, augering and several truck mine operations. The total outlay for wages, royalties and taxes was $3,807,533. The value of the coal at $4.50 per ton was $11,128,000. This leaves a difference of $7,320,467. The amount of taxes paid, although small in comparison to gross income, represents 13.5 percent of the tax income for the county in which the company has its operations. Despite the resources the coal mining counties generate a smaller proportion of their total revenue than the counties in the rest of the Appalachian area.

The corporation having the mineral rights mentioned above is probably the most profitable in America. According to their 1968 Annual Report they netted 65 percent of gross and paid dividends of 40 cents out of each dollar received.[26] Harry Caudill reported the same corporation as netting 61 percent of gross and paying 45 cents on each dollar received in 1964. He compared it with General Motors which reported a profit of 10.2 cents out of each dollar received and paid a dividend of five cents. Caudill claims that this corporation is characteristic of other mineral owning corporations in the area.[27]

Depletion and Depreciation Allowances

Depletion and depreciation allowances give coal companies a very favorable position. Depletion for coal mined is based on the cost of the mineral properties and estimated recoverable tonnage. In some cases the depletion allowance is greater than the taxes on the minerals and the land. Although the original purchases of most of the mineral lands were made before 1900 at 30 cents to $1.00 an acre the depletion is figured on the last price paid. When lands change hands even through a subsidiary the new cost is the basis for the depletion. This is figured as the percentage of the cost of the land which is mined during the year. Kirby points out that this is an incentive to sell. An acre bought for 50 cents can be sold in a year of mining for $5,000 increasing the cost depletion allowance considerably.[28]

Another concession given to coal companies is the tax on mine equipment and machinery. In Virginia, they are taxed at only 10 percent of their value while all others, individuals and businesses, are taxed at approximately one-third of value. Here also resale to subsidiaries can make this even lower for coal companies. A leasing company can sell a $100,000 machine to a mining company it controls for $10,000 and the mining company will pay tax on 10 percent of that or $1,000. Caudill reports a similar situation in Kentucky.[29] Through resale to subsidiaries mining machinery worth $75,000 is valued at $3,000 and taxes are less than a miner pays on his automobile which he drives to work to operate the machine. Blizzard reports taxes low in West Virginia due to the influence of the coal industry.[30] West Virginia has a gross sales tax regardless of profit or loss but coal companies do not pay on sales made at out-of-state markets, which excludes most of the coal sales. Machinery and supplies used for coal mining are also exempt from a sales tax.

Strip Mining—"The Logical Thing, Costwise"

In line with the general tendency of colonists to be exploitative we find that public spiritedness on the part of coal operators is rare in the area. Coal companies in Virginia are suing the counties, claiming that assessing "land under development" at a differential rate is in fact a form of severance tax on mined coal which is unconstitutional. Most of the remarks concerning civic responsibility made by coal company representatives sound like turn-of-the-century rugged capitalism. When asked about decaying coal camps, burning slag heaps or disabled and unemployed miners, coal company executives are heard to say that they have no responsibility to the area or to the people. Their responsibility is to mine coal as cheaply and efficiently as possible and to make a profit for the company and the stockholders. They provide employment and housing when needed to get employees, food stores when necessary to hold employees and they continue these as long as they are either necessary to keep workers or are profitable to the company. Even one of the most public spirited executives of a large mining company said that their decision to begin strip mining is because it is "the logical thing, costwise."[31] This same executive has been quoted in the *Mountain Eagle* and states with great candor in the NET film *Rich Lands Poor People,* "If there is something wrong with what we are doing in Eastern Kentucky, then there is something wrong with the country."

The Economy of Exploitation

Certain income distribution is characteristic of colonialism. Coal mining produces different kinds of distribution of resources than those produced by manufacturing industries. It requires a less complex and a shorter range of skills which leads to an income distribution with a small elite and a large number of people at the bottom. Throughout Appalachia the income system is overwhelmingly lower income class ranging from 38 to 65 percent of the population with incomes under $3,000.[32]

Education distribution and migration patterns also reflect the economy of exploitation. Despite some improvements in schools and a greater number of high school graduates from local schools in recent years, the median education has improved only slightly. The industry attracts the uneducated, and the high school and college trained leave the area. Even with mechanization the skill requirements have not increased to the point of attracting the better educated.

The outside coal interests exert political control in subtle and often unseen ways for the local inhabitant. The protection of investments and property through state legislation and the judicial system began early. Seldom does the outside owner have to deal on the local level with local politicians. He can work through the state capitals, and the state courts and the counties are relatively impotent in ability to tax or control the industry.

The courts have been used to legitimize what were fraudulent, inadequate or at least "inconclusive" leases to property bought at the turn of the century by speculators from the illiterate and unwary mountaineers. In one study of titles in a small area of Eastern Kentucky, Warren Wright has shown how the court legitimized very weak and doubtful leases, some of which were gained by fraud and coercion. In a decision by Judge Palmore in *Blue Diamond Coal Company* versus *Neace,* he said "right or wrong, it would be a grave matter indeed for this Court by overruling it now to upset property rights which have since been vested in reliance upon it."

Counties in Kentucky find themselves unable to ban strip mining in their localities and citizens who try to help enforce the law against overloaded coal trucks find themselves the felons. Local governments and citizens cannot control the industrial practices within their boundaries. One would have difficulty finding a lawyer in the coalfields or a commonwealth or district attorney who is elected to represent the people who is not on a retainer from a coal company.

Writers on Appalachian culture point to the fact that most relationships in the mountains are "personal" including politics. This is usually related to a rural, familistic orientation. One might also relate it to powerlessness of both the people and their local leaders. Local politicians are limited in what they can do. They can help individuals stay out of jail, evade a fine, evade local taxes, get county jobs, etc. So one votes for and elects those who can help with little personal favors. Big deals are left for the state capital and the homelands of Pittsburgh.

Racism and Colonialism

The condition of racism associated with the colonialism model is well illustrated in Appalachia. Memmi points out that it is not only the colonizers but the colonized who go into businesses that engage in this practice.[33] In the region one finds that the smaller independent coal operators are even more conservative in their political and economic ideology than the outsiders. The *Independent Coal Leader* claims to represent the small operators and its contents reflect a general negative evaluation of the local population who are unemployed, and has taken rather dramatic stands against any individual or organization attempting to question the coal industry and its practices. Most of these small operators are dependent upon the larger companies for leases or money for equipment or their coal sales facilities. A number of local millionaires have emerged in the area through strip mining, selling equipment and truck mining. It is interesting to observe how many of these make their money and then retire to Florida. Perhaps Florida serves as the "homeland" for the native who joins the colonists.

Native Colonizers

The natives who become colonizers of their own people must protect themselves with even more disparaging evaluations of the people than the outsider makes. While the outsider may become interested in the esoteric ways of the natives, collecting quilts, mountain folk tales, music, and speak with appreciation about mountain culture, the native exploiter is apt to denigrate his own, speak of laziness and "sorriness" or a "certain class" of people, especially those on welfare or those who are unemployed. They recount stories of the suspicion, untrustworthiness and unreliability of their workers. Since these small operators often pay even less than minimum wages they find themselves in competition with welfare programs.

This is not a new pattern. General John Daniel Imboden was one of the earliest "developers" of the area. In 1880 he bought 47,000 acres of mineral lands in Wise County, Virginia. Later, he bought 21,000 acres for only 35 cents an acre for certain "gentlemen of large means" who were officials of the Baltimore and Ohio Railroad. A list of property made in May, 1880 reveals that Imboden and his son owned one-sixth interest in over 100,000 acres in Wise County. Imboden purchased land, built the railroad into the coal fields and later was a lobbyist in North Carolina for the coal interests. He wrote after a stint at the state capital in Raleigh about the elegant people he was meeting. He said he told them about Wise County and "how nice it was . . . and interested them so much that when our road is built they are coming to see for themselves. They think it must be delightful to see and mingle with such *primitive people!*" [emphasis added][34]

Distrust of Services Colonizer Provides

One test of whether colonization exists is to see if the colonists utilize the same services they provide the colonized. One finds a general distrust of such services in Appalachia, especially toward local doctors and local hospitals. They are mistrusted for they provide services to miners or county people and therefore inadequate service—they, too, are opportunists or exploiters. A local hospital administrator resents the fact that members of their local board travel 100–300 miles eastward to seek "good doctors" or "good medical services" because the "coal camp doctors are not as good." Other local services and professionals who stay in the area are denigrated " . . . they are no good or they would go

elsewhere." Fanon in an essay on "Dying Colonialism" about the native medical service points to the distrust by the native of local medicine, seeing it as an agent of the colonists.[35] Perhaps their judgment is true. The fantastically poor medical service provided in the early days of coal camps in Appalachia has been documented. Today, coal company doctors often refuse to admit the existence of pneumoconiosis or "black lung" and one company doctor was elected to the Virginia House of Delegates and succeeded in getting this disease removed from the Workman's Compensation law. Company doctors are said by many miners to be more likely to report injuries or to diagnose pneumoconiosis in order to protect the company from "getting stuck" with an already disabled miner.

To continue with examples of conformity between the realities of Appalachian life and the colonialism model would be pointless. That the total interests came into the region uninvited; that cultural patterns changed as a result of this intrusion; that the area is controlled by representatives of the industry cannot be disputed; and that racism exists to perpetuate this pattern has been illustrated. Since these conditions exist it would appear that recommendations for change should consider these factors. Changing the values of Appalachians will not change the system of colonialism. Nor will knowledge of the situation.

Changing the Colonial System

Those who view Appalachia in this way present very different solutions to the problems of Appalachia. They emphasize the need to change the structure of society. They advocate the redistribution of goods and resources which would give power to the poor. They see the revolt of blacks in America and rebellion of Mexican-Americans as resulting from the similar colonialism, and they look for and work for a strong movement of the people. They do not look to social work, education and psychiatry or programs designed to change attitudes, to motivate and assimilate the Appalachian into mainstream culture.

Tanner in the *Objector* writes:[36]

The challenge is one of political control, either a powerful public control or the continued control by corporations. Strategies must be devised which will take power from these vested interests. Anything short of this will not accomplish significant change. The power to correct the existing evils cannot be left to the same men and institutions which helped create them. Rather, new political and economic alternatives must be formulated which will represent the people. And these alternatives must have as their ultimate aim to become the dominant political reality.

There is an interest in developing Appalachian pride, reemphasis on the culture as good, emphasis on Appalachian studies to rediscover the lost history of struggle, and to start a revitalization movement and develop an Appalachian identity.

Those who follow this point of view look to parallel organizations for social services or radical alteration of existing dominant institutions with respect to the values, attitudes and interests which they serve. Tanner speaks for the "dismantling of them (political, social and economic institutions) and their replacement by others of a democratic nature." He insists that a belief that our political institutions are basically sound, needing only certain adjustments, is a dangerous error. The government is not one which is fundamentally responsible to the people, except in the most mechanical and superficial way by using democratic processes to protect the fact that colonial industrial interests dominate.

Although some will dismantle and some radically change, all emphasize the need to make the service institutions responsive to the people: the institutions should change, there must be radical shifts in power relationships and the class system. Professionals must learn respect for subcultural systems and recognize the legitimacy and creativity of the subculture rather than regarding them as problems to be changed.

Problems with the Colonial Model

This view, although it seems to address itself more to the causes of Appalachian problems than the first model, does present us with problems when we come to strategies for change. Where is the "homeland" of the exploiters? How can one "throw the bastards out" and take over the resources when one is also part of the same national system? How does one begin a meaningful revitalization movement? Do the colonized always revolt? There is evidence that the most severely oppressed people and subsocieties have seldom rebelled or risen up effectively. Those helpers or change agents who are the proponents of radical change in the mountains are also very expendable, and have little power of their own to back up such a movement. There is also a tendency for them to exaggerate a single cause: it's the coal company, and postulate a nirvana when this one source of trouble is eliminated or conquered. Stop strip mining! Pass a severance tax on coal! Take the resources! This also becomes a rationalization for failure. Since the corporations are so large and powerful and unapproachable, and the institutions so corrupt and unresponsive, little can be done. So they just sit and wait for the revolution and maybe sing a few folk songs while they are waiting. They worry so much about changing society they may forget to help a friend. Some are even calculating enough to be willing to "throw a few bodies" at the system.

There is also a tendency on the part of the revolutionaries to overprotest the deficiency model, and to stereotype all the mountain culture as good. They go native and begin to extoll a life-style, much of which may be an adjustment to oppression. Some would be very reluctant to allow Appalachian people to live a suburban, middle-class style of life even if they wanted to.

Two Views Compared

As we have looked at the two models we find differences in responses to the conditions in Appalachia stemming from the acceptance of one or the other. Those who follow the deficiency or difference approach—the subculture model—work to help to change people. Their object is to change their values and assimilate the Appalachian poor to middle-class culture. Through various programs of social work, education and psychiatry, they hope to change attitudes, to motivate and to assimilate. Those who follow the colonialism model emphasize the need to change the structure of society. They advocate the redistribution of goods and resources which would give power to the poor.

Is there a meeting ground for the two approaches? One can look at Appalachia as a heterogenous subsociety with adaptive subcultures. The area does share norms of the total society but there are variations in different locales and situations. Creative adaptive cultural patterns have developed from historical and situational sources. Some of these are adaptions to oppression and powerlessness. Programs for change must recognize the varieties of Appalachian life-styles and avoid uniform programs to eliminate poverty based on distorted stereotyped pictures of Appalachian life. Change must look toward changing the causes of poverty and not the results of poverty. The compromise or combination model would approach change through:

1. Increase resources and/or control over resources.
2. Radical change of institutions to meet needs and deliver services.
3. Alteration of the total social structure to provide for power and participation by Appalachian poor.
4. Change some subcultural patterns resulting from oppression through education, social work and cultural programs to motivate and stimulate creative activity among all the people.

But, is it possible? Are there enough strengths left in the region to produce creative forms of action for change?

A Paleface Reservation?

Tom Gish, editor of the *Mountain Eagle* in Whitesburg, Kentucky talks about colonialism, outside exploitation of the wealth and the various government programs for amelioration. Although outside corporations still exploit the resources he feels that the period of blatent colonial control and local domination is past. The coal companies can continue to mine the minerals through control over a few politicians, state courts and lawyers and they can control labor through collusion with the United Mine Workers. In the meantime they can ignore and leave behind the many social problems resulting from technological change, illness, injury and long powerlessness and deprivation. These will be handled (along with polluted streams and devastated land) by federal government programs. The early war on poverty programs tried to create political action which was frightening to the local power structure and to the corporate interests. These programs have been co-opted or dropped. The focus is now on economic development, assistance and control. Regional offices of Health, Education and Welfare, Department of Labor, U.S. Corps of Engineers, Office of Economic Opportunity, Department of Agriculture and Department of Interior with headquarters in Atlanta, Baltimore, Philadelphia and Washington funnel in programs of "assistance" through regional economic planning and development organizations. Gish finds these regional organizations developing more and more like the Office of Indian Affairs, to control the natives. Perhaps this is a latter stage of colonialism in which those who are leftover, the land and the people, are now wards of the government, living on a Paleface Reservation.

NOTES

1. Walter Lippman, *Public Opinion,* Macmillan, 1954.

2. I am indebted to Charles Valentine for much of this discussion of views from his critique of the culture of poverty model in *Culture and Poverty,* Chicago, 1968. A paper which he read at the American Psychological Association meeting in 1969 also inspired the title to this paper. His Paper "It's either brain damage or no father," discusses the results of the culture of poverty model on social work in the ghetto.

3. See especially Jack Weller, *Yesterday's People,* Lexington, 1965; Marion Pearsall, "Communicating with the Educationally Deprived," *Mountain Life & Work,* Spring 1966; John Stephenson, *Shiloh: A Mountain Community,* Lexington, 1968.

4. Richard Ball, "A Poverty Case: The Analgesic Subculture of the Southern Appalachians," *American Sociological Review,* December 1968; Paul F. Cressey. "Social Disorganization and Reorganization in Harlan County, Kentucky," *American Sociological Review,* June 1949; Jonathan Williams, "The Southern Appalachians," *Craft Horizons,* June 1966.

5. John Stephenson, *Shiloh;* Jack Weller, *Yesterday's People.*

6. Roger Lesser, "Culture: Toward Tomorrow's People," *Peoples' Appalachia,* March 1970.

7. Thomas R. Ford, "Value Orientations of a Culture of Poverty: The Southern Appalachian Case." Working with Low-Income Families, American Home Economics Association, Washington, D.C.,

1965; and "The Effects of Prevailing Values and Beliefs on the Perpetuation of Poverty in Rural Areas." *Problems of Chronically Depressed Rural Areas,* N.C. University, 1965; Edward E. Knipe and Helen M. Lewis. "The Impact of Coal Mining on the Traditional Mountain Subculture." *Southern Anthropological Society,* 1969.

8. These criticisms are made of the "culture of poverty" concept by Jack L. Roach and Orville R. Gurrslin, *Social Forces,* March 1967.

9. Harry Caudill, *Night Comes to the Cumberlands,* Boston, 1962.

10. C. Vann Woodward, *Origins of the New South,* Baton Rouge, 1951.

11. See especially Albert Memmi, *The Colonizer and the Colonized,* Boston, 1965; Frantz Fanon, *The Wretched of the Earth* and *Dying Colonialism,* New York, 1967; Pierre Jalee, *Pillage of the Third World,* 1965.

12. See *People's Appalachia, Appalachian Lookout. The Objector. Hardtimes, Appalachian South,* ASP.

13. Bob Tanner, "West Virginia: Occupied Colonial Territory," *The Objector,* Sept. 25, 1968.

14. William C. Blizzard, *Appalachian South,* Summer 1966.

15. Barry Barkan and R. B. Lloyd, "Picking Poverty's Pocket," *Article One,* May 1970.

16. Robert Blauner, "Ghetto Revolt: A Case of Colonialism," *Social Problems,* 1964.

17. Appalachian Regional Commission Research no. 9, *Capital Resources in the Central Appalachian Region,* Washington, 1969.

18. Richard Kirby, "Kentucky Coal: Owners, Taxes, Profits: A Study in Representation without Taxation," *Appalachian Lookout,* October 1969.

19. David Walls, Research Bulletins, *Appalachian Lookout,* 1968–1969.

20. Barkan and Lloyd, op cit.

21. Richard Diehl, "Appalachia Energy Elite and How International Energy Elite Rules," *Peoples' Appalachia,* March, April–May, 1970.

22. David Brooks, former chief economist, Bureau of Mines in talks to Appalachian Seminar, Clinch Valley College, Jan. 1970.

23. V. E. McKelvey, *Appalachia: Problems and Opportunities, Mineral Resources of the Appalachian Region,* Geological Survey Paper 580, Washington, D.C., 1968.

24. National Coal Association, Coal Data Book, Washington, D.C., 1968.

25. Virginia Department of Labor and Industry, Annual Report, 1968.

26. Penn Virginia Corporation Annual Report, 1968.

27. Harry Caudill, "Appalachia: The Dismal Land" in Larner and Howe, *Views from the Left,* New York, 1968.

28. Kirby, op cit.

29. Harry Caudill, "Poverty and Affluence in Appalachia," *Appalachian South,* Spring, 1966.

30. Blizzard, op cit.

31. Calvin Trillin, "U.S. Journal: Kentucky, the Logical Thing Cost-wise," *New Yorker,* December 27, 1969.

32. See Roman B. Aquizap and Ernest Vargas, "Technology, Power and Socialization in Appalachia," *Social Casework,* March 1970.

33. Memmi, op cit.

34. Edward L. Henson, "General Imboden and the Economic Development of Wise County 1880–81," *Historical Society of Southwest Virginia,* February 1965.

35. Fanon, *A Dying Colonialism.*

36. Tanner, op cit.

28. ALLIANCE RELEASES LAND OWNERSHIP STUDY FINDINGS:

Land Task Force Urges Community Response

from Mountain Life and Work

Appalachian Land Ownership Study

The Appalachian Land Ownership Study is an attempt to document land ownership patterns in the Appalachian Region and to describe their impact on rural communities. Representing the most comprehensive such study to date, the project was initiated by residents of the region in fall 1978, on the belief that land ownership patterns—especially corporate and absentee ownership—underlie or contribute to many of the policy issues that the region faces—property taxes for local services, poverty, economic development, loss of farmland, inadequate housing, energy production, environmental damage.

Conducted by the Appalachian Land Ownership Task Force, a coalition of community groups, scholars and individuals, associated with the Appalachian Alliance, the seven-volume study has involved the work of some sixty people in six states.

The study consists of seven volumes—a regional overview (Volume I) (see MLW, April 1981), and one volume for each of the six states studied: Alabama (Volume II), Kentucky (Volume III) (See MLW, May 1981), North Carolina (Volume IV), Tennessee (Volume V) (See MLW, September 1981), Virginia (Volume VI) (see MLW, June 1981), and West Virginia (Volume VII) (see MLW, July/August 1981).

Major funding for this study came from the Appalachian Regional Commission.

The project was administered by the Center for Appalachian Studies, Appalachian State University, with research coordinated from the Highlander Research and Education Center, New Market, Tennessee, and conducted by teams of citizens in each state.

—from the Preface

Only one percent of the local population, along with absentee holders, corporations and government agencies controls over one-half of the land surface in 80 counties scattered throughout the Appalachian Region, according to a study released on April 3 by the Appalachian Alliance and the Appalachian Regional Commission (ARC).

The land study released this week records, on a county-by-county basis, the largest landowners in each county, the assessed value of the land, the taxes each large landholder paid and the impact of these patterns on the well-being of local communities.

The study concludes that "land ownership patterns are a crucial element in explaining patterns of inadequate tax revenues and services, lack of economic development, loss of agricultural lands, lack of sufficient housing and the development of energy." As a result, relatively little land is actually available or accessible for use by local residents who are not large land-

holders. (See related article in this issue for more detailed review of findings.)

The two-year study was carried out by the Appalachian Land Ownership Task Force—a group of community organizations, scholars and individuals associated with the Appalachian Alliance, a coalition of groups and individuals which was formed after the 1977 floods in Central Appalachia.

The study is different from previous studies of Appalachia in that it grew directly out of the needs of people within the region who were attempting to understand how land ownership affected their own attempts to improve their communities.

And, unlike most government or academic studies, it was carried out by area residents who may be directly affected by the results. Over 65 individuals participated directly in the project and almost 100 are acknowledged in the forward for their help.

Funded by the Appalachian Regional Commission and private foundations, and supported through in-kind contributions from local and regional organizations, the report is the most comprehensive land study ever attempted in Appalachia. Researchers went into 80 courthouses and used tax rolls and county deed books to compile information on 55,000 parcels of land totaling almost 20 million acres of surface and mineral property acres.

Compiled in over 1800 pages of text and charts, the findings are contained in a regional volume and six other volumes which deal separately with each of the six states studied, including Virginia, West Virginia, Kentucky, Tennessee, North Carolina and Alabama.

Each state report contains a land ownership profile of each county studied in the state which includes: the top ten land owners and taxes paid, the top ten mineral owners and taxes paid, a comparison of whether these top owners live in the county or out of the county (absentee owners) and comparisons of taxes paid by individuals and corporations and of local residents as compared to absentee owners.

In addition, 19 of the 80 counties were selected for special case studies and researchers interviewed government officials, landholders and county residents to obtain an in-depth portrait of each county.

Reprinted from *Mountain Life and Work,* Vol. 57, No. 4 (April, 1981) pp. 13–20. Used with permission.

The study was administered by the Center for Appalachian Studies, of Appalachian State University, Boone, North Carolina, with research coordinated from the Highlander Research and Education Center, New Market, Tennessee.

Land Study Provides Data for Appalachian Study

The hard data on land ownership which forms the basis for the land report will likely attract the attention of regional writers and scholars for years to come. It has already had an impact upon many scholars and researchers throughout the Appalachian area. Some members of the Land Ownership Task Force are members of the Appalachian Studies Conference, a regional network of academics who teach courses on Appalachia at regional colleges and universities.

"I've always been concerned that Appalachian Studies would become a narrow academic discipline, confined to just classroom work and not paying any attention to what is going on in communities," explained Bill Horton, a professor of sociology who was one of the regional coordinators of the study. "This study shows that academics can find ways to work directly with community groups and that scholarly research can benefit local groups."

"What surprised me the most," he continued, "was the high degree of absentee and corporate ownership which we found *throughout* the region. We knew it was high in the coalfields from prior research, but we didn't expect to find it in the Southern mountains."

Horton's concern about absentee and corporate ownership was echoed by Dr. David Walls of the University of Kentucky's Appalachian Center. "It is clearly the first complete study of land ownership in the region and it's the first time anyone has tried to do a comparative study of several states using the same methodology. It gives us an up-to-date framework for understanding the kinds of power that flow from ownership of land and it documents the extent of corporate and absentee ownership of land in Appalachia." Walls himself was not involved in the land study, but he and the Appalachian Center have conducted similar community studies in eastern Kentucky.

Many of the researchers are also people who were involved in community organizing efforts during the 60's as part of the War on Poverty. They have been involved in efforts to regulate strip mining, to build low income housing, and to deal with problems of underfinanced public schools.

Study Builds on Two Decades of Earlier Attempts to Document Region's Status

The land survey may be the largest research project in Appalachia since the *Southern Appalachian Region:*

A Survey, was completed in 1962. That survey, which involved 11 state universities, and several colleges, and government agencies, focused on standard sociological categories such as population growth, manufacturing, tourism, religion, social welfare and health care, and folklore, but largely ignored problems of land ownership.

The importance of land holdings in Appalachia was given little recognition in academic writings on the region until national attention began to focus on widespread poverty and economic hardship in the early 60's.

The first writer to draw widespread attention to the problem of absentee ownership was Harry Caudill in his full-throated attack on corporate power, *Night Comes to the Cumberlands* in 1963. Following his expose of how the coal industry dominated east Kentucky, other writers began to examine the effects of corporate power upon the region and found similar patterns in Tennessee, West Virginia and Virginia.

Some of this interest was fed by attempts to organize the region's poor into a political force during the War on Poverty days of the Johnson Administration.

In 1969, Richard Kirby, a law student working for the Appalachian Volunteers, studied 11 eastern Kentucky coal counties and concluded that 31 individuals and corporations owned about four-fifths of eastern Kentucky's coal. He also concluded that more than 85 percent of the coal was owned by absentee interests and that these large investors paid very little in property taxes to county governments.

Researchers Point to Impact on Entire Appalachian Region

But while these findings have been fairly widely accepted, especially among Appalachian scholars and community activists, there has been little consensus about what the impacts were on the region as a whole or whether governmental action was needed to deal with inadequate taxation or special problems such as the unavailability of land for economic development or new housing.

The new land study attempts to deal with this gap both by describing the problems of land ownership in Appalachia and by recommending a course of action for citizens, as well as state and federal governments.

Community Organizing Efforts, Floods of 1977 Showed Need for Land Ownership Study

Much of the need for the land study grew out of continuing efforts by community groups to build regional coalitions which could argue for more corporate accountability, press for federal legislation dealing with strip mining or push for special assistance going to poor areas of the country.

Top Surface Owners

Source: Appalachian Land Study, 1981

NAME AND ADDRESS OF HEADQUARTERS	PRINCIPAL BUSINESS OF COMPANY	PRINCIPAL LOCATION OF HOLDINGS (TOTAL ACRES)
1. J. M. Huber Corp, Rumson, NJ	diversified products, especially timber and wood	Tennessee/Kentucky (226,805)
2. Bowaters Corporation (Hiwassee Land Co.) London, England	wood products	Tennessee (218,561)
3. N & W Railroad (Pocahontas Land & Pocahontas-KY)Roanoke, VA	railroad, transportation	West Virginia/Kentucky/ Virginia (178,481)
4. Koppers Co., Pittsburgh, PA	diversified chemicals & metals, coal gasification	Tennessee (169,796)
5. U. S. Steel, Pittsburgh, PA	steel	Alabama/Kentucky/West Virginia/Tennessee (168,911)
6. Georgia Pacific, Atlanta, GA	wood products	West Virginia/Virginia/ Kentucky (139,441)
7. Pittston Corporation, New York, NY	coal	Virginia (137,650)
8. Tenneco, Inc., (TN River, Paper and Pulp) Houston, TX	oil, land, packaging	Alabama (98,751)
9. Continental Oil (Consolidated Coal Co.) Stamford, CT	oil, gas, petro-chemicals, coal	West Virginia/Virginia/ Kentucky (84,403)
10. Gulf States, Tuscaloosa, AL	paper & wood products	Alabama (78,054)
11. Chessie Systems, Inc. (Western Pocahontas, C & O Railroad) Baltimore, MD	holding company, trans-port, petrochemical	Kentucky/West Virginia (76,805)
12. Weyerhauser, Settle, WA	wood products	Alabama (65,005)
13. Coal Creek Mining & Manuf. Knoxville, TN	coal and land	Tennessee (64,374)
14. Champion International, Stamford, CT	building materials, paper, furniture	Alabama/North Carolina (63,405)
15. Penn Virginia Corp., Philadelphia, PA	coal land	Virginia (62,893)
16. Berwind Land Co. (Kentland Co.) Philadelphia, PA	coal and natural resources, other diversified products	West Virginia/Kentucky/ Virginia (60,881)
17. Kentucky River Coal, Lexington, KY	coal lands	Kentucky (56,279)
18. Bethlehem Steel, Bethlehem, PA	steel and steel products	Kentucky/West Virginia (47,132)
19. Mead Corporation (Georgia Kraft Co.) Atlanta, GA	paper and wood products	Alabama (46,765)
20. Rowland Land Company, Charleston, WV	coal lands	West Virginia (44,867)
21. Bruno Gernt Estate, Allardt, TN	coal & tember	Tennessee (42,317)
22. Union Carbide, New York, NY	chemicals, carbon products	West Virginia (41,060)
23. Brimstone Co., Dover, DE	coal lands	Tennessee (40,261)
24. Soterra, Inc., Delaware, OH	unknown	Alabama (39,917)
25. Stearns Coal and Lumber Stearns, KY	coal land, timber	Tennessee (38,934)
26. The Southern Co (Alabama Power) Atlanta, GA	utility	Alabama (38,736)
27. Plateau Properties, Crossville, TN	land and mining	Tennessee (38,430)
28. Lykes Resources, Inc., (Youngston Mine) Pittsburgh, PA	steel	West Virginia/Virginia
29. Alabama By-Products, Birmingham, AL	coal, coke, chemicals	Alabama (34,365)
30. Natural Resources (Virginia Iron Coal & Coke) Detroit, MI	gas & coal	Virginia/Kentucky (33,155)

Part of the impetus for the study also came from young scholars in the region, many of whom teach Appalachian Studies, who are searching for new ways to put their academic training to work by analyzing how the region's economic and social problems were created.

Many of these individuals disagreed with the arguments that Appalachia was an underdeveloped or depressed region which needed to be brought into the mainstream of American life. Such popular analysis ran counter to the political and economic realities of activists' own communities. The coalfields, they argued, where much of the poverty and social problems are concentrated, cannot be described as underdeveloped when the region is tied directly to the economic centers of the country by rail, water, and road. This "depressed" area in fact supplies a large percentage of the nation's coal.

In other parts of the mountains outside the coalfields, they found distressingly similar problems which could not be explained solely on the basis of physical isolation. In the 70's, many of these scholars began to examine the impact of corporate power upon rural communities in Appalachia.

Appalachian Alliance Responds to 1977 Flood Disaster

The floods of April, 1977, brought about widespread suffering in many Central Appalachian communities. Many faced a major housing crisis. Two West Virginia counties hit hardest by the flooding, Mingo and Logan, had almost no land on the market suitable for housing. In fact, little land in those counties had changed hands in over 60 years. The efforts of state and federal agencies to respond to the floods were largely ineffective. In southern West Virginia, where 5,000 families were left homeless, local groups charged that state and federal agencies had created a second disaster through government inaction and red tape.

Residents in Mingo County formed the Tug Valley Recovery Center and issued a call for groups from throughout Appalachia to gather in Williamson, West Virginia to respond to the flood crisis. Out of the meeting in April, 1977, the Appalachian Alliance was born.

Communities, Scholars "Team Up" through Alliance Land Task Force

Members of the Appalachian Alliance began to talk about ways in which they could focus attention upon the problems of corporate ownership of land. A Task Force on Land was formed to take responsibility for the effort.

The Appalachian Alliance Task Force on Land Ownership provided a structure through which members of local community groups could work together with scholars on a common goal—to discover what impact land ownership had on other elements of community life.

When task force members learned that the Appalachian Regional Commission was considering a study of land, ownership and settlement patterns, they decided to seek ARC funds to help underwrite their own project.

Somewhat to their surprise, the task force members found the ARC interested in their ideas and they negotiated a contract to provide a study which would document ownership patterns in rural Appalachia looking at such factors as corporate ownership, absentee ownership, principal owners, and the relationships between ownership and land use.

The Task Force also agreed to investigate the impacts of these land ownership patterns upon economic and social developments in rural Appalachia and explore the relationships of land ownership patterns to land use, taxation structures, land availability for housing and industry and economic growth. The Task Force was formed as a coalition of over 50 groups and many individuals concerned about regional problems.

Attempting to deal with the severe housing crisis, local groups began to pressure West Virginia Governor Jay Rockefeller to force land companies to turn over land for housing. The land companies refused and Rockefeller was ultimately forced to start condemnation proceedings against Cotiga Development Company which was owned by a Pennsylvania family.

The West Virginia example was typical of many situations in the central coalfields where land ownership is historically concentrated in the hands of a few owners.

The results, issued April 3 after two years of work, are expected to generate more debate and controversy over the impact of land ownership on local communities.

Appalachian Land Dominated
by Few Outside Owners

Underdevelopment, Poor Housing and Community Services, Environment Linked to Outside Corporate Land Ownership

Ownership of land and minerals in rural Appalachia is concentrated among a few absentee and corporate owners, resulting in little land actually being available to local people, according to the Appalachian Land Study. These findings are crucial to explaining current patterns of inadequate local tax revenues and services, lack of economic development, loss of agricultural lands, lack of sufficient housing, the development of energy and environmental abuse, the study concludes.

The land study documents why Appalachia communities reap few of the benefits from the land and resource wealth in their localities.

Systematic land use planning and regulation are virtually non-existent in most rural Appalachian counties. In their absence, decisions over use of the land are made, *de facto,* by the larger and more powerful owners in terms of their own interests. While such decisions can dramatically affect an area's development, the affected public has little say in how these decisions are made.

The following is a summary of some of the major findings and conclusions of the report.

Land Ownership Patterns

• *The ownership of land and minerals in Appalachia is highly concentrated in the hands of a few owners.*

Only 1 percent of the local population, along with absentee holders, corporations, and government agencies, control at least 53 percent of the total land surface in the 80 counties.

Forty-one percent of the 20 million acres of land and minerals owned by 30,000 owners in the survey are held by only 50 private owners and 10 government agencies.

The federal government is the single largest owner in Appalachia, holding over 2 million acres.

• *Appalachia's land and mineral resources are absentee-owned.*

Nearly three-fourths of the surface acres surveyed are absentee-owned, that is, held by out-of-county and out-of-state owners. Four-fifths of the mineral acres in the survey are absentee-owned.

In one quarter of the survey counties, absentee-owned land in the sample represented over one-half of the total land surface in the county.

Contrary to expectations that absentee ownership would predominate only in the coal counties of central Appalachia, the study found a high level of absentee ownership throughout the 80-county survey area.

• *Large corporations dominate the ownership picture in much of Appalachia.*

Forty percent of the land in the sample and 70 percent of the mineral rights are owned by corporations. Forty-six of the top fifty private owners are corporations.

Corporate ownership, often for energy and resource exploitation, and government ownership, with associated tourism and recreation development, threatens the access people in the region have to the land and the control they exercise over its use.

Taxation of Land and Minerals

• *Mineral taxation.*

Though values of mineral properties have escalated rapidly in Appalachia, local governments have not experienced a corresponding increase of property tax revenues. Generally, in fact, mineral rights are greatly under-assessed for property tax purposes.

• *Taxation of surface rights.*

In general, taxes paid on rural lands are also low when compared to their rising market value. Overall, the amount of taxes paid per acre of surface in the survey is only 90 cents. Almost a quarter of the owners in the study pay less than 25 cents per acre.

In general, the large and the absentee owners tend to pay less per acre than the small, local owners pay.

• *Tax-exempt lands.*

Many counties in the survey contain substantial federal or other government holdings, which are exempt from local taxes. In the case of state-owned lands, no programs were found in the counties studied that compensate counties for the loss of this land from the tax base.

In the case of federal lands, "in-lieu of tax" payments are set at a minimum of 75 cents per acre, but this amount rarely is equal to the average tax paid by private owners.

Taken together, the failure to tax minerals adequately, the underassessment of surface lands, and the revenue loss from concentrated federal holdings has a marked impact on local governments in Appalachia.

30 Top Mineral Land Owners

Source: Appalachian Land Study, 1981

NAME AND ADDRESS OF HEADQUARTERS	PRINCIPAL BUSINESS OF COMPANY	PRINCIPAL LOCATION OF HOLDINGS (TOTAL ACRES)
1. Columbia Gas System Wilmington, DE	natural gas, holding company	West Virginia (342,236)
2. N & W Railroad (Pocahontas– KY. Pochontas Land) Roanoke, VA	railroad transportation	Kentucky/West Virginia (201,950)
3. Continental Oil (Consolidation Coal) Stamford, CN	oil, gas, petro-chemicals, coal	West Virginia/Kentucky (193,061)
4. Pittston Corporation New York, NY	coal	Virginia (185,254)
5. Occidental Petroleum (Island Creek Coal) Los Angeles, CA	gas, oil, petro-chemicals, coal	West Virginia/Kentucky/Virginia (144,741)
6. Berwind Land Company Philadelphia, PA	coal and natural resources	Kentucky (108,561)
7. American Natural Resources (Virginia Iron Coal and Coke) Detroit, MI	gas and coal	Virginia (80,705)
8. U. S. Steel Pittsburgh, PA	steel	Alabama/Tennessee/West Virginia (71,601)
9. Republic Steel Cleveland, OH	steel	Alabama (67,252)
10. Georgia Pacific Atlanta, GA	timber	West Virginia (67,027)
11. First National Bank of Birmingham Birmingham, AL	bank, holding company	Alabama (66,991)
12. Diamond Shamrock (Falcon Seaboard) Cleveland, OH	oil, gas, chemicals, coal	Kentucky (66,928)
13. Deep Water Properties (held through First National Bank, Birmingham) Birmingham, AL	financial trust	Alabama (66,038)
14. Cherokee Mining, Houston, TX	coal	Alabama (60,294)
15. National Steel, Pittsburgh, PA	steel	Kentucky (60,000)
16. Reynolds Metals (Reynolds Minerals) Richmond, VA	ore, chemicals, aluminum	North Carolina (58,000)
17. Wilson and Maryanne Wyatt Louisville, KY	attorney	Tennessee (57,614)
18. Chessie Systems (Western Pocahontas or B & O Railroad) Baltimore, MD	holding company, chemicals, transportation	West Virginia/Kentucky (56,830)
19. Rowland Land Company Charleston, WV	coal lands	West Virginia (54,474)
20. North Alabama Mineral Division Company (no address)	minerals	Alabama (50,141)
21. J. M. Huber, Rumson, NJ	diversified products, extensive timber & wood products	Tennessee (47,759)
22. Quaker State Oil Co. (Kanawha Hocking and Valley Camp Coal) Oil City, PA	oil	West Virginia (47,711)
23. Wesley West, Houston, TX	coal land	Alabama (46,682)
24. Beaver Coal Company, Beckley, WV	coal land	West Virginia (44,807)
25. Plateau Properties, Crossville, TN	land and mining	Tennessee (42,038)
26. Union Carbide, New York, NY	chemical, carbon products	West Virginia (41,689)
27. Alabama By-Products, Birmingham, AL	coal, coke, chemicals	Alabama (41,001)
28. Charleston National Bank Charleston, WV	bank, holding	West Virginia (40,566)
29. Cotiga Development Co. Philadelphia, PA	coal lands	West Virginia (39,648)
30. Mower Lumber, New York, NY	timber, coal lands	West Virginia (36,776)

The effect is to produce a situation in which a) the small owners carry a disproportionate share of the tax burden; b) counties depend upon federal and state funds to provide revenues, while the large, corporate and absentee owners of the region's resources go relatively tax free; and c) citizens face a poverty of needed services despite the presence in their counties of taxable property wealth, especially in the form of coal and other natural resources.

By conservative calculations, improved taxation of coal reserves in the major coal counties in the sample would more than quadruple the mineral taxes currently received. The new tax revenues would equal $16.5 million annually, or about $300,000 per country. Eight million dollars of the new revenue would be generated in eastern Kentucky, where they are desperately needed.

Economic Development

Land ownership patterns vary according to types of counties: corporate ownership is greatest in the counties with the greatest coal reserves; government ownership is associated with tourism and recreation counties; and individual ownership is highest in the major agricultural counties. In each type of county, land patterns affect the course of economic development which occurs.

• *Coal counties.*

In the major coal counties in the sample, 50 percent of the land surveyed is corporately held (compared to 31 percent in agricultural counties and 23 percent in tourism counties).

Some 72 percent of the land and 89 percent of the mineral rights are absentee owned, and the ownership is highly concentrated in the few hands. With absentee ownership, the wealth derived from the land and mineral resources is drained from the region; with concentrated ownership, a few, primarily corporate owners, can dominate the course of a county's development.

These concentrated absentee and corporate land ownership patterns serve as one limiting factor to economic diversification.

Without diversification, the areas become more vulnerable to the "booms and busts" of the coal industry. With "booms" come greater pressures upon limited land for housing, and greater demands upon already strained county budgets for more services. When "busts" occur, few non-coal jobs are available, use of the land for survival is limited for most of the population (even for tilling the hillsides), and, for many, outmigration becomes the only real choice.

• *Tourism and recreation counties.*

Recreation and tourism counties are associated both with large federal holdings (e.g., Forest Service, National Parks) and smaller, individual holdings, usually absentee owners holding the land for speculative purposes or for second-home developments.

The tourism and recreation industry which springs from the use of the land promotes a pattern of low wage and seasonal employment. At the same time, local residents face rising prices for land, housing and other goods due to the spending and speculation of the usually more affluent "outsiders."

• *Agriculture*

A dramatic decline of farming has occurred in the region: in the 80 counties surveyed, well over a million acres of farmland went out of agricultural production and 26 percent of the farming population left agriculture between 1969–74, the latest year for which figures are available.

If these rates continued throughout the 1970s, the new Agricultural Census will show that in a single decade, over half of Appalachia's farmers will have ceased farming and over a third of the region's farmland will have gone out of production.

The decline of farmland in the region is greatest where farmers are competing with other owners who hold the land for non-farm uses. The highest rate of farm decline was found in the survey counties in western North Carolina, with their tourism and second home developments, and eastern Kentucky, with their coal developments.

Housing

Land ownership patterns also are found to be a contributing factor to Appalachia's continuing housing crisis. In general, the greater the degree of corporate ownership, and the greater the degree of absentee ownership in a county, the more overcrowded the housing stock for local residents.

In the coalfield counties, tightly-held ownership of large blocks of land for possible energy development means that land for housing is often simply unavailable. Competition for what land is on the market sends prices soaring out of the reach of many low and middle income residents.

In recreation counties, land speculation connected with tourism and second home development also serves to inflate housing costs.

In the four southern coalfield counties of West Virginia where new housing is desperately needed, for instance, there were 12,579 *fewer* housing units in 1970 than in 1950. In these four counties, almost 90 percent of the land sampled is corporately held, amounting to well over two-thirds of the total surface of these counties.

New Energy Developments and the Environment

• *Large energy interests, primarily multinational ore and energy conglomerates are taking over coal resources in the traditional coalfields.*

The new owners are bringing with them new levels of capital and technology, including such developments as strip mining on a larger scale than ever before in the region, the growth of a synthetic fuels industry, and massive pump storage facilities.

• *Absentee and corporate control of land is extending to new areas.*

Absentee and corporate control of land has extended to such areas as central and northern West Virginia, midwest Virginia, southern Tennessee and northern Alabama. Related energy developments are likely to have major effects on these primarily agricultural areas.

• *Corporate and absentee interests are acquiring new minerals.*

New corporate and absentee ownership of minerals includes oil shale, oil and gas, uranium and bauxite. The extraction of these minerals is also likely to have major environmental consequences for the rural areas in which they are located.

Recommendations

The study provides a number of recommendations for dealing with land ownership patterns and their impacts, based upon a three fold strategy:

• *Land reform.*

Actions must be taken which deal with the underlying problems of concentrated and absentee ownership. Methods must be found by which people of the region can gain more access to, control over and benefit from the land and its resources.

• *Mitigation of impacts.*

Actions must be taken which mitigate the adverse effects of ownership patterns, even though they do not address directly the underlying structures of ownership.

Policies should insure patterns of land use beneficial to the entire community; provide adequate property tax revenue for the delivery of services; promote diverse economic development that is not destructive of local communities.

• *Land retention.*

Policies must be developed to prevent the rapidly occurring loss of local land for local use, including economic and housing development, as well as agricultural use.

29. THE KENTUCKY WAY: RESISTANCE TO DEPENDENCY UPON CAPITALISM IN AN APPALACHIAN REGION

Rhoda H. Halperin

INTRODUCTION

This essay focuses on "the Kentucky way" and resistance to dependency upon capitalism in an unstudied region of Appalachian America. The analysis derives from a six year ethnographic field study in a 10 county region of northeastern Kentucky (Halperin 1990). The region does not fit the conventional stereotypes of Appalachia, however. It is not presently, nor historically has it ever been a coal mining region; it is not mountainous; neither is it geographically isolated. Rather, it is somewhere in between the core and the periphery of economic life in the United States. The basic livelihood strategies operating in this region are generalizable to many other parts of the world where state systems undergo simultaneous industrialization, deindustrialization, urbanization and resistance to urbanization. The rural parts of Europe, areas of the Texas border, even Vermont's Appalachia might be cases in point.

The fieldwork began several years ago when, a very bright student, early in her graduate career one day in my office adopted the tone of a confessional and announced that she spoke two dialects of English:

"country" and "city." She paused, and with some tension in her voice, told me how much she feared lapsing into "country" English while concentrating so hard to speak "city" (standard) English to her university professors. After I assured here that I would think no less of her if she used either dialect, she volunteered that she used "country" English at her parents' home in rural of Kentucky. There she experienced another sort of anxiety. If she slipped into "city" English, her Mom and Dad would consider her snobbish and uppity. The tensions evident in that anecdote—tensions between country and city, urban educational institutions and subsistence farm families, are only some of the many strains people feel as they resist dependency upon capitalism.

All of the key elements of the Kentucky way must be understood in the context of regionally based, three generation extended families. I will begin by describing the activities of one typical extended family in

This article was prepared specifically for the third edition of *Appalachia: Social Context Past and Present*. Used by permission of the author.

this Northeastern Kentucky region. The family is typical because it is three generational in structure, it is involved in a multicentric economy of small family farms and subsistence gardens, factory based wage labor, and an informal periodic marketplace system. Family imperatives dominate people's choices of work tasks, places of residence and overall patterns of life and livelihood. All of the important clues to understanding the relationships between the Kentucky way and resistance to dependency upon capitalism are contained in the following brief scenario:

Harry, a former employee of Coca Cola and Ilene Smith, now retired from her job in the city as a dentist's receptionist, along with their daughter Sue, and son-in-law Nathan, are planning their economic activities for a fall weekend. Harry and Ilene were born and raised in the same county in the country where his family owned a sheep farm and hers were tenant farmers. They now live in one household in a hamlet in an area between the country and the city that I have called the "shallow rural." Shallow rural contrasts with deep rural ("the country") and with urban, "the city". Sue and Nathan (both temporary wage laborers in a nearby factory) live with their two children, a son, four years old, and a daughter, six years old, in another household in a mobile home park six miles from Sue's parents. The following activities must be coordinated. Harry has two housepainting jobs to finish before the weather turns cold; he also has several indoor house-renovating jobs. He and Ilene are regular vendors in the rotating periodic marketplace system (an organized system of "flea markets"), and they are eager to sell off the goods they have accumulated over the summer by attending garage sales and auctions. Harry specializes in selling (illegal) guns, Ilene in quilts and antiques. It is not unusual for Harry and Ilene to clear $400 to $1200 per weekend in market sales. Ilene has a talent for picking up bargains at garage sales. She will then clean her goods, repair them, or combine them with other items to produce highly saleable goods. She can transform old things worth a few dollars into items that sell for $35 or more. Harry has an extensive network of clients for his guns since he is a trustworthy dealer. Harry and Ilene do not report their income.

The best day to sell at the Redside market, a major marketplace in the system, is Saturday or Sunday. Ilene is also very concerned about "putting up" her beans and cucumbers for the winter; if she does not process them in time, both beans and cucumbers will grow too large and tough to be eaten. Ilene's sister is ill, and Ilene must take her some cooked food sometime during the weekend. As temporary wage laborers, Sue and Nathan work six days each week; sometimes they work double shifts.

Ilene and Harry decide to set up their booth at the Redside market on Saturday, the busiest day. They take their grandchildren with them. Sue and Nathan will harvest the beans and cucumbers and prepare food to take to Ilene's sister after work on Saturday. On Sunday they will all go to Sue's aunt's farm in the country for their Sunday dinner.

In the first part of this essay, I will discuss the Kentucky way as a cultural idiom and livelihood strategy for maintaining identity and autonomy in a rapidly changing post industrial economy. I will then illustrate how the strategy works by elaborating upon Nathan's experience as a rural person, carpenter, wage laborer, member of a three generation extended family and, most importantly, as someone who sees himself as a practitioner of the Kentucky way. There are female counterparts to Nathan in this regional system; there are also younger and older people who either have experienced or will experience his work patterns (Halperin 1990). The economic activities of all of these people are firmly embedded in regionally based extended families with ties to land.

THE REGIONAL CONTEXT OF THE KENTUCKY WAY

The region is predominantly agrarian with small holdings. The landholdings in this region are, and have always been small, privately owned, subsistence-oriented units that use the labor of three-generation extended families (Precourt 1983). Only 2% of the farms in the region are larger than 500 acres. The average farm size in the region is 121 acres, and this is considered by most to be a large farm.

The agrarian holdings are themselves diverse, however. Some are small family farms with a few acres devoted to cash crops (primarily burley tobacco) and one or two acres planted in feed for livestock. Other agrarian holdings are homesteads, that is households located on small holdings with subsistence gardens. Still others are combinations of small farms, gardens, and workshops (welding, crafts, furniture, repairs, etc.). The agrarian holdings provide the baselines from which people negotiate their relationships to factory-based wage labor and to the informal economy of a rotating periodic marketplace system.

The "shallow rural" is the most problematic, as well as the most interesting and complex part of the region. It is an unstudied, unnamed, and uncategorized grey area between country and city. Small holdings with substantial kitchen gardens and plots of tobacco sit next to shopping malls, tract housing developments and mobile home parks. The rotating periodic marketplace system is located in the shallow rural along with the factories that employ temporary wage laborers. Thus, in the shallow rural we find the institutional representations of the formal economy of industrial capitalism coexisting alongside the informal economy of periodic marketplaces.

In contrast to the shallow rural, the deep rural is solidly agrarian. In one typical deep rural county, ninety six percent of the 206 square miles of land is farm land. People who live in the shallow rural are migrants from the deep rural parts of the region. A person who speaks "country English" is not at all conspicuous in the shallow rural; in the city, he or she will be labelled a "hillbilly." By the same token, speakers of "city English" are conspicuous as outsiders in the factories and marketplaces of the shallow rural. A complex infrastructure of superhighways and county roads weave their way through the shallow rural, linking it easily to cities in the north and south.

The Kentucky way is not unique to Kentucky or to Appalachia. The economic strategies of the Kentucky way are peasant-like in the sense that they are subsistence oriented and driven by ties to kin and to homeplace. The economic strategies are rural and agrarian. Indeed the same kinds of strategies operate with variations and transformations in many rural parts of the world, for example, what Daniella Weinberg calls, peasant wisdom in Europe (Switzerland) and what James Scott calls "everyday forms of peasant resistance" (1985) in Malaya. The implications of these common peasant strategies have for accomplishing identity, autonomy and a sense of control over life and livelihood are also similar, or at least comparable in many rural cultures. What makes the Kentucky case so compelling is its immediacy and its proximity to urban industrial cities in the U.S.; the Kentucky way is intensifying and transforming on a daily basis.

The practitioners of the Kentucky way are difficult to classify: They work constantly but officially they appear as unemployed, retired, or both. They live in rural areas and many work in factories or commute to jobs in the city, but they are not counted, nor do they define themselves as factory workers. They plant gardens and cash crops, but they are not farmers in the conventional sense of that term. They buy and sell goods in colorful, bustling marketplaces that form a full blown rotating periodic marketplace system of the sort found in many third world countries—Mexico and China— to name two, but they are not traders or merchants. Their work tasks are varied, numerous and constant, however, and these tasks change weekly, seasonally and generationally. These facts about the multiple livelihood strategies of rural working class people provide some of the clues to "the Kentucky way" and to understanding resistance to dependency upon capitalism.

I want to emphasize at the outset that it is not capitalism per se that people resist in rural Kentucky; rather people resist *dependency* upon capitalism. Resistance here is positive, energizing, and it has the effect of denying claims made by superordinate classes and by the state (resistance to proletarianization and to taxation). (1) If anything, it is seen as a revitalization of rural culture. Kin networks and a mosaic of economic processes provide the keys to understanding resistance to capitalist dependency. People use capitalism and its products in ingenious ways and their livelihood strategies combine elements of both capitalist and noncapitalist systems.

"The Kentucky Way"

What is "the Kentucky way" and how does it enable people to resist dependency upon capitalism? The Kentucky way is a cultural idiom that refers to the complex relationships between economy, culture and kinship. The Kentucky way refers to a broad spectrum of practical skills and of knowledge of local resources. People repeat the expression "the Kentucky way" often, sometimes with nostalgia, sometimes with regret, but always with affection and respect. The idiom evokes immediate associations—sympathies between people, common lifestyles, beliefs and sentiments. It identifies people with one another. "You must record" the Kentucky way "before it disappears," said a young country woman. I was flattered by her willingness to give me such a responsibility; I was also taken aback by the task she had assigned to me—namely to salvage something so essential to the culture before it changes or disappears. The Kentucky way provides the template for making a living and for living itself. Often people speak of the Kentucky way in a religious idiom, especially when they are talking about work. People say such things as "The idle body is a sin," or "I am working for the Lord," or "God sits above the government." As a system of local knowledge and practices, doing things "the Kentucky way" allows people to exercise control over their livelihood and provides them with a sense of autonomy that would not be possible were they to confine their economic and social relationships to an urban-based, cash economy.

At its core, "the Kentucky way" is about maintaining livelihood and maintaining rural culture. It includes commitments to kin, to hard work and self-sufficiency, to freedom and to the land, to generosity and reciprocity, and to certain kinds of practical knowledge. Economic knowledge itself is based on rural skills—knowing something about everything within the appropriate male and female domains. Maintaining a general, rather than a specialized repertoire of skills is extremely important. People resist becoming specialists for specialists must rely on others to perform tasks for them (Hicks 1973). Being a generalist is a strategy of self-reliance, a mark of one's versatility and flexibility, and one's ingenuity and cleverness. In this region, self-reliance does not serve to isolate people. It is not individualistic or self-serving. Rather it is a form of outreach to kin and to neighbors in the context of offering multiple goods and services in multiple arenas.

The fact that people are so versatile creates great flexibility for livelihood strategies. Not only can people choose easily between various work tasks, they can switch from one task to another in accordance with the needs of family members and with the opportunities made available through kinship ties.

For both men and women, knowledge of the local ecology is essential for knowing when and how to hunt, fish and gather, as well as for knowing when and how to clear, plant, and harvest. Hunting and fishing are not mere sport in this area; they provide essential protein, which when combined with garden produce and meat from livestock (primarily pigs) when available, add up to a large portion of daily subsistence. Knowledge of the land, its virtues, limitations, and seasonal patterns, are certainly important for all agricultural societies, but "the Kentucky way" reinforces the importance of hunting, fishing and agrarian skills in combination with the mechanical skills necessary for keeping machinery, vehicles and households functioning as self-sustaining units.

Being a "good Kentucky woman" (homemaker and worker in the broadest sense of these terms) is an essential part of "the Kentucky way." Women pass down knowledge of food production (gardening), processing (canning and freezing) and storage techniques from generation to generation. For women as well as for men, knowing how to be resourceful is regarded as the essence of the good person. Women also resist specialization, but in ways that are both similar to and different from that of men. For both men and women, maintaining one's position in trade networks and social groups leads to knowledge about which marketplaces are best for selling or buying particular items. Men and women sell and trade different kinds of things, however, and they engage in different kinds of social groups. Women's social groups are often church-based. Women exchange goods, provide help with children, and donate time for home health care. Men's social groups are smaller and more informal. It is not uncommon to see men gathered in groups of two or three on porches, in the aisles of marketplaces, or almost anywhere.

On another level, "the Kentucky way" signifies certain kinds of ideal relations to the means of production, especially to the land. Owning land, "private property," however small one's plot may be, provides a buffer against dependency upon outsiders. A piece of land large enough for a large subsistence garden and tobacco plot (Tobacco, until recently, was the main cash crop.) is most desirable. In this context, ties to rural homeplaces can be understood not only as sources of land, but as reservoirs of local knowledge and the resources this knowledge provides.

The Kentucky way also indicates relationships to regional and state authorities. It is a form of identity, an attachment to rural lifestyles. Disdain for industrialism and for economic development is part of the Kentucky way. I remember being driven around the region one afternoon when my attention was directed to the posted signs that read: "Let Toyota be your neighbor." "This is terrible," said one of the region's residents. "This is ruining our farms." Many people express strong resentments concerning the defacement of the countryside by foreign industrialists. One hears negative comments about the governor's lack of sensitivity to the traditional needs of the people. In part, the negativism stems from the fact that people do not perceive jobs as providing a secure or sufficient livelihood. A disdain for industry is combined with disdain for those in power and for those who control the means of production. "People are made into machines in those factories," one man told me repeatedly. The Toyota plant, which opened within the last few years, did indeed encompass the entire horizon. I was urged to photograph one particular spot in which the plant spanned the horizon; and barn occupied the background, and a lone horse, the foreground. "See," one man said, "all the trees have been cut down; no berries and no rabbits could live there now."

Participating in the Kentucky way carries certain obligations as well as certain rights. Critical among the obligations are those to family members. Making a living must never interfere with these obligations. If, for example, a young adult chooses to take a job that is located too far for kin to visit easily, he or she will be the object of criticism. Also, staying in school too long for the pursuit of advanced degrees can be negatively regarded. Questions from parents such as, "Haven't you been in school long enough; when are you going to get a *real* job?" are frequently heard.

Perhaps one of the best ways to understand the Kentucky way is as a form of what Daniela Weinberg has called the traditional ideology of "peasant wisdom:" "the wisdom to remain free of outside control by owning and managing a variety of resources, and free of debt by running a self supporting household" (1975:196). The key component of peasant wisdom, Kentucky style, is control over one's day to day life, if not one's destiny. Control requires maintaining a network of people for support in times of need and securing sufficient private property in land such that one does not rely upon the outside for loans. Loans from kin are preferable to loans from banks or loans from non-kin. The kinsperson who is in the best position to lend money and provide work for the unemployed kin is the person who owns a farm.

The bottom line for practitioners of the Kentucky way is that work tasks are oriented towards meeting basic needs without overconsumption or conspicuous consumption. One afternoon in a produce stand the size of an eight by ten shed, people were talking about how "we don't want for anything; we live high on the hog." People are very sophisticated in knowing how to obtain "everything we need and more."

We can begin to see a subtle, but distinct ideology of equality as part of the Kentucky way. It appears in statements such as "We're all kin here" (Bryant 1981, Beaver 1986, Foster 1988). A highly respected judge in the region told me that "it takes awhile to become accepted here, but once you are, people take you in as family." It is not that people do not recognize differences in income, education, and skill, but that these differences are not emphasized. People's resistance to specialization contributes to egalitarianism. On a more subtle level, the ideology of equality operates in the form of people's willingness to give freely and generously of their time and their resources to help kin and neighbors on a regular basis, not just in times of crisis. University students whose families grow burley tobacco are expected to go home to help out with the harvesting and processing of tobacco regardless of how pressing their academic responsibilities might be. Needless to say, there are conflicts for many people who grow up with the Kentucky way. Work responsibilities must be compatible with responsibilities to family. People make constant adjustments to accommodate family needs in accordance with the basic exigencies of livelihood. People without families are objects of pity.

One of the most important features of "the Kentucky way" then, is its emphasis on the benefits of the country, whether this involves living in the country or maintaining close ties to people and land, or both. People see greater opportunities to use a variety of resources in the country. They see themselves as "belonging to the country" and as "country people", even though many of them live less than five miles from a city. Belonging to the country involves the mastery of practical knowledge through apprenticeships and close intergenerational ties. Older Kentuckians lament the proliferation of young "shut ins", a folk term for people who live in apartments, work at unskilled and low-paying wage labor jobs, and watch television and drink beer in their spare time. In analytical terms, these are people who, by refusing to engage in learning the spectrum of practical skills, prevent the production and reproduction of local practical knowledge. From the point of view of older people in the region, these young adults are putting themselves in a very vulnerable position. That is, without practical local knowledge of agrarian skills, people become completely dependent upon cash generated in the wage labor sector. When they are inevitably laid off, unless family members "help them out" they must rely upon the welfare system, something that is an anathema to "the Kentucky way" because it flies in the face of self-sufficiency and local autonomy.

People talk about not putting all your eggs in one basket, an idiom that refers not only to being a generalist, but to operating in multiple economic sectors, in this case, the agrarian, the marketplace, and the wage labor sectors. Nathan is an example of a person who uses his rural skills and his ties to his own and his wife's extended family, to resist participation in the wage labor system, and thus, to resist dependency upon capitalism.

Nathan, now 28 years old, was born on a farm in Southern Kentucky. From the age of 14, he worked as a carpenter's apprentice for a man with whom he had an excellent working relationship. The carpentry business was good, and Nathan worked extremely hard. At the age of 21, Nathan moved to Cincinnati, where he worked as a wage laborer for a wholesale food company. When the food company went out of business, he went to work as a temporary wage laborer for the Goody Company, a large manufacturing firm where he held a similar kind of job maintaining machinery, operating a fork-lift truck, and performing a variety of other tasks in the factory. He obtained this temporary job from an agency in the city. While working for the Goody Company, he met his present wife, Sue, who is also 28 years old. Shortly thereafter, all temporary employees at Goody were notified of termination. Sue quickly found another temporary job at the Rinterline plant and, after one month of employment, learned of a few openings in the machine recycling area. She told Nathan about these jobs. He applied and was immediately hired because of his machine operator's experience at the Goody facility. Because both Sue and Nathan were temporary employees, they could both be hired at Rinterline.

Nathan's job in truck part recycling at the Rinterline plant was dangerous and dirty. Everything in this area of the plant was covered with grease. As a temporary employee, Nathan had to furnish and wash his own work clothes. In this particular work area, a set of clothes lasted approximately two weeks at the most. The wage was $4 per hour with no benefits of any sort. Sue told me that Nathan was exposed to petroleum products and no mask was provided. She said also that the chemical compounds used to clean the recycled parts nearly ruined Nathan's wedding band. The floors were slippery from the grease and this made it difficult to move 70 lb parts from one station to another. Nathan's back became very sore from several bad falls on the floor. Since grinding metal was part of the job, goggles were provided by Rinterline. The metal particles were so small, however, that they still occasionally came behind the goggles. Three weeks into his employment, a piece of metal slipped into Nathan's eye. He was transported to an eye specialist in Fenwick who removed the fragment. The doctor told Nathan and Sue that the cornea was severely scratched, placed a patch over the eye, and sent Nathan back to work. The Rinterline Company paid for the physician's bill, but did not "give Nathan a break work station wise." Sue repeatedly told me that "Nathan really hates Rinterline. He would look out the back door and exclaim that Fenwick had been converted into a moonscape—all the trees plowed down and only brown grass remaining, the horizon was dotted with factories instead of farms." Nathan himself said to me that he "felt dirty, like a peon! I know I can do better for myself."

Nathan walked off the job after four months as a temporary wage laborer at Rinterline. He began self-employment as a painter and carpenter. Much of his work, especially initially was obtained through connections long established by his father in law, Harry Smith who is a veteran wage laborer and now market vendor.

"Country people," particularly men, who quit their wage labor jobs in favor of odd jobs, or who decide to intensify their activities in the agrarian and marketplace sectors, often see themselves as "opting out of the system" or as "working outside the system." Discussions about the dangers of factory work, the lack of concern for safety on the part of owners and managers came out in many cases. People see themselves as resistant to factory work, and their resistance takes many forms. People see their investments in kin networks as providing them with flexibility, with options to leave wage labor jobs and establish other means of livelihood.

I would like to end with the following anecdote because it illustrates some of the rawness manifested by resistance not only to dependency upon capitalism, but to urbanism and everything that urbanism represents. Again, I return to Nathan.

One day I was driven around the countryside by Nathan and Sue. They were in the front seat. I was in the back with one of the students working on this project. We had just finished lunch "Dinner," in folk terms, at a charming old restaurant in the deep rural part of the region where the old soda fountain was still in place, complete with glass goblets with Coca Cola written on them in script. Nathan took great pride in showing us the countryside, almost as though all of it belonged to him.

I knew that Nathan had been working odd jobs with his brother for some time. I also knew that he had had a series of odd jobs since quitting his job at Rinterline. I was not quite sure what kinds of jobs they were, but I know some had been obtained through his brother, and others through his father in law. Since he seemed rather relaxed, yet in full control of the situation, quite literally in the driver's seat, I took the opportunity to ask him some rather pointed questions. He and his brother had been renovating houses. Some of the work had been obtained through a contracting company. He had also told me that he had done some other jobs "on his own", and I was extremely curious to know about the work in detail. He appeared to regard the work with

a degree of flippancy, which aroused my interest all the more. On the one hand, he seemed proud of his control of his working life and of his partnerships working with his brother and father in law. On the other hand, he tried to convey the impression that he did not regard the work with any degree of seriousness. When I asked about how long the renovations would take, and whether the work was difficult, he told me "not very long; it's easy work." Yet, at least at this particular time, his "easy work" occupied the better parts of his days. I could not help but think that he was purposely downplaying his efforts because he was not declaring the income. Since he seemed already to have a chip on his shoulder, I figured I had nothing to lose in pursuing the issues a bit further. He had mentioned a job refinishing floors for a woman in the next town, a job he had obtained through his uncle. "How much can you make on that floor?" I asked him directly, to which he responded. "It's none of your business."

While Nathan's wife seemed to cringe at his apparent rudeness, I was impressed by the power of his convictions—the strength of his voice and his forthrightness. I even felt that it was the first time he was being completely honest with me by resisting my question. With the question about his income, I became to him the voice of urban authority—urban power, the power of standard English. Usually he kept his anger at that authority under a veil of politeness, albeit a politeness with an edge.

The unit of economic organization here is the three generation extended family, not the individual. People in the regionally based kin networks work in the agrarian, marketplace and factory economies and they coordinate their activities through informal systems of exchange. Marketing is only one piece of the Kentucky way, but it is an important piece because it is both flexible and lucrative. Gardening is the most reliable livelihood strategy, but it is not sufficient in and of itself. Cash cropping and factory work are both risky, the former because of declining prices and federal subsidies for tobacco and the latter because of the constant lay-offs and the alienating nature of the work. Resistance to dependency upon capitalism, in a system that is indeed capitalistic, requires all the creative combinations of capitalist and pre-capitalist, formal and informal economies.

The essence of the Kentucky way is not a romantic notion; it is fundamentally practical—meticulously tailored to fit the local economy, ecology, and family structure. Preparedness is essential to the Kentucky way. It is positive and represents a great deal of foresight and planning. In order to be prepared, people marshall resources (including labor through kin networks) and knowledge to deal with a range of eventualities. In the face of plant closings, plummeting tobacco subsidies, a less and less adequate minimum wage, and the seasonal vagaries of agricultural cycles, the Kentucky way represents both continuity with past forms of rural economic organization and some creative solutions to what are becoming widespread economic conditions.

In sum, the Kentucky way is a system of local, practical knowledge that is essentially rural ("country"), and that defines "the way we do things here." The essence of the Kentucky way involves making ends meet in the self reliant, steadfast, Kentucky style. The Kentucky way involves continuities as well as transformations and reinterpretations of kin and community in relationship to livelihood. Probably the most remarkable aspect of the Kentucky way is that it operates, for the people in this study, outside of traditional community contexts. The Kentucky way involves an expansion of the range of kinship ties and an expansion of the tasks of kin network members. It also involves an expanded sense of what is local, for local refers to a region, not a community or even a county. It is clear that local does not include the city. People mobilize their ties to family members in the region as a form of outreach to people with diverse skills, knowledge and resources. One part of the family network quite literally "holds on to the land" (Hall and Stack 1982) while other parts engage in a diverse set of livelihood strategies. People always maintain the option of coming back to the land, either temporarily or permanently. The most important point to realize is that the goal of economic activity is to sustain the family network.

REFERENCES CITED

Beaver, Patricia, Rural Community in the Appalachian South. (Lexington: University Press of Kentucky, 1986.)

Bryant, Carlene, We're All Kin: A cultural study of an East Tennessee Mountain Neighborhood. (Knoxville: University of Tennessee Press, 1981.)

Foster, Stephen William, The Past is Another Country. (Berkeley: University of California Press, 1988.)

Gaventa, John, Power and Powerlessness: Quiescence and Rebellion in an Appalachian Valley. (Urbana: University of Illinois Press, 1980.)

Hall, Robert and Carol Stack (eds.), Holding on the Land and the Lord. (Athens: University of Georgia Press, 1982.)

Halperin, Rhoda H., The Livelihood of Kin: Making Ends Meet "The Kentucky Way." (Austin: University of Texas Press, 1990.)

Hicks, George, Appalachian Valley. (New York: Holt, Rinehart and Winston, 1976.)

Lewis, Helen, The Colony of Appalachia. In Colonialism in Modern America: The Appalachian Case, edited by Helen Matthews Lewis, Linda Johnson, and Donald Askins. (Boone, N.C.: Appalachian Consortium Press, 1978.)

Precourt Walter, The Image of Appalachian Poverty in Alan Batteau (ed.) Appalachia and America. (Lexington: University of Kentucky Press, 1983.) Pp. 86–110.

Scott, James, Weapons of the Weak. (New Haven: Yale University Press, 1985.)

Walls, David, Internal Colony or Internal Periphery: A Critique of Current Models and an Alternative Formulation. In Colonialism in Modern America: The Appalachian Case. Helen Matthews Lewis, Linda Johnson, and Donald Askins. (Boone, N.C.: Appalachian Consortium Press, 1978.)

Weinberg, Daniela, Peasant Wisdom: Cultural Adaptation in a Swiss Village. (Berkeley: University of California Press, 1975.)

Whisnant, Modernizing the Mountaineer: People, Power and Planning in Appalachia. (New York: Burt Franklin and Company, 1980.)

NOTES

1. Scholars are just beginning to address heterogeneity within the Appalachian culture area. While there is no question that Appalachian people have experienced political, economic, and cultural domination, the assumption has been that their responses have necessarily been negative (Gaventa 1980; Whisnant 1980, 1983, Lewis 1978, Walls 1978).

30. ENVIRONMENTAL THREATS IN APPALACHIA

Paul J. Nyden

Charleston Gazette
Charleston, West Virginia

A malevolent Midas, King Coal devastates what it touches. A century ago, coal began molding new communities from the Appalachian wilderness, a process described eloquently by scholars such as Ronald D. Eller and David Corbin. For a century, depressions alternated with booms. When production and employment were up, coalfield families shared some measure of prosperity.

During the 1980s, an irreversible job decline has accompanied rising production. Fewer and fewer miners share in the prosperity enjoyed by the industry today.

An ever-declining percentage of money generated by coal remains in the coalfields.

During the coalfield depression after World War I, 200,000 miners lost their jobs in five years—between 1923 and 1927. When continuous mining machines revolutionized underground production after World War II, another 275,000 jobs disappeared between 1948 and 1965.

Reprinted from *Proceedings of the Conference on Environment in Appalachia,* Appalachian Center, University of Kentucky (1990), pp. 3–13. Used by permission.

Life during coalfield depressions has always been difficult. In 1936, nearly half of all mountain families were on federal relief rolls. [Eller, p. 240.] During the 1950s, tens of thousands of mining families left for the factories of Detroit and the mills of Cleveland.

Job losses since 1980 seem even more permanent. The hollow, the core of coalfield society, is being destroyed—culturally, economically, physically, environmentally—more completely than it was during the 1920s, 1930s, or 1950s.

Is the human and environmental damage from mining worth the costs of mining to society, especially during an era of declining employment?

Go to Gary Hollow, deep in the coalfields of McDowell County. Drive up any one of a dozen hollows near Charleston, the state's most prosperous city. A few houses and boarded-up schools mark towns where hundreds of mining families once lived. Picturesque tipples rust away on rail sidings or are torn down. Where long strings of rail cars once hauled coal out of the hollows, overloaded coal trucks rumble down narrow roads from small drift mines or strip jobs. They dump their coal in unsightly stockpiles in the valley, generating clouds of dust and blackening the Kanawha River with oily sludges.

Look at the mountains. Many are still scarred from unregulated stripping of the 1950s and 1960s. Today, mountains are literally moved by huge draglines that excavate as many as 12 or 14 coal seams from a single mountain. Huge dozers push what is left into nearby hollows and valleys. The resulting "valley fills" in West Virginia and Kentucky are among the largest man-made structures east of the Mississippi River.

Loggers usually precede the strippers, removing trees and leaving bare earth to wash over gardens and under homes. The Surface Mining Control and Reclamation Act of 1977 regulates mining. In the forests, compliance with environmental standards is purely voluntary in many states, including West Virginia.

Oversight of timbering by government officials, environmental groups and the press is virtually non-existent. The Wilderness Society is a notable exception. It regularly publishes studies on the exploitation of national forest lands by private timber interests.

Household trash litters many hills and creeks. More sinister wastes—chemical drums, electric transformers leaking PCBs—pollute others.

Mountain creeks run increasingly acidic from mine drainage and acid rain. The most acidic rain ever recorded in the United States fell in Wheeling, West Virginia. It had a pH of 1.5—as strong as battery acid. Typically, West Virginia rain is 20 times more acidic than natural rainfall. [National Clear Air Coalition]

Drive off the main mountain roads. Oil and gas rigs poke the ground, seeking more mineral wealth to exploit. Where drilling is successful, pipelines leave long, bare trails from wellheads to collection tanks and main pipelines.

Environmental protection was never a primary value of the early coal barons. In Eller's words, "Entering upon a region of serried hills matted in a dense forest of virgin hemlocks, poplars, oaks, and laurel, they left the land scarred and barren, covered with the black residue of coking ovens, coal tipples, and slag piles." (Eller, p. 199.)

Today, potential environmental damage is far greater than it was at the turn of the century, or a generation ago. Stripping is on the rise, and accounts for more than 60 percent of all coal mined nationally. The largest strip mines use drag-lines that can hold small houses in their buckets.

LANDFILLS

The newest environmental threat in Appalachia is posed by the mammoth trash dumps developers hope to place in rural counties throughout the mountains. West Virginia has 30 pending applications for "Class A" landfills, each of which would take in at least 10,000 tons of garbage a day—twice the amount generated by the state's 1.9 million residents. Appalachia's hollows could become a dumping ground for the Northeast.

The developers argue state-of-the-art dumps will protect the environment more effectively than smaller, poorly-run landfills now scattered across the mountains. West Virginia's new solid waste law, passed last year, might open the door to the developers. Tougher regulations are squeezing out the smaller dumps, many of which are operated by cities and counties. The initial capital investment needed to comply with new state standards could squeeze all but the largest companies out of the business.

In some counties, landfill developers are soliciting community support with promises of construction contracts, permanent jobs, free local trash disposal and substantial "tipping fees" for host counties. Millions of dollars in new revenue annually could appeal to officials in poor rural counties.

Some coal companies are becoming interested in the landfill business. West Virginia coal sells for about $30 a ton. Norman Steenstra, a former small coal operator who now handles environmental issues for the West Virginia Citizen Action Group, said $2 a ton is a good profit in today's coal business. The city of Baltimore will pay up to $60 a ton to dispose of trash, Steenstra said. Some New Jersey cities pay between $80 and $100 a ton.

If disposal payments were only $50 per ton, a landfill accepting 10,000 tons a day would generate $156 million a year, if it operated six days a week. Gross revenue from two such landfills would equal the state's $1.74 billion annual budget in just over five years.

Trash could replace coal as the major money-maker for some companies.

Last year, Anker Energy based in Morgantown sold 4.5 million tons of coal. Vice President Kenneth James said his company has already spent $1 million promoting a proposed 600-acre landfill in Upshur County. Anker is prepared to spend up to $30 million before the first ton of trash is dumped on an old strip mine the company owns near Philippi. Anker officials predict annual profits of at least $5 million from the landfill.

The Ashland Independent recently reported 16 percent of all New Jersey's garbage is being buried in Kentucky. Addington Inc., a major coal producer in Kentucky, West Virginia and Ohio, makes 20 percent of its income from landfills, including a controversial 937-acre site in Greenup County, Kentucky. [Coal, April 1989, p. 55.]

Appalachian Mining, owned by the Addingtons, has been the target of ongoing protests since it opened mountaintop removal mines in late 1988 and early 1989 on Campbells Creek and Boomer. Local residents fear Appalachian Mining plans to develop landfills once the mountains are leveled.

GROUNDWATER

Coal mining, timbering, landfills, chemical emissions and wastes, oil and gas drilling, acid rain and acid mine drainage all contribute to what some believe is becoming the major environmental problem in the mountains—groundwater degradation.

Chuck Chambers, Speaker of the West Virginia House of Delegates, is one of the few politicians who is outspoken on environmental issues. Last year, Chambers spoke in favor of a proposed groundwater protection bill, which passed the House, 86 to 14. Gov. Gaston Caperton opposed, calling it too expensive for industry, and the more conservative State Senate killed it.

Chambers said, "Groundwater is a bit unique; it is not like some of the other resources that we talk about. You know, when we pollute the air, it blows away—it goes somewhere else. When we pollute the surface water, we watch it flow downstream and become someone else's problem.

"Groundwater doesn't travel like that," Chambers said. "Groundwater stays under the earth in aquifers of which we have very little understanding. We can't watch it, we can't see how it flows; we can only guess what happens to it. And we know that because it stays there literally year after year in the hundreds or thousands of millions of years. We know that what we put in, stays there. When we contaminate it, that contamination has no place to go—it stays underground."

Groundwater supplies drinking water for half of all West Virginians, and for more than 90 percent of those living in many rural counties. Groundwater is not just a West Virginia, Kentucky or Appalachian issue. The creeks, streams and rivers in the mountains provide water for much of the Eastern United States.

KING COAL THE CORRUPTER

Since the first drift mouth opened, King Coal has corrupted the social and political fabric in the mountains. Coal profits, landfill profits, logging profits—all provide cash for political influence and corruption. Whether the administration is Republican or Democratic seems to make little difference.

Coal operators contributed hundreds of thousands to Republican Arch Moore in 1984, and again in 1988. Coal operators—including many of the same individuals—gave an equal amount to Democrat Gaston Caperton. Caperton is a multi-millionaire insurance executive whose family made its fortune from mines in southern West Virginia. Caperton received most of his coal contributions after he defeated Moore in November 1988.

King Coal's influence guarantees that schools, health care and cultural opportunities in Appalachia's coalfields remain among the nation's poorest.

Ralph Halstead, who recently retired as research director for the West Virginia Department of Employment Security said, "Coal poisons everything it touches. Coal makes it very difficult to bring about economic development that would create prosperity in West Virginia. Is West Virginia a place where managers and professionals and engineers want to live? Look at the hollows, at the mountains, the streams. They are being destroyed. Look at the school system, health care, recreation facilities, cultural development, libraries. We have no chance," Halstead said. "A lot of that has to do with the unwillingness of the coal industry to pay for the destruction it creates."

Writing about regional development between 1880 and 1930, Eller argues the coal barons forged a society they could dominate completely. A society of company-controlled towns prohibits the development of other industries and of a strong regional professional/merchant class. The "condition of growth without development placed the mountains in a highly vulnerable relationship to the larger market system." [Eller, p. 229.]

PRESSURES FOR ENVIRONMENTAL PROTECTION

Twenty years ago, environmental regulation was not a major factor in the coal, or any other, industry. In the 1970s, Congress passed a series of laws, including the act establishing the Environmental Protection Agency in 1970, the Clean Air Act of 1970, the Toxic Substances Control Act of 1976, the Resource Conservation and Recovery Act of 1976 and the Surface Mining Control and Reclamation Act (SMCRA) of 1977.

More federal money has been spent to regulate coal than any other industry, according to environmental lawyer L. Thomas Galloway. Yet more than 12 years after Congress passed SMCRA, and after $1 billion has been spent on enforcement, strip mining abuses might be worse than ever in West Virginia, Galloway said earlier this year.

Within the past two years, coal strippers mined in a cemetery near Morgantown, nearly destroyed an historic house near Fairmont, excavated a 50-foot high wall up to the edge of a residential subdivision in Clarksburg, prospected for coal in the New River Gorge National River and caused mine subsidence that ruined homes, a highway and water tank in the town of Worthington.

What are the prospects for protecting the coalfield environment? To oversimplify things, two major forces are at work.

West Virginia's coal industry constantly seeks ways to cut costs to compete with operators in Kentucky, Pennsylvania and the Western states. Appalachian coal, moreover, competes with Australian coal in Japan, with South African and Polish coal in Western Europe, with Colombian coal in Florida and the Southeast.

Reclamation costs vary widely from region to region. A 1982 study found SMCRA added 54 cents to the price of a ton of coal in the West, $3.07 in the Midwest and $6.14 in Appalachia. [Harvey, pp. 114–115, 196.]

Weak environmental regulation in one state can give its operators a big boost over competitors in other states. Earlier this year, the Lexington Herald-Leader stated, "Reclamation in this country will only be as good as what is found in the weakest state. The competitive demands of the coal market will drive operators to the lowest common denominator of the law—a level now firmly maintained by the state of West Virginia."

Counteracting industry is a growing army of grassroots group. National groups—the National Wildlife Federation, Sierra Club, Wilderness Society and Environmental Policy Institute—conduct environmental studies and sometimes file lawsuits. The NWF won major concessions from coal operators in Kentucky and are now doing the same thing in West Virginia, as a result of suits filed by Galloway.

In addition to national groups, and perhaps even more significant, are local community groups springing up in reaction to specific environmental problems. Despite what coal operators say, the most striking thing about these groups is their diversity.

University professors want creeks near their homes to run clear. Fly fishermen don't want acid mine drainage killing trout. Hunters don't want their woodlands despoiled. Farmers become unhappy to see huge dozers or drilling rigs moving over lands previously untouched by the coal and gas industries. These local groups have names like the 4-H Road Community Association, Homeplace Inc., Mountain Stream Monitors or the Husky Musky Club.

In West Virginia, a strong coalition between the United Mine Workers and local environmental groups has emerged during the past two years, in reaction to the Division of Energy's failure to enforce environmental laws strictly. Without union support, it is unlikely a tougher, new set of mining regulations would have passed the state legislature in April.

Environmental groups, in turn, have begun supporting issues important to the UMW. In November, eight national environmental groups announced their support for the Coal Industry Health Benefit Stabilization Act of 1989, introduced by Sen. Jay Rockefeller, D-W.Va. The bill would require all coal companies who paid into UMW health benefits trust funds before January 1, 1988 to continue doing so. Rockefeller said the bill, which is also supported by the Bituminous Coal Operators Association, would help end the bitter strike against Pittston Coal and prevent coal companies from escaping financial responsibilities to pensioners, disabled miners, widows and children.

Mike Clark, president of the Environmental Policy Institute and Friends of the Earth, said, "Our lengthy experience suggests that a strong union is critical to environmental protection in the coalfields. . . . We have been united on numerous occasions against the environmental ravages, as well as public health and safety threats of illegal coal operations. . . . Over the last decade, we repeatedly have witnessed non-union coal operators among the worst offenders of federal environmental laws."

Sometimes, a single individual can help focus public attention on a particular problem. Last year, a mining technician working for a chemical supplier exposed the dangers of anhydrous ammonia to West Virginia's streams. Anhydrous ammonia, a toxic gas used to neutralize acid mine drainage, is outlawed in some states, including Tennessee and Pennsylvania. Some researchers, such as M. S. Smith and V. P. Evangelou of the University of Kentucky, found the gas neutralizes acid water at its source, but downstream, causes the "eventual generation of more acidity than is neutralized and the addition of nitrate, a potential pollutant, to surface waters." [Smith and Evangelou, p. 2.]

James E. Hiller, the technician who helped expose the danger this chemical poses to West Virginia streams, is hardly a rabid environmentalist or dedicated left-winger. He said he believed the two most important reforms for West Virginia's future are the passage of a right-to-work law and abolition of the Division of Energy.

Environmental concerns are widely felt throughout society. The people fighting damage to the mountains, valleys, and streams often agree on little else. An economically conservative Republican candidate for sheriff of Clay County helped expose mining abuses in that rural county. Citizens active in the Kanawha County textbook protest of 1976, a protest generally opposed by liberal organizations, are today among the state's most outspoken citizens against strip mining.

THE GREAT U-TURN

The pressures to ignore environmental protection are great, especially in an era when American corporations are fighting for markets around the world.

The 1980s witnessed "The Great U-Turn," according to economists Bennett Harrison and Barry Bluestone. This decade has seen a reversal of a trend since the end of World War II that saw a gradual rise in worker incomes and increasing equality for minority groups.

In the 1970s, America's business leaders began facing increasing overseas competition and rising costs of capital, accompanied by an orgy of corporate mergers. Maximum short-term financial returns—not the long-term development of technology and skilled workers—became the major goal in many corporate board rooms.

"This new managerial gospel," wrote Robert Hayes and William Abernathy, "played a major role in undermining the vigor of American industry." Financial wizards and lawyers replaced production specialists.

Losing its long-time dominance over resources, capital and technological expertise, American business leaders began seeking other methods to regain profits. Harrison and Bluestone believe three methods came into prominence—"zapping" labor, reducing costs of complying with government regulations, including environmental regulations, and reducing taxes. [Harrison and Bluestone, pp. 24–25.]

These national trends had a major impact on Appalachia's coalfields. After the 1981–1982 recession, the wave of concession bargaining that hit organized labor throughout the nation also reached the coalfields. Union miners, the ones lucky enough to still have jobs, were forced to accept lower pay increases than those of the 1970s. The less fortunate miners, working for companies like A. T. Massey and Pittston Coal, found themselves targets of union-busting campaigns and out on strike for months.

The job decline gave operators another ideological weapon. Miners, threatened with the unemployment and public assistance lines, become more receptive to arguments that environmental protection destroys jobs.

PRODUCTIVITY IN THE COALFIELDS

In past years, coal provided many more jobs. In 1922, 705,000 coal miners produced 565 million tons of coal.

In 1948, 442,000 miners dug 600 million tons. In 1987, 141,000 miners produced 919 million tons.

Despite what they repeatedly claim publicly, coal operators don't open mines to provide jobs. They open mines to make money. To make more money, they eliminate jobs.

In Appalachia, labor represents half the operating costs for deep mines, but only 21 percent of the costs of operating surface mines. Capital costs are 24 percent and 52 percent, respectively. [Harvey, p. 140.]

During the 1980s, large coal companies streamlined their operations. They installed longwall mining machines that cost up to $10 million each. They bought the draglines that can hold small houses in their steel buckets. Small operators found it increasingly difficult to compete, so they cut corners, by operating non-union and paying workers less. Some small underground mines in Kentucky and West Virginia pay miners as little as $5 an hour, with few hospital, vacation or pension benefits.

Operators also cut corners environmentally. Scores of small operators stripped coal from mountainsides, then disappeared leaving exposed highwalls, bare soil and acid water. Profits rise dramatically when operators fail to pay federal reclamation fees, taxes, unemployment compensation and Workers' Compensation premiums.

Increasingly, smaller operators are put in business by larger companies, such as Island Creek Coal, A. T. Massey, W. R. Grace, Pittston Coal Group, the ITT Corp. Typically, the large companies lease or own the coal lands, obtain mining permits, provide equipment and sell coal for the small operators. Small operators say they are caught in a vise between big companies, on the one hand, and environmental and labor costs, on the other. The small operator often has the choice between making a profit and staying in business—or running safe mines and reclaiming the land.

When small, undercapitalized operators incur major environmental, safety or labor liabilities, the big companies behind them deny responsibility for their troubles. A procession of small operators regularly files through federal bankruptcy courts in Charleston, Wheeling and Lexington.

"The Massey Coal Company Doctrine" is probably the boldest presentation of how large companies can distance themselves from smaller operations. The Massey doctrine is a strategy for insulating the main company from economically marginal subsidiaries and contractors. In a section titled "Corporate Objectives," the document states, "The value system is that of E. Morgan Massey [company president], which involves to a great extent the belief that duty comes before self, but in a hedonistic society, self comes before society at large." [Massey Doctrine, p. 3]

PRODUCTIVITY IN WEST VIRGINIA MINES

During the 1980s, the West Virginia coal industry has reduced costs dramatically, especially labor costs. Since 1981, more than 30,000 West Virginia miners were laid off by an industry producing more coal.

In 1988, West Virginia mines produced 144.9 million tons of coal, the most since 1968. In 1989, production is up slightly again, even with the summer's wildcat walkouts in sympathy with the Pittston strikers.

Total wages dropped by nearly half a billion dollars. Between 1981 and 1988, the average miner's weekly paycheck rose by 48 percent, from $474 a week to $701 a week. But since the number of working miners fell from 55,411 in 1981 to 25,488 in 1988, the industry's total wage bill dropped from $1.4 billion to $929 million. (West Virginia Coal Association).

Productivity, measured by the number of tons produced by each miner each year, rose spectacularly during the 1980s. For decades, annual productivity crept slowly upward, from 755 tons per year in 1900 to 1,217 tons in 1950. As operators began using continuous mining machines, productivity tripled to 3,567 tons per year by 1967.

Productivity declined in the 1970s, as coal prices quadrupled, in part due to the oil embargo, which allowed less efficient mining operations to reappear. "Smaller mines tend to have lower productivity. . . . Also, a younger, inexperienced work force probably depressed productivity growth," stated a 1981 U.S. Bureau of Labor Statistics report.

Each miner's annual production hit a low of 1,498 tons in 1978, a year when the United Mine Workers waged a 78-day contract strike. A decade later, in 1988, the average West Virginia miner produced 5,921 tons, four times as much.

Strip mining, non-existent in West Virginia until World War II, will continue to play a major role in increased productivity. The percentage of coal stripped in West Virginia rose slightly during the past decade, reaching nearly 25 percent of total production and an all-time high of 35 million tons in 1988.

Nationally, strip mining is even more important, reaching 25 percent of all coal mined in 1954, and 50 percent in 1971. With production in Western states soaring, surface-mined coal exceeded 60 percent for the first time in 1981, a level that has since remained relatively constant.

Regulatory authorities in West Virginia have helped the industry's push for greater productivity.

In West Virginia reclamation bonds are $1,000 an acre. In Kentucky, reclamation bonds are $3,000 an acre. In Pennsylvania, they are even more for some mines, especially in acid-producing seams. Lax enforcement by the West Virginia Division of Energy, created in July 1985, has allowed scores of operators to reap millions in extra profits, by permitting them to ignore environmental regulations.

The DOE's own policy statement reads, "It is the explicit purpose of the West Virginia Department of Energy to encourage and direct the exploration, development, production and use of coal, oil, natural gas and other mineral resources. . . . Additionally, the department is committed to the assurance that all federal and state environmental and health and safety regulations . . . will be enforced."

Some critics, including a business-oriented task force appointed by the new governor, see a basic flaw in any department that is both promoter and regulator of an industry. Under two commissioners—Republican Kenneth R. Faerber and Democrat George E. Dials—many abuses were stopped only when the U.S. Office of Surface Mining stepped in and insisted on compliance with federal regulations.

For example, one of the state's most productive strip mines was a mountaintop removal operation owned by G & W Equipment Leasing in Nicholas County. One reason it was so productive is that the company mined coal without doing any reclamation. Only after months of pressure from OSM did DOE order the company to comply with federal standards.

Today, Dal-Tex Corp., a subsidiary of United Coal based in Bristol, Virginia, is mining 14 seams from one mountain in Logan County. OSM inspectors recently cited DOE for failing to enforce environmental laws on reclamation and construction of huge valley fills. DOE is fighting OSM, and the dispute is not yet resolved.

Taxpayers are the ultimate losers. The West Virginia state government pays more than $250,000 a year from its Special Reclamation Fund to treat acid water coming off 3,686 acres stripped in the early 1980s. In 1985, the DLM Coal Corp. negotiated a deal with DOE, giving the state the land and $850,000 in assets in exchange for releasing it from all future environmental liability. Energy Commissioner Kenneth R. Faerber chose not to sue DLM's parent, General Energy Corp., a profitable company based in Lexington, Kentucky. Hydrologists predict that treatment costs will total about $2.5 million every decade. Treatment will be required for centuries.

DLM Coal is a clear example of a company that made extra profits by failing to internalize the costs of mining.

George E. Dials and Elizabeth C. Moore analyzed the costs of mining coal in 1974, 15 years before Dials became Energy Commissioner. "In calculating the social costs of coal," they wrote, "the standards of acceptable reclamation are beyond dispute; after reclamation is complete, the surface-mined land must be at least as economically productive and attractive to the eye as it was before mining began. . . . There is some land that should never be surface-mined at all, since it can never be fully restored, no matter how much money is spent." [Dials and Moore, p. 17.]

Fifteen years ago, Dials and Moore calculated it cost at least $4,000 an acre to reclaim the average strip mine. "If we try to do it for less, we will get just what we pay for: lands that are less productive and frequently far less beautiful than they were before mining took place." [Dials and Moore, p. 19.]

With inflation, reclamation costs would have reached $10,000 this past summer, if the Dials-Moore estimate is used.

In a July 1989 report, the Pennsylvania Department of Environmental Resources reveals it currently spends an average of $10,500 an acre on mine reclamation. In West Virginia, DOE spends $2,800 an acre, according to the most recent federal oversight report. [U.S. Office of Surface Mining, p. 10.] If reclamation in West Virginia were more thorough, and if all abandoned mines were reclaimed, the state's Special Reclamation Fund would quickly go bankrupt.

CARBON FUEL: A CASE STUDY

Nowhere is the destruction of a hollow so stark as on Cabin Creek and Winifrede Hollow, a few miles east of Charleston. Carbon Fuel Company, which operated mines on both hollows, was taken over by the ITT Corp. in 1977. In the 12 years since, jobs, families, communities, mountains and streams have been ravaged.

Between 1979 and 1986, more than 1,200 jobs at 10 Carbon Fuel mines vanished. Environmental carelessness created orange seeps filled with bright green algae, white creek beds and jet black sediment ponds, as iron, aluminum and manganese entered the area's waters. A pH meter reveals the clear waters tumbling down hillsides off the mines have a pH of 3.6, about as acidic as vinegar.

In 1976, the year before ITT Corp. paid more than $200 million to buy Carbon Fuel, the company employed 1,239 miners and produced 1.5 million tons of coal. (Keystone Coal Mine Directory, 1977). During the next decade, employment dwindled to nothing under the successive managements of ITT and U.S. Steel Mining. U.S. Steel signed a burdensome coal contract in 1974, at the peak of the energy shortage. In 1982, U.S. Steel signed a new agreement with Carbon Fuel and began operating the mines itself. Between 1982 and 1986, U.S. Steel operated the mines, lost more money, then negotiated an agreement to break the leases as of early 1988. (Charleston Gazette, Sept. 22, 1987).

This summer, the only miners still working on thousands of acres of Carbon coal lands were 17 surface miners working for non-union Kentucky operator, John A. Adkins. In October, Adkins shut down and began hauling his equipment away. Adkins left major environmental problems at mines operated by 10 different companies he once owned in Eastern Kentucky. Many of these companies forfeited reclamation bonds and owed tens of thousands of dollars in state and federal fines. Adkins said he sold the companies before the problems developed. Kentucky officials are still investigating him and West Virginia authorities are preparing to forfeit his bonds in West Virginia.

Last March, Adkins bought Fields Creek Coal from Carbon Fuel for $1,000 and signed a lease granting him mining rights. Fields Creek had three mining permits covering 915 acres. Adkins agreed to treat acid discharges from more than 500 acres which had already been mined by U.S. Steel. Last spring, he began spending more than $8,000 a month to treat acid water. Six months later, Adkins decided his profits did not even cover growing treatment costs, which he estimated to be several hundred thousand dollars a year.

Before he left for his home in Pikeville, Adkins filed a lawsuit against Carbon Fuel and U.S. Steel Mining, charging that both companies defrauded him by concealing the environmental problems. "Undisclosed environmental problems . . . created such large liabilities that the stock in Fields Creek and the lease with Carbon have no value and are, in fact, a huge net liability," stated a lawsuit he filed on October 13.

U.S. Steel Mining, a USX subsidiary, is still paying Carbon Fuel about $5 million a year, in part to pay for environmental damage, court documents reveal. If Adkins pursues his lawsuit, it will provide a fascinating look into relationships between major corporations and small operators. If Adkins cannot convince the courts to rescind his sale and lease with Carbon Fuel, he may inherit the full legal responsibility for environmental clean-up and be permanently barred from mining—in large part because he cannot afford to treat environmental problems he did not create.

The suit will examine to what extent environmental liabilities can be bought and sold. West Virginia University law professor Patrick C. McGinley wrote, "It is exceedingly difficult to avoid liability by private contract. To put it bluntly, the owner of coal property can rarely, if ever, dispose of its environmental liability by sale or lease; however, the buyer, simply by virtue of assuming ownership, can acquire environmental liability." [McGinley and Webber, p. 666.]

FORCES FOR CHANGE:
A UNION-ENVIRONMENTAL COALITION

The United Mine Workers opposed the Adkins permits from the beginning, in part because Adkins failed to post a wage bond to cover wages and benefits for employees if his company went out of business. Mark March, a UMW official, stated DOE officials "knew there was a major, major problem about acid mine drainage before they gave him a permit. They even told Adkins about it. Why did they let him go in there and mine?"

On issue after issue, the union has joined with community groups in asking that environmental regulations be enforced. Clearly, union support is motivated by the fact that the majority of marginal, outlaw operators are non-union. But sometimes, environmentalists forget that coal miners, more than anyone else, must live in communities damaged by poor mining practices.

During the past two years, the U.S. Office of Surface Mining has taken an increasingly active role in policing the West Virginia industry. The OSM gave the state "primacy" to enforce federal mining laws in 1982. But when state regulators fail to enforce federal standards, OSM can first ask state regulators to take enforcement action, then step in if nothing is done. OSM has been intervening in enforcement in West Virginia with increasing frequency. Federal enforcement actions include the following.

When Fresa Construction finished stripping 37 acres of an eight-foot coal seam, bulldozers hit a 300-foot buffer zone protecting a residential subdivision just outside Clarksburg. Fresa then applied for a coal exploration permit, governed by looser regulations, and DOE issued it. After Fresa cut a 50-foot highwall up to people's backyards, OSM shut the mine down. Earlier this year, new Energy Commissioner George E. Dials supported Fresa's appeals of the OSM shutdown. All have failed.

A.S. & K. Inc., owned by Englishman Brian Jones, began remining a 20-acre coal refuse pile near the town of Osage in early 1989. In May, OSM shut Jones down, stating that water impoundments, one poised above a mobile home park, posed an "imminent danger to the health and safety of the public." DOE called the federal closure order too tough. In June, Jones dewatered the impoundments. On July 11, the area had the heaviest rainfall in 50 years. OSM engineer Michael J. Superfesky said federal intervention actions were "instrumental in preventing . . . catastrophic flooding of the trailer court and other occupied dwellings." Owing wages to employees and reclamation fees to the federal government, Jones went bankrupt in November.

During the past year, OSM ordered three major coal companies—Consolidation, Peabody and Beth-Energy—to reclaim old coal refuse piles. The DOE—under Faerber and Dials—refused to take any enforcement action.

JOURNALISTS AND CITIZEN GROUPS

James Lyon, director of the Citizen's Mining Project for the Environmental Policy Institute, believes the media should play a major role in defending the environment. "In some ways the media is doing its job well. In other ways, environment seems to be a shrinking issue. The general trend of newspapers is to get away from covering environmental issues."

Lyon said "big picture" environmental issues often get more ink and air time than more localized environmental controversies. "Major global environmental issues need leadership, issues such as global warming, destruction of the rain forests, destruction of ozone. But typically, these stories do not hurt local interest groups," Lyon said.

Local issues tend to be more controversial, and therefore less likely to be covered by the press. "Typically, you are taking on state government and local industry. This can generate enormous controversy and political conflict," Lyon said.

Lyon believes citizens and environmentalists have just as much responsibility to pressure the media as they do government agencies, if reporters are not covering environmental issues.

Lyon stresses the great popular appeal environmental issues have. "Millions of people go to the ocean every summer, people from all walks of life. They all go for the purpose of enjoying that environment," he said. "They get angry when they see the effects of ocean dumping, or the effects of overdevelopment. Try polling people sitting on the beach. You'll find a very diverse group of people. The vast majority wants to protect those beaches."

Lyon said not nearly as many Americans visit strip mines every summer. "But I'm sure very few people would stand on top of a devastated mountain, look at an unreclaimed mine, and say, 'What the hell. This generated a little money. It gave a few people jobs.' "

While some newspapers might discourage reporters from writing about environmental issues, especially local ones, I suspect there are a lot of reporters on dailies and weeklies, in television and radio, who would welcome telephone calls and suggestions from interested citizens.

Citizens, who study environmental issues and make their research available to the media, play an instrumental role in protecting the environment. Unfortunately, citizens are often the only environmental watchdogs around when public regulators are in bed with industry.

ACCOMPLISHMENTS

It is amazing what irate citizens, a handful of environmental lawyers, a couple of union organizers, a technical expert and a reporter can do. The most important conferences to enforce mining law do not take place in state office buildings. These meetings take place in kitchens, over a pot of coffee, among citizens armed with telephones, a couple of note pads and a Xerox machine.

In West Virginia, this impromptu coalition has blocked at least two dozen mining permits since 1987, sparked several federal and Congressional investigations into mining abuses and forced the reclamation of several abandoned mines. Since January, non-governmental enforcement efforts have netted nearly $600,000 in fines, fees and reclamation costs.

If a coal operator has outstanding fines, if he forfeited reclamation bonds or had a permit revoked, federal law prohibits that operator from opening another mine anywhere in the country. Yet over and over again, state officials in West Virginia, Virginia and other states fail to check backgrounds of operators who apply for permits. Month after month, citizen groups, lawyers and reporters do the work state regulators should be doing.

The Applicant Violator System, operated by OSM, is a disaster. Data entered into the system is incomplete and inaccurate. Over and over again, the AVS system fails to catch operators with problems in one state who open mines in another. In February, House Interior Committee Chairman Morris K. Udall said, "We have computer systems in this country to keep track of everything from missiles to kindergarten kids who are sick or absent. I can't renew my driver's license without a computer check of my driving record. But the Interior Department can't develop a system, even with the help of $15 million, to keep violators out of the coalfields." An alternative computer system, created by Galloway, the National Wildlife Federation and the United Mine Workers has become the most effective tool there is to identify repeat violators. Galloway is presently trying to sell that system to the federal government.

VIOLATORS CAUGHT BY CITIZENS

Over and over again, DOE has taken no action until forced to do so by citizens and newspaper stories. Here are a few examples:

After digging 13 illegal prospect pits, Black Gold of West Virginia applied for a permit to mine 125 acres of Lincoln County farmland owned by a Pennsylvania doctor. Delbert Burchett, who supervised the operation, forfeited reclamation bonds at five mines in Eastern Kentucky and declared bankruptcy, owing more than $11 million. His debts included $7 million in unpaid environmental fines in Kentucky and $1.5 million in unpaid taxes, according to the federal bankruptcy records in Lexington. When Burchett left Black Gold, DOE granted the permit. Citizen lawsuits against the company are still in the courts.

Templeman Construction, owned by Michael Templeman, a partner of John Adkins in Kentucky, lied about his past on a permit application and began stripping a mountain above Campbells Creek in April 1986. Despite accurate information from union officials that Templeman forfeited permits in Kentucky, DOE officials never investigated his mining history. Within a year, Templeman abandoned a 90-foot highwall around two mountains and forfeited his $25,000 reclamation bond. The bond will cover 11.4 percent of the $219,280 reclamation contract recently awarded by DOE.

Daugherty Coal mined more than 500 acres in rural Preston County, then left it unreclaimed. Two days before DOE forfeited three Daugherty reclamation bonds, DOE sent a new permit application from Hobar Coal out for public advertisement. The wife and daughters of Daugherty Coal officer Howard L. Parsons own Hobar. Lawyer Tom Rodd accused Parsons of a "corporate name-shuffling scam to avoid federal mining laws." After a public outcry, Dials denied the Hobar permit. Parsons is appealing the denial.

Carl N. Graybeal, an operator with a long history of serious mining abuses, violated federal laws limiting the amount of coal to be mined under a prospect permit in the town of Sophia. DOE fined his company, Kodiak Land Company. Graybeal never paid the fine. Kodiak's mine superintendent then created a new company called GEM Mining and applied for a full-scale stripping permit. DOE officials did nothing, until local citizens protested, in part to protect an $8 million flood-control project the U.S. Soil Conservation Service completed in August. Dials denied the permit to strip 13 sites in Sophia, the home town of Sen. Robert C. Byrd, D-W.Va. Graybeal is now blocked from getting new mining permits.

James L. Laurita Sr. and James L. Laurita Jr., Morgantown coal operators, control a tangled web of two dozen coal companies in Wet Virginia and Pennsylvania. In successive applications to DOE, filed under the names of Stone King Coal and Mepco Inc., the Lauritas failed to reveal their history of more than 300 environmental violations in Pennsylvania between 1984 and 1987. DOE did not investigate the Lauritas, until the 4-H Road Community Association protested and filed lawsuits, calling the new companies a "thinly-disguised family mining scam." Under pressure, the Lauritas withdrew both applications.

FINES COLLECTED

Citizens, lawyers and reporters can also collect fines and reclamation fees. Since April, this coalition has collected $600,000. Baltimore coal broker John McCall paid $145,000 in fines in April 1989 owed by the Imperial Corp., a defunct mining company. McCall denied his ties to the company until legal research and newspaper articles exposed them. Democratic state legislator Barbara Warner and her lawyer-partner paid $5,872 in fines in April, after a newspaper article revealed the pair owned an unreclaimed prospect mine with a history of environmental abuses. Kentucky operator John A. Adkins paid more than $40,000 in delinquent federal Abandoned Mine Lands in May, after several articles detailed his past mining abuses.

Virginia coal operator James O. Bunn agreed to post $400,000 reclamation bond to guarantee reclamation of a strip mine abandoned in Leslie County. After Kentucky's Department of Surface Mining Reclamation and Enforcement revoked a Picadilly Coal Company permit in February 1987, Bunn opened new mines in West Virginia and Virginia. Bunn posted the bond in October, after newspaper articles and lawsuits finally spurred West Virginia authorities to threaten to revoke Bunn's mining permits in Mingo County.

The Bunn case was a remarkable one. Bunn was blocked from mining in Kentucky. A call to Kentucky officials revealed that fact. DOE never made that call. Bunn's name also appeared on DOE's own permit-block list. Apparently, no one at DOE even bothered to check the agency's own list. After newspaper articles revealed Bunn's problems, the Energy Commissioner attacked the paper for irresponsible reporting. But within a month, Bunn agreed to post the $400,000 bond. Virginia authorities are now also investigating Bunn's operations in that state.

POLITICAL CORRUPTION

Whenever an industry regulated by government makes big profits, money is available for influence-peddling. Politicians generally respond to the weight of public opinion on a wide range of issues, including the environment. But cash sometimes seems to convince some not to implement the public will.

Gov. Arch Moore created the Department of Energy in 1985, after being elected to his third term as West Virginia governor. The industry wanted "one-stop shopping," a single agency to issue all the permits needed to mine coal. Moore got more than $250,000 in coal contributions between 1984 and 1988. Almost 90 percent came from small and medium-sized operators. Most live in West Virginia. Critics say the small operators bought the Department of Energy.

A list of coal industry contributors to Moore contains several operators in the center of environmental controversies, including the Lauritas; Michael Fresa; Rosa Graybeal; Charles Sorbello, whose mines created subsidence cracks that destroyed homes, roads and the water tank in Worthington; Fred Golden, who opened a controversial prospect mine; officials from Buffalo Coal, a company using anhydrous ammonia; officers of Daniel Boone Coal and Double P Inc., Clarksburg companies that paid the Department of Natural Resources more than $100,000 in 1985 for concocting a fraudulent bankruptcy scheme to avoid environmental liabilities.

Caperton, whose cousin is an officer of Massey Export Services, collected money from many of these same operators—most of it after he was elected governor in November 1988.

Admittedly, coal contributions in West Virginia pale next to contributions from the Addington family in Kentucky. In 1987, the Addington brothers gave candidates $257,000. A record $199,000 went to the campaign, political action committees and inauguration committee of Gov. Wallace Wilkinson. (Louisville Courier-Journal, April 18, 1988). In West Virginia, with limits on campaign contributions, the Addingtons gave $5,000 to Moore and $7,000 to Caperton's campaign and inauguration committees.

Last year, House Speaker Chambers said, "Larger corporations are used to protecting themselves. Smaller companies may feel they are more at the mercy of the DOE. They may perceive the best way to protect themselves is by making large contributions to the governor, who appoints the Energy Commissioner and other important personnel." (Charleston Gazette, July 17, 1988).

John Leaberry, Moore's campaign manager and a former coal company executive, said small operators donate more to political candidates because "they are local people who have grown up in West Virginia. They are part of the local fabric of communities here. With larger companies, people often float around from community to community." (Charleston Gazette, July 17, 1988).

Local coal operators also regularly portray themselves as philanthropists. They sit on college boards, contribute to the United Way, support West Virginia University athletic teams and donate thousands more to local charities.

Cash for philanthropic and charitable activities can be generated readily by avoiding and evading environmental and labor laws. James "Buck" Harless is a multi-millionaire sawmill owner and coal operator based in Mingo County. In 1984, the Charleston Gazette editorial board named Harless West Virginian of the Year. Last year, Harless hired a logging contractor to timber land on Coal Fork of Campbells Creek before another company opened a strip mine. Harless paid Freda Smith $600 to move logs across her property, then hired non-union logging contractor Garnet Dixon. Dixon's Logging Co. never paid Workers' Compensation premiums, despite the fact logging is the most dangerous industry in the state. Last winter, Dixon hauled off big trees, day and night, then left.

When the spring rains fell on Coal Fork, mud covered Freda Smith's garden, oozed under her mobile home and covered part of her family's graveyard. Mud and rocks stopped just short of a stone marking little Elizabeth's grave. "Infant daughter of J.E. & L.G. White. Born and Died Oct. 21, 1910. Budded on earth to bloom in heaven," the marker read.

Perhaps some of the extra cash Harless put in his pocket when Dixon left Coal Fork helped the WVU football team win games this season. Harless and Dixon left an environmental mess in Lincoln County, before moving to Campbells Creek. David and Pamela Litz later sued Harless and two other companies, charging that logging polluted a stream and caused extensive soil erosion on their 78-acre farm near Yawkey.

David Litz had harsh words. "Mr. Harless has no social conscience. Rip, rape and sell. That's Mr. Harless. . . . Mr. Harless does not make heartfelt monetary contributions. They are prudent business investments."

The failure of Moore's Department of Energy to enforce environmental and mine safety laws was a major issue in his losing campaign for a fourth term as governor.

Fifteen years before becoming Energy Commissioner, Dials wrote in 1974, "Without proper reclamation, thousands of square miles of surface-mined 'moonscape' will be left as a legacy to future generations; large portions of some Appalachian states already have this appearance." [Dials and Moore, p. 15.] At the end of the first year of Caperton's administration, it remains unclear whether or not environmental laws will be enforced strictly.

Chambers said, "When you look at the history of this state, many of us have shared the sentiment that we've really been kind of a colony, perhaps like a Third World country. Underdeveloped in terms of our own economy, but supplying raw materials of all kinds to make America what it is. And it troubles me a great deal that while we profess to have this tremendous love and respect for the natural environment, when you look at the history of West Virginia, we haven't kept that commitment. We haven't honored the land that we claim to love."

Chambers asked, "Can anyone imagine a state, a land anywhere with more wealth than West Virginia? Imagine, 200 years ago, had we had the foresight in this country to protect those resources, how much of that wealth would still be here in West Virginia."

What does the future hold for Appalachia's hollows?

Halstead thinks about McDowell County. "After the removal of billions and billions of dollars of high-grade metallurgical coal, and despite the population is half of what it was in 1950, there is an acute shortage of housing. A lot of the housing that is occupied is dilapidated. The county does nothing to dispose of its waste, human and otherwise. Its roads and bridges are a wreck. "It raises a specter," Halstead said. "Are you looking at the future of all the rest of the southern coal-producing counties? It is a frightening prospect, and one that haunts me."

BIBLIOGRAPHY

Bishop, Bill. *Lexington Herald-Leader* editorial, "West Virginia Coal Outlaws Thrive at Kentucky's Expense," March 5, 1989.

Chambers, Robert (Chuck), speech on House of Delegates floor, March 23, 1989. Reprinted in *The Highlands Voice,* 22, 5 (May 1989).

Corbin, David Alan, *Life, Work, and Rebellion in the Coal Fields.* Urbana: University of Illinois Press, 1981.

Dials, George E. and Elizabeth C. Moore, "The Cost of Coal," *Appalachia,* 8, 2 (October–November 1974).

Eller, Ronald D. *Miners, Millhands, and Mountaineers: Industrialization of the Appalachian South, 1880–1930.* Knoxville: University of Tennessee Press, 1982.

Harrison, Bennett and Barry Bluestone, *The Great U-Turn: Corporate Restructuring and the Polarizing of America.* New York: Basic Books, 1988.

Harvey, Curtis E. *Coal in Appalachia: An Economic Analysis.* Lexington: University of Kentucky Press, 1986.

Hayes, Robert and William Abernathy. "Managing Our Way To Economic Decline," *Harvard Business Review,* July–August 1980.

Massey, E. Morgan. "The Massey Coal Company Doctrine," 27 pages, typewritten, July 1982.

McGinley, Patrick C. and Barbara S. Webber, "Pandora in the Coal Fields: Environmental Liabilities, Acquisitions and Disposition of Coal Properties," *West Virginia Law Review,* 87, 3 (Spring 1985), p. 666.

National Clear Air Coalition. "Acid Rain in the South." 1984.

Smith, M. S. and V. P. (Bill) Evangelou. "Improving Water Quality in Sediment Ponds: Consequences of Neutralizing Acidity with Ammonia," *Reclamation News and Views* [Published by the University of Kentucky College of Agriculture], 1, 7 (October 1982).

West Virginia Coal Association. *Coal Facts '88.* Charleston, 1989.

U.S. Bureau of Labor Statistics. "Technology, Productivity, and Labor in the Bituminous Coal Industry, 1950–79," Bulletin 2072, February 1981.

U.S. Office of Surface Mining. "1988 West Virginia Annual Evaluation Report, for the period July 1, 1987 to June 30, 1988 (June 1989).

General Note: Undocumented cases discussed above are based on articles written by the author in *The Charleston Gazette.*

VI. Polity

It has become customary in recent years to make arbitrary divisions for analytical purposes when examining the role of the economic and political institutions in society. It is questionable, however, whether such distinctions are meaningful or justifiable. In the industrial society we see these institutions interact so intensely with each other that it becomes impossible to make meaningful distinctions between them. This is not to deny that each institution has major concerns, but even so, they demonstrate an increasing interdependency. The major thrust of the economic institution is the production and distribution of goods and services, many of which may be "scarce." The very factor of scarcity, whether real or manipulated, necessitates the establishment of rules governing the production and distribution of goods. The establishment of rules and the regulation of production becomes one of the major responsibilities of the political sector. In addition to maintaining order, the political structure also becomes increasingly involved in providing programs and services not provided by other sectors of the society. The following statement by Paul Sites describes the interdependency of these two institutional orders:

> We live in a market society and the *social ordering of all institutional spheres is constrained in many ways by the influence of the market* and the market mentality that develops in a market society. The economic institution, with its market economy and its free enterprise ideology, *is the dominant social institution in American society.* The government regulates and protects the economic institution as part of the reciprocal ordering of control relationships. Other institutions also reciprocally affect it, but the key to understanding American society is to recognize the dominance of the economic institution.*

The articles in this section clearly illustrate the reciprocal nature of these institutional orders. In most cases the articles focus their attention upon the economic problems inherent in the region and the programs initiated at the federal and state level to deal with them. One such program is ARC. The major reason for the creation of ARC was to help resolve many of the problems existing in Appalachia that are directly or indirectly the result of economic conditions. The intent of the program is to funnel money into the area for the purpose of stimulating the area economically and increase economic diversification through a type of public works program. Consequently, the bulk of the funds have been used for projects such as massive highway construction, building of hospitals and schools, construction and development of water and sewage treatment plants, and to a lesser extent, provide funding for some social service programs. The rationale behind this "brick and mortar" program is that these types of projects will attract new industry and stimulate commerce.

*Paul Sites, Control and Constraint, New York: Macmillan Publishing Co., Inc., 1975.

Most critics of ARC feel that even though these projects may benefit the area somewhat, the program does not really get at the root causes of the social conditions, and thus, the sense of powerlessness and alienation persists among the inhabitants of the region. They feel that such feelings will persist and suspicions about government programs will exist as long as the following conditions are present; first, continued exploitation by corporate interest whose primary concern is the maximization of profits, and secondly, the growing centralization and professionalization of the decision-making process. It is felt that as long as industry is accountable only to its stockholders, rather than the public sector, the deplorable social and economic conditions are going to continue in the region. The activities of ARC and other governmental programs which have as their major objective the encouragement of industrial development are seen by many as a perpetuation of the present conditions.

31. WHAT THE NEW FRONTIER AND GREAT SOCIETY BROUGHT

James Branscome

A. Origins of the ARC

Senator John Kennedy's 1960 presidential primary campaign in West Virginia put him and the state on the nation's agenda. Kennedy, by showing a Catholic could win a Protestant state, won the presidency; West Virginia, its sores so obvious, shocked even reporters long familiar with black poverty in the South. David Brinkley stood on a one-lane wooden bridge on Highway 52 in Wayne and told the nation of West Virginia's poverty and Kennedy's promise to "do something" about it. The grateful people of Wayne named the bridge the "David Brinkley Bridge," and hung a sign over it that crashed into the river with the bridge ten years later when an overloaded truck crossed it. Other reporters, too, discovered mountain poverty. Homer Bigart of the *New York Times* wrote movingly about eastern Kentucky children so hungry they ate clay from chimneys. A Scripps-Howard reporter visited a mined-out Bethlehem Steel town in Pike County, Kentucky, and datelined his story "Hellier, Kentucky, where you can sit on your front porch and look into Hell." Appalachia was on the map.

It did not take many figures to tell Appalachia's story. Coal mining employment had declined from a high of 476,859 men in World War II to 198, 488 men in 1960, with production about the same. From 1950–60 railroad employment had dropped 40%. One mountain family in three in 1960 had an annual income lower than $3,000, compared with a national ratio of one in five. Fewer than one-third of the population had completed high school. In a region of nearly 19 million people, 34% of the housing was deteriorating or dilapidated. Three million "economic refugees" had left since World War II to find jobs in the North. In central Appalachia the problem was worse, with floods and starvation wiping out whole families. Men walked the streets of coal towns in eastern Kentucky in December barefooted, their families following them in the same fashion.

Prior to the 1960 campaign, the Appalachian governors had met to draw up a resolution on regional development to use as a leverage point with a new administration. They called for a program to correct transportation facilities (roads) and to control water resources (dams). The governors got a plank in the Democratic platform calling for depressed area relief. The proposals for highways in the mountains had been made before, the first time in 1808 by Albert Gallatin in a report to President Jefferson. As the governors noted, building roads by traffic count rather than development potential had kept Gallatin's proposals from ever being realized; the governors aimed this time to make their point, that Appalachia was underdeveloped and in need of federal uplift.

When he assumed office, Kennedy appointed a special panel on distressed area aid chaired by Senator Paul Douglas of Illinois. That committee recommended a special regional commission for Appalachia that could become a model for solving problems in other regions of the country. The immediate result of Douglas's effort was re-passage of area development legislation that had been vetoed twice by President Eisenhower. Nationally, it provided for loans to businesses, public works grants, manpower training, and the creation of the Area Redevelopment Administration (ARA) in the Department of Commerce. The meagerness of the legislation became readily apparent, however, when a full one-third of the counties in the nation qualified for aid. Seventy-six percent of Appalachia qualified, but the funds were too limited to satisfy the governors. They continued to press for a special Appalachian agency.

Because of the pressure, the ARA commissioned two studies, one by the Stanford Research Institute and another through the University of Pittsburgh, to determine what should be done about the region. A special interagency panel, but including as well representatives of the governors, called the President's Appalachian Regional Commission followed in April 1963, headed by Franklin D. Roosevelt, Jr. Kennedy charged this panel with drawing up an Appalachian plan. By October the plan was finished and Roosevelt launched an eleven-day trip to the region to sell the program, with stops in Atlanta, Lexington, Charleston, Hagerstown, and other places. The Commission report was a shopping list: highways, health centers, vocational schools, timber management, promotion of tourism, and even a program to raise calves in the mountains for shipment west for fattening (later rejected when objected to by western representatives).

It was in essence a public works program stripped of all controversial elements like expanding public power, breaking up land monopolies, and creating public utility districts. Its emphasis that Appalachia was basically an underdeveloped nation, "an island of poverty in a sea of affluence," fitted the national identification of the mountains' problems. While the report used to justify the program cited the poverty of people, the answers proposed were mainly for solving the poverty of things: hospitals, schools, roads. Planning mechanisms

Reprinted from the *Federal Government in Appalachia* by James Branscome, The Field Foundation, 1977, pp. 23–43.

from multi-county districts to Washington, were built in. While President Johnson said the ARC would end porkbarrel, Rep. H. R. Gross of Iowa, a veteran detractor of federal spending, pronounced it "the longest gravy train in history."

B. Implementing the Program

Johnson thought the program would "put this region out on the bright highway of hope." The agency's critics said to do that Johnson had simply given money and power to the same people who had helped create the problems. The act gave power to 13 governors and one federal co-chairman, all equal except that the latter has a veto power; but the it has never been exercised. For federal co-chairman, Johnson named John Sweeney, a Washingtonian with Democratic Party connections. Sweeney had little knowledge of the region, and his greatest impact will probably have been his chance meeting at the White House with a young Coast Guard social aide, Alvin Arnett. Impressed that Arnett was from Kentucky, Sweeney put him on the staff; Arnett later was to be one of the men named by the Nixon administration to dismantle OEO. Sweeney was followed as co-chairman by Pat Fleming, an aide to Senator Fullbright. He was followed by John Waters, an associate of Senator Howard Baker. Waters was followed by Donald Whitehead, a Massachusetts attorney who was a Nixon campaign aide and friend of longtime Nixon political operative, Murray Chotiner. His Democratic replacement is ex-Governor Robert Scott of North Carolina. Whatever else ARC has been, it has not been apolitical.

As their permanent Washington representative the states chose John Whisman, an irrepressible Jaycee from Hazard who made his living at one time selling inflatable buildings, as he traveled the mountains peddling the idea of area development. Whisman had landed an ARA job in Kentucky Governor Comb's administration and by progression became the liaison between the Kennedy aides and the governors; he was retired in 1976 for irregularities in the keeping of his expense accounts.

The executive staff was comprised mainly of former aides to various senators and congressmen. Ralph Widner, executive director, had been an aide to Senator Clark of Pennsylvania. Howard Bray, deputy director, had been an aide to Senator Anderson of New Mexico. The remainder of the staff was and has continued to be from essentially the same background: the Hill, Department of Commerce, private consulting agencies, and the Bureau of Public Roads. Nearly all shared an unfamiliarity with the region. Many staff slots were filled with incompetents put on the payroll because of pressures from Capitol Hill. In the main, the staff was organized to please the public works committees, only secondarily to relate to the region. Reflecting that priority, the public relations and publications staff has always been outnumbered the economic development staff by at least 10 to 1. Research has been mainly directed to proving agency impact, not at objective study of the region's problems. From the start, there was an antagonistic attitude toward OEO and other human resource programs of the Great Society. Disputes between ARC chieftains and those in OEO, the Economic Development Administration, and Health, Education and Welfare were to insure that ARC would quietly spend its money from Connecticut Avenue while the rest of the government went about its own normal business of giving the region the treatment it had come to expect from Washington. As ARC had claimed Appalachia was "a region apart," so the agency was a program apart. As long as the public works committees and the governors were happy, ARC had nothing to fear.

C. Ending the Pork Barrel

As an agency with a "different" approach ARC aimed to be tough minded about its spending. There would be an investment strategy built around growth centers determined by states. Highways would be built for development impact. Hospitals would be built for the same reasons. Porkbarrel was out. In fact, the porkbarrel was rolling about the region as never before.

The highway locations were determined by the states. Hospitals were built as they had always been built. Cities like Beckley, West Virginia, that had a Miner's Hospital to which doctors were hostile, got another, a Hill Burton hospital, through ARC matching. Counties like Wise, Virginia, that had a Miner's Hospital in a central location, got a hospital in Big Stone Gap, Governor Holton's hometown. Businessmen and politicians excluded from OEO's Community Action Agency (CAA) boards were put on ARC boards, and with the coming in the early 1970s of Nixon's "New Federalism" and its charter known as A-95, they began to pass on all aid requests in their multi-county areas. They voted themselves airports, industrial sites, sewer projects, and housing projects to vie with those of OEO. When they failed to get control of a local CAA, ARC gave them a child development program of their own, one that did not have to bother with having the poor on its board. The establishment loved it. Governor Arch Moore won a second term as governor against Jay Rockefeller because he was "West Virginia's Road Building Governor." He also got a track and field "hall of fame" funded with ARC money.

Congress loved it too. The Mississippi senators got sewer and water projects for northeastern Mississippi, an area that hardly met normal ARC criteria. Rep. Joe L. Evins of Tennessee and the House Public Works Appropriations subcommittee got a million dollar craft center that even the ARC staff thought a colossal boondoggle. Senator Robert Kennedy got a highway corridor for southwestern New York. Governors Agnew and Mandel were so effective as Appalachian brokers that Maryland got more aid per capita than any of the other 12 states. Former Governor McNair of South Carolina got consulting contracts, as did the former any somebody who really wanted one.

D. Expertise No Great Advantage

While the ARC has frequently demonstrated it has the technical expertise to define problems, it seldom has exercised the clout to do anything about those problems. It has done studies which demonstrated that the region needs water control, but it has bowed to Corps of Engineers' pressure to interpret that as an argument for dams, dams that destroy the little remaining open space in some areas for housing and farming, another subject on which ARC has frequently lamented but never acted. Its staff defined capital outflow in central Appalachia to be a major developmental problem, pinpointing conservative banking practices as one cause, and then shelved the study. It has described land management in the mountains repeatedly as a disaster, yet—with the single exception of late and lukewarm support of minimal federal strip mine controls—has not, so far as one could tell, even bothered to walk across town to talk to the biggest Appalachian landowner of them all: the Forest Service. While admitting its own housing programs are under-utilized because of lack of available land, it has demonstrated an amazing timidity in approaching coal companies and railroads, which own up to 90% of the surface of some West Virginia counties, to see if they would donate, sell, or otherwise relinquish control for miners' housing.

While the agency has shown some sensitivity to the problems of overdevelopment, i.e., problems like black lung, brown lung, and other industrial diseases, its program approaches to those problems have been basically misdirected and, frequently, comical failures. The agency, for example, hired a $400 a day consultant from Nashville, who had little coal-field experience, to help draw up a plan for spending its black lung money, while the region's and the world's experts (who were all in the region) were ignored. Though the agency's staffers knew from studies that it was cheaper to clean up the mine dust that causes the disease than for the government to pay miners' compensation, it never let the word outside the agency. And while several of its staffers have pushed to keep the agency from making every mountain community into a sure-flop tourist mecca, they have

been shunted aside in favor of tourist promoters in every regional hamlet. In short, the expertise, worthless unless backed by political courage, seldom has been.

E. Who Is Against Motherhood?

ARC's support of 914 vocational schools, 126 libraries, 147 airports, 12,000 housing units, 16,000 erosion control projects, and 144 health construction projects appears on the surface as genuinely supportable as motherhood. Few sensible ARC critics even any longer challenge the need in the region for passable roads, though they differ on ARC's choice of roads. In total perspective, no one can say all of ARC has been a waste. Its problem has been that its potential has always been far above its results, or even its endeavors. It could have done something about mine safety, about strip mining, about land monopolies, about state and local under-taxation of corporations, about governmental accountability about local leadership development, about the maze of fumbling Washington bureaucracies that deal with the region and, in short, it could have behaved as if its constituency were Appalachia, as if its mission were to end porkbarrel, and as if it really believed its own studies were worthy of implementation. It seldom has. It has been an agency apart from its own mission, frequently apart from its own better judgment.

F. Appalachia After a Decade of Development[1]

Population increase tells one of the most dramatic stories in a region accustomed to economically enforced out-migration. It also is one reason why the economic improvement of the last decade has been diluted.

Between World War II and 1965, the region lost three million people to northern cities. In the five and one-half years after 1970, the census showed an 810,000 increase in the region's population. Significantly, 36% of that was for net in-migration. The greatest portion of that change came in the southern half of the region, with Appalachian Georgia leading the way with a 3% per annum growth (the national average is 5%).

Over the five-year period of 1970–75, eastern Kentucky experienced a 9% growth in population, with a net in-migration of 41,000 people. With the exception of central West Virginia, the rest of the southern region experienced a similar increase.

The ARC reports are fond of stating that the regional unemployment rate in 1976 was only 5%. It is an example of how the agency uses statistics to cover the holes. In fact, regionwide from 1970–74 the total number of unemployed persons increased by 10%, and by 16% in southern Appalachia.

While the region gained in its comparative percentage of national income, the variation was dramatic. West Virginians, for example, in 1974 earned 82% of the national per capita income (up from 80% in 1965), but eastern Kentuckians earned only 62% (up from 50% in 1965). For central Appalachia as a whole, the per capita income was 65% of the national average in 1974 (up from 52% in 1965), compared with the whole region's 83%.

Census measures of poverty tell the story even more graphically. The incidence of poverty among Appalachian families in 1970 (the last year for which figures are available) was 39% higher than the national average; the 1959 level, according to the 1960 census, had been 41% higher, hardly a change at all. The relative incidence of poverty among Appalachian black families was 20% higher in 1970 than that for black families nationally and 33% higher for elderly Appalachians than for the elderly nationally. In Appalachian Kentucky 43% of all black families earned below the poverty level; in Appalachian Mississippi, the figure was 59%.

In housing the same story continues: the average value of all homes in Appalachia in 1970 was $14,350, 26% below the national average. Deficient units (no plumbing, etc.) constituted 38% of all occupied dwellings in central Appalachia, ranging to 44% in some counties. In Appalachian Kentucky, 96,631 dwellings lacked plumbing, and in the central Appalachian region (60 counties in four states), the number rose to 303,578. By contrast, nationally only 13% of homes are deficient. With less than 10% of the nation's population, Appalachia has nearly 30% of its deficient homes.

Despite the coal boom that created an estimated 100 millionaires in eastern Kentucky in the 1970's, this is where Kentucky continued to rank according to a number of key indicators:

(1) the state as a whole ranked 44th in the U.S. in per capita income in 1975;

(2) at the end of the fiscal year in 1976, Kentucky had 400,000 of its 3.4 million people (12% of the population) on food stamps. This ranked the state third, above even Mississippi and Louisiana;

(3) during the same period, Kentucky had more than 200,000 people on welfare;

(4) Owsley County, with 5,200 residents, had 2,565 (49%) on food stamps in its isolated mountain hollows; 1,156 people received AFDC (22%). Sixty-two percent of Owsley County families—who are outside ARC growth centers—are below the poverty level, 48% of them in "severe poverty" according to the 1970 census;

(5) the five counties with the lowest incomes in the nation are the following Kentucky mountain counties: McCreary, Owsley, Wolfe, Clay, and Jackson.

Despite the spending of more than $300 million alone since 1965 by the ARC, the regions' health has shown no major improvement. Here are some basic indicators:

(1) the rate of deaths from black lung disease—once hardly calculated—is now estimated by the UMW to be 3,000 per year;

(2) the region's heart disease rate has increased from 105% of the national rate in 1963 to 115% in 1973;

(3) the cancer death rate has increased from 96% of the national rate in 1963 to 102% in 1973;

(4) in 1963 the region had 67% of the national ratio of doctors to patients; in 1973 it had 66%. In 1963 it had 73% as many dentists; in 1973, 73%;

(5) in 1963 the region had 95% as many registered nurses as the nation; in 1973, 91%;

(6) only in infant mortality (deaths per 1,000 live births) did the region show any significant gain, from 111% of the national average in 1963 to 106% in 1972. That rate placed the region around 10th in the world, behind some Latin American countries and East Germany.

Despite ARC's spending of $297.5 million on vocational education and assistance to 921 facilities in the region since 1965, only 39% of Appalachia's 11th and 12th grade vocational enrollees in 1976 were enrolled in "job relevant skills," according to Labor Department statistics. In 1973, 11% were enrolled in office training, 8% in agriculture, 9% in home economics, 5% in distribution, 5% in technical skills, 5% in health, and the remainder in skills loosely defined as trades and industries (58%). The total enrollment in ARC facilities was 109,519 students.

G. Straightening Up

ARC could easily be dismissed as a fourth level of government, yet another intermediary between people and power. It and its local development districts have frequently been that. But it could be an ideal experiment station for figuring out how to make government at all levels work better. Here are some of the things that could be done:

First. The leadership should be persons familiar with the region and dedicated to the advancement of its people. *Otherwise, no structural or process changes, no more or less funding, will matter much, if at all.*

Second. The agency should be given a leading role in planning and coordinating the revival of a deep-mine oriented coal industry, one that is safe for workers.

Third. The local development districts should be subjected to close scrutiny to determine whether they can be made accountable to local citizens.

Fourth. The agency should be given an ombudsman role in Washington to press other federal agencies to tailor their programs to the needs of the region; and the agency should be given at least provisional veto power over federal programs that conflict with the wants and needs of the region (but only provided ARC is itself made into an agency credible in the region).

Fifth. Its expensive consulting contracts with nonregionally experienced firms should be immediately cancelled.

Sixth. A strategy should be developed to get broad-based citizen influence into ways to push ARC into an activist role in promoting cooperative, land management, housing construction, health improvement, and a wide variety of other areas of concern.

THE WAR ON POVERTY

On April 24, 1964, Lyndon Johnson came to Martin County, Kentucky, to dramatize the need for a war on poverty. For the proper effect, Johnson's aides had chosen for the President to visit with Tom Fletcher, an unemployed laborer with eight children, who had earned only $400 in 1963. Sitting on a pile of 2×4's with the President, Fletcher told the once-poor Texan that he needed a job, as did his neighbors in Martin County, then the fourth poorest county in the nation. The President agreed that lack of jobs was the root cause of poverty. Fletcher told reporters he believed Johnson's visit "would bring us some luck." On August 20, 1964, Johnson signed the Economic Opportunity Act of 1964.

A year later, Fletcher and his family were having better luck. The Great Society had signed him up to be trained as an auto mechanic by the Manpower Development and Training program, paying him $42 a week. Fletcher bought a cookstove, some furniture, and new false teeth for himself and his wife.

Seven years later, in 1972, Fletcher was in the same predicament he had been in during 1964. His auto mechanic training had never taught him more than how to change spark plugs. No job ever materialized. All Fletcher had to show from the war on poverty was his disappointment and food stamps. Barring but few exceptions, Tom Fletcher's experience was a microcosm of the war on poverty in Appalachia.

In 1977 Martin County is boom town U.S.A. Thanks to a decision by the N & W Railroad to lease thick seams of coal in its holdings there, the county is prospering. It has less unemployment than counties in Kentucky's rich Bluegrass country.

The designers of the great Society had ample warning that solving poverty in Appalachia would take more than piece-meal programs. In 1962, Harry Caudill had written in *Night Comes to the Cumberlands* that the region was so plagued with problems that they might not be "susceptible of solutions which social and economic planners can devise and which the taxpayers can sustain. So complex and deeply rooted are the region's problems that one may seriously question whether the nation possesses the skill and tenacity to cope with

them successfully." Unfortunately, there is little evidence that Caudill's challenge was taken seriously by the designers of OEO.

While the Sargent Shriver report to the President outlining the war on poverty noted that "the needs of the poor are not the same in Eastern Kentucky and west [sic] Harlem," the program's design did nothing to address Appalachian problems as different from those of Harlem. It was assumed that Community Action Agencies would do for Harlan County what they would do for Harlem and the Hopis. The debatable impact of OEO in other areas aside for the moment, arousing and training people to demand and seek jobs that were not there in Appalachia was hardly a useful service to people, by any measure.

There were other built-in horrors for Appalachia in the OEO package of programs, many that can be traced to misunderstandings of the region. Even the most responsive CAAs found themselves constantly frustrated by that problem at the top in Washington. Instead of proposing bold programs like cooperative coal mines to mine coal for freezing families, the Washington people proposed rabbit coops, feeder-pig coops, feeder-calf coops, craft coops, these and other million dollar programs that were plagued with operational problems even in Deep South agricultural areas. There were other daily frustrations with OEO commanders, which caused most good leadership at the CAAs to abandon ship early in the program; OEO showed little sensitivity to complaints about the entrenched courthouse gangs in the coalfields who were taking over programs for their own benefit. And there were simple frustrations that provided insight into OEO: the Mercer County, West Virginia, CAA director called his regional office to complain that OEO's failure to provide travel funds for community people was limiting his organizing; he was told that $2,000 worth of subway tokens would be sent to him immediately.

Part of the reason that the war on poverty did not address problems like black lung, or a corrupt UMW that denied pensions to deserving miners, or other uniquely regional problems was that the elected leadership of the region did not ask it to. While bringing poor people to a glimpse of the mainstream of the economic order may have worked marginally nationally, it failed to raise the key question in Appalachia: *who has the wealth, the land and its resources, and how can they be made to share it?*

One person who believed that question was what OEO was all about was Everett Tharpe, a disabled Perry County, Kentucky, coal miner who had been a key leader of the "Roving Pickets" movement and recording secretary of the Appalachian Committee for Full Employment. Thanks to an unusual surplus of savvy and some hints picked up in taking law courses by correspondence, Tharpe wrote and obtained funding for one of the first rural CAAs in the nation. He hired miners as organizers and quickly had well organized community groups in all counties. But before he could get his assault on the system into high gear, OEO had helped put him out of office. "They wanted a program that kept quiet, put the women to sewing and the men to sweeping streets," Tharpe said later. "The last thing they wanted was for us to have a piece of America."

Some of Tharpe's organizers became key staff leaders later in other OEO-funded programs like the Appalachian Volunteers, but the four county CAA in the heart of Congressman Perkin's district hardly made a peep after that. Regionwide, OEO was underfunded, uncoordinated with other government programs like ARC, unrelated programmatically to regional economic programs, and hampered, through its own "Green Amendment" (requiring that locally elected officials serve on CAA boards), by the ingrained courthouse gang system in the region. In other ways OEO plainly did not have Appalachia on the top of its agenda: in 1967 there were 39,000 Job Corps applicants from six mountain states for 616 slots in the centers in West Virginia and Kentucky. The mountaineers were sent to northern and western centers, where they achieved a dropout rate equal to that of American Indians. Also in 1967, Kentucky manpower programs were finding jobs for fewer than one-third of those trained, while states like Ohio and Minnesota were finding jobs for two-thirds of their trainees.

That OEO on the whole seems to have failed in Appalachia does not mean that it did not meet with success in some areas and leave some lasting monuments to its passing through the mountains. Some examples:

(1) In Mingo County, West Virginia, an enterprising CAA director Huey Perry, a native of the county, like Everett Tharpe, took OEO's mandate to shake up the establishment seriously. Before the Mingo County establishment put him out, as described in Perry's delightful book, *They'll Cut Off Your Project,* Mingo County citizens had exposed the graveyards that regularly voted in all elections, established a still functioning restaurant employing poor people, and organized a cooperative store that bought shares in A & P to challenge a food stamp program ruling that those poor people who cooperatively owned stores could not use food stamps there. But, in the end, the people, of course, lost.

(2) In several counties in eastern Kentucky the Appalachian Volunteers, a group that grew from a housepainting crew at Berea College into a famous, multimillion dollar OEO program for (initially) college students—many shifting from the civil rights movement to Appalachia in 1966—, provided lasting organized groups and programs. While the Volunteers—headed at the beginning by a native Appalachian, Milton Ogle, and later by a Free Speech Movement leader, David

Walls—did best when assisting separately organized groups like the Appalachian Group to Save the Land and People (the anti-strip mining group), the Volunteers did provide several Appalachian communities with surviving groups. Most disappeared when the AVs were defunded by OEO in 1970, but among those that survived was the East Kentucky Welfare Rights Organization.

In addition to forcing the Floyd County, Kentucky, school system to stop making poor youngsters sit on the school stage and watch more affluent students eat lunch, E.K.W.R.O. has performed a host of other community services. From that group there is still a surviving community clinic at Mud Creek, thanks to Eula Hall, once an AV employee and long a stalwart of mountain causes. To that group also, and to the Appalachian Research and Defense Fund, an OEO-funded legal services program, credit must go for helping to make the black lung movement into an effective regional movement.

(3) In Letcher County, Kentucky, the East Kentucky Housing Corporation, funded originally by OEO and now by its successor, the Community Services Administration (CSA), is building homes for poor families at a cost competitive with the house trailer merchants who plague the region. The homes were designed by Yale architects, the frames for module development were put together by Mainstream workers (OEO), and are built by the same workers for families with incomes similar to their own. Asheville, North Carolina, and several West Virginia counties have also benefited from OEO-funded housing programs.

(4) In several counties of the region OEO-funded economic development programs showed signs of success until the recession and President Nixon axed most funds. Among those that survive and provide jobs is a craft coop in Lenoir, North Carolina, a tomato growing cooperative in southeastern Kentucky, and a furniture factory in Barbourville, Kentucky. But the total number of persons employed is hardly significant, and the cost of creating the jobs is very high.

(5) Across the region OEO programs accomplished much in areas where success is difficult to measure. Head Start, for example, whatever its merits in actually giving a head start, has saved the hearing and health of thousands of mountain youngsters plagued with childhood diseases easily cured with the most rudimentary care. Only the next generation will fully know the impact of Head Start, and other programs like Upward Bound.

(6) A spin-off from OEO funding was the changing of some mountain organizations that had few ties to the mountain poor. One was the Council of the Southern Mountains, an oldtime social service agency taken over in 1969 by OEO funded community groups and OEO salaried individuals. The Council now, while basically broke, assists community groups in self-help programs.

A Council assisted grocery coop in Knott County, Kentucky, unlike its OEO predecessors, is flourishing.

Despite these salutary efforts of OEO in the mountains in many instances, and the widespread "feeling" that something was happening, objective analyses fail to confirm the hope that the mountains were alive with the ferment of basic reform.

The most extensively evaluated war on poverty programs in Appalachia have been in Eastern Kentucky. In 1972 the General Accounting Office released the most comprehensive report done on OEO projects in the region. The study focused on Johnson County, Kentucky, which is next door to Fletcher's Martin County, and also next door to Floyd County, Kentucky, where the AV's were the most active. Their findings:

(1) By 1969 the war on poverty had spent $21.5 million in the county, $243 per resident, and made $6.7 million in loans. Over the decade, however, the number of jobs in the county actually declined.

(2) The number of persons dependent upon basic welfare increased from 1965 to 1969. The rate of poverty jumped from 57% of all families in 1965 to 65% in 1969. (Outmigration over the period was 11%.)

(3) The study found that thee was little or no cooperation between federal programs working in the county, even OEO programs. Job training programs in the county, for example, trained 359 employees for jobs, and apparently few or none of them in county works programs funded by the Economic Development Administration and ARC.

In the midst of the continued depression in Johnson County, the Paintsville Citizen's National Bank reported that deposits jumped from $7 million in 1964 to $20 million in 1969, mostly from growth in the coal industry. Clearly for Johnson County, OEO had not designed the program Caudill said would be needed.

Knox County, Kentucky, was another area where OEO opinion held that things were happening. OEO believed that so much that it hired an evaluation team to study for three years the maverick workings of the CAA, which started the furniture factory previously mentioned, a coop craft shop and restaurant, and led a celebrated poor people's march on Kentucky's Republican Governor, Louie Nunn. The study concluded, "The patterns of [political] alignment existing in the county when the community action programs began were not basically affected." At most, the OEO organizing of the poor merely clarified "the leaders and narrowed the leadership base. The real leaders . . . [have] consolidated their positions and [are] more firmly established than before." CSA in the county today, as OEO's successor, is barely alive. Most of its economic development programs totter on the brink of extinction. For coal mining Knox County—once again—it was the Arabs, not the federal government, who put the county to work, even if it is as destroyers of their own mountains with strip mining.

THE IMPACT OF FEDERAL MONIES ON LOCAL INCENTIVE

While Appalachia as a whole has made progress in improving the capability of local and state government to finance community services that are commonplace in other areas of the country, it still lags far behind the nation in utilizing property and income taxes to finance basic community services. As a result, there is undue dependence on federal and state funding, with the effect of federal funding actually supplanting local effort. In some counties in West Virginia and Kentucky in particular, dependence upon categorical grant-in-aid programs for education has resulted in warehouses full of video equipment, projectors, and central broadcasting units with no software or personnel to make them of use.

Regionwide, a Southern Regional Education Board study done at the University of Tennessee this year showed that all Appalachian states from West Virginia on south underutilized both their property tax and personal income tax potential, while overutilizing the general sales tax. The study, by Dr. Kenneth Quindry, showed that the reservoir of untapped tax potential increased by more than 18% over a period of recent years, while collections rose only 9%.

All coalfield states now have either state severance taxes or local option county taxes. Varying from a 5% per ton selling price tax in Kentucky to 20 cents a ton in Alabama, all the taxes share in common either (a) their pittance character or (b) their mandated payment to the state general fund or mandated use by the counties for special purposes like road repairs.

Local community groups and local governments are buffaloed by the mining industry when an attempt is made to increase the severance tax. Both Virginia and Alabama citizens' groups this year, for example, were beaten by the coal interests who argued that an increase over 15 cents a ton tax would put them out of business. Meanwhile, in Kentucky, the same quality coal was being mined and sold profitably with severance tax as high as $2 a ton. Kentucky collects the tax for its general fund, sharing a portion in return with the counties, but most of that small amount at the local level is spent on roads, not on such needs as schools and health clinics. Letcher County, Kentucky, for example, has spent a million dollars in three years from its share of severance taxes on a park that is not yet open to the public and may remain forever a mudhole in tribute to an effort to reclaim a strip mining area. There still is a correlation in Kentucky between the poorest counties and the counties with the largest share of property owned and operated by coal companies.

A 1973 study by Save Our Cumberland Mountains on taxation in east Tennessee counties and neighboring

263

central Appalachian counties reported (updated where relevant):

—In 1972 Claiborne County, Tennessee, derived only 18% of its county revenues from the property tax. Seventy-five percent of the revenue came from the state and federal governments. One company—the American Association of London, England—owns 17% of the county's land, but pays 3% of the county's property tax on an average of $25 an acre assessment on 44,000 acres of land.

—On the whole, in the central Appalachian area, 48% of the total revenue comes from local sources, as opposed to 65% nationally. Yet the region, according to ARC, continues to have a net capital outflow, the majority of that coming from export coal sales worth more than one billion dollars in 1976.

—Between 1962 and 1967 (the last years studied), as federal funding increased, the percentage of local revenues provided by property taxes decreased. In 1962, 64% of the revenues generated locally in central Appalachia came from property taxes, as compared with 69% nationally. In 1967, only 60% of local government revenues came from the property tax, as compared with 66% nationally. While the value of coal in the ground increased, its value to the county budgets in Appalachia actually decreased.

An Appalachian Volunteers study using data from the 1960s showed that none of the eastern Kentucky coal counties taxed mineral wealth at a ratio that yielded more than 30% of the total locally generated revenue. In most cases the figure was no higher than 10%, and in the case of Floyd County, which has long been the scene of revenue battles fought by community groups, the figure was only 10%. The same study (which has not been updated) showed that 31 individuals and corporations owned 90% of eastern Kentucky's coal reserves.

A 1971 study by attorney J. Davitt McAteer found that in 14 major coal producing counties in West Virginia, 25 landowners owned 44% of the land surface (10 owned 31% of the land); yet their total assessment accounted for one-fifth of the total assessment in the same counties.

A 1973 study of taxation in the six coal mining counties in southwest Virginia by the Concerned Citizens for Fair Taxation showed that the counties contributed 30% of their local budget, while Virginia counties on the average contributed 55%. Wise County, the largest county in the state and one of the largest coal producers in Appalachia, contributed only 30% of its local budget. The county in 1971 produced 8,021,400 tons of coal worth, by very conservative estimate, $66 million (figured at $8.32 a ton). Wise County's total real estate appraisal in 1972 was $114,649,680, of which only $14,354,880 (or 13%) was assessed on minerals. Wise County's taxable wealth per child was 62%

of the state's average. In 1971, the state paid 54% of Wise County's bills and the federal government 16%. If in 1976 Wise County had taxed coal at the same severance rate as neighboring Kentucky, it could have doubled its 1971 revenues while eliminating all other taxes.

THE BLACK LUNG PROGRAM: REGIONAL DEVELOPMENT THE MINER'S WAY

In contrast to regional development programs like the TVA and the ARC, where public works benefits trickle down to the grassroots in often unmeasurable fashion, a compensation program conceived and won by Appalachian coal miners in 1969 has had a far more visible effect on the mountain economy. TVA's only contribution to the black lung program was to buy coal from miners who had or got the disease; ARC's only role in the battle to gain benefits was to ignore the issue.

The black lung movement was as grassroots as any people's movement could ever be. Motivated mainly by the agony of their own daily gasping, and word supplied by VISTA Volunteers that their brethren in England had been compensated for "miner's asthma: (pneumoconiosis) since 1943, a handful of Fayette and Kanawha County, West Virginia, men met in 1968 to form a group to lobby the legislature to make the disease compensable in West Virginia.

It took a strike and the shutdown of the state's mining industry in 1969 to get the state's attention, to convince UMW leader Tony Boyle that miners were serious about the demands, and to get Congress to make the disease compensable.

Winning the compensation was only half the battle. A hostile Nixon administration and the Social Security bureaucracy teamed up to deny benefits to men who clearly felt they had the disease and had supporting evidence from physicians like Dr. Donald Rasmussen of Beckley, West Virginia, (one of the few coalfield doctors who had the knowledge, interest, or equipment to detect black lung) to prove it. To thwart the efforts of the bureaucracies to deny miners compensation, the Black Lung Association (BLA) launched its own education and training programs. With assistance from the Appalachian Research and Defense Fund and other groups in the region, the BLA trained black lung victims themselves as lay advocates to counsel other victims seeking compensation. The program not only reached miners who could not have afforded representation by attorneys—some of whom have now become millionaires as a result of the program—but its lay advocate system, its materials geared to the educational level of miners, and its emphasis on information geared to action represents one of the best examples of effective adult education since the citizenship schools and voter registration programs of the civil rights movement in the South.

Even with government resistance to the program, by June 1974, 37,000 miners in eastern Kentucky—many of whom had no other income—were drawing $7 million per month. By 1976, 497,000 miners nationwide were drawing more than a billion dollars a year from the program. In the seven years of the program's existence, more than $5 billion has been put directly into the pockets of miners, the major portion of it going to Appalachia.

Despite the fact that the government has spent millions of dollars over the past decade studying various experimental "income transfer" programs, it did not take advantage of a more real-life situation to determine how black lung victims would spend their money, particularly those who got back-payments sometimes totaling more than $20,000 in a lump sum. The overwhelming observation of those close to the recipients shows that most miners, if their monthly check (the amount of which is pegged to that paid to disabled federal workers) covered survival expenses, went for housing: frame houses where possible, mobile homes elsewhere. No disapproving party has come forward with any report that the money went down a rat hole or into junkets to Las Vegas.

The black lung battle had other important social and political impacts. Most notably, the movement is credited with the 1972 takeover of the UMW and with placing BLA president Arnold Miller in the union presidency. In addition, the movement was a major spur behind getting both the union and ARC to contribute to health clinics that now dot longforsaken hollows in the coalfields from Clairfield, Tennessee, to Morgantown, West Virginia.

On the disappointing side, the government has yet to get reduced dust levels in the mines to prevent the disease among working miners. The Department of the Interior claims to have reduced dust levels to compliance standards in 80% of the nation's mines, but the UMW claims the figure is no better than 10%. In February, the government revealed that a dust measuring device used in most mines since the inception of the program was faulty, confirming the union's suspicion that the government was not doing all it could to reduce the risks to working miners. And while Congress refuses to approve a regulation granting automatic benefits to miners with more than 20 years experience, the claims filed with Social Security to date show that the overwhelming bulk of those who have been in the mines that long definitely have the disease. A blanket qualification, the BLA claims, would end a system where a sympathetic doctor and administrative hearing officer grant benefits to one miner while another like him will be disqualified in another era. (Social Security has approved 65% of all applicants for benefits; the Department of Labor, which supervises new applicants, is approving only 10%). But even with progress on these fronts, it will not erase the fact that 3,000 miners each year are buried in an early grave because of the disease.

AFTERWORD

In April 1977, two acts—one by God and one by the president—underscored again the point that despite all the planning, all the money, and whatever goodwill, the nation has neither done much nor learned much about this region that has fascinated it for so long.

In early April heavy rainfall—exactly how much is being debated by several state and federal agencies—fell on the region, creating record floods that covered coaltowns in Appalachia with water, leaving behind 25,000 homeless people and a sea of mud and misery. People were still homeless a month later, some sleeping in cars, and coal miners were striking because they felt the government was doing little to aid their plight. But more long-lasting than the drudgery of the cleanup are likely to be the questions of why the flooding was so bad, why the dams and floodwalls did not hold, why the people had been given a false sense of security; in short, why a region so planned for, so vital to the energy of America, was still so fragile.

The region's leaders disagreed on their answers to these questions, but as they debated, President Carter in his energy message called upon the region to rescue the nation from a peacetime Pearl Harbor. As he made the call for a doubling of coal production, officials were totaling up the region's flood impact at one billion dollars, trying to figure out how to get the coal trains running again, and how people could be asked—even if they could afford it—to build houses again in a region so prone to natural and man-assisted disasters. Citizen groups were asking why the President did not connect the record flooding with the denuding of the hills by strip mining. Why, they asked, did he not call for a strip mine bill far stronger than the heavily compromised one that is moving through Congress?

The President's call for a doubling of coal production in ten years raised other questions in the minds of those familiar with mining problems in the region. One reporter, wondering why the energy message did not contain a strong pledge to improve mine safety, called the White House press office and asked to speak with the staff members in charge of mine safety matters. Two days later a press officer called back with the statement, "I hope you won't print this, but we don't have one."

Federal studies have long showed what is obvious to any hillside farmer: take off the trees and topsoil and water runs off faster. Governor John D. Rockefeller IV, of West Virginia, hardly a farmer, said he believed strip mining worsened the flood. Governor Julian Carroll of Kentucky, who is proud of a boyhood farm attachment and whose state got hit the worst by the flooding, disagreed. Most of the region's politicians agreed with Carroll, even though for a precious few days some federal bureaucrats dared to link the flooding to strip mining.

In Knoxville, the TVA issued press releases saluting its dams for holding back the floodwaters. The agency failed to point out that the heavily flooded regions of Virginia that are in the TVA area did not benefit from the dams. The agency also conveniently overlooked any contribution to the flooding made by its denuding through strip mining of Appalachian hills that are outside its region and its flood-control dams. Like the Army Corps of Engineers, TVA took credit for taming some of nature's wrath, but they both self-selected the portions of the region they felt they were obligated to. That added up to a very small portion of the region.

In Washington, the ARC said nothing. On its shelves was a multimillion dollar Corps of Engineers study on Appalachian Water Resources completed several years ago. Meanwhile, in ARC growth centers—none of which appeared any better able to withstand floods than they had been in the flood of 1957—citizens wrestled with the mud and found themselves mired in the red tape of agencies that seemed to have aid for everything except flood victims. ARC's new federalism, its streamlining of government, appeared to have

amounted to nil. The veneer its monies had put over the region's scars of neglect was pulled off in a mere three days.

Citizens groups from around the region, many of them started by OEO funds, called for an investigation by the White House into why the flood was so bad and why the government was so poor at responding to needs. A month later they got a reply in the form of a visit by the head of the Department of Housing and Urban Development, Patricia Harris, who went to the flooded Williamson, West Virginia area, and criticized the citizens for criticizing her department's efforts.

For Appalachian people to ask for yet another study of their problems may seem as incongruous as a slave begging for more lashes, but a new ordering of the institutions of the region has to be undertaken. The continued plight of the region's people should be reason enough to do so but if this nation aims to end its enslavement to the OPEC nations, it has no choice except to liberate the region from the strangleholds that keep it an "island of poverty in a sea of affluence."

NOTES

1. Data, unless otherwise cited, are based on staff reports to the ARC governors and federal co-chairman.

32. POWER AND POWERLESSNESS IN APPALACHIA: A REVIEW ESSAY

Steve Fisher

I

Central Appalachia is a region of poverty amidst riches. Within its borders lie natural resources of enormous wealth, but large, absentee corporate interests, not the region's people, own and benefit from these resources. It is a place of glaring inequalities. Over a third of the families live below the poverty line; well over half the adult population has less than a high school education; problems of unemployment and poor health care persist. In sum, there may be found in central Appalachia examples of the starkest deprivation and most blatant political and economic oppression in American society.

These conditions have existed in central Appalachia for almost a century, yet they usually have not led to major challenges from Appalachians themselves. When resistance has occurred, it has tended to be sporadic and short-lived. Why, in an exploited community, where intuitively one might expect upheaval, does one instead find quiescence? Under what conditions does resistance

begin to emerge and succeed? These are perhaps the two most central questions facing those who are working for fundamental change in the mountains.

The traditional response to these questions links quiescence directly to the apathetic and fatalistic nature of the Appalachian culture. However, John Gaventa's *Power and Powerlessness: Quiescence and Rebellion in an Appalachian Valley* (Oxford: Clarendon Press; and Urbana: University of Illinois Press, 1980) demonstrates the total inadequacy of this response by viewing quiescence as a function of the exploitative power relationships which continue in central Appalachia. Through an examination of the historical development and contemporary workings of power relationships in Middlesboro, Kentucky, and in the surrounding rural areas, Gaventa shows that the quietness typical of central Appalachia's lower and working

Reprinted from *Appalachian Journal,* Vol. 8, No. 2 (Winter, 1981), pp. 142–149. Copyright Appalachian State University/Appalachian Journal. Used by permission.

classes cannot be taken to reflect an acceptance of fate that may be innate in their "culture." In fact, the silence, is not as pervasive as it appears from afar. Generalized discontent is present, but it lies hidden and contained as a result of the character of domination which abounds in the region. For resistance and rebellion to occur, these power relationships must be altered.

Power and Powerlessness provides a significant breakthrough in our efforts to understand the political situation in Appalachia. Like David Whisnant's *Modernizing the Mountaineer: People, Power, and Planning in Appalachia* (New York: Burt Franklin, 1980),[1] this book is a result of a conscious effort to help overcome the inequalities of the region by furnishing information about Appalachian political and corporate controllers. Taken together, these two books should change the nature and tenor of the discussion and debate in Appalachian Studies.[2] They offer models of what scholarly research and writing on Appalachia can and should do and an opportunity to examine more closely the causes and substance of Appalachian poverty and underdevelopment.

Gaventa's book is not easy reading. It is drawn from his Ph.D. dissertation and is, in one respect, a political science study of power theory. Political scientists have largely ignored the Appalachian region, and Gaventa's background and training enable him to employ concepts and theories which have been missing from Appalachian Studies. However, accompanying the concepts and theories is a political science jargon which may make the book difficult going for non-social scientists. The jargon may also make Gaventa's controversial conclusions appear more "scholarly" and thus more acceptable to traditional academics. Unfortunately, what makes the book more acceptable academically renders it less accessible to the people he is writing about. This is certainly not to say that non-academics cannot understand or benefit from the book. Gaventa's main points come through quite clearly, and the historical sections on Appalachia are highly readable.

II

The problem of quiescence in a situation of inequality is significant to classical democratic and Marxist theories alike, for, as Gaventa points out, both share the notion that the action of those oppressed will serve to counter and correct social inequities. Prevailing theories of politics present the absence of resistance as evidence of either the legitimacy of an existing order or the apathy and ignorance of the exploited. Gaventa attempts to show that the appearance of quiescence does not necessarily imply consent or ignorance, nor does it refute the participatory ideals of classical democratic and Marxist theory. Rather, it may reflect the use or misuse of modern-day power.

Relying heavily upon Steven Lukes' *Power: A Radical View,*[3] Gaventa conceptualizes power as having three dimensions, each carrying with it (implicitly or explicitly) differing assumptions about the nature and roots of participation and non-participation. He develops the three dimensions of power into a tentative model for more accurately understanding the generation of quiescence and resistance, and then applies the model to the politics of inequality in a central Appalachian valley. Gaventa's discussion of the nature of power and his tentative model is complex and cannot be presented here in any detail. Yet it is necessary to understand the essence of his arguments in order to appreciate the contributions he makes toward an understanding of Appalachian powerlessness.

In the one-dimensional approach, power is understood primarily in terms of who participates, who gains and loses, and who prevails in decision-making. This approach, commonly called pluralism, assumes that people act for themselves or through leaders upon recognized grievances in an open political system. For pluralists, non-participation or quiescence is not a political problem since citizens, if they were so inclined, can act on their grievances through voting and other acceptable forms of political participation. Pluralists thus attribute inaction to apathy, political inefficacy, cynicism or deficiencies in the culture of the non-participants. In other words, rather than examining the possibility that power may be involved, this approach "blames the victim" for his non-participation.

The pluralist approach has been challenged by a second school which argues that power may work to limit the actions of the relatively powerless through a "mobilization of bias" that prevents certain issues and actors from gaining access to the decision-making process. There may exist in a community "a set of predominant values, beliefs, rituals, and institutional procedures ('rules of the game') that operate systematically and consistently to the benefit of certain persons and groups at the expense of others."[4] Those in control may have the ability to suffocate potential challenges to their power before they are voiced, stop them before they reach the relevant decision-making arena, or, failing those things, divert or destroy the challenges in the implementation stage of the policy process. This may be done through such tactics as the use of force, the threat of sanctions, or the manipulation of symbols (i.e., redbaiting). In the two-dimensional approach, therefore, quiescence is not necessarily the result of the "ignorance," "indifference," or "shiftlessness" of the people, but rather the suppression of the options and alternatives that reflect the needs of the non-participants. As E. E. Schattschneider put it, ". . . whoever decides what the game is about also decides who gets in the game."[5]

The second view has been extended by a third view which suggests that power may not only limit challenges to inequalities from the powerless but also may serve to shape conceptions of the powerless about the nature and extent of the inequalities themselves. In other words, power may prevent demands from even being made by influencing, shaping, or otherwise determining the very wants of the powerless. Such power takes directly observable form through the process of socialization. In addition, there are other more indirect means which involve psychological adaptations to the state of being without power. Gaventa provides several examples of how these "indirect" mechanisms of power's third dimension mold political conceptions. In one instance, the conceptions of the powerless may change as an adaptive response to continued defeat. Such a sense of powerlessness could manifest itself as extensive fatalism or undue apathy and could lead to an internalization of the powerful's values or rules of the game as a means of escaping the subjective sense of powerlessness. A second example has to do with the interrelationships of participation and consciousness. There is evidence to suggest that those denied the opportunity to participate actively in determining their own affairs may not develop political consciousness of their own situation or of broader political inequalities.

The model Gaventa derives from this analysis is essentially designed to reveal that the three dimensions (or faces) of power are interrelated and cumulative in nature. Thus, power in one of its dimensions serves to create power in the others. Concomitantly, powerlessness in the others. Once such power relationships are developed, they tend to be self-sustaining, and attempts at their alteration are inevitably difficult. Challenge, or rebellion, can develop only if there is a shift in the power relationships—either owing to the loss of power of the controlling elites or a gain in the power of the oppressed. Even with such a change in power, the exploited must overcome a number of obstacles derived from the second and third dimensions of power.

The dominant school of Appalachian Studies, by placing the explanation for inaction in the culture or circumstances of the Appalachians themselves, has adopted the pluralist approach to the problem of quiescence. This approach has come under increasing attack, which includes several alternative views illustrating in some manner the second-and-third dimensional approaches to the study of power. From the second dimensional point of view, the works of Robert Coles and Dick Couto have examined barriers to expressed grievances by the powerless in parts of Appalachia. Several of those who compare Appalachia to a colony describe power relationships quite similar to those inherent in the third view of power. However, as Gaventa points out, there has yet to be a specific empirical study of the means and extent to which the multiple faces of power affect the politics of an Appalachian community over time.

In fact, there has been very little empirical testing of the second, and especially the third, face of power in any community or region. This task has been avoided at least partially because of the methodological difficulties involved. How can you study challenges which do not occur? How can you reveal the so-called "hidden faces" of power? What about problems of objectivity, especially in making assumptions about what people would want or do were they not oppressed? Gaventa argues that such problems are surmountable, and, in an important and convincing methodological section, puts forth a series of assumptions and procedures which sets the stage for his empirical study of Clear Fork Valley.

III

Clear Fork Valley is located near the Cumberland Gap, stretching between the Pine and Cumberland Mountains across parts of Tennessee and Kentucky. At the end of the nineteenth century, the American Association, Ltd., boosted by over twenty million dollars of British capital, acquired over 80,000 acres of coal and mineral-rich land in the Valley and, over a period of time, shaped patterns of submission and resistance which continue today.

Gaventa's analysis is divided into three parts. The first part is mainly an historical look at how the Association gained control over the area, how it was able to manufacture an apparent consensus, and why various challenges to the Association's control arose and ultimately failed. After detailing the ways in which the Association acquired the land, Gaventa, in one of the strongest and most intriguing sections of the book, meticulously describes how the Association began to create a pattern of acquiescence. This process involved: (1) the development of a highly stratified class system; (2) the establishment of a political apparatus which incorporated local leaders into the elite and created certain controls and biases which clearly served the interests of the absentee economic elite rather than the mountaineers; (3) the imposition of an ideological apparatus that helped disguise existing inequality and ensure a lack of resistance from local workers, and (4) the development in the coal camps of the 1920's and 1930's of a tight system of control over miners and their families. Challenges emerged when the roots of power shifted, as in the collapse of the economic boom in 1893 and the demise of the coal industry in the late 1920's. Gaventa shows that even with the weakening of the power elite and the emergence of conflict in one dimension of power, the other dimensions of power served to control challenges until the strength of the power-holders was re-established. The entire process, concludes Gaventa, was "like a colonizing process; the development of dominance of one set of values and procedures over another, out of which there emerges a colonial situation in which the dominant set of values and procedures is accepted by the colonized" (p. 82).

Having demonstrated how the basic patterns of quiescence were created in the Valley, Gaventa turns his attention to the present and examines how and why the historically-shaped patterns have been maintained and even strengthened. He does this by looking at the response to inequalities in local politics and the local union. First he asks why potential issues in the Valley such as tax inequality have not been contested and debated as part of the electoral process. Using an innovative but complicated voting model, he is able to show that through processes of coercion there may develop over time a routine of non-conflict within and about local politics—a routine in which actions of challenge (and even conceptions of such actions) by the powerless against the powerful become organized out of the political milieu. Gaventa then asks why programs for social reform during the 1960's and 1970's have had so little influence on the historical local power relationships. He illustrates how these programs have occurred in fields of power controlled by local elites who have the ability to exclude certain issues and participants from the political process. In fact, Gaventa concludes that these programs have probably placed decision-making further away from the local non-elite. Finally, Gaventa investigates the opposition of miners in the Valley to the rank-and-file revolt in the United Mine Workers against Tony Boyle in the late 1960's. He finds that in the Valley's environment of consolidated, multidimensional economic and political domination, the powerlessness of the miners and their families led to dependency upon the union organization to a much greater degree than in other union districts. This dependency manifested itself in uncritical loyalty and allowed the manipulation of the local union by its pro-Boyle leaders for their own ends.

In the final part of his Appalachian case study, Gaventa examines the emergence of challenge in the Clear Fork Valley, setting it against his analysis of the historical development of power relationships and the contemporary workings of power in the previous two sections. He looks first at the formulation of issues and strategies in what he calls "the pre-protest arenas of community conflict"; in particular, he discusses the role of a community development corporation and the use of alternative media (community videotaping and the making of a film about the Association) in shaping alternative consciousness and action upon grievances. He then examines what happened when the Clear Fork citizens attempted to take their grievances beyond the Valley to corporate and governmental powerholders. In so doing, Gaventa indicates the elements of power and powerlessness which must be overcome for protest to germinate, occur, and succeed. First, a process of issue and action formulation must take place to overcome the effects of the third dimension of power. People must develop their own notions of interest and actions, and of themselves as political actors in the process of organizing to challenge injustices. This process of "conscientization" occurred in a small way in the Valley when the community development corporation and the alternative media brought some grievances to the fore-front. The powerless must then develop their own vehicles for challenge (i.e., organization, information, sustaining values) to locate and overcome the barriers which normally deny them access to the decision-making arenas. Only as these multiple aspects of powerlessness in the second and third dimensions are overcome can challenges surface and succeed in the arenas of the first dimension of power. In situations of great inequality as in Clear Fork Valley, conflict rarely reaches such a pluralist stage. The powerful have many resources and can intervene at any point along the process of emerging challenge to restore quiescence. In sum, Gaventa shows that for resistance or rebellion to be successful, it must confront not only the more visible aspects of power; it must also overcome the subtle and accumulated effects of powerlessness. This is a tremendously difficult task, one the struggle over inequalities in Clear Fork Valley has so far been unable to accomplish.

IV

Gaventa's case study of Appalachia is rich in detail. It makes major strides in helping us understand the ways in which challenges by the people of central Appalachia to the massive inequalities they face have been precluded or repelled. But there is still much to be done. Gaventa himself explains that his study does not fully explore the impact of certain socialization institutions—especially education and religion—upon power relationships. These two institutions undoubtedly play a major role in establishing and maintaining patterns of quiescence and deserve serious scrutiny in the future. There are still methodological problems to be solved. Gaventa makes very careful use of historical data, participant observation, and a comparative approach to examine and document the three dimensions of power. However, historical evidence is not always available or clearcut, comparisons with similarly deprived groups facing differing aspects of power are often not possible, and there are limits to use of participant observation (i.e., time, money, objectivity). Similar studies must be conducted of other powerless groups across the country before we can speak with confidence about how the second and third dimensions of power are generated and strengthened.

Gaventa paints a very pessimistic picture of the chances for successful resistance, but a number of questions can be raised concerning his analysis and conclusions. For one thing, the methodology Gaventa employs stresses the process of power which work against change. This probably leads him to underplay the significance and hence the circumstances of the challenges which have occurred. Moreover, Gaventa seems to believe that challenges can arise only after the power field has been altered to a significant degree by some outside force (i.e., the collapse of the economic boom in 1893, the Depression, the passage of labor legislation in 1933). This implies that resistance may be futile until the power field changes, a position that has been argued recently by Piven and Cloward in *Poor People's Movements*.[6] This view neglects the promise of Paulo Freire's process of "conscientization"[7] and raises several questions. How and to what degree must the power field change for resistance to emerge? For example, it is not clear exactly how the power field changed in the 1970's to enable people in the Valley to respond so favorably to the community development corporation. Why are people able to break through the third face of power so quickly after the power field changes? For instance, why did the threats and violence which had worked so well previously not initially deter supporters of the community development corporation's efforts? What should be the nature of deprived people's response to a change in the power field?[8]

There are also unanswered questions concerning what the oppressed can hope to accomplish after challenges have been raised. Gaventa concludes that in order to overcome the biases of power they face, the Valley's people "must gain strength by alliance with similarly deprived groups, or win intervention on their behalf by powerholders elsewhere." How is this to be done? What kind of groups and what type of powerholders? What are the limits and danger of such a strategy? Gaventa sees his work only as a beginning, and it is unrealistic to expect him to provide convincing answers to these and similar questions concerning change. The point is simply that there is much more to be learned about how challenges arise and are maintained.

Finally, as Gaventa recognizes, *Power and Powerlessness* does not seriously consider the question of the boundaries that separate power and structure. This is a very difficult but crucial issue. Gaventa shows clearly how the political consciousness of the people of Clear Fork Valley is dominated by elite interests. But he does not place this process within the broader context of the American political economy. Who are these elites, what

are their interests (in contrast to Appalachian interests), and from whence do these interests come? Gaventa attempts intermittently throughout the book to tie his analysis to the colonial model of Appalachian development. This is not done in any systematic manner and, as David Walls and others have shown, this model itself does not provide an adequate base for understanding the structural foundation of domination in Appalachia.[9] In fact, there is considerable evidence in Gaventa's analysis to suggest that the cultural domination of Appalachia should be seen not as a function of "colonization" but as the class hegemony and legitimation of a peripheral region within an advanced capitalist nation. Gaventa and Whisnant's works provide crucial pieces to the puzzle of underdevelopment and powerlessness in Appalachia. The task now is to build upon and move beyond these analyses to draw the structural links between oppression in Appalachia and the nature and operation of the American and international capitalist economy.

Despite these limitations, Gaventa has written a very significant book. The problem of quiescence is not unique to Appalachia; it is found throughout the country.[10] Thus, what Gaventa offers is not only a better understanding of the politics of inequality within Appalachia, but also an understanding of the processes of power which may be involved in the quiescence which is found in industrial society more generally. Perhaps more important, he has challenged theorists and practitioners of democracy to shift their attention from "blaming the victims" for their own powerlessness to considering how the power relationships of contemporary society can be altered to remove the barriers restricting effective democratic participation on the part of people in their daily lives.

NOTES

1. See my review of Whisnant's book in the *Appalachian Journal*, 8 (Autumn 1980).

2. As such, they serve to further what I and several colleagues have referred to as "praxis." See Jim Foster, Steve Robinson and Steve Fisher, "Class, Political Consciousness, and Destructive Power: A Strategy for Change in Appalachia," *Appalachian Journal*, 5 (Spring 1978), 290–311; and Steve Fisher and Jim Foster, "Models for Furthering Revolutionary Praxis in Appalachia," *Appalachian Journal*, 6 (Spring 1979), 170–94.

3. Steven Lukes, *Power: A Radical View* (London: Macmillan, 1974). Lukes was Gaventa's dissertation supervisor.

4. Peter Bachrach and Morton S. Baratz, *Power and Poverty: Theory and Practice* (New York: Oxford University Press, 1970), p. 43. Bachrach and Baratz are the major proponents of the two-dimensional approach.

5. E. E. Schattschneider, *The Semi-Sovereign People: A Realist's View of Democracy in America* (New York: Holt, Rinehart and Winston, 1960), p. 105.

6. Frances Fox Piven and Richard Cloward, *Poor People's Movements: Why They Succeed, How They Fail* (New York: Pantheon Books, 1977).

7. Paulo Freire, *Pedagogy of the Oppressed* (New York: Seabury Press, 1974). See Gaventa's discussion of this process on pp. 208–9.

8. For example, Piven and Cloward argue that the proper response is disruption rather than organization.

9. David S. Walls, "Internal Colony or Internal Periphery? A Critique of Current Models and an Alternative Formulation," in *Colonialism in Modern America: The Appalachian Case,* ed. Helen Lewis, Linda Johnson, and Donald Askins (Boone: Appalachian Consortium Press, 1978), pp. 319–49.

10. As Gaventa makes clear, what is distinctive about central Appalachia is not quiescence, but "the starkness of the inequalities, the exaggeration of the quiescent patterns, and the relative nonintegration of the region into the nation's political, social or cultural mainstreams" (p. 44).

33. THE WORST LAST: THE PROGRAMS OF THE APPALACHIAN REGIONAL COMMISSION

David Whisnant

O Almighty God, who has given us this earth and has appointed men to have dominion over it; who has commanded us to make straight the highways, to lift up the valleys and make the mountains low, we ask thy blessing upon these men who do just that. Fill them with a sense of accomplishment, not just for the roads built, but for the ways opened for the lengthening of visions. . . .

Bless these, our Nation's road builders, and their friends. . . . Amen.

> Official Prayer of the
> American Road Builder's
> Association

One of the first things I was surprised by was the lack of understanding of roads. My God, I said to myself, don't they know that roads mean economic development?

> John Waters, Federal
> Co-chairman, Appalachian
> Regional Commission

The Appalachian Regional Commission must seem an answer to some road builders' prayers. But the results of its programs (including the highway program itself) suggest that as an answer to the most persistent needs of a majority of the region's people and communities, the Commission leaves a great deal still to be prayed for.

The ARC's highway, industrial development, and vocational education programs (its earliest and largest) remain the most substantial evidence that instead of initiating and controlling enlightened and innovative development, the Commission acts primarily as a rationalizer and facilitator of conventional private development. When after several years' experience in those areas the Commission acts primarily as a rationalizer and facilitator of conventional private development. When after several years' experience in those areas the Commission attempted some "people" programs, such as health care, the results were generally unsatisfactory and in some cases regressive. And as it approached its second decade of operation, some of its projected programs (tourism and enterprise development, for example) remained seriously out of phase with the region's anticipated need for affordable, effective human services; environmental reconstruction; responsive public institutions; and the development of natural resources for the public good.[2]

Quick Start: Rationalizing Private Development

During the 1965 Senate hearings on the act, the executive vice-president of the American Road Builders' Association testified before the Senate Committee on Public Works that "the highway industry is ready to move into this new program without delay." It was not an overstatement. The political bargaining that preceded the passage of the act left highways as virtually the only program no one objected to, and thus highway construction emerged as the principal strategy ARC chose in order to make a "quick start" and an immediately visible impact upon the region.

From its original $840 million authorization for 2,350 miles of "developmental highways" and access roads, the highway program grew in seven years to more than a $2 billion authorization for more than 3,200 miles. Well over half of all ARC money continues to go for highways.[1]

Criticism of the program from outside the Commission has been strong, and even ARC's two in-house analysts. Rothblatt and Newman, have charged that no cost-benefit studies were made; that no one knows whether spending so much for highways is preferable to other economic development alternatives; that construction has been "sluggish" (the system was still less than 24 percent complete as late as June 1973); that transportation alternatives were not considered; and that corridor locations were frequently chosen for political rather than sound developmental reasons. Maryland, for example, which has only three Appalachian counties and more paved roads per square mile (and a higher per capita income) than the national average, gained an early advantage in the bargaining over mileage and routes through its position in the Conference of Appalachian Governors and PARC. As a result, it received the highest per capita allocation of ARC highway money and a principal corridor, Corridor E, the location of which caused West Virginia's Corridor H to be moved south to avoid an embarrassingly close parallel alignment.[5]

Reprinted from *Modernizing the Mountaineer* by David Whisnant, Appalachian Consortium Press, 1980, pp. 153–182. Used by permission.

It was hardly surprising that even stronger criticism of the highway program came from within the region; the Commission's own studies show that the system was designed largely without reference to the wishes of the majority of its people. Locations and design standards were especially criticized. Noting that the standards for the developmental highways had been set below those for the interstate system with which they were supposed to connect, editor Tom Gish called them two-lane "cow-paths to the future."[6]

Like the contemporary designers of urban expressways, the Appalachian highway planners also paid little heed to either the dysfunctional effects of highway construction or its impact upon local communities. The studies assumed that virtually any growth and development were desirable, that highways would produce both, and therefore that social values were hardly at issue.[7] The highways were designed to move raw materials and manufactured goods; human needs were at best secondary considerations.

It is not even clear that the highways produced the narrowly economic advantages claimed for them. In theory the system was intended to "open up" isolated areas to economic development and connect (and thus stimulate) ARC's designated growth centers. In practice however, it appears that most highway-related development inside the region occurred not in the "opened up" areas but at highway interchanges near established urban centers, and that the system therefore stimulated growth not primarily in the growth centers but in peripheral metropolitan areas outside the region (Atlanta, Charlotte, Nashville, Baltimore). An Ohio State University economist and geographer found after three years of study that the ARC highway program in Ohio was ineffective. "The rich areas got richer and the poor areas did not change," Harold L. Gauthier concluded, citing a General Accounting Office study that called the development highway system in the entire region a "patch-work of highway segments which provide no . . . basis for coordinated development."[8]

Since the main justification for building highways was that they would produce the industrial and commercial development through which it was assumed the immediate human needs of the region's people would at length be served, the highway program cannot be understood apart from the Commission's other efforts to stimulate industrial development. Initial direction came from a series of industrial location studies authorized shortly after the passage of the act and prepared by the Fantus Corporation in 1966.

The Fantus studies encouraged Appalachian communities to seek more marginal industries, even though as early as 1960 the report prepared by the Maryland Department of Economic Development for the Conference of Appalachian Governors pointed out that "too

large a portion of the Region's resources have been directed toward attracting weak, low-wage oriented industries such as textiles and apparel."[9] Thus the Fantus report on the capital-intensive and highly profitable chlor-alkali industry discouraged communities from seeking new chlor-alkali plants. But another report in the series called getting a mobile home or apparel plant, "a goal to which more communities can realistically aspire."[10] For the mobile-home industry, communities were advised that labor "must demonstrate good productivity, moderate wage patterns . . . free[dom] from undue wage pressures" and have a high enough selectivity ratio "to permit screening of undesirable influences" (pp. 4, 24). The report also noted that moving plants from the Great Lakes area (where they were then concentrated), would result in large savings to manufacturers in wages and fringe benefits, because wages in the industry averaged thirty-five to sixty cents an hour lower in Appalachia.

Neither the mobile-home nor the apparel report discussed the negative effects of bringing more marginal industries into the region. Instead, they urged communities to go with the trend. Between 1958 and 1963 New York and New Jersey lost 307 apparel plants; in the same period, 184 opened in Appalachian states. In only four years (1962–66), 78 new men's clothing plants appeared in the region. Apparel plants seek, the report said, "areas of basic female under-employment where experience shows that workers respond with positive work and productivity attitudes." Communities showing "a strong commitment to organized labor" were therefore called "less suitable" locations.[11] Thus the region was offered an industry that even the report itself showed was low-wage (averaging less than $2 an hour at the time of the study), unstable (because of seasonality, import competition, frequent style changes, and other factors), labor-intensive, and antiunion.

The apparel report not only encouraged communities to believe that getting such plants was in their best interest economically but also implied that shifting the industry to Appalachia would have a progressive, indeed a civilizing, function. Implicitly blending images of immigrants who stitched away their lives in ghetto sweatshops with those of the pioneers who settled the West, the report said the apparel industry "has often [functioned] as a pioneer blazing a trail in virgin territory. Its importance to Appalachia rests not only on its ability to add purchasing power to the inhabitants, but also to socialize people into the industrial work environment" (p. 40). That ability was presumably important to ARC Executive Director Ralph Widner, who the next winter said that the "hollow culture" of Appalachia produced people "who cannot work on the production line."[12]

Consideration of social costs, environmental or political impact, the preferences of residents, occupational health and safety in the industry (for example, brown lung), or the distribution of profits and earnings on specific industries was absent from the industrial location studies. They paid careful attention, however, to the needs of the industries themselves. Translated into the vernacular, the euphemistic statement that in seeking workers, industries are sensitive to "expectable responsiveness to incentive wage patterns" meant that Appalachian workers would be expected to accept the piecework and speed-up rejected by unionized workers in areas from which apparel factories were fleeing.[13]

The emphases of the early industrial location studies and the direction of ARC's subsequent efforts were at length reflected in the actual results of industrial relocation decisions. A 1970 ARC report claimed ninety-six new plant locations and more than fifteen thousand new jobs in Central Appalachia since the passage of the Act in 1965, but Keith Dix showed that nearly 30 percent of the new plants and more than half the jobs were in textiles and apparel. The majority of other new jobs were in coal mining or other extractive enterprises that had long constituted the other principal industrial activity in the region.[14]

In a final recommendation, which revealed the interdependence of separate ARC programs, the apparel industry report urged (p. 41) that a trained labor force for the factories be provided at public expense through vocational-technical schools. It was a recommendation well attuned to the intent of the 1965 act.

Like the highway program and the industrial development effort, ARC's vocational-technical education program came into being largely because none of the governors objected and because industries wanted it. It became one of ARC's proudest accomplishments, photographed and reported on time after time in *Appalachia,* the Commission's public relations magazine.[15] Appropriations for vocational education totaled $90 million through 1969 and $160 million through 1974, and the Commission's stated goal was to build enough facilities to accommodate half the eleventh- and twelfth-grade high school population of the entire region.[16]

But it was primarily the needs of industries, and not those of the region's people, that had shaped the program. Noting the paradox that vocational training received emphasis in the 1965 act even though the region needed two hundred thousand college graduates to bring its share up to the national average, ARC's former director of youth leadership, James Branscome, said that "Appalachians have a choice of becoming skilled machine laborers, or starving." Thus in 1969 the State of South Carolina, with ARC assistance, having noted that only about one-quarter of its high school graduates had previously gone on to college, decided that college-preparatory courses should be deemphasized in favor of vocational courses.[17]

The underlying premise of the vocational education program is that it is both a public responsibility and a benefit to the region's people to provide at public expense skilled workers trained to the specialized requirements of specific industries. What industry prefers, two of the location studies point out, is "training by requisition," which is candidly defined as "public, on-the-spot training of a work force for specific jobs that must be filled when a new [plant] is about to be established."[18]

But the premise is at variance with some of the values and assumptions upon which public education has been based in the rest of the country. The Jeffersonian principle is that democracy can thrive only when each individual citizen receives an education that liberates and strengthens her or his unique human potential and develops broad critical and analytical abilities. Because the need for such an education is especially critical in an exploited region, the vocational education program is a double disservice to the region's people: It locks them into the fickle job-demand system of marginal industries and deprives them of the analytical skills needed to press for long-term reconstruction of the region.[19]

After Quick Start: People Programs

As the phase-out of the Office of Economic Opportunity proceeded under the Nixon administration and as the limitations of the ARC's own early programs (highways, stimulation of industrial development, vocational education) became manifest, the Commission began a well-publicized attempt to develop human resources or "people" programs. In the two main areas chosen for concentration, health care and education, the results were hardly more satisfactory than with earlier programs.

Health care. Section 202 of the 1965 act authorized $69 million "for the construction, equipment, and operation of multi-county . . . health facilities" in order "to demonstrate the value of adequate health . . . facilities to the economic development of the region." By 1970 health-care programs had come to claim more of the ARC budget (7.4 percent) than any other program except highway construction. Through 1974, $215 million had been spent.

When the Commission set up a Health Advisory Committee in 1965 to begin implementing the provisions of Section 202, health and health-care problems in the region were critical: scarce and outdated facilities, few doctors, high infant mortality, malnutrition, virtual absence of preventive care, high rates of communicable disease, and special occupational diseases such as black lung (among miners) and brown lung (among textile workers). The Committee's recommended emphases (regional service, comprehensive care, demonstration of "new health service techniques") were reasonable enough, but the Commission launched no actual programs for more than two years, and there was scant evidence that health problems would be measurably improved through the new programs.[20]

The Commission's first approach, the building of new hospitals, struck Harry Caudill as a "patent absurdity" before the ink was dry on the ABC legislation. As early as 1964 *Mountain Eagle* editor Tom Gish noted that lack of operating funds had forced three hospitals to close in Letcher County, Kentucky, during the previous seven years.[21] The Advisory Committee's own report noted, in fact, that the need was not for more buildings but more services.[22] In 1967 Congress removed the restriction against supplying ARC operating funds to hospitals not constructed with Section 202 money, but such problems of allocation were only the beginning.

The basic problem of the ARC health program can be succinctly stated: The limits it set in its own guidelines prohibit truly innovative approaches, and even within the narrow limits set by the guidelines the stated objectives were not achieved.

In almost no area of human need in the region have conventional assumptions, approaches, and systems of service delivery proved adequate. But instead of moving outside conventional boundaries, ARC reinforced and extended them. As soon as the Section 202 demonstration health areas were chosen, there arose a "concern within influential segments of medical practice in the Region that the Appalachian Health Program would be a device for overturning the private practice of medicine.[23] The Commission therefore wrote into its guidelines language designed to placate local medical societies by requiring that the "development and operation of any community health service under Section 202 shall preserve and encourage all existing programs and arrangements involving the relationship between the physician and the patient."[24] To insure that the guidelines would be observed, the governing boards of the local health councils were heavily weighted with doctors and "established local leaders." As of 1970 the Commission reported that "no area has successfully obtained effective representation of the disadvantaged" on the health councils, which it said "generally represent the existing power structure."[25]

But within the program's narrow limits, what actually happened in health care? Initial studies indicated that there was little substantial change in the level or quality of available services, that medical care remained beyond the financial means of most families, and that the Commission had not successfully demonstrated any new approaches to medical care. One analyst, generally favorable in his assessment of the Commission, called the health program "a case study in the travails of attempted innovation."[26]

David Danielson's extensive study of the health program in 1970 concluded that the choice of health demonstration districts was made "in a highly politicized atmosphere"; that three years after the program was authorized $20 million in appropriated funds were uncommitted and "nothing had happened"; and that subsequent fears of a budget cut caused the Commission to spend $19.6 million in less than three months on hastily approved projects.[27] Danielson also found that the Commission rejected the usual Public Health Service requirement that health boards have 51 percent consumer representation; that one 202 agency was apparently set up primarily to get a new hospital for a clique of physicians; that 69 percent of health facilities construction money had been spent for conventional hospitals (some of which were called "gold-plated" and "lavish" even by the doctors); that there was little coordination between the multi county demonstration health areas and the multicounty development districts; and that much publicized screening programs had not been followed up by efforts to correct the defects discovered.

Danielson concluded that the 202 program "follow[s] the lead of imperfect State and Federal programs, and buys 'more of the same' rather than trying new paths which could lead the Nation out of the maze of high-cost medical care." A 1974 study by the comptroller-general of twenty-four ARC health projects in Kentucky was more blunt: "A comprehensive regional health network, as defined by ARC," the study concluded, "has not been achieved."[28]

The Commission's black lung program provided a striking example of its inability to cope with a widespread health problem peculiar to the region.

Coal workers' pneumoconiosis (black lung) is caused when miners breathe fine particles of coal dust suspended in the air in coal mines. The dust collects in tiny nodules in the lungs, destroys lung tissue, impairs the transfer of oxygen to the blood, destroys small blood vessels, and eventually leads to enlargement of the heart and early death. Once black lung begins it can progress even without further exposure to coal dust. Ten years' work in a mine is so certain to precipitate the disease that both the United Mine Workers and the Black Lung Association have argued that it should be accepted as definitive proof that a miner has black lung.

Although ARC was not the first public agency to delay attention to black lung, it had less justification for doing so than any other except perhaps the Bureau of Mines. As early as 1813, autopsies had shown that the lungs of coal miners were blackened, and by 1833 some doctors were asserting that the condition was caused by mining. The British government declared black lung a compensable occupational disease in 1943, established a sophisticated screening and treatment program, and by 1965 had reduced the incidence of new cases to four-fifths their former level.[29]

But in the United States it has been a different story. Although by 1950 the Public Health Service had established that coal miners were five times more prone to respiratory diseases than other workers, it did not ascertain the actual incidence of black lung until 1963. Doctors in the United States were reluctant to recognize the disease. Until 1959 Cecil's *Textbook of Medicine* denied that breathing coal dust was dangerous and suggested that it might even benefit miners by slowing silicosis (a disease they were admitted to have). As late as 1966 Harrison's *Principles of Internal Medicine* equivocated on the causes of black lung.[30] It was 1969 before Title IV of the Federal Coal Mine Health and Safety Act recognized black lung as a compensable occupational disease.[31]

The Appalachian Regional Commission did nothing in relation to black lung until the Senate Public Works Committee, in hearings on the 1969 amendments, made clear that it must. In November 1970 John Whisman presented what he called an "action plan on coal mining problems," and in 1971 the Commission initiated a series of studies for a scheduled 1972 conference. One $38,000 study, designed to discover what makes men want to work in coal mines, concluded that they did so because it was the best job available, the pay was good, and the alternatives were scarce. Another showed that black lung cost workers, companies, and consumers $50 million a year but could be prevented for $31 million per year, or a maximum of 13¢ per ton of coal mined. In January 1973, UMWA President Arnold Miller charged in a letter to ARC's Federal Cochairman Donald Whitehead that the Commission's action on black lung had been "criminally slow." A few months later the guidelines were finally approved.[32]

When the Commission finally began a black lung screening and diagnostic program early in 1973, it was beset with problems. Although a comprehensive approach was indicated ("Concentration of miners . . . has more to do with the location of coal seams than with state boundaries," Arnold Miller said), ARC's "federalism" led to a fragmented state-by-state approach. During the first half of 1973, the Commission funded three separate programs in Ohio, West Virginia, and Tennessee.[35]

ARC's black-lung programs also sought to guarantee that the entrepreneurial medical system would not be disturbed. A proposal to establish a black lung clinic at the East Tennessee Chest Disease Hospital noted that the program would be "integrated into the current miner-physician encounter system without disrupting [it] by working with the . . . dedicated but overburdened physician . . . in a supportive way." About the same time, however, the *Louisville Courier-Journal's* Kyle Vance reported that some "dedicated but overburdened" doctors in Kentucky were boosting their incomes by four thousand to ten thousand dollars a month by handling black lung claims for both miners and coal companies.[34]

The most immediate beneficiaries of the Commission's black lung program may in fact have been physicians and consultants. Late in 1972, after working on its guidelines at meetings from which reporters were barred, the Commission let two controversial contracts for assistance with its program. A contract with Macro Systems, Inc., to develop screening and diagnostic services provided a fee for $469 per day for the project director, $322 per day for a "project manager," and $184 per day for a "senior consultant." Even a research assistant was to be paid $70 per day (the equivalent of $20,000 per year). Both Macro Systems and the ARC defended the fees as reasonable.[35]

A second contract authorized American Health Profiles to supply a design for a mobile black lung screening van, a plan for its use, and an "awareness" program for potential users. Doctors working on the design were to be paid $250 per day. Many authorities questioned the suitability of mobile vans for screening because they offered little privacy, caused patients to wait outside in bad weather, were unreliable technically when delicately calibrated equipment was jarred during travel over rough mountain roads, and were perhaps less economical than fixed-site alternatives.[36] But the van was nevertheless built and was unveiled with considerable publicity by the governor of West Virginia. After remaining parked in front of the state capitol for three days (screening no miners), it departed for the midwest. The van remained the property of AHP, leading some critics to charge that the net result of the contract was for the ARC to buy AHP a black lung van.

In early 1972, recognizing the limitations of some of its earlier approaches to health care, the Commission began to place additional emphasis on what had come to be called primary care, defined by one consultant as the care "most of the people need most of the time."[37] During the ensuing two years, the ARC spent more than $7 million on thirty-seven primary care projects in eleven states (less than $95,000 per project per year), which it advertised as evidence that it was capable at last of the boldness and innovation in health care called for by Section 202.

One of the programs of which it appeared proudest was the Hot Springs (North Carolina) Health Program. In fact, however, the Commission had nothing to do with the creation of the highly successful Hot Springs program. Its later commitment of support, though substantial, was hedged with conditions that proved difficult to meet. And some of the most important policy implications of the program had little discernible impact on larger Commission strategies for dealing with health care.

The Hot Springs Health Program was conceived and begun by Linda Mashburn, a nurse who had spent four years in the late 1960s conducting health fairs throughout the region as an employee of church groups and the Council of the Southern Mountains.[38] As a location for an experiment in providing primary health care to low-income people, Hot Springs was appropriate both practically and symbolically. Situated in one of North Carolina's far western counties, where poverty and illness were widespread and health care virtually unattainable, the town took its name from mineral springs whose reputed curative properties had drawn the wealthy to its elegant hotel and baths since the early nineteenth century.

But in the early 1970s the health needs of most of the 5,500 people who lived in Hot Springs and three surrounding townships were little better provided for than they had been 170 years earlier. A small cinder-block clinic, built across a weed-grown field from the old hotel and baths (a faded sign on the wall still advertised baths for $1.50 and a gallon of mineral water for 50 cents) by descendants of the original hotel owner, had stood empty for eight years. The county had four doctors, but none would accept Medicare or Medicaid patients. The nearest general hospital was in Asheville, thirty-five miles away by a winding mountain road.

Within a few weeks after Linda Mashburn arrived in February 1971 (and despite opposition from the county's four-doctor medical society), the old clinic building had been rented and renovated, a community organizational meeting held, and a steering committee formed. On May 1 the clinic opened, its services and policies controlled by a board elected from among community people. From a shoestring operation using all volunteer personnel and with a budget of $5,000 provided by a foundation grant, the clinic grew to a staff of seventeen in eighteen months. By 1974 it had a staff of twenty-five, and two satellite clinics had been opened in outlying areas. More than four thousand patients were paying the clinics more than seventeen thousand visits a year.[39] Services (for which patients paid according to a sliding scale) included treatment for acute and chronic illnesses, physical examinations, dental care, family planning and well-baby care, drugs, home health care, and health education in the local school system. Intensive use of paramedical personnel, especially family nurse practitioners, allowed the program to function adequately with only one full-time physician.

In September 1972, sixteen months after it opened, the Hot Springs Health Program received its first $190,000 grant from the Commission. Two annual grants of $221,000 followed. But the Commission's requirement that its health projects become self-supporting after five years resulted in an anxious visit from the North Carolina governor's ARC stand-in,

J. D. Foust, in January 1975, after data in a new Hot Springs program proposal showed that Madison County could not possibly support a quality medical program solely through patient fees. A subsequent meeting of ARC-funded primary care personnel in Johnson City, Tennessee, produced a resolution stating that it was imperative that the Commission develop a plan for providing long-term support for health care to low-income people. Although long-term funding of neighborhood health centers by HEW was cited as a precedent and analogue, the proposal met with little enthusiasm from ARC planners.

Education. The Commission's first thrust in education was its vocational education program, which complemented its emphasis on highways and industrial development and implemented the early recommendation of its Education Advisory Committee that the whole secondary education curriculum in the region be revised to "increase the relevancy of regular school courses to the world of work."[40]

A later, less heavily funded effort took the form of Regional Education Service Agencies (RESAs), designated as "the first priority for action by the states" and intended to provide "economies of scale" in delivering varied services on a cooperative basis to small school systems. The programs provided by the RESAs—media services, early childhood education, special education, staff development, adult education, research—were vitally needed by Appalachian school children and their families. But the RESAs were not instituted until 1970 and received during that year less than $1 million, as against the $104 million by then committed to vocational education.[41]

The disparity between RESA funding and vocational-education funding suggests that the Commission gravitated to approaches to education not in conflict with either the expressed wishes of industries or a narrowly technocratic approach to human problems. Such a conclusion was confirmed by a recent venture in education carried out by ARC in conjunction with the RESAs: the Appalachian Education Satellite Program (AESP). Though smaller and newer than most of the Commission's other programs, AESP raised issues that had substantial predictive value as the Commission requested renewal of its legislative authorization for what John Whisman called "the payoff decade."

The AESP's history was complicated, but its aims were relatively simple: to use a Fairchild-built Application Technology Satellite (ATS-6) launched on May 30, 1974, to beam 100 hours of instruction in reading and "career education" prepared by the University of Kentucky to 1,200 Appalachian teachers from NASA's Rosman, North Carolina, control center to receiving stations at five of the Commission's RESAs. The satellite ("one swinging spacecraft," a Fairchild executive called it), which cost the public $206 million and was scheduled to remain aloft six years, also was to send programs to the Rocky Mountain states and Alaska before its signals were redirected to Ahmedabad, India.[42] The University of Kentucky assured participants that they would "absorb a solid core of the most reliable, up-to-date knowledge in the fields of reading and career education."

A more immediate beneficiary, however, was Fairchild Industries, which built the satellite as a pilot project for its entry into the commercial satellite business. Fairchild's earnings quadrupled during the second quarter of 1974, partly as a result of revised accounting procedures related to its new commercial satellite operations.[43]

Though sophisticated technologically, AESP was naive in conception and not suited to the region's most pressing educational needs. Several critics suggested that even if its aims were defensible, they could have been accomplished more easily and cheaply by using cable television, inexpensive cassettes, or other conventional means. Even David Larimore, project director for the University of Kentucky, conceded, "We aren't doing anything that can't be done some other way." Asked late in 1974 why cable television was not used for the program, a Clinch-Powell, Tennessee, RESA official told Catherine Foster of the *La Follette Press* that "we just wanted to experiment with the program. And if you put it on commercial television or the cable, just anybody could get it. And nothing kills a program faster than the misinformation that can be spread about it. That's why we wanted to put it on the satellite."[44]

The ARC reacted defensively to the criticism. Harold E. Morse, project director, said, "I was a little suspicious like the mountain man when I first heard about the satellite, but now that I've thought about it, it's the only way to go. . . . I am convinced that telecommunications satellites will be to Appalachia what small landing strips were to outlying villages in World War II." Later Morse called AESP "the forerunner of more ambitious satellite projects to help crack the cultural isolation of Appalachia."[45] But whether the region was in fact culturally isolated, and whether, if it was, that isolation could or should be "cracked" by satellites or any other means remained open to serious question.

Although Morse maintained that "local input" was sought in designing the project, there was little evidence that significant input was obtained. Numerous critics in fact suggested that consultation with local people in Appalachia's tax-starved school districts would almost certainly have placed higher priorities on raising teachers' salaries, buying school books and clothing for children who needed them, upgrading the region's universities, or even establishing a regionwide cable television system.[46]

If one must judge from the naiveté of the program's design and content, even the relatively low-priority needs of the 1,200 middle-class master's degree candidates who received AESP appear not to have been well served. In early 1974, responding to criticism of AESP, Federal Co-chairman Donald Whitehead made public a transcript of a University of Kentucky videotape justifying and explaining the project. It is worth quoting at some length:

> [Each teaching session has] a programmed instruction feature. Each participant, equipped with . . . a panel of four buttons, will listen to hypothetical teaching situations and be asked to choose among alternative approaches to the problem posed. After pressing a button corresponding to one of the four alternatives, he or she will hear a recorded discussion of the merits of that answer. . . . On the afternoon of every fourth television session, the participant can also expect to take part, by . . . telephone, in a live television seminar keyed to the continuing course work. . . . This kind of regular two-way contact [will guarantee that] course work will apply to his or her own teaching situation. . . .
>
> What really sets this program apart, however, is that all participants will [have] access to . . . an information system that will permit [the University of Kentucky] computer center . . . to make specialized searches . . . of all available literature and instructional materials in these fields. [There will also] be telephone terminals to provide rapid access to information stored in the [University of Kentucky] system. . . . All these high-quality services will be available through the RESAs. [The University] is spending a great deal of time, effort, and expertise to insure the reliability of these systems.[47]

Thus the Commission's position remained that "satellite television has a future in Appalachia's educational system. . . . If the project proves feasible, as there is every indication it will, then it will be appropriate to consider whether educational funds available in Appalachia can most wisely be expended by expanding the project." Ironically, the videotape transcript itself warned that "all too often big projects with . . . lots of money end up as relics or curiosities. Leaving little behind, they are soon forgotten. Nor is it unusual for projected technological solutions to human problems to ignore or do violence to the individual's life and work."[48]

Program Design for the Payoff Decade: Out of Touch and Out of Phase

In mid-1973, near the end of its first eight years of operation, the Appalachian Regional Commission launched a "program design effort" calculated both to evaluate its past programs and to project new programs in anticipation of Congressional reauthorization hearings scheduled for early 1975. To accomplish the former aim, it allocated $850,000 for hiring consultants to review existing programs; to design possible new programs, it set up eight subcommittees of its own state representatives, eventually assisted by other consulting firms.[49]

But the Commission's record of improving programs designed by one contingent of consultants and found faulty by a later set was not encouraging. It seemed likely that new programs would therefore be no more useful than their predecessors. Two projected programs that suggested how problematic the "payoff decade" was likely to be in Appalachia were "culture and tourism" and "enterprise [that is, industrial site] development."[50]

Culture and Tourism. During the winter of 1748 George Washington visited the "famed warm springs" at Berkeley Springs, Virginia (now West Virginia). By 1774 the first cabin had appeared at White Sulphur Springs, and by the early nineteenth century tourism was already a growing enterprise in various parts of the region.[51] It brought wealth to a few but demeaned many more. As early as 1860 Frederick Law Olmsted's *A Journey to the Back Country* took note of mountain women picking blackberries to sell to resort hotels northeast of Asheville in the Blue Ridge mountains. In 1905, Emma Bell Miles commented in *The Spirit of the Mountains,* "Too late the mountaineer realizes that he has sold his birthright for a mess of pottage" when the hotels arrive, and "the semblance of prosperity . . . vanishes with the departure of the summer people."[52]

But tourist development has nevertheless continued to be prescribed as a "natural" strategy for improving the lot of Appalachian people, and ARC became its chief exponent after the demise of ARA. John Whisman consistently proposed tourism as a prime development strategy, from his earliest work in eastern Kentucky through the Conference of Appalachian Governors and ARA. In early 1964, before he joined ARC, he spoke enthusiastically of "Cloud City" and "Magic Mountain," two visionary tourist complexes planned for eastern Kentucky but never built.[53] Inside ARC itself, his enthusiasm remained undiminished despite a lengthening series of reports showing that tourism was not a good development strategy.

The first report, a study completed by Robert R. Nathan and Associates only a year after the ARC was formed, pointed out that jobs generated by the tourism industry required low-level skills, that "few . . . pay a living wage," that most (75 percent) were seasonal only, and that almost none were covered by collective bargaining. At Capon Springs, Virginia, where resort activity had been important since the eighteenth century, investigators found women who were heads of households working twelve hours a day for $7.00 plus tips and living during the half-year the resort was closed on $16 per week in unemployment benefits.[54] The report concluded that the usual economic impact of tourist development was "marginal," citing Gatlinburg, Tennessee, as an example of intensive development that benefited few and exploited many. Groping for justifications for continuing such development, the report

ventured that it could "raise the aspirations of local residents whose horizons are broadened by contact with outsiders."

The 1966 Robert Nathan study was actually the first step in a four-phase ARC recreation and tourism plan for the region. In addition to providing an inventory of existing recreational development, it also designated twenty-three "terminal complexes" as "focal points of . . . development over the next two decades" and chose fourteen for further analysis in the second phase market-analysis study, which was released in 1971.[55] The third and fourth phases were to include the preparation of "site development" and "implementation" plans for each of the fourteen complexes.

The 1971 market-analysis report was an ill omen for the region. Discussing the problem of environmental control, it cited Disneyland as a new standard of total environment" to which recreational complexes should aspire.[56] It was an odd recommendation indeed for an area already blighted with more than its share of "theme parks": Hillbilly Worlds, fake Indian villages, and Tweetsie Railroads. For private tourism developers, the report recommended public subsidy. "In those complexes that are not yet developed as recreational centers," it said, "the public sector might have to pioneer the initial construction and operation of recreational facilities, until . . . markets become large enough to justify private investments." One of the terminal complexes chosen for intensive development was Boone, North Carolina, which was already experiencing serious difficulties as a result of uncontrolled private tourism development during the late 1960s. Another was the nearby Mount Rogers, Virginia, area, where local citizens were organizing to oppose further public development.

As the years passed, evidence mounted that tourism was not a desirable basis for economic development, but the Commission's policy of promoting tourism remained unchanged. As early as 1965 a study for the Commission done by Litton Industries concluded that "local income and employment multiplier effects" from such development were "practically nonexistent in areas without a sizeable city" and cautioned that jobs in the industry were seasonal.[57] The warnings were repeated by the Robert R. Nathan study of 1966 and were spelled out in detail by a three-volume study submitted to the Economic Development Administration (EDA) just as ARC formed its Culture and Tourism committee in 1973.[58]

The EDA study, which focused on the economic impact of specific tourist development projects, included five Appalachian projects already in operation. At Carter Caves, Kentucky, 28 percent of the thirty-nine jobs created were permanent, and average annual income for all jobs was $2,206. Only twelve out of one hundred jobs at Greenbo Lake State Resort Park

(Kentucky) were permanent. The eight-eight seasonal employees earned an average of $1,935 per year. The Breaks Interstate Park (Virginia and Kentucky) provided $1,793 average annual incomes for eighty-one employees, only eight of whom worked throughout the year. At the Cass Scenic Railroad (Virginia), average incomes were much higher ($4,877), but workers had raised their incomes only $1,027 on the average, and only twenty out of 140 employees had year-round jobs. At Pipestem State Park in West Virginia, built with about $13 million of ARA and EDA funds, slightly more than a third of the jobs were permanent, and employees earned an average of $2,932 per year.[59]

The chairman of ARC's Culture and Tourism committee insisted in mid-1974 that the committee's work was oriented merely toward "taking stock" rather than actually promoting tourism, but a committee staff member had earlier admitted to a reporter, "Instead of being open to what, if any, role ARC might play, we're starting with the idea of promotion."[60] To have done otherwise would in fact have been inconsistent. The Commission had already designed its highway and vocational education programs partly to reinforce an emphasis on tourist development. And it had been promoting tourism more directly through a series of contract studies stretching over ARC's entire history and costing $500,000. As early as 1969, ARC funds had built a fifty-seven-unit motel-restaurant training complex at the Tri-County Vocational Education High School and Technical Institute at Nelsonville, Ohio, and a smaller "hospitality training center" was later started at the Asheville-Buncombe Technical Institute in western North Carolina.[61] The centers were built to train Appalachian young people as functionaries in the tourism industry—motel operators at best, and maids, janitors, waitresses, and filling station attendants at worst.

Thus the dynamics of the tourism industry itself and the history of the Commission's prior involvement in tourism development both suggest that there will be more promotion and further extrapolation of existing trends. A $50,000 study prepared for ARC in 1974 by Centaur Management Consultants, which had earlier done the tourism study for EDA, recommended, in fact, that the Commission inaugurate a $300,000-a-year market research program and a $2-million-a-year television advertising campaign to provide for "continued development and expansion" of tourism in the region. The study played down environmental problems related to tourist development, which it said were associated almost solely with second-home construction.[62]

What the results of further promotion are likely to mean at the local level can be illustrated by the case of western North Carolina (the site of one of ARC's terminal complexes), where tourism has long been a principal industry.

One of the earliest centers of tourism development in western North Carolina was Watauga County. Blowing Rock became a resort center in the 1880s, and shortly thereafter Moses H. Cone (the "Blue Denim King" from Greensboro) bought and developed a 3,600-acre estate nearby. A small surge of development came with the creation of the Blue Ridge Parkway in the late 1930s, but until the end of the 1950s the county remained mostly an area of small, locally owned farms. In 1960 its population was less than 18,000 (fewer than 55 persons per square mile, compared to nearby Buncombe County's 201).

But beginning in the early 1960s, resort and second-home development boomed in the county. Local developers, such as Grandfather Mountain's Hugh Morton from neighboring Avery County, added their efforts to those of large out-of-state corporations such as Carolina Caribbean to produce the boom. Within the next few years, such large resort developments as Hound Ears, Beech Mountains, and Seven Devils had sprung up. By 1968, in an article on ARC in *Harper's,* John Fischer cited the county as one the Commission had helped save by tourism development, and ARC's 1971 marketing study recommended more tourist promotion, more motels, and new lakes ("flat water recreational resources") to attract more tourists.[63]

But all was not well in Watauga County. By 1974, a meticulous study by the North Carolina Public Interest Research Group showed that 23,350 acres of the county (roughly 12 percent of its total area) were in the hands of corporate and nonlocal owners. About half appeared to have been committed to resort development. The number of second homes had increased by 250 percent between 1960 and 1970. Half-acre lots were selling for $20,000 at the Hound Ears resort; condominiums averaged $80,000.[64]

In nine other counties, patterns were similar. For the ten-county area studied intensively, nonlocally owned land increased 26 percent between 1968 and 1973, and a majority of it was concentrated in large parcels held by out-of-state buyers. During the five-year period there had been a dramatic increase in both the volume of land sales and prices (land that sold for $100–$250 per acre in Cherokee County in 1966 was selling for $2,000–$2,500 in 1974). More than seventy thousand acres were committed to resort development in the counties. Carolina Caribbean, the G. F. Company, and Sugar Mountain owned 16,300 acres in Avery County; Liberty Life Insurance held 20,400 in Burke and Jackson, three Florida firms (Realtec, Jones, and Collier and Gonzalez) owned 26,000 in Jackson and Transylvania; Carolina Ritco, a Miami firm, held title to 35,800 in Jackson; and DuPont had acquired 11,000 in Henderson and Transylvania. There were fifty-seven parcels of more than 2,000 acres each; more than half were wholly or partly owned by out-of-state investors.

The contrast between the living standards of local people and those in the second-home developments and resorts was striking. The ten-county area had acquired 13,000 second homes by 1960 but contained 60,000 substandard locally owned homes. In 1973, there were 400 second homes in Madison County, where 66 percent of the local housing was substandard. In 1970, the median value of all owner-occupied homes was $11,700, but the average cost of a resort lot was $13,000; prices ran up to $50,000 in such places as Avery County's Invershiel.

Economic benefits of resort development to local people, the study said, had been "significantly overstated" by planners and developers. The average large resort hired only twenty-five people; and Macon County, one of the fastest developing, had experienced 27 percent out-migration in the 15- to 30-year age group during the five-year period.

The negative environmental impact was found to be severe: flooding caused by the disruption of existing drainage patterns: increased erosion and siltation from the clearing of large areas for golf courses and ski slopes: a strain on water suppliers: and inadequate sewage treatment. There were, the report concluded, "no real restrictions on what a developer may do to the land." Stanley P. Whitcomb, president of the Realtec Corporation of Fort Lauderdale, which owned the 4,700-acre Connestee Falls resort in Transylvania County, said his company pledged that in its developments "nature shall not surrender to man, but . . . man shall enhance, preserve, and protect nature, our inheritance, with all the resources at our command." But Michael Epley, chief planner for Transylvania County, called the development practices at Connestee Falls "abysmal."[65]

Ironically, about the same time the North Carolina PIRG study documented the negative impact of tourist development upon local people and communities, other evidence suggested that the tourism bubble itself might burst, and ARC might be called upon to bail out faltering developments in order to salvage its own tourist development policy. In late July the Groundhog resort near Hillsville, Virginia—2,600 acres of second-home lots, condominiums, and "tennis chalets"—filed for bankruptcy.[66] Less than a month later, Carolina Caribbean's Beech Mountain resort in Avery County, North Carolina, reported financial difficulties, and Governor Holshouser (at the suggestion of Secretary of Natural and Economic Resources James Harrington, a former executive of the county's 3,000-acre Sugar Mountain resort) asked that Beech Mountain be included in the ARC's upcoming tourism study by Centaur Management Consultants.

Although Harrington insisted that no federal or state aid to Beech or other resorts was contemplated, the *Winston-Salem Journal-Sentinel* reported that the study could "serve as the basis for offers of financial aid." A month later, a *Mountain Eagle* reporter quoted Harrington as saying the Centaur study was "significant because it will document the case for public assistance to troubled resorts." Carolina Caribbean had by then reported a loss of $6 million for 1973 and was $20 million in debt. Beech Mountain's president denied a report of bankruptcy, but in mid-November the parent company admitted losses of $9.3 million for 1974 and announced the sale of its Saint Croix, Virgin Islands, property at a $3.1 million loss.[67]

A report by the *Mountain Eagle* at the end of 1974 strengthened suspicions that despite its repeated disclaimers, ARC contemplated financial assistance to resorts. A $25,000 ARC contract to the Sea Pines Resort Company in fact produced a study that recommended property tax breaks for resorts and a system of land banking "whereby the government would purchase mountain land from hard-pressed landowners and then sell or lease it back to developers." Sea Pines owned 6,750 acres of resort land in North Carolina's mountainous Clay County and had been given the study contract after hosting a May 1974 ARC staff meeting at its Hilton Head, South Carolina, resort.[68]

Thus a significant component of ARC's "program design" effort for the "payoff decade" was tied to a development strategy whose economic value to the region was marginal and whose political, cultural, social, and environmental effects were largely negative. It was a strategy borrowed from, and shown ineffective by, the early days of the Area Redevelopment Administration. Another questionable borrowed strategy surfaced in ARC's program design effort as "enterprise development."

Enterprise development. Prohibited by Section 224(b) of the 1965 act from making direct ARA-type loans or grants for industrial or commercial development, ARC had to rely on its highway and vocational education programs, as well as other indirect means, to implement its growth center and "trickle-down" strategy of serving the interests of businessmen and industrialists first and the majority of the region's people later if at all. But with its enterprise development proposal it moved toward direct subsidies, primarily through industrial site development.

In March 1974, ARC awarded a contract to Katherine Peden and Associates to design the enterprise development program. The firm, asserting quite unaccountably that ARC had "very little contact with the business establishment" in the region since 1965, recommended amending the act to allow direct grants for industrial development. Nearly 82 percent of the $76.4 million expenditure recommended was to go for the acquisition and development of industrial sites.[69] The study also recommended that ARC set up a Private Sector Enterprise Development Advisory Committee to "make the private sector more aware of what the Commission is doing and . . . give the Commission an understanding of how it can help the private sector do more for enterprise development."

Many of the study's recommendations were formulated in a "private sector working seminar" conducted by Peden at Knoxville's Hyatt-Regency Hotel early in May. Among those who joined John Whisman and other ARC staff members for the seminar were vice-presidents of American Electric Power Company and J. P. Stevens (textiles); Beth-Elkhorn's David Zegeer (overseer of the company's Letcher County, Kentucky, strip-mining operations); and representatives of Armco Steel, Consolidated Natural Gas, Columbia Gas System, Pennsylvania Power and Light, Union Carbide, the West Virginia Coal Association, and the Westvaco Corporation.[70] The seminar produced vehement complaints against federal environmental and occupational health and safety regulations. One participant asserted, "There's no such thing as social responsibility in a business that's not making a profit." Others suggested that ARC become an "ombudsman for Appalachian businesses and industries." Although the evils of welfare programs were emphasized, there was consensus on the need for government subsidies for industrial site development.[71]

The contorted logic of the seminar was paralleled by conflicts of interest among its participants. They reached from the local and relatively recent effect of Beth-Elkhorn's influence on ARC's Kentucky River Area Development District, to the broader attempts of an American Electric Power company subsidiary to block public development of the New River's hydroelectric potential, to the long-standing regressive influence of private utilities upon Appalachian development legislation. One participant, the multinational Westvaco Corporation, which had 1973 sales of more than $650 million and operated thirty pulp, paper, and chemical plants in nine of the thirteen Appalachian states, was currently involved in eleven suits charging the company with violating antitrust laws and atmospheric emission regulations and with using discriminatory employment practices.[72]

However useful an enterprise development program might prove to be to Westvaco and others in the "private sector," the potential usefulness of site development in the region was open to question. As early as August 1968 *Mountain Life and Work* reported that a 120-acre Paintsville, Kentucky, site provided with paved roads, parking lots, fire hydrants, and lighting at public expense had been abandoned twice and was growing up in weeds. Repeated efforts had been made by the Kentucky River Area Development District over the next few years to entice a manufacturer to use two sites at Whitesburg and Jackson, also prepared at public expense. But in late 1974, three months after the enterprise development study was released, KRADD's executive director reported that both sites were still unused.[73]

The Future of ARC

Although President Nixon had proposed terminating ARC in his 1971 and 1972 budget messages, Congress continued to provide funding ($272 million for fiscal 1974).[74] But the Commission was increasingly embattled and defensive. An ARC memo of early 1974 suggested that reallocating Commission funds on a subregional basis "could provide the sizzle that sells doubters in Congress and the Nixon administration."[75]

In late 1974 the Commission announced a series of public meetings in each of its seventy local development districts ("ARC's first serious public accounting to and dialogue with Appalachia's residents," Federal Co-chairman Whitehead called them) and hired a Philadelphia public relations firm to explain ARC to the public.

The public meetings afforded scant opportunity for authentic dialogue. Meeting schedules and informational materials were delayed until the last minute, and the number of meetings was vastly reduced. Audiences consisted mainly of LDD staff personnel and local officials, who watched an ARC-prepared slide show and responded to questions designed to project the Commission in a favorable light. At the Bedford, Pennsylvania meeting there were no coal miners or steel workers in evidence: plainsclothesmen were reportedly hired to keep undesirables out of the December 3 meeting in Wise, Virginia. John Whisman spoke repeatedly of the ARC's coming "payoff decade," but in moments of candor he admitted that the growth center strategy "never really worked," that "regional planning and democracy are not necessarily compatible," and that he had no idea how to control strip-mining or keep coal profits in the mountains. Audience response ranged from complaisant in Asheville, North Carolina, to skeptical and restive at Bedford, to openly hostile in Wise.[76]

Legislation to reauthorize ARC until 1979 was introduced in 1975, accompanied by allusions to the Commission's "solid advances" and its "pre-eminent concern for respecting and fostering that special spirit of the Appalachian people."[77] A flurry caused by a *Courier-Journal* report of possible misuse of states' administrative funds by John Whisman subsided rather quickly after a brief investigation by the governors, and the bill moved into committee hearings.[78] The hearings themselves seemed carefully managed to ensure reauthorization. No hostile witnesses were called, and some sessions were conducted before a lone legislative aide. The Senate subcommittee's scrutiny of ARC was confined largely to a series of written questions submitted to governors and Commission officials. The questions were superficial, and answers from the states were so nearly identical in some instances as to suggest that they may have been prepared by ARC itself and merely submitted by the states.[79]

Except for a surprising assertion by West Virginia's Governor Arch Moore that "we must go beyond the outmoded concept of growth centers [because] they do not fit . . . any part of Appalachia with which I am familiar," and a cogent suggestion by Dr. Vernon Wilson of Vanderbilt University that ARC consider taking "health care services to where people live" and allowing them to be planned by the communities themselves, the hearings produced no significant analysis or criticism of the Commission. The dominant motif was expressed by South Carolina's Representative Kenneth Holland to Governor Moore: ARC "is an economic force that you need desperately. And we intend to see that you get it."[80]

On December 31, 1975, the president signed P. L. 94–188 into law, reauthorizing the Appalachian Regional Commission for four years. Congress granted the Commission authority to spend $1.02 billion on highway construction through 1981 and $640 million for non-highway projects through 1979.

NOTES

1. Quoted in Robert Goodman, *After the Planners* (New York: Simon & Schuster, 1971), p. 79, and *People's Appalachia,* 1 (August-September 1970), 14, respectively.

2. Each observation could be substantiated by an analysis of almost any program, and each problem is observable during every period of ARC's history. But for the sake of simplicity I have chosen to consider the problems in a roughly chronological sequence, illustrating each with a specific program or programs drawn from the period in which both the problem and the program were especially prominent in the Commission's activities.

3. U.S. Senate, *Hearings Before the Committee on Public Works, U.S. Senate . . . on S. 3,* 89th Congress, 1st Session, January 10–21, 1965, p. 205.

4. See Monroe Newman, *Political Economy of Appalachia: A Case Study in Regional Integration* (Lexington, Mass.: D. C. Heath, 1972), pp. 113–21; Donald N. Rothblatt, *Regional Planning: The Appalachian Experience* (Lexington, Mass.: D. C. Heath, 1971); and *Annual Report of the Appalachian Regional Commission* (1973), pp. 16 ff.

5. Rothblatt, *Regional Planning,* p. 87. For another critical consultant's study, see Ernest H. Manuel, *The Appalachian Development Highway Program in Perspective* (Washington, D.C.: Appalachian Regional Commission, 1971, mimeo), esp. pp. 4–14, 23, 57. The main critique prior to Manuel's was John M. Munro, "Planning the Appalachian Development Highway System: Some Critical Questions," *Land Economics,* XLV (May 1969), 149–61. Some of Munro's details, but few of his arguments, were challenged by Manuel.

6. *Mountain Eagle,* August 11, 1966.

7. A pertinent example is the ARC-financed study *Capitalizing on New Development Opportunities Along the Baltimore-Cincinnati Appalachian Development Highway* (Washington, D.C.: Appalachian Regional Commission, 1968) (on Corridors D and E).

8. See Rothblatt, *Regional Planning,* pp. 86–87; Carl W. Hale and Joe Walters, "Appalachian Regional Development and the Distribution of Highway Benefits," *Growth and Change,* V (January 1974), 3–11; and *Columbus* (Ohio) *Citizen-Journal,* November 2, 1973, respectively.

9. *The Appalachian Region* (Annapolis: Maryland Department of Economic Development, 1960), pp. 18–22.

10. *Research Report No. 6: Industrial Location Research Studies: The Chlor-Alkali Industry* (Washington, D.C.: Appalachian Regional Commission, 1966), pp. 12–25; *Research Report No. 4: . . . Summary and Recommendations,* p. 8. Subsequent quotations are from *Report No. 11: . . . The Mobile Home and Special Purpose Vehicle Industries* and *Report No. 3: . . . the Apparel Industry.* The reports were prepared under an ARC contract by the Area Research Division of the Fantus Corporation of New York. Technically, these and other consultants' reports cited subsequently do not necessarily represent the Commission's official position, but functionally it is difficult to discern substantial differences between them and official ARC documents, reports, programs, and development grants. In most cases parameters of such studies are set by the Commission before the studies themselves are undertaken.

11. *Report No. 3: The Apparel Industry,* pp. 22–30. In 1964, in order to encourage a certain garment manufacturer to locate in the area, Whitesburg, Kentucky, passed a "right to work" ordinance requested by the company. The ordinance and the company's request were denounced by the *Mountain Eagle,* and the ordinance was later repealed (August 13, p. 1, and August 20, p. 2).

12. *New York Times,* January 6, 1967.

13. *Report No. 4: Summary and Recommendations,* p. 15. "Speed-up" is the practice of running machines or production lines at faster rates than workers have become accustomed to, in order to achieve higher production rates without additional cost to the manufacturer.

14. *Appalachia,* vol. III (April, 1970), and Keith Dix, "Appalachia: Third World Pillage?" *People's Appalachia,* I (August-September 1970), 9–13.

15. Richard Powers's evaluation study, *The Vocational Education Program in Appalachia from Fiscal 1966 Through Fiscal 1969: An Appraisal* (Washington, D.C.: Appalachian Regional Commission, 1971) (mimeo), p. 9, calls the program a success. See *Appalachia,* I (May 1968), 18 ff.; I (August 1968), 28 f.; II (November 1968), 23 ff.; II (February 1969), 13; III (August 1970), 1–8; VI (June-July 1973), 1–21; and *The Status of Secondary Vocational Education in Appalachia* (Washington, D.C.: Appalachian Regional Commission, 1968).

16. *The Appalachian Experiment, 1965–1970* (Washington, D.C.: Appalachian Regional Commission, 1971), p. 57, and 1973 *Annual Report,* pp. 17 and 33, respectively.

17. *People's Appalachia,* I (August-September 1970), 23, Cf. Harry Caudill's objections in "Misdeal in Appalachia." *Atlantic Monthly,* CCXV (June 1965), p. 45, and *State and Regional Development Plans in Appalachia, 1968* (Washington, D.C.: Appalachian Regional Commission, 1969), p. 123.

18. *Report No. 10: . . . Materials Handling Equipment,* p. 29, and *Summary and Recommendations,* pp. 14–25.

19. An alternative analysis of the traditional educational system holds that instead of reflecting the Jeffersonian ideal, its chief function has been to socialize students into the materialistic, nationalistic, and philistine values of the culture. In either case, the ARC vocational-education program extrapolates the less desirable features of our educational philosophy and experience.

20. See *Appalachia,* I (December 1967–January 1968), 1–4.

21. Caudill, "Misdeal in Appalachia," p. 46, and *Mountain Eagle,* January 2, 1964, p. 2 (cf. January 15, 1970, p. 2, for a later criticism of ARC's "bricks and mortar" approach to health care).

22. See *The Appalachian Experiment, 1965–1970,* pp. 62–63. Nevertheless, the report noted 58 percent of the Section 202 funds through fiscal 1970 went for new construction. James Branscome reported in late 1972 that a new hospital built with ARC funds in Jellico, Tennessee, did not open for three years because staff could not be found. *Mountain Eagle* (November 1972), p. 3.

23. *The Appalachian Experiment, 1965–1970,* p. 63. As of 1970 there were twelve 202 areas in all Appalachian states except New York.

24. *Ibid.,* p. 63. Cf. *State and Regional Development Plans in Appalachia in 1968* (Washington, D.C.: Appalachian Regional Commission, 1969), pp. 67–68, and Newman, *Political Economy,* p. 140. Jack E. McVey, "Eastern Kentucky Cardiopulmonary Diagnostic

Program" (mimeo report to ARC, 1973), p. 25, notes that the recommended program "seeks to augment and support the present health care system in Appalachia, not replace it."

25. *The Appalachian Experiment, 1965–1970*, p. 63. A new policy adopted late in 1972 was aimed at making hospital boards (but not health councils) more representative. See *Louisville Courier-Journal*, October 10, 1972, p. B–1. On the political and cultural assumptions and problems associated with changing the health-care system in the region, see an article by James Branscome in *Mountain Eagle*, November 9, 1972, p. 3.

26. Newman, *Political Economy of Appalachia*, p. 140.

27. David A. Danielson, *The First Years of the Appalachian Health Program* (Washington, D.C.: Appalachian Regional Commission, 1970, mimeo), pp. 22 and 44.

28. *Ibid.*, p. 64, and *Review of Selected Activities of Regional Commissions* (Washington, D.C.: Comptroller-General, 1974), pp. 22–24.

29. See Brit Hume, *Death and the Mines: Rebellion and Murder in the UMW* (New York: Grossman, 1971), p. 67, and Estie Stoll, "Coal Mining: The Way to a Dusty Death," *The Sciences*, August–September, 1971, p. 29.

30. Stoll, "Coal Mining," pp. 6, 29–30, and T. R. Harrison (ed.), *Principles of Internal Medicine* (New York: McGraw-Hill, 1966), pp. 935–36. Estie Stoll pointed out that in 1963 the Public Health Service spent $100,000 for a black lung study, and the European Coal and Steel Community spent $9 million in research on the disease. When expenditures in the United states finally totaled $1 million in 1966, the ECSC annual budget was $20 million. For further comparisons between U.S. and European practices, see *Coal Patrol*, no. 13 (May 16, 1971), pp. 1–2, and no. 19 (January 24, 1972), pp. 6 ff.

31. On delays in providing benefits under the act, see Arthur E. Hess, "Disability Procedures: Statement of Steps and Rationale for Action Taken. . ." *Papers and Proceedings of the National Conference on Medicine and the Federal Coal Mine Health and Safety Act of 1969* (Washington, D.C.: 1970), pp. 41–50, and *Louisville Courier-Journal*, June 18, 1974, p. 11.

32. Danielson, *The First Years of the Appalachian Health Program*, p. 24; Bill Peterson, "Action Plan on Coalmine Problems Shows Scant Results," *Louisville Courier-Journal*, April 10, 1973, p. 13; Lucille Langlois, *The Cost and Prevention of Coal Workers' Pneumoconiosis* (Washington, D.C.: Appalachian Regional Commission, 1971, mimeo); and Miller to Whitehead, January 19, 1973 (cf. *Louisville Courier-Journal*, January 19, 1973, p. B–1). In the interim, miners themselves organized the Black Lung Association, struck repeatedly over black lung legislation and benefits, and elected Miller as reform president of the UMWA. See Hume, *Death and the Mines*, pp. 94 ff.

33. McVey's report, "Eastern Kentucky Cardiopulmonary Diagnostic Program," recommended that ARC set up a central Department of Coal Health and Safety in the Region.

34. *Louisville Courier-Journal*, July 21, 1973.

35. See *Mountain Eagle*, October 26, 1972, p. 1. The contract (No. 73–52) was for $39,100. The controversy was reported on in *Mountain Eagle*. January 11, 1973, pp. 1, 19: *Charleston* (W.Va.) *Gazette*, January 16, 1973; and *Louisville Courier-Journal*, January 13, 1973, p. B–16, and March 28, 1973, p. B–1.

36. The American Health Profiles contract was No. 73–64 (for $23,000). Among those objecting to black lung was UMW President Arnold Miller.

37. *The Scope of Primary Care and Emergency Medical Services*, undated ARC mimeo report, ca. April 1974.

38. Information on the Hot Springs program is taken primarily from a series of interviews in August 1974 and February 1975.

39. Priscilla Guild, "Summary Descriptive Report: Hot Springs Health Program," mimeo report, University of North Carolina School of Public Health, April 1974.

40. *The Appalachian Experiment, 1965–1970*, p. 56. The Committee was established in August 1966; its report appeared in December 1967.

41. *Ibid.*, pp. 57 ff. and *Annual Report of the Appalachian Regional Commission, 1970*, pp. 60 ff.

42. Fairchild quotation from *Louisville Courier-Journal*, January 27, 1974, p. 1. Other information on the AESP is from a series of articles by Phil Primack and Anita Parlow in the *Mountain Eagle*, January 17—March 21, 1974; an unpublished investigative report by Anita Parlow: official Commission documents; interviews with Commission officials: *Appalachia*, VII (June 1974), 1–9; and *Communications Technology for Education and Health Care in Appalachia*, prepared for ARC by Washington University's Center for Development Technology in July 1972. The ATS-6 project originated in, and was funded by, the National Institutes of Education (formerly the National Center for Educational Technology in the Office of Education). A $2.2 million grant from the Institutes enabled ARC to participate.

43. *Washington Star-News*, July 24, 1974, p. 16.

44. *Louisville Courier-Journal*, January 27, 1974, p. 1 *La Follette Press* report reprinted in *Mountain Eagle*, October 17, 1974, p. 5. The Center for Development Technology report showed that, as in the rest of the country, about 80 percent of the homes in the region were served by educational television.

45. *Richmond* (Va.) *Times-Dispatch*, January 31, 1974.

46. Cf. *La Follette Press* article cited above, which raises these priorities.

47. *Mountain Eagle*, February 21, 1974, p. 4, partially reprinted in *Appalachia*, VII (June–July 1974), p. 6.

48. *Ibid.*, pp. 7–9, and transcript.

49. For a criticism of ARC's reliance upon consultants, see *Charleston* (W.Va.) *Gazette*, November 23, 1973.

50. Others were health and job development; environment and natural resources; transportation, housing, and community development; education; and institutional and development strategy.

51. See John W. Morris, "The Potential of Tourism," in Thomas W. Ford (ed.), *The Southern Appalachian Region: A Survey* (Lexington: University Press of Kentucky, 1962), p. 138.

52. Emma Bell Miles, *The Spirit of the Mountains* (1905; reprint, Knoxville: University of Tennessee Press, 1975), pp. 195–96.

53. *Mountain Eagle*, February 20, 1964, p. 1.

54. Robert R. Nathan and Associates, *Research Report No. 2: Recreation as an Industry* (Washington, D.C.: Appalachian Regional Commission, 1966), p. 73 and *passim*. See a response by Powell Lindsay, "Tourism Not Answer to Ills of Appalachia," *Knoxville News-Sentinel*, January 22, 1967.

55. *Research Report No. 14: Recreational Potential in the Appalachian Highlands: A Market Analysis* (Washington, D.C.: Appalachian Regional Commission, 1971). See also "Recreation-Areas Designated in Appalachian Highlands," *Appalachia*, II (October 1968), 11–16, and II (August 1969), 18. There is a close relationship between the ARC's tourism and highway programs. *Research Report No. 13: Highway Transportation and Economic Development* (Washington, D.C.: Appalachian Regional Commission, 1970) notes: "Several [highway] corridors were selected to open up large areas of Appalachia with significant potential for recreation development. Corridors A [Atlanta to Asheville] and K [Chattanooga to Asheville] were chosen in part to achieve this objective" (p. 6).

56. *Research Report No. 14*, p. 80. Early in 1974 Tennessee had a request before the Commission to assist with recreation and tourism projects. Plans were to be prepared by Leisure Systems, Inc. (LSI), of Fort Lauderdale, Florida, under the direction of Elliot L. Lewis, who had previously done large-scale work for Disney and whose other recent projects had included ghost towns. LSI's proposal (which led to contract No. 74–117 for $87,120) said the firm could offer a "totally unique . . . synergistic interaction of creative conceptual skills and sound market and financial analysis." They proposed to interview tourist development operators and investors but not citizens of the affected areas.

57. *A Preliminary Analysis for an Economic Development Plan* (Washington, D.C.: Litton Industries, 1965), p. 115.

58. *Evaluation of Tourism/Recreation Projects for the Economic Development Administration* (Washington, D.C.: Centaur Management Consultants, 1973).

59. Figures are from *ibid.*, II, D–23 ff., 34 ff., 267 ff., 278 ff., and 289 ff.

60. Interview with J. D. Foust, July 3, 1974 and *Mountain Eagle,* March 7, 1974, p. 1, respectively.

61. Richard Powers, "The Vocational Education Program in Appalachia from Fiscal 1966 Through Fiscal 1969: An Appraisal" (Washington, D.C.: Appalachian Regional Commission, 1971, mimeo), appendix, p. 2, and interview with J. D. Foust, July 3, 1974, respectively.

62. *Tourism Policy Study for Appalachia* (Washington, D.C.: Centaur Management Consultants, 1975), pp. ii–xi. Centaur noted that its data on promotion were taken partly from Florida "to allow comparison . . . with a well-developed, or mature tourism area."

63. John Fischer, "Can Ralph Widner Save New York, Chicago, and Detroit?" *Harper's,* CCXXXVII (October 1968), 2 ff., and *Recreational Potential for the Appalachian Highlands,* p. 129, respectively.

64. *The Impact of Recreational Development in the North Carolina Mountains* (Durham, N.C.: North Carolina Public Interest Research Group, 1975). The PIRG study was based upon local land ownership records in county court houses, corporate records, and other data.

65. *Ibid.,* p. 26. See also *Southern Exposure,* II (Fall 1974), *passim,* for related articles on tourism in western North Carolina.

66. *Winston-Salem* (N.C.) *Journal-Sentinel,* July 26, 1974.

67. *Ibid.,* August 13, 1974; *Mountain Eagle,* September 12, 1974, p. 3; and *Durham* (N.C.) *Morning Herald,* November 13, 1974. The Centaur study confirmed the probability of bankruptcy for Beech Mountain.

68. James Branscome, "ARC Considering Recreation Study Proposal for Area," *Mountain Eagle,* December 26, 1974, p. 1. Branscome also noted that former South Carolina governor (and ARC states' co-chairman) Robert McNair and Jimmy Konduras (a former ARC governor's representative) were attorneys for Sea Pines.

69. *An Enterprise Development Program for Appalachia* (Louisville: Katherine G. Peden and Associates, 1974).

70. My letter of September 23, 1974, to Katherine Peden and Associates, asking how participants for the seminar were chosen, elicited no reply.

71. *An Enterprise Development Program,* pp. 179–80.

72. *1973 Annual Report: Westvaco on the Move* (New York: Westvaco Corp., 1974), p. 27, and telephone interview with A. T. Brust, Westvaco Public Relations Manager, September 23, 1974, Westvaco's earnings were up 269 percent over the previous year.

73. *Mountain Life and Work (MLW),* XLIV (August 1968), 21, and "Report of Executive Director, Kentucky River Area Development District," October 24, 1974, p. 2.

74. *Louisville Courier-Journal,* January 30, 1973, p. 4, and *Mountain Eagle,* January 18 and February 8, 1973.

75. *Louisville Courier-Journal,* January 27, 1974, p. B–1.

76. See a series of reports in the *Mountain Eagle.* August 8, September 19 and 26, October 3 and 31, November 7, and December 12, 1974.

77. *Congressional Record,* CXXI (April 23, 1975), 6537 ff.

78. On the allegations against Whisman, see *Louisville Courier-Journal,* March 17 and 25, 1975; *Congressional Record,* CXXI (April 23, 1975), 6539; U.S. House of Representatives, *Hearings Before the Subcommittee on Economic Development of the Committee on Public Works and Transportation . . . to Extend the Appalachian Regional Development Act of 1965,* 94th Cong., 1st Session. March 18–20, 1975, *passim;* and U.S. Senate, *Hearings Before the Subcommittee on Economic Development of the Committee on Pubic Works [on] Extension of the Appalachian Regional Development Act,* 94th Congress, 1st Session, March 10–June 3, 1975, Parts I and II, *passim.* Although an audit cleared Whisman of charges that he had mismanaged funds, controversy over his role in the Commission continued. The ARC statute was subsequently revised to deny the states' regional representative veto power over ARC spending, and a three-man committee of governors was appointed to review Whisman's role. The *Louisville Courier-Journal,* May 27, 1976, p. 1, quoted Kentucky Governor Julian Carroll as saying, "My suggestion to [Whisman] is he ought to be looking for a job." See also James Herzog, "Whisman Has Lost Power, May Lose Job in ARC Changes," *ibid.,* April 13, 1976, p. B–5.

79. Senate *Hearings on Extension,* Part II. To a question on the ARC's development plan, identical answers were submitted by Kentucky (p. 35), Maryland (p. 120), Ohio (p. 150), Pennsylvania (p. 174), and West Virginia (p. 268). Identical responses to a question concerning early criticisms of the highway program by Professor John Munro came from Kentucky (p. 52), Maryland (p. 129), Ohio (p. 164), Pennsylvania (p. 183), South Carolina (p. 199), and West Virginia (p. 301).

80. House *Hearings to Extend,* p. 139.

34. APPALACHIAN CULTURE AS REACTION TO UNEVEN DEVELOPMENT: A WORLD SYSTEMS APPROACH TO REGIONALISM

Roberta McKenzie

Introduction

The region called Appalachia in the United States has been defined over the last half century as a culture apart from mainstream America (Billings, Blee, Swanson, 1986). Such perceptions of Appalachia as different from the rest of society has fostered not only volumes of research on the nature and causes of this difference, but a reactionary literature to the negative implications of many analyses.

Since the advent of a coal-boom inspired infrastructure in World War II, the historically isolated mountain region has been perceived, in the extreme, as harboring descendants of criminals who were responsible for their own "backwardness" and poverty (Raitz and Ulack, 1984:336). A softer, and in some ways more exploitative, image of Appalachians is that they were simply behind and needed to "catch up" to the modern world. Two important themes, one pervasive during the 1970s, and a second one which has been developing recently, are intellectual responses to the explanations of

Reprinted from *Mountains of Experience: Interdisciplinary, Intercultural, International: Journal of the Appalachian Studies Association,* Vol. 1, 1989, Appalachian Consortium Press, pp. 93–104. Used by permission.

Appalachians as possessing a culture that is out-of-step with the rest of society: 1) The application of the internal colonialism model to the situation of Appalachians, and 2) the question of an emerging Appalachian ethnic identity. In general, the internal colonial model has been applied to explain the conditions of Appalachian development as due to uneven capitalist relations between the region and the rest of the country (Walls). The question of "Appalachianness" is explored here as a reaction to these uneven relations and to the definition given to Appalachians by outsiders.

The World System and Social Order

World Systems theories are anchored in the premise that the components of the world, i.e., nation-states, governments, groups and individuals, are integrated politically and economically within a system. Whether this notion arises from a perspective which equates internal dynamics with the capitalist mode of production (such as Wallerstein, Feinberg, Frank) or from a view that there are diversified systems in ideological as well as economic conflict (Krasner, etc.), the basic contention is that the peoples of the world interact on an institutional level and that these relationships are often uneven. Imperialism and colonialism are concepts which delineate the exploitative nature of these relationships. Smith (1981:5) defines imperialism." . . . as the effective domination by a relatively strong state over a weaker people whom it does not control as it does its home population, or as the effort to secure such domination." Colonialism is the forced entry into and domination of a region by outsiders and is characterized by cultural and social restructuring and by "racism" (Lewis, 1978:16). In most analyses of such relationships investigators deal with the colonization of a nation or region by a foreign culture (Hechter, 1975:30). The *internal* colonial model is used to analyze a "peripheral" or underdeveloped area *within* the national boundaries of a "core or highly-industrialized area (Hechter, 1976; Lewis, 1978; Walls, 1976). This model was particularly important in Appalachian studies during the 1970's.

In an external colonial situation, less advantaged groups may adopt an ideology in opposition to racist perceptions of their dominators in order to claim economic and political rights. Nationalism since the nineteenth century was forced reaction to the spread of capitalist relations (Nairn, 1977:27). The movement for Scottish separatism within the British Isles, Nairn (1977:126–128) argues, was a "neo-nationalist" response to "relative deprivation." "Neo-nationalism arises at a different much later point in the same general process [of capital expansion] . . . at a far more advanced stage of general development" (Nairn, 1977:128). Likewise, Beers (1979:202) examines ethnic

activism in France in the dual framework of *internal colonialism* and relative deprivation. "While internal colonialism explains the preservation of ethnic regions, rapid economic development and its attendant rising expectations explains the extra-electoral ethnic protests of the present time" (Beers, 1979:217). Hechter (1975) takes a similar view, using the internal colonial model to define nationalism as *ethnic* reactions to domination from the core. The question to be asked is whether or not there can be detected such a tendency among the people of the Appalachian region and what it indicates about institutional relationships. Specifically, is identification with a group a cultural manifestation of the political and economic conditions of a capitalist world economy?

Internal Colonialism

As stated before, colonialism and imperialism are related and sometimes interactive processes. Melizia (1973:130) claims imperialism is not just a capitalist phenomena: "Broadly speaking, imperialism refers to a complex set of unequal relationships—economic, political and cultural, where the strong take advantage of the weak." He (Melizia, 1973:132–134) delineates three types of economic imperialism: 1) Unequal real wage distribution between metropolitan and nonmetropolitan regions; 2) Unequal amounts of profits on same production processes across regions; and 3) unequal market relations.

British expansion in the nineteenth century was still characterized primarily by imperialism that was both a consequence and a motive of British economic policy (Smith, 1981:35). The political dimension of imperialism developed due to competition among Western powers that forced projections into other regions (Smith, 1981). Thus imperialism predicated on capitalism may be seen as an antecedent or previous state of colonialism. "Imperialism was particularly apt to become colonialism in those areas where the native political organization was unable for local reasons to exercise its authority effectively" (Smith, 1981:85).

While overt imperialist expansion and colonialism are no longer part of European and American international policy, the legacies of the processes are still very much a part of the economic world order and colonial relations persist (Smith, 1981). One of the manifestations of these relations is the racial basis of differentiation among groups. This carries over from the colonial justification for dominating and administering to an "inferior" populace. Thus colonialist relations are not only characterized economically and politically, but ideologically. "Colonialism, racialism and racialist ideology are the products and component parts of the capitalist system" (Klaus, 1980:454).

"One of the defining characteristics of the colonial situation is that it must involve the interaction of at least two cultures—that of the conquering metropolitan elite and of the indigenes" (Hechter, 1975:73). Indigenous culture is denigrated and results in the native's will being undermined to resist the colonial regime (Hechter, 1975:73). Ultimately this translates into the "culture of poverty" perspective that the indigenous culture is responsible for its own backwardness. Regarding Appalachia: "Generally, such explanations tend to identify subcultural traits (or behavior) and compare these against some 'norm' usually the larger American culture" (Raitz and Ulack, 1982:341). Thus, the denigration and appropriation of culture is indicative of such an exploitative situation as the appropriation of resources.

Lewis (1978:16) borrows Blauner's rather straightforward distinction between classical colonialism and internal colonialism. In the former, the colonizers move in; in the latter, the colonized are brought into the situation as well. Otherwise, relationships between the dominant group and the subordinate group differ little between the two situations. Internal colonialism occurs in the uneven development of state territory settled by different groups (Hechter, 1975:9). "As a consequence of this initial fortuitous advantage, there is crystalization of the unequal distribution of resources and power between the two groups" (Hechter, 1975:9). This results in a diversified industrial core and a complimentary dependent periphery (Hechter 1975:9).

Emergent Ethnicity

Hechter (1975:28) applies the internal colonialism model to the relationship between the Celtic regions of the British Isles to England as a way to explain the "survival of traditionalism within a sea of modernity." "From the seventeenth century on, English military and political control in the peripheral regions was buttressed by a racist ideology which held that Norman Anglo-Saxon culture was inherently superior to Celtic culture" (Hechter, 1975:342). When one group is denied access to high prestige roles which the superordinate group reserves for its members this "contributes to the development of distinctive ethnic identification in the two groups" (Hechter, 1975:9). Further, . . . "to the extent that social stratification in the periphery is based on observable cultural differences, there exists the probability that the disadvantaged groups will, in time, reactive assert its own culture as equal or superior to that of the relatively advantaged core" (Hechter, 1975:10). The specific form of a culture is incidental to the function culture performs in maintaining social order (Hechter, 1975:35). In this way, an ethnic group is defined by cultural traits

(Hechter, 1975:35). This definition is inadequate to explain social change and the maintenance of cultural differences between groups in close, continued contact (Hechter 1975:35). For Hechter (1975:37), cultural distinctions can be deliberate and purposeful: "It is clear that culture maintenance in the periphery can be regarded as a weapon in that it provides the possibility of socialization, as well as political mobilization that can result when individuals see inequality as a pattern of collective oppression (Hechter, 1975:41–42).

Another way to view ethnicity which may be concommitant to Hechter's (1975) perspective is to see it as a psychological "anchor" for personal identity in a changing world (Obermiller, 1977), an in-gathering of human resources for group economic and political participation (Isaacs, 1975: Glazer, 1983; Eisinger, 1978), or as developing from both processes. Ethnicity becomes more of a rational "option" (Eisinger, 1978). "Rather than viewing it as a primitive holdover, the optionalists conceive of ethnicity primarily as a strategic possibility peculiarly suited to the requirements of political and social mobilization in the modern large-scale state" (Eisinger, 1978:90). However, this may be taken further: ". . . as more groups choose the option of exploiting ethnicity for political mobilization—as American blacks have done most recently—other groups feel compelled to use ethnicity as a defensive response" (Eisinger, 1978:93). It is necessary for survival.

To put this into a simpler framework, the emergence or salience of ethnicity may be seen as based on interactions between distinct groups within facilitating circumstances: ". . . ethnic distinctions do not depend on an absence of social interaction and action, but are quite to the contrary often the very foundations on which embracing social systems are built" (Barth, 1969:10). In this way, ethnicity is more of an instance of active participation distinctly different from anthropological definitions which are based primarily on cultural and geographic distinctions. However, this fact—anthropological definition, that is—may be a part of the process. In other words, pushing a group into a particular definition may spark a reactionary self-definition.

Appalachian Underdevelopment

The cultural definitions of Appalachia are generally limited to the coal-rich Central Plateau in parts of West Virginia, Kentucky, Tennessee, and North Carolina even though the mountains range from upper New York to central Alabama. "Appalachia was not recognized as a distinct sociocultural region until the latter part of the nineteenth century" (Raitz and Ulack, 1984:18). It was delineated first by the "local color movement," then cultural regionalizations and governmental regionalizations (Raitz and Ulack, 1984:26). Even sociologists and anthropologists perpetuated an image of a traditional, isolated society that ran counter to mainstream America.

Pearsall (1959:127) described the folk culture of Appalachia based on fieldwork done in 1949–50:

> "Through continued isolation, the world of the Southern frontier became a folk world of small isolated, homogenous societies with a simpler and almost self-sufficient economy. In such societies there can be little occupational specialization or differentiation of roles beyond those of male and female, adult and child."

However, even then, Pearsall (1959:137) noted the tendencies for missionaries and social workers from the outside "to lump the entire mountain population together, seeing 'quaint' folk traits but also seeing 'appalling' characteristics of a rural lower class." What seemed to be happening was both a process of definition of Appalachians and explanation of their society that was centered in the region and concentrated on Appalachian resistance to outside influence.

In the 1970's, along came an upsurge in studies on the Third World that charged that the age of colonialism is still affecting the political processes and social organizations of Third World countries. This view was "borrowed" to some extent and applied to the Appalachian region as "victim" of uneven capitalist relations to counter the culture of poverty definitions. Whereas the prevailing view in the mid-century was of a traditionalist subcultural "remnant," political and economic interpretations of Appalachia began to replace these views in the 1970's (Billings, Blee and Swanson, 1986:154).

"The internal colonialism model has emerged from a background of the history and theories of colonialism and imperialism, and is most directly related to the theories of neocolonialism and dependency that have been developed in the post-World War II period" (Walls, 1978:234). The model is attractive because of its powerful analysis of the destruction of indigenous culture by the dominators (Walls, 1976:238). Caudill (1965), Walls (1976:237) claims, while not naming it outright, was using it when he outlined the relationship between the coal boom and the discovery of Appalachia: "When the construction gangs laid down their tools . . . the vast, backward Cumberland Plateau was tied inseparably to the colossal industrial complex centering in Pittsburgh, and a dynamic new phase in the region's history had begun" (Caudill 1965:93).

In a similar fashion, but with a different tone, Eller's (1982:xviii) later analysis of Appalachian history discussed the penetration of the industrial North and the disparaging attitudes toward Appalachians as a tendency in core/peripheral relationships:

> "Blaming the victim, of course, is not a uniquely American phenomenon. Rather, it is a misreading that takes international form. French intellectuals talk about the Alps and Spanish intellectuals talk about the Pyrenees in much the same simple if condescending way as urban

Americans talk about Appalachia. Ironically, it was during the same years that the static image was emerging as the dominant literary view that a revolution was shaking the very foundations of the mountain social order."

The nature of the "invasion" of the Appalachian region was a negative one, bringing ". . . bitter civil war followed by vicious exploitation of timber and mineral resources" (Pearsall: 1959:61). Pearsall (1959:58) noted the encounter with the outside left Appalachians not only negatively defined but in a negative economic position.

Along with the coming of railroads, towns and expanding industrialization, ". . . there emerged in Appalachia a constructed political system based upon an economic hierarchy" (Eller, 1982:xxi). Those in economic and political power exploited the region's natural wealth (Eller, 1982:xxi). Behind this transition in political culture lay the integration of the region into the national economy and the subordination of local interests to those of outside corporations (Eller, 1982:xxi).

To get down to a specific instance of outside exploitation and the application of the internal colonial model, Gaventa (1980) analyzed a small coal town in Central Appalachia. He (Gaventa, 1980:52–53) described the appropriation of resources as ". . . the industrial colonization of . . . valleys of the Cumberland Gap region . . ." which was undertaken by the American Association, Ltd.—an English company incorporated in 1887.

Further, Gaventa (1980) contended the valley's apparent disinterest in contesting their unequal treatment was due to past experience, a phenomena not unique to America. "As much of the under-developed area is owned and dominated by a British-based corporation, an understanding of the situation involves examining the contemporary role of the multinational in the affairs of a local community, as well as the means through which protest may emerge against landholders who are corporate and absentee" (Gaventa, 1980:vii-ix.)

The mechanisms by which the multinational, American Association, Ltd., maintained its hold on the community was three-dimensional (Gaventa, 1980:13). The first dimension of power is a straightforward conflict with emphasis on who prevails in decision-making: the second dimension is a "mobilization of bias," the institutionalization of systematic rules in favor of certain groups (Gaventa, 1980:13–14). The third, or "hidden" dimension of power is descriptive of colonial relationships:

> "Their [mechanisms of power] identification, one suspects, involves specifying the means through which power influences, shapes, or determines conceptions of the necessities, possibilities, and strategies of challenge in situations of latent conflict. This may include the study of social myths, language and symbols, and how they are shaped or manipulated in power processes" (Gaventa, 1980:15).

This is tied, then to the ideological aspect and leads to the appropriation of culture, a process which ranges from new place names in an area that reflect outside influence to the control of socializing agencies such as churches and schools (Gaventa, 1980:62).

The evidence of a colonial relationship between Appalachia and the rest of the United States "cannot be disputed" according to Lewis (1978:24). Uninvited coal interests controlled the region from outside and impacted the cultural patterns (Lewis:24). Especially supportive is " . . . the fact that racism exists to perpetuate this pattern . . ." (Lewis, 1978:24). Additionally, Lewis (1978:17) claims the domination of the region is based on technological superiority and the "broad-form" deed. These deeds were instituted during the early industrialization of Appalachia and ceded to coal operators all minerals and rights to remove them any way necessary (Lewis, 1978:17018). Much of the evidence of colonialism is centered around the broad-form deed (Raitz and Ulack, 1984:344–345), the legality of which is still being contested.

Melizia (1973:130) claims a scientific application of the imperialism concept in examining statistics in a non-metropolitan region of Central Appalachia. Despite a lack of statistical support for unequal wage, values of capital and trade between core and peripheral areas, he (Melizia, 1973:132–136) switches to a logical argument: "The region appears to continually suffer from a net drain of economic surplus to other areas without making gains in relative income or productivity growth."

However, Walls (1976:232), while contending that Central Appalachia "is a peripheral region within an advanced capitalist society," claims internal colonialism must be carefully defined to be more than a "catchword" (Walls, 1976:235) and that Lewis' application is "strained" (Walls, 1976:237).

The establishment and maintenance of dominance over others is a pervasive process in America extending to all ethnic and working-class cultures in advanced capitalist societies (Walls, 1986:239). Walls (1976:234–235) says, internal colonialism is popularly useful to counter exploitative situations or to justify what he calls "regional or ethnic chauvinism." "The model suggests the need for an anticolonial movement and a radical structuring of society, with a redistribution of resources to the poor and the powerless." (Raitz and Ulack, 1984–343). Thus, the internal colonial model not only raises the question of ethnic reactions but might be viewed as founded on an agitation for an Appalachian "identity movement."

Billings, Blee and Swanson (1986:155) argue that ethnographic accounts of Appalachia that concentrated on traditionalism looked at communities outside the industrialized regions of coal extraction. "What Pearsall [1959], Stephenson [1968] and to a lesser extent, Brown [1950], frequently saw as *antiquated* behavior were traces of a social logic and a set of values distinct from those of more advanced capitalist societies but nonetheless shaped by economic rationality" (Billings, Blee and Swanson, 1986:156). Whereas Billings, Blee and Swanson (1986:157) see the colonial model as somewhat reactionary to these accounts, what would be more appropriate, they (Billings, Blee and Swanson, 1986:168) conclude, is a " 'second oppositional challenge' " to Appalachian exceptionalism: "that is an historically-based understanding of unique cultural trends and power relationships.

Appalachian Ethnicity?

If the internal colonialism model is a valid perspective on Appalachian underdevelopment and accepted as the basis for ethnic momentum, then two more questions must be asked: First, what are the specific economic and political links to colonialism? Some of this has been explored in defining relationships between the dominant and subordinate groups.

A second question, to be explored briefly, is who among the Appalachian populace will define themselves as uniquely Appalachian?

In many of the studies of colonialism, boundaries set up by conquerors that gave no attention to existing social allegiances and the unequal treatment of and partitioning of resources to the existing groups were facilitating circumstances for ethnic allegiances. A similar process occurs in internal colonialism, however, it may work to dispel ethnic tendencies among certain segments of the indigenous population. Groups in the urban areas within a peripheral region, those who are quicker to adopt "modernization," are viewed differently from the most rural populace. Hechter (1975:122) explores this in Great Britain: " . . . the docility of late eighteenth-century Wales and Scotland was achieved by the co-optation of regional elites, rather than the direct intervention of the state." Likewise, Gaventa (1980), found middle-class elites less resistant to changes in the social order.

An essay by Lewis (1967:7) that predates the development of her internal colonial model charged: "The coming of coal-mining did not open up the mountains. It facilitated three subcultures." One of these subcultures, located in the mountain settlements, was traditionally-minded and presented a solid front to outsiders. This was necessary, she maintains, for security and adjustment in the face of change. She predicted then an eventual breakdown in segregation with full integration of the mountaineer into main stream capitalist culture. "Instead of reticent and retiring, he will become blase, gregarious and sophisticated" (Lewis, 1967:16).

For Obermiller (1977:148,345) . . ."the key issue in urban Appalachian studies in ethnicity . . . Many Appalachians in the cities and mountains need the opportunities afforded by ethnic recognition."

What Billings and Walls (1980:137–138) conclude is that ethnic politicalization and reactions to prejudice are salient to urban Appalachian migrants. "Hillbilly stereotypes cause some migrants to disavow their Appalachian origins, but they also function to pull the group together" (Billings and Walls, 1980:127). There exists in Cincinnati, Ohio, an urban Appalachian Council and an Appalachian Identity Center (Billings and Walls, 1980:127). Returning migrant professionals may also be more ethnically "aware" such as scholars and professors involved in Appalachian Studies in many universities and colleges in the region. On the other hand, Billings and Walls (1980:178) say "Appalachia" is not as an important symbol of identity as are other affiliations. Further, these authors call for a reassessment of Appalachia that synthesizes the traditional subculture view and outside domination (Raitz and Ulack, 1984:346). This could take the form of assessing the difference between "hanging on" to culture and being culturally defined.

Finally, one last point is raised that ties culture to capitalism in a most direct manner. When Stephenson (1984) returned in the 1980's to Shiloh (1968) where he had studied the extension of modernity in mountain culture, he found what he called "culture-brokering." The elites of Shiloh were "commodifying" the place (Stephenson, 1984) by selling it as a traditional community offering escape from the alienated metropolis (Stephenson, 1984).

REFERENCES CITED

Barth, Fredrik, *Ethnic Groups and Boundaries* (Little Brown and Company: Boston 1969.)

Beers, William R., "Internal colonialism and rising expectations: Ethnic activism in contemporary France." *Ethnic autonomy—Comparative Dynamics: The Americas, Europe, and the Developing World.* Raymond L. Hall (ed.). (Pergamon Press: New York 1979.) Pp. 201–233.

Billings, Dwight, Kathleen Blee and Louis Swanson, "Culture, family, and community in pre-industrial Appalachia." *Appalachian Journal,* (Winter 1986.)

Billings, Dwight and David Walls, "Appalachians." *Harvard Encyclopedia of American Ethnic Groups.* Stephan Thernstrom (ed.). (Harvard University Press: Cambridge 1980.) Pp. 125–128.

Brown, James Stephen, "The social organization of an isolated Kentucky mountain neighborhood." Dissertation. Harvard University. Department of Social Relations 1950.)

Caudill, Harry M., *Night Comes to the Cumberlands.* (Little, Brown and Company: Boston and Toronto, 1963.)

Eisinger, Peter K., "Ethnicity as a strategic option: An emerging view." *Public Administration Review,* 38:89–93 (1978).

Eller, Ronald D., *Miners, Millhands and Mountaineers: Industrialization of the Appalachian South, 1880–1930.* 1982.

Gaventa, John. *Power and Powerlessness: Quiescence and Rebellion in an Appalachian Valley.* (University of Illinois; Urbana 1980.)

Glazer, Nathan, *Ethnic Dilemmas: 1964–1982.* (Harvard University Press: Cambridge, 1983.)

Hall, Raymond L., "Introduction." in *Ethnic Autonomy—Comparative Dynamics: The Americas, Europe and the Developing World.* Raymond L. Hall (ed.) (Pergamon Press: New York, 1979.) Pp. xvii–xxxii.

Hechter, Michael, *Internal Colonialism. The Celtic Fringe in British National Development, 1536–1966.* (Berkeley: University of California Press, 1975.)

Isaacs, Harold, *The Idols of the Tribe: Group Identity.* (Harper and Row: New York, 1975.)

Klaus, Ernst, "Racialism, racist ideology and colonialism, past and present. Sociological Theories: Race and Colonialism. UNESCO. (1980) Pp. 453–475.

Lewis, Helen Matthews, Linda Johnson and David Askins (eds.), *Colonialism in Modern America.* (The Appalachian Consortium Press: Boone, North Carolina, 1978.)

Malizia, Emil, "Economic imperialism: An interpretation of Appalachian underdevelopment." *Appalachian Journal,* 1:2 (spring), 1973.

Nairn, Tom, *The Breakup of Britain: Crisis and Neonationalism.* (Humanities Press: London, 1977.)

Pearsall, Marion, *Little Smoky Ridge. The Natural History of a Southern Appalachian Neighborhood.* (University of Alabama Press, 1959).

Obermiller, Phillip, "Appalachians as an urban, ethnic group: Romanticism, renaissance or revolution?" *Appalachian Journal,* 1977. 5(1):150–160.

Raitz, Karl B., and Richard Ulack, *Appalachia: A Regional Geography: Land, People and Development.* (Westview Press: Boulder, 1984).

Smith, Tony, *The Pattern of Imperialism: The United States, Great Britain, and the Late-industrializing World Since 1815* (Cambridge University Press: Cambridge, 1981.)

Stephenson, John B., "Escape to the periphery: Commodifying place in rural Appalachia." *Appalachian Journal,* 1984, 11(Spring):187–200.

———. *Shiloh: A Mountain Community.* (University of Kentucky Press: Lexington, 1968).

Thompson, Richard H., and Mary Lou Wylie, "The professional-managerial class in Eastern Kentucky: A preliminary interpretation." *Appalachian Journal,* 1984, 11(1–2):105–121.

Walls, David S., "Internal colony or internal periphery: A critique of current models and an alternative formulation." *Colonialism in Modern America. Lewis, Helen Matthews, Linda Johnson and David Askins (eds.).* (The Appalachian Consortium Press: Boone, North Carolina, 1978.)

———. "Central Appalachia: A peripheral region within an advanced capitalist society." Journal of Sociology and Social Welfare, 1976. 4(2):232–246.

35. AN ALTERNATIVE DEVELOPMENT STRATEGY FOR APPALACHIA'S FUTURE: APPLICATIONS OF "ANOTHER DEVELOPMENT" AND "SUSTAINABLE SOCIETY" THEMES TO A REGION IN CRISIS

John G. McNutt

Department of Sociology, Anthropology and Social Work
James Madison University

Appalachia is clearly a region in crisis. The land and its people continue to experience the traditional problems of poverty, unemployment, resource depletion, inadequate educational, health, and welfare programs, inequality, and environmental decay. In addition, the region has new difficulties that arise out of its interaction with the world economy and national government. These include capital flight, deregulation of environmental standards, and cuts in Federal programs, as well as a host of related problems (Couto, 1984).

The crisis of Appalachia is also a crisis of development theories. Development policies are a means of dealing with the problems that a society encounters. A crisis occurs when these theories are no longer adequate to deal with the problems. At the same time, many of the problems we face are the consequences of earlier development programs. It seems evident that many contemporary theories lack viability in the present situation.

This essay takes the position that a new set of development theories and policies is needed to respond to the region's problems. I will offer an alternative based on the themes of a "sustainable society" and "another development." Before delineating a different approach, however, it is useful to examine the existing theory base.

THE PRESENT STATE OF APPALACHIAN DEVELOPMENT THEORIES

There is certainly no shortage of theories about Appalachian development, and space does not permit a full accounting here. For the sake of convenience, let us divide the theories into those that follow the Regional Planning and Modernization Schools and those that utilize the Dependency School and Marxist/Neo-Marxist analysis. We will refer to the first group as the Official Development Position and the second group as the Radical Alternative Position.

The official analysis sees the target region as the source of the problems and relies heavily on Modernization Theory. Approaches such as the Culture of Poverty (Weller, 1965; Lewis, 1967) and Regional Planning Model (Walls and Billings, 1977) seem to have their roots in this theory. Let us examine the major assumptions of this approach. Problems are seen as internal to the area in need of development (Lenski and Lenski, 1982). All societies go through a series of stages to reach industrialization, from a traditional state to a highly developed state (Rostow, 1960).

Economic growth is seen as central to the modernization process (Todero, 1985). While much of modernization thinking is economic, there is an important socio-political component. Some institutions are seen as promoting modernization, while others are seen as retarding this process. The former are promoted and the latter are replaced in the process of development (Galbraith, 1964). Even attitudes that do not support the modernization process are slated for change (Hagan, 1967; McClelland, 1962) as a "growth psychology" is promoted. The push for industrialization assured an almost inherently anti-rural bias. In fact, the early work of Arthur Lewis (1954) describes in detail how people are induced to move from the traditional agricultural sector to the modern industrial sector.

Modernization theory treats development as a technical process without a value base. Myrdal (1968) provides a stinging critique of this assumption.

Modernization theory was once the principal guiding force in development (Higgins and Higgins, 1979). In recent years, it has fallen into disrepute in the international development community, but appears to be a strong influence in Appalachian Development Theory. I have argued in an earlier paper (McNutt, 1986) that Appalachian Development continues to employ strategies that are rarely used in our Overseas Assistance Policies. It is fairly obvious that the programs of the Appalachian Regional Commission strongly reflect the ideals of the Official Position. The Growth Center model has a strong urban, industrial, economic growth promotion-oriented bias. The emphasis on infrastructure, development is also in keeping with the official approach.

Reprinted from the *Proceedings of the Conference on Land and Economy in Appalachia,* Appalachian Center, University of Kentucky (1987), pp. 51–58. Used by permission.

Many states and communities also employ the Official Approach. The strategy of outside industrial recruitment seems to assume internal problem causation. Other aspects of local community economic development also reflect such a bias.

The Official Position provides us with a coherent view of the development process (if we accept the assumptions) and a set of policy prescriptions. What are the consequences of the policies that it encourages?

We cannot expect that the official approach would be able to respond very effectively to external economic threat. If one assumes internal causation of underdevelopment and bases one's policy prescriptions on that assumption, it is clear that the policy framework would be inappropriate. In conditions of external problem causation, (clearly the problem of capital flight is an external problem) the present strategy of industrial recruitment only puts communities in competition with each other (Shannon, 1983: Bluestone and Harrison, 1982).

The emphasis on economic growth as development, so aptly critiqued by Seers (1972), leads to additional problems. One would hardly call the wholesale destruction of the ecological system of the coalfields "Development," except in an economic sense. Yet this assumption is in keeping with the official approach.

Whisnant (1980) finds many Appalachian Development Programs "culturally destructive." The preservation of traditional culture is not a priority of the official approach. In fact, many earlier modernization theorists would argue that such cultural destructiveness was inevitable, even desirable. So it would hardly be surprising that policies from the official position would be culturally destructive.

Resource depletion is another problem that the official position aggravates. The assumption that economic growth is development provides an incentive to promote exploitation of non-renewable resources (Schumacher, 1973). This is apparently the case in Appalachia, especially with regard to coal.

The official approach also assumes that consumption must be limited to provide funds for investment which will contribute to economic growth. Expenditures on health, welfare and educational services are consumption and, unless they can be defended as "Human Capital Investment" are proscribed by the theory. This can be seen graphically in areas where such services are cut back in an attempt to attract industry by reducing taxes and the social wage (Bluestone and Harrison, 1982).

We see that cultural destructiveness, reduced social educational and health services, resource depletion, environmental decay, and a host of other problems are made more serious by the official theories. The policy prescriptions of this school thus seem less and less viable. The Radical Alternative, however, provides a different analysis of the region's problems. The radical alternative includes Marxist, Neo-marxist and Dependency Analysis of the Appalachian situation. These theories include the internal colonialism model (Lewis, et al., 1978), the Internal Periphery Model (Walls and Billings, 1977) and a variety of related models.

The principle strand that ties these theories together is the assumption of external exploitation of the region. This analysis places the cause of many of the region's problems outside Appalachia.

The dependency-related theories, which make up much of the theoretical base for the radical alternative, focus on the unequal terms of trade between less developed and more developed areas. The periphery, or underdeveloped region, must remain poor for the core or developed area to remain rich. The analysis is still largely economic. This line of argument was pioneered by South American economists such as Raul Prebisch and Andre Gunter Frank who were looking for an alternative to western explanations of their region's poverty. Helen Lewis' (Lewis, Kobak, and Johnson, 1978; Lewis, 1970) application of internal colonialism to Appalachia is, perhaps, the best representative of this model.

The Radical Alternative Position has provided us with a great deal of scholarly inquiry into the processes of dependency. Recent work on land ownership (Appalachian Land Ownership Task Force, 1983) had documented outside ownership of the land. Gaventa's (1980) careful work on the faces of power provides us with insight into the way Appalachians lost control of their communities. A small but dedicated group of critical scholars continue to explore the methods of external control.

While we can use the analysis of the radical alternative position, there are a limited number of practical policy prescriptions that can be culled from the radical alternative position.

Obviously, if we speak of terms of trade, one option would be to sever those relationships. The People's Republic of China was successful at doing this for many years. This option is not open to Appalachia. The nationalization of industries is another dependency-inspired intervention that is clearly impossible. Appalachia as the third world is largely a metaphor and a metaphor that, as John Friedman (1966) reminds us, has definite limits of usefulness.

There have been a number of proposals for small-scale community initiatives (Shannon, 1984; Fisher and Foster, 1979). These do not, however, create a coherent regional policy. A number of alternatives are described by Whisnant (1980), but these generally fall short of effective public regional-level policy.

There are some additional limits to the radical alternative position. The analysis provided by the radical alternative continues to be largely economic and technical as opposed to global and normative. It provides a limited number of theory-based ideas about ecological destruction. While it does offer some ideas about resource depletion, the ideas are less global and more regional.

Clearly, we must offer another alternative to regional policy making from the official position. I feel that two emergent approaches from the international development literature have the promise of meeting, at least in part, the need for a new Appalachian Development Policy.

A NEW DEVELOPMENT THEORY BASE FOR APPALACHIA

Appalachia finds itself in a position where it must plan development for the future while dealing with the problems created by earlier development efforts. At the same time, it must deal with a world economy that promises to have adverse effects on the region's future.

It seems unlikely that the region will be able to deal with the world economy in any absolute sense. The region's economy is too enmeshed with the world system to hope for more than a partial solution. It is, however, still possible to have the type of development that the region deserves.

In the late sixties and early seventies there was dissatisfaction with the present nature of development (largely Modernization Theory) and a search for alternatives began (Todero, 1985). Dependency theory became popular, but even with sovereign states it was difficult to formulate and apply solutions from the theory (See Hettne, 1983, for additional problems). Some less-developed countries nationalized industry, others united in regional cooperatives, and some attempted to close off trade. Perhaps the most significant expression of dependency inspired policy was the New International Economic Order (NIEO) proposal (Todero, 1985). This proposal called for a radical restructuring of the world's economy, generally in favor of the third world (Todero, 1985). The results have been less than impressive.

There was additional dissatisfaction with dependency theory. Like modernization theory, the analysis was still largely economic. It continued to preserve the myth that development was a technical process rather than a normative process (Myrdal, 1968; see also Whisnant, 1980, on this point). It also fails, as does modernization theory, to deal with the problems of ecological destruction and resource depletion. In many ways the dependency alternative failed to offer anything new.

A number of alternative approaches began to emerge. Two complementary development theories, Another Development and the idea of Building Sustainable Societies, were among these new approaches.

These two theories differ from earlier approaches in the role given to economic growth. While the Modernization and Dependency theories give economic issues a primary role, these new approaches tend to regard economic growth as a secondary issue.

The overall approach of these two theories is more "normative and value based" (Hettne, 1983:261). They call for a reorientation of the economic system toward human needs and values, much in the spirit of Lux and Lutz's "Humanistic Economics" (1979).

Sustainable society thinking is highly concerned with the resource and biological base of society (Brown, 1981; Praiges, 1977). The sustainable society theorists question not only if growth is desirable, but also if it is possible, given the resource constraints. Among the strategies advocated are renewable energy sources, local self-reliance, moving away from automobiles toward more sustainable transportation, changes in agriculture, restructuring the economy, movement away from urbanization, reduced consumption, and recycling. (Brown, 1981:247–284). Workplace democracy and local solutions to global problems are also advocated (Stokes, 1981). To use Brown's (1981:280) phrase, a movement "from growth to sustainability" becomes the goal.

"Another Development" accepts a decidedly normative framework for development as well. Hettne (1983:261) notes that previous approaches were based on the assumption that development was an inherent quality in all societies and that development was a good thing which should be promoted by removing obstacles to it, whether constituted by obsolete social structures or external dependence. In contrast, Another Development would be a process in accordance with contextually defined human needs and values.

Another Development, then, changes development from a technical/economic process to one with a strong value component, much in the tradition of Goulet (1971) and Myrdal's (1968) explorations into the normative bases of development.

Hettne (1983) notes that Another Development prescribes strategies of self-reliance, basic needs fulfillment, participation, and eco-development. Self-reliance refers to the idea of developing self-sufficient units for development. Fulfillment of basic needs means meeting the survival needs of all members of the population in as brief a period as possible. This strategy was adopted by the International Labor Office (1976) and U.S. Foreign Aid Programs during the 1970s. Basic needs have been defined to include not only food, clothing and shelter, but even things like education, social justice, participation, and health care (Baster, 1985).

While participation has a long tradition in community development, participatory development provides an alternative to the top-down strategies of the official strategies (Gran, 1980). Workplace democracy could be considered an aspect of participation. Eco-development has a very strong similarity to sustainable society orientations. It concentrates on resource conservation and ecological concerns (Hettne, 1983).

The strategies suggested in Sustainable Society and Another Development approaches are complementary. The common points of agreement include:

1. a normative, value-centered approach to development;
2. concentration resource conservation and ecological concerns as well as quality of life concerns;
3. small-scale development based on relatively self-reliant local communities;
4. rejection of economic growth as the sole criterion of development;
5. participation in development and production.

Other points suggested by one approach or another include commitment to basic needs fulfillment, overall self-reliance, etc. It is upon these building blocks that we can begin to build a better development strategy for Appalachia.

A NEW STRATEGY FOR APPALACHIAN DEVELOPMENT

We can now begin to speculate about the shape of an Appalachian Development strategy based on this conception of development. The proposed strategy has six elements:

1. a reorientation of goals away from economic growth toward an emphasis on human growth, quality of life, and societal growth;
2. a change in measurement to reflect the above-noted changes in goals;
3. a policy framework to encourage societal development within a sustainable context and to encourage community-level planning =Stokes, 1981);

4. a participatory "bottom-up" planning model, connected to policy framework and working at the community level;
5. a structure for providing technical assistance;
6. a structure for ensuring fulfillment of basic needs.

The relationship between these elements is depicted in Figure 35.1. Let us consider the elements in turn.

Changing the goals of Appalachian Development will require a major rethinking of what the future of the region will look like. Progress in the American mindset is equated with creating clones of the industrial northeast. This model may not be appropriate to the people of Appalachia (or, for that matter, to the people of the northeast), and if it is not, it should be discarded in favor of something more comfortable.

At the very least, a change in orientation should reflect concerns for the quality of life, social development, and the realization of human potential. Ideally, a fair amount of opportunity for participation in goal setting should be accorded to people of Appalachia. This would be a difficult and time-consuming process that may take many years to reach an acceptable level. We can, however, begin to move in this direction.

If there is a change in the way that development is conceived, there must also be a change in the way it is measured. The present economic output indicators fit well with the outcomes prescribed by the official theory. They presume to measure economic growth. While there are a number of criticisms of output measures, such as GNP, they remain appropriate to the task of showing progress in economic growth (Hicks and Streeten, 1979; Nordhaus and Tobin, 1972).

These output measures are not appropriate for the broader definitions of development that are proposed here (Seers, 1972; Morris, 1979; Schumacher, 1973; Brown, 1981). There has been a great deal of work in developing measures of socio-economic development, much of which is relevant to our effort here. (Baster,

Revised Development Goal Orientation

Overall Development Policy Framework

Basic Needs Fulfillment Policies   Local Problem-Solving Support Policies   Regional Level Policies

Area Technical Assistance Network

Community-Level Problem-Solving Efforts

Figure 35.1: Relationship between major strategic elements

1972; 1985; Rao, et al. 1978; Hicks and Streeten, 1979). These measures use either pure social indicators or a combination of social and economic indicators.

Galtung (1976) makes an important point when he suggests that the people be involved in the selection and development of indicators. It seems to make little sense to have a development based on participation measured by an elitist set of indicators.

While the region is very well supplied with economic indicators through the system of national accounts, other development indicators are not as widely available. It seems appropriate for an organization to be set up to gather information about the development of the region as reflected by the new orientation.

Another critical component of this approach is the creation of a policy framework to support and structure the development process. There will be four principal parts of this policy framework:

1. a set of policies dealing with regional level issues such as resource conservation and environmental protection;
2. a set of policies to support the efforts of local communities;
3. a set of policies to insure basic needs fulfillment;
4. a policy to provide technical assistance to community-level groups.

An overall set of policies for regional issues is vital because many problems cannot be dealt with on a local basis. The present policy framework of the official school supports (and even encourages) resource exploitation. Environmental regulation laws have been historically lax in Appalachia, so an overall policy might compensate for the lack of resolve on the part of the states. Those things that need to be done on a regional basis would fall into this category.

One part of the overall policy framework that could have a distinct impact on capital flight and related issues would be policies that would require notice before plants move out of an area or even co-determination (a worker voice on the Board of Directors) as is done in Germany and Sweden (Lux and Lutz, 1979; Bluestone and Harrison, 1982). Shearer (1983–1984) goes so far as to advocate a "Bill of Economic Rights." (See Gil, 1986, for a report of such an effort in Massachusetts). Along the same line, the overall policy framework should press for workplace democracy and employee ownership (Shearer, 1983–84; Stokes, 1981).

A second set of policies supports local efforts. Stokes (1981) notes that, while local efforts are the essence of a sustainable development strategy,

Public policies in support of self-help efforts are often necessary to overcome some of the human and institutional obstacles that stand in the path of people helping themselves.

(Stokes, 1981:123)

This set of policies will attempt to provide the means to obtain technical assistance and resources (such as loans), linkage between local and large-scale projects, and linkages between local projects (Stokes, 1981:123–137).

In terms of technical assistance, it may be useful to set up a sub-regional system to link governmental and academic expertise with local communities through a system of sub-regional centers. These centers will have direct contact with the communities. One possible model, but not the only one, is the use of voluntary associations to provide technical assistance. Franda (1979) discusses one scheme where voluntary associations link village-level workers with young professionals who work and live in a voluntary association setting, much as the Settlement House workers did in the 1880s. This strategy has the potential advantage of putting professional expertise in a more personal package.

The provision of basic needs is another important part of the strategy. Perhaps what is needed is an enhanced community-oriented social welfare system with more emphasis on empowerment and a more secure system of income support. This would also argue for Full Employment Assurance (Gil, 1986) in the overall policy framework.

The final component of the model is the development of participatory bottom-up planning and problem-solving for Appalachian communities. This planning should give the people of the community the opportunity to define their own problems and develop local solutions that are consistent with local cultural and social patterns.

Stokes (1981) provides an extensive discussion of local efforts. These efforts include energy conservation, healthcare, etc. Gran (1980) provides an extensive rational for these types of efforts. The key is not only local efforts, but local efforts connected with regional efforts.

The obvious pitfall here is the power of local elites (Caudill, 1963; 1976; Gaventa, 1980). There is no ready solution to this problem. One might expect that through the involvement and empowerment of local people, some power redistribution might occur.

This completes the model in its entirety. The question is, will it work?

VIABILITY OF THE APPROACH

The ultimate question that can be asked of any development program is, "Can it be successful in the real world?" The answer, while not completely clear, is not unhopeful.

It would be very difficult for this strategy to work in the present socioeconomic climate. There are a number of reasons to expect that this situation will change.

People are afraid of the future of the region. They fear for their families, their jobs, their communities, and their personal future. The present development strategies do little to allay that fear. People are also less trusting of business and government alike. This creates a situation where we will begin to look for new strategies.

Social movements, like the Greens, continue to grow in power. Hettne (1983) notes the consistency between these social movements and the growing popularity of another development in industrialized nations. The most important reason to suggest that this strategy is possible is the likelihood that the present crisis of Appalachia will get worse. There is little chance that Appalachia can deal successfully with the world system. The effects of capital flight will continue to warp local economies and communities. The policy instruments we have for dealing with the world system have an exceedingly slim chance of success. The present system continues to expend non-renewable resources at phenomenal rates—a trend that cannot continue forever (Brown, 1981; Schumacher, 1973). To put it simply, official development cannot continue to function in the present environment.

There is, then, some cause for optimism. Present approaches seem to have reached the end of their utility and the evolving national ideology may provide for a new development in Appalachia.

CONCLUSION

Appalachian Development Theory has experienced a number of problems in dealing with the crisis of Appalachia. The official position provides a set of undesirable policy prescriptions. While the radical alternative provides a somewhat different analysis, it provides only a few usable policies. An alternative development strategy, based on Another Development and sustainable society concepts has been offered here. This model combines local development with a regional policy framework to provide a model of development that is both workable and viable for Appalachia. We can have the kind of future we want for the mountains. It is vital that we move toward that future with every step taken in the cause of regional development.

REFERENCES

Appalachian Land Ownership Task Force. *Who Owns Appalachia?* Lexington: University of Kentucky Press, 1983.

Baster, N. *Measuring Development.* London: Frank Cass, 1972.

———. "Social Indicators Research: Some Issues and Debates". In Hilhorst and Klass, *Social Development in the Third World,* Croom-Helm, 1985.

Brown, Lester. *Building a Sustainable Society.* New York: Norton, 1981.

Bluestone, B. and Harrison. *The Deindustrialization of America.* New York: Basic Books, 1982.

Caudill, Harry. *Night Comes To The Cumberlands.* Boston: Little-Brown, 1963.

———. *Watches of the Night,* Boston: Little-Brown, 1976.

Couto, Richard. *Appalachia: An American Tomorrow.* Knoxville: Commission on Religion in Appalachia, 1984.

Fisher, S. and Foster, S. "Models for Furthering Revolutionary Praxis in Appalachia," in *Appalachian Journal,* 1979.

Franda, Marcus, *India's Rural Development.* Bloomington: University of Indiana, 1979.

Friedman, John. "Poor Nations and Poor Regions," in *Southern Journal of Economics,* 1966.

Gallbraith, John K. *Economic Development.* Cambridge: Harvard University Press, 1964.

Galtung, J. "Toward New Indicators of Development," in *Futures,* 1976.

Gaventa, J. *Power and Powerlessness.* Urbana: University of Illinois Press, 1980.

Gil, David. "Economic Rights: State Takes First Step," in *MASW News,* 1986.

Goulet, D. *The Cruel Choice.* New York: Pantheum, 1971.

Gran, Guy. *Development by People.* New York: Praeger, 1980.

Hagen, E. *A Theory of Social Change.* Chicago: Irwin, 1962.

Hettne, Bjorn. "The Development of Development Theory," in *Acta Sociologica* (26)3/4, 1983.

Hicks and Streeten, "Indicators of Development: The Search for a Basic Needs Yardstick," in *World Development,* 1979.

Higgins and Higgins, *Economic Development of a Small Planet.* New York: Norton, 1979.

ILO. *Employment, Growth and Basic Needs.* New YorK: Praeger, 1976.

Lenski, G. and Lenski, J. *Human Societies.* New York: McGraw Hill, 1982.

Lewis, A. "Economic Development with Unlimited Supplies of Labor," in *Manchester School Journal,* 1954.

Lewis, H. "Fatalism or The Coal Industry," in *Mountain Life and Work,* 1970.

Lewis, H. *et al.,* eds. *Colonialism in Modern America: The Appalachian Case.* Boone: Appalachian Consortium Press, 1978.

Lewis, Kobak and Johnson, "Family Religion and Colonialism in Central Appalachia," in Lewis et al., *Colonialism in Modern America: The Appalachian Case.* Boone: Appalachian Consortium Press.

Lewis, O. "A Culture of Poverty," in *Scientific American,* 1967.

Lux and Lutz. *The Challenge of Humanistic Economics.* Menlo Park, CA: Benjamin/Cumming, 1979.

McClelland, A. *The Achieving Society.* Princeton: Princeton University Press, 1962.

McNutt, J. "Practicing What We Preach; Some Preliminary Observations on the Historical Evolution of Federal Development Policy for Appalachia and the Third World," Paper presented at the 1986 Appalachian Studies Conference, Boone, North Carolina.

Morris, M. D. *Measuring the Conditions of the World's Poor.* New York: Pergamon Press, 1979.

Myrdal, G. *Asian Drama.* New York: Random, 1968.

Nordhans and Tobin. "Is Economic Growth Obsolete?" in Moss (Ed.), *The Measurement of Economic and Social Performance.* New York: National Bureau of Economic Research.

Pirages, C. *Sustainable Society.* New York: Praeger, 1977.

Rostow, W. W. *The Stages of Economic Growth.* New York: Cambridge, 1960.

Rao, M.V.S. et al. *Indicators of Human and Social Development.* Tokyo: United Nations University, 1978.

Schumacher, F. *Small Is Beautiful,* 1973.

Seers, D. "What Are We Trying To Measure?" in *Journal of Developmental Studies,* 1972.

Shearer, D. "Planning with a Political Face," in *Nation,* 1983–84.

Shannon, T. "Appalachia as an Enterprise Zone: Some Speculations on the Future Direction of Federal Policy Toward The Region." Paper presented at the 1983 Appalachian Studies Conference.

—————. "Surviving the 1990s: Inter-Regional Variation in Economic Problems." Paper presented at the 1984 Appalachian Studies Conference.

Stokes, B. *Helping Ourselves.* New York: Norton, 1981.

Todero, M. *Economic Development of the Third World.* New York: Longmans, 1985.

Walls and Billings. "The Sociology of Southern Appalachia," in *Appalachian Journal,* Vol. 7, No. 1, 1977.

Weller, J. *Yesterday's People.* Lexington: University of Kentucky Press, 1969.

Whisnant, D. *Modernizing the Mountaineer.* Boone: Appalachian Consortium Press, 1980.

VII. Family

Echoing the warning made over 20 years ago by James Brown that "the Southern Appalachian Region is not an entirely homogeneous area," we suggest that great variety is found in the family structures of Appalachian families "as well."[1] This variety is not apparent however, if one looks only to "the hollow folks" of Sherman and Henry,[2] Gazaway,[3] Weller,[4] or Fetterman.[5] These studies are locally specific and should not serve as prototypical of the Region. They make an impact, especially on the outside-the-region reader, that is not easily overcome.

Long ago, John C. Campbell suggested that there are three classes of highlanders: the urban and near-urban folk, the prosperous rural folk, and "the holders of small tracts of poorer land."[6] He went to some length to observe that rigid distinctions are hard to make, but the family life gives many clues as to the differences which exist. Campbell's observation may well serve even today to form a useful basis for distinguishing family structures and life-styles throughout the Region which is now a third again the geographic size of the one he knew.

Careful attention to the significant variable is a hallmark of good social science. The children of Campbell's Southern Mountains are the subject of Beaver's descriptive study of rural community. Her focus is on kinship: its centrality in the lives of the folk of Grassy Fork and the ways it is celebrated. Family ties communities together, it gives individuals identity, and helps them to understand where they fit into the social networks. The reading explores this basic social mechanism as practiced in a rural place.

The Tickamyer's article examines more closely one specific variable that affects family life: females as heads of household. Using the case of families in poverty—the persistent Appalachian plight despite millions of Federal (ARC) dollars—they show how this one factor is a significant distinguisher among families in poverty. Students will find the reading useful as a methodological tool as well.

1. James S. Brown and George A. Hillery, Jr., "The Great Migration, 1940–1960" in Ford, *The Southern Appalachian Region, op cit.,* pp. 54.

2. Mandel Sherman and Thomas R. Henry, *Hollow Folks,* New York: Thomas R. Crowell, 1933.

3. Rene Gazaway, *Longest Mile,* New York: Doubleday, 1969.

4. Jack Weller, *Yesterday's People: Life in Contemporary Appalachia,* Lexington, University of Kentucky Press, 1965.

5. John Fetterman, *Stinking Creek,* New York: Dutton, 1967.

6. John C. Campbell, *The Southern Highlander and His Homeland, op. cit.*

The third article stresses the interaction within family life. Noting that the nuclear family is the basic unit, Fitchen stresses its elasticity, i.e., its ability to survive disruptions, stresses, and separation. Her first hand accounts make the task of working out conflict almost come alive. The articles, while being regionally specific, stress coping mechanisms useful for describing the process which is family life.

36. FAMILY, LAND, AND COMMUNITY

Patricia Duane Beaver

In 1898 Amanda moved from the town of Jackson, where she was raised, into the Grassy Fork community to teach school. She married John Miller the next year. For the next forty years until her retirement, Amanda taught the children in the community, including her own eight children and one grandchild. Amanda and John's daughters Betty and Mary married Lewis brothers, and Amanda's own two brothers married two Lewis sisters. Amanda's daughter Mary, now an eighty-two-year-old widow, lives next to her daughter Sarah in a new trailer, put up to replace the old homeplace. Mary's mother-in-law, Lucy Woody, now a widow in her nineties, lives across the road, and three of her children live within sight of her house. Lucy's three brothers and their families live on up the road.

Down the other direction, Mary's daughter Evelyn lives with her husband and son, near Mary's brother's widow, Lynn. Next to Lynn is her son and his family. And so it goes around the community. Most households are connected by blood or by marriage, by close ties and distant, to other households in the community, and these kin ties form a basis for community life. With very few exceptions, families in the community are firmly rooted in extended and extensive networks of kin and in elaborate and often complicated community-wide kin relationships. As Mary noted about her own and her husband's kin relations in the community, "It's a mess. Maybe you can figure it all out."

Kinship and family in the rural mountain community are a highly valued and central part of life. Yet kinship is more than biological or genealogical connectedness; it is a cultural idea through which relationships are expressed and from which community homogeneity is derived. Kin ties connect community residents into a system that gives personal identity through the expression of common roots, common ancestry, shared experience, and shared values; kinship also provides an idiom for people's behavior toward one another and is one of several bases for the actual formation of groups.

The child is born into a set of nurturing, sustaining relationships with a group of relatives. Throughout his or her life, parents, grandparents, siblings, aunts, uncles and cousins are interested in the individual's welfare and freely give love, support, and criticism. The individual matures into a social world in which family offers an atmosphere of trust, and the experiences of daily life give the individual no reason to doubt the constancy of family loyalty.

Glenda Wilson's dad went to Detroit with his brother in the 1920s in search of work. After several years her dad returned home to take up farming, an occupation that he and his son following him still pursue today. His brother stayed in Detroit, and over the years, as correspondence diminished, the family gradually lost track of him. However, contact with the long-lost brother was reestablished during the 1960s; the old uncle, alone and in poor health, was brought back home to live out his last days among his kin. "Nobody had seen him for forty years, but when they brought him home it was like it had been a day." Glenda continues, "Folks around here are that way, they'll take in their black sheep, their wanderers, 'cause they're family, no matter what."

Land and family, place and kinship are intimately interwoven and value laden. Historically, as Eller has written,

> Land held a special meaning that combined the diverse concepts of utility and stewardship. While land was something to be used and developed to meet one's needs, it was also the foundation of daily existence giving form to personal identity, material culture, and economic life. As such, it defined the "place" in which one found security and self-worth. Family, on the other hand, as the central organizing unit of social life, brought substance and order to that sense of place. Strong family ties influenced almost every aspect of the social system, from the primary emphasis upon informal personal relationships to the pervasive egalitarian spirit of local affairs. Familism, rather than the accumulation of material wealth, was the predominant cultural value in the region, and it sustained a lifestyle that was simple, methodical, and tranquil.[1982:38]

Kinship is a cultural value, connecting the individual to other people, to land, to community, to history, and to identity. The "Decoration Day" services, commonly at churches or family cemeteries in many mountain communities, provide a time for recognition and celebration of this continuity of family and place through time. On Decoration Day, descendants of persons buried in family cemeteries congregate to honor the dead and to renew old relationships.

In the Rocky Creek community, Decoration Day is held on one Sunday each year. In addition, because of the overlapping nature of kin ties in the community, it is celebrated on different Sundays for each of the six family cemeteries. Because of the complex, kin-group intermarriages, especially in the past, and thus the overlapping kinship ties connecting members of the community to each other, an individual may have ancestors buried in several of the family cemeteries. Thus one may acknowledge status in several different categories of people who have common ancestry. Consequently, some individuals celebrate several different Decoration Days.

Traditionally, the eldest male of the family, as head of the extended family group, would go with a grandson to the cemetery on the eve of Decoration Day to clean up, cut the grass, and trim around the stones and along the fence surrounding the cemetery. On Decoration Day morning, relatives convene at the cemetery and cover the graves with freshly cut flowers. Prayers are offered by older men of the assembled families; scripture reading and preaching may take place if someone is so moved. The most rewarding activity for most people, who may drive quite a distance to attend these events is the renewing of old acquaintances and the sharing of family gossip. For many, this is the only chance during the year to see out-of-community relatives, even those living close by. In one family, for example, two brothers who lived within fifty miles of each other saw each other only once each year, at this festivity. After spending several hours in the cemetery, family members congregate at the house of the eldest resident family member for a covered-dish dinner. About mid to late afternoon the group breaks up, everyone goes home, and ancestry is put aside for another year.

Decoration Day can also be a time of healing, of mending old wounds between family members. Iris wondered one Sunday morning, "How can I face my mother's grave?" Tensions were running high that morning because of conflicts with her husband's brother and sister-in-law and their children, who lived next door, latent during most of the year but rekindled and stirred by the barrage of visiting relatives from Ohio. Yet face them she did, and the tears that streamed down her face as she embraced her kinfolk in the cemetery sprang from a wealth of emotions: hostility, guilt, anger, and love.

THE KINSHIP IDIOM

Each person is born into a set of kinship relationships—a kindred, a network of individuals. These ties provide a variety of potential relationships that the individual can use when the need arises. Kinship ties thus provide a basis for reciprocal exchange, assistance, and the formation of groups; but kinship also provides an idiom for the way in which people *should* behave toward each other.

When Linda and Larry Douthit moved into Rocky Creek in 1970 they knew no one in the area. J. B. and Iris Blackwelder helped them out in many ways—both in getting them settled in their house and in beginning their farming activities. When Larry's mother, an upper-middle-class urban woman who disapproved heartily of her son's lifestyle, arrived unexpectedly, Iris took a freshly baked cake over to the house so that Linda and Larry would have some refreshments. Linda and Larry feel some strain in the relationship with the Blackwelders because they do not have the means to reciprocate the many favors done for them. They try, however, to do whatever they can to help Iris and J. B. On occasion, Linda has done some bookkeeping for the Blackwelder trucking firm and has helped Iris with canning and freezing. Sometimes Larry helps J. B. in his farming. At other times he drives J. B., who periodically has vision difficulties, to places he needs to go. Linda and Larry have been incorporated into Iris and J. B.'s set of socially important kin and are sometimes referred to as "some more of our young 'uns." Likewise, Larry half-jokingly refers to J. B. as "Uncle J. B."

Women who become close friends through mutual visiting and mutual exchange may refer to each other as being "like a sister to me," and women may refer to their mother's close friends as having been "like a second mother to me." Friends may be incorporated into socially important relationships through the idiom of kinship, specifically through the use of fictive kinship terms. For example, Maxine and Cecil developed a close visiting relationship with the young couple who rented their house. On one occasion, at a large gathering at the high school, Maxine introduced the young renters to her friends as "some more of our young 'uns."

Use of the terms "aunt" and "uncle" is a common means of incorporating people into socially important groups through fictive kinship. These terms are used in respect for older people with whom one has developed socially important ties. Just as Larry refers to the older man as "Uncle J. B.," J. B. refers to his older cousin as "Uncle Jason," the old man Charles Phillips refers to the long-deceased, nonkin woman from whom his father bought his land as "Aunt Jane Wilson," and old John Blackwelder refers to a now-deceased, nonkin neighbor as "Uncle Scott Weldon." These terms of address are thus used to incorporate both kin and nonkin into close kin categories.

Socially important relationships are expressed in terms of an "idiom of kinship." There are certain expected or ideal patterns of reciprocal activity and mutual aid between close kin; kinship provides a prototype for ideal social relationships. The idiom of kinship dominates most social relationships in the community.

To be surrounded by an extensive network of kin, an extended family, is an ideal. Parents want the best for their children and recognize that, to a greater or lesser extent, their children at some point must be on their own and make their own way. If that means leaving the community or even leaving the mountains, then parents can accept it. Yet, to have children and grandchildren close at hand is a fine and highly desirable state of affairs.

When several generations of a family are able to live in the community—when married children can find work close enough at hand to reside locally and when land can be spared or acquired for a house or a mobile home—then families can be residentially clustered near each other. While married children establish a separate household as soon as possible, usually upon marriage, a common pattern for children who can find the means to live locally is for parents who have land to provide them with an acre or two. Because of the high cost of new homes and the scarcity of rental housing, children quite often put up a mobile home on their parents' land.

When such family clusters do occur, extended-family activity groups are the natural result. Cooperation among related families is useful in gardening, farming, building, equipment use and repair, food storage, and a range of other activities. Through their cooperative efforts and residential patterns, the image of a solidary, unified family group is established. Efforts to mobilize and unify the separate nuclear families rest with the older generation, the parents, who have authority by virtue of age, experience, and ownership of property and equipment.

OTHER GROUPS

Members of different nuclear families come together for economic, social, and ritual purposes. Most commonly, people come together in seasonal work groups for agricultural work such as setting out and working tobacco, putting up hay, clearing land, putting up food for winter storage, or harvesting cash crops such as beans, cabbages, or tomatoes. These "activity groups" may or may not be composed of close kin, or even solely of kin; their composition changes often, depending on the activity. Individuals and families may have multiple ties and obligations throughout the community and will work and socialize with different individuals and families at different times and for different purposes throughout the year.

Seasonal work groups usually come together for agricultural work. Close kin who also live near each other commonly share such work, and if extra labor is needed, a close kinsman who lives outside the community may also come to help. Rachel, her sister Ruth, and Rachel's daughter Rebecca frequently work together in farming, harvesting, and food storage and simply enjoy visiting together as well. They are sometimes joined by Amy, also a neighbor, the wife of Rachel's husband's cousin. Rachel, Rebecca, and Ruth gave a wedding shower for Rebecca's son Fred. Rebecca and Ruth make quilts and sew together. The relationship among the three women is one of warmth and great mutual confidence.

Neighbor children will occasionally be hired to help in seasonal work. A residentially close, nonkin neighbor may also join in the work, and the labor will be reciprocated at another time. A man with a harvester may harvest several neighbor's fields, and the neighbors will help him harvest his own and put up his tobacco. A good mechanic will repair a neighbor's car or help pull an engine, and the neighbors will help the mechanic reroof his house.

Andy sought Fred Miller's help on several occasions, since Fred and his son Fred Junior have the equipment, expertise, and spare parts to pull and replace an automobile engine, rebuild a carburetor, or weld a lawn-mower handle back together. When Fred cut his hay, he called on Andy to help, and Andy spent three evenings working with Fred, Fred's wife, Geneva, a neighbor boy, and Fred's cousin. Andy also helped Fred put the roof on Fred's new barn. Andy couldn't anticipate when Fred would call on him, but he had no doubt about his obligation and dropped everything he was doing when Fred called for help with the hay. Andy says, "Fred put down everything he was doing when I needed his help and spent most of the morning helping me with that old engine."

Male kinsmen sometimes come together for ongoing economic enterprises, and the cooperative labor provides support for each household. John Blackwelder is the father of Tom, Walton, J. B., and Johnny and the grandfather of Billy, Mark, Steve, and Bob, all of whom are involved to different degrees in a family trucking business that was built by John. Managerial responsibility has passed from John to his son J. B. and to J. B.'s son Mark, while Tom owns several of the trucks and makes most of his business contracts independently of those made by Mark. Tom's two sons, Steve and Bob, usually work for their father, although they occasionally drive for Mark. Grandson Billy is primarily a mechanic and works in J. B.'s garage, both on the family trucks and on jobs that he has contracted independently.

Participation in such work groups is primarily influences by kinship. Close kin—including lineal relatives (parents, grandparents, great-grandparents, and their children) and their spouses; siblings, their children, and spouses; parents' siblings and their children; spouse and spouse's close kin—are those to whom obligations are felt and on whom one can call for help. A second factor influencing the group participation is residence in the community. Nonkin neighbors may help each other before nonresident kinfolks, particularly when nonkin neighbors are also friends. A third factor is the economic obligation one may have to reciprocate past or anticipated help to a neighbor, as well as the need for help from neighbors.

Several factors may preclude participation in community groups, including public-work obligations, although neighbors will quite often pitch in and help with whatever labor is going on after they get off work. Hostilities or quarrels among close kin may also preclude sharing labor; two brothers or two sisters-in-law may adamantly avoid working together in an otherwise family work group because of an ongoing quarrel.

LAND AND FAMILY

Land is the most valuable resource for the rural community and thus the most controversial object of inheritance. Furthermore, the ideal of the independent nuclear family places a high value on individual property ownership as an added assurance of continuing family independence and as a symbol of financial security. Yet, parents need the help of married children and their families in working the land and also desire to keep children "in the fold," loyal to the family. Likewise, young couples need the help of others because they have not raised a labor force of children and do not always have access to capital for hiring labor or purchasing equipment. Parents, who are often in control of resources, may therefore manipulate potential ownership of land by children in order to assure their children's loyalty and cooperation in collective activities.

A newly married couple's decision to stay in the community after marriage is primarily affected by three factors: the availability of adequate housing, the probability that they will inherit or be able to buy land, and the availability of work. Because of these three factors, many young people leave the community either to reside in another nearby community or to migrate out of the region altogether. In particular, many young people leave the community to find work, recognizing that the prospects are dim for making a living in a rural community with limited job and land possibilities.

Land is most frequently obtained from older family members, often through inheritance. Inheritance ideally involves an equal distribution of property among all children, regardless of age, sex, or other considerations. Such inheritance is, however, an ideal. Eighty-six-year-old Charles Phillips said that, when he was first married, he told his wife: "Now, I want us to live right and raise six children, and I want us to manage to work out six hundred acres of land, give 'em a hundred acres apiece, and build 'em all a good nice home." The reality of their situation deflated his ideal, however, when his wife cut him off with, "Let the God-durned young 'uns work just like we worked."

In a few cases, in spite of dwindling holdings, the ideal of equal inheritance by all children has prevailed, with predictable results. For example, one of the better Rocky Creek farms—one with fertile, flat land and ample water—had lain vacant for a number of years since the death of the owners. The eleven children of the deceased couple inherited equal shares of the 155-acre farm but could not decide on the disposition of the property. On this land stands a 150-year-old cabin; in it, five generations of the family have grown up. Yet, because several of the heirs wanted to farm the land, while several wanted to develop it for real estate purposes, people in the community suspected that the entire farm would be sold to the highest bidder, and the money divided equally. The highest bidder would, no doubt, have been a developer, as none of the farming children (or any of the local farmers) had enough money to purchase the land. The problem was partially resolved when the land was surveyed and divided into eleven equal shares, and the children drew to determine who received which share. Whether one or more of the heirs would be able to buy out the others remained to be seen.

Before the mid-1960s each child's inheritance of some portion of the family estate created no overwhelming difficulties in Rocky Creek. Even though inherited landholdings might be small, the possibilities usually existed for consolidating landholdings through marriage or for expanding holdings through purchase. In addition, although the amount of readily usable (that is, cleared) land was in fact limited, it was and still is, possible to clear forested land. Depopulation of the rural communities since the 1960s and the decline of agriculture have meant that much hillside land that was actively farmed by earlier generations has been allowed to revert to timber. Although sections of the forested land in the community are too severe and rocky for agriculture or pasturage, some forested plots are cultivable.

Several factors may alter the principle of equal inheritance and/or affect the acquisition of land by local families. First, the youngest child is expected to remain closer to the parents than other siblings and to take care of any needs that may arise. Adherence to this practice depends on the age and physical condition of the parents. Thus if the parents are old or unable to assume major responsibilities at the time the youngest child marries or departs from home, parents and older siblings will tend to expect the youngest child, more than any of the others, to remain close to the parents. It is usual for the youngest child who stays close to the parents to inherit more property than his or her siblings. Throughout the mountain area, the "baby" occupies a special position in the family. Yet, at least one person mentioned that the youngest child in a family may be more likely to leave the area altogether, because family responsibilities and expectations, sibling pressures, and threatened loss of independence can become quite overwhelming.

Second, in families in which sons are involved in working the land with their fathers, parents will sometimes deed or sell a greater portion of land to sons than to daughters. The male work patterns established in a family sometimes continue after the son marries. Consequently, if a cooperative economic venture is occupationally feasible for a family group and if, as a result, a married son and his family remain residentially close to the son's parents, the son is apt to receive a greater portion of land than siblings, male or female, who have moved away. In such cases, parents often attempt to compensate other siblings financially. This practice is not limited to the farming family; the Blackwelder family trucking concern has supported six nuclear families in various capacities. Residential decisions are occasionally influenced by the desire to continue male work units in large-scale economic activities. As a result, families tend to live closer to the husband's parents than to the wife's.

A third factor affecting the land acquisition is out-migration. The lure of fortunes to be made in the northern industrial centers, western timber, Kentucky coal, and elsewhere, as well as the lack of work locally, drew many potential inheritors of family property permanently away from the community. The siblings left behind thus received larger shares of the family property. In several families, children inherited land only if they remained in the community; in others, inheritors of family property who left the community sold their portions of the family holdings to siblings left behind, at reasonable rates. Out-migration remains significant in the community, although sale of land to siblings has been greatly affected by the development of a full-scale recreation industry since the 1960s, the popularity of second homes in the mountains, and the resulting rapidly increasing cost of land. For the young family with no equity and only a minimal income, the possibility of purchasing land in the communities in which they grew up is becoming increasingly remote. In two decades, the cost of farmland has jumped from between two hundred and four hundred dollars per acre to well over one thousand dollars an acre, and even hillside land prices have skyrocketed. While large acreage (eighty acres or more) can still be obtained for as little as five hundred dollars an acre or sometimes less, young families and those who want to farm are usually priced out of the market. With the increasing value of farmland have come increasing taxes and increasing land sale by farmers.

> Agriculture, especially at the small scale common (in western North Carolina), often does not generate the income necessary to pay these taxes and farmers feel compelled to sell all or part of their land or to abandon agriculture as an occupation and seek employment in other sectors. ... Just as it is difficult to maintain a farm, it is even more difficult to begin a career in farming. As land prices rise with speculation, young persons wishing to go into farming are priced out of the market for land. As a result, farming has become less of an alternative as both an occupation and lifestyle, and is increasingly maintained by older, well-established farmers. [Appalachian Land Ownership Task Force, 1981:26]

A fourth factor affecting land acquisition is the recent increase in land sale to outsiders. Many people who live in the community consider themselves "land poor" and recognize that the only way to make money off land, particularly land unsuitable for farming or grazing, is to sell it to developers, land speculators, summer people, or outsiders moving in. Consequently, those who remain in the community and wish to buy land for farming often cannot afford to pay the price that outsiders, and particularly land speculators, are able to offer. Individuals who decide to remain in the community have little assurance that kinsmen will sell land to them at prices they can afford.

While most of the rural land in western North Carolina communities is privately owned, an increasing number of owners are nonlocal, and the number of local residents owning large tracts of land is declining. Although an increasing number of nonlocal people are buying land for second-home development or for speculation, corporate interests, including timber, land development, and mining corporations, also control a considerable amount of local land.

Population pressure on the land has not been a factor in ownership or division of farms, since out-migration from rural communities has been occurring since World War II. While out-migration from the region slowed during the 1960s, migration from rural areas to towns continued through the 1970s.

The economic base of rural mountain communities has not been altered significantly with the increase in tourism, particularly in those communities located far from the resort areas of the counties, although the tourism industry has created an inflationary economic situation. Thus many families who, fifteen or twenty years ago, would have been in a position to expand their landholdings, are now trapped in a situation in which the potential for expansion is dismal, while others cannot afford to keep what they have.

Parents, who own the major portion of available land and either do not have children in the household or realistically anticipate the loss of children from the household, need the help of married children and their families in working the land. Parents are therefore reluctant to deed children their share of the inheritance immediately upon marriage, for this would result not only in the splitting up of the larger land unit and the loss of assurance that the products of the deeded land will benefit the parents but also in the threat of losing the labor of the younger family unit and the control over this labor pool, which would represent a threat to the solidarity of the extended family. One way of ensuring family cooperation is for parents to deed or, occasionally, to sell to children a small plot of land on which to build their own houses. Children thus own their own land and help work the parents' land, with the expectation that they will inherit a larger portion of the land than siblings who live farther away. Historically, land was sold to children before there was any significant land pressure. In a family history of one of the earliest families to settle in Rocky Creek, it is recorded that "beginning about 1823, 'broken down' and unable to walk due to 'the rheumatiz' or arthritis, [X] began selling his lands to his children for nominal sums which he used for maintenance of himself and [his wife]." Four different sons were sold 312, 246, 150, and 82 acres, and two sons-in-law were sold 206 and 200 acres. The "homeplace," of undetermined acreage, was given to the youngest son. One of the sons later sold his land to a third sister's husband when the son moved away from the community. After the first passage to the youngest son, the family homeplace was not passed to other youngest children, although it "remained in the hands of [X's] descendants for more than a hundred years after his death, which occurred in 1833 or 34." The present owner of the twelve remaining acres of the eighty-two acre plot is a great-great grandson of the original owner.

Land, the most valuable resource in the community, is the most controversial object of inheritance. The principle of independence of the family of marriage from extended-family obligations and controls reinforces a high value on individual property ownership. Furthermore, the conflict between nuclear-family independence and the necessity for extended-family economic cooperation creates a structural bind. Each nuclear family desires independent landownership. Parents desire cooperation from married children and their families. Parents are in the position to hold land as incentive for the young family to contribute to the solidary, extended-family cooperative unit.

The case of Charles Phillips, who wanted to give each child one hundred acres, reflects this problem. Charles's unmarried daughter has lived with him since the death of his wife, taking care of all the domestic duties and farming. Charles had one married son in the community, Dale Phillips, who had seven children living at home. Dale Phillips and his wife, Rebecca, who owned no land, were renting. Dale and Rebecca had lived with Charles for several years after they married but eventually moved away, into a house next to Rebecca's parents, primarily because Charles and Rebecca could not get along.

In the early fall of 1973, Dale, Rebecca, and the children bought a new mobile home and did move back to the father's land. While fearing the problems that would arise from living near and working with her domineering old father-in-law, Rebecca was eager to have a home of her own. Dale and Rebecca wanted Charles to give them their inheritance, but Charles resisted this idea and was highly resentful of the suggestion by some of his other children, who didn't live nearby, that he make a will.

The move of Dale's family back to his father's land was probably encouraged by the fact that Charles had sold several large tracts of land to outsiders and that he had had a number of good offers for the rest of his land by a local developer (who, incidentally, talked the old man out of making a will when Charles asked him to draw one up). Charles did deed to Dale one acre (out of his 126) when the move was made. Charles considers himself "land poor"—that is, owning land that is not productive without the help of a number of people and worth money only when sold. Moreover, two of Dale and Rebecca's children were working in factory jobs but were unmarried and still living at home, thus contributing both capital and some farm labor to the family. These children were expected to contribute to the cost of the new trailer as long as they remained in residence.

To summarize, Charles wanted to keep his land, continue farming, and have good workers under his thumb, without giving them the freedom that would result from his giving them the land. Dale's family owned only one acre, they wanted to farm and maintain a comfortable, "traditional," independent existence, but they had to satisfy Charles's desires in order to receive a possible share of the inheritance (before the speculator did). They now maintain two separate residences approximately fifty yards apart, and Charles, his daughter Elvira, Rebecca, the younger children when they are not in school, and the older children when they are not at work farm the land together. On the other hand, Fred Miller is one of the largest landowners in Grassy Fork, yet he leases his son the land upon which Fred Junior has built his house and garage.

In the case of the Blackwelders, J. B. and Iris lived with Iris's parents upon marriage and then "were given" five acres by J. B.'s parents, on which they built their house. Similarly, another son and his wife were given seven acres of land. They say that, although the land was given to them, they have paid for it many times over. The problem of land distribution in this particular extended family is more complicated and deserves some attention.

John Blackwelder, patriarch of the extended family, grew up on a farm just outside the community. He married Lisa Profitt, who grew up in the community on a farm now owned by Lisa's nephew. Lisa's father gave John and Lisa a few acres of land and helped them build the house in which John and his second wife, Louise, still live. After several years of marriage, John and Lisa bought approximately 390 acres of land (194 of which John still owns) adjacent to the land on which they were living. Several years later Lisa died, and as the house was in her name, Lisa willed it to her children.

John remarried and had three more children. He persuaded the six children by his first marriage to deed him the house, and he in turn agreed to deed to them

200 acres of land he had bought, an agreement that was never put in writing. In 1969, however, John's grandson-in-law Joe, who lives in Burnsville, talked John into selling him approximately 150 acres of the land in question at a low price and the money from this sale was distributed equally among the six children. Joe then resold the land to another man outside the community at a twenty-thousand-dollar profit to himself. In 1973 John sold another 40 acres of the land for twelve thousand dollars to a land speculator outside the community. John says that he sold the land because he is old and poor and needs the money. The six children feel that they have been cheated of their inheritance because, first, they were not consulted on the matter and would never have allowed it to go for such a pittance; second, they had no intentions of letting the land go anyway; and third, they say that John is by no means poor. Two of the first six children, J. B. and Tom, live on small plots clustered near John, on land that he gave them. As I noted earlier, one son lives just outside the community on John's homeplace, which he inherited from John's brother, and the three remaining children live outside the state. Two of these three had planned to build retirement homes on their share of the land, and all resent the "swindle." The resentment is directed toward John and toward Joe, who is considered quite a wheeler-dealer. The resentment is controlled, however, as no one feels he has the right to interfere; on the surface, relations among the parties involved are quite amicable.

In sum, there is an ideal of equal inheritance, by all children of family property, yet, in practice two factors work against this ideal. First, land prices are inflated with respect to local economic potential. Because of high prices, one's potential inheritance may be sold to people outside the family or community and potential inheritors may be forced to leave the area and thus forfeit their inheritance. Second, inheritance is one element that may, on occasion, be manipulated by those in control of resources in order to ensure the cooperation of the residentially close but supposedly independent families of children. Extended-family cooperation ensures an economic margin of security to cooperating family units, in spite of the primary self-sufficiency of each nuclear family.

SOLIDARITY AND CONFLICT

The nuclear family is supposed to have an element of autonomy or independence from parents and parents-in-law, yet extended families are supposed to act like family, that is, to share resources, labor, time, and love. While newlyweds have come from families expecting family loyalty, the adjustment to the requirements of loyalty and cooperation with a new spouse's family may be difficult to make.

The subtle, and sometimes not so subtle, tensions that arise from family pressures from both the older and younger couple's points of view are dealt with in a variety of ways. Frustration and annoyance are vented through gossip; mounting tensions or continuing, irreconcilable differences are dealt with by avoidance; and occasionally, continuing and mounting hostilities can be dealt with through threats or acts of violence.

If a newly married couple stays in the community, they usually reside in a separate house or trailer close to the parents of one or the other. When the couple settles near the husband's parents, the husband and his male kinsmen continue working together in those agricultural activities requiring cooperative labor or, in some cases, in joint business ventures. The products of the collective labor benefit each separate household. The new wife is expected to merge into the female work unit and to contribute her energy to her new family group. If a couple settles near the wife's parents, the same is expected. The new husband should merge into the male work unit, and the wife should contribute her labor to the female work unit.

If both sets of parents live in the community or if one set lives in the community and the other nearby, the couple may have double obligations and expectations. Friction may arise over the distribution of the new couple's labor and over the expectations of visiting. The promise of land, as well as closer proximity, may reinforce a couple's affiliation with one particular set of kin. However, the more distant parents may pressure the couple to continue in established patterns of visiting and even work sharing.

Hazel and Bob and their seven children live on land given to them by Bob's parents, who live about one-quarter mile away. Bob's job keeps him away from home most of the time, and the burden of family obligation falls squarely on Hazel's shoulders. Maxine and Cecil, Bob's parents, rarely find anything kind to say about Hazel, complaining that Hazel "can throw more out the back door with a teaspoon than her husband can bring in the front door with a shovel." Hazel, who has no relatives nearby, says that her parents-in-law resent the fact that she and the children won't be controlled in the way that Bob has always been controlled. Hazel in turn complains of Bob's overattention to his parents' needs and his neglect of his own family. Hazel copes with an uncomfortable existence by gossip and, as much as possible, by avoidance. While she and the children must help with the family farm work, she says that she doesn't have much to say to her parents-in-law, because whatever she says they'll criticize. Maxine refers to Hazel as "that old slab-sided thing," and Hazel refers to "my mother-in-law, the stubborn old coot."

Women have also dealt with such family frustrations by running away. Running away usually meant returning to the woman's natural household; several women laughingly told of doing this as young brides. One woman, whose parents did not live in the community but whose ancestors for five generations had done so and who had several aunts and uncles nearby, "ran away" on four or five different occasions, as she simply could no longer tolerate her parents-in-law's demands on her labor. She would walk down to the tracks, flag down the passenger train, and travel to her parent's home, about thirty miles away. She likewise told of getting her brothers to lie for her, to tell her husband she was ill so that she wouldn't have to return to him or to say that other family members were ill so that she would have an excuse for being home. On each of these occasions, either her husband would come after her or her parents would insist that she return on her own. As in other such cases, a woman's parents would usually receive her for a short period, but since the attitude is overwhelmingly that nuclear families should stay together if possible, she would be encouraged to return to her husband.

Relationships among unrelated women who marry into the same family may contain an element of strain or potential conflict; in such a case, contacts are usually simply avoided. Thus two women who married brothers each told of conflict with their sister-in-law, brother-in-law, and parents-in-law. Although two sisters-in-law now live next door to each other whose husbands usually work together, neither has visited the other or has been in the other's house for a number of years. Furthermore, one of the women refuses to attend social gatherings, such as family dinners, at the nearby house of parents-in-law. She states that there is always conflict, normally in the form of criticism of her children's behavior, and she simply refuses to tolerate it any more.

Men who are feeling the pressure of being the less-than-perfect or perhaps unsatisfactory in-married spouse occasionally confide in a close, nonaffine friend. One young man complained bitterly to such a friend of the hostility he felt toward his wife's parents, who lived next door and who partially supported his family of three. This man was expected to help his father-in-law with farming, but he resented the control that the older couple had over his family. He eventually left his wife and baby, although whether the separation will be permanent is yet unknown.

Husbands occasionally confide in a sympathetic older child. Furthermore, many middle-aged men in the community work during the week away from the community and therefore have means for venting their feelings away from the domestic scene that are not as available for the older generation of women. Younger and middle-aged women, who are largely employed in local mills, also have the workplace in which to vent frustrations and find support.

The parents-in-law of one man refer to their son-in-law as "that drunken, lazy, good-for-nothing sot" and say that they cannot understand how their daughter could possibly stay married to him. A daughter-in-law of the same parents, who gets along equally poorly with them, says that they offered their daughter money to leave her husband (although the validity of this statement is questionable). Although the son-in-law never complained much, he did have a tendency to go "out with the boys" and to get drunk rather frequently; it was suggested by his in-married sister-in-law that, whenever the parents criticized him for being a "drunken sot," he would get drunk, which would increase their criticism.

As mentioned above, men and women have somewhat different means of dealing with strain, due to different socialization and roles in the system. Violence is an alternative rarely used by either sex, but in the past there had been several cases of men using violence as a means of dealing with overwhelming and increasing expectations and criticism. In one such instance in the 1950s, a couple attended a gathering at one of the two churches in the community, to which the wife's parents came as well. The parents had been attempting to interfere with the couple since they were married and continued to heap abuse on the husband's activities during the social. He left the church and walked the mile up the mountain to his home for his gun, returned to the church, shot his father-in-law and brother-in-law as they emerged from the church, and after he had chased her around the church, finally succeeded in shooting his mother-in-law. He then drove himself to the sheriff's office and turned himself in. This man was released from prison on good behavior after serving seven years and returned to the community, where he was accepted back as a neighbor (although not necessarily one to cross). His wife had divorced him, so he married the widow of his mother's deceased brother, a person in a much safer relationship to him.

In the perspective of the extended family, there are several cases of violence against those who threaten the solidarity of the kin group. In one such case, an outsider to a large extended-family group that was clustered nearby in a single, relatively isolated hollow started courting one of the daughters of the family. In addition, he began to socialize with several of the daughter's brothers. Together, these young men frequently spent time drinking and driving, getting into fights and whatever trouble they could find. One evening the patriarch of the family, an excellent marksman, waited on the side of the mountain and, as the car full of young men rode by, shot and killed the potential affine, thereby eliminating the threat of future disruption to his group. In a recent case, the drunken father and leader of an extended family attempted to push his daughter and son-in-law's mobile home off the side of the mountain, when no one was inside. The restraint that had existed in the tension between the two men had been broken down by alcohol (which perhaps explains the father-in-law's attempting the push with a Volkswagen Beetle—he failed).

For men and women there are basically three alternative solutions to potential conflict. The first is violence, but the consequences of such action are severe and therefore restrictive, whether enforced by law or by community opinion. Furthermore, violence is a dramatic type of interference with another person's life and is ultimately a break in the code of noninterference. Violence most often is preceded by threats of violence, which normally are heeded, so that a second solution—avoidance—is more often followed. In some cases, however, individuals believe that their own independence and therefore their worth has been so damaged or threatened that it can be regained to a degree only through violent destruction of the cause.

Religious ritual is a third, but rarely heeded, strategy. Decoration Day provides a ceremony through which individuals may on occasion seek resolution of difficulties. The frequent spontaneous preaching by members of the group is one means of easing hostilities that may exist between those preaching and other family members. As one person noted, Decoration Day is a time for "clearing the air," so that "if you've done something against somebody and you let it out with the help of the Lord, and ask his help and intervention in public, then nobody can say 'that son-of-a-bitch.' " Decoration Day in some ways serves the function of settling, or at least easing, potential hostilities.

In the face of hostilities, then, avoidance is a solution and God is the only mediator. But where avoidance is not possible and God doesn't listen, then violent action is a logical alternative.

The independent nuclear family is an ideal state of existence, since extended-family cooperation enhances the economic status of all families involved. Independent ownership of land by nuclear families is greatly valued. Land is, however, usually acquired from parents. Parents and married children each need the other's resources, since parents often have land and equipment but need labor and since children often can supply labor but have limited financial resources, land, and equipment. Parents are therefore in a position to influence their married children's lives. Inheritance is one factor that can be manipulated by those in control of resources in order to ensure the cooperation of the residentially close but ideally independent families of children. Affinal strain thus results from the conflict between the ideal independence of nuclear families and the necessity for subordination of nuclear-family interests to those of parents. This strain specifically occurs between in-married spouses and their parents-in-law.

A final qualification must be added: this system, like all rural social systems, is changing. With the decreasing viability of agriculture and the increasing reliance on "public work," as well as the increasing number of occupational and educational possibilities that are becoming real alternatives to the mountain young person, the necessity for extended-family cooperation is decreasing. Affinal strain is becoming increasingly uncommon and, for those who do not choose to leave the community altogether, is more easily handled by simple avoidance when it does occur. Furthermore, as illustrated by a 1973 case of multiple murder in a nearby community, in which the son-in-law killed not only his parents-in-law but also his wife and himself, a violent solution to a problem now represents a case of absolute desperation when no possible alternatives exist.

37. GENDER, FAMILY STRUCTURE, AND POVERTY IN CENTRAL APPALACHIA

Ann R. Tickamyer

Department of Sociology, University of Kentucky

Cecil Tickamyer

Appalachian Center, University of Kentucky

INTRODUCTION

More than two decades after Appalachia was identified as a primary battleground in the "war on poverty," the region remains the quintessential example of persistent poverty and underdevelopment in the United States. This is true despite decades of government interventions promoting growth as well as clear evidence of real growth in aggregate income, industrialization, and improved infrastructure. In this paper we look at how the economic structure of the region differentially influences poverty rates for different segments of the

Reprinted from the *Proceedings of the Conference on Land and Economy in Appalachia,* Appalachian Center, University of Kentucky (1987), pp. 80–90. Used by permission.

population. In particular, we combine the insights from theories of uneven development with those from the emerging feminist analysis of poverty to examine how region, gender, and family structure contribute to our understanding of poverty in the central Appalachian region.

PERSPECTIVES ON APPALACHIAN POVERTY

The persistence of poverty in the United States has re-emerged in the 1980s as a social problem and a political issue after a decade of relative quiescence. In the 1960s poverty was conceptualized largely in terms of region, race, and age—as a problem of the urban ghettos, the elderly, native populations, the deep South, and Appalachia. In the 80s gender and family structure were added to the list as factors recognized as important sources of poverty. The "feminization of poverty" is a phrase that captures the growing recognition that women and children are disproportionately represented in poor populations. To date there is very little research which looks at how region, gender, and family structure interrelate and how the problems of poverty for women and their dependents is influenced by the local economy of particular places. Here we examine how gender and family structure are implicated in the region with some of the most persistent and intractable poverty levels in the U.S.—central Appalachia.

In 1979, when 9.6% of all American families had incomes below the poverty level, the poverty rate for families in the central subregion of Appalachia—the area most clearly identified with the region—was 19.2% (19.9% for nonmetropolitan counties only). This contrasts with a rate of 10.9% for the non-Appalachian counties of the five surrounding states (13.2% for nonmetro counties).

The reasons for this situation remain a matter of debate. Some Appalachian scholars say there is a unique subcultural identity for the region with its own patterns of economic activity, family life, language, and customs which run counter to modern economic values (Brown and Hillary, 1962; Campbell, 1969; Stephenson, 1968). An unsympathetic version of this argument defines this cultural complex as the "culture of poverty" and uses this to explain persistent poverty in the region.

More recently, however, many regional economists and development specialists have questioned the explanatory value of regional labels or subcultural explanations, suggesting that the problems associated with a region are the result of the particular configuration of its regional political economy (Markusen and Schoenberger, 1979). Appalachian poverty and underdevelopment are explained with such factors as class composition, land ownership, industrial base, and lack of urban development (Billings, 1974; Fisher, 1977; Philliber, 1981; Walls, 1978; Walls and Billings, 1977).

Uneven Development: The concept of uneven development entailed in this approach has become an important tool for understanding pockets of regional and subregional poverty which remain endemic to specific locations within advanced capitalist economies such as central Appalachia (Malizia, 1978; Hansen, 1979). Perhaps more to the point, it has also become clear that even in places of large scale economic growth, regional imbalances remain. Traditional socioeconomic theories of development assumed that expanded growth would result more or less automatically in increased benefits for the places and populations involved. Ultimately, even the poorest segments of the population would benefit via a "trickle down" process (Friedman and Weaver, 1978; Hansen, 1974; Higgins, 1977). As the experiences of both third world and regional pockets of poverty in the U.S. and other industrialized nations demonstrate, even vastly expanded growth in income and productivity do not necessarily benefit large segments of society if the benefits of such growth do not get distributed to the population. In this (not uncommon) case, underdeveloped areas remain impoverished or even decline in the quality of life for many residents (Adelman and Morris, 1973; Cline, 1975). Studies of the impact of economic sector and economic growth in Kentucky demonstrate that measures of development and quality of life are influenced both by the nature of the local economy and by the distribution of income and jobs resulting from the type of economic activity found in each county (Tickamyer and Duncan, 1984; Duncan, 1985).

Policies designed to promote development via economic growth are likely to fail if the social relations of production promote maldistribution of income, jobs and resources (Holland, 1976; Markusen, 1979; Bluestone and Harrison, 1982). To understand regional poverty it is not enough to examine the type of local economy and the degree of economic development, although these are very important. In addition, it is crucial to look at how key socio-economic factors affect different groups within a region and how these factors are translated into opportunities for individuals and groups.

Gender and Family Structure: The importance of examining the different impacts of economic structure on different groups and the importance of the distribution of opportunities both highlight one of the key insights of the new feminist scholarship. This is the new recognition of the importance of gender and family structure in the explanation of poverty. In other words, gender takes its place along with race and class and age as a major determinant of poverty status. The last few years have seen massive documentation of the increasing disadvantage of women and the vastly greater likelihood they have of entering poverty, remaining poor, slipping in and out of poverty, and transmitting it to their children (Pearce and McAdoo, 1981). At least three different reasons for this situation have been identified. These are women's disadvantage in the waged labor force, women's predominance in unpaid labor, and government policies towards women's work both paid and unpaid.

Women's poor position in the waged labor force has been documented at length. A summary of factors which contribute to the impoverishment of women include occupational sex segregation with women's jobs concentrated in low wage secondary occupations and peripheral industries; technological obsolescence and deskilling of many traditional women's jobs such as clerical work; and contraction of high wage industries, preventing expansion of women into better paying sectors (Scott, 1984). Many of these trends are particularly appropriate for understanding women's labor market status in central Appalachia, where much of the industrial employment is either in low wage peripheral industries or in the better paid but rapidly declining mining sector.

In addition to their waged labor, women's unpaid labor plays a major role in increasing their vulnerability to poverty. Women shoulder the greatest amount of home work, including major if not sole responsibility for child rearing and household chores (Hartmann, 1981; Berk and Berk, 1979). This "unjust dual role" places major burdens on women as well as limiting opportunities for generating income (Sarvasy and Van Allen, 1984). The disadvantage may extend beyond underpaid waged labor and unpaid domestic duties. The large amount of volunteer work done by women provides important community goods and services but rarely can be translated into income generating activities. Finally, Scott (1984) points out that in the third world, unpaid labor includes out of the house work in the informal sector, i.e., the supply of goods and services to both formal and other informal sector members. Studies of poor people in poor places in the U.S. find the same thing (cf. Stack, 1975; Stack and Semmel, 1975).

Many idealized accounts of Appalachian community life depict the non-market economic activities of women which are crucial for family survival but do little to assist women out of poverty when there are few other sources of income. Considering the strength of traditional family forms in the Appalachian region, the failure to participate in the waged labor force can extract a heavy price in terms of women and their dependents' economic well-being.

Finally, government policies towards women, families and work play a major role in the impoverishment of women. Public family and welfare policies devalue both women's domestic labor and their labor force activity (Folbre, 1984). Comparative studies of how women's labor and family roles are treated show that the U.S. is virtually the only industrialized nation which makes no provision for women's dual role, nor provides any but punitive assistance to poor mothers and their children (Kamerman, 1984). A dual welfare system exists which parallels the segmented labor markets in which women work (Pearce and McAdoo, 1981). In the secondary welfare system which primarily applies to women and children, programs such as Aid to Families with Dependent Children (AFDC) are seen as a privilege rather than a right, coverage is uncertain, stigmatized, and varies from place to place. This is in sharp contrast to entitlement programs such as unemployment compensation and social security for which men are more often eligible. For example, in Appalachian mining communities, many men collect unemployment or disability benefits which are generally defined as earned benefits rather than the "handouts" which are available to impoverished women, such as AFDC. Finally, the experience with the welfare bureaucracy disempowers poor people, increasing their disadvantage and making effective opposition unlikely. This too is more likely with transfers defined as charity compared to entitlements viewed as rights, and therefore more likely to be experienced by women.

These contributions from feminist scholarship make it clear that in order to disentangle the factors contributing to poverty, it is necessary to consider the role of gender and family structure. When we look at information on individuals, the factors creating poverty for women are not always the same for men. At the aggregate level, however, it is not clear how women and men compare. There is no question that women have higher rates of poverty, but it is not known whether local and regional economic factors will influence female poverty rates in the same ways as for males. In fact, there is some reason to think they won't, since women's position in the labor force and local economy is not the same as it is for men. Therefore, our goal is to determine whether and how regional economic structure affects gender-based county poverty levels in central Appalachia.

SOURCE OF DATA ON APPALACHIAN POVERTY

To address these issues we examine 1980 county level census data for the Appalachian region. There are massive problems in trying to find information on socioeconomic structure of subregional areas of the U.S. such as Appalachia. First, the only way of obtaining data for the Appalachian region which does not include large non-Appalachian areas is to use county level data. The major sources of data for individuals such as the public use samples of the census, current population surveys and a variety of large scale surveys geared to issues of income and poverty (e.g., PSID, SIPP, NLS) either do not permit this type of regional breakdown or omit this region entirely from their sampling frame.

Using county data, however, creates additional problems. The most reliable and complete source of data is the summary information tabulated for the 1980 U.S. census. For income and poverty levels, this means using 1979 data. During intercensal periods, especially as the next decennial census looms closer, questions arise about whether the figures are still valid. At this time the information is almost seven years old and during this period there has been a major recession, farm crisis, and decline in energy prices, to name a few of the events that can be presumed to have a major influence on Appalachian poverty. Attempting independent estimates for intercensal years is a risky business, however, and tend to be highly inaccurate. For example, poverty estimates published by the Kentucky Department of Commerce for 1978 are grossly different from the 1979 census figures, and efforts by state agencies in other parts of the country have found the problem equally intractable. Difficulties in projecting total poverty rates make clear the difficulty of obtaining rates for specific population segments.

Given the events during this decade, it seems reasonable to assume that the poverty situation for Appalachian counties is no better than it was in 1979, and it quite likely is worse. However, this is not the end of the problem. There are relatively few tabulations provided by the census of population values for different groups' socio-economic characteristics. For example, it is possible to obtain poverty rates for female-headed households with and without children, but it is not possible to directly obtain poverty rates for women by labor force status. Furthermore, in many cases even where the census does provide information, privacy guidelines mandate suppression of data for any situation where resulting small numbers might violate these rules. Especially in the many small population counties of rural Appalachia, this results in suppression of important information. It would be impossible, for example, to obtain poverty rates for blacks in many Appalachian counties.

The problems do not end with the source of data. There are also difficulties in defining poverty and defining Appalachia. There has long been a debate on the most appropriate way to measure poverty levels. In the two census periods in which this has been attempted, the procedure entails determining the cost of food (the "market basket") for families of various sizes and types and then multiplying this by three on the assumption that in a minimal survival budget, food costs will be a third of total consumption needs. The resulting figure is the poverty level specific for family household size and age in 1980 and also farm status in 1970. In 1979 for a family of four including two related children under the age of eighteen, this was defined as an income of $7356. The specific criteria vary for individuals and families of different sizes and types. It was calculated differently in the 1970 census than in 1980. This means that it is not possible to compare poverty rates directly across the census years. It is also not clear how location influences the actual experience of poverty since prices of basic commodities can vary dramatically from region to region. Similarly, it is not clear that the price of food relative to other commodities has been stable over time and place, raising questions about the multiplier used (3). Finally, there is no way to account for noncash benefits such as food stamps which may influence the meaning of particular income levels and the ensuing quality of life.

An alternative approach to calculating poverty levels is to measure *relative poverty* using the bottom income quintile as the definition of poverty. Using this approach, the rate of poverty in this country jumps dramatically in many areas since by definition it is 20% in the U.S. as a whole. For Appalachia this means a 28.4% rate for the ARC counties of the five state central region (including metro)—more than double the usual and official poverty rate. It should be noted that even though the proportion of families in poverty increases dramatically, the income level is not that much higher. It is $9844, underscoring how close to the margin even officially nonpoor populations live. Critics of this approach say that an arbitrary cutoff point such as the bottom quintile has no intrinsic meaning. It does not incorporate a sense of the submarginal standard of living which poverty is supposed to convey. However, the low income figure represented by the bottom quintile suggests that large numbers of persons who are not officially classified as poor have an impoverished standard of living. Most important, using this approach allows comparisons across time.

A final problem area is the definition of Appalachia. In the mid-sixties with the formation of the Appalachian Regional Commission, counties in thirteen states ranging from New York to Mississippi were designated "Appalachian." However, it is generally, recognized that there were major political considerations employed in the designation of Appalachian status, and that many areas not traditionally defined as Appalachia or not needing the interventions for which the ARC was defined were included. To deal with the problems this creates, the larger Appalachian region is often divided into subregions, including central, southern and northern. Additional definitions of Appalachia have been suggested (cf. Ford, 1967). In this study we have used a number of different definitions of Appalachia to check the validity of our findings and to define the limits of the regional effect. For clarity the emphasis in this study is on the portion of the Appalachian Regional Commission (ARC) defined Appalachian region within the five central states of Kentucky, North Carolina, Tennessee, Virginia, and West Virginia. The non-Appalachian comparisons generally are the non-ARC counties within these states.

APPALACHIAN POVERTY: DATA AND FINDINGS

The data for this study are all from the 1980 U.S. Census and represent the years 1979 and 1980 (U.S. Census, 1982). Counties are the unit of analysis and, include the five states of Central Appalachia described above.

Poverty Measures include a number of different group specific poverty rates. Major emphasis is placed on comparing the percent of female headed families with children to nonfemale-headed (families with a male head or married couple) with children. However, for descriptive and comparison purposes, we also look at the percent of all female and nonfemale-headed families in poverty, as well as various breakdowns by age and family status.

Table 37.1 shows the distribution of persons and families in poverty for various definitions of poverty and family situations. A number of alternative formulations of poverty rates are included. From Table 37.1, it is clear that Appalachia is substantially worse off than the rest of the United States. By far the most impoverished region is central Appalachia, using the central ARC counties of Kentucky, Tennessee, Virginia, and West Virginia. Both the counties which define central Appalachia and the total state figures in which these counties are located present a fairly dismal picture. The Northern and Southern subregions tend to be better off than central Appalachia, with poverty rates similar to non-ARC counties, but still worse than the total nation.

This pattern holds when examining poverty status of different types. It is clear that gender is the major variable affecting poverty status. Female-headed families are by far the worst off; those which include children present a devastating picture.

Measures of Socio-Economic Structure compare ARC and non-ARC nonmetropolitan counties on a variety of social and economic characteristics as shown in Table 37.2 (see page 312). Unemployment is the proportion of persons with any episode of unemployment

TABLE 37.1

Proportion of Nonmetro Persons and Families in Poverty by Region, Family Type, and Definition of Poverty

	Extreme Poverty and Near Poverty: Proportions of Persons Below Specified Percentages of Poverty Level				Proportion of Families in Poverty By Type of Family				
	75%	100%	125%	150%	Total Families	Total Female Headed Families	Female Headed Families with Children	Total Nonfemale Headed Families	Nonfemale Headed Families with Children
U.S. Total (including metro)	.083	.124	.170	.217	.096	.303	.403	.062	.075
Appalachian Subregions in Five State Region:									
Non-ARC	.109	.168	.233	.297	.132	.339	.437	.100	.109
Central Appalachian	.162	.236	.308	.378	.199	.396	.527	.174	.194
Northern Appalachian	.107	.164	.227	.290	.127	.307	.438	.104	.121
Southern Appalachian	.094	.154	.206	.269	.124	.284	.368	.104	.111
State Totals:									
Kentucky	.150	.218	.288	.356	.183	.388	.507	.158	.175
North Carolina	.108	.169	.237	.305	.135	.345	.436	.100	.109
Tennessee	.117	.185	.254	.323	.150	.333	.435	.126	.134
Virginia	.095	.147	.207	.270	.111	.289	.382	.086	.096
West Virginia	.113	.169	.232	.294	.134	.321	.459	.109	.128

TABLE 37.2

**Economic Characteristics of Nonmetro Counties in Five State Region,
By ARC Appalachian Subregion.**

	ARC Appalachian Subregion Within Central Five Region			
	Non-ARC	Central	North	South
Unemployment Rate:				
Female	.192	.214	.195	.197
Male	.162	.252	.228	.177
Labor Force Nonparticipation Rate:				
Female	.432	.594	.567	.446
Male	.207	.299	.266	.219
Proportion Rural	.668	.817	.761	.736
Agriculture Employment (Proportion of Workers)	.057	.045	.029	.036
Mining Employment (Proportion of Workers)	.009	.152	.104	.006
Manufacturing Employment (Proportion of Workers)	.318	.179	.181	.393
Proportion of Persons in Families	.879	.915	.878	.897
Proportion of Families Female Head No Husband	.134	.114	.112	.110
Proportion of Families With No Workers	.120	.202	.174	.130
Proportion of Families With One Worker	.317	.405	.403	.318
Persons in Families In Poverty (Proportion)	.147	.221	.139	.132

during the course of the year. Nonparticipation rate shows the proportion of persons sixteen and over who are not in the labor force. The percent of residents living in rural areas is defined by the Census as persons living in places under 2500 population. Economic base is represented by proportion of workers employed in agriculture, mining, and manufacturing. Finally, characteristics of family structure are shown with proportion of persons in families, proportion of female-headed families, proportion of families with no workers and one worker and proportion of persons in families in poverty.

Table 37.2 provides an interesting profile of Appalachian economy and society. The Central Appalachian subregion is much worse off than the portions of the five-state region which are in the northern or southern subregions. Unemployment rates are higher as are the nonparticipation rate and the proportion rural. The southern subregions look much more like the non-ARC counties than the central region, and the northern region falls in the middle. As to be expected, there is higher mining but lower manufacturing employment in Central Appalachia. Family structure is particularly interesting as there are more persons in families, fewer with female heads/no husband, and many more with no workers or only one worker. In other words, a more traditional family structure prevails in the central Appalachian subregion, alongside a more depressed economy.

Next we use the different economic characteristics to compare male and female-headed families with children for ARC and non-ARC counties in order to see how local and regional economic structure affects gender and family based poverty rates. Each of the economic factors is trichotomized into low, medium, and high levels to characterize counties with different economic profiles. Table 37.3 shows the results (see page 313).

TABLE 37.3

Proportion of Nonmetro Families with Children in Poverty by Family Type and ARC Appalachian Subregion, for Three Levels of Selected County Economic Characteristics

	Proportion of Families with Children in Poverty, By Family Type and Region, By Nonmetropolitan County Economic Characteristics For Five State Region							
	Female head, no husband present				Non-female headed			
	Non-ARC	Central	North	South	Non-ARC	Central	North	South
Unemployment Rate:								
Less than 20%	.430	.433	.443	.334	.103	.140	.109	.094
20%–25%	.460	.526	.409	.422	.125	.179	.113	.135
More than 25	.486	.578	.529	.497	.143	.244	.178	.209
Labor Force Nonparticipation Rate:								
Less than 35%	.416	.441	.370	.347	.097	.139	.088	.096
35%–45%	.489	.506	.428	.400	.136	.198	.114	.132
More than 45%	.455	.558	.497	—	.109	.203	.153	—
Proportion Rural:								
Less than 70%	.426	.501	.373	.366	.097	.157	.101	.100
70%–90%	.438	.524	.462	.361	.113	.184	.117	.107
More than 90%	.484	.551	.494	.393	.143	.227	.153	.145
Agriculture Employment (Proportion of Workers):								
Less than 4%	.365	.530	.431	.361	.075	.181	.120	.102
4%–8%	.461	.499	.455	.379	.114	.192	.116	.125
More than 8%	.491	.569	.467	.430	.146	.267	.143	.171
Mining Employment (Proportion of Workers):								
Less than 5%	.437	.505	.451	.365	.109	.203	.106	.110
5%–15%	.432	.528	.402	.452	.111	.221	.117	.151
More than 15%	.398	.541	.472	—	.115	.177	.139	—
Manufacturing Employment (Proportion of Workers):								
Less than 15%	.400	.533	.442	.321	.090	.178	.127	.096
15%–30%	.465	.535	.432	.364	.115	.216	.120	.114
More than 30%	.424	.491	.455	.369	.108	.208	.100	.111

As expected, ARC counties have higher poverty rates than non-ARC; central Appalachian counties are worse than other ARC counties; as the percent of rural population increases so does poverty, and at every level there are higher female-headed family poverty rates than non-female. Poverty rates increase with higher unemployment rates, with especially dramatic figures for women. The greater the nonparticipation in the labor force rate, the greater the levels of poverty, again especially for female-headed families.

What is very clear is that regardless of the basis of the local economy, women have higher poverty rates, and they are especially at risk in counties with high mining and agricultural employment. Mining is especially interesting, because at the highest levels of mining employment, men's poverty levels drop whereas women's increase. This undoubtedly results from the lack of other employment opportunities in the male dominated resource extraction industries, and the fact that although the mining industry tends to be highly volatile, when employment opportunities exist, the men working in this field make relatively high wages (Tickamyer and Duncan, 1984). Poverty rates are highest in high agriculture employment counties, although again, they are much higher for women. Both male and female rates fall slightly for high manufacturing employment, but the baseline rate remains much higher for women. It is ironic to note that while at the highest level of manufacturing employment, female poverty rates decline somewhat, it is precisely the jobs in low wage manufacturing, frequently held by women, which are declining in the region.

DISCUSSION AND CONCLUSIONS

It is clear that the situation of female-headed families is far more dire than others and female-headed families with children are especially at risk. The situation in Central Appalachia is far worse than in the rest of the country or other portions of Appalachia. However, compared to other areas, it seems safe to conclude that Appalachian poverty problems are not attributable to having large segments of the population at risk. Elsewhere, high poverty rates can at least in part be attributed to the disproportionate presence of groups at risk—the elderly, female-headed families, children, blacks, and other racial or ethnic minorities. In Appalachia, however, these groups are either at or below the expected population levels. Appalachian poverty is clearly identified with the structure of the local economy, the type of employment opportunities, and the degree of isolation which makes economic opportunity scarce. These hit women harder than men, but the same factors are implicated for both.

In an earlier study, we used multivariate statistical techniques to identify and control for factors which have been used to explain differential male and female aggregate poverty rates. We had similar results: the same types of influences were important for both male and female poverty rates, suggesting that there are similarities in the process of producing high poverty levels. However, we were better able to explain the amount of poverty for the nonfemale-headed families than for female-headed families. These results reinforce the idea that there are additional factors which must be considered to explain women's poverty compared to men. It is not that the factors which create male poverty don't apply to women, but rather that women bear additional burdens which increase their risk. In the Appalachian region where there remains a larger proportion of women who are not in the labor force and where there is a strong tradition of husband-wife families with a traditional division of labor (including a higher proportion of single earner families than in the rest of the country), women will be especially vulnerable to spells of poverty when their usual sources of support break down.

We suggest that one reason for the high poverty levels for women and their dependents in Appalachia is that they represent a segment of the population which is most vulnerable to whatever negative economic trends emerge. The more traditional the community and family life (and it is often argued with good evidence that this is a major characteristic of Appalachia), the more limited the opportunities for employment and income generating activities, the harder hit will be those groups in the population who are least economically independent. It would be easy to blame the breakdown of community for the "feminization of poverty," but it is more appropriate to view this trend as an outcome of the problems in the position of women in a society where non-market labor is marginalized and where market opportunities are not readily available. To deal with *all* Appalachian poverty, it is necessary to have more jobs. But it is particularly important to make sure that opportunities of whatever type and location are available to *all* members of the community.

REFERENCES

Adelman, Irma and Cynthia Morris, *Economic Growth and Social Equity in Developing Countries.* (Stanford, Calif.: Stanford University Press, 1973.)

Berk, Richard and Sarah Berk, *Labor and Leisure at Home.* (Beverley Hills, Calif.: Sage, 1979.)

Billings, Dwight, "Culture and poverty in Appalachia: theoretical discussion and empirical analysis." *Social Forces* 53 (Dec. 1974) 315–23.

Bluestone, Barry and Bennett Harrison, *The Deindustrialization of America.* (New York: Basic, 1982.)

Brown, James and George Hillery, "The Great Migration, 1940–1960." In T. Ford (ed.), *The Southern Appalachian Region: A Survey.* (Lexington, Kentucky: University Press of Kentucky, 1962.)

Campbell, John, *The Southern Highlander and His Homeland.* (Lexington, Kentucky: University Press of Kentucky, 1969.)

Cline, W. R., "Distribution and development: a survey of literature," *Journal of Development Economics 1* (Feb. 1975):359–400.

Duncan, Cynthia, *Capital and the State in Regional Economic Development: The Case of the Coal Industry in Central Appalachia.* Ph.D. Dissertation, University of Kentucky, Lexington, Kentucky, 1985.

Fisher, Stephen, "Folk culture or folk role." Pp. 14–25 in J. Williamson (ed.), *An Appalachian Symposium.* (Boone, N.C.: Appalachian State University Press, 1977.)

Folbre, Nancy, "The pauperization of motherhood: patriarchy and public policy in the U.S." *Review of Radical Political Economics* 16 (4):72–88, 1984.

Ford, Thomas (ed.), *The Southern Appalachian Region: A Survey.* (Lexington, Kentucky: University Press of Kentucky, 1967.)

Friedman, John and Clyde Weaver, *Territory and Function.* (London: Edward Allen, 1978.)

Hansen, Niles, *The Future of Nonmetropolitan America.* (Lexington, Mass.: D. C. Heath, 1974.)

———. "The new international division of labor and manufacturing decentralization in the United States." *Review of Regional Economic Studies* 9:1–11, 1979.

Hartmann, Heidi, "The family as the locus of gender, class, and political struggle: the example of housework." *Signs* 6 (3):366–94, 1981.

Higgins, Benjamin, "Economic Change," Pp. 99–122 in M. Nash (ed.), *Essays on Economic Development and Cultural Change in Honor of Bert F. Hoselitz.* (Chicago: University of Chicago Press, 1977.)

Holland, Stuart, *Capital Versus the Regions.* (New York: St. Martin's, 1976.)

Horan, Patrick and Charles Tolbert, *The Organization of Work in Rural and Urban Labor Markets*. (Boulder, Co.: Westview, 1984.)

Kamerman, Sheila, "Women, children and poverty: public policies and female-headed families in industrialized countries." *Signs* 10(2):249–71, 1984.

Malizia, Emil, "Organizing to overcome uneven development: the case the U.S. South." *Review of Radical Political Economics* 10:87–94, 1978.

Markusen, Ann, "Regionalism and the capitalist state." Working Paper 305. (Berkeley, Calif.: Institute of Urban and Regional Development, University of California, 1979.)

Nelson, Barbara, "Women's poverty and women's citizenship: some political consequences of economic marginality." *Signs* 10(2):209–31, 1984.

Pearce, Diana, "Toil and trouble: women workers and unemployment compensation." *Signs* 10(3):439–59, 1985.)

Pearce, Diana and Harriette McAdoo, *Women and Children: Alone and in Poverty*. (Washington, D.C.: National Advisory Council on Economic Opportunity, 1981.)

Philliber, William, *Appalachian Migrants in Urban America*. (New York: Praeger, 1981.)

Sarvasy, Wendy and Judith Van Allen, "Fighting the feminization of poverty: socialist feminist analysis and strategy." *Review of Radical Political Economics* 16(4):89–110, 1984.

Scott, Hilda, *Working Your Way to the Bottom: the Feminization of Poverty*. (London: Pandora Press, 1984.)

Stack, Carol, *All Our Kin*. (New York: Harper and Row, 1974.)

Stack, Carol and Herbert Semmel, "Social insecurity: welfare policy and the structure poor families." Pp. 89–103 in B. Mandell (ed.), *Welfare in America*. (Englewood Cliffs, NJ: Prentice-Hall, 1975.)

Stephenson, John, *Shiloh: A Mountain Community*. (Lexington, Kentucky: University Press of Kentucky, 1968.)

Tickamyer, Ann and Cynthia Duncan, "Economic activity and the quality of life in eastern Kentucky." *Growth and Change* 15(4):43–51, 1984.

Tickamyer, Ann and Cecil Tickamyer, "Gender and poverty in central Appalachia." Presented at the annual meetings of the Southern Sociology Society, New Orleans, La., April, 1986.

U.S. Bureau of the Census, *Census of Population and Housing, 1980: Summary Tape, File 3, Technical Documentation*. (Washington, D.C.: U.S. Dept. of Commerce, 1982.)

Walls, David, *Central Appalachia in advanced capitalism: its coal industry structure and coal operation associations*. Ph.D. Dissertation, University of Kentucky, Lexington, Kentucky, 1978.

Walls, David and Dwight Billings, "The sociology of southern Appalachia." *Appalachian Journal* 10(Autumn, 1977):131–44.

38. MARRIAGE AND THE FAMILY

Janet M. Fitchen

Introduction

This chapter analyzes the structures and processes of marriage and family life in rural poverty enclaves. The analysis includes a description of the characteristic features and a delineation of the underlying goals and cultural values pertaining to marriage and family. The chapter seeks to identify the stresses that bear upon the family, the way these stresses affect marriages and families, and the way people absorb or deal with them. The analysis is based on long-term observations of many families, in Chestnut Valley and in other nearby rural depressed neighborhoods. Whenever quantitative profiles are used, however, they are restricted to the original twenty low-income families from the 1969 sample.

Characteristic Features

Three characteristics of family structure and process stand out. They are: the basic nuclear family model, the elasticity of the household, and the high incidence of marital disruption.

Basic Nuclear Family Model

A principal characteristic of the family structure is its conformity to the "standard" American pattern. In conceptual norms and in actuality, the standard nuclear family of a married couple and their young children clearly predominates. In 1969–70, eighteen of the twenty households contained a core married couple. In the remaining two households a single adult temporarily was living separately from a spouse.

In the twenty households, there were slightly more children (fifty) than adults (forty-five). There were children in fifteen households. (Three households had only grown, departed children; one household did not yet have children; and one household contained only an adult male.) In the fifteen households with children, the average number of children in the home was slightly over three, with a range from one to eight. The total number of children born to a family ranged up to ten; in the three-year period from 1970 to 1973, sixteen babies were born in the twenty households.

Elasticity of the Household

Although the predominant pattern is the nuclear family, the second characteristic is elasticity. Individuals, part-families, and entire nuclear families may be taken into a household temporarily. They may break away later, perhaps drift back, and then leave again, creating a shifting household structure. At any time, at least one-quarter of the families are expanded families, with some extra people in addition to the primary nuclear family. But the expansion does not create a permanent family form: families that are expanded at one time may be nuclear at other times, and vice-versa. In 1970, six of the twenty households were expanded. In 1972, there were five expanded households, but these were not all the same households. Only one expanded household remained that way for the two years; the other five had changed from expanded to simple, nuclear composition, while four previously nuclear families had expanded. Over time, then, the family structure is basically a nuclear unit, with temporary expansions to include extra people.

The most frequent form of expansion is the re-inclusion of a grown daughter with her children, if any. Three of the six expanded families in 1969–70 were of this type, and remained this way for six months to more than two years. In some cases, more than one grown daughter with children were living in the parental home. Occasionally, expansion includes the daughter's husband or boyfriend, but this is usually a short-lived situation. Another common expansion pattern is the inclusion of a sibling, parent, or parents of a principal adult. In a few cases, a grown son and his wife and/or children become part of the parental household for a short time. Occasionally, an unrelated family or individual will be temporarily annexed.

Marital Disruption

A third characteristic of the family is the high incidence of marital disruption. Eighteen of the twenty households contained married couples in 1969–70, but two couples split up soon afterward, and all parties moved out of the neighborhood. One other marriage was in a state of informal separation (in separate domiciles in the neighborhood). In the succeeding five-year period, two more couples broke up. In addition to long-term separations and terminations, five more marriages underwent episodes of serious crisis and temporary separation during the research period.

Evidence of the long-term pattern of marital disruption is also found in those cases where a presently intact nuclear family includes children born of previous marriages. Additionally, the movement of individuals into and out of Chestnut Valley is very often connected to or triggered by episodes of separation or divorce, or by the formation of a new union after dissolution of a prior one.

In addition to the high incidence of actual breakup, there is a much higher incidence of temporary but repeated and serious family disruption. Violent marital fighting, sudden departure of a spouse, mutual agreement to separate, and accusations or open acknowledgement of extramarital relationships are common in fact, ubiquitous in conversation, and pervasive in thought, fear, and suspicion.

Thus, whether one looks at the development of individual families over a period of time, or at situations in the total sample at one point, severe disruptions in marriage relationships appear to be frequent and characteristic. Although marriage and the nuclear family predominate as the modal type, marital breakup and altered family structure are characteristic also. What are the reasons for this paradox? What do people strive for and why? And why does the reality fall so short of the ideal?

Sentiments and Values Perpetuating Marriages

Family stability or instability is a complex phenomenon, and cannot be understood purely in terms of the statistical frequency of separations and breakups. If we merely count the number of broken and breaking-up families we get an exaggerated impression of instability, because we are using only one of several possible indices of family strength or weakness. Statistical counts of marriage dissolution neglect sentiment and values and tend to leave the erroneous or untested inference that the individuals do not place any emphasis on marital and family stability. In fact, although many of these marriages undergo serious disruption, most couples subsequently reunite, with a strong desire to smooth out the trouble and start over again. All three of the couples that broke up in 1969–70 were eventually reunited.

Many separation attempts—a husband or wife leaving the home, even going into court for initial protective or separation or custody procedures—are aborted because of the strong desire to try one more time to keep the marriage going. As one woman said "I keep giving him one more chance, hoping that he'll straighten out." Many of the couples in the study had been married for decades, despite periods of intense stress, disruption, infidelity, and brutality that an outside observer might consider significantly damaging to one or both partners and to the children. All but a few of the disrupted marriages were subsequently reconciled. Those few couples who did finally and permanently divorce reached that point only after many attempts to repair their marriages, and the individuals soon established unions with other partners. The longevity of some marriages, despite serious and periodic disruptions, may be a more significant social fact here than the rate of breakup or disruption of marriages.[1]

Maintaining a stable, intact family is an ideal strongly held by both husbands and wives. While actual family life may periodically or frequently fall far short of being harmonious, the goal of an intact family is tenaciously held, and tremendous emotional effort is spent attempting to achieve it. There appear to be four chief factors that reinforce the goal of "family."

An Intact Family Is Important for Children

Many of the adults of Chestnut Valley whose lives today are most problem-ridden grew up in disrupted homes. Death of a parent, and periods spent in foster homes and institutions are common in the life histories of one or, in many cases, both parents.[2] As these adults reflect on their present difficulties and their probable causes, they invariably cite their childhood family situations.

> I really didn't have any upbringing. I just existed. And it was always a struggle. Before I was fifteen, I was out in the world alone, getting by however I could, always in trouble, constantly fighting.

> I had no family, I've always resented the fact that they didn't care about me to care for me.

> My husband always wanted a relationship with his children that he never had with his father.

> Both my husband and I want so badly for our kids to have the home and childhood that *we* never had.

The lack of a stable family during childhood is viewed as definitely contributory to adult life problems. Now, as parents, men and women fervently hope that their children will have a better life than they had. Providing a two-parent home is considered crucial. Parents believe that as long as a child grows up in his or her own family and, for the most part, receives love and care, periodic upheavals will not seriously harm the child. Parents assume that children are able to see beyond the short-lived fights and squabbles to the overriding fact that their parents love them and that they are doing the best they can to provide a secure home, better than the one in which they were raised.

Fear of Institutional Care for Children

Parents fear the consequences to their children if the family should break up. From their own childhood experiences, from those of friends and relatives, and from experiences with their own children, parents have a deep-seated fear of the possibility of foster homes or institutional care for children. Divorce or separation might lead, eventually, to having the children put into such a foster-care situation, or even to having them "taken away" for good. Most parents, even those few who may appear to have a rather poor relationship with their children, are chilled by that possibility. Their fear of having the children removed, even temporarily, is partly based on negative feelings about the community and its institutions. Parents are convinced that keeping the family together at all costs is preferable to running the risk of having their children brought up by outside agencies, institutions, or individuals. They say, "no matter what it's like, the kids want to be in their own home."

Dependence of Parents on Their Children

Couples appear to perpetuate a marriage despite its stresses because, consciously or unconsciously, they are dependent upon their children. For many parents, the children are an extension of themselves, a means of self-fulfillment, and an important part of their self-image.

> "Without children, there is no family," said one father.

> "Where my children are, that is my home," said a mother.

> "My children mean the world to me. They *are* my world."

Many women consider the role of mother to be far more important than that of wife, and generally far more satisfying and fulfilling. Some men are emotionally dependent on their children because they receive their main acceptance and admiration from their young children. In times of severe family upheaval, both parents may openly express their personal emotional need for their children. (This need is part of the explanation for the phenomenon of a mother's keeping a child home from school when the child is not ill.) Even estranged parents may recognize that they both have a right and need to continue seeing the children. A divorced woman categorized her relationship with her former husband this way: "We are no longer man and wife. But he is and always will be the father of my children, the grandfather of my grandchildren. So I can never completely cut him out of my life, no matter how much I hold against him for the way he treated me." And so it is hard to make a complete break, and the temptation to try once more postpones a decisive parting.

This dependence of the adults on the children keeps a troubled marriage going because each parent fears that in a separation he or she might be the one to lose the children, either by the simple act of the spouse's removing them, or by the processes of court action. Sometimes a husband attempts to keep a wife in line by instilling in her a fear that he could at any time have her declared an "unfit mother" and have the children taken from her. A similar threat is sometimes used by wives against husbands who do not provide support. Fear of losing the children has many times been mentioned explicitly as a reason for not leaving home. Even women who are brutally beaten believe if they run away from home to escape domestic violence, they jeopardize their rights to the children. Thus, the ideal of preserving a two-parent home "for the sake of the children" also includes the unspoken need to preserve an intact home for the sake of the *parents*.

Dependence of Husband and Wife on Each Other

Adults also cling to a frequently disrupted and tension-filled marriage because of dependence on each other. This factor was apparent in several cases of long-term but unsatisfactory marriages and in marriages that only broke up after many years of recurrent fighting. Wives, especially, exhibit this dependence, particularly in cases where many years of married life have entailed virtual confinement to the home. In some cases, the wife has had little opportunity to operate as a responsible, independent individual in the wider world. In local phrasing, she has been kept "barefoot and pregnant." The only life she knows is keeping house, bearing and rearing children, soothing everyone's hurts. Even the meals she cooks may be prepared from food that she has not selected, because her husband is the one who drives, the one with the money, the one who gets the groceries. The decisions and interactions involving the big events and the little day-to-day activities may all be made by the husband: whether to buy that trailer or this car, whether to apply for food stamps, whether to take a child to the doctor. For a wife in this position, the contemplation of establishing a separate existence in a world she hardly knows brings tremendous fear and insecurity. This in turn makes her decide that it is better to stay put and take the inevitable blowups than to leave home and try to make it on her own. Her low self-esteem, her limited experience in the outside community, her fear of failure—all these underlie and are combined with emotional dependence on her husband, and give a woman strong reasons to remain with him. Rather than making a drastic change, she attempts to make the best of a bad situation.

In some cases, a wife stays with her husband mostly out of fear of him. On numerous occasions, an unhappy wife consciously decides against leaving home because she fully believes her husband's threats to harm her, the children, or himself if she should leave. Loaded shotguns are powerful deterrents to leaving home in the heat of marital squabbles.

Husbands, also, may keep a poor marriage going because of their dependence on their wives, a dependence more often based on emotional than practical needs. Although men seldom admit their dependence, it shows up when their women do leave them. In these situations, men exhibit a real state of emotional loss, appear helpless in coping with everyday life, and often go on a protracted alcoholic binge. A man whose wife has left him may claim that he can get along without her, and may boast that he can easily obtain sexual gratification with other women. But he may also go to great lengths to track her down and beg her to come home—which, in many cases, she does.

Mixed in with this dependence, there is usually an undeniable and strong bond of affection, and memories of better times together in the past. These, too, act to prolong even a seriously troubled marriage.

Sources of Family Stress

Despite the strong commitment to maintaining a marriage as central to a good home for children and as emotionally important for the adults, rupture and temporary breakdown are commonplace. The reasons for marital upheaval include both long-term causes and immediate or triggering events.

The triggering event—the last straw—is usually perceived and emphasized by the individuals involved. In most cases, it is a small act by either husband or wife that is reported as having brought on the crisis. The wife may have purchased a relatively extravagant food item, or made an unauthorized purchase for the house. The husband may have refused to fetch the children from the neighbors; or perhaps he has procrastinated in repairing the heater, but is angered by his wife's oblique reference to how cold it is in the house. Sexual promiscuity—actual or imagined, recent or dredged up from years ago—is a frequent fight starter. Either husband or wife may have been seen in some questionable circumstance with someone of the opposite sex, and rumors fly quickly through the neighborhood.

These actions and events, however, are only potential triggering causes: whether or not they actually give rise to a marital fight depends on many factors in the state of the marriage and the individual's emotions. When the marriage has been fairly peaceful for a period, potential triggering events may be overlooked or ignored. However, if one or both individuals are feeling "down" emotionally, or are under the influence of alcohol, small triggering events may be particularly volatile.

Marital fights seem to go through several stages, usually starting with abusive verbal exchanges, goading, and name-calling. Accusations are exchanged concerning factual or fancied marital infidelities of the past or present, and there ensues a general berating and belittling designed to further undermine the fragile ego of the other person. Physical fighting often erupts, and may be brutal, with threats of even greater violence in the future. It is usually the wife who suffers the most physical damage, and furniture and household items are frequently broken. Children, too, may become involved, threatened but seldom physically harmed. They may take sides or merely scream at both parents from the sidelines. Often the row ends in a stormy departure by either husband or wife, and the action and tension subside.

Behind the triggering events that touch off such flareups lie long-run, semipermanent stresses on the family and its members. Couples apparently do not recognize or they underestimate these deeper sources of marital stress, dwelling only on the triggering events. But the underlying stresses are festering irritants, as each partner harbors a longstanding and complex list of grievances and accusations. They explain the fact that very minor events so easily erupt into major battles. At most times, a family is under pressure from several stress sources.

Chronic Economic Problems

As discussed in the previous chapters, rural poor families carry a perpetual burden of money shortage, back debts, unsatisfactory or insecure jobs, worry about where tomorrow's meals will come from, and under-satisfaction of felt needs. The financial squeeze is an ever-present source of tension in some households, and the necessity of coping with it, combined with the inevitability of worrying about it, causes an undercurrent of anxiety and tension.

The economic problem may be the triggering cause of any particular dispute, with many marital arguments arising over the expenditure of money: she spent it on a nonessential for the house; he spent it on booze; and so on. Money is also a cause of arguments between parents and children, and these, too, may trigger marital confrontations: a small child may throw a tantrum because his mother refuses to buy a treat to eat; a teenager may sulk for days because the father wouldn't allow her to buy new shoes. In such cases, the parent-child dispute may well end up as a marital fight when one parent takes the child's side in the argument. There are endless small confrontations over money, and criticisms of the way money is spent often enter into marital squabbles, even when they are irrelevant to the argument.

Even when not the cause of a particular dispute, however, the constancy of money problems causes a general tension and anxiety that erode family life. The economic situation is a seething substratum that is constantly present to fuel other problems in the household, to exacerbate interpersonal tensions, and to drain the strength of individuals.

Unresolved Emotional Problems of Adults

Various emotional problems, rooted in childhood, frequently appear as continuing sources of stress in later life. Most of the adults grew up in difficult situations, and many carry into marriage a residue of unresolved emotional conflicts. Because of factors in their early childhood—disrupted homes, deserting parents, abject poverty, foster homes, or homelessness—some adults may find difficult later in life maintaining close interpersonal relationships. The psychological mechanisms that enabled them as children, to weather the emotional stress of frequently disrupted family life may actually work against them when, as adults, they attempt to establish and maintain close interpersonal connections. Perhaps in childhood it was necessary for self-protection to limit close emotional ties and to withhold trust. But in adulthood, this insulating shield becomes an isolating wall. This effect was apparent in the case of the man whose childhood consisted of a series of "new mothers," each of whom subsequently left or died: he now reports difficulty in getting along well with his second wife, or any other woman, on a long-term basis.

Some marriages suffer from the fact that they began when the partners had not yet reached sufficient maturity to know what they really wanted or expected in a marriage, knowing only that they needed a refuge from personal and family problems in their parental home. But the emotional needs that give rise to an early escape from the parental home are not necessarily satisfied in the marriage. For example, a woman who married at seventeen, in part because of her need to throw off the controlling hand of her parents, finds that in marriage she is no more autonomous or free than she was in her parental home. The couple has recently been going through a difficult period of struggle for authority, with the wife eventually buckling under to her husband's will—but not without seething resentment that occasionally erupts into hostile rebellion. Likewise, a boy of sixteen has quickly found that establishing a household with his girlfriend and their baby has not magically turned him into a man, and that his problems of getting along with other people have not been solved, but have multiplied.

Built-in Tension Points

Tension may be structured into some families as a result of the family's previous history. For example, if the union is a second marriage for either or both partners, there may be problems connected with the former spouses, or with children of former unions. If the children in the family are from previous marriages or from extramarital relationships, these children may provide a built-in source of conflict between husband and wife. They may argue that "his" children or "her" children are getting inferior treatment, or special consideration, in the family. Accusations of favoritism toward one's own children and accusations of sexual advances toward stepchildren can be a continuing and bitter source of marital disharmony.

In-law problems may also cause strain. Relationships with his or her "people," particularly if they live in the same house or nearby, may provide built-in tension sources.

Presence of Extra Individuals in the Household

Stress in the marital relationship sometimes arises as a result of the characteristic flexibility and expandability of the household. Often the household expands to incorporate an elderly grandparent, disabled adult sibling, or grown child or grandchildren. This temporary inclusion of others is seen as a fulfillment of one's obligation to help close relatives who have been unable to make their own way in life, an expression of lasting reciprocal bonds of mutual assistance. But it is viewed as neither the preferred nor the normal household situation. People openly state that such an expanded-family situation tends to cause tensions or provide fuel for existing difficulties. It drains family resources of food and money, often causes extra work, and reduces privacy.

The strains of having extra people living in the house show up particularly in the case of the re-inclusion of a grown daughter with her children, the most frequent form of expansion. The daughter may stay in the home because, without a husband, she needs the advantages of free or cheap room and board, she desires grandparental babysitting, and she seeks emotional and social support. In most cases, the daughter is in an anomalous position in the household, as role relationships, lines of authority, and division of labor are ambiguous.[3] Her father may assume a male authority role over both the daughter and her children, especially if the daughter has no man living with her. The young mother may come into conflict with her own mother with respect to the handling of and responsibility for her children. And in some cases, the lines of affect appear to be unclear, even to the children. A child in such a household may as likely go to grandmother as to mother for comfort, and in some cases may even address grandmother as "Mamma." In addition, the young mother may try to assume a disciplinary role toward her younger siblings in the household, as if they, too, were her children.

This lack of clarity in relationships between the basic family members and the annexed individuals is apt to create tensions that reverberate through the household, strains that are exacerbated by the temporary overcrowding of the home. The problem is even greater if only one member of the parental couple is parent to the daughter, while the other member is a more recent stepparent, officially or unofficially. Eventually, the strains may make the daughter move out, perhaps to a trailer or converted bus beside the house, or perhaps to join her husband or another man elsewhere. In some cases, the daughter may soon again need the refuge of a place to live and a family—and once more she will be taken into the home, with the difficulties and strains of the previous stay forgiven and forgotten. Occasionally, the length of stay may be protracted, and more than one daughter may be living at home at the same time. The strain on the central couple is usually apparent, and was described by one woman.

> My husband and I need a life together, some privacy. We don't even have a chance to sit by ourselves and talk, or to sit in the living room and watch TV.

> And we don't have the time we need to devote to the younger children because my grown girls and their babies are always around. It's so crowded here that my little one still has his bed in with us, and he has no place to play.

But even though parents would like their grown children to move into homes of their own, the parents continue to put up with the strain of an expanded household when necessary because "she is our daughter, and we can't just turn her out." Marital harmony comes second.

Unsuccessful Role Fulfillment

Because of a host of factors in this multigenerational poverty situation, individual adults may be unable to perform their expected roles to the satisfaction of either themselves or their marriage partners.

The male role pattern appears to present considerable difficulty. The adult male is conceived of as head of household, sole sex partner of the wife, earner of the family's sustenance, provider for the family's secondary wants, and chief authority figure in the household, with the power to make decisions and the authority to carry them out and to use sanctions to secure compliance. In actuality, few men attain even an approximation of this ideal. Many of the male heads of households find that in the jobs they hold they cannot earn enough money to provide what the family needs and wants. And so a man's sense of his own worth may be diminished, in his own eyes and in those of family members. Many of the irritating situations of daily life—the "hungry Thursdays," the chill of the cement kitchen floor, the necessity of sharing shoes and a bed with a brother, the blurry picture on the old TV set— are somehow connected to the vague realization that the man is not successful as a provider for his wife and children. This low self-image is a clear contributor to marital problems.

For the wife, the role expectations are less impossible to achieve. In most cases she can provide her husband with sexual satisfaction and bear children. Mother and housekeeper, as well as mate, are roles she can perform with some degree of success. Whatever the margin of separation between her ideal role and her actual performance, that difference is not totally a reflection on her. For example, her performance as housekeeper may fall below role expectations held by her husband, her neighbors, or by the outside community, as well as by herself. However, the brunt of the blame for this shortcoming may not fall directly on her, but on factors beyond her control, such as inadequate facilities—lack of closets, of hot water, of a washing machine; insufficient money for cleaning supplies; and overcrowding in the house. The blame falls diffusely on her husband, on the job situation, on the fact that there are a lot of people in the household, and on the vague explanation of "that's just the way it is around here." Thus, her performance may not be questioned, her ego not threatened. Outside the home, also, a woman usually escapes the constant exposure to defeat and failure that her husband encounters. If she does take a job, it is an extra role, and she has some leeway to be unsuccessful or to quit without causing damage to her self-evaluation or to her husband's evaluation of her.

The greater attainability of woman's role ideals, and the ability to direct blame for unsuccessful role performance away from the self, give rise to a frequently observed pattern in which a wife's ego strength and functioning level appear greater than those of her husband. Although many of the women encounter feelings of failure periodically, and occasionally quite strongly, on the whole the women are less perpetually and consistently assaulted by the sense of failure in fulfilling what they conceive of as their roles.

Although it might seem that this differential success in role fulfillment is a real plus for the women, the imbalance can also be seen as a contributing factor in the tension between husbands and wives. The differential possibility for fulfilling role expectations has been explicitly mentioned by several women, and is apparent in many of the instances of long-term marital strife.

Lack of Roles in the Outside Community

People lack access to secondary social roles in which they could gain a positive evaluation of themselves. This leaves both men and women highly vulnerable to ego damage if their performance in their primary roles (in employment and family) is inadequate. Since there are no other roles open that provide separate gauges of the individual's worth, too much personal evaluation depends on performance of basic husband and wife roles. A man's failure as family provider appears even more crushing than it would be if there were opportunities for him to be successful in other, outside roles. (Even success on a community baseball team or as a member of a volunteer fire department would help. But the men of the rural depressed neighborhoods do not participate in such organizations.)

It was apparent during the course of observations that individual adults, both men and women, function better in their home and family roles when they are provided with some active nonfamily social role to fill. Success in filling even a temporary outside role apparently builds ego-strength and thus enhances performance in the primary roles. It also takes the mind off family problems. Several women, in the midst of a very demanding and stress-filled home life, have earnestly stated that they would like to be able to give some time to helping out in some worthy cause in the community, like a day-care center or a nursing home. While participation in such outside roles might not put more food on the table, the boost to the self-image produces a sense of well-being that results in smoother relationships in the home. (Some small-scale opportunities for this kind of participation were created during the process of fieldwork in Chestnut Valley, and each time it was clear that the women who participated felt a heightened sense of self-worth during and after the events, for they had given some of their own time, skills, energy, and even money for refreshments to help put on a successful activity for the children of the neighborhood.)

The interaction of primary and secondary roles is by no means a classbound phenomenon. In the middle class, active community roles may compensate for or support weak marriages. But the people of the rural poverty enclaves do not have access to such substitute or compensatory roles—and one result is stress in marital relationships.

Discharged Aggression

Frequently, marital upheavals result from the fact that the family serves as the place where frustrations generated by experiences in the outside world are released. The many frustrations derived from experiences on the job, in the community, and at school cannot be expressed outwardly and directly, either because the source of frustration is diffuse and undefined, or because there is no avenue or mechanism for redress. Often the individual fears that direct expression of hostility against the perceived source of frustration would entail a large risk which he or she cannot afford to take. The consequences might involve losing a job, even worse treatment for the children at school, being dropped from welfare, being further looked down upon by the rest of the community. Some individuals fear that if they tried to express their disagreement directly to a boss or caseworker, their anger would boil up into furious, uncontrollable rage, making matters much worse. Instead of taking such a risk, frustrations experienced in the outside world are often held in (except when the individual is under the influence of alcohol), and are later vented in hostility toward the family. A marital blowup is much more likely when such pent-up frustrations are present. But many families appear to be accustomed to such venting, as one wife explained.

> Right now my husband is doing the best he can. So we try not to get upset about his angry rages. If someone or something on the job upsets him, he takes it out at home on the family. Even the kids understand this and try to put up with his bad days. After all, its the same for the kids. If a child has a bad experience at school and he suppresses his feelings about it, he'll take them out on the family when he gets home.

This pattern of discharging aggression within the family is clearly not peculiar to the people of this study, or to people in poverty; certainly the bad-day-at-the-office syndrome is well known in the middle class. But the situation in rural poor families is more destructive of smooth family functioning because of several factors: (1) the frequency of frustration-producing experiences is higher; (2) the tolerance level for frustration may be lower, due to insecurity and low self-image; (3) the channels of redress are less accessible; (4) there are likely to be other sources of stress already at work in the family; (5) there may be a greater tendency to express anger in a violent manner rather than verbally; and (6) with the crowded conditions in the home, there may be no space or manner in which one individual can vent his pent-up frustration and anger without immediately impinging on all other members of the family. Thus, discharged aggression is a factor in marital difficulties.

In summary, these seven sources of stress, singly or in combination, press against the emotions and interpersonal relationships of a married couple and of a family. They provide a constant undercurrent of tension that erodes relationships as it erodes individuals. They provide a ready source of friction to touch off a marital row. In the face of these persistent irritants, the remarkable fact is that the marriages last as long as they do.

Processes in Marital and Family Adjustment

Despite these inescapable stresses and strains, people hold tenaciously to the ideal of marriage and an intact family life. Both young adults and older people expect that a marriage will have its stormy periods, but their hope is that their marriage can be better than that of their parents, that their marriage can withstand disruptions, can outlive the fights and separations. An analysis of the dynamics of family adjustment shows how the ideals are pursued, the hopes perpetuated, despite the strains.

Short Cycles of Fighting and Starting Over

It appears that the climatic blowups, caused by relatively trivial triggering events superimposed on deeper strains, serve to relieve a highly charged marital atmosphere. They force unvoiced problems and tensions out into the open, making each partner more aware of the depth of pent-up rage in the other. The blowups also reaffirm the commitment to the abstract ideals of marriage in terms of obligations, rights, and roles. Many of the battles concern accusations of marital infidelity and of failure to fulfill expected roles within the family. The strength of these accusations reveals to each spouse (as it also reveals to the social scientist observer) the esteem in which the marriage and family ideal is held by the individuals. The marital blowup thus serves several positive functions: it acts as a safety valve; it clears the air; and it reaffirms each partner's commitment to marriage and family life. It also sets the stage for "starting all over again," a theme that is quite common in accounts of family history.

One typical example of this pattern, a relatively common occurrence, is that of the wife who has her husband arrested and put in jail for beating her. To the bafflement of others, the wife goes down to the jail the very next morning to take her husband cigarettes and toilet articles. They appear to be on friendly terms. She refuses to press charges, and arranges to obtain his release.

The results of this episode are that the husband has had "the fear of the law put into him," and each partner has realized his or her dependence on the other. The stage is set for starting over again. A harmonious period in the marriage may ensue, perhaps with a pregnancy initiated at this time.

Thus, both the blowups and the re-formations actually serve to keep marriages going, as an ideal and as a practice. The social analyst must look at the many attempts to perpetuate a marriage, as well as at the forces that tear it apart. In this cyclic view of marital blowups and attempts to start over, it becomes clear that despite the high incidence of marital strife, a strong commitment to marriage and family life is indeed present.

The Long-run Cycle of Adjustment

In the developmental history of each family, these short cycles of breakdown and starting over are epicycles on a long-term cycle of adjustment. The long-run adjustment cycle is essentially a response to the varying degrees of stress engendered by poverty circumstances at different periods in the family's development, and there is a clear pattern, despite variations from one family to the next.

Before a marriage partnership begins, either member may be involved in premarital relationships, perhaps with a child born of the relationship. These involvements do not usually entail serious long-term commitment for the future, but may contain many of the secondary attributes of marriage. For example, the young man or woman may very easily slip into the role of unofficial son-in-law or daughter-in-law in the home of the partner's parents. In some cases this entails a very warm relationship between the young man or woman and the unofficial mother-in-law, who in some cases is clearly serving as a substitute mother, providing a relationship that may be almost as important to the young individual as the love and sex relationship with the partner.

In contrast to this tentative arrangement, a marriage relationship, whether or not it is marked by a wedding ceremony, entails a serious commitment and some feeling of intended permanence. A tentative relationship between two individuals may drift into a permanent marriage, including an official legal ceremony. In other cases, each member of the original tentative relationship finds a different partner for marriage. In either case, the new relationship is recognized as the real marriage.

A new couple starts out with high goals, with each expecting a good deal of the other. By the time the young couple has two or three babies and small children to care for, however, considerable marital strife may have developed as a result of several disappointment areas: the inability of each individual to meet his or her own expectations; the inability of each individual to live up to the expectations of the other; and disillusionment over the benefits of marriage itself. And all of these potential sources are heightened and brought into action by the continuing and/or worsening struggle to make ends meet.

The years when the children are young may be dramatic, with many episodes of upheaval—although these are usually followed closely by attempts to start over, in hopes of keeping the family together "for the sake of the children."

By middle age, after twenty or more years of an often stormy marriage, and as the children are leaving home, the picture brightens. The income of the family may be higher, relative to expenses, and the irregular spending patterns of younger days may be more controlled, so that a greater portion of recurrent expenses can be met without strain. The husband and wife seem more willing to accept what they have. By this time, they perceive themselves as having learned "to make do with the things we have and live within the amount of money available." Thus, there are fewer arguments over "foolish spending," and fewer strains over inability to acquire desired goods. They also have learned to accept the faults or drawbacks of each other and "to know that the world isn't a bed of roses, and other people have had rough times also."

Several people have used analogy to describe the lifelong process of marital adjustment. One woman said that making a marriage work is a continuous balancing of both people's wishes, and she compared this to the process of making ends meet through continuous balancing of desires against dollars. The ability to strike this balance is seen as a sign of maturity, not as resignation. "We have accepted our life." Another woman summed up her observations on her own struggle and the balance she had achieved.

> When you're young, you have an idea. For instance, what kind of home you want. You keep striving towards that. But finally you come to the conclusion that you won't get there. Once you accept that, then you can accept your little shack as home. Then you try to make little improvements on it—paint, curtains, paneling. This will satisfy you, at least for the time being. It may not be the ideal home you had visioned, but it's better than what you started with. You have to compare what you have now with what you had in the beginning, not with the best you'd like to have ideally.

But this acceptance, and the peace it brings, usually comes only in mid-life, after years of marital stress, and after the crucial years of raising young children have passed.

The middle-aged period, however, may also give rise to new sources of stress that can create marital friction. Although the children have grown and left the house, they may themselves be going through the stressful phase of early adulthood, encountering problems with marital crises, babies, and financial burdens. During this period, the grown children and their problems may become a preoccupation and a source of worry or dispute between the parental couple. Grown children may periodically return to the parental home, with their own children in tow, coming back to the security of home after having been beaten in their attempt to forge a life of their own in the outside world. As a result of the parents' involvement, conflicts may arise to threaten the newfound harmony of the parental household. Some men complain that their wives give more time, attention—and money—to their grown-up children than they did when the children were little, and more than they ever did to their husbands. A few women have managed to remain aloof from the problems and squabbles of their grown children, but most find their children's dramas as compelling as the soap operas they watch on TV. And because they are their own children and their own grandchildren, they feel obligated to help in any way they can, even if it creates a strain in their marriages.

Eventually, as most of the grown children settle with their families in independent, if nearby, residences, the older couple may again enjoy a more stable relationship with fewer stresses and less interruptions. Couples look forward to this achievement, to being by themselves, less burdened with the problems of children and grandchildren, and free of the extra economic demands. They anticipate this period as a reward for their years of work and worry, and as it arrives, they may find new marital harmony.

However, this later-life situation is not usually idyllic. For one thing, the lifetime of grinding worry, the cumulative effects of undernourishment and limited health care, of many pregnancies in quick succession, of accidents, injuries, heavy smoking and/or heavy drinking combine to make many people age rather rapidly. (Individuals in their mid-fifties are often perceived by outsiders as being nearly seventy.) Poor health in the later years and deteriorative aging problems may provide yet another set of problems and anxieties. Some people are partially incapacitated for many years. Financially, many elderly people are worse off than ever, often subsisting on very meager payments from Social Security (meager because the salary rate and years of employment that determine their benefits were quite low); a pension of some sort, such as a disability payment; or welfare if necessary. They cannot afford to improve their houses, to modernize, or even to repair. For many, however, there is the offsetting fact that nearby and all around them are their children and their grandchildren, who keep them busy smoothing out problems, soothing hurts, caring for babies, giving advice. An elderly individual whose spouse has died may move in with his or her grown children, although others prefer even an inadequate home of their own to dependence and chaos in their children's homes. For a few individuals, loneliness is a painful part of old age, but for most, the support of young family members all around keeps them going.

This, then, is the long-range cycle of marriage and family, much simplified and generalized, but characteristic.

Conclusions

Despite the eroding effects of long-term economic, social, and emotional stress, the family is of tremendous importance in impoverished rural areas. While certain trends in contemporary society have tended to weaken the American family and usurp some of its former functions, the situation appears to be somewhat different among the rural poor. Here, the family remains the major element in the lives of individuals—if only because there are no other social roles and groupings available to them.

Due to the collapse of the local rural community and the failure of the urban community to become a social substitute, the family in these rural depressed areas has been forced to take on extra functions. Because of the social marginality, the rural multigenerationally poor families must provide for their members most of the social and psychological functions that more affluent members of the community satisfy through a variety of secondary relationships and groups. By default, the family is the only group in which poverty-stricken rural people regularly participate on a sustained basis. It is the only social unit with which individuals identify. And, for better or worse, the individual's reputation is inextricably bound to his family's. In addition, the family is a cooperating economic unit, with continuing responsibilities to offer a home, food, and services to its members, even after they have left the nest. In a striking number of cases, the family provides a temporary or semipermanent home to its elderly, its disabled, and its mentally retarded.

The bonds among family members appear to have a high positive valence and considerable permanence, an ability to survive temporary rifts. The family is a fairly self-contained center of affect, activity, and social interaction, largely because there is no other available grouping, either on the neighborhood level or the community level. But the family's broad functions also result from traditional cultural values: people believe that the family is and should be a strong, lasting unit. Adults believe that a stable home with both parents present is important for the long-term well-being of their children. And they conceive of family as a continuing entity, with life-long bonds of reciprocity and responsibility to its members. Thus, in sentiment and values, as well as in action, the family is the most significant social grouping.

However, the smooth functioning of the family is continually being threatened and undermined by the many stresses that impinge upon it as a unit and upon its component members as individuals. Family disruption results, despite the desire for family survival. Couples repeatedly try to patch up marriages that are fraught with tension and prone to periodic breakdowns.

As the family strives to surmount the stresses and to fulfill within itself the functions that other people have long since delegated to the secondary and institutional community, it tends to become a separated segment, somewhat detached from other families of the neighborhood (particularly when undergoing a rough period), and socially isolated from the people and institutions of the larger community. There is one significant function that the family does not serve. It does not act as a link between its members and the outside world. Parents do not make connections for their children, nor do children forge connections for their parents. The family does not effectively launch its members into the wider community. Instead, the family is a refuge from the wider world.

NOTES

1. The sample was too small, and the time too short, to indicate whether this natural longevity built upon determination to "try one more time" is characteristic of the current generation of young adults. It would seem that the recent marriages of young people are just as tension-filled and rocky as the earlier married years of the previous generation. Whether today's young couples will stick it out remains to be seen. In any case, they seem no more divorce-prone than the rest of society, and possibly less so. Like their parents, young adults from the rural poverty enclaves believe in the importance of keeping the family intact for the sake of their children.

Parents tend to urge their grown children to marry live-in mates, and to give a tenuous marriage one more try. However, the young adults are also a part of their own generation: they seem more accustomed to the fact of unwed motherhood, and they are not as concerned about divorce.

2. The high probability that both husband and wife had difficult childhoods is the result of two factors: (1) the high incidence of family disruption in the preceding generation of rural low-income families, and (2) the pattern of socioeconomic endogamy, in which people from the rural depressed areas are likely to marry people of similar socioeconomic backgrounds.

3. This is in contrast to the more distinct lines and clear understandings between a young mother and her mother in the Black, urban families studied by Stack (1974). There, the very young mother might give over her first baby's care to her mother completely, and in so doing assign over the motherhood role, rights, and responsibilities. Although such an arrangement is not unknown in Chestnut Valley, it is rare, and did not occur during the decade of research.

VIII. Education

Teaching the young is an aspect of socialization, one of the things which must get done in any society. [1] Once a child enters a school, the major place of "teaching" in American society, that local formal organization we call the Board of Education becomes a major agent in the socialization process. How they work, who they hire and what they stand for all affect the learning which may or may not take place in a given classroom. Hence, the process of education may be viewed in the formal setting of the schools. This is the setting in which the educational issues presented in the articles of this section are located.

One educational issue which may be more rural than Appalachian is the town versus state orientation (alternately stated local versus cosmopolitan). Another issue is whether or not the educational system is the great leveler, the great equalizer, in American Society.[2]

With the slow but steady rise in the number of private schools, Christian and otherwise, we may even ask whether Americans want a public school system or not. One further issue—apparently resolved, but bound to be rekindled as neighborhood and cost cutting become prized values—is the local vs. the consolidated school. Few decisions in the past thirty years have done so much to put an end to that rural commercial interacting unit we called the small town as did the educationally sound (?) and economically efficient decision to merge small educational units. The cost to local pride, community interaction and personal identity may have been too high a price to pay.[3]

The reader will quickly realize that critics of Appalachian school systems want for the children there many of the same things that other critics want for ALL American children; they want life-long learning opportunities, cross-cultural experiences, development of self-motivation, and regional or ethnic pride. In one sense, we can see in the Appalachian school systems described herein some of the same issues which face educators throughout the nation.

There is, however, a unique Southern mountain institution dedicated to both the teaching of children and the social welfare of the community. This institution is the Settlement School. The result of a marriage between local expressed need and (usually) Northern beneficent response, settlement schools were created to fill the need for which county government was either unwilling or unable to provide. Although these schools

[1] David F. Aberle, et al., "The Functional Prerequisites of a Society" *Ethics*, 60, (1/50), 100–111.

[2] For an informed discussion of this issue on a national scale see Robert L. Heilbroner's review of Samuel Bowles and Gerbert Gintis, *Schooling in America* in New York Review of Books, April 15, 1976, 13–14.

[3] "Kingdom Come School," Appalshop Films, poses the issue nicely, but suggests no answer.

have now either merged with or been absorbed into the county school system, or "metamorphisized" into folk, craft or art centers, a review of their bright history will serve to accent what variations in a system can do—and might still do.[4]

We may consider the role of class—in the Reck and Reck article—class as closely related to native/non-native status, and consider the role of "consolidated efficiency" by studying the data in the final two articles. These findings are significant and raise some basic questions for school administrators and parents as well.

[4] Several of the mountain settlement schools incorporated in 1970 to form, Settlement Institutions of Appalachia, Inc. For information write Suite 204, Regas Office Building, 318 Gay St., N.W., Knoxville, TN 37917.

39. EDUCATING APPALACHIA'S POOR

James Branscome

In September, CBS began its new television season with the theme "Let's All Get Together." If you watch television on Tuesday nights, you know that who got together, back-to-back, is the stars of three of America's most popular TV programs: The Beverly Hillbillies, Green Acres, and Hee-Haw. Each week millions of Americans gather around their sets to watch this combination which has to be the most intensive effort ever exerted by a nation to belittle, demean, and otherwise destroy a minority people within its boundaries. Within the three shows on one night, hillbillies are shown being conned into buying the White House, coddling a talking pig, and rising from a cornpatch to crack the sickest jokes on TV—all on the same channel only a short while after Eric Sevareid has finished lecturing the American public on decency, integrity, dignity, and all other great virtues to which he and his network supposedly adhere.

If similar programs, even approaching the maliciousness of these (say like Amos and Andy), were broadcast on Blacks, Indians, or Chicanos, there would be an immediate public outcry from every liberal organization and politician in the country and a scathing editorial in the *Times* about the program's "lack of taste." The new culture people would organize marches and prime-time boycotts and perhaps, even, throw dog dung at Eva Gabor as she emerged from her studio. They might even go a step further and deal with the hillbilly-maligning patriot Al Capp. But in this, as in all things Appalachian, silence. America is allowed to continue laughing at this minority group because, on this, all of America agrees: hillbilly ain't beautiful.

The treatment given by the media to Appalachia is only one example of the massive failure of America's institutions for a century to meet the need of the people of the region. Another example can be found in Appalachia's schools, where the dropout rate is almost double the already high national rate—a residuum of disenchanted, frustrated, and, in many cases, alienated young adults who have found too little of value in their schools. Sixty-five percent of Appalachian youth never finish high school, and in some areas the dropout rate has reached 71 percent—a massive vote of no confidence in our public school system by Appalachian youth, an outright rejection of our daylight detention camps' insistence that all of us become nice melting-pot products who behave like Dick and Jane.

The school system has succeeded marvelously in doing what it was designed to do: obliterate differences and adjust children to the technological society as unquestioning, joyless and obedient robots. It is the world's most successful channeling device, Selective Service notwithstanding. But as an educational device, it is hardly as successful. Even President Nixon wondered, in his address to Congress on educational reform, if schools had as much educational impact on our youth as does TV.

Deprived Children

Virtually all the children from lower income and minority groups are in what the schools deem "low-ability" groups: They are deprived—deprived of ego strength, of realistic goal-orientation, of family stability, of secure peer relationships; they lack the serene middle-class faith in the future. They feel confident in their culture, not in the middle-class school. For these reasons, they lack self-control, cannot risk failure, won't accept criticism, can't take two steps back to go one forward, have no study habits, no basic skills, don't respect school property, and didn't read "Cowboy Small."

There are apparently successful Headstart programs in Appalachia, though their success is probably due to the fact that the preschoolers have not yet been told they are incapable of doing something worthwhile or making a significant contribution to society. Yet the Appalachian participation in these programs decreased 15 percent between 1967 and 1969 (the national participation rate decrease was three percent). The greatest decrease in Appalachia, significantly, was in full-year programs—those regarded as most beneficial to poor children.

Once these children reach the public school system, they usually face culturally deficient teachers who refuse to acknowledge the unique cultural heritage of the Appalachian youth. They are immediately embroiled in the classic historical struggle between a nation intent on erasing a minority from its midst and a people intent on preserving their identity and life style. Teachers—who were once "culturally divergent" but have since conformed to the norm—perpetuate the culturally annihilistic aims of the non-divergents against their own. For too long we have defined equal education as the equal opportunity to become carbon copies of ourselves. The educational system must be structured to meet individual needs rather than to insure conformity and administrative efficiency.

For the black, Indian, Puerto Rican, Mexican-American, or Appalachian, the American educational

Reprinted from *People's Appalachia*, Vol. 1, No. 5 (October–December, 1970), pp. 5–8. Used by permission.

process has been inadequate, and it has systematically devaluated and attempted to destroy their cultural uniqueness. Family life is depicted as white, intact, loving, rarely having over four members, with suburban home and briefcase-toting daddy. Middle-class teachers cannot comprehend that the world of Appalachian children or ghetto youth is often more vital than their own. The real trouble with perpetrating the colorless materials from Dick and Jane upon very colorful children is not only that the weak culture it purveys is out of kilter with the one the children already have, but that it also is mediocre by comparison.

James Coleman ("Equality of Educational Opportunities") has pointed out that if we control six factors influencing the child—home, environment, father's income, parents' attitude toward school, etc—we can predict 99 percent of the time whether the child will fail or succeed in school. Coleman also tells us that the most important thing in determining educational success is whether the child feels he has some control over his life, whether the child feels he "belongs." Yet so far, in compensatory education, we have insisted that the child be changed, not the school or the home environment.

Crumbling System

Even by its own standards, the educational system has failed in Appalachia. Standardized tests have shown that the IQs of school children have declined from 1/4 to 1/2 a point annually for 13 years.

Nothing could better typify the image of the crumbling school structure than the dry and deadly basic reading texts used in most schools. Every cliche of bad American children's literature seems to be contained in these books about Betty Jane Brown and Sarah Best and Miss Molly and Fluffy Tail and Miss Valentine of Maple Grove School. Children in black ghetto schools have been hearing for several years about Birmingham and Selma and Newark and teargas and cattle-prods and nightcourts and slumlords and jazz. It is futile to expect these children to care about books which even comfortable suburban children find irrelevant and boring.

But even if all the deadly textbooks were taken away, the teachers who believe in those books are still teaching and until they stop teaching, or stop believing, the assumptions will live on and the dignity of the children will decay. Of young, native Appalachian teachers, nearly 70 percent leave the region after four years of teaching.

Channeling Process

It is a chilling paradox that in a country where the most urgent cultural value is education, the "educational experience itself is surreal and degrading." Our high schools don't educate, they channel. They send some youth to college, some to business school, and some to the war, and too many to welfare rolls. (The unemployment rate among poor youth is 40–50 percent.)

They continue and intensify a channeling process begun by the earliest elementary teacher in areas such as Appalachia to send the culturally different student—ashamed of his background and ill-equipped to meet the needs of his region—into middle-class society outside the region or out of productive society entirely.

Our youth are not allowed to develop creatively; no student initiative is fostered. Thus, upon completion of their formal education, where they have been taught with authoritarian supports for such a significant portion of their lives, they find that they are not capable of teaching themselves, of being autonomous when they are out of school. We fail to recognize that learning is a constant in the life of every individual and that it can't stop with graduation or dropping out. As a result, the educational system produces people who are willing to have things decided for them. It produces poor parents, poor citizens, poor leadership, and inevitably a country in serious trouble.

We cannot, of course, blame the educational system for all our social ills. But this greatest, unaccountable monopoly in American society must begin to take its share of the blame for the job it has not performed.

Vocational and Higher Education

Vocational education, viewed by many as a panacea for Appalachia's educational problems, has also failed. Students are frequently trained for jobs which do not exist, and are not trained for those that are available. Moreover, while Appalachia has 13 percent of the national enrollment in secondary school vocational education, it receives only 7.3 percent of the federal funds available.

Appalachia is heavily populated with institutions of "higher learning" supported by various churches and state governments, but the region's students are no better served here than in the secondary institutions. In fact, the colleges do a great disservice to the region by siphoning off the "cream of the crop"—the valedictorians and salutatorians. Instead of promoting a regional consciousness on the part of this potential leadership, the institutions encourage them to get "educated" so they will be able to get out of the region.

There is not one Appalachian studies program in the region which could begin to rival the offerings in Far Eastern studies or astronomy. English majors seldom if ever hear a work—much less whole courses—on Appalachian literature. Art majors seldom or never study about the beauty and value and history of Appalachian crafts. Economics majors sitting right in the middle of the stripmining country never hear about the economics of Appalachia and what stripmining and the outside corporations mean to the economy of the region and how economists might address these problems. Sociology majors spend four years in institutions in the heart of Appalachia and seldom hear a word about the different life patterns of the Appalachian people. Political science majors graduate without studying Appalachian politics and the effect or noneffect it has had on the plight of the people of the region. Education majors never get instruction on the special problems of Appalachian youth and how to meet these problems with their teaching. Medical students are taught to treat medulla tissue on the brain, but know next to nothing about how to practice in rural areas. Nursing students graduate with experience in urban and local hospitals, but few have real training in public health with field work in the region. History majors learn about English History, "American" History, Indian History, Russian History, Latin American History, and lately sometimes Black History, but not a word about Appalachian History. Home economics majors are taught to cook fine French dinners and to prepare receptions for New York society, but not a word about the dishes of the mountains or nutrition training for poor mothers. In fact, no institution of American society is more divorced from Appalachia than the higher educational system which resides within it.

Concurrently, most colleges and universities are not in the business of granting academic credit to students working to solve immediate and indigenous community problems. But the world of needs beyond the classroom is a learning environment that is grossly under-utilized.

One of the major problems of Appalachia is the loss of young people. A region which needs more than 200,000 college graduates—a minimum of 5,000 physicians, many more thousands of nurses, teachers, businessmen, government leaders, ad infinitum—has lost again in its struggle with America's institutions.

Once they are educated and/or trained, Appalachia's young people move away because they believe that nothing can be done to change the way of life they are escaping, or because they have not been involved in the tedious process of uplifting the region.

Most dropouts and unemployed high school graduates eventually are forced to migrate to find work. In West Virginia, for instance, 70 percent of the young people leave before they reach the age of 24. Usually referred to as migrants, instead of more candidly as economic refugees, these youth join the more than two million other mountaineers who have preceded them in the northern industrial cities like Cincinnati, Chicago, Indianapolis and Detroit. If they have a skill and happen to move during relative economic prosperity, or are willing to accept a job run by the stopwatch and a minimum wage employer, as many do, their chances for survival are good. If, on the other hand, they have to move in with kin in the "back home" ghetto, the situation is different: They never find the textbook world they seek of Dick and Jane and the affluence of America built at Appalachia's expense.

Suggestions for Reform

We have to reinterpret "freedom of choice" to mean giving our youth the right to get a good education and to live in the community they desire, economic considerations notwithstanding. Our cities cannot continue to take the influx of people; our nation cannot tolerate more disenchanted people. We need to see everybody as they really are—just people, no more and no less. And we need to see children as people, young people with individuality, not as some separate group of beings dominated by the adult world. Individuals must have a part in shaping their own destiny. Our educational system might accomplish this by correcting four major failures (For phrasings 1–3 I am grateful to Robert Sigmon of the North Carolina Internship Office):

(1) Our educational system fails to recognize that learning is constant in the life of every individual and that experience itself can be education. Under the present pattern of formal education, we assume that an academic degree certifies a man to be competent to enter public life—that some body of knowledge is automatically communicated to an individual by his exposure to the cultural and intellectual traditions of Western civilization, and that a person appropriates and uses this information to meet the demands of his life.

But to assume that human life proceeds deductively—that is, that human action is always the result of the application of some principle—seems fallacious. On the contrary, philosophical inquiry begins with human experience. For example, although we do not teach it this way, Kant's thought and argument were derived inductively from his attempts to make sense of his experience. Formal education practices frequently fail to recognize that life proceeds inductively.

A more sensible approach to education would be to help students examine their own experiences creatively and critically. Formal education provides little opportunity to learn how to learn or how to solve problems that are not hypothetical. Little attention is devoted to analyzing life styles, to understanding processes, to examining how institutions influence behavior. Most current emphasis is still on factual information, content delivery and the preparation of specific skills. But research now tells us that within five years this kind of education is either forgotten or outdated.

(2) A second deficiency of formal education, which is particularly severe in parts of Appalachia, is the lack of emphasis on cross-cultural experience. Although our exposure to other cultures and life styles through the

mass media is high, our understanding of diverse behavior patterns and cultures is minimal. This paradox is due largely to the fact that exposure to other cultures is passive. Only by living in a different cultural context and by experiencing other behavioral patterns and modes of thought does an individual become aware of cultural distinctions and the values which are uniquely his own.

If the goal of education is to learn how to learn, such experiences are essential. When an individual visits a mental facility, a management arm of a large business, or a black community, he comes to appreciate both genuine differences and shared values.

Educational personnel particularly need these experiences if they are to deal with culturally different children. Such a cross-cultural experience enhances an individual's ability to reason inductively and to conceptualize on the basis of his experience of the world.

(3) The lack of emphasis on developing autonomy and on fostering student initiative is a third deficiency of present-day formal education. Students in our society have been taught with authoritarian support for so significant a portion of their lives that they find it difficult when they are forced by necessity to teach themselves. As it is currently structured, formal education tells students what to do, how to do it, what is important and what is unimportant. This directive approach produces people who are willing to have things decided for them; it does not create confident people whose learning is self-generated.

(4) The fourth deficiency is our insistence that all children must become melting-pot products, especially at a time when the pot is a "boiling cauldron" and we know so little about what "proper behavior" and the "right culture" are all about. The challenge that disadvantaged youth, who it seems are always members of poor minority groups, place before American education is this: Can it allow people to be vertically mobile without stripping them of their differences?

The real goal of education must be to assist each learner to become all that he is capable of becoming. The goal of forcing him to become a mannikin in that nebulous middle-class majority must cease. Our whole society's value system must change.

We must change monocultural schools to bicultural, multi-cultural schools. (Should we "fail" Johnny Middleclass for not knowing about the Navajo nation as we fail Johnny Indian for not knowing about the American nation?) This nation will not fall if Appalachian students continue to say "haint" (as Lady Macbeth did) nor if Chicano youngsters continue to speak Spanish. This nation will not fall if we go a few steps further and recognize black culture and black identity instead of just black skin—nor if we take learning beyond the four walls of isolation into the community where people are—nor if we make our teachers and our schools accountable for their mistakes as the rest of us are accountable for ours. This nation will not fall if we judge every student on the basis of his potential and not his clothing, his speech, or his poor academic past. But it may fall if we don't melt the pot and begin to care for our children as people; just people; God's children.

40. SETTLEMENT SCHOOLS OF APPALACHIA "TO MAKE A LIFE: SETTLEMENT INSTITUTIONS OF APPALACHIA"

Jim Stokely

The idea of the settlement institution was not a new one. During the 19th century, London's working class had found itself caught in the whirlwind of the industrial revolution. Families faced long hours in the factories, poor health conditions, subsistence wages, and little or no education. Imaginative Englishmen plotted an escape from the terrors of this new poverty. In 1854, theologian F. D. Maurice and writer Thomas Hughes founded the Working Men's College, a forerunner of the modern vocational school. Designed to recognize and enlarge the workers' status, the College also encouraged cooperative association among laborers.

Thirty years later, in London's impoverished East End, an Anglican priest named Samuel Barnett gathered a group of university graduates and actually settled in the neighborhood. Toynbee Hall, located next to St. Jude's Church, was the first real settlement institution. Settlers at the Hall participated in local life and worked in such crucial areas as adult education and industrial improvement.

Reprinted from *To Make a Life: Settlement Institutions of Appalachia* by Jim Stokely. Published by Settlement Institutions of Appalachia, Inc., 1975.

Toynbee Hall attracted the attentions of America's earliest social workers. Two visitors to Toynbee Hall, Stanton Coit and Jane Addams, started settlement houses of their own during the late 1880's. Chicago's famous Hull House and Coit's Neighborhood Guild, in New York City's Lower East Side, soon had company after Robert Woods established Andover House in Boston's South End. These houses became vital community centers and served as headquarters for wide-scale activities.

At Hull House, for example, a vacant residence built in 1856 was renovated over thirty years later and expanded to include a nursery, a gymnasium, a college-level curriculum, and a girl's boarding club. A dozen other buildings were later added by Miss Addams and her companion, Ellen Gates Starr. Always energetic and unfailingly compassionate—winner of the Nobel Peace Prize in 1931—Jane Addams believed in a social work that had its basis not in statistics but in human beings. While speaking once on the subject of Chicago's immigrant populations, Jane Addams expressed an attitude which could just as well have been applied to the people of Appalachia or any other part of America.

> If the body of teachers in our great cities could take hold of the immigrant colonies, could bring out of them their handicrafts and occupations, their traditions, their folk songs and folk lore, the beautiful stories which every immigrant colony is ready to tell and translate; could get the children to bring these things into school as the material from which culture is made and would discover by comparison that which they give them now is a poor meretricious and vulgar thing. Give these children a chance to utilize the historic and industrial material which they see about them and they will begin to have a sense of ease in America, a first consciousness of being at home. I believe if these people are welcomed upon the basis of the resources which they represent and the contributions which they bring, it may come to pass that these schools which deal with immigrants will find that they have a wealth of cultural and industrial material which will make the schools in other neighborhoods positively envious.

This approach recognized the good in all individuals and groups. Such open-mindedness helped make the cities' new settlement houses an astounding success.

Yet the true awakening of interest in settlement institutions did not come within the urban centers. It came in an exquisitely rural setting called Appalachia. And it was natural that this should happen, for the continuing frontier ideals of adventure, discovery, and neighbor helping neighbor harmonized exactly with the trusting, risk-taking, work-based methods of the settlements. An Appalachian settlement institution was and is nothing more and nothing less than a non-profit group of people attempting to discover service, and development for the immediate community and perhaps even the region as a whole.

Early east Tennessee academies, such as those at Friendsville and Washington College, had already introduced a more rigorous education for mountain children. In eastern Kentucky, three conscientious citizens had started a school of their own in 1880; Hazel Green Academy would grow with the years and carry on a rich heritage. Several miles to the southwest, a fellow mountaineer by the name of Burns had blazed a decisive trail against feuding and violence when, in 1899, he began the well-known Oneida Baptist Institute.

In the same year, Katherine Pettit also took a stand against the mountain feuds and in favor of education. When a preacher from the small town of Hazard, Kentucky, asked for the services of "a woman, a gentle, womanly woman, a dear old-fashioned woman," she travelled by rail and wagon from Lexington and commenced to teach homemaking there. Miss Pettit had been strongly influenced by the urban settlement houses, but she came equipped with innovations and exciting ideas.

As Lucy Furman has written: "Shortly afterward, on a wooded spot in Hazard, in a tent borrowed from the State Militia, and gayly decorated with flags, pictures, and red cheesecloth, and bright kindergarten chairs, the first rural social settlement ever undertaken was begun by Katherine Pettit, May Stone, and three other young women, with classes in cooking, sewing, home-nursing, singing, and kindergarten, daily bible and temperance readings, and all kinds of 'socials' and play-parties." Just at the outset of a new century, a mountain triumph was itself beginning.

The temperance "missionizing" was, fortunately, only one aspect of a broad program which at once struck enthusiastic response. Late in the summer, Solomon Everidge from Troublesome Creek asked these "quare, fotched-on women from the lowlands" to bring the same work into his community. By this time, Pettit and Stone had enlarged their thinking to include "an industrial school, where hands and minds could be simultaneously trained, and where the young could pay for their board with their labor." The result blossomed forth in 1902: Hindman Settlement School.

Hindman provided education for students of all ages. It offered an infirmary and several travelling clinics. Its steam plant even supplied the town's electricity for nearly thirty years. Community support was strong; after a devastating fire in 1910, residents saved the school by pledging more than $2000 and a thousand days of labor. Such mutual aid was also present at Lost Creek, Kentucky, where five years earlier the Reverend and Mrs. George Drushal had started Riverside Christian Training School on land donated by a local citizen.

Other vital schools were begun on Kentucky's mountainous Cumberland Plateau. In 1909, Rev. William Worthington arrived at Pond Creek, bought a worn-out farm, and began to mold an influential academy now known as Annville Institute. Four years later, Katherine Pettit and a co-worker from Hindman named Ethel deLong journeyed south to the forested slope of Pine Mountain. There, on 95 acres given them by one William Creech, they founded Pine Mountain Settlement School.

Pine Mountain's program was typical of the basic services offered by settlement institutions during the 1920's and the 1930's. As at a host of settlements throughout the southern Appalachian states, Pine Mountain furnished solid education, trained nurses, and the opportunity to work, plus physical and spiritual nourishment. A 1919 dental report stated, in its own unassuming way: "Number of people examined, 135; number of teeth pulled, 140 for 60 people; number of teeth filled, 101 for 30 people; teeth cleaned for 5 people; receipts, $34."

During these years between the world wars, the settlements remained an obvious necessity in Appalachia. After World War II, however, circumstances changed. County and state governments began to take a closer look at their responsibility to meet the needs of the people. Better roads pushed into and through the mountains. Health and child welfare departments established themselves in the larger communities. Most significant of all, public school systems located new facilities throughout their region. Such changes forced the settlement institutions to re-evaluate their own positions. Had their purpose and service been overtaken by public agencies?

The answer was a definite no. The older academies continued their full operations and came to provide a smaller, more familiar alternative to the often impersonal public schools. Several settlement schools founded in the 1920's simply adapted to the transition and thereby strengthened their programs. Red Bird Mission, centered at Beverly, Kentucky, welcomed the opportunity to work with publicly paid teachers at Red Bird High School. This extensive Methodist mission also expanded its well-used hospital. In the nearby town of Frakes, Henderson Settlement turned its educational facilities over to the county and moved into the areas of child and farm demonstration.

In east Tennessee, Sunset Gap settlement gave way to school consolidation but retained its local commitment by becoming an active community center, complete with baseball teams and scouting troops, preschool classes and pot-luck suppers. This impulse to embrace a wider variety of needs and resources lay at the heart of other institutions, such as North Carolina's John C. Campbell Folk School. Named after Appalachia's earliest and most energetic advocate, Brasstown's Folk School grew steadily as an organization dedicated to the goals of work, faith, and craftsmanship.

The unique assets of Appalachia's settlement institutions were underscored during the 1960's. The Federal Government's sudden "war on poverty" descended upon the region with the furor of an unloosed tide. Rather than aiding the already established settlements, the "war" financed new departments and bureaus. In many cases, governmental workers knew little or nothing of the mountain people's traditions, sentiments, and desires. All too often, eager or even stubborn volunteers organized and regulated instead of listening and cooperating.

But the settlements survived this turbulent period of Appalachia's history. Having known and experienced the teachings of the past, they could look toward the future with a perceptive eye. Being middlemen of a sort—independent or denominational shapers on a local level—they could draw their resources from both inside and outside the region. Government programs shrivelled from lack of funds, or simply died from lack of interest; the difficult work of the settlement institutions, its living roots watered by careful human effort, outlasted the "easy money."

These roots spread and proliferated. Hinton Rural Life Center, begun in 1957 near Hayesville, North Carolina, grew into a first-class retreat facility and a forward-looking office for parish development. Bethel Mennonite Center, established a year later at Rowdy, Kentucky, developed a sturdy summer camp program. And in southern Ohio, Jackson Area Ministries Resource and Training Center added yet another element to the spectrum of service. Acting as an "enabler" for change, JAMRATC commenced in 1969 to help plan and find funding for a multitude of local programs ranging from low-cost housing to mental health to rural transportation.

By the 1970's the mountain schools and centers had come to recognize more than ever before, their common goals and diversified strengths. From Georgia to Ohio, settlement institutions were attempting to foster education and community development, physical and spiritual health, and effective Appalachian leadership. In order to provide a regional forum for conferences, workshops, and seminars, leaders from many of the settlements drew together out of a desire for fellowship, jointly initiated projects, and the exchange of ideas.

To this end, Settlement Institutions of Appalachia was incorporated in 1970 and empowered to help finance and coordinate the programs of its members. As a non-profit consortium of schools, agencies, and interested individuals. SIA can receive donations and grants. Besides channeling these much-needed funds directly to the settlement institutions, SIA serves as an invaluable marketplace for the sharing of thoughts and initiatives. Settlement Institutions of Appalachia welcomes new members and expressions of interest from any and all quarters.

The achievement of SIA is determined by the quality of each institution. That quality has been, is, and should remain high. Yet its aspects cannot be fully understood through naked lists of names, addresses, or communities served. For there are patterns of quality which emerge from the collective effort of the settlements. These patterns are not simply labels or baling twine; they are traits and common tenets, grown deep through the years and meant to endure.

First of all, there are no frills. The settlements do not and have never believed that extras on the order of shag rugs or fuel-injection engines help people as much as clean water, for instance, or milk, or penicillin. Fundamentals have always been the keynote of settlement talk and action. At the same time, these schools and centers look upon books, teachers, and counselors as necessities for a full and promising life. In a nation where incidentals are sometimes confused with essentials, Appalachia and its settlements tread the low-road of stability and common sense.

Secondly, the settlement institutions are made up of committed and enthusiastic people. A trained, competent staff working for minimal pay is by definition concerned with something more than a weekly wage. Like high school students, college interns, and other volunteers, staff members at the settlements can rely upon their idealism and their fortitude in order to surmount practical day-to-day problems. Perhaps most important, residents of the communities take a willing interest in their institutions and, ultimately, make them what they are.

The third quality of the settlements also involves the mountain communities. For the settlement institutions are not only located there; they are part of what is there. They are outsiders no more, because they have lived and worked in Appalachia for so long. By attitude and assimilation, they are themselves Appalachian. They are of the region, a resource therein, a segment of the total expression of the southern mountains. The phrase "Appalachia and its settlements" means exactly what it says.

Finally, these institutions have the ability to locate, release, and enlarge the resources around them. As the schools and centers communicate and share among themselves, they also offer a splendid variety of service based upon such principles as health and education, worship and vocation, the making of crafts and the care of children and the appreciation of the environment. This variety is as it should be, for the settlements must and are doing exactly what other agencies will not, or cannot do, and they are doing it well.

The settlement institutions continue to touch the hearts of Appalachia. Committed as they are to the daily life of mountain counties and communities, they provide work as well as workshops, action as well as activity, demonstration as well as assertion. For the historical experience of the region has been this: that a raised awareness is companion to a lowered shoulder; that a spirit of cooperation and individual progress depends upon a joining together in common effort; and that pillars of concrete and roads of asphalt must take a second place to the basic needs and the everyday triumphs of the people themselves. The settlement institutions of Appalachia speak to these needs, contribute to these triumphs.

Annville Institute

The modern-day traveler, riding comfortably in some sleek automobile along Kentucky's main roads, can come upon Annville suddenly and without warning. He or she might give quick attention to the buildings near the highway: a large schoolhouse, a white-frame chapel, a smaller garage for the Pond Creek Volunteer Fire Department. These could be seen from a moving car within the space of a few seconds, and the anxious traveler—searching, perhaps, for a place to spend the night—would soon be able to drive on toward the parkways and the interstates.

But for the individual willing to pause by the side of the road, willing to take a bit of time to discover these buildings and their surroundings, the place called Annville Institute grows steadily. It combines a long history with a vital present.

Annville's 225-acre campus suggests this union of tradition and energy. Even in winter there is a greenness here, stretching from hillside pastures to creek-bottom fields to the very lawns and walks of the high school itself. This peaceful scene seems far removed from the hectic second day of Jackson County Court in May 1858, when the price of vacant land was set at $5 per 100 acres. Yet the present-day farm buildings and equipment, instrumental in the teaching of modern agri-business, also recalls earlier years, when workers at the Institute struggled to build the first concrete silo in the area.

The overall struggle to build Annville Institute did not go unfulfilled—Annville is today a fully accredited high school, offering vocational and academic instruction for almost 100 young men and women in grades eight through twelve. Among the strong variety of subjects taught are regular liberal arts, agri-business, power mechanics, graphic arts, home economics, and woodworking. With a student-teacher ratio of only 4 to 1, Annville succeeds in maintaining that close fellowship which is so essential to progressive education.

During the early years of the 20th century, the state of education in Jackson County was not a great deal different from what it had been 50 years earlier, when the county was formed:

School houses were built of logs, sometimes hewed, sometimes unhewed. Each one had a big stone chimney and a wide fireplace. Often the smoke from these filled the room, this making it very uncomfortable for the pupils who sat upon one-half of a split log, in which was adjusted wooded pegs which supported it at a proper height. In some instances the boards forming the roof were held in place by stones as weights while in other cases the boards were fixed with wooden pegs. Many of these schools were known as "Frog Pond" schools because the pupils were permitted to study aloud.

The vast majority of the county's residents were farmers, growers of corn, grains, and tobacco. They saw no overpowering necessity for schools; their interests were more quickly aroused when an occasional lump of silver was found, or when rumors began of lumber rising in value.

William Allen Worthington of the Reformed Church in America believed in the inherent worth—and the long-term value—of education. Born in Poplar Grove, Illinois, and an alumnus of Rutgers University and New Brunswick Theological Seminary, this eager graduate journeyed during the summer of 1909 to Jackson County "for a short-term work while awaiting my prepared sailing to India as a foreign missionary." While in the county, Worthington served as a student pastor, but he also met and courted another Reformed Church worker. Henrietta Zwemer, Michigan-born principal of McKee Academy for the previous two years, matched the young minister in physical hardiness and spiritual sensitivity. By December, the two were married, and they had decided to settle and teach in the little village of Annville.

Their 75-acre farm, bought for their work through the Mission Board, presented a formidable challenge. One of the oldest on Pond Creek, it was "covered with useless sage grass. Its old barn and sheds were falling down. A little creek ran through the farm, but the few acres of level land along its banks were covered with a dense growth of willows." Writing years later, Rev. Worthington commented with a dry wit upon the transaction: "The soil had been worn out, and the owner, a very pleasant and intelligent mountain lawyer, had been glad to dispose of the farm."

But the land was only a temporary stumbling block. The Worthingtons began housekeeping in a small cabin, established a church, and enrolled local children in Sunday School. A circuit-riding preacher taught William Worthington much about singing the old hymns and "holding services in the hills." The year 1910 saw a 50-pupil grade school plus a normal training class, where qualified students could review 8th grade work and receive teaching certificates. High school grades were added four years later.

The Annville teachers worked hard to prove Rev. Worthington's bold idea that "the training of native leadership for community work is the quickest, most prominent, and most economical method of community development." One boy, laboring awkwardly over the new manual training course at Annville, approached his teacher with a discouraged air:

"What is the matter with this piece of wood?" he asked. "Do I twist it just by looking at it?"

The teacher took the piece of wood and turned it in his rough hands. Then, as he handed it back, he replied:

"Let me give you a bit of advice. Tear loose on your work. Don't be afraid of spoiling a few things. Go at it hard. Tear loose."

The student did indeed tear loose. He won Annville's prize in manual training, went through college, and later returned to eastern Kentucky to teach and work in wood.

The "go at it hard" reply is characteristic of the hope and enthusiasm which Annville Institute has come to stand for in its community. The school has operated a thriving work program since its founding, with girls helping out in the dining hall and boys haying or milking on the farm and assisting in general maintenance. Historically speaking, Annville's pioneering in farm demonstration made an enormous impression on local families, for students were returning home with new ideas for cover crops or drainage or livestock management. Clover- and alfalfa-fed cows, used to paltry sedge grass, began to give almost twice their normal amount of milk. Community canning and poultry clubs were organized and during the 1940's Annville Institute introduced beef cattle and a high-production chicken industry, complete with electric incubator.

Such advancement within the county led to lasting friendships. Said one community leader: "The two biggest things that ever came to Jackson County were a lumber company and Annville Institute. The one took out and left us poorer, the other put in and has left us richer in every way." A comprehensive school health program, organized largely by Chicago-trained nurse Anna Van Dyke, helped immeasurably by ministering to students, educating them in immunization, and establishing mobile X-ray and diagnostic clinics.

Annville has continued its close community ties. The self-supporting Campus Crafts Industries, begun in the spring of 1948 by Emily Heusinkveld and skillfully developed by Berea's Dorothy and Enos Brockman, employs local workers in weaving and woodworking and serves well the purposes of any small-scale business. Student training in the Industries supplements Annville's work program and helps pupils earn their way through school, learn basic business principles, and acquire a sense of pride and worthiness in their labors. Rugs and placemats, candlesticks and bookends, slippers and corn-shuck dolls all attest to the sturdy heritage and enterprise of southern Appalachia.

Heritage and enterprise: the two are felt on Annville's campus, nowhere more intensely than at the busy

Trade Store. By selling high-quality donated merchandise at low prices, the store draws the attention and respect of neighbors throughout the county and beyond. They come in pick-up trucks and campers, jalopies and 4-door sedans, trading pocket-sized knives and outsized stories, not minding the lines, earnestly discussing last week's tornado or next week's tobacco bed. As with the other settlement schools and centers, people are at the heart of Annville, individuals from Idaho and New Jersey and the winding banks of Sinking Creek, human beings from many backgrounds attempting to merge and communicate and bring their visions to a chosen place.

The fire department was such a vision. It started in the village grocery, when conversation among a half-dozen residents and Annville staffers turned to the need for some kind of fire protection. Within minutes the idea progressed from "It sure would be nice" to "I don't see why not" to "How about if we do this?" Annville deeded a small piece of its property for the future department's use and then searched for any Appalachian funding sources which would help finance the project. Finding none, the Institute sought aid from the Reformed Church, who ended up contributing a fire truck from Pennsylvania, a tanker from Michigan, and some fundamental training in fire-fighting techniques. A volunteer service group from the Church in Michigan arrived in Annville during the summer for a week's work camp and constructed a modest building. Afterwards, members of the community painted it, furnished it, manned it, and to this day can look back upon a genuine achievement.

But the main achievement of Annville Institute lies, as always, with its students. The high school operates full-force out of imposing Lincoln Hall and the nearby gymnasium and industrial arts building. Day students from the immediate area learn and share with the boarders, who are housed in Annville's modern dormitories. The "Bulldogs" print *The Eclipse,* a newspaper which goes to every boxholder in the county, twice a month. Having their own concert choir and a touring group known as "The Chinquapins," Annville students also help out with a local children's choir.

These services and benefits, coupled with the primary goals of classroom education, clarify Annville's motto: "Complete living for mountain people." Both the motto and the action grew out of experience-tested attitudes garnered by such people as William and Henrietta Worthington. A 1937 pamphlet tells of these attitudes: "Ruggedness and strength are marked characteristics of these mountain folk. Living close to nature, they seem to have acquired a greatness of soul that lies hidden in the recesses of their being and appears only at times of stress and strain. Underlying all other emotions is their desire for life in fuller measure." Annville Institute is doing its part to find that fuller life.

John C. Campbell Folk School

The mountains of western North Carolina are a study in extremities. Unlike the wide and constant sweep of Kentucky's rough Cumberland Plateau, the ranges of North Carolina vary from the high ridge of the Great Smokies and the rugged slopes of Mt. Mitchell to the tamer valleys of the Blue Ridge. In the extreme southwestern part of the state, near the Georgia border, a village called Brasstown nestles in one of these farming valleys. Brasstown is the home of John C. Campbell Folk School, a school which throughout its history has both broadened the opportunities of rural living and shared with the community and visitors a greater respect for mountain living.

Founded in 1925 and named after Appalachia's earliest and most energetic advocate, the John C. Campbell Folk School has grown steadily as an organization dedicated to the goals of work, faith, and craftsmanship. With 365 acres and a dozen buildings, the Folk School functions as a real community center and encourages the training of quality craftsmanship from both inside and outside the region. The idea of the folk school, taken from Danish social philosophy, encompasses not only the books and classes of a standard education; it also includes more intangible qualities of outlook and tolerance as well as the concrete fundamentals of agriculture and technical work. Such an idea held strong appeal for the open mind of John C. Campbell.

Mr. Campbell was a complex man, gentle but thorough in his efforts to understand people, places, events. Born September 14, 1867 in LaPorte, Indiana, he grew up in Wisconsin and was formally educated at Massachusetts' Phillips Academy and Williams College. After graduating from Andover Theological Seminary, Mr. Campbell married and became the principal of Cullman Academy in Joppa, Alabama. By the turn of the century, he had moved northeast and was supervising education at Tennessee's Pleasant Hill Academy. Within five years, he was named president of Piedmont College in Demorest, Georgia.

This work on the mountain fringes challenged the young minister-teacher and introduced him to a different way of life. He later wrote, referring to his experience as academy principal in "a little mountain hamlet":

> Naturally the post-office was an edifice of importance, for there we called daily for the letter someone might chance to write us, and we never could be sure when the package of seed from our congressman might arrive. But of first importance, and dearest to the hearts of all, were our three emporia that competed with each other in a leisurely way in the sale of coffee, coal oil, sidemeat, sugar, flour, calico, snuff, tobacco, and a few other necessities.

The challenge grew. His wife died in 1905, and a distraught John C. Campbell resigned as Piedmont's president. Later he met Olive A. Dame of Medford, Massachusetts, and married her in the spring of 1907.

The two were quite a combination. Olive Dame Campbell, graduate of Tufts and daughter of a botanist and a musician, complemented her husband's talents and enthusiastically helped him in his travels and lectures. Both believed in the dignity of the mountain region and were convinced of the need for a new kind of education. Headquartered in Asheville, North Carolina, and working with the Russell Sage Foundation, John C. Campbell embarked upon a lengthy study of the Southern Appalachians. He soon wrote of the "questions that confront all rural workers not alone in the Southern Highlands but in almost every part of our land":

> They are, in substance, how to obtain sympathetic understanding of the people and their background, unanimity of spirit rather than discord by reason of the forms that embody it, better public health and sanitation, a kind of school that does not divorce the so-called cultural from the necessary economic life of the neighborhood, and practical co-operation toward all these ends.

"A kind of school. . . ." P. P. Claxton, United States Commissioner of Education, had told the Campbells of a Danish institution called the Folk School. These folk schools, an application of the "spirit of living" philosophy of Bishop N. F. S. Grundtvig, emphasized a thorough knowledge of "the mother tongue" and practiced "that home culture which tells the experiment of what life is all about." Excited and encouraged by the possibility of establishing such a school in the mountains, the Campbells prepared to visit Denmark. But World War I broke out 10 days before they were to sail. Then, in May of 1919, John C. Campbell died from the complications of a heart condition and tuberculosis.

His widow, though grief-stricken, carried on. Olive Dame shared her husband's long-held belief that traditional education sent its best graduates out of the mountains and was therefore but another element of colonization. She was also committed to the idea that "There is a native culture in the mountains that has been too much ignored." With this and other similar insights, John C. Campbell had recalled the sentiments of Jane Addams. He had set the goals for a coming age:

> The culture material of a country's youth need not be imported from foreign lands and ancient times, but lies ready to hand in the speech and life that formed their childhood's environment. By using this, there will be no more break between education and life than there is between the states of nature and grace. For the aim of individual education is not so much intellectual strength and richness, as heart power and will power and a richness of emotional experience.

Olive Dame Campbell rose to the task before her. She completed her husband's sociological study and saw it published by the Russell Sage Foundation as the seminal *The Southern Highlander and His Homeland.* She met and enlisted the aid of an eager partner named Marguerite Butler, a Vassar graduate from Cincinnati who had taught and nursed for eight years as an extension worker at Kentucky's Pine Mountain Settlement School. By 1922, this energetic pair had secured fellowships from the American-Scandinavian Foundation. They spent the next 15 months studying Denmark's adult education, its folk schools and cooperatives.

Thus armed with first-hand information, Miss Butler and Mrs. Campbell returned to the mountains and commenced a 5-state search for a community which would accept and nurture an innovative school. During this time, "O. D." Campbell wrote her own study entitled *The Danish Folk School,* but an even larger accomplishment was at hand. A Pine Mountain colleague of Marguerite Butler's, Ann Ruth Metcalf, suggested North Carolina's Cherokee County was a possible school site. Miss Butler accordingly went to Murphy, the county seat, and was soon visited by Fred and Luce Scroggs of Brasstown. They told her of their small community near the Clay County line, of its location in the fertile valley of the Hiawassee River. And as Marguerite Butler wrote O. D., "They said they wanted a school that would not just make teachers and preachers, but one that would help the country."

So began, in 1925, a lasting association between a town and a vision. The Scroggs family gave 30 acres, and a 60-acre adjacent farm with house was soon purchased. The townspeople, all 100 of them, drew up a legal pledge and donated firewood, building stone, shrubs, trees, telephone poles, over $800 cash, and thousands of days of free labor.

John C. Campbell Folk School has never lost its enthusiasm. Intensive two-week courses in weaving, wood, blacksmithing, enameling, leatherworking, pottery, and other crafts are offered throughout the year. Annual events include folk-dance week, Little Folk School for children, and the Fall Festival of Arts, Crafts, and Music. Even the more informal Family Week carries with it the usefulness of a course; families gather in a vacation atmosphere, swap skills, and contribute among themselves to the special aura of a folk school.

This sharing recalls an earlier session in the Schools' history, when one neighbor remarked of the crowd: "Law, if it had been pretty weather you couldn't have housed them! This is like a revival. The more you come, the more you come." The willingness to come and talk to and do—the sheer willingness to create—is crucial, for creativity is the essence of it all. Creativity lies at the heart of the School's motto, "I Sing Behind the Plow," because of the finding of song and joy within a chosen vocation must stand as the intent and desire of any people, any community.

The charter of incorporation said it: ". . . to enrich the whole content of rural life." Those early workers surely felt it when in the fall of 1972 they completed the great community room, rejoiced in it, and decorated it with "rich red sourwood trees and garlands of greenery." They surely felt it in the first classes, when young teachers taught even younger pupils from maps and documents and textbooks: "Each evening class would close with the singing of Auld Lang Syne as the group would form a circle with hands crossed and clasped, Scotch fashion." And the carvers felt it, those "sons of rest" in front of the Brasstown store whom Oliver Dame Campbell helped organize into the now-famous Brasstown Carvers.

Carving was and is "the simple, non-competitive recreation" that has found its way to the core of John C. Campbell's philosophy. Said one Folk School carver during the economic depths of the Depression: "I just delight in it." "It" was what Olive Dame Campbell termed "whittling with a purpose," the purpose being beautiful products plus a good source of income. Sue McClure, an excited local student, remembered in detail her first carving experience: "I tied up a hen on the back porch and used the hen as a model. The first week I carved I only made thirty cents clear money. I gave three cents at the church and bought sandpaper."

The Folk School matured along with Sue McClure's carving. After O. D. retired as Director in 1946—eight years before she died—an able Dane named Georg

Bidstrup, recently married to co-founder Marguerite Butler, took over the farming, recreational, and educational operations of the School. Numerous new projects were undertaken, among these a literacy program and the growing of experimental trellis tomatoes. The Olive Dame Campbell Scholarships, honoring 10 students each year, were initiated. As time went on, building and policies continued apace to include memorial gardens, a model campground, stone houses of Danish influence, and the bold Internship for Rural living.

There is in the flux of the modern day a feeling of wanting to regain certainties. This feeling is not a regression to dogma but a reaching out toward constancy. Amidst Brasstown and its School, one literally senses the quality: It comes through the smell of breads and cakes and the warm wooden interiors of homes; through the tastes of corn and spice; through the touch of grainy lumber stacked beside a saw mill blade; through the sight of budding rhododendron hugging a cabin chinked with the mud-clay-sweat of its past.

This John C. Campbell Folk School is a center for sights and sounds and experience. It is the site of weekly community dances and occasional lectures on subjects as varied as beekeeping and alternative energy sources. And it is expanding into the areas of art and the theatre. At work among the ranging hills of western North Carolina, the John C. Campbell Folk School stands as the practical composite of one man's dream.

41. PROGRESS IS OUR MOST IMPORTANT PRODUCT: DECLINE IN CITIZEN PARTICIPATION AND THE PROFESSIONALIZATION OF SCHOOLING IN AN APPALACHIAN RURAL COUNTY*

Tom Boyd

Of the 52 states and territories of the Union, on the basis of the number of illiterate white voters of native white parentage, Kentucky is 49, leaving whites in North Carolina, Louisiana, and New Mexico alone lower. (*Biennial Report of Superintendent of Public Instruction 1907–1909*)

Fact: The least-educated adult population in the nation. In 1980 only 56 percent of those 18 and over had a high school diploma. Only 11 percent had a college education. *Fact:* One of the highest high school dropout rates in the nation. In 1981 Kentucky's rate was 33 percent; only eight states did worse. (*Louisville Courier-Journal*, Oct. 30, 1983)

These comments, separated by seventy-five years of change in public education, give evidence of interest in the results of formal education; but their tone also indicates the way lack of educational attainments are

managed as major stigmata in an urban, industrial society. The Commonwealth of Kentucky receives these signs as Saint Francis and others did—light marks symbolic of pain—Appalachian Kentucky carries the very wounds evidencing deep penetration.

Efforts for improved public education in this century carry all the attributes of 'progress': increasing specialization of effort, increasing efficiency in management and administration, even greater expenditures for new plant and equipment. They have also been associated with the decline in citizen participation that

*Funding for some of this research was provided by a James Still Fellowship administered through the Faculty Development Project of the Appalachian Center, University of Kentucky. Write to author for tables.

Reprinted from *The Many Faces of Appalachia: Proceedings of the 7th Annual Appalachian Studies Conference*, Appalachian Consortium Press, 1985, pp. 107–124. Used by permission.

has accompanied the strengthening of external ties binding local communities to a wider society governed by professionals and urban middle class interests.[1] This paper traces the history of change in formal education in Jackson County, Kentucky, a part of central Appalachia.

A number of recent empirical researches carry on the documentation of educational deficiency in the mountains that has long been a part of the national definition of the region as a problem area. These contemporary efforts are noteworthy in that they strive to spread the blame to others than the victim; nonetheless they continue to provide evidence (now in the social science idiom of scales and tests) of the stigma of deficiency when students are examined or measured. DeYoung, Vaught, and Porter have demonstrated that on the Comprehensive Tests of Basic Skills in Kentucky, " . . . the school districts having the higher percentages of below average readers tend to come from Appalachia".[2] In another study developing measures of school inputs, processes, finances, and outcomes DeYoung has concluded:

> Appalachian county school districts in Kentucky have poorer input, process, outcome, and financial characteristics than do non-Appalachian county districts or independent districts.[3]

Rech and Rech in a study of pupils in the Appalachian mountains of Western North Carolina and urban North Carolina used the Piers-Harris Children's Self Concept Scale along with interviews with many children.

> The scores obtained from the application of the self concept scale indicate significant differences between the two populations. The rural Appalachian children possessed a significantly more negative general self concept than did the urban non-Appalachian children.[4]

All of these studies conclude that the source of these problems lies, at least in part, in the separation between schools and the majority of the citizens of the rural areas of Appalachia.

Jackson County in Eastern Kentucky is a very rural county; the 1980 census lists the population as 100 percent rural. One major newspaper in the state marked it in front page detail recently in the following terms:

> Only 28.6 percent of the county's adults have completed high school—the third-lowest ranking among the nation's 3,137 counties.
>
> Fewer than 40 percent have gone beyond the eighth grade. In last year's statewide testing, Jackson County ranked 167th out of the state's 183 school systems. *Many people, including educators, seem to have grown tired of even hoping for better.*[5](emphasis mine)

This fatigue on the part of educators and other observers—if an accurate assessment—is of very recent vintage. Jackson County, as the rest of rural America, has in the past been the object of many "hopes for the better." These efforts from outside the county and from

the profession of education may explain many of the present conditions; they are rarely cited with such figures are given.

The series of Biennial Reports of the Superintendents of Public Instruction in Kentucky from the turn of the century onward give evidence of aspirations for Jackson County schools. From 1899–1919 the section titled "Epistolary Reports of County and City Superintendents" also gives some of the thinking of the county superintendents on this subject. These aspirations and thoughts are all in the direction of centralization of power, consolidation of schools, and the adoption of management techniques as being progress for the county's schools.

In the 1899–1901 report the State Superintendent praises the work of the teachers in the Commonwealth and goes on to say, "next to the work of the teacher in importance is the work of the (county) superintendent".[6] Words of criticism are used when the subject of the management of school affairs is tackled.

> To say the present common school trustee system is an absolute failure would be probably too severe a criticism, but to say the least, it is unsatisfactory.[7A]

The system of local trustee control was under attack for many years. At this time the duties of the local trustees were vast—a list of 16 activities covered everything from school records, maintenance, and teacher employment to a pupil census and the duty "to urge upon parents the necessity of prompt and regular attendance of their children".[7B] The county superintendent received the trustees' reports every year but at this time he had little control over these locally selected citizens.

The 1899–1901 report suggests a better form of management,

> The plan in brief is this: Place all the schools of the entire county . . . under the management of a county board of education, to be composed of the county superintendent, and one member elected from each magisterial district of the county by the voters thereof . . . [8]

The press for centralization of control and management was strong from the turn of the century onward. The Jackson County Superintendent, R. M. Bradshaw, in his report agreed with this direction of change and added further comments as to why it was obviously desirable.

> The present trustee system should be abolished and in its place a county board of education created, consisting of a member from each magisterial district having *an educational qualification,* elected by the people and *exercising the same powers as the boards of education in our cities.*[9](emphasis mine)

Here we first find the juxtaposition of educational qualifications and urban educational practices defined as progressive activity for this entirely rural area.

In 1908 the County Administration Law brought this form of organization to all of Kentucky; it made the county the unit of administration and set up county boards. From 1909 onward Jackson County has had such a school board with six, and now five, citizens elected from the magisterial districts. However, at this time the sub-district trustee still existed. The 1914–15 *Kentucky Educational Directory* said the county had no graded schools and it listed 71 of these citizen-trustees who were to be found residing all over the county. In spite of the existence of county boards the sub-district trustees dominated affairs making it difficult for the county boards to bring about what some observers saw as progress—the consolidation of schools.[10]

In the 1907–1909 Biennial Report the state superintendent explained in detail his concern that the trustee system had an unfortunate tendency to allow "political influence" in school affairs as opposed to what would now be called "professional management" of these activities. His justification for embarrassment is telling:

> The old school district system which has prevailed in Kentucky until recently, *was discarded in the Northern States nearly 75 years ago,* and has been discarded in every Southern State excepting Arkansas.[11](emphasis mine)

The "politics" that derived from citizen involvement, as well as the knowledge that the practice of trustee management was abandoned elsewhere, were major arguments to justify the centralization of power in education and the removal of supervision from the hands of citizens. The issue of educational attainment as a qualification for the exercise of power was evident early on and the final stroke on the bill of indictment of trustees was the matter of cost and the efficiency of popular election.

During the period of trustee control it was pointed out that much of the population of any area, and especially a rural area, was illiterate and it was from such a population that school officials were elected. One observer stated it succinctly.

> These men were good, honest, upright men but they had little or no education, and *therefore they possessed a very limited vision of the possibilities of education.*[12](emphasis mine)

The 1909–1911 Biennial Report records Superintendent Davis of Jackson County giving clear justification and need to reduce citizen participation in the name of economy and efficiency.

> I believe all vacancies in the office of subdistrict-trustee should be filled by appointment by the County Board of Education. I also favor the election of trustees "viva voce" compensating the trustees so elected with the money annually expended for holding school elections.[13]

The argument against trustees were clearly based on the believed superiority of central control; it was also linked with the fact that many citizens were unable, or unwilling, to make the necessary effort to provide a major modern structure for education—the consolidated school.

Early on the Jackson County superintendent praised the idea of consolidation linking it with the graded instruction found in urban areas.

> I . . . believe that we could consolidate several of our districts into one large district . . . and have a school building sufficient for four or five teachers; that is, a room for each grade, and then we might hope to have our schools graded as well as any college or normal school.[14]

The wishes of professional teachers were also used as a justification for consolidation in this period.

> It is my opinion that, with longer terms of schools, we would have more professional teachers, and with our little local schools consolidated, we would have better graded schools.[15]

The State Supervisor for Rural Schools in 1916 chided the citizens of the Commonwealth in terms of being once again behind the rest of the nation—now the new issue was this one of consolidation. He said the only hope for improvement (ie consolidation) was, "the enactment of laws standardizing public school buildings and making the State Department of Education responsible".[16] Consolidation accompanied the transfer of power that had recently replaced the district with the county; but, the way to attain this newest goal for progress in education was to further transfer power from the county to the state level. Superintendent Chapman also invoked the newly popular idea of efficiency as a justification. "Consolidation in its best form [creates] a larger school where more efficient work may be done, or equivalent work at less expense."[17]

During the period 1899–1919 Jackson County attempted to meet these desires to conform to urban America but it was a difficult task and some cases of skepticism as well as despair are notable. Superintendent Davis in 1913 wrote:

> As to consolidation and transportation, it is impractable (sic) because the roads are so poor and there are so many mountains to be crossed by the pupils. The county being one of the poorest in the State, makes consolidation almost impossible. Where possible, it is, in my opinion, the one step needed in our schools.[18]

In 1919 Superintendent Minter echoed this assessment:

> We have no consolidated schools in this county. In most parts of the county the roads are so bad and the population so sparse that consolidated schools are impractical. About half the school population would be unable to attend for at least half the term.[19]

Nonetheless he ended his report on a note of hope lest deviant local conditions be seen as defeating progress. "A sentiment for better roads seems to be growing and this is the first step toward consolidated schools."[20]

Scrutiny of these documents and reports produces one area of stated pride in progress made during this time. A new form of equipment gave the county superintendent a noteworthy event for the 1914–1915 report.

> Since my last report we have built three new school houses and *purchased and installed patent desks and seats* in seventy of the schools in my county. [Our goal is] . . . to have comfortable school houses, with patent seats and desks, in every district of the county.[21](emphasis mine)

In the 1916–1917 report the spread of formal education and this new equipment go hand in hand.

> We have either built or repaired almost every school house in the county, have established nine new districts, and have *furnished every schoolhouse in the county with patent desks during my incumbency.*[22](emphasis mine)

The purchase of manufactured desks and seats was, in this rural timber-producing county, an important symbol of the successful quest for progress on the part of this Superintendent. At least in this effort he could comply with the urban industrial standards sought by the profession of education. The historian Thomas Clark has described how 'patent' goods as symbols of real or imagined modernity spread across the rural South in an earlier period. Drummers and stores were agents of the new industrial age—in this respect so was the increasingly powerful school superintendent.[23]

From 1921 onward statistical tables dominate the Biennial Reports in a new format representing the theme of numerical accounting as an adjunct to efficient management. Statements of events, plans, and achievements—the epistolary reports of county superintendents themselves—disappear. The replacement is prepared by the State Department of Education that is growing in power.

In his 1921 report the state superintendent writes of the county school administration law as the most important school legislation enacted by the General Assembly of 1920. Through this mandate the sub-district trustees are at last removed. Attention is now directed at the qualifications of the rural superintendent as being the major problem of management. The mirror for reflection remains an urban one.

> The county school administration law of 1920 was designed primarily and specifically to give to each county in the state . . . better leadership. The superiority of the city schools to the county schools is primarily due to the better ability, the better preparation, and the better leadership of city superintendents as compared with county superintendents. [This law] . . . makes it possible to secure for the administration of county schools, the same sort of leadership that cities have enjoyed for years.[24]

When problems were described in detail the blame was clearly shifted to a person not having the requisite, new professional skills. "Too many county superintendents were not properly prepared, and did not have the administrative ability and educational leadership the position demanded."[25]

By 1940 the Jackson County School system still had many small schools. County-wide consolidation had proved to be difficult but there were some district level mergers to provide multi-grade and multi-teacher schools. The seventy-three schools in the county were still dominated by the one-teacher school; there were fifty-nine of these with the rest being eleven two-teacher schools, one three-teacher school, and two twelve-grade schools.[26] The report of a teacher working on improvement of instruction illustrates transportation problems.

> The difficulties of transportation enter into teacher reports frequently. Jackson County has no railroad and few improved highways. Many of the rural schools are situated far from the main highways on dirt roads that become impassable in bad weather. The supervisors reached a number of these schools on horseback.[27]

For forty years comments of state, county, and other observers reflect awareness that consolidation is dependent upon road conditions; other aspects of the new structure received more sanguine attention.

The State Superintendent of Rural Schools produced a fourteen page report extolling the virtues of consolidated schools.

> First. The consolidated rural school secures better buildings, better equipment, better teachers, better attendance, more sanitary conditions, greater school spirit and greater efficiency along all lines.
>
> Second. This type of school may become, and almost invariably does become, a community center and a rallying point for all the educational, moral and industrial forces of the community.
>
> Third. While the difference in cost between the one-room school system and the consolidated system is very little, if any, the advantages of the larger school are so much greater that they more than compensate for the difference in cost, should there be any.
>
> After all else has been said, the best argument for consolidation and transportation is that they *get more children into school, keep them there better and for a longer time, and give them opportunity for more rapid progress*[28](emphasis mine)

It was believed that as roads were built consolidation would follow swiftly behind. Just to make sure readers would be aware this was the wave of the future the report concludes on a strong note. "As no successfully consolidated school, so far as is known, has ever returned to the old way . . . consolidation is surely beyond the experimental stage." (Chapman, 1917)

The author of another study of the consolidation process in Kentucky in the 1920's got caught up in the mood of the times. "The history of consolidation in business, in manufacturing, in education has shown the key note of success."[29] It was believed that such a process would attract and hold better teachers, give better instruction to the children, produce better buildings and equipment, and allow the teaching of new subjects.[30] The growth of the consolidation movement could only be hindered by transportation problems, conservatism of people, financial conditions, and inadequate leadership.[31] From the 1920's onward consolidation was seen to be a natural extension of a process that produced efficiency in the growing urban, industrial economy. Outside the lack of physical resources the only things that could prevent it were deficient or inadequate people.

A 1969 history of Kentucky small schools produced by the State Department of Education argued that the larger schools offered,

> . . . better trained teachers, greater variety of curricular and extra-curricular activities, *better adaptation on the part of graduates to the present social order,* and better leadership in business, industry and government, resulting from a broader and better education.[32](emphasis mine)

During a fifty-year period the state abolished 98 percent of the one-teacher schools, most of the remaining ones were found in Eastern Kentucky. Three factors were cited as making this consolidation possible. First there was the obvious growth in the possibility of pupil transportation as school buses were developed. Second, "growth of population in small villages and towns . . . made it necessary to abolish small schools and construct larger ones". And third, "from 1955 to the present, emphasis on accreditation and evaluation has been a large factor in the decline".[33] The population shift away from rural areas aided consolidation, perhaps doing away with the personal inadequacies that led to opposition to the process as well. After 1955 the principle factor was the control of the State Department of Education with professional evaluation and standards being advanced as links with state financing of county educational programs.

In 1961 Jackson County still had 31 schools—a reduction of 41 from the 1940 figure. Sixteen one-teacher schools remained in existence; the rest of the county's schools were five two-teacher, two three-teacher, five general elementary and three twelve-grade schools. The county had been loosing population over the years. From 1940–50 there was a 19.8% loss, from 1950–1960 a 18.5% loss, and from 1960–1970 there would be a 6.3% loss. Efforts to consolidate the Jackson County school system could finally be completed during the decade of the 1960's, roads in the county had been improved somewhat, there was some loss of population in the outlying areas, and federal and state dollars were available for educational expenditure to bring change. This decade brought a further change at the state level; the yearly publication, *Profiles of Kentucky Public Schools* began to publish data that allowed comparison of schools in the rough terms of inputs to educational programs and the results of schooling. Such data collected

for one county system over time allows us to compare time periods using these same variables.

Table 1 gives data on the performance of the county system for the period 1966–67 (the first year such statistics were complete) to the present. Appendix 1 gives the method the State Department of Education uses to develop these educational indicators. Comparison with data for the entire state during the same time period allows us to view any changes relative to a wider norm for performance that is not solely urban. Looking at the change in these figures an assessment of the claims for consolidation can be made in its own terms of better buildings, greater efficiency, getting more children into school, keeping them for a longer time, and giving them opportunity for more rapid progress. Scrutiny of the fourteen-year period from 1966 to 1980 gives a picture of changes in the system as consolidation was completed and as the first group of pupils left schooling having had a full 12 years of the transformed, transportation-oriented rather than neighborhood-oriented, county school system.

In 1980 the county has only five elementary schools and one high school. The elementary schools consist of three major multigraded schools in the larger population concentrations near the most important highway and two smaller more remote schools the State Department of Education has recommended the county close. The single consolidated high school, according to Department of Education figures, is thirty-five miles away from the more distant pupils; many children are on busses at 6 A.M. in order to reach high school by 8:15 A.M. By the 1981–82 school year transportation was 15.4% of total current expenses, and the county was derided by weathermen on television newscasts for being closed so often when ice was on these mountain roads.[34] Figures 1–7 compare county and state figures and chart changes in the educational indicators as the county system has begun to have an educational effort that includes approximately 3,000 miles of total bus travel on any given day.

Facilities for schooling have changed dramatically since 1940, the three newest buildings are recognizable as schools found anywhere in the nation and the high school has had the most recent status benefit of modern construction—expensive removal of asbestos used in the construction of the library. All three have gyms for indoor physical education and the ubiquitous pursuit of prowess in basketball—patent desks and chairs abound.

In 1966–67 the county pupil/teacher ratio was 27.7 to 1 and that was only one more pupil more than the state ratio of 26.6. By 1979–80 the Jackson County ratio declined to 20.7 and the state ratio was reduced to 21.0. In 1966–67 the percentage of students enrolled who were in attendance was 90.8%, the state average was 94%. By 1979–80 the county figure was 89.7% and the state 93%. During this period of culmination for the process of consolidation, the county did not improve its performance relative to the state averages for pupil/teacher ratio and percent attendance.

Throughout the United States the 1960's and 1970's were a period of inflation as well as increasing amounts of money spent on public education. In 1966–67 Jackson County spent $346 per pupil when the annual current expenses were divided by the average daily attendance; by 1979–80 the figure was $1,184. The state change during the same period was from $357 to $1,452. In the initial period, expenditure in Jackson County was 97% of the state average, by 1979–80 it had dropped to 82% of the state figure. When the cost per pupil for instruction alone is considered the figure for Jackson County in 1966–67 was $253; by 1979–80 the amount spent was $772. The state change during the same period was from $280 to $970. The culmination of the consolidation effort led to the county declining from 90% to 80% of the state average of dollars being spent per pupil for instruction. From this view consolidation has not led to an increase in the county expenditure relative to the state average expenditure per pupil. This might be viewed as supporting the claims of greater "efficiency" that were promised by the proponents of the process.

In the 1966–67 school year 57.5% of the Jackson County students entering ninth-grade in 1962 graduated from high school. These young people had come out of any one of twenty-six elementary schools. In 1979–80 the percentage had dropped to 46.2%. The dramatic drop this year may be due to the closing of the small private high school, but in years before this the figure had dropped below 50% five separate times and climbed above 57% only three times. The state figures for this period were 69% and 65%. Jackson County had a percentage point decrease of 11 and the state a decrease of 4 points. The early county figure was eight-tenths of the state percentage and the new figure was a decline to about seven-tenths of the state percentage.

The 1966–67 school year saw 28.7% of the high school graduates entering college and by 1979–80 the figure was 23.9%. Ten times during this time period the percentage was below the initial figure and only three times was it above the figure for the students with the more neighborhood-based elementary education experience. During this same period the state percentage fluctuated much less; the initial figure was 42.4% and ending figure was 42.8%. For Jackson County the early figure was 68% of the state percentage and the later figure was 56% of the state percentage. Such figures do not demonstrate that the process of school consolidation improved the ability of the schools to "hold pupils" or to "motivate and prepare" them for higher education.

The claims of educational improvement through school consolidation have not been supported in this Appalachian county. Things have stayed the same or declined further. More modern buildings have been built, the pupil/teacher ratio and expense per pupil have shifted. But there has been no increase in "getting more children into school", "keeping them for a longer time", and the "opportunity for more rapid progress"—if anything things have gotten worse and these figures don't necessarily show the entire picture. In Kentucky pupils may stop attending school at age 16; many of these dropouts never reached the ninth grade to be counted in the figures for percentage of ninth grade graduating from high school. Nonetheless, as the figures show, the new system did not greatly increase retention of the pupils that did reach the ninth level of state graded educational attainment.

What social processes have gone on during the period from 1961 to the present? There has been increasing centralization in the distribution of educational facilities in this reduction from 31 to six schools. Schooling is, with two exceptions that are condemned to be closed soon, found in the population concentrations. There has also been a centralization of power and participation as the reduction in schools means a longer bus ride for pupils and greater distance for parents to travel to participate in school meetings, events and the like. This 'de-ruralization' of education has taken place in a county where more than two-thirds of the pupils are considered "economically deprived children". The state figure is 32%. These events have been organized, directed and managed by the profession of education from outside the county with some citizens accepting the process as progress.

Opposition has not been totally absent. Some members of the Hisel community have recently thwarted attempts to close their two-teacher elementary school and the school board has supported them by going against the wishes of the Kentucky Department of Education, keeping this school open on a year-by-year basis. However, in some cases this has been used by newspapers, teachers, and educational administrators as further evidence of the backwardness of education in Jackson County rather than a wise decision in the face of a wrong policy.[35]

Evaluations of the effects of consolidation on school systems are not frequent in the social science literature of today. The conventional wisdom seems to be that it has been successful so there is no need for analysis; any problems are the result of incomplete or thwarted consolidation. Another view holds that it is a "natural" process not worthy of scrutiny. As Rosenfild and Sher point out in an article entitled "The Urbanization of Rural Schools, 1940–1970",

By the 1960's consolidation, as a political issue, had ceased to be a legitimate subject of debate or policy analysis. Consolidation and other urbanizing practices were no longer perceived as *reforms* championed solely by the progressive elements of society. Rather, they had become accepted educational *standards* supported not only by the full range of the education profession, but also by the mainstream of American society.[36]

Claims of cost effectiveness abound in terms of "economies of scale" and greater efficiencies in larger schools. But at least one study has shown how after a certain size is reached new diseconomies of scale emerge in more busses, higher fuel costs, faster depreciation and the cost of new administrative specializations.[37]

Studies of the effect of consolidation on participation of citizens and students alike show results similar to the ones found in Jackson County, but such studies are rarely, if ever, cited in state analyses. A study of high school size and student participation published in 1964 found that when students were transferred to a larger county high school they had a *decrease* in their participation in extracurricular activities and the amount of satisfaction associated with, "acquiring knowledge and developing intellectual interests."[38] A case study of a school consolidation struggle in rural West Virginia showed how sides taken are often in terms of "experts versus amateurs", "professional educators versus parents" etc.

For members of the middle class (including professional educators) consolidation is an effective way to strengthen influence and control within the community, while furthering their aspirations for their children. Yet, to the rural poor and working class, consolidation represents an attempt to destroy what is often their only sphere of public influence and their last vestige of control over their childrens' education and socialization.[39]

Decline in participation is impossible to refute. It is often a result of consolidation that is admitted not as a cost but as something desirable in a "complex" world. When, it is admitted as a cost it is frequently justified as being necessary for the educational benefit of improved pupil performance—this study shows that such a benefit is a false assumption.

The early consolidation studies took place in urbanized areas; they did not control for family economic conditions as an effect upon learning and thus showed some positive correlation between school size and student achievement. Recent studies demonstrate that when researchers control for I.Q. and socio-economic status the result is, "a complete reversal of the traditional conclusions about the correlation between size and achievement".[40] A review of the literature, one author claims, shows that not one of the controlled studies demonstrates a positive correlation between size and achievement independent of social class.[41] Jackson County has two-thirds of its pupils in the status the state measures and terms "economically deprived".

We have seen that the impetus for consolidation in rural Kentucky came from comparison with urban areas. This is not unique to Kentucky or Appalachia; the process and the results in terms of participation are similar in areas of the nation having a better reputation.[42] In urban America community control of schools gave way to a "corporate-bureaucratic model" as part of a drive "taking the schools out of politics".[43] A similar theme was sounded in the complaints about Jackson County and other rural areas. In American urban education this happened in a much earlier period, as state and county Superintendents often proclaimed in their early reports, and it was a major transfer of power from parents (many of them recent immigrants and most working class) to professionals.

The professionals were not immune to forces for change themselves. From the turn of the century onward there has been considerable adoption of business values and practices in educational administration. At this time professional administrators in urban areas began to be perceived as business managers rather than educational philosophers.[44] The demise of county "epistolary reports", and the State Superintendent replacing this with statistical reporting methods, in the 1920's, demonstrates this well as do all the surveys and cost accounting material that begins to appear at this time.

In urban America at the turn of the century school boards were being reduced in size and their composition was changing, in that they were increasingly dominated by businessmen.[45] Administrators responded to this pressure on their work in a positive way. A 1916 text book *Public School Administration* explained that businessmen, manufacturers, and bankers made the best school board members and those who would not be adequate were politicians, saloonkeepers, and uneducated or relatively ignorant men.[46] The pressures for change in school board composition in Jackson County was largely from the profession of education not local businessmen! Even today, perhaps due most to the nature of the population in the county, the school board is not dominated by manufacturers, businessmen and bankers. Also, as we have seen, this school board is not pushing as hard as the state and the profession for the remaining consolidation effort.

What does the future hold for Jackson County and the rest of Appalachian Kentucky? The commonwealth has seventy-three elementary schools with less than eight teachers. All of these small schools, having at least one instance of a teacher assigned to more than one grade, are slated to be consolidated into larger graded schools.[47] As part of this the Moore's Creek and Hisel schools in the county will be closed.

For Jackson County the State facilities survey recommends the construction of a new upper elementary school for all 7th and 8th grade pupils.[48] It will be built next to the existing high school and means that two more complete grades will be bussed to the central education facility each day.

Legislation pending in the 1984 Kentucky General Assembly will raise the minimum educational level for new school board members from an eighth-grade to a high school education. Jackson County has 2,313 citizens 18 years old and over who meet this educational qualification. In the future only 28.6% of the population will be eligible for participation as a school board member.

In the 1981–1983 *Biennial Report* the Superintendent of Public Instruction has recommended the following,

> Election of county school district boards of education should be at large rather than by subdistricts so that the boards represent and advocate for *a sound county-wide public education* and not a regional or sub-district one.[49] (emphasis mine)

When implemented this change will at last lay to rest the "problem" of the local interest and sub-district trustee, they have gone from 71 to five in number. With the adoption of this recommendation from the professionals there is no longer any assurance that peripheral areas will be represented and a county-seat population might produce all five school board members.

The educational lights have gone out all over this central Appalachian county. During the past forty years the processes of centralization of power and consolidation have brought urbanization in the provision of schooling, the decline in local participation, and the alienation of citizens that occurs when the universal and whole, in this case socialization, is transferred into the hands of professionals alone. This has not been totally due to professionals. In every Appalachian county some citizens have seen it in their interest to promote this cause. They have accepted the ideology of individual advancement and social mobility and believed that the urban school—"The one best system"—was the way to attain it.[50] They overlooked the fact that in such a distribution someone has to be on the bottom. In terms of stigmata Kentucky carries light marks symbolic of pain, but many Appalachian counties have had profound penetration leaving deep wounds.

APPENDIX 1
Definition of Indicators used in *Profiles of Kentucky Public Schools*

1. *Pupil/Teacher Ratio:* This was calculated by dividing the enrollment obtained from the Superintendent's Annual Statistical Report by the total number of classroom teachers as reported on the federal and state salary schedules.

2. *Percent of Attendance:* Data on the Annual Statistical Report was used to calculate this by dividing the aggregate days attendance by aggregate days membership.

3. *Annual Current Expenses Per Pupil in Average Daily Attendance:* Data obtained from Annual Financial Reports collected by the Division of Finance from the local districts and the Superintendents' Annual Statistical Reports collected by the Division of Pupil Personnel. The total current expenses were divided by the ADA to arrive at the figure. Current expenses include administration, instruction, attendance services, health services, pupil transportation, operation of plant, and fixed charges.

4. *Cost Per Pupil for Instruction:* Instruction costs were calculated by dividing the total spent for Instruction by the average daily attendance. The total for instruction excluded money spent in this area from Title I and IV of ESA. (This exclusion is due to accounting requirements for federal reporting.)

5. *Percent of Ninth Graders Graduating:* The Superintendents' Annual Statistical Report submitted by the local districts to the Division of Pupil Personnel is the basis for this calculation. It lists the total graduates by age and enrollment by grades. The number of graduates was divided by the number of ninth graders enrolled three years ago. **In districts which have merged or experienced a significant enrollment increase or decrease the figures can be misleading.

6. *Percentage of High School Graduates Entering College:* The School Data Form is the source of graduates entering college. High School graduates are reported on the Superintendents' Annual Statistical Report and divided into the number entering college.

7. *Percent of Economically Deprived Children:* This was taken from records of the Office of School Food Services indicating the percentage of children eligible for free school lunch benefits in proportion to total children of school age in the district.

NOTES

1. For a consideration of this process in a single Appalachian rural community see Tom Boyd, "Floating Down The Stream Of Time: An Appalachian Rural Community Confronting Mass Society", unpublished paper presented at the 1982 Appalachian Studies Conference.

2. Alan DeYoung, *et. al.,* "Evaluating Educational Performance in Appalachian Kentucky", *Appalachian Journal,* vol. 9, nr. 1, (Fall 1980) p. 54.

3. Alan DeYoung, "The Status of Formal Education in Central Appalachia", *Appalachian Journal,* vol. 10, nr. 4 (Summer 1983) p. 323.

4. Una Mae Lange Rech and Gregory G. Rech, "Living is More Important than Schooling: Schools and self concept in Appalachia", *Appalachian Journal*, vol. 8, nr. 1, (Fall 1980) p. 20.

5. *The Louisville Courier Journal*, "In Jackson County the schools are failing to end the poverty cycle", p. 1, October 30, 1983.

6. *1899–1901 Biennial Report*, p. 11.

7A. *1899 Biennial Report*, p. 14.

7B. Moses E. Ligon, *A History of Public Education in Kentucky* (Lexington: Univ. of Kentucky Press, 1942) p. 118.

8. *1899–1901 Biennial Report*, p. 17.

9. *1899–1901 Biennial Report*, p. 238.

10. Ligon, *Op, cit.,* p. 214.

11. *1907–1909 Biennial Report*, p. 15.

12. Ligon, *op. cit.,* p. 119.

13. *1909–1911 Biennial Report*, p. 68.

14. *1901–1903 Biennial Report*, p. 160.

15. *1901–1903 Biennial Report*, p. 160.

16. *1916–1917 Biennial Report*, p. 273.

17. *1916–1917 Biennial Report*, p. 277.

18. *1911–1913 Biennial Report*, p. 101.

19. *1917–1919 Biennial Report*, p. 27.

20. *1917–1919 Biennial Report*, p. 27.

21. *1914–1915 Biennial Report*, p. 280.

22. *1916–1917 Biennial Report*, p. 34.

23. Thomas D. Clark, *Pills Petticoats and Plows: The Southern Country Store,* (Bobbs-Merrill, 1944) p. 21.

24. *1920–1921 Biennial Report*, p. 6.

25. Ibid., p. 7.

26. Mary J. Patterson, "A Demonstration in In-Service Education of Teachers", unpublished M.A. Thesis, University of Kentucky (1943).

27. Ibid, p. 66.

28. *Kentucky School Report, 1916–1917,* "Supplementary Report of J. Virgil Chapman, State Supervisor of Rural Schools", pp. 281–282.

29. Hattie C. Warner, "Consolidation of Rural Schools In Kentucky", unpublished M.A. Thesis, University of Kentucky, (1925) p. 21.

30. Ibid, p. 40.

31. Ibid, p. 29.

32. *The Little Red School House in Kentucky,* Division of Pupil Personnel Attendance and Accounting: State Department of Education: (June 1969) p. 2.

33. Ibid, p. 2.

34. Figures calculated from *1981–1983 Biennial Report.*

35. *Jackson County Sun,* August 5, 1982, "Hisel School to remain open" p. 1. *Jackson County Sun,* May 12, 1983, "Hisel gets one-year reprieve" p. 1. *Lexington Herald-Leader,* May 13, 1983, "Tiny School in Jackson gets 1-year reprieve", p. 1.

36. Stuart A. Rosenfeld and Jonathan P. Sher, "The Urbanization of Rural Schools, 1940–1970", pp. 11–42, in Jonathan P. Sher (ed) *Education in Rural America: A Reassessment of Conventional Wisdom,* (Boulder Colorado: The Westvies Press, 1977) p. 40.

37. Jonathan Sher and Rachel B. Tompkins, "Economy, Efficiency, and Equality: The myths of Rural School and District Consolidation", pp. 43–75 in Sher, *op. cit.,* p. 46.

38. Roger G. Barker and Paul V. Gump, *Big School, Small School: High School Size and Student Behavior,* (Stanford University Press, 1964) p. 153.

39. Timothy Weaver, "Class Conflict in Rural Education: A Case Study of Preston County West Virginia", pp. 159–204 in Sher, *op. cit.,* p. 161.

40. Sher and Tompkins, *op. cit.,* p. 63.

41. Ibid, p. 64.

42. Wayne E. Fuller, *The Old Country School: The Story of Rural Education in the Middle West,* (Univ. of Chicago Press, 1982).

43. David B. Tyack, *The One Best System: A History of American Urban Education,* (Harvard Univ. Press, 1974) p. 7.

44. Raymond E. Callahan, *Education and The Cult of Efficiency* (Univ. of Chicago Press, 1962) p. 120.

45. Ibid, p. 150.

46. Ibid, p. 151.

47. Shirley Williams, "Jabez Elementary School: One for all, all for one", *The Louisville Courier Journal,* Jan 9, 1983. Mr. Harmand Bisconti of the State Bureau of Instruction discusses these plans here.

48. *Comparative Facilities Survey of Jackson County Kentucky School District,* June 1973, Department of Education.

49. *1981–1983 Biennial Report,* p. 81.

50. For a discussion of the rise of this vertical view of life as opposed to the horizontal view see: Berton Bledstein, *The Culture of Professionalism,* (Norton 1978).

42. FAMILY AND EDUCATION IN SOUTHERN APPALACHIA

Susan E. Keefe
Una Mae Lange Reck
Gregory G. Reck

Education in the southern Appalachian region is marked by low student achievement levels, high dropout rates, and a low percentage of high school graduates going on to college. For example, the Appalachian Regional Commission's Educational Advisory Committee found the Appalachian dropout rate between grades one and twelve average 65% in 1966 compared to 36% nationally (Parker 1970). A total of 62% of the adult population in Appalachia have not graduated from high school. Thirty percent of the region's population are functional illiterates. Of the population 25 years and older, only 10% in Appalachia had finished college in 1976 compared to 15% nationally (Appalachian Consortium 1981).

Despite the significance of the problem, there have been no comprehensive studies of education in southern Appalachia. Community studies generally include observations about education and the schools, and these suggest that Appalachians face many of the problems

Paper presented at the annual meeting of the Appalachian Studies Conference, Berea, Kentucky, 1985. Used by permission.

familiar to ethnic minorities elsewhere in the U.S. Reck and Reck (1980), for example, have found negative stereotyping of rural mountain youths has a negative consequence on educational decisions. Native writers, such as James Branscome (1976) and Jim Wayne Miller (1977), have emphasized further problems of educational prejudice, alienation, and cultural misunderstanding and conflict.

Our intent was to undertake a holistic study of education in a southern Appalachian county. The research was funded by the National Science Foundation during 1983–84. The focus of the research was the single consolidated high school and the factors contributing to students' success in school and reasons for dropping out. The high school, however, was studied in the context of the larger society, and methods were used to ensure a broad perspective. A questionnaire concerning participation in school clubs, sports and activities was administered at the high school and 1193 students responded. From this a sample of 14 case studies was selected covering variation in cultural background, socioeconomic class, and rural/urban residence. Both students and parents in these families were interviewed with a number of formal interview schedules. Several dropouts and their parents were also interviewed intensively. Interviews were conducted with school administrators, elementary and high school teachers, civic leaders and other residents of the county. The investigators also attended community events and public meetings and observed in the schools.

The site for the research was a county in western North Carolina with a population of approximately 30,000. The county seat is the only urban area in the county with a population of about 12,000 permanent residents. A four-year college is located in this town, boosting the population during the school year to over 20,000. Major sources of employment other than the college are in light industry, tourism, and small-scale agriculture. Like other tourist and recreation counties in southern Appalachia, the town and county has experienced major population growth in the last 15 years. As a result of the population growth and the particular economic base, the town and county population is heterogeneous, including native-born Appalachians and immigrant non-Appalachians, lower class farmers and laborers and upper middle class professionals and entrepreneurs, and rural small-scale agriculturalists and longtime urban dwellers. One of the primary goals of our research was to come to understand the complex interaction of socioeconomic status, rural/urban residence, and ethnicity in Appalachia and their effect on educational achievement.

The application of the concept of ethnicity to white Appalachians is controversial. In fact, the research was undertaken in part to determine the extent to which mountaineers form a distinct ethnic group. A model of ethnicity was developed to include three general aspects: structural, cultural and symbolic. The structural aspect of ethnicity refers to the boundedness and opposition of groups within the larger society. Cultural ethnicity is based on a distinctive pattern of traits shared by members of a group. Lastly, the symbolic approach to ethnicity puts emphasis on ethnic identification and perceived cultural differences. These are distinctive though interrelated aspects of ethnicity in general. According to this definition, then, ethnicity refers to the distinctiveness of two or more groups which are in contact yet set apart in structural, cultural, and symbolic ways.

In order to test the validity of the structural, cultural and symbolic aspects of ethnicity in the Appalachian context, an independent marker of Appalachian ethnicity is needed. The marker we have used is "association with place" defined as three generations born in the mountains. This can be operationalized by asking for the birthplace of the informant and the informant's parents and grandparents. We have used the ARC's definition of the southern Appalachian region to categorize birthplace.

Regional planners estimate that 70% of the recent population growth in western North Carolina is due to the immigration of people born outside the area. According to the results of our survey in the county high school, 36% of the students were born outside the Appalachian region. Clearly, newcomers in Appalachia are different in origins. Some come from the south, some from the north. National heritage and religious affiliation are heterogeneous. On the other hand, some commonalities emerge: most are white, middle class, and have an urban background. Furthermore, newcomers tend to be "mainstream" American, following the cultural norms typically cited as "American." Thus, we can identify essentially two groups by birthplace in the region: (1) native Appalachians whose families are from the mountains and (2) recent non-Appalachian immigrants.

In this paper, we intend to explore some of our findings, specifically regarding the interrelationship of family and education in southern Appalachia. Family and kinship are important for all three aspects of ethnicity. Kinship contributes to the structure of social relations. Rural Appalachia is often described as a kin-based society. Furthermore, numerous writers have found that extended family structure as found in Appalachia forms a distinctive cultural pattern (Brown 1952; Bryant 1981). Finally, family provides the foundation for self-identity and perceptions about the way in which the world outside is organized.

Family, of course, has an important effect on students' attitudes toward and participation in the schools. When asked why students drop out, informants (including students, parents, teachers and school administrators) typically lay blame on the family for lack of emphasis on education. True, in some cases, parents who have dropped out themselves are little interested in education and their children may receive little encouragement in their studies. In some cases, familial problems such as divorce or alcoholism result in little attention paid to the education of the children. But for the most part, we found (like Ford in his regional study in 1962) that most parents see the value of education and desire a good education for their children. Parents who have dropped out who have tried getting jobs in the public sector know the value of a high school diploma. Says one informant, "I don't know what my son will do after high school, but he'll graduate. These days you got to have a diploma to get a decent job. It's the first thing they ask you on an application form. I know because I left school in the 8th grade. I'm trained as a plumber, but I can't get no job in plumbing." (This man works nights as a janitor at the college.) Many of the parents of dropouts regret that their children dropped out of school and hope that their younger children will finish.

While academic performance is related to finishing high school, many of those who drop out or consider dropping out are average or above average students. In fact, they may have had dreams of going to college and eventually getting a professional job. What changes their attitude and their mind is what they confront at the high school. Here are the words of one rural eighteen-year-old girl who dropped out at sixteen:

> I always liked school until I got to high school. I hardly ever missed over here at (my elementary school). The high school was a different story. I never did like it. It was cold, unfriendly I mean. The teachers and all were. It wasn't the same at all. I liked to learn too. I've always loved animals and in elementary school I wanted to be a veterinarian. I really wanted to. When I went to the high school I had the idea to be a vet, to go to college. But I just couldn't take it over there. So I quit. I blame it on them that I'll never get to be a vet. . . .
>
> I just couldn't take it. These kids would try to push all these drugs on you and then they'd call you all these names 'cause you wouldn't do it. It got so bad I didn't go to my classes for three or four weeks. I'd just go sit in the bathroom all day. Just sit there! The town kids would make you feel so inferior—calling you names, looking down their noses at you. You have to see it. So one day I just called my Daddy and told him to come get me. And I quit.

This girl's father echoes her feelings. Asked about other students' attitudes toward rural students at the high school, he replies:

> They treat us like dogs. They think they're better and smarter. Now I don't care who you are or how much you want to go to school, if someone treats you like a dog you ain't going to put up with it. You'll either fight or walk away. It don't do nobody no good to fight. So it's better just to come on back here (the local community) where people accept you for who you are.

What the dropouts and their parents give as reasons for leaving school have to do primarily with the prejudice, discrimination, and indifference of students and teachers at the high school.

Students at the high school are perceived as falling into three social groups, generally viewed hierarchically as an upper, middle, and lower group. The upper group, also called the popular group, the "in" group, snobs, big-shots, and High Society, is primarily distinguished on the basis of socioeconomic class and residence by informants. They have more money, wear more expensive clothes with designer names, and "think they are better than everybody else." They dominate in sports and activities like cheerleading. They go to a lot of parties and drink. They are in the middle or upper track classes; many of the academically gifted are in this group. They live in town where the high school is located, facilitating their participation in sports after school. They tend to have gone to the elementary school in town, but many went to one of the two or three other elementary schools located close in to town. The uppers are also characterized by other kids as "different" in cultural ways, such as having a non-local accent and language patterns. Although it is not verbalized, the fact is that most of the upper group are non-Appalachians, often the sons and daughters of professionals (doctors, university professors) who have moved into the county in the last decade.

The lower group is also referred to as the rednecks, hicks, back-woods, mountain kids, the By-Gods, and the unpopular group. This group is also distinguished primarily on the basis of socioeconomic class and residence. The lowers are poor; they wear old clothes that are not name-brand and they wear the same clothes for days at a time. They are characterized as dirty, not bathing frequently. They are believed to be rough, prone to violence. They typically wear jeans and t-shirts; boys also wear baseball caps with tobacco, beer or manufacturer labels on the front. Girls often wear leather belts with their name printed on them. Rednecks are never involved in athletics. They take the easiest courses, get poor grades, don't care about school, and "are just waiting to get out." They tend to hang out at the smoking area in the high school; most of them smoke or chew tobacco. They tend to live in rural areas in the county and come from schools furthest out from the high school. Culturally, they are characterized as having a mountain accent (such as accentuating vowels), poor grammar, and using "slang" or mountain colloquialisms.

The middle group (also called the average or in-between group) is basically made up of those students not falling into these two smaller, more extreme groups. They are neither wealthy nor poor. Their clothes are "average," not fitting any particular mold. They participate in school activities but do not stand out. They do fairly well in their coursework and take middle or upper track classes. This group is not easily characterized by socioeconomic class, residence or ethnicity. It includes a mixture of students from a wide range of backgrounds.

This all sounds somewhat familiar to anyone who has been to high school in the U.S. The three-level hierarchy in a way replicates the social class system; many of our informants, in fact, compare it to the class system. What makes it different is the overlay of ethnicity as an additional factor in determining social identity. Socioeconomic class is the primary basis for classifying students; there are no poor students in the "popular" group and no wealthy students in the "redneck" group. Residence is an important additional means of classifying students but is secondary to class, so that we find some rural students in the "popular" group if they are middle class and have special attributes such as athletic ability. Similarly, some "rednecks" live in the urban school district and attend the urban elementary school but because they are lower class they have been classified in the lower group. In these cases, the individuals classified into the lower group are inevitably also Appalachian natives. In most of the cases of rural students in the "popular" group, they tend to be non-Appalachian, but exceptions can be found.

Part of the reason for the overlap of ethnicity, class, and residence in characterizing the peer groups is that these traits are correlated in the general population. Appalachian natives are more likely than non-Appalachians to live in blue-collar families in rural areas. For example, according to our survey at the high school, 83% of the natives live outside the town compared to only 67% of the non-Appalachians (p. 000). Only 35% of the natives have fathers with white collar jobs versus 87% of the non-Appalachians (p. 000).

Only 24% of the native students' fathers have had more than 12 years of education compared to 85% of the non-Appalachians' fathers. The town in this particular county is overwhelmingly middle class; there are no neighborhoods which are identifiably poor except for a few trailer parks and the small black section of town. Because of this, in fact, we found it impossible to fill our case study sample categories of "urban-lower class" for either Appalachians or non-Appalachians. The stratification system, then, is one in which Appalachians natives tend to be lower or working class, rural residents while the non-Appalachians tend to be middle or upper-middle class. While non-Appalachians are more likely to live in town than natives, the majority (67%) of non-Appalachians live in rural areas. The town itself is about evenly made-up of both Appalachian and non-Appalachian residents. The rural areas of the county are overwhelmingly populated by natives.

In analyzing the high school questionnaire on students' participation in clubs, extra-curricular activities, sports, and school-sponsored social activities, we found that socioeconomic status is the primary variable which consistently accounts for differences in participation although one or more other variables also contribute to these differences. Clubs are allowed to meet during school time every other Friday, thus allowing maximum participation by students; 77% of the natives and 88% of the non-natives belong to at least one club. Using multiple regression procedures, we could determine 30% of the variance between club participants and non-participants with two independent variables: father's education and high school class (freshman, etc.). Participation in extra-curricular activities (such as student council, chorus, band, cheerleading, the school newspaper and high school annual) is less common, involving only 23% of all natives and 38% of non-natives. Five variables account for 48% of the variance in distinguishing participants from non-participants in extra-curricular activities: mother's education, sex (females more active), graduating elementary school location in the county, father's occupation, an urban/rural residence.

The rate of participation in sports lies between that for clubs and extra-curricular activities; 31% of the natives and 51% of the non-natives are active in sports. Five variables account for 47% of the variance between participants and non-participants: sex (males more active), father's education, high school class, whether or not the student rides the bus, and graduating elementary school location. For attendance at school sponsored social activities (including football game, basketball games and dances), 41% of the variance was accounted for by five variables: riding the bus, father's education, graduating elementary school, high school class, and rural/urban residence.

A total activity scale was created summing participation in clubs, sports, and extra-curricular activities and attendance at school social activities. Five variables account for 53% of the variance in activity participation: father's education, riding the bus, high school class, mother's occupation, and graduating elementary location. Two of these variables are indicators of socioeconomic class while an additional two variables implicate SES *and* rural/urban residence (bus riding and elementary school location). In none of the regression equations does ethnicity (Appalachian birthplace) figure as a statistically significant variable. However, given the significant correlation of ethnicity with father's education ($r = .51$, $p = .000$), father's occupation ($r = .42$, $p = .000$), rural/urban residence ($r = .17$, $p = .000$), graduating elementary school location ($r = .27$, $p = .000$), and riding the bus to school ($r = .14$, p=.000), it is clear that ethnicity is not unimportant in school activity participation. Thus, while the primary factors enabling students to participate in high school activities are high socioeconomic status and residence in town, it is also true that those students most likely to fit this description are non-Appalachians. Evidently, their ethnic background has much less to do with their ability to participate than class and residence. Yet, because ethnicity is strongly correlated with these factors, it is often *perceived* by informants as *the* contributing factor. For example, parents and teachers will often generalize about the needs of "mountain kids" but it is clear that they are specifically referring to rural, lower class natives.

Because of the *perception* of the importance of ethnicity, structural limitations and stereotypes are reinforced which make the educational experience more difficult for Appalachian natives who are middle class. For example, one middle class, rural boy responded this way to the question of whether he had experienced any difference in treatment in school due to his background:

> Maybe because I'm a freshman. Seniors can make it rough on freshmen. Well, maybe just a little because I'm from (out in the county). Some people are labeled rednecks the minute they walk in the door. (Were you?) Well, maybe a little by some. But you got to work through it. After they get to know you it's different. They see you're not a redneck. (What is a redneck?) They lack a good education, the way they talk, not much money. It's someone to pick on. Some town kids think we're all like that until they get to know some of us. You can work through it pretty fast. (How?) Just by getting to know different people. Then they see there's not that much difference between us; that there's a lot of difference between (us and other) people from out here.

Thus, individual acceptance by peer groups involves a process of negotiation upon arrival at the high school. Anyone coming in from a rural area (often discovered by asking what elementary school one graduated from) is labelled a "redneck." This can apply to non-Appalachians as well. It is then up to the student to present certain information and to behave in certain ways which cause social reclassification. This involves exhibiting social, economic, and cultural traits. For example, previous acquaintance with people who live in town indicates similar social circles. The ability to buy expensive clothes, travel, and get to school by other means than the bus indicate high economic status. Accent, vocabulary, and language skills are indicative of both socioeconomic status and cultural background. Thus, non-Appalachians and middle class or urban Appalachian natives have resources with which to negotiate higher status in peer groups. Rural, lower class Appalachians do not have such resources and tend to be consistently classified into the lowest ranked peer group, "rednecks."

Moreover, rural lower class Appalachians often have an ascribed status based on family surname which makes it difficult if not impossible to escape the "redneck" label. There is the recognition by families, teachers, school administrators, and community members in general that certain local surnames are associated with a lower class background and poor success in school. Children entering school with these surnames are automatically labelled potential dropouts and are treated differently throughout their school years. Given the expectation, it is not unusual to find that almost all of these youths do in fact drop out. In these cases, family surname functions as effectively as physical, racial traits in ascribing lower class status.

While the perception of ethnic differences is obviously important in the labelling and status negotiation process, it is important to point out that *real* cultural differences do emerge in a comparison of natives and non-natives. In an analysis of family and kinship, for example, we find that the Appalachian concept of family is patterned differently than for the mainstream American non-Appalachians. For Appalachian natives, "family" is defined as including the nuclear family of procreation (spouse and children) and the family of orientation (parents and brothers and sisters) and generally brothers' and sisters' spouses and children. Typically, the nuclear family is a separate household unit and is the fundamental unit of social organization, but it is not conceived of as an entirely independent unit. Rather than splitting from the family of orientation, new families of procreation are added to the larger family. This family unit, then, is made up of many households. Frequent visiting and exchange takes place between members of these closely related households, most often between parents and their married children and between siblings who live nearby or feel special affection toward one another.

Other relatives fall into two groups: (1) "relatives"/ "kin" who include more distantly related blood kin and their spouses (such as grandparents, aunts, uncles, and cousins) and (2) spouses' kin. Relatives can be a large group but typically informants do not recognize kin beyond the grandparents' ascending generation, grandchildrens' descending generation, and first cousins in their own generation. "Relatives" are seen and exchange goods and services less frequently than "family." They are most often seen at weddings, funerals, and reunions. Spouse's kin are not conceived of as the informant's relatives or kin. Rather, they are referred to as "my wife's family" or "my husband's family." Visiting is less frequent with spouse's kin than with the informant's own "family." Sometime this results in interesting visiting patterns within the nuclear family. One woman, for example, married into her husband's community. One of his brothers lives nearby and they visit daily, often at her house. However, she says, she doesn't really talk to her brother-in-law. Her concern is directed more toward her own "family," particularly her parents whom she visits every Sunday.

This pattern identified as Appalachian is associated with rural residence and geographic stability. It does not appear to vary with SES in rural areas. There are indications, however, that urban, middle class Appalachians are more likely to follow the mainstream American pattern.

Among the non-Appalachians, the most basic social unit is the nuclear family made up of spouse and children. The nuclear family is perceived as an independent unit and frequently this is reinforced by geographic isolation from other kin. A second unit is identified (many times perceived as closely connected to the nuclear family) and referred to as "family"/"relatives"/"kin." As one informant put it, these relatives are "those who really care about you." This group typically includes parents, brothers and sisters and their spouses and children. It may also include: grandparents, aunts, uncles and cousins, and spouse's kin. It is these relatives with whom exchange and visiting takes place. A third group is identified as "relatives"/"distant relatives" and includes blood kin and spouse's kin not included in the second group. These relatives are seen infrequently and rarely participate in the exchange of goods and services.

In sum, family and kinship form different conceptual patterns for Appalachians versus non-Appalachians. Furthermore, as we might expect, patterns of social organization differ for the two groups. From an analysis of social networks, we find that native Appalachians have networks which invariably include relatives as frequent social contacts; relatives are rarely a majority of contacts, however. Nevertheless, those relatives included (generally members of the larger "family" unit) are important for exchange of goods and services. For students, these relatives can have an important influence on their educational goals and success. Typically more numerous as network contacts are friends and co-workers. Neighbors form only a small component of Appalachian social networks even in rural areas. Fellow church members may be as numerous as neighbors. Rural, lower class Appalachians have the most distinctive networks as they tend to be sex-segregated and limited to contact with other native Appalachians. Urban and middle class Appalachians are much more likely to interact with non-Appalachians, although half or more of their social contacts still tend to be other native Appalachians.

Non-Appalachians rarely have relatives in their social networks, not surprising given the fact that all of them are migrants into the region. It is important to note, however, that mainstream Americans in general typically have few if any relatives in their social networks (Keefe 1980). Non-Appalachians' networks are made up of friends and co-workers. Neighbors and church members are few in number. Non-Appalachians' networks are dominated by others of similar cultural background, although an average of 20–30% of their network contacts are Appalachian natives. There appears to be little difference between networks of non-Appalachians living in rural versus urban areas, indicating that location of residence *per se* is less important than rural/urban background in shaping ethnic social organization.

It is apparent that structural, cultural, and symbolic differences separate Appalachians and non-Appalachians as a whole. Members of these two ethnic groups perceive each other as different, have real differences in cultural patterns such as family organization, and interact in fairly distinct social circles. This ethnic difference, however, is mediated to a great extent by socioeconomic class and rural/urban residence. Rural, lower class Appalachians are most distinctive in structural, cultural and symbolic ways. It is this segment of the population which suffers most from discrimination and prejudice in the schools and other social arenas. Urban, middle class Appalachians are much less distinctive. However, they are still affected by the symbolic content of ethnicity and must deal with the perceptions of non-Appalachians and forced identity. Although they may feel pride in their heritage, urban, middle class Appalachian youth may suffer from significant identity problems when faced with the derogatory stereotypes and misperceptions about their people. For those who go on to college, these problems are often resolved by reorientation toward and identification with mainstream America. While this may resolve identity problems, it robs these individuals of their heritage and roots.

In conclusion, it is clear that educational institutions must come to recognize the special needs and problems of native Appalachian students. And while substantial programs are needed to serve the needs of rural, lower class Appalachians, schools must also recognize the importance of reinforcing a positive ethnic identity among all native Appalachians. Finally, it may be just as important for schools to sensitize non-Appalachians. Finally, it may be just as important for schools to sensitize non-Appalachians (especially teachers) to the nature of ethnic prejudice and discrimination in the schools and ways to eliminate these educational barriers.

NOTES

This research was funded by the National Science Foundation, grant number BNS-8218234.

REFERENCES

Appalachian Consortium Newsletter, Appalachians Complete More Years of School, 4(4): 7, 1981.

Branscome, James, A Colonial System of Education. *Mountain Life and Work* 47:14–18, January, 1971.

Brown, James S., The Conjugal Family and the Extended Family Group. *American Sociological Review* 17:297–309, 1952.

Bryant, F. Carlene, We're All Kin: A Cultural Study of a Mountain Neighborhood. (Knoxville: Univ. of Tennessee Press, 1981.)

Keefe, Susan Emley, Personal Communities in the City: Support Networks Among Mexican Americans and Anglo Americans. *Urban Anthropology* 9:51–74, 1980.

Miller, Jim Wayne, Appalachian Education: A Critique and Suggestions for Reform. *Appalachian Journal* 5:13–22, 1977.

Parker, Franklin, Appalachia: Education in a Depressed Area. *Phi Kappa Phi Journal* 50:27–38, 1970.

Reck, Una Mae Lange and Gregory G. Reck, Living is More Important than Schooling: Schools and Self Concept in Appalachia. *The Appalachian Journal* 8(1): 19–26, 1980.

IX. Religion "Just a Closer Walk With Thee"

Thomas O'Dea in his book The Sociology of Religion *describes three fundamental characteristics of human existence:*

First, man lives in conditions of uncertainty; events of crucial significance to his safety and welfare are beyond his prevision. Human existence, in other words, is characterized by contingency. Second, man's capacity to control and affect the conditions of his life, although increasing, is inherently limited. At a certain point, man's condition with respect to the conflict between his wants and his environment is characterized by *powerlessness*. Third, men must live in a society, and a society is an orderly allocation of functions, facilities, and rewards. It requires imperative coordination—that is, some degree of superordination and subordination in the relations of men. Moreover, societies exist and conditions of scarcity—the third fundamental characteristic of human existence.[1]

Religion with its orientation to the "sacred," a realm that transcends the mundane everyday order of things, is often used by man to assist in dealing with these three brute facts of human existence. Religion becomes one of the many alternatives used by man to come to grips with what Max Weber called "the problems of meaning" or Paul Tillich called "the ultimate concerns."

The way in which one experiences these three ultimate conditions will consequently influence to a very high degree the form and content that religious expressions will take. Religion is shaped by the social and cultural milieu of which it is a part and at the same time religion acts upon the social and cultural milieu. Religion and culture become intertwined. If the adherents of a particular religious system are drawn from the privileged status or class in society, the religious expression is most likely to take the form of guarded optimism and this worldliness. On the other hand, a people enduring physical hardships along with social and/or economic deprivation are likely to encompass a religion that emphasizes an otherworldly promise of salvation as a way to escape the suffering and toil of this world.

One point that is frequently made by writers when describing the Appalachian region is the strong degree to which religion permeates the entire cultural milieu and its inhabitants. Loyal Jones states in his article "Appalachian Values" that mountain people are religious but not necessarily in the more restrictive institutional sense of being active church member. They are religious in the sense that religion becomes the source of their values and the meanings they see in life. (See Jones, "Appalachian Values," article in a previous section of this reader.) The rugged social and physical conditions of the early frontier denied an optimistic outlook on life. This denial of optimism has been sustained by contemporary conditions for a

[1] Thomas F. O'Dea *The Sociology of Religion,* Englewood Cliffs, N.J.: Prentice-Hall, Inc., 1966, p. 5.

good many of Appalachia's inhabitants—unemployment, economic exploitation, coal mining and its accompanying disasters, etc. The nature of the Appalachian experience brings into clear focus man's existential confrontation with the problems of contingency, powerlessness, and scarcity. The response is a system of religious beliefs and practices that help to sustain the Appalachian when dealing with the many conditions that are beyond their control. As Loyal Jones writes,

> These beliefs, and variations on them, have sustained us, have given our lives meaning, and have helped us to rationalize our lack of material success. Every group of people must have meaning in their lives, have to believe in themselves. Religion helps to make this belief possible. There are few Appalachian atheists because Appalachians need God.[2]

In addition to the many religious beliefs and values discussed thus far, there were other characteristics of the religious heritage that left their imprint upon the area and still persist in many forms of religious expression today. Beryl Maurer in an essay on religion in the book Mountain Heritage describes five of these: (1) living awareness of an intensely personal relationship with God; (2) a sense of independence (maturity) built upon the security of God's love; (3) the ability to withstand hardship and privation; (4) ability to accept people as they are; (5) the expression of the Gospel in song—"I've Got the Joy."[3]

Those who are interested in the work of the mainline religious bodies in the Appalachian region should consult the references in the bibliography pertaining to the work of CORA (Commission on Religion in Appalachia). CORA consists of a cooperative effort on the part of seventeen religious communions working in cooperaton with other organizations to develop a program designed to minister to the pressing human needs of the people of Appalachia.

[2] Loyal Jones, "Appalachia Values" see section on Appalachian Folk Culture of this reader
[3] Beryle Maurer (ed.), *Mountain Heritage*, Mountain State Arts and Craft Fair, 1974, pp. 109–111.

43. GRACE AND THE HEART OF APPALACHIAN MOUNTAIN RELIGION

Deborah Vansau McCauley

On Route 421, about nine miles from the southwest Virginia border, is Cranks, Kentucky. In the heart of coal country, the nearest large town to Cranks in eastern Kentucky is Harlan. Cranks, Kentucky, is marked mostly by a small grocery store just before crossing the bridge over Cranks Creek. An unpainted cement block church—Cranks Presbyterian Church—complete with monochrome tinted glass windows and a steeple, is on the other side of Cranks Creek just around the curve in the road, a product of Presbyterian home missions in the region earlier in the century. Just after reaching Cranks Presbyterian Church is a single story wood structure painted white. The sign reads, "New Church at Mill Creek." This is an independent holiness church built and maintained by Sister Lydia Surgener, an independent holiness preacher whose half sister, Becky Simpson, runs Cranks Creek Survival Center. A county road with no outlet runs along Cranks Creek just off of Route 421. Three miles down the road is the Survival Center, started by Becky Simpson in 1977 after a treacherous flood considerably worsened by strip mining run off destroyed lives and property It is a self-help effort that has sought to benefit the residents in a five-county area, including two counties in Virginia, with food, clothing, shelter needs such as insulation and roofing, outhouse construction, whatever needs to be done.

Becky Simpson and Sister Lydia Surgener are second cousins to Sister Mae June Hensley, who lives on the county road running along Cranks Creek not far from Cranks Creek Survival Center. Sister Mae June is the founder and church matriarch of Cranks Holiness Church. The story of how Cranks Holiness Church came to be is extremely telling about the nature of church life and traditions in the central Appalachian region in particular. Cranks Holiness Church represents the independent, nondenominational church tradition that stands at the center of the spectrum of mountain religious life. Although mountain religious life is marked by variety and multiplicity, there are also many commonalities characteristic of church traditions in the Appalachian region that independent nondenominational churches have distilled to their essence. Many times Baptist, more often than not holiness, the worship practices, belief systems, and religious traditions of independent nondenominational churches represent traditions reflecting more the practices and belief systems of plain-folk camp-meeting religion in the upland South that was Appalachia during the first half of the 19th century than they do the holiness-pentecostal traditions of the late 19th and early 20th centuries. In turn, the traditions of pietism of the Radical Reformation, Scots-Irish sacramental revivalism, and the Baptist revival in colonial Virginia are some of the major reservoirs of tradition for mountain religious life and are reflected in the traditions of independent holiness churches as well as in more doctrinally developed traditions such as the Old Regular Baptists.

Cranks Holiness Church is a one-room building that stands out as a church building only because of the cross above the doorway. The church building was built by a black Baptist preacher, Brother James L. Turner, and the property was still owned by his family until the summer of 1989, when it was sold to Sister Mae June for a nominal sum. Prior to that, when the black community moved out of Cranks in the late 1960s when times were good, the church was entrusted as a dormant or sleeping church to the care of Sister Mae June. Sister Mae June would sweep out the church building once a week, check on the property, and make sure everything was alright. When a church community moves away, church houses are rarely abandoned. Even though there is a strong distinction between the "church," meaning the people who attend, and the church house, a church house is treated almost like a person, attended to with loving care even though no church community currently occupies the building.

After many years of tending the church building, Sister Mae June says that God laid on her heart that the church building was to be a living church again. So after she would sweep it out, she would sit on the front step and pray, "holding services by myself." At the time, Sister Mae June lived about two miles away down a hollow. One Friday while Sister Mae June was praying on the step, Brother Coy Miser came down the road. Brother Coy is an independent holiness preacher who has founded several churches throughout the central Appalachian region and as far north as southern Ohio. Brother Coy says that he had never been down the Cranks Creek road before. He says that God laid on his heart to come down the road, and he saw Sister Mae June sitting on the step. Brother Coy asked Sister Mae June what she was doing. Sister Mae June replied that she was praying and holding services by herself, because God had laid on her heart that this was to be a

This article was prepared specifically for the third edition of *Appalachia: Social Context Past and Present*. Used by permission of the author.

living church again. So Brother Coy went inside the building and preached to her, and he came every Friday thereafter to preach to Sister Mae June.

One day, Brother Coy had a vision of two angels standing on either side of the doorway of Cranks Holiness Church with people coming in and it was a living church again. So Brother Coy and Sister Mae June anointed with oil and prayed over each bench. The following Friday, people started to come for services and it has been a living church ever since. That was in 1982.

Sister Mae June, through the help of the Survival Center, now lives in a house right beside Cranks Holiness Church. Sister Mae June has lived in the Cranks Creek area all of her life. In her younger years she made split white oak baskets which she sold in Pennington Gap, Virginia, about a half an hour away by car on Route 421. Sister Mae June is now in her mid-sixties. She is considered the matriarch of the church and its principal caretaker. Cranks Holiness Church is frequently referred to simply as "Sister Mae's Church," even though Brother Coy has been its pastor. In the past year or so, Brother Coy has had to step aside as pastor due to failing health. Many preachers come and go at Cranks Holiness Church. Its center of stability is Sister Mae June. She is the central figure of the church or the person most identified with the church. The status of church matriarch is achieved with age and an active religious life. Sister Mae June has spent her entire life going to holiness services throughout the whole area and she has traveled a great deal with Sister Lydia.

Brother Coy Miser is in his early seventies and suffers from black lung disease, a product of his years working in deep mines in the 1940s and 1950s. Brother Coy has also worked as a laborer in construction, when his health no longer allowed him to mine. Brother Coy's father was a subsistence farmer who moved from near Sneedville, in Hancock County, Tennessee, to Pennington Gap, Lee County, Virginia, before Brother Coy was born. Like Sister Mae June, Sister Lydia, and Becky Simpson, Brother Coy and his people have lived in the area all of their lives. Brother Coy is both a preacher and a pastor, although he functions mostly as a pastor. A pastor is someone who oversees a church and who directs its spiritual focus, but he is frequently not its main preacher. Indeed, in Brother Coy's church in Pennington Gap, Red Hill Holiness Church, the main preacher is a man by the name of Brother Loyd Haskell Underwood, but Brother Coy has been seen as its pastor, until recently. Many people in Appalachia understand themselves to be preachers and not pastors, or pastors and not preachers. A pastor will preach, but it is not his or her primary vocation in their own understanding.

This story about the coming to be of Cranks Holiness Church illustrates several features characteristic of mountain religious life: the central place divine inspiration ("God laid on my heart") holds in the active faith life of the believer; the religious credence given to dreams and visions; the spontaneity, autonomy, and religious authority assumed by the individual, whether ordained or not; the absence of institutional or denominational structures for the founding of churches and church communities in a neighborhood. The respect the black Baptist preacher had for Sister Mae June, the respect Sister Mae June had for the unused church house, the respect Brother Coy had for Sister Mae June's conviction of the church building's viability, Sister Mae June's respect for Brother Coy's preaching to an "empty" church house, Becky Simpson's respect for Sister Mae June by helping her acquire a home next to the church house, even though Becky herself is not a church-goer—all of these elements illustrate the respect Appalachian people hold for the *Imago Dei* and for the individual's relationship with God.

The Appalachian tradition of churches "fellowshipping together" is very strong still today. Services at Cranks Holiness Church are on Monday and Friday. At Sister Lydia's New Church at Mill Creek in Cranks services are on Tuesday. Services at Sister Lydia's House of Prayer in Pennington Gap are on Sunday. At Red Hill Holiness Church services are on Wednesday and Saturday. Schedules are arranged so as not to compete with each other. Congregations tend to flow from one church to another, having one church they attend regularly. Because services are scheduled at night covering every day of the week, a church building will often have posted outside the door a sign that reads, "Church here tonight."

The respect for the image of God in the individual, and for the individual's relationship with God, leads to a very wide tolerance and appreciation for other ways of worshiping and praising God, as reflected by the tradition of "fellowshipping" among independent holiness churches, whose members also feel free to attend independent Missionary Baptist churches, Free Will Baptist churches, as well as a host of other traditions. Despite Old Regular Baptists' strict polity about whose churches may be attended and preached in, even among Old Regular Baptist churches themselves, the Old Regular Baptists are also a tradition in the Appalachian region—most characteristic in eastern Kentucky and southwest Virginia—that has a very strong tradition of "fellowshipping." There are theological roots shared by most mountain church traditions that account for this wide streak of tolerance, despite doctrinal differences, and those roots are found most of all in doctrines of *grace*.

Not until the 1980s was any attempt made to explore the historical development and differentiation of Appalachian mountain religion from what became the dominant religious culture in the United States in the 19th and 20th centuries. Any attempt to do so must look at the variety as well as the continuity and historical integrity of worship practices, belief systems, and religious traditions in Appalachia making up a regional religious tradition known as Appalachian mountain religion. Mountain religion is primarily an oral religious tradition, which accounts for its virtual invisibility in the study of American religious history. Nonetheless, Appalachian mountain religion has played an extremely significant role in American religious history, from the continuing traditions of Calvinist theological heritage to the holiness-pentecostal movements, providing the setting for the most dramatic events of the Great Revival period which continued to inform the development of mountain religious life long after the last camp meeting of the era had passed. Moreover, mountain religion has continued traditions of the doctrine of *grace* that remain closer to the sensibilities of Jonathan Edwards than to the conversion and revival traditions of Charles Grandison Finney. These traditions mark what is perhaps most theologically distinctive about Appalachian mountain religion when compared with the broader religious developments of Protestantism in the United States.

This theological distinctiveness goes beyond distinguishing Appalachian mountain religion as a regional religious tradition from mainstream Protestant traditions. It is absolutely necessary to underscore at the outset that mountain religious life and history are also not to be identified or equated with "southern religion" in its many varieties or with the Southern Baptist Convention; nor is it to be identified or equated with the religious ethos of television evangelists, ranging from the fundamentalists independent Baptist tradition represented by Jerry Falwell to the Assemblies of God traditions of Jim and Tammy Faye Bakker or Jimmy Swaggert. At the heart of these differences on a theological plane—differences which cannot be totally extracted from the central elements of land, people, history, and traditions—is the centrality of the doctrine of grace on an experiential level in the worship life of Appalachian church communities, be they Old Regular Baptists or independent holiness.

The centrality of grace—of God's initiative and human cooperation—in mountain religious life points to the line of separation between Jonathan Edwards and James McGready on the one hand compared later to Charles Grandison Finney. In 1796, McGready's Presbyterian churches in Logan County, Kentucky, prayed and waited on God to move in a revival for nearly a year, praying every Saturday night and Sunday morning, and all day on the third Saturday of each month. When their revival finally came in 1797, it gave birth less than three years later to the Great Revival in the Old Southwest (Appalachia and its immediate borders). It is no accident that Free Will Baptists in Appalachia still adhere to a view of grace, of God's initiative and divine providence, in events such as revivals (which precludes any prearrangement or planning to make them happen)—this in spite of the Free

Will Baptists' early historical position on general atonement that led eventually to the full Arminianization of Calvinism for mainstream Protestant churches, meaning in part the shifting of emphasis from divine sovereignty to human responsibility in—and control over—the salvation process. Revivals which had waited for a movement of the Holy Spirit to ignite at any time and any place, now became subject by the 1830s to organizational advance planning and scheduling, i.e. subject to human-centered control rather than God-centered control. For example, Brother Coy Miser recounts how he once went to preach a service in the front yard of a private home in east Tennessee and that the Holy Spirit ignited the meeting and turned it into a three-week revival. Such an illustration contrasts with the practices of many mainstream Protestant churches of scheduling a revival and evangelists for a set period of time.

This emphasis on the centrality of grace is a major characteristic distinctive historically and today of mountain religious life. It stands in contradistinction to the fully Arminianized interpretation of Finney, the "father" of modern revivalism, who by 1835 was calling revivalism a "science," something that now relied on human initiative and God's cooperation. This represented an earth-shaking shift in emphasis, one that accounts most of all for the tenacious resistance of "Old School" Baptists, a majority of whom were in the mountains of Appalachia. Their position gave birth to the anti-mission controversy of the first decades of the 19th century and created the distinctly Appalachian phenomenon of "Missionary Baptists" and Baptists still identified with a more traditional Calvinist understanding of the world, such as Primitive Baptists and Old Regular Baptists. This "Old School" viewpoint was lampooned and caricatured by a host of writers on mountain religious life, starting with the triumphant home missionaries of the Baptist farmer-preacher John Taylor's day in the 1820s, repeated even louder beginning in the early 1880s, and picked up by local color novelists such as Charles Egbert Craddock (a.k.a. Mary Noailles Murfree) in *The Prophet of the Great Smoky Mountains* (1885), the first novel set entirely in Appalachia with no "outsider" characters and focusing on Hiram Kelsey, a mountain preacher. This drumbeat of ridicule and misapprehension about the nature and necessity of grace in Appalachian mountain religion has yet to end in writings on mountain religious life. Its most popular label is "fatalism."

Finney's theological interpretation, while not at all exclusive to Finney at the time, created the lines of development characterizing modern evangelical Protestantism, from Finney to Dwight L. Moody, to Billy Sunday, to Billy Graham and TV evangelists in general. Salvation had become a matter of making a rational "decision for Christ," something to be enacted any time through individual choice, once the individual was sufficiently persuaded; it was no longer a hope-filled wait for the movement of the Holy Spirit in an act of unmerited grace, a "sweet hope in my breast" as the Primitive Baptists call it. The theological traditions of mountain religious life, as reflected especially in their worship practices, pursued a different path of development, a path that parted early on, prior to Finney's "science" of revivalism in the 1830s. A movement of God's grace as the heart of the salvation process remained the same as it had been for the 18th century Consistent Calvinist Jonathan Edwards.

By the turn of the 20th century, the Old Regular Baptists—among the most doctrinally sophisticated of all Appalachian religious traditions—had developed what has become normative as their doctrine of atonement or salvation, a mediating position between Calvinism and Arminianism that very much represents the general Appalachian religious position on grace: the Old Regular Baptist atonement doctrine is summarized as "election by grace," through the "sanctification of the Holy Spirit." It falls between the more Calvinist "particular election" traditions of the Primitive Baptists and the more Arminian "general" or "universal" atonement traditions attributed to the Free Will and Missionary Baptists. However, even for the Primitive Baptists and the Free Will and Missionary Baptists, emphasis is upon religious experience—from the experience of conversion or salvation itself to emotional expressions in a worship service—unmediated by human manipulation.

Throughout mountain religious life, there is a dominant emphasis on the purity of God-generated or God-instituted emotion or religious experience. Expressive and ecstatic worship traditions—singing and praying spontaneously, shouting, shaking hands, crying, thrusting hands heavenward, even testifying and preaching spontaneously—have a very long heritage in mountain religious life, reaching back to the earliest years of settlement on the Appalachian frontier in the 18th century. These emotional expressions, to a greater or lesser degree, cut across almost all mountain church traditions. A preacher is supposed to *experience* emotion while preaching, not generate it or "whip it up." Most television evangelists are seen by mountain people as generators of emotion or religious experience, not leaning on the unmanipulated movement of the Holy Spirit. The same applies to the call to conversion or salvation: one cannot make "a decision for Christ," as evangelical Protestants have come to express it. One can only be open to the experience of saving grace in one's life. The centrality of grace over rational decision in the conversion experience goes hand in hand with the centrality of the Holy Spirit in mountain worship life.

This emphasis on the movement of the Holy Spirit in the community of believers has roots in Appalachian religious traditions not in the late 19th and early 20th century holiness-pentecostal movements, but in classic Calvinist theological tradition reaching back to the Synod of Dort in 1618–1619 and ultimately to Calvin himself. In terms of the traditions of the doctrines of grace and the Holy Spirit, Calvinism is alive and well in mountain religious life. It binds together traditions such as Free Will Baptists and independent holiness and Old Regular Baptists and Primitive Baptists. In Appalachia, these traditions, as well as many others, even many mountain churches representing mainstream Protestant traditions such as the Methodists and Southern Baptists, have more in common with each other than with the larger denominational movements with whom they share their early roots.

Other features complimenting the experiential traditions of the doctrine of grace also distinguish the religious traditions of Appalachia as a regional religious traditions: preachers assume more of a prophetic stance than a charismatic one; free church polity, expressed primarily through a firm belief in democratic equality and the priesthood of all believers, makes church life very much a corporate, collegial reality. This latter fact has much to do with how corporate decisions are reached in rural Appalachian communities about all decisions affecting the group. An emphasis on humility—also a product of the doctrine of grace—makes leadership a subtle, deferential affair in church life on the part of those who are recognized religious leaders, both women and men.

Let's take a closer look at the independent nondenominational church as the center of the spectrum of mountain religious life, before moving on to the broader spectrum of traditions making up Appalachian mountain religion. The American religious historian Catherine L. Albanese makes a telling statement in her study, *America: Religions and Religion* (1981), about what she calls "the fruit of the mountain spirit and the mountain religious traditions" in her study of Appalachian mountain religion as a regional religious tradition:

> . . . as one individual or another (usually male) among the people became convinced that God was calling him to preach and exhort . . . he would set about establishing a church of his own, often on his property, either in his house or a separate building he might construct. Like a patron to his neighbors in a lonely mountain hollow, he invited them to join with him in seeking the Word and will of God. Here all the characteristics of mountain religion came together at their fullest expression: the uneducated preacher, the independent church, the primacy of the Bible, and the strong emotionalism of religious worship. The nondenominational church was the fruit of the mountain spirit and the mountain religious traditions [p. 234].

One may rightly ask, "How accurate is Albanese's portrait?" A major clue is found in the field notes or schedules for Elizabeth R. Hooker's 1931 religious survey housed in Special Collections at Berea College in Kentucky and making up the basis for her 1933 publication, *Religion in the Highlands: Native Churches and Missionary Enterprises in the Southern Appalachian Area.* One summary about a mountain preacher stands out in particular, because it is a good example of much of what the survey uncovered. W. H. Callaway of Avery County, North Carolina, was born in 1858. A farmer with no schooling, he had been pastor of the independent Church of God, the name he gave to the church house he built on his property, for nearly twenty-five years at the time of his interview:

> Mr. Callaway is an elderly farmer who has spent his whole life in this place. He has no education and could not read until after he was grown. He has spent a great deal of time reading the Bible, which he regards as inspired in every detail, and as a result knows it remarkably well. Feeling called upon to preach the Gospel, he set up a building on his own land, at his own expense and with his own hands, and established a church independent of other denominations. At present the church has only 12 resident members, mostly relatives or life-long friends of his. For 24 years he has served as the pastor to the best of his ability, and received almost nothing in return. He is a kindly, lovable old man, always ready to help any who need it, and sometimes is imposed upon. Although his own beliefs are very definite, he very often allows men who differ with him to preach in his building.

There is not the space to comment on each line of this very telling statement, except to note that the parallels between Brother Callaway and Brother Coy Miser, Sister Lydia Surgener, and Sister Mae June Hensley are very strong indeed, despite the fact that they are separated in time by nearly sixty years. The Bible tends to be known primarily as oral literature, even by those who can read and read well. Preacher and pastors generally are not paid for their services, a tradition reaching back to the earliest years of settlement on the Appalachian frontier and well documented by the Virginia-Kentucky Baptist farmer-preacher John Taylor in his *History of Ten Baptist Churches* (1823). "Feeling called upon to preach the Gospel" is equivalent to "God laid on his heart." Brother Callaway took autonomous action to establish a church house on his own property; whether or not he went through any form of ordination is not indicated. Ordination in the independent holiness tradition is not a requirement, only spiritual maturity and the recognition of the people in the area where one attempts to exercise one's "gifts." Religious life is highly autonomous in Appalachia, which is not to be equated with "individualistic"; mountain religion "happens" only within the context of a finely tuned relationship with the local community in which it arises. Brother Callaway has very definite views, but also a wide streak of tolerance: "he very often allows men who differ with him to preach in his building."

The independent nondenominational church tradition represented by independent holiness probably goes back at least to 1840, when plain-folk camp-meeting religion went "underground" into the mountain regions of Appalachia after it was abandoned by the Baptists and Methodists. However, the tradition of the independent church, especially independent Baptist, probably reaches back to the late 18th century; there have always been Baptist churches in Appalachia not in formal affiliation with any association (an organizational structure characteristic of the Baptist tradition that allows for the fellowshipping of Baptist churches within a certain geographic area).

With the claim that the independent nondenominational church—either independent holiness or independent Baptist—stands at the center of the spectrum of mountain religious life, the question arises, What does this spectrum look like beyond the center? The spectrum model is linear or two-dimensional, and so has limited use as a model for purposes of description. Perhaps a circular, three-dimensional model is more appropriate, for the left-right aspects of the spectrum image create difficulties unresolved at this time. On either side of the spectrum's independent, nondenominational center are Appalachian church traditions functioning at the subdenominational level, a level marked by membership in regional associations or some form of loose fellowship, but not in national, denominational, organizational structures. On either side of the independent nondenominational church, then, are Old Regular Baptists, Primitive Baptists, Free Will Baptists, United Baptists, Regular Baptists, and Church of Christ, as well as other traditions involving a regional organizational structure that preserves the autonomy of the local church community. The associations are not hierarchical structures. Membership is for fellowship only, not for the deferral of authority over local church matters. Nearer the ends of the spectrum are denominational traditions that had their origins in the Appalachian region—traditions such as the Church of God (Cleveland, Tennessee), Christian Church, and the Cumberland Presbyterians. Nearing the periphery of the spectrum are mainstream denominational traditions long established in the Appalachian region—United Brethren (a pietist tradition), Southern Baptist Convention, Methodist Church. At the ends of the spectrum are mainstream denominational traditions that have never been established in the mountains except as home mission interests—Presbyterians, Congregationalists, Disciples of Christ (despite the identification of their earlier years with the Church of Christ and Christian Church), Episcopalians, Lutherans, Roman Catholics, and so on. Mainstream denominations are marked much more by a national identity, a national purpose, rather than by a regional identity.

With such variety and historical relativity, how is it possible to speak of Appalachian mountain religion as a regional religious tradition? Certainly mountain religion is not monolithic. However, it is possible to speak of commonalities and repetitions as well as variety.

Catherine Albanese has provided a very useful heuristic device for approaching the quieter, more subtle, and largely undocumented stories of people's inner religious life, because those stories are revealing and of value. This device, which I call the "four c's," provides an approach to the study of Appalachian mountain religion as a regional religious tradition by looking at: *creeds* (what people believe), *codes* (how people live), *cultuses* (how people worship), and *communities* (the people who are bound together by shared traditions, history, and place). Albanese writes that regional religion is "religion born of natural geography, of past and present human history, and of the interaction of the two" (p. 222). For example, creeds can be anything from the Nicene Creed, the backbone of Christian orthodoxy in the western world, to the informal beliefs passed on through oral transmission and oral interpretive traditions. Codes are illustrated by the oft-made claim that Appalachian mountain religion represents a strong variant of "revival religion." There is a great deal of truth to this claim, if we understand revival religion to be made up primarily of the twin aspects of salvation and assurance—that is, salvation by *experience* and assurance by *conduct*. As such, revival religion has to do with status authority, if status authority is understood not in terms of a prestige-loss scheme (as it usually is), but as styles of life or lifestyles through which revival religion has the right to regulate conduct and assign identities. Mountain religion as a strong variant of revival religion is about the power of creating one's own religious identity within the community of believers and in one's wider society. Cultuses or how people worship has to do primarily with worship practices. In mountain religious life there is a strong tradition of expressive and ecstatic worship practices reaching back to the 18th century: Old Regular Baptists as well as independent holiness will shout, weep, throw hands up, testify, and so on. Worship also tends to be a very casual environment, unlike the strict behavior codes found in most mainline churches, including many denominational pentecostal church traditions. Communities are the communities making up the Appalachian region itself, in all its variety. For example, the labor history and geography of eastern Kentucky and southwest Virginia are certainly not that of western North Carolina. Yet there are strong commonalities that make all three of these areas "Appalachia."

One of the key features binding together the variety of traditions making up mountain religious life is the orality of mountain religion: Appalachian mountain religion is primarily an oral religious tradition. Mountain religion is marked very much by its traditional features, yet there is a strong tension between what is conservative and what is dynamic. It is this tension that allows the traditional features of mountain churches to be transmitted through oral transmission and oral interpretive traditions, a process that is more informal than formal. Elaine J. Lawless writes in *God's Peculiar People: Women's Voices & Folk Tradition in a Pentecostal Church* (1988) that traditional religion in such a church community consists of "beliefs, behaviors, practices, and rituals" transmitted from generation to generation and from person to person in an informal, oral style (pp. x, 4). In Appalachia today and throughout its history, mountain religion is characterized by its orality and traditional features, which go hand in hand. Lawless observes further that churches characterized by worship practices and belief systems that are "performed orally by the collective group involved . . . do tend to be autonomous." This autonomy allows for variety and variation, rather than identical expression in churches of the same tradition, while at the same time the nature of oral tradition creates similarity and replication, given the integrity of the transmission process. The oral character of Appalachian mountain religion is both a product and a cause of the overall autonomous character of mountain church life, apart from denominationalism and institutionalism. It is also a product and a cause of the shared features—be they strongly or less pronounced—found in the worship practices, belief systems, religious experiences, and traditions of the variety of church traditions characterizing mountain religious life, apart from ideological, theological, and doctrinal distinctions.

Many clues are also found in the material culture of religious life in the Appalachian region. For example, the single most important piece of religious art in mountain churches and homes is Leonardo da Vinci's "Last Supper." The strong history of Scots-Irish sacramental revivalism suggests why this one piece of art—found in independent holiness churches as well as in Old Regular Baptists churches and in most other mountain churches of a variety of traditions—represents such a pronounced "historical memory" in Appalachian religious life. As an illustration, the following is an account of a foot washing service in Cranks Holiness Church.

On December 31, 1989, I attended a Night Watch service for praying in the New Year at Cranks Holiness Church in Harlan County, Kentucky. This was to be a special occasion, for "sacrament" and footwashing were planned for the night service, which started at 7:00 P.M. and would go until a little after midnight. Brother Coy Miser, Sister Mae June Hensley, and Sister Lydia Surgener were all in attendance. There was preaching, several hours of singing, and praying over those in need along with anointing with oil. When it came time for sacrament, about an hour before midnight, a small table was set up before the pulpit. The pulpit itself had on the front of it a velvet tapestry of Da Vinci's "Last Supper." A white linen cloth covered the table. Matzos were used for the bread and grape juice for the wine. Two chairs were set up on either side of the table. The lay preacher read at length from each New Testament account of Jesus' Last Supper with his disciples, including John 13, where Jesus girds himself with a towel to wash his disciples' feet. At the conclusion of the readings Brother Coy offered a prayer and then invited first the women to come two-by-two to seat themselves at the table where they would be served the elements. Each person who came up to be seated was prayed over and then served. The occasion was very solemn and electric with spiritual energy. Muffled tears, occasional quiet ejaculations, spontaneous prayers all accompanied the serving of the elements during the "sacrament meeting." The vestiges of the Scots-Irish sacramental meeting were writ large in the occasion. The emotionally charged piety and intense solemnity, the spontaneity of the service despite its traditionalism, the table draped in white linen, the communicants seated at the table to receive the elements, the slow, dignified, unhurried pace of the service where there was plenty of room for emotional expression all typified a lineage steeped in religious history in the Appalachian region.

As Howard Dorgan observed in his study of Old Regular Baptists, emotional exuberance—shouts and loud cries—was reserved for the footwashing part of the service in this tiny independent holiness church. A curtain was stretched across the room to separate the women from the men. Basins and towels were distributed. The intensity of love and compassion was almost unbearable for many who were present. Each who had partaken of the communion elements—for not all did so—washed feet and had their feet washed. Sister Hassie Miser, spouse of Brother Coy Miser, was so moved that she cried and prayed out loud through most of the footwashing on the women's side of the curtain. On the men's side the sound was like the rhythmic breaking of a wave on an ocean shoreline. As each man had his feet washed, the men would cry out praying and singing and exclaiming as a group. The intensity of the sounds would rise and fall. At the conclusion of the footwashing, Brother Coy smiled and said, "We had a wonderful time."

Sacramental revivals for the Scots-Irish were a combination of conversionist preaching and eucharistic practice. Their long history set a pattern in Scots-Irish religious consciousness so that when the Presbyterian sacramental season, and Presbyterianism itself, had been overtaken by other revivalist traditions in the Appalachian region, especially those of the revival Baptists, their sacramental consciousness was transferred from the celebration of the Lord's Supper to other practices—namely footwashing and baptism—producing the same ritual patterns and results in the experience of personal and communal conversion. The memory of the powerful sacramental seasons of the Scots-Irish persisted in mountain religious life, its memory enshrined in the myriad of reproductions of Leonardo da Vinci's "Last Supper" in mountain churches and homes. The "Last Supper" is a portrait of a divinely instituted common meal, with participants seated at a table and the bread and wine distributed among them, that had been at the heart of the Scottish sacramental occasion and distinguishing it from the communions of 17th-century Anglicans and Independents, as it had in the late 16th century from the Catholic mass.

In the new sacramental occasions in mountain religious life, just as it had in the early Scots-Irish sacramental meetings or communion seasons themselves, community is revived by the "complementary process" of the conviction of all the participants, followed by the salvation of sinners and the confirmation or renewal of the saints. Just as with the sacramental meetings, the new sacramentalism of the mountains was never aimed at the unconverted only, but was meant to restore and revive the whole community, with the saved renewing their experience of conversion so that they could be strengthened time and again throughout their earthly pilgrimage. For Scots-Irish Presbyterians, salvation and the sacrament, conversion and communion, were inseparable. Although not the original sacramental revivalism of the Scots-Irish, centered as it was on conversionist preaching and the Lord's Supper, mountain religious life has its own sacramental revivalism today. Appalachian sacramental revivalism is centered on conversionist preaching and a collection of ritual practices in mountain worship life, culminating in particular in the public rite of baptism, that break through social distance and confirm community.

During the Baptist revival in colonial Virginia in the late 18th century, many of the worship practices of revival Baptists became normative for the worship services in the church houses making up mountain religious life—baptism, the Lord's Supper, footwashing, the holy kiss, the love feast (testifying what God's grace has meant in your life), dedicating infants, the right hand of fellowship, laying on of hands, anointing the sick. The great public ceremonies—large revival meetings—were transformative: people exchanged their place from the old status order to the new status order, one which emphasized individual equality, where status had to do not with levels of prestige, but with what Max Weber called "styles of life" or lifestyle. If large public revival meetings were transformative, the revival "ceremonies" that occurred within the privacy of church houses were confirmative: spontaneous action is built into revival ceremonies, spontaneous action that emphasizes the autonomy of the individual within the worshiping community. This is a hallmark of mountain religious life throughout its history. Emphasizing the autonomy of the individual within the worshiping community made the individual the principal cultural category. This emphasis on the individual person underscores the worshiping community's concern for individual needs and circumstances, and is the avenue of interpretation by which mountain religious life is perhaps best understood.

If the individual is the principal cultural category, grace is the principal theological focus of mountain religious life. But mountain preachers preach little about grace. Grace is bound up in religious experience and the movement of the Holy Spirit. Instead, the most significant and telling recurrent theme in mountain preaching, from Old Regular Baptists to independent holiness, is that of the broken heart, tenderness of heart, a heart not hardened to the Spirit and the Word of God. Brother Coy Miser says of the holiness people he knows and ministers to, "These are humble people," and their humility resides most of all in their tender-heartedness. Mountain people teach that the image of God in each person lives in the heart, that the Holy Spirit takes up residence in the heart, that the Word of God lodges itself in the heart, and the heart is meant to guide the head, not the other way around. "God speaks to the heart. The Devil speaks to the head," says Brother Coy. For this reason, mountain people with strong religious sensibilities, women and men, tend to be highly intuitive people, listening first to what their hearts speak and trusting what they hear. Hardness of heart—manifested in unkind, selfish, insensitive words and deeds—is the greatest grief one Christian can cause another. It is also the clearest indication that what people do and say, no matter what faith statements they profess with their lips, is not in line with the Word of God, since the Holy Spirit speaks first to the heart of believers whose greatest duty is to humble their will and pride to the gentle nudgings they feel in their hearts and the very quiet voice they hear within. It is not lost on mountain people that the Bible cautions time and again against hardness of heart. They dip deep into the well of prayer to keep their hearts alive and tender.

Rich in historical precedents, the basic ethos of mountain religion is straightforward: Appalachian mountain religion is very much a religion of the heart, and of heart-felt expressions. An oral religious tradition, mountain religion provides little in the way of written documentation apart from preaching, singing, and praying, and apart from the material culture of religious life in the Appalachian region.

Until the late 1980s, most of the material on Appalachian mountain religion was written by home missionaries and social scientists. Social scientists in particular have promoted a subculture of poverty model for understanding religious life and traditions in the Appalachian region. Moreover, social scientists have interpreted Appalachian religious traditions in terms of "alienation," compensation for deprivation, and church-sect typology. Some Appalachians regional scholars in the social sciences have countered this approach by saying that mountain religion is a form of cultural resistance to industrial exploitation. The limitation inherent in both of these approaches is that they fail to see and interpret mountain religious life and history *as religion*. Instead, they see mountain religion as a subunit of a larger social system. A religious studies perspective such as Catherine Albanese's places emphasis first on religious belief systems, and factors in the historical, social, and geographic data that inform religious belief systems themselves. As a religion of the heart, mountain religion is not suited to an objectivistic approach. There is much that remains to be explored in this "invisible" regional religious tradition that has contributed so much to American religious history and the history of the Appalachian region. Only those students, researchers, and scholars who do not fear to be touched deep inside, and probably transformed by what they seek to understand and share with others, are best suited to approach this wide-open field.

44. TRADITIONALISM, ANTIMISSIONISM, AND THE PRIMITIVE[1] BAPTIST RELIGION: A PRELIMINARY ANALYSIS

Melanie L. Sovine

Introduction

Traditionalism has been a powerful theme in the study of Appalachia, and the mythical image of a traditional Appalachian subculture has been a historically pervasive and persuasive interpretive image of the Appalachian region. Few, if any, social behaviors in the region have escaped the descriptive label of "traditional," including religion. In particularly simplistic

ways, religion and culture have been treated as one and the same, and whatever was descriptive of "Appalachian culture" was considered descriptive of "Appalachian religion."[2] The romantic mythology of an Appalachian subculture became a selective mechanism

Reprinted from *Reshaping the Images of Appalachia,* Loyal Jones (ed.), The Berea College Appalachian Center, 1986, pp. 32–44. Used by permission.

for the identification of regionally representative religious groups, and consequently, certain groups were erroneously designated as the embodiment of a mythical Appalachian traditionalism. For example when Appalachia was seen as a traditional subculture, the "Old Baptists" groups, including the Primitive Baptists, were cited as the finest example of religious traditionalism in Appalachia.[3] The traditionalism of the "Old Baptists," then, was assumingly related to the traditionalism of Appalachia, an assumption based on ethnographic and historical accuracies for neither the "Old Baptists" nor Appalachia. Consequently, revisions in the study of the Primitive Baptist Church are not unlike those in the study of culture in Appalachia, and both the Primitive Baptists and Appalachia are in want of a more authentic ethnography and history.[4]

Examining the available histories and ethnographies, the misrepresentations associated with the Primitive Baptists and Appalachia are remarkably similar and, in fact, are not unrelated. Both have been treated as historical oddities, their anomalous positions in the chronicles of American historical development carefully maintained for the benefit of others. Regional characteristics are attributed to both, and the use of regionalism as an explanatory context is employed in similarly pejorative and restrictive ways. People generally wonder why the Primitive Baptists and Appalachians continue to exist as they do, suggesting they are just peculiar, or that both were isolated and are now anachronisms. Or worse, both are dismissed as regressive in their thinking and behaving. Because of poor insight, misunderstanding, or extreme prejudice on the part of those who felt compelled to write about Appalachians or the Primitive Baptists, addressing the history of either entails a process of separating ethnographic and historical accuracies from years of accumulated scholarly error and mythology. Regional scholars and activists are contributing significantly to the revision of Appalachian history, and this paper represents a continuation of the same for the history of the Primitive Baptist Church. In challenging the errors and mythologies associated with this group, a new history will begin to take shape, one admittedly preliminary and descriptive. As with the study of Appalachia, a more authentic history of the Primitive Baptists must begin by dispelling the myths of traditionalism.

The Romance of Traditionalism

The Primitive Baptist Church is an American religious group whose membership extends across the United States, with numerical strength concentrated in the Southeast and Midwest. In the religious community, the Primitive Baptists are known for their strong Calvinistic beliefs, especially the doctrines of Predestination and Election. The Primitive Baptists are described as "very strict" in their interpretation of these two doctrines and those who feel themselves to be more moderate in theology have labeled the Primitive Baptists "hyper-Calvinists." Their so-called hyper-Calvinism is used as an explanation for why they do not proselytize for members. In support of this explanation, it is always noted that they have no Sunday schools to attract and socialize children into church members, nor missionary or religious educational systems for evangelizing, social benevolence, or ministerial training. While certain religious activities are conspicuously absent in the Primitive Baptist Church and the above description therefore correct, these absences have significance beyond theology. Further, the description defines the Primitive Baptist Church in terms of what its members do *not* do, effectively separating the Primitive Baptists from mainstream American religions. This separating definition offered by the religious community is not an arbitrary one, and its significance also extends beyond theology.[5]

They are known popularly, especially among folklorists, ethnomusicologists, and students of American culture, for their religious rituals: the practice of feetwashing, unaccompanied congregational hymn singing, a selectively compiled hymnody, a chanting preaching style utilized by the older elders, and their originally maintained church houses.[6] Again, these descriptions are correct, though problematically, this ritual behavior has come to symbolize "Old Time Religion" in America. The Primitive Baptists delicately preserve and continue to practice these rituals, and as a result a far too simple conclusion is reached about the Church's anachronistic status within the development of American religion: the Primitive Baptists are living religious history.

> A week ago I visited a little Primitive Baptist church in Hopewell, New Jersey, less than a hundred miles from New York City, where we are celebrating the glittering material advances of the age. In Hopewell they celebrated last April the 225th anniversary of the founding of their church with singing of the same folk-hymns which their forefathers brought from provincial Britain more than two centuries ago, songs which they have sung ever since. They sang these songs also in the early manner, without instrumental aid.
>
> While the Hopewell church-goers and a few other likeminded groups have been carrying on the Old-Time Religion and the Old-Time Songs, other sections of the denomination, bearing the same Baptist name, have come to make up one of the largest Protestant bodies in America. This they have accomplished by casting off piecemeal those traditions—the folk-song tradition among them—which hindered their keeping up with the times.[7]

For some, the Primitive Baptist religion is another example of romantic traditionalism in American history. They are thought of as wonderfully pristine, unchanged and unadulterated. Within this perspective the Primitive Baptist Church, and the accompanying sociocultural life consistent with this religion, is a mirror of the romantic religious past. In broad and historically leaping explanations, the history of the Primitive Baptists is reduced to a simple reflection, alienated from an immediate and contemporary setting. Their lives and religion are thought to be appropriate to life as it existed yesterday. Part of this may be attributed to the romantic infatuation with traditionalism experienced by scholars when working among the Primitive Baptists. Experiences of living in lost time, however, are never very productive in scholarship and, if historical and ethnographic accuracy is to be maintained, the romantics must be left behind to fan and sigh by the gramophone.

Rid of its romantic allure for scholars, traditionalism remains positively valued by the Primitive Baptists and a clear understanding of the place of traditionalism in their religion is essential for understanding the Primitive Baptists today. The ritualized context of traditionalism so characteristic of their religious meetings is not achieved through lost time or simple living. Rather an appreciation for things as they were, and are, is purposely cultivated.[8] Religious traditions are therefore ostensibly maintained, and their maintenance is both a historical and political question. It is a historical question in the sense that the decision to maintain an unchanged religious system of belief and behavior was made by the Primitive Baptists nearly one hundred and fifty years ago. It was a critical decision, one which helped the Primitive Baptists, during their formative years, agree upon their religious priorities. An examination of their formative years, 1800–1840, will provide a clearer understanding of the significance of this decision, and consequently, provide insight into the place of traditionalism in their religion. Moreover, their formation took shape around some of the familiar controversial sociopolitical issues of these decades, all of which were debated and resolved at a national level with national consequences. This context of national controversy gives their decision to maintain their original faith and practice a political dimension as well as a historical one. A consideration of this political dimension will place the history of the Primitive Baptist religion in a more inclusive and expansive interpretive context. Their history is integral to the whole of American history and they are neither theological anomalies nor Appalachian curiosities.

The Historical Context of Choice and Action

Historically, the Primitive Baptists chose to maintain the Baptist religious system of beliefs and behaviors operative before the addition of missionary and educational systems. The decision was made in a period of religious change and most religious Americans were adopting these changes. Missionary, educational, and benevolent societies were proliferating within and across denominations and all religious groups, including the Baptists, joined competitively in adding these societies to their regular church activities. The consequences of the Primitive Baptists' decision not to adopt these societies culminated in a Baptist denomination fully divided between opposing and nonfellowshipping factions, the "missionary Baptists" and the "antimissionary Baptists."[9] The antimissionary Baptists quickly selected to call themselves "Primitive Baptists," the name "Primitive" chosen to symbolize continuity. First and foremost, the Primitive Baptists desired to maintain a spiritual continuity with the Apostolic or Primitive Church, following that faith and practice without deviation or change.[10] Secondly, they placed a special sense of value on the history of the Primitive Baptist Church, promoting a cultural continuity with past members of the Church and agreeing to preserve deliberately the much-loved cultural traditions of their forefathers.[11] In the face of imposed changes upon their religious system, spiritual and cultural continuity, which are today labeled "traditionalism," became of primary concern for the Primitive Baptists. Focusing on the importance of continuity and not the importance of change, they separated from those adopting the changes. "Traditionalism" was a matter of choice for the anti-missionary Baptists. It is a matter of choice today for the Primitive Baptists, and a keen watch is kept by the members for the maintenance of spiritual and cultural continuity in the practice of their religion. Thus we see that the Primitive Baptist religion remained unchanged not because of an unchanging time and place, but because they chose to emphasize spiritual and cultural continuity in their religion. The histories of the Primitive Baptists do not describe a context of choice, nor do they attribute a sense of integrity on the part of the Primitive Baptists in placing a value on continuity. Without this historical context of choice, there is a failure to see the Primitive Baptists as conscionable actors within their own history. Consequently, in the more recent histories and ethnographies, they are easily depicted as passively existing within their daily lives, this passive portrayal keeping the interpretations of their religion consistent with the mythologies of traditionalism.

Returning to the comparison of Appalachia with the Primitive Baptists, the role of the image of passivity and ignorance on the part of native Appalachians is now clearly understood for its economic benefits to industrialists and capitalists in the region. The image justified the imposition of sociocultural changes (industrialization) upon Appalachia by absentee owners and outside developers.[12] Similarly, we need a clear understanding of why denominational leaders and historians were successful in erroneously attributing passivity and ignorance to the Primitive Baptists. Part of this success has to do with American history, itself, as a discipline and profession. Until recently, history has been in the service of the elite, lending integrity only to the economically and politically powerful. Telling an attenuated story, most histories do not recount the complexity and diversity of daily life in America, especially the histories of many who believed in ideologies and maintained perspectives differing from those of mainstream America. In the case of alternative groups who could not be ignored, histories were often used as political tools in shaping and perpetuating pejorative or historically nullifying images of these groups.

The images functioned to preserve the integrity of the elite. Further, American history has long recorded the rise and fall of dominant political parties, the tactics of battle and the outcome of war, and described long-passing and forever on-coming eras. There are no people in these histories and therefore life, as the people lived it, does not emerge from them. Writings in American religious history, focused on denominational campaigns and the religiously elite leadership, are consistent with writings in American history, in general. It is easy to recognize an unwillingness on the part of denominational historians to accurately and legitimately address alternative religious groups with belief systems contrasting to the dominant American religious worldview. In the case of Primitive Baptist history, the denominational historians successfully stereotyped their members and streamlined their history, obscuring the sociopolitical context within which the controversies associated with missionary and educational enterprises occurred, and against which the Baptist denominational division took place. Images of the Primitive Baptists being swept along passively and without thought by a few reactionary and ignorant leaders played an important role in clouding this sociopolitical context.[13] It is therefore necessary to re-examine the history of the denominational division, highlighting the political aspects associated with the formation of the Primitive Baptist Church, and documenting the political sophistication that forbade them an authentic place in American history.

The Denominational Historical Legacy

The decades of 1800–1840 were years of transition for the Baptists. During this period they changed from a loosely fellowshipping group of zealous Separatists to a politically active, nationally visible, and tightly articulated American denomination.[14] This change was achieved through the design, implementation, and successful management of organizational structures integrating an otherwise diverse membership, and by investing this membership in national efforts to promote Christian missions and education. The motivation behind the successful completion of this change, if not altogether political, certainly was politically consequential. The Baptists leaders hoped to achieve denominational prominence, assuming a position alongside the major American denominations. This positioning carried with it a potential for political brokering and a possible role in deciding the outcome of American national issues. From a religious perspective, the Baptist denominational objective was to affect the course of politics in the interest of maintaining a Christian moral order that would continue to permeate the whole of American society. This was neither an original nor an untested objective.[15] Actually, the Baptists were imitating other major denominations, such as the Presbyterians and Congregationalists, in designing and implementing highly articulated organizational structures to maintain a Christian moral order and to access the political arenas in which the successful maintenance of this order could be assured. From 1800–1840, the American people and the American government bore a decidedly religious and moral character, the whole of America was ostensibly "Christian."[16] Drawing impetus from the fundamentalist revivalism of the Great Awakening,[17] moral concern was a primary focus.[18] A religious sentiment affected all aspects of national life and in turn, gave shape to mainstream America's ideas on progress and reform.[19] Denominational and political leaders cooperated in maintaining a Christian nation, and as allies conceptualized and implemented the programs of national progress and moral reform. Underneath the moral and progressive rhetoric, however, was a desire to establish and maintain control of a certain American social order with recognizable economic, political, and moral characteristics and consequences.[20] Problematically, there were large populations of people who held views inconsistent with this American social order, and for whom its vision of Protestant equality and democracy did not ring true. Refusing to accept the truly pluralistic makeup of American society, these populations were described one by one as being in need of reform, the essence of which was an Americanization of culturally and socially variable people.[21] Simplistically, these people were viewed singularly as living within social environments preventing them from a successful and complete integration into mainstream American society. Focusing on a need to disrupt or completely alter these social environments, political and religious discussions of the day were centered around the concepts of removal, colonization, and civilization through the implementation of agricultural or industrial changes.[22] These discussions resulted in full-scale social programs empowered by the federal and state governments cooperatively with major American denominations, conceptualized and organized by their respective representatives, and implemented and supported at local levels by the majority of American people. Taken as a whole, these programs and the ideology associated with them are known as American Benevolence, a social movement of national expanse that unleashed a storm of collective reformer energy upon Native American Indians, Afro-American Blacks, and ultimately Appalachian American Whites.[23]

The strength of the concept of benevolence in American Protestantism and Politics had been developing for some time, and the Baptists were actually late in coming to this idea, though to be sure, their denominational leaders seized upon it and recreated the organizational structures within the Baptist denomination necessary to achieve denominational prominence. These structures were the now familiar national and state level religious conventions and boards. They were corporate-like in their design, coalescing in their power, and controlled by denominationally prominent men. Their agenda was the successful promotion of an extensive public campaign for ideologic and economic support of missionary and educational efforts, the mechanisms of American Benevolence.[24] Initially the Baptist membership was reluctant in supporting these efforts, though eventually they swelled fanatically behind the cause of missionary and educational systems, and in so doing, joined the memberships of other major denominations in a driving support of American Benevolence.

Baptist denominational leaders rapidly and successfully formed alliances with other denominational and political leaders by demonstrating their ability to organize and implement large-scale campaigns among an extensive and diverse membership. While most of the local Baptist members felt themselves to be accumulating believers of Baptist theology and simultaneously affecting moral and social uplift, these campaigns extended beyond a simple reading lesson for the nonliterate and a conversion experience for the unregenerate. Missionary and educational efforts were intertwined with political events, and the whole of American Benevolence smacked of elitist social control.[25]

A sense of mistrust grew up around this well-oiled system of American Benevolence. The source of this mistrust had to do with the obvious similarities of denominational organizations to social and political organizations. Moreover, the leadership within these organizations appeared to be overlapping and concentrated among a few. From 1910 through 1840, there were strong voices of opposition that developed as a result of this general sense of mistrust. These voices, through periodicals, newspapers, pamphlets, and public speaking documented the coalescing of religious, social, and political efforts around the national issues of Removal, Colonization, and Civilization.[26] The political character and motives of these coalescing leaders were accurately described and the benevolent cloak shrouding their political goals was made clear. The participants who were eager to establish a selectively

defined American social order were shrewdly pinpointed, and the mechanisms through which these participants intended to maintain control over this social order were identified. People began to question the extent to which the monies accumulated to support missionary and educational efforts were actually supporting selective political efforts. Further, the authenticity of the spiritual motivation behind missionary and educational efforts was questioned. The opposers correctly exposed both the political consequences of these efforts for those who were the recipients of reform, and the political benefits for those who achieved the goals of reform. Collectively, this period of opposition is known as the Antimissionary Movement, a social movement also of national expanse opposing the achievement of social and political ends in the name of "American Benevolence."[2;7]

The opposers within the Baptist denomination, as previously indicated, were the "antimissionary Baptists." Ostensibly and with great deliberation, the antimissionary Baptists chose not to be absorbed, as were other Baptists, into the political-denominational alliances and thoughtfully made the decision not to support American Benevolence. This decision separated the antimissionary Baptists from the mainstream of American religion. In refusing to participate in Christian missions and education, they were rejecting this central-most idea in the dominant American worldview. While Baptist denominational division certainly resulted from this decision, the Primitive Baptists were actually withdrawing their religious fellowship from all denominations supporting the enterprising systems of American Benevolence.[28] In the process of separation and formation, the Primitive Baptists examined their religion and agreed upon selective priorities that remain critical characteristics of their religious belief system today.[29] Setting aside the idea of redesigning and reorganizing the affiliation of one church with another, the Primitive Baptists protected, in an absolute way, the long-held Baptist belief in the autonomy of individual churches. Repudiating a consistency with American political and economic ideologies, and refusing to take advantage of alignments with American political or social societies, they agreed to remain consistent only with the Apostolic Church. They gave priority to continuity rather than accept imposed religious changes and purposely declined to "progress" with other American denominations through these changes. A standard of humility was emphasized, rather than individual merit and achievement or denominational hierarchy and power. Theologically, they highlighted the doctrines of grace in determining the eternal condition of their souls, and declined to accept the relationship of great eternal rewards for great religious efforts on Earth. Persisting in grace and humility, the Primitive Baptists would never compete with the overpowering version of American Protestantism that emerged from these decades of reform and moral concern.

Even while the Primitive Baptists did not desire to compete successfully with American Protestantism, Baptist denominational leaders of the day worked to diminish the very existence of the Primitive Baptists. They behaved publicly as if shocked by an opposition on the part of some of their members to benevolence, shaking their heads as if bewildered. In reality, the denominational leaders were angered by their inability to control these members, and by their ineffectiveness at investing all Baptists in Christian missions and education. Further, they were taken off guard and threatened by the clarity with which the opposers saw through the economic and political motivations of missionary and educational enterprises. Embarrassed in front of their nationally prominent friends, the Baptists ridiculed and pejoratively stereotyped their antimissionary members. They attempted to contain the antimissionary influence among the people by accusing them of espousing an aberrant Calvinistic theology. Their leaders were portrayed as unlettered men who agitated the people into following their ignorant and uninformed scriptural interpretations. These interpretations were given the name "Hardshellism." While attempting to quell the opposition in the face of deleterious effects on the missionary and educational campaign, the Baptists spoke of "breaking the old Hard Shell's back." When the back withstood the rod, the Baptists engaged in loud predictions as to the early and certain extinction of this opposing group.[30] Defying these predictions, the Antimissionary Baptists could not be ignored and the mainline Baptists, in puffed-up tones, began to congratulate themselves for having rid the denomination of the opposing membership.

> So long as those who through selfishness or through a paralyzing type of theology were retained in the bosom of the churches and associations, any forward movement was difficult. When the denomination began to move forward the reactionary began to crystallize and fall out. Our fathers of three-quarters of a century ago were enabled to undertake their divinely given task because the antimissionism was cast off.[31]

Ironically, a diminishment was accomplished as a result of including the Primitive Baptists in Baptist denominational histories. Reviewing them, it is interesting to note the absence of material relating to politically expedient alliances, particularly in reference to the Antimissionary Movement. Through this absence the sociopolitical context of the schism within and beyond the boundaries of the Baptist denomination is unclear and a large social movement is reduced to a denominational schism. On the contrary, men and women across the country found themselves in opposition to American Benevolence long before the Primitive Baptists formed into a separate religious group.

Most of the opposers did not become members of the Primitive Baptist Church and the years of controversy were peopled well beyond the confines of the Baptist denomination. The treatment, however, of the missionary-antimissionary schism by Baptist historians as a somewhat embarrassing in-house event served to obscure its relevance to the controversies associated with American Benevolence, as well as to obscure the role of Baptist denominational leaders in directing the outcome of these issues.[32] Denominational historians imposed a restrictive interpretative boundary around Antimissionism, thereby restricting the interpretations of Primitive Baptist history. There is no mention of Antimissionism as a broadly based, sophisticated, and articulate social movement in America, working to expose the exploitations of American Benevolence. Consequently, any mention of the Primitive Baptists is within the Baptist denominational context. In addressing the Primitive Baptists, the denominational legacy records only an unexpected and unfortunate problem with Hardshellism, a problem the denomination portrays itself as having overpowered, progressing into prominence as if never having experienced opposition. The effects of this denominational legacy were historically deadening. Even the more recent histories of the Primitive Baptist Church continue to interpret their formation within a theological-denominational context,[33] perpetuating a popular image of the Primitive Baptists as the unenlightened, uneducated, and unsophisticated men and women who would not, indeed because of their lower social status could not, progress with other Baptists to a position among the powerful and competitive American denominations.[34] This image of the Primitive Baptists is reminiscent of the image of Appalachians as too ignorant, passive, and poor to progress on their own to a productive integration into mainstream American society.[35] Considering the similarity of these images, it is important to observe that the Primitive Baptists were opposers of American Benevolence and Appalachia an object of American Benevolence.[36] Further, denominationally affiliated men and women, supporters of American Benevolence, perpetuated the image of passivity and unprogressiveness as a stereotype for both.[37] The traits of passivity and unprogressiveness were collapsed into the category of traditionalism, and traditionalism became an encompassing description imposed upon Appalachians and the Primitive Baptists with an obliviousness to ethnographic and historical detail. This obliviousness, in part, accounts for the confused relationship of traditionalism in Appalachia with that in the Primitive Baptist Church. As a further consideration, recall that the vision of "Progress" held by mainstream Americans developed during the early decades of reform, 1800–1840, and that by 1850, the programs of progressive reform were well underway. "Progress" was an idea employed uncritically as a motivation for moving people, forcibly if necessary, along an imagined continuum of traditionalism to modernism and finally to post-modernism. In the process of making the vision of progress a reality, the histories of some Americans were abolished or adulterated so as to make them consistent with a prescribed version of American history. The ethnographic and historical details authentic to recalcitrant populations were obliterated in the process of labeling them all "traditional," simultaneously pulling these populations into the reformers' ideological continuum of Progress, and justifying programmatic changes imposed upon them to affect their Americanization. Having identified the opposer-object relationship of the Primitive Baptists and Appalachia makes more intelligible the sweeping projection of mythical traditionalism upon both of them. Politically and persuasively describing them both as passively and ignorantly living in the past subsumed the Primitive Baptists and all of Appalachia within the rhetoric of American Benevolence and within the reaches of American Reformers.

Having arrived at the so-called stage of post-modernism, we are in the posture of cleaning up the wrecks of this progressive course of time and, simultaneously, involved in recapturing much of the color and shape of American life that remains understated and underwritten. Recapturing a more authentic history brings us to the point at which this essay began, emphasizing the importance of maintaining ethnographic and historical accuracy and critically challenging the errors and mythologies of scholarship, itself. In writing a more authentic history for Appalachia or the Primitive Baptists, we must also recapture a sense of the ongoing, of choice and action in daily life,[39] lending integrity and strength to the course of seemingly common lives who were active participants in the whole of American historical development.

NOTES

1. This paper is based on research supported by two fellowships: an Appalachian Studies Fellowship, administered by Berea College and made possible by a grant from the Andrew W. Mellon Foundation, and an NEH Post-doctoral Fellowship, administered by the American Antiquarian Society and made possible by a grant from the National Endowment for the Humanities. I would like to express my gratitude to Elizabeth M. Rowe for editorial comments and to Donna Cammers for the many typed versions of this manuscript. Mistakes and errors of interpretations are my own.

2. Melanie Sovine, "On the Study of Religion in Appalachia: A Review/Essay," *Appalachian Journal* 6 (Spring 1979): 239–244.

3. John C. Campbell, *The Southern Highlander and His Homeland,* 2nd Ed. (Lexington, Kentucky: The University Press of Kentucky, 1969), pp. 176–194.

4. David S. Walls and Dwight B. Billings, "The Sociology of Southern Appalachia," *Appalachian Journal* 5 (Autumn, 1977): 131–144, and Ronald D. Eller, "Toward a New History of the Appalachian South," *Appalachian Journal* 5 (Autumn, 1977): 74–81.

5. Arthur Carl Piepkorn, "The Primitive Baptists of North America," *Concordia Theological Monthly* 42 (May, 1971): 297–314. This article remains the single best concise historical and descriptive summary of the Primitive Baptists.

6. Representative articles include Brett Sutton, "In the Good Old Way: Primitive Baptist Traditions," *Southern Exposure* V (Summer-Fall, 1977): 97–104; Melanie Sovine Reid, "Religious Ritual in an Absolute Predestinarian Primitive Baptist Church," *Appalachian Heritage* 8 (Winter, 1980): 58–64; William H. Tallmadge, "Baptist Monophonic and Heterophonic Hymnology in Southern Appalachia," *Yearbook For Inter-American Musical Research,* XI (1975): 106–136.

7. George Pullen Jackson, "Some Enemies of Folk-Music in America," *Papers Read at the International Congress of Musicology, New York, September 11–16, 1939* (NY: Music Educators' National Conference for the American Musicological Society, 1944), p. 83.

8. Melanie Sovine Reid, ' "Neither Adding nor Taking Away": The Care and Keeping of Primitive Baptist Church Houses,' in Camille Wells, ed., *The Proceedings of the Vernacular Architectural Forum, 1980 and 1981* (Annapolis, MD: The Vernacular Architectural Forum, 1982).

9. William Warren Sweet, "The Rise of the Anti-Mission Baptists: A Frontier Phenomenon," *Religion on the American Frontier: The Baptists* (NY: Holt and Co., 1931): 62–66. Sweet provides an adequate description of the Baptist denominational division through his interpretation of "Frontierism" is erroneous.

10. Cf., W. J. Berry, *Tracing the True Worship of God* (Elon College, NC: Primitive Publications, 1971).

11. Melanie Sovine, ' "A Sweet Hope in my Breast": Belief and Ritual in the Primitive Baptist Church,' Unpublished M. A. thesis, Department of Anthropology, University of Georgia, Athens, GA, 1978.

12. John Gaventa, "Property, Coal, and Theft," in Helen Lewis, et. al., eds., *Colonialism in Modern America: The Appalachian Case* (Boone, NC: The Appalachian Consortium Press, 1978): 141–159.

13. Sweet, Op. cit., gives a cursory description of the three Baptist leaders generally associated with antimissionism, pp. 62–72.

14. For an excellent reflection by a Baptist on the changes in the Baptist denomination see David Benedict, *Fifty Years Among the Baptists* (NY: Sheldon and Co., 1860).

15. Christian benevolence, implemented through denominationally supported missionary and educational enterprises both in foreign and domestic areas, was introduced to the Baptists by Adoniram Judson and Luther Rice, two Congregationalist missionaries who converted to the belief in baptism by immersion, announcing to the world they were dependent upon support of the Baptist denomination. Baptist denominational leaders rallied behind them, completely reorganizing the denomination to undergird the ideologies of Judson and Rice. Cf., Joan Jacobs Brumberg, *Mission for Life* (NY: The Free Press, 1980): pp. 1–3.

16. Martin E. Marty, *Religious Empire: The Protestant Experience in America* (NY: Dial Press, 1970) and Robert T. Handy, "The Protestant Quest for a Christian America," *Church History* 22 (March, 1953): 8–20.

17. William Warren Sweet, *Religion in Colonial America* (NY: Charles Scribners Sons, 1947).

18. Ralph Henry Gabriel, *The Course of American Democratic Thought: An Intellectual History Since 1815* (NY: Ronald Press, 1940): 26–38.

19. Francis Paul Prucha, "Federal Indian Policy in United States History" in Prucha, ed., *Indian Policy in the United States: Historical Essays* (Lincoln: University of Nebraska Press, 1981): 20–35.

20. Brumberg refers to this American social order as "evangelical-cultural forms [that] were diffused far beyond the confines of those churches commonly considered evangelical, embracing all of American Protestantism." She continues, "While evangelical religious practices remained distasteful to some, it was hard to contain the cultural implications of the evangelical movement." Op. cit., p. 19.

21. Francis Paul Prucha, *American Indian Policy in the Formative Years* (Lincoln: University of Nebraska Press, 1970): "Preface."

22. Cf. Warner T. Wickstrom, "The American Colonization Society and Liberia: An Historical Study in Religious Motivation and Achievement, 1817–1867," Unpublished doctoral dissertation, Hartford Seminary, Hartford, CT, 1958; Francis Paul Prucha, Op. cit., Chapter IX: "Civilization and Removal," pp. 213–249; and, Grant Foreman, *Indian Removal: The Emigration of the Five Civilized Tribes of Indians* (Norman, OK: University of Oklahoma Press, 1932.)

23. James C. Klotter, "The Black South and White Appalachia," *Journal of American History* 66 (1980): 832–849.

24. Cf. I. M. Allen, *The Triennial Baptist Register* (Philadelphia: Baptist General Tract Society, 1836).

25. Clifford S. Green, "Religious Benevolence as Social Control, 1815–1860," *Mississippi Valley Historical Review* XLIV (1957): 423–444.

26. Gaylord Albaugh, "Bibliography of Religious Periodicals 1730–1830," Unpublished manuscript, Library of the American Antiquarian Society, 1944.

27. Bertram Wyatt-Brown, "The Antimission Movement in the Jacksonian South: A Study in Regional Folk Culture," *Journal of Southern History* 36 (1970): 501–529. This is the single best historical description of the Anti-missionary Movement though the interpretations associated with a folk culture and southern regionalism are in error.

28. W. J. Berry, comp. *The Kehukee Declaration and Black Rock Address with Other Writings Relative to the Baptist Separation between 1825–1840* (Elon College, NC: Primitive Publications, n.d.).

29. Melanie L. Sovine, "Studying Religious Belief Systems in Their Social Historical Context," in Allen Batteau, ed., *Appalachia and America* (Lexington, KY: The University Press of Kentucky): especially pp. 51–63.

30. "He [David Benedict] also wrote another history of the denomination, which was published in one volume, in 1848. This was subsequent to the Division; and he then being a "Missionary," advocating all the new schemes of the day, took decided ground against the Primitive Baptists, treated them quite unceremoniously, and declared they were so few and worthless that they would likely become extinct before his book reached his more distant subscribers." Elder Sylvester Hassell, *History of the Church of God* (Reprint by Old School Hymnal Co., Inc. 1973), p. 751.

31. W. W. Barnes, "Who Are The Primitive Baptists, Part II," *Southwestern Journal of Theology* 1 (1917), p. 64.

32. Prucha, Op. cit., cites the Baptist denomination as "memorialists" for the congressional bill requesting forced removal of the Southeastern Indians.

33. Keith R. Burich, "The Primitive Baptist Schism in North Carolina: A Study of the Professionalization of the Baptist Ministry," Unpublished M.A. thesis, The University of North Carolina, Chapel Hill, NC, 1973. This dissertation reviews the historiography of the Primitive Baptist religion, finding pejorative interpretations throughout based largely on the church-sect typology, casting the Primitives erroneously among the less educated, culturally isolated, and lower classes.

34. Cf. Richard Hofstader, *Anti-Intellectualism in American Life* (NY: Alfred Knopf, 1963); T. Scott Miyakawa, *Protestants and Pioneers* (Chicago: University of Chicago Press, 1964); Graylord P. Albaugh, "Antimissionary Movement in the United States," in Vergilius Ferm, ed., *An Encyclopedia of Religion* (NY: Philosophical Library, 1945): 27–28; and Bertram Wyatt-Brown, Op. cit.

35. Jack E. Weller, *Yesterday's People: Life in Contemporary Appalachia* (Lexington: Kentucky Paperbacks, University of Kentucky Press, 1966).

36. Henry D. Shapiro, *Appalachia on Our Mind* (Chapel Hill, NC: The University of North Carolina Press, 978): 133–136.

37. Ibid., pp. 32–58.

38. The following citations address the use of images in Appalachian studies. Melanie L. Sovine, "The Mysterious Melungeons: A Critique of the Mythical Image," Unpublished doctoral dissertation, Department of Anthropology, The University of Kentucky, Lexington, KY, 1982; Ronald D. Eller, "Industrialization and Social Change in Appalachia, 1880–1930: A Look at the Static Image," in Helen M. Lewis, et al., eds., *Colonialism in Modern America: The Appalachian Case* (Boone, NC: The Appalachian Consortium Press, 1978): 35–46; Walter Precourt, "The Images of Appalachian Poverty," in Allen Batteau, ed., *Appalachia and America* (Lexington, KY: The University Press of Kentucky, 1983): 86–110; and, Bob Snyder, "Image and Identity in Appalachia," *Appalachian Journal* 9 (Winter–Spring, 1982): 124–133.

39. Sherry B. Ortner, "Theory in Anthropology since the Sixties," *Comparative Studies in Society and History* 26 (January, 1984): 126–166.

45. HOLINESS PEOPLE

Yvonne Snyder Farley

In most ways the Besoco Church of Jesus in Raleigh County resembles hundreds of other pentecostal and holiness churches scattered across West Virginia. Worship is emotional, with lively music and enthusiastic participation by members. As in many fundamentalist churches, the practices of footwashing and baptism by total immersion are observed. But the Besoco congregation has one belief—that in "taking up serpents," as they understand the Bible to command them to do—which sets them apart. For this belief, church members have suffered the ridicule and morbid curiosity of outsiders. They generally feel that press coverage of serpent-handling religion has been unnecessarily sensationalized, but they agreed to a recent visit by Yvonne Snyder Farley, formerly a religion reporter for a Beckley newspaper. No snakes were present at the service Farley attended, but she did interview members extensively about their beliefs and experiences. Her sensitive report follows.

GOLDENSEAL does not endorse any form of worship over any other, but believes that the snake-handling sects deserve attention as one part of West Virginia's varied religious heritage.

"We don't want to be anything but exactly what we are," said Brother Ray Stewart, pastor of the Church of Jesus in Besoco, Raleigh county. And by their own definition they are *holiness* people. They believe in Jesus

Reprinted from *Goldenseal*, Vol. 5, No. 2 (April–June, 1979) pp. 23–29. Used by permission.

and in holiness living. Holiness living makes for a strict life—close to the church and away from the world. "We're trying to get pure enough to see God," preached Brother Ray at a Wednesday night meeting in March of this year.

The Besoco congregation shares many beliefs and practices with other holiness churches. But while the other churches worship in peaceful obscurity, the world takes notice of the Besoco group because of one of its beliefs—serpent-handling. For church members, snake handling is but one part of a larger form of worship, practiced only at certain times of the year and then not by all worshippers. But they believe it is this practice which has singled them out for curiosity, ridicule, and even persecution by non-believers.

They've read books on serpent handling which they feel unfairly portray them as fanatics. Brother Tom Puckett, a soft-spoken church member, held up a book about serpent handling written from Tennessee. The cover, as he pointed out, was indeed sensational—the frenzied face of a snake handler, a big rattlesnake, and the words "Snake Handlers" dripping down the page in voodoo-like lettering. The book's appendix featured "100 exciting photographs of serpent handling." Brother Tom also had a hardback book which he didn't think was quite as bad as the paperback.

At best they are condescendingly described as naive, misguided Appalachians; at the worst, as psychologically disturbed cultists. To themselves, they are ordinary people living a religious life.

Yet their religion leaves them free from any resentment towards those they feel exploit them. "You'll not find a cold shoulder in a holiness church," said Brother Gary Blankenship, a church member. The men and women at the Besoco church are remarkably friendly, open, and honest. They are confident and sincere in what they believe. Perhaps it is the same sincerity that leads them to follow so literally the passages from the scripture which other Christians reject.

To the dedicated believers at the Church of Jesus, they are simply carrying out the words of Jesus in St. Mark 16:17–18.

"And these signs shall follow them that believe: in my name shall they cast out devils; they shall speak with new tongues; they shall take up serpents and if they drink any deadly thing, it shall not hurt them; they shall lay hands on the sick and they shall recover."

According to Brother Ray, most fundamentalist churches take the healing sign, but very few take the Bible literally on serpent handling. "Believe me," he said, "If it didn't say it, I wouldn't do it."

They do not handle serpents to test their faith. And they don't feel they are "tempting God" as they are frequently accused of doing by other Christians. They wouldn't handle snakes, said one brother, unless they felt that the power of God was sufficient to protect them.

They feel they are protected because they take the Bible as it is written. The five signs mentioned by Jesus are "confirmation of the word."

Church members also observe the signs in faith healing and in speaking in tongues, but they do not purposefully "drink any deadly thing." Brother Ray explained that Jesus said "If"—not "shall." There's a difference, he said. He believes *if* a believer would drink poison, he would not be hurt. However, there are other churches where strychnine and other poisons are taken in the course of worship.

Brother Ray thinks many of the beliefs held by the Besoco church were once held by other fundamentalist churches which have now "fallen away." The Church of God, a large pentecostal denomination, allowed snake handling as recently as 1920, according to one source.

As in other holiness churches, women take an active role in the Raleigh County congregation. It was Sister Violet Halsey Stewart of Besoco who left the Church of God in the early 1950s and along with several other women founded what is today the Church of Jesus. She is, said her son Brother Ray, a kind of "spiritual mother" of the church. The group, which included sisters Margerie Spears, Mildred Mercer, and Erma Justice, first met in their homes.

The practice of handling serpents came to them after attending a meeting of Sister Effie Gilmore's in Pearisburg, Virginia—but no one remembers exactly when that was. The earlier history of serpent handling is, however, well known to church members. The movement was begun in 1909 by George Went Hensley, of rural Grasshopper Valley in East Tennessee. But it was in the 1940s and 1950s that the practice flourished and spread throughout the region. Practitioners suffered jailings and other persecutions for their beliefs, and laws were enacted in many states and municipalities to forbid serpent handling. In West Virginia it is legal.

Brother Ray said he would see a law forbidding the handling of serpents as the starting place for the state to interfere in religion. For him it is an issue of religious freedom. He stated without hesitation that passing a law against the practice would not stop people from handling snakes.

The Church of Jesus has 75 members. The present church building was completed in 1967. There is no name on the outside of the unpretentious grey building lodged between the mountains beside a narrow stream. A blacktop road curves in front of the church. Brother Tom Puckett explained that it's only a building. Tapping his chest, he said, "The real church is here— inside."

The Besoco serpent handlers are not poor people. The interior of their church reflects the prosperity of the membership—plush pew cushions, attractive carpeting, wood paneling, bright red drapes, an electric organ and a good sound system. The membership is a working one—with a high percentage of mine company foremen, union miners, truck drivers and other workers.

Many of the members are related to each other. Many were brought up in the church. Brother Ray said he began handling snakes at age 14 or 15 and has never "known anything else." He emphasized that at the Besoco church no one under 18 is allowed to handle the snakes, however.

No one is required to handle the snakes. In fact, it is possible to belong to the Besoco church and never do it, although most members do. The snakes are kept away from those who do not participate and one member said, "We'd never force it on anyone."

"We don't hang salvation on it," said the preacher.

The Besoco church has much in common with the other holiness churches and fellowships with churches which do not sanction snake handling. Preachers from other churches hold revivals with the Besoco church. And, for five years, the Besoco church went without any serpent handling at all.

When they do have serpents, it's in the summer and fall. The serpents they handle are mostly "mountain rattlers." Brother Ray described the snakes they use: "We believe in wild rattlers. We don't believe in handling fish worms."

Church members capture their own snakes. Two particularly plentiful areas for snake hunting are in Babcock State Park on the cliffs facing the New River in Fayette County, and at Glen Fork in Wyoming County. Brother Ray keeps the snakes locked up near his house. Some snakes are used more than once and others not—depending on their health.

No one at the Besoco church has ever died from a snake bite. Some members have never been bitten. Others have. Bucky Woolwine of Meade was bitten 20 months ago by a black timber rattler, one of the most severe bites anyone at the church has ever suffered. He recovered and is currently working in the mines.

Sister Eva Tucker, 62, was bitten a year ago by a rattler. That was a Friday night, recalled Brother Bill Spencer. By the next Monday morning Sister Eva was outside her house hanging clothes on the clothes line. The mother of 13 living children, Sister Eva has been bitten twice with 20 years between bites. Sister Mildred Mercer, one of the founding members, has never been bitten in 36 years, although once a snake did try to bite her. During one meeting, recalled Brother Ray, three members were bitten by a four-foot long rattler without any ill effects.

Brother Ray, 47, has been bitten four times. He was bitten in the temple two years ago by a rattlesnake. Bitten at 8:30 P.M. on a Saturday night, Brother Ray remembered that he came to church the next day. By Monday he had begun to recuperate. He won agreement from those sitting around him when he described the bites as painful.

The same commitment and devotion that leads them to follow understanding of God's word so faithfully pervades church life. Members of the Church of Jesus don't believe in owning television sets. According to Brother Ray, television promotes violence and fornication. They don't smoke or chew tobacco. They abstain from alcoholic beverages and from soft drinks. Some older members don't drink coffee. And they don't go to ballgames. When they are moved by God to fast, they do so. Holiness women dress modestly in long skirts or dresses. They wear no gold, nor do they cut their hair. Such asceticism is hard to maintain in the modern world, and church leaders say they lose more members because of the high standards of holiness living than they do because of serpent handling.

Members of the Besoco church don't believe in divorce, although a martial problem recently caused some legal difficulties for them. The husband of a woman member attempted to seek custody of their two children in Raleigh County circuit court last year by claiming his wife as not a fit mother because of her church membership. Church members said the father claimed that serpent handling endangered the children's lives and that the church music was loud enough to damage their ears.

The court ruled in the young mother's favor. She said she felt her ability to mother had been called into question because of her religious beliefs. And, Brother Ray fears that the court case opened up all church affairs to legal scrutiny. "We definitely take care of our children," he said. Although the adults may believe in divine healing for themselves, they take their children to doctors. Serpent handling is not permitted to the young.

Like the Baptists, the Church of Jesus believes in baptism by total immersion in water. They baptize in "the name of Jesus" because they believe that Jesus is God in three manifestations. Like many fundamentalist churches they practice foot washing. They do not take communion or the Lord's Supper because, said one member, "when the spirit is within you, you are partaking."

Dedicated to the scripture, members quoted chapter and verse from the Bible when they explained any doctrine. In testimony and preaching, their speech was full of Biblical quotations as reference.

Church members talk freely about their beliefs, discussing them at length with visitors in their homes. But like other religious people they are most content when putting their beliefs into practice in actual worship services. This happens three times weekly at Besoco, on Wednesday, Saturday, and Sunday evenings. At a recent Wednesday service, the church music was happy music. "Every time I think about Jesus, I feel good!" They repeat and sing it, clapping and moving as Brother Ray plays the organ. There is a freewill offering collected in the front of the church.

Some people, said Brother Bill Spencer of East Gulf, "live to put a boat in the water." But for him and his holiness brothers and sisters happiness is going to church. They attend the three weekly services faithfully, and there's no doubt that they rejoice in their worship.

The services move with the spirit, perhaps with singing, clapping, testifying, preaching the word, or speaking in tongues. Speaking in tongues, preaches Brother Ray, is evidence of the Holy Ghost. "A lot of people fight us on that," he said, "but when we hear tongues we have to witness that the Lord is on the inside."

In church the children may sit quietly in their seats, sing with the music, or play away from the front of the church. Some mothers cuddle small children while other adults vibrate the floors with "I'll be Alright Someday." Sister Violet may start singing the old hymn, "Just Over in Glory Land." Or there's a quiet "How Great Thou Art." The religious experience of the participants is personal and involved.

A brother speaks: "Get in the spirit. Quit sitting around. I feel the spirit. God's calling . . . I'm flyin' and I can't see . . . the spirit can see. I praise God! Get in the spirit of God. The only way is for this old man to die. . . . Get in it . . . it's here . . . it won't make you take it. . . . Pray for me, saints!"

A woman in black with long, straight dark brown hair stands and speaks without break . . . "I want to thank Jesus tonight. I praise him for the food on the table, my home, my kids, and my health." Another woman thanks God for her mother and her mother-in-law.

A younger brother in the front speaks. He tells about accidentally running over his small daughter with his truck. She wasn't injured. "It's so simple," he testifies. "It's so simple we miss it. We miss the simplicity of the Gospel trying to get into something deep."

An older sister who sits on the platform stands and begins to testify: "We're not ashamed of the gospel tonight. I praise him because he's been my doctor for many years. God has been my healer. I've suffered two serpent bites. He's healed my body. When we need him, Brother Ray, he's right at our side." Many other members testify God's healing powers in their lives.

The spirit moves another brother to speak: "People think we're crazy because we want to get excited about God! I get excited about the Word of God!" Pacing back and forth he tells how his employer threatened that if he got bitten again by a snake, he'd be fired. "God give it to me and no man can take it away!" Barely pausing, he continues to tell how he was bitten again and that he recovered. "Hallelujah! I want to get up and thank God for being here!"

"We're not some kind of religious fanatics," he testifies while moving back and forth up and down the aisle. "These signs will follow and they're going to follow the believers!"

Now Brother Ray comes to the pulpit. Discharged honorably from the army because he would "salute no man" (St. Luke 10:4) and because he refused to take medicine, Brother Ray guesses that the last time he had a pill was around 1949. A retired mine foreman with black lung disease, he was injured in a mine accident when a rock fell on him several years ago. He was taken to the hospital and X-rayed. The holiness preacher says he refused any treatment and signed himself out of the hospital—even though the doctor told him the ankle was broken. Holding up the ankle for examination, Brother Ray recounted that he was back again preaching on that same foot three weeks later. Members who refuse treatment are denied workman's compensation benefits for work time lost from their jobs.

Brother Ray is a forceful speaker. "The world knows us not, because they know him not." He tells the people that "holiness" is defined in the dictionary as "freedom from sin." And he adds, "I believe God's people can live above sin!"

He begins to preach about the world scene and tells them, "America needs healed tonight! If God don't get us back up, this nation will fall. We've got away from God!" He says there are devil worshippers in California. "Used to be a witch was put to death in this country—now we're sanctioning it!" He asks the congregation if they can call this a religious country. Hitting upon a recent incident where a male teacher was allegedly discovered in sexual activities with a 14-year-old female student, he concludes, "This is not even a religious county!"

Brother Ray believes, as do many fundamentalist Christians, that the world is coming to an end. For him "God's time clock started ticking when Israel became a nation." He predicts fearful days ahead. Drawing from prophecies in the Bible, he believes current Mideast politics signal the Apocalypse. The events of the day are pointing the way to the final battle between God and the forces of evil.

And that is why the saints of the Church of Jesus in Besoco are getting ready. That is why they are trying so hard. They believe there will be no real peace in the world until Jesus comes again. They want to go to heaven. Their understanding of signs in St. Mark assures them that they're on the right road.

Other Sources

The following books, articles, and films offer other views of the religious practice of serpent handling. The two films are available for borrowing from the West Virginia Library Commission, through local public libraries.

Karen W. Calden and Robert W. Pelton, *The Persecuted Prophets*. Cranberry, NJ: Barnes and Company, 1976.

Weston LaBarre, *They Shall Take Up Serpents.* New York: Schocken Books, 1969.

Nathan L. Gerrard, "The Serpent-Handling Religions of West Virginia," *Trans-action* (May, 1968), pp. 22–28. Fayette County snake handling, by a Morris Harvey College professor.

"Jolo Serpent Handlers," 28 minute color film. The Jolo, West Virginia, congregation.

"They Shall Take Up Serpents," 24 minute color film. Serpent handling in Boone County.

TAKING UP SERPENTS

The Besoco Church of Jesus is an independent holiness church, unique in many specifics of belief and practice. Although the church has much in common with other holiness churches and with other serpent handling sects, it would be unfair to generalize about its theology and history. Care has been taken in the accompanying article to adhere to what members describe as the beliefs of their church, and to avoid projecting upon them doctrines which may be found in other churches. Nor would it be fair to project the beliefs and practices of the Besoco congregation upon other holiness churches—certainly few others practice serpent handling, for example.

Despite variation from church to church, however, there does appear to be a common thread of doctrines uniting a large number of holiness churches. Many have sprung from Methodist or Baptist backgrounds, and their staunch congregationalism is perhaps partly a rejection of the more structured organization of those mainstream churches. Certainly, most holiness churches work independently of any denominational organization, and a great variety of names is evident.

The holiness churches are primarily concerned with attaining perfection and holiness itself. Most of them believe in the trinity, original sin, salvation through Christ, the infallibility and divine nature of the scriptures, and the blessings of the Holy Spirit, including divine healing and speaking in tongues. Most are premillenarians, believing that the visible return of Christ will precede his reign of a thousand years on earth. There are usually two sacraments in the church—holy communion, or the Lord's Supper as it is commonly called, and baptism by immersion. Footwashing is a common practice.

The emphasis on direct action of the Holy Spirit and the believers' personal interaction with the Spirit are at the heart of the holiness religion. In the New Testament, after Christ has returned to Heaven, the Holy Spirit descended upon the apostles like a "mighty rushing wind" at the celebration of the Jewish Pentecost (Acts 2:3). Holiness people seek to recapture this pentecostal experience. Individual sanctification, a belief common to many Christian churches, is attained when the believer is set free from sin and exhalted to the true holiness of life.

Serpent handling is a splinter movement within the larger holiness religion. Churches which honor the practice believe that God confers certain powers upon the believers—divine healing, speaking in tongues, drinking of deadly poisons, and casting out devils, as well as handling serpents. Some serpent handlers speak of the "annointing power" of God through the Holy Ghost. They say they are "annointed" to pick up serpents and that without this divine intervention, they would be bitten. The annointing feeling varies from person to person—a numbness of the hands, a tingling somewhere, a great calmness, an inner voice—but no matter what the manifestation, believers recognize it. The facial expression of those handling serpents point to the trance-like state induced by strong, intense emotions.

"God has moved the hedge back," it is said when a believer is bitten, drawing a descriptive metaphor from Ecclesiastes 10:8. Some say that when the serpent bites, it is because God ordained it. He might intend the bite as a sign to nonbelievers to let them know that the snakes are dangerous, or, God may be disciplining a transgressor. One often-bitten snake handler in McDowell County avers that the bite itself is the evil work of the devil, but that God allows the devil to act through the snake. Whatever the reason, when a snake bites, the result is painful swelling, discoloration, and sometimes death. Herpetologists claim that the snakes' venom loses potency in captivity, but there is no doubt that bitten believers suffer great pain. However, in approximately 70 years of serpent handling by hundreds of people, there have been surprisingly few fatalities. Those who believe enough to take up serpents usually do not accept medical treatment, but resort to prayer and faith, believing that the same spirit which moved them to handle snakes can also heal them.

According to religious scholars, the practice of handling serpents is an ancient one whose origins precede Christianity. Probably the best known ancient snake handlers were initiates of the classical Greek mystery cults. In the history of human mythology, the serpent appears as a universal religious symbol. In Christian writings, the snake invariably appears as a representation of evil, beginning with Eve's temptation in the Garden of Evil.

The practice of handling serpents among some southern fundamentalists was begun by George Went Hensely of Grasshopper Valley, Tennessee, in 1909. Hensley traveled throughout the area, introducing the practice to nearby Kentucky at the East Pineville Church of God and at the Pine Mountain Church of God, both near Harlan. The first publicity came in 1938 when an irate husband of a church member brought suit against the Pine Mountain church. The members were acquitted, but snake handling was eventually to be outlawed in all Appalachian states except West Virginia.

Hensley left Tennessee, and the practice of serpent handling had by the early 1920s all but disappeared without his encouraging leadership. Hensley himself died in Florida at the age of 70, of snakebite. It was left to one of his converts, Raymond Hays, to revive Appalachian snake handling, which he did in 1943 at the Dolley Pond Church of God With Signs Following. This church in eastern Tennessee is sometimes referred to as the "mother church of snake handling," although the practice apparently spread to West Virginia by way of Harlan County, Kentucky.

In 1945, the snake handlers again came into the limelight with the death of a man during a Dolley Pond meeting. Around the same time, church members attempted to hold revival meetings in Chattanooga, and were arrested. The accompanying trial and publicity brought the prohibition of religious serpent handling by the Tennessee state legislature in 1947. Following years brought similar sensational publicity and persecution of believers. There were numerous jailings, confiscation of snakes, and trials. Nonetheless, traveling preachers and others spread the practice into most of the southern states and as far away as California. In 1955, nearly 4,000 people gathered for an outdoor meeting in Harlan, Kentucky, which was recorded by photographers for *Life* magazine. Controversy has continued to the present, and a 1973 court case against Carson Springs, Tennessee, church members brought the American Civil Liberties Union to the defense of two preachers.

X. A Selective Bibliography for Appalachian Studies
(Revised, Summer 1990)

Steve Fisher

This highly selective bibliography is designed to aid those teaching Appalachian courses with a social science, political economy, and grassroots perspective.

TOPIC OUTLINE

I. Introductory Works
    A. General Bibliographies
    B. General Anthologies
    C. Introductory Books, Pamphlets, and Articles
    D. Community Studies
    E. Major Surveys of the Region

II. The Concept of Appalachia
    A. The Development of the Concept of Appalachia
    B. Appalachian Identity
    C. Appalachian Studies

III. Regional Diversity
    A. Economic and Geographical Diversity
    B. Ethnic and Racial Diversity
    C. Women in Appalachia

IV. History
    A. Overview
    B. Preindustrial Appalachia
    C. The Industrialization of Appalachia
    D. Labor Relations (Pre-1950)

V. Culture

VI. Agents of Socialization
    A. Family
    B. Religion
    C. Class
    D. Education
    E. Media

VII. The Migrant Experience

VIII. Human Needs and Services: The Quality of Life in Appalachia

A revision and update of a bibliography that appeared in the *Appalachian Journal,* Vol. 9, No. 2–3 (Winter–Spring, 1982). Used by permission.

IX. Models of Development
    A. Subculture Model
    B. Regional Development Model
    C. Colonialism Model
    D. Beyond the Colonialism Model
    E. Gender

X. Corporate and Labor Actors
    A. Coal
        1. Industry Structure, Characteristics, Impacts, and Trends
        2. Health and Safety
        3. Strip Mining
        4. United Mine Workers of America (Post-1950)
    B. Textiles
    C. Other Economic and Labor Actors

XI. Assault on the Land and Water

XII. Political Actors
    A. General
    B. Tennessee Valley Authority
    C. Appalachian Regional Commission

XIII. Resistance and Reconstruction

ABBREVIATIONS

ACP   Appalachian Consortium Press

AH   Appalachian Heritage

AJ   Appalachian Journal

ARC   Appalachian Regional Commission

B   Batteau, Allen, ed. *Appalachia and America: Autonomy and Regional Dependence.* Lexington: UKP, 1983.

CCA   Catholic Committee of Appalachia

E&K   Ergood, Bruce, & Bruce E. Kuhre, eds. *Appalachia: Social Context Past and Present.* 2nd ed. Dubuque, IA: Kendall/Hunt, 1983.

ERS   Economic Research Service (of the USDA)

F   Fisher, Steve, ed. *A Landless People in a Rural Region: A Reader on Landownership and Property Taxation in Appalachia.* New Market, TN: Highlander Center, 1979.

H&M   Higgs, Robert J., & Ambrose N. Manning, eds. *Voices from the Hills: Selected Readings of Southern Appalachia.* New York: Frederick Ungar, 1975.

L   Lewis, Ronald L., ed. *Transformation of Life and Labor in Appalachia. Journal of the Appalachian Studies Association,* Vol. 2. Johnson City, TN: Center for Appalachian Studies and Services, East Tennessee State U., 1990.

LJ&A   Lewis, Helen M., Linda Johnson, & Donald Askins, eds. *Colonialism in Modern America: The Appalachian Case.* Boone: ACP, 1978.

MLW   *Mountain Life and Work*

MR   *Mountain Review*

PA   *Peoples Appalachia*

P&S   Photiadis, John D., & Harry Schwarzweller, eds. *Change in Rural America: Implications for Action Programs.* Philadelphia: U. of Pennsylvania, 1971.

S	Somerville, Wilson, ed. *Appalachia/America: Proceedings of the 1980 Appalachian Studies Conference.* Boone: ACP, 1981.
SE	*Southern Exposure*
TVA	Tennessee Valley Authority
U	University
UKP	U. of Kentucky Press or U. Press of Kentucky
UIP	U. of Illinois Press
UMWJ	*United Mine Workers Journal*
UNC	U. of North Carolina
USDA	United States Department of Agriculture
USGPO	United States Government Printing Office
UTP	U. of Tennessee Press
VPI&SU	Virginia Polytechnic Institute & State U.
W	Williamson, J. W., ed. *An Appalachian Symposium: Essays Written in Honor of Cratis D. Williams.* Boone: Appalachian State U. Press, 1977.
WVU	West Virginia U.

I. INTRODUCTORY WORKS

A. General Bibliographies

Appalachian Bibliography. Morgantown: WVU Library, 1980.

Appalachian Outlook: New Sources of Regional Information. Issued quarterly. Morgantown: WVU Library, 1964–date.

Drake, Richard. "A Bibliography of Appalachian Bibliographies." *Appalachian Notes* 2:3 (1974): 44–48; 3:3 (1975): 47–48; 3:4 (1975): 62–63; 4:2 (1976): 31–32.

Fisher, Steve. "A Selective Bibliography for Appalachian Studies." *AJ* 9 (Winter–Spring 1982): 209–42. Also in E&K, 335–67.

Flynt, J. Wayne, & Dorothy S. Flynt. *Southern Poor Whites: A Selected Annotated Bibliography of Published Sources.* New York: Garland, 1981.

Garrison, Ellen, ed. *Archives in Appalachia: A Directory.* Boone: ACP, 1985.

Kessner, Richard M. "A Bibliographic Survey of Dissertations Dealing with Appalachia." *AJ* 6 (Summer 1979): 277–310.

Kuehn, Jennifer. *People of Appalachia: A Research Bibliography, 1980–1988.* Columbus, OH: College of Social Work, Ohio State U., 1989.

Miller, Jim Wayne. *Reading, Writing, Region: A Checklist, Purchase Guide and Directory for School and Community Libraries in Appalachia.* Boone: ACP, 1984.

Ross, Charlotte T., ed. *Bibliography of Southern Appalachia.* Boone: ACP, 1976.

Schuster, Laura, & Sharyn Mc/Crumb. "Appalachian Film List." *AJ* 11 (Summer 1984): 329–83.

B. General Anthologies

Axelrod, Jim, ed. *Growin' Up Country.* Clintwood, VA: Council of the Southern Mountains, 1973.

Batteau, Allen, ed. *Appalachia and America: Autonomy and Regional Dependence.* Lexington: UKP, 1983.

Beaver, Patricia D., & Burton L. Purrington, eds. *Cultural Adaptation to Mountain Environments.* Athens: U. Press of Georgia, 1984.

Ergood, Bruce, & Bruce E. Kuhre, eds. *Appalachia: Social Context Past and Present.* 2nd ed. Dubuque, IA: Kendall/Hunt, 1983.

Guinan, Edward, ed. *Redemption Denied: An Appalachian Reader.* Wash., DC: Appalachian Documentation, 1976.

Hacala, Joseph, ed. *Dream of the Mountains' Struggle: Appalachian Pastoral Five Years Later.* Prestonburg, KY: CCA, 1980.

Higgs, Robert, & Ambrose Manning, eds. *Voices from the Hills: Selected Readings of Southern Appalachia.* New York: Frederick Ungar, 1975.

Jones, Loyal, ed. *Reshaping the Image of Appalachia.* Berea, KY: Berea College Appalachian Center, 1986.

Lewis, Helen M., Linda Johnson, & Donald Askins, eds. *Colonialism in Modern America: The Appalachian Case.* Boone: ACP, 1978.

McNeil, Nellie, and Joyce Squibb, eds. *A Southern Appalachian Reader.* Boone: ACP, 1988.

Peoples Appalachian Research Collective (PARC), ed. *Appalachia's People-Problems-Alternatives: An Introductory Social Science Reader.* Rev. ed. Morgantown, PARC, 1972.

Photiadis, John D., & Harry Schwarzweller, eds. *Change in Rural Appalachia: Implications for Action Programs.* Philadelphia: U. of Pennsylvania Press, 1971.

Riddel, Frank S., ed. *Appalachia: Its People, Heritage, and Problems.* Dubuque, IA: Kendall/Hunt, 1974.

Walls, David S., & John B. Stephenson, eds. *Appalachia in the Sixties: Decade of Reawakening.* Lexington: UKP, 1972.

Williamson, J. W., ed. *An Appalachian Symposium: Essays Written in Honor of Cratis D. Williams.* Boone: Appalachian State U. Press, 1977.

Proceedings of the Appalachian Studies Conference have been published annually since 1981. The separate volumes are not listed here, but selected articles from these proceedings are cited throughout this bibliography.

C. Introductory Books, Pamphlets and Articles

Appalachian Alliance. *Appalachia in the Eighties: A Time for Action.* 1982.

Appalachian Issues and Resources. 2nd ed. Knoxville: Southern Appalachian Ministry in Higher Education, 1978.

Branscome, Jim. "Annihilating the Hillbilly: The Appalachians' Struggle with America's Institutions." *Katallagete* 3 (Winter 1971): 25–32. Also in LJ&A, 211–27.

Carawan, Guy, & Candie Carawan. *Voices from the Mountains.* Urbana: UIP, 1982.

Catholic Bishops of Appalachia. *This Land Is Home to Me: A Pastoral Letter on Powerlessness in Appalachia.* Whitesburg, KY: CCA, 1975.

Caudill, Harry M. *Night Comes to the Cumberlands: A Biography of a Depressed Area.* Boston: Little, Brown/Atlantic Monthly Press, 1962.

Fisher, Steve. "As the World Turns: The Melodrama of Harry Caudill." *AJ* 11 (Spring 1984): 268–73.

Fisher, Steve, & J. W. Williamson. "An Interview with Harry Caudill." *AJ* 8 (Summer 1981): 249–99.

Kirby, Jack T. *Rural Worlds Lost: The American South, 1920–1960,* Baton Rouge: Louisiana State U. Press, 1987.

Wells, John C., Jr. "Poverty amidst Riches: Why People Are Poor in Appalachia." Ph.D. diss., Rutgers U., 1977.

Wilson, Charles R., & William Ferris, eds. *The Encyclopedia of Southern Culture.* Chapel Hill: UNC Press, 1989.

D. Community Studies

Beaver, Patricia D. *Rural Community in the Appalachian South.* Lexington: UKP, 1986.

Blee, Kathleen, & Dwight Billings. "Reconstructing Daily Life in the Past: An Hermeneutical Approach to Ethnographic Data." *Sociological Quarterly* 27 (Winter 1986): 443–62.

Brown, James. *Beech Creek: A Study of a Kentucky Mountain Neighborhood.* Berea, KY: Berea College Press, 1988.

Bryant, F. Carlene. *We're All Kin: A Cultural Study of a Mountain Neighborhood.* Knoxville: UTP, 1980.

Dunn, Durwood. *Cades Cove: The Life and Death of a Southern Appalachian Community, 1818–1937.* Knoxville: UTP, 1988.

Fetterman, John. *Stinking Creek: The Portrait of a Small Mountain Community in Appalachia.* New York: Dutton, 1967.

Foster, Stephen W. *The Past Is Another Country: Representation, Historical Consciousness, and Resistance in the Blue Ridge.* Berkeley: U. of California Press, 1988.

Gazaway, Rena. *The Longest Mile.* Garden City, NY: Doubleday, 1969.

Hicks, George. *Appalachian Valley.* New York: Holt, Rinehart & Winston, 1976.

Kaplan, Berton H. *Blue Ridge: An Appalachian Community in Transition.* Morgantown: Appalachian Center, WVU, 1971.

Lantz, Herman R. *People of Coal Town.* New York: Columbia U. Press, 1958; rpt. Carbondale: Southern Illinois U. Press, 1971.

Lewis, Helen M., & Suzanna O'Donnell, eds. *Ivanhoe, Virginia: Remembering Our Past, Building Our Future.* Ivanhoe: Ivanhoe Civic League, 1990.

McDonald, Michael J., & William B. Wheeler. *Knoxville, Tennessee: Continuity & Change in an Appalachian City.* Knoxville: UTP, 1983.

Pearsall, Marian. *Little Smokey Ridge: The Natural History of a Southern Appalachian Neighborhood.* University, AL: U. of Alabama Press, 1959.

Plunkett, H. Dudley, & Mary Jane Bowman. *Elites and Change in the Kentucky Mountains.* Lexington: UKP, 1973.

Schwarzweller, Harry, James S. Brown, & J. J. Mangalam. *Mountain Families in Transition: A Case Study of Appalachian Migration.* University Park: Penn. State U. Press, 1971.

Stephenson, John. *Shiloh: A Mountain Community.* Lexington: UKP, 1968.

Weller, Jack. *Yesterday's People: Life in Contemporary Appalachia.* Lexington: UKP, 1965.

Wolfe, Margaret. *Kingsport, Tennessee: A Planned Community.* Lexington: UKP, 1987.

E. Major Surveys of the Region

Campbell, John C. *The Southern Highlander & His Homeland.* New York: Russell Sage Foundation, 1921: rpt. Lexington: UKP, 1969.

Ford, Thomas R., ed. *The Southern Appalachian Region: A Survey.* Lexington: UKP, 1962.

Jones, Loyal. "The Surveys of the Appalachian Region." *AH* 4 (Spring 1976): 25–42.

USDA. *Economic and Social Problems and Conditions of the Southern Appalachians.* Wash., DC: USGPO, 1935.

II. THE CONCEPT OF APPALACHIA

A. The Development of the Concept of Appalachia

Brown, James. "An Appalachian Footnote to Toynbee's *A Study of History*." *AJ* 6 (Autumn 1978): 29–32.

Cunningham, Rodger. *Apples on the Flood: The Southern Mountain Experience.* Knoxville: UTP, 1987.

———. "Signs of Civilization: *The Trail of the Lonesome Pine* as Colonial Narrative." In L, 21–46.

Ergood, Bruce. "Toward a Definition of Appalachia." In E&K, 31–41.

Howell, Benita. "Mountain Foragers in Southeast Asia and Appalachia: Cross-Cultural Perspectives on the 'Mountain Man' Stereotype." In *Mountains of Experience: Interdisciplinary, Intercultural, International*, ed. Parks Lanier, Jr., 114–24. *Journal of the Appalachian Studies Association*, Vol. I. Boone: ACP, 1989.

Klotter, James C. "The Black South and White Appalachia." *Journal of American History* 66 (March 1980): 832–49.

McKinney, Gordon B. "The Political Uses of Appalachian Identity after the Civil War." *AJ* 7 (Spring 1980): 200–09.

McNeil, W. K., ed. *Appalachian Images in Folk and Popular Culture.* Ann Arbor, MI: UMI Research Press, 1989.

Markusen, Ann R. *Regions: The Economics and Politics of Territory.* Totowa, NJ: Rowman & Littlefield, 1987.

Precourt, Walter. "The Image of Appalachian Poverty." In B, 86–110.

Ray, Clyde H. "Images of the Southern Appalachian in America from 1920–1940." *AH* 9 (Fall 1981): 35–49.

Shapiro, Henry D. *Appalachia on Our Mind: The Southern Mountains and Mountaineers in the American Consciousness, 1870–1920.* Chapel Hill: UNC Press, 1978.

Simon, Richard M. "Regions and Social Relations: A Research Note." *AJ* 11 (Autumn–Winter 1983–84): 25–31.

Steiner, Michael, & Clarence Mondale. *Regions and Regionalism in the United States: A Source Book for the Humanities and Social Sciences.* New York: Garland, 1988.

Ulack, Richard, & Karl Raitz. "Perceptions of Appalachia." *Environment and Behavior* 14 (November 1982): 725–52.

Wagner, Melinda B. "Appalachia in America's Future: Alternative Cultural Forms." In *Critical Essays in Appalachian Life & Culture: Proceedings of the 5th Annual Appalachian Studies Conference,* ed. Rick Simon, 88–97. Boone: ACP, 1982.

Walls, David S. "On the Naming of Appalachia." In W, 56–76.

Whisnant, David E. *All That Is Native and Fine: The Politics of Culture in an American Region.* Chapel Hill: UNC Press, 1983.

———. *Modernizing the Mountaineer: People, Power, and Planning in Appalachia.* Boone: ACP, 1980.

Williams, Cratis D. "The Southern Mountaineer in Fact and Fiction." 4 parts, *AJ* 3 (Autumn 1975–Summer 1976).

See also works in I E, II B, III B, V, VI E, & IX.

B. Appalachian Identity

Batteau, Allen. "An Agenda for Irrelevance: Malcolm Chapman's *The Gaelic Vision in Scottish Culture:* A Review Essay." *AJ* 8 (Spring 1981): 212–16.

Best, Bill. "To See Ourselves." *MR* 5 (October 1979): 1–6. See also Best's "Stripping Appalachian Soul." *MR* 4 (January 1979): 14–16; responses to this article are in *MR* 5 (July 1979): 25–28.

Billings, Dwight B., & David S. Walls. "Appalachians." In *Harvard Encyclopedia of American Ethnic Groups,* eds. Stephan Thernstrom, Ann Orlov, & Oscar Handlin, 125–28. Cambridge: Belknap Press of Harvard U. Press, 1980.

Day, Graham. "The Reconstruction of Wales and Appalachia: Development and Regional Identity." In *Contemporary Wales: An Annual Review of Economic and Social Research,* Vol. I. Cardiff: U. of Wales Press, 1987, 73–89.

Depta, Victor M. "Prosody in Revolt." *AJ* 9 (Fall 1981): 65–72.

Einstein, Frank. "The Politics of Nostalgia: Uses of the Past in Recent Appalachian Poetry." *AJ* 8 (Autumn 1980): 32–40.

Foster, Stephen W. *The Past Is Another Country: Representation, Historical Consciousness, and Resistance in the Blue Ridge.* Berkeley: U. of California Press, 1988.

Miller, Jim Wayne. "A Mirror for Appalachia." In H&M, 447–59.

———. "A Post-Agrarian Regionalism for Appalachia." *AH* 8 (Spring 1980): 58–71.

Norman, Gurney, and Lance Olson. "Frankenstein in Palestine or: Postmodernism in Appalachia." In *Pine Mountain Sand & Gravel: Contemporary Appalachian Writing,* ed. Jim Webb, 76–100. New York-Whitesburg, KY: Appalapple Productions, Inc., 1988.

Whisnant, David E. "Developments in the Appalachian Identity Movement: All Is Process." *AJ* 8 (Autumn 1980): 41–47.

———. "Ethnicity and the Recovery of Regional Identity in Appalachia: Thoughts upon Entering the Zone of Occult Instability." *Soundings* 56 (Spring 1973): 124–38.

———. "The Folk Hero in Appalachian Struggle History." *New South* 28 (Fall 1973): 30–47.

See also works in II A.

C. Appalachian Studies

Best, Bill. "From Existence to Essence: A Conceptual Model for Appalachian Studies." Ed.D. diss., U. of Massachusetts, 1973.

Blaustein, Richard. "Regionalism and Revitalization: Towards a Comparative Perspective on Appalachian Studies." In *Remembrance, Reunion, and Revival: Celebrating a Decade of Appalachian Studies. Proceedings of the 10th Annual Appalachian Studies Conference*, ed. Helen Roseberry, 14–20. Boone: ACP, 1988.

The Cratis Williams Symposium Proceedings: A Memorial and Examination of the State of Regional Studies in Appalachia. Boone: ACP, 1990.

Fisher, Stephen L., J. W. Williamson, & Juanita Lewis, eds. "A Guide to Appalachian Studies," *AJ* 5 (Autumn 1977).

Gaventa, John. "Inequality and the Appalachian Studies Industry," *AJ* 5 (Spring 1978): 322–29.

McGowan, Thomas, ed. "Assessing Appalachian Studies." *AJ* 9 (Winter–Spring 1982).

PA 1 (Spring 1971). Special Issue: "Appalachian Studies: A New Look at Ourselves."

See also works in VI D.

III. REGIONAL DIVERSITY

A. Economic and Geographical Diversity

"Appalachia: The Economic Outlook through the Eighties." *Appalachia* 17 (November–December 1983): 1–14.

Bingham, Edgar. "A Bibliography of Appalachian Geography." *AJ* 5 (Autumn 1977): 65–73.

Bowman, Mary Jean, & W. Warren Haynes. *Resources and People in East Kentucky: Problems and Potentials of a Lagging Economy.* Baltimore: Johns Hopkins Press, 1963.

"Comparing Appalachia's Counties with the Nation's." *Appalachia* 19 (Spring 1986): 8–15.

Couto, Richard A. *Appalachia: An American Tomorrow. A Report to the Commission on Religion in Appalachia on Trends and Issues in the Appalachian Region.* Knoxville: Commission on Religion in Appalachia, 1984.

DeLeon, Paul, ed. *Appalachia's Changing Economy: A Reader.* New Market, TN: Highlander Center, 1986.

Lovingood, Paul E., Jr., & Robert E. Reiman. *Emerging Patterns in the Southern Highlands: A Reference Atlas.* Vol. 1, *Introduction.* Boone: ACP, 1985.

Pickard, Jerome. "A New County Classification System." *Appalachia* 21 (Summer 1988): 19–24.

Raitz, Karl B., & Richard Ulack. *Appalachia, a Regional Geography: Land, People, and Development.* Boulder, CO: Westview, 1984.

Shannon, Thomas R. "Surviving the 1990s: Inter-Regional Variation in Economic Problems." In *The Many Faces of Appalachia: Proceedings of the 7th Annual Appalachian Studies Conference*, ed. Sam Gray, 125–37. Boone: ACP, 1985.

Watts, Ann D. "Cities and Their Place in Southern Appalachia." *AJ* 8 (Winter 1981): 105–18.

White, Stephen E. "America's Soweto: Population Redistribution in Appalachian Kentucky, 1940–1986." *AJ* 16 (Summer 1989): 350–60.

B. Ethnic and Racial Diversity

Becker, Edmund R. "Black Bituminous Coal Miners in Southern Appalachia: 1890–1970." *Sociological Spectrum* 4:4 (1984): 461–76.

Berthoff, Rowland. "Celtic Mist over the South." *Journal of Southern History* 52 (November 1986): 532–46.

Cunningham, Rodger. *Apples on the Flood: The Southern Mountain Experience.* Knoxville: UTP, 1987.

———. "Eat Grits and Die: Or, Cracker, Your Breed Ain't Hermeneutical." *AJ* 17 (Winter 1990): 176–82.

Ehle, John. *Trail of Tears: The Rise and Fall of the Cherokee Nation.* New York: Anchor Press/ Doubleday, 1988.

Finger, John R. *The Eastern Band of Cherokees, 1819–1900.* Knoxville: UTP, 1984.

Fischer, David H. *Albion's Seed: Four British Folkways in America.* New York: Oxford U. Press, 1989.

Henige, David. "Origin Traditions of American Racial Isolates." *AJ* 11 (Spring 1984): 201–13.

Hudson, Charles M. *The Southeastern Indians.* Knoxville: UTP, 1976.

King, Duane H. *The Cherokee Indian Nation: A Troubled History.* Knoxville: UTP, 1979.

Lewis, Ronald L. *Black Coal Miners in America: Race, Class, and Community Conflict, 1780–1980.* Lexington: UKP, 1987.

Leyburn, James G. *The Scotch-Irish: A Social History.* Chapel Hill: UNC Press, 1962.

McWhiney, Grady. *Cracker Culture: Celtic Ways in the Old South.* Tuscaloosa: U. of Alabama Press, 1988.

Merrell, James H. *The Indians' New World: Catawbas and Their Neighbors from European Contact through the Era of Removal.* Chapel Hill: UNC Press, 1989.

Montell, William L. *The Saga of Coe Ridge: A Social History.* Knoxville: UTP, 1970.

MLW, October 1982, February 1984, & April–June 1988. Special issues on Black Appalachians.

Purrington, Burt, ed. "New Perspectives on the Cherokee." *AJ* 2 (Summer 1973).

Silver, Timothy H. *A New Face on the Countryside: Indians, Colonists, and Slaves in the South Atlantic Forests, 1500–1800.* New York: Cambridge U. Press, 1990.

SE 13 (November–December 1985). Special Issue: "We Are Here Forever: Indians of the South."

Turner, William H., & Edward J. Cabbell, eds. *Blacks in Appalachia.* Lexington: UKP, 1985.

Walls, David S., & Dwight B. Billings. "The Sociology of Appalachia." *AJ* 5 (Autumn 1977): 131–44. Also in E&K, 41–51.

Williams, Cratis D. "Who Are the Southern Mountaineers?" *AJ* 1 (Autumn 1972): 48–55. Also in H&M, 493–506 & E&K, 54–58.

Wolfe, Margaret R. "The Appalachian Reality: Ethnic and Class Diversity." *East Tennessee Historical Society's Publications* 52 (1980–81): 40–60.

Wood, Peter H., Gregory A. Waselkov, & M. Thomas Hatley, eds. *Powhatan's Mantle: Indians in the Colonial Southeast.* Lincoln: U. of Nebraska Press, 1989.

Wright, J. Leitch, Jr. *The Only Land They Knew: The Tragic Story of the American Indians in the Old South.* New York: Free Press, 1981.

See also works in I D, I E, & II A.

C. Women in Appalachia

Cheek, Pauline, ed. *The Appalachian Woman: Images and Essence.* Mars Hill, NC: Council on Appalachian Women, 1980.

Coles, Robert, & Jane H. Coles. *Women of Crisis: Lives of Struggle and Hope.* New York: Delacorte Press, 1978.

Couto, Richard A. "Women and Poverty in Appalachia." *Forum for Applied Research and Public Policy* 1 (Fall 1986): 101–10.

Ewald, Wendy. *Appalachian Women: Three Generations.* Whitesburg, KY: Appalshop, 1980.

Farr, Sidney S. *Appalachian Women: An Annotated Bibliography.* Lexington: UKP, 1981.

Ganim, Carole. "Herself: Woman and Place in Appalachian Literature." *AJ* 13 (Spring 1986): 258–74.

Hall, V. Aileen. *Poverty and Women in West Virginia.* Charleston: Women & Employment, 1983.

Kahn, Kathy. *Hillbilly Women.* New York: Doubleday, 1973.

Lewis, Helen M., Linda Selfridge, Juliet Merrifield, Sue Thrasher, Lillie Perry, & Carol Honeycutt. *Picking Up the Pieces: Women In and Out of Work in the Rural South.* New Market, TN: Highlander Center, 1986.

Lord, Sharon B., & Carolyn Patton-Crowder. *Appalachian Women: A Learning/Teaching Guide.* Knoxville: UTP, 1979.

Mathews, Alice E. "Tall Women and Mountain Belles: Fact and Fiction in Appalachia." In *Perspectives on the American South,* Vol. 4, ed. James C. Cobb & Charles R. Wilson, 39–53. New York: Gordon & Breach, 1986.

Medlin, Christine L. "The Influence of Significant Others, Fertility and Gender Role Attitudes on the Educational and Occupational Processes of Low-Income Women from Rural Appalachia." Ph.D. diss., U. of Tennessee, 1987.

Miller, Danny L. "Images of Women in Southern Appalachian Mountain Literature." Ph.D. diss., U. of Cincinnati, 1985.

MLW, September 1984. Special Issue: "Women in Non-Traditional Jobs in Appalachia."

Simon, Rick, & Betty Justice. "The Economy of West Virginia and the Oppression/Liberation of Women." In S, 44–56.

Southeast Women's Employment Coalition. *Women of the Rural South: Economic Status and Prospects.* Lexington, KY, 1986.

SE 4 (Winter 1977). Special Issue: "Generations: Women in the South."

SE 9 (Winter 1981). Special Issue: "Working Women: A Handbook of Resources, Rights, and Remedies."

Spence, Beth. *In Praise of Mountain Women.* Whitesburg, KY: CCA, 1988.

Stout-Wiegand, Nancy, & Roger B. Trent. "Sex Differences in Attitudes toward New Energy Resource Developments." *Rural Sociology* 48 (Winter 1983): 637–46.

Timberlake, Andrea, Lynn W. Cannon, Rebecca F. Guy, & Elizabeth Higginbotham, eds. *Women of Color and Southern Women: A Bibliography of Social Science Research, 1975–1988.* Memphis, TN: Center for Research on Women, Memphis State U., 1988.

Weiss, Chris. *Women and Inequality in Appalachia: The Effect of Economic Development.* Charleston, WV: Women & Employment, 1987.

West Virginia Women's Commission. *Missing Chapters: West Virginia Women in History.* Charleston, 1983.

Whisnant, David E. "Second-Level Appalachian History: Another Look at Some Fotched-On Women." *AJ* 9 (Winter–Spring 1982): 115–23.

Other works on women are listed in relevant sections throughout this bibliography. See especially the works on women coal miners in X A 1 and the works on gender in IX E.

IV. HISTORY

A. Overview

Caudill, Harry M. *Night Comes to the Cumberlands: A Biography of a Depressed Area.* Boston: Little, Brown/Atlantic Monthly, 1962.

Crowell, Suzanne. *Appalachian People's History Book.* Louisville: Southern Conference Educational Fund, 1971.

Drake, Richard. *Mountaineers and Americans.* Berea, KY: Berea College, 1976.

Edwards, Everette E. *References on the Mountaineers of the Southern Appalachians.* Wash., DC: USDA, 1935.

Eller, Ronald D. *Miners, Millhands, and Mountaineers: Industrialization of the Appalachian South, 1880–1930.* Knoxville: UTP, 1982.

Salstrom, Paul. "Appalachia's Path toward Welfare Dependency, 1840–1940." Ph.D. diss., Brandeis U., 1988.

Shackelford, Laurel, & Bill Weinberg. *Our Appalachia: An Oral History.* New York: Hill & Wang, 1977; rpt. Lexington: UKP, 1988.

B. Preindustrial Appalachia

Billings, Dwight, Kathleen Blee, & Louis Swanson. "Culture, Family, and Community in Preindustrial Appalachia." *AJ* 13 (Winter 1986): 154–170. See response by Paul Salstrom in *AJ* 13 (Summer 1986): 340–52.

Campbell, John C. *The Southern Highlander & His Homeland.* New York: Russell Sage Foundation, 1921; rpt. Lexington: UKP, 1969.

Caruso, John A. *The Appalachian Frontier: America's First Surge Westward.* Indianapolis: Bobbs-Merrill, 1959.

Crawford, Martin. "Political Society in a Southern Mountain Community: Ashe County, North Carolina, 1850–1861." *Journal of Southern History* 60 (August 1989): 373–90.

Hoffman, Ronald, Thad W. Tate, & Peter J. Albert, eds. *An Uncivil War: The Southern Backcountry during the Civil War.* Charlottesville: U. Press of Virginia, 1985.

Hsiung, David C. "How Isolated Was Appalachia? Upper East Tennessee, 1780–1835." *AJ* 16 (Summer 1989): 336–49.

Inscoe, John C. *Mountain Masters: Slavery and the Sectional Crisis in Western North Carolina.* Knoxville: UTP, 1989.

Kephart, Horace. *Our Southern Highlanders.* New York: Outing Pub., 1913; rpt. Knoxville: UTP, 1976.

McKinney, Gordon B. "Preindustrial Jackson County and Economic Development." In L, 1–10.

Miles, Emma Bell. *The Spirit of the Mountains.* New York: J. Pott, 1905; rpt. Knoxville: UTP, 1975.

Olmsted, Frederick L. *A Journey to the Back Country, 1853–54.* New York: Mason Brothers, 1860; rpt. New York: Schocken, 1970.

Paludan, Philip S. *Victims: A True Story of the Civil War.* Knoxville: UTP, 1981.

Pudup, Mary Beth. "The Boundaries of Class in Preindustrial Appalachia." *Journal of Historical Geography* 15:2 (1989): 139–62.

————. "The Limits of Subsistence: Agriculture and Industry in Central Appalachia." *Agricultural History* 64 (Winter 1990): 61–89. See also Pudup's Ph.D. diss.: "Land before Coal: Class and Regional Development in Southeast Kentucky," U. of California, Berkeley, 1987.

Raine, James W. *The Land of the Saddlebags: A Study of the Mountain People of Appalachia.* New York: Missionary Education Movement, 1924.

Rohrbough, Malcolm J. *The Trans-Appalachian Frontier: People, Societies, and Institutions, 1775–1850.* New York: Oxford U. Press, 1978.

Slaughter, Thomas P. *The Whiskey Rebellion: Frontier Epilogue to the American Revolution.* New York: Oxford U. Press, 1986.

Smith, Edward C. *The Borderland in the Civil War.* New York: Macmillan, 1927.

Trotter, William R. *Bushwackers: The Civil War in North Carolina.* Vol. II, *The Mountains.* Greensboro, NC: Signal Research, Inc., 1988.

Weingartner, Paul J., Dwight B. Billings, & Kathleen M. Blee. "Agriculture in Preindustrial Appalachia: Subsistence Farming in Beech Creek, 1850–1880." In *Mountains of Experience: Interdisciplinary, Intercultural, International,* ed. Parks Lanier, Jr., 70–80. *Journal of the Appalachian Studies Association,* Vol. I. Boone: ACP, 1989.

Wilhelm, Gene, Jr. "Appalachian Isolation: Fact or Fiction?" In W, 77–91.

See also works in I D, II A, III B, IV A, & IV C.

C. The Industrialization of Appalachia

Banks, Alan J. "Coal Miners and Firebrick Workers: The Structure of Work Relations in Two Eastern Kentucky Communities." *AJ* 11 (Autumn–Winter 1983–84): 85–102.

————. "The Emergence of a Capitalistic Labor Market in Eastern Kentucky." *AJ* 7 (Spring 1980): 188–99.

————. "Land and Capital in Eastern Kentucky, 1890–1915." *AJ* 8 (Autumn 1980): 8–18. See also Bank's Ph.D. diss.: "Labor and the Development of Industrial Capitalism in Eastern Kentucky, 1870–1930," McMaster U. (Ontario), 1980.

Barnum, Donald T. *The Negro in the Bituminous Coal Mining Industry.* Philadelphia: U. of Pennsylvania Press, 1970.

Beardsley, Edward H. *A History of Neglect: Health Care for Blacks and Mill Workers in the Twentieth-Century South.* Knoxville: UTP, 1987.

Becker, Edmund R. "Black Bituminous Coal Miners in Southern Appalachia: 1890–1970." *Sociological Spectrum* 4:4 (1984): 461–76.

Billings, Dwight B., Jr. *Planters and the Making of a New South: Class, Politics, and Development in North Carolina, 1865–1900.* Chapel Hill: UNC Press, 1979.

Boyte, Harry. "The Textile Industry, Keel of Southern Industrialization." *Radical America* 6:2 (1973): 4–49.

Buxton, Barry M., & Malinda Crutchfield, eds. *The Great Forest: An Appalachian Story.* Boone: ACP, 1985.

Carlton, David L. *Mill and Town in South Carolina, 1880–1920.* Baton Rouge: Louisiana State U., 1982.

Caudill, Harry M. *Theirs Be the Power: The Moguls of Eastern Kentucky.* Urbana: UIP, 1983.

Clarkson, Roy B. *Tumult on the Mountain: Lumbering in West Virginia, 1770–1920*. Parsons, WV: McClain, 1964.

Cobb, James C. "Beyond Planters and Industrialists: A New Perspective on the New South." *Journal of Southern History* 54 (February 1988): 45–68.

———. *Industrialization and Southern Society, 1877–1980*. Lexington: UKP, 1984.

Dix, Keith. *Work Relations in the Coal Industry: The Handloading Era, 1880–1930*. Morgantown: Institute for Labor Studies, WVU, 1977.

Einstein, Frank H. "Things Fall Apart in Appalachia Too: Hubert Skidmore's Account of the Transition to Capitalism." *AJ* 11 (Autumn–Winter 1983–84): 32–42.

Fishback, Price V. "Did Coal Miners 'Owe Their Souls to the Company Store'? Theory and Evidence from the Early 1900s." *Journal of Economic History* 46 (December 1968): 1011–29.

Gaventa, John. *Power and Powerlessness: Quiescence and Rebellion in an Appalachian Valley*. Urbana: UIP, 1980.

Hahn, Steven. *The Roots of Southern Populism: Yeoman Farmers and the Transformation of the Georgia Upcountry, 1850–1890*. New York: Oxford U. Press, 1983.

Hahn, Steven, & Jonathan Prude, eds. *The Countryside in the Age of Capitalist Transformation: Essays in the Social History of Rural America*. Chapel Hill: UNC Press, 1985.

Hall, Jacquelyn D., James Leloudis, Robert Korstad, Mary Murphy, Lu Ann Jones, & Christopher B. Daly. *Like a Family: The Making of a Southern Cotton Mill World*. Chapel Hill: UNC Press, 1987. Includes a useful bibliography on textile sources.

Harvey, Katherine. *The Best Dressed Miners: Life and Labor in the Maryland Coal Region, 1835–1910*. Ithaca: Cornell U. Press, 1969.

Hearden, Patrick J. *Independence and Empire: The New South's Cotton Mill Campaign, 1865–1901*. DeKalb: Northern Illinois U. Press, 1982.

Johnson, James P. *The Politics of Soft Coal: The Bituminous Coal Industry from World War I through the New Deal*. Urbana: UIP, 1979.

Jones, G. C. *Growing Up Hard in Harlan County*. Lexington: UKP, 1985.

Lawrence, Randall G. "Appalachian Metamorphasis: Industrializing Society on the Central Appalachian Plateau, 1860–1913." Ph.D. diss., Duke U., 1983.

Lemert, Ben. *The Cotton Textile Industry of the Southern Appalachian Piedmont*. Chapel Hill: UNC Press, 1933.

Lewis, Ronald L. *Black Coal Miners in America: Race, Class, and Community Conflict, 1780–1980*. Lexington: UKP, 1987.

Long, Priscilla. *Where the Sun Never Shines: A History of America's Bloody Coal Industry*. New York: Paragon House, 1989.

Maggard, Sally. "From Farmers to Miners: The Decline of Agriculture in Eastern Kentucky." In *Science and Agricultural Development*, ed. Lawrence Busch, 25–66. Totowa, NJ: Allenheld, Osmun, 1981.

Miller, Donald L., & Richard E. Sharpless. *The Kingdom of Coal: Work, Enterprise and Ethnic Communities in the Mine Fields*. Philadelphia: U. of Pennsylvania Press, 1985.

Moore, Tyrel G. "An Historical Geography of Economic Development in Appalachian Kentucky, 1800–1930." Ph.D. diss., U. of Tennessee, 1984.

Munn, Robert F. *The Coal Industry in America: A Bibliography and Guide to Studies*. Morgantown, WVU Library, 1977.

Parkinson, George. *Guide to Coal Mining Collections in the United States*. Morgantown: WVU Library, 1978.

Pope, Liston. *Millhands and Preachers: A Study of Gastonia*. New Haven: Yale U. Press, 1942.

Ross, Malcolm H. *Machine Age in the Hills*. New York: Macmillan, 1933.

Salstrom, Paul. "Subsistence Farming, Capitalism, and the Depression in West Virginia." *AJ* 11 (Summer 1984): 384–94.

Simon, Richard M. "The Labor Process and Uneven Development: The Appalachian Coalfields, 1880–1930." *International Journal of Urban and Regional Research* 4 (March 1980): 46–71.

Speer, Jean H. "Folk Tradition and Industrialization in Appalachia." In L, 11–20.

Sullivan, Charles K. "Coal Men and Coal Towns: Development of the Smokeless Coalfields of Southern West Virginia, 1873–1923." Ph.D. diss., U. of Pittsburgh, 1979.

Thomas, Jerry B. "Coal Country: The Rise of the Southern Smokeless Coal Industry and Its Effect on Area Development, 1872–1910." Ph.D. diss., UNC, Chapel Hill, 1971.

Tudiver, Sari L. "Political Economy and Culture in Central Appalachia, 1790–1977." Ph.D. diss., U. of Michigan, 1984.

Tullos, Allen, *Habits of Industry: White Culture and the Transformation of the Carolina Piedmont.* Chapel Hill: UNC Press, 1989.

Turner, Carolyn C., & Carolyn H. Traum. *John C. C. Mayo: Cumberland Capitalist.* Pikeville, KY: Pikeville College Press, 1983.

Wallace, Anthony F. C. *St. Clair: A Nineteenth-Century Coal Town's Experience with a Disaster-Prone Industry.* New York: Knopf, 1987.

Waller, Altina L. *Feud: Hatfields, McCoys, and Social Change in Appalachia, 1860–1900.* Chapel Hill: UNC Press, 1988.

Williams, John A. *West Virginia and the Captains of Industry.* Morgantown: WVU Library, 1976.

Wood, Phillip J. *Southern Capitalism: The Political Economy of North Carolina, 1880–1980.* Durham: Duke U. Press, 1986.

Wright, Warren. "The Big Steal." In LJ&A, 161–75.

See also works in I D, II A, IV A, IV B, IV D, IX C, IX D, & X.

D. Labor Relations (Pre-1950)

Amsden, Jon, & Stephen Brier. "Coal Miners on Strike: The Transformation of Strike Demands and the Formation of a National Union." *Journal of Interdisciplinary History* 7 (Spring 1977): 583–616.

Aurand, Harold W. *From the Molly Maguires to the UMW: The Social Ecology of an Industrial Union, 1869–1897.* Philadelphia: Temple U. Press, 1971.

Bowman, John R. "When Workers Organize Capitalists: The Case of the Bituminous Coal Industry." *Politics & Society* 14:3 (1985): 289–327.

Brophy, John. *A Miner's Life.* Ed. by John O. P. Hall. Madison: U. of Wisconsin, 1964.

Byerly, Victoria. *Hard Times Cotton Mill Girls: Personal Histories of Womanhood and Poverty in the South.* Ithaca, NY: ILR Press, 1986.

Coleman, McAlister. *Men and Coal.* New York: Farrar & Rinehart, 1943; rpt. New York: Arno, 1969.

Corbin, David A. *Life, Work, and Rebellion in the Coal Fields: The Southern West Virginia Miners, 1880–1922.* Urbana: UIP, 1981.

Derickson, Alan. *Workers' Health, Workers' Democracy: The Western Miners' Struggle, 1891–1925.* New York: Cornell U. Press, 1988.

Dubofsky, Melvyn, & Warren Van Tine. *John L. Lewis: A Biography.* New York: Quadrangle, 1977.

Everling, Arthur C. "Tactics Over Strategy in the United Mine Workers of America: Internal Politics and the Question of the Nationalization of the Mines, 1908–1923." Ph.D. diss., Pennsylvania State U., 1976.

Fink, Gary M., & Merl E. Reed, eds. *Essays in Southern Labor History.* Westport, CT: Greenwood, 1977.

Frankel, Linda J. "Southern Textile Women: Generations of Survival and Struggle." In *My Troubles Are Going to Have Trouble with Me: Everyday Trials and Triumphs of Women Workers,* ed. Karen B. Sachs & Dorothy Remy, 39–60. New Brunswick: Rutgers U. Press, 1984. See also Frankel's Ph.D. diss.: "Women, Paternalism, and Protest in a Southern Textile Community: Henderson, North Carolina," Harvard U., 1986.

Garland, Jim. *Welcome the Traveler Home: Jim Garland's Story of the Kentucky Mountains.* Ed. by Julia S. Ardery. Lexington: UKP, 1983.

Gowaskie, Joe. "John Mitchell and the Anthracite Mine Workers: Leadership, Conservatism and Rank-and-File Militancy." *Labor History* 27 (Winter 1985–86): 54–83.

Green, Archie. *Only a Miner: Studies in Recorded Coal Mining Songs.* Urbana: UIP, 1972.

Hall, Jacquelyn D. "Disorderly Women: Gender and Labor Militancy in the Appalachian South." *Journal of American History* 73 (September 1986): 354–82.

Hall, Jacquelyn D., Robert Korstad, & James Leloudis. "Cotton Mill People: Work, Community, and Protest in the Textile South, 1880–1940." *American Historical Review* 91 (April 1986): 245–86.

Hevener, John W. *Which Side Are You On? The Harlan County Coal Miners, 1931–39.* Urbana: UIP, 1978.

Lane, Winthrop D. *Civil War in West Virginia: The Story of the Industrial Conflict in the Coal Mines.* New York: Huebsch, 1921; rpt. New York: Oriole Editions, 1977.

Lee, Howard B. *Bloodletting in Appalachia: The Story of West Virginia's Four Major Mine Wars and Other Thrilling Incidents of Its Coal Fields.* Morgantown, WVU Press, 1969.

Lunt, Richard D. *Law and Order vs. the Miners: West Virginia, 1907–1933.* Hamden, CT: Archon, 1979.

McHugh, Cathy L. *Mill Family: The Labor System in the Southern Cotton Textile Industry.* New York: Oxford U. Press, 1988.

McLaurin, Melton. *Paternalism and Protest: Southern Cotton Mill Workers and Organized Labor, 1895–1905.* Westport, CT: Negro U. Press, 1971.

Miller, Marc S., ed. *Working Lives: The Southern Exposure History of Labor in the South.* New York: Pantheon, 1980. Includes a comprehensive bibliography on Southern labor history.

Mooney, Fred. *Struggle in the Coal Fields.* Ed. by J. W. Hess. Morgantown: WVU Press, 1967.

Nash, Michael. *Conflict and Accommodation: Coal Miners, Steelworkers, and Socialism, 1890–1920.* Westport, CT: Greenwood, 1982.

National Committee for the Defense of Political Prisoners (Theodore Dreiser, et al.). *Harlan Miners Speak: Report on Terrorism in the Kentucky Coal Fields.* New York: Harcourt, Brace, 1932; rpt. New York: DaCapo, 1970.

On Dark and Bloody Ground: An Oral History of the U.M.W.A. in Central Appalachia, 1920–1935. A National Endowment Youth Grant Report, 1973.

Parton, Mary F., ed. *The Autobiography of Mother Jones.* Chicago: Charles H. Kerr, 1925, 1972. For additional information on Mother Jones, see Linda Atkinson. *Mother Jones: The Most Dangerous Woman in America.* New York: Crown, 1978; Dale Fetherling. *Mother Jones, The Miners' Angel.* Carbondale: Southern Illinois U. Press, 1974; Philip S. Foner, ed. *Mother Jones Speaks: Collected Writings and Speeches.* New York: Monad Press, 1983; Edward M. Steel, ed. *The Correspondence of Mother Jones.* Pittsburgh: U. of Pittsburgh Press, 1985; and Edward M. Steel, ed. *The Speeches and Writings of Mother Jones.* Pittsburgh: U. of Pittsburgh Press, 1988.

Roydhouse, Marion W. " 'Big Enough to Tell Weeds from the Beans': The Impact of Industry on Women in the Twentieth-Century South." In *The South Is Another Land: Essays on Women in the Twentieth-Century South,* ed. Bruce Clayton & John L. Salmond, 85–106. Westport, CT: Greenwood, 1987.

Savage, Lon K. *Thunder in the Mountains: The West Virginia Mine War, 1920–21.* Charleston, WV: Jalamap Publications, 1985.

Tippet, Tom. *When Southern Labor Stirs.* New York: Jonathan Cape & Harrison Smith, 1931; rpt. Huntington, WV: Appalachian Movement Press, 1972.

Titler, George. *Hell in Harlan.* Beckley, WV: BJW Printers, 1973.

Ward, Robert D., & William W. Rogers. *Labor Revolt in Alabama: The Great Strike of 1894.* University, AL: U. of Alabama Press, 1965.

Wardell, Mark, & Robert L. Johnson. "Struggle and Industrial Transformation: The U.S. Anthracite Industry, 1820–1902." *Theory and Society* 16 (November 1987): 781–808.

Yarrow, Michael. "The Labor Process in Coal Mining: Struggle for Control." In *Case Studies on the Labor Process,* ed. Andrew Zimbalist, 170–92. New York: Monthly Review Press, 1979.

Zieger, Robert H. *John L. Lewis: Labor Leader.* Schenectady, NY: Twayne, 1988.

See also works in IV A, IV B, IV C, IX E, X, & XIII.

V. CULTURE

Batteau, Allen. "Appalachia and the Concept of Culture: A Theory of Shared Misunderstandings." *AJ* 7 (Autumn–Winter 1979–80): 9–31. Also in E&K, 109–25.

———. "Rituals of Dependence in Appalachian Kentucky." In B, 142–67.

Beaver, Patricia D., & Burton L. Purrington, eds. *Cultural Adaptation to Mountain Environments.* Athens: U. of Georgia, 1984.

Conti, Eugene A., Jr. "The Cultural Role of Local Elite in the Kentucky Mountains: A Retrospective Analysis." *AJ* 7 (Autumn–Winter 1979–80): 51–68. See also Conti's Ph.D. diss.: "Mountain Metamorphoses: Culture and Development in Eastern Kentucky," Duke U., 1978.

Cunningham, Rodger. *Apples on the Flood: The Southern Mountain Experience.* Knoxville: UTP, 1987.

Ford, Thomas R. "The Passing of Provincialism." In *The Southern Appalachian Region,* ed. Thomas R. Ford, 9–34. Lexington: UKP, 1962. Also in E&K, 129–54.

Jones, Loyal. "Appalachian Values." In *Appalachians Speak Up,* ed. I. Best, 109–21. Berea, KY: By the Editor, 1972. Also in H&M, 507–17. Also in E&K, 125–29.

Lewis, Helen M. "Subcultures of the Southern Appalachians." *Virginia Geographer* 3 (Spring 1968): 2–8.

Lewis, Helen M., & Edward Knipe. "The Impact of Coal Mining on the Traditional Mountain Sub-culture." In *The Not So Solid South: Anthropological Studies in a Regional Subculture,* ed. John Moreland, 25–37. Athens: U. of Georgia Press, 1971.

Miller, Jim Wayne. "Appalachian Values/American Values." 6 parts. *AH* 5 (Fall 1977)—7 (Winter 1979).

Shapiro, Henry D. "The Place of Culture and the Problem of Identity." In B, 111–41.

Welch, Janet G. "A Study of Appalachian Cultural Values as Evidenced in the Political and Social Attitudes of Rural West Virginians." 2 vols. Ph.D. diss., U. of Maryland, 1984.

Weller, Jack. *Yesterday's People: Life in Contemporary Appalachia.* Lexington: UKP, 1965.

Whisnant, David E. *All That Is Native and Fine: The Politics of Culture in an American Region.* Chapel Hill: UNC Press, 1983.

———, ed. "Process, Policy, and Context: Contemporary Perspectives on Appalachian Culture." *AJ* 7 (Autumn–Winter 1979–80).

Whitson, S. Mont., ed. *Sense of Place in Appalachia.* Morehead, KY: Office of Regional Development Services, Morehead State U., 1988.

See also works in I D, VI, & IX A.

VI. AGENTS OF SOCIALIZATION

A. Family

Anglin, Mary. "Redefining the Family and Women's Status within the Family: The Case of Southern Appalachia." In *Feminist Visions: Toward a Transformation of the Liberal Arts Curriculum,* ed. Diane L. Fowlkes & Charlotte S. McClure, 110–18. University, AL: U. of Alabama Press, 1984.

Batteau, Allen. "The Contradictions of a Kinship Community." In *Holding On to the Land and the Lord: Kinship, Ritual, Land Tenure, and Social Policy in the Rural South,* ed. Robert L. Hall & Carol B. Stack, 25–40. Athens: U. of Georgia, 1982.

Brown, James S., & Harry K. Schwarzweller. "The Appalachian Family." In P&S, 85–97.

Bryant, F. Carlene. "Family Group Organization in a Cumberland Mountain Neighborhood." In B, 28–47.

Coles, Robert. *Migrants, Sharecroppers, Mountaineers.* Vol. II of *Children of Crisis.* Boston: Little, Brown/Atlantic Monthly, 1971.

Cox, Arthur J. "Black Appalachian Families." *Journal of Sociology and Social Welfare* 10 (June 1983): 312–25.

Egerton, John. *Generations: An American Family.* Lexington: UKP, 1983.

Ewald, Wendy. *Portraits and Dreams: Photographs and Stories by Children of the Appalachians.* New York: Writers & Readers Pub., 1985.

Ford, Thomas R., Thomas A. Arcury, & Julia D. Porter. "The Impact of Economic Change on Central Appalachian Households and Families." *Sociological Focus* 18 (October 1985): 288–89.

Hirsch, Herbert. *Poverty and Politicalization: Political Socialization in an American Subculture.* New York: Free Press, 1971.

Jaros, Dean, Herbert Hirsch, & Frederick Fleron, Jr. "The Malevolent Leader: Political Socialization in an American Subculture." *American Political Science Review* 62 (June 1968): 564–75.

Jaros, Dean, & John A. Shoemaker. "The Malevolent Unindicted Co-conspirator: Watergate and Appalachian Youth." *American Politics Quarterly* 4 (October 1976): 483–508.

Keefe, Susan E., ed. *Appalachian Mental Health.* Lexington: UKP, 1988.

Lewis, Helen M., Sue E. Kobak, & Linda Johnson. "Family, Religion, and Colonialism in Central Appalachia or Bury My Rifle at Big Stone Gap." In LJ&A, 113–39.

Looff, David H. *Appalachia's Children: The Challenge of Mental Health.* Lexington: UKP, 1971.

Photiadis, John D. *Community and Family Change in Rural Appalachia.* Morgantown: Center for Extension and Continuing Education, WVU, 1983.

Polansky, Norman, Robert D. Borgman, & Christine DeSaix. *Roots of Futility.* San Francisco: Jossey-Bass, 1972.

Ritchie, Jean. *Singing Family of the Cumberlands.* New York: Oak Publications, 1955.

Sloane, Vera Mae. *What My Heart Wants to Tell.* Washington, DC: New Republic Books, 1979.

See also works in I D, V, & IX A.

B. Religion

Abell, Troy D. *Better Felt Than Said: The Holiness-Pentecostal Experience in Southern Appalachia.* Waco: Baylor U. Press, 1982.

Albanese, Catherine L. *America, Religions, and Religion.* Belmont, CA: Wadsworth, 1981. See esp. Chap. 9.

Billings, Dwight B. "Religion as Opposition: A Gramscian Analysis." *American Journal of Sociology* 96 (July 1990): 1–31.

Boles, John B. *The Great Revival, 1787–1805: The Origins of the Southern Evangelical Mind.* Lexington: UKP, 1972.

Bruce, Dickson D. *And They All Sang Hallelujah: Plain-Folk Camp-Meeting Religion, 1800–1845.* Knoxville: UTP, 1974.

Christian Social Action, October 1989. Special issue on Appalachia.

Coles, Robert. "God and the Rural Poor." *Psychology Today,* January 1972, 33–40. Also in E&K, 322–29.

David, Charles T., & Richard A. Humphrey. "Appalachian Religion: A Diversity of Consciousness." *AJ* 5 (Summer 1978): 390–99.

Dickinson, Eleanor, & Barbara Benziger. *Revival.* New York: Harper & Row, 1974.

Dorgan, Howard. *Giving Glory to God in Appalachia: Worship Practices of Six Baptist Subdenominations.* Knoxville: UTP, 1987.

————. *The Old Regular Baptists of Central Appalachia: Brothers and Sisters in Hope.* Knoxville: UTP, 1989.

Johnson, Douglas W. *The Commission on Religion in Appalachia, Inc.: A Case Study.* New York: National Council of the Churches of Christ, 1971.

Johnson, Linda. "The Foot-Washin' Church and the Prayer-Book Church: Resisting Cultural Imperialism in Southern Appalachia." *Christian Century,* 3 November 1976, 952–55. See responses to the article in *Christian Century,* 6 April 1977, 322–25.

Jones, Loyal. "Studying Mountain Religion." *AJ* 5 (Autumn 1977): 125–30.

Kane, Stephen M. "Holy Ghost People: The Snake-Handlers of Southern Appalachia." *AJ* 1 (Spring 1974): 255–62. See also Kane's Ph.D. diss.: "Snake Handlers of Southern Appalachia," Princeton U., 1979.

Lawless, Elaine J. *God's Peculiar People: Women's Voices and Folk Tradition in a Pentecostal Church.* Lexington: UKP, 1988.

Lewis, Helen M., Sue E. Kobak, & Linda Johnson. "Family, Religion, and Colonialism in Central Appalachia or Bury My Rifle at Big Stone Gap." In LJ&A, 113–39.

McCauley, Deborah V. "The Study of Appalachian Mountain Religion." *AJ* (Winter 1989): 138–52.

Peacock, James L., & Ruel W. Tyson, Jr. *Pilgrims of Paradox: Calvinism and Experience among the Primitive Baptists of the Blue Ridge.* Wash., DC: Smithsonian Institution Press, 1989.

Photiadis, John D., ed. *Religion in Appalachia: Theological, Social and Psychological Dimensions and Correlates.* Morgantown, WVU, 1978.

Reinhardt, Robert M. "Religion and Politics: The Political Behavior of West Virginia Protestant Fundamentalist Sectarians." Ph.D. diss., WVU, 1974.

Rosenberg, Ellen M. *The Southern Baptists: A Subculture in Transition.* Knoxville: UTP, 1989.

SE 4 (Fall 1976). Special Issue: "On Jordan's Stormy Banks: Religion in the South."

Sovine, Melanie L. "Studying Religious Belief Systems in Their Social Historical Context." In B, 48–67.

Titon, Jeff T. *Powerhouse for God: Speech, Chant and Song in an Appalachian Baptist Church.* Austin: U. of Texas Press, 1988.

Wallhausser, John. "I Can Almost See Heaven from Here." *Katallagete* 8 (Spring 1983): 2–10.

Weatherford, W. D., & Earl D. C. Brewer. *Life and Religion in Southern Appalachia: An Interpretation of Selected Data from the Southern Appalachian Studies.* New York: Friendship Press, 1962.

See also works in I D, V, & IX A.

C. Class

Batteau, Allen. "Mosbys and Broomsedge: The Semantics of Class in an Appalachian Kinship System." *American Ethnologist* 9 (August 1982): 445–66.

Coles, Robert. *Privileged Ones: The Well-Off and the Rich in America.* Vol. 5 of *Children of Crisis.* Boston: Little, Brown/Atlantic Monthly, 1977. See esp. 157–81.

Fisher, Steve. "Life with Father: Reflections on Class Analysis." *AJ* 11 (Autumn–Winter 1983–84): 154–62.

Long, Tim. "Social Stratification in Appalachia." *AH* 5 (Fall 1977): 54–58.

McDonald, Joseph A. "Union Attitudes and Class Consciousness: The Case of the Tufted Textile Industry." *AJ* 9 (Fall 1981): 38–48.

Portelli, Alessandro. "Patterns of Paternalism in Harlan County." *AJ* 17 (Winter 1990): 140–55.

Roebuck, Julian, & Mark Hickson, III. *The Southern Redneck: A Phenomenological Class Study.* New York: Praeger, 1982.

Smith, Kevin B., & Robert A. Bylund. "Cognitive Maps of Class, Racial, and Appalachian Inequalities among Rural Appalachians." *Rural Sociology* 48 (Summer 1983): 253–70.

Southern Mountain Research Collective, ed. "Essays in Political Economy: Toward a Class Analysis of Appalachia." *AJ* 11 (Autumn–Winter 1983–84).

Tudiver, Sari L. "Political Economy and Culture in Central Appalachia, 1790–1977." Ph.D. diss., U. of Michigan, 1984.

Walls, David S., & Dwight B. Billings. "The Sociology of Southern Appalachia." *AJ* 5 (Autumn 1977): 131–44. Also in E&K, 41–51.

Yarrow, Michael. "How Good Strong Union Men Line It Out: Explorations of the Structure and Dynamics of Coal Miners' Class Consciousness." Ph.D. diss., Rutgers U., 1982.

See also works in I D, IV C, IV D, V, VI A, VI B, VI D (especially the works on the textbook dispute), VIII, IX, X, & XIII.

D. Education

Baldwin, Fred. "AEL: A Laboratory for Better Education." *Appalachia* 23 (Spring 1990); 9–14.

Billings, Dwight, & Robert Goldman. "Religion and Class Consciousness in the Kanawha County School Textbook Controversy." In B, 68–85.

Boyd, Tom, & Alan J. DeYoung. "Experts vs. Amateurs: The Irony of School Consolidation in Jackson County, Kentucky." *AJ* 13 (Spring 1986): 275–87.

Campbell, Roberta, & Alan J. DeYoung. "A Bridge or a Barrier?: Assessing the Usefulness of Public Education for Individual Success in an East Tennessee County." In L, 155–74.

Clark, Mike, Jim Branscome, & Bob Snyder. *Appalachian Miseducation.* Huntington, WV: Appalachian Press, 1974.

Cowan, Paul. "A Fight Over America's Future: Holy War in West Virginia." *Village Voice,* 9 December 1974, 19–23.

Cox, J. Lamarr, Judy Ann Holley, Hayman Kite, & Wanda Y. Durham. *Study of High School Dropouts in Appalachia.* Prepared for the ARC. Triangle Park, NC: Center for Education, Research Triangle Institute, 1985.

Crew, B. Keith. *Dropout and Functional Illiteracy Rates in Central Appalachia.* Appalachia Data Bank Report #1. Lexington: Appalachian Center, U. of Kentucky, 1985.

DeYoung, Alan J. "Appalachian Educational Research in the National Context: Where Have We Been and Where Are We Going." In *Remembrance, Reunion and Revival: Celebrating a Decade of Appalachian Studies. Proceedings of the 10th Annual Appalachian Studies Conference,* ed. Helen Roseberry, 29–49. Boone: ACP, 1988.

————. "The Status of Formal Education in Central Appalachia." *AJ* 10 (Summer 1983): 321–34.

DeYoung, Alan J., & Julia D. Porter. "Multicultural Education in Appalachia: Origins, Prospects and Problems." *AJ* 7 (Autumn–Winter 1979–80): 124–34.

DeYoung, Alan J., Charles Vaught, James J. O'Brien, & Jean A. Brymer. *Educational Performance in Central Appalachia: Statistical Profiles of Appalachian and Non-Appalachian School Districts.* Prepared for the ARC. Lexington: Appalachian Center, U. of Kentucky, 1982.

Gotts, Edward E., & Richard F. Purnell. "Families and Schools in Rural Appalachia." *American Journal of Community Psychology* 14 (October 1986): 499–520.

Horton, Bill. "Images of Classlessness and Berea College." *AJ* 11 (Autumn–Winter 1983–84): 58–66.

Lewis, Helen M. "State College: The Clinch Valley Experience." *MR* 3 (February 1978): 30–34.

Mielke, David N., ed. *Teaching Mountain Children: Towards a Foundation of Understanding.* Boone: ACP, 1978.

Miller, Jim Wayne. "Appalachian Education: A Critique and Suggestions for Reform." *AJ* 5 (Autumn 1977): 13–22.

Moffett, James. *Storm in the Mountains: A Case Study of Censorship, Conflict and Consciousness.* Carbondale: Southern Illinois U. Press, 1988.

Moses, Allan. "Settlement Schools." In E&K, 296–307.

National Education Association, Teacher Rights Division. *Kanawha County, West Virginia: A Textbook Study in Cultural Conflict.* Washington, DC: 1975.

Page, Ann L., & Donald A. Clelland. "The Kanawha County Textbook Controversy: A Study of the Politics of Life Style Concern." *Social Forces* 57 (September 1978): 265–81. See comments on the article in *Social Forces* 57 (June 1979): 1393–98 and 59 (September 1980): 281–84.

Puckett, John L. *Foxfire Reconsidered: A Twenty-Year Experiment in Progressive Education.* Urbana: UIP, 1989.

Reck, Una Mae Lang, & Gregory G. Reck. "Living Is More Important than Schooling: Schools and Self-Concept in Appalachia." *AJ* 8 (Autumn 1980): 19–25. Also in E&K, 284–89.

Schwarzweller, Harry K., & James S. Brown. "Education as a Cultural Bridge Between Eastern Kentucky and the Great Society." *Rural Sociology* 27 (December 1962): 357–73. Also in P&S, 129–45.

Silver, Roy, & Alan J. DeYoung. "The Ideology of Rural/Appalachian Education, 1895–1935: The Appalachian Education Problem as Part of the Appalachian Life Problem." *Educational Theory* 36 (Winter 1986): 51–65.

University of Kentucky, Appalachian Center, ed. *Education in Appalachia. Proceedings from the 1987 Conference on Appalachia.* Lexington, 1988.

Wigginton, Eliot. *Sometimes a Shining Moment: The Foxfire Experience.* Garden City, NY: Anchor Press/Doubleday, 1985.

See also works in I D, II C, V, IX A, & IX B.

E. Media

"Appalshop and the History of Appalachia: Interviews with Herb E. Smith and Helen Lewis." *AJ* 11 (Summer 1984): 410–23.

Bowler, Betty M. " 'That Ribbon of Social Neglect': Appalachia and the Media in 1964." *AJ* 12 (Spring 1985): 239–47.

Branscome, Jim. "Annihilating the Hillbilly: The Appalachians' Struggle with America's Institutions." *Katallagete* 3 (Winter 1971): 25–32. Also in LJ&A, 211–17.

Fisher, Steve "The National Media and the Mountains." *The Plow,* 4 February 1978, 13.

Gaventa, John. *Power and Powerlessness: Quiescence and Rebellion in an Appalachian Valley.* Urbana: UIP, 1980. See Chap. 8.

"Hollywood in the Hills: An Interview with Tom Rickman." *AJ* 10 (Summer 1983): 335–49.

Maggard, Sally W. "Cultural Hegemony: The News Media and Appalachia." *AJ* (Autumn–Winter 1983–84): 67–83.

———. "Newsmaking and Social Change in Eastern Kentucky: 'Why Aren't They Telling Our Side?' " In *The Appalachian Experience. Proceedings of the 6th Annual Appalachian Studies Conference,* ed. Barry M. Buxton, 67–80. Boone: ACP, 1983.

Newcomb, Horace. "Appalachia on Television: Region as Symbol in American Popular Culture." *AJ* 7 (Autumn–Winter 1979): 155–64.

Seltzer, Curtis. *Fire in the Hole: Miners and Managers in the American Coal Industry.* Lexington: UKP, 1983.

Trillin, Calvin. "Jeremiah, Ky.: A Stranger with a Camera." *New Yorker,* 12 April 1969, 178–83.

Underhill, David. "A Report on CBS News and 17 Million Appalachian People." *MR* 1 (Winter 1975): 1–3, 14.

VII. THE MIGRANT EXPERIENCE

ARC. *A Report to Congress on Migration.* Wash., DC: ARC, 1979.

Arnow, Harriet S. *The Dollmaker.* New York: Macmillan, 1954.

Batteau, Allen, ed. *Appalachia and America: Autonomy and Regional Dependence.* Lexington: UKP, 1983. See for several articles on the migrant experience.

Coalition for Appalachian Ministry. *Wayfaring Strangers: Appalachians in the City.* Amesville, OH, 1984.

Coles, Robert. *The South Goes North.* Vol. III of *Children of Crisis.* Boston: Little, Brown/ Atlantic Monthly, 1972.

Fowler, Gary L. *Appalachian Migration: A Review and Assessment of the Research.* Prepared for the ARC. Chicago: U. of Illinois at Chicago Circle, 1980.

Gitlin, Todd, & Nanci Hollander. *Uptown: Poor Whites in Chicago.* New York: Harper & Row, 1970.

Greenberg, Stanley B. *Politics and Poverty: Modernization and Response in Five Poor Neighborhoods.* New York: Wiley, 1974.

Howell, Joseph T. *Hard Living on Clay Street: Portraits of Blue Collar Families.* Garden City, NY: Anchor, 1973.

Kirby, Jack T. "The Southern Exodus, 1910–1960: A Primer for Historians." *Journal of Southern History* 49 (November 1983): 585–600.

Miller, Jim Wayne. *The Mountains Have Come Closer.* Boone: ACP, 1980. See esp. Part III, "Brier Sermon."

MLW, September 1983. Special issue on urban Appalachians. *MLW* regularly carried information on the activities of urban Appalachians.

Obermiller, Phillip J. *An Annotated Bibliography on Urban Appalachians.* Cincinnati: Urban Appalachian Council, 1984. Also in E&K, 169.

———. "Appalachians as an Urban Ethnic Group: Romanticism, Renaissance, or Revolution? And a Brief Bibliographical Essay on Urban Appalachians." *AJ* 5 (Autumn 1977): 145–52. Also in E&K 164–168.

Obermiller, Phillip J., & William W. Philliber, eds. *Too Few Tomorrows: Urban Appalachians in the 1980s.* Boone: ACP, 1987.

Philliber, William W. *Appalachian Migrants in Urban America: Cultural Conflict or Ethnic Group Formation?* New York: Praeger, 1981.

Philliber, William W., & Clyde B. McCoy, eds. *The Invisible Minority: Urban Appalachians.* Lexington: UKP, 1981.

Schwarzweller, Harry K., James S. Brown & J. J. Mangalam. *Mountain Families in Transition: A Case Study of Appalachian Migration.* University Park: Penn. State U. Press, 1971.

SE 17 (Spring 1989). See for several articles on Appalachian migrants.

Thomas, John C. *Between Citizen and City: Neighborhood Organizations and Urban Politics in Cincinnati.* Lawrence: U. Press of Kansas, 1986.

Tucker, Bruce. "An Interview with Michael Maloney." *AJ* 17 (Fall 1989): 34–48.

Tudiver, Sari L. "Country Road Take Me Home: The Political Economy of Wage-Labor Migration in an Eastern Kentucky Community." In *And the Poor Get Children: Radical Perspectives on Population Dynamics,* ed. Karen Michaelson, 221–45. New York: Monthly Review Press, 1981.

Weiland, Steven, & Phillip J. Obermiller, eds. *Perspectives on Urban Appalachians: An Introduction to Mountain Life, Migration, and Urban Adaptation, and a Guide to the Improvement of Social Services.* Cincinnati: Urban Appalachian Awareness Project, 1978.

White, Stephen. "Return Migration to Eastern Kentucky and the Stem Family Concept." *Growth & Change* 18 (Spring 1987): 38–52.

Zehner, Robert B., & F. Stuart Chapin, Jr. *Across the City Line: A White Community in Transition.* Lexington, MA: Lexington Books, 1974.

VIII. HUMAN NEEDS AND SERVICES: THE QUALITY OF LIFE IN APPALACHIA

Appalachian Alliance. *Appalachia in the Eighties: A Time for Action.* 1982.

Appalachian Landownership Task Force. *Who Owns Appalachia? Landownership and Its Impact.* Lexington: UKP, 1983.

Beardsley, Edward H. *A History of Neglect: Health Care for Blacks and Mill Workers in the Twentieth-Century South.* Knoxville: UTP, 1987.

Bishirjian, Terry. "Rural Health Care in the 1990s: Decade of Decision and Change." *Appalachia* 22 (Spring 1989): 31–37.

Brown, J. Larry, & H. F. Pizer. *Living Hungry in America.* New York: Macmillan, 1987. See Chap. 3.

Center for Economic Competitiveness. *Building Appalachia's Capacity to Compete.* Prepared for the ARC. Wash., DC: SRI International, 1987.

Commission on Religion in Appalachia. *Economic Transformation: The Appalachian Challenge.* Knoxville, 1986.

Couto, Richard A. "Appalachian Innovation in Health Care." In B, 168–88.

Deaton, Brady J., & Charles E. Hanrahan. "Rural Housing Needs and Barriers: The Case of Central Appalachia." *Southern Journal of Agricultural Economics* 5 (July 1973): 59–67.

Duncan, Cynthia, & Ann R. Tickameyer. "Comparison of the Quality of Life in the Coal and Manufacturing Counties of Eastern Kentucky." *AJ* 10 (Spring 1983): 228–43.

Eller, Ronald D. "Looking to the Future: The Problems and Promise of Regional Life." *AH* 13 (Fall 1985): 32–39.

Ellis, Betty. *A Comprehensive Bibliography of Health Care in Appalachia.* Lexington: Appalachian Center, U. of Kentucky, 1988.

Gall-Clayton, Nancy. *Not Poor in Spirit: Hope for Kentucky's Low-Income Families and Children.* Louisville: Kentucky Youth Advocates, 1988.

Gaventa, John. "The Poverty of Abundance Revisited." *AJ* 15 (Fall 1987): 24–33.

Gaventa, John, Barbara E. Smith, & Alex Willingham, eds. *Communities in Economic Crisis: Appalachia and the South.* Philadelphia: Temple U. Press, 1990.

Goss, Rosemary C., & Savannah S. Day. "Housing Conditions and Satisfactions of Central Appalachian Coal Miners." *Home Economics Research Journal* 13 (March 1985): 278–91.

Hanson, William E. "Building Houses in Appalachia: The Non-Profit Motif." *Appalachia* 13 (January–February 1980): 38–48.

Highlander Economics Education Project, ed. *New Directions: Responses to the Rural Economic Crisis.* Abingdon, VA: Creekside Press, 1986.

Johnson, Kenny, & Marilyn Scurlock. "The Climate for Workers: Where Does the South Stand?" *Southern Changes* 8 (October/November 1986): 3–15.

Kraybill, David S., Thomas G. Johnson, & Brady J. Deaton. *Income Uncertainty and the Quality of Life: A Socio-Economic Study of Virginia's Coal Counties.* Virginia Agricultural Experiment Station Bulletin 87-4. Blacksburg: VPI&SU, 1987.

Lazere, Edward B., Paul A. Leonard, & Linda L. Kravitz. *The Other Housing Crisis: Sheltering the Poor in Rural America.* Wash., DC: Center on Budget and Policy Priorities & the Housing Assistance Council, 1989.

Newman, Anne. "The ARC Health Program: Twenty Years of Pioneering Success." *Appalachia* 18:6–19:1 (Fall 1985): 22–31.

Nolan, Robert L., & Jerome Schwartz, eds. *Rural and Appalachian Health.* Springfield, IL: Charles C. Thomas, 1973.

O'Hare, William P. *The Rise of Poverty in Rural America.* Wash., DC: Population Reference Bureau, 1988.

Parlow, Anita. "Pikeville: Millionaires and Mobile Homes." *SE* 3 (Winter 1976): 25–30.

Richard, Patricia B., & Joy Huntley. "Are They Better Off Than They Were Four Years Ago? Reaganomics and the Women of Athens County." *AJ* 12 (Summer 1985): 306–23.

Rowles, Graham D. *The Elderly in Appalachia.* Appalachian Data Bank Report #3. Lexington: Appalachian Center, U. of Kentucky, 1986.

———. "Place and Personal Identity in Old Age: Observations from Appalachia." *Journal of Environmental Psychology* 3 (December 1983): 299–313.

Rucker, George. "Public Transportation: Another Gap in Rural America." *Transportation Quarterly* 38 (July 1984): 419–32.

Seltzer, Curtis I. "Two Conclusions about Cows and Some Thoughts about Appalachian Economics." In *Appalachia Looks at Its Future: A Regional Forum,* ed., J. Paxton Marshall, 12–20. Blacksburg: Extension Division, Cooperative Extension Service, VPI&SU, 1978.

Southeast Women's Employment Coalition. *Women of the Rural South: Economic Status and Prospects.* Lexington, KY, 1986.

SE 6 (Summer 1978). Special Issue: "Sick for Justice: Health Care and Unhealthy Conditions."

SE 8 (Spring 1980). Special Issue: "Building South."

Tickameyer, Ann R., & Cecil Tickameyer. *Poverty in Appalachia.* Appalachian Data Bank Report #5. Lexington: Appalachian Center, U. of Kentucky, 1987.

UMWJ, 16–29 February 1976. Special section on "Housing Crisis in the Coalfields."

U.S. Congress. House. Select Committee on Hunger. Domestic Task Force. *Appalachia: Rural Women and the Economics of Hunger.* 99th Congress, 1st session, 22 October 1985. Wash., DC: USGPO, 1986.

U.S. President's Commission on Coal. *The American Coal Miner: A Report on Community and Living Conditions in the Coalfields.* Wash., DC: USGPO, 1980.

U. of Kentucky, Appalachian Center. *Health in Appalachia. Proceedings from the 1988 Conference on Appalachia.* Lexington, 1989.

———. *The Land and the Economy of Appalachia. Proceedings from the 1986 Conference on Appalachia.* Lexington, 1987.

———. *The Status of Pre-School Children and Their Support Systems in Central Appalachia.* Appalachian Data Bank Report #7. Lexington, 1988.

Van Willigen, John. *Gettin' Some Age on Me: Social Organization of Older People in a Rural American Community.* Lexington: UKP, 1989.

Whisnant, David E. "Growing Old By Being Poor: Some Cautionary Notes about Generalizing from a Class Phenomenon." *Soundings* 57 (Spring 1974): 101–12.

White, David B. "A Social Epidemiological Model of Central Appalachia." *Arete* 12 (Summer 1987): 47–66. See also White's Ph.D. diss.: "A Social Epidemiological Analysis of Central Appalachian Economic Distress," U. of Pittsburgh, 1982.

Zierath, David L. "The Quality of Life of People in Poor, Rural Southern and Appalachian Areas." Ph.D. diss., U. of Kentucky, 1982.

See also works in I D, III A, IV, X, & XI.

IX. MODELS OF DEVELOPMENT

A. Subculture Model

Ball, Richard A. "Poverty Case: The Analgesic Subculture of the Southern Appalachians." *American Sociological Review* 33 (December 1968): 885–95. Also in P&S, 69–79.

Billings, Dwight. "Culture and Poverty in Appalachia: A Theoretical Discussion and Empirical Analysis." *Social Forces* 53 (December 1974): 315–23.

Erikson, Kai T. *Everything in Its Path: Destruction of Community in the Buffalo Creek Flood.* New York: Simon & Schuster, 1976.

Fisher, Stephen L. "Victim-Blaming in Appalachia: Cultural Theories and the Southern Mountaineer." In E&K, 154–63. Shortened version in W, 14–25.

Goshen, Charles E. "Characterological Deterrants to Economic Progress in People of Appalachia." *Southern Medical Journal* 63 (September 1970): 1053–61.

Lewis, Helen M. "Fatalism in the Coal Industry?" *MLW,* December 1970, 4–15. Also in E&K, 180–89.

Louv, Richard. "Appalachia Syndrome." *Human Behavior* 6 (May 1977): 40–47.

Maloney, Mike, & Ben Huelsman. "Humanism, Scientism and Southern Mountaineers." *PA* 2 (July 1972): 24–27.

Rabow, Jerome, Sherry L. Berkman, & Ronald Kessler. "The Culture of Poverty and Learned Helplessness: A Social Psychological Perspective." *Sociological Inquiry* 53 (Fall 1983): 419–34.

Tincher, Robert. "Night Comes to the Chromosomes: Inbreeding and Population Genetics in Southern Appalachia." *Critical Issues in Anthropology* 2 (1982): 27–50.

Weller, Jack. *Yesterday's People: Life in Contemporary Appalachia.* Lexington: UKP, 1965.

See also works in I D, II A, V, & VI. Some of the works in IX C & IX D offer a critique of this model.

8. Regional Development Model

See XII C. See also works in VIII. Some of the works in IX C & IX D offer a critique of this model.

C. Colonial Model

Appalachian Landownership Task Force. *Who Owns Appalachia? Landownership and Its Impact.* Lexington: UKP, 1983.

Caudill, Harry M. *Night Comes to Cumberlands: A Biography of a Depressed Area.* Boston: Little, Brown/Atlantic Monthly, 1962.

Fisher, Steve, ed. *A Landless People in a Rural Region: A Reader on Land Ownership and Property Taxation in Appalachia.* New Market, TN: Highlander Center, 1979.

Gaventa, John. *Power and Powerless: Quiescence and Rebellion in an Appalachian Valley.* Urbana: UIP, 1980.

Giardina, Denise. "Third World in America." In *Appalachia's Changing Economy,* ed. Paul DeLeon. New Market, TN: Highlander Center, 1986.

Goodstein, Eban. "Landownership, Development, and Poverty in Southern Appalachia." *Journal of Developing Areas* 23 (July 1989): 519–33.

Langman, R. C. *Appalachian Kentucky: An Exploited Region.* New York: McGraw-Hill Ryerson Ltd., 1971.

Lewis, Helen M., Linda Johnson, & Donald Askins, eds. *Colonialism in America: The Appalachian Case.* Boone: ACP, 1978.

Lewis, Helen M., & Edward E. Knipe. "The Colonialism Model: The Appalachian Case." In LJ&A, 9–31.

Lewis, Helen M., Sue E. Kobak, & Linda Johnson. "Family, Religion and Colonialism in Central Appalachia or Bury My Rifle at Big Stone Gap." In LJ&A, 113–39.

Nyden, Paul J. "An Internal Colony: Labor Conflict and Capitalism in Appalachian Coal." *Insurgent Sociologist* 8 (Winter 1979): 33–43.

PA. Writers for this journal were among the first to popularize the idea of Appalachia as a colony. See especially Vol. I.

Turner, William H. "Race: The Ignored Dimension of the Colonial Analogy as Applied to Powerlessness and Exploitation in Appalachia." *Journal of Black Studies* 7 (Spring 1983): 10–25.

See also works in IV & XI. See works on coal landownership and taxation in X A 1. Some of the works in IX D & IX E offer a critique of this model.

D. Beyond the Colonial Model

Arnett, Douglas O. "Eastern Kentucky: The Politics of Dependence and Underdevelopment." Ph.d. diss., Duke U., 1978.

Banks, Alan, & Jim Foster. "The Mystifications of Post-Industrialism." *AJ* 10 (Summer 1983): 372–78.

Batteau, Allen. "A Contribution to the Critique of Political Economy." In *The Many Faces of Appalachia. Proceedings of the 7th Annual Appalachian Studies Conference,* ed. Sam Gray, 41–46. Boone: ACP, 1985.

Clavel, Pierre. *Opposition Planning in Wales and Appalachia.* Philadelphia: Temple U. Press, 1983.

Curran, Daniel. "Dead Laws for Dead Men: The Case of Federal Coal Mine Health and Safety Legislation." Ph.D. diss., U. of Delaware, 1980.

Duncan, Cynthia L. "Capital and the State in Regional Economic Development: The Case of the Coal Industry in Central Appalachia." Ph.D. diss., U. of Kentucky, 1985.

Fisher, Steve. "The Nicaraguan Revolution and the U.S. Response: Lessons for Appalachia." *AJ* 14 (Fall 1986): 22–37.

Fisher, Steve, & Jim Foster. "Models for Furthering Revolutionary Praxis in Appalachia." *AJ* 6 (Spring 1979): 171–94.

Foster, Jim, Steve Robinson, & Steve Fisher. "Class, Political Consciousness and Destructive Power: A Strategy for Change in Appalachia." *AJ* 5 (Spring 1978): 290–311.

Gaventa, John, Barbara E. Smith, & Alex Willingham, eds. *Communities in Economic Crisis: Appalachia and the South.* Philadelphia: Temple U. Press, 1990.

Legeay, Stephen P. "The Development of Advanced Capitalism: A Case Study of Retired Coal Miners in Southern West Virginia." Ph.D. diss., U. of Notre Dame, 1980.

Lewis, Helen M. "Industrialization, Class, and Regional Consciousness in Two Highland Societies: Wales and Appalachia." In *Cultural Adaptation to Mountain Environments,* ed. Patricia D. Beaver & Burton L. Purrington, 50–70. Athens: U. of Georgia, 1984.

Lewis, Helen M., & Myles Horton. "The Role of Transnational Corporations and the Migration of Industries in Latin America and Appalachia." In S, 22–33.

Lohman, Rodger A. "Four Perspectives on Appalachian Culture and Poverty." In L, 76–91.

McNutt, John G. "An Alternative Development Strategy for Appalachia's Future: Applications of 'Another Development' and 'Sustainable Society' Themes to a Region in Crisis." In *The Land and Economy of Appalachia, Proceedings from the 1986 Conference on Appalachia,* ed. Appalachian Center, U. of Kentucky, 51–58. Lexington, 1987.

Malizia, Emil. "Economic Imperialism: An Interpretation of Appalachian Underdevelopment." *AJ* 1 (Spring 1973): 264–72. Also in E&K, 189–99.

Matvey, Joseph J. "Central Appalachia: Distortions in Development, 1750–1986." Ph.D. diss., U. of Pittsburgh, 1987.

O'Toole, Thomas. "Culture and Development: Through Romantic Relativism into the Emerging Present." *AJ* 6 (Summer 1979): 264–72.

Plaut, Tom. "Appalachia and Social Change: A Cultural Systems Approach." *AJ* 6 (Summer 1979): 250–63.

―――. "Extending the Internal Periphery Model: The Impact of Culture and Consequent Strategy." In L&A, 351–64.

Pudup, Mary Beth. "Land before Coal: Class and Regional Development in Southeast Kentucky." Ph.D. diss., U. of California, Berkeley, 1987.

Reid, Herbert G. "Appalachian Policy, Social Values, and Ideology Critique." In *Policy Analysis: Perspectives, Concepts and Methods,* ed. William N. Dunn, 203–22. Greenwich, CT.: JAI Press, 1986.

Salstrom, Paul. "Appalachia's Path Toward Welfare Dependency, 1840–1940." Ph.D. diss., Brandeis U., 1988.

Simon, Richard M. "The Labor Process and Uneven Development: The Appalachian Coalfields, 1880–1930." *International Journal of Urban and Regional Research* 4 (March 1980): 46–71. A slightly different version of this article appears in *AJ* 8 (Spring 1981): 165–86. See also Simon's Ph.D. diss.: "The Development of Underdevelopment: The Coal Industry and Its Effect on the West Virginia Economy, 1880–1930," U. of Pittsburgh, 1978.

Southern Mountain Research Collective, ed. "Essays in Political Economy: Toward a Class Analysis of Appalachia." *AJ* 11 (Autumn–Winter 1983–84).

Tudiver, Sari L. "Political Economy and Culture in Central Appalachia, 1790–1977." Ph.D. diss., U. of Michigan, 1984.

Walls, David. "Central Appalachia: A Peripheral Region Within an Advanced Capitalist Society." *Journal of Sociology and Social Welfare* 4 (November 1976): 232–47. Also in LJ&A, 319–49. See also Walls' Ph.D. diss.: "Central Appalachia in Advanced Capitalism: Its Coal Industry Structure and Coal Operator Associations," U. of Kentucky, 1978.

Wells, John C. Jr. "Poverty amidst Riches: Why People Are Poor in Appalachia." Ph.D. diss., Rutgers U., 1977.

See also works in II A, IV, VI C, IX C & IX E.

E. Gender

Anglin, Mary K. " 'A Lost and Dying World': Women's Labor in the Mica Industry of Southern Appalachia." Ph.D. diss., New School for Social Research, 1990.

———. "Working Women: The Intersection of Historical Anthropology and Social History." *AJ* 16 (Winter 1989): 154–63.

Bokemeier, Janet L., & Ann R. Tickameyer. "Labor Force Experiences of Nonmetropolitan Women." *Rural Sociology* 50 (Spring 1985): 51–73.

Borman, Kathryn M., Elaine Mueninghoff, & Shirley Piazza. "Urban Appalachian Girls and Young Women: Bowing to No One." In *Class, Race, and Gender in American Education,* ed. Lois Weis, 230–248. Albany: State U. of New York, 1988.

Fiene, Judith I. "Gender, Class and Self-Image." In *Appalachian Mental Health,* ed. Susan E. Keefe, 66–80. Lexington: UKP, 1988. See also Fiene's Ph.D. diss.: "The Social Reality of a Group of Rural Low-Status Appalachian Women: A Grounded Theory Study," U. of Tennessee, 1988.

Hall, Jacquelyn D. "Disorderly Women: Gender and Labor Militancy in the Appalachian South." *Journal of American History* 73 (September 1986): 354–82.

Maggard, Sally W. "Class and Gender: New Theoretical Priorities in Appalachian Studies." In *The Impact of Institutions in Appalachia. Proceedings of the 8th Annual Appalachian Studies Conference,* ed. Jim Lloyd & Anne G. Campbell, 100–13. Boone: ACP, 1986.

———. "Eastern Kentucky Women on Strike: A Study of Gender, Class, and Political Action in the 1970s." Ph.D. diss., U. of Kentucky, 1988.

Pudup, Mary Beth. "Beyond the 'Traditional Mountain Subculture': A New Look at Pre-Industrial Appalachia." In *The Impact of Institutions in Appalachia. Proceedings of the 8th Annual Appalachian Studies Conference,* ed. Jim Lloyd & Anne G. Campbell, 114–27. Boone: ACP, 1986.

Tice, Karen, & Amy Pabon. "From 'Fotched-on' Women to the New Feminism: A Review of Women in Social Service Delivery for Women in Appalachia." In *Remembrance, Reunion and Revival: Celebrating a Decade of Appalachian Studies,* ed. Helen Roseberry, 57–67. Boone: ACP, 1988.

Tudiver, Sari L. "Political Economy and Culture in Central Appalachia, 1790–1977." Ph.D. diss., U. of Michigan, 1984.

Whites, LeeAnn. "The DeGraffenried Controversy: Class, Race, and Gender in the New South." *Journal of Southern History* 54 (August 1988): 449–78.

Yarrow, Mike. "Capitalism, Patriarchy and 'Men's Work': The System of Control of Production in Coal Mining." In *The Impact of Institutions in Appalachia. Proceedings of the 8th Annual Appalachian Studies Conference,* ed. Jim Lloyd & Anne G. Campbell, 29–47. Boone: ACP, 1986.

Yount, Kristen R. "Women and Men Coal Miners: Coping with Gender Integration Underground." Ph.D. diss., U. of Colorado at Boulder, 1986.

See also works in III C, IV, VI & IX D.

X. CORPORATE AND LABOR ACTORS

A. Coal

1. Industry Structure, Characteristics, Impact, and Trends

Ackerman, Bruce A. & William T. Hassler. *Clean Coal/Dirty Air or How the Clean Air Act Became a Multibillion Dollar Bail-Out for High-Sulphur Coal Producers and What Should Be Done About It.* New Haven: Yale U. Press, 1981.

Alm, Alvin L. *Coal Myths and Environmental Realities: Industrial Fuel-Use Decisions in a Time of Change.* Boulder, CO: Westview, 1984.

Appalachian Land Ownership Task Force. *Who Owns Appalachia? Landownership and Its Impact.* Lexington: UKP, 1983. Includes an extensive annotated bibliography on coal landownership & property taxation.

Arble, Meade. *The Long Tunnel: A Coal Miner's Journal.* New York: Atheneum, 1976.

Balliet, Lee. *"A Pleasing Tho' Dreadful Sight:" Social and Economic Impacts of Coal Production in the Eastern Coalfields.* Prepared for the Office of Technology Assessment, 1978.

Bagby, Jane W., ed. *Environment in Appalachia. Proceedings from the 1989 Conference on Appalachia.* Lexington: Appalachian Center, U. of Kentucky, 1990.

Baratz, Morton S. *The Union and the Coal Industry.* New Haven: Yale U. Press, 1955.

Batt, Laura. *Coal Industry Research Guide.* Lexington: East Kentucky Chapter, National Lawyers Guild, 1980.

Bell, Brenda, & June Rostan. *Pregnant and Mining: A Handbook for Pregnant Miners.* Oak Ridge, TN: Coal Employment Project, 1982.

Braunstein, H. H., E. D. Copenhaver, & H. A. Pfuderer, eds. *Environmental, Health, and Control Aspects of Coal Conversion: An Information Overview.* 2 vols. Oak Ridge, TN: Oak Ridge National Laboratory, 1977.

Calzonetti, Frank J., Timothy Allison, Muhammad A. Choudhry, Gregory G. Sayre, & Tom S. Witt. *Power from the Appalachians: A Solution to the Northeast's Electricity Problems?.* Westport, CT: Greenwood, 1989.

Carpenter, Donna S. *Coal Industry Taxes.* New York: McGraw-Hill, 1981.

Charles River Associates, Inc. *The Economic Impact of Public Policy on the Appalachian Coal Industry and the Regional Economy.* 3 vols. Prepared for the ARC. Wash., DC, 1973.

Clemens, John M., & Francis E. Kazemek. *Citizens' Coal Haul Handbook.* Corbin, KY: Appalachia-Science in the Public Interest, 1978.

Coal. Chicago: McLean Hunter Pub. (monthly).

Coal Company Monitoring Project. *". . . in the mines, in the mines, in the Blue Diamond Mines. . .".* Knoxville, 1979.

Coal Data. Wash., DC: National Coal Association (annually).

Conrad, Robert F., & R. Bryce Hool. *Taxation of Mineral Resources.* Lexington, MA: Lexington Books, 1980.

Council of State Governments. *State Coal Severance Taxes and Distribution of Revenue.* Lexington, KY, 1976.

Couto, Richard A. "Changing Technologies and Consequences for Labor in Coal Mining." In *Workers, Managers and Technological Change,* ed. Daniel B. Cornfield, 175–202. New York: Plenum, 1987.

Dix, Keith. *What's a Coal Miner to Do? The Mechanization of Coal Mining.* Pittsburgh: U. of Pittsburgh Press, 1989.

Donovan, Arthur. "Carboniferous Capitalism: Excess Productive Capacity and Institutional Backwardness in the U.S. Coal Industry." *Materials and Society* 7: 3–4 (1983): 265–78.

Dotterweich, Douglas. *Property Tax Effort in Eastern Kentucky Counties: Implications for Financing Public Services.* Morehead, KY: Appalachian Development Center, Morehead State University, 1982.

Dow, Alan. *Synthetic Fuels from Coal and Coal Shale.* Lexington, KY: Appalachia-Science in the Public Interest, 1981.

Duncan, Cynthia L. *Coal and Economic Development in Central Appalachia: A New Framework for Policy.* Berea, KY: Mountain Association for Community Economic Development, 1986.

Elliot, Thomas C., & Robert Schwieger, eds. *The Acid Rain Sourcebook.* New York: McGraw-Hill, 1984.

Energy Ventures Analysis, Inc. *Labor Productivity Changes in Appalachian Coal Mining.* Berea, KY: Mountain Association for Community Economic Development, 1986.

Facts about Coal. Wash., DC: National Coal Association (annually).

Fisher, Steve, ed. *A Landless People in a Rural Region: A Reader on Land Ownership and Property Taxation in Appalachia.* New Market, TN: Highland Center, 1979.

Froehlich, Larry G. "A Study of Public School Tax Revenue Losses Due to Current Tax Appraisals of Selected West Virginia Coal Lands." Ed.D. diss., WVU, 1984.

Gordon, Richard L. *Coal in the U.S. Energy Market: History and Prospects.* Lexington, MA: Lexington Books, 1978.

Hall, Betty Jean. *Women in the Coal Industry.* Oak Ridge, TN: Coal Employment Project, 1978.

Harvey, Curtis E. *Coal in Appalachia: An Economic Analysis.* Lexington: UKP, 1986.

Harvey, Curtis, Herbert G. Reid, David S. Walls, & Ann-Marie Yanarella. *Coal and the Social Sciences: A Bibliographical Guide to the Literature.* Lexington: Social Science/Technology Development Group, U. of Kentucky, 1979.

James, Peter. *The Future of Coal.* New York: Macmillan, 1982.

Kaufman, Paul J. "The Horse Creek Story: A Model for the Coal Industry." *AJ* 5 (Winter 1978): 194–97.

Kentucky Fair Tax Coalition. *Taxing Unmined Minerals in Kentucky: Questions and Answers.* Lovely, KY, 1983.

Keystone Coal Industry Manual. New York: McGraw-Hill (annually).

Kolbash, Ronald L. "A Study of Appalachia's Coal Mining Communities and Associated Environmental Problems." Ph.D. diss., Michigan State U., 1975.

Kroll-Smith, J. Stephen, & Stephen R. Couch. *The Real Disaster Is Above Ground: A Mine Fire & Social Conflict.* Lexington: UKP, 1990.

Lenzi, Raymond C. "The Relationship of Coal Severance Tax Allocations to Coal County Socio-economic Conditions." Ph.D. diss., Southern Illinois U. at Carbondale, 1985.

Levy, Builder. *Images of Appalachian Coalfields.* Philadelphia: Temple U. Press, 1989.

Lewis, Helen M. *Coal Productivity and Community: The Impact of the National Energy Plan in the Eastern Coalfields.* Prepared for the Department of Energy, 1978.

Long, Priscilla. *Where the Sun Never Shines: A History of America's Bloody Coal Industry.* New York: Paragon House, 1989.

McCormick, John L. *Facts about Coal in the United States.* Rev. ed. Wash., DC: Environmental Policy Center, 1975.

McGinley, Patrick C., & Barbara S. Webber. "Pandora in the Coal Fields: Environmental Liabilities, Acquisitions, and Dispositions of Coal Properties." *West Virginia Law Review* 87 (Spring 1985): 666–85.

McMartin, Wallace, Virgil Whetzel, & Paul R. Myers. *Coal Development in Rural America: The Resources at Risk.* Rural Development Research Report-29. Wash., DC: ERS, USDA, 1981.

Miller, Saunders. *The Economics of Nuclear and Coal Power.* New York: Praeger, 1976.

Mirvis, Kenneth W. "A Phenomenological Analysis of Two Appalachian Coal-Producing Counties." Ed.D. diss., Boston U. School of Education, 1981.

Munn, Robert F. *The Coal Industry in America: A Bibliography and Guide to Studies.* Morgantown: WVU Library, 1977.

Murray, Francis X., ed. *Where We Agree: Report of the National Coal Policy Project.* 2 vols. Boulder, CO: Westview, 1978.

Nelson, Robert H. *The Making of Federal Coal Policy.* Durham: Duke U. Press, 1983.

Noyes, Robert, ed. *Coal Resources, Characteristics and Ownership in the U.S.A.* Park Ridge, NJ: Noyes Data Corporation, 1978.

Peterson, Bill. *Coaltown Revisited: An Appalachian Notebook.* Chicago: Henry Regnery, 1972.

Regens, James L., & Robert W. Rycroft. *The Acid Rain Controversy.* Pittsburgh: U. of Pittsburgh Press, 1988.

Research Triangle Institute, North Carolina State U., & ARC. *An Assessment of the Effects of Coal Movement on the Highways in the Appalachian Region.* Wash., DC: ARC, 1977.

Ridgeway, James. *Who Owns the Earth.* New York: Collier Books, 1980.

Rivers, Francis J. *People and Jobs in the Southwestern Virginia Coalfields.* A Report prepared for the Commission on Religion in Appalachia and the Community College Ministries. Knoxville, 1986.

Rosenbaum, Walter A. *Coal and Crisis: The Political Dilemmas of Energy Management.* New York: Praeger, 1978.

Sachs, Patricia. "Together We Work, Together We Grow Old: Life, Work and Community in a Coal Mining Town." Ph.D. diss., City U. of New York, 1986.

Schlottmann, Alan M. *Environmental Regulation and the Allocation of Coal: A Regional Analysis*. New York: Praeger, 1977.

Schwenke, William, ed. *Natural Resource Taxation: Perspectives, Resources & Issues*. Wash., DC: Economic Development Project, Conference on Alternative State & Local Policies, 1980.

Seltzer, Curtis. *Coal Employment: Trends and Forecasts, 1975–1995*. Berea, KY: Mountain Association for Community Economic Development, 1986.

————. *The Coal Industry After 1970: Cost Internalization, Good Works, and Public Planning for Development*. Berea, KY: Mountain Association for Community Economic Development, 1986.

————. *Fire in the Hole: Miners and Managers in the American Coal Industry*. Lexington: UKP, 1985.

Seltzer, Curtis, & Cynthia Duncan, eds. *Industry Perspective on Development: Transcripts of Interviews with Coal Industry Leaders*. Berea, KY: Mountain Association for Community Economic Development, 1986.

Sims, Richard. *A Public Sector Income Statement for the Coal Industry in Kentucky, 1985–2000*. Berea, KY: Mountain Association for Community Economic Development, 1986.

Smith, Duane A. *Mining America: The Industry and the Environment, 1800–1980*. Lawrence: U. of Kansas Press, 1987.

Smith, Janet M., David Ostendorf, & Mike Schechtman. *Who's Mining the Farm?* Herrin, IL: Illinois South Project, 1978.

Stinson, Thomas F., & George S. Temple. *State Mineral Taxes, 1982*. Rural Development Research Report-36. Wash., DC: ERS, USDA, 1983.

Thompson, Richard H. "Let's Make a Deal." *AH* 10 (Winter–Spring 1982): 70–80.

Trent, Roger B., & Nancy Stout-Wiegand. "Attitudes toward Women Coal Miners in an Appalachian Coal Community." *Journal of the Community Development Society* 18:1 (1987): 1–14.

U.S. Department of Energy. *The Changing Structure of the Coal Industry, 1976–1986*. Wash., DC: USGPO, 1988.

U.S. Department of Justice. *Competition in the Coal Industry*. Wash., DC, 1978.

U.S. President's Commission on Coal. *The American Coal Miner: A Report on Community and Living Conditions in the Coalfields*. Wash., DC: USGPO, 1980.

Vescey, George. *One Sunset a Week: The Story of a Coal Miner*. New York: Saturday Review Press, 1974.

Vietor, Richard H. *Energy Politics in America since 1945: A Study of Business-Government Relations*. New York: Cambridge U. Press, 1984.

————. *Environmental Politics and the Coal Coalition*. College Station: Texas A&M Press, 1980.

Walls, David S. "Central Appalachia in Advanced Capitalism: Its Coal Industry Structure and Coal Operator Associations." Ph.D. diss., U. of Kentucky, 1978.

Walls, David S., Dwight B. Billings, Mary P. Payne, & Joe F. Childers, Jr. *A Baseline Assessment of Coal Industry Structure in the Ohio River Basin Energy Study Region*. Wash., DC: Office of Research and Development, U.S. Environmental Protection Agency, 1979.

Wardell, Mark L., David L. Smith, & Charles Vaught. *Coal Miners and Coal Mining in Southwestern Virginia: An Organizational Study*. Blacksburg: Department of Sociology, VPI&SU, n.d.

White, Connie L., ed. *Coal Employment Project Training Manual*. Rev. ed. Oak Ridge, TN: Coal Employment Project, 1980.

Wilkinson, Carroll W. "A Critical Guide to the Literature of Women Coal Miners." *Labor Studies Journal* 10 (Spring 1985): 25–45.

Witt, Matt. *In Our Blood: Four Coal Mining Families*. New Market, TN: Highlander Center, 1979.

Yanarella, Ernest J., & Randal H. Ihara, eds. *The Acid Rain Debate: Scientific, Economic and Political Dimensions*. Boulder, CO: Westview, 1985.

Yarrow, Mike. "Miner's Wisdom." *AJ* 15 (Winter 1988): 162–72.

See also works in I D, III A, IV C, IV D, VIII, IX C, IX D, X A 2, X A 3, & X A 4.

2. Health and Safety

Althouse, Ronald. *Work, Safety, and Life Style among Southern Appalachian Coal Miners: A Survey of the Men of Standard Mines.* Morgantown: WVU, 1974.

Amandus, Harlan. *The Appalachian Coal Miner Mortality Study: A Fourteen-Year Followup.* Morgantown: National Institute for Occupational Safety and Health, Epidemiological Investigations Branch, Division of Respiratory Disease Studies, 1982.

Barth, Peter S. *The Tragedy of Black Lung: Federal Compensation for Occupational Disease.* Kalamazoo, MI: W. E. Upjohn Institute for Employment Research, 1987.

Bethell, Thomas N. *The Hurricane Creek Massacre.* New York: Harper & Row, 1972.

Bethell, Thomas N., & J. Davitt McAteer. "The Pittston Mentality: Manslaughter on Buffalo Creek." *Washington Monthly,* May 1972, 19–28. Also in LJ&A, 259–75.

Braithwaite, John. *To Punish or Persuade: Enforcement of Coal Mine Safety.* Albany: State U. of New York Press, 1985.

Citizen Committee to Investigate the Buffalo Creek Disaster. *Disaster on Buffalo Creek: A Citizens' Report on Criminal Negligence in a West Virginia Mining Community.* Charleston, WV, 1972.

Clague, Ewan, ed. *The Health-Impaired Miner under Black Lung Legislation.* New York: Irvington Pubs. 1973.

Curran, Daniel. "Dead Laws for Dead Men: The Case of Federal Coal Mine Health and Safety Legislation." Ph.D. diss., U. of Delaware, 1980.

David, John P. "Earnings, Health, Safety, and Welfare of Bituminous Coal Miners since the Encouragement of Mechanization by the United Mine Workers of America." Ph.D. diss., WVU, 1972.

Dials, George E., & Elizabeth C. Moore. "The Cost of Coal: We Can Afford to Do Better." *Appalachia* 8 (October–November 1974): 1–29.

DeMichiei, John M., John F. Langton, Kenneth A. Bullock, & Terrence C. Wiles. *Factors Associated with Disabling Injuries in Underground Mines.* Wash., DC: Mine Safety & Health Administration, U.S. Department of Labor, 1982.

Dillon, Lacy A. *They Died in the Darkness.* Parsons, WV: McClain, 1976.

——. *They Died for King Coal.* Winona, MN: Apollo, 1985.

Drury, Doris M. "A Study of the Literature on Accidents in Coal Mines of the United States with Comparisons of the Records in Other Coal-Producing Countries." Ph.D. diss., Indiana U., 1965.

Erickson, Kai T. *Everything in Its Path: Destruction of Community in the Buffalo Creek Flood.* New York: Simon & Schuster, 1976.

Fitzpatrick, John S. "Underground Mining: A Case Study of an Occupational Subculture of Danger." Ph.D. diss., Ohio State U., 1974.

Foster, Jim. "Health and Safety versus Profits in the Coal Industry: The Gateway Case and Class Struggle." *AJ* 11 (Autumn–Winter 1983–84): 122–41.

Friedl, John. "Explanatory Models of Black Lung: Understanding the Health-Related Behavior of Appalachian Coal Miners." *Culture, Medicine and Psychiatry* 6 (March 1982): 3–10.

Graebner, William. *Coal-Mining Safety in the Progressive Period: The Political Economy of Reform.* Lexington: UKP, 1976.

Guidotti, T. L. "Coal Workers' Pneumoconiosis and Medical Aspects of Coal Mining." *Southern Medical Journal* 72 (April 1979): 456–66.

Jackson, Carlton. *The Dreadful Month.* Bowling Green, OH: Bowling Green State U. Press, 1982.

Judkins, Bennet M. *We Offer Ourselves as Evidence: Toward Workers' Control of Occupational Health.* New York: Greenwood, 1986.

Kent, William H. *An Analysis of Appalachian State Coal Mine Health and Safety and Workmen's Compensation Programs: Recommendations for Improvement.* Wash., DC: ARC, 1973.

Key, Marcus M., Lorin E. Kerr, & Merle Bundy. *Pulmonary Reactions to Coal Dust: A Review of the U.S. Experience.* New York: Academic Press, 1971.

Lewis-Beck, Michael S., & John R. Alford. "Can Government Regulate Safety? The Coal Mine Example." *American Political Science Review* 75 (September 1980): 745–56.

Lopatto, John. "The Federal Black Lung Program: A 1983 Primer." *West Virginia Law Review* 85 (1983): 677–704.

McAteer, J. Davitt. *Coal Mine Health and Safety: The Case of West Virginia*. New York: Praeger, 1973.

———. *Miner's Manual: A Complete Guide to Health and Safety Protection on the Job*. 3rd ed. Wash., DC: Center for Law & Social Policy, 1985.

———. "You Can't Buy Safety at the Company Store." *Washington Monthly,* November 1972, 7–19.

McAteer, J. Davitt, & L. Thomas Galloway. "A Comparative Study of Miners' Training and Supervisory Certification in the Coal Mines of Great Britain, the Federal Republic of Germany, Poland, Romania, France, Australia and the United States: The Case for Federal Certification of Supervisors and Increased Training of Miners." *West Virginia Law Review* 82 (1980): 937–1018.

McClure, Barbara. *Federal Black Lung Disability Program*. Wash., DC: Library of Congress, 1981.

Matthes, Dieter. "Regulating the Coal Industry: Federal Coal Mine Health and Safety and Surface Mining Policy Development." Ph.D. diss., U. of Pittsburgh, 1977.

Moore, Marat. "A Shameful Record: Senate Probes MSHA in Oversight Hearings." *UMWJ* 98 (June 1987): 8–10.

National Research Council. *Fatalities in Small Underground Coal Mines*. Wash., DC: National Academy Press, 1983.

———. *Mineral Resources and the Environment, Supplementary Report: Coal Workers' Pneumoconiosis—Medical Considerations, Some Social Implications*. Wash., DC: National Academy of Sciences, 1976.

———. *Toward Safer Underground Coal Mines*. Wash., DC: National Academy Press, 1982.

Smith, Barbara E. *Digging Our Own Graves: Coal Miners and the Struggle over Black Lung Disease*. Philadelphia: Temple U. Press, 1987.

Stoltzfus, Emilie. "Diesels Underground: At What Cost to Our Safety?" *UMWJ* 100 (November 1989): 5–11.

U.S. Department of the Interior, Coal Mines Administration. *A Medical Survey of the Bituminous Coal Industry*. Wash., DC: USGPO, 1947.

Ward, Robert D., & William W. Rogers. *Convicts, Coal and the Banner Mine Tragedy*. Tuscaloosa: U. of Alabama Press, 1987.

Wardell, Mark L., Charles Vaught, & David L. Smith. "Underground Coal Mining and the Labor Process: Safety at the Coal Face." In *The Rural Workforce: Non-Agricultural Occupations in America,* ed. Clifton Bryant, Donald J. Shoemaker, James K. Skipper, Jr., & William E. Snizek, 43–58. South Hadley, MA: Bergin & Garvey, 1985.

Williams, David P. "The Political Economy of Coal Mine Safety and Its Contribution to the Theory of the Welfare State." Ph.D. diss., Brandeis U., 1987.

Zahorski, Witold W., ed. *Coal Workers' Pneumoconiosis: A Critical Review*. Hanover, NH: U. Press of New England, 1974.

See also works in IV C, IV D, X A 1, & X A 4.

3. Strip Mining

Austin, Richard. *Spoil: A Moral Study of Strip Mining for Coal*. Cincinnati: Board of Global Ministries, 1976.

Baber, Bob H. "Blue Knob: Gone But Not Forgotten." *AJ* 17 (Winter 1990): 156–74.

Branscome, James. "Paradise Lost." *SE* 1 (Summer–Fall 1973): 29–41.

Caudill, Harry M. *My Land Is Dying*. New York: Dutton, 1971.

Center for Law and Social Policy & Environmental Policy Institute. *The Strip Mine Handbook: A Citizen's Guide to the New Federal Surface Mining Law, How to Use It to Protect Your Community and Yourself*. Wash., DC, 1978.

Chambers, H. Harold, Jr. *Citizen Participation in the Battle against Strip-Mining under the West Virginia Surface Mining and Reclamation Act of 1971*. Charleston: Appalachian Research & Development Fund, 1975.

Dials, George E., & Elizabeth C. Moore. "The Cost of Coal: We Can Afford to Do Better." *Appalachia* 8 (October–November 1974): 1–29.

Doyle, John C., Jr. *State Strip Mining Laws: An Inventory and Analysis of Key Statutory Provisions in 28 Coal-Producing States*. Wash., DC: Environmental Policy Institute, 1977.

Elliott, Charles L. "The 1977 Surface Mining Control and Reclamation Act: A Wildlife Benefit or Barrier?" In *Environment in Appalachia. Proceedings from the 1989 Conference,* ed. Jane W. Bagby, 63–68. Lexington: Appalachian Center, U. of Kentucky, 1990.

Finnissey, John C., Jr. "The Politics of Protests: People and Strip Mining in Western Maryland," Ph.D. diss., Temple U., 1987.

Fritsch, Albert J., Dennis Darcey, Gerard McMahon, Elaine Burns, & Brian Ulrickson. *Strip Mine Blasting: A Study of Vibrational Pollution in the Eastern and Midwestern Coalfields.* Wash., DC: Center for Science in the Public Interest, 1977.

Fritsch, Albert J., Mark L. Morgan, Glenn G. Yanik, Thomas J. Conry, & David E. Taylor. *Enforcement of Strip Mining Laws in Three Appalachian States: Kentucky, West Virginia, and Pennsylvania.* Wash., DC: Center for Science in the Public Interest, 1975.

Hardt, Jerry. *Harlan County Flood Report.* Corbin, KY: Appalachia-Science in the Public Interest, 1978.

Harris, Richard A. *Coal Firms under the New Social Regulation.* Durham: Duke U. Press, 1985.

Kalt, Joseph P. *The Costs and Benefits of Federal Regulation of Coal Strip Mining.* Cambridge: Energy and Environmental Policy Center, John F. Kennedy School of Government, Harvard U., 1982.

Kentucky Department of Natural Resources and Environmental Protection. *The Floods of April: A Report of the April 1977 Flood in Southeastern Kentucky.* Frankfurt: Commonwealth of Kentucky, 1977.

Landy, Marc K. *The Politics of Environmental Reform: Controlling Kentucky Strip Mining.* Wash., DC: Resources for the Future, 1976.

McElfish, James M., Jr., & Ann E. Beier. *Environmental Regulation of Coal Mining: SMCRA's Second Decade.* Wash., DC: Environmental Law Institute, 1990.

Maneval, David R. "Coal Mining vs. Environment: A Reconciliation in Pennsylvania." *Appalachia* 5 (February–March 1972): 10–41.

Menzel, Donald C. "Redirecting the Implementation of a Law: The Reagan Administration and Coal Surface Mining Regulation." *Public Administration Review* 43 (September–October 1983): 411–20.

Morgan, Mark L., & Edwin A. Moss. *Citizens' Blasting Handbook.* Corbin, KY: Appalachia-Science in the Public Interest, 1978.

Mountain Community Union, Land Use and Environmental Rights Committee. *You Can't Put It Back: A West Virginia Guide to Strip Mine Opposition.* Fairmont, WV, 1976.

Munn, Robert F. "The Development of Strip Mining in Southern Appalachia." *AJ* 3 (Autumn 1975): 87–93.

———. *Strip Mining: An Annotated Bibliography.* Morgantown: WVU Library, 1973.

National Research Council. *Surface Mining: Soil, Coal, and Society.* Wash., DC: National Academy Press, 1981.

Rasnic, Carol D. "Federally Required Restoration of Surface-Mined Property: Impasse between the Coal Industry and the Environmentally Concerned." *National Resources Journal* 23 (April 1983): 335–49.

Rowe, James E., ed. *Coal Surface Mining: Impacts of Reclamation.* Boulder, CO: Westview, 1979.

Runner, Gerald S., & Edwin H. Chin. *Flood of April 1977 in the Appalachian Region of Kentucky, Tennessee, Virginia, and West Virginia.* Report prepared jointly by the U.S. Geological Survey and the National Oceanic and Atmospheric Administration. Wash., DC: USGPO, 1980.

Sherman, John. *Water Problems & Coal Mining: A Citizens Handbook.* Nashville, TN: Student Environmental Health Project, Center for Health Services, Vanderbilt U., n.d.

Shover, Neal, Donald A. Clelland, & John Lynnwiler. *Enforcement or Negotiation: Constructing a Regulatory Bureaucracy.* Albany: State U. of New York Press, 1986.

Squillace, Mark. *The Stripmining Handbook: A Coalfield Citizens' Guide to Using the Law to Fight Back against the Ravages of Strip Mining and Underground Mining.* Wash., DC: Environmental Policy Institute & Friends of the Earth, 1990.

Steel, Gary. *But When Will It Be Reclaimed? A Study of Strip Mining in Laurel County, Kentucky on the Eve of the Federal Surface Mining Control and Reclamation Act's Tenth Anniversary.* Livingston, KY: Appalachia-Science in the Public Interest, 1986.

Tompkins, Dorothy. *Strip Mining for Coal.* Berkeley: Institute of Governmental Studies, U. of California, 1973.

Veith, David. *Literature on the Revegetation of Coal-Mined Lands: An Annotated Bibliography.* Wash., DC: U.S. Department of the Interior, Bureau of the Mines, 1985.

Vietor, Richard H. *Environmental Politics and the Coal Coalition.* College Station: Texas A&M Press, 1980.

See also works in X A 1, XI, XII B, & XIII.

4. United Mine Workers of America (Post-1950)

Armbrister, Trevor. *Act of Vengeance: The Yablonski Murders and Their Solution.* New York: Saturday Review/Dutton, 1975.

Berney, Barbara. "The Rise and Fall of the UMW Fund." *SE* 6 (Summer 1978): 95–102.

Bethell, Thomas N. "Conspiracy in Coal." *Washington Monthly,* March 1969, 16–23, 63–72.

———. "The UMW: Now More than Ever." *Washington Monthly,* March 1978, 12–23.

Black, Kate. "The Roving Picket Movement and the Appalachian Committee for Full Employment, 1959–1965: A Narrative." In L, 110–27.

Brett, Jeanne M., & Stephen B. Goldberg. "Wildcat Strikes in Bituminous Coal Mining." *Industrial and Labor Relations Review* 32 (July 1979): 465–83.

Brunstetter, Maude P. "Desperate Enterprise: A Case Study of the Democratization of the United Mine Workers in the 1970's." Ph.d. diss., Columbia U., 1981.

Caldwell, Nat, & Gene S. Graham. "The Strange Romance Between John L. Lewis and Cyrus Eaton." *Harper's* 223 (December 1961): 25–32.

Citizens' Public Inquiry into the Brookside Strike. *Proceedings of the Citizens' Public Inquiry into the Brookside Strike, March 11 and 12, 1974, Harlan County, Kentucky.* Evarts, KY, 1974.

Clark, Paul F. *The Miners' Fight for Democracy: Arnold Miller and the Reform of the United Mine Workers.* Ithaca: New York State School of Industrial and Labor Relations, Cornell U., 1981.

Couto, Richard A. *Redemptive Resistance: Church-based Intervention in the Pursuit of Justice.* Whitesburg, KY: CCA, n.d.

Finley, Joseph E. *The Corrupt Kingdom: The Rise and Fall of the United Mine Workers.* New York: Simon & Schuster, 1972.

Green, Jim. "Holding the Line: Miners' Militancy and the Strike of 1978." *Radical America* 12 (May–June 1978): 3–27.

Harris, V. B. *Kanawha's Black Gold and the Miners' Rebellion.* Ann Arbor, MI: Brown-Brumfield, 1987.

Hodel, Martha. "Children of the Mines." *SE* 18 (Summer 1990): 36–39.

Hollyday, Joyce. "Amazing Grace." *Sojouners,* July 1989, 12–22.

Hopkins, George W. "The Wheeling Convention of Miners for Democracy: A Case Study of Union Reform Politics in Appalachia." In S, 6–22. See also Hopkins' Ph.D. diss.: "The Miners for Democracy: Insurgency in the United Mine Workers of America, 1970–1972," UNC, Chapel Hill, 1976.

Hume, Brit. *Death and the Mines: Rebellion and Murder in the United Mine Workers.* New York: Grossman, 1971.

Jenson, Richard J. "Rebellion in the United Mine Workers: The Miners for Democracy, 1970–1972." Ph.D. diss., Indiana U., 1974.

Judkins, Bennett M. *We Offer Ourselves as Evidence: Toward Workers' Control of Occupational Health.* New York: Greenwood, 1986.

Levy, Elizabeth, & Tad Richards. *Struggle and Lose, Struggle and Win: The United Mine Workers Union.* New York: Four Winds Press, 1977.

Lewis, Ronald L. *Black Coal Miners in America: Race, Class, and Community Conflict, 1780–1980.* Lexington: UKP, 1987.

Marshall, Daniel. "The Miners and the UMW: Crisis in the Reform Process." *Socialist Review,* no. 40–41 (July–October 1978): 65–115.

Mills, Nicolaus. "Solidarity in Virginia: The Mine Workers Remake History." *Dissent* 37 (Spring 1990): 237–42.

———. "War in Tug River Valley: A Long and Bitter Miners' Strike." *Dissent* 33 (Winter 1986): 45–52.

Moore, Marat. "Cleaning Out the Courthouse: Rank-and-File Political Victory in Mingo County, W. Va." *UMWJ* 98 (February 1987): 11–15.

Mulcahy, Richard P. "Organized Medicine and the UMWA Welfare and Retirement Fund: An Appalachian Perspective on a National Conflict." In L, 92–109. See also Mulcahy's Ph.D. diss.: "To Serve a Union: The United Mine Workers of America Welfare and Retirement Fund, 1946–1978," WVU, 1988.

Nyden, Paul J. "Miners for Democracy: Struggle in the Coal Fields," Ph.D. diss., Columbia U., 1974.

Perry, Charles R. *Collective Bargaining and the Decline of the United Mine Workers.* Philadelphia: Industrial Research Unit, Wharton School, U. of Pennsylvania, 1984.

Seltzer, Curtis. *Fire in the Hole: Miners and Managers in the American Coal Industry.* Lexington: UKP, 1985.

Simon, Richard M. "Hard Times for Organized Labor in Appalachia." *Review of Radical Economics* 15 (Fall 1983): 21–34.

Sinclair, Hamish. "Hazard, Ky.: Document of the Struggle." *Radical America* 2 (January–February 1968): 1–24.

Smith, Barbara E. *Digging Our Own Graves: Coal Miners and the Struggle over Black Lung Disease.* Philadelphia: Temple U. Press, 1987.

Takamiya, Makoto. *Union Organization and Militancy: Conclusions from a Study of the United Mine Workers of America, 1940–1974.* Meisenheim am Glan: Anton Haig, 1978.

Taplin, Ian M. "Miners, Coal Operators, and the State: An Examination of Strikes and Work Relations in the U.S. Coal Industry." Ph.D. diss., Brown U., 1986.

UMWJ. Wash., DC (monthly).

Ury, William L. "Talk Out or Walk Out: The Role and Control of Conflict in a Kentucky Coal Mine." Ph.D. diss., Harvard U., 1982.

"Women and the UMWA: From Mother Jones to Brookside." *UMWJ* 87 (March 1976): 10–27.

Woolley, Bryan, & Ford Reid. *We Be Here When the Morning Comes.* Lexington: UKP, 1975.

Yates, Michael D. "From the Coal Wars to the Pittston Strike." *Monthly Review* 42 (June 1990): 25–39.

See also works in IV C, IV D, X A 1, X A 2, & XIII.

B. Textiles

Avery, David, & Gene D. Sullivan. "Changing Patterns: Reshaping the Southeastern Textile-Apparel Complex." *Economic Review,* November 1985, 34–44.

Bouhuys, A., J. B. Schoenberg, G. J. Beck, & R. S. F. Schilling. "Epidemiology of Chronic Lung Disease in a Cotton Mill Community." *Lung* 154 (1977): 167–86.

Burritt, Chris. "Textile Industry Catches Up." *Appalachia* 21 (Spring 1988): 14–20.

Cobb, James C. *The Selling of the South: The Southern Crusade for Industrial Development, 1936–1980.* Baton Rouge: Louisiana State U. Press, 1982.

Conway, Mimi. *Rise Gonna Rise: A Portrait of Southern Textile Workers.* Garden City, NY: Anchor/Doubleday, 1979.

Earle, John R., Dean D. Knudsen, & Donald W. Shriver, Jr. *Spindles and Spires: Religion and Social Change in Gastonia.* Atlanta: John Knox Press, 1976.

Fredrickson, Mary. "Four Decades of Change: Black Workers in Southern Textiles, 1941–1981." *Radical America* 16 (November–December 1982): 27–44.

Hall, Bob. "The Brown Lung Controversy." *Columbia Journalism Review* 16 (March–April 1978): 27–35.

Hodges, James A. *New Deal Labor Policy and the Southern Cotton Textile Industry, 1933–1941.* Knoxville: UTP, 1986.

Judkins, Bennett M. *We Offer Ourselves as Evidence: Toward Worker Control of Occupational Health.* New York: Greenwood, 1986.

Leiter, Jeffrey. "Continuity and Change in the Legitimation of Authority in Southern Mill Towns." *Social Problems* 29 (June 1982): 540–50.

———. "Reactions to Subordination: Attitudes of Southern Textile Workers." *Social Forces* 64 (June 1986): 948–74.

Liefermann, Henry P. *Crystal Lee: A Woman of Inheritance.* New York: Macmillan, 1975.

McAteer, J. Davitt. *Textile Health and Safety Manual: A Complete Guide to Health and Safety Protection on the Job.* Wash., DC: Occupational Safety and Health Law Center, 1986.

McConville, Ed. "A Step Forward, Two Steps Back: J. P. Stevens Contract." *Nation* 232 (21 March 1981): 330–32.

McDonald, Joseph A. "Textiles: The Political Economy of a Peripheral Industry." *Humanity and Society* 5 (June 1981): 100–19. See also McDonald's Ph.D. diss.: "Textile Workers and Unionization: A Community Study," U. of Tennessee, 1981.

——. "Union Attitudes and Class Consciousness: The Case of the Tufted Textile Industry." *AJ* 9 (Fall 1981): 38–48.

McDonald, Joseph A., & Donald A. Clelland. "Textile Workers and Union Sentiment." *Social Forces* 63 (December 1984): 502–21.

Miller, Marc S., ed. *Working Lives: The Southern Exposure History of Labor in the South.* New York: Pantheon, 1980.

Mullins, Terry, & Paul Luebke. "Symbolic Victory and Political Reality in the Southern Textile Industry: The Meaning of the J. P. Stevens Settlement for Southern Labor Relations." *Journal of Labor Research* 3 (Winter 1982): 81–88.

Newman, Dale. "Work and Community Life in a Southern Textile Town." *Labor History* 19 (Spring 1978): 204–25.

Olson, Richard P. *The Textile Industry.* Lexington, MA: D.C. Health, 1978.

Rowan, Richard L., & Robert E. Barr. *Employee Relations Trends and Practices in the Textile Industry.* Philadelphia: Industrial Research Unit, Wharton School U. of Pennsylvania, 1987.

Schulman, Michael D., Rhonda Zingraff, & Linda Reif. "Race, Gender, Class Consciousness and Union Support: An Analysis of Southern Textile Workers." *Sociological Quarterly* 26:2 (1985): 187–204.

Simpson, Richard L. "Labor Force Integration and Southern U. S. Textile Unionism." In *Research and Sociology,* Vol. 1, ed. Richard L. Simpson & Ida H. Simpson, 381–401. Greenwich, CT: JAI Press, 1981.

Tolchin, Susan J., & Martin Tolchin. *Dismantling America: The Rush to Deregulate.* New York: Oxford U. Press, 1983. See Chap. 4.

Truchil, Barry E. *Capital-Labor Relations in the U.S. Textile Industry.* New York: Praeger, 1988. Includes a good bibliography on textile sources.

Zingraff, Rhonda, & Michael D. Schulman. "Social Bases of Class Consciousness: A Study of Southern Textile Workers with a Comparison by Race." *Social Forces* 63 (September 1984): 98–116.

See also works in IV C, IV D, & XIII.

C. Other Economic and Labor Actors

Agarwal, Anil, Juliet Merrifield, & Rajesh Tandon. *No Place to Run: Local Realities and Global Issues of the Bhopal Disaster.* New Market, TN: Highlander Center & Society for Participatory Research in Asia, 1985.

"Appalachian Crude." *Dun's Review Magazine,* October 1980, 37–42.

"Aquaculture: An Industry with a Future for Appalachia." *Appalachia* 23 (Winter 1990): 17–21.

Bagby, Jane W., ed. *Environment in Appalachia. Proceedings from the 1989 Conference on Appalachia.* Llexington: Appalachian Center, U. of Kentucky, 1990.

Basset, James S. "The Asheville Citizen Strike: An Example of the Ineffectiveness of Appalachian Labor." *AJ* 11 (Summer 1984): 403–09.

Bernard, Jacqueline. "Organizing Hospital Workers." *Working Papers* 4 (Fall 1976): 39–48.

Cherniack, Martin. *The Hawk's Nest Incident: America's Worst Industrial Disaster.* New Haven: Yale U. Press, 1986.

Cobb, James C. *The Selling of the South: The Southern Crusade for Industrial Development, 1936–1980.* Baton Rouge: Louisiana State U. Press, 1982.

DeLeon, Paul, ed. *Appalachia's Changing Economy.* New Market, TN: Highlander Center, 1980.

Egerton, John. "A Big Job for a Little Town." *Progressive* 45 (April 1981): 45–48.

Franklin, Ben A. "In the Shadow of the Valley." *Sierra* 71 (May/June 1986): 38–44.

Garber, Carter. *Saturn: Tomorrow's Jobs, Yesterday's Wages and Myths, A Case Study of Industrial Recruitment in Rural America.* Wash., DC: Rural Coalition, 1985.

Gaventa, John. *From the Mountains to the Maguiladoras: A Case Study of Capital Flight and Its Impact on Workers.* New Market, TN: Highlander Center, 1988.

Gaventa, John, Barbara E. Smith, & Alex Willingham, eds. *Communities in Economic Crisis: Appalachia and the South.* Philadelphia: Temple U. Press, 1990.

Gilmer, Robert W. "Structural Change in Southern Manufacturing: Expansion in the Tennessee Valley." *Growth and Change* 20 (Spring 1989): 62–70.

Goldstein, Joyce, & Michael Parsons. *Knockin' on Heaven's Door: Health & the Chemical Industry, Kanawha Valley, West Virginia.* Kanawha Valley Committee on Occupational and Environmental Health, 1979.

Highlander Research & Education Center. *Watch Out! A Handbook of Safety & Health for Furniture Workers.* New Market, TN, 1979.

Junkerman, John. "Nissan, Tennessee: It Ain't What It's Cracked Up to Be." *Progressive* 51 (June 1987): 16–20.

Kenneally, Sharon, Shane Rock, & Meg Wilcox. *Tennessee Right-To-Know: A Guide for Communities.* Nashville: Student Environmental Health Project, Center for Health Services, Vanderbilt U., n.d.

Kenny, Maxine. *"I'm afraid for the children": A Report on Health and Industrial Pollution in Upper East Tennessee.* Kingsport: Kingsport Environmental Health Study Group, 1979.

Kingsport Study Group. "Smells Like Money." *SE* 6 (Summer 1978): 59–67.

Klimasewski, Theodore. "Corporate Dominance of Manufacturing in Appalachia." *Geographical Review* 68 (January 1978): 94–102.

Liden, David. *Rights: Yours and Theirs. A Citizens' Guide to Oil and Gas Development and Leasing in Appalachia.* New Market, TN: Appalachian Alliance, 1983.

Marshall, Ray. "Southern Unions: History and Prospects." In *Perspectives on the American South,* Vol. 3, ed. James C. Cobb & Charles R. Wilson, 163–78. New York: Gordon & Breach, 1985.

Merrifield, Juliet. *Putting Scientists in Their Place: Participatory Research in Environmental and Occupational Health.* New Market, TN: Highlander Center, 1989.

———. *We're Tired of Being Guinea Pigs! A Handbook for Citizens on Environmental Health in Appalachia.* New Market, TN: Highlander Center, 1980.

Miller, Marc S., ed. *Working Lives: The Southern Exposure History of Labor in the South.* New York: Pantheon, 1980.

MLW, May 1983. Special Issue: "Toxics."

Mull, Brenda C. *Blue Ridge: The History of Our Struggle against Levi-Strauss.* Boston: New England Free Press, n.d.

Overton, Jim, ed. "Tower of Babel: A Special Report on the Nuclear Industry." *SE* 7 (Winter 1979): 25–120.

Petro, Sylvester. *The Kingsport Strike.* New Rochele, NY: Arlington House, 1967.

Robinson, Craig. "Family, Community and Occupational Health: A Look at Rural Industrial Workers in Central Appalachia." Highlander Pamphlet Series No. 8. New Market, TN, 1977.

Schlesinger, Tom. "Crossing State Lines: The South's Jumbo Banks." *SE* 15 (Summer 1987): 33–36.

Schlesinger, Tom, John Gaventa & Juliet Merrifield. *How to Research Your Local Military Contractor.* New Market, TN: Highlander Center, 1983.

Schlesinger, Tom, with John Gaventa, & Juliet Merrifield. *Our Own Worst Enemy: The Impact of Military Production on the Upper South.* New Market, TN: Highlander Center, 1983.

SE 1 (Summer/Fall 1981). Special section on Southern Power Companies.

SE 9 (Winter 1981). Special Issue: "Working Women: A Handbook of Resources, Rights, and Remedies."

Strange, Walter G. "Job Loss: A Psychological Study of Worker Reaction to a Plant-Closing in a Company Town in Southern Appalachia." Ph.D. diss., Cornell U., 1977.

Wells, John C. "Organized Labor in Central Appalachia." In *The Land and the Economy of Appalachia. Proceedings from the 1986 Conference on Appalachia,* ed. Appalachian Center, U. of Kentucky, 123–29. Lexington, 1987.

Wise, Leah, & John Bookser-Feister. *Betrayal of Trust: Stories of Working North Carolinians.* Durham, NC: Southerners for Economic Justice, 1989.

See also works in III A, IV C, IV D, VIII, XI, & XIII.

XI. ASSAULT ON THE LAND AND WATER

Anderson, Robert G. *Agriculture in Appalachia: A Planning Study for Small Farms.* Prepared for the Farmers Home Administration. Berea, KY: Human/Economic Appalachian Development Corporation & the Bluegrass Development District, 1979.

Appalachian Land Ownership Task Force. *Who Owns Appalachia? Landownership and Its Impact.* Lexington: UKP, 1983. Includes an extensive annotated bibliography on a variety of land issues.

Austin, Richard C. "The Battle for Brumley Gap." *Sierra* 69 (January–February 1984): 120–24.

———. *Reclaiming America: Restoring Nature to Culture.* Abingdon, VA: Creekside Press, 1990.

Bagby, Jane, ed. *Environment in Appalachia. Proceedings from the 1989 Conference on Appalachia.* Lexington: Appalachian Center, U. of Kentucky, 1990.

Beaver, Patricia D. "Appalachian Families, Landownership and Public Policy." In *Holding on to the Land: Kinship, Ritual, Land Tenure, and Social Policy in the Rural South,* ed. Robert L. Hall & Carol B. Stack, 146–54. Athens: U. of Georgia Press, 1982.

———. "Participatory Research on Land Ownership in Appalachia." In B, 252–66.

Bingham, Edgar. "The Impact of Recreational Development on Pioneer Life Styles in Southern Appalachia." *Proceedings of the Pioneer America Society* (1973): 59–68. Also in LJ&A, 57–69.

Blanton, Bill. "The National Recreation Area: What Will It Mean?" *The Plow,* 1 June 1978, 15–18, 24–26.

———. "Not by a Dam Site: Brumley Gap, Virginia—How One Community Fought Back." *SE* 7 (Winter 1979): 98–106.

Boerner, Deborah A. "Monongahela Revisited." *American Forests* 92 (February 1986): 16–19, 49–53.

Branscome, Jim, & Peggy Matthews. "Selling the Mountains." *SE* 2 (Fall 1974): 122–29.

Buxton, Barry M. "Mountaintop Construction in North Carolina Sparks Controversy." *Appalachia* 17 (January–April 1984): 15–19.

Campbell, David, & David Coombs. "Skyline Farms: A Case Study of Community Development and Rural Rehabilitation." *AJ* 10 (Spring 1983): 244–54.

Cary, William, Molly Johnson, Meridith Golden, & Trip Van Noppen. *The Impact of Recreational Development: A Study of Land Ownership, Recreational Development and Local Land Use Planning in the North Carolina Mountain Region.* Durham: North Carolina Public Interest Research Group, 1975.

Clark, Mike. "How Can You Buy or Sell the Sky?" *Mountain Eagle,* 23 June 1977. Also Highlander Reports Pamphlet Series No. 7.

Clark, Thomas D. *The Greening of the South: The Recovery of Land and Forest.* Lexington: UKP, 1984.

Coalition for Appalachian Ministry, ed. *ERETS: Land. The Church and Appalachian Land Issues.* Amesville, OH, 1984.

Dodsen, Jerome E. "The Changing Control of Economic Activity in the Gatlinburg, Tennessee, Area, 1930–1973." Ph.D. diss., U. of Tennessee, 1975.

D'Souza, Gerard E. *The Role of Agriculture in the Economic Development of West Virginia: An Input-Output Analysis.* Morgantown: Agriculture and Forestry Experiment Station, MVU, 1988.

Duerr, William A. *The Economic Problems of Forestry in the Appalachian Region.* Harvard Economic Studies No. 84. Cambridge: Harvard U. Press, 1949.

Dunn, Durwood. *Cades Cove: The Life and Death of a Southern Appalachian Community, 1818–1937.* Knoxville: UTP, 1988.

Fisher, Steve. "Land Reform and Appalachia: Lessons from the Third World." *AJ* 10 (Winter 1983): 122–40.

———, ed. *A Landless People in a Rural Region: A Reader on Landownership and Property Taxation in Appalachia.* New Market, TN: Highlander Center, 1979.

Fisher, Steve, & Mary Harnish. "Losing a Bit of Ourselves: The Decline of the Small Farmer." In S, 68–88.

Foster, Stephen W. *The Past Is Another Country: Representation, Historical Consciousness, and Resistance in the Blue Ridge.* Berkeley: U. of California Press, 1988.

Foster, Thomas H. "The Economic State of Agriculture in the Tennessee Valley." *Forum for Applied Research and Public Policy* 1 (Summer 1986): 69–70.

Fritsch, Albert J. *Communities at Risk: Environmental Dangers in Rural America.* Wash., DC: Renew America, 1989.

Fritsch, Albert J., & John R. Davis., eds. *Land Ethics in Appalachia. Proceedings from a Conference on Ethical Values Related to Land.* Livingston, KY: Appalachia-Science in the Public Interest, 1982.

Frome, Michael. *Promised Land: Adventures and Encounters in Wild America.* New York: Morrow, 1985.

Garrison, Charles B. "A Case Study of the Local Economic Impact of Reservoir Recreation." *Journal of Leisure Research* 6 (Winter 1974): 7–19.

Gaventa, John, & Bill Horton. "Land Ownership and Land Reform in Appalachia." In *Land Reform, American Style,* ed. Charles C. Geisler & Frank J. Popper, 233–44. Totowa, NJ: Rowman & Allanheld, 1984.

Godschalk, David R., Francis H. Parker, & Charles E. Roe, eds. *Land Development in the North Carolina Mountains: Impact and Policy in Avery and Watauga Counties.* Chapel Hill: Department of City & Regional Planning, UNC, 1975.

Goodstein, Eban. "Landownership, Development, and Poverty in Southern Appalachia." *The Journal of Developing Areas* 23 (July 1989): 519–33.

Gottfried, Robin. "Observations on Recreation-Led Growth in Appalachia." *American Economist* 21 (Spring 1977): 44–50. See also Gottfried's Ph.D. diss.: "The Impact of Recreation Communities on Land Prices in the Local Community: The Case of Beech Mountain," UNC at Chapel Hill, 1981.

Hall, Bob. *Who Owns North Carolina?* Report of the Land Ownership Project under the Auspices of the Institute for Southern Studies. Durham, NC, 1986.

———, ed. *Environmental Politics: Lessons from the Grass Roots.* Durham, NC: Institute for Southern Studies, 1988.

Hardt, Jerry. *The Feasibility and Design of a Central Appalachian Land Bank.* Berea, KY: Human/Economic Appalachian Development Corporation, 1979.

Horton, Bill, Dave Liden, & Tracey Weis. *Who Owns It? Researching Land and Mineral Ownership in Your Community.* Prepared for the Appalachian Alliance. Prestonsburg, KY: Mountain Printing Co., 1985.

"An Interview with Zell Miller." *Foxfire* 22 (Spring 1988): 46–53.

Jackson, Laura E. *Mountain Treasures at Risk: The Future of the Southern Appalachian National Forests.* Wash., DC: Wilderness Society, 1989.

Johnson, Leland R. "A History of the Operations of the Corps of Engineers, United States Army, in the Cumberland and Tennessee River Valley." Ph.D. diss., Vanderbilt U., 1972.

Jolley, Harley E. *The Blue Ridge Parkway.* Knoxville: UTP, 1969.

Jones, Lindsay, ed. *Citizen Participation in Rural Land Use Planning in the Tennessee Valley.* Nashville: Agricultural Marketing Project, 1979.

Jordan, James. "Frontier Culture, Government Agents, and City Folks." In B, 239–51.

Jubak, Jim. "West Virginia's Water Watchers." *Environmental Action* 23 (July/August 1981): 16–19.

Kahn, Si. *The Forest Service and Appalachia.* New York: John Hay Whitney Foundation, 1974. See also "The Government's Private Forests." *SE* 2 (Fall 1974): 132–44. Also in LJ&A, 85–109.

Katuah Journal. Leicester, NC, quarterly.

Liden, David. "Pulling the Pillars: Energy Development and Land Reform in Appalachia." In *Land Reform, America Style,* ed. Charles C. Geisler & Frank J. Popper, 101–16. Totowa, NJ: Rowman & Allanheld, 1984.

Lovingood, Paul E., Jr., & Robert E. Reiman. *Emerging Patterns in the Southern Highlands: A Reference Atlas.* Vol. 2, *Agriculture.* Boone: ACP, 1985.

Massey, David. "Over a Barrel: Southern Waterways and the Army Corps of Engineers." *SE* 8 (Spring 1980): 92–100.

Mastran, Shelly S., & Nan Lawerre. *Mountaineers and Rangers: A History of Federal Forest Management in the Southern Appalachians, 1900–81.* Wash., DC: USGPO, 1983.

Nathan (Robert R.) Associates. *Recreation as an Industry* 2 vols. Prepared for the ARC and issued as Research Report No. 2. Wash., DC, 1966.

Ormsby, Peg. "Residents Oppose Stonewall Jackson Dam: Dam Madness in West Virginia." *MLW,* November 1978, 12–15. *MLW* regularly carried information on citizen resistance to dam projects.

Otto, John S. "The Decline of Forest Farming in Southern Appalachia." *Journal of Forest History* 27 (January 1983): 18–27.

Parlow, Anita. *The Land Development Rag: The Impact of Resort Development on Two Appalachian Counties, Watauga and Avery in North Carolina.* Knoxville: Southern Appalachian Ministry in Higher Education, 1976. Excerpt in LJ&A, 177–98.

PA 1 (August–September 1970). Special Issue: "The Developers: Partners in Colonization."

Perdue, Charles L., Jr., & Nancy J. Martin-Perdue. "Appalachian Fables and Facts: A Case Study of the Shenandoah National Park Removals." *AJ* 7 (Autumn–Winter 1979–1980): 84–104.

Schlesinger, Tom. "The Fruits of Corporate Forestry." *Environmental Action* 24 (March 1982): 11–16.

Schoenbaum, Thomas J. *The New River Controversy.* Winston-Salem, NC: John F. Blair, 1979.

Schweri, William F., II. & John Van Willigen. *Organized Resistance to an Imposed Environmental Change: A Reservoir in Eastern Kentucky.* Research Report No. 10. Lexington: Water Resources Research Institute, U. of Kentucky, 1978.

Selfridge, Linda, John Gaventa, Juliet Merrifield, & Rob Currie. *Water: "You Have to Drink It with a Fork".* New Market, TN: Highlander Center, 1985.

Smith, Barbara E. "Questions about Tourism." *SE* 14 (September–October 1986): 40–42.

Smith, Michael. *Behind the Glitter: The Impact of Tourism on Rural Women in the Southeast.* Lexington, KY: Southeast Women's Employment Coalition, 1989.

Soden, Dennis. "Past Commitments, Current Problems, and Future Choices: Water Use in Appalachia." In *Contemporary Appalachia: In Search of a Usable Past. Proceedings of the 9th Annual Appalachian Studies Conference,* ed. Carl Ross, 65–82. Boone: ACP, 1987.

SE 2 (Fall 1974). Special Issue: "Our Promised Land."

SE 10 (January–February 1982): 32–52. Special Section: "Who Owns Appalachia."

SE 16 (Spring 1988). Special Issue: "Unsettling Images: The Future of American Agriculture."

Southern Land Economics Research Committee. *Farmland Tenure and Farmland Use in the Tennessee Valley.* Pub. No. 9, n.p., n.d.

Spurr, Stephen. "Clearcutting on National Forests." *Natural Resources Journal* 21 (April 1981): 223–43.

Stephenson, John B. "Escape to the Periphery: Commodifying Place in Rural Appalachia." *AJ* 11 (Spring 1984): 187–200.

Stewart, Fred J., Harry H. Hall, & Eldon D. Smith. "Potential for Increased Income on Small Farms in Appalachian Kentucky." *American Journal of Agricultural Economics* 61 (February 1979): 77–82.

Trent, Roger B., Nancy Stout-Wiegand, & Dennis K. Smith. "Attitudes toward New Development in Three Appalachian Counties." *Growth and Change* 16 (October 1985): 70–86.

U.S. General Accounting Office. *The Federal Drive to Acquire Private Lands Should Be Reassessed.* Wash., DC: USGPO, 1979.

U. of Kentucky, Appalachian Center. *The Land and the Economy of Appalachia. Proceedings from the 1988 Conference on Appalachia.* Lexington, 1987.

Virginia Food System Project. *Harvesting Our Choices: A Study of the Virginia Food System.* Richmond: Rural Virginia, 1984.

Wagner, Melinda B., Donna Lynn Batley, Kai Jackson, Bill O'Brien, & Liz Throckmorton. "Appalachia: A Tourist Attraction?" In *The Impact of Institutions in Appalachia. Proceedings of the 8th Annual Appalachian Studies Conference.,* ed. Jim Lloyd & Anne G. Campbell, 73–87. Boone: ACP, 1986.

Walp, Neil. "The Market for Recreation in the Appalachian Highlands." *Appalachia* 4 (November–December 1970): 27–36.

Whisnant, David E. "A Case Study in Appalachian Development." *New South* 28 (Spring 1973): 34–43.

———. *Modernizing the Mountaineer: People, Power, and Planning in Appalachia.* Boone: ACP, 1981.

Zimet, Kristin C. "Making Peace with Earth." *Appalachian Peace Education Center News,* no. 42 (September–October 1989).

See also works in X A 1, X A 3, XII B, & XIII.

XII. POLITICAL ACTORS

A. General

Banks, Andrew. "Electing Our Own." *SE* 12 (January–February 1984): 67–69.

Barkey, Frederick A. "The Socialist Party in West Virginia from 1898–1920: A Study in Working Class Radicalism." Ph.D. diss., U. of Pittsburgh, 1981.

Bass, Jack, & Walter DeVries. *The Transformation of Southern Politics: Social Change and Political Consequence since 1945.* New York: Basic Books, 1976.

Blakey, George T. *Hard Times and the New Deal in Kentucky, 1929–1939.* Lexington: UKP, 1986.

Busson, Terry. "Federal Budget Cuts in Appalachia: Policy Implications for Rural America." *Forum for Applied Research and Public Policy* 1 (Fall 1986): 91–100.

Caudill, Harry M. *The Senator from Slaughter County.* Boston: Little, Brown/Atlantic Monthly, 1973.

———. *The Watches of the Night.* Boston: Little, Brown/Atlantic Monthly, 1976.

Couto, Richard A. "Political Silence and Appalachia." *AJ* 5 (Autumn 1977): 116–24.

———. *Poverty, Politics and Health Care: An Appalachian Experience.* New York: Praeger, 1975.

Dodd, Joe. *World Class Politics: Knoxville's 1982 World's Fair. Redevelopment and the Political Process.* Salem, WI: Sheffield, 1988.

Duncan, Cynthia. "Myths and Realities of Appalachian Poverty: Public Policy for Good People Surrounded by a Bad Economy and Bad Politics." In *The Land and Economy of Appalachia. Proceedings from the 1986 Conference on Appalachia,* ed. Appalachian Center, U. of Kentucky, 25–32. Lexington, 1987.

Fenton, John H. *Politics in the Border States: A Study of Political Organization and Political Change Common to the Border States—Maryland, West Virginia, Kentucky, and Missouri.* New Orleans: Hauser Press, 1957.

Gaventa, John. *Power and Powerlessness: Quiescence and Rebellion in an Appalachian Valley.* Urbana: UIP, 1980. See Chap. 5.

Grant, Phillip A. "Appalachian Congressmen during the New Deal." *AJ* 2 (Autumn 1974): 72–77.

Grantham, Dewey W. *Southern Progressivism: The Reconciliation of Progress and Tradition.* Knoxville: UTP, 1983.

Grimes, Richard. *Jay Rockefeller: Old Money, New Politics.* Parsons, WV: McClain, 1984.

Hall, Bob, & Will Coviello. "Where Will the Hawks Roost?" *SE* 15 (Summer 1987): 11–15.

Hall, Bob, & Lorisa Seibel. "The South in Congress." *SE* 15 (Summer 1987): 15–19.

Johnson, Gerald W. "Research Note on Political Correlates of Voter Participation: A Deviant Case Analysis." *American Political Science Review* 65 (September 1971): 768–76.

Kahn, Si. *Who Speaks for Appalachia, 1972.* Mineral Bluff, GA: Cut Cane Associates, 1972. For an update of the data in this article, see: Steve Fisher. "Some Thoughts on Appalachia and the 1976 Election." *AJ* 4 (Spring–Summer 1977): 190–94; C. David Sutton. "Appalachia and the 1980 Election." *AJ* 8 (Winter 1981): 150–54; C. David Sutton. "Election '82: Democratic Resurgence in Appalachia." *AJ* 10 (Spring 1983): 294–98; C. David Sutton. "Election '86: All Politics Is Local." *AJ* 14 (Spring 1987): 262–67; & C. David Sutton. "Incumbent Appreciation Day: The 1988 Election in Appalachia." *AJ* 16 (Winter 1989): 176–82.

A Kentucky Legislator. "How an Election Was Bought and Sold." *Harper's* 221 (October 1960): 33–38.

Key, V. O., Jr. *Southern Politics in State and Nation.* New York: Knopf, 1949.

Lee, K. W. "Fair Elections in West Virginia." *Appalachian Lookout* 7 (April 1969): 21–28.

Long, Kate. "Almost Broke, West Virginia." *SE* 16 (Fall 1988): 56–59.

McKinney, Gordon B. *Southern Mountain Republicans, 1865–1900: Politics and the Appalachian Community.* Chapel Hill: UNC Press, 1978.

Miller, Wilbur R. "The Revenue: Federal Law Enforcement in the Mountain South, 1870–1900." *Journal of Southern History* 55 (May 1989): 195–216.

Nyden, Paul. "Pay Dirt." *SE* 17 (Winter 1989): 20–24.

Peirce, Neil. *The Border South States: People, Politics and Power in the Five Border South States.* New York: Norton, 1975.

Perry, Huey. *"They'll Cut Off Your Project": A Mingo County Chronicle.* New York: Praeger, 1972.

Photiadis, John D. "The Economy and Attitudes toward Government in Appalachia." In **P&S**, 115–28.

Ritt, Leonard G. "Presidential Voting Patterns in Appalachia: An Analysis of the Relationship between Turnout, Partison Change, and Selected Socio-Economic Variables." Ph.D. diss., U. of Tennessee, 1967.

Rivkin, Dean H. "The Institutional Setting in Appalachia: Of Scapegoats and Caricatures." In *Appalachia Looks at Its Future,* ed. J. Paxton Marshall, 21–30. Blacksburg: VPI&SU, 1978.

Ryan, John P. *Cultural Diversity and the American Experience: Political Participation among Blacks, Appalachians and Indians.* Beverly Hills, CA: Sage Professional Papers in American Government, 1976.

Sparks, Phil. "Coalfield Elections: For Sale to the Highest Bidder?" *UMWJ* 87 (16–30 November 1976): 6–8.

Sutton, Willis A., Jr. "Visible, Symbolic, and Concealed Leaders in a Kentucky County: A Replication and Comparisons with Other Communities." *Sociological Quarterly* 13 (Summer 1972): 409–18.

White, Theodore H. *The Making of the President.* New York: Atheneum, 1961.

Woodruff, Nan E. *As Rare as Rain: Federal Relief in the Great Southern Drought of 1930–31.* Urbana: UIP, 1985.

B. Tennessee Valley Authority

Barnes, Peter. "Back-Door Socialism: Reflections on TVA." *Working Papers,* Fall 1974, 26–35.

Branscome, James. *The Federal Government in Appalachia.* New York: Field Foundation, 1977.

Brookshire, Michael L., & Michael D. Rogers. *Collective Bargaining in Public Employment: The TVA Experience.* Lexington, MA: Lexington Books, 1977.

Caldwell, Lynton K., Lynton R. Hayes, & Isabel M. MacWhirter. *Citizens and the Environment: Case Studies in Popular Action.* Bloomington: Indiana U. Press, 1976.

Callahan, North. *TVA: Bridge over Troubled Waters.* South Brunswick, NJ: A. S. Barnes, 1980.

Chandler, William U. *The Myth on TVA: Conservation and Development in the Tennessee Valley.* Cambridge, MA: Ballinger, 1984.

Clapp, Gordon R. *The TVA: An Approach to the Development of a Region.* Chicago: U. of Chicago Press, 1955.

Couto, Richard A. "TVA, Appalachian Underdevelopment and the Post-Industrial Era." *Sociological Spectrum* 8 (1988): 323–47.

———. "TVA's Old and New Grass Roots: A Reexamination of Cooptation." *Administration and Society* 19 (February 1988): 453–78.

Creese, Walter. *TVA's Public Planning: The Vision, the Reality.* Knoxville: UTP, 1990.

Droze, W. H. "TVA and the Ordinary Farmer." *Agricultural History* 53 (January 1979): 188–202.

Durant, Robert F. *When Government Regulates Itself: EPA, TVA, and Pollution Control in the 1970s.* Knoxville: UTP, 1985.

Dwyer, Lynn Ellen. "The Anti-Nuclear Movement in Middle Tennessee." Ph.D. diss., American U., 1977.

Grant, Nancy L. *TVA and Black Americans: Planning for the Status Quo*. Philadelphia: Temple U. Press, 1989.

Hargrove, Erwin, & Paul Conkin, eds. *TVA: Fifty Years of Grass-roots Bureaucracy*. Urbana: UIP, 1983.

Hubbard, Preston J. *Origins of the TVA: The Muscle-Schoals Controversy, 1920–1932*. Nashville: Vanderbilt U. Press, 1961.

Jacobs, Jane. "Why TVA Failed." *New York Review of Books* 31 (10 May 1984): 41–47.

Lilienthal, David E. *The Journals of David E. Lilienthal*. 4 vols. New York: Harper & Row, 1964–69.

———. *TVA: Democracy on the March*. New York: Harper & Brothers, 1944; rpt. Westport, CT: Greenwood, 1977.

McDonald, Michael J., & John Muldowny. *TVA and the Dispossessed: The Resettlement of Population in the Norris Dam Area*. Knoxville: UTP, 1982.

McGraw, Thomas K. *Morgan vs. Lilienthal: The Feud within the TVA*. Chicago: Loyola U. Press, 1970.

———. *TVA and the Power Fight, 1933–1939*. Philadelphia: J. B. Lippincott, 1971.

Matthiessen, Peter. "How to Kill a Valley." *New York Review of Books* 27 (7 February 1980): 31–36.

Moore, John R., ed. *The Economic Impact of TVA*. Knoxville: UTP, 1967.

Morgan, Arthur E. *The Making of TVA*. Buffalo, NY: Prometheus Books, 1974.

Overton, Jim. "Taking on TVA: Tennessee Valley Ratepayers Protest Soaring Utility Charges." *SE* 11 (January–February 1983): 22–28.

Owen, Marguerite. *The Tennessee Valley Authority*. New York: Praeger, 1973.

Selznick, Philip. *TVA and Grass Roots: A Study in the Sociology of Formal Organization*. Berkeley: U. of California Press, 1949.

Shannon, Thomas. "Appalachia and the State." *AJ* 11 (Autumn–Winter 1983–84): 143–53.

Talbert, Roy, Jr. *FDR's Utopian: Arthur Morgan of the TVA*. Jackson: U. Press of Mississippi, 1987.

Wengert, Norman I. *Valley of Tomorrow: The TVA and Agriculture*. Knoxville: Bureau of Public Administration, U. of Tennessee, 1952.

Wheeler, William B., & Michael J. McDonald. *TVA and the Tellico Dam, 1936–1979: A Bureaucratic Crisis in Post-Industrial America*. Knoxville: UTP, 1986.

Whisnant, David E. *Modernizing the Mountaineer: People, Power and Planning in Appalachia*. Boone: ACP, 1981.

C. The Appalachian Regional Commission

Appalachia: A Report by the President's Appalachian Regional Commission, 1964. Wash., DC: USGPO, 1964.

"Appalachian Highways Are a Catalyst for Change." *Appalachia* 15 (November/December 1981–January/February 1982): 8–17.

ARC. *Appalachia*. Wash., DC, bimonthly.

———. *Appalachia: Twenty Years of Progress*. Wash., DC, 1985.

———. *Appalachian Development Districts: A Status Report*. Wash., DC, 1983.

———. *The Appalachian Experiment, 1965–1970*. Wash., DC, 1971.

Bingham, Edgar. "Some Questions about the ARC's Past and Its Possible Future." *AJ* 10 (Spring 1983): 286–93.

Branscome, James. *The Federal Government in Appalachia*. New York: Field Foundation, 1977.

Bray, Howard. "Appalachia: The View from Washington." *Progressive* 39 (February 1975): 31–34. Also in E&K, 234–37.

Burlage, Robb. "ARC's First Six Year Plan: A Critical Interpretation." *PA* 1 (August–September 1970): 14–29.

Caudill, Harry. *The Watches of the Night*. Boston: Little, Brown/Atlantic Monthly, 1976.

Clavel, Pierre. *Opposition and Planning in Wales and Appalachia*. Philadelphia: Temple U. Press, 1983.

Conn, Philip W. "The Appalachian Regional Commission: An Experiment in Intergovernmental Management." *AH* 11 (Fall 1983): 49–58.

Fisher, Steve. "A Selectively Annotated Bibliography of the Appalachian Regional Commission (ARC)." *AJ* 8 (Summer 1981): 300–07.

Friedmann, John R. "Poor Regions and Poor Nations: Perspectives on the Problem of Appalachia." *Southern Economic Journal* 32 (April 1966): 456–73.

Gauthier, Howard L. "The Appalachian Development Highway System: Development for Whom?" *Economic Geography* 49 (April 1973): 103–08.

Haeberle, Steven H. "The Appalachian Regional Commission: Evaluating an Experiment in Creative Federalism." Ph.D. diss., Duke U., 1981.

Hansen, Niles M. *Intermediate-Size Cities as Growth Centers: Applications for Kentucky, the Piedmont Crescent, the Ozarks, and Texas.* Lexington, MA: Lexington Books, 1973.

————. *Rural Poverty and the Urban Crisis: A Strategy for Regional Development.* Bloomington: Indiana U. Press, 1970. See pp. 59–106.

Little (Arthur D.) Inc. *Regional Economic Development in Appalachia.* Prepared for the ARC. Cambridge, 1982.

Newman, Monroe. *The Political Economy of Appalachia: A Case Study in Regional Integration.* Lexington, MA: Lexington Books, 1972.

Parlow, Anita, Jonathan Sher, & Phil Primack. *Appalachian Regional Commission: Boon or Boondoggle?* Wash., DC: ARC Accountability Project, n.d. [1974].

Primack, Phil. "Hidden Traps of Regionalism." *Nation* 217 (24 September 1973): 272–76. Also in LJ&K, 295–305.

Rothblatt, Donald N. *Regional Planning: The Appalachian Experience.* Lexington, MA: Lexington Books, 1971.

Rovetch, Warren, & John J. Gaskie. *Program Budgeting for Planners: A Case Study of Appalachia with Projections through 1985.* New York: Praeger, 1974.

Shannon, Thomas R. "Appalachia as an 'Enterprise Zone': Some Speculation on the Future Direction of Federal Policy toward the Region." In *The Appalachian Experience. Proceedings of the 6th Annual Appalachian Studies Conference,* ed. Barry Buxton, 199–204. Boone: ACP, 1983.

————. "Appalachia and the State." *AJ* 11 (Autumn–Winter 1983–84): 143–53.

Sprague, Stuart S. *ARC from Implementation to Payoff Decade and Beyond.* Research Report No. 11. Morehead, KY: Appalachian Development Center, Morehead State U., 1986.

U.S. Congress. Senate. Committee on Environment and Public Works. *Summary and Analysis of the Legislative History of the Appalachian Regional Development Act of 1965 and Subsequent Amendments.* Wash., DC: USGPO, 1985.

U.S. General Accounting Office. *Should the Appalachian Regional Commission Be Used as a Model for the Nation?* Wash., DC: USGPO, 1979.

Watts, Ann D. "Does the Appalachian Regional Commission Really Represent a Region?" *Southeastern Geographer* 17 (May 1978): 19–36.

Whisnant, David E. *Modernizing the Mountaineer: People, Power and Planning in Appalachia.* Boone: ACP, 1981.

XIII. RESISTANCE AND RECONSTRUCTION

Adams, Frank, with Myles Horton. *Unearthing Seeds of Fire: The Idea of Highlander.* Winston-Salem, NC: John F. Blair, 1975.

Appalachian Alliance. *Appalachia in the Eighties: A Time for Action.* New Market, TN, 1982.

Appalachian Community Fund. *A Guide to Funders in Central Appalachia and the Tennessee Valley.* Knoxville, TN, 1988.

Arnold, E. Carroll. "Appalachian Cooperatives: Economies of the Third Kind." *Appalachia* 11 (December 1977–January 1978): 20–27.

Baker, Deborah M. "Flood without Relief: The Story of the Tug Valley Disaster." *SE* 6 (Spring 1978): 20–27.

Beaver, Patricia. "You've Got to Be Converted: An Interview with Helen Matthews Lewis." *AJ* 15 (Spring 1988): 238–65.

Billings, Dwight B. "Religion as Opposition: A Gramscian Analysis." *American Journal of Sociology* 96 (July 1990): 1–31.

Bookser-Feister, John, and Leah Wise, eds. "Everybody's Business: A People's Guide to Economic Development." *SE* 14 (September/October–November/December 1986).

Braden, Anne. "American Inquisition, Part II: The McSurely Case and Repression in the 1960s." *SE* 11 (September–October 1983): 20–27.

Branscome, James G., and James Y. Holloway. "Non-Violence and Violence in Appalachia." *Katallagete* 5 (Winter 1974): 32–42.

Carawan, Guy, and Candie Carawan. *Voices from the Mountains.* Urbana: UIP, 1982.

Clavel, Pierre. *Opposition and Planning in Wales and Appalachia.* Philadelphia: Temple U. Press, 1983.

Couto, Richard, Pat Sharkey, Paul Elwood, and Laura Green. "Relevant Education: Sharing Life's Glories." *SE* 14 (September/October–November/December 1986): 60–61.

Crittenden, Beth. "West Virginia Elders Make a Difference." *SE* 13 (March–June 1985): 52–56.

Daley, Nelda, and Sue Ella Kobak. "The Paradox of the 'Familiar Outsider'." *AJ* 17 (Spring 1990): 248–60.

Davis, Donald. *Empowering the South: A Bibliography for Community Organizing.* Maryville, TN: Southern Empowerment Project, 1990.

Fisher, Steve. "Economic Development Strategies for Appalachia in the Eighties." In *Appalachia's Changing Economy: A Reader,* ed. Paul DeLeon. New Market, TN: Highlander Center, 1986.

Fisher, Steve, and Jim Foster. "Models for Furthering Revolutionary Praxis in Appalachia." *AJ* 6 (Spring 1979): 170–194.

Garland, Anne W. "Tell It on the Mountain: Marie Cirillo Helps People in Appalachia Take Charge of Their Lives." *Progressive* 52 (July 1988): 22–25.

Gaventa, John. *Power and Powerlessness: Quiescence and Rebellion in an Appalachian Valley.* Urbana: UIP, 1980.

Gaventa, John, Barbara E. Smith, & Alex Willingham, eds. *Communities in Economic Crisis: Appalachia and the South.* Philadelphia: Temple U. Press, 1990.

Glen, John. "The Council of the Southern Mountains and the War on Poverty." *Now and Then* 5 (Fall 1988): 4–12.

———. *Highlander: No Ordinary School, 1932–1962.* Lexington: UKP, 1988.

Highlander Research and Education Center: An Approach to Education Presented through a Collection of Writings. New Market, TN: Highlander Center, 1989.

Hoffman, Edwin D. *Fighting Mountaineers: The Struggle for Justice in the Appalachians.* Boston: Houghton Mifflin, 1979.

Horton, Myles, with Judith Kohl & Herbert Kohl. *The Long Haul: An Autobiography.* New York: Doubleday, 1990.

Howard, Thomas F. K. "Moving Mountains." *In These Times,* 16–26 July 1980.

Kahn, Si. "New Strategies for Appalachia." *New South* 25 (Summer 1970): 57–64.

———. *Organizing: A Guide for Grassroots Leaders.* New York: McGraw-Hill, 1982.

Kobak, Sue Ella, and Nina McCormack, with assistance from Nancy Robinson. *Workshop on Developing Feasibility Studies for Community-Based Business Ventures.* New Market, TN: Economics Education Project, Highlander Center, 1988.

Lewis, Helen M. "Backwood Rebels: Resistance in the Appalachian Mountains." In *Conflict & Peacemaking in Appalachia,* ed. Coalition for Appalachian Ministry, 16–26. Amesville, OH, 1987.

———. "Maxine Waller: the Making of a Community Organizer." *Now & Then* 7 (Spring 1990): 12–14.

Lewis, Helen M., and John Gaventa. *The Jellico Handbook: A Teacher's Guide to Community-Based Economics.* New Market, TN: Economics Education Project, Highlander Center, 1988.

Long, Kate. "Progressive Network/Progressive Gains." *SE* 12 (January–February 1984): 60–67.

Luttrell, Wendy. *Claiming What Is Ours: An Economics Experience Workbook.* New Market, TN: Economics Education Project, Highlander Center, 1988.

McDonald, Kevin. "Outreach and Outrage: The Student Health Coalition." *SE* 6 (Summer 1978): 18–23.

Martin, Linda. "The Politics of School Reform in the Eighties." In *Education in Appalachia. Proceedings from the 1987 Conference on Appalachia,* ed. Appalachian Center, U. of Kentucky, 59–63. Lexington, 1988.

Moran, Jane. "Is Everyone Paying Their Fair Share? An Analysis of Taxpayers' Actions to Equalize Taxes." *West Virginia Law Review* 85 (Winter 1982–83): 209–37.

MLW, June 1983. Special Issue: "Nonviolent Organizing in Eastern Kentucky."

Neely, Jack. "Grassroots Power: Tennesseans Fight for Social Justice." *SE* 13 (March–June 1985: 40–45.

Nigro, Carol A., and Ann M. Ventura. "Making a Career of Community Involvement: An Interview with Edna Compton." *Appalachia* 21 (Summer 1988): 25–29.

O'Connell, Barry. "Whose Land and Music Shall Ours Be? Reflections on the History of Protest in the Southern Mountains." *AJ* 12 (Fall 1984): 18–30.

Peddle, Dorothy H. "To Do What's Right: Interviews with Eula Hall and Mike Sheets." *SE* 11 (March–April 1983): 39–43.

PA 3 (Spring 1973). Special Issue: "Getting from Here to There—Together."

PA 3 (Summer 1974). Special Issue: "New Federalist Papers."

Pignone, Mary M. "Development and Theology in Central Appalachia." *Saint Luke's Journal of Theology* 22 (March 1979): 87–102.

Plaut, Thomas. "Conflict, Confrontation, and Social Change in the Regional Setting." In B, 267–84.

———. "Political Alienation and Development: A Perspective from Appalachia." In E&K, 295–303.

Rural Community Education Cooperative, Mountain Women's Exchange. *Claiming Our Economic History: Jellico, Tennessee.* Jellico, TN, 1987.

Simon, Richard, and Roger Lesser. "A Working Community Commonwealth: A Radical Development Strategy for the Mountains." *PA* 3 (Spring 1973): 9–15.

Smith, Stephen B. "A Ministry to God's Backyard: Development of the Appalachian People's Service Organization, Inc. (APSO) 1965–1983." *Historical Magazine of the Protestant Episcopal Church* 52 (December 1983): 405–26.

Staub, Michael. " 'We'll Never Quit It!' Yellow Creek Concerned Citizens Combat Creekbed Catastrophe." *SE* 11 (January–February 1983): 43–52.

Szakos, Joe. "They're Not All Sitting Back and Taking It: Fighting for Change in Eastern Kentucky." In *The Land and Economy of Appalachia: Proceedings from the 1986 Conference on Appalachia,* ed. Appalachian Center, U. of Kentucky, 91–96. Lexington, 1987.

Szakos, Kristin L. "Schools and Taxes: Making Industry Pay Its Way." *SE* 14 (September/ October–November/December 1986): 24–27.

Szakos, Kristin L., and Joe Szakos. " 'The Older I Get the Closer I Get to the Ground': An Interview with Everett Akers." *SE* 13 (March–June 1985): 68–71.

Tudiver, Neil. "Why Aid Doesn't Help: Organizing for Community Economic Development in Central Appalachia." Ph. D. diss., U. of Michigan, 1973.

Whisnant, David E. "Controversy in God's Grand Division: The Council of the Southern Mountains." *AJ* 2 (Autumn 1974): 7–45. See responses to this article in *AJ* 2 (Spring 1975): 171–91.

———. "Finding New Models For Appalachian Development." *New South* 25 (Fall 1970): 70–77.

———. "The Folk Hero in Appalachian Struggle History." *New South* 28 (Fall 1973): 30–47.

———. *Modernizing the Mountaineer: People, Power and Planning in Appalachia.* Boone: ACP, 1981.

Many of the books and articles listed throughout this bibliography offer strategies of change and examples of citizen resistance. See especially the works on the UMWA, textile organizing activities, and groups fighting to protect their land (IV D, X, & XI).

XI. Audio-visual Materials

Available from:
APPALSHOP FILMS
BOX 743
Whitesburg, Kentucky 41858
Phone   606/633–5708

	VHS Video Purchase with Public Performance Rights	16MM Film Purchase	16 MM Film Rental
Appalachian Genesis	$100.00	$425.00	$ 50.00

1973/Directed by Bill Richardson with David Adams and Ben Zickafoose
Appalachian young people talk about the frustrations and pleasures of adolescence in the coal mining region of central Appalachia.

Artus Moser of Buckeye Cove	100.00	Video Only	

1985/Directed by Anne Johnson
A renaissance man of the mountains, Artus grew up on the Biltmore Estate near Asheville, N.C., where his father worked for the estate forester. Artus was an early collector of ballads for the Library of Congress, college and high school teacher, singer, storyteller, actor, painter, sculptor, and naturalist.

The Big Lever	100.00	750.00	80.00

1982/Directed by Frances Morton
The film focuses on the career of County Judge-Executive Allen C. Muncy, the man who invited Nixon to Leslie County, and subsequently sought re-election despite a federal conviction of vote fraud conspiracy. The focus of the film is country electioneering: hollow to hollow vote-hunting, family squabbles over candidates, patronage promises, and courthouse steps speechmaking.

Buffalo Creek Flood: An Act of Man	100.00	550.00	60.00

1975/Directed by Mimi Pickering
On February 26, 1972, a coal-waste dam at the head of a crowded hollow in southern West Virginia collapsed. The dam belonged to the Pittston Coal Company, and when it collapsed, a wall of sludge and water slashed through the valley killing 125 people and leaving 4000 homeless. Buffalo Creek Flood: An Act of Man is Appalshop's first look at the disaster and the ensuing controversy about Pittston's liability.

Buffalo Creek Revisited	100.00	500.00	55.00

1984/Directed by Mimi Pickering
Buffalo Creek Revisited looks at the second disaster on Buffalo Creek, in which the survivors' efforts to rebuild the physical and emotional community shattered by the flood have been thwarted by government insensitivity and a century-old pattern of corporate control of the region's land and resources.

Catfish: Man of the Woods   100.00   450.00   50.00
1975/Directed by Alan Bennett

> Astrologer, herb-gatherer, holistic healer, mountain nutritionist, marriage counselor, possessor of 67 nicknames, social commentator, and occasional nudist, Clarence "Catfish" Gray is a good man to know if you feel your life has gone out of balance; his spirit is a tonic for troubled times.

Chairmaker   100.00   400.00   45.00
1975/Directed by Rick DiClemente

> Filmed in the hills near Sugarloaf Hollow, Kentucky, 80-year-old Dewey Thompson discusses and demonstrates his particular craft of furniture building.

Clinchco: Story of a Mining Town   100.00   40.00 (filmstrip)
1982/Directed by Susie Baker

> A series of photographs, many from family albums, that chronicles the boom and bust of a bi-racial coal camp in the hills of Virginia.

Coal Miner: Frank Johnson   100.00   200.00   25.00
1971/Directed by Ben Zickafoose

> The testimony of a man who has been a coal miner since he was 15 years old. In the film Frank addresses both the difficulty miners have had in unionizing and the ongoing problem of enforcing mine safety standards.

Coalmining Women   100.00   650.00   70.00
1982/Directed by Elizabeth Barret

> Interviewed at home and on the job, women coal miners tell of the social and economic conditions that led them to seek jobs in the strenuous, male-dominated coal mines.

Dreadful Memories: The Life of Sarah Ogan Gunning   100.00   Video Only
1988/Directed by Mimi Pickering

> Dreadful Memories: The Life of Sarah Ogan Gunning is an uncompromising look at one of the most powerful of all the labor organizing folk-singers of the 1930's, Sarah Ogan Gunning from Knox County, Kentucky.

The Feathered Warrior   100.00   200.00   25.00
1973/Directed by Ben Zickafoose with Gene DuBey and Bill Hatton

> In this film a cockfighter describes the business and provides color commentary on a live cockfight.

Fixin' To Tell About Jack   100.00   425.00   45.00
1975/Directed by Elizabeth Barret

> Ray Hicks is a mountain farmer from Beech Mountain, N.C. with genius for telling traditional folktales or "Jack Tales." In his film, Ray tells "Whickety-whack, Into My Sack" (also known as "Soldier Jack") at home and with a group of children.

Frontier Nursing Service   100.00   Video Only
1984/Directed by Anne Johnson

> A look at the pioneering rural nurse and midwifery service in Leslie County, Kentucky.

Grassroots Small Farm   100.00   Video Only
1988/Directed by Anne Johnson
    The Grassroots Small Farm Project has worked with over 260 families to
    teach subsistence farming methods.

Hand Carved   100.00   1,350.00   150.00
1981/Directed by Herb E. Smith
    "The film's succession of grand pictures is about the Chester Cornett who
    makes chairs with high craft and unbelievable skill. Chester Cornett is a
    hero, a gentle survivor of hard times, bad luck, lost love and a kitchen that
    must be the most colossal mess of any place outside the Federal Budget
    Office."—Karl Hess, author of **Community Technology.**

Hard Times in the Country: 100.00   Video Only
The Schools
1988/Directed by Anne Johnson
    One of a proposed six-part series on the impact of the War on Poverty in
    Appalachia, this program looks at the pros and cons of building large, con-
    solidated schools and closing small, community-based schools.

Harriette Simpson Arnow: 100.00   550.00   55.00
1980–1986
1988/Directed by Herb E. Smith
    This documentary portrait, filmed shortly before Arnow's death, is com-
    posed of interviews shot in and around the author's home, and will be of
    interest to anyone interested in Arnow's work as well as those interested
    in the creative process and the workings of a writer's mind.

I'm What This Is All About   100.00   Video Only
1985/Directed by Anne Johnson and Mimi Pickering
    Co-produced with a rural West Virginia parents group, this program pre-
    sents an overview of the complex issues residents of the state faced when
    the courts ruled the schools unconstitutional.

In The Good Old-Fashioned   100.00   450.00   50.00
Way
1973/Directed by Herb E. Smith
    Examines the life of the spirit in the Old Regular Baptist Churches of
    Letcher, Knott, and Perry counties in Kentucky.

In Ya Blood   100.00   300.00   30.00
1971/Directed by Herb E. Smith
    Appalshop's first dramatic narrative follows Randy as he tries to decide
    between working the mines and going away to college.

John Jacob Niles   100.00   Video Only
1978/Directed by Bill Richardson with Mimi Pickering and Ben Zickafoose
    Made just a few years before Niles' death, this film captures the dynamism
    of one of the better-known folk musicians of our time.

Judge Wooten and   100.00   175.00   20.00
Coon-on-a-Log
1971/Directed by Herby E. Smith
    Judge George Wooten of Leslie County, Kentucky talks about life and pol-
    itics as area hound dogs try to knock a raccoon off a log in the middle of
    a pond.

The Kingdom Come School   100.00   400.00   45.00
1973/Directed by Dianna Ott
> A visit to one of the last one-room schoolhouses in the country—on Kingdom Come Creek in Letcher County, Kentucky. At Kingdom Come School, learning took place in an intimate atmosphere of love and familiarity.

Lily May Ledford   100.00   Video Only
1988/Directed by Anne Johnson
> Interviews and performance footage with the "banjo-picin' girl" who led the Coon Creek Girls, stars of the Renfro Valley Barn Dance, and the first all-woman band on radio.

Long Journey Home   100.00   825.00   90.00

Lord and Father   100.00   700.00   75.00
1983/Directed by Joe Gray, Jr.
> Documents the conflicting viewpoints of father and son over profitability and morality in the operation of a Kentucky tobacco farm.

Mabel Parker Hardison   100.00   Video Only
Smith
1985/Directed by Anne Johnson
> Transplanted to Harlan County, Kentucky, in the early 1900's, Mabel recollects the life of a black Appalachian miner's family while archival and personal photos illustrate her colorful narration.

The Millstone Sewing   100.00   200.00   25.00
Center
1972/Directed by Mimi Pickering
> Millstone was an exercise in grassroots economic development—Mabel Kiser's effort to organize alternatives to welfare programs by providing a center for local women to sew clothes for the communities of Letcher County, Kentucky. Great film for providing historical insight into the strength of one community of Appalachian women in the end days of the War on Poverty.

Mine War on Blackberry   100.00   Video Only
Creek
1986/Directed by Anne Johnson
> A series of Vignettes of a long and bitter strike by members of the United Mine Workers of America against a unit of the A. T. Massey Coal Co.— a subsidiary of large multinational corporations.

Minnie Black's Gourd Band   100.00   Video Only
1988/Directed by Anne Johnson
> A Video portrait of the first lady of gourd art.

Mountain Farmer   100.00   150.00   20.00
1973/Directed by Shelby Adams and Mimi Pickering
> A visit with Lee Banks, one of the last of the old-style mountain farmers— a man who grew his own and "never bought no meat nor lard in 50 years." A horse and a wooden plow, a vegetable garden, and a few hogs sustain Lee and his family.

Mud Creek Clinic   100.00   Video Only
1986/Directed by Anne Johnson
    This film shows how a health clinic was established—against formidable odds—by residents of Floyd County, Kentucky.

Nature's Way   100.00   400.00   45.00
1974/Directed by John Long with Elizabeth Barret
    Aunt Etta Banks takes the viewer through the preparation of her family's special salve, certain of its superiority to any doctor medicine she's ever had. Another man hawks his natural remedies, while another gentleman discusses the preparation of the cancer cure medicine that saved his wife. Nature's Way ends with a dramatic scene in which a midwife talks about the 5000 babies she has brought into the world as she delivers a set of twins.

Nimrod Workman: To Fit   100.00   500.00   55.00
My Own Category
1975/Directed by Scott Faulkner and Anthony Slone
    Nimrod's reminiscences about early union organizing and the life of a coal miner are interposed with the traditional ballads and original compositions for which he is famous. Features an armchair performance of Nimrod's original classic, "Watergate Boogie."

Oaksie   100.00   400.00   45.00
1979/Directed by Anthony Slone
    A portrait of basketmaker, fiddler, and harp player Oaksie Caudill from Cowan Creek in Letcher County, Kentucky.

On Our Own Land   100.00   Video Only
1988/Directed by Anne Johnson
    On Our Own Land looks at the dying days of the broad form deed in Kentucky and the peoples' fight to kill it.

One Ring Circus   100.00   Video Only
1987/Directed by Andrew Garrison
    A behind-the-tents look at the one of the last travelling circuses touring the mountain towns.

Ourselves and That Promise   100.00   425.00   45.00
1978/Directed by Joe Gray with Gene DuBey and Scott Faulkner
    Four Kentucky artists—writers James Still, Robert Penn Warren, Ronnie Criswell, and photographer Billy Davis—discuss their work and its relationship to their environment.

Portraits and Dreams   65.00   35.00
                                                           (filmstrip)

Quilting Women   100.00   475.00   50.00

Ramsey Trade Fair   100.00   300.00   35.00
1973/Directed by Scott Faulkner
    This beauty of a film is a visit to a weekly trade fair in Southwestern Virginia. Ramsey Trade Fair is a fleamarket; it's an institute in the gentle art of barter; it's a place to swap songs and stories, produce and pocketknives. Ramsey Trade Fair is a short cinematic seminar in rural economics.

Red Fox/Second Hangin'   49.95   Video Only
1984/Directed by Don Baker
> Roadside Theater has produced this videotape of their acclaimed play, which mixes historical drama and intrigue in their unique storytelling style. Set along the border of Virginia and Kentucky shortly after the Civil War—a time of feuds and the arrival of the coal and timber barons from the East—the play turns around the character of Doc Taylor, "The Red Fox of the Cumberlands." doctor, preacher, U.S. Marshal, and the second man hanged in Wise County, Virginia.

Sarah Bailey   100.00   Video Only
1984/Directed by Anne Johnson
> Folk artist Sarah Bailey makes dolls and flowers from corn shucks, and does her own weaving. She is seen at work and teaching in an Elderhostel in this piece.

So Was Einstein: A Look at   100.00   Video Only
Dyslexic Children
1988/Directed by Anne Johnson
> Four Eastern Kentucky students and their families are the focus of this show about how families, schools, and special programs like one in Hindman, Kentucky can work together to help dyslexic children.

Sourwood Mountain   100.00   475.00   50.00
Dulcimers
1976/Directed by Gene DuBey
> In this film, I. D. Stamper, a master dulcimer maker and player, and John McCutcheon, one of the most talented of the next generation of dulcimer players, play together, swap tunes, and discuss musical traditions and history.

Sunny Side of Life   100.00   845.00   90.00
1985/Directed by Scott Faulkner, Anthony Slone, and Jack Wright
> Sunny Side of Life looks at the past and celebrates the living legacy of the Carter family country music dynasty.

Strangers & Kin   100.00   825.00   90.00
This film shows the development and effects of stereotypes in a region where technological change collides with tradition. The film traces the evolution of the "hillbilly" image through Hollywood films, network news and entertainment shows, popular literature and interviews with contemporary Appalachians.

Stripmining: Energy,   100.00   750.00   75.00
Environment, and Economics
1979/Directed by Frances Morton and Gene DuBey
> This film details the beginnings, growth, and consequences of the method of mining which accounts for over 50% of the coal produced in the Appalachian region.

Stripmining In Appalachia   100.00   425.00   45.00
1973/Directed by Gene DuBey
> Appalshop's earlier look at the most problematic of coal recovery techniques.

The Struggle for Coon   100.00   200.00   25.00
Branch Mountain
1972/Directed by Mimi Pickering

> The story of the fight to improve the roads and schools of McDowell County, West Virginia. This film looks at the political and bureaucratic roadblocks thrown up in front of the parents and children in one West Virginia community and the way the people fought back.

Tell Me A Story, Sing   100.00   Video Only
Me A Song
1985/Directed by Dudley Cocke, Anne Johnson, and Susan Wehling

> (A Headwaters Program) Three independent theater companies, A Free Southern Theater, A Traveling Jewish Theatre, and Roadside Theater, gather for a three-way tour.

Three Mountain Tales   100.00   Video Only
1982

> Three mountain folk tales as told by the members of Roadside Theater. Illustrated with pastel drawings by taleteller Angelyn DeBord.

Tomorrow's People   100.00   350.00   40.00
1973/Directed by Gene DuBey

> I.D. Stamper, Coy Morton, and Lee Sexton supply the soundtrack to a swirl of images of mountain life.

Tradition   100.00   375.00   40.00
1973/Directed by Bill Hatton and Anthony Slone

> Moonshining and the law's effort to stop it are the two time-honored Appalachian traditions examined in this film.

Unbroken Tradition: Jerry   100.00   475.00   50.00
Brown Pottery

UMWA 1970: A House   100.00   200.00   25.00
Divided
1971/Directed by Ben Zickafoose and Dan Mohn

> A short film that captures the struggle of rank-and-file union members to clean up the union during the Tony Boyle era.

War, Taxes, and The   100.00   Video Only
Almighty Dollar

Waterground   100.00   350.00   40.00
1977/Directed by Frances Morton

> A stoneground mill in the middle of the mountains of Western North Carolina—one of the last waterpowered grist mills in existence—is the focus of Waterground.

Whoa, Mule   50.00   Video Only

| **Woodrow Cornett: Letcher** | 100.00 | 175.00 | 20.00 |

County Butcher

1971/Directed by Bill Richardson and Ben Zickafoose

Watch in amazement as Woodrow takes a hog from hoof to ham.

| **Yellow Creek, Kentucky** | 100.00 | Video Only |

1984/Directed by Anne Johnson

Co-produced with the Yellow Creek Concerned Citizens, this program documents their efforts to stop a commercial tannery's dumping of toxic wastes into the creek that flows through their southeast Kentucky community.

Appendix

Demographic Characteristics: Summary for the United States and Appalachia.

	1965	1970	1975	1980	1985	1990	Latest Data
Unemployment Rate (%)							(1991 Avg Ann)
United States	4.5%	4.9%	8.5%	7.1%	7.2%	5.5%	6.7%
Appalachia	5.0%	5.4%	8.7%	8.5%	9.4%	6.2%	7.5%
Civilian Labor Force (Bureau of Labor Statistics)							
United States	74,455,000	82,715,000	92,613,000	106,940,000	115,461,000	124,787,000	125,303,000
Appalachia	6,492,000	7,108,000	7,851,000	8,915,000	9,191,000	9,790,944	9,870,800
Number Employed							
United States	71,088,000	78,678,000	84,783,000	99,303,000	107,150,000	117,913,000	116,877,000
Appalachia	6,167,000	6,723,000	7,169,000	8,158,000	8,330,000	9,184,043	9,134,000
Population (Data in thousands)							**1991**
United States	193,451	203,799	215,457	226,546	238,036	248,710	252,177
Appalachia	17,940	18,262	19,374	20,352	20,583	20,702	20,929

Total Personal Income Per Capita (Bureau of Economic Analysis)

	1965	1970	1975	1980	1985	1990	1991
United States	$2,772	$3,945	$5,842	$9,916	$13,899	$18,696	$0
Appalachia	$2,166	$3,176	$4,858	$8,195	$11,096	$15,316	$0
Appalachia as % of US	78.1	80.5	83.2	82.6	79.8	81.9	00.0

Source: Appalachian Regional Commission

Transfer Payments-Federal Outlays for Six Major Welfare Programs (in thousands of dollars)

	1965	1970	1975	1980
United States		8,073,736		39,054,025
Appalachia		756,949		3,427,868

Infant Mortality (Infant deaths per 1,000 live births)

	1960	1968	1973	1975	1980	1985	1990	1988–90
United States	26.0	21.8	17.7	16.1	12.5	10.6	9.1	9.7
Appalachia	26.5	22.9	19.2	17.0	10.5	10.5	9.3	9.6

Poverty Status (1960 from OEO data; 1970, 1980, & 1990 from Census of Population)

	1960 Number of Persons in thousands and %		1970 Number of Persons in thousands and %		1980 Number of Persons in thousands and %		1990 Number of Persons in thousands and %	
	U.S.	App.	U.S.	App.	U.S.	App.	U.S.	App.
	38,684.5	5,446.6	27,125.0	3,228.4	27,383	2,770.9	32,581	3066.8
	22.1%	31.2%	13.7%	18.1%	12.4%	14.0%	13.1%	15.2%

Migration

	1950–1960		1960–1970		1970–1980		1980–1990	
	U.S.	App.	U.S.	App.	U.S.	App.	U.S.	App.
Net Migration		−2,189,000		−1,106,000		1,078,000	5,205,852	−448,371
Percent		−12.7		−6.2		5.9	2.3%	−2.2

Education Attainment for Persons 25 Years Old or Older (Bureau of Census)

| | 1960 | | 1970 | | 1980 | | 1990* | |
	U.S.	App.	U.S.	App.	U.S.	App.	U.S.	App.
Less than High School Education	58.9%	67.2%	47.7%	56.2%	33.5%	46.2%	24.8%	31.6%
Four or More Years of College	7.7%	5.4%	10.7%	7.3	16.2%	11.2%	20.3%	14.3%

*Some definitional changes in 1990 Census.

Education Attainment for Youths 18–24 Years Old (Bureau of Census)

| | 1960 Number of Persons in thousands and % | | 1970 Number of Persons in thousands and % | | 1980 Number of Persons in thousands and % | |
	U.S.	App.	U.S.	App.	U.S.	App.
Less than High School Education			6,396	629	7,162	649
			27.4%	31.5%	23.9%	25.3%
One or More Years of College			5,524	436	9,385	704
			23.6%	21.8%	31.4%	27.5%

Condition of Housing (Bureau of Census)

| 1960 Deteriorating & Dilapidated (in thousands) | | 1970, Lacking One or More Plumbing Facility and Overcrowded (in thousands) | | 1980, Lacking One or More Plumbing Facility and Overcrowded (in thousands) | |
U.S.	App.	U.S.	App.	U.S.	App.
10,968.0	1,238.0	8,237.0	1,034.0	5,706.1	508.4
18.8%	26.0%	12.9%	18.3%	7.1%	7.2%

Population: Appalachian State Parts and United States 1970, 1980, 1990, and 1991.

Appalachian State Part	1970 Population	1980 Population	1990 Population	1970–80 Net Change	1970–80 % Change	1980–90 Net Change	1980–90 % Change
Alabama	2,137,278	2,430,244	2,529,623	292,966	13.7	99,379	4.1
Georgia	813,596	1,103,971	1,508,030	290,375	35.6	404,059	36.6
Kentucky	875,922	1,077,095	1,045,357	201,175	22.9	(31,738)	−2.9
Maryland	209,349	220,132	224,477	10,783	5.1	4,345	2.0
Mississippi	433,267	498,374	510,597	65,107	15.0	12,223	2.5
New York	1,056,367	1,083,241	1,088,470	26,874	2.5	5,229	0.5
North Carolina	1,037,212	1,217,732	1,306,682	180,520	17.4	88,950	7.3
Ohio	1,237,660	1,376,130	1,372,893	138,470	11.2	(3,237)	−0.2
Pennsylvania	5,930,303	5,994,240	5,769,410	63,937	1.1	(224,830)	−3.8
South Carolina	656,126	793,040	888,057	136,914	20.9	95,017	12.0
Tennessee	1,733,661	2,073,834	2,146,992	340,173	19.6	73,158	3.5
Virginia	470,094	549,888	517,816	79,794	17.0	(32,072)	−5.8
West Virginia	1,744,237	1,950,183	1,793,477	205,946	11.8	(156,706)	−8.0
Appalachia	18,335,072	20,368,104	20,701,881	2,033,032	11.1	333,777	1.6
United States	203,304,000	238,739,200	248,709,873	35,435,200	17.4	9,970,673	4.2

Source: 1970 and 1980 revised population data from U.S. Bureau of the Census. 1990 data from STF 1 files, U.S. Bureau of the Census
1991 data are U.S. Bureau of the Census estimates

Sources of Population Change: Appalachia and United States.

Appalachian State Part	1980 Revised Population	1990 Census Population	1980–90 Sources of Population Change			
			Net Change	Natural Change*	Net Migration!	Percent Net Migration
Alabama	2,430,223	2,529,623	99,400	127,128	(27,728)	−1.1
Georgia	1,103,964	1,508,030	404,066	106,674	297,392	26.9
Kentucky	1,077,095	1,045,357	(31,738)	53,072	(84,810)	−7.9
Maryland	220,124	224,477	4,353	4,918	(565)	−0.3
Mississippi	498,374	510,597	12,223	33,016	(20,793)	−4.2
New York	1,083,241	1,088,470	5,229	46,721	(41,492)	−3.8
North Carolina	1,217,732	1,306,682	88,950	40,932	48,018	3.9
Ohio	1,376,130	1,372,893	(3,237)	65,852	(69,089)	−5.0
Pennsylvania	5,994,240	5,769,410	(224,830)	113,689	(338,519)	−5.6
South Carolina	793,039	888,057	95,018	48,691	46,327	5.8
Tennessee	2,073,737	2,146,992	73,255	77,278	(4,023)	−0.2
Virginia	549,888	517,816	(32,072)	11,698	(43,770)	−8.0
West Virginia	1,950,186	1,793,477	(156,709)	52,610	(209,319)	−10.7
Appalachia	20,367,973	20,701,881	333,908	782,279	(448,371)	−2.2
Appalachian Nonmetropolitan Counties	9,189,174	9,240,633	51,459	354,881	(303,422)	−3.3
Appalachian Metropolitan Counties	11,187,799	11,461,248	273,449	427,398	(144,949)	−1.3
United States	226,542,204	248,709,873	22,167,669	16,961,817	5,205,852	2.3

*Number of births minus the number of deaths.

!U.S. Bureau of the Census calls this column residual change to account for population undercounts and births reported to incorrect county of residence.

Per Capita Income: Appalachian State Parts and United States 1970, 1980, and 1990 and Annual Average BEA Income Data as of May 1992.

Appalachian State Part	1970 Per Capita Income	TP170 (000)	1970 Index US = $4,051	1980 Per Capita Income	TP180 (000)	1980 Index US = $9,919	1990 Per Capita Income	TP190 (000)	1990 Index US = $18,696
Alabama	3,051	6,533,384	75	7,964	19,403,101	80	15,615	39,552,108	84
Georgia	2,954	2,424,560	73	7,892	8,767,683	80	16,295	24,761,623	87
Kentucky	2,371	2,087,380	59	6,601	7,127,862	67	11,760	12,291,659	63
Maryland	3,347	701,245	83	8,204	1,802,430	83	15,371	3,456,975	82
Mississippi	2,484	1,042,948	61	6,507	3,149,970	66	12,232	6,250,316	65
New York	3,627	3,842,111	90	8,072	8,744,946	81	15,381	16,746,354	82
North Carolina	3,156	3,290,183	78	7,941	9,702,867	80	16,127	21,122,508	86
Ohio	3,145	3,904,983	78	7,915	10,907,496	80	13,346	18,452,819	71
Pennsylvania	3,702	21,974,472	91	9,287	55,669,668	94	16,779	96,783,411	90
South Carolina	3,239	2,134,503	80	8,198	6,525,659	83	16,121	14,368,583	86
Tennessee	2,971	5,174,719	73	7,549	15,702,815	76	14,738	31,680,382	79
Virginia	2,670	1,260,515	66	7,494	4,126,299	76	14,128	7,300,058	76
West Virginia	3,077	5,375,309	76	7,915	15,458,842	80	13,744	24,601,612	74
Region	3,252	59,746,312	80	8,195	167,089,638	83	15,316	297,566,298	82
UNITED STATES	4,051		100	9,919		100	18,696		100

Average Annual Employment: Appalachian State Parts and United States 1970, 1980, 1990, and 1991

Appalachian State Part	1970 Number Employed	1970 Number Unemp.	1970 Civilian Labor Force	1970 Unem Rate	1980 Number Employed	1980 Number Unemp.	1980 Civilian Labor Force	1980 Unem Rate
Alabama	767,500	33,830	801,330	4.2	959,763	98,872	1,058,635	9.3
Georgia	261,640	13,320	274,960	4.8	498,217	37,754	535,971	7.0
Kentucky	231,083	22,219	253,302	8.8	381,393	40,383	421,776	9.6
Maryland	79,315	5,495	84,810	6.5	89,355	10,849	100,204	10.8
Mississippi	157,370	8,220	165,590	5.0	201,344	18,167	219,511	8.3
New York	344,500	21,000	365,500	5.7	447,431	34,008	481,439	7.1
No. Carolina	423,730	19,690	443,420	4.4	552,305	38,663	590,968	6.5
Ohio	418,500	23,300	441,800	5.3	489,238	52,116	541,354	9.6
Pennsylvania	2,226,500	108,700	2,335,200	4.7	2,417,464	238,790	2,656,254	9.0
So. Carolina	296,350	11,750	308,100	3.8	367,787	23,998	391,785	6.1
Tennessee	669,940	33,920	703,860	4.8	819,010	71,368	890,378	8.0
Virginia	150,950	8,584	159,534	5.4	220,442	17,913	238,355	7.5
West Virginia	589,910	39,630	629,540	6.3	714,003	74,004	788,007	9.4
Appalachia	6,617,288	349,658	6,966,946	5.0	8,157,752	756,885	8,914.637	8.5
United States	78,678,000	4,093,000	82,771,000	4.9	99,303,000	7,637,000	106,940,000	7.1

Appalachian State Part	1990 Number Employed	1990 Number Unemp.	1990 Civilian Labor Force	1990 Unem Rate	1991 Number Employed	1991 Number Unemp.	1991 Civilian Labor Force	1991 Unem Rate
Alabama	1,140,781	79,529	1,220,310	6.5	1,135,358	84,577	1,219,935	6.9
Georgia	716,947	42,371	759,318	5.6	708,636	38,841	747,477	5.2
Kentucky	387,755	32,418	420,173	7.7	375,751	42,027	417,778	10.1
Maryland	99,743	8,249	107,992	7.6	102,236	10,183	112,419	9.1
Mississippi	224,645	19,873	244,518	8.1	225,116	23,493	248,609	9.4
New York	485,135	23,852	508,987	4.7	472,827	33,604	506,431	6.6
No. Carolina	656,828	29,218	686,046	4.3	654,564	38,746	693,310	5.6
Ohio	557,286	41,966	599,252	7.0	558,403	48,391	606,794	8.0
Pennsylvania	2,552,373	168,706	2,721,079	6.2	2,544,810	210,171	2,754,981	7.6
So. Carolina	447,439	20,254	467,693	4.3	441,482	26,253	467,735	5.6
Tennessee	981,874	58,461	1,040,335	5.6	981,985	75,282	1,057,267	7.1
Virginia	225,236	18,008	243,244	7.4	231,872	23,232	255,104	9.1
West Virginia	708,001	63,996	771,997	8.3	701,000	82,006	783,006	10.5
Appalachia	9,184,043	606,901	9,790,944	6.2	9,134,040	736,806	9,870,846	7.5
United States	117,913,000	6,874,000	124,787,000	5.5	116,877,000	8,426,000	125,303,000	6.7

Poverty Rates

Appalachian State Part	1960 Percent of Population Living in Poverty	1960 Number of People Below Poverty Level	Appalachian State Part	1970 Percent of Population Living in Poverty	1970 Number of People Below Poverty Level
Alabama	38.8	762,251	Alabama	22.1	463,306
Georgia	38.5	258,812	Georgia	16.9	135,957
Kentucky	58.4	536,079	Kentucky	38.8	334,373
Maryland	24.9	47,939	Maryland	14.8	30,214
Mississippi	56.0	225,941	Mississippi	33.8	138,594
New York	17.1	165,110	New York	11.5	116,917
North Carolina	37.2	341,949	North Carolina	18.8	190,440
Ohio	26.1	287,115	Ohio	16.0	176,373
Pennsylvania	19.3	1,126,903	Pennsylvania	11.4	663,877
South Carolina	34.0	195,940	South Carolina	16.2	104,010
Tennessee	39.9	632,555	Tennessee	22.4	381,061
Virginia	24.4	229,184	Virginia	24.4	113,214
West Virginia	34.6	636,794	West Virginia	22.2	380,113
Appalachia	31.2	5,446,612	Appalachia	18.1	3,228,449
United States	22.1	38,684,545	United States	13.7	27,124,985

Appalachian State Part	1980 Percent of Population Living in Poverty	1980 Number of People Below Poverty Level	Appalachian State Part	1990 Percent of Population Living in Poverty	1990 Number of People Below Poverty Level
Alabama	16.6	394,851	Alabama	15.8	391,301
Georgia	12.3	134,202	Georgia	10.0	148,200
Kentucky	26.0	274,796	Kentucky	29.0	296,431
Maryland	11.9	25,296	Maryland	12.4	26,481
Mississippi	22.1	104,599	Mississippi	22.5	112,207
New York	12.0	124,156	New York	12.9	133,032
North Carolina	13.8	164,175	North Carolina	12.4	158,185
Ohio	12.9	170,105	Ohio	17.4	232,297
Pennsylvania	10.0	586,629	Pennsylvania	12.4	696,729
South Carolina	12.6	96,995	South Carolina	11.6	99,634
Tennessee	16.6	337,437	Tennessee	16.1	337,709
Virginia	15.2	82,703	Virginia	17.6	89,529
West Virginia	15.0	286,995	West Virginia	19.7	345,093
Appalachia	14.0	2,782,939	Appalachia	15.2	3,066,828
United States	12.4	27,383,000	United States	12.4	32,581,000

Note: 1960 data file furnished by the Office of Economic Opportunity. 1970 and 1980 data compiled by ARC from fourth count tabulations, 1970 and 1980 U.S. Census of Population. 1990 data from U.S. Bureau of the Census estimated household population data.

Infant Mortality Rates: Appalachian State Parts and United States 1960, 1970, 1980, and 1990.

Appalachian State Part	1960* Births	1960* Deaths	1960 IM Rate	1970 Births	1970 Deaths	1970 IM Rate	1980 Births	1980 Deaths	1980 IM Rate	1990# Births	1990# Deaths	1990 IM Rate
Alabama	46,844	1,450	31.0	39,973	940	23.5	37,250	525	14.1	38,183	407	10.7
Georgia	15,166	442	29.1	16,692	322	19.3	17,689	200	11.3	25,645	255	9.9
Kentucky	21,480	663	30.9	16,531	334	20.2	17,414	221	12.7	14,717	129	8.8
Maryland	4,048	101	25.0	3,467	73	21.1	2,840	38	13.4	2,794	28	10.0
Mississippi	9,884	325	32.9	8,108	237	29.2	8,589	148	17.2	8,452	123	14.6
New York	20,634	553	26.8	18,142	412	22.7	15,198	155	10.2	15,306	72	4.7
North Carolina	22,746	513	22.6	17,783	395	22.2	14,740	189	12.8	17,605	192	10.9
Ohio	24,246	582	24.0	20,045	379	18.9	20,083	265	13.2	19,480	158	8.1
Pennsylvania	123,240	2,946	23.9	93,922	1,842	19.6	77,649	970	12.5	74,346	639	8.6
South Carolina	13,922	384	27.6	12,440	284	22.8	11,898	144	12.1	13,383	149	11.1
Tennessee	35,366	980	27.7	31,373	665	21.2	28,442	353	12.4	29,134	251	8.6
Virginia	10,554	327	31.0	8,108	174	21.5	7,483	124	16.6	6,118	47	7.7
West Virginia	39,474	1,005	25.5	30,194	705	23.3	29,438	347	11.8	21,613	218	10.1
Appalachia	387,604	10,271	26.5	316,778	6,762	21.3	288,713	3,679	12.7	286,776	2,668	9.3
United States	4,257,850	110,873	26.0	3,731,386	74,667	20.0	3,612,258	45,552	12.6	4,179,000	38,100	9.1